THE
DODGERS ENCYCLOPEDIA

3rd Edition

THE
DODGERS ENCYCLOPEDIA

3rd Edition

by

William F. McNeil

SPORTS
PUBLISHING

Sports Publishing books may be purchased in bulk at special discounts for sales promotion, corporate gifts, fund-raising, or educational purposes. Special editions can also be created to specifications. For details, contact the Special Sales Department, Sports Publishing, 307 West 36th Street, 11th Floor, New York, NY 10018 or sportspubbooks@skyhorsepublishing.com.

Sports Publishing® is a registered trademark of Skyhorse Publishing, Inc.®, a Delaware corporation.

Visit our website at www.sportspubbooks.com

10 9 8 7 6 5 4 3 2

Library of Congress Cataloging-in-Publication Data available on file.

ISBN: 978-1-61321-066-6

Printed in Canada

This book is dedicated to Dodger fans everywhere, and to the memory of all the outstanding baseball players who plied their trade in baseball parks named The Capitoline, Eastern Park, Washington Park, Ebbets Field, The Coliseum, and Dodger Stadium

Contents

Contents

Acknowledgments

The author would like to thank the following people and organizations who provided him with valuable assistance during the preparation of this book.

Tot Holmes; Shirley Mullin Rhodes; Brent Shyer, Barry Stockhamer, and John Olguin, Los Angeles Dodgers; Mark Rucker, Transcendental Graphics; Bill Burdick, National Baseball Library, Cooperstown, NY; Bill Martin, New York Daily News; Julie Moffat, Archivist, Brooklyn Public Library; John Thorn and Pete Palmer, Editors, Total Baseball V; Vince Walsh, Princeton Desktop Publishing, Inc.; Bob Carroll, Walt Wilson, Mary Brace, Brace Photo; and Yuyo Ruiz, La Esquina Del Left Field.

I would also like to thank Mike Pearson, Lisa Peretz, and Susan McKinney, at Sagamore Publishing, without whose efforts, this book would still be in manuscript form. And a special thanks you to Mark Zulauf, Developmental Editor for Sports Publishing L.L.C., whose dedicated work ethic and meticulous editing of the second edition was invaluable.

THE DODGERS ENCYCLOPEDIA

3rd Edition

CHAPTER 1

THE HISTORY OF "DODGER" BASEBALL

"Meketre winds and pitches. Menes swings and drives the ball deep to right center field. Sinuhe is off at the crack of the bat, but the ball is over his head. It rolls toward the overflow crowd ringing the outfield. The swift first baseman of the Memphis Tigers races around the bases without breaking stride, and crosses home plate with the winning run before the ball can be retrieved. Memphis wins the Upper Egypt Championship for the third straight year." The date is 2013 B.C.

"Marcus Vinicius is in deep trouble. The Pompeii Panthers have the bases loaded with two men out in the last of the ninth. The underdog Rome Renegades still cling to a slim 3-2 lead in the final game of the European World Series. The dangerous Claudius Fabius, power hitting outfielder of the Panthers is at the plate, having hit one home run already today. He works the count full against Vinicius, three balls, two strikes. Marcus takes his stretch, eyes the runners, and comes to the plate. Claudius Fabius

swings. He misses. It's strike three. The game is over. Rome ends eight years of frustration, and wins its first European championship with a stirring come-from-behind victory in Game Seven." The date is A.D. 13.

Far fetched? Perhaps. These scenarios might not be accurate, but ball games, of one type or another, have been played around the world for as long as civilization has existed. The British Museum in London houses a small leather ball that was used in Egypt around 2000 B.C. Wall paintings on ancient Egyptian tombs depict ball games being played on the banks of the Nile River over 4,500 years ago.

Roman and Greek histories speak of ball games being played in those ancient empires before the birth of Christ.

It is not clear exactly who invented the good old game of American baseball, but it definitely wasn't Abner Doubleday as previously reported. The game of baseball,

24. CLUB-BALL.—XIV. CENTURY.

Club-Ball, another predecessor of American baseball, was played in England as early as A.D. 1344, as shown in this drawing. In addition to the pitcher and batter shown here, the original drawing had several defensive players, stationed behind the pitcher, who were apparently waiting to catch the ball after it was hit. (Transcendental Graphics)

as it is played today, with all its innovations and complicated strategies is certainly an American game. It reflects the spirit and personality of the American people.

The roots of the game, however, are not American. Neither are they English. Their beginnings are shrouded in the ancient civilizations of Mesopotamia and Egypt. The first ball probably still lies buried in the yellow-brown clay of Sumeria; the first bat hidden beneath the shifting sands of the Sahara Desert.

The game, as we know it, most certainly evolved over a period of hundreds of years, passing from country to country across the European continent. It, or its ancestor, came across the water from Europe to Colonial America during the 18th century. A game called baseball was being played in England as long ago as A.D. 1700. In fact, a book titled, *A Little Pretty Pocket Book*, published in England in 1744 contained an ink drawing of a baseball game with the following poem.

> " The ball once struck off
> Away flies the boy
> To the next defin'd post
> And then home with joy."

Numerous variations to this game existed in both England and America. Rounders was a popular English ball game, as was stool ball. In the American Colonies, the favorite game in the 18th century was town ball, which eventually evolved into American baseball, around the 1840s.

As the game of baseball grew in popularity, the Establishment feared that this new national sport might be associated with England. Having only recently thrown off the yoke of oppressive rule by British tyrants, and filled with a new-found sense of national pride, baseball's founding fathers were determined to claim the game of baseball as a purely homegrown invention.

During the last half of the 19th century, discussions relating to the origin of baseball became loud and emotional in taverns and social clubs across the continent. Finally, in 1905, A. G. Spaulding, one of the pioneers of the game, suggested a committee be formed to once and for all determine the true origin of baseball. Unfortunately, the seven-man committee appears to have been heavily biased in favor of America for Americans. Relying exclusively on the recollections of old-timers around the Colonies, and of one old timer in particular, the committee concluded that the game of baseball was invented in Cooperstown, New York, in 1839 by a West Point cadet named Abner Doubleday. Doubleday, himself, had no such recollection. At least he never mentioned having invented baseball in his memoirs.

Henry Chadwick, a New York sportswriter, insisted the game of baseball was a natural evolution of earlier games played in England and the Colonies; games like rounders and stool ball. Chadwick, who appears to have been more open-minded about the origin of baseball than most of his contemporaries, eventually became known as the "Father of Baseball", for his many contributions to the game in the late 19th century. One of his innovations was the box score, introduced in "The New York Clipper" on July 16, 1853, following a game between the Knickerbocker and Gotham baseball clubs of New York. The Knickerbockers won the game, 21-1 in six innings.

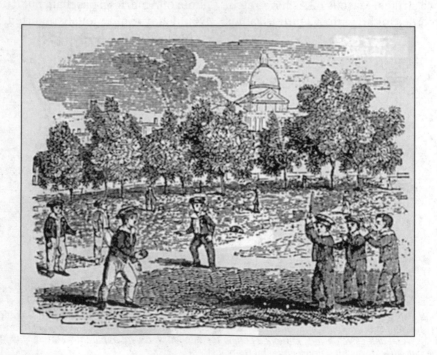

This drawing, from A Little Book of Sports, *published in 1834, shows a group of boys engaged in a game of baseball on Boston Common. (Transcendental Graphics)*

Alexander J. Cartwright, another early pioneer of the game, formulated the first set of baseball rules for his team, the Knickerbocker Baseball Club of New York City, the first recognized baseball club in America. Among the more important rules adopted in 1845 were these:

- The playing field was standardized in the well known diamond-shape. Previously the field was laid out in a variety of shapes, from oblong to square.
- The number of players were limited to nine per side.
- The distance between bases was set at 90 feet.

One year later, Cartwright's Knickerbockers participated in the first recorded baseball game in history. Accepting a challenge from the New York Nine, the Knickerbockers travelled to Hoboken, New Jersey on the morning of June 19, 1846. There, on Elysian Field, the two teams locked horns in mighty battle for the bragging rights of New York City. As recorded in the archives, the New York Nine prevailed by the lopsided score of 23-1, in a game limited to four innings. According to the rules of the day, the game ended when one team scored 21 aces (or runs).

From that momentous event, the game has evolved into the game of today, the recognized national pastime, with 50 million fans passing through major league turnstiles every season.

As the years passed, baseball continued to be refined and improved upon. The Knickerbockers unveiled the game's first uniforms in 1849. Eight years later, the first organized amateur league was formed, The National Association of Baseball Players (NABP). New rule changes did away with the 21-run rule and made the standard length of the game nine innings. Three strikes were out, but it still took nine balls to be awarded a free pass to first base.

Brooklyn and New York teams were in the forefront of the rapidly developing sport from its earliest days, each city fielding four superior teams. Brooklyn was represented by the Atlantics, Excelsiors, Putnams, and Eckfords, but it was the Excelsiors who were the trailblazers in this new athletic competition. The hard-hitting Brooklyn Nine excited the imagination of fans everywhere with their long-distance hits and high-scoring games. Their feats were legendary up and down the eastern seaboard, from Maine to North Carolina, and westward from New York to Ohio. The Excelsiors were the first team to take their show on the road, touring New York State during the summer of 1860. The prodigious Brooklyn scoring machine drew record crowds all along the route, from Albany to Niagara Falls. In Buffalo, they routed the powerful home town Niagaras, 50-19, setting a new record for most runs scored in a game by one team. That record lasted only a matter of days before they annihilated the Newburgh Nine, 59-14. Another "road trip" took the pride of Flatbush as far south as Maryland and Delaware. Their victims included Baltimore (51-6) and Philadelphia (15-4).

The first World Series of baseball can be traced back to a challenge hurled at the New York clubs by their adversaries in Brooklyn in 1858. Both sides assembled all-star teams from their respective cities, and a three-game series was scheduled for a neutral field, the Fashion Race Course on Long Island.

The Excelsiors of Brooklyn were one of the premier baseball teams of the early days. They were almost unbeatable when James Creighton (holding the ball) was on the mound. (Transcendental Graphics)

Several thousand fans attended the competition, which was lively and high scoring, as was the practice of the day. The momentum swung back and forth continuously in Game One, with the New York team finally eking out a hard-fought 22-18 victory. The Brooklyn All-Stars, not discouraged by the defeat, bounced back to rout their adversaries from across the East River in Game Two. The score was 29-8. In story book fashion, New York took the rubber game, 29-18, establishing a habit of New York dominance over Brooklyn teams that would last for 97 years. Johnny Podres finally put the ghost to rest once and for all on a comfortable October day in 1955.

The Excelsiors, for a time, enjoyed the services of baseball's first genuine superstar, a 19-year-old pitcher

the best teams in the country during this period, winning national championships in 1864 and 1866. They succeeded the Brooklyn Eckfords who copped the title in 1862 and 1863.

Eighteen hundred and sixty seven saw a development that revolutionized this new game. William Arthur "Candy" Cummings, star pitcher of the Excelsiors, in a game against the Harvard Baseball Club in Boston, unveiled a new pitch, a ball that curved as it approached the batter. The curveball, however, did not become a popular pitch until the 1880s. In Cummings' time the distance from the mound to home plate was only 45 feet, and the ball had to be thrown underhand. Under these conditions, the curve ball was not an easy pitch to master. With the

The Brooklyn Atlantics were the greatest team of the 1860s. This was the team that ended the powerful Cincinnati Red Stockings' 80-game undefeated streak. (Transcendental Graphics)

with a blazing fastball. His name was James Creighton. For several years, he was the top drawing card in baseball, with his innocent good looks and his winning smile. Whenever the Excelsiors played on the road, street posters would announce Creighton as the pitcher, and people would come from miles around to see this young phenom throw the ball past the home town hitters. He never disappointed them. Tragically, the Brooklyn star did not live to see his 22nd birthday. On October 14, 1862, Creighton collapsed at the plate after hitting an inside-the-park homer against the Unions. He was taken to his home on Henry Street, but never recovered. Four days later, the pride of Brooklyn was dead.

In its infancy, baseball was primarily an East Coast game but, thanks to the pioneering efforts of clubs like the Excelsiors, the game spread west to Ohio and Illinois during the 1860s. The Brooklyn Atlantics fielded one of

advent of the overhand pitch and the establishment of the 60'6" pitching distance, the curveball came of age.

By 1869, professionalism had entered the arena of American baseball. The Cincinnati Red Stockings recruited the best baseball players in the country, and paid them to play ball full time. From March 15 through November 15, these superstars, led by shortstop George Wright, steamrolled all opposition. They went undefeated for almost two years, piling up an 80-game undefeated streak. The streak ended dramatically on June 14,1870, when the Brooklyn Atlantics beat the Cincinnati team 8-7 in 11 innings.

In the fall of the same year, the Cincinnati baseball team was disbanded. The next year, 1871, the first professional baseball league was formed, the National Association of Professional Baseball Players. The Brooklyn

The Brighton trolley was one of the many different electric trolley cars that traversed the streets of Brooklyn, beginning about 1890. According to local historians, these electrical monsters, driven by unskilled former horse and buggy drivers, were killing an average of one pedestrian a week by 1895. (Brooklyn Public Library)

Eckfords became league members during the first season, but their records were later stricken from the books after it was determined they had registered too late.

Five years later, the National League was formed. In 1882, another professional league arrived on the scene, the American Association. And, in 1884, Brooklyn joined the Association to give the Flatbush faithful their first bonafide major league baseball team. The team was called simply, the Brooklyns, although many people referred to them as the Grays after the color of their uniforms.

The city of Brooklyn was in the throes of a population explosion during the last half of the nineteenth century, and transportation was one of the major problems. The 1850 population of 70,000 would increase to over one million in the short span of 50 years. The old horse-drawn cars were no longer adequate to handle the demands of a rapidly expanding community. A new invention, the electric trolley car, was sweeping the country at this time, and had proven successful in alleviating traffic congestion in Kansas City as well as Richmond, Virginia. The "trolley" was the first modern rapid transit system, something the City of Churches desperately needed. Trolley car tracks were soon decorating every street in Brooklyn, and crisscrossing every intersection. They were at their worst in front of Eastern Park where a confluence of tracks made life especially dangerous for baseball fans who had to dodge the trolleys as they crossed the busy thoroughfares on their way to the game. It wasn't long before the citizens of Brooklyn were being dubbed "Trolley Dodgers" by amused visitors to the quaint city. In time, the team itself was called the Trolley Dodgers, although the name didn't stick until after the Wilbert Robinson era, in 1932.

The Brooklyns played their first home game in ramshackled Washington Park, on 5th Avenue, on April 12, 1884. The park consisted of an old wooden grandstand, rickety bleachers, and a flimsy wooden fence that encircled a cow pasture-type outfield. But it was home.

It, and similar old wooden parks, would be home for 28 years until Ebbets Field opened in 1913. The Brooklyn professional debut was inauspicious as they were beaten at home by the Cleveland Spiders, 5-1. It was three weeks later, on May 5, when they won their first home game. They walloped the Washington team, 11-3, no great feat since Washington dropped out of the league before the season ended, finishing with a record of 12 and 51.

Charlie Ebbets joined the Brooklyn franchise in 1884, a bright young man of 25 in search of his fortune. Charlie was ambitious and was willing to do anything to advance his career. Nothing was too difficult. Nothing was too demeaning. For Brooklyn, Charlie was the Jack-of-all-trades. He collected tickets, ushered people to their seats, and raked the infield. Then he cleaned the park after the game was over. Whenever possible, he purchased stock in the club. Within 20 years, Charlie Ebbets was President of the team–and in full control of its destiny.

The Brooklyns won only 40 games their first year, finishing ninth in a 13-club league. They improved their position year by year until, in 1889, the team, now called the "Bridegrooms" because six of their players had gotten married during the off-season, captured their first professional baseball championship. Robert Lee "Parisian Bob" Caruthers, a tiny right-handed pitcher, was their first star, leading the team to the pennant with a record of 40-11. The Bridegrooms lost the World Series that year to the New York Giants, the champions of the National League, six games to three.

The next year, the Bridegrooms stepped up in class, joining the more renowned National League. To prove their American Association title was no fluke, Manager Bill McGunnigle's crew raced home in first place, capturing the National League title by two games over Cap Anson's Chicago Cubs. Bob Caruthers had another fine season on the mound, contributing 23 victories to the cause. Tom Lovett (30-11) and Bill Terry (26-16) combined with "Parisian Bob" to give Brooklyn the best pitching staff in the league. Unfortunately, the Louisville Colonels of the American Association played them tough in the World Series, which ended in a 3-3-1 draw.

As the twentieth century approached, the Brooklyn team received help from an unexpected source. Harry Von der Horst, owner of the famed Baltimore Orioles, was embroiled in financial problems with his franchise. Fearing the loss of his best players in a court battle with creditors, the wily Von der Horst purchased a controlling interest in the Brooklyn ball club. He then proceeded to transfer the Baltimore manager, Ned Hanlon, and most of the star players to Brooklyn. The Bridegrooms received such immense baseball talents as "Wee Willie" Keeler, Joe Kelley, and Hughie Jennings. This infusion of skills turned a tenth-place team into an instant winner. From a 54-91 record in 1898, the Bridegrooms won 88 games against only 42 losses in 1899, a turnaround of 41 1/2 games, one of the greatest flip-flops in major league history. Brooklyn romped to the title by eight games, led by the aforementioned Keeler (.377), Kelley (.330), and Jennings (.299), and ably supported by former Baltimore pitchers Jim Hughes (28-6) and Doc McJames (19-15). There was

When Ebbets Field opened on April 9, 1913, it was the most modern, and the most beautiful baseball stadium in the country.

no World Series that year as competition between the National League and the American Association had ceased in 1890, and a postseason playoff between the top two teams in the National League, which was instituted in 1894, was dropped after the 1897 series.

The Bridegrooms repeated as pennant winners in 1900. By this time they were called the Superbas. A popular vaudeville act of the time, called "Hanlon's Superbas"

was touring the country, and the name was a natural fit for manager Ned Hanlon's charges. Keeler at .368 and Kelley at .317 were supported by the strong pitching of "Iron Man" Joe McGinnity whose 29-9 record kept Brooklyn on top. Reverting to old times, the second-place Pittsburgh Pirates challenged the Superbas to a "World Series." Ned Hanlon's boys quickly picked up the gauntlet and, behind the clutch pitching of McGinnity who won two games, they easily subdued Honus Wagner's Buccaneers three games to one.

The upstart American League was formed in 1901 and it immediately raided the existing franchises, siphoning off many of the top players of the senior circuit. "Iron Man" McGinnity took his 26 wins to Baltimore and the Superbas slipped to third place. Within two years, the Brooklyn franchise had been stripped of most of its ex-

Wilbert Robinson assumed the managerial reins of the Brooklyn club in 1914. During a notable 17-year playing career, he was a member of the famed Baltimore Orioles of the 1890s. When he retired from active play in 1902, he left behind a .273 batting average.

perienced ballplayers, and the team languished in the second division for 12 long years.

The rebuilding process had to be accomplished through the farm system, and it was a slow, frustrating process. By 1908, Charlie Ebbets had gained full control of the Brooklyn franchise and he set about building a new baseball stadium worthy of the people of Brooklyn. It took four long years to obtain the property and construct the park, but on April 5, 1913, before 25,000 of the Flatbush faithful, Charlie Ebbets unveiled his new $750,000 pride and joy. Ebbets' daughter, Genevieve, threw out the first ball, and the Superbas beat the New York Highlanders in an exhibition game, 3-2, on a Casey Stengel home run.

Wilbert Robinson, the old Baltimore Oriole catcher, was hired by Ebbets to be the new Brooklyn manager. Unfortunately, the team soon became known as the Robins, a sobriquet hung on them by clever sportswriters. For a few years after Ebbets Field opened, Dame Fortune smiled on the Robins. Sparked by a group of home grown players like Stengel, Zack Wheat, Jake Daubert, Jeff Pfeffer, Sherry Smith, Jimmy Johnston, Hy Myers, and Burleigh Grimes, the Robins captured National League flags in 1916 and 1920. The 1916 edition lost the World Series to the Boston Red Sox and a slick southpaw pitcher named Babe Ruth. In 1920, the Cleveland Indians, led by Elmer Smith's grand slam home run, Bill Wambsganss unassisted triple play, and Stan Coveleski's three victories, dominated Uncle Robby's boys, five games to two.

Elsewhere in the major leagues, 1920 was a tragic year for club owners and fans alike. The notorious "Black Sox" scandal rocked the country, and in September, eight members of the Chicago White Sox were indicted for throwing the 1919 World Series to the Cincinnati Reds. Eventually, all eight, including the great "Shoeless Joe" Jackson, were barred from baseball for life.

On the bright side, the 1920 regular season witnessed one of the all-time great pitching feats, a 26 inning, 1-1 tie between the Brooklyn Robins and the Boston Braves. Both starting pitchers, Leon Cadore of Brooklyn and Joe Oeschger of the Braves toiled the entire 26 innings in as gutty a pitching exhibition as has ever graced a major league field.

As 1921 unfolded, mediocrity joined the Brooklyn team as a permanent member. The pitching staff collapsed

that year and the Robins limped home in fifth place. Three years later, in 1924, Brooklyn unexpectedly challenged for the title, finishing a close second to the New York Giants. The team was led by Zack Wheat and Dazzy Vance. The 37-year-old Wheat enjoyed one of his finest years, batting .375 and knocking in 97 runs. Vance, at 33, had a "career" season, winning 15 games in succession, setting a National League single-game strikeout record with 15, walking away with the "most valuable player" award, and leading the league in wins (28), strikeouts (262), and earned run average (2.16).

But 1924 was only a mirage. Every other year between 1922 and 1929 Uncle Robby's boys held down sixth place. The era of the "Daffyness Boys" was in full bloom in Brooklyn. It continued unabated through most of the thirties as the Brooklyn team saw the light of the first division only four times between 1922 and 1938. One day, three Robin baserunners arrived at third base at the same time. On another day, an outfielder in full flight after a

Dixie Walker struggled for nine years, trying to win a steady job in the American League. The journeyman ball player, hampered by shoulder and knee injuries, was rescued by Larry MacPhail in 1939, and went on to become a legend in Brooklyn.

Hack Wilson, a member of the Daffyness boys, was a demon with the bat, but fielded like a man wearing boxing gloves. He was also fond of napping on the bench during the game.

fly ball stopped to pick up his hat, while the baserunner gleefully ran out a triple. Reports of ballplayers making out the lineup, reading magazines during the game, and even managing the team from time to time, were widely publicized in the nation's newspapers.

The talent on the ball club was, for the most part, mediocre. With the exception of Vance, Wheat, and Babe Herman, the rest of the roster was more like a side show than a professional baseball team. One pitcher had a habit of letting out a piercing hog call after every strikeout. Fortunately, "Pea Ridge" Day lasted only one year with the big club. Outfielders, at times, caught more balls with their shoulders than with their gloves. And the pitching staff had a proclivity for giving up the long ball. A pitcher named Beck was even nicknamed "Boom Boom", to imitate first the sound of the bat striking the ball, then the sound of the ball striking the outfield fence. Beck's best year was 1933 when he won 12 games against "only" 20 losses.

The era of the"Daffyness Boys" lasted for 18 long years. An entire generation of baseball fans grew up in Brooklyn without ever experiencing the thrill of winning a pennant, or the excitement and satisfaction of a World Championship.

The most notable event of this period was the permanent adoption of "Dodgers" as the team nickname. In 1933, Dodgers was stitched across the front of the team jersey for the first time.

Dodger fortunes began to change in 1937 when the Dodger owners hired Larry MacPhail to be President of the club. Given a free reign to bring a pennant winner back to Brooklyn, the dynamic MacPhail set a course that would eventually bring a dynasty to the baseball starved fans of the third largest "city" in the United States.

The big redhead was just what the doctor ordered. An astute baseball man who was not afraid to invest money in the future of the club, he set about to improve the facilities and to obtain the players necessary to win a pennant. Within four years he had set the Brooklyn express on the pennant track.

MacPhail was a hard working, no-nonsense, wheelerdealer, often referred to as "Hurricane Larry." He had introduced night baseball to the major leagues in Cincinnati in 1935. He also pioneered baseball radio broadcasts, hiring Red Barber to do the play-by-play of the Reds' games. As soon as he had settled into the general manager's chair in the big office on Montague Street, he began to attack the stagnant conditions in Dodger Land. He renovated Ebbets Field, brought night baseball to the big city, corralled the "old redhead" to describe the Dodger action to all fans within reach of a radio, and initiated the much envied and frequently copied Dodger farm system. As a stop-gap measure, to produce a winner while the farm system was developing, he went out on the open market and purchased several established stars and other major and minor league players he thought had potential. These included Dolph Camilli, Pee Wee Reese, Dixie Walker, Kirby Higbe, Whitlow Wyatt, Mickey Owen, and Hugh Casey.

MacPhail then promoted shortstop Leo Durocher to field manager. All the pieces were now in place. The Dodgers were ready to make their move toward the top of the National League. Fifty years later, the Dodgers are still the dominant team in the league. And Leland Stamford MacPhail was the prime mover—the father of Dodger baseball.

Brooklyn finished third in 1939, second in 1940. Then in 1941, the Dodgers grabbed the brass ring. By then, Reese was solidly entrenched at short, and Lippy Leo was a full-time bench manager. The 22-year-old outfield sensation, "Pistol Pete" Reiser lit up the National League with his sizzling hitting, his dazzling speed, and his daring outfield play. He led the league in batting with a .343 average, the youngest player ever to win the title. Higbe and Wyatt piled up 22 victories each, and "Dem Bums" won 100 games and hoisted a National League pennant over Ebbets Field for the first time in 21 years. The World Series was disappointing, however, as Durocher's boys fell to the hated New York Yankees, four games to one. Mickey Owen's dropped third strike on Tommy Henrich was the turning point of the Series.

Carl Furillo's sacrifice fly scored Gil Hodges as Brooklyn beat Pittsburgh, en route to the 1949 pennant.

The following year, Durocher's crew racked up 104 victories, but had to settle for second place when Billy Southworth's Redbirds won 106. The Dodger season essentially ended on July 19, when Pete Reiser, hitting a lusty .356, crashed into the center field wall in St. Louis and had to be carried from the field on a stretcher. "Pistol Pete", suffering from dizzy spells the rest of the year, courageously stayed in the lineup, but could muster only a .220 batting average down the stretch. The Dodger hopes died when Reiser went down.

Branch Rickey, who replaced Larry MacPhail as President of the Brooklyn club in 1942, maintained MacPhail's aggressive policies, and even improved upon some of them. He expanded the Brooklyn farm system and developed the training facilities until, by 1948 Dodger farm teams, numbering 26 with over 600 players, shared spring training facilities with the major leaguers in the brand new Dodgertown training camp in Vero Beach, Florida.

In his constant search for new talent, the "Mahatma" focused in on the Negro Baseball Leagues, which he called the greatest untapped source of raw baseball talent left in the country. On August 28, 1945, in an historic event, Branch Rickey signed Jackie Robinson, a black shortstop with the Kansas City Monarchs, to a professional baseball contract, thereby breaking the 60-year-old color barrier.

World War II interrupted the Dodger march to glory temporarily, but in 1946 the boys returned home and the golden era of Brooklyn baseball began. Carl Furillo attended his first spring training camp in Florida, joining "Pee Wee" Reese as the first two "Boys of Summer." Surprisingly, the fuzzy-cheeked Brooklyn brigade fought the heavily favored Cardinals tooth and nail, finishing the season in a dead heat with Eddie Dyer's club. The spirited Dodgers were finally overpowered by a superior St. Louis team, two games to none, in the first playoff series ever held in the major leagues.

Between 1947 and 1949, Furillo and Reese were joined by Don Newcombe, Carl Erskine, Preacher Roe, Billy Cox, Gil Hodges, Roy Campanella, Jackie Robinson, and the Duke of Flatbush, Donald Edwin Snider. The "Boys of Summer" were on the prowl.

Over the next ten years, the Dodger wrecking crew wreaked havoc on National League pitchers as they won six National League flags, lost one playoff for a league title, and lost another pennant on the last day of the season. The 1947 champs lost the Series to the Yanks four games to three, but left their fans with some memorable moments. In Game Four, pinch hitter Cookie Lavagetto, lined a two- run double to right field with two out in the bottom of the ninth, to break up Yankee right-hander Bill Bevens bid for a no-hitter. The hit also won the game for the Brooks, 3-2.

In Game Six, substitute outfielder Al Gionfriddo raced to the bullpen in distant left field to make a sensational catch of Joe DiMaggio's bid for a game-tying, three run homer. After a disappointing third-place finish in 1948, the Flatbush Flock prevailed once again in 1949, only to see the Yanks take the Series once again, 4 to 1.

1950 was another heartbreak year in Dodger land. Faced with the opportunity to force a playoff for the National League pennant on the last day of the season, Brooklyn couldn't pull it off.

First, lead-footed Cal Abrams, carrying the winning run, was thrown out at home by chicken-winged Richie Ashburn in the bottom of the ninth. Then, both Carl Furillo and Gil Hodges came up with the bases loaded but were unable to deliver the game winner.

Burt Shotton's boys never got another chance; Dick Sisler saw to that. The big Phillie first baseman put the ball into orbit with two on in the tenth, and the Whiz Kids went to the Series.

The following year was another disaster, the year of the "shot heard round the world." Leading by 13 1/2 games on August 13th, the Dodgers saw Leo Durocher's Giants go on a rampage in the last six weeks of the season, winning 36 of their last 44 games to force a playoff. As everyone now knows, Bobby Thomson's three-run homer with two out in the bottom of the ninth inning carried New York to the title and frustrated the Brooklyn gang one more time.

In 1952, Charlie Dressen's team put it all together, winning the pennant by 4 1/2 games, only to bite the dust at the hands of Casey Stengel's Yanks, four games to three. Billy Martin's shoestring catch of Jackie Robinson's pop fly choked off the tying runs in the seventh inning of Game Seven to clinch it.

One year later, the pride of Flatbush fielded its greatest team and, perhaps, the greatest team in National League history. Led by MVP Roy Campanella, the Brook-

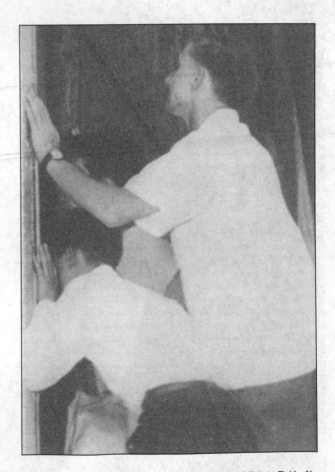

A sign of old age is evident in this 1955 photograph of Ebbets Field. Non-paying customers are able to view the game through a hole in the fence, proving that the once proud Brooklyn showplace had finally outlived its usefulness.

lyn bashers won a team-record 105 games on the strength of a scoring attack that averaged over six runs per game. Six players scored over 100 runs. Duke Snider with 42 home runs and Roy Campanella with 41 spearheaded a Dodger attack that slugged 208 round-trippers in 154 games. Five men batted over .300, led by Carl Furillo,

Walter O'Malley, President of the Brooklyn Dodgers, and founder of the 50-year-old baseball dynasty, reluctantly relocated his club to Los Angeles after he was unable to find a suitable new home for them in Brooklyn.

whose .344 average led the NL. Campy, with 142 RBIs, was one of five Dodgers who drove in over 90 runs each. Behind this devastating onslaught, the Big Blue Machine romped home 13 games in front of second-place Milwaukee. Still, they could not master the New York Yankees, and the Bronx Bombers won the World Series in six games. "Wait till next year" became the anguished cry of the Flatbush faithful.

In 1955, Brooklyn finally scaled the summit. Behind second-year manager Walter Alston, the dynamite Dodgers swept to 22 victories in their first 24 games, and opened a nine-game bulge over the Giants by early May. From there, Campanella and crew coasted home, clinching the pennant on September 8, the earliest clinching date in National League history. The momentum carried over into the World Series for the frustrated Brooks. Riding the courageous left arm of 23-year-old Johnny Podres, who won two games, the Dodgers finally won their first World Championship, defeating the Yankees in seven games. Little Sandy Amoros, the Cuban dandy, saved Game Seven for Alston's crew when he made a spectacular catch of an extra base bid by Yogi Berra, then turned it into a fast, 7-6-3 double play. It would be the Dodgers' only world title as a representative of the fair borough of Brooklyn.

Their attempt at another world title in 1956 was thwarted by those same New Yorkers, who beat down the National League Champions in seven games. Don Larsen's perfect game in Game Five sparked Casey Stengel's team to victory.

Walter O'Malley had ushered in a new era in Dodger history when he succeeded Branch Rickey to the presidency in 1950. Convinced that the Dodgers had outgrown the cozy confines of Ebbets Field, O'Malley petitioned the city of New York to build a new stadium. After four fruitless years of negotiating with the New York bureaucracy, Mr. O'Malley packed his bags and relocated his championship baseball team to the sunny environs of southern California. With that tragic chain of events, the sun disappeared from the skies over Brooklyn, and the days have been dark ever since.

On the other side of the country however, the citizens of Los Angeles were in a festive mood. They had obtained a major league baseball team. In fact, they corralled the most colorful, most successful baseball team in all of America. The fans turned out by the thousands to welcome the Dodgers to the land of surf and sun. Walter O'Malley beamed. He had everything he could possibly want, everything except a place for his athletes to play.

For the first four years, the Brooklyn expatriates were forced to play their home games in the Los Angeles Coliseum, a stadium originally constructed for the 1932 Olympic Games. As a baseball field, it was a monstrosity. The left-field fence was only 252 feet from home plate. It was topped by a 40-foot-high screen. The right-field fence, on the other hand, was 440 feet distant. Carl Erskine won the honor of pitching the home opener on April 18, 1958,

and he came away a 6-5 winner, on the strength of Dick Gray's seventh-inning home run.

The "Boys of Summer" were on the decline now, and the early years in L.A. were ones of transition, but the 1959 patchwork lineup surprised everyone by capturing the National League flag in a playoff with the Milwaukee Braves. Then Larry Sherry and Chuck Essegian, et.al, topped off their fantastic season by winning the World Championship; stopping the Chicago White Sox in six games. Sherry won two games and saved two others in an impressive one-man show.

During the 60s, the Los Angeles Dodgers established their own unique identity. Anchored by the pitching duo of Koufax and Drysdale, the Dodgers shed their brawling, rough house hobo image and developed a California style all their own. Instead of brute force, the L.A. attack was based on balance. Backed by an outstanding pitching rotation, ably supported by Johnny Podres, Claude Osteen and Ron Perranoski, the team relied on pitching, defense and speed, more than on power. With the likes of Maury Wills, Tommy Davis, and Willie Davis, the Hollywood nine could gallop around the bases in record time. Most of the power in the lineup was supplied by big Frank Howard, all 6'7" of him. The 250-pound strongman was known to drive balls into the left field pavilion with one hand.

The Los Angeles contingent had their first unpleasant brush with destiny in 1962. The season started on a high note when Dodger President Walter O'Malley, dedicated the new Dodger Stadium on April 10. Sandy Koufax pitched the first victory in the new park, downing the Reds, 6-2, the following day. From then until the end, the season was one of ups and downs. Despite winning 102 games, Walter Alston's crew was beaten by their arch ri-

Los Angeles mayor Norris Poulson is shown pitching to San Francisco mayor George Christopher in the opening game in the Coliseum, on April 18, 1958. The Dodgers won the game, 6-5.

vals, the San Francisco Giants, in an exciting finish. The Dodgers first blew a four-game lead during the last week of the season, then lost a two-run lead and the pennant in the last inning of the last playoff game.

Still, there were some bright spots for L.A. during the season. Little Maury Wills startled the baseball world by stealing 104 bases, surpassing Ty Cobb's "unbreakable" 47- year-old record of 96. Wills' achievement earned him the National League's Most Valuable Player award, and popularized the stolen base for years to come. Dodger left fielder Tommy Davis was the league's offensive player of the year, leading the NL in batting (.346), runs batted in (153), and hits (230).

In 1963, Los Angeles was determined to make amends for their disappointing finish the year before. Tommy Davis once again led the league in batting with an average of .326, and Sandy Koufax finally blossomed into a great pitcher, topping the league in victories (25), strikeouts (306), and earned run average (1.88). With Wills leading the league in stolen bases once again, L.A. captured the National League flag by six games. They main-

John Roseboro is welcomed back to the Dodger dugout after smashing a three-run homer against the New York Yankees' Whitey Ford in Game One of the 1963 World Series.

tained their momentum in the World Series, sweeping the proud New York Yankees in four straight. This was Los Angeles' finest hour.

Two more National League flags flew over Dodger Stadium during the sixties, one in 1965 and another in 1966. The World Championship banner also fluttered proudly in the breeze over L.A. in '65, thanks to a 2-0 victory over the Minnesota Twins in Game Seven of the Series. A three-hit shutout by Sandy Koufax, and a game-winning home run by "Sweet Lou" Johnson ended the season on an exciting note.

1966, though, was a sad year for Los Angeles fans. First, their beloved Dodgers were humiliated in the World

Series; a four-game sweep by the Baltimore Orioles. Then, on Friday, November 18, the saddest blow of all was struck. Sandy Koufax announced his retirement from baseball. The 30- year-old southpaw was forced out of the game by an arthritic elbow, leaving a list of achievements that may last forever. His career record of 165-87 was overshadowed by his phenomenal accomplishments during his last four years. From 1963 through 1966, Koufax was almost untouchable, piling up 97 victories against only 27 losses for a winning percentage of .782. He struck out 1,228 men in 1,192 innings, while fashioning a miniscule earned run average of 1.85. Over that same period, the magnificent Koufax hurled four no-hitters, including one perfect game. Five years after retiring, the great Dodger lefty was voted into baseball's Hall of Fame, the youngest player ever so honored. Sandy Koufax may well have been the greatest pitcher who ever lived. And he retired at the peak of his game.

As the '60s wound down, big Don Drysdale carried on the great Dodger pitching tradition started by he and Koufax. In 1968, "Big D" pitched an amazing 58 2/3 consecutive scoreless innings, breaking Walter Johnson's record of 56, established 55 years earlier.

Willie "3 Dog" Davis closed out the decade in fine style, hitting in 31 consecutive games in 1969, a new Dodger record. The old record of 29 was set by Zack Wheat back in 1916.

Dodger legends Roy Campanella and Jackie Robinson are reunited at Dodger Stadium in 1970.

June 13, 1973, was an historic day in major league baseball. On that date, "The Infield" was born. Steve Garvey, Davey Lopes, Bill Russell, and Ron Cey jogged onto the field as an infield unit for the first time. They stayed together for eight years, four months and five days, a major league record. The previous Dodger record, was five years for those glorious "Boys of Summer", Hodges, Robinson, Reese, and Cox.

The decade of the '70s was a time of success for the Los Angeles organization, both on the field and in the front office. The Dodgers were the dominant team in the National League, winning three league titles, never finishing below third place. They still relied on a balanced attack to accomplish their goals. It was team speed, defense, and great pitching that brought enemies to their knees. Six times the outstanding Dodger pitching staff led the National League in earned run average.

Led by Don Sutton, Burt Hooton, Doug Rau, Mike Marshall, Charlie Hough, and Tommy John, L.A. was strong from top to bottom. The pitchers were ably supported by a staunch defense headed by catcher Steve Yeager and "The Infield". On the bases, speedsters like Willie Davis, Davey Lopes, and Bill Russell created havoc for enemy catchers.

Still there were the disappointments. L.A. looked more like "Brooklyn versus the Yankees" in the World Series, losing all three encounters with American League

rivals. In 1974, Charlie Finley's Oakland Athletics, resplendent in their dazzling green and gold uniforms, stood astride the baseball world like the Colossus of Rhodes. They crushed Los Angeles underfoot in five games, enroute to their third straight World Championship. Led by Joe Rudi, "Catfish" Hunter, and Rollie Fingers, the Oakland band was one of the American League's all-time great teams.

In 1977, and again in 1978, the Dodgers met their perennial foes, the New York Yankees, in the fall classic. L.A. lost both Series, but they deserved a better fate. They were not outgunned. They were out-lucked. In '77, a bad call on Steve Garvey's attempt to score in the sixth inning of Game One kept the Dodgers from jumping out to a quick 2-0 lead. They subsequently lost the Series, four games to two. The following year, Reggie Jackson's famous "hip shot", a flagrant violation that was ignored by the umpiring staff, prevented Tommy Lasorda's crew from taking a 3-1 lead in games. This time they lost in six. The famous Welch-Jackson duel was the highlight of the Series for Dodger fans.

Two years later, the Dodgers began perhaps the strangest decade in their history. The '80s would be remembered as the swan song of "The Infield", exciting pennant races in 1980,81,82,83,85 and 88, World Championships in 1981 and 1988, and adrenaline pumping comebacks in 1980-81 and 82.

During the first three years of the decade, Tommy Lasorda's crew earned the moniker of "The Comeback Kid" because of their ability to claw their way back into contention from the brink of elimination, and challenge for the pennant. "The Comeback Kids" were born in 1980. After fighting the Houston Astros tough all year, the never-say-die L.A. crew found themselves with their backs to the wall—three games behind the Texas team with only three to play. As fate would have it, the final three-game series matched the Dodgers against the Astros in Dodger Stadium. In a remarkably gutty performance, the Dodgers swept the series from the stunned Astros to move into a first-place tie. A 19-year-old Mexico native with ice water coursing through his veins, starred in the series. Young Fernando Valenzuela, recently called up from the minors, racked up one victory and one save. Ron Cey's two-run homer in the eighth inning of Game Three carried the Dodgers to a 4-3 victory and a share of first place. LA's luck ran out the following day, however. In a one-game playoff, first baseman Art Howe powered Houston to a 7-1 win and the Western Division title.

The disappointment was soon forgotten in the excitement of the 1981 season. In a campaign designed to eliminate the faint of heart, and to test the mettle of their staunchest fans, L.A.'s "Team of Destiny" grabbed the brass ring. Led by 20-year-old rookie pitcher, Fernando Valenzuela, who won his first eight games, tossed four shutouts and compiled a 0.50 ERA by mid-May, the 1981 Dodgers scratched and clawed their way to the title. Lasorda's boys won the first half of a strike-shortened

Al Downing marched (or pitched) into baseball history on the evening of April 8, 1974. It was on that night that Hank Aaron of the Atlanta Braves sent a Downing fastball over the left field fence for home run # 715, breaking Babe Ruth's record, and becoming the major league's all-time home run king.

season, by edging the Cincinnati Reds by 1/2 game. They met the Houston Astros, the second-half winners, in a Western Division playoff. Ironically, the Reds, who owned the division's best overall record, didn't make the playoffs, finishing second in both halves of the season.

In a scenario they would play over and over, LA's "Comeback Kids" lost the first two games of the five-game playoffs to Houston. Then, behind the gutty pitching of Hooton, Valenzuela and Reuss, who limited Houston to a total of two runs in three games, the Dodgers fought back to claim the Western Division crown. In the National League Championship Series with the Montreal Expos, L.A. found themselves on the brink of elimination again. Down two games to one in the best-of-five series, the

56,236 enthusiastic Dodger fans crowded into Dodger Stadium to witness Game Three of the 1981 World Series. The Dodgers won the game, 5-4, to begin their rousing comeback from an 0-2 game deficit to win the World Championship.

Dodgers had to play the final two games in Montreal. Once again, pulling themselves up by their bootstraps, Lasorda's never-say-die band of warriors roared back. They captured Game Four, 7-1, to deadlock the series. In the finale, clutch pitching by Valenzuela and a dramatic ninth-inning home run by Rick Monday gave Los Angeles it's eighth National League pennant.

Fittingly, the L.A. opponent in the World Series was none other than Bob Lemon's New York Yankees. In typical Yankee fashion, the Bronx Bombers jumped out to a quick two-games-to-none lead over the slow-starting Dodgers. But the "Comeback Kids" were poised and waiting to make their move. Fernando Valenzuela halted the slide in Game Three by outduelling New York rookie Dave Righetti, 5-4, cutting the Yankee lead to two games to one. Game Four was the turning point of the Series. The New

Yorkers pulled out all the stops in their attempt to bury the Dodgers once and for all. But they couldn't drive that last nail in the coffin. Each time the Yankees jumped to a lead, Lasorda's boys clawed their way back into the game.

An early 4 - 0 Yankee lead was cut in half in the last of the third inning. Then, a 6-3 lead failed to hold up in the sixth. Jay Johnstone's pinch-hit two-run homer highlighted a three-run Dodger rally that tied the game. Hits by Baker, Monday, and Lopes gave the Dodgers their first lead in the seventh, and they held on to win, 8-7. From there it was all downhill. The "Comeback Kids" were on a roll now. Back-to-back homers by Pedro Guerrero and Steve Yeager gave Jerry Reuss a 2-1 victory in Game Five. Then a three hit, five-RBI performance by Guerrero in Game Six, clinched the World Championship as Burt Hooton coasted, 9-2.

1982 was more of the same, but in spades. Lasorda's band of athletes spent the first four months of the season trying to get untracked. Nothing worked. "The Infield" was no more, Davey Lopes having moved on to Oakland. The pitching was erratic, the offense sputtered, and the defense struggled. The Atlanta Braves, meanwhile, were on a roll. They began the season in a blaze, winning their first 13 games. And they never looked back—until July 29th that is. On that day, the Los Angeles Dodgers began the greatest comeback in the history of baseball. They moved into Atlanta for a four-game series, trailing the sizzling Braves by 10 1/2 games. After falling behind by five runs in the first game of the series, the Dodgers clawed their way back to win. They also won the next three games from the suddenly disorganized Braves, and the lead was cut to a "mere" 6 1/2 games. The following weekend, Lasorda's crew completed another four-game sweep of the reeling Atlanta team and were poised to take the top spot. Two days later, on August 9, L.A. defeated Cincinnati, 11-3, to move into first place in the Western Division. Never had a team come from so far back in so short a period of time to claim first place. The Dodgers had gained 11 games on the Braves in a span of only 12 days.

As often happens in cases like this, the Dodgers couldn't sustain the momentum. A disastrous eight-game losing streak in mid-September dropped Lasorda's crew into third place, as they, San Francisco and Atlanta jockeyed for position. The final series of the season decided the race. The Dodgers eliminated the Giants in head-to-head competition on the next-to-last day of the season. Then, on the final day, needing a victory to force a playoff with the Braves, the Dodgers were beaten by the Giants, as little Joe Morgan stroked a three-run home run in the seventh inning. The cry of "'wait till next year" wafted eerily through the streets of Los Angeles.

As 1982 faded into history, so too did an era in Dodger baseball. "The Penguin," Ron Cey, and "Mr. Reliable" Steve Garvey, both departed during the winter, leaving the infield chores up to names like Brock, Sax, and Guerrero. Things would never be the same in Dodgerland, as Peter O'Malley, Al Campanis, and Tommy Lasorda struggled to rebuild the team. But stability would be a long time coming. It would not happen during the remainder of the '80s.

L.A. struggled with their defense for five years. The move of Pedro Guerrero to third base proved to be a disaster, as the porous Dodger infield became the joke of the league. The once proud Los Angeles farm system lay in tatters, as one highly touted player after another failed with the big club, and some highly rated talents were traded away for "quick fixes." Somehow the Dodger magic still carried O'Malley's team to division titles in 1983 and 1985, but they lost both National League Championship Series, first to Philadelphia, then to Whitey Herzog's Redbirds.

In between, the pride of Los Angeles finished fourth in 1984, fifth in 1986 and fourth again in 1987. In a crazy kaleidoscopic world of minor league phenoms and major league free agents, General Manager Fred Claire tried to buy time for his farm system to reestablish itself by going out into the marketplace and picking up superstars Kirk Gibson and Alfredo Griffin, as well as veterans Rick Dempsey and Mickey Hatcher.

And suddenly, another miracle was born in Chavez Ravine. With Kirk Gibson as the catalyst and Mickey Hatcher as the spirit of the Dodgers, Tommy Lasorda's patchwork lineup worked wonders during the '88 campaign. For the first time in six years, the defense was an asset instead of a liability. The offense was adequate, especially when Gibson was in the middle of it. And the pitching was superb as usual. During the torrid stretch run, Dodger ace, Orel Hershiser broke Don Drysdale's consecutive-inning scoreless streak, finishing the campaign with 59 straight zeroes.

Dramatic performances by Hershiser, Gibson and Mike Scioscia in the National League Championship Series, catapulted Los Angeles past the highly favored New York Mets, four games to three. In the World Series, Kirk Gibson's storybook home run in the bottom of the ninth inning to win Game One, sparked the Dodgers to a five game drubbing of the mighty Oakland Athletics. The inimitable Mickey Hatcher slugged two home runs and led the team with a .368 average in the Series.

As the Los Angeles Dodgers approached the 21st century, the team was, once again, in transition. The patchwork lineup of 1988 was only a memory, as Mickey Hatcher retired, age caught up with Dempsey and Gibson, and arm miseries shelved both Orel Hershisher and Fernando Valenzuela. Also, the young hopefuls, players like Jose Gonzalez, Franklin Stubbs, and Jeff Hamilton, failed to achieve their potential.

This turn of events forced General Manager Fred Claire back into the free agent market, as a stop gap measure. For a time, it appeared as if Claire had pulled another rabbit out of the bag, with the acquisition of veterans Eddie Murray, Darryl Strawberry, Kal Daniels, Juan Samuel, Brett Butler, and Kevin Gross. The Big Blue Machine dominated the National League during the first half of the 1991 season, but a young and hungry Atlanta Braves outfit, led by Tom Glavine, Steve Avery, and Dave Justice, caught them at the wire, depriving them of the coveted West Division flag.

After a disastrous last place finish in 1992, the Dodgers first cellar occupancy in 87 years, Tommy Lasorda's boys bounced back the following year, finishing fourth. In '94 and '95 they captured the National League's Western Division title once more, and in '96 they finished a close second, after leading the division by two games with just three games left to play.

The legendary Dodger farm system, that had been decimated during the 80s was again the talk of the major leagues. Five consecutive National League Rookies-of-the-Year marched out of the Dodgers' minor league baseball factory between 1992 and 1996: Karros, Piazza, Mondesi, Nomo, and Hollandsworth.

The announcement, early in 1997, that Peter O'Malley intended to sell the franchise cast a temporary pall over the club, but his genuine concern for the fans of Los Angeles, and his stated objective of locating a worthy buyer, boded well for the long term fortunes of "America's Team". O'Malley's farewell season began on a promising note and the team headed into the final two weeks of the season with a two-game lead over the San Francisco Giants, but then with just thirteen days remaining in the season, the wheels came off the Dodger pennant express and

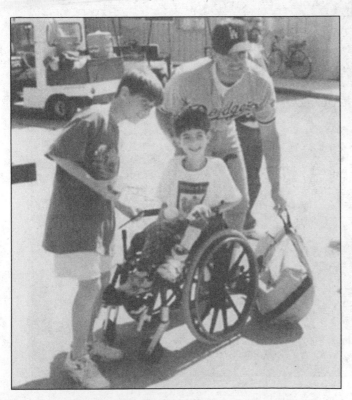

Mike Piazza, the National League's 1993 Rookie of the Year, takes time out to pose with a couple of fans during spring training. (W. McNeil)

Dodger President Peter O'Malley, shown with manager Tommy Lasorda, put the baseball team up for sale after 47 years of family control. During his tenure, and that of his father, the Dodgers were the most dominant team in the National League, with six World Championships, 13 National League pennants, and 9 Western Division titles, to their credit.

their two-game lead turned into a two game deficit. A dejected Dodger team limped home in third place after dropping seven of their last eleven games.

During the off season, the O'Malley family sold their baseball franchise to the Fox Group, a unit of News Corporation, owned by Australian businessman Rupert Murdoch. The 1998 and 1999 seasons were expected to be rebuilding seasons for Murdoch's management team. Their long-term goal was clear—to restore the Dodgers to their glory days of the 1950's through the 1980's, and to make Los Angeles the dominant major league team of the first decade of the 21st century—but carrying out the program did not go as smoothly as anticipated. Chaos reigned in the early going. Major trades sent all-world receiver Mike Piazza, Hideo Nomo, and the Dodgers top rookie, Paul Konerko, packing. Manager Bill Russell and General Manager Fred Claire were fired. The Dodgers finished a distant third, 15 games behind the San Diego Padres.

On the bright side, in December L.A. signed one of baseball's greatest pitchers, Kevin Brown, to a $105 million, seven-year contract, giving them a solid anchor on which to base their future pennant hopes.

The situation began to stabilize in 1999 behind Brown's 18-win season, but it was all a mirage. After four more sub-par years, the Fox Group called it quits and sold the team to Boston real estate developer Frank McCourt, Jr. who immediately took steps to move the Dodgers to the top of the National League Western Division. He gave the city of Los Angeles their first division title in ten years in 2004 behind manager Jim Tracy, and repeated as division leaders in 2006, 2008, and 2009. Los Angeles advanced to the League Championship Series the last two years, but a World Series reservation continued to elude them.

Kevin Brown won 18 games for the Dodgers in 1999, and led the league in ERA in 2000. (Los Angeles Dodgers)

THE 2011 SEASON

In 2011 the Dodgers, under first year manager Don Mattingly hoped to return the team to respectability, but Frank McCourt's personal problems threatened to compromise the team's efforts. General Manager Ned Colletti made several off-season moves to strengthen the team and correct some of the weaknesses. He shored-up several positions on the team through free agent signings, including second baseman Juan Uribe, a 24-home run slugger with San Francisco in 2010, pitchers Jon Garland, a 14-game winner with San Diego and Matt Guerrier who had appeared in 74 games for the Minnesota Twins, and veteran infielders Jamey Carroll and Aaron Miles, both of whom came armed with dangerous bats. Colletti's strategies were outstanding but fate proved unkind. Before long, three-quarters of the Dodgers infield, Uribe, Rafael Furcal, and Casey Blake, went down with injuries. They appeared in just 177 of a scheduled 486 games during the season. In all, Dodger players lost more than 1000 games to injury by the time the curtain came down on the season in September. Fortunately, Colletti's foresight brought welcome relief to the inner garden as Carroll and Miles appeared in 146 games and 136 games respectively, providing reliable defense and solid hitting for beleaguered manager Don Mattingly. Further adding to the Dodgers' woes was the painful knee injury to one of their top hitters Andre Ethier, who had hit 31 home runs as recently as 2009. L.A.'s slugger hobbled through most of the season until going down permanently on September 9. He had gotten off to his usual fast start, putting together a 30-game hitting streak between April 2 to May 6, stinging the ball at a .411 clip with three home runs and 17 RBIs. He reached his high-water mark of .388 on April 22, but from then on, the pain in his knee seriously affected his swing, and reduced his power to almost nothing. For the year, Ethier would hit a respectable .292 in 487 at-bats but would have just 11 home runs and 62 RBIs, a far cry from his 2009 season.

L.A. limped through the first month of the season with a 14-14 mark, leaving them in second place, 4½ games off the top, but as the wounded made their way to the Disabled List, Dodger fortunes imploded. The team went 12-16 in May and an even worse 10-16 in June. On July 6, they were firmly ensconced in the Western Division basement,

Andre Ethier's injured knee hampered him most of the season. (Los Angeles Dodgers)

didn't have any long winning streaks, but they did go 25-10 after August 21 including an 11-1 run from August 22 to September 3.

There were numerous heroes to the Dodgers' late season success, not the least of which, were Clayton Kershaw and Matt Kemp. Kershaw inserted himself into the middle of the Cy Young Award race with brilliant pitching the entire season, and Matt Kemp made an exciting run for the Triple Crown, something that hadn't been accomplished in the National League since 1937. There was also Guerra, a handsome Texan, who was called up from Double-A Chattanooga in the Southern League following Broxton's injury and who collected his first save on June 4 in an eleven-inning 11-8 victory in Cincinnati. The 200-pound right-hander had the confidence and poise needed to close games, and he had a full repertoire of pitches that included a 95 mile per hour cut fastball, a good slider, and a changeup. He went on to record 20 more saves during the season against just two blown saves for an excellent 91% save percentage. He appeared in 47 games for the Dodgers during the year, with a 2-2 record and a 2.31 ERA in 46 2/3 innings pitched. Kenley Jansen, a 23-year old power pitcher called the "Strikeout Machine," was a converted catcher, only two years removed from wearing the tools of ignorance, and he was sensational, posting a 2-1 record in 51 games and establishing a new major league record of 16.1 strikeouts for every nine innings pitched. His cut fastball, that normally hovered around the 95 mph mark but occasionally topped the 100 mph mark, was his out pitch and he threw it 90 percent of the time, with an occasional slider mixed in.

There seemed to be a different hero every day as the rejuvenated Dodgers roared down the homestretch. Matt Kemp began the charge on July 7 with a two-run double in the sixth inning to pace Kershaw's 6-0 whitewash of the Mets. De La Rosa and Billingsley hurled their shutouts on the eighth and ninth. And on the tenth, Andre Ethier sent two solo home runs into the upper atmosphere in support of Ted Lilly's 4-1 victory over the Giants. Matt Kemp was the focus of attention on August 26 in a historic game against the Colorado Rockies in Dodger Stadium. Mattingly's charges pushed over six runs in the bottom of the seventh inning to overcome a 1-0 Colorado lead, the last run coming on Kemp's 30th home run of the season to the cheers of 38,960 of the Dodger faithful. Combined with his 33 stolen bases, he became only the second 30-30 player in Dodger history, joining Raul Mondesi who accomplished the feat twice, once in 1997 and again in 1999. And the Dodger slugger was back at it the next night, smashing an eleventh-inning walk-off homer to sink the Rockies by a 7-6 score. He went two-for-six in the game and drove in his 100th run of the season. Casey Blake had a single, two doubles, and two RBIs and James Loney was two-for-six with an RBI.

As the season turned to September, the Dodger

with a 37-51 won-loss mark, fourteen games under .500 and twelve games behind the high flying San Francisco Giants. In addition to the injuries mentioned previously, closer Jonathan Broxton didn't pitch after May 4, leaving with an elbow injury that would eventually require surgery, and Hong-Chih Kuo missed a significant part of the season with an anxiety disorder. The left field platoon experiment was deemed a failure and the duo of Marcus Thames and Jay Gibbons were released.

Then, quite unexpectedly, Dodger fortunes improved. Colletti and Mattingly made several moves that would help the team, not only in 2011, but in future years as well. They plucked a number of players from L.A.'s minor league system, and the moves paid off handsomely. They found a closer in 25-year old Javy Guerra, an exciting shortstop in Dee Gordon, a solid catcher in A. J. Ellis, as well as outfielder Jerry Sands, infielder Justin Sellers, and pitchers Nathan Eovaldi and Josh Lindblom. On July 7, Dodger ace, Clayton Kershaw, a Sandy Koufax clone, got the "new" 2011 season underway with a 6-0 shutout over the New York Mets in Dodger Stadium. The Dodgers followed that masterpiece with two tension-packed 1-0 victories over San Diego behind 22-year old right-hander Rubby De La Rosa and Chad Billingsley, giving the Padres permanent possession of the cellar as well. The team finished the month with a 12-13 record that had them positioned in fourth place, 12½ games from the top, but they finished the season in a blaze of glory. They

express gained steam. They took the measure of the Atlanta Braves by an 8-6 count on the second of the month, behind the timely hitting of their electrifying 5', 11", 150-pound shortstop Dee Gordon who punched out three hits in five trips to the plate, scored three runs, and stole two bases. Juan Rivera, an important mid-season pickup by Ned Colletti, had two hits and three RBIs and Javy Guerra recorded his 14th save. One week later, Don Mattingly's never-say-die contingent scored single runs in the eighth and ninth innings to steal a game from the San Francisco Giants in AT & T Park in the Bay Area. The game was a brilliant pitching duel between potential Hall of Famers Clayton Kershaw and Tim Lincecum with both pitchers at the top of their game. San Fran touched Kershaw for an unearned run in the bottom of the first inning on an error and a two-out single. The game remained a 1-0 Giant lead until the eighth inning when L.A. tied the score on a topped ball single down the third base line by Kemp, a stolen base, and a seeing-eye single through the middle of the infield by Rivera. In the Dodger ninth, Rod Barajas hit a line drive single to right-center field, moved to second base on a well-placed bunt by Justin Sellers, took third on a wild pitch, and carried home the eventual winning run on a fielder's choice grounder by Jamey Carroll. Guerra retired the side in order in the bottom of the ninth on three ground balls to give Kershaw his eighteenth victory of the season. The next night, another Colletti pickup, Dana Eveland kept the Giants under wraps with a 3-0 shutout, giving the Dodgers their 15th victory in their last 18 games.

The following week, they enjoyed one of their more relaxed games, a 15-1 laugher over the Pittsburgh Pirates. The game produced 23 base hits by the west coast crew, led by James Loney's four singles and a double, Jerry Sands four base hits including a home run, and four RBIs, Juan Rivera's three hits and four RBIs, and Matt Kemp's three hits with a double and a home run. Chad Billingsley was the recipient of L.A.'s offensive explosion to record his eleventh win of the season. And the rejuvenated Dodgers finished their season in fine style. Clayton Kershaw won his 20th game of the season on September 20, another 2-1 win over Tim Lincecum, and in so doing he became the first L.A. pitcher in 65 years to beat the Giants five times in a season. Sands home run in the second inning proved to be the game-winner. Kemp, who hit home run number 37 in a 2-0 victory over the San Diego Padres, was 16 for 29 for a .552 batting average during a seven-game hitting streak that included four doubles, four homers, and nine RBIs. And five days later, he powered his 39th home run as Don Mattingly's cohorts closed out the season with a satisfying 7-5 victory over the division leader Arizona Diamondbacks.

The season, that began with a disappointing and frustrating series of mishaps and losses in April, May, and June, ended with a flourish as the team pulled itself out of the cellar and finished in third place. After finding itself fourteen games under .500 in July they went 45-28 from July 7 to the end of the season, giving them hope for a successful 2012. Matt Kemp, who challenged the record books to become the first Triple Crown winner since Ducky Medwick in 1937 fell just short of his goal, finishing third in the batting race with an average of .324, but he still won the home run crown with 39 and the RBI crown with 126. His sensational season was recognized by the baseball community when he was selected as the recipient of the 2011 Hank Aaron Award as the most outstanding offensive player in the National League. He was just the seventh player in major league history to be ranked in the top three for batting average, home runs, runs-batted-in, and stolen bases, joining Hall of Famers Ty Cobb, George Sisler, Honus Wagner, Chuck Klein, Willie Mays, and Hank Aaron. His counterpart in the pitching department, Clayton Kershaw, walked off with the pitcher's Triple Crown, leading the league in victories (21, tied with Ian Kennedy), strikeouts (248), and earned-run-average (2.28). He is the 16th National League pitcher to win the Triple Crown and the first Dodger since Sandy Koufax in 1966. He is also, at 23 years of age, the youngest to win the crown since Dwight Gooden in 1985. Kershaw was also the recipient of the 2011 Warren Spahn Award as the most outstanding left-handed pitcher in the major leagues. Both Kemp and Kershaw were selected for the Sporting News National League All-Star team.

The Los Angeles Dodgers discovered a wealth of young talent in their farm system during the year and added several key veterans to the mix to give them excellent balance up and down their lineup.

Twenty-three year old Clayton Kershaw completed his fourth major league season in 2011. (Los Angeles Dodgers)

And the pitching staff was particularly impressive. During their first half malaise, Dodger hurlers sported a hefty 3.89 earned-run-average, but down the stretch their pitchers held the opposition to a meager 3.02 earned runs per game. Significant contributions were made by Kershaw, Billingsley, Hiroki Kuroda (3.07 ERA), Javy Guerra (2.31 ERA with 21 saves), Kenley Jansen (2.85 ERA), Ted Lilly (3,97 ERA), Scott Elbert (2.43 ERA), Josh Lindblom (2.73 ERA), Dana Eveland (3.03 ERA), and Nathan Eovaldi (3.63 ERA). Matt Kemp needs only to repeat his 2011 performance to be the team leader Don Mattingly expects; Andre Ethier is expected to return to the high average, long ball hitter he was prior to his injury; and James Loney appears to have found the power that has avoided him since he became a major leaguer. In addition to the core of the lineup, the Dodgers also discovered a shortstop in the fleet-footed Dee Gordon (a .304 batting average and 24 stolen bases in 56 games), a possible second baseman in 25-year old Justin Sellers who sported a .993 fielding percentage in 35 games, a left fielder in Juan Rivera who drove in 46 runs in 62 games after joining the Dodgers, and a potential power hitting outfielder in big, 6', 4", 220-pound Jerry Sands who hit several important home runs for Mattingly's crew after his September call-up.

2012—THE DODGERS HAVE NEW OWNERS

The big news in major league baseball in early 2012 was the sale of the Los Angeles Dodgers by Frank McCourt, Jr. to Guggenheim Baseball Management LLC, a group that includes Mark R. Walter, CEO of Guggenheim Capital LLC, Stan Kasten, former President of the Atlanta Braves and the Washington Nationals, and Magic Johnson, the legendary star of the Los Angeles Lakers professional basketball team and a beloved hero in the Los Angeles area. The purchase price was $2.15 billion, 25 percent higher than the next highest bidder, and the highest price ever paid for a North American sports franchise. The purchase price includes the team, the stadium, and the surrounding land.

Mark Walter is the controlling partner of the team. Stan Kasten, who will be the CEO and President of the Dodgers, is a proven winner, having been the architect of the Atlanta Braves dynasty during the 1990's when the team won 14 division titles in 15 years. And Magic Johnson will be significantly involved in Community Relations in L. A., and will assume other responsibilities in the Dodgers day to day operations.

The three most visible members of Guggenheim Baseball Management LLC are all committed to winning in Los Angeles, and sooner rather than later. They are committed to adding key players, if needed, before the June 30, 2012 trading deadline, and they are expected to be a major player in the free agent market at the end of the season. Magic Johnson, for one, has said he will be on the phone with free agents as soon as the market opens.

With sufficient funds and an attitude that emphasizes winning, the future looks bright for the Los Angeles Dodgers.

Magic Johnson in Los Angeles. (AP Images)

"DUSTY" BAKER

Dusty Baker was an important cog in the Los Angeles Dodgers pennant machine from 1976 through 1983. During his eight-year career with Lasorda's crew, the team captured four league championships, three National League flags, and one World Championship.

Born Johnnie B. Baker Jr. on June 15, 1949, in Riverside, California, Dusty was an all-around athlete at Carmichael High School, excelling in baseball, football, basketball, and track. Snatched up by the Atlanta Braves after graduation, the tall, good-looking youngster spent five years riding buses from town to town in the Braves' minor league farm system.

Dusty Baker

When he was finally promoted to the major league team in 1972, Hank Aaron's heir apparent responded with a solid .321 batting average, 17 home runs, and 77 runs batted in. For the next three years, the talented Baker was a solid performer. He could run, throw, field, and hit with power. Unfortunately, he was not Hank Aaron, and the fickle Atlanta fans never let him forget it.

When he was traded to Los Angeles in 1976, it proved to be a rebirth for the six-foot-two slugger. After a year of adjustment, Dusty Baker became a full-fledged star in the Dodger outfield. In 1977, he joined Ron Cey, Steve Garvey, and Reggie Smith as the first quartet of players to hit 30 home runs for the same team in the same season in major league history. Dusty's entrance to the club was quite dramatic, slugging home run number 30 on his last at bat of the season.

In all, Dusty stroked a total of 144 home runs during his Dodger tenure. In 1,117 games, he knocked in 586 runs, with a high mark of 97 in 1980. And he hit with consistency, putting together back-to-back .320 and .300 seasons in 1980 and 1981. He finished his career with the Oakland Athletics in 1986.

His major league career spanned 19 seasons, during which time he batted a solid .278 with 1981 hits, 242 home runs, and 1,013 runs batted in.

Baker was at his best when the National League pennant was on the line. Playing in four post-season playoffs, he boasted a combined batting average of .371, hitting at a .357 pace during the 1977 NLCS, .466 in 1978, .316 in 1981, and .357 in 1983.

He was a star on a team of stars, and his contributions to four league championships were vital to the Dodgers' success.

CHAD BILLINGSLEY

Chad Ryan Billingsley was born in Defiance, Ohio on July 29, 1984. He signed a professional baseball contract with the Los Angeles Dodgers out of Defiance High School in 2003 and received his baptism of fire in organized baseball with Ogden in the Pioneer League that same year, going 5-4 with a 2.83 ERA. The 6', 1", 240-pound right-handed pitcher was put on the fast track by Dodger executives after they witnessed his poise and the command he had of his pitches. He was considered to have the best control and the best curveball in the Dodger farm system. In Ogden he walked only 15 batters in 54 innings to go along with 62 strikeouts. The same pattern followed him to Vero Beach, Jacksonville, and Las Vegas, between 2004 and 2006, although his walk total did increase slightly as he moved from Class-A ball through Double-A and up to Triple-A.

Chad Billingsley (Los Angeles Dodgers)

He started the 2006 season with Las Vegas in the Pacific Coast League, but with the Dodgers battling for a playoff spot and in need of starting pitching, the 21-year old Ohio native was called up to the parent club on June 14. He made his major league debut the following day, pitching 5.1 innings in a no-decision outing and allowing just two runs with three strikeouts. He also drove in two runs with a single in his first official major league at-bat. Billingsley started 16 games during the season with a 3.80 ERA and 59 strikeouts in 90 innings pitched. He was 0-2 at the All-Star break but picked it up down the stretch, winning seven of his last nine decisions. The only blip on the scope was his 58 bases on balls, an average of almost six walks a game. That was considered to be an aberration that he would correct, and the following season he walked just 64 batters in 147 innings. Billingsley started the season with a flourish, going 7-0 to July 23. That day, he tossed his first career complete game, a 10-2 victory over the Houston Astros, and he went on to record a 12-5 won-loss record for the season, with 20 starts, 147 strikeouts, and a 3.80 earned-run-average. The 2008 season was the 23-year old hurler's high-water mark as he reached the pinnacle of pitching excellence, going 16-10 in 201 innings over 35 games with 201 strikeouts and 80 bases on balls. Two of his best games that year were pitched during the heat of the summer. On July 13, he defeated the Florida Marlins 9-1 before a large crowd in Dodger Stadium, throwing seven innings with 13 strikeouts and no walks. That brought his record to 9-8. From there to the end of the season, he went 7-2. On the 30th of July, again in L.A., he threw a complete game shutout at the San Francisco Giants as 41,282 frenzied Dodger fans cheered his every pitch. His 4-0 masterpiece included eight strikeouts, no walks, and just five base hits. Russell Martin's two singles and two RBIs paced the Dodger attack.

Billingsley's career seemed to plateau after the 2008 season. He went 12-11 in 2009 with a 4.03 ERA, 12-11 the following year with a 3.57 ERA, and 11-11 in 2011 with a career-high 4.21 ERA. Manager Don Mattingly believes his big right-hander loses focus during games causing him to give up runs in bunches. He still had some big games over the past three years, most notably an 11 strikeout, no walk, 11-1 shellacking of San Francisco on April 13, 2009, a complete game 2-0 shutout of San Francisco on July 21, 2010, and a 13 strikeout, seven inning no-decision against Arizona on September 26, 2010. Dodger fans are looking for a return of the 2008 Chad Billingsley, or perhaps an improved model, in 2012 and beyond.

FRENCHY BORDAGARAY

Frenchy Bordagaray was a member of Brooklyn's famed "Daffy Dodgers" contingent. He spent six years of his 11 year major league career in the City of Churches, between 1935 and 1945. During his first tour of duty at Ebbets Field, in 1935 and '36, he tortured manager Casey Stengel with his off-beat antics. As noted in chapter 9, in the section "The Daffyness Boys," the zany French Canadian marched to a different drummer. Even though the Brooklyn management had a rule against facial hair, Bordagaray arrived in spring training camp one year sporting a mustache and a goatee. After a short meeting with Stengel, during which time the Dodger manager explained the facts of life to his centerfielder, Bordagaray shaved off the forbidden facial hair.

On the field, Bordagaray was a talented player, when the mood struck him. But, as noted in *The Ballplayers,* edited by Mike Shatzkin, the mood didn't always strike him. "Gifted but erratic, he mixed brilliant plays with bonehead ones. He ran when he wanted, failed to slide when he should have, and ignored signs."

Frenchy Bordagaray

The 5'8", 170-pound right-handed hitter pounded the ball at a .282 clip as a 25-year-old rookie in 1935. The next year, he hit a respectable .315, with 28 extra base hits in 372 at bats, then was traded to the St. Louis Cardinals in the off-season. After spending seven years with the Cardinals, Reds, and Yankees, Frenchy returned home to Brooklyn to stabilize the Dodgers outfield situation during the last three years of World War II. He joined a miscast lot of major league retreads like 42-year-old Babe Herman, and fuzzy-cheeked kids like 16-year-old Tommy "Buckshot" Brown and 17-year-old Eddie Miksis. The old veteran put together averages of .302, .281, and .256 from 1943 through 1945, helping the Dodgers to two third-place finishes. He retired from active duty when the boys returned home from military service.

Frenchy Bordagaray was a decent major league player who compiled a .283 batting average over a successful 11 year career. But in Brooklyn, he will always be remembered as one of the "Daffy Dodgers," a group of lovable losers who made the perennial sixth-place finishes of the 1930s, not only bearable, but enjoyable

RALPH BRANCA

Ralph Branca will always be known as the man who threw "the ball."

But there was a lot more to Ralph Branca than October 3, 1951. The "Hawk," so named because of his prominent nose, broke into professional baseball with Olean in the Pony League in 1943 – at the tender age of 17. Rushed through the Dodger farm system at breakneck speed because of World War II, the big, strapping 6'3" youngster toed the rubber in Ebbets field for the first time one year later.

Blessed with a blazing fast ball, the kid from Mt. Vernon, New York, almost carried the Dodgers to a pennant single-handedly in 1947, winning 21 games at the tender age of 21! He added another victory in the World Series, winning Game Six in relief.

It may be that Ralph Branca pitched too much, too soon. The strain of throwing 280 innings at 21 years of age may have destroyed a great pitching arm. The truth is, he never again matched his 1947 performance. In 1948, the Hawk racked up eight straight victories before the season was two months old. Then the injuries caught up with him, miseries set in and struck him down. He finished the year with a disappointing 14-9 record, and followed it with victory totals of 13, 7, 13, 4, and 0.

For awhile it appeared as if the likable Branca might be on the road back. In 1951, pitching 204 innings in 42 games, the big right-hander showed flashes of his old form as he finished with a 13-12 record and a respectable 3.26 E.R.A. When the Dodgers and Giants finished in a flatfooted tie for the pennant, Branca was rewarded for his

Ralph Branca

fine work by being given the starting assignment in Game One of the three-game playoff by manager Charlie Dressen. He pitched a fine game, only to lose 3-1 on a two-run homer by Bobby Thomson.

Clem Labine snapped Brooklyn out of its doldrums the next day, coasting home an easy 10-0 winner. In Game Three, Dressen handed the ball to big Don Newcombe. Durocher countered with "The Barber," Sal Maglie. The two teams battled on even ground for seven innings; then the Brooks erupted for three big runs in the top of the eighth for an apparent pennant-winning cushion.

Newk retired the Giants in order in the bottom of the eighth, but tired in the ninth, he yielded three hits while retiring only a single batter. Dressen walked slowly to the mound, pondering his pitching selection. He had both Carl Erskine and Ralph Branca warming up in the bullpen. He called for Branca.

The rest is history.

Big Ralph retired in 1956, having compiled a wonloss record of 88-68 over a 12-year period. If talent, heart and courage determined a player's record, Ralph Branca would have been a shoo-in for the Hall of Fame. Unfortunately, luck also comes into play. And The Hawk's luck was all bad.

JIM BREWER

Walter Alston called Jim Brewer the best relief pitcher he ever had. Strong praise indeed from a man who held the reigns of the Brooklyn and Los Angeles Dodgers for 23 years, and who managed such bullpen stalwarts as Hugh Casey, Clem Labine, Mike Marshall, and Ron Perranoski.

Jim Brewer was something special. Born in Merced, California, the easy-going Brewer entered the major league scene in 1960 as a 22-year-old rookie with the Chicago Cubs. His main claim to fame that year was that Billy Martin attacked him on the mound after a close pitch and put him in the hospital with a broken jaw. After two more nondescript seasons in the Windy City, the 6'1" southpaw was dealt away to the Los Angeles Dodgers.

The following year, 1964, on a tip from Warren Spahn, Brewer developed a nasty screwball that eventually turned him into the top relief pitcher in the National League. First, however, he had to pay his dues. He worked as setup man for Ron Perranoski, a job he performed admirably for four years. When Perry was traded to Minnesota after the '67 season, the talented Brewer stepped in to fill the breach.

And fill it he did. In 1968, the slim southpaw appeared in 54 games, compiling an eight and three record with 14 saves and a sparkling 2.49 earned run average. For six years, Jim Brewer answered the call whenever a Dodger starter faltered. His save totals from 1969 through 1973 were 20, 24, 22, 17, and 20. His earned run averages were even more impressive, totalling 2.56, 3.13, 1.89, 1.27, and 3.00.

Jim Brewer had the ideal temperament for a relief pitcher. He was a great competitor, intense yet cool and calm during times of strife. A pleasant man off the field, the screwball pitcher was all business when he stood on the mound staring down at an opposing batter. Although his darting screwball was beaten down into the dirt more often than not, it was also elusive enough to account for

Jim Brewer (Los Angeles Dodgers)

an average of seven Ks for every nine innings pitched over a 17-year career.

The handsome southpaw retired to his home in Broken Arrow, Oklahoma, following the 1976 season. His 17-year record showed 69 wins against 65 losses, with 132 saves and a 3.07 earned run average in 584 games. His 125 saves in Los Angeles was a Dodger record until 1997.

In the fall of 1987, he worked as a coach in the Arizona Instructional League. When the season ended, Brewer packed his bags and headed east, back to Broken Arrow and his family.

He never arrived. The likable relief ace was killed instantly in a head-on automobile collision in Carthage, Texas. The date was November 16, 1987. Jim Brewer was 50 years old.

BILL BUCKNER

Bill Buckner is remembered as the man who made the error in the 1986 World Series.

That is unfortunate, because Bill Buckner was a hardnosed baseball player who gave 110% every time he stepped on the field. There aren't many players today who have Buckner's combination of talent and dedication. As far as the 1986 Series is concerned, it should be remembered that Buckner's error only allowed the New York Mets to tie the Series with the Boston Red Sox, at three games apiece.

In Game Seven, Boston led 3-0 after 5 1/2 innings. The Mets came back to win the game, 8-5, but Buckner didn't blow that one. The Sox pitching staff did.

Bill Buckner

Bill Buckner, a native of Vallejo, California, began his professional baseball career as an 18-year-old first baseman with the Ogden Dodgers of the Rookie Pioneer League in 1968. He advanced to the Los Angeles roster by 1970, along with Bill Russell. By 1973, Buckner was part of a kiddie infield that included Lopes, Russell, and Cey. He was eventually bumped by Steve Garvey, with that quartet forming the all-time longest-running major league infield.

Buckner played the outfield and first base for Alston's crew for eight years, batting a combined .289, with three .300 seasons. He did whatever it took to win, including stealing a base if necessary. He swiped 31 of them in 1974, and 28 in 1976.

The 6'1", 182-pound left-hander was traded to the Chicago Cubs in 1977, for outfielder Rick Monday. He put together eight solid seasons in the Windy City, batting over .300 four times. He captured the National League batting title in 1980 with an average of .324. He also led the league in doubles twice in 1981 (35) and 1983 (38). Then it was on to Boston, where his destiny awaited. Buckner was a major contributor to the Red Sox pennant drive, pounding out 39 doubles, two triples, and 18 home runs, and driving home 102 teammates.

Bill Buckner retired in 1990 after a very productive 22-year career. His statistics included 1,077 runs scored, 2,715 base hits, 721 extra base hits, 1,208 runs batted in, and a .289 batting average. He struck out an average of only 26 times a year. His 2,715 hits is the 40th highest hit total in the history of major league baseball.

Bill Buckner was major league all the way.

"OYSTER" BURNS

The handsome, compact Burns led the Brooklyn Bridegrooms to the National League pennant in their first year in the league. Born Thomas P. Burns on September 6, 1862, in Philadelphia, Pennsylvania, he looked more like an accountant than a ballplayer off the field. Standing only 5'7" tall and adorned with a handlebar mustache, the 183-pound Burns was very distinguished looking when dressed in a morning suit.

On the field however, he was a speedy outfielder with a solid bat. He began his pro career as a Ditcher with Harrisburg in the Interstate League in 1883 After several major league trials with the Baltimore Orioles, Burns' contract was transferred to Brooklyn by Chris Yon der Horst, who owned both clubs. He immediately became a fixture in the Bridegroom outfield.

"Oyster" Burns, who got his nickname by selling shellfish in the off-season, was a crowd favorite in Washington Park. To the colorful residents of Flatbush, he was "Erster Boins," one of their own. Batting in the third position in the batting order, Burns sparked the Grooms to

"Oyster" Burns

the American Association pennant in 1889, batting .315 with 104 runs scored and 100 runs batted in. In the ensuing World Series against the National League champion New York Giants, Burns starred in a losing cause. He hit a three-run home run in the darkness to win Game Four, 10-7, giving the Brooklyn contingent a 3-1 lead in games. That lead didn't hold up, however. New York rallied to win the final five games to take the Series, six games to three. Burns hit another home run in Game Eight, and finished with a team leading 11 RBIs.

In 1890, the Brooklyn Bridegrooms became members of the National League. Proving that their A.A. title was no fluke, the Grooms took the National League flag by six games over Cap Anson's Chicago Cubs. Once again, "Oyster" Bums led the way. He led the league with 13 home runs and 128 RBIs, while crossing the plate 102 times himself. In the ensuing post-season classic against the Louisville Cyclones, the stocky Burns once again led the way, hitting a two-run homer in the top of the first inning of Game One, to spark the Grooms to a 9-0 victory. The seven-game series ended in a 3-3-1 tie, as inclement weather forced the cancellation of additional games.

The stocky outfielder continued to anchor the Brooklyn offense for another four years, hitting around the .300 mark and averaging 83 runs batted in a year. In 1894, at the age of 32, "Oyster" had his last big year, stroking the ball at a .354 clip and driving home 107 runs. His major league career spanned 11 seasons. Over that time, he batted a solid .310 in 1,186 games, with 1,451 hits, 869 runs scored, and 673 RBIs.

Thomas "Oyster" Burns retired in Brooklyn after his playing days were over. He died there November 11, 1928. He was 64 years old.

Brett Butler is one of the outstanding leadoff men in baseball. The star outfielder for the Los Angeles Dodgers has a lifetime on-base percentage of .379, and has averaged 92 runs scored for every 550 at bats, after 17 years of major league competition.

The slightly built left-handed batter has excellent bat control, with an uncanny ability to foul off pitches until he finds one to his liking. His skill at chopping the ball into the ground and beating the infielder's throw to first base has given him dozens of base hits every year. He's picked up another 15-20 hits a year as a result of his bunting skills.

In addition to his offensive strengths, the speedy Butler is one of baseball's top center fielders. His great speed allows him to run down balls that would normally drop for extra bases. He once played 307 consecutive games without an error, and has committed just 41 errors in 5,294 career chances, a .992 fielding average.

Brett Morgan Butler was born in L.A. on June 15, 1957. He made his major league debut with the Atlanta Braves in 1981, after a sensational, three-year minor league career. He joined his hometown team, the Dodgers, in 1991. Over the next six years, he helped Tommy Lasorda's crew to three Western Division championships with his hustling all-around play.

In 1993, the 5'10", 160-pound sparkplug helped lift the Dodgers out of the cellar with a .298 batting average, 80 runs scored, and 39 stolen bases. He handled 375 total chances in center field without an error.

The following year, as L.A. took their first Western Division crown in six years, Butler once again showed the way, rapping the ball at a .314 clip, with a league-leading 9 triples, 79 runs scored, and 27 stolen bases. After signing a free-agent contract with the New York Mets in 1995, he returned to L.A. in a trade on August 18, just in time to help them edge out the Colorado Rockies by a single game in the West.

Butler's 1996 season came to a shocking halt on May 1, when he was stricken with throat cancer. Although his life was in jeopardy and his baseball career was thought to be over, the courageous born-again Christian never gave up. After surgery and a debilitating regimen of radiation treatments, the 39-year-old ballplayer vowed to return to the Dodger lineup before the year ended. Brett Butler kept his promise. He stepped out onto the grass at Dodger Stadium again in full uniform on September 6, just four months after surgery. And, in true Hollywood fashion, he scored the winning run on a sacrifice fly, in the last half of the eighth inning, as the Dodgers nipped the Pittsburgh Pirates, 2-1. Butler's comeback was short lived however. He broke his hand five games later, after being hit by a pitched ball.

The courageous Butler came back one more time, closing out his major league career in fine style. He played a full season in 1997, and batted a solid .283.

Brett Butler was the sparkplug of the Dodger attack from 1991 through 1997. (W. McNeil)

DOLPH CAMILLI

Adolf Louis Camilli was one of the first ballplayers Larry MacPhail obtained when he began to rebuild his Brooklyn Dodger organization. The 5'10", 185-pound first baseman was an established star when MacPhail paid the Phillies $50,000 for his contract. Dolph broke into the National League with the Chicago Cubs in 1933 at the age of 26. The next year he was traded to Philadelphia, where he achieved star status. In 1936, the left-handed slugger hit .315 with 28 homers and 102 RBIs. The next year, his average soared to .339. He drove in 80 teammates with 27 homers, and scored 101 runs himself.

When he arrived in Brooklyn, the Dodgers were a mediocre team, perennial tenants of sixth place. Still, they were better than the cellar dwellers he left. In Dolph's first year in Flatbush, Burleigh Grimes' team was still mired in sixth place, but they were getting better. Camilli was a big reason for the improvement as he slugged 24 home runs, scored 106 runs and drove in another 100 himself. His 119 bases on balls led the league. Over the next two years, the Dodger pennant contender began to take shape. Camilli was joined by veterans Kirby Higbe, Whitlow Wyatt, Dixie Walker, and Joe Medwick,

and rookies "Pee Wee" Reese and Pete Reiser. The team gradually crept up the league ladder, improving their position to third place in 1939, then to second place in 1940.

Camilli followed up his initial Brooklyn success with two more solid years, socking 26 homers with 104 RBIs in 1939, and 23 homers and 89 RBIs in 1940. He once again led the league in bases on balls in 1939 with 110. Both Camilli and the Dodgers were poised to make their move in 1941. It was a great pennant race all summer with Brooklyn and St. Louis laying the groundwork for a rivalry that would last throughout the '40s. The Cardinals won a total of 97 games, but Leo Durocher's crew took the pennant with an even 100 victories, wrapping things up by taking two out of three in St. Louis in mid-September.

The Dodgers received superb performances from many players. "Pistol Pete" Reiser became the youngest batting champion in National League history when he won the crown with a .343 average at the tender age of 22. Joe Medwick hit .313 and Dixie Walker chipped in with a .311 average. On the mound, the Brooks were blessed with two 22-game winners, Kirby Higbe and Whitlow Wyatt.

But it was Dolph Camilli who was the star of stars during the pennant chase. The graceful first baseman led the league with 34 home runs and 120 RBIs. His powerful performance sparked the team to victory after victory, and earned him the National League's Most Valuable Player award for the season. The Dodgers lost the World Series to the powerful New York Yankees in five games, but that defeat could not put a damper on Brooklyn's most exciting season in 21 years.

Dolph Camilli

In 1942, another torrid pennant race ensued, with the Dodgers and Cardinals once again going at it tooth and nail. This time the Gods were against Durocher's crew. After building a big ten-game lead the Dodgers seemed to have the pennant locked up. But the Cardinals were not to be denied. Even though Brooklyn put together one of the greatest seasons in its history, winning 104 games, they still finished two games behind Billy Southworth's fired up crew.

Dolph Camilli once again led Dodger hitters in slugging, as he finished with 26 home runs and 109 runs batted in. That was Dolph's swan song. The following season he was traded to the New York Giants and subsequently retired. Camilli's major league stats showed a total of 239 home runs and 950 runs batted in over a period of 12 years and 1490 games. He hit 20 or more home runs eight times in his career, and drove in over 100 runs five times. He retired with a career batting average of .277.

The Brooklyn-Los Angeles dynasty has endured for more than 50 years since its beginning in the early 1940s. And Dolph Camilli was one of its founding fathers.

ROY CAMPANELLA

Roy Campanella

Roy Campanella, the son of a black mother and an Italian father, was born in Nicetown, an integrated section of Philadelphia, on November 19,1921. Roy was an exceptional high school athlete, especially in track, where he starred in the 100-yard dash. Recruited by the baseball coach to try out for the team, Campy donned the catcher's mask because no one else wanted the job. The rest is history.

The stocky catcher turned professional at the tender age of 15, touring the northeast states with the Bacharach Giants on weekends. He moved up to the Baltimore Elite Giants of the Negro National League in 1937, spending the next nine years there. He developed into one of black baseball's superstars by the time he was 24. Signed by Branch Rickey in 1946, the happy-go-lucky Campanella followed closely in the footsteps of Jackie Robinson as one of the black pioneers of organized baseball. Starting in Nashua, New Hampshire of the New England League, Roy moved on to Montreal, then St. Paul of the American Association, before being brought up to Brooklyn to stay in 1948.

Campanella established himself as a full-fledged major league star immediately. He arrived in Brooklyn from St. Paul on July 2, just in time for a three-game set with the New York Giants. All he did against the hated Giants was collect nine hits in 12 at-bats, including a double, a triple, and two home runs. Brooklyn was in last place when Campy arrived. By Labor Day, they were first.

During his ten-year major league career, Campy won the Most Valuable Player trophy three times, tying a National League record. When healthy, he was a feared .300 hitter, capable of hitting 30 to 40 home runs a year, and driving in over 100 runs. Unfortunately, he was forced to play hurt many years, and his batting average suffered as a result.

Through it all, Roy Campanella was the consummate catcher. He brought an exceptional all-around athletic ability to the game. Even though he was an outstanding hitter, he was an even better defensive catcher. He was one of the best handlers of pitchers in the game, and his squat 5'9" build hid the reflexes of a cat. He was death on high foul balls directly overhead, and on infield grounders he often beat the baserunner to first base, while backing up the play.

Campy's shotgun arm was the talk of the league. During his first two years with Brooklyn, he gunned down 45 of 70 baserunners who attempted to steal, an amazing 64%, once going 51 consecutive games without allowing a stolen base. One day, during an enemy uprising with the bases loaded and no one out, the daring catcher picked two runners off base to end the rally.

Campanella's most unforgettable day in the major leagues was August 26, 1950, in Cincinnati's Crosley Field. Facing left-hander Ken Raffensberger, Brooklyn's slugging catcher deposited three baseballs on the roof of the laundry behind the left-field fence, to drive in six runs in a 7-5 Dodger victory. He often relieved the tension during a tough game with his little boy pranks. Once he poured sand into Willie Mays' shoe while Willie was batting. The Giant center fielder complained loudly to the umpire and to his manager Leo Durocher, while Campy squatted innocently behind the plate and chuckled silently to himself.

Tragically, in the twilight of a memorable career, the Dodger catcher crashed his car into a tree on an icy winter road on Long Island. The accident trapped him in his car for four hours, and left him paralyzed from the neck down. Confined to a wheelchair for the rest of his life, Campanella responded in typical fashion, fighting off the depression and bitterness of his injury, and setting an example in courage for all to follow.

On the night of May 7, 1959, before an exhibition game with the New York Yankees in the mammoth Los Angeles Coliseum, former Dodger captain Pee Wee Reese pushed Campanella's wheelchair onto the playing field as 93,103 appreciative fans stood and applauded the man who gave so much of himself to baseball. It remains the largest crowd ever to witness a major league game.

The courageous and bubbly Dodger catcher, the man who was an inspiration to countless individuals of all ages, ended his valiant fight on June 26, 1993. He died of a heart attack at his home in Los Angeles at the age of 71.

"PARISIAN BOB" CARUTHERS

Robert Lee Caruthers was one of the most versatile players of the nineteenth century. Not only was he was one of the top pitchers in the American Association and the National League year after year; he was also a capable outfielder with a lifetime batting average of .302. It was on the mound, however, where he excelled, compiling a won-loss record of 217-101 over a ten-year period. His winning percentage of .682 is the third highest in baseball history.

Caruthers was 5'10" tall but skinny as a rail, tipping the scales at only 138 pounds in his prime. Not a fastball pitcher, he relied on deception and finesse to stop the opposition: he out-thought them rather than overpowered them. Twice during his short career, the slim southpaw won 40 games, leading the league in victories and winning percentage each time. In ten years he played on five championship teams, three in St. Louis and two in Brooklyn.

"Parisian Bob" Caruthers

Robert Lee Caruthers played the outfield for Cedar Rapids in the Northwestern League as a fuzzy-cheeked 19-year-old. Two years later he was pitching for the St. Louis Browns in the American Association, then a major league. He helped pitch the Browns to three consecutive American Association titles between 1885 and 1887, winning 40 games as a 20-year-old rookie, then following up with seasons of 30 wins and 29 wins. His pitching partner, Dave Foutz, won 33, 41, and 25 over the same period as the Browns' outdistanced the opposition by a minimum of 12 games each year. Eighteen eighty seven was, perhaps, Caruthers' finest season. He won 29 games against only nine losses, leading the league in winning percentage at .742. He also played 59 games in the outfield, hitting a whopping .357 with 23 doubles, 11 triples and eight home runs. And to top it off, he stole 59 bases.

Caruthers was a fun-loving individual who gravitated toward the city night life. He was a devoted card player, a pool shark, and a party man. He picked up his nickname, "Parisian Bob" after a rousing off-season trip to the French capital.

Chris von der Ahe, the schizophrenic owner of the Browns, disregarding his three straight league championships, considered Caruthers to be a bad influence on the team and sold him to the Brooklyn Bridegrooms for $8,250 after the 1887 Series. He sold Foutz for another $13,500. The Browns, after the departure of Caruthers and Foutz, managed one more pennant in 1888, then had to wait 56 years for another.

The 34-year-old lefty helped Brooklyn to a second-place finish in the Association in 1888 by winning 29 games. The following year he won a league-leading 40 games as the Bridegrooms came home two games ahead of the pack. He also led in shutouts with seven. In the post-season classic against New York, won by the Giants six games to three, Caruthers was 0-2 with a 3.75 ERA.

Moving over to the National League for the 1890 season, both Brooklyn and Caruthers showed their Association pennant was no fluke. The Grooms won the National League flag by six games over Chicago with "Parisian Bob" contributing a 23-11 record. The heavy pitching strain of the past six years, however, was beginning to tell on Caruthers arm, and he was unable to play in the World Series as Brooklyn and Louisville battled to a 3-3-1 draw.

In 1891, Caruthers pitched over 300 innings for the seventh consecutive year, but he was losing his effectiveness and his record fell to 17-17. He pitched in only 16 games in 1892, winning two and losing eight with a dead arm. He finished his career as a minor league outfielder in the Western Association in 1896.

"Parisian Bob" Caruthers was like a meteor streaking across the evening sky. He illuminated the heavens in a brilliant glow for a brief instant, then quickly burned out and disappeared from view.

HUGH CASEY

Hugh Thomas Casey was a hard drinking, hard living Irishman. Born in Atlanta, Georgia on October 14, 1913, the tall, blue-eyed Casey grew up a loner, having few friends and preferring it that way. He embarked upon a professional baseball career with his hometown Atlanta Crackers of the Southern Association in 1932. There he came in contact with former Brooklyn Dodgers manager, Wilbert Robinson, then president of the Atlanta team. Robinson took the 6'3" curveballer under his wing, teaching him control and discipline on the mound.

Casey was a starting pitcher in his early days, spending seven uneventful years making the rounds of various minor leagues, with four years being spent in the Southern Association. After compiling a mediocre 13-14 record with the Crackers in 1937, he was bought by Larry MacPhail, who spotted some qualities in the big right-hander that other people missed.

Pitching for Brooklyn in 1939, the 26-year-old rookie won 15 games and lost only 10, as the Dodgers raced home in third place, their highest finish in seven years. The following year, the curve ball artist put together an 11-8 record.

As 1941 unfolded, the Dodgers strengthened their pitching staff by acquiring fireballer Kirby Higbe from Philadelphia. With Higbe, Wyatt, and Curt Davis in the starting rotation, Hugh Casey inherited the closer role in the bullpen, an ideal assignment for him. The tall Southerner had the perfect attributes for a relief pitcher. He was mean and intimidating on the mound. And he was blessed with two outstanding breaking pitches, both of which broke sharply down and away from a right-handed batter. One was a hard slider, the other a slower, wide breaking curve ball.

Casey was an important cog in the Dodger 1941 pennant machine as he appeared in 45 games, winning 14 games and saving another seven. In the World Series he pitched three times, losing two games in spite of a splendid 2.38 ERA. The name Hugh Casey will always be associated with the 1941 Series. It was he who threw the curve ball to Tommy Henrich in the ninth inning of Game Four; the pitch that eluded catcher Mickey Owen and led to a four-run, game-winning Yankee rally.

The big Georgian won six games and saved 13 in 1942, then spent the next three years in the United States Navy, serving his country in the South Pacific. Back from the war in 1946, the 33-year-old Casey picked up where he left off, winning 11 and saving five in 46 appearances.

Hugh Casey, a private man, had few close friends on the Brooklyn team. He was an affable teammate in the clubhouse, although given to periodic fits of anger. When the team was on the road, Casey hung out with Kirby Higbe, his drinking buddy. Most of Hugh's free time was spent in his hotel room, reading western novels, smoking big cigars and drinking whiskey.

Nineteen forty seven was the portly Casey's best season. He trudged in from the bullpen 46 times, compiling a 10-4 record and saving 18 games as Brooklyn's Boys of Summer captured their initial post war pennant. The indefatigable reliever then went on to set a World Series record by appearing in six games, winning two and saving one. He allowed only five hits in 10 innings, in posting a glittering 0.87 earned run average.

Hugh Casey

Casey's career lasted only three more years. He was traded to Pittsburgh following the '48 season, spent a few months with the New York Yankees, then hurled for the Atlanta Crackers one more time, in 1950.

Hugh Casey spent nine years in the major leagues, finishing with an outstanding 75-42 won-loss record. His 51-20 relief record, a winning percentage of .718, is an all-time major league record.

After an unsuccessful comeback with Brooklyn in 1951, the big Southerner returned to Atlanta. Beset with marital problems, and with no visible means of support, the tormented Casey checked into an Atlanta hotel, and there, on the night of July 3, 1951, he put a shotgun into his mouth and pulled the trigger. He was 37.

RON CEY

Ronald Charles Cey, affectionately known as "The Penguin" for his stocky build and waddling gait, held down the hot corner for the Los Angeles Dodgers from 1971 through 1982. During that time, LA won four National League titles and one World Championship. They finished in second place five times. Cey's solid play, both defensively and offensively during that period, earned him the honor of being the all-time Brooklyn-Los Angeles Dodger third baseman, edging out Billy Cox in a close race.

"The Penguin" broke into professional baseball with Tri-City in the Northwest League at the age of 20, leading the league in fielding and RBIs. Progressing systematically through the Dodgers farm system, with stops in Bakersfield, Albuquerque, and Spokane, the talented Cey joined LA to stay in 1973. On June 13 of that year, in the second game of a doubleheader, Ron Cey found himself playing alongside shortstop Bill Russell, second baseman Davey Lopes, and first baseman Steve Garvey for the first time. That combination stayed together as a unit for almost nine years, the longest-running infield in major league history.

Cey quickly established himself in the hearts of the Dodger faithful by his exciting infield play and his long ball power. An outstanding if unspectacular fielder, The Penguin led the league in fielding twice. On offense, he was a major contributor. An excellent low fastball hitter, he could hit the ball out of any park in the league. Ten times he hit 20 or more home runs in a season, with a personal high of 30 in 1977. Twice he knocked in over 100 runs, and three other times he exceeded 90. He was particularly dangerous in the clutch, and could be counted on to drive in the game-winning run if given the opportunity. And he was just as likely to do it with a home run as with a single.

In 1977, the native of Tacoma, Washington had an April to remember. Coming out of the gate like a bolt of lightning, The Penguin carried the Dodgers single-handedly for one solid month. He set a major league record by driving in 29 runs for the month, on the strength of nine homers and a stratospheric .425 batting average.

Four years later, in 1981, Ron Cey and his never-say-die teammates reached the pinnacle of their illustrious careers, going all the way to the World Championship of baseball. Pitted against their arch rivals, the New York Yankees, the Dodgers quickly dropped the first two games of the Series in Yankee Stadium. Then, behind the motivational magic of manager Tommy Lasorda, they fought back to tie the Series at two games apiece in Dodgertown. Cey's three-run homer led the way to a 5-4 Dodger victory in Game Three, and his two RBIs helped salvage an 8-7 win the next day. In the eighth inning of Game Five, the 5'9" fireplug was beaned by a Goose Gossage fastball and left the field on a stretcher.

In typical Frank Merriwell fashion, Cey, suffering from a severe concussion, dragged himself out of his hospital bed, and made his way to Yankee Stadium to be with his teammates. Lasorda, never one to miss a psychological edge, immediately inserted The Penguin into the cleanup slot in the starting lineup. Cey responded brilliantly, igniting a three-run Dodger fifth with a run-scoring single as LA finished off the demolition of the Bronx Bombers with a convincing 9-2 victory. In recognition of his .350 batting average and six RBIs, Ron Cey was voted CO-MVP of the Series, along with Pedro Guerrero and Steve Yeager.

Ron Cey's statistics reflect a solid 16 year-career as one of the finest third basemen in the National League. Six times a National League All-Star, The Penguin played in 2,073 games. Included in his 1868 hits were 328 doubles, 21 triples, and 316 home runs. He drove home 1,139 teammates and scored 977 runs himself.

The sight of the stocky third baseman circling the bases with his straight-legged waddling gait, arms bent, elbows held out away from his body like a bird striving for flight, will be remembered in Dodger Stadium as long as baseball is played there.

"WATTY" CLARK

William Watson "Watty" Clark, a native of St. Joseph, Louisiana, was a capable major league pitcher from the mid 1920s to the mid 1930s. The tall, slender southpaw, a finesse pitcher, usually worked with a large plug of tobacco protruding from his left cheek.

His stock in trade was a capable fastball, a curveball mixture combined with pinpoint control. The crafty Clark seldom beat himself, issuing an average of only two bases on balls per game.

For most of his 12-year career, the six-foot, 175-pound Clark had the misfortune of pitching for second division teams, mostly in Brooklyn. From 1927 through 1936, Clark played on five sixth-place

Ron Cey

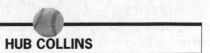

HUB COLLINS

"Watty" Clark (Brace Photo)

teams, one that finished seventh, and another that held down fifth place. The Dodgers finished in the first division only three times during Clark's tenure, never higher than third place.

The hard-working Clark pitched over 200 innings five times in his major league career, leading the National League in innings pitched in 1929 with 279. In spite of the lack of talent on the Dodgers, Clark managed to win in double figures six times. His best year was 1932, when he won 20 games. As the ace of a staff that included Van Lingle Mungo, Dazzy Vance, and Sloppy Thurston, the 30-year-old southpaw propelled Brooklyn into the thick of the pennant race. The team won a total of 81 games before finally succumbing to the superior talents of the pennant-winning Chicago Cubs and the Pittsburgh Pirates. They finished the year in third place, nine games behind Chicago.

Watty Clark won a total of 111 games against 97 losses during his career. He displayed a fine 3.66 earned run average while tossing 206 complete games. It is conceivable that, with a contending ball club, Watty Clark could have been a 200-game winner.

Hub Collins was a fiery little second baseman who stole bases in bunches and covered the ground like no other Dodger second baseman before or since. He was destined to be the greatest second baseman in Brooklyn history before an insidious disease cut him down in the prime of his life. Instead of fame and Hall of Fame recognition he became another of those haunting memories of what might have been.

Hubert B. Collins was born in Louisville, Kentucky, on April 15, 1864. By the time he was 24 years old, the fleet-footed Collins was playing major league baseball for the hometown Louisville Cyclones of the American Association. As fast as greased lightning, Collins covered left field like a shadow, handling 2.7 chances per game in 1888.

Traded to the Brooklyn Bridegrooms midway through the '88 season, the .308 hitter was quickly converted to a second baseman by manager Bill McGunnigle, desperately in need of infield help. He immediately tightened up the Groom inner defense, helping the team jump from seventh place all the way to second. The next two years, the kid from Kentucky sparked the Brooklyn team to successive league championships. Blessed with blazing speed, he excelled both offensively and defensively. In 1889, he batted .286, scored 139 runs, and stole 65 bases. In the field he showed outstanding range by handling an average of 6.2 chances per game. The following year, he led the league in runs scored with 148, finished second in stolen bases with 85, third in doubles with 32, and fourth in bases on balls with 85. His batting average was a solid .278.

Hub Collins

Hub Collins was at his best in post-season play. In two World Series, covering a total of 16 games, he hammered the ball at a .344 clip, with 22 hits including three doubles, a triple and a home run. He also drew 10 bases on balls, scored 20 runs, and stole eight bases. His .371 average in 1889 led the team.

On the brink of a brilliant baseball career, Hub Collins was struck down with typhoid fever four weeks into the 1892 season. He succumbed to the disease on May 21, 1892. He was 28 years old. During his brief seven-year career, the speedy Collins left many indications of what might have been. Playing in only 680 games, Collins scored 653 runs, an average of 0.96 runs per game. This figure is the fourth highest in baseball history, although Collins didn't play enough games to qualify for official recognition. A lifetime .284 hitter, he stole 335 bases during his career, 195 of them with Brooklyn. His stolen base per game average is one of the highest ever recorded. He is fifth on the all-time Dodger list, in spite of the fact that he played in only 407 games in the City of Churches. In the field, his lifetime 6.1 range factor is the best of any Dodger second baseman.

TOMMY CORCORAN

Thomas William Corcoran, a slender, handsome Irishman came out of New Haven, Connecticut, in 1890 to begin his professional career with the Pittsburgh club in the Players League. When the league folded, the 21 year-old shortstop moved to the American Association. It also failed, closing its doors after the '91 season.

The bare-handed fielder caught on with the Brooklyn Bridegrooms in 1892, beginning a distinguished five-year career in Flatbush. Corcoran was a demon in the field, finishing his 18-year career with a 5.63 range factor, #9 all-time. He out-fielded the great Honus Wagner in three of the four years they opposed each other.

Tommy Corcoran

Tommy, or "Corky as he was called by his teammates, loved to hit. The 5'9", 164-pound infielder seldom walked, choosing rather to swing at anything even close to the strike zone. Although he averaged only 24 walks a year, he was a good contact hitter, striking out only 20 times a year. His best year at Brooklyn was 1894, when the pitchers were trying to adjust to the new 60'6" pitching distance. It was a hitter's year and Tommy Corcoran, like most hitters, took advantage of it. He batted .300 for the only time in his career, chipping in with 21 doubles, 20 triples, and five home runs. He set personal highs in runs scored with 123 and RBIs with 92.

His .256 lifetime batting average was deceptive. Corcoran was an aggressive batter and a good clutch hitter. He could be counted on to score 80 runs a year, and drive in another 80. He batted in over 70 runs in nine different seasons.

After playing five years in a Brooklyn uniform, "Corky" was traded to Cincinnati where he excelled at shortstop for ten years, serving as team captain most of that time. He retired in 1907 at the age of 38, having played in 2,200 games with 1,184 runs scored, 2,252 hits, and 1,135 runs batted in.

Tommy Corcoran remained in the game after hanging up his glove as an active player, he became an umpire.

The square-jawed Yankee passed away in Plainfield, Connecticut, in 1960 at the ripe old age of 91.

BILLY COX

Billy Cox has been called the man with the golden glove. He is Brooklyn's all-time third baseman, the keeper of the hot corner for the "Boys of Summer."

There is a story about Casey Stengel that defines Billy Cox's rightful place in baseball history. During a spring training Game One year, Stengel yelled out to Brooks Robinson, "You're the second greatest third baseman of all time". "Who's the best?" puzzled Brooks. "Number Three over there in Brooklyn", was the reply. "He was the best of all time." Stengel should know. He saw every major league third baseman from 1910 through 1975, a period of 65 years.

Born in Newport, Pennsylvania, the wiry little infielder came up to the Pittsburgh Pirates as a 22-year-old shortstop in 1941, playing ten games at the end of the season. Within months he found himself in the United States Army and, for the next four years, he tramped through the sands of Africa and the mud of Sicily and Italy, enduring the many hardships and horrors of war. Stricken with malaria and battle fatigue, the 5'10" Cox returned home a 130-pound skeleton. He never fully recovered his health.

Billy Cox

Billy Cox was the premier third baseman in the major leagues from 1948 through 1954, although his career was severely limited by nagging health problems. In addition to recurrent attacks of war-induced battle fatigue and malaria, Cox was injury prone. Problems with his back, his arm, and his leg kept him out of the lineup for extended periods of time. During his seven years in Brooklyn, he never came to bat more than 455 times in any one season, and only once played in more than 119 games.

A healthy Billy Cox would have enjoyed a long, distinguished career and most likely would have earned a permanent niche in baseball's Hall of Fame. Compared to his American League counterpart, Brooks Robinson, Cox had better range and a stronger arm. There has not been another defensive third baseman like him. As Roger Kahn so aptly put it, Billy Cox was "the most glorious glove on the most glorious team that ever played baseball in the sunlight of Brooklyn."

In 1946, Cox became the regular Pirate shortstop. After two successful seasons in Pittsburgh, during which time he hit .290 and .274 and fielded like a demon, he was traded to the Brooklyn Dodgers along with his roommate, Preacher Roe. It turned out to be the best trade ever made by Branch Rickey, as Cox and Roe combined to help the "Boys of Summer" snatch three pennants in six years, finishing second twice and third once.

Nicknamed "Horse" because of his long narrow face and sad eyes, the 28-year-old infielder was moved to third base by Dodger manager Leo Durocher. He immediately became a hot corner legend with the glove. When his buddy Preacher Roe pitched, Cox would tell him, "Let 'em hit it to ole Hoss, Preach. I'll snip it for ya." Cox didn't field the ball smoothly like most infielders. He was blessed with great hands and outstanding reflexes, and he would snatch at the ball rather than taking it in one fluid motion. Once he had it, he would hold it for what seemed an eternity, studying the seams, before throwing it to first. In spite of the fact that Cox had a cannon for an arm, his shortstop companion, Pee Wee Reese, would constantly implore him to get rid of the ball. Cox would just glance at Reese, smile, and say, "Ole Hoss has got 'im." And he did.

Although he was only a .262 lifetime hitter, the 150-pound third baseman was a dangerous man with the bat. In three World Series, he stroked the ball at a .302 clip. His brightest hour occurred in the 1953 Series when he led the Dodgers with six RBIs. He smashed three doubles and a home run in six games. His fielding performances against Casey Stengel's Yankees caused the Old Professor to complain, "He's not a third baseman, he's a blankety-blank acrobat."

ROGER CRAIG

The Brooklyn Dodgers won only one World Championship in their 66-year National League tenure. In 1955, they ran off 22 victories in their first 24 games, en route to a convincing pennant run. But, in midsummer, they did have some moments of concern when their almost insurmountable lead began to disappear. When that happened, manager Walter Alston beckoned two right-handed pitchers from the Dodgers' wealthy minor league system. Don Bessent and Roger Craig righted the Brooklyn ship, with Bessent going 8-1, with two saves, in 24 games, and Craig winning five games against three losses, also with two saves, in 21 games.

Both pitchers also made valuable contributions to the Dodgers' World Series triumph. Bessent appeared in three games in relief, without allowing a run. Roger Craig appeared in only one game, but it was a key to the championship. The master of the split-fingered fastball started game five, with the Series deadlocked at two games apiece. He proceeded to shut down the mighty New York Yankees on two runs over six innings, leaving with a 4-2 lead. Dodger closer Clem Labine made it hold up for a big 5-3 victory.

Roger Craig pitched for the Dodgers, in both Brooklyn and Los Angeles, for seven years. In 1956, he won 12 games against 11 losses, as the Dodgers repeated as National League champs. After two sub-par years, he bounced back to win 11 games against only 5 losses, with a sparkling 2.06 earned run average, for the Los Angeles entry, as Walter Alston's boys won another World Championship.

Roger Craig

The tall 6'4", 190-pound right-hander went 8-3 in 1960, then slipped to 5-6 the following year. The years 1962 and 1963 are two years Roger Craig would rather forget. As the ace of Casey Stengel's pathetic New York Mets (losers of 120 games against only 40 victories), he took the brunt of the shellackings handed out to the expansion team day after day. He led the National League in losses both years, going 10-24 in 1962 and 5-22 in 1963.

Fortunately he was rescued by the St. Louis Cardinals in '64, winning 7 games for the World Champions, and picking up a critical victory with 4 2/3 innings of stellar relief in game four of the Series, as the Cardinals rallied from a 3-0 deficit to capture the game, 4-3.

Roger Craig's major league career came to an end after the 1966 season, but he continued to play a vital role in the dugout, managing both the San Diego Padres and San Francisco Giants over a 10-year period. He won two division titles with the Giants, and one National League flag.

WILLIE CRAWFORD

Willie Crawford first put on a Los Angeles Dodger uniform in 1964, before he was old enough to shave. The 17-year-old phenom signed a $100,000 bonus contract out of L.A.'s Fremont High School, as both the Dodgers and Willie, were hoping he was a future superstar. But such was not the case. Willie Murphy Crawford was a hard working, talented baseball player, who could intimidate minor league pitchers, but in the majors, he just couldn't get untracked.

The big, 6'1", 205-pound left-handed slugger tormented California League pitchers with a .326 batting average in 1964. Two years later, he pounded out 20 doubles, a league leading 14 triples, and 15 home runs in 140 games, with Albuquerque. In 1967, he hit .305 with 21 homers with the Dukes and, in '68, he batted .295 for Spokane.

Willie Crawford became a Los Angeles regular in 1968, at 21 years of age, and with four years of professional baseball already behind him. The speedy outfielder appeared in 61 games with the Dodgers, hitting .251 in 175 at bats. Except for a .281 season in 1972, his average never exceeded .251 during his first five years in L.A. He was still only 25 years old.

Willie Crawford (Los Angeles Dodgers)

In 1973 Crawford spanked the ball at a .295 clip with 14 home runs and 66 RBIs in 457 at bats and, the next year, he helped Walter Alston's club win the National League pennant, by hitting .295 again, with 11 homers and 61 runs batted in. The handsome Californian saw action in three games in the World Series against the Oakland Athletics, pinch hitting in two games and starting in right field in another. His big thrill came in game 3 when he hit a ninth inning home run into the right field stands in the Oakland Coliseum.

Willie Crawford was traded to the St. Louis Cardinals in 1976, hitting .304 in 120 games. After a disappointing year with the Houston Astros and Oakland Athletics in 1977, during which he hit a paltry .216 in 101 games, he retired from the game. His career totals show a .268 batting average, with 921 base hits and 86 home runs, over a 14 year career.

JAMES CREIGHTON

James Creighton was the star pitcher for the Brooklyn Excelsiors during the mid-1800s. The handsome, slightly built right-handed hurler was the games first celebrity, and its first bonafide superstar.

Born in Brooklyn, New York, in 1841, Creighton was a star cricket player as well as an outstanding baseball player during his youth. Blessed with a blazing fast ball, he had an imperceptible, and illegal, snap to his wrist as he released the ball, causing it to move at an incredible velocity. As a result, he was almost unhittable at the official pitching distance of 45 feet, even though he had to throw the ball underhand.

As a 17-year-old phenom, he was recruited by the Brooklyn Excelsiors, one of the top amateur baseball clubs in existence. Two years later, in 1860, the Excelsiors became the first baseball team to embark on a road trip. During that summer, they toured New York State from Albany to Buffalo, as well as parts of Pennsylvania, Maryland, and Delaware. Wherever they went, large posters were prominently displayed on poles and trees, as well as in store windows, announcing their playing date. The circulars also proclaimed that Excelsior star James Creighton would pitch.

Fans flocked to the games by the thousands to see their local heroes do battle with the great Creighton and his teammates. The scores were usually high scoring, such as their 50-19 crushing of the highly regarded Buffalo Niagaras. Regardless of the opponent, the outcome was always the same, an Excelsior victory. In all, the Brooklyn contingent played 15 games on their highly publicized tour. James Creighton pitched in every game, and the team won them all. Their visits and their skillful performances did much to advance the popularity of baseball throughout the eastern part of the country.

James Creighton was the idol of baseball fans everywhere from 1858 to 1862. Handsome, single, and a powerful hitter as well as a star pitcher, the athletically built Creighton was adored by young girls from New York to Ohio. Unfortunately, the young man's celebrity was short lived. During a match with the Unions of Morrisania in Brooklyn on October 14, 1862, the 21-year-old pitcher suddenly collapsed while batting. Suffering from an internal injury, he was carried to his home at 307 Henry Street, where he died four days later. The Brooklyn Eagle, in reporting his demise, said that "Creighton was familiar in baseball and cricket circles as one of the best players in the Union."

He was buried in Greenwood Cemetery, his grave marked by a large, gaudy, granite tombstone erected by his teammates. The stone contained carvings of many baseball articles, including two crossed bats, a base, a baseball cap and a scorebook. Above all was the single word, "Excelsior." The stone was crowned with a granite baseball.

James Creighton (Transcendental Graphics)

"CANDY" CUMMINGS

William Arthur "Candy" Cummings is regarded as the inventor of the curveball, the most significant innovation in the game of baseball during the 19th century. The entire truth behind the development of the revolutionary pitch is clouded in mystery, with several people laying claim to the discovery, but on the strength of testimony by contemporary baseball experts like Henry Chadwick, credit for the invention was given to William A. Cummings. Election to the Baseball Hall of Fame, in 1939, was his ultimate reward.

Candy Cummings was born in Ware, Massachusetts, on Boston's south shore on October 18, 1848. As a youth, Cummings spent many summer days frolicking on the beaches near his home. It was on one such day that Cummings claims to have invented the curveball while scaling clamshells out into the water. According to Cummings, the different trajectories on the shells, caused by variations in his throwing motion, stirred a curiosity within the teenager. He soon began to wonder if a similar phenomenon could be transmitted to a baseball.

"Candy" Cummings (Transcendental Graphics)

Cummings was hardly the image of the ideal baseball player. Standing 5'9" tall, he weighed a scant 120 pounds, his sparrow-like legs seemingly unsuitable for supporting his upper torso. Still, he was a good baseball pitcher and played with the highly regarded Brooklyn Excelsiors during the late 1860s. One day in 1867, the Excelsiors traveled to Boston to engage the Harvard baseball club. The tall, skinny Cummings, having spent four years developing his trick pitch, unveiled it against the unsuspecting Harvards.

Much to his surprise and glee, many of the Harvard batters were unable to make contact with the new pitch. Over the next few years, he kept perfecting his execution and improving his control of the pitch. By 1870 he was considered by many baseball men to be the best pitcher in country. It was during this time that he acquired the nickname "Candy," 19th century slang for "the best."

As professional baseball was born, the highly regarded Cummings became one of its first stars. Playing for the New York Mutuals of the National Association in 1872, "Candy" was one of the league's top pitchers. Playing for four different teams over a period of four years, he strung together won-loss records of 33-20, 28-14, 2826, and 35-12. When the National League came into existence in 1876, Cummings moved to the new league as a member of the Hartford Blues.

His 18 and 6 record helped the Blues to a third-place finish, and his .750 winning percentage was fifth best in the league. On September 9 of that year, "Candy" Cummings became the first professional pitcher to hurl both ends of a doubleheader. As it turned out, that was his swan song. The following year, playing for the last place Cincinnati Red Stockings, the curve ball specialist won only five games against 14 losses.

During the 1877 season, realizing his pitching skills had deteriorated, the 29-year-old hurler accepted the position of President of the International Association, the first minor league. He pitched briefly but ineffectually for several teams in the IA over the next two years, finally hanging up his glove for good in 1878 after compiling a record of 1-11.

The baseball pioneer passed away in Toledo, Ohio, in 1924 at the age of 75.

TOM "TIDO" DALY

During the last decade of the 19th century, the Brooklyn Bridegrooms spent most of their days mired deep in the second division. Plagued by a thin and ineffective pitching staff and burdened with a mediocre offense, the Grooms struggled against overwhelming odds to taste the rarified air of the first division. One of their few strengths was their double-play combination of shortstop Tommy Corcoran and second baseman Tom Daly.

Thomas Peter Daly, nicknamed "Tido," was one of the finest second baseman in Brooklyn history. Born in Philadelphia in 1866, the 5'7" Daly broke into the National League in 1887 as a catcher with the Chicago White Stockings. He was rated as a good defensive catcher, but his weak throwing arm kept him from becoming a first-string receiver. After bouncing around the league for three years, Daly finally found himself in Brooklyn. In 1892, after the untimely death of second baseman Hub Collins, Daly was chosen as his replacement. It turned out to be the perfect move; negating his weak arm and utilizing his great range and his solid bat.

Tido Daly was an outstanding all-around second baseman. He had excellent range; his 6.0 range factor being #9 on the all-time list. He holds the Dodger all-time season and lifetime range factor records with 6.3 and 6.0 respectively. Early in his career, he led the league in errors, but once he learned his position, he became one of the best. Twice he led the league in range factor, in 1899 and again in 1901. He also led in double plays in 1899.

Tom "Tido" Daly

It was on offense, however, where Tido Daly excelled. He was an outstanding hitter, averaging .305 during the nine-year period from 1893 through 1901. Hitting from the fifth spot in the Brooklyn lineup, Daly was especially tough with men in scoring position, driving in an average of 81 runs per year. His bat-handling prowess seemed to increase with age, as he hit .329, .313, .312, and .315 during his last four years in Brooklyn. He led the league in doubles with 38 at the age of 35. The following year he was traded to Chicago, retiring in 1903 after hitting .293 for Cincinnati in 80 games.

The switch-hitting second baseman enjoyed his finest season at the plate in 1894 when his bat sizzled to the tune of .341. His 40 extra base hits drove in 82 teammates, and he scored another 135 runs himself. And just to prove he was no slouch on the basepaths, the 170-pound speedster swiped a career-high 52 bases. He is #9 on the all-time Dodger stolen base list, and #59 in baseball history.

Tido Daly is a rarity in Dodger baseball lore. While in Brooklyn he played on three pennant winners – and he never lost a World Series. In 1890, as a backup catcher, Daly played in the 3-3-1 series with the Louisville Cyclones. Nine years later, the tough little second baseman hit a solid .313, knocked in 88 runs and stole 43 bases as the Brooklyn team, now known as the Superbas, finished eight games ahead of the Boston Beaneaters. There was no World Series that year. In 1900, Daly once again contributed to a Flatbush pennant parade. His .312 batting average was third on the team behind Keeler and Kelley, although he was limited to 97 games because of injuries. He came back to play in the Chronicle-Telegraph Cup Series against Pittsburgh, won by Brooklyn, three games to one.

During his 16-year major league career, Tido Daly batted .278, amassing a total of 1,582 hits in 1,564 games. He scored 1,024 runs, drove in another 811, and stole 389 bases. After his playing days were finished, Daly managed in the minor leagues for years, then became a scout for the New York Yankees and the Cleveland Indians. He died in Brooklyn at the age of 73.

"GENTLEMAN JAKE" DAUBERT

Throughout their history, the Dodgers have been noted for their slick-fielding first basemen. Modern fans recall the likes of Gil Hodges, Ron Fairly, Wes Parker and Steve Garvey; but the first of Brooklyn's defensive magicians was a slim, graceful acrobatic first baseman named Jacob Elsworth Daubert.

Jake Daubert was born in Shamokin, Pennsylvania, in the heart of coal country, on April 17, 1884. His father and two brothers spent their lives in the mines and, when he was 11 years old, young Jacob joined them. But his heart wasn't into coal mining. His ambitions lay elsewhere, on the local baseball fields where he excelled, first as a pitcher, then as a first baseman. By the time he was 23 years old, Jake was good enough to turn pro, and he signed a contract with Kane in the Inter-State League. Three years later, after hitting a solid .314 for Memphis in the Southern League, the slim, left-handed hitting Daubert was drafted by the Brooklyn Superbas to replace Tim Jordan, the National League home run leader who was forced into retirement by knee injuries.

Along the way, Jake Daubert acquired the moniker "Gentleman Jake" because of his quiet leadership and his well-dressed demeanor. Intelligent, unassuming, and stylish, the Dodger first baseman added a touch of class to a blue-collar team from a blue-collar town. Starting his career in the cozy confines of Washington Park, he quickly emerged as a steadying influence in the infield and one of the top hitters on the team. In his second year, he blossomed into a solid .300 hitter, stinging the ball at a .307 clip.

"Gentleman Jake" Daubert

In 1916, the pride of Pennsylvania then captain of the team, sparked the Robins to their first pennant in 16 years, leading the league in fielding with a .993 average, and stroking the ball for a .316 average. The Brooklyn front office, however, still smarted from their star's exorbitant salary demands and, when the situation arose, they shuttled him off to Cincinnati in a highly publicized trade for Tommy Griffith. His last year in Brooklyn, Daubert led the league in triples with 15.

Jake Daubert was a shining star in the early history of the Brooklyn Dodgers. A lifetime .303 hitter, he amassed a total of 2,326 hits, including 165 triples, over a 15-year career. His 19,634 putouts at first base places him in seventh place on the all-time major league list. He was the greatest first baseman in Brooklyn history during its first 60 years in the National League, and second only to Gil Hodges as Brooklyn's all-time best.

TOMMY DAVIS

In good times or in bad, Jake Daubert was a solid performer. The perfect second-place hitter, he could do it all with the bat. His ball placement on hit-and-run plays was impeccable, and his unselfish nature resulted in a league-leading 392 sacrifice hits during his career. Playing during the dead ball era, one run often meant the ball game, and Daubert was always ready to give himself up for the good of the team. But if the situation warranted it, the smooth-swinging lefty could send a line drive up the gap as well as anyone. At 160 pounds, he was not a long-ball hitter, but his consistent performance at the plate kept the offense moving, setting the table for Stengel and Wheat to drive in the winning runs.

In the field, Daubert had no equals. His dazzling infield play set the standard for all first basemen. In 1912, he led the league in fielding with a mark of .993. The following year, 1913, Charlie Ebbets opened his new modern stadium, Ebbets Field, and Jake Daubert christened it with a flourish. He had a career season at the plate, winning the batting title with an average of .350 and carrying off the coveted Chalmers Award as the most valuable player in the National League.

He repeated as the batting champ in 1914, stinging the ball at a .329 clip. In the field, his eight errors were the fewest in the league, while his .993 fielding average was second only to Ed Konetchy. Jake Daubert was firmly entrenched as the premier first baseman in the National League. After threatening to jump to the new Federal League in 1914, Daubert became the league's first superstar, corralling a salary of $9,000 a year for five years, a figure that was five to seven times the normal salary.

Tommy Davis, better known as "T.D.," may have been the purest hitter ever to grace a Dodger uniform. The Brooklyn native entered professional baseball in 1956, a fuzzy-cheeked 17-year-old high school star full of wide-eyed enthusiasm and unlimited talent. Not only was he a solid line drive hitter with power, but he had blazing speed to boot and was an outstanding defensive outfielder.

Playing in 43 games for Hornell in the Pony League in his pro debut, the 6'2" 195-pound slugger was an immediate success, stinging the ball at a .325 clip. The following year, in Kokomo, Indiana, he dominated the Midwest League's offensive statistics, leading in runs (115), hits (185), total bases (251), stolen bases (68), and batting average (.357). Then, after a .304 season with Victoria, T.D. capped off his minor league career with another batting title, hitting .345 at Spokane and leading the top minor league with 211 hits and 315 total bases as well.

The handsome right-handed hitter was promoted to Los Angeles in 1960, spending the next two years trying to break into the regular lineup. When he finally established himself as the team's left fielder in 1962, Davis carried the Dodgers to within three outs of the pennant with his sizzling bat. At 23 years old, he became one of the youngest batting champions in National League history, winning the title with an average of .346. His league-leading 230 hits are second only to Babe Herman's 241 in Dodger history, while his 153 RBIs, the most in the National League in 25 years, remain an all-time Dodger record.

Tommy Davis became the youngest player in National League history to win back-to-back batting titles when he captured the championship again in 1963 with an average of .326. He stayed hot during the World Series, batting .400 with two triples as the Dodgers raced to an historic four-game sweep of the New York Yankees.

After an off year offensively, tragedy struck the sensational youngster early in 1965. Sliding into second base in an attempt to break up a double play against San Francisco, Davis' spikes caught in the dirt, shattering his right ankle, and sidelining him for the season. Coming back in 1966, the Brooklyn native showed he had not lost his batting eye by smashing the ball at a .313 clip, but he never regained his quickness afoot, becoming a liability both on the bases and in the field.

He was traded to the New York Mets in 1967; then made the circuit of eight other teams over the next ten years, serving as a designated hitter and a pinch hitter. When he finally retired in 1976, Tommy Davis had compiled the highest pinch-hitting batting average in major league history, .320, with 63 hits in 197 pinch hitting appearances. He played a total of 18 years in the Big Leagues, finishing with a career .294 batting average, 1,052 RBIs and 136 stolen bases. His 2,121 hits included 272 doubles, 35 triples and 153 home runs. T.D. batted over .300 six times, three of them with the Dodgers, where he compiled a lifetime batting average of .304 during his eight-year Los Angeles career.

Tommy Davis

Tommy Davis is still a member of the Dodger family, working for their Community Services Team to foster good community relations throughout the California area. He is also the resident expert batting instructor at the Dodgers Adult Baseball Camp in Vero Beach, Florida, where he passes his hitting philosophy on to his middle-aged students. "Snap your wrists. Follow through. Keep your head on the ball. You've got to sit to hit."

He should know. Tommy Davis could always hit.

WILLIE DAVIS

For 17 years, Willie Henry Davis was the fastest man in baseball. The lithe, 6'1" 185-pound speedster was a blur on the bases, and he covered centerfield like a frightened fawn. Born in Mineral Springs, Arkansas on April 15, 1940, Willie broke into professional baseball at the age of 19, and immediately set the minor leagues on its ear. Playing for Reno of the California League in 1959, the young gazelle led the league in five categories; runs (135), hits (187), doubles (40), triples (16), and batting average (.365). Moving up to Spokane of the Pacific Coast League, Davis was voted the minor league player of the year, leading the league in runs (126), hits (216), triples (26), stolen bases (30), and batting average (.346).

The following spring, Manager Walter Alston brought the 20-year-old Arkansas flash up to the big club, where he became a center field fixture for the next 14 years. Willie was always an outstanding defensive outfielder and an electrifying baserunner, but he had his ups and downs as a major league hitter, particularly during the first half of his career. During his first nine years in L.A., the "man of a thousand stances" often looked confused at the plate, changing his batting stance almost as often as he changed his socks. From 1960 through 1968, Willie Davis compiled a mediocre .265 batting average, mixing solid .284 seasons with such pitiful totals as .238 and .245.

Then, in 1969, at the age of 29, the slender left-handed hitting outfielder made a complete turnaround. He found a permanent batting stance and proceeded to drive the ball with authority. His final five years in L.A. showed averages of .311, .305, .309, .289, and .285. After 14 years of service with the Dodgers, Willie Davis left many vivid memories. In 1969, the "new" Davis put together a 31 consecutive-game hitting streak, the longest streak in the major leagues in 24 years and an all-time Dodger record. Of his 154 Dodger career home runs, five were of the electrifying inside-the-park variety, including one on a ground ball over first base! Willie holds Los Angeles Dodger career records in at bats (7,495), runs (1,004), hits (2,091), triples (110), total bases (3,094), and extra base hits (585). He is second in games

Willie Davis with "The Boss," Peter O'Malley.

played, RBIs, and doubles, third in stolen bases, fourth in home runs, and 10th in batting average (.279).

There was one embarrassing incident in Davis' career that will never die. In the 1966 World Series against the Baltimore Orioles, Willie made three errors in one inning; two on successive dropped fly balls and a third on a wild throw. Those miscues sent three runners across the plate and saddled Sandy Koufax with the loss in his final major league appearance.

Willie Davis played 18 years in the major leagues, finishing with a total of 2,561 base hits, 1,053 RBIs, 398 stolen bases, and a batting average of .279.

In Los Angeles and other Dodgers way stations, he will always be part of Dodgers lore. It will be Willie, hat off, outrunning a long fly ball. Or Willie, a blue blur racing from first to third in the cool California night air. Or Willie, a bemused batter trying out a new batting stance in hopes of breaking out of a prolonged slump. Sometimes called "three dog" because of his uniform number, his speed, and his penchant for greyhound racing, Willie Henry Davis will always be remembered fondly as one of the most exciting players ever to wear Dodger blue.

DON DRYSDALE

Overpowering stuff, blazing fast, and mean as a junkyard dog. That could well have been Don Drysdale's major league epitaph. Born Donald Scott Drysdale in Van Nuys, California, on July 23, 1936, the big right-hander soon grew into an oversized kid and a star athlete.

By 1956, "Big D" stood 6'6" tall, weighed 208 pounds, and was a 19-year-old major league pitcher with the Brooklyn Dodgers of the National Baseball League. He quickly established himself as one of the most dominating pitchers in the league, as well as the most feared. Don Drysdale, an affable giant off the field, was mean and nasty when he toed the rubber. He threw a 90-mile-an-hour fastball, and he delivered it with a sidearm buggywhip motion seemingly from the third base dugout. In addition, he felt as if the plate was his personal property, and he was not averse to using a brush back pitch on anyone who moved too close to it. Many a terrified batter found himself on the seat of his pants after an encounter with "Big D," some of them nursing big red welts. Over a 14-year career, the big Californian set a major league record by hitting 154 batters, one every 22 innings.

In conjunction with Sandy Koufax, he gave the Dodgers one of the great pitching combinations in major league history. He was known for always pitching tough, although the Dodgers of the early sixties did not always give him much run support. He may well have lost more 1-0, 2-1, and 3-2 games than any other pitcher. But he always kept the Dodgers in the game. Beginning in 1967, "Big D" won 17,12,17,15,13,25,19,18,23,13,13, and 14 games. His

14 year career showed a record of 209 wins and 166 losses. He struck out 2,486 batters and had an excellent 2.95 earned run average. He was also a workhorse on the mound. Over a 12-year period he averaged 40 starts and 273 innings pitched per year. He threw more than 300 innings four years in a row.

In 1957, the 21-year-old Drysdale put together a record of 17-9 with a 2.69 ERA. Five years later, he had a career season, finishing 25-9, and 2.84. He led the league with 314 innings pitched, 25 victories, and 233 strikeouts, and was the recipient of the Cy Young Award as the major league's best pitcher. The big Dodger right-hander won 20 games again in 1965, compiling a glossy 23-12 record. In 1968, he capped his magnificent career by throwing 58 consecutive shutout innings, breaking Walter Johnson's 55-year-old record. The streak included a record six consecutive shutouts.

Don Drysdale

Don Drysdale was just as tough in the World Series as he was during the regular season. He appeared in four post-season classics, with a 3-3 won-loss record, and a sparkling 2.95 earned run average. In 1963, as the Dodgers finished off the Yanks in four straight, Big Don won Game Three, 1-0, with a three-hit masterpiece. He would later refer to it as the best game he ever pitched. His catcher, John Roseboro, said, "He was one of the most complete pitchers I've seen. He was determined, aggressive, mean, stable."

In eight All-Star Games, Drysdale pitched 19 innings, fanned 19 batters, had a 2-1 won-loss record and a 1.40 ERA.

In addition to his pitching prowess, Big D was an excellent fielder and an awesome hitter. He holds the Dodger season record for home runs by a pitcher with seven, a total he reached twice during his career. He also leads Dodger pitchers in five other season hitting categories, including at bats, runs, hits, triples, and runs batted in. He led National League pitchers in home runs four times, finishing with a career total of 29, second only to Warren Spahn's National League record of 35.

In 1984, Donald Scott Drysdale was elected to Baseball's Hall of Fame in Cooperstown, New York. Nine years later, on July 3, 1993, while serving as a sportscaster for the Los Angeles Dodgers, Don Drysdale suffered a fatal heart attack in a Montreal hotel room. He was 56 years old.

The sight of Don Drysdale standing on the mound, staring in for a sign, struck fear in the hearts of many a National League batter. Big D was big and mean, and his buggywhip sidearm motion intimidated the most fearless hitters. As one notable opponent put it, "The trick is to hit Drysdale before he hits you."

CARL ERSKINE

When the names of the guttiest players ever to play for the Dodgers are bandied about, Carl Erskine's name will be near the top of the list.

Carl Erskine pitched for the Dodgers for 12 years, most of them in constant pain. The slightly built right-hander hurt his pitching arm during the 1951 season and never fully recovered. He pitched with a knot the size of a golf ball behind his right shoulder most of the time, unable to throw much between starts, and forced to endure the pain of stretching out the injury on game day. His roommate, Duke Snider, marvelled at the courage exhibited by the little right-hander.

Erskine's stock in trade was the overhand curve ball, better known as a drop in the old days. He also owned the best change of pace in the league, plus a "sneaky" fast ball. During his 12 year career with the Dodgers, most of them in Brooklyn, he posted a won-loss record of 122-78, a winning percentage of .610. In 1953 he won 20 games against only six losses, leading the league with a winning percentage of .769. He won 18 games in 1954, 16 games in 1951, 14 in 1952, and 13 in 1956. The Brooklyn fans loved their little pitcher, yelling their support from the stands as only they could do. "We're witcha Oisk." Stick it in his ear Oiskin."

"The Master of the Overhand Curveball" played on six pennant winning teams in twelve years, five with Brooklyn and one with Los Angeles. He won a World Championship ring in each city, winning two games and losing two. His two victories were Series masterpieces. In 1952, pitching against the New York Yankees in Yankee Stadium, "Oiskin" took a 4-0 lead into the fifth inning,

only to see the Bronx Bombers fight back with five big runs. Three singles, a walk, and a Johnny Mize home run did the damage. A lesser pitcher would have quit right there, but the tough little Hoosier just sucked it in and went back to work.

Two innings later, his roomie Snider tied the game with his second homer of the game. Erskine threw goose eggs at the Yanks in the 6th, 7th, 8th, 9th, and 10th innings, retiring the side in order each time. In the Dodger 11th, a Duke Snider double scored Cox with the go-ahead run. Erskine then proceeded to nail down the hard-fought victory by retiring Mantle, Mize, and Berra, 1-2-3, striking out the dangerous catcher to end it. After Mize's home run in the fifth, the Dodger hurler retired the last 19 batters.

In 1953, the Brooklyn righty threw a World Series gem, defeating Yankee ace Vic Raschi in a great pitchers' duel, 3-2.

The Dodgers won the game on an eighth-nning home run by Roy Campanella, but it was Erskine's pitching that was the talk of the town. He broke Howard Ehmke's 24-year-old World Series strikeout record by fanning 14 New Yorkers enroute to the victory. The great Mickey Mantle went down on strikes four times, as did first baseman Joe Collins.

Carl Erskine

In spite of his World Series achievements, Carl Erskine's greatest pitching performances were reserved for the regular season. He pitched two no-hit games during his career, the first coming within a hair of a perfect game. It took place in Ebbets Field against the Chicago Cubs on June 19, 1952, under threatening skies. In his hurry to complete five innings before the storm hit, the little Hoosier walked the opposing pitcher in the third inning. He was Chicago's only baserunner as Erskine throttled Chicago, 5-0, retiring the last 19 batters.

His second no-hitter, against the New York Giants, was also pitched in Brooklyn, this one on May 12, 1956. Relying on his control and a good change-up, Erskine struck out three and walked two, winning 3-0 on a long double by Duke Snider and a single by Campanella. He retired the last 18 men in a row.

Carl Erskine's career was a study in courage and determination. Armed with an excess of talent, but burdened with a physical handicap, the gritty Midwesterner gave it all he had for as long as he could. When the pain became too intense, he retired from the game without regret, returning to his roots in Indiana. He served as President of the First National Bank of Madison County for many years.

ANDRE ETHIER

One of the best trades the Los Angeles Dodgers ever made was obtaining Andre Ethier from the Oakland Athletics in exchange for troublesome outfielder Milton Bradley. Ethier, a 6', 1", 210-pound left handed hitter, blessed with good power and an excellent batting eye, had come up through the Oakland farm system, displaying his talents in such way stations as Kane County, Vancouver, and Midland, Texas. The Dodgers spotted him in the Texas League and managed to reel him in thanks to General Manager Ned Colletti. The 24-year old Phoenix, Arizona, native spent the first month of the 2006 season with Las Vegas where he scorched the ball at a .349 clip in 25 games, bringing about his promotion to Los Angeles on May 2. He celebrated his new diggings with a double in a 10-8 loss to Arizona, and went on to have a fine rookie season with the Dodgers, batting .308 with 11 home runs, and 55 runs-batted-in, in 396 at-bats.

Ethier hit .284 and .305 with 13 homers and 20 homers respectively over the next two years, and displayed his superb defensive capabilities with a perfect 1.000 fielding average in 2008. He experienced a break-out season in 2009, playing 160 games with a .272 batting average, 42 doubles, 31 homers, and 106 RBIs, helping the Dodgers win their second consecutive Western Division pennant. His best day as a Dodger was May 19. In an 8-2 victory over the Seattle Mariners, he sent three home runs into the distant reaches of Dodger Stadium while the hometown fans screamed with delight. The sweet-swinging lefty crushed a three-run homer in the second inning to give Clayton Kershaw a 3-0 lead, put another ball into the right-field seats with one man on in the sixth, and hit a solo shot in the eighth. He went on to hit a torrid .500 in the NLDS as Joe Torre's cohorts took the measure of the St. Louis Cardinals in three straight, and he posted a respectable .263 average in the five-game loss to Philadelphia in the NLCS. He was presented with a Silver Slugger Award as the top hitter at his position in the off-season. Another fine season followed for the handsome right-fielder in 2010 as he batted .292 with 23 homers and 82 RBIs, but Los Angeles fell to fourth place, twelve games behind San Francisco.

Andre Ethier (Los Angeles Dodgers)

Andre Ethier was hoping to have a career-year in 2011, but an injury scuttled his hopes. He hurt his right knee early in the season and was never able to go at top speed. The 29-year old slugger got off to his usual fast start when the bell rang and was hitting a robust .388, with a .456 on-base percentage and a .550 slugging average on April 22 after going one-for-two in a 12-2 thumping of the Chicago Cubs in Wrigley Field. He put together a 30-game hitting streak between April 2 and May 6, hitting .411 with three homers and 17 RBIs in 112 at-bats. Although his bat speed was good, it was obvious that his power stroke was missing. Ethier's batting average began to tail-off in mid May and he finished the month with a .327 average. It finally dipped below .300 for the first time on July 18. Manager Don Mattingly was disappointed with his star outfielder's offensive output and thought he was getting frustrated and losing focus at the plate. And Mattingly may have been right.

Certainly Ethier's injured knee was subject for concern, especially in view of the fact that no definite diagnosis was ever made and some of the Dodger coaching staff thought he might be dogging it. The matter came to a head on August 28 when he was out of the lineup with a reported sore knee. He returned to the lineup in September and played five games, going three for 16 with no home runs, before going on the Disabled List on the ninth of the month. Five days later he underwent arthroscopic surgery to clean up his knee, with a projected recovery time of six to eight weeks. Even with his knee problems, Ethier remained in the upper echelon of National League defensive right fielders, and in 2011 he had his second perfect season, flaunting a 1.000 fielding average and earning him his first Gold Glove.

Andre Ethier batted .292 in 487 at-bats in 2011, with just 11 home runs and 62 runs-batted-in. He is expected to be up to speed and in top physical condition by the start of spring training in February 2012, and he is looking forward to having his best year in the major leagues, both from a batting average standpoint and a power standpoint. If the 30-year old slugger can put it all together again, manager Don Mattingly and the entire Los Angeles Dodger organization will benefit from his resurgence with another Western Division pennant.

RON FAIRLY

Ron Fairly came out of the University of Southern California with a shock of flaming red hair and the sweetest swing this side of Beverly Hills. A Georgia native, Ronald Ray Fairly was born in Macon on September 9, 1938. Twenty years later he was roaming the outfield for Des Moines in the Western League, a Los Angeles affiliate.

The affable 5'10" 175-pound left-handed swinger earned a trip to the majors in a little over a year, becoming a regular in 1961. Fairly, deathly slow afoot, was converted to a first baseman by Walter Alston, who wanted to keep his timely bat in the lineup. In a short time, the stocky redhead became one of the top defensive first basemen in the game.

His career with the Dodgers lasted 12 years, during which time he batted .260. Never a high average hitter in the big leagues, Ron was nevertheless known as a consistent clutch hitter, averaging over 13 home runs and 80 RBIs a year. He had an excellent eye at the plate, coaxing more than 80 bases on balls a year. Appearing in four World Series, he sported a .300 Series batting average. In the 1965 Series, his .379 batting average led both teams, as did his six RBIS. His eleven hits included six singles, three doubles and two home runs. Fairly is one of those rare Dodger players who wears three World Championship rings; from 1959, 1963, and 1965.

Following his outstanding career with Los Angeles, the freckle-faced Californian went on to star with the Montreal Expos for another six years; then played for St. Louis, Oakland, Toronto, and California, before retiring from the game in 1978. His 21-year major league statistics show a total of 7,184 at bats, with 1,913 hits, 307 doubles, 33 triples, 215 home runs, 1,044 RBIs, and a .266 batting average.

Like many other former major league players, Ron Fairly became a color analyst and play-by-play radio broadcaster after hanging up his uniform.

JOE FERGUSON

Joe Ferguson was another of the stellar defensive catchers the Dodgers developed over the past fifty years, players like Roy Campanella, John Roseboro, and Steve Yeager. The tough 6'2", 200-pound Ferguson gave the Dodgers some outstanding defense as well as above average power during his 11 years with the club.

He played on three pennant winners and one World Championship team. Although his postseason batting average was not very high, he enjoyed two shining moments in the spotlight. In the 1974 Series against the Oakland Athletics, Ferguson hit a mighty two run homer over the center field fence off Vida Blue in game 2 to give Walter Alston's club a hard fought 3-2 victory. Six years later, when the Dodgers came from three games back in the final three games of the season, to tie the Houston Astros for first place, the right-handed bomber hit a towering 10th inning bomb to left field to win the first game of the final series, 3-2.

Joe Ferguson enjoyed an excellent 14 year career in the major leagues, 11 of those years in Los Angeles.

Ron Fairly

Joe Ferguson

Ah, but with his bat ... With his bat, all the damage was done to the opposing team. Breaking in with Aberdeen-Seattle in the Northwest League in 1908 at the tender age of 15, he began his journey to the big time. It took him a couple of years to get untracked but, by the time he reached Moose Jaw in the Western Canadian League in 1911, he was ready to break loose.

The 18-year-old Frenchman tore the Canadian League apart that year, slugging a whopping .377, while leading the league with 106 runs scored, 149 hits, 28 doubles, and 19 triples. What went unnoticed were the 40 errors he made at first base. The Chicago White Sox purchased his contract but regretted the deal when they saw his glovework. In spite of the fact that he hit .311 and .322 in the Windy City and led the American League in slugging in 1915 with a percentage of .491, the 6', 190-pound Fournier found himself back in the minors again in 1917.

He had a quick look-see with the New York Yankees in 1918, batting .350 in 27 games, but couldn't stick. He finally went up to the majors for good in 1920, joining Rogers Hornsby on the right side of the St. Louis Cardinal infield. He batted a solid .306 that year, but led the league's first basemen in errors with 25. A .343 season in 1921 did not satisfy his manager, Branch Rickey. With Sunny Jim Bottomley standing in the wings, the leaky-gloved Fournier was expendable, and he was traded to the Brooklyn Robins in 1923.

When he first became the Dodgers catcher, in 1973, he set a major league record by committing only three errors during the season. He led the league that year in fielding average and double plays.

Joe Ferguson did not hit for a high average in the Big Time, compiling a lifetime batting average of just .240, but he exhibited outstanding power with 22 home runs and 80 runs batted in, for every 550 at bats.

JACQUES (JACK) FOURNIER

Once upon a time, as legend has it, a bouncing baby boy was born in the upper peninsula town of Au Sable, Michigan, clutching a baseball bat in his tiny hand. As the boy grew, he and the bat were one; and the boy learned to handle the bat as no one else before him.

The boy was Jacques Fournier, one of the great natural hitters of all time. Fournier could hit any pitcher in any league at any time. Unfortunately, in his haste to master the theory of hitting, he completely neglected the art of defense. It was always a question of whether Jack would knock in more runs than he let in.

Jacques (Jack) Fournier (Brace Photo)

He came into his own as a hitter in Brooklyn, although his fielding was still an adventure. The big left-handed slugger played four years in the comfortable confines of Ebbets Field and he gave Wilbert Robinson some of the best offense the manager had seen in years. He stroked the ball at a .351 clip in '23, knocking in 102 runs on the strength of 30 doubles, 13 triples, and 22 home runs. The next year he directed the Robins on a merry pennant chase, giving the mighty New York Giants fits before settling into second place during the last week of the season. Fournier's contribution was a .334 batting average, 116 RBIs, and a league-leading 27 homers.

In 1925, the happy French Canadian once again dominated offensive statistics in Flatbush. His .350 batting average included 21 doubles, 16 triples, and 22 home runs. He drove home 130 runners and led the league in bases on balls with 86, giving him an on-base percentage of .446.

Slowed down by injuries, the 34-year-old Fournier was traded to the Boston Bees in 1927, where he played his final major league season. Fournier's career statistics are impressive. Over a 15-year span, the sweet-stroking Canadian batted .313, amassing 1,631 hits, with 252 doubles, 113 triples, and 136 home runs. He also accumulated the generous total of 215 fielding miscues, most of them at first base.

Jacques Fournier's career batting average in four years in Brooklyn was .337, third only to Willie Keeler and Babe Herman!

DAVID "SCISSORS" FOUTZ

David "Scissors" Foutz is fondly remembered in Brooklyn as the slugging first baseman of the championship teams of 1889 and 1890. In major league baseball circles, however, he is more familiar as the winningest pitcher of all time. Pitching for the St. Louis Browns and the Brooklyn Bridegrooms from 1884 through 1894, Foutz compiled a won-loss record of 147-66, an all-time-high winning percentage of .690! His teammate in St. Louis, Bob Caruthers, holds down third place with a percentage of .688.

David Luther Foutz was born in Carroll County, Maryland on September 7, 1856. He was a late bloomer as far as major league baseball was concerned, kicking around the semi-pro and minor league circuits for almost ten years. By the time his contract was purchased from Bay City, Michigan, by Chris Von der Ahe of the St. Louis Browns, he was a 27-year-old string bean of a pitcher, standing 6'2" tall and tipping the scales at a svelte 162 pounds. His nickname "Scissors" fit his profile.

Paired with "Parisian Bob" Caruthers in the Browns pitching rotation, the right-hander was an immediate winner. He finished the 1884 season with a 15-6 record,

his teammate Caruthers coming in at 7-2, as the St. Louis entry finished fourth. From then on, there was no stopping the powerful Browns. They proceeded to win three straight American Association championships, in 1885, '86, and '87. Their winning margins were a comfortable 16 games, 12 games, and 14 games. They were, quite frankly, in a class by themselves.

David "Scissors" Foutz (Los Angeles Dodgers)

Foutz and Caruthers won 99 games each over the three-year stretch, with Foutz finishing at 33-14, 41-16, and 25-12. The three-year pitching binge, however, ruined Foutz' arm completely. From 1885 through 1887, "Scissors" pitched in 146 games, throwing an outrageous 1,251 innings. At the end, his arm was dead. The wily Von der Ahe, suspecting the worst, sold his star pitcher to Brooklyn for the exorbitant price of $13,500.

After winning only 12 games for the Brooklyns, Foutz was converted into slugging first baseman finishing the year with a .277 batting average, 99 RBIs, and 91 runs scored. He teamed with Oyster Burns and Darby O'Brien to power a Brooklyn offense that went on to capture two successive league pennants. In 1889, he repeated his .277 average, this time driving home 113 runners, and scoring another 118. The Brooklyn team, now known as the Bridegrooms, edged out St. Louis for the American Association pennant.

Moving over to the National League in 1890, the Grooms proved it was no fluke by finishing first again. The lanky first baseman once more anchored the attack, hitting .303, scoring 106 runs, and knocking in another 98.

Time was running out on the slender Foutz as the last decade of the 19th century began, but he still had something to prove. In 1892, the 36-year-old competitor took one last turn on the mound, pitching 203 innings, throwing 17 complete games, and turning in 13 winning efforts. In 1894 he batted .307, but that was his swan song. After a four-year fling at managing the Brooklyn team, Dave Foutz was struck down with a respiratory ailment, and died on March 5, 1897.

One of the greatest pitchers ever to toe the rubber, a slugging first baseman on two pennant-winning teams, and a winning major league manager; David "Scissors" Foutz could do it all.

JOHNNY FREDERICK

Johnny Frederick was one of the great outfielders in Brooklyn Dodger history. Also one of the unluckiest. John Henry Frederick was born in Denver, Colorado, on January 26, 1901, with steel springs in his legs. As a youngster he was discouraged from aspiring to play professional baseball because of his slight build. He stood 5'11" tall but weighed only 165 pounds. Still, he loved the game, and he played sandlot ball at every opportunity.

In 1922, he signed his first professional contract to play baseball with Regina in the Western Canada League. Seven years later, the speedy outfielder became a member of the Brooklyn Dodgers. His rookie season was nothing short of sensational. He gave Wilbert Robinson some center field play that hadn't been witnessed in Flatbush since the days of Hy Meyers. He had great range, so good in fact, that he still ranks in the top ten in major league history. His success was a combination of speed and anticipation.

But it was at the plate where he made his reputation. He consistently made contact with the ball, striking out only 34 times in 628 at bats. Balls rocketed off his bat like they were fired from a cannon, splitting the outfielders, bouncing off fences, or sailing over the high screen onto Bedford Avenue. The left-handed slugger took no prisoners. Included in his 206 hits were 52 doubles (still an all-time Dodger record), six triples, and 24 home runs. He drove in an amazing 75 baserunners while batting in the leadoff position, and crossed the plate 127 times himself. His .328 batting average capped off one of the finest seasons in Dodger history.

Johnny Frederick did not suffer from the sophomore jinx at the plate. On the contrary, his .334 batting average, 206 hits, 120 runs scored, 44 doubles, 11 triples, 17 home runs, and 76 RBIs, kept the Brooklyn entry in the pennant race until the last week of the season. Playing with such offensive stalwarts as Babe Herman, Glenn Wright, and Del Bissonette, Frederick helped the team finish with an aggregate .304 team batting average.

His luck did begin to fail him with regard to his health, however. On September 13, while attempting a backhanded shoestring catch of a sinking line drive off the bat of Cincinnati's Leo Durocher, the brilliant Dodger centerfielder crashed heavily to the turf, his right ankle twisted grotesquely under his body. Although he managed to limp off the field under his own power, he suffered a broken ankle, and missed the last two weeks of the season. From that point on, Johnny Frederick's fortunes went downhill. His leg problems worsened with each passing game, eventually reducing him to the role of a part-time player.

He still had some zip in his legs in 1931, posting a .270 batting average with 17 homers and 71 RBIs and giving Brooklyn fans continued excitement with his daring outfield play. But by 1932, he was seriously hobbled, his once great range only a memory. In the batters box he could still sting the ball, putting together season marks of .299, .308, and .296, but he was unable to run the bases or cover the outfield in a satisfactory manner. More and more he had to sit on the bench and watch his teammates in action, his legs heavily taped, his body aching.

Johnny Frederick

Still, 1932 was a year that Johnny Frederick fans will always remember. In that year, Frederick became a pinch-hitter extraordinaire. In 30 pinch-hit appearances, he slugged six pinch-hit home runs, in just 29 at bats, good for a .310 average.

Two years later, Johnny Frederick laced on his spikes in the Brooklyn locker room for the last time. He was traded to Sacramento of the Pacific Coast League after the '34 season, ending a short but brilliant major league career. Frederick continued to play minor league ball for another six years, and his bat never failed him. He put together batting averages of .363, .352, .301, .319, .326, and .306.

His Brooklyn career lasted only six years; still his accomplishments will always be recalled whenever old Dodger fans reminisce and discuss the glory days that used to be. He left Flatbush with a lifetime batting average of .308, 11th on the all-time Dodger list. He holds the major league record for pinch-hit homers in a season (six), the Dodger record for most doubles in a season (52), and the highest range factor for Dodger outfielders.

Johnny Frederick had unlimited talent but suffered through some bad breaks. He was a gutty, determined ballplayer who gave it everything he had. As his granddaughter said, "He just kept plugging".

CARL FURILLO

Carl Anthony Furillo was first and foremost a baseball player. He was born to play baseball. He was a solid, consistent contact hitter, yet one capable of hitting the long ball, and driving in runs in bunches. Furillo's baseball prowess did not end with his hitting however. He was known as "The Emperor of Right Field" during his playing days in Brooklyn, for his uncanny ability to play the crazy concrete and wire barrier that fronted Bedford Avenue. No one ever played it any better. But strange as it seems, his most potent weapon was neither his bat nor his glove. The deadliest weapon in his entire arsenal was his strong right throwing arm; an arm so accurate and so powerful that few baserunners had the temerity to challenge its capabilities. And when they did test it, they were, more often than not, thrown out by a wide margin. His prowess at throwing a baseball earned him the sobriquet of "The Reading Rifle" early in his career, a nickname he wore with honor.

Carl Furillo was a Hall of Fame baseball player, although he has yet to be accorded the honor of official membership in that exalted society. The son of an Italian immigrant, he was born in the small town of Stony Creek Mills, Pennsylvania, near Reading, on March 8, 1922. Two years after he began his professional career, the Japanese bombed Pearl Harbor, igniting World War II, and the patriotic Furillo rushed off to defend his country. He subsequently distinguished himself in action in the Pacific theatre of operations. Engaging the Japanese in combat in such bloody skirmishes as Guam and the Philippine Islands, the tough infantryman received three battle stars and a purple heart.

Returning home after 38 months in the service, he resumed his baseball career at the highest level. He joined the 1946 Brooklyn Dodgers in spring training in Vero Beach, Florida, and quickly earned the center field position with his outstanding play. Pee Wee Reese was there to greet him. Slowly, over the next two years, they were joined by Jackie Robinson, Duke Snider, Roy Campanella, Gil Hodges, Billy Cox, Preacher Roe, Don Newcombe, and Carl Erskine, to form the nucleus of "The Boys of Summer;" one of the greatest baseball teams in National

League history. They would rule the National League for the next ten years.

The mighty Brooklyn juggernaut captured six National League flags during the decade, missing two others on the last day of the season. And Carl Furillo was a major factor in their success. Consistency was his forte, and he always managed to save his greatest achievements for those times when his team needed help the most. In late summer, the heat and humidity took its toll on most baseball players, and their overall performances began to suffer. At times like these Carl Furillo rose to the fore.

- In 1949, he single-handedly carried the Dodgers to the pennant, collecting 78 hits in 181 at bats over the last 46 games, an average of .431!
- In 1954, Carl knocked in 48 runs in the last 48 games.
- In 1955, Carl started the season with seven home runs during the first two weeks, as the Dodgers jumped way out in front of the pack with a 22-2 record, and an imposing lead of nine games over second-place Milwaukee. Late in the summer, as Brooklyn began to stagger, Furillo stormed back again, batting .465 over a five-week period.

Cal Furillo played 15 years for the Dodgers, both in Brooklyn and in L.A. And, except for 1952 when he was bothered by eye problems, he never hit less than .284. His .344 average in 1953 won him the National League batting title.

When he retired in 1960, he left behind some impressive lifetime batting statistics.

Carl Furillo (R) and Carl Erskine, enter the clubhouse arm in arm, after the Dodgers had captured their first World Championship, in 1955. Furillo had eight hits in seven games.

YEARS	G	AB	R	H	D
15	1,806	6,378	895	1,910	324

T	HR	RBI	BB	SO	BA
56	192	1,058	514	436	.299

Broken down into an average season, Carl's performance would rank among the tops in the league in any era.

G	AB	R	H	D	T
162	638	90	191	32	6

HR	RBI	BB	SO	BA
19	106	51	43	.299

Just imagine what a major league team would pay today for a player who could bat .300, hit 19 home runs, and drive in 106 runs, while only striking out 43 times in 638 at bats. And who possessed unparalleled defensive skills to boot.

Cooperstown, what are you waiting for?

STEVE GARVEY

Steve Garvey, the all-time Los Angeles Dodger first baseman, was the greatest clutch hitter in LA history. The clean-cut, smooth fielding, smooth swinging Garvey always rose to the occasion when the chips were down and the game was on the line. Born in Tampa, Florida, young Steve, whose father drove the Dodger team bus in Vero Beach during spring training, became a Dodger fan after serving as the team batboy. Following graduation from Michigan State University, he entered the Los Angeles farm system and, after tearing up the minor leagues with four consecutive .300 + seasons, he joined the big club.

On June 13, 1972, Steve Garvey joined Davey Lopes, Bill Russell, and Ron Cey in the Dodger infield, forming a unit that would establish a major league record for longevity by playing together for a total of eight years, three months and 17 days. The second longest-running Dodger infield combination were also Dodgers, the famous Boys of Summer; Hodges, Robinson, Reese and Cox. They performed as a unit for five years.

During Steve Garvey's 19-year career he established numerous National League and major league records, the most significant of which is his NL mark of having played in 1,207 consecutive games over a seven year period. He also holds the National League record for most consecutive chances handled by a first baseman without an error, 1,633. His major league records include highest season fielding percentage by a first baseman (1.000), fewest errors (0), and highest career fielding average (.996tie with Wes Parker). He led the NL in games played six times, in put outs six times, fielding average five times, and hits twice. He won the

National League Most Valuable Player award in 1974.

In spite of his longevity record and his fielding prowess, Steve Garvey is best remembered as a slugging first baseman and the games premier clutch hitter. The "Senator," as he was called because of his political aspirations, had a smooth, compact swing that usually put the ball in play and, more often than not, resulted in line drives to the distant recesses of the park.

Garvey's career .294 batting average included 2,599 base hits, 755 extra base hits, 1,143 runs scored, and 1,308 RBIs. His 14-year stay in LA was a model of consistency; his batting average ranging from .282 to .319. He batted over .300 seven times, and knocked in over 100 runs on five occasions. He led Los Angeles to four National League pennants and one World Championship in 14 years, then added another NL flag and a World Championship in five years with San Diego. In 1978, Steve Garvey joined Dusty Baker, Reggie Smith and Ron Cey as the first foursome in major league history to hit 30 or more home runs in the same season.

Garvey was not only "Mr. Clutch" during the regular season. His outstanding performances carried over into post-season play as well. In five National League

Steve Garvey

Championship Series, the right-handed slugger batted an astronomical .356 in 22 games, while smashing eight home runs and driving home 21 teammates, both NLCS records. The Senator's four-hit, two home run-performance led the Dodgers to a 12-1 rout of the Pittsburgh Pirates in the 1974 NLCS finale. Four years later, he slugged two homers and a single and drove in four runs to propel the LA contingent to a 9-5 win over the Philadelphia Phillies in the Championship Series opener. He homered in a losing cause in Game Three, then hit another roundtripper in Game Four as Los Angeles captured the title, 4-3, in 10 innings. In Game Four of the '81 playoff with Montreal, the Dodgers were down two games to one and facing elimination when Garvey snapped a 1-1 tie with a two-run, game-winning homer in the eighth inning. They wrapped up the National League pennant the next day, 2-1, on Rick Monday's dramatic 9th inning shot.

Garvey slowed down only slightly in the World Series, but still compiled a solid .319 average in 28 games, hitting .381 in 1974, .375 in 1977, and a team leading .417 in 1981 as the Dodgers swept to the World Championship. His All-Star game record was just as impressive. The 5'10", 190-pound first baseman hit .393 in 10 All-Star game appearances, and holds the all-time high slugging percentage, with .955.

Steve Garvey was a class act, and every inch an all-star. He is still the Los Angeles Dodgers all-time most valuable player.

JAMES "JUNIOR" GILLIAM

James "Junior" Gilliam was Mr. Versatility for the Dodgers for 14 long years, both in Brooklyn and in Los Angeles. He was the Dodgers true transition player, spending his first five years in Brooklyn, then toiling in LA for another nine. The slick-fielding infielder starred for both teams, not only during the regular season, but in the World Series as well. During his 14-year tenure, the Dodgers won seven National League titles. His four World Championship rings are the most ever won by any Dodger player in the team's history.

James William Gilliam was born in Nashville, Tennessee on October 17, 1928. As a young boy, he found the doors of major league baseball closed to him and to all members of his race. As a result, the 16-year-old black boy began his baseball career as a second baseman for the Nashville Black Vols of the Negro League, moving on to star for the Baltimore Elite Giants from 1945 through 1950. As the youngest member of the Baltimore team, he naturally acquired the nickname of "Junior." In 1951, the talented Gilliam, thanks to the efforts of Jackie Robinson et al., was recruited by the Brooklyn Dodgers to play for their Montreal farm team.

After two years in the minor leagues, Jim Gilliam became the Dodgers' regular second baseman in 1953,

displacing the aging Robinson, who moved over to third. He was an immediate hit in Brooklyn, helping Charlie Dressen's team to another National League flag. In addition to teaming with Pee Wee Reese to give the Brooks one of the best double-play combinations in the league, the versatile Gilliam hit a solid .278, drove in 63 runs, scored 125 runs, drew 100 bases on balls, stole 21 bases, and led the league in triples with 17. He was selected as the National League's Rookie of the Year for his fine performance. He continued his superior play in the World Series, batting .296. The switch-hitting infielder set a rookie record by slugging home runs from both sides of the plate in the Series.

When the Dodgers moved to Los Angeles in 1958, the 30-year-old Gilliam was beginning to slow down a step or two, and was shifted to third base. In the 1965 World Series against the Minnesota Twins, the move paid dividends tenfold. With Sandy Koufax pitching a 2-0 shutout in the seventh game, Gilliam choked off the Twins' last rally with a great defensive play. In the fifth inning, with one out and runners on first and second, Twins shortstop Zoilo Versalles hit a shot over the third-base bag that looked like a sure game-tying double. Not so. The determined Gilliam made a sensational diving backhand stop of the ball behind third, scrambled to his feet, and beat the runner to the bag for a forceout. That

James "Junior" Gilliam

was all the help the great Dodger lefty needed. He retired 13 of the last 14 batters to clinch another World Championship for the City of Angels.

James "Junior" Gilliam could do it all: field, hit and run. He was not a superstar, but he was a genuine major leaguer who starred at both second base and third base for the great Dodger teams of the 50s and 60s. A lifetime .265 hitter, he enjoyed only one .300 season, in 1956, but he had a superb on-base percentage of .361 on the strength of 150 hits and 80 bases on balls a year. A heady baserunner who was always a threat to take an extra base, the speedy Gilliam stole 203 bases in his career (#8 on the all-time Dodger list). His other career totals showed 7,119 at bats (#5), 1,163 runs scored (#4 on the all-time Dodger list), 1,889 hits (#8), 304 doubles (#7), 2,530 total bases (#8), and 440 extra base hits (#10).

Following his playing career, the quiet, unassuming Gilliam took over the third base coaching chores for the Dodgers, an assignment he held for 12 years. His untimely death of a brain hemorrhage in 1978 at the age of 49 cast a pall over the Dodgers' World Series appearance that year. The following year, in memory of his many contributions to the team, Jim Gilliam's number 19 was permanently retired.

SHAWN GREEN

Shawn Green was born in Des Plaines, Illinois on November 10, 1972, and became a professional baseball player in the Toronto organization in 1992, swatting the ball at a .273 clip in 114 games with the Dunedin Blue Jays in the Florida State League. The following year, the 6', 4", 210-pound slugger made his first appearance in a major league uniform, playing three games with Toronto, and in 1995 he took over as the Blue Jays permanent right fielder. The smooth-swinging left hander stroked the ball at a hefty .288 clip as a rookie, with 15 home runs and 54 RBIs in 379 at-bats, and he reached the pinnacle of his career three years later when he pounded the ball to the tune of .278 with 33 doubles, 35 home runs, 106 runs scored, and 100 RBIs, adding 35 stolen bases to his resume for good measure. He had another breakout season in 1999 when he enjoyed his first .300 season, batting .309 with a league-leading 45 doubles, 42 homers, 134 runs scored, 123 RBIs, and 20 stolen bases. That was all the Los Angeles Dodgers needed to see. They acquired the 27-year old slugger on November 8, 1999, for Pedro Borbon and Raul Mondesi, and he went on to give Dodger fans five outstanding years, not only with his bat but with his glove as well.

His first year in Dodger blue, he hit .269 with 24 homers and 99 RBIs for Davey Johnson's second place club. The next three years under manager Jim Tracy the club finished third twice and second once, but Shawn Green more than held up his end of the Dodger attack. He had a sensational year in 2001, hitting .297 with a franchise record 49 home runs to go along with 121 runs scored, 125 runs-batted-in, and 20 stolen bases. He followed that up with a .285 season in 2002, with 42 homers, 110 runs scored, and 114 RBIs., and he joined the immortals along the way, turning in the best

single game offensive display in major league history. On the night of May 23, in Miller Park, Milwaukee, with 26,728 stunned Brewer fans staring quietly at the historic events unfolding before them, the Dodger slugger sprayed six base hits around the park, including four home runs, a double, and a single, good for 19 total bases, a figure that is still the major league benchmark. His last home run, coming in the ninth inning, was a monstrous 450 foot shot that came to rest in a walkway beyond right-center field, bringing the score in the Dodger assault to 16-3. He went on to hit three more home runs against Arizona's Curt Schilling and Randy Johnson over the next two games, becoming the first major leaguer to hit seven home runs in three games. He also set a National League record with nine home runs in one week.

Green's career began to wind down after 2002, but he was still a major contributor to the Dodgers' successes. He batted .280 with 19 homers and 85 RBIs in 2003 and .266 with 28 home runs and 86 RBIs in 2004, and he had some big hits in the latter year that helped propel Jim Tracy's crew to the division pennant. The Dodgers were engaged in a season-long struggle with the San Francisco Giants and the San Diego Padres in 2004 before taking the Giants by two games and the Padres by six games at seasons-end, and Green, like his team, came on strong down the stretch. Los

Shawn Green (W. McNiel)

Angeles struggled during the first half of the season, falling three-and-a-half games behind San Diego on July 2 with a 40-37 won-loss record, and their big right-fielder was limping along with a .254 batting average and just 9 home runs and 35 RBIs in 283 at-bats. Then, as the weather warmed up, so too did the Dodger bats. Jim Tracy's cohorts went 24-6 over the next 30 games to open up a 6½ game lead in the pennant race, and Shawn Green, in support of hot-hitting Adrian Beltre, hit .283 with four homers and 18 RBIs.

The Des Plaines native came through big time in September, particularly in two critical games over the final two weeks of the season. With L.A. nursing a 1½ game lead over San Francisco on the 19th, Green climaxed a stirring Dodger rally by slamming a two-out, two-run, ninth inning homer to carry the Dodgers to a 7-6 victory over the Colorado Rockies, wiping out a 5-0 deficit after six innings. Five days later, he launched a two-run homer in PacBell Park to give his team a 3-2 victory over San Francisco, opening up a 2½ game lead with nine games remaining. L.A. hung on to win the Western Division title but was eliminated by the St. Louis Cardinals three games to one in the National League Division Series. The Dodgers embarked on a youth program in the off-season and Shawn Green was one of the victims of that strategy. He was traded to the Arizona Diamondbacks on January 11, 2005. His five-year L.A. legacy showed a .280 batting average with 33 doubles, 30 home runs, and 93 runs-batted-in for every 550 at-bats.

MIKE GRIFFIN

Mike Griffin, a solidly built 5'7", 173-pound outfielder from Utica, New York, starred in the major leagues for 12 years, including eight years in Brooklyn. Unfortunately, his stay with the Dodgers was during one of their long droughts; they finished fifth or below seven times.

Griffin began his pro career with the Utica team of the New York State League as a 20-year-old right-handed slugger in 1885. Two years later, his contract was purchased by the Baltimore Orioles of the American Association, then a major league. Griffin literally tore the league apart. Blazing through the most spectacular rookie season on record, he stroked the ball at a .368 clip, while scoring 142 runs on 214 base hits, including 32 doubles, 12 triples, and four home runs. His 94 stolen bases set a rookie record that stood for 98 years, until Vince Coleman pilfered 110 in 1985.

Griffin cooled off considerably after his electrifying start, but he remained a .300 hitter throughout his career. After jumping to the Player's League in 1890, the young New Yorker caught on with the Brooklyn Bridegrooms, where he remained for eight years, until his retirement in 1899.

The compact left-handed hitter batted over .300 five times for the Grooms, including a sizzling .365

Mike Griffin

in 1894, and .335 in 1895. He scored more than 100 runs in nine of his 12 big league seasons and, in 1891, he led the league with 36 doubles. The speedy Irishman was no slouch as a centerfielder either, leading the league's outfielders in putouts in 1891 and 1895, in fielding average in 1891, 1892, 1893, 1895, and 1898, in range factor in 1891, and in double plays in 1895. His 3.0 range factor in 1891 and again in 1894 are second on the all-time Dodger list, behind Jigger Statz' 3.16 in 1917.

Griffin was a solid line-drive hitter, and a heady baserunner who stole 549 bases. He was a formidable offensive threat who scored a phenomenal 60% of the time he reached base. His scoring average of .94 runs scored per game is #6 on the all-time major league list. Leader Billy Hamilton, averaged 1.06 runs per game during a 14year career. Griffin's average offensive statistics are truly impressive. Of the more than 1,200 ballplayers who have toiled for the Dodgers over the years, his on-base-percentage of .388 is second only to Jackie Robinson's .410.

Averages based on a 154-game schedule:

GAMES	AT BATS	RUNS	HITS	D
151	596	140	178	32

T	HR	RBI	BB	SO	BA
11	4	63	81	30	.307

After the 1898 season, Mike Griffin was sold to the St. Louis Perfectos. He refused to report, choosing to retire instead. He passed away in his hometown of Utica in 1908, at the young age of 43.

BURLEIGH GRIMES

Burleigh Arland Grimes, known as "Old Stubble-beard," never shaved on game day. The resulting two-day growth gave the big right-hander a dark and sinister look, a visage he cultivated to his advantage. Grimes was naturally mean and surly, and on the mound, his disposition worsened. The mound was his kingdom, and the plate his private territory, and woe to the batter who dug in too deep. The poor fellow might be wearing a cowhide earring after the next pitch.

When the spitball pitch was outlawed in 1920, the 17 active major league spitball pitchers were permitted to continue using the pitch throughout their careers. For everyone else, it was illegal. Burleigh Grimes, one of the 17, was the last of the spitball pitchers, keeping it in his repertoire until his retirement in 1934.

Grimes was born in Emerald, Wisconsin, in 1893, and began his professional pitching career with Eau-Claire in the Minnesota-Wisconsin League in 1912. After paying his dues for four years in the minors, the stocky spitballer was promoted to the Pittsburgh Pirates at the tail end of 1916. A 3-16 rookie season brought him a quick trade to the

Burleigh Grimes (Brace Photo)

Brooklyn Robins in what must have been one of Wilbert Robinson's most successful deals. Old "Boily" as he was called in Brooklyn, turned it completely around the next year, and finished with a glittering 19-9 record for the fifth-place Robins.

The kid from Wisconsin found a home in the City of Churches, and he spent the next nine years there, winning a total of 158 games and tossing 20 shutouts. Grimes was Brooklyn, a blue-collar pitcher in a blue-collar town. The citizens of the country's second largest city could relate to old Boily. He was surly and belligerent, a man who hated the enemy and who would do whatever it took to win. He fought with everyone, opposing players, umpires, and even teammates. Most people disliked him intensely. Flatbush loved him.

In his third year in Brooklyn, as the ace of the staff, he won 23 games against 11 losses, and led the Robins to the National League title, finishing seven games ahead of the Giants. The next year, Grimes was even better, finishing with a record of 22-13, but the rest of the Brooklyn pitching staff was mediocre, and the team played to a disappointing fifth-place finish. Little did the fans of Flatbush know it at the time, but their beloved Robins (and Dodgers) would finish in the second division 14 times over the next 18 years, a record of futility unknown in Dodgerland before or since.

The 5'10", 190-pound hurler racked up 21 and 17 wins over the next two seasons for sixth-place clubs. When Robby's boys made an unsuccessful run for the crown in 1924, Boily went 22-13, pitching a league-leading 311 innings. After two sub-par seasons, he was shunted off to the New York Giants, where he won 19 games in 1927. The following year, in a Pittsburgh uniform, the 35-yearold spitball artist finished with a dazzling record of 25-14, and an ERA of 2.99. He led the National League in games (48), and innings pitched (331), as well as victories. The old veteran had three more strong years, winning 17, 16, and 17, before his talent faded into the sunset. He helped pitch the St. Louis Cardinals to pennants the last two of those years.

Over a 19-year major league career, Burleigh Grimes proved to be a rugged competitor, an early day Don Drysdale. It was said that he would brush back his mother if she crowded the plate. The strategy must have worked because he finished an outstanding career with 270 victories, placing him 27th on the all-time victory list. The durable right-hander pitched over 300 innings five times in his career. He won ten or more games 14 times, 20 or more games five times.

In addition to his pitching prowess, old Boily had a career batting average of .248, batting over .300 twice. He is generally considered to be one of the ten best fielding pitchers of all time. The wily competitor was recognized for his many contributions to the game in 1964 when he was voted into baseball's Hall of Fame.

PEDRO GUERRERO

Pedro Guerrero was one of many major league stars who were weaned in San Pedro de Macoris in the Dominican Republic. Amazingly enough, at one time in the early '80s, six of the 26 major league shortstops were natives of the tiny village. Guerrero came to Los Angeles by way of Cleveland. Dodger Vice President Al Campanis, in one of his most profitable deals, plucked the 6', 190-pound slugger from the Indian farm system in exchange for pitcher Bruce Ellingsen.

The big right-handed hitter spent the better part of six years working his way through the Dodger's vast minor league farm system, honing his skills in such out-of-the-way places as Bellingham, Danville, Waterbury, and Albuquerque. By 1980, Guerrero had proven himself to be a solid .300 hitter in the high minors, thus convincing manager Tommy Lasorda to make room for him on the big club.

It wasn't long before the handsome Dominican outfielder became the star of the team, sparking the Los Angeles contingent to three division titles and one World Championship in eight years. The pitching thin Dodgers were on their way to a fourth Division Title in 1988 when Guerrero was traded to the St. Louis Cardinals for a badly needed starting pitcher, southpaw John Tudor.

During Pedro's heyday, the Big Blue Machine was always in the chase for the flag. In addition to the three division flags, Tommy Lasorda's boys lost the 1980 title in a one-game playoff with the Houston Astros, and finished one game behind the Atlanta Braves in 1982 after leading by four games in mid-August.

During the glorious season of 1981, the year the Dodgers earned the title of "The Comeback Kids" by fighting back, time after time, to win, first the Western Division title, then the National League flag, and finally the World Championship, Pedro Guerrero blossomed into a bonafide star. After finishing the regular season with a batting average of .300, the 25-year-old youngster struggled through postseason play, hitting a meager .176 in the Division Series and a barely visible .105 in the NLCS. In the World Series, he started off 0-7 in the first two games, both of which the Dodgers lost, and the experts were beginning to question his heart and his head. Then he got hot, slugging the ball at a torrid .500 clip over the final four games, as L.A. swept to the title. His hits included a double, a triple, and two home runs, good for seven RBIs, and earned the young slugger a share of the Series' MVP award.

For the next four years, Guerrero was one of the major league's premier stars. He batted .304 with 32 homers and 100 RBIs in 1982, and followed that with seasons of .298-32-103; .303-16-72; and .320-33-87. In 1985, the Dodger left fielder tied a major league record by hitting 15 home runs in the month of June. At one stretch, he reached base 14 consecutive times, two short of Ted Williams' record. The following year, as the Dodgers prepared to defend their Western Division title, Guerrero's world came crashing down around his shoulders. He shattered his knee sliding into third base during a spring training game, and was lost for the better part of the season.

He bounced back in '87, slugging the ball at a .338 pace, while socking 27 homers and driving in 89 runs, but his speed was gone and his age was beginning to show. Despite another workmanlike job in 1988, he became expendable when the pennant race heated up and the need for another starting pitcher became paramount.

The hero of San Pedro de Macoris retired after the 1992 season, leaving behind a .300 career batting average. His 15-year stats include 1,618 base hits, 215 home runs and 898 runs batted in.

In each decade, certain players are indelibly associated with specific teams. In the decade of the '80s, when the Los Angeles Dodgers are discussed, the name of Pedro Guerrero will be at the top of the list. He was the heart and soul of the Dodger offense.

Pedro Guerrero (Los Angeles Dodger Photo)

BABE HERMAN

Floyd Caves "Babe" Herman was the greatest hitter in the history of Dodger baseball. Period!

Over the years, the easy-going Herman has been made the butt of countless jokes. The media characterized him as a clown, but the exact opposite is true. Babe Herman was a talented, all-around baseball player who possessed one of the most natural swings ever seen in the major leagues. The 6'4" left-handed batter was a consistent power hitter who smashed vicious line drives to all areas of the field, driving in runs in bunches. Unlike the modern day long-ball hitters who fan 25% of the time, the big, rawboned Californian struck out only once for every ten at bats. In addition to his prowess with the bat, Brooklyn's Babe, through hard work, developed into a capable outfielder with a strong, accurate throwing arm; one that led the league in double plays in 1932. He was a fast and talented baserunner as well, stealing 56 bases over one three-year period and running out 110 triples during a 13-year major league career.

Born on June 26, 1903, in Buffalo, New York, and raised on the west coast, the gangling youngster began his quest for major league stardom with Edmonton in the Western Canadian League at the tender age of 17. He got off the mark quickly, hitting a whopping .330 in 107 games, and leading the league with 18 triples, proof of his swiftness afoot. Over the next four years, he punished minor league pitching to the tune of .340, earning himself a promotion to the "Bigs" along the way.

Babe Herman

The Brooklyn Robins purchased his contract from Seattle in 1926, and he immediately made his presence felt in the City of Churches, socking the ball at a .319 clip, and chipping in with 57 extra base hits. In spite of his electrifying start, Babe Herman's image as a buffoon was already developing. The good-natured first baseman was good copy, and reporters buzzed around him like bees to honey, looking for another juicy tidbit to pass on to their readers. Nineteen twenty-six was the year of the "three-men-on-third" episode and, in spite of the fact that Babe's hit drove in the game-winning run, the press corps made him out to be an empty-headed oaf.

At the plate, however, there was never any question as to Babe Herman's capabilities. In 1929, and 1930, the big left-handed hitter put together the two finest seasons ever recorded in either Brooklyn or Los Angeles. In 1929 the 26-year-old hitting machine pounded the ball at a torrid .381 clip, with 42 doubles, 13 triples, and 21 home runs. He scored 105 runs and knocked in 113. The following year he actually raised his batting average 12 points, finishing at an astronomical .393. His 241 hits included 48 doubles, 11 triples, and 35 home runs. He crossed the plate 143 times himself, and batted in 130 teammates. The 241 hits, .393 batting average, 416 total bases, and 143 runs scored are still all-time Dodger records.

During Babe's six-year tenure in Brooklyn, Wilbert Robinson's team, lovingly dubbed the "Daffyness Boys," fumbled their way through one season after another, finishing fourth twice and limping home in sixth place four times. After leaving the cozy confines of Ebbets Field, the big slugger bounced around the National League for six more years, playing for four different teams before moving back down to the minors in 1938.

The Babe hit for the cycle three times during his illustrious career, one of only two men to have accomplished that feat in over 100 years. He is the only man to do it twice in the same year, pulling off the double-cycle in 1931. He hit for the cycle again in 1933. Herman also had a three-homer day, as a Chicago Cub in 1933, and had the honor of hitting the first home run in a night game, as a member of the Cincinnati Reds in 1935.

Brooklyn's beloved Babe Herman finished his career with a .324 lifetime batting average, placing him 34th on the all-time hitter's list. In the hearts of Dodger fans everywhere, however, "The Babe" will always be #1.

OREL HERSHISER

In 1988, Orel Leonard Hershiser IV put together one of the most overpowering seasons ever witnessed in Dodgerland. Nicknamed "Bulldog" by manager Tommy Lasorda for his tenacity on the mound, the lanky right-hander pitched Lasorda's group of misfits to the World Championship, leading the National League in innings pitched with 267, and in victories with 23.

During the postseason triumphs, he won another three games and saved one, with a glittering 1.06 earned run average. In recognition of his outstanding achievements, the New York native was awarded the National League Cy Young award as the league's best pitcher, the National League Championship Series most valuable player award, and the World Series most valuable player award. He also copped a gold glove as the NL's top fielding pitcher.

During his "career" season, when the stretch run heated up, Hershiser went it one better. Beginning in late August, the sinkerball specialist finished the season with 59 consecutive scoreless innings, breaking Don Drysdale's major league record of 58. In the month of September, the Dodger ace compiled a spotless 5-0 record with a 0.00 ERA; a standard of pitching perfection that will never be broken.

His momentum carried through the postseason play, as he went 1-0 with one save and a 1.10 ERA in the NLCS against the favored New York Mets, blanking them 6-0 in Game Seven. He topped off his magical season with a perfect 2-0 record and a 1.00 earned run average against the powerful Oakland Athletics. Again he captured the final game of the series, winning Game Five, 5-2 with a strong four hitter. Rubbing salt into the A's wounds, Bulldog led all hitters in the Series with a 1.000 batting average, going 3 for 3 with 2 doubles.

Hershiser had a once-in-a-lifetime year in 1988,

but he was not a one-season pitcher. He arrived in the major leagues in 1983 after doing three years of apprenticeship in the Dodgers' minor league farm system. The 6'3" hurler burst into national prominence with a glittering 19-3 record in 1985, capping it off with an earned run average of 2.03 and a league-leading winning percentage of .864. His record at home was even more impressive, as he went 11-0, 1.08 at Dodger Stadium!

Shockingly, Los Angeles' top pitcher was struck down with arm problems in 1990, missing the last five months of the season after surgery to repair a damaged shoulder. In typical Bulldog fashion, Hershiser returned to the starting rotation ahead of schedule, and ran up a fine 7-2 record during the last half of 1991.

After three more sub-par years in L.A., Hershiser signed a free agent contract with the Cleveland Indians in 1995. He spent five years with the Cleveland Indians, San Francisco Giants, and New York Mets before returning to the Dodgers in 2000 to close out his career. He finished an outstanding and occasionally brilliant 18-year career with a record of 204 victories against 150 losses.

KIRBY HIGBE

When Brooklyn Dodger President Larry MacPhail was wheeling and dealing in the late 1930s and early 40s to rescue the Brooklyn franchise from impending bankruptcy, one of his first moves was to obtain the services of right-handed pitcher Kirby Higbe from the Philadelphia Phillies. The 23-year-old fireballer cost MacPhail three players and $100,000 in cash, but he was worth every penny of it.

In his first year in a Brooklyn uniform, "Higgleby," as the hometown fans called him, sparked the Dodgers to their first National League pennant in 21 years, leading the league in games pitched with 48, and tying for the lead in victories with teammate Whitlow Wyatt. With each pitcher contributing 22 wins to the Brooklyn cause, Leo Durocher's battling Bums finished 2 1/2 games in front of Billy Southworth's St. Louis Cardinals.

Higbe followed up his outstanding season with a 1611 year in 1942; then went 13-10 the following year before entering the U.S. Army for wartime service. Two years of active duty didn't diminish his skills in the slightest, and on his return to Flatbush, he paced the '46 club with a 17-8 mark and a 3.03 ERA.

The big right-hander was traded to the Pittsburgh Pirates in 1948 for personal reasons, but was never as effective as he had been in Brooklyn. Used primarily in relief, he spent three mediocre seasons with the Pirates and Giants, finally retiring after the 1950 season. He left behind an enviable 118-101 record compiled over a 12-year major league career.

Orel Hershiser (W. McNeil)

Higbe, a native of Columbia, South Carolina, was a hard-living individual, a legendary carouser. When the team went on the road, Higbe roomed with Hugh Casey, another good-old-boy from Dixie. Together, they formed a hard-drinking, bar-hopping night brigade that kept their manager on his toes. It is said that when Higbe checked into a hotel, his baggage contained only liquid refreshment. He purchased all the necessities at the hotel gift shop; tooth brush, toothpaste, razor, etc. After a quick shower and shave, two sandwiches and two shots of booze, Hig and Hughie were ready for a night on the town.

Kirby Higbe

On the mound, the hard throwing right-hander asked no quarter and gave none. He led the National League in bases on balls four times, and set the pace in strikeouts once. The "conveniently wild" pitcher always kept the batters loose at the plate, frequently dropping them in the dirt with a high hard one if they seemed to be digging in too much.

Old Higgleby died in 1985 at the age of 70. The handsome flamethrowing right-hander will always be remembered in Flatbush for his competitiveness and his innate skills. His 70-38 record in a Dodger uniform is one of the highest winning percentages in Brooklyn history. At .648, he trails only Preacher Roe and Don Newcombe. Fittingly, he is immediately followed by his old teammates Hugh Casey and Whitlow Wyatt.

GIL HODGES

From 1947 through 1956, the Brooklyn Dodgers fielded the most awesome lineup in National League history, the fabled "Boys of Summer." One of the most consistent performers on that team was Gil Hodges, considered by many to be the greatest first baseman in Dodger history. Arriving in Brooklyn as a third-string catcher, the 6'1" slugger was converted into a first baseman by manager Leo Durocher. In short order, he became the best defensive first baseman in the National League, leading his counterparts in fielding five times, and winning gold gloves in 1957, 58, and 59. He was a graceful performer around the bag, had exceptionally large hands, a long stretch, and outstanding footwork. He was particularly adept at digging bad throws out of the dirt.

Hodges was the stereotypical strong, silent type. He rarely said much; choosing to let his bat and his glove do his talking for him. And talk they did. Over the course of 18 major league seasons, 16 with the Dodgers, Hodges batted a solid .273, piled up 1,921 hits, hit 370 home runs, scored 1,105 runs, and batted in 1,274 runs. He knocked in more than 100 runs seven years in a row, with a high

Gil Hodges

of 130 in 1954. During his career in Brooklyn and Los Angeles, the Dodgers captured seven National League pennants, and lost two others on the last day of the season. In the second game of the 1959 playoffs with the Milwaukee Braves, Hodges carried home the pennant-winning run in the twelfth inning on a single by old Brooklyn buddy Carl Furillo.

Gil hit over 20 home runs 11 consecutive years; six times going over 30, and twice exceeding 40, with a high of 42 in 1954. As a member of seven pennant winners, he appeared in 39 World Series games, batting .267 with five home runs and 21 RBIs. The low point in his career came in the 1952 World Series when he drew the collar against the New York Yankees, going an embarrassing 0-for-21 with six strikeouts. He bounced back from that debacle with a vengeance, to hit .364, .292, .304, and .391 in his last four Series.

Hodges, considered by many to be the strongest man in the National League, had his greatest day as a major leaguer on August 31, 1950, during the heat of a pennant race. In a game against the Boston Braves, with Hall of Fame pitcher Warren Spahn on the mound for Billy Southworth's team, the Brooklyn slugger smashed four home runs into the far reaches of Ebbets Field, his fourth one a two-run shot into the upper left field seats in the bottom of the eighth. He also stroked a seventh-inning single, giving him 17 total bases for the game, sparking the Dodgers to a 19-3 rout of the fourth-place Braves, and sending 14,226 Flatbush fans home happy. Gil Hodges was the sixth major leaguer, and fourth National Leaguer, to hit four home runs in one game. He followed in the footsteps of another first sacker, New York Yankee great Lou Gehrig, who accomplished the feat in 1932.

He established a National League mark, since broken, of hitting 14 career grand slam home runs. Willie McCovey and Hank Aaron, later, both finished with 16.

Gil Hodges closed out his playing career with the New York Mets in 1963, and began his managerial career the same year, in Washington. After five years in the nation's capital, the quiet leader returned to New York where he led the "Miracle Mets" to the World Championship in 1969, rolling over the mighty Baltimore Orioles in five games. Three years later, on April 2, 1972, during a spring training golf game, the big first baseman suffered a fatal heart attack. He was 47.

BURT HOOTON

The man with the woeful expression was fittingly dubbed "Happy" by his manager, Tommy Lasorda. And Happy made Dodger fans happy for ten years as he rolled up 112 victories against only 84 defeats, helping the Big Blue Machine of Los Angeles win three National League flags, and one World Championship.

Burt Hooton (Los Angeles Dodgers)

Burt Carlton Hooton, was born in Greenville, Texas on February 17, 1950. Twenty-one years later, the 6'1", 210-pound, right-handed pitcher was given a bonus of $50,000 to sign a professional baseball contract with the Chicago Cubs. In his fourth major league start, on April 16, 1972, the big rookie, wild but effective, threw a no-hitter at the Philadelphia Phillies, winning 4-0. He struck out seven and walked seven in his masterpiece.

In 1975, Burt Hooton was traded to the Los Angeles Dodgers. After going 6-7 during his first three months in L.A., the master of the knuckle-curve reeled off 12 straight victories to finish the season 18-9 (he had been 0-2 in Chicago prior to the trade).

Two years later, Happy Hooton produced a 12-7 record as the Dodgers won the National League pennant. The low point in Hooton's career occurred that year, in the NLCS against the Philadelphia Phillies. In Game Three, with the series deadlocked at one game apiece, Hooton lost his cool completely over home plate umpire Harry Wendelstedt's ball-strike calls. As the crowd became more and more abusive, the Dodger hurler issued bases-loaded walks to pitcher Larry Christensen, Bake McBride, and Larry Bowa, giving the Phils a 3-2 lead. Fortunately, his Los Angeles teammates fought back, scoring three times in the ninth for a 6-5 victory.

The Dodgers went on to take the pennant, three games to one, and earn the right to meet the New York Yankees in the World Series. Hooton compiled a 1-1 record in the Series, pitching a complete game 6-1 victory over Billy Martin's team in Game Two.

The following year, the man from Texas had his best season, leading the L.A. staff with a 19-10 record and a 2.71 ERA. Once again Hooton had a 1-1 record in the Series, winning Game Two against New York, 5-3. Unfortunately, for the second straight year, Hooton and the rest of the Dodgers had to watch as the New Yorkers hauled in the winner's share of the purse.

The script changed, however, in 1981. This time, "Team Comeback" would not be denied. Los Angeles, winners of the first half, in a strike-shortened season, met the Houston Astros, the second-half winners, in the Western Division playoff. With the Dodgers down two games to none in the best of five series, Burt Hooton stepped to the fore, and got his team rolling with a 6-1 three-hitter. When Valenzuela took Game Four 2-1, and Jerry Reuss bested Nolan Ryan, 4-0, in Game Five, Tommy Lasorda's boys were off to the NLCS.

Once again the Dodgers got off the mark slowly. After Hooton took Game One, 5-1, L.A. hit the skids, dropping the next two games at home, and putting themselves in a big hole. But again, Hooton came to the rescue. With his knuckle-curve darting in and out all afternoon, the big righty evened the series with a strong effort, winning 7-1 when the Dodgers scored two in the eighth and four in the ninth. Valenzuela closed it out in Game Five, winning 2-1 on Rick Monday's dramatic home run in the ninth.

The World Series was no different. The New York Yankees caught the Dodgers cold once again, and had them down two games to none at the start. Hooton pitched six strong innings in a 3-0 loss in Game Two, leaving after having yielded only one unearned run. This time Fernando stopped the slide, defeating rookie Dave Righetti, 5-4, with a gutty pitching performance. Tommy Lasorda's scrappers fought back time after time in Game Four, overcoming a four-run deficit and a three-run deficit, before winning, 8-7. Jerry Reuss took Game Five 2-1 to put the Big Blue Machine on top for the first time in the Series, three games to two. Happy Hooton never let the Bronx Bombers back in. He pitched a solid game, winning the finale 9-2, with relief help from Steve Howe.

A major cog in the Los Angeles Dodgers three miracle comebacks, the big Texan produced a combined record of 4-1, with a spectacular 0.82 earned run average. It was his finest hour.

Hooton retired in 1985, after 15 years in the big show, with 151 wins, 136 losses, and a 3.38 earned run average.

CHARLIE HOUGH

There's an old saying in baseball that knuckle ball pitchers can pitch forever. Charlie Hough, the man with the butterfly pitch, put that theory to the test.

Charles Oliver Hough was born in Honolulu, Hawaii, on April 5, 1948. Hough began his professional baseball career in 1966, with the Ogden team of the Pioneer league. His debut was inauspicious, a lukewarm 5-7 wonloss record. After bouncing around the minors for four years with mediocre success, Hough learned the knuckleball pitch from Los Angeles scout Goldie Holt, and his future suddenly got much brighter.

Hough gradually worked his way up to the Dodgers, earning a full-time spot in their bullpen in 1973. For the next eight years, the man from Honolulu was the major cog in the L.A. relief corps, holding down the middle relief role for a time, then taking over as the closer when Mike Marshall went down with an injury in late 1975. The butterfly specialist did a yeoman's job for the next two years, appearing in 77 games with 18 saves and a 2.20 ERA in 1976, and pitching in 70 games with 22 saves in 1977.

Charlie Hough (Los Angeles Dodger photo)

Hough's effectiveness as a reliever tapered off after the '77 season, and he was traded to Texas midway through 1980. Ranger manager Don Zimmer converted the 34year-old Hough to a starting pitcher and, over the next nine years, he became the most productive starting pitcher in Texas Ranger history, starting over 30 games each year, and compiling a won-loss record of 132-130. He led the team in wins, complete games, and innings pitched for six consecutive years. Over that span, he never pitched less than 230 innings in any year.

The 43-year-old Hough changed uniforms once again in 1991, donning the black and white of the

Chicago White Sox. On the Sox, he teamed up with 44-yearold Carlton Fisk to form one of the oldest major league batteries in history. Two years with the Florida Marlins ended Hough's major league career. He finished with a 216-216 record, and 61 saves over a 25-year career. His 858 game appearances stand #11 on the all-time list.

FRANK HOWARD

If ever a man with a bat struck fear into the hearts of opposing third basemen, that man was big Frank Howard. Standing a towering 6'7" high and tipping the scales at 255 pounds, the man called Hondo was a fearsome sight at the plate. And when he swung, he was more frightening. He ripped line drives with a fury seldom seen in the big leagues. Many times his vicious shots tore the glove completely off the third baseman's hand. Occasionally, the force of the blow was enough to spin the fielder completely around. From the time Hondo broke into professional baseball with an MVP season at Green Bay in the III League, there was never any question about his ability to crush a baseball. He impressed everyone with his awesome power.

Howard, an Ail-American basketball player at Ohio State University, spent only two years in the Dodger's minor league farm system. After his spectacular debut at Green Bay; he led the league in games (129), runs (104), home runs (37), and runs batted in (119), while hitting a lusty .333, – he split the 1959 season between three clubs; Victoria in the AA Texas League, Spokane in the AAA Pacific Coast League, and Los Angeles. The towering slugger devastated Texas League pitching, with 27 homers and a .356 batting average in 63 games. He went on to blast 16 more home runs while hitting .319 in 76 games with Spokane, the Dodgers' top minor league entry, and he added another round tripper, his 44th of the season, in a short stint in L.A. He was named "Minor League Player of the Year" by *The Sporting News* in recognition of his achievements.

In 1960, Frank was in Dodger blue for good, hitting prodigious home runs for the enjoyment of the California fans. He belted one tape measure job in Pittsburgh that fans are still talking about. The ball cleared the 400foot fence in left field with plenty to spare, travelling another 160 feet before coming to rest an estimated 560 feet from the plate. Another time he blasted a game-winning grand slam home run off Bob Buhl in Milwaukee, the ball disappearing into a clump of pine trees behind the center field fence. Howard's crowning achievement came when he was voted National League Rookie of the Year after hitting 23 homers and driving in 77 runs in 117 games.

In 1962, as the Dodgers made an unsuccessful bid for the National League pennant, Howard was a major contributor to the attack He hit a solid 296, smashed 31 home runs, and drove in 119 runs. He also set a Dodger record for runs batted in a month, when he knocked in 41 runs during the August stretch drive.

The following year, in spite of injuries that sidelined him for 40 games, the right-handed power hitter still accounted for 28 round trippers, as the Dodgers rolled to the National League pennant. In the World Series sweep against the Yankees, the big right fielder rapped the ball at a .300 clip. In the bottom half of the fifth inning of Game Four, the 6'7" slugger hit a monstrous home run into the upper deck of left field at Dodger Stadium, off Yankee ace Whitey Ford, a 450-

Frank Howard (Los Angeles Dodger photo)

foot shot-and he hit it with only one hand on the bat!

The Dodgers, in need of a quality left-handed starting pitcher, traded Howard to the Washington Senators in 1965 for Claude Osteen. Big Frank Howard went on to glory in the nation's capital. He hit 237 home runs in just seven years, including 48 in 1969. He led the league with 44 home runs in both 1968 and 1970. He also led the league in RBIs in 1970 with 126, and in bases on balls with 132.

In 1968, the fearsome slugger set several long-ball records that still stand. He holds the major league record for

- most home runs in six consecutive games (10);
- most home runs in five consecutive games (8) twice; and
- most home runs in four consecutive games (7) tie.

When Hondo finally hung up his spikes in 1973 after a 16-year major league career, he left behind a .273 batting average and 382 home runs. His career home run percentage of 5.89 is 17th on the all-time list.

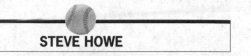

STEVE HOWE

Steve Howe is a tragic example of unlimited potential wasted. The hard-throwing southpaw had all the necessary mental and physical attributes required of a world class closer, but his unsuccessful struggle against a deadly drug habit destroyed a possible Hall-of-Fame career.

The cocky 22-year-old Howe, one year out of the University of Michigan, arrived on the Dodger scene with little fanfare in 1980, but with a 94-miles-per-hour fastball and an overabundance of confidence, he quickly became the closer on the Los Angeles team. He appeared in 59 games for Tommy Lasorda's club, going 7-9 with a 2.65 earned run average, and breaking Joe Black's rookie record for saves, with 17. His outstanding performance earned him National League Rookie of the Year honors.

In 1981, the handsome 6'1", 180-pound fire-baller continued his rise to the top. His 5-3 record in 41 games included 8 saves and a 2.50 ERA. He appeared in three games in the World Series, pitching 7 innings, and winning the crucial fourth game over the New York Yankees, 8-7, with three strong innings of relief. In one of the most exciting World Series games on record, L.A. rallied from 4-0 and 6-3 deficits behind Jay Johnstone's electrifying sixth inning home run, and Howe's clutch pitching. Steve also picked up a save in the sixth and final game, with 3 2/3 innings of strong relief. Earlier, the crafty lefty had pitched in a total of four games in. the Division Series and the League Championship Series, recording four shutout innings.

By 1982, Steve Howe was firmly established as the Dodger closer, and he responded with his finest season. The 26-year-old Michigan native won 7 games against 5 losses, in 66 games, with 13 saves and a blistering 2.08 ERA. The following year, on March 4, Howe admitted to using cocaine, but claimed he was now free of the habit. However, after

running up a brilliant 1.44 earned run average with 18 saves, in 46 games, he ran afoul of Los Angeles management, being fined $54,000, and suspended for the remainder of the season. On December 15, baseball commissioner Bowie Kuhn suspended the Dodger reliever for one full year for tarnishing the image of the game.

Steve Howe made more than a half dozen comebacks from his substance abuse, but was never able to shake the deadly habit permanently. In his last comeback, he put together several outstanding years for George Steinbrenner's New York Yankees, compiling season earned run averages of 1.68, 2.45, and 1.80 along the way. When he fell from grace for the last time after the 1996 season, his career log showed a 47-41 won-loss record, with 91 saves and a 3.03 earned run average, in 497 games over 12 seasons.

Steve Howe (Los Angeles Dodgers)

JAY HOWELL

The Dodgers, both the Brooklyn and Los Angeles varieties, were blessed with great relief pitchers over the years, beginning with old number 46, Hugh Casey. Jay Canfield Howell was a recent addition to the Dodgers "Bullpen Hall of Fame."

Jay Howell was born in Miami, Florida, on November 26, 1955. He began his professional career with Eugene, Oregon as a bushy-tailed 20-year-old intent on becoming a starting pitcher. He went 5-4 in 13 games in his pro debut in the Northwest League. For the next eight years, the big right-hander bounced around between the majors and minors, compiling a sorry 5-8 record and a stratospheric earned run average over parts of four seasons in the big time.

In 1984, Jay Howell became a relief expert, and was an immediate success with the New York Yankees, appearing in 61 games, with a 9-4 record, seven saves, and a glossy 2.69 ERA. After the season, he was dealt to the Oakland Athletics for Ricky Henderson. He spent the next three years with the A's, honing his relief skills, and accounting for 61 saves along the way. His success as a closer brought him to Los Angeles in the Bob Welch deal in the winter of 1988.

The 6'3", 220-pound fast ball pitcher was a major factor in the Dodgers "miracle" World Championship. He made 50 mound appearances in '88, with 21 saves, and a brilliant 2.21 earned run average. His postseason performance was notable on several counts, the most memorable being his ejection from an NLCS game against the New York Mets when pine tar was discovered in his glove.

In the World Series, the 33-year-old hurler was the losing pitcher in Game Three when he threw a home run ball to the As Mark McGwire in the bottom of the ninth inning. He reaped revenge the following night however, when he retired McGwire with the bases loaded in the bottom of the seventh to save the game for Tim Belcher.

The L.A. closer piled up 28 saves in 1989, followed by 16 in each of the next two years, before an arm injury laid him low. Howell remained active with the Dodgers through the '92 season, although he spent the better part of that year on the disabled list. After brief flings with Atlanta and Texas, He hung up his glove in 1994.

In his five years in L.A., the hard-throwing relief ace compiled a 22-19 record with a spectacular 2.07 ERA. He was also credited with 81 saves, stamping him as one of the most effective relief pitchers in Dodger history. He is presently #4 all-time, behind Todd Worrell, Jim Brewer, and Ron Perranoski.

Jay Howell (W. McNeil)

JIMMY JOHNSTON

Jimmy Johnston, a 5'10" outfielder-third baseman was an Eddie Stanky-Mickey Hatcher type of ballplayer; a player of limited ability who got by on determination, energy, teamwork, and flexibility. The native of Cleveland, Tennessee bounced around the minor leagues for several years, playing for seven different ballclubs, before he attracted the attention of manager Wilbert Robinson of the Brooklyn Robins in 1916. The hustling Johnston paid immediate dividends, helping the Robins capture their first National League flag in 16 years, edging out Pat Moran's Phillies by 2 1/2 games.

The 160-pound slap hitter stayed in the City of Churches for ten years, contributing to another Robin pennant in 1920, and proving himself to be an invaluable player. He was no standout, but during his sojourn in Brooklyn, he played every position except pitcher and catcher, and did a creditable job wherever he played.

When Johnston shifted to the infield, playing third base regularly, his offensive production took a turn for the better. From 1921 through 1923, the man from the Volunteer state had batting averages of .325, .319, and .325, and runs scored totals of 104, 111, and 110. Batting from the leadoff or second spot, he kept the ball in play, as shown by the fact that he struck out only 58 times in 1,816 times at bat, an average of only 19 times a year.

Jimmy Johnston

ERIC KARROS

Eric Karros was a vital cog in the Dodgers' Big Blue Machine of the 1990s. The native of Hackensack, New Jersey joined the Los Angeles organization in 1988, after being drafted in the sixth round of the Free Agent Draft.

The 20-year-old first baseman found the Pioneer (Rookie) League to his liking as he pounded the ball at a .366 clip for the Great Falls, Montana, Dodgers, with 12 home runs in just 66 games. A .303 year with Bakersfield in the Class A California League was followed by .352 at San Antonio, and .316 at Albuquerque. His performance with the Dukes, including 22 home runs and 101 runs-batted-in, won him a promotion to Los Angeles.

When spring training began in 1992, the 6'4", 216pound youngster was the #3 first baseman, behind Kal Daniels and Todd Benzinger. After spending the first six weeks of the season platooning, Karros won the position outright after hitting a three-run, pinch-hit home run off Stan Belinda of the Pittsburgh Pirates, in a 5-4 Dodger victory, on May 23. Karros' bat caught fire in the second

Jimmy Johnston, because of his hustle and his determination to win at any cost, was a huge fan-favorite in Ebbets Field. He was a smart baserunner, in addition to his other strengths, stealing 169 bases during his major league career. On September 22, 1916, the Robin outfielder stole second, third, and home in the same game. He hit for the cycle in 1922, quite a feat considering he hit only 22 home runs in his entire career.

The darling of Flatbush was traded to the Boston Braves in 1926, went to the Giants a couple of months later; then retired from active play when the season ended. He coached the Robins for awhile after retirement, then managed in the minor leagues for several years.

Johnston played in the major leagues for 13 years, during which time he accumulated 1,493 hits, good for a .294 batting average. The best tribute that could be paid to James Harle Johnston was "he was a winner."

Eric Karros (W. McNeil)

half of the season, particularly in clutch situations. From the All-Star game to the end of the season, the handsome right-handed slugger led the National League in runs-batted-in, with 55. He finished the year with a Los Angeles Dodger rookie record of 88 RBIs, to go along with 20 home runs and a .257 batting average. His performance earned him the National League's Rookie of the Year award, the 12th time a Dodger won the award.

In 1993, the handsome Greek helped pull the Dodgers out of the cellar. His 23 dingers and 80 runs-batted-in gave Tommy Lasorda's boys some badly needed punch, although his .247 batting average was a slight drop from his rookie season.

With the addition of Piazza and Mondesi to the Los Angeles lineup, the Dodgers became an offensive-minded unit as the decade approached the halfway mark. They showed their class in the strike-shortened 1994 season by winning the Western Division pennant.

They won the division again in 1995 and finished a close second to San Diego the following year. And Eric Karros was a big reason for their success. In '95, he just missed the .300 mark, batting .298 with 32 home runs and 115 RBIs. He almost duplicated that effort in '96 when he hit .260 with 34 homers and 111 RBIs.

He continued his onslaught against opposing pitchers over the next four years, smashing 119 home runs and driving in 409 runners. Back problems hampered his run production in 2001 and 2002, but he remained a valuable contributor to the team's pennant drives with many key hits.

Karros left his mark on many Los Angeles Dodger records, including games played, base hits, home runs, fielding average, putouts, and assists. He was traded to the Chicago Cubs in December 2002.

"WEE WILLIE" KEELER

Wee Willie Keeler, standing only 5'4" tall in his stocking feet, was a giant among men. The Brooklyn Irishman was the finest bat mechanic the major leagues have ever seen. He choked up on the bat a full 6", using his quick hands to punch the ball over the infield. He could do everything with a bat; bunt, hit and run, or swing away. When asked his secret, he replied, "Keep your eye on the ball an' hit 'em where they ain't."

The left-handed hitting Keeler played in the major leagues for 19 years, amassing 2,955 hits along the way. His .345 batting average is #12 on the all-time list. He led the league in hitting twice. In 1897 he piled up 243 hits in only 128 games and hit .432, the third highest season average in major league history. The following year he "slumped" to .379, still good enough to be number one. In 1897, he set a major league record of hitting safely in 44

"Wee Willie" Keeler (Brace Photo)

consecutive games. That mark stood until Joe DiMaggio hit in 56 straight games in 1941. His National League mark was later tied by Pete Rose.

Wee Willie could pick 'em up and lay 'em down too, as attested to by his 519 career stolen bases. He swiped 73 bases in 1896, and 63 bases in 1897.

The little man began his baseball career with Binghamton in the old Eastern League in 1892, and immediately gave promise of what was to come when he led the league in batting with an average of .373. Two years later, he found a permanent home in Baltimore with Ned Hanlon's famed Baltimore Orioles. Along with players like John McGraw, Fielder Jones, and Wilbert Robinson, the diminutive Keeler helped revolutionize the game of baseball, popularizing new strategies like the bunt, hit-and-run, Baltimore Chop, and heady baserunning. The Orioles converted their ingenuity into three consecutive National League pennants, in 1894-9596.

Three years later, when Hanlon shifted his talents to the borough of Brooklyn, he took several of his players with him, including the 27-year-old Keeler. The revamped Dodgers immediately won two consecutive National League pennants, giving Hanlon a record of five pennants and two second-place finishes in seven years. In the 1900 Chronicle-Telegraph Cup Series, the forerunner of the World Series, the Superbas defeated the Pittsburgh Pirates, three games to one. Keeler hit a resounding .353 in the four games.

Wee Willie Keeler demonstrated his batting prowess in Flatbush for four years before jumping to the New York Highlanders of the newly formed American League. He pummeled the ball at a sizzling .358 clip for Hanlon's Superbas, as they were being called, and carried a total of 456 runs across the plate in the four years, including a league-leading 141 runs in 1899. His 820 hits included a league-leading total of 208 in 1900.

The speedy outfielder played in the American League for seven years, but he was not the same hitter he had been earlier. Although still a superior batsman, his AL batting average of .295 couldn't hold a candle to the lofty .377 average he had accumulated during his 12year National League career.

Wee Willie Keeler was one of a kind. John McGraw, who played with and managed some of the greatest players ever to grace a ballfield, once said, "except for Ty Cobb, Keeler was the greatest player I ever saw." The friendly, easy-going outfielder was elected into baseball's Hall of Fame in 1939, alongside Cobb, Ruth, and Wagner.

MATT KEMP

Matt Kemp has the potential to be a five-tool player, one who can hit for average, hit with power, run, field, and throw. He showcased that type of player in 2011 and is on track to continue to play at a high level, both offensively and defensively, over the rest of his career.

Matthew Ryan Kemp was born in Midwest City, Oklahoma, on September 23, 1984. He was signed to a professional baseball contract by the Los Angeles Dodgers out of high school in 2003 at the age of 18 and began his rise to the top of the baseball world with the Gulf Coast Rookie League Dodgers that same year, hitting a respectable .270 in 42 games. The following year, he split his time between Columbus in the South Atlantic League and Vero Beach in the Florida State League, hitting .288 for Columbus in 112 games and .351 for Vero Beach in 11 games. He returned to Vero Beach in 2005 where he batted .306 with 27 home runs in 109 games, and then was fast-tracked to AA Jacksonville for 48 games before being called up to Los Angeles on May 28 after hitting .327 for the Suns. Kemp made his major league debut on the 28th in Nationals Park in Washington, D.C., going one for four in a 10-4 loss to the Nats. He went on to hit eight home runs in his first 18 days in the major leagues, becoming just the first Dodger and fifth major leaguer to accomplish that feat. He batted .253 in 52 games for Grady Little's crew, but the Dodgers, who were struggling to stay afloat in the tough Western Division race, couldn't afford to force-feed the 21-year old youngster at the big league level, and they optioned him to Las Vegas for more experience on July 14. He went on to rattle the fences in the Pacific Coast League, batting a torrid .368 over the last 44 games.

Matt Kemp began the 2007 season with Los Angeles, but after five games he went on the Disabled List with a shoulder separation and was optioned to Las Vegas to rebuild his strength and regain his batting eye. He spent six weeks with the 51s where he hit .329, returning to the Dodgers on June 8. From there to the end of the season, he tortured opposing pitchers to the tune of .342, the fourth highest single-season batting average in Los Angeles Dodger history. He also chipped in with 10 homers and 42 RBIs in 292 at-bats. He hit a solid .290 in 155 games for his new manager, Joe Torre, in 2008, slamming 18 homers and driving in 76 runs along the way while helping his team to a Western Division pennant. The next year, he upped his batting average to .297, hit 26 homers, and drove in 101 runs, as the Dodgers captured another pennant. He won Gold Glove and Silver Slugger Awards in 2009, and was selected for the National League All-Star Team. But darker days lay ahead.

Matt Kemp (Los Angeles Dodgers)

As the 2010 season approached, Kemp appeared to have been mesmerized by the bright lights and the teeming night life of the big city. He began a relationship with pop star Rihanna late in 2009 and, between the two of them they attracted paparazzi by the busload. The relationship took its toll on the Dodger center fielder as winter turned to spring and the baseball season got underway. He seemed to be on edge most of the season, had a contentious relationship with management, and appeared to lose focus frequently on the field. He missed catching balls that he would normally put in his pocket, and his looping throws to the infield resulted in only three assists all season. He was also lost on the bases, getting picked off first base on a regular basis, and watching his stolen base percentage plummet from 78% to an embarrassing 56%. He even got thrown out on a steal while standing up. The 6', 3", 220-pound right-handed hitter lost concentration at the plate as well, swinging at pitches in the dirt, fanning 170 times in 602 at-bats, and limping home with a .249 batting average, 50 points below his career average.

Matt Kemp and Rihanna parted company in December 2010 and the 26-year old outfielder rededicated himself to becoming the player everyone predicted he could be. He raised his level of play in 2011 while challenging for the Triple Crown title most of the season. He finished the year in third place in the batting race with a .324 average but he led the league in both RBIs with 126 and home runs with 39. He also joined the 30-30 club, adding 40 stolen bases to his home run total and becoming just the second Dodger player to achieve that honor, the other being Raul Mondesi. Kemp's stolen base success in 2011 was partly due to his work with Dodger coaches, and former major league stolen base champions, Maury Wills and Davey Lopes, who mentored him in all aspects of the art of base stealing including how to maximize his lead and what to look for in a pitcher's moves. He also became, once again, one of the top defensive center fielders in the National League, exhibiting outstanding speed, a reliable glove, and a strong, accurate throwing arm that gunned down eleven runners trying to take an extra base. Kemp finished the season as arguably the best all-around player in the National League and maybe in both leagues.

The Oklahoma native performed like a superstar in 2011, earning him the Hank Aaron Award as the National League's most outstanding offensive player. He also earned a Player's Choice Award as the league's most outstanding player, a Gold Glove as the league's top defensive center fielder, and a Silver Slugger Award as the league's best hitting center fielder. He was also selected for the Sporting News National League All-Star Team, and was one of the top contenders for the league's Most Valuable Player Award. If he can continue to perform at this high level, or come reasonably close to it, for another decade or so he will probably be welcomed into the hallowed halls of Cooperstown with open arms, sometime around the year 2029.

WILLIAM "BRICKYARD" KENNEDY

In 1892, a 23-year-old brickmaker walked off his job in Bellaire, Ohio, and began to carve out a reputation for himself in the hurly burly world of professional baseball. His name was William V. Kennedy, better known as "Brickyard." The hard-throwing youngster joined manager Monte Ward's Brooklyn Bridegrooms that year and immediately became their number-three starter, behind George Haddock and Ed Stein. He won 13 games his first season in the big leagues and, within a year, had moved up to the number-one spot.

"Brickyard" Kennedy was an intense competitor with an explosive temper, characteristics that carried him to great achievements on the mound. They also got him into hot water from time to time, particularly with members of the umpiring staff.

Kennedy stood 5'11" tall, but weighed only 160 pounds. His job as a brickmaker, however, gave him a strong, sinewy body, with bulging biceps, attributes that caused his fastball to literally explode as it crossed the plate.

In 1893, the Ohio native established himself as a quality major league pitcher. On his way to a 25-20 season, the ace of the threadbare Brooklyn pitching staff volunteered to pitch both ends of a doubleheader on two separate occasions. On May 30, he tossed a double victory against the hapless Louisville Colonels, throwing a two-hit shutout at them and beating them 3-0 in Game One, then coming back with a 6-2 five-hitter in the nightcap. Less than two months later, he attempted to repeat the feat against the great Cy Young of the Cleveland Spiders. He dropped a decision to Young in Game One, but bounced back to win the second game, 7-3.

Brickyard's big season was one of eight straight years in which he won 16 or more games. From 1894 through 1900, he piled up victory totals of 24, 19, 17, 18, 16, 22, and 20, pitching the Brooklyn team, now called the Superbas, to National League pennants in 1899 and 1900.

William V. Kennedy, in addition to being a fierce competitor, was also a fun-loving Irishman who occasionally caused his manager great consternation. Like Rube Waddell of the Philadelphia Athletics, and many other turn-of-the-century athletes, Kennedy was just a boy in a man's body. The youngster from Bellaire loved to pitch, and it didn't matter where. One day, Kennedy stayed home from a game, complaining of a sore arm. The next morning, manager Ned Hanlon almost choked on his coffee when he spotted the following account of a sandlot baseball game in the local newspaper, "Yesterday, the Shriner's baseball team lost the game in spite of a fine pitching performance by Brooklyn's ace pitcher, William Kennedy."

Brickyard Kennedy toiled in a Brooklyn uniform for ten years, during which time he was the workhorse of the team. His 176 victories over that span distinguish him as Brooklyn's top pitcher of the nineteenth century, and place him fourth on the all-time Dodger win list, behind Don Sutton's 230, Don Drysdale's 209, and Dazzy Vance's 190.

Kennedy was also a fine hitter, finishing his career with a .261 batting average. He hit over .300 four times, putting together seasons of .304 in 1894, .307 in 1895, .301 in 1900, and a sizzling .362 in 1903. He holds Dodger hitting records for pitchers in several categories, including most hits in a career (294), most hits in a season (49), and most career RBIs (126).

William "Brickyard" Kennedy

CLAYTON KERSHAW

Sandy Koufax is the greatest pitcher in Dodger history and one of the three greatest southpaws in the history of major league baseball. And 23-year old Clayton Kershaw appears to be a clone of the legendary hurler. The new Dodger southpaw was born in Dallas, Texas on March 19, 1988. He was recognized as one of the country's best high school pitchers in 2006 when he posted a perfect 13-0 record for Highland Park High School in Dallas, and threw an all-strikeout perfect game in a playoff game that year. L.A. quickly signed the young phenom to a contract following his graduation and sent him to the Gulf Coast Rookie League for experience. He pitched in ten games for the Gulf Coast Dodgers, going 2-0 in 37 innings with 54 strikeouts, five bases on balls,

and a 1.95 ERA. His development continued at an accelerated pace as he passed through the Rookie League, Class-A, and Class Double-A, impressing Dodger brass at every way-stop.

Clayton Kershaw (Los Angeles Dodgers)

He began the 2008 season with Jacksonville in the Double-A Southern League, where he was rated as having the league's best fastball, best breaking ball, and for being the best prospect in the league. After going 2-3 with a 1.91 ERA in 13 games with the Suns, his contract was purchased by the Dodgers and he made his major league debut on May 25, firing two-run ball over six innings in an eventual 4-3 ten inning Dodger victory. At 20 years and 65 days old, he became the fourth youngest starting pitcher in Los Angeles Dodger history. L.A., being conscious of the youngster's age and his long-term potential, handled him with kid gloves the rest of the year. He appeared in 22 games for L.A., pitching 108 innings and posting a 5-5 won-loss mark. He was given a little more free rein in 2009, pitching 171 innings in

31 games with an 8-8 record, 185 strikeouts, 90 bases on balls, and a 2.79 ERA.

The 6', 3", 215-pound fireballer continued to work on his command in the off-season and was ready to go when the Dodger brass turned him loose on opposing batters in 2010. He was armed with an impressive arsenal—a 93-96 mph four-seam cut fastball with late movement, a 91-93 mph two-seam fastball, a hard slider, a 12-6 curveball, and a circle change-up—and he used all of them to his advantage. On April 15 he fanned 13 batters in a 5-4 no-decision against the San Francisco Giants in Dodger Stadium. The smooth working left-hander threw seven innings in that game, leaving with a 2-1 lead but the bullpen blew the lead before recovering to win it in ten. He had another notable no-decision game in the Great American Ball Park in Cincinnati on August 30, going seven innings and striking out eleven batters in a 3-2 twelve-inning Dodger victory. For the year, he won 13 games against 10 losses in 204 innings, with 212 strikeouts and a fine 2.91 ERA. And he continued to improve his command and reduce his bases on balls, issuing just 81 walks for an average of 3.6 walks per game.

Clayton Kershaw, who was still just 23-years old in 2011, catapulted into the rarified atmosphere of Dodger ace as it all came together for him. His full repertoire of pitches was working to perfection and his command was near perfect as he struck out an average of 9.6 batters for every nine innings pitched while walking just two. He began the year with a brilliant effort against San Francisco ace Tim Lincecum and he came away with a 2-1 victory over the two-time Cy Young Award winner, yielding no earned runs while striking out nine Giant batters and issuing a single base on balls. The game was one of five victories he registered over the Giants during the season, three of them against Lincecum, two by scores of 2-1, and one by a 1-0 margin. He beat the Giants again on April 11 by a 6-1 score, but then went without a win for three weeks before stopping the Chicago Cubs 5-2 on May 2. He took the measure of the New York Mets by a 4-2 mark in Shea Stadium on the 8th, and defeated Arizona 4-3 five days later with an 11 strikeout performance. He fanned ten batters in an 8-0 shutout of the Florida Marlins on May 29, struck out 11 batters in a complete game 4-0 shutout over the Detroit Tigers on June 20, and fanned another eleven batters in a 3-2 win over the Los Angeles Angels six days later.

The Kershaw express roared to the finish line as summer faded and September approached. By Labor Day his record stood at 17-5. The flame-throwing Texan took the measure of the Giants again on September 9, beating Santiago Casilla, 2-1. He outpitched Dan Hudson of Arizona, 3-2, on the fourteenth, defeated Lincecum for the third time, 2-1, on the twentieth, and closed out his season with a 6-2 victory over the San Diego Padres. His season statistics were awesome. He went 21-5, pitching 233 innings over 33 starts, with 248 strikeouts, 54 bases on balls, and a 2.28 earned-run average. He led the league in victories (tied with Ian Kennedy), strikeouts, and ERA to become the Dodgers first Triple Crown Winner since Sandy Koufax in 1966.

After the season ended, the awards came in fast and furious. First he walked off with the Warren Spahn Award as the major league's top southpaw pitcher. Then he won a People's Choice Award as the best pitcher in the National League, earned a Gold Glove for his exceptional fielding skills, and was selected for the Sporting News National League All-Star Team. To top it off he captured the National League's Cy Young Award as its most outstanding pitcher. At the age of 23, the world is his oyster. His potential is unlimited and his future place in the history of the game is, barring injury, up to him. Based on his fantastic 2011 season, Clayton Kershaw is in line to join Matt Kemp in Cooperstown, claiming a pedestal sometime around the year 2033.

SANDY KOUFAX

Whenever the greatest pitchers in baseball history are discussed and debated, Sandy Koufax's name always comes up. The stylish 6'2" southpaw dominated major league baseball for five consecutive seasons, from 1962 through 1966. Over that period, the former Brooklyn wild man led the league in earned ran average every year. He also led the league in victories three times, and in strikeouts four times. The workhorse of the Los Angeles Dodger pitching staff hurled more than 300 innings three times. No pitcher in the history of major league baseball, with the exception of Lefty Grove, ever dominated the sport so thoroughly.

Sandy Koufax

The totality of Koufax's dominance of his profession is evident in his four-year statistics, from 1963 through 1966.

YEARS	W	L	PCT.	IP	CG
1963-66	97	27	.782	1,192	89

SHO	SO	BB	ERA
31	1,228	259	1.82

Broken down, his yearly averages were:

W	L	PCT	IP	CG
24	7	.782	298	22

SHO	SO	BB	ERA
8	307	65	1.82

Early in his career, Koufax was considered to be a gifted athlete, but one who was unable to harness his immense talent. Signed off the University of Cincinnati campus by the Brooklyn Dodgers in 1955, the 19-year-old fireballer showed periodic flashes of brilliance, such as the two-hit shutout he threw at the Cincinnati Reds in his second National League start, 14 Redlegs going back to the bench on strikes. Unfortunately, performances like this were few and far between during Koufax's first six years in the majors. More often than not, the scatter-armed youngster's inconsistency would prove to be his downfall. He averaged almost six walks per game.

In June 1959, he fanned 16 Philadelphia batters. Then, in late August he shattered the National League single game strikeout record by fanning 18 San Francisco Giants. He also set National League records for the most strikeouts in two games (31), and in three games (38).

The glory days were infrequent, however. From 1955 through 1960, his career record was a mediocre 36-40 with a 4.03 earned run average. His strikeout average was an impressive 9.5 per game, but his 5.6 walks per game prevented him from realizing his potential.

Then one day in 1961, things began to turn around for the Brooklyn native. During a spring training "B" game, catcher Norm Sherry suggested that Koufax take a little off his fast ball, rather than trying to throw it through the backstop on every pitch. Miraculously, the lean southpaw discovered that he could ease up on his motion without losing any effectiveness. His control improved and he developed confidence in his other pitches, rather than just relying on his fastball. He discovered that his sharp breaking curveball was the most devastating curve ball in the league, and his change of pace was a back breaker.

After two transition years, the Dodger ace went on a four-year roll. His achievements were monumental.

- He was voted the National League most valuable player for 1963.
- He won the National League Cy Young award in 1963, 1965, and 1966.
- He was voted the World Series' most valuable player in 1963 and 1965.
- He was voted the major league player of the decade, 1960-69.
- He pitched four no-hitters, one each in 1962-64 and 65, topping it off with a perfect game against the Chicago Cubs on September 9, 1965. His total of four career no-hitters is a National League record.

In the 1963 World Series, the overpowering southpaw won two games against the New York Yankees in a four-game Dodger sweep, fanning a record 15 of the Bronx Bombers in a 5-2 opening game win, then besting Whitey Ford, 2-1, in the finale. In 1965, Koufax blanked the Minnesota Twins twice, beating them 7-0 in Game Five with a four-hit, 10-strikeout performance, then coming back in Game Seven to whitewash them again, 2-0, scattering two hits and fanning 10.

In four World Series appearances, during which the Dodgers won three World Championships, Sandy Koufax compiled a 4-3 record with a magnificent 0.95 ERA, and two shutouts. He fanned 61 batters in 57 innings.

The handsome 31-year-old hurler was forced to retire at the end of the 1966 season because of arthritis in his pitching elbow, ending his fabulous career just as it reached its peak. In his final season, he went 27-9 with 317 strikeouts and a 1.73 earned run average.

Fittingly, he was elected to the Baseball Hall of Fame in his first year of eligibility, 1972. At 32, he is the youngest player ever elected to the shrine.

Sandy Koufax's career needs no embellishment. He was simply the best. As one teammate appropriately put it, "Sandy Koufax belongs in a higher league."

CLEM LABINE

Clement Walter Labine was born in Lincoln, Rhode Island, on August 6, 1926, of French-Canadian parents. The handsome crewcut right-hander began his professional career with Newport News in the Piedmont League in 1944, compiling a 2-4 record in 12 games.

Working his way through the Brooklyn farm system after World War II, he was used alternately as a starter and a reliever. In 1948, at Pueblo, he went 13-10 as a starter. The following year, in St. Paul, the curveball pitcher appeared in a league-leading 64 games, all but one in relief. He won 12 and lost six with many important saves.

With Chuck Dressen's team engaged in a bitter dog-fight with Leo Durocher's Giants in 1951, Labine was recalled from St. Paul to beef up the beleaguered Dodger pitching staff. Down the stretch, the cocky rookie won five games against a single loss, topping off his excellent showing with a masterful 10-0 whitewashing of the Giants in the second game of the playoffs.

By 1953, the 6' right-hander had become the team bullpen stopper. Two years later, as the "Boys of Summer" swept to their first World Championship, the sinkerball specialist appeared in a league-leading 60 games, won 13 and saved another 11. He chipped in with three home runs to boot. In the World Series against the Yankees, Labine pitched in five games, winning one and saving another.

The following year, he led the league in saves with 19, while appearing in 62 games, with a 10-6 won-loss record. In the World Series against New York, Labine

Clem Labine

appeared in only two games, but one of them was a gem. In Game Six, with the Dodgers down three games to two, the gutty relief ace started against Bullet Bob Turley, and pitched ten strong innings, retiring the last eight men in order. He came away with a dramatic 1-0 victory when Brooklyn pushed across a run in the bottom of the tenth on walks to Gilliam and Snider, and a game-winning single by Jackie Robinson.

Labine led the league in saves once again in 1957, piling up 17 of them but, after two declining seasons in Los Angeles, the 34-year-old pitcher was traded to Detroit. He retired from the game in 1962, finishing with a record of 77-56, and 96 saves. He appeared in 513 major league games in his 13-year career, 38 as a starter, 475 as a reliever. In addition to his saves, he had seven complete games as a starter, with two shutouts.

The Rhode Island native played in four World Series, pitched 27 innings in ten games, had a 2-2 record with two saves, and a sparkling 1.65 ERA.

Clem Labine will always be remembered as a valuable member of "The Boys of Summer." When Brooklyn fans let their thoughts drift back to another time, to the time of their glorious dynasty, one picture will remain vividly clear; that of a tall, handsome, crewcut pitcher sporting number 41 on his back, strutting in from the bullpen to save another game for Carl Erskine or Preacher Roe. Nor will the Flatbush faithful ever forget his two memorable starts, shutouts against the Giants in the 1951 playoffs and against the Yankees in Game Six of the 1956 World Series.

In addition to his other many achievements in Brooklyn, Labine accomplished one other thing that endeared him to the patrons of Ebbets Field. He retired Dodger nemesis and Hall-of-Fame slugger Stan "The Man" Musial 49 consecutive times.

KEN LANDREAUX

Ken Landreaux was a Los Angeles native who took a circuitous route to Dodger Stadium, but when he finally arrived in 1981, he stayed for seven years, helping Tommy Lasorda's contingent capture one World Championship and two division titles.

The 21-year-old Landreaux, in just his second year in professional baseball, slammed Pacific Coast League pitching for a .359 average, on his way to winning the 1977 Sporting News Minor League Player of the Year award, as well as a promotion to the California Angels. Three years later, with the Minnesota Twins, Landreaux ran off a 31-game hitting streak, the longest in the American League in 30 years. The 1980 all-star also showed his great speed by running out three triples in one game, tying a major league record. The following year, he was on the move again, this time to the Los Angeles Dodgers, for Mickey Hatcher. One of his most memorable moments in a major league uniform occurred on April 12 of that year when he hit a game winning home run off Vern Ruhle of the Houston Astros, in Dodger Stadium. The roar of the home crowd that day was something special for a Los Angeles boy.

The 5'10", 160-pound centerfielder gave the Dodgers outstanding defensive play, as well as blinding speed on the bases, during his tenure with the club. He hit only

.251 in the strike shortened '81 season, but stole 18 bases in 99 games and led the league in fielding with a perfect 1.000 fielding average, as the Dodgers swept to the World Championship.

Surprisingly, the slender right-handed batter also exhibited above average power at the plate, giving Lasorda a comfortable mix of speed and punch in the number two slot in the batting order. The speedy Landreaux swiped 31 bases in 1982. In '83 he stole 30 more and also rapped out 17 round trippers, along with a .281 batting average, as the Dodgers claimed the Western Division crown.

In 1985 Ken Landreaux hit a respectable .268 with 12 homers and 15 stolen bases, as the Lasordamen once again finished first in the west. He rose to the occasion in the National League Championship Series against the St. Louis Cardinals, by pounding the ball at a .389 clip, with 3 doubles in five games. But, in the year of Ozzie Smith and Jack Clark, the Big Blue Machine went home empty handed.

The 32-year-old Landreaux was released by the Dodgers after the 1987 season, finishing his 11-year major league career with 1,099 base hits, 91 home runs, 145 stolen bases, and a .268 batting average.

HARRY "COOKIE" LAVAGETTO

Harry "Cookie" Lavagetto was a dependable baseball player who spent ten years in the major leagues with Pittsburgh and Brooklyn. He missed four more years due to military service in World War II.

Lavagetto began his major league career in Pittsburgh in 1934, as a 21-year-old second baseman, after batting .312 and driving in 100 runs for the Oakland Oaks of the Pacific Coast League. After three mediocre seasons in the Steel City, the California native was traded to Brooklyn in 1937, where he became the Dodgers' regular third baseman for the next four years. In 1941, he was a big factor in bringing the borough of Brooklyn its first National League pennant in 21 years. He hit a solid .277 during the pennant drive and knocked in 78 runs, batting from the sixth slot.

At the peak of his career, the war broke out, and the 6', 170-pound infielder marched off to serve his country in the U.S. Navy, one of the first major leaguers to enlist. Returning to baseball in 1946 after a four-year absence, the 33-year-old Lavagetto was relegated to the status of a part time player. He played in only 88 games in '46, hitting a paltry .236 as the Dodgers came within

Ken Landreaux

Cookie Lavagetto

one game of the pennant. The following year, with Jackie Robinson and Carl Furillo on the team, Burt Shotton brought them home in first place, five games ahead of Eddie Dyer's St. Louis Cardinals. Lavagetto, by this time, had lost his job to "Spider" Jorgensen, and was a utility player and pinch hitter. In 41 games, the grizzled veteran batted .261.

The Brooklyn Bums paired off against the New York Yankees in a bitterly contested World Series. Although the Bronx Bombers won the Series in seven games, Cookie Lavagetto became a baseball legend when he smashed a two-out, game-winning double off the right field wall in Ebbets Field, in the bottom of the ninth inning of Game Four, depriving Yankee pitcher Floyd Bevens of a no-hitter. Lavagetto's pinch hit was one of the most dramatic hits in World Series history. Neither Lavagetto nor Bevens ever played in another major league game.

Cookie went on to play minor league ball for several years with the Oakland Oaks. He returned to the majors as a coach for the Dodgers and Washington Senators, then managed the Senators and Minnesota Twins for five years. He retired from baseball in 1967.

Lavagetto suffered a fatal heart attack at his home in Orinda, California, on August 10, 1990. He was 77 years old.

Cookie Lavagetto was a solid major league third baseman, a tough hitter, and a decent RBI man. During his 10-year career, the right-handed batter piled up 945 hits to go along with a .269 batting average. He played in two All-Star games, in 1940 and 41. As long as baseball is played, the name of Cookie Lavagetto will never die. He will always be remembered in Brooklyn as the man who made THE HIT!

JAMES LONEY

James Anthony Loney, out of Houston, Texas, was a fancy fielding, smooth swinging first baseman who joined Kemp, Ethier, and Billingsley, on the Los Angeles team in 2006 to give Grady Little's charges four world class rookies as they fought their way into a tie for the Western Division Crown with the San Diego Padres. The team was eliminated by the New York Mets in three games in the National League Division Series, but it set the groundwork for division titles in 2008 and 2009, with perhaps more to come. And James Loney was a major factor in the Dodger successes. He had his biggest day in the major leagues on September 6, 2006, when he went four-for-five at the plate with a double and a home run, and he drove in nine runs to set a Los Angeles Dodger record and tie Brooklyn's Gil Hodges for the all-time franchise record. He finished his rookie season with a fine .284 batting average, stroking 15 extra base hits in 102 at-bats, and he carried his batting

stroke into the post-season, ripping the ball at a .750 clip against the Mets in the NLDS. The 6', 3", 220-pound left handed hitter split the 2007 season between Los Angeles and Las Vegas, hitting .279 in the Pacific Coast League and a sizzling .331 with the big club, smashing 18 doubles and 15 homers in 344 at-bats.

James Loney (Los Angeles Dodgers)

Loney became a fixture in the Dodger lineup beginning in 2008, and has been a consistent run producer since that time, but the long ball output that was expected of him based on his 2007 statistics has not surfaced. He hit .289 with 13 homers in 2008, .281 with 13 homers in 2009, and .267 with ten homers the following year, but in 2011, after 439 at-bats through August, the 27-year old Texan had only nine home runs to show for his efforts. L.A.'s hitting instructor, Dave Hansen, spent untold hours with Loney during the season, working on his rhythm, his wrist speed, his balance, and his weight shift, and teaching him how to elevate the ball after contact. All the hard work seemed to pay dividends in September as Loney, who was hitting just .276 on August 31 with 19 doubles in addition to his nine home runs, ripped the ball at a .348 clip in September with 11 doubles, three home runs, and 17 RBIs, in 92 at-bats. He had one three-game stretch, against the Pittsburgh Pirates from September 16 to September 18, when he stroked eight base hits in 11 at-bats, including two doubles and two home runs, while driving in three runs in each of the contests. Time will tell if the Dodgers finally have a long-ball-hitting first baseman in their lineup. They need one badly.

James Loney will become one of the Dodgers more valuable players if he can take advantage of his innate batting skills and drive the ball with authority, because he is already one of the premier defensive first basemen in the league, with excellent range, quick hands, and a sure glove. He fielded a glittering .996 in 2011 with just five errors in 1208 chances.

Lopes' 557 career stolen bases ranks 19th on the all-time list. He led the National League in thefts with 77 in 1975 and 63 in 1976. He stole five bases in one game in 1975 and, the same year, established a major league record, since broken, of 38 consecutive steals. He holds the National League Championship Series record with nine steals in 17 games, and is #3 in World Series competition with 10 stolen bases in 23 games.

When the chips were down, little Davey rose to the occasion. During the Dodgers' exciting World Championship experience in 1981, Lopes was unstoppable. He swiped five bases in the NLCS against the Montreal Expos, and followed that with four thefts against the Yankees in the Series.

The compact 170 pounder was more than a base stealer, however. He could do it all. When the situation called for it, Lopes could play long ball better than most. His 155 career home runs included 17 in 1978, 28 in 1979, and 17 in 1983. One of his most impressive power performances occurred in the 1978 World Series. He hit two home runs and drove in five runs to spark Tommy

DAVEY LOPES

During the 1970s, a group of Los Angeles Dodgers formed the longest playing infield in major league history. Steve Garvey, Davey Lopes, Bill Russell, and Ron Cey performed as a unit from the middle of 1973 through the 1981 season, a run of 8 1/2 years. Their contribution to Dodger legend included four National League pennants and one World Championship. Their teams finished second four times and third once, a record of success seldom seen in professional baseball.

Second baseman Davey Lopes was the sparkplug of the unit, doing whatever was necessary to rattle the opposition and win the game. Lopes was an ideal lead-off man; someone who could hit, and hit with power if necessary, or could squeeze out a base on balls to ignite a rally. Once on, the 5'9" speedster was unnerving to the opposing pitcher. He was one of the most effective base stealers in major league history, stealing 83% of the bases he attempted, #3 on the all-time list.

Davey Lopes (Los Angeles Dodger Photo)

Lasorda's team to an 11-5 romp m Game One; then hit another homer in a losing cause in Game Six, finishing the Series with seven RBIs and a .308 batting average.

A converted outfielder, Lopes developed into a solid defensive second baseman. The pride of East Providence, Rhode Island, won a gold glove in 1978.

Davey Lopes began his professional career with Daytona Beach in the Florida State League in 1968, moving systematically through the Los Angeles organization to Spokane and Albuquerque. After leading the Pacific Coast League in stolen bases with 48 in 1972, the 26-year-old infielder was promoted to the big club in September 1972. He stayed in the "Bigs" for 16 years, finally retiring in 1987 at the age of 42.

Although a late arrival in the major leagues, the speedy Lopes left behind some impressive statistics. He played in a total of 1,812 major league games, accumulating 1,671 hits, 437 extra base hits, 557 stolen bases, and a batting average of .263.

Davey Lopes played during an exciting period in Los Angeles Dodger history. The team was the class of the league during his tenure in California, and he was a major factor in their success. As a member of "The Infield" his achievements will never be forgotten.

AL LOPEZ

Alfonso Ramon Lopez was a tough kid who ate and slept baseball. When he was ten years old, he took a ball flush in the face, knocking him cold and breaking several bones, but he was back on the field again as soon as he healed. His baseball skills made him a local celebrity even in high school and, as soon as he turned 16, he traded in his school books for a mask, chest protector, and mitt, signing a professional contract with his home town Tampa team in the Class D Florida State League.

One of the highlights of his life was catching Walter Johnson in an exhibition game in Tampa after the 1925 season.

Al Lopez rose rapidly through the professional ranks, joining the Brooklyn Dodgers in 1928 shortly after his 20th birthday. He became the Dodgers regular catcher two years later, beginning a notable 19-year career. His first full year in the majors was known as "the year of the hitter" because changes in the construction of the baseball had made it difficult for pitchers to throw a curveball, and easy for batters to lay the wood to it. National League teams hit .303 for the year, still the league record, and Chicago Cubs slugger Hack Wilson drove in 191 runs, another mark that has survived the test of time. The 5'11" 165-pound Brooklyn backstop joined the hit parade that year, rapping the ball to the tune of .309, a mark he never reached again. He also caught 128 games, the first of 12 seasons in which he caught more than 100 games.

Lopez was known as an outstanding defensive catcher, with a fine arm, and a keen mind. He was death on bunts and pop-ups, and the take-charge guy in the infield. When he was traded to the Boston Braves in 1936, Dodger pitcher Van Lingle Mungo lamented, "I won 18 games and I would have won 25 if we hadn't traded Lopez. Nobody could work with a pitcher the way Al could. He knew the hitters and he studied them just like a manager." Over his long career, with Brooklyn, Boston, and Pittsburgh, Al Lopez set numerous records, including most career games caught major leagues (1,918), most years catching 100 or more games NL (12), and most games caught without a passed ball NL (114). He led National League catchers in fielding average four times, and in assists four times. And he was rated the seventh best defensive catcher of all time in a poll of retired major league players, conducted in the mid 80s, according to *The Ballplayers*.

Following his retirement as a player, the man known fondly as El Señor embarked upon a memorable 17-year managerial career, which included two American League pennants, and 10 second-place finishes. His teams finished out of the first division only three times in 17 years, giving him the ninth highest winning percentage in baseball history, at .584. In 1959, his American League champion Chicago White Sox, known as the Go-Go Sox because of their penchant for running wild on the bases, stole 113 bases, 45 more than the second place team.

Al Lopez

Al Lopez retired to his Tampa home and the golf links after the 1969 season, but he made one more public appearance, when he was inducted into the National Baseball Hall of Fame in Cooperstown, NY in 1977.

MIKE MARSHALL – PITCHER

Michael Grant Marshall was one of the most extraordinary relief pitchers in major league history. He was also one of the most controversial players of his day, constantly feuding with his managers, trainers, and teammates.

The stockily built, 5'10", 180-pounder started his professional baseball career as an infielder in the Philadelphia organization, but soon switched to pitching where he slowly but surely worked his way up the minor league ladder. After six years in the horse-and-buggy circuit, Marshall finally found his niche in Montreal, as a relief pitcher. Under manager Gene Mauch, the Michigan State graduate developed into the National League's foremost closer. He appeared in a league-leading 65 games in 1972, finishing with 18 saves, a 14-8 record, and a 1.78 ERA. The following year he led the league in both appearances (92) and saves (31). He pitched an unheard of 179 innings out of the bullpen.

Mike Marshall-Pitcher

A 1974 trade sent Willie Davis to the Expos, and brought Marshall to L.A. With big Mike came the pennant. A devout believer in, and professor of Kinesiology, the rugged reliever preached that, with proper muscle exercise, a pitcher could pitch every day. In 1974 he put that theory to the test. As Walter Alston's finely tuned unit fought its way to the pennant, the human pitching machine worked overtime. He set major league records for relief pitchers that may last forever, including most games pitched in relief (106), most innings pitched in relief (208), most games finished (83), and most consecutive games pitched (13). His amazing effort was rewarded with the National League Cy Young award as the league's best pitcher for 1974. He capped off his extraordinary season by appearing in all five World Series games, pitching nine innings with one save and a 1.00 ERA in a losing cause.

Marshall struggled through an injury-plagued season in 1975, pitching in only 57 games, with 13 saves, and 109 innings pitched. Fearing that he had lost his effectiveness, the Dodgers traded the 33-year-old reliever to Atlanta in 1976. Two years later he was back on top, rejoining his old Montreal manager, Gene Mauch, in Minnesota. In 1978, Marshall appeared in 54 games with the Twins, with 21 saves and a 2.45 earned run average. In '79, the big reliever led the American League with 90 appearances and 32 saves, with a 2.64 ERA.

The Michigan native ended his 14-year career with the New York Mets in 1981. He appeared in 723 games as a major leaguer, 699 of them in relief, finishing with a 97-122 won-loss record, 188 saves, and a fine 3.14 ERA. His superhuman achievements in 1974, pitching in 208 innings in 106 games, all in relief, may never be equalled. They are not of this world.

MIKE MARSHALL – OUTFIELDER

Known to some by the nickname "Moose", Mike Marshall was an imposing sight at the plate, standing a distant 6'5" from the ground and tipping the scales at a solid 215 pounds. The big right-handed slugger clubbed his way through the Los Angeles farm system in three short years, leaving a trail of devastation everywhere. In Lethbridge in 1978, he hit .324 and drove in 70 runs in 65 games. In Lodi, his .354 batting average produced 24 home runs and 116 runs batted in 137 games. At San Antonio he hit .321, with 16 homers and 86 RBIs. Then, at Albuquerque in 1981 he exploded. The Minor League Player of the Year crushed the ball at a .373 clip, smashed 34 homers and drove in 137 runs. He was whisked off to L.A. in a hurry.

Unfortunately for Marshall, and for the Dodgers, his major league career was peppered by prolonged periods on the disabled list. His medical record includes a foot operation, an appendectomy, back problems, a beaning, wart removal, and food poisoning. His nine years in Los Angeles were a tortuous trek through trainers rooms and doctors' offices, with brief glimpses of "what might have been." The troubled outfielder was never able to reach his potential. In his later years, he was accused of being a malingerer; a stigma that alienated him from many of his teammates. Two years with the New York Mets and the Boston Red Sox did not quiet the rumors, and he saw little action with either team.

In the beginning, the 6'5" power hitter was welcomed into the Dodger clubhouse with open arms. He became an L.A. regular in 1983 and showed promise, batting .284 with 17 home

Mike Marshall-Outfielder (W. McNeil)

runs and 65 runs batted in. A Jeff Reardon fastball almost stopped him before he got going, but Marshall bounced back from the beaning quickly to regain his batting eye. In 1984, a foot operation put him on the sidelines for a month, and he never got untracked at the plate, finishing with 21 homers, 65 RBIs, and a .257 batting average. The next year, in spite of a mid-season appendectomy, the big guy hit the ball at a decent .293 clip, with 28 homers and 95 RBIs, as the Dodgers rolled to the Western Division title.

His star began to set after that season. He appeared in more than 105 games only once over the next four years. That was in the penant year of 1988

when Big Mike got into 144 games, with 20 homers, 82 runs batted in, and a .272 batting average. He hit .273 in the NLCS, and smashed a key three-run homer in the World Series as the Dodgers spanked the mighty Oakland A's in five games to capture the World Championship.

Mike Marshall left the major leagues for Japan after the 1990 season. During his ten-year career in the big time, Marshall spent time on the disabled list in every one of his last seven years. He missed a total of 247 games in his last six years in L.A., an average of 41 games a year.

In spite of all the physical and emotional turmoil swirling around the big slugger, he produced respectable numbers when he was ready to play. He participated in 1,011 games over a 10-year period, batting .270 with 953 hits, 147 home runs, and 523 runs batted in.

RAMON MARTINEZ

Ramon Jaime Martinez was born in Santo Domingo, Dominican Republic, on March 22, 1968. He joined the Los Angeles Dodgers organization in 1985, as a tall, skinny 17-year-old fireballer. After an impressive debut with Bradenton, the 6'4", 160-pounder breezed through Bakersfield, Vero Beach, San Antonio, and Albuquerque, in short order.

He burst on the major league scene in 1988, not long after his 20th birthday. He won his first major league victory on August 29, pitching seven innings

Ramon Martinez (W. McNeil)

in a 2-1 win over Montreal. The next year, splitting his time between Albuquerque and L.A., the youngster went 10-2 in AAA, and 6-4 with the big club.

In 1990, he came of age, winning 20 games against only six losses, tossing four shutouts, and finishing with a 3.27 earned run average. His 20th victory was a 2-1 complete game decision over the San Diego Padres in his final start of the year, on October 1. The highlight of his season came on June 4 when he fanned 18 Atlanta Braves, while pitching a three-hit, 6-0 shutout.

He appeared to be tossing a duplicate season in '91, running up a 12-3 record by the All-Star break. Then, his world came crashing down, as hip and arm problems threw his pitching motion out of kilter. He struggled through the last half of the season, winning only five games against 10 losses.

The next three years were painful ones for the handsome Dominican, as he struggled to regain his former arm strength and rhythm. He went 8-11 in '92, followed by 10-12, and 12-7.

Slowly his arm returned to normal, and in 1995 he posted an excellent 17-7 record. On July 14 of that year, Martinez reached the pinnacle, with a brilliant 7-0, 8 strikeout, no-hitter against the Florida Marlins. After the All-Star break, he went 9-1, finishing the season with a six-game winning streak.

He went 15-6 in '96 and 10-5 the following year, before arm miseries sent his career into decline. He retired in 2002 after compiling an enviable 135-88 won-loss record. He will always be remembered as one of the Los Angeles Dodgers greatest pitchers. He is #7 on the Dodger all-time victory list, #6 in strikeouts, and #9 in both innings pitched and shutouts.

Otto Miller

OTTO MILLER

Lowell Otto Miller was born in Minden, Nebraska, on June 1, 1889. By the time he was 21 years old, he was a major league ballplayer, the backup catcher to Bill Bergen, on the Brooklyn Superbas.

After a two-year apprenticeship, Miller replaced the good field-no hit (.170 lifetime) Bergen in the Brooklyn lineup. He was an immediate success. Although not a big banger himself, his .245 batting average was a big improvement over Bergen. In fact, in his first year as the regular catcher, he hit a respectable .278, with 20 extra base hits, and 31 runs batted in, in 316 at bats.

The 6', 196-pound backstop, called Moonie because of his round face, was an exceptional defensive catcher. He had great rapport with his pitchers, and he was noted for his excellent pitch calling. His great sense of humor, helped keep his pitchers loose in difficult situations.

Otto Miller was the Superbas catcher for 13 years, from 1909 through 1922. During that time, he helped Brooklyn capture two National League flags. In the 1916 Series, he went one for eight in two games as the Boston Red Sox defeated his Superbas four games to one. Four years later, catching six of seven games, he batted .143 as Cleveland took the measure of his Superbas, five games to two.

Miller became part of baseball history in the 1920 Series. In the fifth inning of Game Five, with Brooklyn trailing 7-0, the Superbas staged a rally. Kilduff and Miller opened the inning with singles. Clarence Mitchell, the next batter lined a pitch back over the mound for an apparent base hit. Lady Luck didn't shine on the Superbas however. Cleveland second baseman Bill Wamsganss, racing to his right, gloved the ball for out #1. He then stepped on second for out #2, and tagged a stunned Otto Miller, standing only three feet away, with mouth agape, for an unassisted triple play, the only one in World Series history.

When he retired after the 1922 season, Moonie Miller had caught in 927 major league games, all with Brooklyn, with 2836 at bats, 695 base hits, and a .245 batting average.

He died in his adopted home town Rof Brooklyn on March 29, 1962.

RICK MONDAY

Rick Monday will always be remembered for two noteworthy events in Dodger history, the rescue of the American flag from two dissidents in Dodger Stadium, Rick Monday will always be remembered for two noteworthy events in Dodger history, the rescue of the American flag from two dissidents in Dodger Stadium, when he was a member of the Chicago Cubs, and his pennant winning home run in Montreal in 1981. But there was much more to Rick Monday than those two events.

The Arizona State baseball star and ex-marine had a long and successful 19-year career in the Big Show. He was an 11-year veteran when he joined the Los Angeles Dodgers in 1977, having played with the Athletics in both Kansas City and Oakland, as well as with the Cubs in the Windy City. On defense, Monday was an outstanding outfielder with a good glove and a strong, accurate throwing arm. At the plate he was a dangerous clutch hitter with grandstand power, but also with a proclivity for striking out.

The 6'3", 200 pound slugger joined the Dodgers in January 1977, in a trade for Bill Buckner. He went on to spend eight years in Dodger blue, mostly as a spare out-fielder and pinch hitter, giving Tommy Lasorda important bench strength, both offensively and defensively. Monday was particularly valuable in 1977 and '78, when the Dodgers won successive National League flags. His 34 home runs and 105 runs batted in over those two years helped push the Big Blue Machine past the powerful Cincinnati Reds in the tough Western Division.

From 1980 to '82, the smooth swinging south-paw smashed 31 homers, drove in 92 runs and batted .275 in 534 at bats. When he retired after the 1984 season, to enter the field of network sports broad-casting, he had accumulated 1619 base hits, of which 245 were home runs, in 6,136 at bats.

Rick Monday will begin his 10th full season as a play-by-play broadcaster for the Los Angeles Dodgers in 2003, but when Dodger fans think of him, it will be in a different setting. Their thoughts will be of Olympic Stadium in Montreal, on a raw October day in 1981. And they will relive, once gain, the thrill of Monday's historic pennant winning home run off Steve Rogers, in the ninth inning of the last playoff game.

Rick Monday (Los Angeles Dodgers)

RAUL MONDESI

Raul Ramon Mondesi had all the prerequisites to be a Dodgers' superstar; superior batting skills, power, speed, and defensive magic.

Mondesi, a native of San Cristobal, Dominican Republic, joined the Dodger organization in Santo Domingo in 1988. He proceeded through the minor league training grounds in the usual manner, touching all the bases en route. Finally, in 1993, he made the big jump up to the parent club. He finished the season in L.A. playing in 42 games, and producing a .291 batting average with four home runs and 10 RBIs.

His 1994 season was a smashing success. Playing in 106 games in the strike-shortened season, the stocky 5'11", 212-pound slugger rapped the ball at a .306 clip, with 16 home runs, 56 runs-batted-in, and 11 stolen bases. His season highlights included two triples against Colorado on August 5, a game-winning home run off Shane Reynolds of Houston on May 11, and another off John Wetteland of Montreal on June 22. He also led the major leagues in outfield assists with 16. As a result of his all-around performance, he was voted the National League's Rookie of the Year.

Raul Mondesi (W. McNeil)

WALLY MOON

Wally Moon patrolled the outer garden for Los Angeles for seven years, helping the Alston-men win three World Championship trophies along the way. The native of Bay, Arkansas, played his first three years in L.A. in the infamous Coliseum, with its 250-foot left-field wall surmounted by a 40-foot-high screen. Although the right-field foul pole was only 301 feet from the plate, the field opened up rapidly, to a cavernous 390 feet, just 15 feet inside the foul pole. The right center field fence was 440 feet from the plate, while deep center field was 420 feet away. Right field was death on left-handed hitters.

Moon, a lefty, knew his future wasn't toward right field, so he invented the cleverly efficient inside-out stroke that allowed him to hit pop flies over the short left field screen. They were called Moon-shots by the media, and they soon became part of the Dodger baseball lexicon. Wally Moon hit a total of 49 home runs between 1959 and 1961.

The strong-armed outfielder was an important cog in the Big Blue Machine's lineup through 1999. His powerful right wing kept base runners honest, and his bat accounted for 163 home runs and 518 RBIs in 3,487 at bats.

He was traded to the Toronto Blue Jays in 2000 for Shawn Green, subsequently finding his way to the New York Yankees two years later.

Wally Moon (Los Angeles Dodgers Photo)

Thirty-seven of them were hit in the Coliseum.

Wallace Wade Moon joined his first major league team, the St. Louis Cardinals, in 1954. He homered in his first major league at bat, and went on to beat out Hank Aaron for the National League Rookie of the Year award, thanks to 50 extra base hits, 76 runs batted in, and a .304 batting average.

Moon was traded to the Dodgers in 1959, after a solid, five-year career with St. Louis. His first year in L.A., the handsome 6', 169-pound outfielder helped the ragtag Dodgers (who had finished in seventh place in 1958), capture the National League flag, by banging the ball at a .302 clip, with 93 runs scored, 26 doubles, a league-leading 11 triples, 19 home runs, 15 stolen bases, and 74 runs batted in. The Dodgers went on to dump the favored Chicago White Sox in the Series, four games to two, after being clobbered in the Series opener, 11-0. Wally Moon batted .261 with a home run and two RBIs.

Moon was also a member of the fantastic 1963 squad that embarrassed the New York Yankees four straight, and the 1965 team, that overcame a two-game-to-none deficit, to defeat the Minnesota Twins, four games to three.

In addition to his offensive spark, he was also a fine defensive outfielder, and a Gold Glove winner.

When he retired after the '65 season, Wally Moon had accumulated 1,399 base hits, good for a .289 career batting average.

Manny Mota (Los Angeles Dodgers Photo)

MANNY MOTA

Manuel Raphael "Manny" Mota is baseball's all-time pinch-hitting king. A veteran of 20 years in the major leagues, the slender 5'10" contact hitter carved out a reputation for himself during his later years as a pinch-hitter extraordinaire, accumulating a total of 150 pinch hits before retiring in 1982 at the age of 44.

Manny Mota was born in Santo Domingo, Dominican Republic on February 18, 1938. Beginning his professional career with Michigan City in 1957, the skinny 19-year-old impressed everyone with his keen batting eye. Six years of grooming in the minor leagues brought him to the majors to stay in 1963. He played with the Pittsburgh Pirates for eight years, batting .332 in 1966 and .321 the following season.

Joining Walter Alston's Los Angeles Dodgers in 1969, the affable Mota played the outfield for four years, before gradually settling into his valuable niche as utility outfielder and number-one pinch hitter. The 160-pound punch hitter batted .323 for Alston in 1969; then went .305, .312, .323, and .314 over the next four years. From 1974 through 1979, the sharp-eyed Mota was the man they kept for pressure-packed pinch-hitting assignments in the late innings of close ballgames. And the man from Santo Domingo responded brilliantly, smashing 10 or more pinch hits for six straight seasons.

There was a joke that circulated for several years about a Manny Mota doll. All you had to do was wind it up and it would punch out a base hit. That wasn't too far from the truth. Over his Dodger career, Mota piled up 105 pinch hits in 332 at bats, for a .316 average. His major league pinch-hitting totals showed 150 hits in 502 at bats, for a .297 average.

The Dodgers' premier pinch hitter had his most memorable day during the 1977 NLCS against the Philadelphia Phillies. With the two teams tied at one game apiece in the best-of-five series, Tommy Lasorda's boys found themselves down 5-3 with two men out and no one on base in the ninth. After Vic Davalillo beat out a bunt, the 39-year-old Mota fought off several 0-2 pitches before doubling off the left field wall to plate Davilillo with run number four. Mota later came in on a single by Lopes to tie it. The Dodgers went on to win the game on a single by Bill Russell, en route to the National League pennant.

Manny Mota played in the major leagues for 20 years, compiling a lifetime batting average of .304, with 1,149 base hits. His proudest achievement was his 150th pinch hit, in 1980, setting the standard for all other pinch hitters to shoot at.

Manny Mota continued to depend on his batting ability after retirement, serving as a Dodger batting instructor.

VAN LINGLE MUNGO

Van Lingle Mungo

Van Lingle Mungo, the man with the rhythmical name, was a high-kicking, hard-throwing, right-handed pitcher for Brooklyn during their "Daffy Dodger" days. Mungo was blessed with immense talent and was considered to be the equal of any pitcher in the major leagues during the 1930s. Unfortunately, he played with a no-talent group that was unable to win even half its games.

Mungo's most productive years were from 1933 through 1936 when he won a total of 68 games while losing 60; this for a team that had a mere .446 winning percentage over the same period. Brooklyn finished in the second division every one of those four years, with sixth place their usual home.

In 1934, the 23-year-old Brooklyn flamethrower racked up 18 wins for a team that won only 71 games all season. He led the league in innings pitched that year with 315, struck out 184 batters, and hurled 22 complete games. The following year, Casey Stengel's bunglers compiled a record of 70-83, finishing 29 1/2 games behind the pennant-winning Chicago Cubs. Van Lingle Mungo was one of the Casey's few bright spots, accounting for 16 of those victories, against only 10 losses.

The hard-luck pitcher, part Dutch and part American Indian, was born in Pageland, South Carolina on June 8, 1911. He was signed to a Brooklyn contract in 1929 by legendary Dodger southpaw Nap Rucker. After two years of minor league ball with Fayetteville in the East Carolina League where he went 10-9, and with Hartford in the Eastern League where he was 15-5 with a 2.12 ERA, the rangy 6'2", 185-pounder made his way to the City of Churches. In his first major league start, late in 1931, he threw a 2-0 shutout at the Boston Braves, contributing a single and a triple to the meager Dodger attack.

Within a year, Van Lingle Mungo was the ace of manager Max Carey's staff. In addition to victory totals of 13, 16, 18, 16, and 18 over the next five years, the big pitcher also led the league with four shutouts in 1934, and 238 strikeouts in 1936. He helped knock the New York Giants out of the 1934 pennant race with a brilliant 5-1 effort on the next to last day of the season. The victory was particularly satisfying because it answered Giant manager Bill Terry's query, asked six months previous, "Is Brooklyn still in the league?" Mungo answered with a resounding "yes."

On June 25, 1936, Van Lingle Mungo's blazing fast ball sent seven successive batters down on strikes, tying a major league record at the time. The next year he achieved a game-high 15 strikeouts against the Philadelphia Phillies.

Pitching in his second All-Star game in 1937, the 26-year-old fast ball pitcher injured his arm, essentially ending his promising career. Over the next seven years, with Brooklyn and New York, he won a grand total of only 13 games. Returning for one brief moment of glory in the war year of 1945, the 34-year-old pitcher was 14-7 with a 3.20 earned run average for the fifth-place Giants.

Van Lingle Mungo was a brilliant pitcher; fast, wild, and mean. He tried to strike out every batter he faced, probably because of the inept defense behind him in Brooklyn. His fast ball, which was once clocked at 118 mph, earned him a spot in the Brooklyn Hall of Fame, alongside Dazzy Vance, Nap Rucker, Burleigh Grimes, and Brickyard Kennedy.

HY MYERS

Henry Harrison Myers was born in East Liverpool, Ohio on April 27, 1889. The young ballhawk made two trips to Brooklyn for cups of coffee in 1909 and 1911, before becoming a permanent outfield fixture in 1914. He replaced Jack Dalton in the Robin outfield that year, playing between Casey Stengel and Zach Wheat.

Myers stood only 5'9" and weighed 170 pounds soaking wet, but he could shag flies with the best of them. In fact, he is fourth on the all-time Brooklyn range factor list for outfielders. The little right-handed hitter played on two pennant winners during his 11-year sojourn in Flatbush, 1916 and 1920.

In the 1916 World Series against the Boston Red Sox, Hy Myers, after hitting only three home runs all season, slammed an inside-the-park job off Sox ace Babe Ruth with two men out in the top of the first inning. That would prove to be the only run Wilbert Robinson's boys would score off the Boston southpaw all afternoon. The Red Sox tied the score in the third on a triple by Ev Scott and an infield out, and won it in the bottom of the 14th on a pinch hit by Del Gainer.

The Brooklyn outfielder was a late bloomer with the bat, his average hovering around the .260 mark during his first five years in the lineup. Then, beginning in 1919, the 30-year-old Myers suddenly became an offensive threat. That year, he hit a solid .307, and led the league with 73 RBIs, 14 triples, and a .436 slugging average. In 1920, he put together his best season in the majors, as the Robins won the pennant by seven games. The Brooklyn centerfielder was the team's offensive spark-plug, batting .304 with 36 doubles, a league-leading 22 triples, and 80 RBIs.

After hitting .288 and .317 the next two years, the 33-year-old outfielder was traded to the St. Louis Cardinals where he finished out his 14-year career three years later.

Hy Myers played in 1,310 games from 1909 through 1925, with 1,380 hits, and a lifetime batting average of .281. He died in Minerva, Ohio, on May 1, 1965.

Hy Myers

CHARLIE NEAL

Charlie Neal was a hard-hitting, smooth-fielding second baseman for Walter Alston's Brooklyn and Los Angeles Dodgers in the late '50s. He made his first appearance in a Dodger uniform for Brooklyn in 1956, playing in 62 games, and batting a solid .287, as the Dodgers captured the National League pennant by one game over the Milwaukee Braves.

Neal won the regular second base job from Junior Gilliam in 1958, and led the league in double plays that year. The next year, he had a career season, which won him National League All-Star honors and a Gold Glove. Defensively, he led the league in double plays, putouts and fielding average. With the bat, he led the league in triples with 11, banged out 30 doubles and 19 home runs, stole 17 bases, scored 103 runs, drove in 83 teammates, and hit .287. He was literally a one-man show. And he finished off his spectacular season in fine style. Over the last three games of the season, including two playoff games with the Milwaukee Braves, he pounded out seven base hits, with two triples and two homers.

Charlie Neal's greatest moments came in the 1959 World Series against the Chicago White Sox. Putting the finishing touches on his outstanding season, the native of Longview, Texas, rapped 10 base hits in six games, including two doubles and two home runs, with six RBIs. After the Dodgers took an 11-0 drubbing at the hands of Early Wynn in the Series opener, Neal got the ball rolling for L.A. in game two. With the team down 2-0 in the fifth inning, he hit a home run into the lower left field stands to cut the deficit to one run . Then, two innings later, with the score deadlocked at 2-2, the clutch-hitting in-fielder launched a two-run, 400-foot shot into the White Sox bullpen in center field, spearheading a 4-3 L.A. victory.

He continued his onslaught in game 3, hitting a single and a double, scoring the first run of the game and driving in the last, as Alston's boys prevailed 3-1. In the Series finale, he came through again, lashing out three hits, scoring one run and driving in two, as the Big Blue Machine finished off Al Lopez's Go-Go Sox, 9-3, capturing the Series four games to two.

The tall, slender right-handed batter had surprising power, thanks to lightning fast wrists. Weighing only 160 pounds, he averaged 16 home runs a year for the Dodgers, from 1956 through 1961, with a high of 22 in 1958. He ended his 8-year major league career in 1963, after accumulating 858 base hits, good for a .259 batting average.

Charlie Neal (Los Angeles Dodgers)

York. He also led all National League pitchers at the plate, with 22 hits and a .229 average.

In the World Series against the New York Yankees that fall, the 23-year-old youngster pitched a masterpiece in the opener, only to lose 1-0 on a ninth inning home run by Tommy Henrich.

Don Newcombe followed up his brilliant start by going 19-11 in 1950, and 20-9 in 1951, as the bedeviled residents of Flatbush watched both pennants disappear on the last day of the season. In 1951, Big Newk handcuffed the New York Giants for 8 1/3 innings in the final game of the National League playoffs, leaving with a 4-2 lead. But, just when Dodger fans were beginning their pennant celebration, Bobby Thomson pulled the rug out from under them.

Two years of military service took the Dodger righty out of the lineup temporarily but, after he returned, he put together two of the most overpowering seasons ever realized by a Brooklyn pitcher. In 1955, as the "Boys of Summer" broke from the gate with a sizzling 22-2 record, holding down first place from start to end, Big Newk led the league with an .800 winning percentage on a 20-5 record. He was even more imposing at the plate, smashing the ball at a torrid .359 clip, with nine doubles, seven home runs, and 23 RBIs. As a pinch hitter, he batted .381!

Walter Alston's outstanding ball club repeated as National League champi-

DON NEWCOMBE

During the Brooklyn Dodgers' 68-year stay in the National League, very few pitchers dominated their profession like Big Don Newcombe. "Newk", as he was called, was a giant of a man, standing 6'4" tall and weighing 220 pounds. The native of Madison, New Jersey, began his career in organized baseball in 1946 after spending two years with the Newark Eagles of the Negro National League where he had a combined record of 21-10.

After signing a contract with the Brooklyn Dodgers, the 19-year-old right-handed pitcher spent three years in the minor leagues, with Nashua of the New England League, and Montreal of the International League. Early in the 1949 season, with the Dodgers floundering in fourth place, a call for help brought Don Newcombe up to the majors. His first start, against the Cincinnati Reds, was a 3-0 shutout, with Newcombe singling in two of the runs himself. The big man went on from there to run up an impressive 17-8 record over the last 4 1/2 months of the season, helping Burt Shotton's team edge out the St. Louis Cardinals by a single game for the National League pennant. En route to Rookie of the Year honors, Newcombe hurled a league-leading five shutouts, tossing 32 consecutive scoreless innings at one stretch, including shutouts over St. Louis, Pittsburgh, and New

Don Newcombe

ons in 1956, with Don Newcombe having a career season on the mound. The fireballing right-hander once again led the league in winning percentage, at .794. This time, he racked up 27 victories against only seven defeats, as the Flatbush Flock nipped the Milwaukee Braves by one game at the wire. His great effort, not only gave him the major league Cy Young award, but also earned him the National League Most Valuable Player award, as well.

During his 10-year National League career, Don Newcombe won 149 games while losing only 90, for an excellent .649 winning percentage. In addition to his explosive fastball, big Newk also had outstanding control, walking an average of only two men per game. In 1955, the Dodger ace walked only 38 men in 234 innings, and the following year, he issued only 46 bases on balls in 268 innings.

One of the highlights of Big Newk's career occurred on September 6, 1950, when he attempted to win both ends of a doubleheader against the first-place Philadelphia Phillies. His Iron Man effort brought back memories of the rugged turn-of-the-century pitchers who hurled both ends of a doubleheader routinely. The big right-hander shut out the league-leading Phils 2-0 in the first game; then pitched seven strong innings in the nightcap, only to leave the game trailing 2-0. The Brooks rallied to win but, unfortunately, Newk was not the beneficiary of the rally.

Don Newcombe is still associated with baseball today, serving as the Director of Community Relations for the Los Angeles Dodgers.

TOM NIEDENFUER

Tom "Buff" Niedenfuer was a baseball prodigy of sorts, beginning his professional career in 1981 with the San Antonio Missions of the AA Texas League, and finishing the year with five strong innings in the World Series. Niedenfuer's big break came when Los Angeles Dodgers vice president Al Campanis visited Texas to recruit pitching help for the Dodgers stretch run. The big, strong 21-year-old right-hander dazzled the V.P. by fanning seven batters in a row, striking out the side on nine pitches in one inning.

Thomas Edward Niedenfuer was an imposing figure on the mound, standing a full 6'5" tall and weighing 225 pounds. With his big, burly build and bushy brown mustache, he was compared to a menacing buffalo by amused teammates, who quickly dubbed him "Buff."

After his rookie season, in which he went 13-3 with a 1.80 earned run average at San Antonio, and 3-1, 3.81 in Los Angeles, the youngster was sent down to Albuquerque to start the season in 1982. He was recalled almost immediately, and appeared in 55 games for L.A., posting a 3-4 record with a 2.71 ERA

and nine saves.

By the following year, the hard-throwing right-hander was the Dodgers' bullpen closer, blowing his 94-mile-per-hour fastball past opposing batters with monotonous regularity. The 23-year-old youngster put it all together in 1983, with 66 game appearances, 11 saves, an 8-3 record, and a 1.90 ERA. In the NLCS against the Philadelphia Phillies, Niedenfuer pitched in two games, earning one save.

He came back the next year to save another 11 games, despite missing half the season with an elbow injury. In 1985, the big right-hander pitched in 64 games, with 19 saves, and a 2.71 earned run average. He fanned 102 enemy batters in 106 innings of relief.

The NLCS against the St. Louis Cardinals that year was something big Buff would just as soon forget. Tommy Lasorda's boys jumped out to a quick 2-0 lead in games behind the pitching of Fernando Valenzuela and Orel Hershiser. Niedenfuer was credited with a save in Game One.

Tom Niedenfuer (Los Angeles Dodger Photo)

After the Redbirds tied the series at two games apiece, L.A.'s relief ace entered Game Five in the bottom of the ninth inning of a 2-2 tie. With one out, Ozzie Smith, a notoriously weak singles hitter, pulled a Niedenfuer fastball down the right field line for a dramatic game-winning home run. The next day, Jack Clark hit an even more dramatic pennant-winning, three-run homer off the righty with two out in the ninth.

Niedenfuer's effectiveness fell off in 1986, although he still came out of the bullpen 60 times. His saves fell to 11, and his earned run average exploded to 3.71, one run per game higher than the previous year. He was traded to Baltimore for John Shelby early in 1987, but his skills had deteriorated to the point where he became a nomad, bouncing around from team to team, from the majors to the minors, for the next several years.

Tom Niedenfuer pitched for the Dodgers for seven years. He appeared in 440 games, while posting a 36-28 record, with 64 saves, and a 2.76 earned run average. He can be proud of his accomplishments. His 64 saves is number six on the all-time Dodger list, both Brooklyn and L.A., trailing only Todd Worrell, Jim Brewer, Ron Perranoski, Clem Labine, and Jay Howell.

HIDEO NOMO

Hideo Nomo (Los Angeles Dodgers)

The year 1981 was the year of Fernandomania, when the Latino population of southern California, the media, and Dodger fans across the country, became caught up in frenzied excitement whenever Mexican pitcher Fernando Valenzuela took the mound for the Los Angeles Dodgers.

Fourteen years later, the surrealistic atmosphere returned to the west coast. Nomomania exploded on the baseball scene on February 13, 1995, when Dodger President Peter O'Malley announced the signing of Hideo Nomo, one of the premier pitchers in the Japanese professional leagues. Almost immediately the Japanese media descended on the City of Angels, shadowing the new Dodger pitcher, and sending an avalanche of photos and stories back to Japan. Whenever Nomo pitched, several hundred Japanese writers swarmed around the ballpark to cover the event.

Back home, large screen television sets were constructed in more than a dozen of Japan's largest cities so the populace could watch their hero challenge American batters. Nomo was the first native born Japanese ballplayer to play in the major leagues.

The 26-year-old strikeout pitcher had dominated the Japanese Pacific League his first four years in the league, before an arm injury shelved him in 1994. He led the Pacific League in strikeouts four times, averaging 10.3 strikeouts per game. His five-year totals showed 78 victories against only 46 losses.

In the United States, it took him a little while to get untracked. He had a no decision in each of his first five starts, then was beaten by Montreal on May 28.

On June 1, his record stood at 0-1. The next day, he racked up his first major league victory, a 2-1 decision over the New York Mets. After that, he was unstoppable. He blazed through June like a freight train, going 6-0, with a stunning 0.89 earned run average, and two shutouts. He fanned 16 Pittsburgh Pirates on June 14, 13 Giants on the 24th, and 13 Rockies on the 29th. During the season, he fanned ten or more batters 11 times, a feat exceeded only by Sandy Koufax.

Hideo Nomo finished his rookie season with an excellent 13-6 record, four shutouts, and a 2.54 ERA. His 236 strikeouts led the National League. He was rewarded for his fine season by being presented with the National League Rookie of the Year award.

Nomo, known as "The Tornado," because of his twisting, back-to-the-plate delivery, continued to shine in 1996 and '97, with records of 16-11 and 14-12. His three-year strikeout average of 10.1 strikeouts per game, was the most by any active National League pitcher.

Hideo Nomo topped off his 1996 season with a most improbable no-hitter. He tossed his 9-0 gem at the heavy hitting Colorado Rockies in, of all places, the hitters paradise at Coors Field.

The dedicated Japanese fireballer was traded to the New York Mets in 1998, and spent the next four years shuttling between four teams. In 2001, pitching for the Boston Red Sox, he tossed his second major league no-hitter, blanking the Baltimore Orioles 3-0 on April 4. He went on to enjoy a fine season in Beantown, winning 13 games against 10 losses.

He returned to Los Angeles in 2002, and had an exceptional season with Jim Tracy's crew, going 16-6, with a excellent 3.39 ERA. His stats included 220 innings pitched and 193 strikeouts.

Hideo Nomo showed his true warrior mentality in 2002 as he battled for every out, and every inning, often pitching out of difficult situations, to keep the Dodgers in contention. There may be pitchers with more talent in the major leagues, but there are none with more heart. Nomo retired after the 2005 season after compiling a record of 123 victories against 109 losses, with two no-hitters to his credit.

Darby O'Brien

DARBY O'BRIEN

Darby O'Brien had a short six-year career in the major leagues, but he packed a lot of excitement into just 709 ballgames. He played in two no-hit games thrown by Brooklyn hurlers, started in left field in the first home game Brooklyn ever played in the National League, and sparked the Bridegrooms to two successive pennants.

William D. O'Brien was born in Peoria, Illinois on September 1, 1863. The slender 6'1", 186-pound outfielder came to the major leagues via the Metropolitans of New York, an American Association entry. In his only year with the original Mets, O'Brien hit a resounding .301 with 48 extra base hits and 97 runs scored in 127 games. His offensive prowess didn't make a big difference however, as the lowly Mets stumbled home in seventh place, 50 games behind the St. Louis Browns.

When the New York club folded after the 1887 season, Brooklyn owner Charlie Byrne signed the right handed hitter to play left field for his American Association ball club. O'Brien's first year in Flatbush was a big success. He batted .280 with 35 extra base hits, and scored 105 runs in 136 games. The Brooklyns improved upon their sixth-place finish of the previous year, coming in a respectable second, 6 1/2 games behind the Browns. They actually led the league briefly in mid-season but couldn't sustain the momentum.

In 1889, the Bridegrooms as they were now called, came of age, dethroning the St. Louis Browns

to win the American Association pennant by two games. St. Louis had won the previous four Association championships. The Groom offense was led by Darby O'Brien, Hub Collins, and Dave Foutz. O'Brien hit .300, scored 146 runs, stole 91 bases, and drove in 80 runs with 46 extra base hits.

The Grooms lost the World Series to the National League Champion New York Giants, six games to three. O'Brien, although held to a measly .161 batting average in nine games, drew 12 bases on balls, stole six bases, and scored eight runs.

The following year, the Bridegrooms joined the National League.

Proving their Association pennant was no fluke, the Grooms waltzed off with the championship, beating the Chicago Cubs by six games. Darby O'Brien smacked the ball at a .314 clip although a leg injury limited his play to 85 games. He still scored 78 runs and drove in 63 in only 350 at bats. He also stole 38 bases.

Brooklyn's fortunes nose-dived after the 1890 pennant run, and the team plummeted to sixth place. Darby O'Brien's offense fell off also, as he hit only .253. The one bright spot in 1891 was provided by Tom Lovett on June 22 when he no-hit the New York Giants by a score of 4-0. O'Brien stroked three hits, scored two runs, and saved the no-hitter with a sparkling catch in right field.

The 1892 entry finished third, their last visit to the first division for six years. O'Brien, in spite of a .243 batting average, still scored 72 runs, batted in 56, and stole 57 bases.

Tragically, the young outfielder was stricken

with typhoid fever early in 1893. He died at his home in Peoria on June 15 of that year. He was 29 years old.

IVY OLSON

Ivan Massie Olson was a rowdy street kid from Casey Stengel's old stomping grounds in Kansas City, Missouri. A former grade school bully, the youngster was weaned on mischief and mayhem. He grew into a tough competitor, as well as a hustling major league shortstop.

Olson played baseball as if his life depended on it. He asked no quarter, and he gave none. Any base runner who came into second base with spikes flying was likely to wake up wearing a baseball for an ear ornament.

Signed to a professional contract by the Cleveland Indians, the stocky 175-pounder broke into the majors in 1911 at the age of 25 hitting a solid .263. Unfortunately, the incomparable Ray Chapman arrived on the scene the next year, forcing Olson to assume a utility role. After seeing limited service over the next four years, Olson was acquired by the Brooklyn Robins to shore up their leaky infield. He quickly became a fixture in Flatbush, giving manager Wilbert Robinson ten years of solid defense, coupled with a fierce desire to win.

Ivy Olson loved to hit. He wanted to get a hit every day, and he was miserable whenever he drew the collar. Naturally, he hated to sacrifice, because bunts took away an opportunity to swing the bat. One day, during the "Daffy Dodgers" period, Olson came to the plate in a sacrifice situation. Manager Robinson kept trying to get Olson's eye to give him the bunt sign, but the wily shortstop carefully avoided looking in the manager's direction. After several exasperating minutes, Robinson just shrugged his shoulders and said, "Ah, the hell with it."

Along the way, while he stabilized the Robin infield and destabilized his manager's psyche, Ivy Olson helped the Robins win two National League flags, in 1916 and 1920. The shortstop had a mediocre World Series in 1916 hitting only .250 and committing four errors. He turned it around four years later however, as he pounded the ball at a .320 clip and handled 32 chances in the field flawlessly.

Playing in Flatbush was not all fun and games, as the kid from Missouri found out. One year, when things were going bad, the Brooklyn boo-birds got on him unmercifully. Finally, in desperation, the kid stuffed cotton in his ears before all home games.

Ivy Olson had a long 14-year career in the majors, 10 of them in Brooklyn. His .258 batting average included 1,575 hits, 156 stolen bases and 730 runs scored. Although not a high average hitter, the right hander was a good contact hitter, striking out

Ivy Olson (Brace Photo)

an average of only 22 times a year. His overwhelming desire to lay the bat on the ball is reflected in the fact that he walked only 28 times a year. Olson's defensive capabilities were not always appreciated in Brooklyn during his playing days. He made a lot of errors, which explains why he had to stuff cotton in his ears occasionally. But his contemporaries, two of whom are in the Hall of Fame, also made their share of errors. Dave "Beauty" Bancroft, and Rabbit Maranville, noted for their defense, played against Olson five full seasons and, in those years, the Dodger shortstop made fewer errors than his famous counterparts in three of them.

Ivy Olson was quick and covered acres of ground, which accounted for many of his errors. In fact, he had the greatest range of any shortstop in Dodger history, based on the number of chances he accepted per game. He holds the all-time single-season Dodger record of 6.08 chances per game in 1921. The Dodger shortstop was a spectacular performer. He was no Bancroft or Maranville-but he wasn't far behind.

Following his playing days, Ivy Olson remained in baseball for some time, serving as a coach in both Brooklyn and New York; then managing in the minors. He died on September 1, 1965, in Inglewood, California, at the age of 79.

CLAUDE OSTEEN

Claude Osteen (Los Angeles Dodger Photo)

During their long history in Los Angeles, the Dodgers have relied on pitching to be successful. At no time was that more evident than during the mid-'60s when Koufax and Drysdale ruled the hill. After their World Championship season in 1963, it became apparent that Walter Alston's boys needed more pitching help if they were to continue to dominate the National League. Johnny Podres was nearing the end of a fine career, and the farm system had no one ready to replace him.

Walter O'Malley solved the problem by obtaining left-handed pitcher Claude Osteen from Washington in a trade for big Frank Howard. Osteen was just what the doctor ordered, a cagy craftsman with a rubber arm, whose off speed deliveries complemented the smoke dished up by Koufax and Drysdale.

Osteen had just completed an outstanding 15-13 season with the ninth-place Senators when L.A. grabbed him. Although slight of stature at 5'11" and 160-pounds, the man from Caney Springs, Tennessee, was a real work-horse. He pitched over 200 innings a year for eleven straight years, including a personal high of 321 innings for the Dodgers in 1969. He also won in double figures all nine years he pitched for Alston.

The stylish southpaw won a total of 147 games with Los Angeles against 126 losses. His best years were 1969 when he went 20-15, and 1972 when he was 20-11. In '72, Osteen's pitching record included an earned run average of 2.64. He also helped himself at the plate, batting .276 with seven extra base hits and eleven RBIs. Two of the RBIs were game winners.

He pitched in two World Series, winning one World Championship. In 1965, against the Minnesota Twins, Osteen was asked to stem the tide after Sam Mele's boys had knocked off both Koufax and Drysdale to take a two-game-to-nothing lead in the Series. The cool-headed Irishman responded brilliantly, tossing a five-hit shutout at the Twins, to win 4-0. That was the lift the Dodgers needed. Big D. won his next start, and Koufax blanked the Twins twice, 7-0 in Game Five, and 2-0 in the Game Seven clincher.

The following year, Osteen tossed a three-hitter at the Baltimore Orioles in Game Three of the Series, but was beaten 1-0 as Baltimore right-hander Wally Bunker threw a six-hit shutout at L.A. It was a Series that Walter Alston and his crew would rather forget, an exercise in futility. Earl Weaver's team swept the Series in four straight, limiting the Dodger offense to a total of just two runs, and shutting them out over the last 33 innings.

The Dodger southpaw pitched in two All-Star games, throwing three scoreless innings to win the 1970 game, 5-4, and pitching two shutout innings in 1973.

Nicknamed "Gomer" because of his resemblance to a television character of the period, the man from the Volunteer state retired in 1975 after a 7-16 season with the hapless Chicago White Sox. The hard-luck hurler compiled a record of 196-195 with a 3.30 earned run average during a commendable 18-year career. His win total would have been higher, except for the fact that his teams were shut out 47 times when he was on the mound. He pitched a total of 3,459 innings in the big time and racked up 40 shutouts of his own, giving him a 41st place tie with Sandy Koufax on the all-time shutout list. In the World Series, Claude Osteen responded brilliantly, holding the opposition to a barely visible 0.86 ERA in 21 innings. His record of 1-2 was caused by the nonexistent Los Angeles offense which failed to score a run for him over his last 15 innings.

The slender southpaw could not only pitch, but

he could hit as well. He was often used as a pinch hitter during his career, as he compiled a career batting average of .188. His 207 career hits included eight home runs.

Osteen remained in baseball after his retirement, serving as a pitching coach for several teams.

WES PARKER

Wes Parker was another in the long line of outstanding Dodger first baseman. Like his predecessors, Daubert, Hodges, and Fairly, the man from Illinois was a defensive wizard around first base. Piling up six straight gold gloves during the course of a nine-year career, the stylish blonde compiled a major league leading career fielding percentage of .996. He committed only 47 errors in his entire major league career!

The tall, handsome left-handed hitter started his professional career with Santa Barbara in the California League at the age of 23. Two years later, he was a fixture in L.A. The 6'1" 180-pounder was poetry in motion around first base, often making his fellow infielders look good with sensational glove-work and footwork.

During the Dodgers' two pennant seasons, in 1965 and 1966, Wes Parker combined with second baseman Jim Lefebvre, shortstop Maury Wills, and third baseman Jim Gilliam, to form the only switch-hitting infield in major league history. Not noted as an offensive threat, his batting average wallowed under the .250 mark during his first five years in the league.

According to both Parker and Duke Snider, the first baseman found it difficult to devote himself solely to base-ball. He had many outside interests, including family matters and business ventures. In 1970, he dedicated himself to the game 100% for the entire season to find out what he could accomplish under those conditions. Not unexpectedly, the smooth-swinging left handed batter had a career season. He became the Dodgers' primary offensive threat, batting a solid .319, the fifth best average in the league. His 197 hits included a league-leading 47 doubles and 11 home runs. He batted in 111 runs, and scored 84 runs himself. Nor did his fielding suffer. He once again led the league in fielding with a percentage of .996, committing only seven errors in 161 games.

Wes Parker's biggest day at bat came on May 7, 1970, when he hit for the cycle against the New York Mets in Shea Stadium. He doubled and homered off Ray Sadecki, singled off reliever Cal Koonce, and tripled off Jim McAndrew. He remains the only Dodger to hit for the cycle in the last 37 years.

Parker was proud of his achievements in 1970,

Wes Parker

but he decided the price was too much to pay for the reward. During his last two years in the League, he reverted to his previous performance level, batting .274 and .279, with 62 and 59 runs batted in respectively.

The 32-year-old infielder retired after the '72 season to pursue other interests, including acting and TV broadcasting. He came out of retirement briefly to play baseball in Japan, with Nankai in 1974. Proving he hadn't lost his skills, the smooth-swinging left hander hit .301 with 14 home runs.

Wes Parker knew his offensive limitations. He also knew his defensive strengths. He once said, "If they had a Hall of Fame for fielders, I'd be the number one guy." No one can argue with that.

DICKEY PEARCE

Dickey Pearce was born Richard J. Pearce in Brooklyn, New York, on January 2, 1836. He was one of the pioneers of professional baseball, playing with amateur teams in and around Brooklyn as early as the mid 1850s. When the Atlantics of Brooklyn were formed on August 14, 1855, Dickey Pearce was a charter member, playing with them from 1856 through 1870.

The diminutive Pearce stood only 5'3" in his stocking feet, and weighed a pudgy 160 pounds. He was the Atlantics shortstop at a time when the shortstop played in short left field. The Brooklyn infielder soon changed that tradition and, in so doing, revolutionized the game of baseball. He positioned himself between second base and third base, making himself a fourth infielder rather than a fourth outfielder. He initiated several defensive innovations to the game such as dropping a fly ball in order to get a double play.

The right-handed batter also contributed numerous original plays to baseball's offensive game as well. For instance, he invented the "tricky hit", or bunt. He also mastered the "fair-foul" hit, which was a ball that landed fair when it was hit, then rolled into foul territory away from the fielders. Many rules changes had to be made to eliminate some of Pearce's tricks, both defensive and offensive.

During Pearce's 15 years with the Brooklyn Atlantics, he appeared in many historic encounters. In 1858, he participated in the first "World Series" against the New York All-Stars at the Fashion Race Course Grounds. The speedy infielder scored six runs in Game Two, as Brooklyn romped to a 29-8 victory. In Game Three, won by New York 29-18, Pearce crossed the plate three times.

The Atlantics won the National Championship in both 1864 and 1865, going undefeated in 1864. In 1866, they played the Philadelphia Athletics for the National Championship. The Atlantics won the series, two games to one.

In 1868, the *St. Louis Times* called the brilliant Atlantics shortstop unequaled. He was considered the premier shortstop in the country, even better than the more famous George Wright.

In 1870, Dickey Pearce played in the most famous game of the 19th century, the contest between the Atlantics and the legendary Cincinnati Red Stockings. The Red Stockings came to Brooklyn on the wings of an 80 game undefeated streak, consisting of 79 wins and one tie, but the Atlantics ended that streak with a hard-fought 8-7 victory in 11 innings.

Professional baseball came to the United States in 1871 with the formation of the National Association, and little Dickey Pearce was on board as a member of the Brooklyn Mutuals. The roly-poly shortstop played with the Mutuals from 1871 through 1874, then joined the St. Louis Brown Stockings in 1875. The baseball pioneer, although way past his prime at 40 years old, played for St. Louis in the National League's premier season, 1876. He batted only .206 in 102 at bats, and retired the following year after playing in only eight games.

Dickey Pearce played amateur and professional baseball for a total of 22 years, including five years in the National Association and National League. He batted .254 as a professional in the twilight of his career. During his heyday, Pearce was noted as a brilliant fielder and a solid singles hitter.

Following his retirement, Pearce umpired for many years. He died in Onset, Massachusetts, on Cape Cod, at the age of 72.

Dickey Pearce was one of the founders of the game of baseball as we know it. He took a colonial game and made it better. We will forever be in his debt.

RON PERRANOSKI

On the Los Angeles Dodgers relief pitching scale, Ronald Peter Perranoski has to rank 1-2. The 6', 180-pound southpaw was the key man in Walter Alston's bullpen for six years, 1962 through 1967. During that time, the Dodgers won three National League pennants and two World Championships.

Born Ronald Peter Perzanowski in Paterson, New Jersey, on April 1, 1936, the stylish lefthander originally signed a professional contract with the Chicago Cubs in 1958. He came to Los Angeles in a trade for Don Zimmer, and was soon converted from a starting pitcher to a reliever.

In his first year in L.A., 1961, The Michigan State graduate appeared in 53 games, with a 7-5 record, six saves, and a 2.64 ERA. The following year, he became the ace of the bullpen, a position he held until 1968.

Dickey Pearce

Over that period, the crafty sinker ball specialist was outstanding and, occasionally, brilliant.

He led the league in games pitched three times, with 70 in 1962, 69 in 1963, and 70 in 1967. In 1963, he put together one of the most overpowering relief pitching performances in baseball history. In addition to his league-leading 69 appearances, the tireless lefty also led the league with an .842 winning percentage on a 16-3 won-loss record. His earned run average of 1.67 was, by far, the lowest in the league but, unfortunately, he didn't pitch enough innings to qualify for the title.

Two years later, as the Dodgers battled the Giants, Braves and Reds down the stretch, the handsome relief ace caught fire. Over the final two months of the season, Perranoski breezed through his last 21 relief appearances, allowing only two earned runs and 24 hits in 47 2/3 innings. His earned run average was a microscopic 0.38. In what most players considered the turning point of the season, the Milwaukee Braves battered Sandy Koufax for six early runs and a 6-2 lead on September 22. At the time, the Dodgers trailed the San Francisco Giants by three games with only ten games left. They couldn't afford any more losses. Perranoski took care of that problem by hurling six scoreless innings, holding Bobby Bragan's troops in check until the Dodgers could push over the game winner in the eleventh. L.A.'s seventh consecutive victory gave them the impetus they needed. They rolled to another six straight wins after Perry's gutty performance, clinching the pennant along the way.

After another brilliant year in 1967, in which the 31-year-old bullpen ace pitched in 70 games, with 16 saves and a 2.45 ERA, he was traded to the Minnesota

Twins to make way for Jim Brewer. Proving that his skills were still intact, the New Jersey native went on to win the fireman of the year award twice in the American League, in 1969 when he saved a league-leading 31 games with a 2.10 earned run average, and in 1970 when he saved a league-leading 34 games with a 2.43 ERA.

When he finally hung up the spikes in 1973, he had pitched in 737 games over a 13-year period, with 179 saves and a dazzling 2.79 lifetime earned run average. Perranoski served as Tommy Lasorda's pitching coach from 1981 through 1995. Helping the team win four Western Division titles, and two World Championships.

JEFF PFEFFER

Big Jeff Pfeffer, all 6'3" and 210 pounds of him, is the all-time Dodger leader in earned run average, at 2.31. Nap Rucker, at 2.43, and Sandy Koufax, at 2.76, are his nearest rivals.

Edward Joseph Pfeffer, called Ed, was nicknamed Big Jeff after his older brother, who pitched for the Chicago Cubs and the Boston Braves between 1905 and 1911. The strong-armed right-hander had a blazing fast ball and pinpoint control. His fastball wasn't a strikeout pitch however, lacking a big hop, but he made it work for him by pitching the batters tight. He never let anyone dig in at the plate.

The kid from Seymour, Illinois, pitched briefly with the St. Louis Browns as a 23 year old rookie in 1911, then moved to Brooklyn in 1913 where he quickly established himself as the ace of the staff. In his first full season, 1914, Pfeffer went 23-12 with a 1.97 ERA for a losing team. In 1916, he pitched Wilbert Robinson's team to the National League pennant, winning 25 games against 11 losses, with a 1.92 ERA. He went 0-1 with one save and a 1.69 earned run average in the World Series. Strangely, manager Robinson decided to go with all southpaw starters in the Series against the predominantly right handed hitting Red Sox, keeping his ace in the bullpen until game five.

Pfeffer helped the Robins win another pennant in 1920, compiling a 16-9 record with a 3.01 ERA. In the fall classic, he saw limited action, pitching in one game and yielding one run in three innings of relief.

Playing for the St. Louis Cardinals in 1922, the 34-year-old veteran still had enough to win 19 games against 12 losses.

He retired after the 1924 season with a career record of 158-112, and a 2.77 earned run average. He completed 194 of his 280 starts with 28 shutouts.

His Brooklyn totals were 113-80. As the ace of the staff, Big Jeff Pfeffer had victory totals of 23, 19, 25, 11, 1, 17, and 16. He served in the naval reserve

Ron Perranoski

Jeff Pfeffer (Brace Photo)

Babe Phelps

in 1918, pitching a shutout in his only start of the year. The workhorse right-hander pitched over 300 innings twice, averaging 264 innings a year in his six full seasons in Brooklyn. His 157 complete games in a Robins uniform ranks sixth on the all-time Dodger list. His 25 shutouts is eighth.

Big Jeff Pfeffer was in the Don Drysdale mold, a big, strong right-handed pitcher who kept the batters loose at the plate, and who was willing to pitch as often as possible to help the team.

Men like that are hard to find.

BABE PHELPS

Babe Phelps was a chubby, 6'2", 225-pound receiver for the Brooklyn Dodgers during the 1930s and early '40s. He began his career in the American League in 1931, joined the Chicago Cubs in '33, and was traded to the Dodgers two years later.

He enjoyed a seven year career in Brooklyn, and was around long enough to see Leo Durocher's crew win the first Brooklyn pennant in 21 years, in 1941. Phelps' nickname was "The Blimp" because of his heft. After it was learned that the hypochondriac

catcher refused to fly, he was tabbed "The Grounded Blimp" by amused opponents.

Babe Phelps' most famous moment was, unfortunately, a negative one. On August 26, 1939, NBC televised the first major league baseball game, with Red Barber doing the play-by-play. The Cincinnati Reds defeated the Brooklyn Dodgers in Ebbets Field by a score of 5-2. A 2-0 Brooklyn lead evaporated in the eighth inning, as Phelps made two critical errors before a network television audience. The first error, a dropped pop fly, started the Reds rally. The second, a dropped throw from the outfield, allowed the winning run to score.

The native of Odenton, Maryland was an average defensive catcher with below average speed. But he could always wield the timber. The right-handed batter had a career batting average of .310 over 11 years. His Brooklyn average was four points higher. He also had above average power with 15 home runs for every 550 at bats.

In 1935 and '36, Phelps put together two of the greatest offensive seasons ever produced by a major league catcher. In '35, he hit .364, but had only 121 at bats. The next year, in a full season, he pounded the ball at a .367 clip, still the highest single-season batting average for a catcher in major league history.

MIKE PIAZZA

Mike Piazza is the unlikeliest of superstars.

Born Michael Joseph Piazza, in Norristown, PA, on September 4, 1968, Piazza was signed by the

Los Angeles Dodgers in the 62nd round of the 1988 Free Agent Draft, as a favor to Piazza family friend, Tommy Lasorda. Dodger brass didn't hold Piazza in very high regard at the time.

After two mediocre seasons in the Dodger farm system, the 6'3", 210-pound slugger began to blossom in 1991. Playing with Bakersfield, he hit a respectable .277 with 80 runs batted in. His 20 home runs were the most by any Los Angeles minor leaguer. He was voted to the Class A all-star team, leading all Class A players in slugging percentage (.540), and extra base hits (58).

The following year, Piazza's bat exploded. He murdered Texas League pitching, pounding the ball at a .377 clip for San Antonio, before moving up to Albuquerque after only 31 games. With the Dukes, the big right hander continued his abuse of pitchers. In 94 games, he racked up a solid .341 batting average, with 16 home runs and 69 RBIs in 94 games. He finished the season in Los Angeles, batting .232 in 21 games.

Piazza's big bat quickly won him a starting job

Mike Piazza (W. McNeil)

with the Dodgers in 1993, over slick-fielding Carlos Hernandez. The 24-year-old phenom got off the mark quickly, hitting .304 with four homers in April. He followed that up with monthly averages of .344, .302, .290, .333, and .330, managing to avoid any prolonged batting slumps.

When the smoke cleared, the handsome Pennsylvanian had walked of with National League Rookie of the Year honors, on the strength of a .318 batting average, 35 home runs, and 118 runs batted in. His 35 homers and 118 RBIs, both Dodger rookie franchise records, were the third-highest rookie totals in major league history.

To show he was not a one-dimensional player, Piazza threw out 58 would-be base stealers, another Dodger franchise record. At one point in the season, he gunned down seven consecutive runners. His 58 "kills" were the highest in the major leagues, and his 35% accuracy rate was the third highest in the National League.

Mike Piazza continued his offensive fireworks without letup in 1994-95-96. Disdaining the sophomore jinx in 1994, he pounded the ball at a .319 clip, with 24 homers and 92 RBIs. Among his home runs were a 477-foot blast in Florida, and a 458-foot shot in Atlanta. He also crushed two grand slams.

In '95, in spite of injuries that put him on the disabled list for almost a month, he hit a rousing .346 (.377 before the all-star break). His 32 home runs knocked in 93 teammates.

The following year, his bat was on fire for the first half of the year. His .363 batting average led National League batters by a wide margin, but the wear and tear of catching took its toll on his body, and he relinquished the batting lead as the season came to a close. Still, he finished with a fine .336 mark, number three in the National League. In 1997 he slugged the ball at a .362 clip.

Mike Piazza caught over 140 games in 1995, and again in 1996. Both are all-time Dodger records. As an example, Roy Campanella never caught more than 140 games in a season in his entire career. Nor has any other Dodger catcher. And the young backstop has absorbed more than his share of bumps, bruises, and broken bones along the way. As Campy liked to say, "It goes with the territory."

When the Rupert Murdoch group purchased the Dodgers in 1998, Mike Piazza was suddenly and shockingly traded to the Florida Marlins for Gary Sheffield and Charles Johnson. The big slugger, who moved on to the New York Mets almost immediately, continued to raise havoc around the National League for another ten years, hitting a hard .293 with 250 home runs and 772 RBIs in 4204 at-bats, over that period. He retired in 2007 as one of the greatest hitting catchers in the history of the game.

GEORGE PINCKNEY

George Burton Pinckney was born in Orange Prairie, Illinois on January 11, 1862. He began his major league career with the Cleveland Blues of the National League, moving to the Brooklyn team of the American Association when the Blues folded following the 1884 season. As a member of the Blues, the 5'7" 160-pound infielder played shortstop and second base during his debut season. The next year, playing in the City of Churches, the 23-year-old ballplayer was installed at third base, a position he held down for the next seven years. Although not fleet of foot, the Brooklyn third baseman had quick reflexes, and was near the top of his profession as a defensive player. At the plate, the little right-handed batter got the maximum mileage out of his efforts. Although his batting average was erratic, fluctuating between .246 and .309, his run-producing talents remained consistent. Capable of drawing upwards of 80 bases on balls a year, and stealing 60 bases, Pinckney averaged 75 runs scored per season. He scored over 100 runs five years in a row.

In 1886, the Brooklyn leadoff man led the league with 70 bases on balls, and scored 119 runs while batting .261. Over the next four years, he scored 133 runs, 134 runs (to lead the league), 103 runs, and 115 runs.

Brooklyn, now called the Bridegrooms, moved from the American Association to the National League in 1890. An indication of the level of play in the two leagues is reflected in Pinckney's stats for that two-year period. In 1889, in the American Association, Pinckney scored 103 runs and drove in 82, with 36 extra base hits. The following year, in the National League, the third baseman crossed the plate 115 times, drove in 83 runs, and had 36 extra base hits.

George Pinckney played in two World Series with the Brooklyns. In 1889, he was a member of the Bridegroom contingent that lost to the New York Giants, six games to three. The right-handed batter hit .258 in the Series, with two doubles, two runs scored, and three RBIs. The following year, in the 3-3-1 tie with the Louisville Cyclones, Pickney batted a solid .357, with four runs scored, two triples, and three runs batted in.

Pinckney left Brooklyn after the 1891 season, spending one year in St. Louis and another in Louisville before retiring in 1893. During his ten-year major league career, seven of them in Brooklyn, George Pinckney batted .263 with 1,212 hits in 4,610 at bats, he scored 871 runs, accumulated 247 extra base hits, and stole over 300 bases. He died in Peoria, Illinois, on November 10, 1926, at the age of 64.

George Pinckney

JOHNNY PODRES

Johnny Podres, the cocky, young southpaw from Witherbee, New York, will be a legend in Brooklyn as long as baseball is played there. For it was he, on October 4, 1955, who shut out the mighty New York Yankees 2-0 to give the fair borough of Brooklyn its first and only World Championship. Later, when being interviewed by the press about his success against Casey Stengel's sluggers, the brash 23-year-old pitcher uttered the famous statement, "I can beat those guys seven days a week." Johnny Podres was a true Brooklynite.

The 18-year-old southpaw signed a Dodger contract in 1951, then had an eye-opening debut as he went 21-3 at Hazard, leading the league with 228 strikeouts and a 1.67 earned run average. The youngster made the jump to the big leagues two short years later going 9-4 in 18 starts. He brought with him everything a manager could want in a pitcher, a good fast ball, a great curve, an outstanding change-up, good control, and the poise of a seasoned veteran.

Podres enjoyed a splendid 15-year career in the major leagues, 13 of them with the Dodgers. He won twelve or more games seven straight years, from 1957 through 1963. Never a big winner during the regular season, the smooth south-

Johnny Podres

paw exceeded 14 wins only twice in his career. He went 18-5 in 1961, leading the league with a .783 winning percentage, then came back with a 15-13 year in '62. In 1957, he led the league with six shutouts and a 2.66 earned run average. In 1962, in his finest major league effort, he retired the first 20 Philadelphia batters to face him, fanning eight men in a row, en route to a 5-1 victory.

Podres was traded to Detroit in 1966, and finished his career with San Diego two years later.

He helped pitch his Brooklyn and L.A. teams to four pennants and three World Championships in 13 years. After being ko'd in his only 1953 Series start, the cocky lefty beat the Yanks twice in '55, stopping them in Game Three, 8-3, with Brooklyn down two games to none; then coming back in Game Seven to toss a shutout at the Bronx Bombers. His fine pitching efforts earned him the Series Most Valuable Player award and a new sports car. Four years later, he took the measure of the Chicago White Sox 8-3 in Game Two with L.A. down one game to none. He started the sixth and final game of the Series, leaving in the fourth inning with an 8-3 lead. The Dodgers eventually won the game 9-3, but Podres didn't pitch long enough to get credit for the victory. In 1963, as the Dodgers humiliated the Bronx Bombers in a four-game sweep, the 31-year-old veteran came away a 4-1 winner in Game Two.

Johnny Podres' name is on many of the Dodgers all-time lists. He is eighth in career wins with 136, tenth in games pitched with 366, seventh in games started with 310, sixth in strikeouts with 1,331, ninth in innings pitched with 2,030, and ninth in shutouts with 23.

His major league totals were 148-116.

"PEE WEE" REESE

The little marble shooting champion of Louisville, Kentucky, was nicknamed "Pee Wee" after his favorite "pooner." In addition to shooting marbles, the youngster also played baseball. He eventually put his marbles away for good, but he kept plugging away at baseball until he developed into one of the finest shortstops in the major leagues.

Harold Henry Reese originally signed a professional contract with the Boston Red Sox organization, playing two years in his hometown of Louisville with the AAA Colonels of the American Association. Even though he was the top shortstop in the Boston minor league chain, the 21-year-old infielder was prevented from displaying his skills in front of the Boston fans by shortstop-manager Joe Cronin, who wasn't yet ready to relinquish his job. As a result, the wily Larry MacPhail was able to pry Reese away from Tom Yawkey's club for the bargain price of $50,000.

In 1941, Reese helped the Dodgers win their first National League pennant in 21 years, when they edged the St. Louis Cardinals by 2 1/2 games. After World War II ended, Brooklyn assembled its famed "Boys Of Summer" wrecking crew, and Pee Wee Reese was installed as the team captain. From 1947 through 1956, the "Boys of Summer" wreaked havoc around the National League. Averaging 95 wins a year, they won six pennants in ten years, and lost two others on the last day of the season.

Pee Wee Reese was the glue that held the team together. His value to the club far exceeded his baseball statistics. As team captain, he was the player the other players went to for advice. He was the man who cooled tempers and soothed bruised egos. He was the first Dodger player to accept Jackie Robinson as a member of the team. He stood by Robinson both on and off the field, making Jackie feel wanted, and discouraging the red necks in the clubhouse and around the league. In his leadership capacity, he also was directly involved with individual personalities, such as Duke Snider. The Duke, a Hall of Fame baseball player, was a moody player throughout his career. Reese had to alternately, cajole, scold, and advise the Dodger center fielder in order to keep him motivated. Pee Wee did his job in a superlative manner.

On the field, Reese was a leader as well, directing traffic, positioning outfielders, and caressing pitchers. Defensively, the Little Colonel could do it all. He wasn't the fastest shortstop around, and he didn't have the strongest throwing arm. He just did the job better than anyone else. He led the league shortstops in fielding once, in double plays twice, assists once, total chances

"Pee Wee" Reese

accepted three times, and put outs four times.

At the plate, he was the perfect #2 man in the batting order. He had outstanding bat control. He could bunt, hit-and-run, hit behind the runner, or swing away. The Little Colonel was a consistent .270-.280 hitter who could show some power when necessary. He led the league with 104 bases on balls in 1947, 132 runs scored in 1949, and 30 stolen bases in 1952.

Reese was never the most valuable player in the league, but he was often near the top. He finished in the top ten in MVP voting eight times, a true measure of his value to the team.

The former marble-shooting champion enjoyed a 16-year major league career, all with one team-the Dodgers. He smashed out 2,170 hits in 8,058 at bats, for a .269 batting average. He had 536 extra base hits, including 126 home runs, scored 1,338 runs, batted in 885 runs, and stole a Brooklyn-record 232 bases.

In seven World Series, the Captain batted .272, including .304 in 1947, .316 in 1949, and .345 in 1952. When the Dodgers won the whole thing in 1955, Reese hit .296 and scored five runs in seven games.

Harold Henry Reese was voted into baseball's Hall of Fame in 1984.

Roy Campanella put it best. "He could do everything to beat you; running, fielding, throwing, stealing, and hitting. Reese was the captain of our team for ten years. He had real class."

PETE REISER

"Pistol Pete" Reiser exploded on the major league baseball scene like a character out of a dime novel,

a larger-than-life hero; Jack Armstrong, Superman, and Frank Merriwell all rolled into one.

In 1939, the 19-year-old rookie walked into the Brooklyn Dodgers spring training camp for the first time; caught manager Leo Durocher's eye, and was inserted into the starting lineup. His debut in a Dodger uniform has never been equaled. He reached base his first nine times at bat, smashing three home runs and five singles, and drawing one base on balls. All told, in 30 spring training games, he crushed the ball at a lusty .450 clip.

The talented Reiser could do it all; play infield or outfield, hit with power from either side of the plate, throw with either arm, and run with blinding speed. He had good looks, youthful exuberance, and an overabundance of baseball instinct. He had everything a young man could want. With one exception. All his luck was bad.

The 5'11" phenom spent the next year and a half with Elmira in the Eastern League. In July, 1940, after hitting .378 in 67 games for the Pennsylvania team, the youngster was promoted to the big club as a shortstop. He got into 58 games with the Dodgers, and hit a respectable .293. The following spring, with Pee Wee Reese firmly entrenched at shortstop, the kid from St. Louis was converted into a center fielder. His assessment of the job was candid. "You mean all I gotta do is chase fly balls and catch them? That's easy."

It was easy for Reiser in 1941. He led the Brooklyn Dodgers to their first pennant in 21 years, quickly becoming the best defensive center fielder in the National League. Offensively, he dominated the statistics, leading the league in batting average (.343), runs scored (117), doubles (39), triples

(17) total bases (299), and slugging percentage (.558). Baseball experts like Leo Durocher and Branch Rickey called him the greatest natural ballplayer they had ever seen; and that included the likes of Ty Cobb, Babe Ruth, and Honus Wagner.

Even in victory, however, the bad luck that was to finally destroy the young superstar was already in evidence. A variety of beanings and injuries kept Pistol Pete on the sidelines for 17 games. In late April he was hit in the face with an Ike Pearson fast ball and awoke in the hospital. In June, he went down with a sprained ankle. In July he was hospitalized with sciatica. And, in August, Boston pitcher Dick Erickson hit him on the head with a pitch.

As the 1942 season got underway, Harold Patrick Reiser made his assault on Baseball's Olympus. After a slow start, "Pistol Pete" got his bat untracked and proceeded to claw his way to the top of the heap. His average climbed steadily during the first half of the season and stood at .356 as the sun rose on July 19.

That Sunday brought Pete Reiser's magnificent career to a tragic and premature end in the green grass of Sportsman's Park. After St. Louis took the opener of a doubleheader, 8-5, the Dodgers and Cardinals struggled into the 11th inning of the nightcap, deadlocked at 6-6. With two men out, Enos Slaughter hit a Johnny Allen fastball to deep center field. Pistol Pete drew a bead on the ball and took off in hot pursuit. He didn't see the concrete wall in front of him. The collision was sickening as Reiser crashed into the immovable barrier at top speed, the ball popping out of his glove on impact.

Instinctively, the Dodger centerfielder chased the ball and threw it back to the infield before collapsing unconscious with a fractured skull.

The indomitable Reiser returned to the lineup only six days later, but he was plagued by headaches and dizzyness the rest of the season. He hit only .230 over the last two months, finishing with a .310 mark.

After spending the next three years in military service, Pete Reiser returned to Brooklyn, showing spurts of his former self in 1946 by stealing home seven times to set a new major league record, but he was never able to put it all together over a full season. His last season as a regular was 1947 when he hit .309 for Brooklyn. His talents declined rapidly after that, and he retired in 1952 after bouncing around between Boston, Pittsburgh, and Cleveland for four years.

The cold statistics say that Harold Patrick Reiser's major league career covered ten years, during which time he batted .295, with 786 hits in 861 games. The true story is more dramatic.

Pistol Pete Reiser flashed across the heavens like a blindingly beautiful meteor. For one brief moment, his dazzling brilliance illuminated the baseball world. Then he was gone, and only a memory remained.

Pete Reiser's career was snuffed out brutally before he could realize his full potential, but for 727 days, from his major league debut on July 23, 1940, until his tragic collision with the outfield wall in St. Louis on July 19, 1942, Pistol Pete Reiser was the greatest baseball player who ever lived.

Pete Reiser

JERRY REUSS

Jerry Reuss, a 6'5" 227-pound southpaw may have been the number-one prankster in the clubhouse, but on the mound he was all business. Over a 20-year career with the Cardinals, Astros, Pirates, Dodgers, Reds, and Angels, the big mustachioed blonde won a total of 220 games against 191 losses. He was never a 20-game winner, but he racked up 18 victories on three occasions and won 16 games twice.

Born in St. Louis, Missouri on June 19, 1949, Reuss signed his first professional contract with his hometown Cardinals at the age of 18. Three years later, he was in the big leagues to stay. After a 14-14 season with the Red-birds in 1971, he moved on to Houston. Two years later, following a 16-13 season with the Astros, Reuss was traded to the "Steel City," where he curbed his wildness and settled in as the ace of the Pirate staff. He led Pittsburgh to two division titles, going 16-11 in 1974 and 18-11 in 1975.

The fun-loving lefty came to the Dodgers in 1979 after an injury-plagued year, and helped his new team to three division titles and one World Championship in eight full seasons. During the '80s, he was one of Tommy Lasorda's top pitchers, going 18-6 in 1980, followed by 10-4, 18-11, 12-11, 5-7, and 14-11.

Jerry Reuss' greatest day in baseball came on June 27, 1980, when he hurled an 8-0 no-hitter at the San Francisco Giants in Candlestick Park. A first-inning infield error deprived the 31-year-old pitcher of a perfect game. Davey Lopes with three hits, Dusty Baker with a three-run homer, and Steve Garvey with a solo shot, spear-headed the Dodger attack.

Nineteen eighty was a big year for Reuss in more ways than one. In addition to pitching a no-hitter, he captured the National League's Comeback of the Year Award. After a disastrous 7-14 debut in Los Angeles in 1979, the big blonde led the Dodger staff with an 18-6 record while tossing a league-leading six shutouts.

Reuss' biggest disappointment as a major leaguer was his inability to pitch effectively in the League Championship Series. He appeared in the NLCS five times, finishing with an 0-7 record in seven games. He made a major contribution however, to the Dodgers miracle World Championship in 1981. Facing the Houston Astros twice in the division playoffs, he pitched nine scoreless innings in Game Two with no decision, then threw a 4-0 shutout at the Astros in Game Five to clinch the Western Division title. After his usual siesta in the Championship Series, the gutty southpaw returned to form in time to outduel Ron Guidry of the New York Yankees, 2-1, in the pivotal fifth game of the Series. L.A. won the championship the next day, 9-2, behind Burt Hooton.

Off the field, the mischievous blonde was a terror to his managers, constantly harassing the likes of Tommy Lasorda, Danny Murtaugh, and Red Schoendienst. Once, in spring training, he locked Lasorda in his room while the trainer waited patiently to begin the day's activities. Another time, in Chicago, when the Yankees were in town, Reuss went to Comiskey Park, strode into the Yankee dressing room with his equipment bag in his hand, and announced to manager Lou Piniella, "Hi, I'm your new pitcher"

The gregarious southpaw was a tireless worker, pitching more than 200 innings ten times, and winning ten or more games on 11 occasions. A control pitcher with a live fast ball, he was a competitor who always gave a maximum effort.

Jerry Reuss was an asset to any team, both on and off the field.

Jerry Reuss (Los Angeles Dodger Photo)

JACKIE ROBINSON

Jackie Robinson was not just a great baseball player, Jackie Robinson was a great human being. His tremendous competitiveness, his grace, and his fiery spirit belied his humble beginnings in a sharecropper's shack.

Born in Cairo, Georgia, on January 31, 1919, Jack Roosevelt Robinson knew both poverty and prejudice from his early days. After his father, Jerry Robinson, deserted the family when Jackie was six months old, his mother, Mallie took the five Robinson children to Pasadena, California to start a new life. The prejudice was still there, but the opportunities for success were better. Jackie grew up with a burning outrage against the social injustice he witnessed daily. This, coupled with his innate sense of competitiveness, created a burning desire to excel in every struggle, whether on the athletic field or in the field of academics. These characteristics would mold Robinson, the man, into a leader, who would show his people the way out of bondage and into the light, in the arena of professional baseball.

Jackie's vast natural talent made him a star athlete, first at John Muir Technical High School, then at Pasadena Junior College, and finally at UCLA. In college, he excelled in football, basketball, baseball, and track, becoming the school's first four-letter athlete. Jackie broke his brother Mack's national collegiate long jump record during his sophomore year. He also won honorable mention on the NCAA All-American football team.

It was at UCLA that Jackie met his future wife, Rachel Isum, who was to become a stabilizing force in his life. After college and a three-year tour of duty with the U.S. Army in World War II, Jackie began his professional baseball career with the Kansas City Monarchs of the Negro American League. His Negro League career was short-lived however. He was recruited by Branch Rickey, President of the Brooklyn Dodger Baseball Club, to participate in, what Rickey referred to, as "The Noble Experiment."

Branch Rickey created a furor of major proportions when he announced to the press on October 23, 1945, that he had signed Jackie Robinson, a black baseball player, to a professional contract. The sparks from that single deed almost created a flame that could have brought major league baseball to its knees, but dedicated men like Rickey and Commissioner of Baseball, Happy Chandler, nipped all potential revolts in the bud.

For his part, Jackie's first three years in professional baseball; one in Montreal, and two in Brooklyn, were pure hell. It was a never-ending nightmare that would have destroyed most men. Vicious insults and threats were spat at him from

Jackie Robinson

the dugout, the stands, and the field itself. Opposing players went out of their way to spike him or to knock him down. Hotels in visiting cities refused him rooms. Restaurants would not serve him. Some teammates isolated him.

It took a special person to not only survive the vilification, but to perform at the highest level of his profession at the same time. Jackie Robinson was such a man. And all the while, his faithful wife Rachel was at his side, sharing his torment with him and comforting him at the same time.

The Montreal Royals won the International League pennant handily in 1946, then disposed of the Louisville Colonels of the American Association, in the Little World Series. Jackie won the batting title with an average of .349, and led the league in runs scored (113), and fielding average for second basemen (.985). He also stole 40 bases.

During spring training in 1947, Robinson remained on the Montreal roster. In seven exhibition games between Montreal and Brooklyn, the black star put on quite a show. He hit a blazing .625 and stole seven bases. Then, on April 10, 1947, Jackie Robinson's contract was purchased by the Brooklyn Dodgers. He was a major leaguer at last.

In spite of all the abuse heaped on him around the league, Jackie hit a commendable .297, fielded his new position at first base like a veteran, and helped the Dodgers win the National League pennant. In recognition of his fine season, the league voted him Rookie of the Year honors.

Jackie moved to his natural position, second base, in 1948, and had another fine season, batting .296 and knocking in 85 runs, but the Dodgers finished a disappointing third behind Boston and St. Louis. By now, the pressure was beginning to ease on Jack Roosevelt Robinson. There were several blacks in the majors now, including Larry Doby and Satchel Paige of the Cleveland Indians. The Dodgers themselves had three other black players in addition to Jackie. It was time for Branch Rickey to remove the shackles. Beginning in 1949, the real Jackie Robinson revealed himself, asking no quarter and giving none.

Jackie exploded in 1949. He walked off with the National League batting title with an average of .342, led the league in stolen bases with 37, cracked 203 base hits, scored 122 runs, and batted in 124. He was voted the Most Valuable Player in the National League for 1949. And the Dodgers won another National League pennant.

During Jackie's ten years in a Brooklyn uniform, the Dodgers won six National League championships, and lost two others on the last day of the season. In 1955, they achieved the ultimate goal, winning the World Championship from the New York Yankees.

Jackie Robinson was a dynamic all-around player. He was a fine defensive second baseman, a solid .300 hitter who hit with power, and a base stealer nonpareil. In an era when base stealing was a lost art, Robinson stole home 19 times, a figure exceeded by only four other men in the history of the game. There was an old saying, "If the game lasts long enough, Robinson will win it for you."

Jack Roosevelt Robinson was elected to baseball's Hall of Fame in 1962. Suffering from diabetes, and slowly going blind, the valiant baseball pioneer succumbed to a heart attack at his home in Stamford, Connecticut in 1972. He was 53 years old.

In a sport that has existed on the professional level for over 120 years and, in which, literally thousands of players, both black and white, have performed their magic before vast audiences of interested spectators, Jackie Robinson stood alone.

Jack Roosevelt Robinson was a man for all ages. His like will never be seen again.

"PREACHER" ROE

Elwin Charles "Preacher" Roe hailed from the Ashflat, Arkansas, hillbilly country. The well-educated, smooth-talking Roe conned the New York press for years, playing the country yokel with tongue-in-cheek as the naive reporters took down his every word.

The 6'2" stringbean began his professional career in the St. Louis organization, but he came to the major leagues as a 29-year-old rookie with the lowly Pittsburgh Pirates in 1944. He led the National League in strikeouts in 1945, winning 14 games with a 2.87 earned run average. A fractured skull suffered in a fight, while officiating a basketball game, reduced his effectiveness in 1946 and '47, and he was dealt to Brooklyn, along with Billy Cox, after a combined two-season record of 7-23. It was one of the best trades Branch Rickey ever made.

During a seven-year career in Brooklyn, the crafty southpaw compiled a brilliant 93-37 record, giving him an all-time Dodger winning percentage of .715. After a 12-8 season in 1948, Roe led the National League in winning percentage in 1949 with .714, on the strength of a 15-6 record. He topped off his outstanding year by pitching a gem in the

"Preacher" Roe

World Series, outdueling Vic Raschi of the New York Yankees 1-0 in Game Two. Two years later, the lanky pitcher once again led the league in percentage with a lofty .880 mark. His 22-3 record brought him National League pitcher of the year honors. Over a three-year period, from 1951 through 1953, his combined 44-8 mark has never been equaled in Dodger history. In 1952, Roe once again tamed the Yankees in the World Series, besting his friend Ed Lopat 5-3 in Game Three.

Roe spent a total of 12 years in the major leagues, seven of them in Brooklyn, winning 127 games against only 84 losses, a .602 winning percentage. The tall southpaw had a complete pitching repertoire, plus pinpoint control. He was sneaky fast, had a good curve ball and an excellent change of pace. He also possessed a working knowledge of the outlawed spitball, a fact that wasn't widely known until after he retired as an active player.

Preacher Roe's greatest thrill in a baseball uniform came at the plate, not on the mound. Roe, a notoriously poor hitter, with a lifetime batting average of .110, stepped to the plate against Pittsburgh pitcher Bob Hall in the third inning of the second game of a doubleheader on July 7, 1953, and promptly cracked a home run, his only one in the majors. His Dodger teammates were so impressed they laid a carpet of towels from the dugout to the plate for him to walk on. His roommate Billy Cox refused to go out onto the field for the next inning until Roe promised him he would never do that again.

Preacher Roe was a graduate of Harding College in Searcy, Arkansas, and once taught high school mathematics, but it was as a hillbilly raconteur that he gained prominence. The entertaining athlete once told an autograph seeker, "I don't write too well, but I got a kid goin' to school, and he'd be glad to sign it for you."

According to the book, *The Ballplayers,* Roe once said his best pitches were, "my change, my change off my change, and my change off my change off my change."

Preacher Roe was a joy to have on the ball club. Realizing that, after all, baseball is still just a game, he brought entertainment, as well as outstanding baseball skills, to the ballpark. He was an interesting conversationalist; smooth, informed, and well spoken. On the mound, he was a thinking man's pitcher, relying on timing, deception, and finesse. To Roe, pitching was like a chess game. It was him against the batter.

More often than not, "Old Preach" came out the winner.

ED ROEBUCK

Edward Jack Roebuck was born in East Millsboro, Pennsylvania on July 3, 1931. He began his professional career in the Brooklyn organization in 1949, going 8-14 with Newport News. A six-year journey through the vast Dodger minor league chain culminated in an 18-14 season at Montreal in the International League, and won the 6'2", 185-pound pitcher a trip to the majors.

Manager Walter Alston immediately converted

Ed Roebuck (Los Angeles Dodger Photo)

the tall right-hander into a relief pitcher, pairing him with Clem Labine to give Brooklyn a potent one-two punch out of the bullpen. Roebuck's 12 saves in 1955, combined with Labine's 11, were major factors in the Dodgers' pennant drive.

The sinkerball specialist pitched for Brooklyn and Los Angeles for nine years, winning 40 games against only 22 losses, and accounting for 44 saves out of the bullpen. He pitched in two World Series, including the 1955 World Championship Series, yielding one run in 6 1/3 innings for an excellent 1.43 ERA. In 1959, Los Angeles' first World Championship season, he sat out the entire year with a shoulder injury.

He returned to the wars in 1960, winning eight games and saving eight others. In 1962, the big right hander appeared in 64 games, compiling a 10-2 record with nine saves. He was traded to the Washington Senators midway through the '63 season, along with Frank Howard, for pitcher Claude Osteen. A year later, he went to Philadelphia where had two fine seasons. In 1964, he pitched in 60 games for the Phils, with a 5-3 record, 12 saves, and a 2.22 earned run average. The next year he pitched in 44 games, with a 5-3 record.

Roebuck retired from baseball after the 1966 season. He finished his 11-year major league career with 52 wins against 31 losses. He pitched in 460 games with 62 saves and an earned run average of 3.35.

JOHN ROSEBORO

John Roseboro was one of the finest catchers to ever don Dodger blue. During his 11 »year career with the Dodgers, the 5' 11 1/2" receiver set a record for most games played by a Dodger catcher, 1,218, since broken by Mike Scioscia. He also set major league marks for most putouts by a catcher; garnering 848 in 1959, then breaking his own record with 877 in 1961. He led all National League catchers in putouts four times, and double plays twice. After moving to the Minnesota Twins, he led the American League in double plays in 1969.

Roseboro was Sandy Koufax's favorite catcher, twice catching no-hitters thrown by the L.A. superstar.

The native of Ashland, Ohio, came up through the Los Angeles farm system, with stops in Sheboygan, Great Falls, Pueblo, Cedar Rapids, and Montreal. Arriving in Brooklyn late in 1957, Roseboro played in 35 games in Ebbets Field, before the club relocated to sunny California. Playing in the Coliseum in 1958, with its distant right field barrier, Roseboro hit 14 home runs, but 12 of them came on the road.

Never noted as an offensive threat, Roseboro had some big hits in his career. In 1959, the Dodger catcher won the first National League playoff game against the Milwaukee Braves with a tie-breaking, sixth-inning home run, giving Larry Sherry a 3-2 victory. In the 1963 World Series against the New York Yankees, the left-handed batter hit a first-inning three-run homer into the upper right field deck in Yankee Stadium against Whitey Ford to spark the Dodgers and Sandy Koufax to a 5-2 victory in Game One, setting the stage for a four-game sweep. Two years later, against the Minnesota Twins, Roseboro smashed a two-run single in the fourth inning against Camilo "Little Potato" Pascual, to break open a scoreless tie, and give Claude Osteen all the runs he needed in a 4-0 shutout victory. The victory brought the Dodgers back from a two games-to-none deficit, and put them on the road to an eventual seven-game triumph.

John Roseboro was the center of one of the ugliest incidents ever witnessed in a major league park. In a game against the San Francisco Giants in Candlestick Park on the night of August 22, 1965, Roseboro was attacked with a bat by Giant pitcher

John Roseboro (Los Angeles Dodger Photo)

Juan Marichal, after Marichal thought the Dodger catcher's return throws to the pitcher were coming too close to his head. The clubbing did not seriously injure Roseboro, but it triggered a 14-minute free-for-all that emptied both benches and led to the ejection of Marichal. His subsequent nine-game suspension proved costly as the Giants blew a five-game lead with only two weeks left in the season. L.A. took the title by two games.

John Roseboro's major league career spanned 14 years, 11 with the Dodgers, two with the Minnesota Twins, and one with the Washington Senators. He played in 1,585 games, with 1,206 hits, 338 extra base hits, and a .249 batting average. Blessed with better-than-average speed, the big catcher stole 67 bases in his career, including 12 in 1961 and 11 in 1958.

Roseboro was an outstanding defensive catcher, winning the gold glove for six successive years, from 1961 through 1966. He caught in over 100 games 12 successive years, and was one of the best game callers in the business.

In a sport that requires dedication, concentration and maximum effort, John Roseboro was a winner. He played on five division winners in 14 years, and helped the Dodgers to four National League flags and three World Championships.

NAP RUCKER

George Napolean Rucker, a handsome, easy-going Georgia boy with a deep southern drawl, was one of the greatest pitchers of his day. Pitching for the hapless Brooklyn Superb as during the early part of the century, the 5'11", 190-pound southpaw won 134 games against 134 losses for a club that never finished higher than fifth during his first eight years

Nap Rucker

in the league. Thirty-eight of his victories came via the shutout route.

From 1907 through 1914, Rucker put together seasons of 15-13, 18-20, 13-19, 17-19, 22-18. 18-21, 14-15, and 7-6, accounting for 25% of his team's victories. His career earned run average of 2.42 is still #19 on the all-time pitching list.

The good-looking Irishman was born in Crabapple, Georgia, on September 30, 1884, playing sandlot ball around Alpharetta around the turn of the century. He acquired his nickname, "Nap," from his appetite for an ice cream confection that was popular at the time.

Nap Rucker began his professional career with the Atlanta Crackers of the Southern League at the age of 19, moving on to Augusta of the South Atlantic League the following year. His teammates in Augusta included the league batting champion, Ty Cobb, and future Black Sox pitcher, Ed Cicotte. Connie Mack

of the Philadelphia Athletics had first crack at the stylish left hander, after he put together a sizzling 27-9 record in 1906, but Mack already had two Hall of Fame southpaws, Rube Waddell and Eddie Plank, so he opted for a right-handed pitcher instead. Charlie Ebbets of the Brooklyn Superbas got the bargain of the year, picking up the redheaded pitcher's contract for a measly $500.

As a 23-year-old rookie, the fireballing left hander won 15 games for a fifth-place ball club, and topped it off with a glittering 2.06 earned run average. The next year, he pitched one of the greatest games in major league history, throwing a 6-0 no-hitter at the Boston Beaneaters, and establishing a new National League strikeout mark of 14 along the way.

On July 24, 1909, he bettered that mark, striking out 16 St. Louis Cardinals.

Rucker was primarily a fast ball pitcher his first six years in the National League, backing his heat up with a crackling curve ball. An arm injury in 1913 deprived the great pitcher of his overpowering fast ball, and hastened his retirement from the game. He pitched for three more years, with erratic results. After averaging 17 wins a year during his first seven years with the Superbas, the Georgia Cracker won only 18 more games before calling it a day.

The good-natured Rucker was a work horse in his prime, never pitching less than 275 innings a year, with 23 or more complete games. In 1910, he led the league with 27 complete games and 320 innings pitched.

Nap Rucker's last year as a major league pitcher was 1916, the year Wilbert Robinson's Brooklyn team won their first National League pennant in 16 years. In Game Four of the World Series, with the Boston Red Sox on top 6-2, Robinson inserted the 32-year-old veteran into the lineup to finish the game. Rucker hurled two shutout innings, fanning three Boston batters along the way. It was the last major league game he ever appeared in.

In the gallery of great Dodger players, Nap Rucker joins Sandy Koufax, Dazzy Vance, and Don Drysdale, as the top four Dodger pitchers of all time.

He stands alone as the greatest left-handed pitcher in Brooklyn history.

BILL RUSSELL

Bill Russell was a member of the longest-playing infield in major league history. Teaming with Steve Garvey, Davey Lopes, and Ron Cey, for 8 1/2 years, the handsome blonde shortstop helped the Los Angeles Dodgers win four National League pennants and one World Championship over that period.

In all, the slim six-footer played 17 years in the major leagues, all for Los Angeles. From 1969

Bill Russell (Los Angeles Dodger Photo)

through 1986, his teams won six division titles and finished second seven times. His career total of 2,181 games played is exceeded only by Zack Wheat's 2,322 games played, in the Dodger record books.

William Ellis Russell was born in Pittsburg, Kansas, on October 21, 1948. He was a basketball star at Pittsburg High School, but didn't play baseball because the school didn't have a team. Still, the Los Angeles Dodgers, aware of his sandlot credentials, and recognizing his basic athletic talents, signed him to a professional contract and sent him to Ogden, Utah to learn the rudiments of the game.

Russell spent four years in the minor leagues developing his skills as a fleet-footed center fielder. When he finally arrived in L.A. at the tender age of 20, he was carefully nurtured by manager Walter Alston, who treated him more like a son than a ballplayer. In 1972, Alston, with uncanny prescience, converted the youngster from a center fielder to a shortstop. It was an ideal move. Russell had speed, a good arm, and natural athletic ability, but he lacked the power necessary to be a successful major league outfielder. The manager also moved Davey Lopes from the outfield to second base, and turned Steve Garvey from a third baseman into a gold-glove first baseman.

The Dodgers, with their new infield performing as a unit for the first time, walked off with the National League championship in 1974. They repeated as Senior Circuit champs in 1977 and 1978, but lost the World Series in each of those years.

Along the way, however, Bill Russell earned the reputation of being a clutch hitter in the League Championship Series. He always seemed to rise to the occasion when the pennant was on the line. Playing in five NLCS, the Kansas native hit the ball at a .337 clip in 21 games, with eight crucial runs batted in. In Game Three of the '77 playoffs against Philadelphia, Russell stepped to the plate with two out in the ninth inning of a tie game. The Dodgers had just fought back to tie the game, scoring two runs off Phillie stopper, Gene Garber, after two men were out. Russell climaxed the rally by driving a ball back through the middle, plating Davey Lopes with the eventual game-winning run. L.A. won the pennant the next day with a 4-1 victory.

In 1978, against these same Phillies, Bill Russell drilled a two-out single to center field in the bottom of the ninth inning of game four, to score Ron Cey from second base with the pennant-winning run. In the World Series against the New York Yankees, the right-handed hitter led both teams at bat with 11 hits, good for a .423 average.

Three years later, the Dodger shortstop hit a respectable .263 in postseason play as Tommy Lasorda's "Comeback Kids" overwhelmed Houston, Montreal, and the New York Yankees, en route to the World Championship.

Bill Russell retired from active play after the 1986 season, but remained with the Dodger organization as a coach and minor league manager. In 1996, he was promoted to manager of the team following the retirement of Tommy Lasorda. The handsome Nebraskan compiled a record of 162-138 over the next two years, finishing second and third in the National League Western Division. He was replaced as manager by Glenn Hoffman on June 21, 1998.

STEVE SAX

Steve Sax was an all-out, hell-bent-for-leather baseball player. The hyperactive second baseman was wired to do whatever it took to win.

Born in Sacramento, California, Sax signed a professional contract with the Los Angeles Dodgers in 1978 at the age of 18. He made the usual trek through the boonies, honing his skills in places like Lethbridge, Clinton, Vero Beach, and San Antonio, before earning a promotion to Los Angeles.

Arriving in Dodger Stadium in 1981 at the age of 21, the young second baseman got his first taste of pennant pressure, spelling Davey Lopes down the stretch, as Tommy Lasorda's boys clawed their way to the World Championship. When Lopes was traded to the Oakland Athletics over the winter, Sax became a regular. In his first full season in the majors, the youngster played in 150 games, stole 47 bases, hit .282, and ran off with the National League Rookie of the Year award.

He duplicated his offensive statistics as a sophomore, but the sophomore jinx still left its mark on him. Mid-way through the season, he began making wild throws to first base. The more he thought about it, the wilder his throws became. It got so bad, people in the first base grandstand wore baseball gloves, and Sax's teammates even joked about his problem. Pedro Guerrero, who was having his own defensive problems at third base, when asked what he thought about just before the pitcher released the pitch, replied, "Just before the pitcher throws the ball, I look up and I say, 'please God, don't let him hit the ball to me.' Then I look around the infield, and I say, 'and don't let him hit it to Sax either.'"

Tommy Lasorda stuck with his young infielder through all the turmoil, and eventually things returned to normal, and Sax's throws became straight and true once more. Through it all, the kid known as "Mr. Hustle" was his usual offensive threat. Except for an off year in 1984, his batting average fluctuated between .277 and .332, and his stolen bases averaged 41 a year. In 1986, when he batted .332, he just missed the National League batting title, trailing Montreal's Tim Raines by a mere .002 points.

Steve Sax played with the Los Angeles Dodgers for eight years, helping them to four Western Division titles, and two World Championships. As might be expected, he was tough in postseason play. In four NLCS, he hit .273, including .300 in 1985. In his only World Series (not counting one at bat in 1981), Sax hit .300, with one stolen base and three runs scored in five games.

The 29-year-old veteran became a free agent following the 1988 season, and signed a contract with the New York Yankees. After three strong seasons in the Big Apple, he was traded to the Chicago White Sox for pitcher Melido Perez.

Steve Sax played major league baseball for 14 years, accumulating 1949 base hits, 444 stolenbases, and a .281 batting average.

MIKE SCIOSCIA

Michael Lorri Scioscia holds the record for most games played in a career by a Dodger catcher. The hardnosed backstop appeared in 1,395 games for Los Angeles during his career. The previous record holders were John Roseboro (1,218) and, before him, Roy Campanella (1,183).

The 6'2", 220-pound athlete was the ideal man behind the plate, because he asked no quarter and he gave none. He was the best plate-blocking catcher of the era, and some executives have called him the best of all time.

Mike Scioscia, from Upper Darby, Pennsylvania, came up through the Dodger farm system, arriving in Los Angeles in 1980 after five years of minor league preparation. Like Steve Sax and several other youngsters, Scioscia found himself in a hot pennant race in 1981, and he performed admirably, giving Steve Yeager a muchneeded breather down the stretch.

He took over the reins as the first-string catcher the following year, and except for an injury-plagued '83 season, he bore the brunt of the long summer schedule until 1995. Scioscia was an outstanding defensive catcher. He had a strong arm, called an excellent game, and was like a wall of granite to baserunners trying to score. Surprisingly, the big catcher was not a power hitter, averaging under ten home runs a year. He did have a good eye at the plate however, striking out only 36 times a year, and combining a .259 batting average with 80 bases on balls a year, to give him a respectable lifetime .353 on base percentage. Scioscia's best year at the plate was 1985 when he hit .296 and drew 77 bases on balls, giving him an on base percentage of .409, second best in the National League to teammate Pedro Guerrero.

During his career in Los Angeles, Mike Scioscia

Steve Sax (W. McNeil)

played on four division winners, and two World Championship teams. He was a member of the "Miracle Dodgers" of 1988, a ragtag group of scrappers who were much maligned in the press, but who rose to the mythical heights to defeat the highly favored New York Mets in the National League Championship Series; then took the mighty Oakland Athletics to task in five games in the World Series.

Mike Scioscia (Los Angeles Dodger Photo)

Scioscia's most memorable day in baseball occurred during the League Championship Series. The New York Mets had defeated Tommy Lasorda's team 10 times in 11 meetings during the regular season, and were odds-on favorites to polish them off quickly in the playoff. The odds seemed to be appropriate as the New Yorkers took two of the first three games, and were leading in game four, 4-2 after 8 2/3 innings, with 18-game winner Doc Gooden on the mound. Gooden, inexplicably, issued a two-out walk to John Shelby. Then Mike Scioscia hit a dramatic two-run homer into the right-field stands to deadlock the game at four runs apiece. Kirk Gibson

won the game with a home run in the twelfth, and L.A. went on to win the NLCS in seven games, behind the pitching of Belcher and Hershiser.

Scioscia retired in 1995. The comments of the Los Angeles executives tell more about the mild mannered Scioscia than mere statistics ever could. Executive Vice President Fred Claire called Scioscia "the ultimate team player," and Tommy Lasorda added, "He is a tremendous young man and he is one of the finest competitors that has ever worn a Dodger uniform."

JIMMY SHECKARD

Jimmy Sheckard was a turn-of-the-century ballhawk who broke into major league baseball with the Brooklyn Superbas in 1897. The native of Upper Chanceford, Pennsylvania, was a good outfielder, possessing outstanding speed and a strong throwing arm. He was also an offensive threat, compiling a .274 batting average over a 17year career.

Sheckard's Brooklyn career spanned eight years, from 1897 through 1905, except for 1899 when he played in Baltimore. The 5'9" speedster was a .300 hitter for Charlie Ebbets' teams, batting .300 in 1900, .353 in 1901, and .332 in 1903. His finest year in Flatbush was 1901. In addition to his .353 batting average, the 23-year-old outfielder led the league in triples with 21 and slugging average with .534. He also scored 116 runs, hit 31 doubles, 11 home runs, drove in 104 runs, and stole 35 bases.

Two years later, he led the National League in home runs with nine, outfield assists with 39, and stolen bases with 67. It was his second stolen base crown. He had stolen 77 bases with Baltimore in 1899.

Sheckard helped the Superbas win the National League pennant in 1900, then watched helplessly as the club became a second division operation over

Jimmy Sheckard (Transcendental Graphics)

the next five years. After a last-place finish in 1905, when the Superbas went 48-104, finishing 56 1/2 games behind the pennant-winning New York Giants, Sheckard was traded to the Chicago Cubs. It was the best break of his life. The hustling centerfielder played in the Windy City for seven years, sharing in four National League celebrations and two World Championships. In 1911, as a 33year-old veteran, Jimmy Sheckard led the league with 121 runs scored, 147 base on balls, and a .434 on base percentage. The next year, he led in walks again, this time with 122.

Sheckard retired from baseball in 1913, having roamed the National League outfields for 17 long years. During that time, he accumulated 2,091 hits, 548 of them for extra bases, scored 1,295 runs, and batted in 813 runs. His 465 stolen bases included 212 in Brooklyn, giving him fourth place on the all-time Brooklyn list, behind Pee Wee Reese's 231.

LARRY SHERRY

Larry Sherry was the hero of the Los Angeles Dodgers miracle pennant of 1959. The transplanted Brooklynites had finished a miserable seventh in 1958, their first year on the west coast, and the media experts didn't give them much chance of improving their position in 1959.

To the surprise of everyone, the Big Blue Machine not only improved on its previous year's performance, it went on to become World Champions. Walter Alston has called the 1959 ball club his favorite; a team with average talent, but with dedication, perseverance, and an overabundance of heart.

The hero of the pennant drive was an obscure 24year-old minor league pitcher named Larry Sherry. The 6'2" fast ball pitcher had kicked around the Dodger farm system for seven years, mostly as a starting pitcher, and was 6-7 at St. Paul midway through the '59 season. Alston, in need of another starting pitcher, and embroiled in a dogfight for first place in July, recalled the cocky righthander.

Sherry dropped his first start, to the Cubs, 2-1, and his second start to Cincinnati 4-3. He didn't lose another game. On September 11, the 24-year-old rookie blanked Pittsburgh 4-0 in an 11-strikeout performance. That was his last start. The wily Alston assigned Sherry to the bullpen as his stopper, and the brash Californian proved more than worthy. In 14 games, he went 5-0 with three saves, and posted a 0.74 earned run average over 36 1/3 innings.

Down the stretch, Sherry was amazing. In one game, he dazzled his manager with a performance Alston called the "greatest one-man show ever put on by a pitcher." He relieved Johnny Podres in the first inning against St. Louis, with the Cards up, 3-0. He proceeded to shut the Redbirds down without a run over the last 8 2/3 innings, and knocked in three

runs himself with two singles and a home run, en route to a 4-3 victory.

After the Dodgers and Milwaukee finished the sea son in a flat-footed tie for first place, the indefatigable reliever took over for starter Danny McDevitt in the second inning of the first playoff game, with the Braves up 2-1. Once again, he was almost perfect, blanking Fred Haney's crew over the last 7 2/3 innings, and coming away a winner when John Roseboro hit a sixth-inning home run.

In the World Series against the Chicago White Sox, Sherry appeared in four of the six games, holding the Go-Go Sox to a 0.71 ERA over 12 2/3 innings. He won two games, saved two others, and captured the Most Valuable Player trophy for his outstanding effort.

Larry Sherry pitched in the major leagues for 11 years, six with the Dodgers, four with the Detroit Tigers, and finishing with Houston and California.

Larry Sherry (Los Angeles Dodgers)

His Los Angeles record showed a 34-25 won-loss record, and 39 saves. In Detroit, the big righty was 18-17 with 37 saves.

Lawrence Sherry, a native of Los Angeles, California, was an average major league pitcher, winning 53 ballgames and losing 44 others, with a 3.67 earned run average over an 11-year career. But for one brief moment in time, from mid-September through early October of 1959, Larry

Sherry was the greatest pitcher the world had ever seen. For five weeks, the cocky relief ace compiled a record of 10-0 with five saves and an earned run average of around 0.50. He pitched his team to the championship of the world.

No pitcher ever did more.

BILLY SHINDLE

Billy Shindle held down the hot corner for Dave Foutz's Brooklyn Bridegrooms during the 1890s. In addition to being an offensive threat, the slightly built Shindle could also field with the best of them. His 3.7 lifetime range factor makes him the number-one defensive third baseman in Dodger history. For comparison, Billy Cox, the great third baseman of "The Boys of Summer," had a lifetime average of 2.97. Shindle twice had season range factors of 4.0, in 1894 and 1898.

William Shindle was born in Gloucester, New Jersey, on December 5, 1860. He began his major league career with the Detroit Wolverines of the National League in 1886, playing alongside all-time greats like "Big Dan" Brouthers and "Big Sam" Thompson. In the dead ball era, the pair of six-footers both hit more than 100 career home runs, with Thompson blasting 20 in 1889.

The third baseman also played with the Baltimore Orioles, and Philadelphia Phillies before coming to Brooklyn in 1894. He spent five years in the City of Churches, during which time the Bridegrooms finished fifth, ninth, sixth, and tenth. The 1894 and '95 teams were the aging remnants of the 1890 pennant winners. Thereafter, the 'Grooms just fielded bad teams. Pitcher

"Brickyard" Kennedy, one of Brooklyn's all-time great pitchers, suffered along with Shindle during that frustrating period.

Billy Shindle didn't let quality of play around him affect his own play, however, as he gave Foutz and his successors excellent offense and defense, year in and year out. In 1894, the 34-year-old third baseman hit .296 with 94 runs scored and 96 runs batted in. He scored 92 runs in 1895. Two years later, the New Jerseyan hit .284, scored 83 runs and drove in 105.

Shindle retired after the 1898 season at the age of 38. In all, his major league career spanned 13 years. He left a .269 career batting average behind him, along with 1,562 hits, 355 extra base hits, 993 runs scored, 758 runs batted in, and 316 stolen bases. The 5'8", 158-pound third baseman was major league all the way.

REGGIE SMITH

Carl Reginald Smith had a long and distinguished 17-year major league career. He began his career as an outfielder for the Boston Red Sox, in 1966, and the following year helped them capture the American League pennant, Boston's first flag in 22 years. He hit two home runs in the ensuing World Series, a losing effort against the St. Louis Cardinals.

Smith was not only a powerful hitter, he was also an outstanding defensive outfielder with a strong throwing arm. He won a Gold Glove in center field in 1968, batted over .300 three times, and hit between 21 and 30 home runs five times.

After eight years in Boston, and two and a

Billy Shindle (Transcendental Graphics)

Reggie Smith (Los Angeles Dodgers)

half in St. Louis, Reggie Smith found his way to Los Angeles, where the smooth-swinging switch hitter helped Tommy Lasorda's crew take the National League pennant in both 1977 and 1978. He was a charter member of the Dodgers

four-man, 30 home ran club in '77, along with Dusty Baker, Ron Cey, and Steve Garvey. They were the first major league quartet to accomplish that feat.

Smith hit 32 home runs in 1977, and rapped three more in the World Series against the New York Yankees. In 78, he hit 29 homers and batted .295. Injuries slowed him down during his remaining three years in L.A., but in 1980, when he hit .322 with 15 homers in 311 at bats, baseball writer and sportscaster Bud Furillo called him the best right-fielder in Los Angeles Dodger history. "Watching him throw runners out at the plate (from 1977 to 1980) became a big part of the excitement of Dodger baseball."

The Reggie Smith era was a proud time in Los Angeles Dodger history.

SHERRY SMITH

Sherry Smith

Sherrod Malone Smith was born in Monticello, Georgia, on February 18, 1891. The Georgia Cracker followed in the footsteps of another great pitcher, Nap Rucker. Both hailed from the Peach Tree State, both were southpaws, and both had their greatest days on the mound in a Brooklyn uniform.

Sherry Smith was a 6'1", 170-pound block of granite. In *The Ballplayers,* he is called "strong as a horse and tireless as a Missouri mule." In seven years with the Robins, the big lefty gave Brooklyn fans some of their most memorable moments.

Smith arrived in Brooklyn in 1915 after spending five years in the minors, and parts of two seasons with the Pittsburgh Pirates. He joined Jeff Pfeffer, Larry Cheney, and Rube Marquard on the Robin pitching staff, going 14-8 in 1915, then 14-10 in 1916 as the Robins won the National League title. After a 12-12 season in 1917, the strapping 26-year-old pitcher enlisted in the service, missing the entire 1918 season. In 1920, Sherry Smith won 11 games against nine losses with a sparkling 1.85 earned run average, as the Robins once again brought home the National League pennant.

Smith's greatest mound performances were saved for the World Series. In 1916, facing the great Boston Red Sox southpaw, Babe Ruth, Smith surrendered a game-tying run to the Bo-Sox in the bottom of the third on a triple by Everett Scott and an infield out by Ruth. He then proceeded to throw goose-eggs at Bill Carrigan's team for ten long innings, but the Robins could not gain him the victory. In the bottom of the 14th inning, Boston scored the game winner on a base on balls, a sacrifice, and a one-out single by Del Gainor.

In 1920, the gutty southpaw tossed a three hitter at the Cleveland Indians, beating 20-game winner Ray Caldwell, 2-1. The victory gave the Robins a 2-1 lead in games in the Series. They didn't win another game as Tris Speaker's boys ran off four consecutive wins to take the nine-game series, five games to two. Sherry Smith came back to pitch again in Game Six, but his outstanding effort was wasted as he lost a nail-biter to Duster Mails, 1-0. The only run of the game crossed the plate in the bottom of the sixth inning on a two-out single by Speaker and a ringing double off the left field wall by George Burns. Smith scattered seven hits and yielded only one walk in pitching a complete game.

In three World Series games, Sherry Smith produced one of the lowest earned run averages in Series history, a meager 0.89 for 32 innings. His 1-2 Series record belies his magnificent pitching performances.

Sherry Smith pitched in the major leagues for 14 years, winning 114 games and losing 118. His Brooklyn record was 69-70 with a outstanding 2.91 ERA. He will be remembered by Dodger fans for his three outstanding World Series efforts, including pitching in the longest game in World Series history.

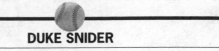

DUKE SNIDER

Edwin Donald "Duke" Snider was the greatest center fielder in Dodger history, perhaps the greatest all around player in Dodger history. He could do it all, both offensively and defensively. At the plate, the left-handed hitting Snider had a picture book swing that drove base-steel springs in his legs, allowing him to cover vast expanses of ground quickly, gracefully and effortlessly, and suit of a potential home run ball. He teamed with right with some of the most exciting outfield play ever witnessed in the major leagues. The picture of Snider scaling the barrier in deep center field to snare a long drive is indelibly imprinted in the minds of Brooklyn fans everywhere

As an all-around player, the Duke of Flatbush had no equal. Playing in the same city with contemporaries Wille Mays and Mickey Mantle, the Los Angeles native more than held his own. He matched them in batting average , home runs, and runs batted in, and he out-fielded both of them. In one five-year period, from 1953 through 1957, the Duke stood alone at the top of his profession. He tied a National League record by hitting 40 or more home runs for five consecutive years, his 43 round-trippers leading the league in 1956. He also led the league in runs scored in three of those years, with 132 in 1953, 120 in 1954, and 126 in 1955. Snider's RBI totals for the five years were 126, 130, 136 to lead the league, 101, and 92. His five-year batting average of .310, included averages lead the league, 101, and 92. of .336 in 1953 and .341 in 1954, when he lost the batting title to Wille Mays on the last day of the season. He was voted *The Sporting News Player of the Year* for 1955

The smooth-swinging left hander was well suited to the cozy confines of Ebbets Field with its 298-foot right field wall surmounted by a 19-foot-screen. Snider's high drives sailed over the 38-foot barrier onto Bedford Avenue with monotonous regularity. Two of his greatest days in baseball took place before the home fans. On May 30, 1950, against the Philadelphia phils, the Duke crushed three home runs in his first three at bats, one to each field. In his fourth at bat, he hit the hardest ball he hit all day, a rising liner to right field. The ball struck the screen one foot from the top, traveling with such speed that the fleet-footed Sinder was held to a single. Five years later, against Milwaukee, the big slugger hit three home runs and a double, driving in six runs in an 11-8 rout of Charlie Grimm's Braves.

Duke Snider appeared in a total of six World Series, five in Brooklyn. He was on two World Championship teams, the famous 1955 Dodgers, and the miracle Los Angeles Dodgers of 1959. In 36 games, the graceful Californian batted. .286 with 11 home runs and 26 runs batted in. His 11 homers places him fourth on the all-time World Series list, and is #1 in the National League. He is sixth in slugging percentage (.594), tenth in runs scored (21), sixth in total bases (79), sixth in doubles (8), and seventh in runs batted in (26).

Duke Snider played a total of 18 years in the National League, accumulating 2,116 hits. With 407 home runs (#22 all-time), 1,259 runs scored, 1,333 runs batted in, and a .295 batting average.

Edwin Donald Snider's proudest moment came in 1980 when he was inducted into baseball's Hall of Fame in Cooperstown, New York.

The Duke is now enshrined with the immortals.

EDDIE STANKY

Eddie Stanky was a hustling hard-nosed infielder for the Broooklyn Dodgers from 1944 through 1947. Manager Leo Durocher, speaking of his tough little second baseman, once said, "He can't run. He can't hit. And he can't field. All he can do is win." Stanky helped the Dodgers win the National League pennant in 1947, then played on the Boston Braves' National League champions in 1948. When Durocher took over the managerial reins of the New York Giants, he obtained Stanky from Boston, and the New Yorkers captured the flag in 1951 and 1954.

Eddie Stanky, known as "The Brat" or "Mugsy" for his pugnacious attitude, came up to the majors with the Chicago Cubs in 1943 as a 27-year-old rookie. He drew 92 bases on balls and scored 92 runs for the fifth-place Cubs, and he led all National League second basemen in total chances per game with 6.1. He moved to Brooklyn in 1944, and was quickly adopted by the blue-collar Brooklyn fans for his aggressive play.

The 5'8" 170-pound infielder was just an average hitter, but he had no equal at drawing bases on balls out of the opposing pitcher. His accentuated crouch made him a difficult batter to pitch to. "The Walking Man" led the National League in walks three times, with 148 in 1945,137 in 1946, and 144 in 1950. In all, he coaxed 996 walks out of the enemy in his career, an average of 125 walks per year.

Stanky averaged 101 runs scored per year over an Il-year period. He also got the job done in the field, leading National League second baseman in putouts three times, double plays twice, assists once, fielding average once; and chances per game twice. He was named to the National League all-star team twice, in 1947 and 1950.

Duke Snider

Eddie Stanky

In 1947, the Brooklyn Dodgers brought second baseman Jackie Robinson up to the big club, and Stanky's days in Flatbush were numbered. Dodger management put Robinson on first base his rookie season to take some of the pressure off him, but in 1948 he was moved to second and Stanky was traded to Boston.

Eddie Stanky finished his 11-year major league career as player-manager with the St. Louis Cardinals in 1953. His 1,154 career hits produced a ,268 batting average, with 811 runs scored.

ED STEIN

Edward F. Stein was born in Detroit, Michigan on September 5,1869. He made his major league debut with the Chicago Cubs at the age of 20

The tall, slender right-handed pitcher made an Impressive debut in the Windy City, winning 12 games against only six losses as Cap Anson's team battled Bill McGunnigle's Brooklyn Bridegrooms for the National League pennant The 'Grooms pre-

vailed by 6 games behind the outstanding pitching of Tom Lovett (30-11), Adonis Terry (26-161, and Bob Caruthers (23-11).

Stein slumped to 7-6 in 1891, then moved on to Brooklyn, where he became the club's leading pitcher for the next four years. Unfortunately for him, the 'Grooms were a mediocre team during that period, reducing his pitching prospects considerably.

In 1892, Gentleman George Haddock compiled a record of 29-13, while the 5'11" 170-pound Stein was close behind at 27-1 6, with six shutouts. The two hurlers were primarily responsible for Brooklyn's third place finish, a neighborhood the Brooklyn players wouldn't visit again for seven long years.

In 1893, professional baseball made a radical rules change, lengthening the pitching distance from 50 feet to 60 feet. The increased distance spelled disaster for many major league pitchers. Haddock, for instance, dropped from 29 victories in 1892 to eight victories in 1893. He won four games in '94, then was gone from the major league scene at the age of 28. Ed Stein however, successfully made the transition. In the first year of the change, Stein was 19-1 5 for the sixth-place 'Grooms

The next year, the 24-year-old hurler had a fine 27-14 record for Dave Foutz's Brooklyn club, but the team still managed a fifth-place finish. Stein supplemented his won-loss record by pitching 359 innings in 45 games, an average of eight innings per game. His 9.93 hits allowed per nine innings, was third best in the league.

Ed Stein (Transcendental Graphics)

Ed Stein's greatest day in baseball came on June 2, 1894, at Eastern Park, when he no-hit the Boston 'Beaneaters 1-0 in a rain-shortened six-inning game. A two-out triple by left fielder George Treadway and a single to right by Mike Griffin scored the only run of the game. Stein, as usual, was wild, walking five men, but he had the Beaneaters hitting the ball into the ground all day, and was in control the entire game.

Ed Stein's career declined after the '94 season. He was still good enough for 15-13 in 1895, then fell to 3-6 the following year. He was out of baseball in 1897, came back briefly in '98, losing two games without a victory, then faded from the scene.

Ed Stein pitched in the major leagues for eight years, five in Brooklyn. He won a total of 110 games against 78 losses, pitching 159 complete games in 184 starts over that period.

Stein died in his hometown of Detroit, Michigan, on May 10, 1928, at the age of 58.

DON SUTTON

Don Sutton

The Dodgers have had many outstanding pitchers during their long and glorious professional baseball history. Donald Howard Sutton ranks up there with the best of them.

The 6'1" curveball specialist holds almost every significant Dodger pitching record, including 550 games pitched, 533 games started, 3,815 innings pitched, 2,690 strikeouts, 52 shutouts, and 233 career wins.

Sutton, a native of Clio, Alabama, began his professional career at Santa Barbara in the California League. The 20-year-old right-hander's 8-1 record won him a quick promotion to the Dodgers top minor league club at Albuquerque, where he won another 15 games, against only six losses. The combined 23-7 minor league stats were good enough for Dodger management to bring the youngster up to the big club after only one year in the minors.

In his rookie season in L.A. Sutton went 12-12 to win the National League Rookie of the Year honors. His 209 strikeouts were the most by a rookie pitcher in 55 years. Sutton pitched for Walter Alston and Tommy Lasorda for the next 15 years, winning 233 games, and helping the Dodgers to three National League Championships. In every one of those years, the durable righthander catalogued more than 200 innings pitched. His forte was conditioning. He was a fanatic on staying in shape. In 23 major league seasons, he never spent one day on the disabled list. He had only one 20-victory season in Los Angeles, going 21-10 in 1976, but he won more than 10 games every year he pitched for the Dodgers, except for 1988 when he was brought back as a 43-yearold veteran, nearing retirement.

Don Sutton won 19 games against nine losses in 1972, went 19-9 again in 1974, and had an 18-10 record in 1973. He pitched spectacular baseball in the League Championship Series, compiling a 3-1 record with an excellent 1.73 earned run average. In the World Series, Sutton had a 2-2 record, winning one game in 1974, one game in 1977, then going 0-2 in 1978.

After leaving Los Angeles in the free agent draft in 1981, Sutton pitched for four different teams over the next eight years, winning 94 games and losing 81. He returned to L.A. to close out his career in 1988.

Don Sutton was not an overpowering pitcher. His best pitch was his curveball. He supplemented that with a good fastball, and a sharp screwball. He was also an intelligent pitcher. A Baltimore scout once said, "Sutton isn't a pitcher. He's an artist."

When Don Sutton's magnificent 23-year career ended, the 43-year-old right-hander had established some memorable records. He started a total of 756 games in the major leagues, a figure exceeded only by the legendary Cy Young. He ranks #12 on the all-time victory list with 324, #8 in shutouts with 58, and #6 in innings pitched with 5282. He holds the major league record for most consecutive years with 100 or more strikeouts-21.

Although he never pitched a no-hitter, the Alabama native hurled five one-hitters, and seven two-hitters.

Don Sutton became a sportscaster for the Atlanta Braves after retiring from play, and was elected to Baseball's Hall of Fame in 1998.

ADONIS TERRY

William H. "Adonis" Terry was born in Westfield, Massachusetts, on August 7, 1864. The handsome right handed pitcher began his professional career with the Brooklyn's of the Inter-State Association in 1883, although he didn't appear in any games.

In 1884, with Brooklyn now a member of the American Association, Terry's pitching career got off to a rather inauspicious start. The Church City Nine were a pitiful ball club their first year in the Association, winning only 40 of 104 games, and finishing ninth in the 13-team league. Since Terry was Brooklyn's ace, even though he was only a rookie, he took the brunt of the pounding. Starting 57 of the team's 104 games, the 19-year-old curve ball specialist limped home with a sorry 20-35 record.

The next year, hampered with injuries, the youngster finished at 6-17. By now, however, both he and the Brooklyn team were on the rise. In 1886, Brooklyn finished third, and Adonis Terry had his first winning season, finishing with 18 wins and 16 losses. More important, he pitched a no-hit, no-run game against the champion St. Louis Browns on July 24.

After a 16-16 season in 1887, Adonis Terry compiled a 13-8 record in '88, and crowned it with

"Adonis" Terry

another no-hitter. This time the victims were the Louisville Cyclones, one of the doormats of the league. Terry shackled Mordecai Davidson's bumbling crew 4-0, fanning eight and issuing three base on balls en route.

Bill McGunnigle's boys, now known as the Bridegrooms, put it all together in 1889, winning the American Association pennant by two games, and breaking the St. Louis Browns' four-year domination. Terry pitched in 41 games, winning 22 and losing 15. In the World Series against the National League champion New York Giants, the Brooklyn workhorse started five of the nine games, throwing four complete games, and finishing with a 2-3 record.

In 1890, the Grooms joined the National League and, proving their American Association pennant was no fluke, they dethroned the New York Giants to win the National League pennant in their first attempt. Adonis Terry had one of his finest years in a Brooklyn uniform, going 26-16 with a 2.94 earned run average. The postseason classic matched the Grooms against the American Association entry, the Louisville Cyclones. The Series was very competitive, but cold weather forced a premature end to the competition before a champion could be crowned. The games stood at 3-3-1 at Series end. Adonis Terry finished at 1-1-1, with one shutout. After a tough 6-16 season in 1891, Terry moved on to Pittsburgh for two years, then finished his career in Chicago.

William "Adonis" Terry was more than a pitcher. He was the first matinee idol in professional baseball. Women swooned at his chiseled features and flowing mustache. Whenever he was scheduled to pitch, women pushed their way through the turnstiles in record numbers. Adonis Terry was a gold-plated drawing card.

In addition to his pitching expertise, Adonis Terry also played other positions in the major leagues. He appeared in a total of 668 games over the course of his career, but only 441 of them were on the pitcher's mound. He played 216 games in the outfield, 16 games at shortstop, 15 games at first base, and one game at third. His batting average of .249 included 76 doubles, 54 triples, and 15 home runs in 2,393 at bats.

On the mound, his 14-year stats showed 197 victories against 195 losses, with 368 complete games in 407 starts.

He died in Milwaukee, Wisconsin, on February 25, 1914, at the age of 49.

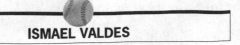

ISMAEL VALDES

Ismael Valdes, the pride of Tamaulipas, Mexico, may have been one of the best natural pitchers ever to don Dodger blue. The 6', 3", 207-pound right hander arrived on the scene with a complete repertoire of pitches, including a live fastball, and a sharp-breaking curve. He was also blessed with outstanding control, averaging only two bases on balls a game, as opposed to six strikeouts. And to top it off, he had the poise of a seasoned veteran.

The handsome Mexican was signed to a Dodger contract at 17 years of age by renowned scout Mike

Ismael Valdes (W. McNeil)

Brito. Even as a youngster, he had all the tools-the pitches, the control, and the poise. He didn't allow a home run during his first two years in professional baseball.

After a sensational year at Mexico City in 1993 where he went 17-8, and a fast start with AA San Antonio the next year, Valdes was called up to the Dodgers on June 8, 1994, a full-fledged major leaguer at the age of 20.

The big right hander had an excellent rookie season in 1995, finishing with a 13-11 record, although he could well have racked up 16 or 17 victories if he had received any offensive support. He teamed with another rookie, Hideo Nomo, to give the Dodgers one of

the most explosive pitching staffs in the major leagues. Valdes and Nomo went 11-1 during the month of June, with Valdes contributing a 5-1 record and an ERA under 2.00. For the year, his 3.05 earned run average was #4 in the league, as was his opponent batting average of .228.

The year 1996 was a coming-of-age year for the big pitcher. He was the stopper on the staff, pitching in 33 games, with 225 innings pitched, 173 strikeouts, 54 bases on balls, and a record of 15-7

In '97 he Continued to be the stopper for the Dodgers, but his offensive support was atrocious. His 10-11 record was not indicative of his value to the team, as evidenced by his miniscule 2.65 earned run average.

Ismael Valdes was plagued with arm problems in 1998 and 1999, and was subsequently traded to the Chicago Cubs for Eric Young. The big right-hander finished the 2002 season with the Seattle Mariners after starting the season with the Texas Rangers. He played another three seasons in the major leagues with fading skills, retiring after the 2005 season with 104 victories against 105 losses, pitching in 325 games with 288 starts.

FERNANDO VALENZUELA

The year was 1981, and a strange phenomenon was sweeping the country. Dodger fans, in passing, winked at each other and whispered the phrase that guaranteed another Dodger victory, "Fernando goes tonight." Fernandomania was sweeping the baseball community like a raging brushfire.

The object of all the furor was a chubby 20-year-old Mexican southpaw named Fernando Valenzuela. El Toro, as he was called, came up to the Dodgers late in 1980, and gave L.A. fans a preview of things to come when he went 2-0 down the stretch, pitching 18 shutout innings out of the bullpen.

Valenzuela was given the 1981 opening-day starting assignment when Jerry Reuss, the scheduled pitcher, suffered a pulled calf muscle. The young screwball pitcher responded brilliantly, blanking the Houston Astros 2-0, and a legend was in the making. On May 14, Fernando edged the Montreal Expos, 3-2, on a ninth-inning home run by Pedro Guerrero. That victory gave him a glittering 8-0 record, with seven complete games, five shutouts, and a 0.50 earned run average.

When the strike-shortened season ended, Valenzuela had posted a 13-7 record and a 2.48 ERA. He topped the league in innings pitched with 192, in strikeouts with 180, and in shutouts with eight. His dominance in the pennant race was rewarded when he won, not only the Rookie of the Year award, but the Cy Young trophy as well.

In postseason play, Fernando continued his exciting pitching. In the western division playoff against Houston, he was 1-0 with a 1.06 ERA in 17 innings. Against the Montreal Expos in the National League Championship Series, the kid from Sonora compiled a 1-1 record with a 2.40 earned run average, winning the fifth and deciding game, 2-1, on a dramatic ninth-inning home run by Rick Monday.

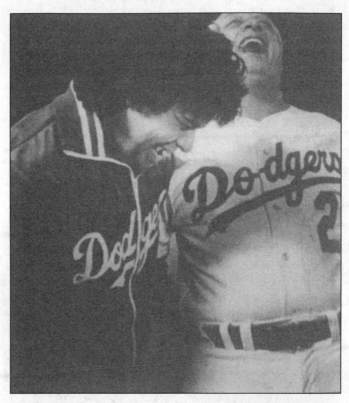

Fernando and Tommy Lasorda share a joke after the 1981 World Series.

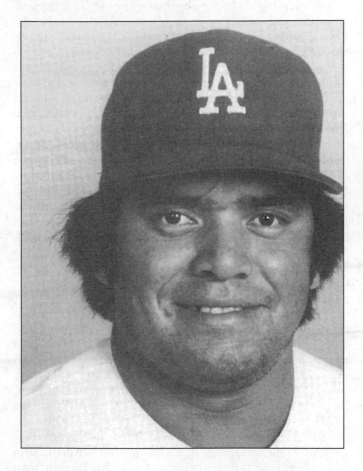

Fernando Valenzuela

In the World Series against the New York Yankees, the Dodger southpaw bested another rookie, Dave Righetti, 5-4 in Game Three. Fernando was touched up for nine hits and seven bases on balls, but he was tough in the clutch, posting a gutty, route going performance.

Nineteen eighty one was a once-in-a-lifetime season for Fernando Valenzuela, but there were still many glory days ahead. Over the next 17 years, the chubby southpaw won 173 games against 153 losses, including a league-leading 21 wins in 1986. tie was still active in 1997, pitching for The San Diego Padres and St. Louis Cardinals

The Dodgers won the National League Western Division title four times in Fernando's tenure; 1981, 1983, 1985, and 1988. The screwball artist always pitched brilliantly when the chips were down. In four Championship Series, Fernando posted a 3-1 record, with an excellent 1.95 earned run average for 37 innings.

In 1985, the 24-year-old southpaw set a major league record by not allowing an earned run for 41 innings at the start of the season. Ironically, his won-loss record was a mediocre 2-3 thanks to Dodger defensive lapses.

Valenzuela topped off his memorable career with a no-hitter against the St. Louis Cardinals on June 29,1990. With Hubie Brooks and Juan Samuel supplying roundtrip power, the Dodger lefty waltzed home an easy 6-0 victor.

Fernando was also outstanding in All-Star competition. He appeared in five All-Star games, pitching seven innings without allowing a run. In the 1985 classic, he struck out the side in the fourth inning, fanning Dave Winfield, Reggie Jackson, and George Brett in order. In 1986, he tied the 52-year-old record of Carl Hubbell by fanning five consecutive batters.

Although Fernando was no longer a Dodger when he retired in 1997, he left his mark on the Dodger record books. He is number eight on the all-time Dodger win list with 141, number six in starts with 320, number six in strikeouts with 1,759, number eight in innings pitched with 2,348, and number seven in shutouts with 29.

His overall major league record was 173-153.

More important than years pitched or records set is the impact the young screwball pitcher had on those around him. The smiling Mexico native was a genuine hero to millions of Hispanics in Southern California. He filled them with pride, and gave them hope for their own futures. He was a good husband, a doting father, and an exemplary role model to youngsters of every nationality.

Fernandomania was a phenomenon that will always be part of Dodger lore.

He was a legend in his own time.

DAZZY VANCE

Tall, freckle-faced, Dazzy Vance was an intimidating figure on the mound, standing 6'2" tall, with an 83" reach and a high-kicking motion, the Iowan farm boy with the blinding speed was, at times, almost impossible to hit. He was conveniently wild and just a tad mean, which made the batter's job even more difficult. The most frightening thing for a National League batter was facing a Dazzy Vance

Dazzy Vance

fastball in the late afternoon shadows, before the advent of artificial lighting. Baseball people referred to the pitch as his "ghost ball," because "very few batters saw it." He was frequently compared to the "Big Train," Walter Johnson, for sheer velocity. But,

where Johnson would never pitch inside for fear of hitting a batter, Vance used the brushback pitch to great advantage.

But the big redhead had more than just an overpowering fastball; he also possessed a crackling, sharp breaking curve ball, that supplemented his "ghost ball". And, if that wasn't enough, the big right-hander sat by his locker before every start and carefully cut the right sleeve of his sweatshirt to shreds. Every time he threw a pitch, his tattered sleeve fluttered in the breeze. Trying to hit a Vance fastball was difficult enough, but trying to focus on it as it came out of the flapping strands of a tattered sweatshirt was nigh on to impossible. Today, such a tactic would be illegal, but in Dazzy's day, all was fair in love, war, and baseball.

Dazzy Vance began his storied major league career with the Pittsburgh Pirates in 1915 at the age of 24. Two short stints with the New York Yankees followed, but wildness and arm miseries hampered his progress, and he bounced around the minor leagues for the next seven years. Dame Fortune finally smiled on the cherubic pitcher in 1922. Brooklyn was in need of a catcher, so they went out and purchased Hank DeBerry from Mobile. Thirty-one-year old Dazzy Vance went along as a throw-in, in the deal. The rest, as they say, is history.

Given a new lease on life, Vance would not be denied again. He immediately set the National League on its ear, winning 18 games for the sixth place Brooklyn entry, and leading the league in strikeouts. The next year, he won 18 again. He followed that up with 28 and 22 victories. In addition, he won the strikeout title each of his first seven years in the Bigs.

Nineteen twenty four was perhaps his greatest season. That year he won 28 games while losing only 6. At one point in the season, the Dazzler ran off 15 consecutive victories, still a Dodger record. On August 1, he tied a major league record by fanning seven Chicago batters in a row, en route to a 4-0 whitewashing of the second place Cubs. Three weeks later, against this same Chicago team, Vance set a new National League record by striking out 15 batters, including six in a row. The Cubs wouldn't have cared if they never laid eyes on Vance again.

The Robins, as they were called in those days, missed winning the pennant by the slimmest of margins, losing to the New York Giants by only 1 1/2 games. Still, Dazzy Vance had a season to remember. He led the league in victories (28), complete games (30), strikeouts (262), and earned run average (2.16). He also set two National League strikeout records, and walked away with the league's Most Valuable Player trophy.

The next year, the 34-year-old fireballer achieved baseball immortality, by pitching a no-hit game against the Philadelphia Phillies. The date was September 13, an unusually hot, late summer day, and old Dazzy was overpowering. Only two Philly

Dixie Walker

batters reached base, one on a leadoff walk in the first inning, the other on a two-base error in the second. The second runner eventually came around to score on a sacrifice fly. The game itself was never in doubt, as the Robins scored four runs in the first inning, then came back with four more in the third en route to a 10-1 shellacking of the seventh-place Phils. Vance set nine Philadelphia batters down on strikes, and retired the last 24 men in a row after the second-inning error.

Vance had another 20-game season in 1928, finally retiring from the game in 1935, at the age of 44. Clarence Arthur (Dazzy) Vance was elected to the Hall of Fame in 1955, as Brooklyn's greatest right-handed pitcher.

DIXIE WALKER

Fred "Dixie" Walker, also known as "The People's Choice," or "Da Peeple's Cheerce" in Brooklynese, was one of the most popular players ever to don a Brooklyn uniform. A journeyman player in the American League for nine years, the hard-hitting outfielder was picked up on waivers by Larry MacPhail in 1939. He was batting .305 for Detroit at the time, after having hit .308 the previous year. In 1936, with the White Sox, Walker had batted .302 and led the American League in triples with 16.

The cagy MacPhail, ignoring Walker's shoulder and knee problems, was in the process of turning the perennial sixth-place Dodgers into a bonafide pennant contender, and Walker's big bat was a key ingredient in the plan.

With a revamped lineup of aging veterans, fuzzy-cheeked rookies, and journeymen ballplayers, the Brooklyn Dodgers jumped from seventh-place in 1938 to third place in 1939. With Walker, Camilli, Reese, Wyatt, and Casey on board, Leo Durocher's crew moved into second place in 1940. After several new additions in 1941, including pitcher Kirby Higbe and a 22-year-old hitting sensation named "Pistol Pete" Reiser, the Dodgers had the talent they needed to capture their first National League crown in 21 years.

Dixie Walker was a major contributor to the pennant drive. Down the stretch, the good-natured blonde came through again and again in game situations, endearing himself to the Flatbush fans. It was during this period that Walker earned the sobriquet, "Da Peeple's Cheerce."

With six games to go in the season, and the Dodgers caught up in a first-place tie with the St. Louis Cardinals, Walker struck an 11th-inning single to defeat the Cardinals, 5-4, and break the tie. Two days later, he doubled in the eighth inning of a scoreless tie and carried home the winning run on a hit by Billy Herman. In Boston for the final series of the season, "The Peeple's Cheerce" won the opener with a bases-loaded triple in the eighth inning, pulling the Dodgers from a 4-2 deficit to a 5-4 victory over the Bees. In the finale, Walker singled and scored in the first inning. He singled again in the second, leading to another Dodger run. In the eighth, the 6'1" slugger's third hit preceded a Reiser home run, as Brooklyn cruised 6-0, winning the pennant by 2 1/2 games over St. Louis.

Dixie Walker had hit .308 for the 1940 Dodgers, and .311 for the 1941 National League Champions. He then hit, in succession, .290, .302, .357, .300, .319, and .306. His .357 average in 1944 won him the batting title. The following year he led the league in RBIs with 124.

Traded to Pittsburgh after the 1947 season, Dixie Walker hit .316 and .282 for the Bucs before retiring at the age of 38. His major league career spanned 18 years, from his first at bat in a New York Yankee uniform in 1931, until his last at bat in the Steel City Walker played in 1,905 games in the majors, stroked 2,064 hits, including 577 for extra bases, scored 1,037 runs, batted in 1,023, and left behind a career batting average of .306.

He is on many of the Dodger all-time hitting lists. His lifetime Dodger batting average of .311 places him in an eighth-place tie with Jackie Robinson. He is 13th in hits (1,395), 11th in runs batted in (725), and 10th in doubles (274).

BOB WELCH

Bob Welch was a big, hard-throwing right-handed pitcher who toiled in a Los Angeles uniform for ten years, during which time the Dodgers won four division titles, two National League Championships, and one World Championship. The 6'3" 190-pound fireballer was a major contributor to those titles.

Robert Lynn Welch was born in Detroit, Michigan on November 3, 1956. He signed a professional baseball contract with the Los Angeles Dodgers out of Eastern Michigan University in 1977. His outstanding talent and poise on the mound earned him a Los Angeles uniform after less than one year in the minors. On June 19, 1978, the 21-year-old hurler struck out Mike Fischlin of the Houston Astros in his major league debut.

Bob Welch went on to compile a 7-4 record in his rookie season, pitching in 23 games with a stingy 2.03 earned run average. His most memorable day in baseball occurred shortly thereafter when he faced Reggie Jackson in the World Series. Welch relieved Terry Forster in the bottom of the ninth inning of Game Two, with the Dodgers ahead, 4-3, two Yankees on base and only one out. Welch retired the first bat-

Bob Welch (Los Angeles Dodger Photo)

ZACK WHEAT

Zack Wheat, part Cherokee Indian, was on the warpath for 18 years in the city of Brooklyn, New York. When he finally put his favorite bat, "Black Lightning" away in 1926, the handsome 5'10" slugger owned essentially every Dodger (or Robin) batting record. He is still #1 in games played with 2,318, at bats with 8,859, hits with 2,804, doubles with 464, triples with 171, and total bases with 4,003. He is second in runs scored with 1,255, third in RBIs with 1,227, second in extra base hits with 766, and fourth in batting average with .317.

Zack Wheat raised havoc around the National League. Purchased by Charlie Ebbets from Mobile in the Southern League for $1,200 in 1909, the 21-year-old, smooth-swinging lefty, was soon stinging line drives to all corners of Washington Park. He batted

ter, Thurman Munson, on a fly to right. Then the dangerous Reggie Jackson, "Mr. October," stepped to the plate, determined to put a serious hurt on the rookie pitcher. It was a mammoth battle between two giants. Jackson already had four hits in seven at bats in the two games, with four RBIs. Now it was heat against heat, fast ball pitcher against fast ball hitter. The count went to 3-2, with Jackson fouling off four balls. Pitch number nine was another fast ball, high and inside. Reggie took a mighty swing-and missed, to end the game.

Overall, Welch was hit hard in postseason play in Los Angeles, going 1-2 with a 5.40 ERA in the NLCS, and 0-1 with a 10.47 ERA in the World Series. He was more successful after he moved to Oakland.

Bob Welch struggled through a miserable 5-6 season in 1979, as he battled a growing alcohol problem. Following rehabilitation at The Meadows in Arizona early in 1980, the 23-year-old righty bounced back with a 14-9 record and a 3.28 ERA. He then put together seasons of 9-5, 16-11, 15-12, 13-13, 14-4, 7-13, and 15-9. Welch did not always get the support he should have at the plate, frequently losing low-scoring games.

In 1988 the fastball pitcher was traded to the Oakland Athletics, where he achieved stardom. Following 17-9 and 17-8 seasons, Bob Welch put it all together in 1990, winning the Cy Young award on the strength of a fabulous 27-6 record with a 2.95 earned run average. When he retired after the 1994 season, Welch had pitched in 506 games, winning 211 of them, and losing only 146.

Zack Wheat

.304 in 23 games in his debut season, then went on to record 13 .300 + seasons, including a league-leading .335 in 1918.

In 1916, he established a Brooklyn record by hitting in 29 straight games. He was finally stopped by Fred Toney of Cincinnati.

His batting eye seemed to improve with age and with the advent of the lively ball. The owner of a .301 batting average after ten years in the National League, Zack Wheat went on a rampage from 1920 through 1926. He stung the new, livelier ball at a .349 clip during those six campaigns. In 1923, the 35-year-old veteran hit his high-water mark at the plate with a sizzling .375 batting average. He duplicated that feat the following year, with 41 doubles, 14 home runs, and 97 runs batted in. Wheat had a career season in 1925 at the age of 37, hitting .359, with 121 runs scored, 221 hits, 42 doubles, 14 triples, 14 home runs, and 103 RBIs.

Buck Wheat, as he was called, not only performed admirably at the plate, he was an outstanding outfielder as well. A fleet ball hawk with great hands, the 170 pound speedster led the league in fielding average in 1912 and 1922, and in putouts in 1914.

The easygoing outfielder played in two World Series with the Brooklyn Robins. Overall he batted .281 in 12 Series games, losing efforts to the Boston Red Sox in 1916 and the Cleveland Indians in 1920. Wheat batted .333 against Tris Speaker's Indians, with two doubles.

Zachariah Davis Wheat was born on a Missouri farm, in Hamilton, on May 23, 1888. He remained a farm boy his entire life. Quiet but intense, Wheat was never thrown out of a major league game in 19 years. A crowd favorite, the mild-mannered outfielder was voted New York's most popular player, in spite of the fact that Babe Ruth was playing with the Yankees.

When his Brooklyn career ended in 1926, he played one year with the Philadelphia Athletics, then played out the string with Minneapolis in the American Association.

Following his playing days, Wheat returned to his roots in Missouri, where he held numerous jobs, including bowling alley proprietor and policeman.

The Dodgers' number-one player was elected to baseball's Hall of Fame in 1959.

He died in Sedalia, Missouri, on March 11, 1972.

STAN WILLIAMS

Stan Williams was a big, strong, hard-throwing right-hander whose wildness kept him from becoming an outstanding pitcher. During his 14-year major league career, the 6'4", 230-pounder won 109 games against 94 losses, averaging 7 strikeouts and 4 walks a game.

Williams was a Los Angeles product, who burned up the Dodgers' minor league system, leading the Class B Piedmont League in six pitching categories in 1955, including complete games (18), strikeouts (301), and earned run average (2.42), to go along with 18 victories. He won 19 games for the Dodgers AAA affiliate in St. Paul in 1957, winning a promotion to the big club.

In the 1959 National League playoff against the Milwaukee Braves, Williams was the winning pitcher in the second and final game, pitching three scoreless innings in relief, as Los Angeles overcame a 5-2 ninth inning Braves lead, finally winning 6-5 in twelve. Williams also pitched two scoreless innings against the White Sox, in his only Dodger World Series appearance.

Stan Williams won 14 games for the Dodgers in 1960, 15 in '61, and 14 again in '62. In 1961 his 205 strikeouts were second in the league behind teammate Sandy Koufax. In '62 the Dodgers once again finished in a dead heat with their upstate rivals, the San Francisco Giants, forcing a three game playoff. It was 1951 all over again. The Giants pummeled Walter Alston's boys 8-0 in the opener, behind southpaw Billy Pierce. In game 2, down 5-0 in the bottom of the sixth the Dodger" finally exploded, scoring seven runs, enough for an 8-7 victory. When game three reached the ninth inning with L.A. on top 4-2, the corks began to come out of the champaign bottles all over Los Angeles. Then the axe fell. Dodger reliever Ed Roebuck was touched for two hits and two

Stan Williams (Los Angeles Dodgers)

walks in 1/3 inning, bringing Stan Williams onto the scene. The L.A. flamethrower gave up a game tying sacrifice fly to Orlando Cepeda, then proceeded to walk both Ed Bailey and Jim Davenport to force in the pennant winning run for Alvin Dark's Giants. It was one of the darkest moments in Dodger history.

Stan Williams was an important cog in the Los Angeles Dodger machine from 1958 through 1962. He was a hero of one pennant chase, a victim in another. Ironically, he pitched against the Dodgers in the 1963 World Series, as a member of the New York Yankees, hurling three shutout innings, with five strikeouts and no walks.

Stan Williams finished out his major league career as a reliever and, in 1970, he went 10-1 with 15 saves and a 1.99 ERA for the Minnesota Twins.

MAURY WILLS

Maurice Morning Wills, the Los Angeles Dodgers' dynamic shortstop for 12 years, single-handedly revolutionized the game of baseball. When Little

Maury Wills (Los Angeles Dodger Photo)

Maury arrived in Los Angeles in 1959, baseball was a cautious, close-to-the-vest, one-base-at-a-time game, with little attention paid to the running game, particularly the stolen base.

The year Wills broke in with the Dodgers, Willie Mays led the National League in stolen bases with 27. Wills stole 50 his first year as a regular, to lead the league. The next year he swiped 35. Then, in 1962, he set the baseball world on its ear as he broke Ty Cobb's "unbreakable" major league stolen base record of 96. Wills had set himself a goal of 50 stolen bases for the year. He captured his 50th base on July 27.

As the pennant race heated up, Wills began to steal at every opportunity. He broke Bob Bescher's 51-year-old National League record of 81 stolen bases on September 7th, swiping four bases in a winning effort against the Pittsburgh Pirates. He stole his 97th base, passing the great Ty Cobb, in game #156, the same number of games that Cobb played. The game was stopped temporarily while the 29-year-old record breaker was presented with second base. During his historic chase, Wills was caught stealing only 13 times. Cobb had been gunned down a total of 38 times.

Wills went on to steal his 100th base in game #159, then pilfered four more in the playoffs against the San Francisco Giants, giving him the incredible total of 104 stolen bases, the first man to break the 100 mark in this century. His fantastic adventure earned him the National League's Most Valuable Player award for 1962.

Maury Wills was an unlikely record breaker. Entering the Dodger farm system with Hornell in 1951, the Washington, D.C. native bounced around in the minors for almost nine years. A consistent .280-.300 hitter, the young infielder had a reputation as a mediocre fielder. Finally moving up in class in 1957, first at Seattle, then at Spokane, Wills batting average dropped to .260, but his fielding improved, and his speed on the bases continued to intimidate opposing pitchers.

As the Dodgers battled the Braves and Giants for the 1959 pennant, Wills was rushed into the chase to replace the slumping Don Zimmer. He earned his keep with his fielding for several weeks, until his bat got hot. Then he blazed his way down the stretch with a .389 batting average in September.

Mousey, as he was called by his teammates, didn't play in his first major league game until he was 26 years old, but he still managed to stay around to see his 40th birthday approach, 14 years later. During his first six full years in a Dodger uniform, the nimble-footed shortstop gave opposing pitchers fits, leading the league in stolen bases every year. His winning totals were 50, 35, 104, 40, 53, and 94.

Finally, at the age of 33, the legs began to fail the little thief, and his stolen base count dropped off to 38, 25, and 28. Wills spent two years with Pittsburgh and part of a year with Montreal in the late '60s, but he returned to Dodger Land to run out his career in 1969.

He played in four World Series with the Los Angeles Dodgers, helping them capture three World Championships. Only Junior Gilliam with four, played on more championship Dodger teams. In the 1965 World Series against the Minnesota Twins, Wills tied two Series records; most hits in a game (four in Game Five-two singles and two doubles), and most double plays by a shortstop (three in Game Five).

Wills' major league totals include 2,134 hits, 1,067 runs scored, 586 stolen bases, and a .281 batting average. He stands #10 on the all-time Dodger list for games played, #10 in at bats, #10 in runs scored, #10 in hits, and #1 in stolen bases.

TODD WORRELL

Todd Worrell was a premier major league closer for 11 years. If he had not been hampered by arm miseries for the better part of five years, he would be sharing the podium with Lee Smith and Dennis Eckersley. As it is, the big Californian still has more than 250 saves, placing him in a category with only a select few.

Worrell, a huge 6'5", 222-pound power pitcher, whose sinkerball exploded at the feet of unsuspecting batters, broke into organized ball with Erie, Pennsylvania, in the N.Y.-PA. League in 1982. After spending three years as a starting pitcher, Worrell moved to the bullpen, and almost immediately made the jump up to the big club, the St. Louis Cardinals.

The right-handed pitcher dominated the Se-

nior Circuit in his rookie year, leading the league in saves with 36 while appearing in 74 games, with a 2.08 earned run average. He was voted the National League's Rookie of the Year for 1986.

After two more overpowering seasons, with 33 and 32 saves, and 75 and 68 game appearances, overwork apparently caught up with the rugged reliever. On September 4, 1989, he injured his elbow in a game against Montreal. Shoulder miseries followed. Over the next two years, he had surgery on both his elbow and his shoulder, pitching in a total of only three games during that time. In 1992, he made a remarkable comeback, pitching in 67 games for the Cardinals, with a 2.11 ERA but by that time Lee Smith was the St. Louis closer, and Todd Worrell was relegated to setup man.

After joining the Los Angeles Dodgers as a free agent in 1993, Worrell was again sidelined with arm problems. Once again he struggled, with just 16 saves over a two-year period, and an earned run average around 5.00.

By 1995, the old Worrell was back. As the Dodgers' closer, the big right hander piled up 32 saves, with a 2.02 ERA. He followed that up with a Dodger-record 44 saves, and a 3.03 ERA, in 1996, and 35 saves in 1997.

Todd Worrell retired after the '97 season, finishing with a career record of 50 wins against 52 losses, with 256 saves. He was the all-time Dodger saves leader until Jeff Shaw passed him in 2001.

WHIT WYATT

Whit Wyatt was a washed-up former major leaguer toiling in the minors when the Brooklyn Dodgers rescued him in 1939. Wyatt had spent parts of nine seasons in the majors, with Detroit, Chicago, and Cleveland, between 1929 and 1937, compiling an ignominious 26-43 record. Following his return to the minors, the tall, slender pitcher learned to throw the slider, and the devastating pitch made him a big winner overnight.

Wyatt used the new pitch to great advantage with Milwaukee in the American Association, winning the league's Most Valuable Player award on the strength on a 23-7 record and a 2.37 earned run average.

Brooklyn president Larry MacPhail drafted the 32-year-old hurler in 1939, and the move paid immediate dividends. Wyatt helped the Dodgers to a third-place finish that year, going 8-3 with a 2.31 ERA. After a 15-14 performance with a league-leading five shutouts the following year, the stylish right-hander helped pitch the Dodgers to their first National League pennant in 21 years, leading the league in victories with 22, against only 10 losses, while posting an excellent 2.31 earned run average

Todd Worrell (W. McNeil)

over 288 innings. He led the league in shutouts again, this time with seven.

Wyatt and the Dodgers almost repeated in 1942 but, in spite of the fact that Wyatt ran up a 19-7 record and the Brooklyn team won a total of 104 games, they still lost the pennant to the St. Louis Cardinals by two games.

The 36-year-old veteran managed one more outstanding season in 1943, with a 14-5 won-loss mark. Then, after suffering an arm injury, his career went downhill quickly. He was 2-6 with the Dodgers in '44, and ended his major league career with a 0-7 season with the last-place Phillies.

Whitlow Wyatt's resurrection in Brooklyn was sensational. His 80-45 record over a six-year period earned him four all-star assignments. In the World Series against the New York Yankees in 1941, the soft-spoken Georgian defeated DiMaggio and Company, 3-2, in Game Two, in a complete-game effort. Coming back in Game Five, the finale of the Series, the Dodger ace pitched another complete-game gem, only to lose, 3-1, to right-hander "Tiny" Bonham.

The tall, slender Wyatt was a quiet, gentle man off the field, but a fierce competitor on it. His high, inside fastball sent numerous batters sprawling in the dirt, earning him a reputation as a headhunter. After his retirement from baseball, he served as pitching coach in Philadelphia and Boston and, according to *The Ballplayers,* he encouraged his pitchers to throw at hitters. Joe DiMaggio called him, "the meanest man I ever saw."

When Whitlow Wyatt pitched in the major leagues for 16 years, winning 106 games against 95 losses. He posted 17 shutouts and an earned run average of 3.78 over 1,762 innings pitched.

When Whitlow Wyatt is remembered by Dodger fans it will bring back memories of the great '41-'42 clubs of Reese, Reiser, Higbe, Camilli, Casey, and Dixie Walker. But none of them will shine any brighter than the man from Kensington, Georgia, John Whitlow Wyatt.

STEVE YEAGER

Steve Yeager was a hard-nosed defensive catcher for the Los Angeles Dodgers between the years of 1972 and 1985. He played the last year of his 15-year major league career, 1986, in Seattle.

The 6', 190-pound Yeager entered professional baseball with the Dodgers' Ogden affiliate in 1967. Six years later, he worked his way into the Los Angeles lineup. He batted .274 in 35 games, an average he never reached again as a major leaguer.

Although not much of an offensive threat, the man from Huntington, West Virginia, had better than

Whit Wyatt

Steve Yeager

average power, as demonstrated by his 102 home runs in. 3,584 career at bats. Six times in his long career he hit over ten home runs.

But it was behind the plate that Steve Yeager excelled. He was known as an intelligent catcher, and an outstanding game caller. During his playing days, he had the most accurate throwing arm in the National League.

The nephew of test pilot Chuck Yeager, he was a team leader for 14 years, helping the Dodgers win six divisional titles, four National League pennants, and one World Championship. He was named a tri-MVP on the 1981 World Championship team, thanks to his game-winning home run off Ron Guidry of the New York Yankees in the seventh inning of Game Five. His long drive into the left center field bleachers gave Tommy Lasorda's team a vital 3-2 lead in games. They wrapped up the Series the following day, with a convincing 9-2 rout.

Steve Yeager performed at his best in the World Series. Catching in four fall classics, Yeager batted a healthy .298 in 57 at bats, with four doubles, four home runs, and 10 runs batted in.

His career stats were less impressive. He played in 1,269 games, with 816 hits, good for a .228 batting average. He stands fourth on the all-time Dodger list for games played by a catcher, his 1,181 games trailing Mike Scioscia (1395), John Roseboro (1218), and Roy Campanella (1183).

Yeager suffered a freak accident in 1976, when several jagged pieces of wood from a broken bat opened a nasty wound in his neck while he knelt in the on-deck circle, waiting for his turn to bat. Shortly thereafter, he introduced a new safety device for catchers, the neck protector, which is attached to the bottom of the catcher's mask.

Steve Yeager was more than a pile of statistics. He was an outstanding defensive catcher, intelligent and sturdy. He was also a team leader, and another in the long line of great Dodger defensive catchers, from Campy to Scioscia.

Steve Yeager was a winner.

GEORGE "THE CHARMER" ZETTLEIN

George "The Charmer" Zettlein was one of the early heroes of Brooklyn baseball. Born in Brooklyn on July 18, 1844, Zettlein served in the U.S. Navy during the Civil War, then returned home to begin a career in baseball.

Zettlein was small by today's standards, standing 5'9" tall and weighing 162 pounds, but he was one of the best pitchers of his day. He was reputed to have the best fast ball in organized baseball. "The Charmer" starred for the mighty Brooklyn Atlantics from 1864 through 1870. He was the winning pitcher in the historic 11-inning duel that ended the Cincinnati Red Stockings' 80-game undefeated streak.

In the bottom of the eleventh, with the score tied at 7-7, and the winning run on first, Zettlein hit a hard smash in the hole between first and second. First baseman Charley Gould bobbled it momentarily, then recovered and threw to second in an attempt to force the baserunner, Bob Ferguson. The throw was wild, rolling into left center field, and Ferguson raced all the way home with the winning run.

When professional baseball finally evolved, with the formation of the National Association in 1871, the 27-year-old star pitcher quickly signed up. He played with the Chicago White Stockings the first year, going 18-9 for a club that finished in second place, two games behind the pennant-winning Philadelphia Athletics. In addition to losing the pennant, the White Stockings also lost their ball park, which burned down in the great Chicago fire. Over the next four years, Zettlein starred in the National Association, putting together records of 15-15, 36-14, 2730, and 12-8.

When the National League came into existence in 1876, the 32-year-old hurler joined the Philadelphia Athletics. The team finished seventh in the eight-team league, with a record of 14-45. The best Zettlein could do was 4-20. He retired shortly thereafter.

"The Charmer" passed away in Patchogue, New York, on May 23, 1905 at the age of 60.

George "The Charmer" Zettlein (Transcendental Graphics)

CHAPTER 3
FAMOUS DODGER MANAGERS

WILBERT ROBINSON

When Brooklyn fielded its first professional base-ball team in the American Association in 1884, the manager was George Taylor, a 29-year-old former outfielder. It was Taylor's only managerial experience, as his team limped home ninth in a 12-team league, with a record of 40-64.

Over the next 30 years, The Brooklyn Club employed 15 different managers as they struggled to build a successful franchise. Finally, in 1914, owner Charlie Ebbets hired New York Giant coach Wilbert Robinson. Uncle Robby, as he was fondly called, stayed around for 19 years, through two National League Championships, 12 second-division finishes, and the hilarious misadventures of the "Daffyness Boys."

Wilbert Robinson was born in Bolton, Massachusetts, on June 29, 1863. He played major league baseball for 17 years, starring for the famed Baltimore Orioles of the 1890s. On the field, catcher Wilbert Robinson was the team leader, calling the game and directing other players positions. In addition to being an outstanding defensive catcher, Robinson also became a solid hitter. After compiling a batting average of only .228 during his first seven years in the majors, the 5'8", 215-pound right-handed hitter improved to .267 in 1892. He soared to .334 the next year, and followed that with a sizzling .353 mark. After an off-year in 1895, Robby hit .347 in another Oriole pennant drive.

Robinson's most memorable day at the plate came on June 10, 1892, when he established a major league record by stroking seven hits in seven at bats, in a single game. His six singles and a double drove in 11 runs as the Orioles destroyed the St. Louis Browns, 25-4.

Wilbert Robinson

When Robby retired from active play, he had accumulated 1,388 hits along with a respectable lifetime batting average of .273. He left with the reputation of being an astute baseball man, an outstanding trainer of young men, and a calming influence on a team.

The old Oriole catcher spent seven years in Massachusetts, running a butcher shop, until his old friend, John McGraw, enticed him back into baseball as the pitching coach of the New York Giants. Robby helped the Giants to three successive National League Championships by developing several of their pitchers into big winners. In 1913, the two old friends had a bitter falling out, and Robinson moved on to Brooklyn, as the new manager of the Superbas.

The large, good-natured manager, now tipping the scales at a hefty 250 pounds, inherited a team that had finished sixth in the National League in 1913, and had 11 straight second-division finishes behind it. In just three years, the cagy Robinson gave the Brooklyn fans a pennant winner. He did it primarily by rebuilding the pitching staff. The old catcher developed young pitchers Jeff Pfeffer and Sherry Smith, and acquired three supposedly over-the-hill veterans, Larry Cheney, Jack Coombs, and Rube Marquard. Together, the five of them won a total of 82 games, led by Pfeffer's 25 and Cheney's 18. He repeated his magic four years later, capturing the National League pennant with a staff consisting of veteran Al Mamaux, youngster Burleigh Grimes, journeyman Leon Cadore, and mainstays Pfeffer, Smith, and Marquard.

In 1921, with his pitching staff nearly decimated, Robby's "Robins," as they were now called, plummeted to fifth place. Except for 1924, when the Robins treated their fans to an exciting pennant race before finishing a close second to John McGraw's Giants, they never saw the light of the first division from 1921 through 1929.

It was the era of the "Daffyness Boys." Led by the inimitable Babe Herman, Uncle Robby's misfits made humorous news copy all over the country. Herman's famous "three men on third" episode was typical Robin fare. Players read the newspaper in the dugout. Some took naps during the game. A few even carried guns. Sportswriters made out the lineup card. Waiters selected starting pitchers. One player was scratched from the starting lineup because Robinson couldn't spell his name when making out the lineup card.

The roly-poly Robinson made the best of a bad situation, managing one group of misfits after another to second-division finishes, yet constantly teaching the youngsters the fundamentals of the game, and striving to maintain morale in the face of impending disaster.

Wilbert Robinson managed Brooklyn for 18 years, and Baltimore for another year, compiling a record of 1399-1398. His Brooklyn record of 1,375-1,341 places him third on the all-time list for most victories. Uncle Robby is also third to Alston and Lasorda in years managed (18) and games managed (2,716).

In addition to his managerial responsibilities, Uncle Robby also held down the presidency of the Brooklyn club from 1926 through 1929. Following his retirement from major league baseball, Robby returned to his favorite home, his hunting lodge in Dover Hall, Georgia, where he fished and hunted to his hearts content, playing cards and swapping tall tales with his old drinking buddies during the winter. He managed the Atlanta Crackers briefly in 1933, and served as the president of the club in 1934. Then it was back to the lodge.

Uncle Robby died in Atlanta on August 8, 1934, he was 71 years old. He is buried at Sea Island near all his buddies.

LEO DUROCHER

Leo "The Lip" Durocher grew up a juvenile delinquent on the streets of Springfield, Massachusetts. He hung around the pool hall hustling marks wherever he found them. He was a brawler and a gambler, and was headed for a life of crime before fate stepped in and saved him.

Durocher loved baseball. Kicked out of high school in the ninth grade for unruly conduct, the young hoodlum went to work for the electric company, playing baseball on the company team. His outstanding talent on the diamond brought him a professional contract, and before long he was discovered by a scout for the New York Yankees.

The 22-year-old shortstop reached the major leagues in 1925, a swaggering and arrogant tough guy. He ridiculed teammate Babe Ruth in the clubhouse, and constantly fought with the other players. On the field, he belittled and berated opposing players, once telling 41-year-old Ty Cobb to "get out of the game old man. You're all washed up."

The flashy dresser spent over two years in the big city, and enjoyed every minute of it. He did not impress the Yankee management with his dedication to the game, however, seeming to prefer Manhattan night life to the American League pennant race. Leo loved women. He loved gambling. He loved the nightclub scene, baseball came second. Three years with Durocher was all that General Manager Ed Barrow could take, and the youngster was finally shipped off to Cincinnati in the National League.

Over the next decade, Leo Durocher settled down to become the best defensive shortstop in the league. He excelled as a member of the St. Louis Cardinals' "Gas House Gang" helping them to a thrilling seven-game victory over the Detroit Tigers in the 1934 World Series. The

"Gas Housers" played to win at all costs. They hit the ball hard, fielded hard, and ran the bases with abandon. Their pitchers sent batters sprawling in the dirt with boring regularity. Durocher fit right in. He loved a fight, and a baseball pennant race was a fight. As he would say later, "Nice guys finish last." Leo Durocher was not a nice guy.

Durocher's managerial talents were developed on the sun-baked fields of St. Louis. They blossomed in the concrete jungle called Brooklyn. Dodger General Manager Larry MacPhail promoted the pugnacious infielder

Leo Durocher

to playing manager of his new Dodgers in 1938. It was a perfect choice. The 33-year-old skipper, a fiery competitor and a skillful motivator, molded the Dodger team, a mixture of fuzzy-cheeked kids, over-the-hill veterans, and minor league journeymen, into a pennant contender almost overnight. Taking over a seventh-place club, the rookie manager swept into third place in '39. The next year, he moved up to second. Then, in 1941, Leo Durocher took the Dodgers to their first National League pennant in 21 years.

The Dodgers under Durocher were a hard-drinking, hard-playing bunch. Kirby Higbe and Hugh Casey were just like their manager, mean as junkyard dogs on the field, and hard-drinking, carousing, women chasers at night. Freddy Fitzsimmons was another fast ball pitcher who would just as soon stick the ball in the batter's ear as throw a strike. The cast of characters even invaded the front office, in the person of General Manager Larry MacPhail. MacPhail, the hot-headed Scot and Durocher, the quick-tempered Frenchman, fought like cats and dogs. At one count, MacPhail fired Durocher a dozen times in less than two years. He always forgot about it the next day after he sobered up.

During the eight years that Durocher managed the Dodgers, there was never a dull moment in Flatbush. After beating the St. Louis Cardinals for the 1941 pennant, the Brooklyn contingent came back to win 104 games the following year, but still fell two games short of the high-flying Redbirds, who went 43-9 after August 6. Leo "The Lip" took another group of young upstarts to a National League playoff in 1946, missing the pennant by a single game. The following spring, as the newly emerging Boys of Summer were ready to spread their wings for the first time, their field leader was suspended from baseball, for the season, for consorting with gamblers.

General Manager Branch Rickey, a teetotaler, was disgusted with his manager's behavior, both on and off the field, and he fired the loquacious Durocher midway through the '48 season. The controversial field leader packed his gear, drove uptown to the Bronx, and assumed the managerial reins of the New York Giants, the Dodgers' hated cross-town rivals.

Success followed the dynamic Durocher to Coogan's Bluff. For the next seven years, The Lip battled the Dodgers toe to toe. Brooklyn won pennants in 1949, 1952, 1953, 1955, and 1956. Durocher scuttled the Dodger ship in 1951, winning the pennant with "The Shot Heard Round The World," then captured the World Championship in 1954 with a four-game sweep of the Cleveland Indians, a team that had won 111 games during the regular season.

Leo Durocher left some impressive statistics behind him when he finally retired to the rocking chair. As a player, he spent 17 years on the field, as one of the best defensive shortstops in the National League. Over the years, he accumulated 1,320 hits in 5,350 at bats, for a .247 batting average. He led the league in fielding average in 1933, 1936, and 1938.

As a field manager, The Lip won 2,008 games against 1,709 losses over a 24-year career, a .540 winning percentage. In the process, he captured three National League pennants and one World Championship.

Leo Durocher had a long and tempestuous career. Brash, argumentative, and cocky, the man from Massachusetts fought with everyone; his teammates, fans, opposing players, and umpires. Over the years, Durocher had numerous run-ins with National League umpires, and he lost them all. He was probably ejected from more games than anyone in the history of baseball.

Leo Durocher was a fiery and emotional individual. People either loved him or hated him. In Brooklyn and New York, he was adored. The Durocher days in Ebbets Field and the Polo Grounds were times of excitement, thrilling pennant races, and dazzling World Series extravaganzas.

Many things can be said about Durocher, some good and some bad. He might not always have been a nice man, but he had uncanny baseball instincts, and a tremendous will to win. In his 24 years as a baseball manager, Leo Durocher finished in the first division 20 times. His victory totals are exceeded only by five men: Connie Mack, John McGraw, Joe McCarthy, Bucky Harris, and Walter Alston.

Leo Durocher will be remembered in the history books as one of the greatest field managers in baseball history.

WALTER ALSTON

Walter "Smokey" Alston was one of the deans of American baseball managers, sharing the spotlight with the legendary Connie Mack, John McGraw, Bucky Harris, Casey Stengel, Leo Durocher, and Joe McCarthy. The man from Darrtown, Ohio, was a member of the elite.

Alston's career statistics are impressive. His 24 years of managerial service have been exceeded by only five men. He is #5 in total games managed (3,568), #4 in victories (2,040), #5 in pennants won (seven), and #4 in World Championships won (four). He stands alone in the National League with four World Titles. The great John McGraw, toiling for the New York Giants for most of his 33 years as manager, won a record ten National League pennants, but could capture just three World Championships.

Walter Emmons Alston was born in Venice, Ohio, on December 1, 1911. A product of the St. Louis Cardinals farm system, the 6'2" 210-pound left-handed swinger was a long-ball hitter in the lower minors, leading leagues in home runs four times. His exploits won him a trip to St. Louis for a look-see. He struck out in his only time at bat in the majors. Alston's batting skills were limited to the AA level. Triple A pitchers overpowered him. In 1946, the 35-year-old first baseman joined the Dodger organization, as player-manager with Nashua in the New England League. Shortly thereafter, he joined the managerial ranks permanently, moving on to St. Paul, then to Brooklyn's top minor league farm club in Montreal. Along the way, he developed such talents as Don Newcombe and Roy Campanella.

In 1954, Walter Alston received the call he had been working for, a promotion to the big club in Brooklyn. Manager Charlie Dressen, after leading the Dodgers to the '53 pennant, had been fired in a contract dispute with Brooklyn President Walter O'Malley, and the 42-year-old former school teacher was thrown into the cauldron. Alston was unknown to most people, including the inhabitants of New York, and the press gave him an early broadside, referring to him as "Walter Who?" Even the Dodger players took him to the wall. As the "Boys of Summer," many of them felt they were the class of the National League and didn't need a rookie manager telling them what to do. An early locker room confrontation with Jackie Robinson quickly established who was boss in the Dodger clubhouse. Walter Alston proved himself to be a

Walter Alston (Los Angeles Dodger Photo)

quiet, fair disciplinarian, and he soon gained the respect of the entire team.

His first year as Dodger manager was a disappointing one for Alston. His ball club, favored to repeat as National League champions by most experts went into a prolonged mid-season slump and finished second, five games behind the New York Giants. The following year, however, was one of the highlights of his illustrious career. His well-disciplined Dodgers broke from the gate with ten consecutive victories, went 22-2 over the first month of the season and, leading the league from wire to wire, clinched the pennant on September 13, the earliest clinching in National League history. The momentum carried over into the World Series, where Flatbush's beloved Bums captured their first and only World Championship, with a stirring come-from-behind victory over Casey Stengel's mighty Yankees.

After the Dodgers moved to the west coast in 1958, Alston's managerial success continued, with five more National League pennants and three more World Championships, although with a different type of ball club. Gone were the thunderous bats of the "Boys of Summer," the 200+ home runs per year sent into orbit by the Sniders, the Hodges, the Furillos, and the Campanellas. The big boom was gradually replaced by the pitching perfection of Don Drysdale, Sandy Koufax, and Ron Perranoski, and the blinding speed of Maury Wills and Willie Davis. Instead of a three-run homer, an L.A. Dodger rally was said to consist of a walk, a stolen base, a sacrifice, and a wild pitch.

Walter Alston proved his managerial skills by adapting to his new team structure, without missing a beat. In what he has called his proudest moment, the 1959 Los Angeles Dodgers, picked to finish in the second division, won the National League pennant in a stirring, season-long race with the San Francisco Giants and Milwaukee Braves. The underdog Dodgers defeated the Braves in a two-game playoff for the title, then went on to beat the Chicago White Sox in the Series behind relief ace Larry Sherry and a cast of 24.

"Smokey" Alston was a class act. Working on 23 consecutive one-year contracts, he won a total of 2,040 games against only 1,613 losses. In the process, he guided his teams to seven National League pennants and four World championships. He won the only World Championship in the 68-year history of the Brooklyn National League franchise.

During his career, he was named National League Manager of the Year three times; in 1955, 1959, and 1963. He is also the all-time All-Star game manager, winning seven games in eight tries.

Walter Alston was a quiet, scholarly baseball tactician, whose innate understanding of human behavior won the respect of his players. Former Dodger coach, Monty Basgall once said, "The first thing I noticed about Alston was how well he ran a ball game. He didn't miss anything. He was two innings ahead of everybody else with his strategy." Center fielder Willie Davis, who chose Walter Alston as his favorite manager, said it best. "Walter treated everyone equal. And he always treated you like a man." Walter Alston, called "The Quiet Man" for his low-key personality, was elected to baseball's Hall of Fame in 1983. He passed away in Oxford, Ohio, on October 1, 1984, just ten months after his induction into the Hall.

TOMMY LASORDA

Thomas Charles Lasorda was born on September 22, 1927, in Norristown, Pennsylvania. He broke into organized ball in 1945 at the age of 17, compiling a 3-12 record with Concord. The 5'9" southpaw had a blazing fastball, a nickle curve, and a problem with wildness. Over the next 15 years, Lasorda bounced around the minors, spending nine of those years with the Dodgers top minor league club in Montreal. He still holds the all-time International League record for wins with 125. Earlier in his career, he struck out 25 batters in a 15-inning game in the New York State League.

Lasorda pitched in the majors, with Brooklyn and Kansas City, parts of three seasons, going 0-4 with a 6.52 earned run average.

His wildness was his downfall, as he walked 56 batters in 58 innings.

The 37-year-old hurler turned to managing in 1965, taking the reins of the Dodgers' Pocatello farm club. He managed in the Los Angeles minor league system for eight years, winning five pennants along the way, then moved up to L.A. as a coach for Walter Alston. Carefully groomed as Alston's replacement, the gung-ho Lasorda stepped in smoothly when "The Quiet Man" stepped down after the 1976 season.

The noisy and theatrical Lasorda won National League pennants his first two years at the helm, losing to the New York Yankees in the World Series both times. Then, in 1981, he got redemption, as he brought the city of Los Angeles its first World Championship in 16 years, in an exciting drive down the stretch. First his Dodgers defeated the Houston Astros in a come-from-behind victory in a Western Division playoff. Next, they captured the National League flag by winning the final two games of the NLCS in Montreal. And, finally, they came from two games back to knock off the Yankees in six in the Series.

The decade of the eighties was an exciting period for Dodger fans everywhere. They won four Western Division titles, two National Leagues pennants, and two World Championships. In addition, they lost the 1980 Western Division title to the Houston Astros in a one-game playoff.

The 1988 World Championship was one of Lasorda's most cherished moments. Winning the Western Division title with a so-called mediocre ball club, his Dodgers were supposed to collapse before the onslaught of the New York Mets, a team that had beaten them 10 times in 11 meetings during the regular season. Surprisingly, the Los Angeles team, behind the outstanding pitching of Orel Hershiser, took the National League flag in seven games. Then, ignited by Kirk Gibson's heroic ninth-inning home run in the World Series opener, Lasorda's boys went on to upset the powerful Oakland Athletics, four games to one.

Tommy Lasorda went on to win two more Western Division titles, in 1994 and 1995. Then, in June of 1996, the 68-year-old skipper was struck down with a heart attack, in the midst of yet another exciting pennant race. Although he fully recovered from his attack, he decided to retire to the safety of a Vice President's desk, in the best interest of his family. He left behind an enviable record of 1,599 wins against 1,442 losses, over a period of 20 years. He stands 13th on the all-time victory list for major league managers. Lasorda teams won eight Western Divison titles, four National League pennants, and two World Championships.

The feisty Lasorda was always a garrulous baseball cheerleader, whose genuine love for the game, knowledge of inside baseball, and "win-one-for-the-Gipper" attitude helped him win titles, even when he had a questionable talent pool. He still talks about "The Big Dodger in the Sky" and swears that he bleeds Dodger Blue. He loves to eat, particularly pasta (although his diet has been severely curtailed since his attack), hobnob with Hollywood celebrities, and travel the country giving motivational speeches during the off-season.

Tommy Lasorda squeezed the maximum effort out of his teams year after year. His development of team spirit, dedication and never-say-die attitude was successful for more than 20 years.

You could never count a Lasorda team out.

In recognition of his achievements, Tommy Lasorda was enshrined in Cooperstown, alongside baseball's other immortals, on August 3, 1997.

Tommy Lasorda (Los Angeles Dodger Photo: Jon Soohoo)

JIM TRACY

When Tommy Lasorda retired in 1997, the Los Angeles Dodgers manager's position became a game of musical chairs. After a period of more than 43 years with just two managers, the Dodgers went through three managers in just over three years. Then, on November 1, 2000, Chairman Bob Daly and President Bob Graziano introduced Jim Tracy as L.A.'s new manager. Tracy, who had been the Dodgers bench coach the previous two years, succeeded Davey Johnson, who was fired on October 5.

The announcement of Tracy's promotion brought the expected "Jim who?" comments from Los Angeles Dodger fans across the country. The last time a similar question was asked, it referred to Walter Alston, a relatively unknown, who assumed the reigns of the Brooklyn Dodgers in 1954 after serving his apprenticeship as a minor league manager for 14 years. Alston went on to manage the Dodgers for 23 years. Dodger management was hoping that lightning strikes twice, and that Jim Tracy's tenure would be a long and successful one, but such is not the rule in the major leagues today

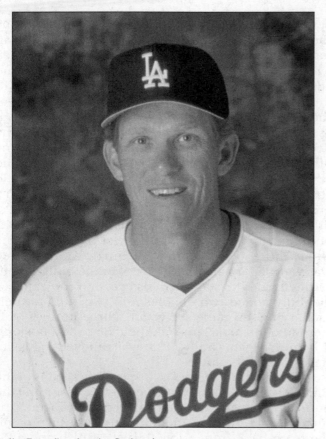

Jim Tracy (Los Angeles Dodgers)

Jim Tracy was born in Hamilton, OH. On December 31,1955. The slightly built athlete became a three-letter man at Badin High School, and gained NCAA Division III All-America honors at Marietta College. Drafted by the Chicago Cubs as a first baseman in 1977, Tracy began an eight-year career as a professional baseball player. It was less than memorable.

He began his managing career in 1987, guiding the Class-A Peoria Chiefs of the Midwest League to a second place finish. Six years later, he led the Harrisburg Senators to the Eastern League title, and in 1984, after bringing the Montreal Expos Triple-A affiliate in Ottawa, home in second place, he joined the major league coaching staff under manager Filipe Alou. He subsequently joined the Dodgers as bench coach in 1999 and actually managed the team for four games in 2000 while manager Davey Johnson was ill, taking home a 3-1 record.

During his time at the helm of the Dodgers, Jim Tracy exhibited superior managing skills, often keeping his team in contention in spite of crippling injuries to key players on the team. He was, in some ways, a mirror image of Walter Alston, who also hailed from the Buckeye state. He was low key, an excellent communicator, and a strong field leader. His game strategies were exceptional, and his motivational skills were well above average. In 2001, his top three pitchers—Brown, Ashby, and Dreifort—all went down with season ending arm injuries. Still, he had the Big Blue Machine in the lead in the wild card race as late as September 7. In 2002, he did even better.

With an almost completely revamped pitching staff, Tracy had the Dodgers in first place by 2½ games at the All-Star break. Although the realities of the game caught up with the team down the stretch, they never gave up. In fact, they made five stirring come-from-behind rallies to win games over the last week of the season, and weren't officially eliminated from the wild card race until game 161. Jeff Shaw may have put it best when he said, "The thing about Tracy is that he's put his heart and soul into everything he's done in this game. Not everyone does that, but that is definitely one thing that separates him."

The Dodgers suffered through a painful season in 2003 when they finished second to the San Francisco Giants, a distant 15½ games off the Giants pace. They led the National League in ERA at 3.16 that year, but their offense was non-existent as they finished dead last in runs scored, a full 68 runs behind the next worst team. The 2004 season was a different story. It was a nail-biter that wasn't decided until the bottom of the ninth inning of the 161st game when Tracy's cohorts overcame a three-run San Francisco Giant lead by pushing seven runs across the plate, the last four on Steve Finley's pennant-winning walk-off grand slam. Their postseason experience was unfortunately brief as they fell to the St. Louis Cardinals in four games in the National League Division Series. The Dodgers well-balanced attack included above average hitting and excellent pitching. Adrian Beltre had a career season, slugging the ball at a .334 clip with a league-leading 48 home runs and 121 runs-batted in. Shawn Green provided additional offensive fireworks by smashing 28 homers and driving in 86 runs. The starting pitching of Weaver, Ishii, and Lima, was bolstered by the sensational exploits of all-world closer Eric Gagne, who completed his historic run of 84 consecutive saves on June 5. He saved 45 games in 47 save opportunities during the year and was ably supported by setup men Duaner Sanchez and Giovanni Carrara.

Jim Tracy was fired after finishing fourth in 2005, a common fate among major league managers, but he has gone on to sharpen his managerial skills in both Pittsburgh and Colorado. His five-year tenure in Los Angeles showed 427 victories against 383 losses, a .527 winning percentage.

GRADY LITTLE

Grady Little (Los Angeles Dodgers)

Grady Little was born in Abilene, Texas on March 3, 1950. After an excellent high school career as a catcher, the 5', 10", 190-pound right handed hitter was drafted by the Atlanta Braves, but he played minor league ball for just six seasons before putting his glove away for good in 1973 after posting a .207 career batting average. He began a minor league coaching career in 1971 while still a player, but left the baseball stage for five years to be a cotton farmer in Texas beginning in 1975.

Returning to the game he loved in 1980, Little took over the managerial reins of the Bluefield Orioles in the Class-A Appalachian League, finishing second to the Norfolk Tides in the Western Division. He continued to manage in the minors for another 16 years before he was signed by the San Diego Padres as a coach in 1996. He was a bench coach in Boston from 1997 through 1999 and coached the Cleveland Indians in 2000 and 2001. He filled in as a substitute manager with the Indians, posting a 19-12 won-loss record during that time.

The 52-year old grandfather received his first opportunity to manage in the major leagues when the Boston Red Sox signed him in 2002. He continued the Back Bay trend of finishing second to the New York Yankees in the American League Eastern Division, a position they filled for six consecutive years between 1998 and 2003. The latter year proved to be Grady Little's downfall. He guided his team to a 95-67 record that year but still finished a full six games behind the Bronx Bombers. For a time, in the postseason playoffs, it looked as if Boston's fortunes had changed. They disposed of the Oakland Athletics in five games in the American League Division Series and overcame a three-games-to-two lead by the hated Yankees before collapsing. Down 6-4 after six innings in Game Six, Little's charges pushed over three runs in the seventh to take a 7-6 lead and added another brace of runs in the top of the ninth to seal the bargain. Boston fans were confident that the Curse of the Bambino would finally be broken as they had their all-world starter on the hill for the deciding game. Pedro Martinez, who was coming off a 14-4 season with a 2.22 ERA, was rested and ready to go, but the Curse of the Bambino would strike them down one more time. The Sox led 5-2 entering the bottom of the eighth inning when Pedro's tank went dry. He was touched up for two hits and one run after retiring the first batter, bringing Grady Little to the mound. Southpaw Alan Embree was warmed up and ready to go, in the bullpen, but Little decided to stay with his ace, and the Yankees gleefully added two doubles and two runs to their total, tying the game at five-all. Three innings later Aaron Boone took Tim Wakefield deep and Boston's dream was over. Grady Little was relieved of his duties shortly thereafter.

He spent two years as a special assistant to the Chicago Cubs General Manager, before assuming the duties of manager for the Los Angeles Dodgers. His first year in L.A. was a memorable one as he brought the team back from a fourth place finish and a 71-91 won-loss record in 2005 to a tie for the National

League Western Division pennant in 2006 with an 88-74 mark. General Manager Ned Colletti put together a bumper crop of rookies including Chad Billingsey, James Loney, Matt Kemp, Andre Ethier and Russell Martin, and complemented them with veterans like Nomar Garciaparra, Kenny Lofton, and Greg Maddux. And Grady Little managed them with the necessary care and with patience. The season, as it turned out, was a roller coaster ride from start to finish. The team went on a long losing streak in early July dropping 13 of 14 games to fall 7½ games behind San Diego. Then, just as suddenly as the streak began, it changed direction with Little's Big Blue Machine running off 17 wins in 18 games. A key pickup at the trading deadline sparked the surge. Greg Maddux, who was obtained in a trade with the Chicago Cubs an hour before the trading deadline, won two of the 17 games and received a no-decision in another Dodger victory. Two games in September typified the Dodger season. On September 18, with the Dodgers trailing the San Diego Padres 9-5 in the bottom of the ninth inning, they exploded for four consecutive home runs to pull even at nine-all. Then, after falling behind by a run in the tenth, they went home a winner when Nomar Garciaparra smashed a two-run walk-off homer. Ten days later, rookie first baseman James Loney tied a Dodger franchise record set by Brooklyn's Gil Hodges by driving in nine runs in a 19-11 blowout in the light air in Colorado. And the craziness continued right down to the last day. Grady Little's charges blew a four-game lead in early September to fall two games behind the Padres but finished strong, winning their last seven games and nine of ten to give them a share of the division lead. They entered the postseason as the wild card entry based on their record against the Padres, and the New York Mets sent them home early with a three game sweep in the Division Series, winning by scores of 6-5, 4-1, and 9-5. Jeff Kent was one of the few bright spots in the losing effort, stinging the ball at a .615 clip, going 8 for 13 with a double, a homer, and two RBIs.

Unfortunately for Little, he could not duplicate his 2006 magic. In spite of outstanding seasons from Loney, Kemp, and Billingsley, the Dodgers fell back into fourth place with an 82-80 won-loss record in 2007, and Little was released in the off-season. His two-year won-loss record with the Dodgers was 170-154 for a .525 winning percentage.

JOE TORRE

Joe Torre was a baseball rarity, an outstanding player who metamorphosed into one of the games most renowned managers. The Brooklyn, New York,

native entered the major leagues with the Milwaukee Brewers in 1960 and stayed in the Big Show for 18 seasons as an active player. His most productive years were with the St. Louis Cardinals in the early 1970s and, after manager Red Schoendienst relieved him of his catching duties and installed him in the infield at either first base or third base, Torre responded with his greatest season in 1971 when he led the National League in batting (.363), base hits (230), and runs-batted-in (137). He also captured the league's Most Valuable Player trophy that year. By the time he hung up his glove for the last time, he had accumulated 2342 base hits with 252 home runs and 1185 RBIs, to go with a .287 batting average.

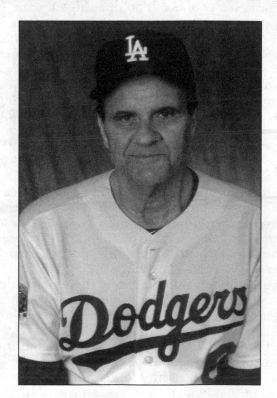

Joe Torre (Los Angeles Dodgers)

Following his retirement as a player with the hapless New York Mets early in 1977, Torre replaced Joe Frazier as the manager of the team, but was unable to make a silk purse out of a sow's ear during his six years as skipper. He brought the team home in fourth place once, fifth place twice, and sixth place three times. The husky New Yorker then moved on to Atlanta for three years and St. Louis for six years before entering the sunlight of championship baseball with the famed Bronx Bombers in 1996. He won the American League pennant by four games over the Baltimore Orioles that year, and went on to defeat the Atlanta Braves in six games to claim the World Championship. Joe Torre managed the Yankees for twelve years, winning six American League pennants and four World Championships along the way.

He left New York in a salary dispute after the 2007 season and was quickly signed by the Los Angeles Dodgers to see if he could work his managerial magic on the west coast. He inherited a fundamentally sound ballclub in 2008, with a core of young players that were just entering their prime. The kiddie brigade, all under 25 years of age with one exception, included catcher Russell Martin, pitchers Chad Billingsley and Jonathan Broxton, first baseman James Loney, and outfielders Andre Ethier and Matt Kemp. They were ably supported by Hiroki Kuroda from the Japanese league, and veterans Jason Schmidt, Rafael Furcal, and Juan Pierre. The team got off the mark quickly as Brad Penny blanked the San Francisco Giants 5-0 on opening day but, beset by injuries to Schmidt, Furcal, and Kuroda, they soon became a .500 team, winning a few and losing a few. They had an eight-game winning streak in late April but it still left them in second place, four games behind the Arizona Diamondbacks in the Western Division. Matt Kemp had two big games during the streak. On April 26, he drove in five runs, four of them coming on a grand slam home run in an 11-3 rout of the Colorado Rockies. And six days later, he went two for five with two doubles and four RBIs as Torre's troops once again decimated the Rockies by an 11-6 count. L.A. languished in second place during the entire summer, but they came to life down the stretch, winning 17 games against 8 losses in September to edge the Diamondbacks by two games for the division title. They met the Chicago Cubs in the NLDS and swept the Windy City contingent in three straight, but they met their match in the Championship Series, dropping four games to the Philadelphia Phillies, with Hiroki Kuroda giving them their only victory.

Joe Torre was optimistic as the team began spring training in their new facility, Camelback Ranch, located in sunny Glendale Arizona. They opened the National League season with a 4-1 victory over the San Diego Padres behind the strong pitching of Hiroki Kuroda and they posted a 10-3 log by the time the sun went down on April 19. As the month came to an end, the Dodgers stood atop the National League Western Division with a 15-8 log, 3 ½ games better than the Padres. The highlight of the month took place on April 13 when Orlando Hudson hit for the cycle. He was four-for-five in the game with three runs scored and two runs-batted-in, sparking L.A. to an 11-1 rout of the hated Giants. Six days later, Matt Kemp pounded out three base hits including a double and two homers with five RBIs in a 14-2 win over Colorado. The big Dodger slugger had three more games with five RBIs during the season and one game with four RBIs. Torre's team had jumped out front as soon as the season got underway and were never threatened. They finished the season with a 95-67 won-loss record, three games ahead of the fast-closing Rockies. The post-season was almost a repeat of the 2008 post-season. They swept the St.

Louis Cardinals three straight, but were eliminated by Philadelphia again in five games. Only Vicente Padilla's gutty performance in game two when he pitched 7 1/3 innings yielding only one run saved the Dodgers from a sweep. L.A. pushed over two runs in the bottom of the eighth inning to make a winner out of Hong-Chih Kuo.

After bringing the Dodgers home in fourth place in 2010, Joe Torre left the managerial ranks to accept a position with the Major League Baseball front office.

DON MATTINGLY

Don Mattingly was a slugging first baseman for the New York Yankees for six years until back problems reduced his power to a fraction of its former level. The Evansville, Indiana native, a three-sport star in high school was signed to a professional baseball contract by the New York Yankees after his graduation in 1979 and broke into organized baseball with Oneonta in the New York-Penn League that same year, batting .349 in 53 games.

Three years later, the 21-year old first baseman made his major league debut, playing seven

Don Mattingly (Los Angeles Dodgers)

games with the Yankees at the end of the season. He split the next year between Columbus in the International League and New York, and claimed the vacant first base position on the Yankee squad in 1984, ripping the ball at a league-leading .343 clip with 23 homers and 110 runs-batted-in. The following year he was named the American League's Most Valuable Player after batting .324 with 35 homers and 107 runs scored and leading the league with 48 doubles and 145 RBIs.

The six foot tall, 180-pound left-handed hitter was soon being recognized as the best first baseman in the major leagues. He combined outstanding power with an excellent batting eye that produced a high average with less than 35 strikeouts a year. He was also the game's most graceful defensive player who led the league in fielding average seven times and is currently ranked number three in career fielding average. According to the tome, *The Ballplayers,* Mattingly "fielded his position at first base with brilliance and displayed a work ethic and charisma reminiscent of Yankee greats of the past." He soon became a "smart two-strike hitter and learned to look for the inside pitch that he might drive into Yankee Stadium's short right-field porch." The Yankee idol hit a combined .337 his first four full years in Yankee pinstripes, averaging 26 home runs and 106 RBIs for every 550 at-bats. Unfortunately back problems robbed him of his powerful batting stroke, and his numbers declined over his last six years in the majors to a .291 batting average with 13 homers and 75 RBIs a year. He retired after the 1995 season with a career .307 batting average and 2153 base hits.

Mattingly served as a special instructor at the Yankees spring training complex for seven years before returning to the game full time in 2004. He was the Yankee's hitting coach for three years, and their bench coach for one year before joining his old manager Joe Torre in Los Angeles in 2008. He was the Dodgers hitting coach for three years and received his baptism by fire as a manager in the 2010 Arizona Fall League. When Torre retired from managing after the 2010 season, Don Mattingly was given the opportunity to take the reins of the team in 2011. It was a frustrating introduction to major league managing for the former Yankee, as his team shot itself in the foot at every turn in April, May, and June, but he turned things around over the final two months of the season to give Dodger fans hope for a successful 2012. On July 7, 2011, the Dodgers record stood at 37-51 after a five-game losing streak, and they trailed first place San Francisco by 14½ games. Then, on July 7, Clayton Kershaw blanked the New York Mets 6-0 and a new, more determined Los Angeles team emerged from the ashes and went on a rampage over the final two months of the season. They compiled a record of 45-28 from July 7 to September 28, climbing from the cellar to third place in the tough National League West Division.

Don Mattingly exercised excellent managerial skills during his first year on the job. He exhibited the patience that is needed to develop young players, he instilled in his players the confidence they need to succeed at the big league level, and he educated them in the work ethic that separates the outstanding player from the average player. Hopefully, the Mattingly Era will be a long, successful one.

CHARLIE EBBETS

Charles Hercules Ebbets was the founding father of Dodger baseball. He also lived the American dream; a young man who rose from modest beginnings to become the owner and president of a major league baseball franchise.

Charlie Ebbets was born in New York in 1859. As a young man, he investigated numerous professions, including draftsman, State Assemblyman, and publisher, before gravitating toward his first love, baseball. In 1883, a group of Brooklyn businessmen purchased a franchise in the Interstate League, and 24-year-old Charlie Ebbets became one of their first employees.

The hard-working Ebbets made himself invaluable to his new employers by becoming a jack-of-all-trades. In addition to keeping the books, Ebbets also collected tickets, mowed the outfield grass, cleaned the stadium after games, and did 101 other jobs that needed doing.

He also invested his money wisely, purchasing stock in the Brooklyn franchise whenever he could afford it. The team's fortunes gradually improved, and Ebbets investment grew along with it.

After one year in the Interstate League, the Brooklyn Grays moved up to the major league level, joining the American Association in 1884. Their debut season resulted in a tenth-place finish in the 13-team league, but their fortunes improved year by year. In 1889, the Brooklyn Bridegrooms, as they were then called, won the Association Championship in a stirring battle with the perennial Champion St. Louis Browns.

The following year, the 'Grooms joined the National League, where they once again captured the championship. At the same time, Ebbets fortunes prospered. His responsibilities with the ball club increased regularly until, in 1896, he was elected secretary of the corporation. Two

Charlie Ebbets

years later, following the death of one of the owners, the 39-year-old businessman was elevated to the presidency.

The Brooklyn team, now known as the Superbas, won the National League pennant in 1899 and 1900, but their fortunes declined thereafter when the newly formed

American League pirated their players. The first decade of the twentieth century was a disappointing one for Charlie Ebbets and the inhabitants of Brooklyn. Beginning in 1903, the Trolley Dodgers finished in the second division for 14 straight years.

Still, Charlie Ebbets worked hard to give the Brooklyn fans a ball club they could be proud of. In 1908, he undertook a major project, the construction of a new stadium in Brooklyn, to replace dilapidated Washington Park. The project took over five years to complete. The land, an eyesore called Pigtown, in the Flatbush section of Brooklyn, was selected for the site of the park. When the final parcel of land was purchased in 1912, construction of the stadium finally got underway.

Ebbets Field, the finest steel stadium of the day, opened to the public on April 5, 1913. The Dodgers defeated the New York Highlanders in an exhibition game, 3-2, with a run in the bottom of the ninth. Miss Genevieve Ebbets, the owner's daughter, threw out the ceremonial first ball before a boisterous crowd of 30,000.

The Dodgers' fortunes improved during the early years of Ebbets Field. With Wilbert Robinson at the helm, the Dodgers, also called the Robins after their manager, captured National League flags in 1916 and again in 1920.

The years of hard work began to wear on Charlie Ebbets in the early twenties, and his health declined rapidly. The stress and overwork associated with running a major business culminated in a massive heart attack following spring training in 1925. The president of the Brooklyn Dodgers died in his New York hotel room on April 18, 1925, after serving Brooklyn baseball for more than 42 years. He joined a ragtag minor league team as a youngster and, through shrewd business acumen and good old hard work, he turned it into a thriving business and a proud representative of the borough of Brooklyn.

Charlie Ebbets was an industrious, conservative businessman, whose love of baseball and appreciation of the Brooklyn fans gave baseball some of its most memorable teams and unforgettable characters.

He was Brooklyn baseball.

LARRY MACPHAIL

If Charlie Ebbets was the founding father of Dodger baseball, Larry MacPhail was certainly the father of modern Dodger baseball. Arriving in Flatbush in 1938, the dynamic baseball executive renovated Ebbets Field, initiated night baseball in Brooklyn, began the first daily broadcasts of Dodger games, and started what was to become the finest farm system in major league baseball.

Leland Stanford MacPhail, a native of Cass City, Michigan, earned a law degree from George Washington University in 1911. For the next 19 years, with one year out for World War I, MacPhail practiced law in Columbus, Ohio. Fate stepped in in 1930, when MacPhail's father invested $100,000 in the Columbus baseball team at the urging of Branch Rickey, President of the parent St. Louis Cardinals. As part of the package, 40-year-old Larry MacPhail became General Manager of the minor league Redbirds.

Larry MacPhail (Los Angeles Dodger Photo)

The flamboyant, abrasive, hard-drinking MacPhail, although disliked by many, was an astute baseball man, and he turned the Columbus franchise around, making it the jewel of the St. Louis farm system. His reputation as a management genius spread, and in 1933 he was hired by the Cincinnati Reds to save their dying franchise. Among his innovations in Cincinnati were the introduction of night baseball to the major leagues, the use of commercial airlines instead of railroads on road trips, and the first radio broadcasts of major league baseball games. A young, 26-year-old southern boy by the name of Red Barber was hired to be the Cincinnati announcer. MacPhail did his job so well, that the Redlegs won National League pennants in 1939 and 1940.

The Brooklyn Trust Company, owners of a Dodger franchise that had finished in the second division 13 times over the previous 17 years, brought Larry MacPhail to the City of Churches to work his magic. And work it he did. Armed with a virtually unlimited bank account, the baseball promoter set about to revitalize Dodger baseball. The creaky old ballpark was freshly painted, the grounds groomed, and the new park attendants given clean uniforms and instructions in customer relations.

Floodlights were installed around the stadium in 1938, and the first night game was played on June 15 of that year. It was an historic occasion for more than one reason. Cincinnati southpaw Johnny Vander Meer christened night baseball in Brooklyn by tossing his second consecutive no-hitter, a 6-0 masterpiece.

The big, beefy redhead spent money like water in support of his personal philosophy, "You have to spend money to make money." He brought in Red Barber to broadcast Dodger baseball games, the first major league games broadcast in New York City. He hired a dozen scouts to canvass the country in search of new talent, and he signed working agreements with several minor league baseball teams, the beginning of the Dodger farm system.

On the field, he set about to buy National League pennants until his farm system matured. He purchased first baseman Dolph Camilli for $50,000, pitcher Kirbe Higbe for $100,000 and catcher Mickey Owen for $60,000. He promoted Leo Durocher to player-manager, signed Babe Ruth as first base coach, and rescued a number of former major leaguers who were languishing in the minors.

The mammoth reclamation project was eminently successful. In three short years, the doormat Dodgers rose from seventh place to second. Then, in 1941, the Brooklyn Dodgers won their first National League pennant in 21 years, a hard-fought 2 1/2 game victory over the St. Louis Cardinals.

The patriotic MacPhail, a veteran of World War I, left his Brooklyn position in 1942 as World War II heated up, enlisting in the U.S. Army. He later spent two years in the New York Yankee organization, before retiring from baseball in 1947.

He was elected to baseball's Hall of Fame in Cooperstown, New York, in 1978.

MacPhail worked the impossible wherever he went. From Columbus to Cincinnati to Brooklyn, the dynamic executive inherited franchises that were in shambles, molded them in his personal image, and left them as models of sound baseball management.

Larry MacPhail was a hard drinking, free-spending egomaniac, with an uncanny knack for taking a mediocre baseball team and turning it into a sound winner. He will always be remembered in Brooklyn as one of the most important men in Dodger history.

He started them on the road to success. The fantastic achievements of the Brooklyn and Los Angeles franchises over the last 57 years are directly attributable to the efforts of the Michigan magician, Larry Stanford MacPhail.

BRANCH RICKEY

Branch Rickey was the architect of the celebrated Dodger dynasty of the past 50 years. The "Mahatma," as he was called because of his keen mind and puritanical air, replaced his former student, Larry MacPhail, as president of the Brooklyn Dodgers in 1942, and immediately expanded the big redhead's baseball development programs. He took the fledgling Brooklyn farm system and converted it into a baseball factory that turned out prospects by the dozens. He also broke baseball's heinous color barrier, hiring Jackie Robinson to be the first black to play professional baseball in almost 60 years.

Wesley Branch Rickey was born in Lucasville, Ohio on December 12, 1881, the son of devout Methodist parents. As a young man he played major league baseball for four years, coached the sport at the University of Michigan, and earned a law degree from the same school in 1911. Two years later, the 32-year-old baseball enthusiast was hired to manage the St. Louis Browns of the American League. Rickey managed in the major leagues, both with the Browns and the St. Louis Cardinals, off and on, for ten years, with mediocre success. His lifetime managing record of 597-664 included only two first-division finishes.

Branch Rickey, the man who initiated the plan to tear down baseball's heinous color barrier, is shown with Jackie Robinson and Dodger manager Burt Shotton, as Jackie signs his 1949 contract.

In 1916, Branch Rickey moved into the executive branch of the St. Louis Brown organization, as vice president. One year later, he moved across town to the Cardinal front office, where he stayed for 25 years. From the beginning, the 35-year-old baseball aficionado proved himself to be an outstanding judge of baseball talent, an innovative teacher of baseball fundamentals, and a shrewd, tight-fisted businessman. He invented the concept of the farm system while serving as president of the St. Louis franchise from 1925 through 1942. The Mahatma built the Redbird farm system to a point where it controlled over 600 players on 32 teams. His efforts produced six National League pennants and four World Championships in 17 years.

Brooklyn chief executive Branch Rickey discusses the upcoming pennant race with his manager Leo Durocher, in 1942.

Among the many pioneering advances Rickey advocated were:

- The sliding pit.
- The stringed strike zone over the plate for pitchers to use to improve their control.
- Batting helmets.
- Pitching machines.

The Brooklyn Trust Company hired Rickey to be President of the Dodgers in 1942 after Larry MacPhail left to join the army. MacPhail introduced his former mentor's business philosophies into Brooklyn baseball during his five years as President. Rickey built on them, creating a baseball dynasty that has lasted for over 50 years.

Branch Rickey was a complex individual. The frugal, bushy-eyed Brooklyn president lived and dressed simply, presenting a disheveled countenance to the outside world. But to business associates, he was a shrewd and purposeful businessman, who was mentally always two steps ahead of everyone else. Rickey's only vice, a love of large-expensive cigars, distracted opponents while he soft talked them into deals that benefitted only him. One of his slickest trades brought Billy Cox and Preacher Roe to Brooklyn in exchange for 37-year-old Dixie Walker and two journeymen pitchers.

The Mahatma's salary negotiations with his ball players were legendary. Preacher Roe, an avid hunter, tells of the year that a blank contract arrived at his house the same day that two expensive hunting dogs, presents from Rickey, were delivered. Roe was so overcome at the sight of the priceless hounds that he signed the contract for a minimum raise. He claims that, as soon as he put the contract in the mail box, the dogs headed north and were never seen again. Another player, leaving Rickey's office after a salary negotiation, was seen smiling from ear to ear. When a reporter asked him if he received a raise, he said, "No, but I didn't take a cut, either."

In 1948, the Dodger president opened Brooklyn's magnificent Dodgertown baseball facility in Vero Beach, Florida. The major leaguers, as well as their farm hands, over 600 players in all, lived and trained together for two full months each year, the only major league team to share quarters with it's minor league affiliates.

Perhaps Rickey's greatest legacy however, was the breaking of baseball's long-standing color barrier. Long chagrined by baseball's refusal to admit blacks into the game, and realizing the vast untapped array of talent available in the Negro Leagues, the Bible-quoting Methodist took steps to end the discrimination. His search for the ideal black ballplayer required an individual with, not only outstanding baseball talents, but with strong personal character as well. He found his man in Jack Roosevelt Robinson, and the rest is history.

Robinson, Campanella, Newcombe, Gilliam, Joe Black, and many other graduates of the Negro Leagues helped create a Dodger dynasty that spanned a decade, and gave the Flatbush faithful the most exciting baseball ever seen.

Branch Rickey left Brooklyn in 1950 after a dispute with Walter O'Malley. His later career included an eight-year stay in Pittsburgh, followed by an abortive effort to form a third major league. He died in Columbia, Missouri on December 9, 1965, 11 days before his 84th birthday.

His peers, recognizing his great contributions to the game of baseball, elected him into the Hall of Fame in 1967.

Branch Rickey was the creator of the modern Dodger farm system, the man who gave us "The Boys of Summer," and the humanitarian who made baseball a game for all men, regardless of color.

Branch Rickey was more than a great baseball executive. He was a great human being.

WALTER O'MALLEY

Walter O'Malley was the last member of the great Brooklyn triumvirate of baseball executives. Larry MacPhail was the entrepreneur, the man who brought the Brooklyn franchise back from the brink of bankruptcy and put it on the road to success. Branch Rickey was the architect of the famed Dodger farm system, the creator of a dynasty, and the man who broke the color barrier. Walter O'Malley was the consummate businessman, the visionary who forged a new frontier on the west coast, and who made the Dodgers the most successful and the most envied franchise in the history of baseball.

Walter Francis O'Malley was born into a wealthy family in New York City in 1903. The son of the New York Commissioner of Public Markets was educated in the best private primary and secondary schools, including the prestigious Culver Academy. He then matriculated at the University of Pennsylvania, where he finished #1 in his engineering class. In 1920, he received a law degree from Fordham University.

The ambitious young Irishman established a law practice in New York City, where his assets grew into the millions over a 20 year period. One of his clients, the Brooklyn Trust Company, had controlling interest in the Brooklyn Dodgers baseball team and, in 1941, they named him the team's attorney. Over the next few years, the astute lawyer bought up large blocks of Dodger stock. Finally, in 1950, he dislodged Branch Rickey in a power struggle, and was named president of the Brooklyn Dodgers. The O'Malley era had begun.

Walter O'Malley was a shrewd and calculating businessman. As the decade of the fifties got underway, it was obvious that the baseball team was badly in need of a new home. Ramshackled Ebbets Field, with its limited seating capacity and lack of adequate parking facilities, was no longer acceptable as a major league stadium. Charlie Ebbets steel wonder had had its day. And its day had passed. O'Malley began negotiating with the City of New York to help him acquire land for a new stadium, preferably a domed facility.

As the years passed, it became obvious that O'Malley and the city fathers were not going to be able to come to an agreement on finding a new home for the Dodgers. O'Malley wanted the city to help him acquire land at

Walter O'Malley (Los Angeles Dodger Photo)

Atlantic and Flatbush Avenues for his stadium, but city officials continually refused his requests. The attitude was different on the west coast, where the city of Los Angeles, California, offered the Dodger president 300 acres of land in Chavez Ravine on which to build his stadium. The Dodgers moved west.

From the beginning, the Dodger-Los Angeles love affair blossomed. Walter O'Malley continued to support and nurture the Dodgers farm system and, that system in return continued to provide the big club with pennant-contending baseball teams. Over a period of 39 years, the transplanted Brooklyn franchise captured nine Western Divison titles, nine National League pennants and five World Championships. They lost two other pennants in playoffs.

From a business standpoint, the coast-to-coast move was an unqualified success. In Brooklyn, home attendance at Ebbets Field hovered around the 1,000,000 figure. In 1955, when the "Boys of Summer" captured the World Championship in a mad wire-to-wire romp, only 1,033,589 fans showed up to lend their support to the rout. On the other side of the country, the attendance has always exceeded 1,500,000, with a National League record of 3,608,881 paid customers pushing their way through the turnstiles in 1980. In fact, for the past 18 years, the attendance figures have always exceeded 2,500,000 patrons.

Walter O'Malley provided stability in other areas of the business as well. For the first 42 years of the O'Malley era, including the presidency of his son Peter, the Dodgers have had only two field managers, Walter Alston and Tommy Lasorda. In the radio and TV booth, Vin Scully has held forth as the patriarch since 1950.

Under O'Malley's direction, the Dodgers have given the fans of Los Angeles not only a championship baseball team, but a showplace as well. The Los Angeles franchise is one of the most efficient operations in baseball. Dodger Stadium is considered one of the cleanest, most comfortable ballparks in the major leagues. Its employees are the most cordial and their hot dogs are the tastiest.

Walter O'Malley died in Rochester, Minnesota, on August 9, 1979, at the age of 75. During his life, he was a smooth, conservative financial expert, whose background and business acumen not only perpetuated the National League's most successful franchise, but molded it into a fiscally sound business that has been called one of America's 100 best-run corporations.

He was a visionary who saw the need for major league baseball on the west coast, and who convinced New York Giant owner Horace Stoneham to move his own team to San Francisco in order to continue the Giant-Dodger rivalry. The move was a great success, not only for the two owners, but for baseball as well. It changed the face of baseball permanently from a regional game into a truly national pastime.

Walter Alston, the long-time manager of the Dodgers paid his former boss the ultimate compliment, when he said, "He was the fairest man I ever met in baseball."

PETER O'MALLEY

Peter O'Malley was born in New York City in 1937, the son of Brooklyn Dodger club attorney, Walter O'Malley. Young Peter, following in his father's footsteps, pursued a degree in law, after finishing a disciplined secondary education at LaSalle Military Academy in Oakdale, N.Y.

O'Malley majored in Business Law at the Wharton School of Business and Finance at the University of Pennsylvania, receiving a Bachelor of Science degree in Economics in 1960. Shortly after graduation, the reserved Irishman joined the Dodgers, now owned by his father, as Director of their spring training facility in Vero Beach, Florida.

Under the watchful eye of the elder O'Malley, Peter worked his way up the Dodger administrative ladder over a period of eight years. Following a three-year sojourn in Dodgertown, he spent two years in the field, as president and general manager of the Spokane Indians, the Dodgers' AAA farm team in the Pacific Coast League. Moving up to the home club in 1967, the 30-year-old executive assumed the title of vice president in charge of stadium operations. One year later he was promoted to executive vice president of the Los Angeles Dodgers–in effect, training for the presidency.

Within a short period of time, on St. Patrick's Day 1970, to be exact, Dodger president Walter O'Malley, confident that the family business would remain in competent hands, retired to the sedentary life at the age of 67. He was succeeded by Peter, an astute businessman with a sense of responsibility, not only to the Dodgers and their fans, but to the Los Angeles area as well. One era had passed into history with Walter O'Malley's decision, but a new era had begun.

Peter O'Malley celebrated his 27th anniversary as Dodger president on March 17, 1997. He has carried the torch higher and burned it brighter than his father could have imagined. During his reign, the Dodgers have remained the envy of major league baseball. Their Dodgertown spring training facility is still the most efficient and most visible facility of its kind in the U.S. Dodger Stadium in L.A. is rated as the most beautiful park in the major leagues. And only a couple of years ago, the Los Angeles Dodgers organization was rated as one of the 100 best run companies in the United States.

More importantly, the Los Angeles Dodgers continue to produce the kind of championship baseball teams the O'Malley family promised their fans way back in 1950 when they first acquired ownership of the franchise. Under Dodger president Peter O'Malley, the Big Blue Machine has captured nine Western Division crowns, five National League pennants, and two World Championships. They have finished second ten times, and third twice. They have finished lower than third only six times in 24 years.

The popularity of baseball has now spread beyond the western hemisphere and the Orient to encompass the entire globe. It appears to be only a matter of time before professional baseball becomes a truly universal sport, with annual tournaments to decide a bonafide world champion. In promoting the sport worldwide, Peter O'Malley has become a twentieth century pioneer. He has been active on an international scale for years, sending Dodgers representatives to such places as The People's Republic of China, Mexico, Nicaragua, Russia, and Korea. The Dodgers have training facilities in the Dominican Republic and Venezuela, as well as two professional teams in the Dominican Summer League. In 1994, as in other years, a foreign baseball team, this one from Waseda University in Japan, trained at Dodgertown. A Russian delegation also visited the Florida complex recently.

On January 14, 1994, the astute O'Malley signed Korean pitcher Chan Ho Park to a Dodger contract. One year later, he corralled Japanese star Hideo Nomo. As the 1997 baseball season approached, the Los Angeles Dodgers' starting pitching candidates looked like a meeting of the United Nations. Park and Nomo were joined by Pedro Astacio and Ramon Martinez, both from the Dominican Republic, Tom Candiotti of the United States, and Ismael Valdez from Mexico. Other members of the team included relief pitcher Antonio Osuna (Mexico), Raul Mondesi (Dominican Republic), Wilton Guerrero (Dominican Republic), Juan Castro (Mexico), and Karim Garcia (Mexico).

Peter O'Malley, like his father before him, has been a credit to the game, and an outstanding ambassador for the national sport. Much to the dismay of Los Angeles Dodger fans, Mr. O'Malley announced early in 1997, his intention to sell the Dodger franchise. His 27 years of leadership, compassion, and integrity, are a perfect example of how a successful business can be run by caring individuals.

FRANK McCOURT, JR.

In 1997 The Los Angeles Dodgers were purchased by the entertainment giant, The Fox Group, owned by Rupert Murdoch's News Corporation. It was obvious from the start that the Fox executives, who might have been excellent businessmen, were not familiar with the business of running a major league baseball team. Over the next six years the Dodgers languished in either second or third place in the five-team National League West Division. Finally, admitting they had made a mistake in trying to manage a sports enterprise, The Fox Group sold the Dodgers to Boston billionaire Frank McCourt, Jr.

Frank McCourt was born in Boston on August 14, 1953, the fifth generation of one of Boston's premier real estate developers. His grandfather, John McCourt, an Irish immigrant, settled in Boston from

Peter O'Malley has always been a "hands-on" executive.

Frank McCourt, Jr.

County Tyrone, Ireland, in the 1870's and founded the John McCourt Construction Company in 1893. Over the years the company became one of Boston's premier construction companies, known for building the runways at Logan Airport and for paving part of the Central Artery. Frank Jr. graduated from Georgetown University in 1975 with a degree in Economics and joined his father's company the same year. Two years later, with financial assistance from his father he founded The McCourt Company and was instrumental in developing many real estate projects in the greater Boston area including the waterfront and Back Bay. Early in the new century, the young entrepreneur, whose grandfather had been part owner of the Boston Braves, attempted to purchase the Boston Red Sox but was outbid by the John W. Henry group. Following that disappointment, his eyes turned westward and he made a successful offer to purchase the Los Angeles Dodgers from The Fox Group for $430 million. He assumed control of the team in 2004 with the intention of making the Dodgers, once again, the most admired team in professional sports.

With manager Jim Tracy at the helm, McCourt brought the team home in first place in 2004 with a record of 93-69, but his joy was temporarily tempered by the four-game loss to the St. Louis Cardinals in the National League Division Series. In the seven years since he purchased the team, McCourt saw his team capture three Western Division pennants and participate in two National League Championship Series. In 2009 they became the first Dodger team to reach back-to-back Championship Series since 1977-78. Unfortunately, McCourt's personal problems interfered with the team's baseball operations and put him in a heated battle with Bud Selig and Major League Baseball. The situation was finally resolved when McCourt agreed in early November, 2011 to sell the team to the highest bidder. The transaction is expected to be completed by the beginning of the 2012 season, giving the Dodgers a full season under their new owners.

NED COLLETTI

Ned Louis Colletti was born in Chicago, Illinois in 1955 and graduated from Northern Illinois University in 1982. He began work with the Chicago Cubs that year in media relations and later moved into baseball operations where he handled salary arbitration cases and assisted in player acquisitions and contract negotiations. He won the Robert O. Fishel Award for Public Relations Excellence in 1990. Four years later he moved on to the San Francisco Giants, eventually assuming the position of assistant general manager, a post he held for nine years. Dur-

ing his San Francisco sojourn, the team recorded an 813-644 won-loss mark, an excellent .558 winning percentage.

Frank McCourt plucked Colletti off the Giants roster in 2006 to become the Los Angeles Dodgers new general manager, and manager Grady Little's club welcomed him to the fold by finishing in a tie with San Diego for the National League Western Division pennant. It was a good start for the Chicago native even though the Dodgers were eliminated by the New York Mets in the first round of the postseason playoffs. The 2007 season was a forgettable one for Colletti as the team crawled home in fourth place, a distant eight games behind Clint Hurdle's Colorado Rockies. But thanks to a strong crop of young players (most of them home-grown products like Matt Kemp, James Loney, Russell Martin, and Chad Billingsley) and supported by players acquired by Ned Colletti, (such as Andre Ethier, Takashi Saito, Hiroki Kuroda, Manny Ramirez, Juan Pierre, and Casey Blake) the Dodgers became the first Dodger team in 21 years to participate in back-to-back Championship Series.

Ned Colletti, held back by budget restraints in recent years, has tried to get the most bang for his buck by continuing to demonstrate his legerdemain when acquiring new players, either through free-agent signings or trades. He collared all-star second baseman Orlando Hudson and Vicente Padilla in 2009, added Jamie Carroll and Ted Lilly, in 2010 and Juan Uribe, Aaron Miles, Jon Garland, and Matt Guerrier, in 2011. And to the mix, he has relied to a large extent on players who have come up through the bourgeoning Dodger farm system including Dee Gordon, Rubby De La Rosa, Jerry Sands, and Nate Eovaldi. The 57-year old Colletti has had a good track record for player development and acquisition in Los Angeles to date. And as a result of his success the club seems poised to make another run at the National League pennant in 2012, with the promise of a World Series reservation to follow.

Ned Colletti

CHAPTER 5
DODGER SPORTSCASTERS

Walter Lanier "Red" Barber will forever be remembered as the "Voice of the Brooklyn Dodgers." The "Ol Redhead" brought the thrill of major league baseball to millions of people in the New York area when he was hired by Larry MacPhail, to broadcast Brooklyn Dodger home games over the radio, in 1939. Prior to that time, radio broadcasts of the Dodgers, Giants, and Yankees games were prohibited by agreement of the team owners. MacPhail broke that agreement, and the face of baseball in the metropolitan area was changed forever–for the better.

Red Barber was born in Columbus, Mississippi on February 17, 1908, but was raised in Tallahassee, Florida. He was smitten with the broadcasting bug as a teenager, when radios became consumer products. He heard his first radio broadcast in 1924 at a neighbor's house, and was immediately captivated by the magical box. While attending the University of Florida, Barber took a job with the local radio station, eventually leaving school to devote his full time to his first passion.

In 1934, the 26-year-old announcer was hired by Cincinnati Reds owner Powell Crosley, for $25 a week, to do play-by-play broadcasts of Reds home games. The young Floridian was an immediate success. His erudite manner and unique colloquialisms, captivated fans throughout the Ohio Valley. In addition to describing Cincinnati baseball games, Barber also did football games for the University of Cincinnati and Ohio State.

Five years later, in 1939, the "Ol Redhead" moved to Brooklyn to help usher in a new era in Brooklyn Dodgers baseball. As part of Larry MacPhail's grand plan to rejuvenate the Brooklyn franchise, Barber's broadcasts helped educate Brooklyn fans in the excitement and intricacies of the manly game of baseball. His rich southern drawl and mellifluous tones were in stark contrast to the harsher

Brooklynese utterances but, as in Cincinnati, his laid-back manner and quaint expressions captivated his audience.

In Barber-ese, when the Dodgers had a big lead, they were "in the catbird's seat." An argument on the field was a "rhubarb." A Dodger rally meant they were "tearin' up the peapatch." A home run was an "Old Goldie" after the cigarette company sponsor. And, when the bases were loaded with Dodgers, they were F.O.B., "full of Brooklyns." His colorful deliveries became part of Brooklyn lore, as was his exhuberant "Oh Doctor," when something extraordinary happened on the field.

"Red" Barber

Walter Lanier Barber became a Brooklyn institution over the years; as much a part of the city as the churches, the subways, or Ebbets Field. The "Ol Redhead" was not only a broadcaster; he was a student of the profession, a keen stickler for details. He spent several hours a day in the Dodger clubhouse, the front office, or the park, prior to the game, studying the little-known aspects of the game, and seeking out the accompanying human drama.

Barber was the Brooklyn Dodger announcer for 15 years, from 1939 through 1953. He became the most well known play-by-play announcer in baseball, one of the pioneers of the game. In addition to initiating radio broadcast in New York City, Barber broadcast the first major league night game, and broadcast the first major league telecast.

Red Barber visits Vin Scully in the Dodger broadcasting booth during the 1981 World Series.

The "Ol Redhead" left Brooklyn in 1954, moving uptown to Yankee Stadium. After 13 years as the sportscaster for the New York American League entry, Walter Lanier Barber packed his bag one last time, and returned to his native Florida, blowing one last kiss in the direction of Brooklyn before he departed.

Red Barber remained active in retirement, authoring six books, writing a newspaper column; even returning to his first love, radio, in 1981, to host a weekly sports show. His contributions to the game of baseball were rewarded in 1978, when he received the Ford J. Frick award for broadcasting, an honor that secured his place in baseball's Hall of Fame in Cooperstown, New York.

The Ol Redhead passed away on October 22, 1992 in Tallahassee, Florida, leaving behind a legion of mourn-

ers. He was 84 years old. The man from Mississippi and Florida was a true southern gentleman, friendly, easy going, and well spoken. It is doubtful that Red Barber ever had an enemy in the world. Hatred was not part of his vocabulary, a fact he realized in 1946 when Jackie Robinson first joined the Brooklyn organization. At first opposed to the idea of a black man playing baseball on the same field with whites, Barber's innate humanity surfaced and, as the years passed, the white Southerner and the black Californian became close friends.

Red Barber is gone, but his legacy lives on in people like Vin Scully and scores of other sportscasters, radio personalities, writers, and just average fans.

The "Voice of the Brooklyn Dodgers" is broadcasting from a new stadium today. Oh, Doctor!

CONNIE DESMOND

Red Barber joined the Brooklyn Dodgers in 1939 as their first radio sportscaster. He was joined in the booth four years later by Connie Desmond.

Desmond was born in Toledo, Ohio in 1909. After graduating from the University of Notre Dame in 1931, he joined radio station WSPD in Toledo, broadcasting Toledo Mud Hens baseball and Big Ten football. He also had a brief career as a crooner for big name bands in the early '30s, but eventually settled in as a full-time sportscaster.

The handsome Irishman moved to the big city in 1942, working as a radio play-by-play man for the Giants and Yankees. The following year he joined the Brooklyn Dodgers as the number two man in the broadcast booth. He immediately picked up a loyal following with a delivery that was soothing, comfortable, and pleasing to the ear.

Connie Desmond had the world on a string by the mid-forties. He was a handsome, thirty-something celebrity with a beautiful wife, two children—a boy and a girl—and a lovely home on Long Island Sound. He had it all. But personal demons kept gnawing at his insides, and eventually brought him crashing to earth.

Desmond was a member of the Brooklyn Dodger broadcast team from 1943 through 1954. He was present at the birth of the Boys of Summer and watched them grow into the most powerful juggernaut in National League history, but he left just before they captured their only World Championship in the City of Churches. He broadcast two losing league playoff series, in 1946 and 1951, and saw another pennant slip away on the last day of the 1950 season. On a brighter note, he cheered the Bums on to National League titles in 1947, '49, '52, and '53, covered no-hitters by Ed Head, Rex Barney, and Carl Erskine, watched Duke Snider and Roy Campanella blast three home runs in a game in 1950, and described Gil Hodges four–home run day against the Boston Braves the same year.

In 1954, Connie Desmond was promoted to the #1 man in the broadcast booth when Red Barber left. He was assisted by Vin Scully, who had joined the team in 1950. Scully always said that his training under Barber and Desmond shaped him into the broadcaster he became. Barber was like a father figure, and a stern taskmaster. He made sure Scully did his homework prior to each game, and he gave the youngster a scathing tongue lashing when the situation warranted. Desmond, the big brother, was always around to console Vin, and to make sure Vin's morale didn't suffer.

Tragically for Desmond, his personal demons got the best of him in 1954, and he was released by the Dodgers at the end of the season. He hung around New York for another six or eight years, but his career continued its downward spiral. He couldn't hold a job, his marriage ended in divorce, and his friends all drifted away. He finally moved back to Toledo in the sixties, did some sportscasting for station WSPD, and died a broken man in 1983.

Connie Desmond, decked out in the popular 1952 version of the Harry Truman Key West style sport shirt.

Connie Desmond was a genuinely good person who could not handle the celebrity world. As Red Barber said, "I never worked with a better person. . . . He had a warm personality, a warm, pleasant voice. He knew his business impeccably." Vin Scully added, "The thing he had better than almost anyone, he could chuckle on the air, and it came over so warm, that you could relate to it. . . . He had a remarkable flair."

Frank Gilhooly, a Toledo sportscaster who gave the eulogy at Desmond's funeral, summed it up when he said, "He was a super guy who goofed."

VIN SCULLY

If Red Barber was "The Voice of the Brooklyn Dodgers" then, without a doubt, Vin Scully will always be the "Voice of the Los Angeles Dodgers." In fact, when Angelino fans were asked to select the most memorable personality in L.A. baseball history, they overwhelmingly chose the handsome redhead over the likes of Sandy Koufax, Don Drysdale, Maury Wills, or Steve Garvey.

Vincent Scully was born and raised in New York City, attended Catholic schools, and graduated from Fordham University. As early as the eighth grade, he knew what he wanted to do in life; write about and broadcast sporting events. He was the sports editor on both his high school and college newspapers.

In 1949, the young Fordham graduate broadcast CBS football games with Brooklyn legend Red Barber. One year later, when the Dodgers were searching for a broadcaster to back up Barber and Connie Desmond in the Ebbets Field radio booth, the "Ol Redhead" recommended the 22-year-old Scully. After serving a three-year apprenticeship under the master, Vin Scully was named Brooklyn's number-one broadcaster. He has remained number one for more than 40 years.

The secret of Vin Scully's success lies in his smooth-flowing and descriptive delivery of the events taking place before him. Sportswriter Bud Furillo said of Scully, "Word pictures are the backbone of radio. Baseball's best photographer is Vin Scully."

He is often called a master of the English language. Like his predecessor, Red Barber, he is a low-key announcer, with an all-encompassing understanding of both events and language. He accompanied the Dodgers to Los Angeles in 1958, broadcasting the first major league game ever played in southern California. His knack for painting word pictures, and his finely timed delivery captured the imagination of the west coast fans, and helped to develop the immense market the Dodgers subsequently captured.

Vin Scully (Los Angeles Dodger Photo)

Over a period of 48 years, Scully has broadcast many historic baseball games, both regular season and post season. Included in his accomplishments are covering three perfect games, 18 no-hitters, Don Larsen's perfect game in the 1956 World Series, two 18-strikeout games by Sandy Koufax and one by Ramon Martinez, Brooklyn's historic 1955 World Championship, the 1963 World Series sweep of the New York Yankees, Kirk Gibson's dramatic home run in the 1988 fall classic, Hank Aaron's 715th home run, the shutout streaks of both Don Drysdale and Orel Hershiser, and Maury Wills successful season-long attack on Ty Cobb's stolen base record. He has broadcast a total of 12 World Series and six All-Star games.

Outside of baseball, the redheaded raconteur has broadcast National Football League games, as well as the PGA golf tour. Honors and awards gravitate to him like bees to honey. He has been named the outstanding sportscaster in the country four times, and the California sportscaster of the year 21 times. In 1987, he received the Ronald Reagan Media Award from the United States Sports Academy.

In 1982, Vin Scully joined his mentor, Red Barber, in Baseball's Hall of Fame. He also had his star placed on Hollywood's Walk of Fame the same year.

In 1997, he began his 51st year behind a Dodger microphone, sharing broadcasting duties with Rick Monday and Ross Porter.

Like good wine, Vin Scully gets better with age. And the hundreds of thousands of Los Angeles Dodger baseball fans are richer for having shared his experiences.

JERRY DOGGETT

Jerry Doggett was the unsung hero of the Dodger broadcast team for 32 years. A fixture in both Brooklyn and Los Angeles from 1956 through 1987, the friendly redhead provided outstanding baseball game coverage to Dodger fans all across the country. Unfortunately, he was always overshadowed by broadcast legend Vin Scully.

Jerry Doggett was born in Moberly, Missouri, on September 14, 1916. After attending Northwestern University for one year, the youngster spent a three-year hitch in the U.S. Navy, dividing his time between shore duty stations in Dallas, Houston, and Honolulu.

His first radio broadcasting job was with station KFRO in Longview, Texas, in 1938. Moving on to WRR in Dallas three years later, Doggett began a 15-year career as the play-by-play announcer for the Dallas Spurs of the Class AA Texas League. In addition to baseball, he also covered football, basketball, and ice hockey.

Broadening his horizons, Doggett teamed with Gordon McLendon to broadcast major league baseball games on the Liberty Broadcasting System for three years. He also did Western Union re-creations for the same network.

The Missouri native joined Vin Scully and Al Helfer on the Brooklyn Dodger radio-and-television broadcast team on Labor Day weekend in 1956, beginning a major league career that would witness more high drama than that provided by any other franchise in the history of American sports. Two weeks after he arrived in Brooklyn, Doggett worked Sal Maglie's pressure-packed 5-0 no-hitter against the Philadelphia Phillies in the heat of a pennant race. Over the years, the Missouri native covered them all; seven National League pennants, three World Championships, four Sandy Koufax no-hitters, including one perfect game, no-hitters by Bill Singer, Jerry Reuss, and John Candelaria, the infamous National League playoff with the San Francisco Giants, the memorable playoff victory over the Milwaukee Braves in 1959, and Dusty Baker's record-setting 30th home run in 1977.

He was there when Hank Aaron spanked his record-setting 715th career home run off Al Downing. He rooted for Don Drysdale when "Big D" ran up a string of 58 consecutive scoreless innings. He saw the birth of "The Infield," and the retirement of Sandy Koufax. Larry Sherry, Willie Davis, Tommy Davis, Frank Howard, Claude Osteen, Ron Perranoski, and Maury Wills were all part of the Doggett era, a golden era in Dodger history.

Jerry Doggett

Don Drysdale, Vin Scully, and Ross Porter. (Los Angeles Dodger Photo)

Throughout his fascinating baseball career, Jerry Doggett remained a devoted family man. He and his wife, Jodie, celebrated their golden wedding anniversary on April 13, 1990. The day after they were married in 1940, Jodie sat in the stands in Longview, Texas, watching her first baseball game as Jerry handled the broadcast duties. The affable redhead retired from the broadcast booth after the 1987 baseball season to spend more time at home, and to enjoy his daughter, Sandra, and his granddaughter Paige.

He also managed to find time to do a little fishing and play a few rounds of golf.

Jerry Doggett passed away on July 7, 1997. He was 80 years old.

The sports world will miss Jerry Doggett's colorful accounts of Los Angeles Dodgers baseball games. He was a true professional.

JAIME JARRIN

Former Brooklyn sportscaster Red Barber and Brooklyn and Los Angeles sportscaster Vin Scully are legends in the United States. Their names are familiar to baseball fans across the country, especially to Dodger fans of all ages. Both men are presently enshrined in the Baseball Hall of Fame in Cooperstown, New York for their unique presentations of major league baseball games.

Jaime Jarrin is also a Dodger sportscasting legend, and is also enshrined in Cooperstown. He is less well known by fans in the United States however, because he is the father of the Dodger Spanish broadcasts. His name is very well known to Hispanics from California to New York, as well as to the citizens of Mexico, Central and South America, and the Caribbean basin. On a purely numerical basis, Jaime Jarrin's name may be recognized by more people than either Red Barber or Vin Scully.

Jaime Jarrin (Jaime Jarrin)

ter the team's arrival from Brooklyn. Later, especially after the spectacular debut of Fernando Valenzuela in Los Angeles, he spread the good news to everyone in Latin America. Over the years, he has become a legend throughout the Spanish-speaking communities of the western hemisphere.

His pioneering efforts in broadcasting were finally rewarded on July 26, 1998 when he was inducted into the broadcasters wing of the Baseball Hall of Fame in Cooperstown, New York. The honor was, according to Jarrin ". . . unbelievable, fantastic, incredible. This is like winning the Nobel Prize, because there is nothing higher in my profession. . . . I feel like this is a dream."

Plaudits came from all corners of the Dodger baseball world, including former Los Angeles owner Peter O'Malley, who said, "Jaime deserves credit for introducing Dodger baseball to millions of fans throughout Southern California and Latin America." Vin Scully added, "He deserves to be *numero uno.*"

In addition to his Hall of Fame induction, Jaime Jarrin has received many other awards and honors over the years. In 1970, he became the first Latin American announcer to win a Golden Mike award, which he won again in 1971. In 1992, he received the government of Ecuador's highest medal, "La Orden Nacional al Merito en el Grado de Comendador". And, in 1998, he was awarded a star on the Hollywood Walk of Fame.

Also in 1998, the final touch was put on Jaime Jarrin's fantasy career: a street was named after him in Dodgertown, "Avenida Jaime Jarrin."

Jaime Jarrin was born in Quito, Ecuador, on December 10, 1935. After graduating from the Universidad Central of Ecuador in 1954, Jarrin emigrated to the United States in hopes of making a better life for himself and his family.

He began broadcasting Los Angeles Dodger baseball games, as "the Spanish voice of the Dodgers," for radio station KWKW 1330 AM, in Pasadena in 1959. Fourteen years later, he was employed by the Los Angeles Dodger Baseball Club as their #1 Spanish announcer. And, in 1989, he became Vice President, News and Sports, for Lotus Communications Corporation and Radio KWKW.

Jaime Jarrin literally brought Los Angeles Dodger baseball into the homes of the Hispanic community for the first time af-

Jaime Jarrin at the 1998 Dodgertown ceremony dedicating a street in his name. (W. McNeil)

ROSS PORTER

According to the Los Angeles Dodgers Media Guide, Ross Porter joined Vin Scully and Jerry Doggett on the Dodgers radio and television broadcast team in 1977. By that time, he was a true veteran of the broadcast world.

Porter always wanted to be a sportcaster and, in fact, did his first play-by-play broadcast when he was only 14 years old. The University of Oklahoma graduate subsequently spent ten years as a sportscaster for KNBC-TV in Los Angeles, doing nightly sports programs. And he won an Emmy for his efforts. He also broadcast National Football League games for seven years.

Over the past 21 years, the handsome Sooner has experienced more than his share of baseball thrills. He broadcast the 1977 and 1978 World Series on CBS Radio, over more than 600 stations worldwide. He covered the 1988 World Series for the Dodger flagship station KABC, and described the 1984 National League Championship Series for the CBS Radio network.

Ross Porter set a record for broadcast endurance when he covered the 22-inning game between the Dodgers and the Montreal Expos, single-handed. The August 23, 1989 game took six hours and 14 minutes to complete, and it is still the longest game ever broadcast by a single person. In recognition of his achievement, the Southern California Sports Broadcasters Association (SCSBA) presented him with a Special Achievement Award.

During the season, Porter is the host of KABC Dodgertalk pre-game and post-game shows. The show won him the 1992 Tom Harmon Award for Radio Sports Anchor, and the Radio Talk Show Host Award, both given by SCSBA.

The energetic announcer still keeps busy year round. In the fall, he broadcasts college football games, as well as doing the "Dodger Focus" show. He remains the only announcer to broadcast the games of a World Series Champion and an NCAA basketball champion, when he covered both the 1981 and '88 Dodgers and the 1990 University of Nevada at Las Vegas Runnin' Rebels.

In his spare time, he is one of the 24 judges of the Jim Thorpe Award, given annually to the top defensive back in college football.

Ross Porter, now in his 21st year as a Los Angeles Dodgers broadcaster, is hoping to broadcast another World Series from his home park.

RICK MONDAY

Rick Monday was an outstanding major league baseball player whose career spanned 19 years, including 8 years with the Los Angeles Dodgers. His playing career is covered in chapter 2, "Players Roll Call." During his last five years with the Dodgers, he prepared for his post baseball career by working for ABC-TV in the offseason.

Following his retirement as an active player in 1984, Monday began a broadcasting career on KTTV in Los Angeles, at the same time doing play-by-play of Dodger games on Dodger Vision and Z Channel. He was nominated for an Emmy in 1988 for his work on the Dodg-ers pre-game show, *Dodger Central*, on KTTV. He was also a color commentator for CBS TV at the College World Series championship game in 1988.

The next year, Monday moved to San Diego, and did play-by-play broadcasts for the Padres, on both radio and television. He also hosted *Padretalk* on KFMB.

The former outfielder joined the Dodger broadcast team in 1993, broadcasting Dodger games on radio and TV. Soon after, he began hosting *Dodgertalk* on KABC and KXTA, and serving as co-host for *The Dodger Dugout*, a pre-game show on KXTA. In 2001, Monday won an Emmy for his work on *Dodger Baseball*.

Over the years, the former Arizona State star has won a host of National Awards, including Patriotism Awards from the Fraternal Order of Police, the American Legion, the Pearl Harbor Survivors Association, the Boy Scouts of America, and the Military Order of Purple Hearts. In addition, he has received a Presidential Commendation from President Gerald R. Ford, for "Service to Others," and was the recipient of the 1st Humanitarian Award presented by Major League Baseball. He was also selected as West Coast Father of the Year.

Rick Monday shed his uniform for a sportscasters business suit in 1985. (Rick Monday)

CHAPTER 6
THE WORLD SERIES EXPERIENCE

BROOKLYN AND LOS ANGELES DODGERS
CHAMPIONSHIP TEAMS

YEAR	TEAM	LEAGUE	ACHIEVEMENT
	AMATEUR CHAMPIONSHIP TEAMS		
1858	BROOKLYN ALL STARS	IND.	LOST TO N.Y.A.S.
1864	BROOKLYN ATLANTICS	NABP	NATIONAL CHAMPIONS
1866	BROOKLYN ATLANTICS	NABP	NATIONAL CHAMPIONS
	MAJOR LEAGUE CHAMPIONSHIP TEAMS		
1889	BROOKLYN BRIDEGROOMS	AA	AA CHAMPIONS
1890	BROOKLYN BRIDEGROOMS	NL	NL CHAMPIONS
1899	BROOKLYN SUPERBAS	NL	NL CHAMPIONS
1900	BROOKLYN SUPERBAS	NL	NL CHAMPIONS
1916	BROOKLYN ROBINS	NL	NL CHAMPIONS
1920	BROOKLYN ROBINS	NL	NL CHAMPIONS
1941	BROOKLYN DODGERS	NL	NL CHAMPIONS
1947	BROOKLYN DODGERS	NL	NL CHAMPIONS
1949	BROOKLYN DODGERS	NL	NL CHAMPIONS
1952	BROOKLYN DODGERS	NL	NL CHAMPIONS
1953	BROOKLYN DODGERS	NL	NL CHAMPIONS
1955	BROOKLYN DODGERS	NL	WORLD CHAMPIONS
1956	BROOKLYN DODGERS	NL	NL CHAMPIONS
1959	LOS ANGELES DODGERS	NL	WORLD CHAMPIONS
1963	LOS ANGELES DODGERS	NL	WORLD CHAMPIONS
1965	LOS ANGELES DODGERS	NL	WORLD CHAMPIONS
1966	LOS ANGELES DODGERS	NL	NL CHAMPIONS
1974	LOS ANGELES DODGERS	NL	NL CHAMPIONS
1977	LOS ANGELES DODGERS	NL	NL CHAMPIONS
1978	LOS ANGELES DODGERS	NL	NL CHAMPIONS
1981	LOS ANGELES DODGERS	NL	WORLD CHAMPIONS
1988	LOS ANGELES DODGERS	NL	WORLD CHAMPIONS

SUMMARY

YEARS IN MAJOR LEAGUES	114
DIVISIONAL TITLES	26
LEAGUE TITLES	22
WORLD CHAMPIONSHIPS	6

THE FIRST WORLD SERIES—1858

The first World Series of baseball can be traced back to a challenge hurled at the baseball clubs of Hoboken and New York by their adversaries in Brooklyn during the spring of 1858. There was no love lost between Brooklyn's top teams; the Eckfords, Atlantics, Excelsiors, and Putnams, and the big city boys.

The New Yorkers quickly picked up the gauntlet, and selected an all-star team from the Knickerbockers, Gotham, Empire, Eagle, Harlem, and Union nines. The two groups agreed to a three-game series, to be held on a neutral field, the Fashion Race Course on Long Island. The games were scheduled to be played over a three-month period, one game each, in July, August, and September.

The first game was held on July 20, amid a genuine World Series atmosphere. Fans from both cities flocked to the ballpark decked out in their Sunday finery. The ferries from Manhattan were packed to the gunwales with exuberant New Yorkers. The Flushing Railroad had to add extra cars to their trains to accommodate the hordes of people headed for Long Island. Large, horse-drawn buses, decorated with colorful banners, flags, and streamers, converged on the Fashion Race Course from all directions. Even the respective baseball clubs arrived in style. The Excelsior club entered the grounds in a gaily decorated bus pulled by 14 smartly groomed horses with fancy feathered headresses.

By game time, 8,000 people had jammed the Course. The entire infield and outfield was ringed with private carriages as well-to-do spectators jockeyed for ringside seats. The play in Game One did justice to the championship billing of the series. The fielding and hitting were outstanding on both sides, as first one team then the other gained momentum. Great defensive plays abounded, yet the game was high scoring, as was the practice of the day. The Brooklyn All-Stars jumped to the lead in the first inning, scoring three quick runs. Second baseman Holder smashed the longest ball of the day, a home run to deep center field. They added two more runs in the second, and another pair in the third, for a 7-1 lead. After New York tied the game at 7-7, the Brooklyn nine moved out in front again, with four runs in the top of the fifth. Grum and P. O'Brien made fine running catches in the outfield to squelch New York rallies, and short fielder Pidgeon robbed several batters of base hits.

Soon however, the Flatbush fans fell silent as the boys from Hoboken and New York unleashed their big guns. A big fifth-inning uprising led by Hoyt, Van Cott, and Pinckney, netted the Gothams seven runs and a 14-11 lead. Middle fielder Davis frustrated two Brooklyn batters with fine running catches, while the tight infield play of Wadsworth and Bixby helped to protect the lead. In the eighth, Brooklyn came back one more time, scoring four runs to recapture the lead, 18-17. But pitcher Mickey O'Brien couldn't hold New York in check. Wadsworth, Hoyt, Van Cott, Pinckney, and Benson, all scored in a big five-run eighth-inning surge. Pitcher Van Cott dug in and blanked the Brooklyn All-Stars in the ninth to protect the thrilling 22-18 victory.

Brooklyn All-Stars	3 2 2 0 4 2 1 4 0 - 18
Hoboken-New York All-Stars	0 1 2 4 7 2 1 5 0 - 22

The Brooklyn All-Stars, not discouraged by the defeat, bounced back to rout their adversaries from across the East River in Game Two on August 17. The score was 29-8. It was a pleasant day for a game, as the hot morning sun disappeared behind a comfortable cloud cover by game time. Occasional sprinkles refreshened the afternoon air. The Brooklyn nine, led by Pinckney, who drove in the first run with a long drive to right field, came out of the blocks with a six-run first inning, and were never headed. Right fielder Grum, of the Eckford club, was unstoppable for Brooklyn. He was retired only once all day, and scored six runs in an impressive offensive display. Pidgeon, who had played such a fine game at short field in Game One, handled the pitching duties for the Brooklyn All-Stars in Game Two, and stifled the New York offense much of the game. Only short fielder Gelston proved a puzzle for Pidgeon, who kept the rest of the high-powered sluggers off the bases.

Brooklyn All-Stars	6 0 5 6 2 3 4 2 1 - 29
Hoboken-New York All-Stars	2 0 1 0 0 0 1 0 4 - 8

The rubber game took place on September 10, in a frenzied environment of championship dimensions. Five thousand rabid fans, mostly men, attended the game. It was the first baseball game to receive front page coverage in the *New York Times*, illustrating the importance of the event. Pidgeon, from the Eckford club, once again took the mound for Brooklyn, while New York countered with Thorn, ace pitcher for the Empire nine. A two-run outburst by Brooklyn in the first, sent their fans into a wild demonstration. The advantage was quickly lost, however, as New York bounced back with seven runs in the same inning. Pidgeon was treated roughly by the Gotham hitters, as Gelston, Benson, and Thorn all tore into his offerings with gusto. The Flatbush team closed to within 7-4 in the fourth, but could get no closer, as the New York bats continued their cannonading. The Manhattanites scored in every inning after the third, en route to a convincing 29-18 victory, and the World Championship.

Brooklyn All-Stars	2 0 0 2 0 2 4 4 4 - 18
Hoboken-New York All-Stars	7 0 0 3 3 2 5 3 6 - 29

This series established a pattern of New York dominance over Brooklyn teams that would last for 97 years. Johnny Podres finally put the ghost to rest once and for all, on a comfortable October day in 1955.

BROOKLYN BRIDEGROOMS (AA) V.S. THE NEW YORK GIANTS (NL)–1889

The mighty New York Giants captured the National League title by one game over the Boston Beaneaters. The Giants were a team of big men, led by 6'3" Roger Connor and 6'2" Mike Slattery. One day, as the team was leaving the field following another Giant victory, an ecstatic Giant manager, Jim Mutrie, was heard to remark, "They're my boys–my giants." The name stuck.

The 1889 team had five future Hall of Famers on the roster; catcher Buck Ewing, perhaps the greatest all-around player of the nineteenth century, slugging first baseman Roger Connor, the all-time home run leader with 137 until Babe Ruth and the lively ball came along, outfielder "Orator Jim" O'Rourke, a lifetime .310 hitter, pitcher "Smiling Mickey" Welch, winner of 307 career victories, and pitcher Tim Keefe, who won 342 games over a 14-year period.

Keefe, the ace of Jim Mutrie's staff with a 28-13 record, had pitched 364 innings during the season and, like his teammate Mickey Welch, was worn out by the time the Series started. Ironically, he and Welch started only one game each in the postseason classic. The shrewd Mutrie relied on the fresh arms of Ed Crane and Hank O'Dea to quiet the Brooklyn bats.

The Giants' opponent, the Brooklyn Bridegrooms, had captured the American Association championship in a close race with St. Louis, slipping past the Browns by two games. Thomas "Oyster" Burns led the Brooklyn hitters during the season with a .304 average. Darby O'Brien and William "Adonis" Terry, both at an even .300, were close behind. On the hill, "Parisian Bob" Caruthers, the diminutive right hander, carried a dazzling 40-11 record into the World Series. "Adonis" Terry was at 22-15, while Tom Lovett won 17 games against 10 losses.

The New York oddsmakers had installed the Giants as overwhelming 3-1 favorites. Although Brooklyn's record was much better than the Giants, the caliber of play in the American Association was suspect. In Game One, at least, Mutrie's boys took the opposition too lightly. The fired-up Bridegrooms jumped on ace right hander Tim Keefe for five big runs in their first at bat. The Polo Grounds fell deathly silent as 8,445 Giant rooters looked on in disbelief. According to the *New York Times*, the feelings between the two towns was heated even at this early date. "The rivalry between New York and Brooklyn, as regards baseball, is unparalleled in the history of the national game ... old men, middle aged men, beardless youths, small boys, and even members of the gentler sex, have the fever, and when the champions of the two teams meet, heated arguments ... are sure to follow."

New York fought back to gain the lead from McGunnigle's crew with a five-run outburst in the seventh, but Brooklyn would not be denied. Trailing 10-8, the Grooms pounded Keefe's changeup for four runs in the bottom of the eighth to snatch victory from certain defeat. The game was called on account of darkness at the end of the eighth. The *Times* reporter chastised the behavior of the Brooklyn rooting section, claiming the Brooklyn minority "shouted, cheered, hissed, yelled, stamped their feet, clapped their hands, and acted as only baseball 'cranks' can."

Hub Collins' second-inning home run sparked the Groom attack.

New York Giants	0 2 0 2 1 0 5 0	- 10	- 11 - 3
Brooklyn Bridegrooms	5 1 0 0 0 0 2 4	- 12	- 14 -6

Reality settled in for New York after Game One, and the Giants viewed the Brooklyn club with a new respect. Edward "Cannonball" Crane faced the Bridegrooms in game two before a capacity crowd of 16,000 at the Polo Grounds. The frenzied Giant fans overflowed onto the field and formed a ring around the outfield. The 204-pound Crane, responding to the partisan crowd, pitched like a man possessed. His fast ball exploded across the plate, and his roundhouse curve had the Brooklyn batters beating the ball into the dirt all day. Second baseman Danny Richardson's 14 assists were visible proof of Crane's effectiveness.

The Giants drew first blood, with a nifty squeeze bunt by Buck Ewing plating George Gore in the first inning. Gore scored, what turned out to be the game winner, in the third, when he singled, stole second, and came home on an error by shortstop Germany Smith.

Brooklyn Bridegrooms	1 1 0 0 0 0 0 0 0	- 2	- 4 -8
New York Giants	1 1 1 1 2 0 0 0 0	- 6	- 9 - 4

Bill McGunnigle managed the Brooklyn Bridegrooms for three years, winning two pennants, and finishing second once.

There was no World Series game on Sunday, but the Bridegrooms played anyway. They defeated the Baltimore Orioles in an exhibition game at Ridgewood Park, 6-2. Right hander Tom Lovett was the winning pitcher, hurling a three-hitter.

Having drawn even at one game apiece, the old cockiness returned, and the New Yorkers began to strut like peacocks again. Captain Buck Ewing was quoted as saying, "It's a hundred dollars to a toothpick we win today." Several hours later, Ewing had to eat his remark.

A couple of "Micks" squared off in Game Three; "Smiling Mickey" Welch for the Giants, and Mickey Hughes for the Grooms. Neither of the "Micks" was around at the finish, however, as it turned out to be a hitter's day. "Smiling Mickey," whose repertoire included a curveball, change of pace, and screwball, was pounded ruthlessly by the Brooklyn hitters, lasting only five innings.

The Grooms, leading 8-7, and hoping that darkness would end the game, stalled at every opportunity. They still clung tenaciously to the lead as the ninth inning began. With the sun setting rapidly in the west and a Giant rally underway, the tension mounted. Finally, with one out and the bases loaded, the umpires moved in and signalled an end to the proceedings. The Giants were furious, particularly Captain Buck Ewing, who threatened to pull his team off the field if the umpires showed any further favoritism toward the Brooklyn club. The *New York Times* would only say, "The players from the other side of the bridge made the haughty Giants lower their colors once more."

New York Giants	2 0 0 0 3 2 0 0 - 7 - 15 - 5
Brooklyn Bridegrooms	0 2 3 1 2 0 0 0 - 8 - 11 - 3

Brooklyn was on a roll now, and they had the mighty New Yorkers on the defensive. Game Four saw William "Adonis" Terry on the hill for McGunnigle's crew, facing tough "Cannonball" Crane. But this time Crane was ineffective. Unable to grip the ball properly in the chilly air, Crane was hammered early and often by the Association champions. His teammates also let him down by playing an atrocious game in the field. They piled up more errors than hits, making 10 miscues while hitting safely only nine times.

The Bridegrooms took an early 7-2 lead, but Mutrie's boys tied the game with a five-run rally in the top of the sixth. The setting sun was nearing the horizon as Brooklyn came to bat for the last time, in the bottom of the inning. The Grooms quickly put two runners on base, and clutch-hitting "Oyster" Burns stepped to the plate. The squat 185-pounder got all his weight into a Crane fastball, and drove it on a high arc to left field. Jim O'Rourke was unable to see the ball in the twilight, and all three runners circled the bases. The umpires immediately stopped the contest, with Brooklyn on top, 10-7.

New York Giants	0 0 1 1 0 5 - 7 - 9 - 10
Brooklyn Bridegrooms	2 0 2 0 3 3 - 10 - 7 - 1

Brooklyn now had a commanding lead in the Series, 3 games to 1, and it looked like a major upset was in the making. But the Giants were made of sterner stuff. Mutrie's boys may have been cocky, but they had an excess of talent, and more than their share of character.

Dave Foutz, a former star pitcher with the St. Louis Browns, was a slugging first baseman with the American Association champions. His 113 RBIs paced the team.

Three thousand Bridegroom fans paid their way into Washington Park, hoping to see their boys put another nail in the New York coffin. Instead they witnessed an impressive display of both hitting and pitching on the part of the fired-up Giants.

"Cannonball" Crane, back for his third shot at the Bridegrooms, tossed a seven-hitter and frustrated Brooklyn hitters all day with his heavy fastball and roundhouse curve. New York batters had no such problem. They found Bob Caruthers' deliveries much to their liking, and dispatched them to various parts of the outfield with lightning-like speed. When it was all over, the New York wrecking crew had completely destroyed the pride of Brooklyn, to the tune of 11-3. The Grooms slunk home to lick their wounds, hoping that tomorrow would be a better day.

New York Giants	0 0 4 0 4 0 0 2 1 - 11 - 12 - 3
Brooklyn Bridegroom	0 0 0 1 1 1 0 0 0 - 3 - 7 - 2

The Giants had the adrenalin flowing now, and they turned up the intensity another notch. For the rest of the Series, the fans witnessed the real New York team, "Mutrie's Giants." They were a sight to behold. And to admire.

Manager Bill McGunnigle selected William "Adonis" Terry to stem the surging New York tide in Game Six, hoping to protect the Brooklyn lead. His opponent, Hank O'Dea, was a journeyman right hander, obtained late in the season to help out in the pennant drive. It was a masterful move as O'Dea won nine games in 10 decisions down the stretch, and was now poised to make a major contribution to an impending New York Giant World Championship.

Game Six was the first real pitching duel of the Series, as both O'Day and Terry were at their best. Terry entered the ninth inning protecting a slim 1-0 lead, but a two-out error by shortstop Jim Davis allowed the tying run to score. The Giants scored the winning run in the 11th, when Mike Slattery raced home from second on an infield out.

Brooklyn Bridegrooms 0 1 0 000 000 00 - 1 - 6 - 4
New York Giants   000 000 001 01 - 2 - 6 - 1

Brooklyn desperately needed a lift. They hoped that Tom Lovett would give it to them. But Lovett was not up to the task. New York raked him for nine runs in two innings, en route to an 11-7 triumph. "Cannonball" Crane and Tim Keefe throttled McGunnigle's boys on five hits, as the Giants swept to their third consecutive win, and their first lead in the Series, four games to three.

Brooklyn Bridegrooms 0 0 4 030 000 - 7 - 5 - 2
New York Giants   1 8 0 001 10x - 11 - 15 - 3

The Series was now beginning to resemble a snowball rolling downhill. With each succeeding victory, the Giants' confidence grew, and the momentum became increasingly more difficult to stop.

"Adonis" Terry was back on the hill for the Grooms in Game Eight, his fourth start of the Series. He had won his first two starts, before losing the 11-inning heartbreaker to Hank O'Dea, in Game Six. This time, however, he didn't have it, lasting only four innings. By the time he departed, Mutrie's sluggers had combed him for 12 runs, while building up an insurmountable 12-2 lead.

Big Roger Connor, the Giant first baseman, led the New York hit parade with three hits, including a triple. Mike Tiernan added a home run for New York, as they rolled to a convincing 16-7 win.

New York Giants   5 4 1 203 001 - 16 - 15 - 4
Brooklyn Bridegrooms 2 0 0 000 023 - 7 - 5 - 4

Brooklyn was down to its last gasp. They needed a miracle to get them back into the Series, trailing five games

to three. But miracles are hard to come by on cold October afternoons when the bones are tired and the arms are weak. Gutty little "Adonis" Terry volunteered to try to stem the tide one more time, his fifth start of the Series.

Terry gave it his all, matching Hank O'Dea pitch for pitch for six innings. In the seventh inning, with the score tied 2-2, Terry's luck once again deserted him. With a Giant runner on third and two out, the Brooklyn right hander struck out the final batter. Or did he? In a scene reminis-

Monte Ward, the New York Giant team captain, batted .417 for the series, and stole 10 bases in nine games. He later managed the Bridegrooms in 1891 and '92.

cent of the Mickey Owen incident, the third strike eluded catcher Doc Bushong and rolled to the backstop, allowing the tie-breaking run to score.

That run turned out to be the game winner, as Hank O'Dea slammed the door in Brooklyn's faces at every juncture. The Giants, deservedly, were the World Champions, coming back from a three-game-to-one deficit, to win the Series six games to three. For their part, the Bridegrooms deserved a better fate. If it had not been for the critical error by Davis in the ninth inning of Game Six, and by Bushong in Game Seven, McGunnigle's team might still be in the driver's seat. But such is fate.

Brooklyn Bridegrooms 2 0 0 000 000 - 2 - 4 - 2
New York Giants   1 0 0 001 10x - 3 - 8 - 4

BROOKLYN BRIDEGROOMS (NL) V.S. LOUISVILLE CYCLONES (AA)—1890

Brooklyn's debut in the National League got off to an ignominious start on April 19, when they were beaten by the Boston Beaneaters at South End Grounds in Boston, 15-9. Fortunately for the former American Association champions, the opening game was not indicative of things to come. Determined to prove their Association title was no fluke, the Bridegrooms soon battled their way into contention in the National League pennant chase. They swept past the Cincinnati Reds on July 11 to move into first place, and went on to capture the pennant by a solid six games over Cap Anson's Chicago White Sox.

Individually the season had many highlights. On the mound, the 5'7", 138-pound Caruthers finished with a fine 23-11 record. He was surpassed however, by "Adonis" Terry at 23-6, and Tom Lovett at 30-11.

Hub Collins, an outstanding second baseman, led the National League in runs scored with 148, and finished second in stolen bases with 85, third in doubles with 32, and fourth in bases on balls with 85. Tragically, his death in 1892, at the age of 28, snuffed out a promising career.

Right fielder Thomas "Oyster" Burns topped the league in runs-batted-in with 128. Burns, a stocky 5'8" outfielder, was a line-drive hitter who was adept at hitting the ball in the alleys for extra bases.

The league-leading Brooklyn attack was led by outfielder Darby O'Brien (.314), third baseman George Pinckney (.309), and first baseman Dave Foutz (.303).

The Bridegrooms opponent in the World Series was the Louisville Cyclones, winners of the American Association pennant. With Brooklyn out of the league, the Cyclones dominated the pennant race. They jumped out front quickly and romped to the title, finishing a whopping ten games ahead of the Columbus Colts.

The Cyclones had big guns of their own. Outfielder William Van Winkle "Chicken" Wolf led the league in batting with an average of .363. Pitcher Scott Stratton hit a robust .323, and first baseman Harry Taylor followed at .306. On the hill, Stratton finished at 34-14, and Red Ehret won 25 games against only 14 losses.

The World Series opened in the Louisville's Eclipse Park on October 17. Brooklyn led off with 26 game winner William "Adonis" Terry. Manager Jack Chapman countered with his ace, 34-game winner, Scott Stratton. The 21-year-old Stratton, suffering from opening game jitters, was rocked by three Brooklyn runs in the first inning. The Grooms added three more runs in the fifth, and closed out the scoring with another trio of runs in the seventh.

Terry meanwhile, had the Cyclones eating out of the palm of his hand. His sharp breaking curveball kept the hitters off stride all day, and the Bridegrooms won easily, 9-0, much to the dismay of the 5,563 home town spectators. The game was halted after eight innings because of darkness.

Brooklyn Bridegrooms	3 0 0 0 3 0 3 0	- 9 - 11 - 1
Louisville Cyclones	0 0 0 0 0 0 0 0	- 0 - 2 - 6

The Brooklyn Bridegrooms won the National League pennant their first year in the league.

Top row, L to R. Germany Smith, Pop Corkhill, Adonis Terry, Dave Foutz, Darby O'Brien, Doc Bushong, and Joe Visner. Front row, George Pinckney, Bob Caruthers, Hub Collins, Bill McGunnigle, Oyster Burns, Boileryard Clark, and Tom Lovett. Seated front, Mickey Hughes.

Oyster Burns was Brooklyn's top gun for seven years. Over that period, he hit .303 and averaged 13 triples, seven home runs, and 106 runs batted in a year.(Transcendental Graphics)

In Game Two, Brooklyn ace Tom Lovett (30-11) bested Ed Daily (6-3) by a score of 5-3. Daily pitched well enough to win most games, but his teammates let him down with shoddy defense. According to the *New York Times*, third baseman Harry Raymond played a "wretched" game, and was solely responsible for the Cyclone's loss. Another good crowd of 5,800 sat in stunned silence as their beloved team fell behind 2-0 in the Series.

Brooklyn Bridegrooms	0 2 0 2 0 1 0 0 0 - 5 - 9 - 3
Louisville Cyclones	1 0 1 0 0 0 0 0 1 - 3 - 6 - 5

To the Cyclone's credit, they did not roll over and play dead after two straight losses in their home park to the National League Champions. The third game was a thriller from start to finish. "Adonis" Terry and Scott Stratton were hit freely during the contest as, first one team, then the other, unlimbered their big guns. Brooklyn scored early and often. Two runs in the second, grew to a 6-1 lead at the halfway point, but Jack Chapman's crew dug in and held their ground from then on. Their valiant stand was the turning point of the Series.

The 6', 180-pound Stratton settled down and contained the Grooms after the fifth inning. His teammates

meanwhile, pounded Terry from pillar to post. A single run in the fifth, and two more in the sixth closed the margin to 6-4. Then, after Brooklyn made it 7-4 in the top of the eighth, Louisville roared back with three runs to tie the game, as darkness fell. The tying run scored on a passed ball as the visibility was down to nothing. The umpires wisely called it quits at the end of the inning, and both teams went to the clubhouse unhappy, with a 7-7 tie.

Brooklyn Bridegrooms	0 2 0 1 3 0 1 0 - 7 - 10 - 2
Louisville Cyclones	0 0 1 0 1 2 0 3 - 7 - 11 - 3

Game Four, still in Louisville, gave the fans something to cheer about for the first time. With a sparse crowd of 1,000 people looking on, 22-year-old Philip Sidney "Red" Ehret pitched the Cyclones to their first victory, 5-4. The tall, sandy-haired right hander, winner of 25 games during the season, blanked McGunnigle's boys over the last six innings, and the Cyclones broke a 4-all tie with a single run in the seventh, to win.

Brooklyn Bridegrooms	0 3 1 0 0 0 0 0 0 - 4 - 7 - 2
Louisville Cyclones	3 0 1 0 0 0 1 0 x - 5 - 9 - 2

Dave Foutz, shown pitching, was one of the premier pitchers in the National League early in his career. By 1890,however, his arm was gone, and he had become a slugging first baseman. That year, he hit .303 with 98 RBIs.(Transcendental Graphics)

After playing four games in Louisville, the Series moved to Washington Park on October 25. Brooklyn ace, Tom Lovett, pitching before 1,000 chilled diehards, on a raw fall afternoon, threw a five-hitter at Jack Chapman's team. The Grooms, meanwhile, treated Ed Daily like a long-lost brother. With one out in the first inning, little "Oyster" Burns smashed a screaming line drive to right field for a two-run homer. A wild demonstration followed, and Burns was forced to take several curtain calls before the game could continue.

First baseman Dave Foutz hit a two-run triple in the fourth to extend the lead to 5-1. Catcher Tom Daly chipped in with two doubles, as the Bridegrooms made the most of their seven hits.

```
Louisville Cyclones      0 1 0  0 1 0  0 0 0 - 2 - 5 - 6
Brooklyn Bridegrooms     2 1 0  2 0 0  2 0 x - 7 - 7 - 0
```

Brooklyn now led the Series three to one, with one tie. But once again, the never-say-die Cyclones dug in. Facing "Adonis" Terry on a raw, windy, fall afternoon before a scant 300 huddled spectators, the Louisville batters pecked away inning after inning, opening up a 5-1 lead at the halfway point. After watching Brooklyn tie the score with four runs off Stratton in the bottom of the sixth, Jack Chapman's boys hung Terry out to dry in the seventh and eighth, scoring two runs in each inning, for a 9-5 lead. They fought off a late Brooklyn rally to win, 9-8.

One note of interest from the game report. The Louisville catcher, was fined $25.00 for making obscene remarks to the umpire.

```
Louisville Cyclones      0 1 2  1 0 1  2 2 0 - 9 - 13 - 3
Brooklyn Bridegrooms     1 0 0  0 0 4  0 3 0 - 8 - 12 - 3
```

Game Seven, and the final game of the Series, took place in Washington Park on Tuesday, October 28. Once again, the weather was miserably cold, raw, and windy, more suited to football than baseball. Red Ehret faced Tom Lovett for the second time, and for the second time, he came away a winner.

Lovett could not control his curve ball in the 50-degree weather, and the Louisville hitters smashed his offerings to all corners of the ballpark. Red Ehret was touched up for two runs in the first inning, then settled down and pitched shutout ball the rest of the way. The Cyclones won the game handily, 6-2, to tie the Series at three games all.

```
Louisville Cyclones      1 0 3  0 0 0  0 2 0 - 6 - 8 - 3
Brooklyn Bridegrooms     2 0 0  0 0 0  0 0 0 - 2 - 4 - 1
```

The remainder of the Series was cancelled with the agreement of both teams. The wintry weather held the crowds down to a few hundred fans, and made it difficult for the teams to play up to their capabilities.

It was a disappointing finish for the Bridegrooms who had jumped out to an early 2-0 lead in games, and led 3-1 at one point. Lovett and Ehret won two games each for their respective clubs. The leading hitters were Patsy Donovan (.471) for the Bridegrooms, and "Chicken" Wolf (.360) for the Cyclones.

BROOKLYN SUPERBAS–
NATIONAL LEAGUE CHAMPIONS–1899

Fate smiled on the Brooklyn National League team during the winter of 1898-99. Coming off a dismal 10th-place finish in 1898, the Bridegrooms had little to look forward to the next year. Until, that is, a wealthy brewery owner named Harry Von der Horst, happened on the scene. Von der Horst was also the owner of the Baltimore Orioles, one of the most successful franchises in the National League. Under fire by creditors in Baltimore, and

Ned Hanlon won pennants his first two years at the helm of the Brooklyn team, in 1899 and 1900. He managed the team five more years without another pennant. Player defections to the new American League decimated his team.

fearing the loss of his star players, Von der Horst obtained controlling interest in the Brooklyn team, and immediately transferred several members of the Baltimore club to Flatbush.

Leading the way was manager Ned Hanlon. He was joined by "Wee Willie" Keeler, a .379 hitter in Baltimore, Joe Kelley who batted .328 the previous year, Hughie

Jennings (.328), and pitchers Jim Hughes (23-12), and Doc McJames (27-15). When combined with Brooklyn veterans Fielder Jones (.302), Brickyard Kennedy (16-21), Jack Dunn (16-21), and new shortstop Bill Dahlen, obtained from Chicago, they gave Brooklyn an immediate pennant contender.

Enthusiasm was at a fever pitch in the "City of Churches" as the season got underway. After an opening day loss, the team, now known as the Superbas, corraled its first victory of the season, defeating the Boston Beaneaters, 4-1, behind the four-hit pitching of Jack Dunn. More than 5,000 excited fans turned out to view Brooklyn's new "Baltimore" look. Dunn won his own game with a two-out, bases-loaded single in the second inning. Bill Dahlen sparkled in the field for Hanlon's charges, handling eight chances flawlessly, some of them very difficult plays.

Second baseman Tom "Tido" Daly was a threat, both offensively and defensively. He led all second baseman in double plays and total chances per game, while hitting .313 with 88 RBIs.

The Superbas soon asserted control in the National League pennant race, and took over the undisputed lead on May 22. They clung to the lead for the rest of the season, fighting off challenges from the St. Louis Cardinals and Boston Beaneaters along the way.

As the season wound down, the Brooklyn lead hovered between six and eight games. The final game of the season, at Washington Park, ended in a violent dispute. Jimmy Sheckard, Baltimore outfielder, was ejected from the game after accosting umpire Hunt after a play at second base. When Sheckard refused to leave the field, and was supported by Oriole manager John McGraw, the game was forfeited to Brooklyn, 1-0, giving Hanlon's team its 100th victory in a most unusual way.

Following the forfeiture, a makeup game was played. Despite Baltimore's constant attempts to delay the game until dark, the necessary five innings were played, with Brooklyn winning, 8-3. Once again Brooklyn bats spoke loud and clear, as they peppered Baltimore pitching for 10 hits in five innings. Keeler, Daly, and Zeke Wrigley, chipped in with two hits each as Brickyard Kennedy coasted to the victory.

The fine Brooklyn Superba team, thanks to the generous influx of talent from Baltimore, made one of the greatest turnarounds in major league history. Coming off a dreadful 54-91 record in 1898, Ned Hanlon's team won 101 games against only 47 losses, a flip-flop of 45 1/2 games! They won the pennant by a convincing eight games over the Boston Beaneaters.

Offensively and defensively, the Superbas were devastating. They had four .300 hitters–Wille Keeler (.377), Joe Kelley (.330), Deacon McGuire (.318), and Tom Daly (.313). Four other players batted over .280. On the mound, Brooklyn had four solid starters; Jim Hughes (28-6), Jack Dunn (28-13), Brickyard Kennedy (22-8), and Doc McJames (19-15).

There was no World Series after the 1899 season. The American Association had disbanded after the 1891 season, and the Temple Cup Series, which matched the first and second place teams in a Championship Series beginning in 1894, ended in 1897. The American League was still two years away from reality.

All things considered, the Brooklyn Superbas of 1899, were an outstanding baseball team. Blessed with a wealth of talent, both at the bat, on the mound, and in the field, they had no visible weakness. World Series or no, they were, without a doubt, World Champions.

BROOKLYN SUPERBAS V.S. THE PITTSBURGH PIRATES–1900

The Brooklyn Superbas were beset with pitching problems as the 1900 season got underway. They lost three of their top four starting pitchers. Jack Dunn lost his effectiveness, winning only three games before being traded to Philadelphia in mid season. Jim Hughes sat out the season in a salary dispute. And Doc McJames retired to practice medicine. It was a far cry from 1899 when the trio won 70 games between them, including McJames league leading 28.

Only Brickyard Kennedy and his 22 victories remained from the pennant-winning crew of 1899. The future looked bleak for Hanlon's boys as the new season approached. Fortunately, owner Chris Von der Horst came to the rescue. He was able to obtain two world-class pitchers from Baltimore when the Orioles dropped out of the league. Joe "Iron Man" McGinnity (28-17), and Frank Kitson (22-16), gave the Superbas the depth they needed to defend their crown in the tough National League.

Bill Dahlen at shortstop, anchored the Brooklyn defense from 1899 through 1903. "Bad Bill" enjoyed a notable 21-year playing career. He later managed Brooklyn from 1910 through 1913.

The Superbas were blessed with a devastating offensive attack and, although the pitching did not match up to that of the 1899 staff, finishing sixth in the league, the Brooklyn entry still proved to be the cream of the crop. Willie Keeler led the Flatbush hit parade with a sizzling .368 average. He was followed by Joe Kelley (.319), Tom Daly (.312), Fielder Jones (.309), and Jimmy Sheckard (.300). The secret of the Superbas success was balance. There were no soft spots in the lineup. From top to bottom, each man was dangerous, and each could knock in a game winner. Seven men batted in over 50 runs, with Joe Kelley's 91 leading the way.

On the hill, Joe McGinnity dominated the league with a record of 29-9 and an ERA of 2.90. His cohorts, blessed with explosive bat support, survived with respectable pitching records in spite of sub par earned run averages. Brickyard Kennedy won 20 games against 13 losses, while Frank Kitson finished at 15-13.

The Pittsburgh Pirates, behind Honus Wagner's league-leading .381 batting average and 100 RBIs, and 20-victory seasons from Jesse Tannehill and Deacon Philippe, fought the Superbas tooth and nail. The Philadelphia Phillies also made a race of it, behind hitters like Nap Lajoie (.337), and "Big Ed" Delahanty (.323), and a well-balanced, deep pitching staff.

When the smoke had cleared at season's end, the pride of Flatbush had outlasted their worthy opponents, finishing 4 1/2 games ahead of Fred Clarke's Pirates, and 8 games ahead of the Phils. The Pittsburgh team was poised on the brink of greatness, and would capture the National League crown the next three years, 1901-1903. But in 1900, the best they could do was second place.

It had become habit over the previous decade, for the second place team to challenge the pennant winner to a playoff at the conclusion of the regular season; the objective being to determine a world champion. The Temple Cup Series, played from 1894 to 1897, was such a challenge. After a two-year hiatus, the *Pittsburgh Chronicle-Telegraph* donated a silver cup for a "World Championship" series, to prove that their beloved Pirates were the number-one team in the world. Von der Horst's cohorts quickly picked up the gauntlet, and the battle was on.

All games were played in Pittsburgh, where the series originated. Honus Wagner, considered by many experts to be the greatest shortstop in the history of the game, still had not found his permanent position at this time. He spent his first five years in the league alternating between first base, second base, third base, and the outfield. In this series, he patrolled right field. The next year, he would move to shortstop, where he would remain a fixture for 16 years.

Game One, at Exposition Park, matched Rube Waddell against the "Iron Man", Joe McGinnity, as the pitching rich Pittsburgh Pirates tried to defuse the dynamite Brooklyn slugging machine. Waddell, who was one of the premier southpaws in major league annals, had not yet reached his peak in 1900. In only his third major league season, the eccentric Waddell had posted a mediocre 8-13 record for the second place Pirates. The following year, Waddell would jump to the new American League, where he would achieve greatness with the Philadelphia Athletics.

The opener was a typical Superbas victory. The cunning McGinnity kept the Pirates off balance the entire game, with his various assortment of curves and change of speeds. Ned Hanlon's boys, on the other hand, jumped on the 24-year-old Waddell early with their usual balanced

"Iron Man" Joe McGinnity, shown here in a Newark uniform in 1909, played professional baseball for 33 years, 11 of them in the majors. He won 247 major league games, to go along with 235 victories in the minors. He pitched his last game, for Dubuque, IA, in 1925, at the age of 54.

attack. Six hits rattled off Brooklyn bats in the third inning and, when the dust had settled, the Superbas were comfortably in front, 3-0. They added single runs in the fourth and sixth to extend their lead to 5-0, quieting the 4,000 Pirate fans in attendance.

McGinnity, meanwhile, was rolling along with a three-hit shutout. An incident in the eighth-inning however, brought the Brooklyn bench to its feet, as their star pitcher came close to being incapacitated. Pirate hurler Rube Waddell was caught in a rundown between third base and home, with Joe McGinnity in the middle of the action. As McGinnity lunged at the elusive Waddell, he fell against Waddell's knee, knocking himself unconscious. The sight of their star pitcher laying motionless along the third base line sent chills up the backs of the Brooklyn players. Fortunately, after some first aid and a brief rest, McGinnity was able to resume his duties.

In the ninth inning, still shaken from his ordeal, the "Iron Man" was touched up for two runs on a walk, a hit batter, and a pair of singles. He finished the game, however, coming away an easy 5-2 winner. True to form, the 13 Brooklyn hits were divided among all nine players, with Deacon McGuire, Bill Dahlen, Fielder Jones, and Willie Keeler picking up two each.

```
Brooklyn Superbas    003 101 000 - 5 - 13 - 1
Pittsburgh Pirates   000 000 002 - 2 - 5 - 4
```

Game Two matched a pair of 15-game winners, righthanders Sam Leever and Frank Kitson. The crowd was small, with only 1,800 fans braving the blustery autumn weather. For Leever, who stands #24 on the all-time earned run average list, with a lifetime ERA of 2.47, it was an agonizing day. His teammates kicked the ball around the infield in a manner most unbecoming a championship team. Nine errors were charged to the erratic Pirate defense, including four by third baseman Jimmy Williams, whose wild throws kept the first base fans on their toes all afternoon.

Hanlon's charges scored the first run of the game in the second inning on a walk, and one of William's patented tosses. After Pittsburgh tied the score in the third, Brooklyn bounced back with three in the sixth, two of them unearned, to grab a 4-1 lead.

Kitson, a tall stringbean right hander, made the four runs hold up, as he coasted to a four-hit, 4-2 victory, giving the Superbas a comfortable 2-0 lead in games in the five-game series.

```
Brooklyn Superbas    010 003 000 - 4 - 7 - 0
Pittsburgh Pirates   000 100 100 - 2 - 4 - 9
```

With a commanding lead in games, Brooklyn manager Ned Hanlon was able to gamble on his pitching assignment for game three, in order to give McGinnity another day of rest before throwing him back into the fray. Since Brickyard Kennedy was unavailable for duty,

Hanlon nominated Harry Howell to start. Howell, a spot starter, had compiled a 6-5 record in ten starts during the year. He was opposed by Deacon Philippe, a big, rawboned, 28-year-old right hander out of Rural Retreat, Virginia.

Philippe, an 18-game winner for Fred Clarke in only his second year of major league ball, was just coming into his own as a National League star. Before hanging up his spikes in 1911, he would win 186 games, compiling five 20 victory seasons along the way.

On this day, the Deacon was unhittable. The twentieth century's top control pitcher stopped the hard-hitting Superbas dead in their tracks, throwing a nifty six-hit shutout at them, while striking out five and walking only two. His teammates meanwhile, were raking Harry Howell for 13 safeties which, when combined with two bases on balls and two Brooklyn errors, were good for ten runs. The Pirates left no doubts about their intentions from the first cry of "play ball." They combed the beleagured Howell for three runs in the very first inning, and another in the second, to take a commanding 4-0 lead. They continued to build on that lead, adding two runs in the fifth, another in the seventh, and three more in the eighth. Left fielder Tommy Leach and center fielder Ginger Beaumont led the suddenly rejuvenated Pittsburgh attack with three hits each.

```
Brooklyn Superbas    000 000 000 - 0 - 6 - 2
Pittsburgh Pirates   310 020 13x - 10 - 13 - 1
```

Pittsburgh hoped their third-game demolition of Brooklyn would give them the momentum they needed to come back and win the series. But it was not to be. The 1900 Brooklyn Superbas were not to be denied. With "Iron Man" Joe McGinnity on the mound for Game Four, Ned Hanlon's boys were unbeatable. They jumped on Sam Leever for a single run in the first inning, as 2335 die-hard Pirate fans groaned with disappointment.

McGinnity kept the Pittsburgh batters at bay over the first three innings with his tantalizing underhand curveball. He protected the slim 1-0 lead into the fourth, when the Superbas broke through for three big runs to give him some breathing room. The "Iron Man" took it from there, yielding only a single run in the sixth, en route to a convincing 6-1 victory. Third baseman Lave Cross led the way for Brooklyn, with three hits. Honus Wagner had two in a losing cause.

```
Brooklyn Superbas    100 311 000 - 6 - 8 - 0
Pittsburgh Pirates   000 001 000 - 1 - 9 - 3
```

Brooklyn proved its right to the World Championship as it dominated every facet of the series, combining a potent offense with brilliant defense. Their pitching, except for Game Three, was overpowering, particularly McGinnity. The "Iron Man" won two games, yielding just three runs and 14 hits in 18 innings, with an ERA of 1.50.

BROOKLYN ROBINS (NL) V.S. BOSTON RED SOX (AL)—1916

After 1900, Brooklyn's fortunes declined. The fledgling American League staged numerous raids on National League rosters, and no one team felt the impact any more than the Superbas. They lost the heart and soul of their lineup, including Joe Kelley, Willie Keeler, Fielder Jones, and Iron Man Joe McGinnity. And Brickyard Kennedy retired.

Charlie Ebbets spent the next decade rebuilding. He filled the roster with new faces, mostly young–and mostly hungry. Twenty-one-year-old Zack Wheat took over left field in 1909, and 26-year-old "Gentleman" Jake Daubert, a slick-fielding first baseman and a .300 hitter, joined the team a year later. Twenty-five year old George Cutshaw was brought in to play second base. Twenty-year-old Hy Myers and 22 year old Casey Stengel, two solid all-around ballplayers, joined future Hall of Famer Wheat in the outfield. Otto Miller, a standout defensive catcher replaced anemic hitting Bill Bergen and helped settle down the pitching staff. Veteran shortstop Ivy Olson was obtained from Cincinnati to solidify the infield. And big Jeff Pfeffer, a 6'3", 210-pound fireballer, with a blur for a fastball, came aboard in 1913 to claim a place in the starting rotation.

Charlie Ebbets opened his magnificent new stadium that same year and, the following year, he hired Wilbert Robinson, the old Oriole catcher, to manage the team. Things continued to improve under Robinson. The team, occasionally called the Robins in deference to their manager, edged up from sixth place in 1913, to fifth in 1914, then third in 1915, when they celebrated their first winning season in 12 years.

The 1916 Brooklyn entry was a well-balanced club. Their fine pitching staff led the league with an earned run average of 2.12. Pfeffer (25-11), veterans Rube Marquard (13-6), Larry Cheney (18-12), and Jack Coombs (12-8), and hard-luck Sherry Smith (14-10) carried most of the load. Nap Rucker, Brooklyn's greatest left handed pitcher, reached the end of the line in 1916.

Brooklyn's defense was above average, if not brilliant. And their offense led the league in average and slugging percentage, while finishing second in runs scored. Zack Wheat, as usual, was the focal point of the lineup, batting .312. Daubert chipped in with .316, and the rest of the lineup performed admirably, from top to bottom.

In spite of the dominant statistics, the Robins were involved in a dogfight right down to the wire. The Philadelphia Phillies, defending National League champions, with Gavvy Cravath and Grover Cleveland Alexander, refused to quit. Brooklyn finally clinched on October 3, with just two games remaining on the schedule.

The Robins' opponents in the World Series were Bill Carrigan's Boston Red Sox, led by the American League's top southpaw pitcher, George Herman Ruth. The 21-year-old "Babe" established himself as one of the premier pitchers in the game in 1916, as he topped the league with an earned run average of 1.75, while running up a 23-12 won-loss record. His supporting cast, although not quite as strong as Brooklyn's, included 19-game winner Carl Mays, and 18-game winner, Dutch Leonard. The Boston defense

The 1916 Brooklyn Robins.

Top row, L to R., Casey Stengel, George Cutshaw, Duster Mails, Rube Marquard, Sherry Smith, Artie Dede, Wheezer Dell, Middle row, Ed Appleton, Chief Meyers, Jeff Pfeffer, Larry Cheney, Nap Rucker, Ivy Olson, Gus Getz, Zack Wheat.. Sitting, Jack Coombs, Ollie O'Mara, Hy Myers, Wilbert Robinson, Jake Daubert, Jimmy Johnston, Hack Miller, Mike Mowrey.

was outstanding, but the offense was mediocre, relying on speed to outscore the opposition. Third baseman Larry Gardner, at .308, was the only regular with a batting average over .271. The BoSox were decided underdogs against the pride of Brooklyn.

The World Series got underway in Beantown on a cool, cloudy fall day. Robins manager, Wilbert Robinson, surprisingly named Rube Marquard to oppose Boston starter, 15-game winner Ernie Shore. The gallant Marquard gave Boston a battle for six innings, but trailed, 2-1, entering the seventh. After Brooklyn went down quietly in the top half of the inning, the Sox broke through in the stretch half. Second baseman Hal Janvrin led off with a sizzling double down the left field line and, almost immediately, the Robin infield self destructed. Errors by Ivy Olson and George Cutshaw plated Janvrin, and left runners on first and second. A sacrifice bunt, a fielders choice, and a sacrifice fly completed the scoring–three runs on one hit and two costly Brooklyn errors.

Manager Wilbert Robinson obtained pitcher Larry Cheney from the Chicago Cubs on waivers in 1915. Cheney went on to win 18 games, with a sparking 1.92 ERA, in the 1916 pennant drive.

Carrigan's boys added a single tally in the bottom of the eighth to take a 6-1 lead into the ninth. It almost wasn't enough. Jake Daubert, leading off, worked Ernie Shore for a walk. Two singles, a hit batter, a Boston error, and another walk followed, and all of a sudden the Robins had three runs in and the bases loaded with two men out. Bill Carrigan rushed Carl Mays in from the bullpen to stem the Brooklyn tide. The score was 6-4 with the tying

run at second and the dangerous Hy Myers at the plate. Myers hit a squibbler to second base and beat Janvrin's throw to first by an eyelash as Mike Mowrey came across with the fourth run of the inning. The Brooklyn fans were in a frenzy now as "Gentleman Jake" strode to the plate with the tying run only 90 feet away and the lead run perched on second. Every player in the Robin dugout was on his feet exhorting Daubert to tie into one. The big first baseman ripped a shot between third and short but the sure-handed Everett Scott ran it down at deep short to end the rally and the game.

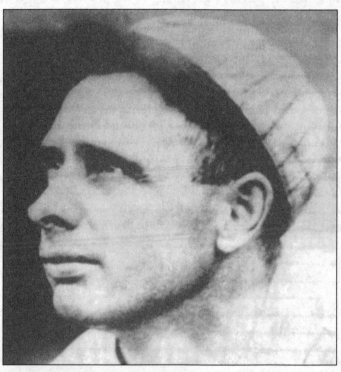

George Cutshaw, the top defensive second baseman of the period, was also a clutch hitter, who rarely struck out. He averaged almost 30 stolen bases a year from 1912 to 1923.

Brooklyn Robins	000 100 004 - 5 - 10 - 4
Boston Red Sox	001 010 31X - 6 - 8 - 1

Game Two was one of the classic games in World Series history. It matched hard luck Sherry Smith of Brooklyn against the inimitable Babe Ruth. Brooklyn drew first blood in the initial frame when Hi Myers slammed a Ruth curve ball into the gap in right center field. The Robin speedster circled the bases with an inside the park home run before Tilly Walker could run the ball down. Boston retaliated in the third. Everett Scott tripled to deep left center and carried the tying run across the plate on a ground ball by Ruth.

From there, the game settled down to a pitchers' duel with both Smith and Ruth breezing through the opposition inning after inning. Over the next ten frames Brooklyn batters were held to just four hits by the Boston southpaw, but Ruth's teammates could do no better with Sherry Smith's slants. The play of the game occurred in the bottom of the ninth inning when the Red Sox threatened to end the game. With Hal Janvrin on third base and no one out, Doc Hoblitzel hit a line drive to Hy Myers in center field. Janvrin, unwisely, tried to score on the play. Myers caught the ball coming in and fired a strike to Otto Miller, who put the tag on the sliding Janvrin, to end the threat.

In the fourteenth, Wilbert Robinson's boys once again went out meekly, one, two, three. In the Boston half, first baseman Doc Hoblitzel walked for the fourth time in the game. After a sacrifice moved him to second, he carried home the winning run on pinch hitter Del Gainer's line drive single over third.

Veteran catcher Chief Meyers, obtained from the New York Giants over the winter, helped guide the Brooklyn pitching staff to 94 wins in 1916.

The Robins' stellar outfield of Zack Wheat, Hy Myers, and Casey Stengel, were solid both offensively and defensively.

Babe Ruth's 13 shutout innings began a streak of 29 consecutive scoreless innings by the slick Boston southpaw, encompassing the World Series of 1916 and 1918. It was the Babe's most precious record, and lasted for 43 years until Whitey Ford broke it in 1961.

Brooklyn Robins	1 0 0	0 0 0	0 0 0	0 0 0 0 0 - 1 - 6 - 2
Boston Red Sox	0 0 1	0 0 0	0 0 0	0 0 0 0 1 - 2 - 7 - 1

The Series moved to Brooklyn with the snake-bit Robins down two games to none. A raucous crowd of 21,067 pushed their way into Ebbets Field on October 10 to root for the home team. Veteran Jack Coombs, a 33-year-old retread from the Philadelphia A's, got the call from manager Wilbert Robinson. Coombs was up to the task. He blanked the Boston team for five innings while his teammates piled up a 4-0 lead. The Robins pushed one run across the plate in the third on singles by Daubert, Stengel, and Cutshaw. They scored another marker in the fourth on singles by Olson and Coombs, and upped the margin to 4-0 in the fifth on two walks and a booming triple off the left field wall by Ivy Olson.

The gallant Coombs tired in the sixth and was replaced by 25-game winner Jeff Pfeffer who retired eight men in a row to preserve Brooklyn's first victory

Boston Red Sox	0 0 0	0 0 2	1 0 0	- 3 - 7 - 1
Brooklyn Robins	0 0 1	1 2 0	0 0 0	- 4 -10 - 0

The Flatbush Flock began Game Four as if they were going to run away with the rest of the Series. Jimmy Johnston led off the game with a resounding triple to deep right center field. Hy Myers plated the Robin right fielder with a single to right, then scored himself on a walk, a force play, and an infield error. But that was to be the only offense Brooklyn could muster against lefty Dutch Leonard. He handcuffed Robby's boys on just three hits the rest of the way. Robin starter Rube Marquard, on the other hand, lasted only four innings, surrendering four runs on five hits, including Larry Gardner's three-run homer in the second. When the dust had settled the National Leaguers found themselves on the short end of a 6-2 score, and one game away from elimination.

```
Boston Red Sox     0 3 0  1 1 0  1 0 0 - 6 -10 - 1
Brooklyn Robins    2 0 0  0 0 0  0 0 0 - 2 - 5 - 4
```

Returning to Boston for Game Five, the Red Sox gave their fans plenty to cheer about. They pecked away at Brooklyn starter Jeff Pfeffer for four runs in seven innings. Duffy Lewis hit a line drive to left field in the second. When the ball took a bad hop over Wheat's head, Lewis raced all the way to third, where he scored on a sacrifice fly by Gardner. In the third, two singles, a walk, and a botched double play by Ivy Olson gave Boston two unearned runs. They capped their scoring with another run in the fifth on a single by Hooper and a long double to center by Hal Janvrin. That was all the offensive support Ernie Shore needed. He three hit the Robins, holding them to a single run as Boston took the Series four games to one.

```
Brooklyn Robins    0 1 0  0 0 0  0 0 0 - 1 - 3 - 3
Boston Red Sox     0 1 2  0 1 0  0 0 X - 4 - 7 - 2
```

BROOKLYN ROBINS (NL) VS CLEVELAND INDIANS (AL)– 1920

Following the 1916 World Series the Robins' fortunes took a decided turn for the worse. Nineteen seventeen saw them tumble all the way to seventh place, the biggest collapse by a pennant winner in the history of major league baseball. The problem was not all of their own doing, however. World War I was underway in all its fury in Europe and, by 1917, America was in the thick of it. The patriotism in the country was at a fever pitch, and many players left the security and comfort of the big leagues to enlist in the war effort. The Robin pitching staff was decimated by defections as Jeff Pfeffer, Leon Cadore, and Clarence Mitchell all went off to serve their country.

In order to reconstruct the pitching rotation, manager Wilbert Robinson was forced to trade some of his established stars. Casey Stengel and George Cutshaw were shuttled off to Pittsburgh for the live arms of Al Mamaux and Burleigh Grimes. Then Jake Daubert was unloaded to Cincinnati for outfielder Tommy Griffith.

Slowly the team began to come together. The seventh place finish of 1917 turned into the fifth-place finish of 1918. After another fifth-place finish in 1919 it was evident more help was needed in order to make the team a pennant contender. The inner defense needed tightening so Pete Kilduff was brought in from the Chicago Cubs to play second base, with Jimmy Johnston moving over to third.

The Robins were not expected to be serious contenders in 1920, usually being picked to finish somewhere between third and fifth. Their start did nothing to change the expert's minds. After taking the season opener 9-2 behind the steady pitching of Leon Cadore and the hitting of first baseman "Big Ed" Konetchy, the Robins settled into a mediocre pattern. They sputtered and floundered for the first couple of months of the season–but they stayed within sight of the leaders.

The month of May brought about one of the strangest weekends of baseball ever witnessed, and one of the most frustrating in Brooklyn history. On Saturday, May 1, the Robins and Braves met in Boston, with Cadore duelling Boston ace, Joe Oeschger. Twenty-six innings later, with the same two pitchers on the mound, darkness descended over Beantown forcing a halt to the festivities with the score deadlocked at 1-1. The following day, in Brooklyn, the Robins played another extra inning contest, only to lose to the Philadelphia Phillies, 4-3, in 13 innings. Then, on Monday, a tired group of Brooklyn ballplayers dragged themselves back to Boston for a return engagement with the Braves. This time they struggled for 19 long innings, but the result was no better. The Robins lost, 2-1. Over the three-day period, after playing three games and 58 innings of baseball, Uncle Robby's boys had nothing more to show for it than one tie and two losses. It was truly a lost weekend.

Spring passed into summer, and still the Robins hung in the pennant race. Late in June they put together a winning streak that saw them take 20 of 23 games, moving them closer to the New York Giants and Cincinnati Reds. When they ran off ten victories in a row in early September they finally slipped past the other contenders and into first place. Day by day they increased their lead until, on September 26, they beat the Giants, 4-2, to clinch a tie for the pennant. The next day, when McGraw's team was beaten by Boston, the Robins were crowned National League Champions.

The victory had been, in all respects, a team effort. Brooklyn finished third in batting, with Zack Wheat at .328, Ed Konetchy at .308, and Hy Myers at .304 their only .300 hitters. The tight infield defense was anchored by shortstop Ivy Olson and second baseman Pete Kilduff. The smooth working middle fielders pulled off 34 more double plays than their predecessors had the year before. But it was on the mound where the The Robins excelled. Uncle Robby's pitching staff led the league in earned run average with a sparkling 2.62. Sherry Smith had an ERA of 1.85 to complement his 11-9 record. Big Burleigh Grimes, the 26-year-old spitballer, was the ace of the staff, rolling up a record of 23-11. He was followed by Jeff Pfeffer (16-9), Leon Cadore (15-14), Al Mamaux (12-8), and Sherry.

The Brooklyn fans showed their appreciation for the fine team effort by flocking to the ballpark in record numbers. Charlie Ebbet's team set a new Brooklyn attendence figure as 808,000 excited fans pushed their way through the turnstiles.

Over in the American League, it had been both an exciting and a traumatic summer. The excitement was caused by George Herman Ruth. The big, barrel-chested slugger, in his second season as a full-time outfielder, and in his first year in a New York Yankee uniform after being traded by the Boston Red Sox, shook the game to its very foundation with his mammoth 42-ounce bat. In 1919, Ruth had broken Ned Williamson's 35-year-old home run record by hammering 29 round trippers in Boston. Now, in his new home in the Bronx, the Bambino crashed the unheard-of total of 54 home runs, revolutionizing the game forever. Heretofore, baseball had been a pitcher's game, with low-scoring efforts dominating the summer pastime. Suddenly the home run became paramount, and the game would never be the same again.

But tragedy also dogged the American League season. First, Ray Chapman, the outstanding shortstop of the Cleveland Indians, died after being hit by a pitched ball. Chappie, a nine year major league veteran at 29, was at the peak of his career, and hitting a solid .303 when he was felled by an errant fastball from submarine pitcher Carl Mays of Boston on August 16. He was carried from the field unconscious and died the next day.

Several weeks later the Black Sox scandal broke. A Chicago grand jury indicted eight members of the defending champion Chicago White Sox for throwing the 1919 World Series to the Cincinnati Reds. The players were suspended from the team with two weeks left in the season, effectively handing the 1920 pennant to the Cleveland Indians. Gone from baseball forever were the likes of "Shoeless" Joe Jackson, a lifetime .356 hitter, all-star third baseman Buck Weaver, and 208-game winner Ed Cicotte.

The pennant-winning Indians were an outstanding team in their own right, and were favored to defeat the Brooklyn Robins in the Series. Led by "The Gray Eagle" Tris Speaker who batted .388, the Indians had a team batting average of .303. Seven players finished over the magic .300 mark. The Indians were dominant in every aspect of the game, finishing second in their league in all departments, batting, fielding, and pitching. Jim Bagby had a career season, winning 31 games against only 12 losses. He was ably supported by Stan Coveleskie (24-14) and Ray Caldwell (20-10).

The 1920 World Series was a nine-game affair, initially adopted in 1919. The new format was unpopular with fans and lasted only three years. The Series opened amidst an atmosphere of gaiety and anticipation in Brooklyn's majestic stadium, Ebbets Field. Charlie Ebbets, his family, and assorted dignitaries were on hand to kick off the festivities. The band played the usual marches, colorful bunting circled the playing field, and American flags waved proudly throughout the grandstand.

Game One matched 24-game winner Stanley Coveleskie against the Robins aging veteran, Rube Marquard. The 23,573 fans in attendance were treated to an outstanding pitching duel between the two old masters. Cleveland got on the board first thanks to a little luck and a fielding blunder by Robin first baseman, Ed Konetchy. George Burns dropped a Texas leaguer into short right field leading off the second inning. The ball was run down by Konetchy who, in his anxiety to cut down Burns at second, threw the ball over Olson's head. The Cleveland first baseman circled the bases as Olson chased the ball all the way to the left field stands. Cleveland added a second run on a walk to Joe Wood and a double by Steve O'Neil before the side could be retired.

Coveleskie, meanwhile, sent the Robins down quietly over the first three innings, retiring all nine batters.

Rube Marquard, a 10-game winner during the season, opened the World Series for manager Wilbert Robinson. Rube tossed a strong five-hitter, but lost a heartbreaking 3-1 decision.

Wood and O'Neil combined for another Cleveland run in the top of the fourth on a pair of doubles. That was more than old Stanley needed. Mixing his fastball, curve and spitball masterfully, he kept the Robins off balance all day. He pitched a five-hitter and allowed only a single run. That came when Zack Wheat ripped a long double to the wall in right center field, and came around to score on two ground balls.

```
Cleveland Indians    0 2 0  1 0 0  0 0 0 - 3 - 5 - 0
Brooklyn Robins      0 0 0  0 0 0  1 0 0 - 1 - 5 - 1
```

Neither the Robins, nor their fans, were discouraged by the disappointing loss to Cleveland in Game One. After all, "Boily" was going in Game Two. Burleigh Grimes, the hard nosed spitball artist was ready to challenge player-manager Tris Speaker's cohorts in the city of churches. His opponent was 31-game winner, Jim "Sarge" Bagby.

As expected, both pitchers were stingy with the base hits, each yielding seven. Brooklyn however, made better use of theirs. In the bottom of the first, after the Indians were retired, Brooklyn brought the partisan crowd to its feet screaming. Jimmy Johnston beat out a hit to deep short, moved around to third on a stolen base and an infield out, and scored when Zack Wheat lined a double into right center.

The Robins scored again in the third on a single by Grimes and a double by Tommy Griffith. They plated their final run of the game in the fifth. Ivy Olson grounded a single past second. He moved to second as Johnston grounded out, then scored when Griffith poked a single past short.

Grimes issued four bases on balls in addition to the seven hits he allowed, but he was tough in the clutch. He recorded only two strikeouts but had Speaker's boys pounding the ball into the ground all day. He, himself, had four assists and, in the second inning, he trapped Gardner off second after fielding a grounder. He was also backed by some fine defensive plays by Kilduff, Griffith, and catcher Otto Miller. All in all it was a great day in Brooklyn, and 22,559 fans went home happy.

```
Cleveland Indians    0 0 0  0 0 0  0 0 0 - 0 - 7 - 1
Brooklyn Robins      1 0 1  0 1 0  0 0 x - 3 - 7 - 0
```

In Game Three, still in Brooklyn, left hander Sherry Smith faced off against big right hander "Rube" Caldwell. Another packed house of over 25,000 Brooklynites were on hand to cheer their boys on. Smith, who had pitched a masterpiece against Boston in the 1916 Series, only to lose a heartbreaker to Babe Ruth in 14 innings, was up to the task at hand.

He disposed of Speaker's boys in the top of the first on three ground balls. Then the Robins went to work on Caldwell. Ivy Olson led off with a walk and was immediately sacrificed to second by Johnston. In quick succession, an error by Joe Sewell and singles by Wheat and Myers plated two runs and drove Caldwell to cover. Relief pitcher Duster Mails came on to quell the Brooklyn rally, but Sherry Smith had all the runs he needed.

The smooth-working lefty would have pitched a shutout except for some uncharacteristically sloppy outfield play by Zack Wheat. With one out in the fourth, Tris Speaker sliced a double down the left field line and, when Wheat misplayed it, the Gray Eagle continued on around the bases to score Cleveland's only run. Sherry Smith finished the game with a neat three hitter, giving Wilbert Robinson's boys a 2-1 lead in the Series.

```
Cleveland Indians    0 0 0  1 0 0  0 0 0 - 1 - 3 - 1
Brooklyn Robins      2 0 0  0 0 0  0 0 x - 2 - 6 - 1
```

Following Game Three, the two teams caught the first train to Cleveland where the next four games were scheduled. On Saturday, October 9, Leon Cadore, the fourth Robin pitcher to start a World Series game was matched against first game winner Stanley Coveleskie. It was no contest as the Indians scored early and often against the embattled Cadore. A walk and two singles plated two runs in the home half of the first. Consecutive singles by Bill Wamsganss, Speaker, and Elmer Smith scored two more in the third.

A Brooklyn run in the fourth was matched by another Cleveland marker in the sixth. From there, Coveleskie, the Pennsylvania coal miner, went on to an easy five-hit 5-1 victory, his second win of the Series.

```
Brooklyn Robins      0 0 0  1 0 0  0 0 0 - 1 -  5 - 1
Cleveland Indians    2 0 2  0 0 1  0 0 x - 5 - 12 - 2
```

The postseason classic was knotted at two games apiece as Sarge Bagby squared off against Burleigh Grimes in a rematch of Game Two. Game Five was destined to go down as the most memorable game of the Series thanks to three record-breaking achievements; the first grand slam home run in Series history, the first home run by a pitcher, and the only unassisted triple play in World Series history.

Grimes had been the winner in his first encounter with Bagby, but he didn't have it this time around, and the vaunted Cleveland attack tore into him with a vengeance. Charlie Jamieson, a lifetime .303 hitter, led off the game with a one base hit to right field. Wamsganss followed with a solid single to center, and the Indians were in business. Things got worse for Grimes almost immediately when Speaker, attempting to sacrifice, pushed the ball towards third. The Brooklyn pitcher slipped coming off the mound and all hands were safe, loading the bases with nobody out. The next batter was the cleanup hitter, Elmer Smith. The big left handed hitting right-fielder had just completed a career season, setting personal highs in batting average (.318), doubles (37), and runs batted in (103). He also contributed 10 triples and 12 homers to the Indian offense.

Grimes, upset with the turn of events, tried to blow a fast ball by Smith–a big mistake. The Cleveland slugger jerked it on a line to right field where it cleared the screen for the first grand slam home run in World Series history.

Three innings later, things got even worse for the Robin ace. With one out and two men on base, the Cleveland pitcher drove a ball to the far reaches of the park. It settled into the center field stands for a home run, the first homer by a pitcher in a World Series. After another single by Jamieson, Grimes was gone–and so were Brooklyn's hopes.

Zack Wheat, Brooklyn's all-time batting leader, had another outstanding season in 1920, batting .328 with 48 extra base hits. He hit a solid .333 in the World Series. (National Baseball Hall of Fame Library, Cooperstown, NY)

The most unusual play of the game, however, was yet to come. Down 7-0 in the fifth inning, the Robins tried to mount a comeback. Pete Kilduff and Otto Miller led off with singles, putting men on first and second with no outs. Clarence Mitchell stepped to the plate. The Robin hurler, often used as a pinch hitter, knew how to handle a bat, as witnessed by his lifetime .252 batting average. He tied into a Bagby delivery, and sent a screaming liner toward center field as 26,884 Cleveland fans watched in hushed silence. Kilduff and Miller were off with the pitch, sensing another hit and a Brooklyn run. But Indian second baseman Bill Wamsganss had other ideas. He broke to his right at the crack of the bat, made a desperate leap, and snared the ball in his outstretched fingertips. His momentum carried him to second base where he tagged the bag, doubling Kilduff who was already rounding third. Then, turning to his left, Wamsganss spied a stunned Miller standing only three feet away. He quickly tagged the immobilized Brooklyn catcher to complete the only unassisted triple play in World Series history.

From there, Sarge Bagby coasted 8-1 and the Indians were in the drivers seat in games, 3-2.

| Brooklyn Robins | 000 000 001 - 1 - 13 - 1 |
| Cleveland Indians | 400 310 00x - 8 - 12 - 2 |

Cleveland now had the momentum. They were determined to close the Series out quickly, and the Brooklyn Robin was a bird ready to be plucked. The team seemed demoralized by the turn of events in Game Five. The snap was gone from their bats and the swagger from their walk. They behaved like a condemned man just waiting for the axe to fall.

Hardluck Sherry Smith drew the starting assignment for Wilbert Robinson's crew, opposing left hander Duster Mails. The 29 year old native of Monticello, Georgia, could have sued his mates for non support. Typical of his World Series experiences, the tall skinny southpaw threw another gem. He limited Tris Speaker's powerful club to seven base hits and a single run. It still wasn't good enough. His teammates could garner only three harmless hits off the slants of Mails.

The winning run scored in the sixth inning. With two men out Tris Speaker sliced an outside pitch to left field for a single. Minutes later, he raced all the way home on a screaming double to the left field fence by George Burns.

| Brooklyn Robins | 000 000 000 - 0 - 3 - 0 |
| Cleveland Indians | 000 001 00x - 1 - 7 - 3 |

Brooklyn's last gasp came on October 12. Burleigh Grimes was on the hill for the Robins, while Stanley Coveleskie was after his third win of the Series for Cleveland. It was a well pitched game on both sides, but Coveleskie had all the better of it. He held Brooklyn to only five hits, and two of those resulted in outs. In the third, Jack Sheehan got credit for a single when his ground ball struck a baserunner. The next inning, Zack Wheat hit a line drive off the right field wall and was thrown out trying to stretch it into a double.

Cleveland's seven hits meanwhile, were used efficiently. Two singles and a Brooklyn error gave Speaker's boys a run in the fourth. They scored again the next inning on a single by Jamieson and a booming triple by Speaker. The final run of the game came across in the seventh. Catcher Steve O'Neil crashed a double to deep left center. After Coveleskie reached on a fielder's choice, with O'Neil being caught in a rundown, the pitcher came in to score when Jamieson doubled down the right field line.

| Brooklyn Robins | 000 000 000 - 0 - 5 - 2 |
| Cleveland Indians | 000 110 10x - 3 - 7 - 3 |

The 1920 Series ended on a disappointing note, with Uncle Robby's charges dropping the last four games, and scoring only two runs in the process. Even worse, although unknown at the time, it was to be the Robins' (or Dodgers') last trip to the World Series for 21 years. Overnight they became a second-division team, a lovable bunch of clowns who couldn't play ball very good but who could entertain a crowd with their wacky antics. Known as the "Daffyness Boys," they finished in the second division 14 times in an 18-year period from 1921 to 1938.

BROOKLYN DODGERS V.S. THE NEW YORK YANKEES–1941

Twenty-one years after their last World Series appearance against the Cleveland Indians, the Brooklyn Baseball Club once again represented the National League in the fall classic. Now known as the Dodgers, the men of Flatbush squared off against Joe McCarthy's mighty New York Yankees.

New York was in the midst of baseball's longest and most awesome dynasty. Since 1921, the Bronx Bombers had captured 11 American League flags and eight World Championships, including four consecutive World Championships between 1936 and 1939.

The 1941 edition of Murderer's Row, back on top again after finishing third in 1940, included such sluggers as "Joltin' Joe" Dimaggio, Bill Dickey, Tommy "Old Reliable" Henrich, Joe "Flash" Gordon, and Charlie "King Kong" Keller. Dimaggio was the league's MVP, hitting a titanic .357 with 30 home runs and a league-leading 125 RBIs. He also established one of baseball's "untouchable" records, as he hit safely in 56 consecutive games. Charlie Keller chipped in with 33 homers and 122 runs batted in; while Henrich (.277, 31-85), Gordon (.276, 24-87), and Dickey (.284, 7-71) rounded out the vaunted attack. The pitching staff boasted no 20-game winners, but it had seven pitchers who won nine or more games. It was competent and it was deep; the best staff in the American League. Lefty Gomez (15-5), Red Ruffing (15-6), Marius Ugo Russo (14-10), and Spurgeon "Spud" Chandler (10-4) carried the bulk of the pitching load. The New Yorker's made a travesty of the American League pennant race, winning 101 games, and leaving the second-place Boston Red Sox in the dust, a distant 17 games back.

Brooklyn's route to the Series was not quite as easy. They had to battle the classy Saint Louis Cardinals tooth and nail the entire summer, with neither team wilting under the pressure. A crucial three-game series in St. Louis in mid-September saw the Brooklyn crew win two out of three, with Whitlow Wyatt eking out a nerve wracking 1-0 victory in the finale. The resulting two-game lead held up over the next two weeks and, when Wyatt threw another shutout, 6-0 over the Boston Braves on September 25, the Dodgers were home free, the 1941 National League champions.

Led by fiery manager Leo "Lippy" Durocher, the Brooks had begun their trek to the top of the baseball world in 1939, when they shocked the experts by climbing all the way from 7th place to 3rd, only their sixth first division finish in 22 years. The following year, they edged even closer to the top, finishing in second place, 12 games behind Cincinnati. In the spring of 1941, they were poised to make their move. President Larry MacPhail had spared no expense to give his manager the players he needed to make a run for the pennant. In addition to fresh young faces from the minor leagues like "The Gold Dust Twins," "Pee Wee" Reese and Pete Reiser, the astute MacPhail raided his major league counterparts for valuable veterans such as Kirby Higbe, Dolph Camilli, and Joe Medwick. He also recognized the potential in several minor league retreads, purchasing the contracts of pitchers Whitlow Wyatt and Hugh Casey. One of the veterans, first baseman Camilli walked off with the National League's Most Valuable Player award, on the strength of a league-leading 34 home runs and 120 runs batted in.

Another old pro, "Ducky" Medwick, contributed a .318 batting average, 18 homers and 88 runs batted in. But the star of the Brooklyn pennant parade was a 22-year-old phenom named Harold Patrick Reiser, one of the most exciting players ever to don a baseball uniform. "Pistol Pete", as he was fondly called, became the youngest batting champion in National League history with an average of .343. He also led the league in most other offensive categories, including doubles (39), triples (17), runs scored (117), total bases (299), and slugging average (.558). His sidekick, Pee Wee Reese anchored a tight infield defense, while Dixie Walker (.311), Billy Herman (.291), and Cookie Lavagetto (.277) gave both offensive and defensive support. The league's strongest pitching staff was led by Kirby Higbe (22-9), Whitlow Wyatt (22-10), Hugh Casey (14-9), and Curt Davis (13-7).

Brooklyn Dodgers–1941 National League Champions

As one might imagine, the fair borough of Brooklyn was sheer bedlam after the Dodger pennant clincher. Twenty-one years of pent-up frustration was loosed on the evening of Thursday, September 25, 1941. The celebration continued, day and night, for a full week, right up to the Series opener the following Wednesday. Confident Yankee fans flocked to the House That Ruth Built on October 1, joined by thousands of wild-eyed Brooklyn fanatics who made the trek across the bridge to root for their heroes. Manager Joe McCarthy, selected his ace, 15-game winner Red Ruffing, to start on the mound for the Yankees. Leo Durocher, skipper of the Johnny-Come-Lately Dodgers, countered with 38 year old Curt Davis.

Hard-throwing Kirby Higbe, picked up in a trade with the Philadelphia Phillies, led the National League in victories (22 - tie), and games pitched (48).

The 6'2", 185-pound right-hander out of Greenfield, Missouri, had performed nobly for Durocher during the year in spot assignments, winning 13 games and compiling an outstanding 2.97 earned run average. Davis and the 37 year old Ruffing were one of the oldest pitching matchups in World Series history.

Ruffing prevailed in a tight pitcher's duel, 3-2. The Yankee attack was led by Joe Gordon, who had a single and a home run, and Bill Dickey, who singled and doubled. Reese had two singles, and Mickey Owen slugged an RBI triple for Durocher's Dodgers.

Brooklyn Dodgers	0 0 0 0 1 0 1 0 0 - 2 - 6 - 0
New York Yankees	0 1 0 1 0 1 0 0 x - 3 - 6 - 1

Game Two, before another packed house in Yankee Stadium, pitted two Georgia boys against each other, New York's Spud Chandler and Brooklyn's Whitlow Wyatt. Chandler, who would post two 20 victory seasons for the Yankees before he retired in 1947, compiled the highest career-winning percentage in major league history; .717 on the strength of 109 wins against only 43 losses. His mound opponent, a 6'1" 185-pound right-hander, was coming off his best season, a league-leading 22 wins and a miniscule 2.34 ERA.

The contest was a repeat of Game One, but this time the Dodgers won. An RBI single by Mickey Owen tied the game at 2-2 in the fifth, after the Yankees had broken on top, 2-0. Dolph Camilli knocked in the game winner with a single in the sixth.

Whitlow Wyatt mixed his pitches masterfully to keep the New Yorkers off balance most of the game.   He scattered nine hits effectively, with seven of them coming in the first four innings.

Brooklyn Dodgers	0 0 0 0 2 1 0 0 0 - 3-6-2
New York Yankees	0 1 1 0 0 0 0 0 0 - 2-9-1

Game Three was a dazzling pitchers duel between lefty Marius Ugo Russo and "Fat Freddie" Fitzsimmons. The game might still be going if the fickle finger of fate had not intervened. For seven brilliant innings the two adversaries matched pitch for pitch.

It was in the seventh that fate entered the picture. Fitzsimmons, working easily, retired Dickey on a grounder to second. After Joe Gordon walked, Phil Rizzuto moved the runner along with another easy hopper to second. Then Marius Russo jumped on a Fitzsimmons fastball and lined it back to the mound. It struck the big pitcher in the knee and deflected to short where Reese caught it on the fly. The inning was over, but so was Fitzsimmons' World Series experience. The blow shattered his kneecap, putting him on the sidelines, and depriving the Dodgers of valuable pitching experience.

The importance of the injury soon became evident. Manager Durocher brought relief pitcher Hugh Casey in from the bullpen to replace the injured Fitzsimmons. Casey wasn't around long, facing only five batters. After retiring Sturm, he was touched up for successive singles by Rolfe, Henrich, Dimaggio and Keller. By the time Larry French got to the mound, New York was on top , 2-0. That was all Russo needed. After yielding a double to Dixie Walker in the eighth, and a run-scoring single by pinch hitter Augie Galan, Russo ended the game by retiring the final four batters.

New York Yankees	0 0 0 0 0 0 0 2 0 - 2-8-0
Brooklyn Dodgers	0 0 0 0 0 0 0 1 0 - 1-4-0

Freddie Fitzsimmons, whose pitching was limited to 13 games in 1941, gave Leo Durocher a 6-1 record, with a fine 2.07 earned run average.

If fate was unkind to the Flatbush faithful in Game Three, what she did to them in Game Four would haunt them forever. Sunday, October 5, was partly cloudy and unseasonably hot. The temperature reached a sweltering 90 degrees by mid afternoon.

Still, 33,813 rabid Dodger and Yankee fans filled the little park along Sutton Place. Atley Donald, 9-5 during the season faced Brooklyn ace Kirby Higbe, 22-9. Donald, a tall right-hander, pitched eight years for the Yankees, usually as the fourth or fifth man in the pitching rotation, and he won a total of 65 games against only 33 losses. Higbe, a hard-throwing, hard-living right-hander out of Columbia, South Carolina, was as mean as a junkyard dog on the mound–and off the mound too.

New York struck first in the historic game, piling up a 3-0 lead after 3 1/2 innings.

The Brooklyn contingent showed their great heart by fighting back in the bottom of the fourth, striking for two runs, on a double by Jimmy Wasdell following two walks. Then, in the fifth, lightning struck. Dixie Walker sliced a double down the left field line, and "Pistol Pete" Reiser, the Dodgers' rookie sensation, caught a Donald pitch on the fat part of the bat and sent it in a high arc over the scoreboard in right center field. It was Brooklyn's first World Series home run in 25 years. The Dodgers had the lead at 4-3, and Atlee Donald joined Kirby Higbe in the locker room.

Hugh Casey had come on to pitch for Brooklyn with two out and the bases loaded in the fifth inning, and proceeded to shut the door on Joe McCarthy's boys through the sixth, seventh, and eighth innings, yielding only two harmless singles. As the ninth inning began, the Brooklyn fans sensed a glorious come-from-behind victory. Sturm grounded to second as 33,813 crazed Brooklyn fans screamed with delight. Red Rolfe hit the ball back to Casey and the big right-hander threw him out. The ballpark was sheer bedlam now. Tommy Henrich stepped to the plate. With a full count on the Yankee hitter, Hugh Casey threw him a wide-breaking curveball. Henrich swung and missed, an apparent strikeout victim, but the ball somehow eluded catcher Mickey Owen and, by the time he retrieved it near the top step of the Dodger dugout, Henrich had crossed first base safely. The Dodger battery should have taken time to regroup at this point, to let Casey regain his composure; or manager Leo Durocher should have gone to the mound himself to calm down his flustered pitcher. Neither of these things took place and, before anyone realized what was happening, the Bronx Bombers took advantage of the situation. With Casey pitching as if he were in a trance, the Yankee Clipper rifled a single to left. Charlie Keller jumped on an 0-2 pitch and sent a ringing double off the top of the right field wall. The ball ricocheted high in the air as both Henrich and DiMaggio scored, giving New York a 5-4 lead. After Dickey walked, Joe Gordon ripped another 0-2 pitch into the left field corner for a double and two more runs. That was it. The Dodgers went quietly in the bottom of the ninth, and an apparent victory had suddenly turned into a devastating 7-4 loss. Many Brooklyn fans wondered if the sun would ever shine over Ebbets Field again.

New York Yankees	1 0 0 2 0 0 0 0 4 -	7-12- 1
Brooklyn Dodgers	0 0 0 2 2 0 0 0 0 -	4- 9- 1

After their heartbreaking loss of the previous day, the Dodgers were a demoralized team as they took the field against the Yankees in Game Five, down three games to one. Ebbets Field was quiet as Leo Durocher handed the ball to 22-game winner, Whitlow Wyatt. The big Georgian pitched a creditable game, holding the Bronx Bombers to just three runs on six hits. But the Brooklyn attack was non-existent. They managed only four safeties, and a single run off Tiny Bonham.

New York Yankees	0 2 0 0 1 0 0 0 0 -	3-6-0
Brooklyn Dodgers	0 0 1 0 0 0 0 0 0 -	1-4-1

For the New York Yankees it was another shining chapter in their long supremacy of major league baseball. For the men of Flatbush, it was a tragic and frustrating end to a glorious season. The Fitzsimmons injury and Mickey Owen's missed third strike would never be forgotten in the borough of churches, but better days were ahead. After the short interruption caused by World War

Mickey Owen, a superb defensive catcher, ended up as the goat of the 1941 World Series for his muff of this third strike on Tommy Henrich. It was rumored that Hugh Casey crossed Owen up by throwing a spit ball. Casey insisted it was a sweeping curveball.(Transcendental Graphics)

II, Brooklyn would possess its own baseball juggernaught, one that would rule the National League for more than a decade. They would be affectionately known as "The Boys of Summer."

BROOKLYN DODGERS (NL) VS THE NEW YORK YANKEES (AL)–1947

The 1947 World Series would go down in history as one of the most exciting Series ever played. Two great teams squared off against each other in the cool crisp autumn air, each one determined to wear the crown. Both lineups were studded with future Hall of Famers like "Joltin' Joe" DiMaggio, Yogi Berra, Jackie Robinson, Duke Snider, Roy Campanella, and "Pee Wee" Reese. But it was the unknowns who stole the fall show. When the '47 Series is discussed, it is Cookie Lavagetto, Al Gionfriddo, and Floyd Bevens whose exploits are re-lived again and again.

Eddie Stanky, with manager Leo Durocher and president Branch Rickey, signs his 1947 contract. It was Jackie Robinson's first year in a Brooklyn Dodger uniform, and he was stationed at first base. The next year, Stanky was traded to the Boston Braves, and Robinson settled into his normal position at second base.

The New York Yankees under manager Bucky Harris, had reclaimed the superiority of the American League in 1947 after a wartime hiatus of three years. The vaunted Bronx Bombers, who had captured 14 American League flags between 1921 and 1943, won the pennant going away, finishing 12 games ahead of second-place Detroit. The

offense was spearheaded by DiMaggio, who batted .315 with 20 home runs and 97 runs batted in, George McQuinn (.304, 13, 80), Tommy Henrich (.287, 16, 98), and third baseman Bill Johnson (.285, 10, 95). On the mound, big Allie Reynolds led the way with a 19-8 record, followed by Spec Shea (14-5), and relief ace Joe Page (14-8 with a league leading 17 saves). New York completely dominated the league- leading in runs scored, batting average, and earned run average.

Across the river, the Brooklyn Dodgers, suddenly aroused by their near-pennant the previous year, surged to a National League Championship in 1947. The inimitable Jackie Robinson, the first black to play in the major leagues in 63 years, broke into the starting lineup at first base, and went on to win Rookie of the Year honors on the strength of a .297 batting average, 48 extra base hits, and a league leading 29 stolen bases. Burt Shotton's boys were strong up the middle as usual, with Bruce Edwards behind the plate, Eddie Stanky at second, Reese at short, and "The Reading Rifle" Carl Furillo, covering center field. Dixie Walker led the Dodger attack with a .306 batting average and 94 runs batted in. Furillo chipped in with a .295 batting average and 88 RBIs, and Edwards hit a solid .295 and drove home 80 runners. Twenty-one-year old Ralph Branca won 21 games against 12 losses, lefty Joe Hatten went 17-8, and bullpen stopper Hugh Casey had a 10-4 record and a league-leading 18 saves.

John "Spider" Jorgensen gave the Dodgers solid third base play in 1947 and batted a tough .274 with 67 runs batted in. An injury to his throwing arm curtailed a promising career.

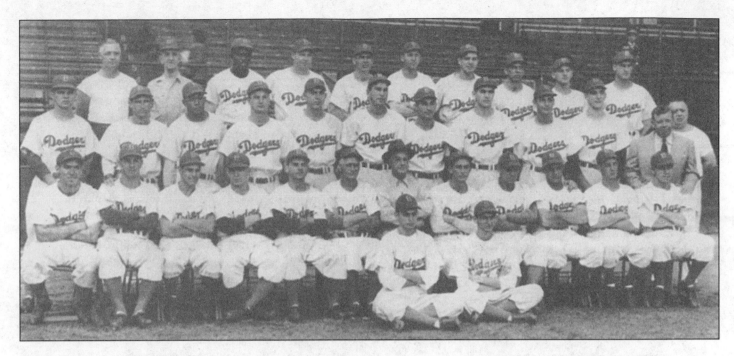

Brooklyn Dodgers–1947 National League Champions

The 1947 season was not without its turmoil. Robinson's promotion to the big team created temporary dissension on the club. The southern element, led by Kirby Higbe and Dixie Walker, circulated a petition to keep Robinson off the team. Management took immediate and decisive action. Higbe and four other players were quickly shuttled off to Pittsburgh for outfielder Al Gionfriddo. Walker would follow him over the winter, going to the same Pittsburgh team for Billy Cox and Preacher Roe. And, if the racial crisis was not disturbing enough, the Dodgers also lost their manager for the entire season on April 9. Leo Durocher was suspended by baseball Commissioner Happy Chandler for associating with professional gamblers. He was replaced by 62-year-old Burt Shotton, who managed in street clothes.

Brooklyn, behind Branca, Walker, and Robinson, broke loose from the pack in June, compiling an 18-11 record for the month, and closed in on first place. They took over the top spot on July 6 and never relinquished it clinching the pennant on September 22, finishing a comfortable five games in front of St. Louis.

The 43rd World Series opened in Yankee Stadium on September 30 with 21-game winner Branca on the mound for the visitors and rookie right-hander Spec Shea toeing the rubber for Bucky Harris' crew. The big intercity rivalry brought the fans out in droves, with 73,365 ticket holders establishing a new Series attendance record.

Branca was the epitome of perfection for four innings, 12 up and 12 down. But, in the fifth, he self destructed. DiMaggio became the first Yankee baserunner, beating out a hit to deep short. The 21-year-old Branca then succumbed to the suffocating pressure of postseason play. He walked first baseman George McQuinn and hit Billy Johnson to load the bases. Left fielder Johnny Lindell then knocked in two runs with a ringing double to left. After walking Rizzuto and falling behind Bobby Brown 2 and 0, the shell-shocked Branca was mercifully replaced by Hank Behrman. Behrman completed the walk to force in a third run. Tommy Henrich then capped off the rally by singling for runs four and five. Relief ace Joe Page hurled the final four innings for the Bronx Bombers to earn the save.

Brooklyn Dodgers	1 0 0 0 0 1 1 0 0 - 3 - 6 - 0
New York Yankees	0 0 0 0 5 0 0 0 x - 5 - 4 - 0

Game Two pitted Brooklyn's diminutive southpaw, Vic Lombardi, against hard-throwing Allie Reynolds. Superchief, a nickname that reflected his Creek Indian ancestry, was the Yankee ace, having led the American League in winning percentage with .704 on the strength of a 19-8 record. Little Vic was no puzzle to the Chief's teammates. They tattooed him for nine hits in five innings, scoring single runs in the first, third, and fourth, and a pair of runs in the fifth. They continued the barrage against Hal Gregg and Behrman, running up a total of 10 runs. Their 15 hits included triples by Johnson, Lindell and Stirnweiss and a home run by Henrich.

Brooklyn Dodgers	0 0 1 1 0 0 0 0 1 - 3 - 9 - 2
New York Yankees	1 0 1 1 2 1 4 0 x -10 -15 - 1

Cookie Lavagetto, in one of the most dramatic moments in World Series history, lines a two-out double off the right field wall at Ebbets Field in the bottom of the ninth inning of Game Four, ruining Floyd Bevens's bid for a no-hitter, and sending the Bucky Harris' troops down to defeat.

The scene shifted to the cozy confines of Ebbets Field for Game Three, much to the relief of Burt Shotton's beleaguered warriors. With the Dodgers trailing two games to none, the Brooklyn faithful held their collective breaths wondering if their charges could avoid a sweep. The answer came quickly. In the bottom of the second inning, the Brooks jumped on starter Bobo Newsome for six big runs as 33,098 Flatbush Fanatics screamed with delight. Bruce Edwards' one-out double plated the first run and, before the Yanks could close the flood gates, five more runs poured across. Singles by Reese, pitcher Joe Hatten, and Robinson, and doubles by Stanky and Furillo did the damage.

The victory would come, but it wouldn't be easy. Hatten, the Dodgers 17-game winner, couldn't stand prosperity. He was KO'd in the fifth inning, when New York closed the gap to 9-6. Rotund Hugh Casey, the National League's top fireman, entered the game in the seventh, after Yogi Berra had slammed a pinch-hit home run to right field to trim the margin to a single run, 9-8. Old Hughie pitched out of a two-on, no-out situation in the eighth by inducing Joe DiMaggio to hit into a double play, then retired the vaunted Bronx Bombers 1-2-3 in the ninth to pick up the win.

New York Yankees	0 0 2	2 2 1	1 0 0	- 8 -13 - 0
Brooklyn Dodgers	0 6 1	2 0 0	0 0 x	- 9 -13 - 1

On Friday, October 3, the Yanks and the Dodgers squared off in Game Four of the 1947 World Series. It turned out to be one of the classic encounters in Series history. Big right-hander Floyd "Bill" Bevens (7-13) was the Yankee pitcher. He was opposed by Harry Taylor (10-5).

The 6'3", 210-pound Bevens was wild but overpowering as the game progressed. He walked batters at a better-than-one-per-inning clip but, otherwise kept the Brooklyn bats silent. As the ninth inning got underway, 33,443 tense Dodger rooters sat on the edge of their seats in silence, contemplating Bevens potential no-hitter. The strong, silent right-hander from Hubbard, Oregon, trudged to the mound in the bottom of the ninth trying to protect a 2-1 lead, and to preserve his place in history. He needed only three more outs to become the first pitcher to hurl a no-hitter in World Series play. He is still waiting for out number 3.

After Bruce Edwards, flied to deep left center field, Bevens issued his ninth base on balls of the game, walking Carl Furillo. He then retired Spider Jorgensen on a foul to George McQuinn behind first, for out number 2. A stolen base by pinch-runner Al Gionfriddo, and an intentional walk to Pete Reiser followed. Burt Shotton then beckoned to Cookie Lavagetto to grab a bat, and the wily veteran marched up to home plate, and into baseball legend. Lavagetto jumped on an 0-1 pitch from Bevens, and drove it off the right field wall, ruining Bevens no-hitter, and driving in the tying and winning runs.

New York Yankees	1 0 0	1 0 0	0 0 0	- 2 - 8 - 1
Brooklyn Dodgers	0 0 0	0 1 0	0 0 2	- 3 - 1 - 3

After watching Bill Bevens pitch the day before, the Dodgers countered with a wild man of their own in game five, twenty two year old Rex Barney. A reporter once said of Barney, "He would be the greatest pitcher in the world if the plate were high and outside." Barney had been used sparingly by Shotton during the season. In 28 games, he had compiled a 5-2 record, walking 59 batters in 77 innings, an average of seven per game.

Barney's opponent was Spec Shea, the winning pitcher in the opener.

Shea had the Dodger batters eating out of his hand during the game, but Barney flirted with disaster inning after inning. In the second, he walked one man and uncorked a wild pitch. In the third, he walked two. In the fourth, he passed two more, and one of them finally came around to score on a single by Shea himself. Joe D. hit a long homerun into the left field stands with one out in the fifth and, when Barney issued his ninth base on balls of the game to Johnson, he was lifted in favor of Joe Hatten.

Spec Shea pitched a 2-1 complete game victory, scattering four hits.

New York Yankees	0 0 0	1 1 0	0 0 0	- 2 - 5 - 0
Brooklyn Dodgers	0 0 0	0 0 1	0 0 0	- 1 - 4 - 1

The Series returned to the Bronx for Game Six, with the Yankees hoping to end it. But the Dodgers were not through yet. Game Six turned into the type of game the Dodgers loved–a real donnybrook. The Flatbush Flock jumped out in front quickly, with two runs in the first, off Superchief Allie Reynolds.

Southpaw Vic Lombardi shut the Yankees down during the first two innings, but six Yankee hits in the bottom of the third, erased a 4-0 Dodger lead, and gave Mr. Lombardi an early shower.

With Joe Hatten on to pitch, manager Burt Shotton made two key defensive changes, putting Cookie Lavagetto on third and installing little Al Gionfriddo, a left handed fielder, in left field. The Yankees touched Hatten for a walk and a single, putting men on first and second with two out, and setting the table for Joe D. The Yankee Clipper wasted no time. He lashed out at the first pitch and sent a long drive screaming toward the bullpen in deep left field. It looked like a three-run homer as it left the bat, but Gionfriddo took off at the crack of the bat. Almost outrunning the ball, little Al reached out at the last instant and made a sensational, twisting, gloved hand catch of the ball at the 415-foot mark, his back brushing the bullpen fence as he came down. The laconic DiMaggio, who very rarely showed any emotion on the ballfield, kicked the dirt in frustration after rounding second. That was the game as far as New York was concerned. They managed one more run off Joe Hatten in the bottom of the ninth, but Hugh Casey came on to snuff out the rally and pick up the save.

| Brooklyn Dodgers | 2 0 2 0 0 4 0 0 0 - 8 - 12 - 1 |
| New York Yankees | 0 0 4 1 0 0 0 0 1 - 6 - 15 - 2 |

Al Gionfriddo was a journeyman outfielder, who played in the major leagues for only four years. He batted .266 in 228 games.

Vic Lombardi won 12 games against 11 losses, with a 2.99 ERA during the season.

Now it all came down to Game Seven. This all-New York Series had proven to be one of the most exciting classics ever played. The pitching-thin Brooks were forced to go with Hal Gregg, only 4-5 during the season, while Bucky Harris was able to bring back Spec Shea, making his third start of the Series. Shea had already won two games, and had a dazzling earned run average of 1.29. Gregg had pitched in two games himself. He had no record, but he had kept the Yanks in check in Game Four prior to the Dodgers' ninth-inning heroics. And his E.R.A. was an equally impressive 2.00.

For awhile, it looked like it might be the Dodgers' day. They got rid of Shea in a hurry, driving him to cover in the second. Gene Hermanski started things off with a one-out triple to right. Bruce Edwards brought him in with a single to left. Another single by Furillo brought Harris to the mound and a new pitcher on the scene. Spider Jorgensen greeted Bill Bevens with a double to right and the Brooks were on top, 2-0. Two walks and a single by Rizzuto cut the margin to one in the bottom half of the inning.

The Bronx Bombers disposed of Gregg and grabbed the lead in the bottom of the fourth. The hard-throwing right-hander issued a base on balls to Billy Johnson in between two strikeouts, but was unable to close out the inning. A single by Rizzuto and a double by Bobby Brown tied the game and chased the Dodger starter. Reliever Hank Behrman proceeded to walk Snuffy Stirnweiss before yielding a tie breaking single to Tommy Henrich.

Joe Page took over the mound chores at the start of the fifth inning as manager Bucky Harris decided not to take any chances on losing the lead with second-line hurlers. It proved to be a good decision as the Yankee relief ace pitched one hit ball over the final five innings. The big 6'3", 200-pound fast ball hurler retired the first 13 batters before Eddie Miksis touched him up for a single with one out in the ninth. Page quickly returned the favor, forcing Bruce Edwards to hit into a Series-ending double play, Rizzuto to Stirnweiss to McQuinn. With that play, the New York Yankees became champions of the whole world.

There was one final ironic note to this exciting Series. The three players who will be most remembered whenever great World Series moments are discussed–Bill Bevens, Cookie Lavagetto, and Al Gionfriddo–never played in another major league game.

| Brooklyn Dodgers | 0 2 0 0 0 0 0 0 0 - 2 - 7 - 0 |
| New York Yankees | 0 1 0 2 0 1 1 0 x - 5 - 7 - 0 |

BROOKLYN DODGERS (NL) V.S.
THE NEW YORK YANKEES (AL)—1949

Nineteen forty-nine produced spine-tingling pennant races in both leagues, with the two champions being crowned on the final day of the season.

After their exciting effort in 1948 when they drove from the cellar to the top of the league during "62 days of glory," the Brooklyn Dodgers were poised for greatness as the 1949 season got underway. They teamed with their perennial rivals, the St. Louis Cardinals, to give the fans another nail-biter, a race that stayed tight from wire to wire.

Manager Burt Shotton had most of the pieces of his "Boys of Summer" Dodger dynasty in place as the season got underway. Roy Campanella arrived in 1948 to claim the catcher's spot. Campy's arrival and the acquisition of third baseman Billy Cox, permitted Shotton to juggle his personnel to get the best athletes in the lineup on a daily basis. The result was an all-star infield that would play as a unit for seven years, through four National League pennants and one World Championship. Gil Hodges moved from catcher to first base, where he became the finest all-around first baseman in the game. Jackie Robinson went from first to second. Reese held down shortstop as usual, and teamed with Robby to form the league's deadliest double play combination. Billy Cox went on to create a Brooklyn legend with his defensive genius at the hot corner.

Carl Furillo was firmly entrenched in right field where his sizzling bat and defensive prowess made him the game's top right fielder. "The Duke of Flatbush" had arrived in Ebbets Field in 1947 to dazzle the inhabitants of Flatbush with his graceful defensive performances and his lightning fast bat. Gene Hermanski, a solid-hitting, long-ball threat, was the first of several left fielders to serve with the "Boys of Summer" over the next eight years.

If the Dodgers had an Achilles heel as the 1949 season got underway, it was on the mound. The starting rotation of Branca, Barney, Hatten, and Roe was shaky at best, and the bullpen was bare with the retirement of Hugh Casey. But help was on the way. Big Don Newcombe arrived on May 20 and quickly won a starter's job, piling up 17 big victories along the way. Carl Erskine, the little Hoosier, came up from Fort Worth in mid-July to run off eight consecutive wins as the Dodgers battled the Redbirds down the stretch. Preacher Roe added another 15 wins to the Dodger cause, and rookie Jack Banta surprised everyone with stellar performances, both starting and relieving. His greatest contribution came on the final day of the season when he tossed 4 1/3 scoreless innings as the Bums clinched the title. Branca won 13 games, and lefty Joe Hatten chipped in with a dozen more.

It was a great pennant race. Eddie Dyer's team was still a force to be reckoned with. They had the top pitching staff in the league with Howie Pollet (20-9), George "Red" Munger (15-8), Harry "The Cat" Brecheen (14-11), and Al Brazle (14-8). Schoendienst, Marion, Musial, and Slaughter were all back to give the Cards outstanding defense and solid offense. Stan "The Man" was in his prime, hitting .338 with 36 homers and 123 RBIs. Slaughter was close behind at .336, 13 and 96.   First baseman Nippy Jones (.300) and third sacker Eddie Kazak (.304) made St.

Brooklyn Dodgers–1949 National League Champions.

Louis the top hitting team in the league with a team batting average of .277.

Brooklyn was not to be outdone however. Their pitching staff was a close second to the Cards, and their .274 batting average was also near the top. In the other important team categories the Dodgers were the class of the league. Their defense excelled. Campy, Hodges, Robinson, Reese, Cox, Furillo, and the Duke were all defensive geniuses, with Gil and Robby winning gold gloves. Their offense also showed the way, as they led the league in slugging average (.419) and home runs (152). Dodger bombers scored 879 runs, or 5.7 runs per game!

The Dodger-Cardinal battle went down to the wire, with Brooklyn holding a slim 1/2-game lead entering the final game of the season. Shotton's boys claimed the title on the strength of a 9-7, 10-inning victory over the Philadelphia Phillies. Duke Snider singled in the pennant-winning run.

The Dodgers' opponent in the World Series was, once again, the New York Yankees. Casey Stengel's boys captured the flag in a similar wild, hair-raising pennant race, overcoming a one-game Boston Red Sox lead, by sweeping the Sox in the last two games of the season in Yankee Stadium. The scores were 5-4 and 5-3.

The World Series opened in Yankee Stadium on Wednesday, October 5, with big Newk facing 17-game winner, Allie Reynolds. Both hurlers were at their best for this most important showdown. Inning after inning went by without the threat of a score. Shotton's men had only seven baserunners in the game. For the most part "Superchief" was in complete control, tossing a neat two-hitter, and fanning nine Dodgers in the process.

On the other side of the field, the 6' 4" Newcombe matched Reynolds pitch for pitch. He allowed only five baserunners, two less than the Yankee right-hander, and he sent 11 of Stengel's sluggers back to the bench with their bats on their shoulders. After 8 1/2 innings, the game was still scoreless. It looked like it would go on forever, the way these two were pitching. But "Old Reliable", Tommy Henrich, took care of that possibility in short order. After Big Newk fell behind Henrich 2 and 0, he came back with a low curveball, but the Yankee slugger was waiting for it. He tomahawked it on a line to right field. Newcombe didn't even bother to watch it. He

Ralph Branca wraps up one of his 13 victories, a 2-1 decision over the New York Giants (L to R Billy Cox, Pee Wee Reese, Branca, Jackie Robinson).

Jack Banta won 10 games for Burt Shotton's club, including the pennant clincher against Philadelphia, on the last day of the season. He pitched 4 1/3 innings of scoreless ball, and Brooklyn won in the tenth, 9-7, on RBI hits by Snider and Olmo.

turned his back on the ball and started off the field before the game-winning home run had settled into the deep right field stands.

The trauma of that one hit haunted Don Newcombe for the rest of his career. Weighted down by the nightmare of that crushing defeat, he never again pitched a creditable game in the World Series. In three Series, spanning a total of five games, his earned run average was 8.59. In his last Series, 1956, his ERA ballooned to 21.21!

Brooklyn Dodgers	000 000 000 -	0 - 2 - 0
New York Yankees	000 000 001 -	1 - 5 - 1

Game Two looked like a repeat of Game One. Only the numbers on the pitchers' uniforms had changed. Like their predecessors, the Dodgers' crafty southpaw, Preacher Roe and the Yankee's 21-game winner, Vic Raschi, overpowered the hitters.   Brooklyn did manage to break through for one run in the second, however, on a double by Robinson and a two-out single by Gil Hodges. The 1-0 lead held up inning after inning as the skinny 6'2" Roe kept Stengel's men off balance all afternoon with a tantalizing mixture of curve balls and change-ups. Through the first seven innings, the Bronx Bombers never had more than one man on base at a time. In the eighth, after a leadoff single by pinch hitter Johnny Mize, an error by Pee Wee Reese gave the Yanks two baserunners with only one out, but old Preach settled down and retired Henrich and Bauer on easy plays.

The Yankees' last shot, in the ninth, was no contest. Roe was untouchable.   After Joe DiMaggio beat out a slow roller to third,   Johnny Lindell struck out, Billy Johnson popped to second, and Gerry Coleman ended the game with a fly ball to Furillo in right.

Brooklyn Dodgers   0 1 0 0 0 0 0 0 0 - 1 - 7 - 2
New York Yankees   0 0 0 0 0 0 0 0 0 - 0 - 6 - 1

As the scene shifted to Brooklyn's Ebbets Field for the next three games, the atmosphere in Flatbush was exhilarating. The players were quietly confident of ultimate victory. The fans, on the other hand, were obnoxiously boisterous. It didn't take the New York contingent long to bring them back to earth. In Game Three, the bats were still silent for eight long innings. Yankee southpaw, Tommy Byrne, 15-7 during the season, hooked up with 13-game winner Ralph Branca in still another pitching duel.

New York broke the scoring ice with a single run in the third, and the Dodgers tied it with a run in the fourth. The score was still 1-1 as the ninth inning got underway.

New York Yankee slugger Tommy Henrich, who was hitless in three previous at bats, has just connected for a ninth-inning, game-winning home run off Don Newcombe.

Big Don Newcombe, Brooklyn's brilliant rookie pitcher, racked up 17 wins during the season, and was selected by manager Burt Shotton to pitch the opening game of the World Series.

It looked like Branca was still in command as he retired Henrich and DiMaggio on routine plays. Then, with two out and a runner on first, the roof caved in. Bobby Brown ripped a single to right. Woodling walked to load the bases, and pinch hitter Johnny Mize, the "Big Cat," smashed a two-run single against the right field wall. Gerry Coleman greeted relief pitcher Jack Banta with another run-scoring single and, suddenly, the Brooks were down, 4-1. They didn't go quietly, however. Luis Olmo hit a one-out homer into the left field stands in the bottom of the ninth, and Roy Campanella followed suit one-out later. But that was all. Page settled down and struck out pinch hitter Bruce Edwards to end the game.

New York Yankees   0 0 1 0 0 0 0 0 3 - 4 - 5 - 0
Brooklyn Dodgers   0 0 0 1 0 0 0 0 2 - 3 - 5 - 0

The Yanks had the momentum now and they capitalized on it. Shotton tried to come back with Newcombe, on only two days rest, for Game Four, but Big Don was not up to the task. Matched against the Yankee "Junk Man", Eddie Lopat, the Dodger ace escaped a two-hit, two-walk first inning without allowing a run, but his luck ran out in the fourth. With one out and the game still scoreless, third baseman Bobby Brown lashed a long double to left center field. Following a base on balls to Gene Woodling, lefty Cliff Mapes sliced a double down the left field line, scoring both Brown and Woodling. Lopat himself added insult to injury by doubling home Mapes with the third run, and driving Newcombe to the safety of the clubhouse. New York struck for three more runs in the top of the fifth against relief pitcher Joe Hatten.

In the Brooklyn sixth, Shotton's sluggers rapped Lopat hard and often, finally knocking him out of the box with a run of five consecutive singles. Reese and Cox opened the inning for the Dodgers with one base hits. After Duke Snider rapped into a short to first double play, the hits came like raindrops. Robinson singled to left for one run. Hodges lined a single to center. Hits by Olmo, Campanella and Hermanski drove in three more runs, and brought big Allie Reynolds to the rescue. The Chief promptly ended the Brooklyn hopes by striking out pinch hitter Spider Jorgensen on a called third strike.

New York Yankees   000 330 000 - 6 -10 - 0
Brooklyn Dodgers   000 004 000 - 4 - 9 - 1

The Yankees made short work of the Dodgers in Game Five. Shotton, forced to go with the erratic Rex Barney in this crucial game, saw his hopes go down the tube quickly. Three walks and a single netted the Yanks two runs in the first. After an uneventful second, the Bronx Bombers drove the Dodger wildman to cover in a three-run third. Two walks, and singles by Woodling, Coleman and Raschi did the damage.

Once again, Brooklyn fought back, but it was a case of too little, too late. After Stengel's crew had widened their lead to 10-2 after six, the gallant Dodgers came roaring back in the seventh. Snider, who had doubled off the right field wall in the sixth inning and scored the Dodgers second run, singled behind a one-out walk to Jorgensen. One run scored on a sacrifice fly, and three more came across on a walk to Hermanski and a home run into the left field stands by the Brooklyn strongman, Gil Hodges.

Joe Page, the major league's premier fireman, came on to strike out Luis Olmo to end the inning. He proceeded to lock up the World Championship for New York with 2 1/3 innings of shutout ball. He finished with a flourish, fanning Snider, Robinson and Hodges to end the game and the Series.

As gloom settled over the City of Churches, and Dodger fans tried to drown their sorrows in the nearest pub, the familiar drone of the Brooklyn rally cry could be heard from Canarsie to Williamsburg, "Wait Till Next Year." Next year wouldn't arrive until 1955.

New York Yankees   203 113 000 - 10 - 11 - 1
Brooklyn Dodgers   001 001 400 - 6 - 11 - 2

BROOKLYN DODGERS (NL) V.S. THE NEW YORK YANKEES (AL)–1952

Following the Dodgers' loss to the Yankees in the 1949 World Series, two years of frustration and disappointment followed. In 1950, Dick Sisler's tenth-inning home run on the last day of the season gave the Philadelphia "Whiz Kids" the pennant over Burt Shotton's crew. The next year was even worse. Bobby Thomson's "Shot heard round the world" in the ninth inning of the third game of the National League playoffs, snatched a certain pennant away from the Flatbush Flock, driving half of Brooklyn into a deep depression. Many loyal fans even contemplated suicide.

As 1952 got underway, the Brooklyn team was fighting mad, and thirsting for revenge. A managerial change brought the fiery Chuck Dressen to Ebbets Field to harness the tremendous talent that Branch Rickey had gathered together. Dressen, a master strategist and a consummate egotist, often implored his team, "Hold 'em for eight innings an' I'll think of something."

The "Boys of Summer" were now a seasoned squad on the verge of greatness. The Giants managed to stay close to the top for about six weeks, then Dressen's crew pulled away, leading by as many as ten games at one time, and finishing a comfortable 4 1/2 games in front.

Brooklyn's success was the result of its well-oiled offense, a wrecking crew that was dangerous from the top of the batting order to the bottom. Gil Hodges was the Dodgers' main gunner with 32 home runs and 102 runs batted in. His capable supporting cast included Roy Campanella (.269, 22, 97), Duke Snider (.303, 21, 92), left fielder Andy Pafko (.287, 19, 85), and Jackie Robinson (.308, 19, 75). The Flock led all National League teams in runs scored with 775, an average of 5 + runs per game.

The Dodgers' stalwart defense again led the National League in fielding with an average of .982, committing only 106 errors in 154 games. Catcher Roy Campanella and third baseman Billy Cox, two of the team's defensive magicians, won gold gloves at their positions.

Not to be outdone, the pitching staff once again was more than adequate, finishing second behind Philadelphia's fine staff led by Robin Roberts and Curt Simmons. In addition to Erskine (14-6, 3.12), Roe (11-2, 3.12), and Ben Wade (11-9, 3.60), two rookie hurlers, Billy Loes (13-8, 2.69) and Joe Black (15-4), made significant contributions to the pennant race. Brooklyn born Loes, a brash young right-hander with the mentality of a southpaw, started 21 games and relieved in 18 more en route to a fine rookie season. Joe Black, overnight, became the top relief pitcher in the league, saving 15 games, winning another 15, and sporting an exceptional 2.15 earned run average.

Mickey Mantle was close behind with 23 round trippers and 83 RBIs on the strength of a .311 batting average. Joe Collins hit 18 home runs and Hank Bauer had 17, while Gene Woodling and Gil McDougald hit 12 and 11 respectively.

Brooklyn Dodgers–1952 National League Champions

As usual, the Dodgers antagonist in the World Series was Casey Stengel's New York Yankees. The Bronx Bombers found themselves in a real dogfight with the pitching strong Cleveland Indians for most of the season. Seldom more than two or three games separated the two teams as the hot summer months dragged on. Cleveland, with three 20-game winners, Bob Lemon (22-11), Early Wynn (23-12), and Mike Garcia (22-11), actually took over the lead briefly on August 22, but didn't have the firepower to hold it. Unfortunately for Cleveland, an off season by future Hall-of-Famer Bob Feller (9-13), prevented Al Lopez's contingent from winning it all.

The Yankees, however, did not back into the pennant. Their pitching staff actually outperformed the Cleveland trio, leading the league in earned run average with a slick 3.14. The Yankees had the kind of staff best suited to short series matchups such as the World Series. It was talented and it was deep. Where Cleveland had basically a four-man staff, the Yankees could throw seven or eight capable pitchers at you. The "Super Chief" Allie Reynolds, as usual, was the ace, piling up a 20-8 record. Vic Raschi followed with 16-5. Eddie Lopat at 10-5 and National League castoff Johnny Sain, at 11-6 rounded out the starting rotation. Joe Page was gone, but the Yankees thrived on a "bullpen by committee."

Yogi Berra led a potent Yankee attack. He batted a solid .273 while slugging 30 homers and driving in 98 runs.

The World Series opened in Ebbets Field on October 1 and, for once, the Dodgers got off to a fast start. Joe Black, Brooklyn's rookie relief ace, was manager Charlie Dressen's surprise starter, and he rewarded his manager's confidence with a sterling pitching effort. Opposed by Allie Reynolds, Black matched the Yankee ace pitch for pitch through five innings. Dressen's crew opened the scoring with a single run off Reynolds in the bottom of the second on a Jackie Robinson home run into the lower left field stands. New York countered in the top of the third on a round tripper by Gil McDougald.

As the bottom of the sixth got underway, the score was still deadlocked at one run apiece, but it didn't stay that way for long. With two out, Pee Wee Reese rifled a single to left field. Then Duke Snider caught an Allie Reynolds fast ball and drove it high over the right field scoreboard and onto Bedford Avenue as 34,861 victory-starved Brooklyn fans sent the little ballpark into a frenzied demonstration not witnessed for several years.

With a 3-1 lead to work on, Joe Black had the game well in hand. He did yield a leadoff triple to Woodling in the eighth that resulted in the Yanks second run, but he slammed the door on them after that, retiring the last six men in order.

New York Yankees	001 000 010	- 2 - 6 - 2
Brooklyn Dodgers	010 002 01x	- 4 - 6 - 0

Hopes ran high as Game Two got underway in Brooklyn. Dodger ace Carl Erskine was well rested and ready to add to the one-game advantage. The little Hoosier did get off to a strong start as he blanked the Bronx Bombers over the first three innings. And his teammates gave him a lead in the bottom of the third, pushing over the first run of the game off fireballer Vic Raschi. Singles by Reese, Snider and Campanella did the damage. As it turned out, those were the only hits Brooklyn would get all afternoon.

Willard Mullin's famous Dodger "Bum," developed in the 1940s, has a cocky expression on his face, as he waltzes into the World Series after disposing of Leo Durocher's Giants in the National League pennant chase. (Shirley Mullin Rhodes)

Erskine meanwhile, couldn't stem the Yankee attack. They tied the game in the fourth on a long double to right by Mickey Mantle and a sacrifice fly. They pushed across the lead run in the fifth on a walk, a stolen base, and a single by second baseman Billy Martin. Then, in the sixth, they broke the game wide open, sending the Dodger ace to the showers before a man was retired. A three-run homer by the pesky Martin capped a five-run inning.

New York Yankees   0 0 0 1 1 5 0 0 0 - 7 - 10 - 0
Brooklyn Dodgers   0 0 1 0 0 0 0 0 0 - 1 - 3 - 1

The Series shifted to Yankee Stadium for Game Three with a thinking man's pitching matchup. Eddie

"The Junk Man" Lopat was on the mound for the Stengel men while Preacher Roe was given the ball by Charlie Dressen. The two southpaws got by on the craft and guile. Neither of them could overpower a batter, but they were both experts at keeping hitters off balance with an assortment of curve balls and changeups. An occasional heater could freeze a batter in his tracks.

Old Preach was nicked for a run in the second, much to the delight of the overflow crowd of 66,698. Lopat himself was the culprit, touching his buddy, Roe, for a run-scoring single to right center. The Flatbush contingent came right back in the third with a run of their own. Carl Furillo led off with a one-bounce double into the right field boxes, later scoring on a sacrifice fly by Jackie Robinson. Brooklyn took the lead in the top of the fifth on singles by Cox and Reese. They extended the lead with another tally in the eighth on singles by Robinson and Campanella and a sacrifice fly by Andy Pafko.

Down 3-1, the New Yorkers pulled closer on a Yogi Berra home run, but the Dodgers, once again, fought back. In the top of the ninth, singles by Reese and Robinson, and a double steal, put men on second and third with two out. Both runners crossed the plate when Yogi Berra let a pitch get away for a passed ball. The lanky Roe gave up a harmless one-out homer to Mize in the bottom of the ninth, before retiring Rizzuto and Sain to end the game.

Brooklyn Dodgers   0 0 1 0 1 0 0 1 2 - 5 - 11 - 0
New York Yankees   0 1 0 0 0 0 0 1 1 - 3 - 6 - 2

Fresh from a Yankee Stadium victory, Charlie Dressen's crew were determined to maintain their momentum. Joe Black, the winner in Game One, came back on two days rest to face Allie Reynolds again. This time however, the "Super Chief" had the upper hand. It was a tight pitchers' duel all the way, with Reynolds tossing a four-hitter, and Black holding the Bronx Bombers to only three safeties in seven innings. New York scored the only run that mattered in the fourth on a home run by Johnny Mize. They made it 2-0 in the eighth on a triple by Mantle and a throwing error by Reese.

Brooklyn Dodgers   0 0 0 0 0 0 0 0 0 - 0 - 4 - 1
New York Yankees   0 0 0 1 0 0 0 1 x - 2 - 4 - 1

Game Five of the 1952 World Series was one of the classic pitching performances in Series history. The little Hoosier, Carl Erskine, got the call from manager Charlie Dressen while Casey Stengel countered with former Cincinnati great, Ewell "The Whip" Blackwell. Blackwell, a 22-game winner for the Reds in 1947, was in the twilight of an injury-riddled career. He would pitch only eight more major league games after this year. In his prime, the tall, lanky Blackwell, standing 6'6" tall and weighing only 195 pounds, was almost unhittable. He threw with a herky-jerky buggywhip motion similar to Don Drysdale,

Joe Black, Dressen's one-man pitching staff, appeared in three games in the Series. He was 1-2 with an excellent 2.53 earned run average in 21 1/3 innings.

his blazing fast ball appearing to come at the batter from the vicinity of the third base dugout. Now, at 30 years of age, and wracked with arm ailments however, his repertoire was no longer overpowering.

Brooklyn nicked him for a run in the second on a walk and two singles. Three innings later, the Dodger wrecking crew lengthened their lead on a sacrifice fly and a two run shot into the right center field seats by Duke Snider. The Yankees, never out of a game, almost drove Erskine to cover under a blistering four-hit attack in the bottom of the fifth. A leadoff walk to Hank Bauer got them going. Then a barrage of singles by Martin, Irv Noren, and Phil Rizzuto brought in two runs, cutting the Dodger lead to 4-2. After Mickey Mantle fouled out to Billy Cox for the second out, Johnny Mize stepped to the

Andy Pafko goes high in the air to rob Gene Woodling of a home run in the second inning of Game Five.

plate. "The Big Cat", at 6'2" tall and 215 pounds, was an awesome sight as he stood in the batter's box. A great clutch hitter and Dodger killer, he immediately lifted an Erskine delivery into the lower right field stands for a three-run home run and a 5-4 New York lead.

The game remained 5-4 until the seventh when the Dodgers got even on an infield hit by Cox and a single by Snider. Now the game turned into a pitchers' duel between Erskine and curveball specialist Johnny Sain. As it turned out, Carl Erskine did not allow another Yankee baserunner after Mize's homer. He retired 19 men in a row from the fifth inning through the eleventh. Sain stayed with him for several innings, but in the 11th, the Boys of Flatbush broke through. One-out singles by Cox and Reese put men on first and third, and a Duke Snider

double plated the game winner. It was one of the greatest victories in Brooklyn's long and illustrious National League history, and a courageous pitching effort on the part of Carl Erskine, who went all the way.

```
Brooklyn Dodgers   010 030 100 01 - 6 - 10 -0
New York Yankees   000 050 000 00 - 5 -  5- 1
```

The Dodgers were now in the drivers seat, up three games to two, and heading home to Ebbets Field for the final two games. The feeling was good. Optimism was high that this would be the championship year. The pitching matchup was Raschi, the winner of Game Two, against right-hander Billy Loes. The game, another low-scoring affair, was marked by two of the most bizarre plays ever witnessed in a World Series.

The two righthanders kept the opponents at bay through the first five and a half innings. Then, much to the delight of the Brooklyn faithful, their boys broke out on top. The Duke of Flatbush brought the crowd to its feet as he unloaded on a Raschi fastball and sent it on a high arc over the right field screen.

The lead didn't hold up for long however, as Stengel's cohorts bounced right back in the top of the seventh, aided by two bizarre plays. Yogi Berra led off the inning, and promptly followed Snider's lead by hitting a home run over the screen and onto Bedford Avenue. Gene Woodling followed with a single to center. Seconds later he was awarded second base on a balk when the ball slipped out of Loes' glove on the mound. After the game, the eccentric right-hander explained the mishap by saying he had "too much spit" on the ball. Later, in the same inning, Raschi sent a ground ball back to the mound. It caromed off Loes' leg and rolled into right field as Woodling raced across with the go-ahead run. Loes claimed he didn't stop the grounder because "he had lost the ball in the sun."

An inning later, Mickey Mantle extended the lead to 3-1 with a long homer into the left center field stands. Brooklyn bounced back again in the bottom of the inning when "The Duke" rewarded his fans with his second home run of the game, another high drive over the screen in right. A two-out double by George "Shotgun" Shuba put the tying run on base, but Old Case brought Reynolds in to face Campanella, and "Superchief" did his job. Campy went down swinging to end the rally.

```
New York Yankees   000 000 210 - 3 - 9 - 0
Brooklyn Dodgers   000 001 010 - 2 - 8 - 1
```

It all came down to Game Seven. Eddie Lopat, the Game Three loser to Preacher Roe, was on the mound for New York. Joe Black, with a 1-1 Series record, was Dressen's choice for the big game. The first three innings were uneventful, as Shuba's second-inning single was the only hit for either side. In the fourth, New York took a 1-0 lead on a double by Rizzuto and a single by Mize. Brooklyn came right back in the bottom of the inning, knocking Lopat out of the box in the process. When the Dodgers loaded the bases with none out on singles by Snider, Robinson and Campanella, Stengel was quick to react. Realizing there was no tomorrow, the Yankee manager beckoned Allie Reynolds from the bullpen, the Chief's fourth appearance in the Series. The first batter to face the Yankee ace, Gil Hodges, hit a line drive to left field. Woodling caught it, but Snider tagged up and scored the tying run. The Dodgers failed to capitalize any further however, as Shuba fanned and Furillo grounded out, third to first.

The Bronx Bombers recaptured the lead minutes later when Woodling homered to right. Again Brooklyn bounced back. Billy Cox, an underrated clutch hitter, doubled off the right field wall, and scored moments later on a hit by Reese. For the third time in as many innings, the Stengelmen took the lead, this time on a round-tripper by Mantle.

The score widened to 4-2 in the seventh on hits by McDougald and Mantle. As the stretch half of the inning got underway, the Flatbush faithful began a rhythmic hand clapping, trying to spur their team to action one more time. It almost worked. With Vic Raschi on the hill for the Yanks, Brooklyn proceeded to load the bases on a single by Cox and walks to Furillo and Reese with only one out. Lefty Bob Kuzava was rushed in from the pen to relieve the beleaguered Raschi. He retired the first batter he faced, the dangerous Duke Snider, on a weak pop-up to third base. Then disaster almost struck the New York contingent. Jackie Robinson hit a high infield fly to the right of the mound. The Yankee players seemed frozen in their tracks, with no one making a move on the ball. Two Brooklyn runners headed home with what would have been the tying runs. At the last instant, second baseman Billy Martin, hat flying in the breeze, made a desperate race for the ball. He caught it with one final lunge, just inches from the ground. With that play, the Dodger hopes were dashed once again. Kuzava, the journeyman southpaw, retired the Brooks without a hit over the final two innings. The New York Yankees were the World Champions again, their fourth consecutive World Title.

| New York Yankees | 000 111 100 - 4 - 10 - 4 |
| Brooklyn Dodgers | 000 110 000 - 2 - 8 - 1 |

BROOKLYN DODGERS (NL) V.S. THE NEW YORK YANKEES (AL)–1953

The 1953 Brooklyn Dodgers were one of the most devastating wrecking crews in major league history. Despite the fact that they didn't win the World Series, the '53 Dodgers were the greatest team ever assembled in either Brooklyn or Los Angeles. Winners of 105 games during the regular season, they dominated most offensive categories. They led the league for the fifth consecutive time in runs scored (955, an average of 6.2 runs per game), home runs (208), slugging average (.474), and runs batted in (887). Their .474 slugging average is still the second-highest average in National League history, trailing only the 1930 Chicago Cubs of Hack Wilson fame, who powered the ball at a .481 clip. Their 208 home runs remains the fifth best in the Senior Circuit. Showing that power wasn't their only offensive weapon, Brooklyn also led the league in stolen bases for the eighth year running.

Their defense continued to be rock solid, as they led the league in fielding for the third straight time, committing only 118 errors in 154 games, a .980 average. Five players, Campanella, Hodges, Robinson, Reese, and Cox, at one time or another, were gold glove recipients. On the mound, they led the league in strikeouts for the sixth consecutive season with 819, and were third in team ERA.

Individually, the "Boys of Summer" were awesome. Six players scored over 100 runs. Three players knocked in more than 100 runs. And eight players contributed 10 or more home runs to the Dodger attack. They were an unselfish team of all-stars. Today, four of them reside in baseball's Hall of Fame in Cooperstown, New York: Campanella, Robinson, Reese, and Snider. Hodges and Furillo also deserve recognition in that hallowed Hall.

Rookie pitcher Billy Loes threw a gutty game against the Yankees in Game Six, tossing six shutout innings, before yielding, 3-2.

Brooklyn Dodgers–1953 National League Champions

Campanella, the Dodgers' rotund catcher, had a career season in 1953. His .312 batting average, 41 home runs and league-leading 142 runs batted in, brought him his second National League Most Valuable Player award, his first coming in 1951. The 26-year-old Snider, in the prime of his career, was a complete ball player. The man with "steel springs in his legs" was a defensive genius who could outrun and outjump most other outfielders in the majors. At the plate he hit a torrid .336 with 42 home runs and 126 runs batted in. He led the league with 132 runs scored and a .627 slugging average. Carl Furillo, the "Reading Rifle," possessed one of the strongest throwing arms in baseball and was considered to be the National League's premier right fielder. Coming back from a sub-par 1952 season that concluded with eye surgery, Skoonj led the league in hitting with an average of .344, while smashing 21 homers and knocking in 92 runs. An on-field brawl with New York Giant manager, Leo Durocher, sidelined Furillo for the last three weeks of the season, and hampered him through most of the Series.

Gil Hodges was one of the all-time great National League first basemen. The Brooklyn strongman, with arms like anvils, hit .302 and propelled 31 balls out of various National League parks during the season, driving in 122 runs in the process. Jackie Robinson, now 34 years old and slowing down, was still the team's driving force. He batted .329, with 12 homers and 95 RBIs, and

stole 17 of the Dodgers league-leading 90 stolen bases. Anchoring the team at third base was "The Golden Glove", Billy Cox. Considered by many to be the greatest fielding third baseman in National League history, Cox was also a tough competitor at bat, and a feared clutch hitter. He contributed a .291 batting average and 10 home runs to the Brooklyn attack. Pee Wee Reese, the captain and team leader, scored 108 runs and led the team with 22 stolen bases.

Reese's second base partner was James "Junior" Gilliam, a six-year veteran of the Negro National League. Junior won Rookie of the Year honors in the National League in 1953 on the strength of a .278 batting average, 100 bases on balls, 21 stolen bases, 125 runs scored, and a league leading 17 triples.

The benefactors of this explosive offense, the Dodger pitching staff, had a most joyous summer. Carl Erskine had a career best 20-6 record, a league-leading .769 percentage, to lead the staff. He was followed by Russ "Monk" Meyer (15-5), Billy Loes (14-8), Preacher Roe (11-3), and relief ace, Clem Labine (11-6).

As might be expected, the Big Blue Machine ran away and hid from the rest of the league, clinching the pennant on September 12 when Carl Erskine dumped the Braves 5-2. It was the earliest clinching in National League history. Indicative of their scoring prowess was the fact that, while they were shutout only once all season, they scored in double figures on 26 separate occasions. Their victory margins totaled 266 runs by season's end. Some of the performances were notable. In one game, they crushed St. Louis 20-4, scoring 12 runs in the 7th inning. In other games, they buried the Cards 14-0, 14-6 and 12-5. Another 12-run rally, this one in the 8th inning, stopped Philadelphia 16-2. An Erskine one-hitter zipped the Redlegs, 10-0. Chicago was a victim, 15-4. Pittsburgh fell by the wayside by scores of 14-2 and 14-6. And the hated Giants felt the Dodger wrath four times, by scores of 12-4, 12-4, 16-7 and 10-0.

Jackie Robinson moved to left field in 1953 to make way for rookie Junior Gilliam to play second base.

Across town, Casey Stengel's New York Yankees were enjoying the summer almost as much as were the Dodgers. Breaking away from the pack in mid-May, the Bronx Bombers continuously widened their lead, racking up 99 wins and finishing 8 1/2 games ahead of Cleveland. Leading the powerful Yankee offense was Yogi Berra with 27 homers and 108 runs batted in. Mickey Mantle, in his third season with New York and still learning his trade, chipped in with 21 round-trippers and 92 RBIs. It was on the mound however, where Stengel's secret weapons were stored. Their usual deep pitching staff was led by second year man Whitey Ford who, returning from the service, compiled an 18-6 record. He was ably supported by "Steady Eddie" Lopat (16-4), 36-year-old Johnny Sain (14-7), Vic Raschi (13-6) and Allie Reynolds (13-7).

As the World Series got underway Brooklyn fans everywhere were justifiably optimistic about the outcome. Their team was unbeatable. Perhaps on paper they were. And perhaps, over the strenuous 154 game regular season, they were. But, in a short series, pitching is paramount. The team with the best concentration of pitching talent usually wins the short series–and the Yanks had the pitching edge.

Pee Wee Reese played his usual flawless defensive game during the Series, but was held to a .208 batting average by the Yankee pitching staff.

Game One, in Yankee Stadium, pitted Allie Reynolds, with a 6-2 record in 13 World Series appearances, against Dodger ace Carl Erskine. It was no contest as "Oisk" got bombed out in the first inning. Hank Bauer tripled in Collins who had walked. Then, after two more free passes loaded the bases, little Billy Martin cleared them with a booming triple over Jackie Robinson's head in left center field.

Visiting Dodger fans were stunned and silent as their unbeatable team got shelled. To Brooklyn's credit, they fought back tenaciously, scoring one run in the fifth on rookie Junior Gilliam's home run to right, then driving the "Superchief" to cover with a three-run barrage in the sixth. A solo homer by Gil Hodges and a two-run shot by "Shotgun" Shuba spelled doom for Reynolds. Singles by Campanella, Hodges and Furillo knotted the count in the top of the seventh, and the Dodgers had runners on second and first, still with no one out. They could not pull the trigger, however, as Yankee pitching toughened. Johnny Sain, a veteran of many wars with the old Boston Braves and the Yankees, kept his cool and frustrated the Brooklyn sluggers. Bunts by Cox and Labine ended up in force plays at third, and Gilliam fouled out to Berra to end the threat.

A Joe Collins home run off Labine in the bottom half of the inning put the Yanks on top for good, and they iced it with three more in the 8th, on three hits and a walk. Johnny Sain's two-run double did most of the damage.

Brooklyn Dodgers	000 013 100 - 5 - 12 - 2
New York Yankees	400 010 13x - 9 - 12 - 0

Game Two was a rematch of the third game of the 1952 Series, pitting the two crafty southpaws, "Steady Eddie" Lopat and Elwin "Preacher" Roe against each other. In '52, the Arkansas hillbilly prevailed over the city slicker by a count of 5-3. The New York-born Lopat, a mainstay of the Yankee's five consecutive American League titles and four World Championships beginning in 1949, sported a 3-1 Series record coming into this fall classic, and he was intent on reversing his lone loss. Roe, on the other hand, at 2-0 in Series play, intended to remain undefeated.

The game was a typical Lopat-Roe encounter, a low-scoring affair distinguished by many baserunners but few runs. In the '52 pitching duel, a 5-3 Brooklyn victory, the two teams left a combined total of 18 runners stranded, 10 by the Dodgers. This year Dressen's crew once again missed numerous opportunities as they left another ten men on base. New York, on the other hand, made the most of their chances, converting nine baserunners into four runs, good enough for a 4-2 win. A seventh-inning home run by Billy Martin and a two-run shot by Mickey Mantle in the eighth, sealed Roe's fate.

Carl Erskine celebrating his record-breaking strikeout performance in Game Three.

Brooklyn Dodgers	000 200 000 - 2 - 9 - 1
New York Yankees	100 000 12x - 4 - 5 - 0

Down two games to none, the power laden Brooklyn Dodgers, conquerors of all they surveyed in the National League, slunk back across the river to regroup, and to plan their future strategy. As 35,270 apprehensive Brooklyn fans crammed into the little park along Bedford Avenue for Game Three, Manager Charlie Dressen considered his choices, then announced that his ace, Carl Erskine, would try to stop the slide. Erskine, the Dodgers' 20–game winner in the regular season had lasted only one inning in game one, yielding four runs on two hits and three bases on balls.

In Game Three, the little Hoosier was overpowering, pitching a tight six-hitter and fanning 14 Yankee batters to break Howard Ehmke's 24-year-old strikeout record. Erskine, the master of the overhand curveball, and the possessor of the game's best change-up, kept the Bronx Bombers off balance all afternoon. He started quickly, striking out McDougald and Collins in the first inning and getting Bauer on a grounder to short. His strikeout total mounted inning after inning, as his curveball crackled and his changeup worked to perfection, setting up his sneaky fast ball.

Yankee pitcher, Vic Raschi, after matching goose eggs with Erskine for four innings, could not stand prosperity. A one-out double off the right field wall by Jackie Robinson quickly produced the tying run. After Robby forced Raschi into a balk move, giving him third base, he raced home on a squeeze bunt by Billy Cox. An inning later, Brooklyn broke into the lead when Robinson's two-out single brought Snider in from second.

The two teams traded runs in the eighth and, as the ninth got underway, Carl Erskine was one strikeout away from tying Howard Ehmke's World Series record of 13. That plateau was reached quickly as "Oisk" disposed of pinch hitter Don Bollweg on three fastballs. The next batter, representing the tying run, was Dodger killer Johnny Mize. This time Old John was no puzzle for the Brooklyn righty and, he too, swung and missed at an overhand curveball, giving Erskine the record. It was fitting that, after damaging Brooklyn so often in the past, "The Big Cat" was the record-breaking 14th strikeout victim.

New York Yankees	000 010 010 - 2 - 6 - 0
Brooklyn Dodgers	000 011 01x - 3 - 9 - 0

Erskine's strikeout-filled victory gave Charlie Dressen's crew some badly needed momentum, and they continued to feed off it the next day. Jumping on Whitey Ford for three big runs in the bottom of the first, the Dodgers gave Billy Loes a working lead he never relinquished. Gilliam led off the festivities by slicing a ground-rule double to right field. A one-out single by Robinson scored the first run of the game and, minutes later, a ringing double off the right-field screen by Duke Snider, batting sixth against the left-handed Ford, brought in two more.

Loes never faltered, tossing an efficient eight-hitter for eight innings, and fanning eight more Yankees in the process. The boys from the Bronx did manage to touch up the Brooklyn righty for two runs in the fifth on a home run by Gil McDougald, but the Bums were on top 4-0 by that time thanks to a fourth-inning, run-scoring double by Junior Gilliam. The Dodgers added two more in the sixth on a Snider homer, a Cox double, and a sacrifice fly by Gilliam. They extended it to 7-2 in the seventh on a run-scoring double by the Duke, his third extra base hit of the game. Gilliam also chipped in with three extra base hits, all doubles.

Billy Cox, the Dodgers' Gold Glove third baseman, batted .304 during the series, with six runs batted-in.

The New Yorkers closed out the scoring in the ninth, loading the bases with no one out against Loes, then pushing across a run on a two-out single by Mantle. Billy Martin, also trying to score on the hit, was thrown out at the plate, Thompson to Campanella, ending the game. Going unnoticed in the Brooklyn success, was Billy Martin's impressive hit total. He was quietly amassing a record-breaking number of base hits, pushing his total up to eight in four games, with a single and a triple.

New York Yankees	000 020 001	- 3 - 9 - 0
Brooklyn Dodgers	300 102 10x	- 7 - 12 - 0

Brooklyn hoped to make it a clean sweep at home as they threw rookie southpaw Johnny Podres against Jim "Hotrod" McDonald, a journeyman right-hander with a 9-7 record. The 21-year-old Podres, later a renowned Yankee killer, was not yet a polished big league hurler. In just his third year of professional baseball, the native of Witherbee, New York, was awed by the riotous atmosphere in Ebbets Field, and awed by the Bronx Bombers as well.

After Gene Woodling led off the game with a home run, Podres settled down momentarily. But, in the third, the youngster's world collapsed. He became unglued after a two-out error by Gil Hodges let in the lead run. A hit batter and a walk loaded the bases for New York, and the Brooklyn lefty was quickly yanked in favor of right-handed "Monk" Meyer. Meyer threw Mantle a curveball, and the Mick hit it a mile, a grand slam into the upper deck of the left-field stands.

Billy Cox's three-run homer in the Dodger eighth and Junior Gilliam's solo shot in the ninth was a case of too little, too late, as the Bronx Bombers regained the momentum with an 11-7 triumph, heading home.

New York Yankees	105 000 311	- 11 - 11 - 1
Brooklyn Dodgers	010 010 041	- 7 - 14 - 1

The Yankees wasted no time getting the jump on their cross town rivals in Game Six. Before the 62,370 paid patrons could get settled in their seats, Casey Stengel's boys had pushed over two runs on Dodger ace Carl Erskine. Yogi Berra's double got the first one in and the second run came across on an error by the usually reliable Junior Gilliam. Two singles and a sacrifice fly made the tally 3-0 in the second.

The Dodgers finally broke the scoring drought in the sixth when Jackie Robinson hit a double off the left-field wall and came around to score on a stolen base and an infield out. New York lefty, Whitey Ford, pitched an outstanding game, limiting the hard-hitting Brooks to a single run on only six hits in seven innings. Seven Dodgers went down on strikes before Ford's assortment of curve balls, fast balls, and changeups, and his usual pinpoint control resulted in only one free pass.

The "Old Professor," thinking his ace was tiring, and wanting a strong, fresh arm to close out the Series, brought Allie Reynolds in from the bullpen. It looked like curtains for Charlie Dressen's contingent when the "Chief" breezed through the eighth, yielding a harmless, two-out single to Robinson. In the ninth, with one out, Duke Snider nursed the Yankee right-hander for a base on balls. Carl Furillo, still bothered by the broken wrist he suffered in his fight with Durocher, stepped to the plate. His timing off as a result of his late season inactivity, "Skoonj" drilled a Reynolds' fast ball to the opposite field. It settled comfortably into the lower right field stands for a game-tying two-run homer and, suddenly, the sun shone again in Brooklyn.

Confidence filled the Brooklyn dugout because their ace reliever, Clem Labine, was on the mound, and the top of the batting order was scheduled up in the top of the tenth. But the top of the tenth never came. Labine, working carefully to slugger Hank Bauer, walked him leading off the bottom of the ninth. After Yogi Berra lined out to Furillo in right, Mickey Mantle, the "Commerce Comet" beat out an infield bouncer to put two men on. Billy Martin, with a count of 1-1, ended the suspense by staying with a Labine sinker and grounding a base hit over second base to drive in Berra with the winning run of the Series, and giving the New York fans an unprecedented fifth consecutive World's Championship.

Brooklyn Dodgers	000 001 002	-3- 8-3
New York Yankees	210 000 001	-4-13-0

Martin's hit, his twelfth of the Series, set a record for most hits in a six-game Series, and tied the record for a seven-game Series. The Yankee second baseman led all batters with an average of .500, and his eight RBIs tied teammate Joe Collins. On the Dodger side, the awesome "Boys of Summer" protected their reputation by combining for a team batting average of an even .300. They were led by Gil Hodges (.364), Carl Furillo (.333), Duke Snider (.320), Jackie Robinson (.320), and Billy Cox (.304).

It was pitching (expected) and defense (unexpected) that did Brooklyn in. Their team earned run average was a dreadful 4.91, with none of the regulars under 3.38.

Carl Furillo, out of the lineup for three weeks with a broken hand, hit a dramatic game-tying home run in the ninth inning of the last game of the Series.

Seven errors by the usually solid Dodger defense let in five unearned runs, all of them scoring in the key fifth game.

BROOKLYN DODGERS (NL) V.S. THE NEW YORK YANKEES (AL)—1955

Wait till next year!

The rallying cry of the frustrated Brooklyn Dodger fan reverberated through the bustling streets of Flatbush, across the green expanse of Prospect Park, and along the boardwalk at Coney Island. It was only a faint murmur when Leo Durocher's surprising band of castoffs and rookies battled the mighty New York Yankees for world supremacy in 1941. It became louder as defeat followed disastrous defeat to those same Yankees in 1947 and 1949. And it grew to a loud plaintive wail as 1952 became 1953 and still the championship eluded the Dodger faithful.

WAIT TILL NEXT YEAR!

The Brooklyn Dodgers had something to prove in 1955. Favored to win their third straight National League flag in 1954, the Dodgers were sidetracked by a fired-up New York Giant club sparked by Willie Mays' 41 home runs and Johnny Antonelli's 21 victories.

As 1955 dawned, the "Boys of Summer," graying slightly at the temples, rededicated themselves to the quest for the elusive World Championship. Five times in eight years, the Dodgers had led the way home in the National League struggle. Five times they came away from the Series empty handed. Under second-year manager, Walter "Smokey" Alston, they vowed it would not happen again. From 37-year-old Pee Wee Reese to 25-year-old Sandy Amoros, the Boys of Flatbush drove themselves as never before.

The work, the pain, and the sacrifice eventually paid off. When the dust settled in late September, the Brooklyn Dodgers had proven that, while they were old compared to their counterparts, they were still the class of the National League. And, when the sun set over Yankee Stadium on October 4, and Gil Hodges had squeezed the last out of the 1955 World Series, the "Boys of Summer" were finally exonerated. The *New York Daily News* splashed it across the front page in bold, black headlines:

THIS IS NEXT YEAR!

The story behind the most glorious chapter in Brooklyn Dodger history began in Flatbush on a blustery April afternoon when 32,000 of the Brooklyn faithful crammed into little Ebbets Field to welcome a new season, and to cheer for "Oisk," Duke, "Pee Wee," and the rest. Carl Furillo hit a three run homer, Carl Erskine tossed a tight seven hitter, and the "Boys of Summer" coasted to an easy 7-1 triumph over the visiting Pittsburgh Pirates. Eight days later, Duke Snider hit one out with two on as the Dodgers routed Robin Roberts and the Phils 14-2.

Brooklyn Dodgers–1955 World Champions!

Home runs jumped off Dodger bats like snowflakes. Furillo slammed seven round-trippers during the first three weeks. Even pitcher Don Newcombe got into the act, poling two homers in one game. Flatbush fans were ecstatic as their beloved Bums won their first ten games, a major league record, lost one, then streaked to another 12 of 13, giving them a 22-2 record and a big nine game lead over the hated Giants. Alston's wrecking crew continued to lengthen their lead through the month of May. A three-homer effort by Snider downed the Milwaukee Braves 11-6 to get June off on the right foot. Injuries slowed the Dodgers down somewhat as the season neared the halfway mark, but the pitchers and the bench helped the team maintain a healthy 14 1/2 game lead over the Milwaukee Braves. Leo Durocher's 1954 World Champion Giants were mired in fifth place, 18 1/2 games out.

Brooklyn's 55-22 record was the result of a total team effort. Big Don Newcombe, the ace of the staff once again, boasted a sizzling 14-1 record, not to mention a .418 batting average and six home runs. Duke Snider had hammered 27 home runs and had driven in 84 runs in only 77 games. Roy Campanella had 19 homers and 64 RBIs.

A mild slump in July raised some concern in the Brooklyn front office, but the lead never dropped below ten games. With the walking wounded outnumbering the healthy, Walt Alston dipped into his minor league reservoir and brought up two young pitchers, Don Bessent and Roger Craig, to help the team during the stretch run. Both men contributed mightily; Bessent with an 8-1 record and Craig with five wins against three defeats.

Through August and into September, the Brooklyn juggernaught rolled on, thanks to Carl Furillo. Skoonj hit at a torrid .465 clip over a five-week period to carry the club through the summer. At one time, in mid-August, the Dodger lead dwindled to a mere ten games, but a 19-year-old, baby-faced southpaw by the name of Sandy Koufax stopped the slide with a 14-strikeout, 7-0 whitewashing of the Cincinnati Reds.

On September 8, Walter Alston's dedicated crew walloped the Braves 10-2 to clinch the National League pennant, the earliest clinching in league history. The previous record, of September 13, was set by the '53 Dodgers. Roy Campanella walked off with his third Most Valuable Player trophy, finishing the year with a .318 batting average, 32 homers and 107 runs batted in. Duke Snider hit .309 and walloped 42 homers, while leading the league with 126 runs scored and 136 RBIs. Gil Hodges was .289, 27, 102, while Furillo came in with .314, 26, 95. Big Newk had a big, big season, finishing with a 20-5 record on the mound, and also showing the way at bat, with an average of .359, seven home runs, and 23 RBIs.

Fittingly, Brooklyn's opponent in the World Series was their perennial nemesis, the New York Yankees. Casey Stengel's mighty bombers, after a one-year hiatus, recaptured the American League flag, although it was not an easy task. Throughout most of the summer, it was a four-team race, with defending champion Cleveland, Boston, and Chicago, all vying for the top spot. Finally, in mid-September, the New Yorkers broke away from the pack, sweeping a three-game series from the Red Sox while Detroit was knocking off Al Lopez's Indians three straight.

Pitching, once again, carried the Yanks to victory, as they led the American League with a team ERA of 3.23. The "Chairman of the Board" Whitey Ford was the ace, with a league-leading 18 wins against only seven losses. "Bullet Bob" Turley followed with 17-13, and 210 strikeouts. Tommy Byrne, the league's winning percentage leader was 16-5, while five other pitchers had between seven and nine victories. Jim Konstanty, the old Philadelphia Phillie closer, anchored the bullpen, going 7-2 with 11 saves and a 2.32 ERA. As usual, the Yankee offense

Wlillard Mullin's "Bum" sends out a warning to National and American League opponents alike, in 1955. Walter Alston's team dedicated itself to a World Championship, in spring training. Then they made their dream come true. (Shirley Mullin Rhodes)

was led by Yogi Berra (.272, 27, 108), Mickey Mantle (.306, 37, 99), and Hank Bauer (.278, 20, 53). The Mick's 37 round-trippers led the league.

The Series began in Yankee Stadium, and the opening foray immediately cast a pall over Dodger land. In a period of 27 hours, the Brooklyn forces found themselves down, two games to none, a position from which no team had ever recovered. Their ace, Don Newcombe, got roughed up in the opener, 6-5, as four Yankeee home runs KO'd the big righty in the sixth inning.

```
Brooklyn Dodgers   0 2 1  0 0 0  0 2 0 - 5 - 10 - 0
New York Yankees   0 2 1  1 0 2  0 0 x - 6 -  9 - 1
```

In Game Two, a neat five-hitter by the cagey lefty, Tommy Byrne, beat Billy Loes, 4-2.

```
Brooklyn Dodgers   0 0 0  1 1 0  0 0 0 - 2 - 5 - 2
New York Yankees   0 0 0  4 0 0  0 0 x - 4 - 8 - 0
```

As the scene shifted across the river to Flatbush, even the most ardent Dodger fan was pessimistic about the team's Series chances. Nineteen fifty-five looked like more of the same old story, a National League pennant, a World Series defeat at the hands of the New York Yankees, and a sheepish promise of "Wait till next year." But the team itself didn't give up, particularly a brash 23-year-old southpaw named Johnny Podres. Podres, a native of Witherbee, New York, was handed the ball for the critical Game Three by manager Walter Alston in spite of a mediocre 9-10 regular season record. Alston chose Podres because of the youngsters great determination and because he refused to wilt under pressure. It turned out to be the best managerial decision in Alston's 23-year-major league career.

As 34,209 screaming fans tried to get their team's adrenaline flowing with a riotous welcome, the slick Dodger southpaw with the league's best change of pace, set the New Yorkers down 1-2-3 in the first. Roy Campanella, the Dodgers roly-poly catcher, jumped on a Bob Turley fast ball and sent it screaming into the left center field stands with Reese on base in the bottom of the first. Then, in Podres' only bad inning of the Series, he was touched up for two runs on three hits in the second. After Mantle hit a long home run into the left center field stands, New York tied the game on a double by Moose Skowron and a single by Scooter Rizzuto.

That was the game as far as the Yanks were concerned. Podres tamed the Stengelmen with a single run on four hits over the final seven innings. Brooklyn, meanwhile, continued to pound Yankee pitching. They took the lead for good in the bottom of the second, scored two more runs off Tom Morgan in the fourth, and iced the game with a pair of runs in the seventh.

The final score was 8-3.

```
New York Yankees   0 2 0  0 0 0  1 0 0 - 3 -  7 - 0
Brooklyn Dodgers   2 2 0  2 0 0  2 0 x - 8 - 11 - 1
```

Given a flicker of hope, Alston's sluggers charged out in Game Four, bent on tying the Series. With Hilda Chester's cow bell and Brooklyn's Sym-Phony Band leading a loyal cheering section 36,242 strong, Ebbets Field was a riotous place on the afternoon of October 1. As the score mounted in the Dodgers' favor, the noise grew louder and louder. Brooklyn starter Carl Erskine was not at his best on this day, a situation that quieted the crowd momentarily. The Yanks drew first blood, scoring single runs in the first and second innings. Brooklyn got one back in the third on a walk and a double by Junior Gilliam, but the Yanks matched it in the fourth as they KO'd Erskine

Jackie Robinson, in a daring maneuver, steals home against Whitey Ford, in the eighth inning of Game One. Robinson was safe when Berra held the ball behind the plate. Pinch hitter Frank Kellert watches the action.

with none out. A single by Berra and a walk to Collins finished the little Hoosier, and brought Bessent on the scene. A bloop single by Billy Martin brought in the run.

In the bottom of the fourth, Alston's charges brought the crowd back into the game as they took the lead for the first time with a long-ball barrage against righthander Don Larsen. Campanella, leading off, hit his second home run of the Series, a line drive into the left-field seats. After Furillo beat out an infield hit, big Gil Hodges smashed a tremendous home run over the scoreboard in right center field.

New York closed the gap to 7-5 with a brace of runs in the sixth, but singles by Campanella, Furillo and Hodges made it 8-5 an inning later. Labine, after surrendering the two runs in the sixth, shut down the Yankee attack without a hit over the final 3 2/3 innings to pick up the victory.

```
New York Yankees     1 1 0 1 0 2 0 0 0 - 5 - 9 - 0
Brooklyn Dodgers     0 0 1 3 3 0 1 0 x - 8 - 14 - 0
```

The momentum had suddenly shifted on the wings of two straight Dodger victories. Brooklyn fans once again walked around with a swagger in their step, and a wise crack on their lips. It was pandemonium along Bedford Avenue as a noisy crowd descended on Ebbets Field for Game Five. Rookie righthander Roger Craig faced Yankee Bob Grim in a key game of the Series.

Craig, who went 5-3 in Brooklyn during the regular season, after compiling a 10-2 record for the Dodgers' Montreal farm team, kept the mighty Yanks in check in his first Series start. Alston's Big Blue Machine jumped on Grim in the bottom of the second to take a two-run lead. Sandy Amoros, the little Cuban left fielder, jerked a Grim fastball over the right field screen with two out and Gil Hodges on base. An inning later, Duke Snider also took the Yankee righty downtown, with a leadoff shot onto Bedford Avenue. New York narrowed the margin to 3-1 in the fourth as they touched Craig up for two singles and a walk.

The Duke of Flatbush got the run back in the 5th with another homer over the screen. It was Duke's fourth home run of the Series and gave him the distinction of being the only man to hit four home runs in more than one Series. Even the mighty Babe never accomplished that.

Yogi Berra made the score 4-3 with a homer in the eighth, but Brooklyn closed out the scoring with a run in the bottom of the inning on singles by Furillo and Robinson.

New York Yankees   0 0 0 1 0 0 1 1 0 - 3 - 6 - 0
Brooklyn Dodgers   0 2 1 0 1 0 0 1 x - 5 - 9 - 2

Hoping to wrap it up in six, manager Alston gambled on fireballer "King" Karl Spooner to stifle the New York bats. It had been Spooner, the sore-armed southpaw, who had pitched the pennant-clincher against Milwaukee. Against the Yankees however, King Karl was no mystery. Back in the friendly confines of their own park, Stengel's men wasted no time in exerting their superiority. After Spooner had sandwiched two bases on balls around a strikeout, Yankee thunder struck. Berra lined a

Southpaw Johnny Podres starts the Dodgers on their historic comeback with an 8-3 victory in Game Three.

single to center scoring the first run of the game. Hank Bauer followed with a single to left for another run. Then Moose Skowron quickly emptied the bases with a three-run homer into the right field stands. Before the crowd had settled into their seats, New York had an insurmountable 5-0 lead with Whitey Ford on the mound, and Karl Spooner was in the shower, having retired only one batter.

Two singles and a base on balls brought in Brooklyn's lone run in the fourth, but the game ended 5-1 as Ford tossed a four-hitter.

Brooklyn Dodgers   0 0 0 1 0 0 0 0 0 - 1 - 4 - 1
New York Yankees   5 0 0 0 0 0 0 0 x - 5 - 8 - 0

Tuesday, October 4, dawned partly cloudy and cool, with a mid-day temperature reaching 69 degrees. It was perfect baseball weather as 62,465 fans pushed their way through the turnstiles at Yankee Stadium. A determined band of Brooklyn Dodgers and a just-as-determined group of New York Yankees squared off in the seventh and final game of the 1955 World Series to decide which team would wear the crown of World Champion.

Walt Alston, the Dodgers' 43-year-old manager from Darrtown, Ohio, had lefty Johnny Podres, the winning pitcher in Game Three, ready to go. Casey Stengel countered with southpaw Tommy Byrne, who had pitched his team to a complete-game victory in Game Two. The big finale had all the earmarks of a pitchers' duel, and it did not disappoint. Hits were few and far between as the 23-year-old Podres and the 35-year-old Byrne locked horns in mortal combat.

Three innings passed without a score. Brooklyn, after going hitless in the first three innings, finally broke through in the top of the fourth. After Snider went down swinging, Roy Campanella laced a double down the left-field line. One out later, Gil Hodges brought the crowd to its feet with a single to left, scoring Campy and giving the Bums a 1-0 lead.

The young lefty from Witherbee, New York, protected the lead over the next two innings. Berra opened the Yankee fourth with a Texas League double to center, a ball that dropped between Snider and Gilliam when they got their signals crossed. Podres, undaunted, retired the next three batters in order. A 1-2-3 Yankee fifth followed.

In the Dodger sixth, things heated up again. Reese led off with a single to center. Snider sacrificed and was safe at first when he knocked the ball out of Skowron's hands for an error. After Campy sacrificed, Carl Furillo was purposely passed to load the bases, giving New York a play at any base. Gil Hodges foiled the strategy by lifting a sacrifice fly to deep right center field, Reese scoring easily after the catch.

Tensions mounted as the bottom of the sixth got underway with Brooklyn up 2-0. Dodger players began to squirm on the bench, several pacing back and forth, too nervous to sit. Brooklyn fans everywhere were apprehensive, many quietly waiting for the axe to fall. In the New York sixth, it almost did. Manager Walter Alston made a key defensive change after the Dodgers batted, inserting left-handed Sandy Amoros in left field in place of Junior Gilliam. That move, as it turned out, saved the game, and the championship, for Brooklyn.

Billy Martin leading off the sixth, coaxed a walk out of Johnny Podres. Gil McDougald then dropped a bunt down the third-base line and beat it out, putting two men on with no one out. The dangerous Yogi Berra stepped to the plate, batting a hefty .455 for the Series. Podres started him off with a high outside fastball. Berra sliced it down

Sandy Amoros, the Cuban dynamo, makes the catch of the century, as far as Brooklyn Dodger fans are concerned, to rob Yogi Berra of an extra base hit, and give the citizens of Flatbush their first and last World Championship.

the left-field line, away from Sandy Amoros, who was swung around to right for the left-handed batter. It looked like a game-tying double when it left the bat, but Amoros never gave up on it. Racing toward the left field line at top speed, the little Cuban seemed to outrun the ball. Reaching out with his gloved hand at the last instant, Amoros speared the ball just three feet away from the left-field stands, at the 301 mark. Whirling, he quickly fired the ball to the cutoff man, Pee Wee Reese, who relayed it to Gil Hodges at first, doubling McDougald off base. It was one of the greatest catches in World Series history, and it saved the Dodgers from certain disaster.

Hank Bauer ended the inning by grounding to short. Two innings later, in the bottom of the eighth, the Bronx Bombers mounted their last threat. Phil Rizzuto led off with a single to left-center field. With one out, McDougald

Seconds after Gil Hodges gloved Pee Wee Reese's throw, for the final out of the Series, Don Hoak and Roy Campanella converge on winning pitcher Johnny Podres, and the celebration is on.

hit safely to left, putting runners on first and third. Again the menacing Yogi Berra came to bat. This time he hit a soft fly to short right that Carl Furillo gathered in for out number two. Hank Bauer worked the count to 2-2, then fanned on a high fast ball as the crowd let go with a deafening cheer.

A 1-2-3 ninth ended with Elston Howard going out Reese to Hodges, as all hell broke loose in Yankee stadium. The rush of fans onto the field, the noise, the yelling, the screaming, was incredible. "Them Dodgers was champions of the whole World!"

| Brooklyn Dodgers | 000 101 000 – 2 – 5 – 0 |
| New York Yankees | 000 000 000 – 0 – 8 – 1 |

Art Smith, in the *New York Daily News*, described the scene in Brooklyn better than anyone. "Everything was crazy in Brooklyn last night....nobody went home to supper. Nobody talked any sense....Everybody walked around with goofy expressions on their pans... For the unbelievable, the incredible, the impossible had come about....them Dodgers had put them Yankees away under the Stadium sod and now they was champions of the whole world. Saloonkeepers gave away booze to guys they

Don Newcombe and Duke Snider erase eight years of frustration, as they finally get to feel what the atmosphere is like in the winner's locker room.

never saw before...Candy store owners played the big treat to neighborhood kids who'd been robbing 'em for years....Women kissed neighbors they wouldn't be caught dead talking to....Men hollered and slugged strangers on the back and guys who hadn't been known to lift a geezer in years rolled off the wagon and barked at the crescent moon."

That's the kind of night it was in Brooklyn on October 4, 1955–the year the Brooklyn Dodgers won their first and only World Championship.

BROOKLYN DODGERS (NL) V.S.
THE NEW YORK YANKEES (AL)–1956

The Brooklyn Dodgers arrived at their Vero Beach spring training camp as the defending World Champions, a title they intended to keep for one more year. They knew it would not be easy, however. There were rumblings coming from Wisconsin way, where the Milwaukee Braves were building a potential World Championship team of their own. Led by second-year player, 21-year-old "Hammering Hank" Aaron, the Braves finished second in 1955, 13 1/2 games behind Alston's aging "Boys of Summer."

As the season got underway, it was a five-team race early, with the Cincinnati Reds, St. Louis Cardinals and Pittsburgh Pirates all joining in the festivities. Less than five games separated the five teams through June; then the Cards and Pirates slowly drifted back into the pack, leaving the struggle to the Dodgers, Braves and Reds.

The Flatbush Flock hovered barely above the .500 mark through the first half of the season, although there were some memorable occasions. On April 19, Walter O'Malley's forces played their first home game in Jersey City, New Jersey, winning a ten-inning thriller from the Phillies, 5-4. The Jersey City strategy was intended to force the politicians in Brooklyn into building a new stadium for their beloved team. When that failed, the Brooklyn owner transplanted his team to the sunny climes of Los Angeles two years later.

Carl Erskine, the Dodgers' sore-armed darling, pitched his second career no-hitter on May 12, stopping the New York Giants, 3-0. Erskine went on to win 13 games during the regular season, in what would be his swan song in the majors. Hampered by arm woes, the 29-year-old hurler won only nine more games before retiring in 1959.

Milwaukee held the top spot from early July until mid-September. The Reds, who stayed neck and neck with the Dodgers during that period, eventually settled back into third place, leaving the Braves and Dodgers to duke it out for the pennant.

The last three weeks of the season turned into a heated dogfight. Brooklyn and Milwaukee were tied for the lead seven times, with both teams on top at one time or another. A key man in the Dodger stretch run was none other than old enemy, Sal "The Barber" Maglie, former New York Giant pitcher and renowned Dodger killer. Maglie won 13 games for Walter Alston, including a crucial 5-0 no-hitter against Philadelphia on September 25. A three-game sweep of the Pittsburgh Pirates on the last weekend of the season catapulted the Dodgers into the National League pennant. The 8-6 clincher, on the final Sunday, included two home runs each by Snider and Amoros, and a singleton by Jackie Robinson.

Brooklyn had many heroes in 1956, but none larger than Don Newcombe. Big Newk finished with an amazing 27-7 won-loss record, and walked off with both the Cy Young award and the Most Valuable player trophy. Craig (12-11), Maglie (13-5), Erskine (13-11), and Labine (10-6 with a league leading 19 saves), provided Alston with capable pitching. Offensively, Junior Gilliam was the lone .300 hitter, but the long ball was still a potent weapon. Duke Snider hit a league-leading 43 round-trippers accompanied by 101 RBIs. Gil Hodges was 32 – 87, Carl Furillo was 21 – 83, and Roy Campanella chipped in with 20 homers and 73 ribbies in an injury plagued season.

As usual, Walter Alston's charges were matched against Casey Stengel's New York Yankees in the Series. It was their seventh meeting in 15 years. The Series started the same way the '55 Series ended. Brooklyn seemed unbeatable. Casey Stengel's Bombers jumped on 39-year-old Sal "The Barber" Maglie for two runs in the top of the first, before the Dodger righty had a chance to get warm. A two-run shot over the right field screen by Mickey Mantle was the damaging blow. That was the only thing New York fans had to cheer about on this cool October afternoon however, as the ace of their staff, Whitey Ford, proved to be no puzzle to the Brooklyn hitters. A homer by Jackie Robinson, a single by Gil Hodges, and a double by Carl Furillo, quickly tied the game in the bottom of the second. An inning later, Alston's crew finished off the Yankee southpaw with a three-run barrage. Singles by Reese and Snider set the table for the Brooklyn strongman, Gil Hodges and the big first baseman didn't disappoint. He deposited a Ford delivery into the lower left field seats for the game winner. A Billy Martin home run finished the Yankee scoring, as Maglie hurled a complete game 6-3 victory, liberally sprinkled with 10 strikeouts.

```
New York Yankees      2 0 0 1 0 0 0 0 0 - 3 - 9 - 1
Brooklyn Dodgers      0 2 3 1 0 0 0 0 x - 6 - 9 - 0
```

Two righthanders named "Big Don" faced off in Game Two, Larson of the Yankees and Newcombe of the Dodgers. Neither man saw the third inning. Big Newk was touched up for a run in the first on two singles and a walk. An inning later, the roof caved in on the 6'4" 220-pound giant. Singles by Martin, Coleman and Larson made the score 2-0, and left runners on first and second. A base on balls to Mantle loaded the bases for Yogi Berra, and the Yankee catcher promptly unloaded them with a towering home run onto Bedford Avenue. In a flash, New York was up 6-0, and Newcombe was on his way to the shower.

Don Larsen, however, fared no better. His six-run lead lasted less than twenty minutes. Alston's determined charges quickly filled the bases on a single, an error, and a walk with no outs. One run scored on a sacrifice fly. Then, with two outs, another walk reloaded the bases. Reliever Johnny Kucks was greeted with a two-run single by Pee Wee Reese and Tommy Byrne was brought on to pitch to Duke Snider. The pride of Flatbush promptly tied the game with a three-run blast over the right-field screen.

Brooklyn un-tied the game in the third on a run-scoring single by relief pitcher Don Bessent. After Stengel's boys made it 7-7 in the fourth, the Dodgers gradually pulled away. Singles by Snider and Robinson, and a double by Hodges, gave the Brooks a 9-7 lead in the bottom of the fourth. A two-run double by Hodges upped

Brooklyn Dodgers–1956 National League Champions

the margin to 11-7 an inning later, and they added still another pair in the eighth. Berra's homer in the ninth brought the final tally to 13-8. Bessent, pitching seven strong innings in relief of Newcombe, earned the victory.

New York Yankees	1	5 0	1 0 0	0 0 1	- 8 - 12 - 2
Brooklyn Dodgers	0	6 1	2 2 0	0 2 x	-13 - 12 - 0

As the scene shifted to Yankee Stadium, it looked like an easy Series for the Dodgers. New York seemed to be outclassed, having lost six of the previous seven games to the Brooks, going back to 1955. They also had history against them. Only once in 53 Series had a team come back from a two games-to-none deficit to win the Series. That happened the previous year when Brooklyn won its first World Championship. It was not likely to repeat itself.

Casey Stengel, a little desperate at this point, brought Whitey Ford back on only two days' rest. The slightly built lefty was a tough competitor, and he welcomed the challenge to halt the Yankee slide. Matched against Roger Craig, the "Chairman of the Board" fought the Brooklyn hitters for every out. It was not an easy game. The aging "Boys of Summer" scratched out the first run on a walk, a single and a sacrifice fly in the top of the second. The Yanks got on the board in the same inning on a homer by the pesky Billy Martin, his fifth homer against Brooklyn in 23 World Series games. His career average was less than one homer for every 55 at bats.

Alston's boys reclaimed the lead in the top of the sixth when Reese ripped a triple past Mickey Mantle in right center field, and Snider brought him in with a sacrifice fly. The lead didn't hold up long, however, as Yankee batsman finally got to the 6'5" stringbean in the bottom of the inning. A two-out, three-run homer into the lower right field seats by Enos "Country" Slaughter was one of the few bad pitches Craig made all day, but it did him in. The Dodgers could not come back against Ford. They managed one run in the seventh on an error by Andy Carey, but the Yankee lefty shut them down thereafter, winning 5-3 and putting New York back into the hunt.

Brooklyn Dodgers	0 1 0	0 0 1	1 0 0	- 3 - 8 - 1
New York Yankees	0 1 0	0 0 3	0 1 x	- 5 - 8 - 1

Twenty-six-year-old Tom "Snake" Sturdivant, was Stengel's choice to start the crucial Game Four. The six-foot right-hander won 16 big games for the Old Professor during the season and he was ready to go. Dodger favorite Carl Erskine, who had given Brooklyn fans some of their most exciting World Series moments over the years, could not stem the tide this time. The Bronx Bombers touched him for a single run in the first on a double by Joe Collins and a single by Yogi Berra. After Brooklyn tied it in the fourth on Snider's double and Hodges' single, Stengel's sluggers pushed over two more runs on two bases on balls and a single by Martin.

New York extended the lead to 4-1 in the sixth against reliever Ed Roebuck on a long home run into the right center field bleachers by the Commerce Comet, Mickey Mantle. Two more Yankee runs came across in the seventh when Hank Bauer sent a Don Drysdale fastball into the left-field seats. Sturduvant meanwhile, held the Bums in check. He yielded a run in the ninth on a double by Robinson and a single by Campanella, but finished with a six-hitter and a well-earned 6-2 win, tying the Series at two games apiece.

| Brooklyn Dodgers | 0 0 0 1 0 0 0 0 1 - 2 - 6 - 0 |
| New York Yankees | 1 0 0 2 0 1 2 0 x - 6 - 7 - 2 |

Game Five belonged to a nondescript righthander named Donald James Larsen. The hard-throwing Hoosier never won more than 11 games in a season, and recorded only 81 victories over a 14-year career, but for one day he was the greatest pitcher who ever toed the rubber. On Monday, October 8, 1956, in "The House That Ruth Built", Larsen became the only pitcher in World Series history to throw a perfect, no-hit, no-run, no-reach game, as the Yankees edged the Dodgers 2-0 to take a 3-2 lead in games before 64,519 delirious fans in Yankee Stadium.

Relief pitcher Don Bessent retired the last five batters to preserve Big Newk's pennant clinching victory over Pittsburgh.

The 27-year-old hurler, throwing from his newly discovered no-windup stance, handcuffed the Brooklyn team on just 97 pitches. He set seven Dodger batters down on strikes, including pinch hitter Dale Mitchell to end the game. Several balls were hit hard against the 6'4" 215-pound Larsen, but he had outstanding defensive support and the required amount of luck.

In the Dodger fourth, Duke Snider smashed a long drive to right that had home run written all over it, but the ball drifted foul into the stands. Gil Hodges and Sandy Amoros came closest to breaking Larsen's string, both attempts coming in the top of the fifth. With one out, Hodges hit a long drive to left center field that was corraled by Mickey Mantle after a long run. Amoros, the next batter, drilled a Larsen pitch down the right field line but, once again, the ball curved foul at the last instant.

Sal "The Barber" Maglie, who pitched a no-hitter during the last week of the season, was manager Alston's choice to open the World Series. He responded with a complete game 6-3 victory.

Sal Maglie, Larsen's mound opponent, pitched an outstanding game himself, holding the Bronx Bombers to two runs on only five hits, but that was enough for Larsen on this day.

You could hear a pin drop in cavernous Yankee Stadium as Don Larsen walked slowly to the mound to start the ninth. Over 64,000 people were in the stands. Yet Don Larsen was alone. He peered in to Yogi Berra for the sign. His first pitch of the ninth inning hurtled plateward. Carl Furillo fouled it off. The Dodger right fielder kept the crowd squirming by fouling off three more pitches. Then he eased the tension slightly by sending a fly ball to Hank Bauer in right. Twenty-five down–two to go. The dangerous Roy Campanella stepped in. After hitting a foul ball, the Dodger slugger swung at a low outside pitch and sent a roller to Billy Martin at second. Out number two. One to go. Manager Walter Alston sent left-handed hitter Dale Mitchell up to bat for Sal Maglie. Mitchell, a lifetime .312 hitter, was a slap hitter, known around the league as a contact hitter. Larsen worked him carefully. With a count of 1-2, the big righthander threw a fastball low and away. Mitchell watched it but did not offer. Home plate umpire Babe Pinelli's right arm shot up. Strike three.

Pandemonium broke loose in Yankee Stadium as catcher Yogi Berra raced to the mound and embraced the stunned Larsen. 65,000 fans tried to scale the wall to mob their newest hero. Don Larsen had just thrown the first perfect game in the major leagues in 34 years, and the first ever in a World Series. Don Larsen, a journeyman pitcher heretofore, had immortalized himself with a magnificent pitching exhibition under the most trying conditions. His name would go down in baseball history, along with the names of Babe Ruth, Walter Johnson, and Ted Williams.

BROOKLYN

		AB	R	H	E
Gilliam	2B	3	0	0	0
Reese	SS	3	0	0	0
Snider	CF	3	0	0	0
Robinson	2B	3	0	0	0
Hodges	1B	3	0	0	0
Amoros	LF	3	0	0	0
Furillo	RF	3	0	0	0
Campanella	C	3	0	0	0
Maglie	P	2	0	0	0
Mitchell	PH	1	0	0	0
Totals		2	0	0	0

NEW YORK

		AB	R	H	E
Bauer	RF	4	0	1	0
Collins	1B	4	0	1	0
Mantle	CF	3	1	1	0
Berra	C	3	0	0	0
Slaughter	LF	2	0	0	0
Martin	2B	3	0	1	0
McDougald	SS	2	0	0	0
Carey	3B	3	1	1	0
Larsen	P	2	0	0	0
Totals		26	2	5	0

Don Larsen has just released the 97th and last pitch of his perfect game. Billy Martin watches intently in the background.

```
Brooklyn Dodgers      0 0 0  0 0 0  0 0 0 - 0 - 0 - 0
New York Yankees      0 0 0  1 0 1  0 0 x - 2 - 5 - 0
```

Don Larsen's superb effort had given the New Yorkers tremendous momentum as they moved to Brooklyn for Game Six. Casey Stengel selected "Bullet Bob" Turley to try to wrap up the World Championship. Dodger manager Walter Alston countered with relief ace Clem Labine, making one of his infrequent starts. The crew-cut right-hander from Woonsocket, Rhode Island, gave his team an unforgettable effort. The scoreboard showed nothing but goose eggs through eight innings.

It began to look as if a break would decide the game, as both pitchers appeared to be unbeatable. The Yanks went out in order again in the ninth, while the Dodgers could do no more than a harmless one-out walk. Labine was in a groove now, as he retired the side in order again, for eight in a row. With one out in the bottom of the tenth, Turley issued his seventh base on balls. After Reese sacrificed the runner, Gilliam, to second, Duke Snider was passed intentionally to bring up number 42. It was once said of Robinson, "If the game lasts long enough, he'll win it for you." It was never truer than on this day. Jackie lined a Turley fastball over Enos Slaughter's head in left field, sending Junior Gilliam racing home with the game winner.

```
New York Yankees      0 0 0  0 0 0  0 0 0  0 - 0 - 7 - 0
Brooklyn Dodgers      0 0 0  0 0 0  0 0 0  1 - 1 - 4 - 0
```

It all came down to Game Seven, for the fourth time in seven meetings between these two rivals. This time, however, Game Seven was anticlimactic. It was strictly no contest. Dodger starter Don Newcombe was ineffective, as Casey's boys bombarded him for five runs on as many hits, in a little over three innings.

Johnny Kucks, the Yanks #2, was on target as he shut down the vaunted Dodger attack on three harmless singles. A seventh-inning uprising against Roger Craig, sparked by a Moose Skowron grand slam, brought the final tally to 9-0, and sent 33,782 of the Dodger faithful home in despair.

New York Yankees   2 0 2 1 0 0 4 0 0 - 9 - 10 - 0
Brooklyn Dodgers   0 0 0 0 0 0 0 0 0 - 0 - 3 - 1

They didn't know it at the time, but Brooklyn would never see another pennant winner, nor would they ever again cheer a World Championship team. One year down the road, owner Walter O'Malley would uproot America's team and set them down in California.

Good-bye Brooklyn. We loved ya.

LOS ANGELES DODGERS (NL) V.S. THE CHICAGO WHITE SOX (AL)–1959

Following their 1956 World Series loss to the New York Yankees, Brooklyn suffered through a sub-par season in 1957. At the end of the season, President Walter O'Malley announced he was moving the team to Los Angeles, California for the 1958 season.

Nineteen fifty-eight proved to be a disaster of the first order for the new Los Angeles Dodgers. Alston's charges were forced to play their home games in the Coliseum, a track and field stadium built for the 1932 Olympics. It was a monstrosity as a baseball park. The outfield dimensions contributed to the team's poor performance. Duke Snider, coming off five consecutive 40+ home run seasons, was confronted with a 440-foot fence in right field, and his home run production promptly plunged to 15. Thirty-six-year-old Carl Furillo's legs gave out in the vast Coliseum outfield, and he was limited to part-time duty.

The Dodgers got off the mark slowly, dropped into the cellar in mid-May, and held down the bottom rung of the ladder through the summer. It was only a complete collapse by the Philadelphia Phillies that prevented the ignominy of the Dodgers' first last-place finish since 1905.

As 1959 dawned, the Los Angeles management looked forward to a long rebuilding process. The "Boys of Summer" were old and gray. Most had long since retired. Some had moved on to other teams. Only six remained from the glory days of Brooklyn; 36-year-old Carl Furillo, 35-year-old Gil Hodges, 33-year-old Duke Snider, 32-year-old Clem Labine, and veterans Podres and Gilliam. Miraculously, the team made a complete about face from '58 and thrilled their fans with sharp defense and a much-improved pitching staff.

Los Angeles Dodgers, 1959 (Los Angeles Dodger Photo)

Spring training began with a touch of the occult, an eerily accurate prediction of the National League pennant race. Peter Hurkos, the Dutch psychic, toured the league's training camps on assignment from *Parade* magazine. Hurkos, a neophyte in the baseball arena, stated that the Milwaukee Braves were the best team in the league, but they would not win the pennant. The San Francisco Giants would lead the league most of the season, but they would not finish first either, according to the man who helped solve the Boston strangler murders. When Hurkos predicted that the Los Angeles Dodgers would win the pennant during the last week of the season, he had few disciples.

As the season unfolded, Hurkos' prediction remained vividly imprinted on the minds of Dodger fans from coast to coast. The first crucial series of the year took place in San Francisco with a week to go in the season, and the Dodgers stunned Billy Rigney's all-stars with a three-game sweep. After winning the first two by scores of 4-1 behind Craig and 5-3 behind Drysdale, L.A. pounded the last nail in the Giant coffin with an 8-2 rout of "Sad Sam" Jones. The Giants proceeded to fade from the race with devastating losses to Chicago and Pittsburgh.

L.A. and Milwaukee, meanwhile, went down to the wire, nose to nose. Alston's crew split the St. Louis series with Roger Craig shutting them out after the Redbirds

had numbed the Dodgers, 11-10, the day before. Four days later, the 6'4" righty ended the season with a 7-1 win over the Cubs, setting up a three-game playoff with the Braves who beat Philadelphia 5-2.

The first game was played in Milwaukee the day after the regular season ended. Southpaw Danny McDevitt started the big game for the Dodgers, and was given a one-run lead in the first on an RBI single by Norm Larker. The lead didn't hold up long, however, as Fred Haney's boys nicked McDevitt for two runs in the second. Alston, realizing that he had to pull out all the stops in a short series, quickly brought hard throwing Larry Sherry in from the bullpen to stem the tide. The Dodger reliever did just that, shutting the Braves down without a run over the last 7 2/3 innings. Sherry's batterymate, John Roseboro, hit a sixth-inning home run to give his team a crucial 3-2 victory.

The next day, in the City of Angels, the two teams locked horns again. This time the pressure was on Milwaukee, as they had to win to stay alive in the playoff. Twenty-one game winner Lew Burdette got the starting assignment for the visitors, while Walter Alston countered with 17-game winner, Don Drysdale. Things looked bleak for LA when the Braves scored single runs in the fifth and eighth, opening up a 5-2 bulge. It seemed unlikely that the Dodgers could come back against their long-time nemesis, Lew Burdette. But this was a team of destiny, its fate predicted by psychic Peter Hurkos six months previous, and strange things happened. Duke Snider, waiting in the on-deck circle as Wally Moon headed up to

Chuck Essegian is greeted by the Dodger dugout, after his pinch-hit home run in the seventh inning of Game Two, started L.A. on the comeback trail.

Charlie Neal's second home run of the game, a two-run shot, catapults the Dodgers to a 4-3 victory in Game Two. Junior Gilliam and Wally Moon wait to congratulate the young slugger.

the plate, also had a premonition, "I have a feeling we're going to get five hits this inning." He was right. Moon, Snider, and Hodges all stroked singles to load the bases and knock Burdette out of the box. Milwaukee's ace reliever, Don McMahon, was rushed to the mound. McMahon had pitched in 60 games during the campaign, with a league-leading 15 saves. This time he couldn't do the job. Left-handed first baseman Norm Larker sliced his third pitch off the left field screen for two runs as the Coliseum crowd screamed with delight. McMahon went out, and the ace of the staff, 38-year-old Warren Spahn was called upon to save the game. Alston sent Carl Furillo up to bat for Roseboro, and Skoonj came through with a game-tying sacrifice fly.

The game went into extra innings with overpowering but erratic Stan Williams on the mound for LA and big Bob Rush on the hill for Fred Haney's crew. Williams

An excited fan, watching Neal's homer settle into the left field stands, accidentally spills his beer on Chicago White Sox left fielder Al Smith.

was on target as he handcuffed the Braves without a hit for three innings. In the bottom of the twelfth, Rush managed to retire the first two batters before he hit the wall. Gil Hodges, another of the old gang, coaxed a base on balls out of Rush who was trying to keep the ball away from Gil's power. Catcher Joe Pignatano followed with a single, sending Hodges to second. Carl Furillo, the hero of the ninth-inning rally, came up again. This time he slashed a ground ball up the middle. Shortstop Felix Mantilla caught up with the ball, but his off-balance throw to first bounced past Frank Torre and rolled toward the dugout. Hodges raced home with the pennant-winning run as Vin Scully screamed into his microphone, "We go to Chicago."

Dutch psychic Peter Hurkos had predicted the scenario of the pennant race back in March–and it all happened just the way he said it would.

The Dodgers' opponents in the World Series were the Chicago White Sox, a team that relied on pitching, defense, and speed to win games. They finished sixth in their eight-team league in runs scored, but their pitching staff was outstanding, yielding almost 60 runs less than the next best team. And their base runners struck sheer terror into the hearts of opposing catchers. Known as the Go-Go Sox, their 113 stolen bases were almost double that of the next team. Team leader Luis Aparicio stole more bases (56) than six other American League teams.

The World Series opened in Chicago on October 1 with 39-year-old Early Wynn toeing the rubber for the Sox. The grizzled old veteran, like old man river, just kept rolling along in 1959, leading the league in victories (22) and innings pitched (256). Roger Craig, one of the Dodger mainstays down the stretch, got the nod from skipper Alston. The tall, lanky right-hander's 2.06 ERA was far and away the best in the National League, although he didn't pitch enough innings to qualify for the league ERA title.

October 1, however, was not Roger Craig's day. Al Lopez' Go-Go Sox jumped all over the Dodger starter early and often. Two singles and a walk got Chicago off the mark quickly in the first inning. Then, in the third, they lowered the boom. A one-out double down the right field line by little Nellie Fox was converted into a run on a subsequent single by Jim Landis. Former Cincinnati first baseman, Ted Kluszewski, then followed with a towering home run into the right field stands, and the rout was on. Before reliever Chuck Churn could stem the tide, a total of seven runs had poured across the plate, opening up an insurmountable 9-0 lead. Another two-run shot by Big Klu in the fourth ended the scoring, as the White Sox breezed 11-0.

Los Angeles Dodgers	000 000 000	-0	-8-3
Chicago White Sox	207 200 00x	-11	-11-0

The experts immediately began to question whether or not the Dodgers were in the same class with Chicago. After all, the Sox won 94 games, and led the pack for much of the summer. Los Angeles, on the other hand, struggled all season. Their final .564 winning percentage (88-68) was the lowest in National League history. Strangely, in the Dodger clubhouse, the atmosphere was one of quiet confidence. Walter Alston's boys considered themselves to be a team of destiny, and they never let the thought of losing enter their minds.

As Game Two got underway, with 18-game winner Bob Shaw of Chicago facing southpaw Johnny Podres of the Dodgers, it looked like the same script as game one. A double, a walk, and an error, produced two runs for Al Lopez' boys in the opening stanza. Meanwhile, the 6'2" Shaw breezed through the first four innings, blanking the

Dodgers on five well-spaced singles. In the fifth, L.A. got it's first ray of hope as Charlie Neal slammed a solo home run into the left field stands to narrow the margin to 2-1.

Podres settled down after his first inning troubles, and shut out the Sox on three hits over the next five innings. In the Dodger seventh, former football player Chuck Essegian, pinch hitting for Podres, hit a prodigious home run into the upper left field stands to knot the count. Shaw appeared rattled as he walked Junior Gilliam; then nervously fed Charlie Neal a hanger that the little second baseman rocketed 415 feet into the White Sox bullpen in center field.

With a save opportunity staring him in the face, rookie reliever Larry Sherry took the mound for Alston's crew in relief of Podres. After a 1-2-3 seventh, the cocky Dodger righthander came close to disaster in the eighth. Singles by Kluszewski and Sherm Lollar put men on first and second with no one out. Left fielder Al Smith then smashed an apparent game-tying double to left center field. Pinch runner Earl Torgeson scored easily, but the slow-moving Lollar was out at the plate on a fine relay from Moon to Wills to Roseboro, frustrating Chicago's hopes. Al Smith, still representing the tying run, died on third when Sherry fanned Billy Goodman and retired Jim Rivera on a foul pop to Roseboro. The 6'2" Dodger fireballer then retired the side in order in the ninth to protect the victory and tie the Series at one game apiece.

| Los Angeles Dodgers | 000 010 300 - 4 - 9 - 1 |
| Chicago White Sox | 200 000 010 - 3 - 8 - 0 |

Game Three was an historic event in major league baseball, the first World Series game ever played west of St. Louis. With the Dodgers playing their home games in the Los Angeles Coliseum, a park built for track and field events, not baseball, an all-time World Series crowd of 92,394 jammed into the odd shaped stands on a sweltering October afternoon to cheer on their new heroes. Don Drysdale, the 6'5" buggy whip righthander was Alston's choice to start Game Three. Big D had compiled a 17-13 record during the season, while leading the league with 242 strikeouts. His opponent, Dick Donovan, a solid major league pitcher who had struggled through a mediocre 9-10 season, had an outstanding slider and kept opponents off balance with his varied pitching repertoire.

It was a game worthy of any World Series as both Drysdale and Donovan were at their best. Donovan, in particular, was impressive as he faced only the regulation 18 batters over the first six innings. Drysdale, meanwhile was touched up for six safeties over the same period, but the Los Angeles defense continued to frustrate the Go-Go Sox.

As the seventh inning got underway, the game was still scoreless. Big D left two Sox stranded when he fanned Jim Landis for the third out. In the Dodger half, Charlie Neal got the ball rolling with a one-out single off the short left field screen. One out later, Donovan inexplicably lost

his control, walking both Norm Larker and Gil Hodges to load the bases. Manager Al Lopez quickly went to his bullpen for relief ace Gerry Staley. Staley, a sinkerball specialist, led the American League with 67 appearances during the season, limiting the opposition to 2.24 earned runs per game. Alston countered Lopez' move by replacing free-swinging Don Demeter with contact hitter, Carl Furillo. It turned out to be a good move as the 37-year-old Furillo sent a ground ball back through the middle for two big runs.

Larry Sherry appeared on the scene in the eighth to squelch another Chicago rally and save another game. The Dodger closer struck out the side in the ninth to preserve a 3-1 victory. It was a bitter defeat for the Chicago contingent, who put 17 men on base during the afternoon, but could not convert that offense into but a single run.

| Chicago White Sox | 000 000 010 - 1 -12 - 0 |
| Los Angeles Dodgers | 000 000 21x - 3 - 5 - 0 |

Game Four was a rematch of Game One, pitting hard-throwing veteran, Early Wynn, against young Roger Craig. The 39-year-old Wynn had tossed seven shutout innings in Chicago's 11-0 opening day rout, while Craig was hammered for five runs in just 2 1/3 innings of work. This was a different day, however, and Roger Craig had his split-fingered fast ball working to perfection. His effort was not without its problems as Chicago put two or more men on base in four of the first six innings, but Craig was tough in the clutch, tossing six scoreless innings.

Los Angeles took command of the game in the bottom of the third, scoring four runs on two-out singles by Moon, Larker, Hodges, Demeter, and Roseboro. Craig made the lead stand up through six, but tired badly in the seventh, as the Go-Go Sox roared back to tie the game. Catcher Sherm Lollar slammed the game-tying three-run homer over the 42-foot-high left-field screen.

As the game progressed, it became a battle of relievers, with Sox relief ace Gerry Staley facing the Dodger magician, Larry Sherry. Gil Hodges, L.A.'s Mr. Reliable, became the hero of the game when he slugged his fifth World Series home run into the left-field seats leading off the bottom of the eighth. Sherry made the lead stand up once again as he retired the Sox in order in the ninth.

| Chicago White Sox | 000 000 400 - 4 -10 - 3 |
| Los Angeles Dodgers | 004 000 01x - 5 - 9 - 0 |

Another record Series crowd of 92,706 pushed their way into the Coliseum for Game Five, hoping to see their beloved heroes close out the pesky Sox four straight. They were disappointed, however, as Chicago manager Al Lopez pulled out all the stops, throwing three starting pitchers at the Dodgers in a desperate attempt to salvage the Series. Bob Shaw, who made two bad pitches in Game Two, and saw both of them disappear into the Comiskey Park

Larry Sherry and his catcher, John Roseboro, meet on the Comiskey Park mound to celebrate Los Angeles' first World Championship.

seats, was on top of his game on this day. Matched with up-and-coming southpaw, Sandy Koufax, the Sox righty kept the Dodgers in check through six innings. Their only threat was a one-out triple by Hodges in the fourth inning, but Shaw retired Demeter on a tap to the mound, and forced Roseboro to hit a soft pop up to short.

The 23-year-old Koufax, still two years away from becoming the game's greatest lefty, pitched an outstanding game. His only trouble came in the fourth when he yielded lead-off singles to Fox and Landis, putting runners on the corners. Fox scored as Sherm Lollar hit into a Neal to Hodges dp. As it turned out, it was the only run of the game. Koufax shut down the Sox with one harmless single over the next 4 1/3 innings, but Shaw was just as stingy, blanking the L.A. contingent for 7+ innings. Dick Donovan came on in relief in the eighth to quell a Dodger rally and save the game for Shaw.

Chicago White Sox	000 100 000 - 1 - 5 - 0
Los Angeles Dodgers	000 000 000 - 0 - 9 - 0

The skies were much brighter for Al Lopez' crew in Chicago, and hopes were high once again. Twenty-two game winner Early Wynn was Lopez' choice to even the Series. Wynn, a fiery competitor, was noted for brushing back hitters to keep them loose at the plate. A reporter once suggested that he would even knock his own grandmother down, to which Wynn replied, "I would if she crowded the plate."

Neither Wynn nor his mound opponent, Johnny Podres, lasted four innings. L.A. drew first blood when Duke Snider, the aging Silver Fox, crashed a two run homer into the distant left center field seats, a 400-foot drive. It was Snider's 11th career Series homer, a National League record. Wynn was routed in the fourth when the Dodgers pushed across six more runs, two of them on a home run by Wally Moon.

Unfortunately, Podres was unable to protect the 8-0 lead, and he was relieved by Larry Sherry after Ted Kluszewski hit a mammoth three-run homer into the upper right field stands. Sherry slammed the door on the Go-Go Sox after that, scattering four hits over the last 5 2/3 innings as the Miracle Dodgers presented their delirious fans with their first World Championship.

Los Angeles Dodgers	002 600 001 - 9 -13 - 0
Chicago White Sox	000 300 000 - 3 - 6 - 1

Larry Sherry captured the Most Valuable Player award for his magnificent pitching performance. He appeared in all four Los Angeles victories, winning two and saving the other two. His 0.71 ERA over 12 2/3 innings of pitching led both teams. On offense, Gil Hodges .391 batting average led the Dodger attack, followed by Charlie Neal's .370. The losing Chicago White Sox were led by Ted Kluszewski's .391 average and Nellie Fox's .375. Big Klu also set a new RBI record by driving in 10 runs in the six game Series.

Thanks to the tremendous seating capacity in the Los Angeles Coliseum, the Series also set an attendance record that may never be broken. Four hundred and twenty thousand, seven hundred and eighty-four people witnessed the six-game event, an average of 70,131 per game!

Walter Alston managed six National League Championship teams and four World Champions, but the 1959 contingent was always his favorite. In his autobiography, *A Year at a Time*, Alston was quoted as saying, "They may not have had as much talent as others, but they had tremendous desire. They played like a championship team all the way. They were a manager's dream team."

LOS ANGELES DODGERS (NL) V.S. THE NEW YORK YANKEES (AL)–1963

Nineteen fifty-five was the most glorious year in Brooklyn Dodger history. In that year, Walter Alston's Beloved Bums not only won their first World Championship; they did it at the expense of the hated New York Yankees.

Nineteen sixty-three was the most glorious year in Los Angeles Dodger history. In that year, Walter Alston's great pitching combination of Koufax, Drysdale, Podres, and Perranoski, humbled the New York Yankees, sweeping the World Series in four straight and holding the once mighty Bronx Bombers to four runs in four games, a Series record for futility.

Nineteen sixty-three began as a year of hope and of redemption for the Dodgers. The previous year, Alston's crew blew a certain pennant when they were defeated by the San Francisco Giants in a three-game playoff, after leading the league most of the season. The Dodgers entered the 1963 season as the favorites to win the pennant, and they were determined not to repeat the collapse of '62. The year began quietly, however, as the team hovered around the .500 mark for the first month. The Giants jumped out in front, and held the lead well into June. A 20-6 run in late June catapulted Alston's boys to the top of the heap for the first time. Then, on July 2, Don Drysdale tossed a 1-0 shutout at the St. Louis Cardinals, and the Dodgers went back into first place, where they stayed for the rest of the season.

San Francisco faded from the scene as the summer heat settled over the ballparks, but Johnny Keane's pesky Redbirds couldn't be shaken off. St. Louis finally put it all together in late August and went on a rampage that produced 19 wins in 20 games. As fate would have it, the Los Angeles Dodgers flew into St. Louis on September 16 to do battle with the red-hot Birds, their once comfortable lead down to a single game. This time, the Dodgers were up to the challenge.

Johnny Podres, L.A.'s premier clutch pitcher for almost ten years, gave his team the advantage in the opener of the three-game series with a hard-fought 3-1 victory. A

two-run Dodger ninth settled the issue, after Stan Musial's 7th inning home run had tied the game. The "unhittable" Sandy Koufax followed Podres to the rubber, and he was even tougher as he breezed to his 24th win of the season, 4-0. Game Three was the clincher. Down 5-1 after three innings, L.A. fought back to tie the game with three runs in the eighth and one in the ninth. Rookie Dick Nen's one-out home run to the top of the right field roof in the ninth tied it. Then Ron Perranoski, en route to a career season, pitched six shutout innings, winning the game in the 13th on a single by Willie Davis and a ground ball by Maury Wills.

For all intents and purposes, the race was over when Davis crossed the plate, but Don Drysdale made it official six days later when he defeated the New York Mets 4-1 before the home town fans. It had been a satisfying season for Walter Alston's crew, with the pitching staff dominating as expected. Sandy Koufax led the league with 25 victories (against only five losses), a 1.88 ERA, 11 shutouts, and 306 strikeouts. Don Drysdale went 19-17 with a 2.63 earned run average, while Johnny Podres was 14-12, 3.54. Ron Perranoski was the league's premier relief pitcher, winning 16 games against only three losses, and saving another 21 games in the process. The great sinkerball pitcher led the league in games pitched (69) and winning percentage (.842) while posting a miniscule 1.67 ERA.

The Dodgers' 99 victories came on pitching and speed. Their offense and defense were only average, but their pitching staff led the league with a 2.85 ERA, 24 shutouts, and 1,095 strikeouts. Maury Wills topped the league with 40 stolen bases and Willie Davis chipped in with 25 more as Los Angeles swiped a total of 124 bases, almost double the league average. Left fielder Tommy Davis won his second consecutive batting title with a .326 average and contributed 16 home runs and 88 runs-batted-in to the limited Dodger offense. Only big Frank Howard with 28 homers and 88 RBIs and Ron Fairly with 12 homers and 77 RBIs provided additional long-ball support. Maury Wills hit .302 and Junior Gilliam hit .282 to complete the Dodger offense, but it was on the mound where the pennant was won.

In the American League, the New York Yankees ran roughshod over their opponents, winning their fourth consecutive pennant, by ten-and-a-half games over the second-place Chicago White Sox. Their 104 victories were surpassed by only seven teams in American League history, with the 1954 Cleveland Indians' 111 wins leading the way. Frank Chance's 1906 Chicago Cubs hold the major league record with 116 victories against only 36 losses.

Ralph Houk's Yankees were a fine all-around club, finishing second in the league in batting, fielding, and pitching. The "Chairman of the Board", Whitey Ford was the ace of the mound corps, compiling a 24-7 record and a 2.74 ERA. Jim Bouton (21-7), Ralph Terry (17-15), and Al Downing (13-5), rounded out the starting four. The big-gun offense was led by Elston Howard (.287, 28, 85), Joe Pepitone (.271, 27, 89), Tom Tresh (.269, 25, 71), and Roger Maris (.269, 23, 53). Johnny Blanchard (16), Mickey

Los Angeles Dodgers, 1963 (Los Angeles Dodger Photo)

Mantle (15), Hector Lopez (14), and Clete Boyer (12), also produced homers in double digits.

New York was installed as 8-5 favorites to win the World Series, but the Dodgers were confident. The cocky Podres expressed the feelings of many L.A. players when he said, "We'll win it in 5. No, better change that. We might do it in four." The opener, in Yankee Stadium on Wednesday, October 2, was a baseball fan's dream matchup; the two top southpaws in the game, 25-game winner Sandy Koufax against 24 game winner Whitey Ford. It was a beautiful fall afternoon, with the temperature hovering around the 76 degree mark, and 69,000 raucous New York fans filling the "House that Ruth Built" to watch their beloved Bombers dispose of the upstart Dodgers. Yankee fans were convinced the Californians were the same old Dodgers they had embarrassed six times in seven previous encounters. They came to jeer their perennial foes, but they left extolling the skills of the L.A. team, particularly Sandy Koufax, who re-wrote the record books by fanning 15 of the proud New Yorkers.

Both pitchers got off the mark quickly, as Ford struck out two Dodgers in the first inning, and the great Koufax fanned the side. In the L.A. second, the Hollywood entourage jolted the Bronx Bombers and their ace, Whitey Ford with four big runs. With one out, Frank Howard strode into a Ford pitch and drove the ball completely over the monuments in dead center field for a 460-foot double. A single by former Yankee, Bill "Moose" Skowron plated the first run and, after a Dick Tracewski single put runners on first and second, a three-run homer into the upper right field deck by catcher Johnny Roseboro, completed the onslaught.

That would prove to be all the runs the brilliant Koufax would require. The kid from the Brooklyn sandlots was overpowering. With his crackling curveball working to perfection, and his blazing fastball keeping the hitters back on their heels, Koufax was untouchable. When the day ended, the National League Champion's 25-game winner owned a new World Series strikeout record, breaking Carl Erskine's old mark of 14 strikeouts by one.

Koufax owned 14 K's after eight innings, and held a safe 5-2 lead. As the ninth inning got underway, the huge New York crowd suddenly changed allegiance. Instead of rooting for the home team to rally, they were screaming for the handsome southpaw to set a new record. Howard opened the ninth with a soft liner to second. Pepitone followed with a single to right. Then Clete Boyer hit a fly ball to center field where Willie Davis pulled it in for out number two. Harry Bright was the next batter, pinch hitting for the pitcher. It was Koufax vs. Bright for the record. On a 2-2 count, the Dodger ace fired a fastball down the middle. Bright swung and missed, an instant frozen in time. Koufax had the record. The Dodgers had the game. And the mighty Yankees had to regroup.

The downcast Bright had the quote of the day after the game. "I waited 15 years to get into a World Series, and when I finally did, 70,000 of our own fans were rooting for me to strike out."

Los Angeles Dodgers	0 4 1 0 0 0 0 0 0 - 5 - 9 - 0
New York Yankees	0 0 0 0 0 0 0 2 0 - 2 - 6 - 0

Ralph Houk's sluggers didn't know it at the time, but their first-game power display was to be their greatest offensive output of the Series. In Game Two, they had to face the cocky southpaw from Witherbee, New York, their tormentor from the '55 Series. Podres got all the runs he needed in the very first inning. Little Maury Wills led off the game with a single and promptly stole second on pitcher Al Downing. Gilliam singled to right and, when the throw went home to hold Wills at third, the alert Gilliam continued on to second. Willie Davis then lined a double to right, and the L.A. crew was up 2-0.

Johnny Podres kept the Yanks off balance all day with his fastball, curve and outstanding changeup, all in the groove. He kept Houk's sluggers at bay through eight innings, spacing five hits over that distance, never more than one per inning. L.A. meanwhile, had added to their lead. A Moose Skowron home run into the right-field stands in the fourth made it 3-0, and a double by Willie Davis and a triple by Tommy Davis in the eighth upped the margin to 4-0.

When Hector Lopez bounced a one-out ground rule double into the left field stands in the ninth, manager Walter Alston went to the bullpen for a well-rested Ron Perranoski. After yielding a run-scoring single to Howard, Perry retired Pepitone and Boyer to end the game.

Los Angeles Dodgers	2 0 0 1 0 0 0 1 0 - 4 - 10 - 1
New York Yankees	0 0 0 0 0 0 0 0 1 - 1 - 7 - 0

Roseboro crosses the plate after crushing a three-run homer off Yankee ace, Whitey Ford, in the second inning of Game One. Moose Skowron and Dick Tracewski are the welcoming committee.

The scene shifted to Los Angeles for Game Three with the Dodgers comfortably in the drivers' seat. Up two games to zero, Walter Alston was sitting pretty with Drysdale and Koufax in the wings. Big D's opponent in Game Three was the capable Jim Bouton, the Yanks' 21-game winner, and a dogged competitor. The game turned out to be one of the best pitched games in World Series history, with a total of only seven hits being credited to the batsman. L.A. got to "Bulldog" Bouton for a single run in the first on a walk to Gilliam, a wild pitch, and a single by Tommy Davis.

Both pitchers kept the lid on after that outburst, although Drysdale was more overpowering. While Bouton scattered four hits, he also walked five men. Drysdale, on the other hand, held the powerful Yankees to three harmless singles, and only one base on balls. Nine New Yorkers went back to the bench dragging their bats behind them. The Yankees only serious threat came in the second when they loaded the bases with two out, on a bunt, a hit batter, and a walk, but pitcher Jim Bouton struck out to end the inning.

Drysdale closed out his masterful 1-0 shutout in style, setting New York down 1-2-3 in the ninth.

New York Yankees   0 0 0 0 0 0 0 0 0 - 0 - 3 - 0
Los Angeles Dodgers   1 0 0 0 0 0 0 0 x - 1 - 4 - 1

The outcome looked bleak for New York after Drysdale's overpowering performance. In spite of the fact they had Whitey Ford going for them, they knew they had to face the "Great Koufax" once again, and they would be decided underdogs. It would take a monumental effort for them to prevent a Dodger sweep, but they were champions, and they were not about to quit. The first half of the game went quickly as both teams posted goose-eggs inning after inning. Koufax held the Yanks to two harmless hits through five innings, while Ford limited the Dodgers to a lone single through four.

In the home fifth, Alston's boys jumped out in front, 1-0, on a mammoth home run by Frank Howard. The 6'7", 250-pound giant put a Whitey Ford pitch into orbit. Swinging with one hand after his back hand slipped off the bat, Howard hammered a high drive to left-field. The ball settled into the loge area of the left-field stands, 450 feet from home plate. Mickey Mantle, batting right handed, got the Bombers even in the top of the seventh with his 15th World Series homer, tying Babe Ruth's mark. It was a 420-foot drive into the seats in left center.

That was it as far as New York was concerned. They had fired their last broadside. In the bottom of the seventh, the L.A. contingent wrapped up the Series without the benefit of a hit. Junior Gilliam led off the inning with a high hopper to third base. Clete Boyer's perfect throw to first was lost in the midday glare by first baseman Joe Pepitone and, by the time the embarrassed Pepitone could run the ball down, the speedy Gilliam was standing on third. Seconds later, the Dodger third baseman carried the winning run across the plate as Willie Davis lofted a long sacrifice fly to Mickey Mantle in center.

It was an unfortunate ending to a classic pitching matchup. Both hurlers were outstanding on this hot, California afternoon. The Dodgers managed only two hits off the crafty Yankee southpaw, both by Frank Howard. Ford walked only one and struck out four as the Dodgers had no baserunners left on base, the first time that had happened since Don Larsen's perfect game in 1956. Koufax was touched up for six hits, but the smooth Dodger lefty had perfect control, walking no one and sending eight batters back to the dugout on strikes.

Frank Howard, drives a Whitey Ford pitch 450 feet into the second deck of the stands at Dodger Stadium, in the fifth inning of Game Four, to give L.A. a 1-0 lead.

New York Yankees   0 0 0 0 0 0 1 0 0 - 1 - 6 - 1
Los Angeles Dodgers   0 0 0 0 1 0 1 0 x - 2 - 2 - 1

Dodger Stadium was sheer bedlam as Sandy Koufax leaped off the mound with joy. Not only had the Dodgers swept the mighty New York Yankees under the rug in four straight, but their magnificent pitching staff had held Houk's Bombers to a World Series-record low of four runs. Elston Howard at .333 was the only New York batter to hit above .300. On the Dodger side, Tommy Davis led both teams with an average of .400, while Bill Skowron followed with .385, and Frank Howard hit an even .300. Dick Tracewski was outstanding on defense for the Dodgers, turning several potential hits into easy outs.

On the mound, the L.A. pitching staff was almost perfect. Sandy Koufax, at 1.50, had the highest earned run average on the team!   Johnny Podres at 1.08, and Don Drysdale and Ron Perranoski at 0.00, contributed to the team ERA of 1.00, the classiest pitching performance in World Series history.

Ron Fairly (#6) leaps in the air, as the whole Dodger team mobs Sandy Koufax on the mound, after Hector Lopez is retired, Wills to Skowron, ending the 1963 fall classic.

The efficiency of the Los Angeles team effort was reflected in the fact that Walter Alston used only 13 players in the entire Series, including only four pitchers.

No matter how long baseball is played in the City of Angels, and no matter how many pennants or World Championships are won, the 1963 World Series will always be something special.

This was their finest hour.

New York first baseman Joe Pepitone starts in pursuit of a ball that got by him when he lost it in the sun. It was the key play of the Series, as it put the eventual Series winning run on third base.

LOS ANGELES DODGERS VS THE MINNESOTA TWINS–1965

After their glorious World Series victory in 1963, the Los Angeles Dodgers came apart at the seams in 1964, finishing a disastrous sixth with a record of 80 wins against 82 losses. Injuries to Sandy Koufax and Johnny Podres decimated the pitching staff, while season-long slumps by Junior Gilliam and Tommy Davis wrote finis to any hopes of a Dodger pennant.

In 1965, with Koufax healthy again, and with the addition of southpaw Claude Osteen to the pitching staff, Walter Alston's mound corps was, once again, the class of the league. Like their 1963 counterparts, the '65 edition of the Dodgers won the pennant with pitching and speed. Their offense was almost non-existent; their defense was just average. Ah, but their pitching was magnificent, and their speed revolutionized the game.

Strangely, the Dodgers' season appeared to be over almost before it began. On May 1, in a game against the San Francisco Giants, Tommy Davis, L.A.'s primary offensive threat, went down for the season with a broken ankle, suffered in a sliding accident at second base. The next day, however, the ebullient Lou Johnson arrived from Spokane to take over the left-field slot, and he turned out to be the sparkplug that would carry Walter Alston's crew all the way to the World Championship.

As the season progressed, the Dodgers found themselves in another dogfight for the National League title. Five teams jockeyed for position through most of the summer, with Los Angeles clinging to the top spot, followed closely by the Cincinnati Reds and the San Francisco Giants. Koufax and Drysdale won 70% of their games with one outstanding pitching performance after another.

On August 22, one of the ugliest episodes in baseball history unfolded before a packed house in San Francisco's Candlestick Park. Giant pitcher, Juan Marichal, enraged by John Roseboro's actions behind the plate, attacked the Dodger catcher with his bat, inflicting painful injuries on his victim. The 14-minute free-for-all that ensued was one of the most violent ever witnessed in a major league park. Marichal was subsequently suspended for eight games during the final days of the pennant race, a punishment that might have cost the Giants the title. They finished two games behind the leaders.

The stretch drive began in earnest on September 7 with the Dodgers and Giants locked in a flat-footed tie for the top spot. Many strange things happened before the title was decided four weeks later. On the 9th, Sandy Koufax hurled his record-breaking fourth no-hitter, this one a perfect game, against the Chicago Cubs. Cubs pitcher, Bob Hendley, limited the L.A. contingent to a single safety, making this one of the most superbly pitched games in major league history. Ironically, the winning run scored in the fifth inning without the benefit of a hit. Lou Johnson walked, reached second on a sacrifice, and carried home the lone run of the game when he stole third and continued in on a wild throw by catcher Chris Krug. The game's only hit came two innings later when Johnson sliced a double down the right field line.

The no-hitter was thrilling, but it didn't discourage the Giants. They proceeded to run off 14 consecutive wins to open a big five-game lead over their down-state rivals, a lead that looked insurmountable with only 16 games left on the docket. But baseball is a strange game. As the Giant streak ended, a similar Dodger streak began. Beginning on September 16, Walter Alston's cohorts won 13 in a row, and finished the season 15-1. The key game of the streak, and the key game of the season for Los Angeles, was played on September 22. On that day, with Los Angeles sporting a five-game winning streak, Sandy Koufax was shelled from the mound in less than three innings, his worst performance of the year. The Milwaukee Braves owned a 6-2 lead at the time, and had the game well in hand against the Dodgers' pop-gun attack. But, on this day, Alston's crew showed the character required of a pennant winner. The team that averaged 3.8 runs per game during the season tied the game with two runs in the fourth and three in the fifth, and eventually won it in the 11th inning on a time-proven formula. Maury Wills beat out a bunt, stole second, and came around to score on a single by Lou Johnson.

Don Drysdale won the last game of the winning streak, a 4-0 shutout over Milwaukee, that gave the Dodgers a two-game lead with only three to play. Big D's mound partner, Sandy Koufax, pitching with two days rest, clinched the pennant two days later with a 3-1, 15-strikeout performance against the same Braves. Fittingly, Lou Johnson, the "Cinderella Man," carried home the winning run.

In the American League, the Minnesota Twins won their first pennant, winning 102 games, and finishing seven games ahead of the White Sox. Unlike the Dodgers, Sam Mele's thumpers were offensive minded, leading the league in batting average, runs scored, and doubles. They had a strong mound corps to support their sluggers, but their defense was their achilles heel, as they committed 172 errors in 162 games.

The World Series opened in the Twins' park on October 6 with Don Drysdale facing "Mudcat" Grant. After L.A. scored the first run of the Series in the top of the second on a leadoff home run by Ron Fairly, Minnesota came back with a vengeance. The Twins touched Big D. for a single run in the second when Don Mincher pulled a home run into the right field bleachers. One inning later, Sam Mele's team raked the Dodger righty over the coals, driving him to cover under a six-run barrage. Second baseman Frank Quilici started the rally with a double inside third. Moments later, Zoilo Versalles poled a three-run homer into the left-field stands. Four more hits and a base on balls finished Drysdale, and gave Grant a comfortable 7-1 cushion.

| Los Angeles Dodgers | 0 1 0 0 0 0 0 0 1 - 2 -10 - 1 |
| Minnesota Twins | 0 1 6 0 0 1 0 0 x - 8 -10 - 0 |

Minnesota's confidence was at a peak after the drubbing of Drysdale. Next, they went after his cohort, Sandy Koufax, in Game Two. The Dodger southpaw matched goose eggs with 18-game winner Jim Kaat for 5 1/2 innings. Then, with Minnesota up in the bottom of the sixth, the game broke open. Junior Gilliam's error on a ground ball by Versalles opened the floodgates. A subsequent double by Tony Oliva and a single by Harmon Killebrew put the Twins up, 2-0. That proved to be more than enough for Kaat. The Dodgers did get one back in the seventh on singles by Fairly, Lefebvre and Roseboro, but Kaat settled down and limited Alston's boys to a solitary single over the last 2 2/3 innings. The Twins added three runs against the Los Angeles bullpen in the seventh and eighth, for a final score of 5-1.

| Los Angeles Dodgers | 0 0 0 0 0 0 1 0 0 - 1 - 7 - 3 |
| Minnesota Twins | 0 0 0 0 0 2 1 2 x - 5 - 9 - 0 |

The Dodgers were on the ropes as they returned home to Dodger Stadium. The shelling of both Drysdale and Koufax in successive games left the team slightly shellshocked. They needed a lift, something to renew their confidence. They got that lift from Claude Osteen, their number-three starter who had rescued them on more

Los Angeles Dodgers, 1965 (Los Angeles Dodger Photo)

than one occasion during the season. Osteen tossed a masterful five-hit shutout at the Twins in Game Three, besting Camilo "Hot Potato" Pascual, 4-0.

Minnesota Twins	000 000 000 - 0 - 5 - 0	
Los Angeles Dodgers	000 211 00x - 4 -10 - 1	

That one win was all the Dodgers needed. They were back on track, with Drysdale and Koufax rested and waiting. Big D. got his chance in Game Four, renewing his rivalry with Mudcat Grant. This time the Dodgers were off and running, in typical Dodger style. Maury Wills ignited the attack in the very first inning when he beat out an infield hit, stole second, and came in to score the first run on an infield single and a force play. The flying Dodgers did it again in the second. Wes Parker beat out a bunt down the first base line, leading off the inning, and immediately stole second. He advanced to third on a wild pitch, and scored on an error by the Twin infield.

Minnesota came back in the fourth to narrow the margin to 2-1 on a solo homer by Harmon Killebrew. L.A. got that one back quickly in the bottom half of the inning

Vice President Hubert H. Humphrey tosses out the first ball to open the 1965 World Series, in Metropolitan Stadium, Minneapolis, Minnesota, as opposing managers Sam Mele of the Twins, and Walter Alston of the Dodgers, look on. Baseball Commissioner Ford Frick is third from the left.

when Wes Parker lost one in the right field seats. Although Tony Oliva brought the Twins within one again in the top of the sixth with a roundtripper, Don Drysdale was in command. Except for the two homers, he limited the Twins to only two other hits over the first six innings, and he fanned seven men along the way.

Alston's boys put the game out of reach in the bottom of the sixth when they drove Grant to cover, and

roughed up Minnesota's bullpen contingent for three big runs. Relief ace, Al Worthington took the brunt of the Dodger attack, as he was touched up for two singles, good for all three runs. With a big 6-2 lead to protect him, Big D. coasted from there. Over the final three innings, the Dodger righty held the Twins to one hit, while fanning four. He struck out the last two batters, Jimmie Hall and Don Mincher, giving him 11 K's for the game.

Lou Johnson closed out the scoring with a solo shot into the left-field stands in the eighth.

Southpaw Claude Osteen pulled the Dodgers back from the brink of defeat, by throttling the Twins 4-0, with a tight five-hit, two-walk effort. Osteen receives well-deserved embraces from Koufax and Drysdale, the losing pitchers in Games One and Two.

Minnesota Twins	000 101 000 - 2 - 5 - 2	
Los Angeles Dodgers	110 103 01x - 7 -10 - 0	

Now it was the Twins who had their backs to the wall. Even though the Series was still tied at two games apiece, Sam Mele's boys did not want to return home trailing 3-2. Yet that was the fate that awaited them as they faced off against Sandy Koufax.

Jim Kaat tried to stem the Los Angeles tide, but to no avail. The Dodgers were on a roll, and they were playing at home in front of 55,801 frenzied fans.

L.A. jumped on the Minnesota starter before many of the fans had even reached their seats. After Koufax had turned the Twins away 1-2-3 to start the game, Maury Wills ignited the Dodger offense by lifting a ground-rule double into the right field seats. Junior Gilliam then rifled a single to right and, just like that, the Dodgers were up, 1-0. Gilliam scored moments later when a sacrifice by Willie Davis was turned into a three base error on a wild throw by third baseman Harmon Killebrew.

Walter Alston's fired-up charges increased their margin to 4-0 in the third. Willie Davis hit a one-out single to right, stole second, and raced home on a single by Lou Johnson. "Sweet Lou" came around to score the fourth run on a double by Ron Fairly, chasing the beleaguered Kaat from the mound after a brief 2 1/3 inning outing. L.A. closed out the scoring with another run in the fourth and two more runs in the seventh.

Meanwhile, Sandy Koufax was his old self on the mound–unhittable. He faced a minimum of 18 batters over the first six innings, limiting the Twins to a bloop single, while striking out seven batters. The lone Twin baserunner was quickly cut down on a 6-4-3 double play.

Koufax ended the game with a flourish. After the Twins opened the ninth with their third and fourth hits of the game, the kid from Brooklyn fanned Zoilo Versalles for the first out; then forced Joe Nossek to line into a game-ending double play, Wills to Tracewski. It was a typical Koufax effort–a four-hit, one-walk shutout, liberally sprinkled with 11 strikeouts.

Minnesota Twins	000 000 000	- 0 - 4 - 1
Los Angeles Dodgers	202 100 20x	- 7 -14 - 0

Minnesota slipped out of Dodger Stadium like a whipped dog. They had dropped three straight games in the unfriendly confines of California, including two shut-outs. In the process, they were outscored, 18-2. Return-ing home to Metropolitan Stadium, manager Sam Mele handed the ball to his ace, James Timothy "Mudcat" Grant. There was no tomorrow now. It was win or out.

Lou Johnson receives the glad hand from first baseman Ron Fairly after smashing a solo home run in the eighth inning of Game Four.

The hard-throwing righthander from Lacoochee, Florida, put on a one-man show before 49,578 adoring fans in Game Six. For three innings, Grant was locked in a scoreless pitching duel with Game Three winner, Claude Osteen. Then, in the fourth, the Twins broke through against the Dodgers' slender southpaw. Bob Allison did the damage with a two-run homer into the left-field seats. After Osteen left for a pinch hitter in the sixth, Sam Mele's sluggers went to work on L.A.'s relief corps, particularly Howie Reed. Two walks, to Allison and Quilici, set the stage for Mudcat's final theatrics. With two out and two on, the colorful Twin pitcher iced the game with a three-run shot into the far reaches of the left center field stands.

Ron Fairly's round tripper in the seventh prevented a Twin shutout, but Mudcat coasted to an easy 5-1 win, deadlocking the Series at three games apiece, and mak-ing the finale a toss-up. Minnesota had the home-field advantage, but L. A. had the pitching edge with both Drysdale and Koufax ready to go.

Los Angeles Dodgers	000 000 100	- 1 - 6 - 1
Minnesota Twins	000 203 00x	- 5 - 6 - 1

Manager Walter Alston pondered his starting pitcher for most of the night. It was Drysdale's turn, but there was only one Sandy Koufax, and he was itching for the ball. The Dodger skipper went with Koufax after the slen-der southpaw implored him, "If you want to win, you'll give me the ball". Alston knew he had to go with his best, even on two days' rest, but he had Drysdale in the bullpen, just in case.....

Game Seven was a nail-biter. Although Minnesota starter Jim Kaat didn't stay around long, the bullpen kept the Twins in the game. After three scoreless innings, Lou Johnson, the Cinderella Man, put his team in front when he hit a line drive off the left-field foul pole, leading off the fourth. When Ron Fairly followed with a double and Wes Parker hit a run-scoring single, Kaat was gone and Al Worthington came on in relief. With that move, the Dodger offense died. They managed just two harmless safeties over the last six innings.

Koufax, meanwhile, kept the Twins at bay over the first four innings, yielding but a single hit, and fanning six. His sharp-breaking curveball had the Minnesota bat-ters waving at thin air, his fastball was a blur in the mid-day glare, and his control was pinpoint perfect as usual.

The Twins' biggest threat came in the fifth inning. With one out, Frank Quilici smashed a Koufax delivery off the left center field screen for two bases. Pinch hitter Rich Rollins then worked the Dodger southpaw for a base on balls, putting the tying runs on base, and bringing up the tough Zoilo Versalles. The American League's MVP threatened to tie the game when he rifled a shot down the third base line, ticketed for two bases. Third baseman Junior Gilliam saved the day however. With cat-like quick-ness, the 13-year veteran lunged to his right and snared the ball backhanded in the webbing of his glove. Then, righting himself quickly, he raced to third in time to force Quilici. The rally died moments later when Nossek hit into a force play, Wills to Tracewski.

Sam Mele's crew never had another chance. Koufax retired ten in a row until Killebrew singled with one out in the ninth. Drawing on his reserves one last time, the Dodger ace ended the game by fanning both Earl Battey and Bob Allison, strikeouts no. 9 and 10 for the game.

Los Angeles Dodgers	000 200 000	2 - 7 - 0
Minnesota Twins	000 000 000	0 - 3 - 1

Sandy Koufax receives congratulations from (L to R) John Kennedy, Wes Parker, and John Roseboro, after shutting down the Twins 2-0, to clinch another World Championship for the city of Los Angeles, their third title in seven years.

Thirty-six year-old Junior Gilliam, showing his reflexes haven't slowed down at all, makes a great backhand stop of a line drive off the bat of Zoilo Versalles, to kill a Twins rally.

Winning the World Championship was a noteworthy achievement for Walter Alston's often maligned crew. Some rival managers accused Alston of doing it with mirrors. Alston himself, maintained it was a combination of pride and determination that carried his team to the top of the baseball world.

In reviewing the entire season, beginning with Tommy Davis' unfortunate injury, and ending with their World Championship, the Los Angeles Dodgers were a team that wouldn't accept defeat. Much of the credit for their success can be attributed to the arrival of Lou Johnson. He brought hope to the team in the midst of despair. He brought enthusiasm, and a positive attitude, and an air of cheerfulness to the clubhouse.

Sandy Koufax said it best when the accolades began pouring in. "Johnson's the guy. If it had not been for the job he did, we might not be here today."

LOS ANGELES DODGERS V.S. THE BALTIMORE ORIOLES—1966

If 1963 was the most glorious year in Los Angeles Dodger history, then 1966 was the year they would most like to forget. It was the year of the humiliating World Series loss to Hank Bauer's Baltimore Orioles. The pitching rich O's not only swept the Series in four straight; they crowned the Alston-men with a new record for ineptness, a 2-run total for a four-game series, three consecutive shutouts, and 33 consecutive scoreless innings.

The year began on a higher note, as the Dodgers celebrated their 1965 World Series championship, and went to spring training full of confidence for the new season. The player personnel were basically the same as the previous year, but the Los Angeles management felt that the offense would be improved with another year of experience. They were wrong. The 1966 Dodgers finished next to last in runs scored, scoring two fewer runs than their predecessors, but the pitching staff improved, holding the opposition to 31 fewer runs. The result was another pennant, with a 95-67 record outlasting their perennial rivals, the San Francisco Giants, by 1 1/2 games.

The game of the year took place on July 27 when the Philadelphia Phillies visited Chavez Ravine. Sandy Koufax faced off against Jim Bunning, in a matchup of perfect game pitchers, the first matchup of its kind in baseball history. Both men lived up to their press clippings, as they toiled to a 1-1 tie through 11 innings. Bunning had 12 k's after 11, but the Dodger lefty led the way with 16. L.A. finally won the game in the 12th, 2-1, with relief ace Phil Regan getting the nod over Darold Knowles. The trade that brought closer Regan from Detroit for infielder Dick Tracewski proved to be an ultimate pennant winner.

By September 27, the L.A. express had compiled a record of 19-7 for the month, and still held onto first place. "Sweet Lou" Johnson was one of the main reasons for the surge as he slugged six homers during the month, giving him 17 for the season. On the last day of the season, with Pittsburgh officially eliminated from the race, the Dodgers need one win to clinch the pennant as they faced the Phils in a season-ending double header. Philadelphia did not make things easy as they took the opener, 4-3. Alston quickly went to Sandy Koufax to wrap it up in Game Two, even though Sandy had only two days' rest. That was all the great lefthander needed, however, as he pitched a 10-strikeout, complete-game victory, 6-3.

Tommy Davis, coming back from his broken ankle, batted .313, and produced some key hits along the way. Lou Johnson batted .270 with 17 homers and 73 RBIs, while Jim Lefebvre hit .274 with 24 homers and 74 RBIs. On the mound, it was all Koufax as he had a career season. His league-leading categories included 27 wins (against only nine losses), a 1.73 ERA, 323 innings pitched, 317 strikeouts, and five shutouts.

L.A.'s opponent in the World Series was the slugging Baltimore Orioles, a team that led the American League in batting average (.258), slugging average (.409), doubles (243), and runs scored (755). Their attack was evenly spread throughout the lineup, with seven men batting over .256, and four men slugging more than 20 home runs. The big sticker was Frank Robinson who led the league with a .316 batting average, 49 home runs, and 122 runs batted in. Third baseman Brooks Robinson hit .269 with 23 homers and 100 RBIs, while Boog Powell batted .287 with 34 homers and 109 RBIs. Outfielder Curt Blefary finished at .255 with 23 homers and 64 RBIs.

Baltimore also fielded one of the best defensive teams seen in the Series in many years. Led by shortstop Luis Aparicio and third baseman Brooks Robinson, both of whom led the league in fielding at their positions, the O's committed the fewest errors in the league, and finished first in fielding average.

Baltimore pitching was adequate as they finished fourth in the league in ERA, and led the league in saves with their bullpen aces, Stu Miller (9-4, 18 saves, 2.25 ERA), and Eddie Fisher (5-3, 13 saves, 2.64 ERA). The staff however, had great potential with their talented but unproven "Kiddie Korps" of 23-year-old Dave McNally, 21-year-old Jim Palmer, and 20-year-old Wally Bunker. McNally, an imperturbable southpaw with outstanding

Los Angeles Dodgers, 1966 (Los Angeles Dodger Photo)

control, finished the season with a 13-6 record and a 3.17 ERA. Palmer, a smooth-working righthander, had just completed his first full season in the majors and, at 15-10, was on the verge of greatness. The baby of the staff, Wally Bunker, burst on the American League scene at 19, when he won his first six games, and compiled a 19-5 record for the year. Arm problems slowed him down after that.

On paper, the Series appeared to be a showdown between Dodger pitching and Baltimore slugging. As it turned out, the Series was strictly a showcase for Baltimore's strong young pitching arms. Game One, in Los Angeles, matched McNally and Don Drysdale. Neither pitcher lasted through the third inning. Hank Bauer's O's rocked Big D early with an attack of long ball. After Russ Snyder walked with one out in the first, Frank Robinson jumped on a Drysdale fastball and sent it rocketing into the left field stands for a two-run homer. The next batter, Brooks Robinson, sent a drive into the same area, making the score 3-0 before two men had been retired.

Baltimore added another run in the second on a walk and Russ Snyder's single to left. L.A. bounced back in the bottom of the inning on a 400-foot home run into the left center field stands by Jim Lefebvre. In the third, they narrowed the gap further, to 4-2, and disposed of McNally in the process. The control pitcher, inexplicably, ran into a streak of wildness, walking Johnson, Tommy Davis, and Lefebvre, to load the bases with one out. Moe Drabowsky relieved McNally and walked Jim Gilliam to force in the Dodgers' second run.

Strangely, that was the end of the Dodgers' offense for the entire Series. They never scored again. Alston's ineffectual slashers established a new record for futility as they were held to two runs in four games. Embarrassingly, their second and final run resulted from four bases on balls.

Drabowsky pitched a masterful game in relief for Hank Bauer's team. He limited Los Angeles to one hit over the final 6 2/3 innings, walked only two, and fanned 11.

Dave Johnson doubled off the left-field screen leading off the fourth, and came around to score Baltimore's 5th and final run on two ground balls.

Baltimore Orioles   3 1 0 1 0 0 0 0 0 - 5 - 9 - 0
Los Angeles Dodgers   0 1 1 0 0 0 0 0 0 - 2 - 3 - 0

Dodger fans were still confident as Game Two began. After all, they were playing at home, and they had the world's greatest pitcher going for them. But, on this day, even Sandy Koufax couldn't prevent them from self-destructing. For four innings it was a ballgame as Koufax and high-kicking Jim Palmer matched pitch for pitch. Then, in the top of the fifth, L.A.'s world collapsed as center fielder Willie Davis experienced the most embarrassing inning in World Series history. The 26-year-old ballhawk made three errors, and Baltimore took advantage of them for a 3-0 lead.

The great Dodger lefty yielded his only earned run of the game in the sixth on Frank Robinson's triple to right center field and Boog Powell's single in the same direction. The O's closed out the scoring with two runs in the eighth against Ron Perranoski, on a walk and singles by Brooks Robinson and Dave Johnson.

Palmer, meanwhile, had the Dodgers eating out of his hand. He scattered four hits, while striking our six and walking three. The Dodgers came close to scoring only in the second inning when they had men on second and third with one out. After Roseboro popped to short, Palmer walked Wes Parker intentionally to load the bases, then retired Koufax on a pop to second.

Baltimore Orioles   0 0 0 0 3 1 0 2 0 - 6 - 8 - 0
Los Angeles Dodgers   0 0 0 0 0 0 0 0 0 - 0 - 4 - 6

Don Drysdale is congratulated by catcher Jeff Torborg after blanking the Chicago Cubs 4-0 on September 23. The victory, Drysdale's 13th, gave the Dodgers a 2 1/2-game lead with a week remaining in the season.

The momentum was all in Baltimore's favor after the debacle in Los Angeles. Alston's crew had more errors (six) than hits (four) in Game Two, they hadn't scored a run in 15 consecutive innings, their two best pitchers had been beaten, and the Series was moving to Baltimore for the next three games.

The first game in Baltimore produced a stirring pitchers' duel as lefty Claude Osteen hooked up with the baby of the Oriole pitching staff, Wally Bunker. The first four innings were scoreless, with each pitcher limiting the other team to just two hits. Hank Bauer's boys broke the ice in the fifth, as center fielder Paul Blair blasted a 400-foot home run into the left-field stands. That was all the support Bunker needed as he continued to shut down the L.A. attack through the sixth, seventh, and eighth innings, yielding a single hit in each inning, but never getting in trouble. In the ninth, he polished off California's hitless wonders 1-2-3, retiring Fairly on strikes, and getting Lefebvre and Johnson on harmless infield grounders.

```
Los Angeles Dodgers    000 000 000 - 0 - 6 - 0
Baltimore Orioles      000 010 00x - 1 - 3 - 0
```

Paul Blair, slides home in the fifth inning of Game Two. Blair had reached second base on a two-base error by Dodger center fielder, Willie Davis, and came around to score on a wild throw by Davis, Willie's third error of the inning.

The Dodgers appeared to be anxious to go home as Game Four got underway. Dave McNally and Don Drysdale were back in a rematch of Game One and, this time, both pitchers were at the peak of their game. The Oriole lefty breezed through three innings of hitless ball, a single walk marring his effort. Big D. was almost as good, as he held Bauer's crew to one single and racked up two strikeouts. After McNally breezed through another easy inning in the fourth, Baltimore went on the attack. With one out in the bottom of the inning, Frank Robinson, who had homered off Drysdale in the first game, did it again, and to the same spot in the left-field stands, only deeper this time.

Don Drysdale pitched a magnificent game, yielding only the home run to Frank Robinson, scattering four hits, and walking only one batter. It was not good enough, however, as Dave McNally blanked the Dodgers on four harmless singles and two bases on balls. The agony ended for Walter Alston's boys just one hour and fifty-five minutes after the first pitch, when Lou Johnson flied out to Paul Blair in center to end the game.

```
Los Angeles Dodgers    000 000 000 - 0 - 4 - 0
Baltimore Orioles      000 100 00x - 1 - 4 - 0
```

The statistics bespoke of the futility of it all for the pride of California. They scored two runs in four games, were shut out for the last 33 innings, managed just 17 hits for the Series including four extra base hits. Their top hitter, at .267, was Lou Johnson, as only three hitters batted over .200. The team batting average was a barely visible .142. Baltimore's offense was only slightly better, as they scored only 13 runs on 24 hits, with eight extra base hits, and batted a weak .200.

The pitching on both sides excelled. The Dodgers, in a losing cause, had a team ERA of 2.65, led by Claude Osteen at 1.29 and Sandy Koufax at 1.50. The high flying O's used only four pitchers, and their performance may never be matched in the World Series. The team earned run average of 0.50, was comprised of Dave McNally's 1.59, Wally Bunker's 0.00, Moe Drabowsky's 0.00, and Jim Palmer's 0.00. The three consecutive shutouts tossed by Bunker, Palmer, and McNally, may also never be equalled.

It was an overpowering pitching performance by Hank Bauer's "Kiddie Korps" that wrote the most glorious chapter in Baltimore Oriole history.

LOS ANGELES DODGERS (NL) V.S. THE OAKLAND ATHLETICS (AL)–1974

The Los Angeles Dodgers of the 1960s, winners of three National League flags and two World Championships, were built around pitching and speed. After the 1966 season, the Dodgers fortunes took a nose-dive. L.A. finished the 1967 season in eighth place, an embarrassing 28 1/2 games behind the high-flying St. Louis Cardinals.

It took O'Malley and Alston three years to bring their team back to contender status again. In 1970, with the league now split into an Eastern and Western Division, L.A. climbed into second place, but they were still 14 1/2 games from the top. Slowly, the new Dodgers began to take shape. Bill Russell (1970), Steve Garvey (1971), Davey Lopes (1973), and Ron Cey (1973), arrived on the scene to form the longest-playing infield unit in major league history.

By 1974, the new Los Angeles Dodgers were ready to make their move. In addition to the kid infield, nick-named the "Mod Squad" after a favorite television show, Walter Alson had the strongest catching corps in the league in Steve Yeager and Joe Ferguson. In the outfield, he had .300 hitting Billy Buckner and slugging Jimmy Wynn. On the mound, he was solid as usual. His starters included Andy Messersmith, Don Sutton, Doug Rau, and Tommy John. In the bullpen, relief ace Mike Marshall, fresh from a record-setting 92 appearances with Montreal in 1973, held forth, ably supported by 25-year-old south-paw, Doug Rau.

L.A. got off the mark quickly as the season opened, and led their division most of the season. By early July they were 10 games ahead of the defending champion Cincinnati Reds. They went on to win their division by four games, finishing with a record of 102-60, the third highest victory total in their history. Twenty-five-year old Steve Garvey, having found a home at first base, had an MVP season, batting a solid .312, with 21 home runs and 111 runs-batted-in. Jimmy Wynn, the "Toy Cannon," slugged 32 homers and knocked in 108 runs. Five other players had 10 or more round-trippers, including "The Penguin" Ron Cey (18), Joe Ferguson (16), Steve Yeager (12), Willie Crawford (11), and Davey Lopes (10).

The Dodgers did it all in 1974. They led the league in runs scored, as well as in fewest runs allowed. At the plate, they were first in home runs and slugging average. On the mound they were first in ERA (2.97), strikeouts, and fewest bases on balls. Andy Messersmith led the mound corps with a record of 20-9. Don Sutton finished at 19-9, while Tommy John (13-3), and Doug Rau (13-11), gave strong backup. In the bullpen, Mike Marshall set a record that may never be broken. He pitched in a major league record 106 games, all in relief, saving 21 and winning 15 more.

The championship wasn't secure with their division title however. The Dodgers still had to play the Eastern Division pennant winners in the League Championship Series (LCS), to determine the overall National League Champion. Alston's boys raced to the title in convincing fashion, destroying the Pittsburgh Pirates, three games to one. Don Sutton blanked the Buccaneers, 4-0, in the opener in Pittsburgh, and Andy Messersmith followed with a workmanlike job in Game Two, winning 5-2, as Ron Cey contributed a single, two doubles, and a home run to the attack. After Pittsburgh salvaged Game Three, 7-0, behind Bruce Kison, the series moved to Los Angeles

where the Dodgers thrilled 54,424 home town fans with a 12-1 rout of Danny Murtaugh's crew in Game Four. Don Sutton cruised to his second victory of the series, as Steve Garvey smashed four hits, including two homers, and drove in four runs in the carnage.

The Dodgers' opponents in the World Series were the powerful Oakland Athletics, winners of four straight American League Western Division titles, three straight American League Championships, and two straight World Championships. The battling A's were a colorful cast of

Steve Garvey

characters, both on and off the field. Dressed in garish gold and green uniforms and wearing white shoes, Charlie Finley's boys fought with each other as often as they fought with the rest of the league but, when the chips were down, they pulled together as a team. They knew how to win–and they loved to win–a deadly combination.

After sweeping to the Western Division title by five games over the Texas Rangers, Alvin Dark's team annihi-lated the Baltimore Orioles three games to one, holding Earl Weaver's squad to one run over the last three games.

Like the Dodgers, the A's thrived on pitching. Like the Dodgers, they led the league in ERA, fewest runs allowed, and fewest bases on balls allowed. Jim "Catfish" Hunter, was the pride of the league, piling up a league leading 25 victories, against 12 defeats. Lefty Ken Holtzman finished at 19-17, and Vida Blue came in at 17-15. In the bullpen, the A's were blessed with future Hall-of-Famer Rollie Fingers, whose league-leading 76 appearances resulted in 18 saves and nine victories. Their slugging offense was led by third baseman Sal Bando who hit 22 homers and drove in 103 runs, Reggie Jackson (29, 93), Joe Rudi (22,99), and Gene Tenace (26,73).

The 71st fall classic opened in the National League city, the first all-California Series. Andy Messersmith was given the honor of throwing out the first pitch for the Dodgers, while Alvin Dark handed the ball to hard-throwing southpaw Ken Holtzman in what would turn out to be a pitchers' series from start to end. In Game One, as 55,974 Dodger fans sat back in polite respect, the A's drew first blood as flashy Reggie Jackson drove a Messersmith fast ball deep into the stands in left center field. The stocky righthander was touched up for another run in the top of the fifth, thanks to Holtzman himself. With one out, the Oakland hurler pulled a Messersmith delivery down the left-field line for two bases. He scored moments later on a wild pitch and a squeeze bunt by Bert Campaneris.

When the Dodgers threatened to tie the game in the bottom of the fifth, Dark dipped into his bullpen for Rollie Fingers. The lanky Oakland relief ace, handlebar mustache shining in the sun, was equal to the task. He fanned Steve Garvey and retired Ron Cey on a fly to left, leaving two Dodger runners stranded.

Fingers, normally a two-inning pitcher, hurled into the ninth. He appeared to be closing the door on Alston's crew when, with two men out, Jimmy Wynn, the "Toy Cannon" drilled a ball over the left-field wall for a home run, narrowing the gap to 3-2. When Steve Garvey followed with a single, Dark, not wanting to let the game slip away, replaced the rapidly tiring Fingers with his ace, "Catfish" Hunter. The big North Carolinian ended the drama by fanning the dangerous Joe Ferguson, as a quiet crowd of Los Angelinos filed out of Dodger Stadium, murmuring something about their bad luck.

Oakland Athletics	010 010 010	- 3 - 6 - 2
Los Angeles Dodgers	000 010 001	- 2 -11 - 1

It was a disappointing loss for the Dodgers, but it didn't shake their confidence any. They still felt they had the superior team. Game Two matched southpaw Vida Blue against L.A.'s Don Sutton. The Dodger righty, fresh from two wins in the LCS, was still in peak form. He

Los Angeles Dodgers, 1974 (Los Angeles Dodger Photo)

threw nothing but goose eggs at Darks' sluggers for 8 + innings, as his teammates forged a comfortable 3-0 lead.

Mike Marshall was rushed into the game in the top of the ninth after Sutton hit Bando with a pitch, and gave up a ringing double to his nemesis, Reggie Jackson. "Iron Mike" was given a rude welcome as Joe Rudi lined a single to center, good for two runs. Now, with the score 3-2, the tying run on first and still no one out, the Dodger closer rose to a new level. He sent first baseman Gene Tenace back to the bench, a strikeout victim. Then Oakland manager Alvin Dark, trying to manufacture the tying run, countered by inserting Herb Washington into the lineup to run for Joe Rudi. Washington, a former Michigan State track star, was the game's only professional pinch runner. He appeared in 105 games over a two-year period, but never had an at-bat to show for it. Used only as a pinch runner, Washington stole 31 bases in his short career and scored 33 runs. Against Mike Marshall, however, he was overmatched. Marshall caught the eager 22-year-old speedster leaning the wrong way, and promptly picked him off base, for out number two. He then struck out Angel Mangual to end the game.

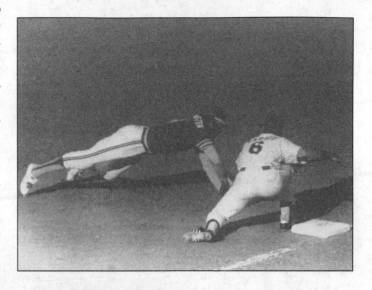

Pinch runner Herb Washington, representing the tying run, is picked off first base by Mike Marshall, in the ninth inning of Game Two. Dodger first baseman Steve Garvey applies the tag.

Bill Buckner, a "Kirk-Gibson type" ballplayer, patrolled the outfield for the Dodgers, and hit .314 with 83 runs scored and 31 stolen bases.

| Oakland Athletics | 000 000 002 - 2 - 6 - 0 |
| Los Angeles Dodgers | 010 002 00x - 3 - 6 - 1 |

The Series moved upstate to the bay area for Games 3, 4, and 5, deadlocked at one game apiece. In the first two games, pitching prevailed. It continued that way. Catfish Hunter, another of Dark's battle hardened veterans, took the mound in the Oakland Coliseum before a friendly sea of green and gold. The righthander from Hertford, North Carolina, was a clutch pitcher. During the season he won 20 or more games for the fourth consecutive year, capturing the Cy Young award along the way. His opponent was 33-year-old Al Downing, a classy southpaw in the twilight of a successful career.

On this day, little Al deserved a better fate. He pitched well, but his defense let him down. In the bottom of the third of a scoreless game, with two on and two out, catcher Joe Ferguson booted a ball in front of the plate as a run scored. A second unearned run came in minutes later on a single by Joe Rudi. The A's made it 3-0 in the fourth when Campaneris singled in second baseman Dick Green who had walked.

With one out in the eighth, and Oakland up 3-0, Billy Buckner slammed a home run into the right field stands, spelling finis for the Oakland starter. Rollie Fingers, seeking his first save of the Series, took the mound. A Jimmy Wynn single was quickly erased when Steve Garvey lined into a second to first double play.

For a time in the ninth, it looked as if Los Angeles might pull the game out. Willie Crawford took a Rollie

Davey Lopes was just coming into his own as a base stealer in 1974. After swiping 59 bases during the season, he pilfered another five in the playoffs and World Series. When he retired in 1987, he had 557 stolen bases to his credit, #19 on the all-time list. (Los Angeles Dodger Photo)

Fingers delivery downtown, depositing it into the right field stands for the Dodgers' second run of the game. When Campaneris fumbled Ferguson's ball, the rhythmic applause from Dodger fans could be heard around the Coliseum. It quieted moments later when "The Penguin" Ron Cey, struck out. And it died altogether when Bill Russell hit a ground ball to second base. Dick Green gobbled it up, and fed it to Campaneris, who relayed it to Tenace for a game-ending double play. Again, Walter Alston's cohorts had fought the good battle, but once again they came out on the short end of the stick, dropping their second 3-2 decision in three games. The cloud that hung over Los Angeles that night was one of despair, not smog.

Los Angeles Dodgers	000 000 011	- 2 - 7 - 2
Oakland Athletics	002 100 00x	- 3 - 5 - 2

The next day the two teams were back at it again, with Game One adversaries Ken Holtzman and Andy Messersmith ready to do battle. The first time, Holtzman dodged bullets for 4 1/3 exciting innings, escaping with but a single run scored against him, in a no-decision outing. Messersmith pitched better, but was the losing pitcher to Rollie Fingers in a tight 3-2 opener.

Now the Dodgers were in desperate need of a lift, down two games to one in the enemy park. As with the other games, this one started out as if one run might make the difference. In the bottom of the third, with the game still scoreless, Holtzman aided his own cause. With one

out, the Oakland hurler, a lifetime .158 hitter with two career home runs, picked out a Messersmith serve to his liking and sent it sailing into the left field stands for a 1-0 lead.

L.A., displaying the character that brought them 102 wins during the regular season, bounced back in the top of the fourth to claim the lead. Steve Garvey lined a one-out single to right field to ignite the rally. After Holtzman gave Joe Ferguson a free pass, he bore down and fanned the dangerous Ron Cey. Then, just when it seemed he might escape unscathed, the roof caved in. Bill Russell, one of the Dodgers most consistent clutch hitters, smashed a line drive to the gap in right center field for three bases. As the ball rolled to the wall, both Garvey and Ferguson scored to put Los Angeles on top 2-1.

The game remained that way until the bottom of the sixth when Messersmith's wildness let the game get away. The Dodger righty walked Bill North to open the inning, then threw wild on an attempted pick-off play to move the runner to second. The A's quickly capitalized on the Dodger mistake when Sal Bando singled to right to tie the game. A rattled Messersmith then walked Reggie Jackson. Joe Rudi's sacrifice and an intentional pass to Claudell Washington loaded the bases for pinch hitter Jim Holt. The six-foot lefty, with just six pinch hits during the season, came through with a single to right, scoring Bando and Jackson with runs three and four. An infield grounder by Dick Green plated Washington, and the A's had a comfortable 5-2 lead.

Mike Marshall set relief records in 1974 that may never be broken—106 games pitched, 208 innings, and 13 consecutive appearances. He also finished every game of the World Series, pitching nine innings with a 1.00 earned run average.

```
Los Angeles Dodgers    000 200 000 - 2 - 7 - 1
Oakland Athletics      001 004 00x - 5 - 7 - 0
```

It was gut-check time as Walter Alston's harried band of warriors took the field for Game Five. Nothing less than a three-game sweep would suffice. The Big Blue Machine had used up all its allowable losses. Don Sutton, the winner in Game Two, was confident that he could add another victory scalp to his belt. He had accumulated three already in postseason play, including two in the LCS. His mound opponent, Vida Blue, the A's flamethrowing southpaw, was just as confident.

Alvin Dark's crew got on the board first, with single runs in the first and second. L.A. tied it in the sixth on two hits and a walk. Steve Garvey's two-out single plated Lopes with the tying run.

"Iron Mike" Marshall took the mound in the bottom of the sixth, trying to keep L.A. in the Series. The big righthander retired the side in order in that inning but, in the seventh, he grooved one to Joe Rudi, and the right handed slugger promptly sent it screaming into the left-field stands for the tie breaking run. It turned out to be the championship run as Rollie Fingers retired the last five Dodgers in order.

```
Los Angeles Dodgers    000 002 000 - 2 - 5 - 1
Oakland Athletics      110 000 10x - 3 - 6 - 1
```

It was a hard fought Series between two evenly matched teams. The Oakland Athletics won the Series because they executed better, and because they were opportunists. Every time the Dodgers left the door open a crack, the A's moved right in. The Dodgers, on the other hand, put men on base more frequently than their adversaries, 57 to 50, but they couldn't get the big hit when they needed it. Four of the five games were decided by one run. It was a Series that could have gone either way.

LOS ANGELES DODGERS (NL) V.S. THE NEW YORK YANKEES (AL)—1977

After a two-year hiatus, during which time Cincinnati's Big Red Machine dominated the major league scene, the Los Angeles Dodgers returned to the top. Since their previous National League Championship, the Blue Crew had made several personnel changes of note. First and foremost, they had a new manager. Walter "Smokey" Alston, their field leader and their last link to Brooklyn, retired after 23 consecutive one-year contracts. His replacement was Tommy Lasorda, one-time minor league southpaw, and a pitcher whose one claim to fame was that he was returned to the minors so Brooklyn could retain another southpaw on the big club. The other man's name was Sandy Koufax.

The other major changes on the team were in the outfield where L.A. picked up Dusty Baker, Rick Monday, and Reggie Smith in trades, giving them three competent ballhawks with outstanding power. The new Blue Crew turned the pennant race into a shambles, winning 17 of their first 20 games, and leaving the rest of the league choking on their dust. Even Cincinnati's band of sluggers couldn't stem the tide. Lasorda's boys opened up a 10-game lead by early May, and made it stand up the rest of the season. Their 98-64 record was 10 games better than the Reds, who never mounted a serious challenge.

As had been a Dodger habit for almost 20 years, their pitching staff led the league in earned run average, while allowing the fewest total runs and the fewest bases on balls. Smooth-working Tommy John, fully recovered from the torn ligament that threatened to end his career three years previous, finished with a 20-7 record and a 2.78 ERA. Rick Rhoden (16-10), Don Sutton (14-8), Doug Rau (14-8), and Burt Hooton (12-7), rounded out the starting corps. Knuckleballer Charlie Hough was the mainstay of the bullpen, appearing in 70 games, and saving 22 of them.

The Los Angeles offense was awesome. They not only led the league with 191 home runs; they became the first team in major league history to field four men with 30 or more home runs. Steve Garvey led the way with 33 round trippers, followed by Reggie Smith with 32, and Ron Cey and Dusty Baker with 30 each. Baker hit his 30th on the last day of the season off Houston Astro ace, J.R. Richard. The four sluggers knocked in 115, 87, 110, and 86 runs respectively. Steve Yeager (16), Rick Monday (15), and Davey Lopes (11), contributed double digits to the Los Angeles home run total.

The Dodgers' opponents in the League Championship Series were the Philadelphia Phillies, a team who won 101 games on power, Steve Carlton, and a deep bullpen. The LCS opened in Los Angeles on Tuesday, October 4, before 55, 968 energetic Dodger fans. The two aces, Steve Carlton (23-10) and Tommy John, faced off against each other, but neither man had much on the ball, and the game turned into a real donneybrook. A Dodger error, and a home run by Greg Luzinski put the Phils up, 2-0 in the first. Two more runs came across in the fifth on another Dodger miscue. By the time the bottom of the seventh rolled around, Tommy John was enjoying a hot shower and Steve Carlton was coasting, 5-1. The Dodgers were not quite dead, however. The Philadelphia southpaw suddenly went wild, walking Jerry Grote and Reggie Smith, and yielding a single to Davey Lopes, to load the bases with two out. "The Penguin", Ron Cey worked the count full, then fouled off three pitches before driving Carlton to cover with a game-tying grand slam. Unfortunately, Lasorda's boys could not stand prosperity, and singles by McBride, Bowa, and Schmidt off reliever Elias Sosa in the ninth, gave the Phils a big 7-5 opening game victory.

L.A. bounced back in Game Two, winning 7-1 behind "old reliable" Don Sutton. The Big Blue Machine hit their second grand slam in two days when Dusty Baker connected in the fourth to break open a 1-1 tie. When the best-of-five series shifted to Philadelphia for the final three games, things looked rosy for Ozark's crew. They had won 60 of 81 games in the friendly confines of Veterans Stadium during the season, including four of six against the Dodgers, and they were confident of continuing the pattern in the LCS.

Game Three matched 19-game winner Larry Christensen against Burt Hooton, and disaster befell Lasorda's team before the fans were settled in their seats. The Dodgers staked Hooton to an early 2-0 lead, but the University of Texas graduate couldn't hold it. With two out and two on in the bottom of the second, a visibly distressed Hooton, upset over the ball-strike calls of plate umpire Harry Wendlestedt, walked three men in a row with the bases loaded, giving Philadelphia a 3-2 lead.

L.A. fought back to forge a tie in the third inning, but Danny Ozarks' crew jumped back on top, 5-3, with a two-run eighth. What happened next will be remembered as long as baseball is played. Gene Garber, working his third inning of relief, retired the first two Dodgers in the ninth. One out away from extinction, Tommy Lasorda went to his bench in search of a magic potion. He found it in 38-year-old Vic Davalillo, who surprised the Phila-

delphia infield with a drag bunt single. Next it was pinch-hitter extraordinaire Manny Mota's turn, and the little lefty spanked an 0-2 pitch over the outstretched glove of left fielder Greg Luzinski at the wall. Davilillo scored and Mota raced to third when second baseman Ted Sizemore bobbled the relay. An infield hit by Davey Lopes scored the tying run as Philadelphia fans sat in stunned silence. Garber, feeling the tightness in his throat, much as Hooton had seven innings earlier, threw wild on a pickoff attempt, and Lopes moved up 90 feet, into scoring position. The next batter was Bill Russell, the much-maligned Dodger shortstop, whose two errors paved the way for the Phils' first-game victory. Now it was pay-back time, and Russell cashed in on it, lining a base hit back over the mound and into center field, sending Lopes home with the eventual winning run.

The Phils were a demoralized crew as they left the stadium in the dusk, and they were not able to pull themselves together for Game Four. With Tommy Johns sinker working to perfection, and Steve Carlton as wild as a March hare, Los Angeles moved into the World Series with a steady 4-1 triumph. Dusty Baker's two-run homer in the second was all the support John needed, as 64,924 dejected Philadelphia fans watched the debacle through a steady downpour. It even rained inside the homes in Philadelphia that night, but that rain was tears of sadness.

Los Angeles Dodgers, 1977 (Los Angeles Dodger Photo)

While all the excitement was going on in the National League, the New York Yankees were wrapping up their second consecutive American League title. After edging out the Baltimore Orioles and Boston Red Sox in a three-team dogfight, Billy Martin's Bombers came from behind with three runs in the ninth inning of the fifth and final game to defeat the tough Kansas City Royals in the LCS.

The World Series opened on upper Manhattan island, in a section of the city known as The Bronx. It

Steve Garvey, the National League's Most Valuable Player, was a dangerous clutch hitter. His postseason batting average was .335.

brought back memories of past Subway Series to many of the players and thousands of New York and Brooklyn fans. Billy Martin selected former Cincinnati pitcher Don Gullet to open for the pinstripers, while manager Tom Lasorda handed the ball to righthander Don Sutton. L.A. jumped on the sore-armed Gullet for two runs in the top of the first on a walk to leadoff hitter Davey Lopes, a triple to left center by Bill Russell, and a sacrifice fly by Ron Cey. The Yanks came right back in their half of the inning. Two-out singles by Munson, Jackson, and Chambliss did the damage.

Billy Martin's street fighters tied the game in the bottom of the sixth when little Willie Randolph jumped

Lee Lacy was a valuable utility man for Walter Alston's team. His ninth-inning single drove in the tying run for the Dodgers in Game One.

on a Sutton fast ball and drove it into the left-field stands. Two innings later, the New Yorkers broke the tie. Randolph opened the inning with a walk and raced all the way home on a two-bagger by Thurman Munson. Lasorda rushed lefthander Lance Rautzhan in from the bullpen to face the meat of the Yankee batting order. Rautzhan walked Jackson and Nettles to load the bases with one out, then fanned Piniella for out number two before getting Dent to hit into a force play.

Lee Lacy's single in the ninth with two men on tied the game once again, and sent it into extra innings. Dodger reliever Mike Garman and Yankee stopper Sparky Lyle battled on even terms for three scoreless innings as 56,668 fans squirmed nervously in their seats. As the bottom of the twelfth rolled around, Rick Rhoden took over the mound chores for L.A. The game ended minutes later before the Dodger righty could retire a single batter. The pesky Randolph led off and cracked a double into the left-field corner. After Munson was intentionally passed, Paul Blair sent the fans home happy with a game-winning single to center.

The key play of the game, from the Dodger perspective occurred in the sixth inning. With one out, Steve Garvey beat out a bunt down the third base line. After Baker flied out, Glenn Burke stroked a single to right center field. Garvey attempted to score all the way from first, but was thrown out at the plate on a perfect relay from Mickey Rivers to Thurman Munson. Replays of the action showed that Garvey had actually beaten the throw with, what would have been, the deciding run. If only the right call had been made ......

left-field fence. They touched the big righthander for another run in the second on a four-bagger by Steve Yeager; then drove the him to cover under a two-run barrage in the third. After Bill Russell lined a one-out single to left, Reggie Smith sent Hunter to an early shower with a homer into the right center field bleachers.

Hooton, meanwhile, had the Yanks eating out of the palm of his hand. Over the first three innings, his pitching log showed a single hit yielded, no bases on balls, and six strikeouts. The New Yorkers did manage a run in the fourth on two singles and a double-play grounder, but that was the extent of their attack. The final run of the game came in the ninth when Steve Garvey hit L.A.'s fourth home run of the game. Burt Hooton finished with a tidy five-hitter, liberally sprinkled with eight strikeouts.

Los Angeles Dodgers   2 1 2 0 0 0   0 0 1 - 6 - 9 - 0
New York Yankees   0 0 0 1 0 0   0 0 0 - 1 - 5 - 0

Back home in Los Angeles, Tommy Lasorda's boys were a confident lot, but the thought of the game that got away still lingered in many minds. They were in a good position, tied at one game apiece with three home games coming up, but they could have been up 2-0 except for the bad call on Garvey.

Ron Cey makes an unsuccessful dive for a line drive off the bat of Thurman Munson in the first inning of Game One.

Rick Rhoden, a 16-game winner during the season, was used in the bullpen in the Series, going 0-1 with a 2.57 ERA.

Los Angeles Dodgers   2 0 0 0 0 0   0 0 1   0 0 0 - 3 - 6 - 0
New York Yankees   1 0 0 0 0 1   0 1 0   0 0 1 - 4 -11 - 0

Down one game to none, the Californians went to the master of the knuckle curve to get them even in Game Two. And Burt Hooton was more than equal to the task. Once again L.A. bolted into the lead in the top of the first. With two out, Reggie Smith hit a long double off the center field wall. Then the "Penguin", Ron Cey welcomed Catfish Hunter to the Series with a two-run shot over the

Big Mike Torrez, at 6'5" and 220 pounds, dominated Game Three as the Bronx Bombers moved back into the lead in the Series. The New Yorkers raked Dodger starter Tommy John over the coals in the first inning to stake Torrez to a big 3-0 lead.

As expected, the Dodgers didn't roll over and die. In fact, they came back to tie the game in the bottom of the third on singles by Reggie Smith and Steve Garvey, and Dusty Baker's big home run into the left-field bullpen. Unfortunately, Tommy John was not at his best, and the New Yorkers pecked away at him for two more runs over the next two innings. The eventual game winner came home in the fourth on singles by Nettles and Dent, and a

Charlie Hough was an excellent relief pitcher for Los Angeles for 11 years, piling up 47 victories and 60 saves. After leaving the Dodgers, the knuckleball expert became a starting pitcher for several major league teams. In all, he racked up 216 victories in 25 years. (Los Angeles Dodger Photo)

ground ball by Mickey Rivers. They added another run in the fifth on a walk and singles by Piniella and Chambliss.

That was all Mike Torrez needed. He settled down after the third-inning uprising, holding Lasorda's team to two singles over the final six innings, none in the last three. He struck out nine and walked three in pitching a complete game victory.

| New York Yankees | 3 0 0 1 1 0 0 0 0 - 5 -10 - 0 |
| Los Angeles Dodgers | 0 0 3 0 0 0 0 0 0 - 3 - 7 - 1 |

Once again, the Dodgers had their backs to the wall. Manager Tommy Lasorda picked 14-game winner Doug Rau to stem the tide, while Billy Martin had his ace, Ron Guidry well rested and raring to go. The 28-year-old Dodger southpaw didn't survive the second inning. After a scoreless first, the Yankees made quick work of Rau in the second. A leadoff double by Reggie Jackson inside third, a single to right by Lou Piniella, and another double by Chris Chambliss, drove the shell-shocked Rau to the safety of the clubhouse. Rick Rhoden, the losing pitcher in game one, came on to yield a run-scoring single to Bucky Dent, as the opportunistic New Yorkers took a 3-0 lead into the third.

The resilient Dodgers fought back again, scoring twice in the third to pull within a run of a tie. Rhoden helped his own cause with a one-out double down the left field line. Davey Lopes then accounted for the two runs with a long home run over the center field fence. The dangerous Reggie Jackson upped the margin to 4-2 in the sixth with a dinger to left center field.

Rick Rhoden performed admirably for manager Tommy Lasorda, giving him seven sparkling innings of relief; yielding but a single run on two hits. Unfortunately, "Louisiana Lightning" was even better, as he slammed the door on the Dodgers inning after inning. When Dusty Baker lifted a fly ball to Mickey Rivers to end the game, Guidry had fashioned an impressive four-hitter, fanning seven men along the way.

| New York Yankees | 0 3 0 0 0 1 0 0 0 - 4 - 7 - 0 |
| Los Angeles Dodgers | 0 0 2 0 0 0 0 0 0 - 2 - 4 - 0 |

The noose was drawn tighter around the Dodgers' neck as they found themselves in the unenviable position of being down three games to one, after losing two successive home encounters. If they were to win the 1977 World Series, they not only had to take Game Six at home; they also had to go back to New York and whip the Bronx Bombers in their own back yard, a monumental task to say the least. Don Sutton got them on the first step back with a complete-game victory in game six. His opponent, Don Gullet, survived the first three innings with a minimum of damage, but couldn't get out of the fifth. L.A. staked their pitcher to a one-run lead in the first inning on a triple to left field by Lopes and a single by Russell.

They broke the game wide open in the fourth, with four runs against the Yankee southpaw. Hits by Garvey and Baker, an error, and a long home run by Steve Yeager, did the damage. With an 8-0 cushion, Don Sutton paced himself for a complete game. He was touched up for four runs over the last three innings, but coasted to an easy 10-4 victory.

New York Yankees	000 000 220 - 4 - 9 - 2
Los Angeles Dodgers	100 432 00x -10 -13 - 0

Los Angeles Dodgers	201 000 001 - 4 - 9 - 0
New York Yankees	020 320 01x - 8 - 8 - 1

Game Six matched two righthanders, knuckle-curve artist Burt Hooton and fireballer Mike Torrez, both of whom had posted a previous victory in the Series. Torrez beat the Dodger hurler with a route-going performance, but it was big Reggie Jackson who put on a one-man show for the 56,407 baseball enthusiasts in attendance.

In the fourth, with the Dodgers leading 3-2, Reggie Jackson jumped all over Hooton's first pitch and lined a two-run homer into the right field stands. An inning later, with two out, and Mickey Rivers on first with a single, Jackson took Elias Sosa's first pitch downtown, a two-run shot that upped the count to 7-3.

It was all over now except for the final tally. Mike Torrez had found a groove and wasn't about to lose a big four-run lead. The big news of the day came in the eighth. Reggie Jackson, batting against Charlie Hough, slammed the first pitch deep into the right-field bleachers for his third homer of the game and his fifth of the Series. In the process, the Yankee right fielder had created a new nickname for himself. He would, forever more, be known as "Mr. October." Jackson had, amazingly, hit three successive home runs, on three successive pitches, off three different pitchers. His three home runs in one World Series game tied Babe Ruth's record, while his five home runs in one Series established a new mark for future sluggers to shoot for.

Teamwise, the 1977 Series was virtually even. The Dodgers actually outscored their east coast adversaries, but a couple of timely hits - and one mammoth bad break - did them in.

LOS ANGELES DODGERS (NL) V.S. THE NEW YORK YANKEES (AL)–1978

Nineteen seventy-eight was deja vu as far as the Dodgers and Yankees were concerned. When the dust had settled from the long hot summer, and the field of battle was again quiet in the two major leagues, New York and Los Angeles stood alone at the pinnacle of their respective mountains.

In the National League, Tommy Lasorda's cohorts, not only had to fight off the charge of Sparky Anderson's mighty Redlegs; they also had to defeat Joe Altobelli's rejuvenated San Francisco Giants. A seven game winning streak in late August propelled Lasorda's team into first place for the first time since May as both the Reds and Giants faltered. They clinched the pennant with a week to go, when rookie Bob Welch blanked the San Diego Padres 4-0.

The Los Angeles franchise passed an important milestone on September 15 when they became the first

Los Angeles Dodgers, 1978 (Los Angeles Dodger Photo)

team in major league history to break the 3,000,000 home attendance figure. Over 47,000 fans jammed Dodger Stadium to watch Don Sutton shut out Atlanta 5-0, sparked by Lee Lacy's two run homer. L.A. finished the season with a record home attendance of 3,347,845.

As in 1977, Tommy Lasorda's boys faced the Philadelphia Phillies in the League Championship Series. Danny Ozark's team had nosed out the Pittsburgh Pirates again, outlasting Chuck Tanners fast closing Buccaneers by the slim margin of 1 1/2 games. This time the series opened in Veterans Stadium, Philadelphia, with manager Danny Ozark predicting a three game sweep for his team. The Dodgers proceeded to make a mockery of that prediction as they jumped on starter Larry Christenson for four runs in the third inning of the opener, for a 4-1 lead. Steve Garvey's 3-run homer was the key blow. The Dodger first sacker hit another four bagger later in the game, and Davey Lopes and Steve Yeager added home runs of their own, as Bob Welch, in relief of Burt Hooton, coasted to a 9-5 victory.

The next day was even worse, as Tommy John, his sinker in high gear, blanked Mike Schmidt & Co. 4-0. Lopes' leadoff home run in the top of the fourth, got L.A. on the board, and they added two in the fifth and another run in the seventh, as they opened up a 2-0 lead in games. Lopes, the Dodger second sacker, was the batting star with a single, triple, home run, and three runs batted in.

As the scene shifted to Los Angeles for Game Three, Tommy Lasorda's boys stood one game away from the title. The Phils were not about to fold, however, especially with their ace, Steve Carlton on the hill. The tall, gangly lefthander brought his team back from near extinction with a gutty 9-4 win. Actually, it was his bat, more than his arm, that did the Dodgers in. In the second inning, with Philadelphia leading 1-0 and two men on base, the 6'4" Carlton, a lifetime .205 hitter, slammed a Don Sutton fast ball over the center field fence for a three-run homer.

Game Four, matching southpaw Randy Lerch, 11-8 during the season, against lefty Doug Rau, 15-9, was a gem. Rau got off to a shaky start as the Phils loaded the bases with no one out in the first on a double by Mike Schmidt, a walk to Larry Bowa, and a single by Garry Maddox. The Dodger starter settled down in the nick of time, however, fanning Greg Luzinski for the first out, then retiring Jose Cardenal on a liner to short and right fielder Jerry Martin on a foul pop to Steve Yeager.

Except for a two-run homer by Greg Luzinski, and singletons by Ron Cey, Steve Garvey, and Bake McBride, pitching dominated. The score stood at 3-3 at the end of nine innings. Tug McGraw, who entered the game in the ninth, had retired five in a row when Cey walked with two down in the bottom of the tenth. The next batter, Dusty Baker, hit a drive right at Garry Maddox in center field. The gold glove fielder dropped the easy fly, and the Dodgers had a life, with runners on first and second. Bill Russell promptly made the Phils pay for the error as he stroked a pennant-winning single to center field.

Over in the Junior Circuit, the New York Yankees had their hands full with Don Zimmer's Boston Red Sox. In fact, by mid-July, New York was mired in fourth place, 14 games behind the rampaging Red Sox, who were 60-28. Manager Billy Martin was replaced by Bob Lemon just as the Yanks got hot. On July 19 the Yanks began to move upward as the Sox faltered. The Bronx Bombers didn't stop winning until they had propelled themselves into a 3 1/2-game lead, with just 15 games left in the season. It said a lot for the Red Sox character that they could, just as suddenly, reverse their direction, and win 12 of their last 14 games to finish the season in a flat-footed tie with New York for first place.

Reggie Jackson and Steve Garvey were the anchor men of their respective teams. In this Series, Jackson won the battle running up a .391 mark to Garvey's .208.

A one-game playoff was played in Fenway Park the day after the regular season ended. The Yankees won the game on the gutty pitching of their ace, Ron Guidry, and a come-from-behind, three-run homer by Bucky Dent into the short left-field screen at Fenway. Dent's dramatic blow, off former Yankee Mike Torrez in the top of the seventh inning, brought Bob Lemon's team from 2-0 down into a 3-2 lead. Goose Gossage, the game's premier reliever, retired Carl Yastrzemski on a foul pop to third base with two men on base, to end the game.

New York went on to defeat the Kansas City Royals, three games to one, in an anti-climatic LCS. The World Series finally opened in the City of Angels on October 10 with southpaw Tommy John facing righthander Ed Figueroa, a 20-9 pitcher during the season. Tommy Lasorda's boys were a confident lot as they faced off against the Bronx Bombers, and their home-field advantage seemed to be working as they exploded for three runs in the bottom of the second. Dusty Baker led off with a long fly ball to left that disappeared over the left field wall for a 1-0 lead. Minutes later, the score mounted to 3-0 on a Rick Monday double and a two-run shot to left by Davey Lopes.

In the fourth, they upped the margin to 6-0 when that same Lopes, dedicating the Series to Dodger hero James "Junior" Gilliam, who passed away just two days before the Series opened, slammed his second home run of the game, a three-run blast to left center. Another run

Bob Welch, the young fireballer, compiled a 7-4 record during the season. He became part of World Series lore after his dramatic duel with Reggie Jackson in Game Two.

scored in the fifth on singles by Cey and Baker, and a wild pitch. The smooth-working John, meanwhile, kept the Yanks at bay with a low sinker that had the batters hitting the ball into the ground all day. The final score was 11-5.

New York Yankees	000 000 320 -	5 - 9 - 1
Los Angeles Dodgers	030 310 31x -	11 - 15 - 2

A loose band of Los Angeles Dodgers took the field in Game Two, determined to build their lead in the Series. Burt "Happy" Hooton, the Dodgers' biggest winner during the season, took the mound for L.A., while Jim "Catfish" Hunter, a veteran of World Series competition, was handed the ball by manager Bob Lemon. Hooton beat Hunter in a pitchers' duel, 4-3. The "Penguin" Ron Cey connected with a Hunter fast ball and sent it rocketing into the left-field stands for the winning run in the sixth inning.

The game, however, is more famous for one particular incident than it is for the 4-3 Dodger victory. One of the great pitching duels in World Series history took place in the top of the ninth inning when Reggie Jackson stepped up to the plate with two men on and two men out. On the mound for the Dodgers was 21-year-old Bob Welch, a youngster well poised beyond his years. The 6'3" rookie stared down the mighty Jackson, and fed him nothing but fast balls. It was strength against strength, as Jackson, a notorious fast ball hitter tried to catch up to Welch's blazer. Jackson worked the count to 3 and 2, fouling off four pitches along the way. The crowd was on its feet screaming as Welch served up more heat. Jackson took a mighty swing–like Casey-at-the-bat–and missed, a moment frozen in time. Mighty Casey had struck out and, as the Dodger bench exploded in joyous celebration, the big Yankee rightfielder slammed his bat down in disgust, the loser in a titanic battle.

New York Yankees	002 000 100 -	3 - 11 - 0
Los Angeles Dodgers	000 103 00x -	4 - 7 - 0

It was a happy band of Dodgers that boarded the plane for New York, up two games to none, and in a commanding position to win it all. Fate was about to step in, however, in the form of one Graig Nettles, third baseman extraordinaire. The Yankee human vacuum cleaner was about to put on one of the greatest fielding exhibitions ever witnessed in World Series play. Similar to the magic performed by another third baseman, Brooks Robinson, in the 1970 Series, the 1978 Series would be remembered as "The Nettles Series."

Game Three matched "Rocket Ron" Guidry against Don Sutton. Guidry had just completed, not only a career season, but one of the most dominating seasons any pitcher ever had. The Cy Young award winner finished the season with a record of 25-3, while leading the league in victories, winning percentage (.893), earned run average (1.74), and shutouts (9).

Guidry's explosive sinker was on target all day, as batter after batter pounded the ball into the ground, accounting for 14 infield assists. Nettles had five assists himself, many of them of the unbelievable variety. In the third inning, with New York ahead 2-0, L.A. struck. Billy

Tommy John gave Tommy Lasorda a sterling effort in the Series. He pitched in two games, winning one, with a 3.07 earned run average in 14 2/3 innings.

North walked, stole second, and went to third on an in-field out. After Bill Russell drove in North with a hit to deep short, Reggie Smith threatened to tie the game with a hot smash over the third base bag. But it was not to be. Nettles made a spectacular backhand stop of the ball behind third, whirled, and threw a strike to first to retire the side and frustrate the Dodgers.

The next Dodger rally came in the fifth, with the same result. With two men on and two out, Reggie Smith hit another shot over third to apparently tie the game, but that man Nettles was Johnny-on-the-spot again. He knocked the ball down, holding Smith to a single and preventing a run from scoring. The run never did score as Guidry forced Garvey to hit into a force play.

The very next inning, Lasorda's Blue Crew was back on the attack again. Baker and Lacy singled, and Mota walked, loading the bases with two out. Then Davey Lopes drove a hot shot over third for, what should have been, a double. But Nettles, getting into the habit of it by now, made a sensational back hand stab, and threw the ball to Brian Doyle for an inning-ending force out at second.

Joe Ferguson was a hard-nosed catcher for L.A. for 11 years. In the '78 Series, he was two for three, with two doubles.

Guidry settled down after the sixth inning, scattering just two hits over the final three innings. Thanks to the great defensive efforts of Graig Nettles that saved five or six runs, the Yankees and their ace pitcher escaped with a deceptive 5-1 victory.

Los Angeles Dodgers   0 0 1 0 0 0 0 0 0 - 1 - 8 - 0
New York Yankees   1 1 0 0 0 0 3 0 x - 5 -10 - 1

Game Four produced another turning point in the Series. Where Game Three was dominated by the defensive wizardry of Graig Nettles, Game Four was highlighted by the deception of one Reginald Martinez Jackson, and by the failure of the umpiring crew to punish the crime. Tommy John and Ed Figueroa battled through four scoreless innings, before the Dodgers broke through in the top of the fifth. Steve Yeager doubled to right center field with one out and Davey Lopes walked. After Russell struck out, Reggie Smith unloaded on the big righthander, sending a ball deep into the right-field seats for a 3-0 L.A. lead.

One inning later, came the play that may well have decided the Series. With one out in the Yankee sixth, White singled, Munson walked, and Jackson singled for a run. The next batter, Lou Piniella, then hit a ball to short for, what appeared to be, an inning ending double play. Bill Russell gloved the ball, stepped on second for the force on Jackson, and threw toward first. The wily Jackson, halfway between first and second, threw his right hip into the ball, sending it ricocheting into right field as a run scored. Manager Tommy Lasorda, and the rest of the Dodgers argued that Jackson had intentionally interfered with the ball and that Piniella should be called out for the third out, with no run scoring. The umpires ruled otherwise.

With Tidrow and Gossage keeping the Dodgers in check, the Yanks came back to win, 4-3 in ten innings.

Los Angeles Dodgers   0 0 0 0 3 0 0 0 0 0 - 3 - 6 - 1
New York Yankees   0 0 0 0 0 2 0 1 0 1 - 4 - 9 - 0

The Yankees had the momentum now and, apparently, the luck also. Everything they did came up heads. It seemed as if they were destined to win the Series no matter what the Dodgers did. Game Five was a blowout. Maybe both teams realized that the Series was essentially over. In any case, New York rookie Jim Beattie, pitching the first complete game of his big league career, throttled the Lasorda-men, 12-2, behind a blistering 18 attack.

L.A. did draw first blood as they scored in the first inning on singles by Lopes and Smith. They upped the advantage to 2-0 in the third when Lopes singled and Russell doubled him home. From that point on, the game belonged to the Yankees as they racked up 12 runs on 17 hits in the next six innings. They shelled Hooton to cover during a four-run barrage in the third. His replacement, Lance Rautzhan, was routed in the fourth.

Charlie Hough, the third Los Angeles pitcher, became the third pitcher to be roughed up as the Bronx Bombers erupted for four more runs in the seventh. A final run in the eighth closed out the scoring.

Los Angeles Dodgers   1 0 1 0 0 0 0 0 0 - 2 - 9 - 3
New York Yankees   0 0 4 3 0 0 4 1 x -12 -18 - 0

The Dodgers returned home, bruised and battered, after seeing their two game to none advantage dissolve into nothingness. Now trailing three games-to-two, the team hoped that a good dish of home cooking would be the lift they needed for a final charge to the title. They forgot that teams that are destined to win a Series, always win the Series, even if they don't deserve it. And in 1978, the New York Yankees appeared to be that team of destiny.

Yankee starter "Catfish" Hunter was touched up for one run in the first as Davey Lopes, in his memorial to Junior Gilliam, slammed his third home run of the Series. But that was it for Lasorda's contingent. The Dodger starter, Don Sutton, after being hammered for three runs in the second, lasted into the sixth, when another outburst sent him to the showers. Lemon's boys closed out the scoring with a pair of runs in the seventh, off Bob Welch. With one out and one on, Reggie Jackson, still smarting from the duel with Welch in game one, hit a fastball to the opposite field, sending it high up into the left-field seats.

New York Yankees	0 3 0 0 0 2 2 0 0 - 7 -11 - 0
Los Angeles Dodgers	1 0 1 0 0 0 0 0 0 - 2 - 7 - 1

The New York Yankees were, once again, World Champions, although this time they were sparked by two very unusual heroes. Second baseman Brian Doyle, a .192 hitter during the regular season, stung the ball at a torrid .438 pace during the Series. His double-play partner, Bucky Dent, a regular .243 hitter, batted .417 when the chips were down. Reggie Jackson led the team with two home runs and eight runs batted in, on the strength of a .391 batting average. In all, seven Yankees hit over .300, as they sported a lusty .306 team batting average.

On the losing side, the Dodgers were led by Bill Russell's .423 batting average. Davey Lopes hit .308 with three homers and seven runs batted in.

In the warm breeze that wafted in off the Pacific, a soft murmuring sound rumbled across Southern California; an eerie whisper with an almost human quality to it. As Dodger fans lamented their second consecutive loss to the Yankees, the celestial messenger, with an accent strangely Brooklynese, consoled them with words of hope, "Wait till next year,... wait till next year."

"Next year" did return again, in 1981, and it was just as sweet the second time around.

Los Angeles Dodgers, 1981 (Los Angeles Dodger Photo)
Front Row: (L to R) Steve Yeager, Davey Lopes, Mike Scioscia, Ron Perranoski, Mark Creese, Manny Mota, Tommy Lasorda, Monty Basgall, Danny Ozark, Bobby Castillo, Derrel Thomas, Pepe Frias. Second Row: Bill DeLury, Bill Buhler, Steve Garvey, Bill Russell, Joe Ferguson, Rick Monday, Pedro Guerrero, Jay Johnstone, Reggie Smith, Dusty Baker, Ron Cey, Ken Landreaux, Paul Padilla, Jaime Murillo. Third Row: Terry Forster, Burt Hooton, Dave Goltz, Rick Sutcliffe, Jerry Reuss, Fernando Valenzuela, Joe Beckwith, Dave Stewart, Steve Howe. Seated in front: Carlos Murillo, Victor Murillo.

LOS ANGELES DODGERS (NL) V.S.
THE NEW YORK YANKEES (AL)–1981

If the New York Yankees were a team of destiny in 1978, then there's no doubt that the Los Angeles Dodgers were destiny's darling in 1981. The magic began to unfold on April 9, when a fuzzy-cheeked 20-year-old southpaw named Fernando Valenzuela took the mound in the season opener against the Houston Astros. A late replacement for the injured Jerry Reuss, the kid from Sonora, Mexico tossed a 2-0 shutout. Five weeks later, the Dodgers were in first place, and Fernando was 8-0, with four shutouts and an almost perfect 0.50 ERA. Fernandomania had blanketed the west coast.

By May 23, Tommy Lasorda had his team comfortably ensconced in first place with a 29-11 record, and a 6 1/2-game lead over second-place Cincinnati. The Dodger mound corps was sensational during this period, with Burt Hooton, 6-0 with a 2.11 ERA, and Jerry Reuss, 4-1 with a 1.50 ERA, filling in the gaps behind Fernando.

The 1981 baseball season was marred by a players' strike that began on June 12. At the time of the walkout, the Dodgers held a scant 1/2-game lead over the surging Reds. Their 36-21 record edged Cincinnati by the margin of one victory, both teams having 21 losses. It was an important win for Los Angeles, because, when the strike ended two months later, Commissioner Bowie Kuhn declared the Dodgers to be the winner of the first half of the season; with a second half yet to be played. In the second half, the Houston Astros romped home in first place, with the Dodgers a distant third, six games behind.

Post-season play promised to be a long ordeal for Tommy Lasorda's cohorts. First there was a five-game playoff with the Houston Astros to determine a Western Division winner, then another five-game series to crown the National League champion. The Western Division playoff opened in the Houston Astrodome with Valenzuela, the eventual Rookie of the Year and Cy Young Award winner, facing fireballing Nolan Ryan, the all-time major league strikeout leader. Ryan, who owned a 1.11 ERA in the Astrodome, had just no-hit Los Angeles, 5-0, on September 26, the fifth no-hitter of his illustrious career. The game, as expected, was a pitchers duel. Steve Garvey's 400 foot home run in the seventh pulled the Dodgers into a 1-1 tie, but the Astros won it in the ninth against reliever Dave Stewart, when Alan Ashby hit a two-out, two-run homer.

Seconds after Rick Monday's dramatic ninth-inning home run gave Los Angeles a 2-1 lead in the final NLCS game, the Dodger outfielder is mobbed at the plate by the entire bench.

Game Two was another nail-biter with Joe Niekro and Jerry Reuss tossing goose eggs at each other for eight innings. The Astros pulled it out again in the ninth, winning 1-0 on a two-out, bases-loaded single by Denny Walling. Dave Stewart was the losing pitcher for the second straight game.

As the series moved to California for the final three games, the Dodgers were down to their last loss. Nothing less than a three-game sweep would give them the title. Tommy Lasorda went to Burt Hooton to keep the series alive, sending his other starter, Bob Welch, to the bullpen,

Houston Astro's third baseman Art Howe is picked off first base during the Western Division playoff. Steve Garvey applies the tag.

to shore up the weak link in the L.A. attack. The Dodgers, happy to be home, and on natural grass again, jumped on starter Bob Knepper for three big runs in the first inning. Dusty Baker's double brought the first run across, while Steve Garvey's homer to left-field plated the last two. That was all the runs "Happy" Hooton needed, as he coasted to an easy 6-1 win.

Fernando Valenzuela was back on the hill in Game Four, this time facing Astro righthander Vern Ruhle. The 20-year-old southpaw had the Houston batters chasing his screwball all night long, as he strung together another string of zeros. Ruhle, after retiring 14 consecutive batters to start the game, threw a homerun ball to Pedro Guerrero for a 1-0 Dodger lead. The Dodgers added another run in the seventh on singles by Garvey and Russell to take a 2-0 lead into the ninth. Houston reached Fernando for one run on a two-out single by Tony Scott, but the poised lefty bore down and retired Jose Cruz on a pop to Scioscia to end the game.

The finale of the dramatic series, before 55,979 screaming Dodger fans, matched the great Nolan Ryan against lefty Jerry Reuss. For five innings the game was scoreless as Ryan struck out six and limited Los Angeles to one hit. Reuss was almost as good, holding the Astros to two safeties over the same distance. In the bottom of the sixth of a scoreless tie, the Dodgers finally broke through against the mighty Ryan. A walk to Dusty Baker gave L.A. a jump start. Subsequent singles by Garvey, Monday, and Scioscia, combined with an error by Walling gave Reuss three runs to work with. He only needed one of them. A double by Landreaux and a long triple by Garvey upped the margin to 4-0 in the seventh, and the Dodgers were home free. Reuss fanned two Astros in the eighth; then retired the side in order in the ninth, striking out Dave Roberts to end the game.

The dramatic, come-from-behind victory in the Western Division playoff was the basis for the legend of "Team Comeback," by which name the Los Angeles Dodgers of 1980-81-82 would come to be known. The character of "Team Comeback" actually evolved from the '80 squad who swept the final three games of the regular season against Houston to catch the Astros at the wire. Unfortunately, the '80 team could not sustain its momentum, losing a one-game playoff for the title.

The Western Division Champion Dodgers met the Montreal Expos in the best-of-five NLCS, with the first two games played in Dodger Stadium. The Expos, fresh from a victory over Philadelphia in the Eastern Division Series, opened with 22-year-old Bill Gullickson, a six-game winner over the last half of the season, and a winner against the Phils. Burt Hooton, the Dodger starter, already had a strong effort under his belt against the Astros, and he was ready to go. Lasorda's boys didn't waste much time getting to Gullickson, as they shelled him for two runs in the second.

Happy Hooton was in a groove, as his knuckle-curve darted in and out, up and down, giving opposing batters fits. He was relieved by Bob Welch in the eighth, with the Dodgers up, 2-0. The Big Blue Crew added three more runs in the eighth when Pedro Guerrero slammed a two-run homer and Mike Scioscia followed with a solo shot. The Astros scored a run in the ninth, making the final tally 5-1.

Ron Cey began the Dodgers' World Series comeback by blasting a three-run homer in the first inning of Game Three.

Dodger thoughts of a sweep disappeared in the heavy California air when big righthander Ray Burris outdueled Fernando Valenzuela for a well-deserved 3-0 victory, sending the Montreal team home to Canada in the driver's seat. Jim Fanning's team tightened their grip on the National League Championship with a 4-1 victory in Game Three, as 54,372 rabid Expo fans screamed for their team in two languages. Steve Rogers, the Montreal ace, beat Jerry Reuss when Jerry White hit a three-run homer in the sixth inning.

For the second time in a week, the Big Blue Machine was down to its last loss, only this time they had to win two straight in the enemy's park, a difficult task at best. Game Four was another duel between Bill Gullickson and Burt Hooton. The Dodger righty had taken the first encounter, 5-1, but this one was tougher. Each team scored an unearned run in the early going, and the game moved into the eighth tied 1-1. Dusty Baker gave the Dodgers a start with a one-out single to left. "Old Reliable" Steve Garvey then took matters into his own hands, sending a long drive over the left field fence for a 3-1 L.A. lead. Lasorda's boys put the game away for keeps in the top of the ninth, scoring four runs behind a five-hit attack that included singles by Yeager, Thomas, Baker, Cey, and Smith. Steve Howe came on in relief to nail down Hooton's well-deserved 7-1 victory.

Fernando Valenzuela, in as gutty a performance as he ever gave the Dodgers, won Game Three, 5-4, with a nine-hit, seven-walk, struggle.

Once again, a Dodger title came down to a single game. As Montreal geared for an expected World Series, Fernando Valenzuela stood before them them like Leonidas at Thermopylae. It was fitting that, with baseball now an international sport, a Mexican pitcher should hurl for an American team in a National League Championship game in Canada. The Expos reached the young

southpaw for a single run in the first, scoring on a double-play grounder, but that was the extent of the Montreal offense. Fernando found his groove and threw nothing but goose eggs at Jim Fanning's boys after the first. L.A. meanwhile, had its own problems with the 6'5", 225-pound Burris. The winner of Game Three showed no signs of slowing down as he blanked the Dodgers over the first four innings. Then, in the fifth, he yielded his first run. Rick Monday and Pedro Guerrero opened the inning with singles, and Monday scored on an infield out by Valenzuela.

The 1-1 tie continued into the ninth as 36,491 fans sat chilled in the frosty 41-degree Canadian air. Fanning, after pinch hitting for Burris, brought his ace, Steve Rogers, into the game. The big righthander, 12 and 8 during the strike-shortened season, retired the dangerous Steve Garvey and Ron Cey, as the crowd breathed a sigh of relief. Right fielder Rick Monday was the Dodgers' last chance in regulation play, and he strode to the plate determined to keep the inning alive. With a count of 3-1 on the batter, Rogers made a fatal mistake. Trying to hit the outside corner for strike two, he accidentally laid a fastball down the middle. The Dodger slugger, momentarily surprised at his good fortune, lashed out at the cripple, and sent it on a high arc to right center field. Center fielder Andre Dawson, off with the crack of the bat, raced back and to his left as far as he could, then watched dejectedly as the ball disappeared over the fence for a home run.

Bob Welch relieved Valenzuela with two on and two out in the bottom of the ninth, and retired Jerry White for the last out. "Team Comeback" had done the impossible again, coming from a two games to one deficit to win the National League Championship. Rick Monday, who's dramatic two-out, ninth-inning, home run won the pennant, earned his place in Dodger legend, alongside such heroes as Cookie Lavagetto, Sandy Amoros, and Kirk Gibson. But more was yet to come.

The Dodgers' opponents in the World Series were, fittingly, the New York Yankees. Bob Lemon's team won the first half of the split season, then captured the Eastern Division title by defeating the Milwaukee Brewers in the playoff. The American League Championship Series was a cakewalk for the Bronx Bombers, as they swept the Oakland Athletics, three games to none.

The Yankees were installed as 9-5 favorites as the fall classic opened in Yankee Stadium on October 20. The weather was a crisp 54 degrees as the Bronx Bombers took the field against "Team Comeback." In the battle of southpaws, "Louisiana Lightning," Ron Guidry had much the better of it against Jerry Reuss. While Bob Lemon's boys were disposing of the Dodger starter in less than three innings, Guidry kept L.A.'s sluggers at bay with a sharp-breaking sinker and pinpoint control.

New York broke from the blocks quickly, piling up three big runs in the first. They added another run in the third on two singles, KO'ing Reuss in the process. A fourth run crossed the plate against Bobby Castillo in the fourth on four bases on balls.

All the while, Guidry had the Dodgers eating out of the palm of his hand, scattering two singles and striking out four men in four innings. Lasorda's boys finally broke the scoring ice in the fifth on a towering blast to right field by catcher Steve Yeager. They narrowed the margin to 5-3 in the top of the eighth after Guidry had departed, but they could get no closer, as Goose Gossage shut them down with one hit over the final two frames.

```
Los Angeles Dodgers  000 010 020 - 3 - 5 - 0
New York Yankees     301 100 00x - 5 - 6 - 0
```

Game Two was not much better for the California crew. Righthander Burt "Happy" Hooton pitched a strong game for manager Lasorda, but his teammates were helpless against the wily southpaw, Tommy John. John's pitches were slow, slower, and slowest, but he mixed up his deliveries well, keeping the L.A. batters off balance all day. For seven innings it was a superb pitchers' duel, with John holding a scant 1-0 lead. The only run of the game scored in the bottom of the fifth when Willie Randolph reached first on an error by second baseman Davey Lopes and, with two men out, came in to score on a double by Larry Milbourne. The Yankees iced the game with a brace of runs against Dodger reliever Steve Howe in the eighth.

Steve Yeager, after putting a Ron Guidry fast ball into orbit to win Game Five, 2-1, doffs his hat to the Dodger Stadium crowd.

```
Los Angeles Dodgers  000 000 000 - 0 - 4 - 2
New York Yankees     000 010 02x - 3 - 6 - 1
```

It was a disappointed band of Dodger players who arrived back at Los Angeles International Airport during the evening of October 21. They were down, but they were far from out. Many teams would have packed it in after suffering two heartbreaking defeats, such as the Dodgers suffered in New York. But this was "Team Comeback," and they thrived on adversity.

Over 56,000 fans pushed their way into Dodger Stadium for Game Three to see if their team could manufacture a miracle one more time. The feeling was upbeat, both in the stands and in the dugout, as 20-year-old superstar Fernando Valenzuela faced 6'2" southpaw, Dave Righetti, in a battle of rookies. Valenzuela was not sharp on this day, but he gutted it out, pitching out of one scrape after another, en route to a complete-game 5-4 victory.

Righetti didn't last past the third. The Dodgers scored three runs off the rookie righty in the first, when Ron Cey took a low fast ball downtown, with two on. The Yankees moved into the lead when they scored two runs in each of the second and third innings. George Frazier, who had relieved Dave Righetti in the third, looked strong as he pitched his way into the fifth. Then the bottom fell out. Steve Garvey beat out an infield hit behind third. After Cey walked, Pedro Guerrero slammed a double to left for one run, with Cey holding third. Monday was walked intentionally to load the bases, and Rudy May came on to relieve Frazier, still with no one out. The Penguin scored, what proved to be the winning run, when Mike Scioscia hit into a fast, 4-3 double play.

Valenzuela got tougher as the game wore on. He yielded a harmless walk in the sixth, retired the side in order in the seventh, then escaped from a two-on, none-out situation in the eighth on a clutch play by Ron Cey. Pinch hitter Bobby Murcer, trying to sacrifice the two runners along, popped a bunt down the third base line. Cey, charging the ball at full speed, made a spectacular diving catch in foul territory; then fired the ball to Steve Garvey to double up a surprised Milbourne at first. It was one of the key plays of the Series.

That was all Fernando needed. He set the last four batters down in order, getting Lou Piniella swinging for the last out of the game.

```
New York Yankees     022 000 000 - 4 - 9 - 0
Los Angeles Dodgers  300 020 00x - 5 -11 - 1
```

Fernando's clutch victory gave the Dodgers a badly need lift. In Game Four, with the adrenaline coursing through their veins once again, they braced themselves for another come-from-behind performance. Game Four was the pivotal game of the Series, and the Dodgers' tenacity spelled the difference. The Yankees gave Lasorda's boys every chance to fold under the pressure, but the Dodger players had only thoughts of victory on their

Pedro Guerrero put the icing on the cake, in Game Six, with an eighth-inning home run. Pete went three for five in the title game, with a single, a triple, and a home run.

minds. Pitching was definitely not the order of the day in this key game. In fact, L.A. starter, Bob Welch, failed to retire a single batter, retiring before a two-run Yankee attack.

The New Yorkers made it 3-0 in the second when Randolph took Dave Goltz deep, hitting a home run to right center field, then upped the margin to 4-0 in the third on two singles and a walk. The Dodgers fought back, scoring two runs off Yankee Starter Rick Reuschel in the third. They narrowed the margin to 4-3 in the fifth when Garvey doubled, and Cey rescued him with a single to left. The Bronx Bombers applied the pressure again in the top of the sixth, pushing over two runs for a 6-3 New York lead.

Again the Dodgers failed to fold. In their typical style, they scratched and clawed their way back. In the bottom of the sixth, Mike Scioscia drew a one-out walk. Jay Johnstone, pinch hitting for pitcher Tom Niedenfuer, made, what may have been, the key hit of the entire Series, hitting a long home run to right center field. Suddenly, Tommy Lasorda's boys were back in the game once more. They still trailed 6-5 but, in their minds, they had the lead. They tied the game moments later when Reggie

Jackson dropped Davey Lopes' fly ball down the right field line for a two-base error, and Bill Russell, atoning for an earlier miscue, brought home the tying run with a line-drive single to left.

The momentum had shifted. The atmosphere was electric. The Dodgers were on the move, and they couldn't be stopped. Such was the feeling on the Dodger bench and throughout Dodger Stadium. In the bottom of the seventh, that feeling became a reality as the Blue Crew pushed across the game winners against Yankee reliever, George Frazier. Frazier, who was the losing pitcher in Game Three, was on his way to setting the unenviable record of losing three times in one World Series. Dusty Baker started the rally against Frazier with a hit to deep short. Rick Monday then blooped a double to center field, with Baker racing around to third. Pedro Guerrero was walked intentionally to load the bases, and Tommy John relieved the beleagured Frazier. Pinch Hitter Steve Yeager brought home the eventual winning run with a sacrifice fly to right field. A second run scored minutes later when Davey Lopes beat out an infield grounder to plate Monday with run number eight.

Steve Howe, the Dodger closer, had entered the game in the top of the seventh, and he protected the lead the rest of the way to pick up the victory. Reggie Jackson nicked the cocky southpaw for an eighth inning home run, but that was all the Yankees could get. L.A. won 8-7.

New York Yankees	2	1 1	0 0 2	0 1 0	-	7	-13	- 1
Los Angeles Dodgers	0	0 2	0 1 3	2 0 x	-	8	-14	- 2

In what was the key game of the 1981 World Series, the Los Angeles Dodgers, not willing to accept defeat, fought back time after time, grasping the momentum on a dramatic home run by Jay Johnstone, then winning the game on a sacrifice fly by Steve Yeager, to deadlock the Series at two games apiece. Now they were ready to take command.

Game Five paired Ron Guidry against Jerry Reuss in a rematch of Game One. The first time around, "Louisiana Lightning" got the better of it, 5-3. But this was a new day. The Bronx Bombers did nick the Dodger starter for a run in the second on a ground rule double by Jackson, an error, and a single by Lou Piniella, but that was the extent of their offense. The big blonde from St. Louis, Missouri scattered three hits over the final seven innings to record a complete-game victory.

The game remained 1-0 New York through 6 1/2 innings thanks to the overpowering pitching of Ron Guidry. The Yankee lefty fanned eight Dodger batters over the first six innings, including the side in the fourth, while scattering two hits. It was an awesome performance, but it didn't last. In the bottom of the seventh, "Gator" struck out Dusty Baker, leading off. Then he hung a slider to Pedro Guerrero, and Pete sent it screaming over the left center field fence to tie the game. The next batter, catcher Steve Yeager, jumped on a Guidry fastball and lined it into the left-field seats for another homer, and a 2-1 Dodger lead.

Reuss, standing 6'5" tall, and tipping the scales at an even 200 pounds, had the game under control. He set the Yankees down easily in the eighth, retiring Milbourne, Winfield, and Jackson in order. Lou Piniella tagged the southpaw for a one out single in the ninth, but Reuss was equal to the task. He retired Rick Cerone on a fly to center for out number two, and struck out Aurelio Rodriguez to end the game.

Dodger closer Steve Howe is greeted at the mound by batterymate Steve Yeager and first baseman Steve Garvey after Bob Watson flied out to Ken Landreaux in center field, to end the Series.

A potential tragedy occurred in the bottom of the eighth. Goose Gossage, the man with the 94-mile-an-hour fastball, threw an inside pitch to Ron Cey. The Penguin was unable to get out of the way of the speeding pellet, and took the full impact of the shot on the left temple. After several nervous minutes, the game Dodger third baseman was able to leave the field under his own power, suffering nothing more than a concussion.

```
New York Yankees       0 1 0 0 0 0 0 0 0 - 1 - 5 - 0
Los Angeles Dodgers    0 0 0 0 0 0 2 0 x - 2 - 4 - 3
```

The scene shifted back to Yankee Stadium for Game Six, and the Bronx Bombers were confident that good old home cooking would restore their winning ways. Also,

they had money pitcher, Tommy John, rested and ready to go. The smooth-working lefty set the Lasorda-men down without a run over the first three innings, scattering three hits along the way. The Yanks, meanwhile, took a 1-0 lead over Dodger starter Burt Hooton in the third when Willie Randolph deposited a 1-0 pitch into the left field bleachers.

L.A. quickly knotted the count in the top of the fourth on singles by Baker, Monday, and Yeager. An inning later, manager Bob Lemon made a decision that has been second guessed ever since. With two men on and two out in a 1-1 game, Lemon sent a pinch hitter in for pitcher Tommy John. The strategy failed as Bobby Murcer flied to deep right. The Yankee skipper compounded the problem by bringing George Frazier in from the bullpen. The big Oklahoman had been the losing pitcher in Games Three and Four, and was in a deep slump.

It didn't take Lasorda's crew long to take advantage of the blunder. Lopes led off the fifth with a ground single to left. After Russell and Garvey had been retired, Ron Cey, gaining a measure of revenge for his beaning three days previous, singled through the middle, scoring Lopes with the go-ahead run. After Dusty Baker singled to center, Pedro Guerrero slammed a long triple to left center field, driving in both Cey and Baker.

The handwriting was on the wall for the Yankees as the Los Angeles juggernaught pushed across four more runs in the top of the sixth, for a comfortable 8-1 lead. Hooton lost his rhythm after the long delay, and was replaced by Steve Howe after loading the bases with only one out in the bottom of the sixth. One run scored on a single by Piniella, before the Dodger reliever settled down and retired both Randolph and Mumphrey without further damage. The final three innings were anticlimatic as Howe kept the Bronx Bombers under control. L.A. scored once more in the top of the eighth, when Guerrero, capping off an outstanding game, hit a home run into the left-field seats. It was Pedro's third hit of the game and gave him five runs batted in.

```
Los Angeles Dodgers   0 0 0 1 3 4 0 1 0 - 9 - 13 - 1
New York Yankees      0 0 1 0 0 1 0 0 0 - 2 -  7 - 2
```

It was a great victory for "Team Comeback," the last chapter in their unbelievable postseason heroics. They trailed the Houston Astros two games to zero in the National League Western Division playoff before coming back to sweep the last three games. They trailed the Montreal Expos two games to one in the National League Championship Series before rallying to win the final two games. And they trailed the New York Yankees two games to zero in the World Series before bouncing back to sweep four in a row.

It was an incredible year, one manager Tommy Lasorda called "the greatest thing that ever happened to me in baseball." Fittingly, the Dodgers had a tri-MVP in the Series, as Ron Cey, Steve Yeager, and Pedro Guerrero shared the honors. Cey batted .350 with a home run and six RBIs. Guerrero hit .333, slammed two homers, and knocked in nine runs. And Steve Yeager caught an outstanding Series, and hit .286 with two homers and four RBIs. His seventh-inning home run in Game Five was the game winner.

LOS ANGELES DODGERS V.S. THE OAKLAND ATHLETICS—1988

The Los Angeles Dodgers and their highly touted farm system fell into disrepair during the mid 1980s. The deterioration was hardly noticeable during the first half of the decade because the remnants of "Team Comeback" managed to win two division titles during that period, losing the NLCS to the Philadelphia Phillies in 1983; then dropping a heartbreaker to the St. Louis Cardinals in 1985. Still, the decay progressed imperceptibly.

A team noted for its solid defense committed 163 errors in 1984, followed by 166, 181, and 155 miscues during the next three years. After finishing a dismal fourth in 1987 with a record of 73-89, 17 full games behind the San Francisco Giants, it was obvious that key moves had to be made. The new General Manager, Fred Claire, made the moves. In his most important deal, he went into the free agency market to pluck the dynamic Kirk Gibson from the Detroit Tigers. Gibson was known in the trade as a winner, a player who gave 110% all the time. A potential All-World player, the speedy outfielder was slowed down by gimpy knees, a souvenir of his linebacker days for the Michigan State Spartans. Still, when Gibson was healthy, there was none better. He was a franchise player.

In addition to the acquisition of Gibson, Claire made several monumental trades that shook up the Dodger lineup from top to bottom. He traded pitcher Bob Welch to the Oakland Athletics for shortstop Alfredo Griffin and relief ace Jay Howell. And he signed free agents Mickey Hatcher and Rick Dempsey. Gibson's fire and determination set the tone in spring training, and Mickey Hatcher's off-beat antics kept the team loose, a combination that proved unbeatable during the summer.

The Dodgers got off the mark quickly in April, with Hershiser rolling up a 5-0 record. Their 13-7 mark found them only a 1/2 game behind the Houston Astros. Gaining momentum as the weather warmed, Lasorda's boys played cat and mouse with manager Hal Lanier's cohorts for three weeks before moving into first place with a hard-fought, come-from-behind victory in Philadelphia. Mickey Hatcher's ninth-inning single knocked in the go-ahead

Los Angeles Dodgers, 1988 (Los Angeles Dodger Photo)

run as L.A. scored three times for a 10-8 triumph. Los Angeles continued to widen the gap over their rivals, until it reached a comfortable eight games on July 18.

The month of September belonged to Hershiser. The lanky righthander reeled off five successive shutouts, en route to a major league record 59 consecutive shutout innings. His statistics for the month showed:

GAMES	IP	W	L	PCT.	ERA
6	55	5	0	1.000	0.00

The Dodgers clinched the Western Division title on September 26, as Mickey Hatcher's eighth-inning single propelled L.A. to a 3-2 victory over the San Diego Padres. Alejandro Pena picked up the win with three innings of shutout relief.

Tommy Lasorda's team had a huge mountain to climb in the National League Championship Series. Their opponents, the New York Mets, had taken their measure 10 times in 11 meetings during the regular season. The Dodgers did, however, have two secret weapons; the unbeatable Orel Hershiser, and the fiery Kirk Gibson. For eight innings in game one of the NLCS, it looked like the Hershiser magic would continue. Davey Johnson's charges found themselves on the short end of a 2-0 score as the ninth inning began. Then the complexion of the game changed swiftly. Greg Jeffries opened the inning with a single, his third hit off the Dodger ace. One out later, a bloop double by Darryl Strawberry produced the first run off Hershiser in 68 innings. Relief ace Jay Howell was rushed into the game, but he couldn't stem the tide. He proceeded to walk the first man he faced, Kevin McReynolds. After Howard Johnson struck out, Gary Carter hit a dying quail to center field. John Shelby got a late jump on the ball, then just missed a shoe-string catch as both Strawberry and McReynolds scored to give the Mets a stirring 3-2 win.

The Dodgers appeared to be snake-bit as they watched a sure victory turn into a gut-wrenching loss. A lesser team would have packed it in for the winter at that point, but the Gibsonites were not yet ready to quit. Bouncing back in Game Two behind rookie fireballer Tim Belcher, L.A. hammered David Cone for five runs in two innings, en route to a 6-3 win. The key hits were produced by Steve Sax, Mickey Hatcher, and Mike Marshall. Moving to New York for Game Three, Lasorda's boys quickly found themselves down two games to one, as a two-out double by Backman and a single by Mookie Wilson keyed a five-run outburst in the eighth inning, and an eventual 8-4 victory.

Things looked bleak the next day as Met ace Dwight Gooden took a 4-2 lead into the ninth inning. After disposing of the first two batters, the big righty, working cautiously, walked Shelby to bring the tying run to the plate in the form of Mike Scioscia. The Dodger catcher then foiled the predicted script by stroking a two-strike pitch into the right-field stands for a game-tying homer. Three

innings later, Gibson hit a game-winning round-tripper to deadlock the series.

Suddenly the momentum had shifted west, and the L.A. contingent was not about to lose it. They unloaded early on New York starter Sid Fernandez in Game Five, scoring three runs in both the fourth and fifth innings. Rick Dempsey's double was the big blow in the fourth inning uprising, while Gibson's 3-run homer did the damage in the fifth. Tim Belcher won his second game of the NLCS with help from Brian Holton.

David Cone, thirsting for revenge after his second-game disaster, kept the New Yorkers in the hunt with a 5-1 win in Game Six to tie the series once again. Unfortunately for Davey Johnson's crew, L.A. had Orel Hershiser waiting in the wings. Pitching with three days' rest, and under intense pressure, the Big O rose to the occasion, keeping the New York bats silent inning after inning while his teammates attacked Met hurler Ron Darling with a flourish. Steve Sax opened the game for L.A. with a single to center. He advanced to third on a double by Hatcher, and scored the first run of the game on a sacrifice fly by Gibson. In the second, the Met defense self-destructed. Critical errors by Jeffries and Backman led directly to runs as the Californians piled up a big 6-0 lead. That was all Hershiser needed. The Dodgers won by that score, and moved on to the World Series.

Their opponents in the fall Classic were the Oakland Athletics, conquerors of the Boston Red Sox in the ALCS, and the powerhouse team of the major leagues. The Athletics, winners of 104 games during the regular season, were led by 21-game winner Dave Stewart, and sluggers Jose Canseco, the major league's first 40-40 man, and first baseman Mark McGwire. Canseco finished the season with a .307 batting average, 42 home runs, 124 RBIs, and 40 stolen bases. His counterpart, McGwire, hit .260 with 32 homers and 99 RBIs. Former Dodger pitcher, Bob Welch, contributed 17 wins to the A's total, while the major's top reliever, Dennis Eckersley saved a record 45 games.

The Dodgers were given little chance of taking the measure of the A's. Their victory over the Mets was considered a fluke more than anything else, and the experts looked for a quick sweep by Tony LaRussa's boys. Once again, the experts forgot about the Big O and Kirk. In Game One, Dave Stewart was paired against Dodger righty Tim Belcher. L.A. drew first blood when the enthusiastic Hatcher smashed a two-run homer into the left-field stands and raced around the bases in record time. The "Bash Boys" bounced back in the second when Canseco took advantage of a Belcher mistake, lining a 400-foot home run off a television camera in dead center field, good for a 4-2 Oakland lead. Stewart made the lead stand up for eight innings, although L.A. narrowed it to 4-3 in the sixth on a run-scoring single by Mike Scioscia.

As the ninth inning got underway, LaRussa beckoned Eckersley from the pen to close it out. After disposing of the first two batters easily, Eckersley walked pinch

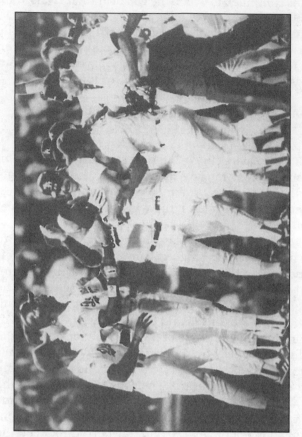

Kirk Gibson brings the Dodgers from the brink of defeat, to victory, in Game One, with his dramatic ninth-inning home run. (Los Angeles Dodger Photo)

hitter Mike Davis to keep the game alive. Then, in one of the most electrifying moments in World Series history, a gimpy Kirk Gibson, sidelined with a hamstring pull, limped to the plate dragging his bat behind him. The Los Angeles crowd exploded in a mighty roar, expecting a miracle to unfold before their eyes. Eckersley wasted no time on Gibson, quickly putting him into an 0-2 hole. Gibson's swings were feeble, and it was obvious he couldn't get his legs into the pitch to drive it. Mike Davis suddenly surprised the crowd, as well as the A's, as he stole second base on ball one. Gibson hung tough, working the count to 3-2. Eckersley, pitching exactly as the Dodger scouts had predicted, tried to sneak a back door slider past the Dodger hitter, but Gibson was ready for it. Swinging only with his arms and wrists, the 6' 3" slugger jerked the ball to right field on a high arc. As the A's ace reliever watched in disbelief, and 55,983 fans leaped to their feet with screams and whistles, the ball settled into the right-field stands for a game-winning home run, the most dramatic home run in World Series history.

The Los Angeles Dodgers had snatched victory from defeat on the evening on October 15 and, suddenly, they began to feel, for the first time, that they were a team of destiny. They felt as if they could defeat the Oakland Athletics and, in the process, capture the coveted World Championship.

Game Two was all L.A. as the unbeatable Orel Hershiser pitched another memorable game. Lasorda's boys jumped on A's starter, Storm Davis, for five big runs in the third inning, led by none other than Orel Hershiser. The 6'3" Dodger righty led off the inning with a single to center. Then, on a daring piece of baserunning, the gutty hurler raced all the way around to third on a single to right by Steve Sax. Minutes later, he scored the first run of the game on another single by Franklin Stubbs. Hatcher's hit rescued Sax; then big Mike Marshall closed out the scoring with a three-run smash to left center.

Hershiser's double to right plated Alfredo Griffin with the sixth run in the bottom of the fourth to close out the scoring for the day. The Big O cracked another double in the sixth as he not only outpitched the A's, but also outhit them. The clearcut 6-0 victory further convinced the Los Angeles contingent that 1988 was their year.

```
Oakland Athletics      0 0 0  0 0 0  0 0 0 - 0 - 3 - 0
Los Angeles Dodgers    0 0 5  1 0 0  0 0 x - 6 -10 - 1
```

As the Series moved to Oakland for Game Three, Tony LaRussa looked to former Dodger Bob Welch to give his team a life. The big righthander did just that. On a day when he did not have his best stuff, the Oakland hurler battled the Dodger hitters every step of the way. Disaster struck the Los Angeles team in the bottom of the second when pitcher John Tudor's elbow blew out, finishing him for the Series. His replacement, Tim Leary, was touched up for a run in the third when Glenn Hubbard singled, stole second, and scored on a single by Ron Hassey.

L.A. tied the score in the fifth on a single by Jeff Hamilton and a double by Franklin Stubbs. They had a chance to break the game open in the sixth when they loaded the bases against Welch with no outs, but they came away empty handed. Reliever Greg Cadaret came on in a tough situation, and retired Mike Scioscia on a foul pop. Right hander Gene Nelson then retired both Hamilton and Griffin without a run scoring, sending the Dodger bench into deep depression.

The game continued 1-1 through the sixth, seventh, and eighth, as both bullpens doled out goose eggs. Dodger closer Jay Howell entered the game in the bottom of the ninth, still tied at 1-1. The first batter, Jose Canseco, was an easy out, lifting a pop fly to second. Mark McGwire stepped to the plate and, on a 2-2 pitch, he lined a shot over the left field fence for a game-winning home run. Oakland fans were deliriously happy, and they were confident that their team would sweep the next three games from the upstart Dodgers.

The effervescent Mickey Hatcher races around the bases on his first-inning home run in Game One. He hit his second homer of the Series in Game Five, after going deep only once during the entire regular season. (Los Angeles Dodger Photo)

```
Oakland Athletics      0 4 0  0 0 0  0 0 0 - 4 - 7 - 0
Los Angeles Dodgers    2 0 0  0 0 1  0 0 2 - 5 - 7 - 0
```

Los Angeles Dodgers   000 010 000 - 1 - 8 - 1
Oakland Athletics   001 000 001 - 2 - 5 - 0

A capacity crowd of 49,317 bay area fanatics crammed into the Oakland Coliseum for Game Four, to watch Dave Stewart match fastballs with rookie Tim Belcher. Both pitchers had started Game One and, although Stewart had gotten the better of that matchup, neither pitcher was involved in the decision. This time, both would be. Spurred on by TV announcer Bob Costas' statement that the L.A. lineup was the weakest in World Series history, the Dodgers raced onto the field yelling, "Kill Costas. Kill Costas."

Lasorda's boys started quickly. Steve Sax opened the game with a base on balls. A subsequent single by Hatcher and a fielder's choice plated two runs for the weak hitting visitors. The "Bash Boys" countered with a run of their own in the bottom of the inning. Luis Polonia singled, and came around to score on a passed ball and two infield outs. L.A. upped the margin to 3-1 in the third. First baseman Franklin Stubbs lined a double to right center field, eventually scoring on an error.

Once again, the A's fought back. A two-out, sixth-inning single by Carney Lansford, knocked in Dave Henderson, who had doubled. Alfredo Griffin drew a one-out walk in the top of the seventh and, when Sax sent him scurrying to third on a single, manager Tony LaRussa yanked Stewart in favor of Cadaret. The big lefty almost escaped unscathed, but a double play just missed, and Griffin scored run number four. The scrappy Oakland team cut the margin back to one in the bottom of the seventh on a single by Walt Weiss and a double by Dave Henderson. By this time, Jay Howell was back in the game, still smarting from McGwire's blow of the previous night. Fans on both sides wondered if the Dodger closer could block the memory of that blast from his mind. The answer wasn't long in coming. A walk to Canseco and an error by Griffin loaded the bases for McGwire. This time, with the game on the line once again, Howell got even. He retired the Oakland slugger on a pop fly to Tracy Woodson at first base.

The eighth inning passed without incident, and the L.A. crew went quietly in the top of the ninth. As the bottom of the ninth got underway, every fan was on the edge of his seat, anticipating a dramatic ending to the game. The Dodger relief ace disposed of Polonia on a fly to left. After Dave Henderson stroked a single, his fourth hit of the game, Howell bore down and fanned Jose Canseco for out number two. Dave Parker, at 6'5" and 230 pounds, now stood between Jay Howell and an L.A. victory. Howell was equal to the task, retiring the big lefty on a pop-up to third base.

Los Angeles Dodgers   201 000 100 - 4 - 8 - 1
Oakland Athletics   100 001 100 - 3 - 9 - 2

The Oakland Athletics had their backs to the wall in more ways than one as Game Five got underway. Not only were they one game away from extinction, but they would have to defeat Dodger ace, Orel Hershiser, twice in three games if they were to claim the crown—a super-human feat, to say the least.

The uncertainty didn't last long. Lasorda's boys came out loose and aggressive. Franklin Stubbs drilled a single to right field with one out and the irrepressible Mickey Hatcher rescued him with a home run, a 360 foot shot to left. The A's finally dented the plate against Hershiser in the third inning, after going scoreless through their first 11 innings against him. Lansford and Tony Phillips led off the inning with singles, and Lansford scored on a sacrifice fly.

Mike Marshall's three-run homer in Game Two iced the game for Orel Hershiser. (W. McNeil)

In the Dodger fourth, a piece of Lasorda strategy gave his team some breathing room. With two out, and Mickey Hatcher on first after a single, Lasorda gave Mike Davis the green light on a 3-0 pitch, and the designated hitter promptly hit a 360 foot homer to right field for a 4-1 lead. With Hershiser on the mound, a three-run lead looked as good as 300 on this day. To make certain however, the Big Blue Machine added another insurance run in the sixth on a walk to Davis and a double by Rick Dempsey.

Hershiser, meanwhile, was moving methodically through the Oakland lineup. After retiring ten men in a row, number 55 walked leadoff man Tony Phillips in the eighth. A one-out single by Julian Javier scored Phillips with Oakland's second run. A temporary lapse of concentration by the Dodger hurler resulted in a walk to Henderson; then a wild pitch put runners on second and third with only one out, and Dodger rooters began to squirm uneasily in their seats. With the bullpen up, and the tying run at the plate in the person of Jose Canseco, the "Bulldog" called on his reserves. He retired the Cuban slugger on a pop to first, then fanned the dangerous Dave Parker on a 55-foot curve ball.

In the bottom of the ninth, Hershiser faced McGwire, Hassey, and Lansford. He retired the baby-faced McGwire on a long fly ball to Shelby in deep center field. Hassey was caught looking for strike three, but the pesky Lansford kept the game alive with a ground-ball single through the shortstop hole, his second hit of the game. Tony Phillips worked the count full, then went down swinging at a Hershiser fastball to end the game and the Series.

```
Los Angeles Dodgers    2 0 0  2 0 1  0 0 0 - 5 - 8 - 0
Oakland Athletics      0 0 1  0 0 0  0 1 0 - 2 - 4 - 0
```

The World Championship of 1988 was truly a team effort. Almost every player contributed to the glorious victory. From Kirk Gibson's game-winning home run in game one, the list of heroes included Sax, Hatcher, Dempsey, Stubbs, Marshall, Hershiser, Belcher, Howell, Pena, Holton, Leary, and Mike Davis. Mickey Hatcher led all hitters with an average of .368 including two home runs and five runs batted in. Sax hit the ball at a .300 clip, while Stubbs was close behind at .294. Hershiser, the Series MVP, was 2-0 with an ERA of 1.00. Leary had an ERA of 1.35 for 6 2/3 innings, and Pena, Holton, and Tudor were perfect.

On the losing side, Terry Steinback was the top batter at .364. Dave Henderson hit a solid .300, but the failure of McGwire (1 for 17 for .059), and Canseco (1 for 19 for .053), spelled doom for the LaRussa-men. Bob Welch led the mound corps with an ERA of 1.80 for his five innings of work, but Dave Stewart (3.80), Storm Davis (11.25), and Dennis Eckersley (10.80) were treated roughly by the banjo-hitting Dodgers.

The 1988 World Championship was one of the greatest achievements in the long history of the Dodgers. It ranks up there with the first and only World Championship in Brooklyn in 1955, with the miracle title in 1959, with the magnificent sweep of the hated Yankees in 1963, and with the thrilling exploits of "Team Comeback" in 1981.

To many Dodger fans across the country, the 1988 World Championship was the sweetest one of all.

Dempsey, Hershiser, Hatcher, and Jeff Hamilton meet at the mound to begin the World Championship party.(Los Angeles Dodger Photo)

CHAPTER 7
PENNANT RACES AND PLAYOFFS

THE 1924 PENNANT DRIVE

The year 1924 was not a championship season in Brooklyn. But it was one of the most exciting pennant races in the club's history. After their last National League pennant in 1920, their fortunes took a turn for the worse. In the nine-year period from 1921 through 1929, the Robins held down sixth place seven times. They finished fifth once. But in 1924, a miracle of sorts unfolded in the little ballpark along Sullivan Place. As the season got underway, there was little hope that Uncle Robby's boys could improve their sixth-place finish of 1923. Their pitching was spotty and their defense was leaky.

Besides, John McGraw's New York Giants had already been conceded the National League pennant by most experts. The early twentieth century Giants dominated the Senior Loop like no team has since. In the 21-year period from 1903 through 1923, the Gothamites finished in the first division 20 times, including nine National League titles, and eight second-place finishes.

The Giants were coming off pennants in 1921, 1922, and 1923. They were the top offensive club in the league, averaging seven .300 hitters a year. The batsmiths were led by "Highpockets" George Kelly who batted .314 and knocked in 332 runs over the three-year period, Ross Youngs who averaged .341, and Emil "Irish" Meusel who stung the ball at a .313 clip. Their stalwart defense was anchored by catcher Frank Snyder, second baseman Frankie Frisch, and shortstop Dave "Beauty" Bancroft. Not to be outdone, the pitching staff was also number one in the league. The ace of the staff was Art Nehf who piled up 47 wins in three years. He was ably supported by a bevy of strong arm pitchers that produced nine 13-to-18 game winners.

But strange things happen in the heat of a pennant race, and the Brooklyn Robins had a pocketful of surprises in store for the Giants as well as their fans in 1924. Much to the delight of the Flatbush faithful, the Robins played

winning baseball during the early part of the season. By the end of June they were comfortably settled in third place with a record of 35-29, eight games behind the front running New York Giants. A feeling of euphoria filled every heart along Bedford Avenue. If only they knew what lay ahead.

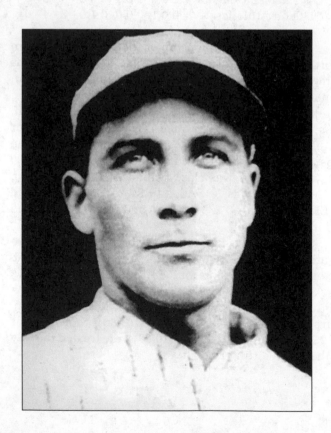

Rookie Rube Erhardt won five games down the stretch for the Robins.

254

As July ran its course, the Robins stumbled a bit. Their 16-17 month dropped them into fourth place, eleven games out. But there was still hope for a respectable finish. Dazzy Vance had gotten hot as the summer progressed, and was in the midst of a four-game winning streak. His 16-4 record led all National League hurlers. The Robin front office, in an attempt to bail out their beleagured pitching staff, brought rookie pitcher Rube Erhardt up from the minors, and obtained right-hander Bill Doak in a trade with the St. Louis Cardinals. Those two moves were pivotal in the Brooklyn drive for the flag.

On August 1, Dazzy Vance quietly put away his fifth straight victory, a 4-0 whitewashing of the Chicago Cubs. Six days later, the Brooklyn hitting machine finally got untracked. A four-run rally in the fifth, highlighted by Bernie Neis' bases-loaded triple, rescued Burleigh Grimes, as the Robins shot down Chicago, 9-6. Uncle Robby's boys went on to win eight of their next ten games, and suddenly the once insurmountable Giant lead was down to only seven games.

Everyone contributed to the Big Blue onslaught. First baseman Jack Fournier's 24th home run sparked an exciting eight-run rally in the fifth inning that allowed the Robins to overtake St. Louis, 11-9. Ray Blade's homer in the ninth beat the Cardinals again, 2-1. Vance won two games during the streak, as did "Old Stubblebeard," Burleigh Grimes.

Brooklyn kept the pressure on for the next eight days, winning six and losing only three. With each new victory, the players' confidence grew. "Lucky Eddie" Brown, the

Dazzy Vance, the greatest right-handed pitcher in Brooklyn Dodger history, almost pitched the Dodgers into the World Series in 1924, winning 28 games, including 15 in a row.

Robin center fielder, was a key player in the pennant drive. His eighth-inning homer pulled one out for Vance as the Robins nipped Pittsburgh, 4-3. The next day he doubled in the eleventh inning of a 1-1 tie, and came around to score the winning run against those same Pirates. Bill Doak was the winning pitcher, outduelling Pittsburgh ace Remy Kremer.

Rookie Rube Erhardt shut out Chicago, 2-0, on August 21 for his second win of the season. Eddie Brown knocked in Wheat with the winning run in the very first inning for the Robins' sixth win in a row. A mild slump saw the Flatbush Flock drop three of their next four, but as they approached an important three-game series with the hated Giants, they were still only seven games out of first.

It was cardiac time in the City Of Churches, as the citizenry of Brooklyn was delirious to be in another pennant race. McGraw's players were stunned when they entered the dugout in Ebbets Field. A World Series atmosphere permeated the little ballpark along Sullivan Place. Giddy young ladies in their Sunday finery flitted around the grandstand. Their gentlemen escorts were gaily adorned in their best straw hats, ready to scale them out onto the field at the first opportunity, as was the habit of the day. Twenty-two thousand baseball fanatics pushed their way into the park, spilling over onto the field before the gates could be closed, leaving several thousand more fans on the outside, looking in. When the game started, the big crowd fell silent almost immediately as Giant ace, Virgil Barnes, outpitched Brooklyn flamethrower Dazzy Vance for seven innings, and nursed a one-run lead at that juncture. But in the eighth, the Robins came to life. "Black Lightning," Zack Wheat, playing his 16th season in a Brooklyn uniform, whistled a double off the right-field wall, to knock in the tying run. Eddie Brown's single plated two more, and Vance took the opener, 3-1.

The next day, Bill Doak struggled to an 8-5 victory, beating 14-game winner Hugh McQuillen. Game Three matched 14-game winner, Art Nehf, against Burleigh Grimes, and "Old Stubblebeard" got the best of it. The game was scoreless until the fifth, when Eddie Brown hit a pop-fly double to left field. A walk and Tommy Griffith's single plated the first run and, when Grimes hit a double to score two more, straw hats showered the field once again. The game had to be held up for ten minutes while groundskeepers cleaned up the debris. New York came back with single runs in the sixth and eighth, but it wasn't enough. The Robins won 3-2. The lead was down to four!

The Giants left Brooklyn in a daze, losers of 11 of their last 17 games. They were still reeling the next day as the lowly Braves held them to a split. Brooklyn meantime, swept Philadelphia in a pair to trim another game off the lead. Wheat smashed a single and a double in Game One, a 7-2 win. Then, in the nightcap, after Fournier hit an early homer, "Black Lightning" cemented the 6-3 win with a two-run shot in the ninth.

Hysteria replaced euphoria in the fair borough of Brooklyn now as the reality of the situation began to sink in. The much-maligned Robins could actually win the pennant. They were as hot as the weather, having won 20 of their last 25 games. They had the Giants on the run, and only three slim games separated them from the top spot.

The gap narrowed to two as Uncle Robby's boys once again swept the Phils, 12-9 and 4-3. Vance was ko'd in the first inning of Game One. The Robins trailed 8-1 after

Eddie Brown hit .308 with a basketful of big hits in the Robin's exciting pennant drive.

three, but they stormed back to tie in the ninth, then pushed over three runs in the 10th, to win. Wheat took care of the second game, with a two-run homer in the fifth.

On September 3, Brooklyn whipped the Phils twice more, 7-6, and 7-0. Grimes survived a rocky start to notch his 20th win of the season in the opener, and the Robins won it with single runs in the seventh, eighth, and ninth. Bill Doak made it easy in the second game, throwing a shutout for his sixth straight win.

The next day, the rampaging Brooklyns took their fourth doubleheader in four days, a major league record, as they belted the Boston Braves, 5-1 and 9-1. Dazzy Vance won his 12th straight in the opener, striking out 11 Braves en route. Eddie Brown cracked the big hit once again, a double, and Milt Stock chipped in with another double, a two-run shot. Dutch Reuther threw a five-hitter in the nightcap. The Robins' 18-hit attack was lead by Zack Taylor and Reuther, with four hits apiece. Brown and Andy

High added three each. The sweep, their 13th win in a row, left them in a virtual deadlock for first place, only three percentage points behind the Giants.

Brooklyn took their 14th in a row the next day, as Rube Erhardt threw a five-hitter at Boston and shut out the Braves, 4-0, for his fourth straight victory. During his streak, the young right hander allowed only two earned runs in 37 innings. On the same day, New York finally began to show signs of life in the pennant race. The proud defending champions were not ready to roll over and play dead for the upstarts from across the river. They stopped Philadelphia twice, 6-5 and 15-3, dropping Uncle Robby's team 1/2 game behind.

On Saturday, the sixth, Bill Doak pitched his second straight shutout, blanking the Braves, 1-0, with a slick two-hitter, for the Robins' 15th win in a row. Boston's Johnny Cooney tossed a four-hitter, but two of the hits came in the seventh, when Brooklyn pushed across the only run of the game. The Robins were finally brought back to earth in Game Two, as the Braves eked out a 5-4, 10-inning victory. For a time, it looked as if Uncle Robby's boys would add another win to their skein. A double by Andy High and a single by Zack Wheat scored one run in the top of the tenth to put the Robins in front, 4-3. But this time, their luck ran out. In the bottom of the inning, Brooklyn pitcher, Art Decatur, threw a potential double play ball into center field. Moments later, a Casey Stengel single and a sacrifice fly brought the streak to an end.

Thirty-six-year-old Zack Wheat enjoyed his most productive season in 1924. His .375 batting average included 41 doubles, eight triples, and 14 home runs. He scored 92 runs and drove in 97.

The next day, the Giants visited Ebbets Field intent on planting Robins' hopes under the Flatbush sod once and for all. They almost accomplished their purpose. New York broke open a 3-3 game in the eighth inning of the series opener, routing Burleigh Grimes with a five-run rally, and sending the Robins down to defeat, 8-7. New York's lead was up to 1 1/2, but they couldn't put the final nail in the Brooklyn coffin. Dazzy Vance rescued his mates the next day, outpitching Art Nehf, 7-2.

On September 10, John McGraw's charges buried Boston under an avalanche of runs, 22-1 and 8-0, but the Robins hung in, defeating Philadelphia 5-1 as Zack Wheat hit a single, a double, and a two-run homer. Ten days later, with Brooklyn still clinging to within 1/2 game of New York, the Pittsburgh Pirates stopped Dazzy Vance's 15-game winning streak with a 5-4, 10th-inning win.

But, just when things looked bleak, one more thrill remained. On the 21st, Chicago blanked New York 3-0 while Brooklyn slipped past Pittsburgh 2-1 in ten innings. A two-out single by Eddie Brown scored Andy High with the game winner. The next day, a Zack Wheat double in the 12th inning beat the Cubs, 2-1, and suddenly, the Brooklyns were within percentage points of the Giants, with only four games left to play.

Robin ace, Dazzy Vance took the mound to face the Cubs in the final game of the series. The big redhead loomed larger than life on the mound, with a record of 27-5, but the fifth-place Cubs were not impressed by old Daz's credentials. They teed off on him early. Hard-hitting second baseman, George Grantham hit homers in the first and third innings, as Chicago jumped out to a 4-3 lead. Uncle Robby's boys fought back to tie the game in the eighth. Then, only two innings later, Dazzy's world collapsed and with it Brooklyn's pennant hope for the year. Hall of Fame catcher Gabby Hartnett propelled one of Vance's fastballs into orbit in the tenth inning, and Chicago prevailed, 5-4. A New York victory gave McGraw's team a one-game lead with only three to play.

Two days later, Boston pitcher Johnny Cooney outpitched Bill Doak, 3-2, and Brooklyn's dream of glory came to an end.

The Robins made a valiant run at the powerful New Yorkers, and they almost pulled off the upset of the decade. They didn't win the flag, but they did give their fans a lifetime of thrills with their heart-stopping, come-from-behind rallies. And some of their individual performances were memorable.

Dazzy Vance set a Brooklyn record with 15 victories in succession. In one game he fanned a league-high fifteen batters. In another, he established a major league mark by striking out seven batters in a row. These accomplishments, plus his 28-6 record, 262 strikeouts, and 2.16 earned-run-average, earned him the National League's Most-Valuable-Player trophy.

1930—THE YEAR OF THE HITTER

1930 will forever be known as the year of the hitter in the National League. Six National League clubs had team batting averages in excess of .300. The other two clubs, bogged down at the .281 mark, dragged the league-average down to .303. Manager Wilbert Robinson's Brooklyn contingent hit a solid .304, but trailed the league leading New York Giants by 15 points.

Individual batting averages, of course, skyrocketed. Giant first-sacker Bill Terry was the top batsman with an astronomical .401 batting average, the last National Leaguer to hit .400 in the twentieth century. Brooklyn's own Babe Herman was a close second with an average of

Del Bissonette enjoyed a career season in 1930, batting .336 with 16 homers, 102 runs scored, and 116 runs-batted-in.

.393; followed by Chuck Klein (.386), Lefty O'Doul (.383), and Freddy Lindstrom (.379).

Blame for the extraordinary improvement in the offensive capabilities of National League hitters was placed on the baseball itself. Supposedly, the balls manufactured for the National League in 1930 had recessed seams rather than raised seams. As a result, pitchers could not grip the ball correctly. Consequently, they could not put the proper rotation on the ball to make it curve. It is an age-old adage that hitters love fast balls that don't move and curveballs that don't break. In 1930, the hitters took advantage of just such a situation and had their most enjoyable and productive season ever. Needless to say, much to the relief of some 80 or 90 beleaguered pitchers who suffered through the long season, the baseball manufacturing process was adjusted over the winter to produce baseballs with raised seams once again.

But for one glorious season, it was a hitter's paradise. Nineteen-thirty also produced another thrilling pennant race; this time involving the Brooklyn Robins, the Saint Louis Cardinals, the Chicago Cubs, and the New York Giants. Chicago, the 1929 pennant winner, was the favorite to repeat. Strangely, the Brooklyn Robins, after a sixth-place finish the year before, were picked for second place. One reason for their lofty selection was their pitching staff, which was the strongest in the league. Brooklyn's greatest all-time hurler, Dazzy Vance, headed up the staff, backed up by 16-game winner, Watty Clark. They were supported by two off-season additions, 17-year veteran

The two greatest sluggers in the major leagues compare notes. Babe Ruth hit a robust .359 in 1930, with 49 home runs. Brooklyn's Babe hit .393 with 35 homers.

Dolph Luque, obtained in a trade with Cincinnati, and 26-year-old rookie, Ray Phelps.

The defense was solid up the middle with rookie Al Lopez behind the plate, veteran Glenn Wright at shortstop and the speedy Johnny Frederick patrolling center field. Offensively, the Robins stacked up with the best of them. Led by slugger Babe Herman (.381–21–113 in 1929), the Flatbush crew was intimidating. Rookie Johnny Frederick hit at a .328 pace with 24 homers and 75 runs batted in. Left fielder Rube Bressler hit .318, while Wally Gilbert chipped in with .304. Spirits were high in the City

of Churches as the season got underway. Pennant fever had once again gripped the citizens of Flatbush, the first time in six years.

The season opened in Ebbets Field on April 15 before an overflow crowd of 30,000 crazed fans. As usual, it was a gala event, made all the more festive by the opposition, the hapless Philadelphia Phillies. On this day, however, the Brooklyn bats went silent and a great pitching effort by Dazzy Vance went for naught. Manager Burt Shotton's Philadelphia contingent squeaked out a hard-fought 1-0 victory. It wasn't until five days later that the Robins won their first game. Then they did it in a big way. They steamrolled the Boston Braves, 15-8, behind Del Bissonette's grand slam homer and three-run triple, and Johnny Frederick's four hits. In spite of that big win, the April blahs continued to plague the team, and they finished the month dead last.

Beginning in early May, things began to jell for the Brooklyn club, particularly in the pitching department. They played bang-up baseball for almost seven weeks, hovering around first place most of the month, in a neck-and-neck struggle with Gabby Street's St. Louis Cardinals.

A double-header sweep of the lowly Phils on Memorial Day moved Brooklyn into first place as St. Louis dropped two to the red-hot Chicago Cubs by scores of 2-0 and 9-8. The month ended on a quiet note when the Phils rose up and beat Dazzy Vance again, 3-1. Hap Collard, a lifetime six-game winner, pitched a game to remember as he outduelled the Robin ace. Del Bissonette accounted for the lone Brooklyn run, depositing his eighth home run of the year onto Bedford Avenue in the second. In spite of the loss, the Robins' 25-15 record gave them a two-game lead over St. Louis, who lost to Chicago again, this time by a 6-5 score. Babe Herman was off to a sizzling start, hitting the ball at a lofty .414 clip. On the mound, Vance led the way with a 6-3 record, while the crafty Cuban, Dolph Luque, was undefeated at 4-0.

June started off as another big month for Wilbert Robinson's boys as they ran up an excellent 14-7 record through the 26th. Johnny Frederick sparked the offense with a .340 batting average, but it was the pitching that kept them on top. Vance, Phelps and Luque sported a combined 18-8 won-loss record. The Cards dropped temporarily out of contention by losing 15 of 25 games, with their position in the standings being taken by the red-hot Chicago Cubs.

The Cubbies slipped into first place as the month ended, by taking three of four from Uncle Robby's crew.

Brooklyn's losing streak reached four as they were routed by the St. Louis Cardinals, 15-7, under a withering 17-hit attack. Watty Clark was bombed out in the third inning when the Redbirds pushed over 11 runs. Frederick, the only bright light in the Brooklyn lineup during the drought, slammed a home run in the ninth. The following day, Babe Herman approached manager Wilbert Robinson in the clubhouse and asked if he could make out the lineup. Robinson, never one to miss a bet, handed the big right fielder the score card and a pencil. The ploy worked. The Robins bounced back to nip St.Louis, 6-5, on hits by Bissonette, Herman, and Frederick and a home run by Wally Gilbert. Ray Phelps had just enough of a lead to withstand two late home runs by "Sunny Jim" Bottomley and a two-run double by Andy High in the ninth.

Brooklyn immediately went on another tear, led by the indomitable Brooklyn Babe. Herman hit in fourteen straight games before he was stopped. According to Tot Holmes, "He had 12 hits in the final four games of his streak, and six of them were for extra bases." Herman, after a long June slump that dropped his batting average 25 points to .389, had regained his batting eye. He finished the month at the .397 mark, thanks to a final day 5-5, that included two singles, two doubles and a home run. In spite of his streak, he still trailed both Terry and Klein who were socking the ball at a .400 + clip.

Although the batting race heated up as the season progressed, it appeared as if the pennant race was cooling off. The Robins, back on top as the dog days of August arrived, stumbled on the road. Their pennant hopes flickered and faded during a long road trip that saw them drop five straight games to the seventh-place Cincinnati Reds. Flatbush was in mourning as the team arrived home, 5 1/2 games behind front-running Chicago. The Robins beat Philadelphia, 14-3, behind a 23-hit attack to finish the month on an up note, but their 12-19 August debacle left their most rabid fans thinking about next year.

As the September stretch run began, the standings looked like this.

	W	L	GB
Chicago	77	51	–
New York	71	55	5
Brooklyn	72	58	7
St. Louis	71	58	7 1/2

After losing two out of three to the Braves in Boston, the Flatbush Flock slipped back into fourth place and were quickly dismissed from any further pennant consideration by the news reporters and so-called baseball experts. Although the obituary had already been composed, Uncle Robby's boys weren't ready for the family plot just yet. Instead, they turned it around one more time, and went on an 11-game winning streak.

Brooklyn regained the momentum at the right time. The league-leading Chicago Cubs moved into town for a crucial three-game series. It turned out to be a cake walk for Uncle Robby's boys as their pitching was overpowering. Ray Phelps, Dolph Luque and Dazzy Vance combined to hold the Windy City Sluggers to a total of just one run. Phelps led off with a scintillating 3-0 shutout, pulling the Brooklyn crew to within 2 1/2 games of the top. Johnny Frederick scored the first run after leading off the game with a triple. Babe Herman got the big blow, a home run in the fifth. As he circled the bases, grinning from ear to

The Brooklyn Dodgers made another valiant pennant run in 1930, led by L to R, Babe Herman (.393), Johnny Frederick (.334), Del Bissonette (.336), Jake Flowers (.320), and Al Lopez (.309).

ear, the *New York Times* reported that "a veritable snowstorm of straw hats, score cards, and torn newspapers, cascaded and swirled onto the field."

Pennant fever was back. And Dolph Luque kept it smoldering as he blanked the Cubs again, this time 6-0. A five-run first routed Root. Babe Herman, hitting in his 14th straight game, had three hits, including a double. The victory was costly, however, as Rube Bressler went down for the season. A line drive off the bat of Hack Wilson struck Bressler on the bare hand as he caught the ball. A fractured finger put him on the bench.

Dazzy Vance finished off Chicago's hopes in game three, fanning a National League-high 13 batters, en route to a hard-fought 2-1 win. Glenn Wright's 20th home run into the left-field circus seats with Herman on base in the first inning was all the big redhead needed. A solo four-bagger by Hack Wilson kept Chicago from suffering the ignominy of a triple whitewashing.

The Cincinnati Reds were the next visitors to the City of Churches, and they were treated no better than their predecessors. The Robins swept four straight by scores of 7-3, 4-3, 8-3, and 13-5. It was an expensive series however. Center fielder Johnny Frederick broke his ankle trying to make a diving catch in Game Two, and was lost for the rest of the season. His .334 batting average, 72 extra base hits, and superior defensive skills, were sorely missed.

On September 16, the sun shone brightly in the fair borough of Brooklyn, and hearts were happy as the second-place St. Louis Cardinals moved into town for a crucial three-game series. As hot as the Robins were, Gabby Street's Redbirds were even hotter. Since August 1, they had rolled up a record of 34-11, picking up 10 games in the standings.

It was fitting that the top hurlers on each staff should meet in the opener of such an important series, so Redbird ace "Wild Bill" Hallahan faced off against the big redhead, Dazzy Vance. The game itself was everything it was advertised to be. It was a quick-moving affair, with goose egg after goose egg being hung on the scoreboard. The game was still scoreless in the eighth when Brooklyn got its first hit, a single by Harvey Hendrick. He was immediately erased on an attempted steal. In the top of the tenth, pinch hitter Andy High sliced a double down the right-field line and came around to score the first run of the game on a looping single by Taylor Douthit. The Flatbush Flock fought back gamely in the bottom half of the inning, loading the bases with one out. Al Lopez, the next batter, hit a shot that bounded away from shortstop Sparky Adams. Adams recovered quickly however, and converted it into a game-ending 6-4-3 double play.

The Robin's lead now stood at one game, with Dolph Luque given the assignment to protect it against 12-game winner Sly Johnson. Outfielder Ike Boone put Brooklyn on top 3-2 with his third homer of the year, but the chunky Cuban righthander couldn't stand prosperity. St. Louis tied the game in the eighth; then won it in the ninth when little Andy High slammed a two-run double. The Brooklyn momentum had suddenly died. Gabby Street's high-flying Redbirds were now in first place by .002, and were positioned for the kill against the Frederick-less Robins. To add insult to injury, former Brooklyn spitball artist, Burleigh Grimes, was on the mound for the Cards in Game Three, and he put another nail in the Flatbush coffin with a 4-3 victory. Babe Herman slammed a home run in the eighth inning, but he was loudly booed by the Flatbush faithful, after suffering through a frustrating 1 for 12 series.

St. Louis was on a rampage, having gone 37-11 over the past seven weeks, while picking up 13 games in the standings. Wilbert Robinson's crew was reeling like a drunken sailor after being manhandled by the Cards. They were still only two games behind, but they couldn't seem to regroup. They were scuttled by Pittsburgh, 6-2 and 7-6, dropping them into third place. An 8-2 loss to John McGraw's Giants, and a 6-3 embarrassment at the hands of the Phillies finished the job. The Robins settled into fourth place, losing five of their final seven games, and finishing six games behind the pennant– winning St. Louis Cardinals.

Babe Herman tried his best to stave off the final curtain by hitting .417 down the stretch, but his failure in the crucial St. Louis series, slumps by other key players, and the injuries to Bressler and Frederick, all took their toll. In addition, the pitching staff ran out of gas just when it was needed the most. The league's top–rated crew surrendered 37 runs during the disastrous seven game losing streak. On top of everything else, the Babe lost the batting title in a close race with Bill Terry, .401 to .393.

The 1930 Brooklyn Robins didn't grab the brass ring, but they did give their fans their money's worth. The exciting pennant drive attracted record crowds to Ebbets Field and helped establish a new season's attendance record of 1,100,000. The Robins exhibited outstanding pitching, solid defense and timely hitting. They scored runs in bunches. They showed an indomitable spirit with the ability to bounce back from adversity time after time. It was a glorious year and, if it had not been for the injury gremlin that struck down both Johnny Frederick and Rube Bressler during the heat of the stretch drive, they might have gone all the way.

1942–ONE HUNDRED AND FOUR WINS FOR SECOND PLACE

In 1941, the Brooklyn Dodgers and St. Louis Cardinals established a rivalry that would endure for more than a decade. Leo Durocher's Bums captured the National League flag that year by winning 100 games, but it was not easy. The Redbirds fought them wire to wire, and came

Vetern Billy Herman was acquired from the Chicago Cubs in 1941 to stabilize the infield. Herman was a valuable contributor to Brooklyn's success in '41 and '42.

up only 2 1/2 games short. In 1942, manager Billy Southworth was determined to make up that shortfall.

The champion Dodgers stood pat with their winning lineup, as well they might have. They had an outstanding blend of youth and experience, and they fully expected additional progress in '42. The 23-year-old "Gold Dust Twins", Pee Wee Reese and "Pistol Pete" Reiser, with a full season of major league ball under their belt, were expected to improve. There seemed to be no limits to what Reiser, the youngest batting champion in National League history, could achieve. He had everything; speed, power, and desire. The supporting cast, led by Dixie Walker, was solid from top to bottom; and the pitching staff, already the best in the league, was strengthened in late 1941 by the addition of Larry French.

St. Louis, aware of their opponents' strengths, dug deep into their extensive farm system for help. And they

World War II was underway, and the big league players were leaving their clubs to serve their military service. Pee Wee Reese would enter the U.S. Navy after the season and would miss the next three years.

came up with several diamonds-in-the-rough; third baseman Whitey Kurowski, who would tighten up the left side of the infield while contributing some offensive punch, outfielder Stan Musial, a future Hall of Famer, who would hit .315 with 52 extra base hits and 72 RBIs as a rookie, and pitcher Johnny Beazley, who would have a career season, winning 21 games with a glittering 2.13 earned run average. The Cards already had the nucleus of a championship team. They could match talent with anybody up the middle, boasting of hard-hitting Walker Cooper behind the plate, Marty Marion, the human vacuum cleaner at short, and Terry Moore, a brilliant

Joe Medwick, an 11-year major league veteran, batted .300 and drove in 96 runners, for Leo Durocher's Dodgers.

defensive outfielder and a consistent .280 hitter in center. Cooper, an outstanding handler of pitchers as well as a dangerous hitter, was the National League all-star catcher every year from 1942 through 1950.

Brooklyn got off the mark quickly when the season started, and looked like they might make a runaway of the National League race. After a slow personal start, Pete Reiser got untracked in May and pushed his average up

to the .340 mark. On May 17, he stole home to break a 1-1 tie in a win over Chicago. Then as the month neared its end, Pistol Pete's bat got as hot as the weather. In a double-header sweep of the Boston Braves, the 23 year old phenom went six for eight. In the opener, he had a single, double and home run, good for three RBIs and four runs scored, to spark a 10-3 Dodger romp behind Curt Davis. In the second game, he stroked two singles and a triple and scored a run as Whitlow Wyatt pitched a masterpiece in a 2-1 Brooklyn win.

That was only the beginning. Leo Durocher's boys moved into Forbes Field and immediately scuttled the Pirate's ship, 17-2. Their 20 hits and 32 total bases made a winner of Les Webber. Reiser was 5-5 with three doubles, a home run, four RBIs and three runs scored, to bring his batting average up to a lofty .366. The Dodgers moved on to Wrigley Field where they took the measure of Jimmie Wilson's Cubs four out of five games. Reiser went six for eight in a Sunday doubleheader, bringing his eight game total to a sizzling 19-35, a .543 pace. His hits included four doubles, a triple, two homers, 11 RBIs, and 12 runs scored. Flatbush was delirious with pennant fever as their boys could do no wrong. The Redbirds were languishing in second place, seven games behind the leaders.

The Brooklyn express picked up speed in June and, on the 18, when the pride of St. Louis visited the cozy confines of Ebbets Field to do battle with "Lippy" Leo's gladiators, emotions were at a fever pitch. In the series opener, before 23,643 wild-eyed Dodger fans, the tension hung heavy in the air. It finally exploded in the sixth inning when Joe Medwick tried to advance to second base on a passed ball. Medwick slid into shortstop Marty Marion spikes high, bringing second baseman Creepy Crespi to his partner's defense. Medwick and Crespi went at it like Ali and Frazier, with both benches spilling on to the field. When order was restored, the Dodgers broke open a 2-2 tie, pushing across two runs in the eighth on a squeeze bunt by Billy Herman and a double by pitcher Larry French.

Brooklyn captured Game Two, 4-3, behind Whitlow Wyatt, who won his fifth straight game. Johnny Rizzo's second-inning homer was the big blow, but Pete Reiser, who went 2-4, stole home in the fourth inning to put the frosting on the cake. On Saturday, Joe Medwick smashed four hits to raise his batting average to .350, one point better than his teammate Pete Reiser. The Dodgers won the game, 10-4, behind a fine relief effort by Hugh Casey.

Billy Southworth's crew salvaged one game of the five-game series as they took the first game of a Sunday twin bill, 11-0 behind a neat five-hitter by Mort Cooper. Kirby Higbe took the measure of rookie Howie Pollet in Game Two, winning 5-2 behind the hitting of Reiser, who had two doubles in three at bats, and Joe Medwick who hit in his 25th straight game. St. Louis left town quietly after losing four of five and falling a distant 8 1/2 games behind.

Three weeks later, the cocky Brooks strutted into

Sportsman's Park, confident they would put a few more nails in the Cardinal coffin. The big series began with a Saturday double, and the Redbirds drew first blood by pounding out a 7-4 victory in the opener. The Flatbush Flock fought back to take the nightcap, 4-3, in a cliffhanger. The following day, the same two teams were back at it for another doubleheader. Once again, the Cardinals copped Game One, 8-5. They did it by driving Dodger ace Whitlow Wyatt to cover in the third inning, and by shutting down slugger Pete Reiser, who went 0-5. Mort Cooper picked up the win.

In Game Two, the Dodgers suffered not only the loss of the game but their sparkplug Pete Reiser and, perhaps, the pennant as well. The game was another thriller. Kirby Higbe was ko'd in a five-run Cardinal third, but the Brooks fought back with four runs of their own in the

Once again, Mickey Owen gave the Dodgers brilliant defense, plus a timely bat. He led all National League catchers in putouts and assists in 1942.

fourth. The game was tied 6-6 as the bottom of the 11th began. Then, with two out, Enos "Country" Slaughter hit a long drive to straightaway center field. Reiser was off in pursuit immediately, and had it squarely in his sights. He caught the ball going away from the plate at top speed but, as soon as his glove caressed the horsehide, he hit the concrete wall with a sickening thud. His instincts forced him to recover the ball and throw it back to the

cutoff man before he collapsed unconscious. Slaughter circled the bases with the game-winning home run as teammates rushed to Reiser's side. He was carried from the field with a fractured skull, and spent the night in a St. Louis hospital before entraining for Brooklyn. Typical of the man, he returned to the lineup six days later, but he never regained his mid-season form. Bothered by double vision and dizzy spells, the courageous Reiser struggled at bat, hitting a paltry .220 over the last two months, and watching his season average plummet from .356 to .310.

The Dodger pennant hopes didn't collapse all at once. In fact, they stretched their lead to 10 games by August 4. Then the lead began to evaporate, but it wasn't a Brooklyn collapse that brought it about. It was a spectacular stretch run by Billy Southworth's cohorts. As August came to a close, the lead was down to 3 1/2. Brooklyn's two-month performance showed an outstanding 40-20 record, but they lost five games off their lead. St. Louis was 47-17. And they weren't through yet.

As the September stretch run began, both teams turned the intensity up a notch. Each loss was a disaster. Brooklyn swept Pittsburgh. St. Louis matched them. The Dodgers then swept the Cincinnati Reds, 3-2 and 2-0. After dropping two of three to their cross-town rivals in the Bronx, the Brooks moved to Boston where they split with the Braves in a twin bill, winning the opener 11-4 behind Dolph Camilli's single, homer, and three RBIs, and the pitching of Les Webber, then dropping a 5-3 decision in the nightcap as Bobo Newsome took a drubbing. The next day, Ed Head escaped a bases-loaded jam in the first inning, then settled down to toss a four-hit shutout, 4-0. Billy Herman, Joe Medwick, and Mickey Owen collected two hits each, with Herman notching hit #2000 in his distinguished career.

On September 11, the Redbirds were in town again, and the Flatbush faithful turned out in droves to welcome them back with catcalls, and good old Bronx cheers. It didn't phase the Cardinals, however, and they took the opener, 3-0, behind big Mort Cooper. He not only pitched a shutout, but he was the hitting star as well, with two hits and two runs scored. The 6'2" 220-pound fastballer was completing an MVP season, with a 22-7 record and an infinitesimal 1.78 ERA. In Game Two, lefty Max Lanier won his fifth game of the year over the Dodgers, 2-1. Whitey Kurowski gave Lanier all the offensive support he needed when he followed a Walker Cooper single with a long home run into the corner of the lower left-field stands in the second inning. The Dodger run came in the second also, as Reese doubled off the right center field wall to score Mickey Owen. Manager Leo Durocher was ejected from the game for arguing a call. The two-game sweep catapulted the St. Louis team into a first-place tie, with both teams standing at 94-46. The next day, the Cards took over the top spot for good as they split with Philadelphia while Brooklyn was dropping two to the Reds before a stunned Ebbets Field sellout of 32,655. The suddenly tame Flock was held to six hits in the two games, a performance the *New York Times* categorized as "fighting with the ferocity of rabbits."

Another loss followed, a 7-3 drubbing at the hands of the Phils in the first game of a doubleheader. The five-game losing streak was their longest of the year. It was also their last loss of the year. Turning it around one last time, Durocher's men went on a season-ending eight-game winning streak. Trailing now by 3 1/2 games, it was gut-check time. And the Brooks responded. A 4-2 victory over Philadelphia behind Bobo Newsome was sparked by a big three-run first inning that included hits by Dixie Walker, Arky Vaughan, Pete Reiser, and Augie Galan. The lead was back to 2 1/2 as St. Louis lost to Chicago 3-0. Kirby Higbe closed out the Philadelphia series by fanning 11 in a 3-1 win. Again, it was first-inning fireworks that spearheaded the attack. A single by Dolph Camilli followed two errors by Nick Etten. Then a Galan double and a Mickey Owen single brought home the runs.

On the last Tuesday of the season, before a large Ebbets Field turnout, Brooklyn took the measure of the hated New York Giants, 9-8 in 12 innings as Dolph Camilli cracked his 25th home run of the season onto Bedford Avenue. St. Louis dumped Pittsburgh 9-3 to stay 2 1/2 up. Next, the Dodgers clubbed the Phils again, 6-0 behind Larry French's brilliant one-hitter. Reiser with two singles and a double, and Camilli with a single and a triple, led the barrage.

On September 24, Mort Cooper two-hit the Reds 6-0, to clinch a tie for St. Louis. Brooklyn had to win its final four games and hope that St. Louis would lose its final two. Trailing 3-1 as the news of the impending Cardinal victory was posted on the scoreboard, Durocher's boys fought their way back, rallying for four runs in the sixth. Whitlow Wyatt gained credit for the victory, as 19,062 diehards screamed with delight. Brooklyn took the next game also, 6-5 in 11 innings, on an error by Sibby Sisti. Camilli contributed his 26th to the cause.

On the next to last day of the season, the Cards were rained out and would have to play two games on the final Sunday. The Flatbush Flock took advantage of the situation to put a little more pressure on Southworth's crew. On a cold, miserable day, they routed Philadelphia, 8-3, before a meager gathering of 2,874 chilled fans. A big six-run sixth inning broke the game open. A bases-clearing double by Dolph Camilli and a two-run triple by Pee Wee Reese did most of the damage. It all came down to the final Sunday, with St. Louis leading by 1 1/2.

On the final day, Brooklyn did its part as they slipped by Philadelphia, 4-3, for their eighth win in a row. Kirby Higbe won his 16th game, and Dixie Walker led the parade with three hits, but it all went for naught. The Cards responded to the challenge, and swept Chicago, 9-2 and 4-1.

It was a great pennant race, and one in which the losing team did not blow the pennant. The winning team won it outright. St. Louis found themselves 10 games behind the Brooklyn Dodgers on the morning of August sixth. From that point to the end of the season, Billy Southworth's boys won a phenomenal 43 games against only nine losses. Once they gained the league lead on September 13, they ensured the final victory by winning 10 of the remaining 11 games. Brooklyn managed a 16-10 record down the stretch, but it was no match for the Cards' September mark of 21-4!

Still, it was a season that the Dodgers could be well proud of. They won a total of 104 games, the second-highest victory total in Brooklyn history.

St. Louis capped off its fine season by taking the New York Yankees to task, four games to one. Brooklyn's drive to dynasty status was delayed several years by World War II, but St. Louis repeated as National League Champions in 1943 and 1944. When the war ended in 1946, the Dodgers and Cards picked up where they left off in 1942, engaging in another ferocious battle for the flag, this one culminating in the first postseason pennant play-

The Dodgers obtained Arky Vaughan from Pittsburgh in a trade after the 1941 season. The 30-year-old infielder played a solid third base, and hit .277, in 1942.

off in major league history. Things were never dull when the Dodgers and Cardinals got together during the '40s.

1946—ONE YEAR AWAY

World War II ended. The troops came marching home to their families, their friends, and their jobs. Hundreds of young athletes happily donned baseball flannels once again, and threw away the drab khaki uniforms they had been wearing for the past three years. Every major league team was excited to have its roster intact again; but none were more excited than the Brooklyn Dodgers.

The Dodgers had been on top of the baseball world when the war intervened. Instead of pennants, the Brooklyn fans had to suffer through two third-place finishes and one dismal seventh place performance. But that was all forgotten now. The boys were home from the war. Billy Herman, Pee Wee Reese, Pete Reiser, Hugh Casey, and Kirby Higbe.... and thoughts of National League championships filled the heads of small children and not-so-small children all over Flatbush.

In fact, the Dodgers stood on the brink of greatness, but they were still a year away from establishing a dynasty. The St. Louis Cardinals had survived the war in much better shape than the Dodgers. Their three-year record showed two pennants and one second place finish, and they were not ready to step aside for Leo Durocher's young up-starts. Eddie Dyer's Redbirds fielded a great team in 1946, one of the best National League teams of the 20th century, and they were confident of capturing their fourth pennant in the last five years.

The St.Louis lineup was impressive with Stan Musial at first base, Red Schoendienst at second, Marty Marion at Short, Whitey Kurowski at third, Enos Slaughter, Terry Moore and Harry Walker in the outfield, and Joe Garagiola behind the plate. The pitching corps consisted of Harry Brecheen, Howie Pollet, Murray Dickson, and Al Brazle. Brooklyn, in 1946, was a team in transition. Ed Stevens and 6'6" Howie Schultz platooned at first base, (Gil Hodges was still two years away and Jackie Robinson wouldn't join the team until '47). Eddie Stanky was on second, Pee Wee covered short, and Cookie Lavagetto held down third. The outfield consisted of Dixie Walker, rookie Carl Furillo, and Pete Reiser. Bruce Edwards was the catcher as Campy was still two years away. The pitching staff included Casey, Higbe, Joe Hatten, Vic Lombardi, and Hank Behrman. The Dodgers were not considered to be serious contenders by the experts, but they fooled everybody. They made a horse race of it, and, like many horse races, it ended in a photo finish.

With Leo Durocher cracking the whip, the Brooklyn team got off the mark like a jackrabbit. By May 31, the Flatbush Flock had piled up a 25-12 record, good enough for a two-game lead over the St. Louis Swifties. Dixie Walker ,"The People's Cherce", was leading the league in hitting with an average of .379. Reese, the fuzzy-cheeked kid shortstop, found himself in the rarefied at-

mosphere of the top ten, #3 actually, with an average of .344. Kirby "Higgleby", happy to be back in the good old U.S. of A., had an unblemished 3-0 record, as did little Art Herring. Ed Head stood at 3-1.

On June 2, the Bums swept Cincinnati by scores of 2-1 in 11 innings, and 1-0. A superb pitching effort by Les Webber in the opener was rewarded when Ed Stevens singled home Augie Galan, who had tripled. In the second game, Art Herring and Hugh Casey combined to blank the Reds. Herring had to leave the game after five innings when his arm tightened up. Dixie Walker singled in Eddie Stanky with the game winner in the first inning. Ed Stevens, who had two hits in the opener, added three more in the nightcap.

Brooklyn Dodger legend Dixie Walker hit a resounding .319 in 1946, and led the club with 116 runs batted in.

June was a good month for the Bums, as they rolled up 18 big victories and opened up a 5 1/2-game lead over Dyer's Redbirds. On the 30th, Rex Barney fired his first complete game of the year, winning 4-3 over Boston. At the same time, the cellar-dwelling Pirates rose up and dumped St. Louis twice, 4-3 and 1-0. Pittsburgh scored the game winner in the nightcap in the last of the ninth when Bill Baker looped a single to right field to plate little

Hard-nosed rookie Bruce Edwards gave the Dodgers outstanding backstopping in 1946. In 1947, he was selected for the National League All-Star team. After Campanella arrived in 1948, Edwards was relegated to a back-up role. He was traded to the Cubs in 1951.

Al Gionfriddo. Harry "The Cat" Brecheen took the loss.

The Dodgers ran their winning streak to seven games before the Giants brought it to a halt in the first game of a July 4 doubleheader, 7-5. Brooklyn bounced back to take the second game, 8-5 for Vic Lombardi's ninth win. Reiser and Walker were the big clubbers, knocking in three runs each. Walker's performance hoisted his batting average to a lofty .373 and his RBIs gave him a league leading 59. Pistol Pete finally moved into the top ten with an average of .320. Brooklyn's lead over St. Louis reached seven games with the victory, but the Cardinals were just getting warmed up.

As the month drew to a close, Eddie Dyer and his crew moved into Ebbets Field to lock horns with the pride of Flatbush, with only 2 1/2 games separating the two antagonists. Musial and Company were poised for the kill as the series got underway, but Brooklyn drew first blood, winning the series opener to extend their lead to 3 1/2 games.

The next day, little Murray Dickson faced off against southpaw Joe Hatten. Brooklyn moved out on top again, much to the delight of the 33,661 faithful who had crammed into the little park. In the bottom of the fourth, hits by Stanky, Reiser, and Walker plated two runners, as Governor Thomas E. Dewey roared his approval. The Cards, however, were not ready to fold. They were made of sterner stuff. Their answer came swiftly and convincingly. Triples by Red Schoendienst and Whitey Kurowski and a double by Erv Dusak drove the Dodger southpaw to cover under a five-run barrage. They went on to win Game Two by a final count of 10-3.

The finale of the series was all St. Louis, as their pitchers shut down the Dodger attack again, this time by a 3-1 score. The loss was much worse than a mere game however. In the fifth inning, Whitey Kurowski smashed a long drive to left field. Reiser, in his typical reckless fashion, gave chase without any consideration for his own safety. He crashed head first into the left field wall, and fell unconscious as the ball bounced away for a double. It was an all-too-familiar sight as the field crew carried Reiser off the field on a stretcher. He spent the night in familiar surroundings; Peck Memorial Hospital.

The season was two-thirds over and it was a donnybrook, just as everyone suspected. Brooklyn held a slim 1 1/2 game lead. Dixie Walker still led the hit parade at .382, and showed the way in RBIs with 78. St. Louis' 25-year-old super star, Stan Musial, was close behind at .357, and Dodger second baseman Eddie Stanky was surprising everyone as he hung in at .311. Another bonus was the hitting of rookie Carl Furillo who was swinging a potent bat, averaging .297. Leo Durocher's pitching staff was enjoying a successful summer, with diminutive Vic Lombardi showing the way with a 10-6 record. Kirby Higbe (9-3), Hugh Casey (8-4), Hank Behrman (7-3), Art Herring (6-1), and Hal Gregg (5-1), provided the manager with considerable depth.

On August 8 Reiser returned to the wars with a bang. He marched into the Polo Grounds and hit a home run into the lower right-field stands in the first inning. Then, after a Willard Marshall homer tied the game in the sixth, Pistol Pete smashed a two-run triple in the tenth to win the game for Hugh Casey, who had tossed 3 2/3 innings of shutout ball in relief.

The summer was fading. So too were the Dodgers. A three game losing streak had the Brooks on edge. So much so, in fact, that their third loss, to the Giants, turned into a free-for-all. Kirby Higbe faced Monte Kennedy, a

Tall, lanky Ed Stevens had some big hits in the pennant race. He slammed 10 home runs and had 60 RBIs in just 310 at bats.

lanky 24-year-old southpaw from Amelia, Virginia. As the fifth inning got underway, with New York leading, 2-1, Goody Rosen hit a line drive to right field. He tried to stretch it into a double, but a good throw from Dixie Walker cut him down at second. Rosen came in with his spikes high. Stanky tagged him high, and the fight was on. When the smoke cleared, both Rosen and Stanky were excused from further activity. The Giants held on, 2-1, and the Dodgers suddenly found themselves in an unusual position, in second place, 2 1/2 games behind St. Louis. The high-flying Redbirds had rolled through August with a 22-9 record, picking up five games on the Dodgers in the process. As the stretch run began however, the momentum shifted again, and Durocher's Dandys made one final charge. They went 17-5 during the first three weeks of September, but, as the season entered its final week, they still trailed the sizzling Cardinals by one game. Both teams cooled slightly at the end, as the also-rans got some measure of revenge. Brooklyn went 4-3 in the final seven games, while St. Louis dropped to 3-4. The season ended with the two teams in a flat-footed tie for first place, setting up the first playoff in National League history. Game One took place in Sportsman's Park, St. Louis on Tuesday, October 1. The midweek afternoon game drew only 26,012 spectators under a cloudless sky. Leo Durocher nominated 20-year-old Ralph Branca to start the historic game. The big, hard-throwing righthander had pitched only 67 innings during the season, but was well rested. It was a big gamble for Durocher, and one that he would lose. Branca had a history of wildness, a weakness that proved to be his undoing, as he failed to last three innings in this critical game. Manager Eddie Dyer handed the ball to southpaw Howie Pollet, the bellwether of the Cardinal pitching staff. The 25-year-old Pollet was the top pitcher in the National League during the season; leading the league in victories (21), earned run average (2.10), and innings pitched (266).

The stylish lefthander kept Dodger bats in check all afternoon, scattering eight hits over the distance. The Redbirds got off the mark quickly in the first inning.

Hard-throwing Hal Gregg posted a fine 6-4 record, with a 2.99 ERA in 26 games.

Singles by Terry Moore and Enos Slaughter, plus a walk to Whitey Kurowski, loaded the bases with two out. The next batter, Joe Garagiola, hit a ground ball in the hole between third and short. A great stop and throw by Reese just failed to nip the Cardinal catcher as Moore scored. Howie "Stretch" Schultz, Brooklyn's towering 6'6" first baseman, tied the game in the third with a long home run to left. Then the roof caved in on Branca. A one-out walk to Musial started the rally. Subsequent singles by Slaughter, Garagiola, and "Harry the Hat" Walker (Dixie's brother), drove Branca to cover, and plated two runs, giving the Cards a 3-1 lead. They never looked back, winning by a final score of 4-2.

The scene shifted to Ebbets Field for Game Two, with lefty Joe Hatten (14-10) facing the Cardinals' diminutive righthander, Murray Dickson (14-6). Brooklyn's Beloved Bums brought their 31,437 screaming fans to their feet in the very first inning as they pushed across a run after two men were out. Third baseman Augie Galan beat out an infield roller to second base. After Dixie Walker drew a base on balls, first baseman Ed Stevens slashed a single back through the box to score Walker. That was it as far as the Dodgers were concerned until the dramatic ninth. They were held hitless by Dickson over the next 7 1/3 innings.

The Redbirds however, came roaring back against the southpaw slants of Hatten. With one out in the second, left fielder Erv Dusak smashed a long drive off the left-field wall, and pulled into third with a triple. He scored minutes later when Marty Marion hit a fly ball to Carl Furillo in center. Catcher Clyde Kluttz singled to center with two out; then Dickson surprised everyone by hitting a line drive to right center field for three bases. Kluttz scored the go-ahead run. St. Louis kept adding to their lead throughout the game, and were comfortably in front, 8-1 through 8 1/2.

As the bottom of the ninth began, the great heart of the '46 Dodgers began beating with greater intensity, and they came charging back one last time. A double by Galan, a triple by Stevens, two singles, and two walks, had Ebbets Field in an uproar. All at once, the score was 8-4, and the Dodgers had the tying run at the plate with only one out. Eddie Stanky, the pesky little second baseman tried to coax a base on balls out of Cardinal relief pitcher, Harry "The Cat" Brecheen, but the crafty southpaw slipped a screwball over the outside of the plate for a called third strike. Howie Schultz, Brooklyn's final batter, had the power to tie the game with one swing, but he was greatly overmatched against Brecheen. He fanned with three mighty swings and the season finally came to an end.

The St. Louis Cardinals, the National League Champions, went on to defeat the Boston Red Sox in seven games in the World Series. Harry "The Cat" Brecheen won three games, while fashioning a 0.43 ERA over 20 innings.

The Brooklyn Dodgers went on to form a dynasty.

1948– SIXTY-TWO DAYS OF GLORY

For the first half of the season, the 1948 Brooklyn Dodgers were the worst team in baseball. Over the final month, they were nothing more than a .500 ballclub. But for 62 electrifying days, from July 2 through August 30 they blazed a path of glory that carried them all the way from the National League basement to the top of the league. It was a miraculous drive reminiscent of the 1914 Boston Braves, who had gone from last place in mid-July to first place by the end of the season. The Braves won the National League title going away, leaving John McGraw's New York Giants a distant 10 1/2 games behind. Then they followed it up with a four-game sweep of the Philadelphia Athletics in the World Series.

Brooklyn's drive to the top was just as exciting. Unfortunately, the team was still too young and too inexperienced. They couldn't sustain the momentum after those 62 glorious days, and they slipped back to third place, finishing 7 1/2 games behind the pennant winning Boston Braves. Brooklyn's thrilling effort began on July 2. The defending National League champions, beset by managerial problems, and in the throes of a transition to a new personnel roster, dropped into last place after suffering their sixth consecutive loss, this one a 6-4 defeat at the hands of the New York Giants.

From the ashes of defeat however, arose a glimmer of things to come. The Dodgers had just recalled catcher Roy Campanella from their St. Paul farm club, and he had a sizzling debut in a losing cause. Campy went 3-4 with a double. The next night, day one on the road to glory, the roly-poly receiver smashed out three more hits, including a triple, as the Bums pushed across five runs in the seventh inning to overcome the Giants, 7-5. The win allowed the Flock to sneak out of the cellar by half a game.

July 4 brought a different kind of fireworks to Ebbets Field, the kind that only a Dodger-Giant donnybrook could create. Thirty-seven players got into the game, and a total of 25 runs and 30 hits rattled around the Bedford Avenue hippodrome before the smoke cleared. For awhile, it looked as if the game belonged to New York, as they led 8-3 after six. But this was a new Dodger team, and they would not be denied. A steal of home by Jackie Robinson in the seventh inning, ignited the offense. The Brooks scored three runs in the seventh, and three more in the eighth to grab the lead ,9-8. After the Giants pushed over four big runs in the top of the ninth to regain the lead by a comfortable 12-9 score, the boys of Flatbush went to work again. Roy Campanella hit a home run with Gil Hodges on base to trim the lead to 12-11. Then with Dick Whitman and Pee Wee Reese sitting on second and third, "Pistol Pete" Reiser, fresh out of a hospital bed, limped to the plate on two badly sprained ankles and promptly drove in the winning runs with a pinch-hit single. Campanella finished the day 2 for 4, including two home runs and four RBIs. For the three-game series, his baptism of fire in the National League, Campy had smashed out nine hits in 12 at bats, with a double, a triple, and two homers.

He also drew one base on balls. His batting average, after three days in the National League, was a lofty .750.

Other changes were made by General Manager Branch Rickey during the first half of July in an attempt to stabilize the team. Manager Leo Durocher was replaced by kindly old Burt Shotton, who quietly established the feeling of confidence the Dodgers needed, in order to mount an all-out assault on the first-place Boston Braves. Pitcher Carl Erskine was called up from the Fort Worth Cats of the AA Texas League, where he had piled up an enviable 15-7 record. And outfielder George "Shotgun" Shuba was rescued from the Mobile Bears where he was hitting .389.

The pieces of the team puzzle gradually fell into place. Catching was finally set with Campanella in control behind the plate. Gil Hodges was in his first full season at a new position, and was still learning the ropes (11 home runs, 70 RBIs .249 batting average). Ditto Duke Snider in center field (5, 21, .244 in 53 games). Jackie Robinson, in his second season, was shifted from first base to second, and was just getting the feel of the keystone sack. Pee Wee Reese was the old pro at short, a six-year veteran. Billy Cox, obtained during the winter from Pittsburgh, was still suffering the effects of wartime malaria, and was limited to only 88 games. In 1949, he would be at

Ralph Branca, a 22-year-old, fireballing right hander, followed up his 21-victory campaign in 1947, with a creditable 14-9 record in '48.

full throttle. Carl Furillo, in his third year in Dodger blue, had relinquished center field to the Duke, and was learning to play the crazy right-field wall in Ebbets Field. Gene Hermanski gave the Dodgers a workmanlike effort in left field, with 15 home runs, 60 runs batted in, and a .290 batting average. Preacher Roe, who had come to the Dodgers along with Cox, was coming of age (12-8). Carl Erskine would contribute six big wins to the drive. Branca (14-9), Rex Barney (15-13), and Joe Hatten (13-10) kept the Dodgers in the race. This was the beginning of the famous "Boys of Summer", but they had not quite jelled into a team at this point.

Still, they were good enough to make the Braves squirm a little. After the big New York series, the Brooks began to roll. They swept the Phils three straight. They won the opener of a twin bill 4-3 in ten innings, as Jackie

Gene Hermanski was one of several different left fielders to play for "The Boys Of Summer." The left-handed slugger was a regular from 1947 through 1950, hitting between .275 and .299, with better than average power.

Robinson, with a beautiful fade away slide, eluded the tag by catcher Andy Seminick to score the winning run. Reese and "Shotgun" Shuba had three hits each in the nightcap to trigger a 10-1 romp behind Rex Barney's five-hitter. The next day, Hank Behrman eight-hit the Phils, 8-0. Shuba smashed his first major league home run, a 360-footer over the right field wall.

That was the way it went the rest of July. Although they closed out the month on a losing note, dropping a 5-2 decision to lowly Pittsburgh, the Brooklyn juggernaught rolled up a 21-8 record after July 2, and moved into third place, only 6 1/2 games behind Billy Southworth's Redskins. Gene Hermanski was leading the team in batting at .310, Robby stood at .307, and Reese was close behind at .304. On the mound, Ralph Branca was 12-7, while Rex Barney and Joe Hatten had identical 7-6 records.

Burt Shotton's bombers continued their drive to the top with a come-from-behind victory over Chicago on August 4. Down 4-2 after five innings, the Dodgers brought the Ebbets Field faithful to their feet as they scored single runs in the seventh, eighth, and ninth. Bruce Edwards' single scored Gene Hermanski who had doubled, with the winning run. The next day, Hermanski enjoyed his greatest day in a Brooklyn uniform. His three home runs and five RBIs sparked the team to a 6-4 win over the same Cubs.

The Dodgers continued to creep up on the slumping Braves, with win after win, each one producing a new hero. Robinson hit a two run homer to down Cincinnati 4-1. Joe Hatten whipped the Reds, 10-2, behind Gil Hodges' two home runs and five RBIs. Duke Snider doubled and scored on a seventh-inning single by Reese to dump Philly, 2-1. The Duke slid under the catcher's tag to bring home the game winner. Rookie Carl Erskine won his fourth game with a five-hitter.

The excitement of a full-blown pennant race boiled over during the last two-weeks of August as the Dodgers and Braves met head-to-head in a big three-game series in Ebbets Field. The Bums took the opener of a double-header on August 21, 8-7, to move into first place. Brooklyn knocked Boston ace Johnny Sain out of the box in the first inning with five big runs. A Jackie Robinson homer in the second extended the lead to 6-0, but Joe Hatten couldn't stand the prosperity. The Braves sent him to an early shower by scoring four times in the fourth. Billy Southworth's crew continued to peck away at the Brooklyn lead, but key defensive plays by Robinson in the sixth and seventh innings saved the game.

The Braves may have lost the first battle, but they were not about to lose the war. They bounced back to take the second game, 2-1, behind Warren Spahn's four-hitter, and reclaim first place. They extended the lead to three full games by winning the final two games of the series, 4-3 and 3-2 in 14 innings. A Clint Conatser home run off Erv Palica won Game Three. A Connie Ryan double spelled defeat in the finale.

The Dodgers suffered a major loss during the series when pitcher Ralph Branca was lost for two weeks with a leg infection. Branca, whose 13-7 record led the Brooklyn staff, won only one game over the final seven weeks.

The Brooklyn team, like Boston's, had character, and they were not about to roll over and play dead after their disappointing home stand. After a 9-1 blowout at the hands of the lowly Pirates, they bounced back stronger than ever.

Lefty Joe Hatten pitched for Brooklyn for five years, winning 59 games against 39 losses. He never had a losing season.

Harry Taylor went 10-5 in 1947, but arm problems plagued him the rest of his career. In 1948, he finished at 2-7.

An eight-game winning streak catapulted them to the top of the league again before month's end. An 18-hit attack led by Stan Rojek and Bruce Edwards, got the ball rolling with an 11-9 win over Pittsburgh. A three-game sweep of Cincinnati followed, with outstanding pitching performances the order of the day. Lefty Joe Hatten tossed a six-hitter at the Reds, to win 6-2. Pee Wee Reese homered. Rex Barney followed with his 12th victory, 3-2. Then it was Preacher Roe, hurling a three-hit masterpiece, to blank the Redlegs, 2-0. Brooklyn was back in the hunt, in third place behind Boston and St. Louis, but only two games out.

While Boston visited Pittsburgh, the Dodgers moved into the hostile environs of Sportsman's Park to engage Eddie Dyer's Cardinals in a short, two day, four-game series. It was Brooklyn's finest hour. On Sunday August 29, the Pirates made Boston walk the plank twice, by scores of 6-1 and 5-2. Shotton's crew didn't miss their golden opportunity. They hammered St. Louis in the opener, 12-7, as Jackie Robinson hit for the cycle, with two singles, a double, a triple, and a home run in six at bats. They took the nightcap also, 4-3, on a tenth-inning single by Arky Vaughan.

The following day, the same two teams were at it again in another double header. Once again, the darlings of Flatbush won both games. The Bums trailed 5-2 after eight innings in the opener, but rallied with four big runs in the ninth. Doubles by Snider and Reiser, and singles

by Hermanski, Vaughan, and "Shotgun" Shuba, stunned the Redbird congregation of 33,508. Joe Hatten put another nail in the Cardinal coffin, tossing a five-hitter to win the second game, 6-1. Hatten, Hodges, and Eddie Miksis had two hits apiece to pace the victory. Meanwhile, old friend Dixie Walker slugged a two-run homer off Johnny Sain in the first inning to sink Boston, 2-1.

At day's end, the standings showed a strange sight. The warriors of Burt Shotton were firmly entrenched atop the National League.

	W	L	GB
Brooklyn	68	51	-
Boston	69	55	- 1 1/2
St. Louis	64	54	- 3 1/2

Brooklyn's drive to the top, covering a period of 59 days, produced an amazing .719 winning percentage. Following their abysmal 27-35 record on July 2, the Dodgers went on to win 41 of their next 57 games to claim first place. But, as everyone knows, glory is fleeting, and enemies appear in the strangest places.

Filled with a feeling of euphoria, the high-flying Dodgers floated into Wrigley Field to do battle with the last-place Chicago Cubs. It was to be a continuation of their eight-game winning streak, and an extension of their league lead, but manager Charlie Grimm and his maligned Bruins had other ideas. Right hander Hank Borowy, a four-game winner, blanked the suddenly passive Brooks, 3-0, on a one-hitter. The second game was just as embarrassing, as Doyle Lade triumphed 7-2. Ralph Branca, trying to come back from the disabled list, failed miserably. He walked the bases full in the second, and light-hitting Emil Verban brought them all home with a double. Boston's win in Cincinnati deadlocked the pennant race.

Brooklyn got a temporary respite the next day as Preacher Roe whitewashed the Cubbies 6-0 for his second consecutive shutout. Jackie Robinson's two doubles got the ball rolling, and Gene Hermanski's 400-foot homer off the top of the center field wall put the icing on the cake. A Boston split dropped the Braves a half-game behind. On Thursday, September 2nd, with 17,210 Wrigley Field enthusiasts screaming their heads off, Chicago rallied to tie the game on a two-run homer by Eddie Waitkus in the sixth, then went on to a 7-6 victory over the Dodgers as Johnny Schmitz hurled four scoreless innings in relief to record his 16th win.

Brooklyn returned home to the friendly confines of Ebbets Field on the 3rd, but facing them were the hostile forces from New York, now managed by Leo Durocher. The Lip had a score to settle with the Brooklyn front office, and there was no better way to do it than to knock their team off their lofty perch. Brooklyn's momentum was gone, and try as they might, they couldn't regain it. Before a quiet crowd of 33,090, Burt Shotton's crew bit the dust twice, 7-5 and 6-3. Sid Gordon's 28th and 29th home runs offset a round tripper by Duke Snider to win the first game. In the second game, Carl Erskine was routed on a home run by Wes Westrum. Boston's 3-1 win over Philly, gave them a 1 1/2 game lead.

Sheldon Jones blanked the Dodgers, 3-0, the next day, and it was all downhill after that. The fighting Brooks did manage to win the series finale, 4-3 in 12 innings on a double by "Shotgun" Shuba, but it was too little, too late. On September 6, Labor Day, Brooklyn made the trek up to Braves Field for a last-ditch stand. Awaiting them were the likes of Warren Spahn and Johnny Sain. A favorite 1948 ditty, reflecting on Boston's thin pitching staff went, "Spahn and Sain and pray for rain." Boston didn't need rain on this day as the two aces shut down the Brooklyn attack with barely a whimper. The southpaw, Spahn, took the 14-inning opener, 2-1, with a steady, workmanlike effort. His right-handed counterpart, Old John, tossed a five-hitter as he blanked the Flatbush Flock, 4-0.

Brooklyn's great run was essentially over. They drifted back into the pack, finishing in third place, 7 1/2 games behind the pennant winning Boston Braves. After August 30, they won 16 games and lost 15, while Billy Southworth's crew went 22-7.

The season ended on a disappointing note for the Brooklyn team, but for 62 glorious days they lived an exciting dream. The city of Brooklyn felt pennant fever for many weeks before reality set in. And it was also a valuable learning experience. The young players like Gil Hodges, Jackie Robinson, Carl Furillo, Duke Snider, Roy Campanella, and Carl Erskine experienced the thrills and the pressures of their first pennant race. In the years to come, they would benefit from that experience.

1950—A RUMBLE WITH THE WHIZ KIDS

The 1950 Brooklyn Dodgers were on the verge of greatness. Molded by the astute baseball genius, Branch Rickey, the fabled "Boys of Summer" took shape following World War II. After a disappointing playoff loss to the St. Louis Cardinals in 1946, the Dodgers won the National League pennant in 1947, finished third in 1948, and copped another title in 1949. They were favored to repeat in 1950.

Brooklyn had squeaked out the '49 National League flag by one game over Eddie Dyer's Redbirds. The Philadelphia Phillies finished a distant third, 16 games off the pace. Quietly, however, and almost unnoticed, manager Eddie Sawyer had built a contender, a young, aggressive team that would be known as the "Whiz Kids" before the summer was over. Anchored by the mound duo of Robin Roberts and Curt Simmons, the Kiddie Korps included center fielder Richie Ashburn, shortstop Granny Hamner, second baseman Mike Goliat, and third baseman Willie "Puddinhead" Jones.

Don Newcombe and Roy Campanella celebrate another Dodger victory. Campy's 31 homers and Newk's 19 victories kept Brooklyn in the pennant race until the last day.

The Flatbush Flock got off to an erratic start in April with Newcombe, Branca, and Bankhead all hampered by sore arms. In an early game against Philadelphia in Shibe Park, Newk was ko'd in the second after yielding four runs. The noisy home crowd sent him to the showers amidst jeers and catcalls. The team struggled, with seven different pitchers winning games in the first month.

As Memorial Day rolled around, the Brooks were locked in a dogfight with the Cards and Phils. A big holiday morning-afternoon doubleheader brought some relief, as Burt Shotton's team swept both games from Phila-

Erv Palica had his finest season in a Brooklyn uniform in 1950, winning 13 games against eight losses. Arm problems curtailed a promising career.

delphia. In the morning game, under cloudy skies, Preacher Roe hurled five strong innings in relief and the Dodgers prevailed 7-6 in 10 innings. Furillo's strong throw nipped the potential winning run at the plate in the ninth. Then, in the bottom of the tenth, two walks and a wild throw by Granny Hamner scored Bobby Morgan with the game winner. Duke Snider took care of the afternoon game single-handedly, as he smashed three home runs and a single, with Jack Banta defeating Russ Meyer, 6-4. Snider's single, a sizzling line drive that struck the right-field wall one foot from the top, was the hardest ball he hit all day.

Brooklyn's 23-13 record through May put them atop the NL standings, one game up on St. Louis, and 1 1/2 ahead of Philadelphia. The three teams continued to jockey for position during the summer, with first one team, then another claiming first place. Injuries and slumps decimated the Flatbush team in July, and they dropped into third place, 4 1/2 games behind the "Whiz Kids." Their 15-14 record for the month paled beside the "Whiz Kids'" 22-13 mark. Jackie Robinson, who was hitting .372 at the end of July, injured his shoulder, and his average dropped 42 points in a month.

As the dog days of summer drew to a close, Dodger bats heated up. On August 26, in Cincinnati's Crosley Field, Roy Campanella smashed his 25th, 26th, and 27th home runs, good for six RBIs, in Brooklyn's 7-5 win over the Redlegs, their tenth consecutive victory. Four days later, the Brooklyn strongman, Gil Hodges, did Campy one better. In a 19-3 romp over Warren Spahn and the Boston Braves, big Gil blasted four round-trippers, tying the modern major league record for one game. When the smoke had cleared, Hodges had added a single to his total, and had accounted for nine runs batted in.

Despite the heroics of Campanella and Hodges, and a fine 19-10 record in August, Brooklyn slipped further behind as the Phils went 20-8, giving them a 42-21 record since July 1. In early September, the Beloved Bums moved into Philadelphia for a critical series with Eddie Sawyer's upstarts. Because of a severe pitching shortage, Don Newcombe volunteered to pitch both ends of a double header. He almost pulled off a double victory. In the opener, Big Newk outpitched Bubba Church, 2-0, with a neat three-hitter. In the nightcap, his outstanding effort went unrewarded, as he left the game for a pinch hitter in the eighth inning, trailing 2-0. The Dodgers came back to win the game for reliever Dan Bankhead, scoring three runs in the ninth off Philadelphia closer, Jim Konstanty. The sweep moved the Dodgers to within 5 1/2 games of the high-flying Phils, and set the stage for a dramatic stretch drive.

As September 19 dawned, Brooklyn's pennant hopes appeared to be lost, as the team was mired in third place, a distant nine games behind. Suddenly, the unbelievable happened. The Dodgers got hot again, the Phillies got stone cold, and the nine-game lead dwindled to but one in 12 short days. The rally began with a sweep of a doubleheader against Pittsburgh. Snider and Hodges hit two home runs apiece in support of Don Newcombe in the opener, and big Newk cruised to his 18th victory of the season, 14-3. Erv Palica hurled the Brooks to a sweep with a 3-2 victory in the nightcap, his 10th win of the season. The next afternoon, Carl Erskine took the measure of the hapless Pirates, 7-2 behind Gil Hodges' grand slam, and the following day the Dodgers completed the four-game sweep with a hard-fought 10-8 win. Brooklyn rapped Bill Werle and Mel Queen for 10 runs and 11 hits in five innings. After the Pittsburgh rout, Burt Shotton's demolition crew travelled to Philadelphia to meet the league

leaders in a "crushful" two-game series. The Flock won both games as Dodger fans went crazy with renewed pennant fever. First, Newcombe took the measure of the "Whiz Kids" 3-2 behind Hodges' three-run homer in the second. Then 22-year-old Erv Palica polished them off, 11-0, with a two-hitter, hitting a grand slam homer to add

Dick Sisler was a smooth-fielding, hard-hitting first baseman, who played in the major leagues for eight years, batting .276 with 55 home runs.

Dan Bankhead was 9-4 in 41 games for the Dodgers in 1950. Bankhead was the first black pitcher in the major leagues, joining Brooklyn in 1947. He homered in his first major league at bat.(Larry Fritsch Cards)

salt to the Phils' wounds. The once-insurmountable nine-game lead was down to five, and the Phils looked ready for the taking.

After taking the Giants to task twice in three games, the Brooks were faced with the unenviable chore of playing three consecutive doubleheaders against the Boston Braves. In spite of splitting the first two doubleheaders, Shotton's crew found themselves only three games in arrears as the Phils continued their slide with doubleheader loss to Leo Durocher's Giants. Brooklyn increased the pressure on Eddie Sawyer's boys as they swept the final twin bill, 7-5 and 7-6. Roe captured his 19th victory in the opener, as the Dodgers fought back from a 5-2 deficit. In the nightcap, Carl Erskine won in relief as the Brooklyn offense once again rescued the shaky pitching staff. This time, home runs by Robinson and Campanella overcame a 6-3 deficit, and made "Oisk" the winner, 7-6. Robby's

blast into the lower left center field stands in the seventh was the game winner.

The season came down to the last weekend and, as fate would have it, the Phils were in town for a final two-game series, trying to protect their now precarious two-game lead. Eddie Sawyer's boys needed only a split to be crowned National League Champions, while the Dodgers had to sweep both games to force a playoff. On Saturday, young Erv Palica stopped the Phils for the second time in a week, winning 7-3, and backing the "Whiz Kids" to the brink. The Little Colonel, Pee Wee Reese, broke open a scoreless tie with a run-scoring triple in the fifth. Snider followed with his 31st home run, a high drive over the right field wall onto Bedford Avenue. With the game still tight in the eighth, Campanella deposited his 31st into the center field seats with a man on, to ice it.

As the final Sunday dawned, the aces of the respective pitching staffs stood ready to do battle; 24-year-old Robin Roberts (19-11) and 24-year-old Don Newcombe (19-10). Both teams were poised for the final confrontation. Momentum and the home park advantage were on the Dodgers' side. Over the past two weeks, the Brooks had won 12 of 14 games, while the Phils were imitating their hapless predecessors in losing nine of 12.

The crowds formed early on Sullivan Place and, when the gates were opened, 35,073 fanatical Dodger fans filled the little park to capacity. It was a warm, sunny fall day with the temperature hovering around the 88-degree mark, and the starting pitchers were as hot as the weather.

For five innings the game was scoreless. Then, in the sixth, the Phils broke out on top on two-out singles by Dick Sisler, Del Ennis, and "Puddinhead" Jones. Brooklyn tied the game in the same inning when a high fly ball to right field by Pee Wee Reese lodged on top of the right field wall for an automatic home run.

The game remained tied through 8 1/2 innings as both pitchers shut down the other team's offense. In the bottom of the ninth, the Bums threatened to win it, but fate ruled otherwise. Cal Abrams, a good hitter but, perhaps the world's slowest runner, led off the bottom of the ninth by drawing a base on balls. The next hitter, Pee Wee Reese, after failing to bunt twice, lined a single to left field, sending Abrams to second. Duke Snider then rifled an apparent game-winning hit to center field, as the stands exploded in anticipation.

The celebration was premature. Center fielder Richie Ashburn, noted for his weak arm, was playing shallow for just such an eventuality. Charging the ball flawlessly, the speedy Ashburn fired a strike to catcher Stan Lopata. Abrams lumbered around third on a green light from coach Milt Stock, and headed home. When he arrived, the ball was waiting for him.

Still, the Dodgers had the game-winning run on third with only one out. Roberts issued an intentional pass to Jackie Robinson to load the bases and give his team a play at any base. Stepping into the box was Carl Furillo, a contact hitter with long-ball potential. Skoonj swung at the first pitch, but could produce nothing more than a weak fly ball to Eddie Waitkus behind first, with the runners holding. The Dodger's final hope, Gil Hodges, sent a long fly ball to deep right center field, but Del Ennis chased it down in front of the scoreboard to end the threat.

Given a life, the "Whiz Kids" made the most of the opportunity. Pitcher Robin Roberts, a good hitting pitcher, lined a single to center, leading off the tenth. Waitkus followed with a pop fly single to center, putting men on first and second. Ashburn, attempting to sacrifice, forced Roberts at third. That brought up Dick Sisler, the son of Hall-of-Famer George Sisler, a good first baseman in his own right, and a long-ball threat. The big left-handed slugger swung and missed Newk's first pitch; then fouled off the next one to fall into an 0-2 hole. Working the count to 2-2, Sisler drove a Newcombe fastball to the opposite field. Cal Abrams gave pursuit, but pulled up at the 348-foot mark and watched the ball drop into the stands for a pennant-winning, three-run homer.

Robin Roberts retired Campanella, Jim Russell, and Tommy Brown in order in the bottom of the tenth, and the Phils were National League Champions.

Philadelphia Phillies 0 0 0 0 0 1 0 0 0 3 - 4 -11 - 0
Brooklyn Dodgers   0 0 0 0 0 1 0 0 0 0 - 1 - 5 - 0

The Dodger clubhouse was naturally quiet as the sun fell over Flatbush, but the team was not overly depressed. It felt it had given its best, and had come up

short. In the end, it was their lack of pitching that did them in. The pitching staff started and ended with Newcombe, Roe, and Palica. They were tied for fifth in staff ERA, a full 0.78 runs per game behind the Philadelphia staff.

Offensively, the Dodgers dominated the league. As a team they led the league in runs scored, home runs, batting average, and slugging average. In the field, they were number one in fielding average, fewest errors, and most double plays. Individually, they were led by Duke Snider (.321, 31, 107), Gil Hodges (.283, 32, 113), Roy Campanella (.281, 31, 89), Jackie Robinson (.328, 14, 81), and Carl Furillo (.305, 18, 106).

Don Newcombe and Preacher Roe both finished the season with 19-11 records, while young Erv Palica piled up 13 wins against eight defeats. Dan Bankhead won nine games, and no one else won more than seven.

The 1950 pennant race went to the best team that year. The Dodgers, with their pitching staff decimated through injuries, fought the good fight. They gave their fans a lot to cheer about down the stretch, but they came up one out short.

1951—THE MIRACLE AT COOGAN'S BLUFF

The year 1951 will forever live in infamy in the hearts of Brooklyn Dodger fans. It was the year of "The Miracle at Coogan's Bluff," climaxed by "The Shot Heard

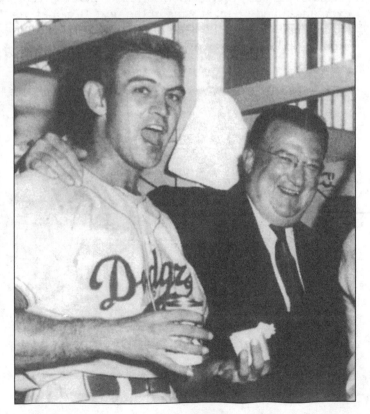

Clem Labine (with Dodger President Walter O'Malley), gave the Dodgers an outstanding rookie season, both starting and relieving. His 5-1 record and 2.20 ERA, almost carried O'Malley's team to the pennant.

Round the World," Bobby Thomson's dramatic pennant-winning home run. It was a year of excitement turned to disbelief, a year of hope, then despair. It was the ultimate nightmare.

The year started off optimistically enough, with Charlie Dressen's fired-up charges dedicating themselves to re-capturing the National League pennant that had slipped from their grasp on the last day of the 1950 season. The Brooklyn Baseball Club presented an awesome lineup, one of the most devastating in National League history. The team had everything; a league-leading offense, the top-rated defensive unit, and better-than-average pitching. They were the "Boys of Summer," nearing the peak of their skills.

The 1951 roster was essentially the same one that came within one game of the title the previous year. President Walter O'Malley, hoping to fortify his pitching staff with players from within his own farm system, made only one roster change over the winter, and that was in the dugout. He replaced kindly old Burt Shotton with dynamic Charlie Dressen, as the team manager. Dressen was the consummate strategist, who once told his team, "Hold 'em for eight innings and I'll think of something." He was brash, daring, and egotistical. And he was a great manager.

After a vigorous six weeks at Dodgertown, the Flatbush Flock opened their pursuit of the title on April 17 with a disappointing 5-2 loss in the season opener at Ebbets Field. They righted themselves the next day, however, and rolled up eight wins in the next 11 games. As April neared an end, the hapless New York Giants came to town, in the throes of an 11-game losing streak. They

Jackie Robinson receives a thank you from manager Charlie Dressen after his pennant-tying home run in Philadelphia.

Don Newcombe, pulling a wishbone with Charlie Dressen, is hoping for a pennant in 1951. His wish didn't come true. And the horseshoe didn't help either.

quickly ended the streak with an 8-5 win over the Dodgers behind Sal "The Barber" Maglie.

The April standings did not yet reflect the exciting pennant race that was to come.

TEAM	W	L	GB
BOSTON	10	5	–
ST. LOUIS	6	3	-1
BROOKLYN	8	5	-1
NEW YORK	3	12	-7 (LAST PLACE)

The Giants under fiery Leo Durocher had finished only five games behind the first-place Phillies in 1950, and they were geared for an assault on the top. The one missing link in their lineup was an offensive sparkplug. A take-charge guy who could ignite an entire team. Lacking that field leader however, the New Yorker's floundered, struggling to find a rhythm.

As May got underway, the Dodger juggernaught hit the road, piling up seven wins in a 10 game span, and moving into first place by mid-month. The Giants, still battling to reach the .500 plateau, called up 20-year-old Willie Mays from their AAA farm team in Minneapolis, where the speedster had hit .477 in 35 games. It turned out to be the key move of the season. The slugging center fielder from Alabama was the inspirational player the

Giants so desperately needed, and the field leader manager Leo Durocher sought. In conjunction with Mays' promotion, Durocher shook up his lineup, inserting Mays in center, moving Bobby Thomson to third base, sending Monte Irvin to left field, and putting Whitey Lockman on first. It took awhile for the "new" Giants to jell. Mays, for instance, went 0-12 in his debut, then, after getting his first hit, went 0 for his next 14. Durocher had to work overtime, sweet talking the dejected youngster, to keep his spirits up.

Brooklyn finished the month of May in first place, two games ahead of the St. Louis Cardinals, and 4 1/2 games ahead of the fourth-place Giants. In spite of their all-star lineup, the Dodgers still had a gaping hole in left field where the slow footed Abrams roamed. They corrected that weakness on June 15 by acquiring slugger Andy Pafko from the Chicago Cubs. The big righthander fit right in, and contributed 18 home runs over the last 84 games.

Dressen's charges extended their lead through the hot summer months. After a fine 18-10 record in June, the Boys of Summer rolled up a 21-7 mark in July, to move nine games in front of the pack. Pitching dominated the Brooklyn streak, led by Roe (15-2), Newcombe (15-5), Clyde King (12-5), Carl Erskine (12-8), and Ralph Branca (9-3). Robby was #2 in the batting race, hitting .344 behind Stan Musial's .373. Campy stood at .331, with Reese (.317) and Furillo (.314) close behind.

The Giants, in spite of a respectable 59-51 record, found themselves in second place, a distant 13 1/2 games behind the red-hot Dodgers (70-35) after the first game of a doubleheader on August 11. Even worse, they stood 16 games behind in the all-important loss column with only 44 games left in the season. After a three-game sweep of the Giants in early August, Dressen gloated, "It's over. They'll never bother us again. The Giants is dead." As usual, his words came back to haunt him.

On August 12, the Gothamites began a 16-game tear and, slowly, the once insurmountable lead began to dwindle. The Dodgers went 12-9 over the last three weeks of August, but the Giants' 17-2 run put them within seven games of the top. Suddenly the laughter became deadly serious. The pennant race was on.

An omen of things to come occurred on September 1 when the Brooks invaded the Polo Grounds for a short two-game series. Maglie tossed a seven-hitter as the Giants upended Brooklyn, 8-1, on a chilly overcast afternoon. Don Mueller's three home runs and five RBIs did the damage. In the fifth, with New York up 5-1, the Dodgers rallied, putting men on first and second with none out. The next batter, Pee Wee Reese, hit a liner to the left of shortstop Al Dark. Dark gloved the ball instinctively, tossed to Stanky to double up Abrams who was on his way to third, and Stanky then tagged Furillo coming down from first for an inning-ending triple play. When New York also took Game Two, 11-2, the lead stood at five.

"The Shot Heard Around The World" is frozen forever in this photograph. *Bobby Thomson has just completed his swing, and the ball (circled) is beginning its historic journey into the left-field stands. Ralph Branca is still following through, and is not yet aware of the disastrous result of the pitch.*

Brooklyn momentarily righted itself on September 8 when Big Newk tossed a two-hitter at the "Jints," routing them, 9-0, before a raucous Ebbets Field crowd of 23,171. Jackie Robinson spearheaded the attack with three hits and three runs scored. With a chance to put the New Yorkers away for good, Dodger bats suddenly went silent the next day and Ralph Branca's fine pitching effort was wasted in a tough 2-1 loss. It still left the Brooks with a solid 6 1/2 game lead, eight games in the loss column, with only 17 games to play, but the door was still open a crack–and the sizzling Durocher-men made the most of it.

On September 11, the Dodgers finally began to unravel. Over the next 17 days, their record was a miserable 6-11. They never won more than one game in a row as Snider and Furillo both slumped badly, and Campy was sidelined from a beaning in Chicago. Clem Labine, the red hot rookie pitcher who had reeled off four key victories in succession, got in Dressen's doghouse on the 21st by throwing a grandslam homer in the first inning at Philadelphia in a tough 9-6 loss. The kid from Woonsocket, Rhode Island was not allowed to pitch over the last three weeks of the season, a decision that has been second guessed ever since.

As the final weekend of the season got underway, the Dodger lead was a mere 1/2 game. Moving into Philadelphia on the final Friday, the cmbattled Brooks jumped out to a 3-0 lead behind Erskine. Roy Campanella had a single and a homer and one RBI, while Robby contributed a single and a double and an RBI. The little Hoosier couldn't hold the lead, however. Andy Seminick's home run in the bottom of the ninth tied the game at 3-3; then a line single by "Puddinhead" Jones past a diving Billy Cox scored Richie Ashburn with the game winner.

Now the drama began to unfold. As Saturday dawned, the Dodgers and Giants were tied for the top spot, with Dressen's team playing their final two games in Philadelphia and Durocher's charges visiting Boston. Both teams won on Saturday. Newcombe, pitching with only two days rest, blanked Eddie Sawyer's team, 5-0, for his 20th win of the season. Campanella's double and Andy Pafko's long home run into the upper left-field stands sparked a three-run Dodger third. Sal "The Barber" Maglie matched Big Newk's performance with a shutout of his own, beating Warren Spahn, 3-0, to run his record to 23-6.

On the final day of the season, New York prevailed once again, edging the Braves, 3-2, behind Larry Jansen's 22nd. The afternoon was so dark and overcast the game had to be played under the lights. In Philadelphia the Dodger fortunes were at a low ebb. With the Giant score staring them in the face, Dressen's cohorts found themselves down 6-1 to the fired-up Phils after three innings. The overworked Roe lasted only 1 2/3 innings, leaving under a four-run barrage.

The Dodgers showed their mettle in this game, battling back to score three runs in the top of the eighth, to tie the game at 8-8. At this point, Don Newcombe and Robin Roberts, both of whom had pitched on Saturday,

were rushed into the game by their respective managers, realizing there was no tomorrow. Big Newk pitched one-hit ball for 5 2/3 innings, from the eighth into the 13th. Roberts, the eventual loser, pitched brilliantly for 6 2/3 innings.

In the bottom of the 12th, the Phils almost ended the Dodgers' season. With darkness falling, the Whiz Kids loaded the bases against Newk with two out. The next batter, Eddie Waitkus, smashed a low line drive back through the middle for an apparent game-winning hit. Jackie Robinson saved the day, however, by racing to his right and throwing his body full length to backhand the ball behind second base for the third out. Two innings later, the fiery second baseman hit a home run into the left-field stands, and the Dodgers held on to win 9-8 in one of the greatest games in Brooklyn history.

The regular season ended with the Dodgers and Giants in a flat-footed tie, each with 96-58 records. A three-game playoff to decide the eventual National League pennant winner got underway the following day, Monday October 1, in Ebbets Field, with Games Two and Three to be played in the Polo Grounds the following two days. In the opener, 30,707 Dodger fans sat in stunned silence as Big Jim Hearn overpowered their heroes, winning 3-1 behind a tight five-hitter. The Brooks took a 1-0 lead in the second on a home run by Pafko, but Bobby Thomson's two-run shot off Ralph Branca in the fourth proved to be the game winner.

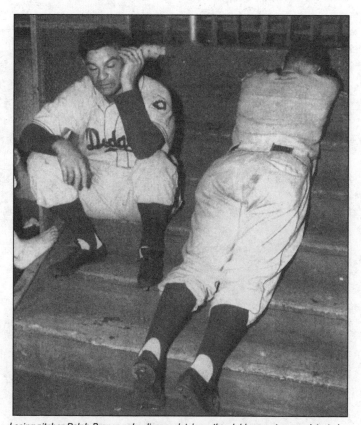

Losing pitcher Ralph Branca sobs disconsolately on the clubhouse steps as dejected Dodger coach Cookie Lavagetto tries to comprehend the magnitude of the Brooklyn disaster. (Barney Stein)

```
New York Giants      000 200 010 - 3 - 6 - 1
Brooklyn Dodgers     010 000 000 - 1 - 5 - 1
```

When the scene shifted to the Polo Grounds for Game Two, manager Charlie Dressen, his pitching staff depleted, was forced to release rookie Clem Labine from his doghouse. The sinkerball artist responded with a masterful six-hit shutout, winning easily, 10-0. Robby got the rout underway in the top of the first, hammering a two-run homer, his 19th, into the lower left-field deck. A double by Snider and a single by Robinson made it 3-0 in the fifth, and a three-run sixth, spearheaded by Gil Hodges' 40th home run, upped the margin to 6-0. Everything went the Dodgers' way on this day. Andy Pafko hit a round-tripper in the seventh, and Rube Walker, filling in for the injured Roy Campanella, completed the scoring with a two-run shot in the eighth.

```
Brooklyn Dodgers     200 013 202 - 10 - 13 - 2
New York Giants      000 000 000 - 0 - 6 - 5
```

The final game of the 1951 National League playoff was one of the greatest games in baseball history; the only time a pennant was ever decided by a home run on the last pitch of the season. A courageous Don Newcombe took the hill for Dressen's team, opposed by Dodger nemesis Sal Maglie. Big Newk had already pitched 23 2/3 innings over the previous seven days, but he was ready to try it again. And try it, he did.

The strapping 6'4" righthander held the mighty Giants in check for 8 1/3 innings, bringing his pitching total to an astonishing 32 innings in eight days. He pitched in four of the Dodgers' last seven games in 1951. Brooklyn drew first blood off Maglie, scoring a run in the top of the first on a walk to Reese and a single by that man Robinson again. The Giants fought back to tie the score off Newk in the seventh when Monte Irvin doubled, and later came in to score on a sacrifice fly by Bobby Thomson.

The Brooks routed "The Barber" with a three-run rally in the eighth. With one out, singles by Reese and Snider put runners on first and third. Pee Wee scored the tie-breaking run on a wild pitch and, after Robinson was intentionally passed, Andy Pafko hit an infield single to plate the second run of the inning. Billy Cox then lined a hit to left for yet another run.

The pennant looked secure for Dressen's juggernaut as Big Newk breezed through the bottom of the eighth, setting the Giants down, 1-2-3. As the bottom of the ninth inning got underway, New York fans squirmed in their seats, fearing the worst. Alvin Dark, leading off, beat out an infield hit to give the New Yorkers a life. The next batter, Don Mueller, lined a single between first and second and, all of a sudden, the tying run was at the plate. Monte Irvin fouled out to Hodges for out number one, but a rapidly tiring Newcombe finally ran out of gas. After Whitey Lockman sliced a double down the left field line to narrow the margin to 4-2, and put the tying runs

on second and third, manager Charlie Dressen waved Ralph Branca in from the bullpen.

Big number 13, the loser in Game One on a Bobby Thomson home run, faced his nemesis again, with a chance to redeem himself. His first pitch was a fast ball down the middle for strike one. His second pitch never reached the plate. The slugging Scot jumped all over it, and sent a high drive down the left-field line. Andy Pafko gave chase and, with his back to the wall, was positioned to make the catch, but the Dodger left fielder ran out of room as the ball settled into the stands for a pennant-winning, three-run homer.

Big #13 turned and, head down and shoulders hunched forward in despair, slowly made his way to the Dodger clubhouse in deep center field. Second baseman Eddie Stanky rode manager and third base coach Leo Durocher piggyback from third to home in pursuit of the grinning Thomson. Giant radio announcer Russ Hodges announced the unbelievable to the world, "The Giants win the pennant. The Giants win the pennant. The Giants win the pennant."

```
Brooklyn Dodgers     100 000 030 - 4 - 8 - 0
New York Giants      000 000 104 - 5 - 8 - 0
```

Wednesday, October 3, 1951, was, without a doubt, the darkest day in Brooklyn Dodger history.

1962—ANOTHER PLAYOFF LOSS TO THOSE BLASTED GIANTS

The Los Angeles Dodgers of 1959, in only their second year of baseball on the west coast, rewarded their fans with a "miracle pennant" and a World Championship. The following year, however, reality set in. Los Angeles was a team in transition, and they settled back into the pack in 1960. Most of "The Boys of Summer" had faded from the scene, and the youngsters were still several years away. The nucleus of the pennant-winning teams of the '60s was underway, however. Maury Wills had settled in at shortstop, while big Frank Howard and Tommy Davis worked their way into the outfield. After a fourth-place finish in 1960, manager Walter Alston's cohorts moved up to second place in 1961, adding swift Willie Davis to the outfield ranks, and breaking in flashy-fielding Ron Fairly at first base. It was on the mound, however, where the backbone of the future World Champions was being formed. Sandy Koufax, the 24-year-old southpaw fireballer had finally completed the metamorphosis from a thrower into a pitcher. The good-looking Koufax went 18-13 in '61, a portent of things to come. "Big D," Don Drysdale, won 13 games, while Stan Williams finished at 15-12, and veteran Johnny Podres won 18 games against only five losses. Larry Sherry and Ron Perranoski anchored the bullpen.

The 1962 season began with unbridled enthusiasm in the Dodger front office. Everyone, from Walter O'Malley

Junior Gilliam with Vin Scully and Walter Alston. Gilliam, a ten-year veteran, gave Alston another solid season of second-base play. He also hit .270 and scored 83 runs.

down to the janitor expected a National League flag come October. To the experts, it looked like a three-team race. The favored defending champion Cincinnati Reds sported a solid all-around lineup. Their pitching staff, anchored by Bob Purkey (16-12) and Joey Jay (21-10), led the league in fewest runs allowed, shutouts, and saves. Their potent offense centered around Frank Robinson (.323, 37, 124), Vada Pinson (.343, 16, 87), Gene Freese (.277, 26, 87), and Wally Post (.294, 20, 57).

The San Francisco Giants fielded a devastating wrecking crew led by 23-year-old sophomore Willie McCovey (.271, 18, 50), "The Baby Bull," Orlando Cepeda (.311, 46, 142), and the incomparable Willie "Say Hey" Mays (.308, 40, 123). The pitching of Mike McCormick, Jack Sanford, Juan Marichal, and Stu Miller, was the equal of any in the league.

The Dodgers, for their part, knew they would live or die on their strong pitching arms. Their offense centered around the blazing speed of Maury Wills and Willie Davis. The crafty Wills revolutionized the game of baseball in the early sixties, turning it from a one-base-at-a-time sluggers' contest, back into the exciting running game of the early part of the century. A typical Dodger game ended with a 1-0, 2-1, or 3-2 score. A "rally" consisted of a walk, a stolen base, an infield out and a sacrifice fly.

April 10 was an historic day in southern California. The Los Angeles Dodgers christened their new baseball showpiece, Dodger Stadium, a park considered to be the most beautiful park in the major leagues. The opening game, however, was one the Dodgers would rather forget. Johnny Podres earned the honor of opening the new

stadium before 52,564 festive Angelenos. Unfortunately, the visiting Cincinnati Reds did not follow the script. Behind righthander Bob Purkey, the Redlegs overwhelmed the boys of Alston, 6-3. Wally Post's three-run homer in the seventh, the first home run in Dodger Stadium, accounted for the winning runs.

Sandy Koufax got the Dodgers off on the right foot the next day, stopping the Reds on four hits, 6-2. Thirty-three-year-old Junior Gilliam, one of the "Boys of Summer", gave the Dodgers the lead by slamming a long home run into the right-field pavilion.

The third game in the three-game series was also an historic event. Rookie pitcher Pete Richert, in his first National League game, tied a major league record by fanning the first six batters he faced in the majors. The 22-year-old southpaw came on in the second inning with the Dodgers down, 4-0, and struck out Frank Robinson to end the inning. In the third, he struck out four men, one batter reaching first on a passed ball. Another Red went down on strikes in the fourth, before pitcher Joey Jay ended the streak by grounding out to first. Richert hurled 3 2/3 innings of hitless ball, and was credited with the victory when the Dodgers came back to win, 11-7.

Sandy Koufax racked up his third win of the season on April 24 as Los Angeles drubbed the hapless Chicago Cubs, 10-2, behind home runs by Andy Carey, Tommy Davis, and Duke Snider. The Dodger lefty liberally sprinkled his dazzling effort with 18 strikeouts, establishing a new National League record and tying the major league mark set by Bob Feller in 1938.

The Dodgers struggled early, falling behind the league-leading San Francisco Giants by as much as four games in mid-May. Then things began to click, with Koufax and Drysdale racking up victory after victory behind a well-rounded L.A. offense. Alston's buzzsaw roared through the west, destroying the Pirates, Cubs, Cardinals, and Astros along the way. Greyhounds Wills and Willie D. swiped everything but the opposing teams' uniforms, and catcher Doug Camilli, Wally Moon, the Duke, and the Davis boys supplied the punch as the Dodger rampage progressed. As May ended, L.A.'s 12-game winning streak upped their record to 34-15, a scant 1/2 game behind the Giants. Maury Wills' 27 stolen bases in 49 games had him on track to break the National League mark of 80 set in 1911.

In June, the Big Blue Machine picked up the pace. New heroes popped up almost daily. Big D., Koufax, Stan Williams, Joe Moeller, Larry Sherry, racked up wins, with Sandy pitching the Dodgers into first place with a 6-3 win over Philadelphia. On June 18, Koufax and the Cardinals' Bob Gibson hooked up in a classic pitching duel. With both future Hall of Famers throwing B-B's, the game stayed scoreless into the ninth. Then, 23-year-old Tommy Davis, en route to the National League batting championship, deposited a Gibson fastball into the distant left-field bullpen for a 1-0 win.

Two weeks later, Sandy Koufax took another step toward baseball immortality when he threw his first no-hitter, shutting out the New York Mets, 5-0. The 6'2" south-paw fanned 13 men along the way, as he recorded his 11th win of the season. The Dodgers jumped on Bob Miller for four runs in the first inning, sparked by Willie Davis' triple and singles by Tommy Davis and big Frank Howard. Howard closed out the scoring with a long home run into the left field seats in the seventh. T.D. ended the month with a solid lock on both the league batting (.339) and RBI titles (81).

A potentially outstanding season suddenly turned tragic when, it was announced, Sandy Koufax was lost for the balance of the season with a rare circulation problem in the index finger on his pitching hand. Without the 14 game winner in the rotation, Dodger pitching became overworked. The team managed to stay afloat for awhile, but the pressure caught up with them before the champagne could be popped.

Sandy Koufax and Don Drysdale are caught in a lighter moment with Roy Campanella. It was not a pleasant season for Koufax, who was lost with a finger injury, in mid-July, after running up a 13-3 record.

Big Frank Howard carried the team single-handedly for 29 games, from late June to late July, during which time he batted .382 and drove in a staggering 47 runs. Hondo's 41 RBIs for the month of July established an all-time Dodger record. Tommy Davis continued his torrid pace also, as he racked up his 100th RBI on July 20. Dur-

ing one stretch, Alston's courageous crew won 13 of 16 games to increase their lead over Alvin Dark's Giants to four games. As the month ended, L.A. had a nine-game winning streak, including a three-game sweep of the Giants. Podres beat Marichal, 3-1, behind Howard's three-run homer. Big Frank knocked in five runs the next day, and reliever Ed Roebuck ran his record to 7-0, as L.A. hung on for a hard-fought 8-6 win. Drysdale nailed down the sweep with his 19th victory, as L.A. pummeled San Fran ,11-1.

Big D. won his 20th on August 3, but time was beginning to catch up with the beleagured Dodger pitching staff. A slump early in the month, including a three-game sweep by the hated Giants, brought Walter Alston's co-horts back to the pack once again. A late-August surge opened the lead to 2 1/2 games as the stretch run began, but two losses to San Francisco and another to Pittsburgh cut the margin to a slim 1/2 game.

On September 8, the embattled blue and white made their last valiant charge. Little Maury Wills, the Dodgers' electrifying base stealer, swiped four sacks in a win over Pittsburgh to break Bob Bescher's 51-year-old National League record of 80. From there, L.A. reeled off seven wins in succession to open up another four-game lead. Six different pitchers picked up W's, an indication of the disintegration of the Dodger pitching staff.

The last two weeks of the season were a complete disaster. Sandy Koufax, attempting to come back after two months on the disabled list, was pummeled by the Cardinals, 11-2. His pitching partner, Don Drysdale, after hurling over 300 innings during the pennant race and piling up 25 victories along the way, finally ran out of gas, and the Redbirds manhandled him also, 12-2. In all, the Los Angeles team dropped 10 of their final 13 games, to finish the regular season in a tie for first with San Francisco.

The lone bright spot for the Dodgers was Maury Wills' drive to the stolen base title. He finally broke Ty Cobbs "untouchable" record September 22, by stealing bases #96 and #97.

The first playoff game, in San Francisco on October 1, saw Sandy Koufax still trying to regain his form after his long layoff but, once again, he was ineffective. Billy Pierce tossed a tight three-hitter at L.A. and the Giants prevailed in a laugher, 8-0. Willie Mays slugged two home runs, and Orlando Cepeda and Jim Davenport each hit one to spearhead the San Francisco attack.

One interesting sidelight to the game was Alvin Dark's attempt to deter Maury Wills from stealing bases in San Francisco. Dark had the ground crew soak the basepaths prior to the game to slow down the mercurial Wills. The effort didn't go unnoticed by the umpires, however. Jocko Conlon spotted puddles of water in the basepaths during his pre-game inspection, and immediately ordered the ground crew to cover the paths with dirt. The strategy proved to be unnecessary as Pierce threw the collar at little Maury.

```
Los Angeles Dodgers    0 0 0  0 0 0  0 0 0 - 0 - 3 - 1
San Francisco Giants   2 1 0  0 0 2  0 3 x - 8 - 10 - 0
```

Game Two in Los Angeles pitted the aces of the respective staffs against one another. Don Drysdale (25-9) took the mound for L.A., while Jack Sanford (24-7) got the nod from manager Al Dark. For five innings it was a tight pitchers' duel. The Giants drew first blood with a run in the second off Big D., and the score stood 1-0 after five. The Dodgers' scoreless streak had reached 35 innings, and even the most faithful fans were beginning to wonder if their team would ever score again.

When San Fran routed Drysdale with a four-run sixth, the Dodger season appeared to be over. But, once again, the battered and bloodied men of L.A. picked themselves up and fought back. Down 5-0 in the bottom of the sixth, the Alston-men mounted a valiant rally. Gilliam drew an opening walk. When Duke Snider doubled and Tommy Davis hit a sacrifice fly, the Dodgers had their first run in 36 innings. That broke the ice. Six more runs poured across the plate before the fourth Giant pitcher could stem the tide. Singles by Howard and Doug Camilli, and a double by Lee Walls were the key hits.

After San Francisco tied the game at seven-all in the eighth, L.A. pushed over the game winner in the bottom of the ninth on three walks and Ron Fairly's sacrifice fly.

```
San Francisco Giants   0 1 0  0 0 4  0 2 0 - 7 - 13 - 1
Los Angeles Dodgers    0 0 0  0 0 7  0 0 1 - 8 - 7 - 2
```

The 1962 season came down to the final game with both teams dead tired. Juan Marichal (18-11), and a noted Dodger killer, was on the hill for Darks' cohorts, while 15-game winner Johnny Podres got the call from Alston. Once again the Giants got off the mark first when they pushed over two runs against the Dodger lefty in the third inning. Two Dodger errors contributed to the scores. L.A. got one of the runs back in the bottom of the fourth, then took the lead in the sixth when Snider singled and Tommy Davis hit a two-run homer.

In the seventh, Wills singled, then proceeded to steal both second and third. He scored when catcher Ed Bailey's throw to third went wild. The score stood at 4-2 L.A., as the ninth inning got underway. With the spector of 1951 hanging over their heads, the Dodgers relied on Ed Roebuck to keep the Giants at bay. Roebuck however, was dead tired. He had pitched in all three playoff games for a total of eight innings, including three in this game, and his tank was empty. After a pinch single by Matty Alou, Roebuck managed to get Harvey Kuenn to hit into a force play. That was the last out he recorded. He walked both McCovey and Felipe Alou to load the bases, then was touched for an infield single by Mays. With L.A. up 4-3, the bases loaded and only one out, manager Walter Alston called in Stan Williams from the bullpen. The big, wild righthander retired Orlando Cepeda on a long sacrifice fly to right field to tie the game, then wild pitched the lead run to third, intentionally passed Ed Bailey to load the bases, and walked Jim Davenport unintentionally to force in the go-ahead run. A fourth run scored on an error by second baseman Larry Burright.

Down to their last three outs, the Dodgers had used up their last miracle. Sixteen game winner Billy Pierce, the shutout victor in Game One, came on to retire Wills, Gilliam, and Walls, in order to give the Giants another miracle pennant.

```
San Francisco Giants   0 0 2  0 0 0  0 0 4 - 6 - 13 - 3
Los Angeles Dodgers    0 0 0  1 0 2  1 0 0 - 4 - 8 - 4
```

It was another tragic and frustrating loss for Los Angeles. In the history of major league baseball there had been only five postseason playoffs, and the Dodgers had been involved in four of them, losing to the Cardinals in 1946, to the Giants in both 1951 and 1962, and defeating the Milwaukee Braves in 1959.

The Dodgers won 102 games. It was not enough.

As sad as the season was teamwise, it was filled with individual accolades. In addition to the single-game histrionics of Richert, Koufax, and Podres, seasonal accomplishments abounded. Don Drysdale walked off with the Cy Young award on the strength of an overpowering 25-9 season. He led the N.L. in victories, innings pitched (314), and strikeouts (232). His left-handed counterpart, Koufax, showed the way in earned run average with a sparkling 2.54. Ron Perranoski led the league in games pitched with 70, and finished second in saves with 20, behind Pittsburgh's Roy Face, who had 28. Maury Wills, on the strength of his record-shattering 104 stolen bases, edged out Willie Mays as the league's Most Valuable Player. Tommy Davis captured most of the offensive awards, leading the league in batting (.346), runs batted in (153), and hits (230).

Overall, the Los Angeles Dodgers had a spectacular season. Willie Davis led the league with 10 triples, stole 32 bases, hit 21 homers, and knocked in 85 runs. Frank Howard hit 31 homers and drove in 119 runs. Wills scored 130 runs, four behind Frank Robinson.

THE 1980 MIRACLE FINISH

After winning two successive National League pennants in 1977 and 1978, the Los Angeles Dodgers struggled through an injury-plagued year in 1979, finishing in third place, 11 1/2 games behind the Cincinnati Reds, and 10 games behind the revitalized Houston Astros.

The amazing Astros had improved their record by 15 games in 1979, and were positioned to challenge for the division title in 1980. Strengthened by the addition of future Hall of Famer Nolan Ryan to an already outstanding pitching staff, Houston seemed poised to take it all.

They got off the mark quickly in April, winning 16 of their first 22 games and, by May 5, had opened up a 2 1/2-game lead on Lasorda's crew. It was nip and tuck for the first two months, with Houston maintaining a slim lead over the rest of the pack. Then disaster struck the Texas contingent. The ace of their pitching staff, J.R. Richard, sporting a sparkling 10-4 record, was cut down with a crippling blood clot, ending his major league career in the blink of an eye. Bill Virdon's team had every right to fold then and there. But they didn't. They regrouped, dedicated their season to J.R., and went back to business as usual. Vern Ruhle, Joe Niekro, and Nolan Ryan, picked up the slack left by the devastating injury to Richard, and kept the focused Astros in first place.

One by one, the contenders dropped by the wayside. As Labor Day came and went, only the tenacious Dodgers remained in the hunt. Anchored by their record-breaking infield of Garvey, Lopes, Russell, and Cey, Los Angeles hung tough. Their pitching had bounced back dramatically from their injury-ridden 1979. Jerry Reuss led the way with 18 victories, followed by Hooton (14-8), Welch (14-9), and Don Sutton (13-5).

Catcher Joe Ferguson slammed a game-winning home run in the first game of the crucial season-ending series with Houston.

Twenty-two-year-old Steve Howe won the closer's job, by pitching in 59 games, with 17 saves and a 2.65 earned run average.

September 15 found the two teams tied for the top spot with identical records of 82-61. Don Sutton put the Dodgers one up on the 17th with a 2-1 victory over San Diego. Two days later, the Western Division leaders entered the lair of the defending National League champion Cincinnati Reds, who were out of the race and thirsting for revenge. Sparky Anderson's boys annihilated the Californians in a series sweep by scores of 10-7, 10-2, and 7-2. When Atlanta followed with a 7-2 scalping of the suddenly impotent Dodgers, things looked bleak at 1000 Elysian Park Avenue. Still, the team that would earn the nickname "Comeback Kids," because of their never-say-die rallies in 1980, 1981, and 1982, would not quit.

Facing the San Francisco Giants in the next to last series of the year, the Dodgers looked like anything but champions. They were lucky to take the first two games of the series, as they committed nine errors in the process. When the Giants bounced back to win the third game, their position looked hopeless. They had to go home to face the Houston Astros in the season's finale, trailing the league leaders by three games with just three to play. Lasorda's team needed a sweep just to force a one-game playoff.

The first game of the big series pitted veteran Don Sutton against Bob Forsch, two hard-throwing right-handers. It was a tight pitchers' duel, fitting of the circumstances. Houston held a slim 2-1 lead in the bottom

Ron Cey's dramatic seventh-inning home run in the last game of the season forced a one-game playoff in the National League Western Division.

ers, Bobby Castillo and rookie Fernando Valenzuela came on to silence the Astro's big bats and keep their team in the chase.

As the seventh inning got underway, L.A. was still down by only two runs, 3-1. Then, pinch-hitter Manny Mota did what he does best. He stroked a single to the outfield to score Pedro Guerrero with the Dodgers' second run. Still, they trailed 3-2 as the bottom of the eighth came around. They were only two innings from extinction when Enos Cabell bobbled Steve Garvey's ground ball. With more than 50,000 fans sitting nervously on the edge of their seats, Ron Cey fouled off a pitch trying to sacrifice. He fouled off a second pitch. He didn't foul off the third one. Getting a low fast ball from relief pitcher Frank LaCorte, the Penguin sent it deep to left field for a two-run homer, setting off a demonstration that threatened to bring down the walls.

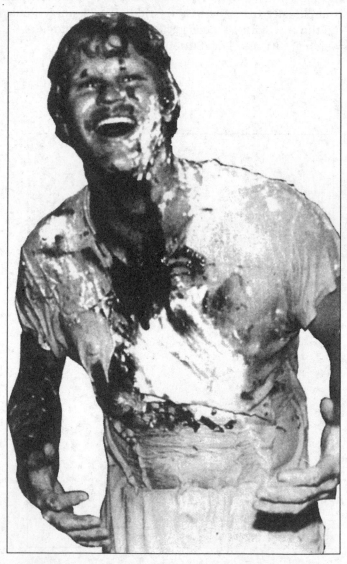

Jerry Reuss was "lathered" by his teammates after the 1981 World Series. He lathered the opponents pretty effectively in '82, winning 18 games.

of the eighth inning when the "Penguin," Ron Cey, slashed a single up the middle to tie the score. Two innings later, catcher Joe Ferguson hit a towering home run to left field off Forsch to win the game, 3-2, and send 49,642 Dodger fans home happy. A baby-faced, 20-year-old rookie left hander named Fernando Valenzuela pitched two shutout innings in relief of Sutton to pick up the win, his second in the major leagues.

The next day, Jerry Reuss toed the rubber for Los Angeles, facing the flame-throwing righthander of Bill Virdon's staff, Nolan Ryan. Once again, runs were hard to come by. L.A. pushed across one in the second, but Houston came back with a run in the top of the fourth to tie. In the bottom of the same inning, "Mr. Clutch," Steve Garvey, caught hold of a Ryan fastball, and drilled it 360 feet into the Dodger bullpen. That was all Reuss needed. He shut down the Astros the rest of the way, striking out seven men en route.

Suddenly the momentum had shifted. Now, it seemed, the pressure was on Houston. Los Angeles was on a roll, and would be hard to stop from here on. Dodger Stadium was rocking as Game Three got underway, with 52,339 sun worshippers packing every nook and cranny of the big park. Houston wasted no time in taking the crowd out of the game, knocking Burt Hooton out of the box in a two-run second inning. Fortunately for the Dodg-

The unbelievable had happened. The Dodgers, who had trailed Houston by three games on Friday, now found themselves in a flat-footed tie for first place as the season came to a close on Sunday evening. The entire season now came down to a single playoff game, to be held in Dodger Stadium on Monday, October 6 at 1 PM.

The playoff was anti-climatic. Houston did not fold. And the Dodgers could not sustain their momentum. Joe Niekro, the 35-year-old knuckleballer handcuffed the L.A. offense with his tantalizing array of pitches, and his teammates hammered Dodger starter Dave Goltz unmercifully in his three innings of work. Big first baseman Art Howe provided the fireworks for Bill Virdon's team, with a two-run homer in the third and a two-run single in the fourth. Houston won easily, 7-1.

It was a disappointing finish to a thrilling season, but Tommy Lasorda's team covered themselves with glory in a lost cause. They never quit. Even when they were laid low with injuries to Reggie Smith and Bill Russell down the stretch; even when the injury jinx struck Lopes, Baker, and Cey on the last weekend; and even when the Penguin was lost for the playoff, the Dodgers believed they could win it all. They almost did.

1982—THE FIFTEEN-DAY MIRACLE

The year 1982 provided another chapter in the exciting annals of "Team Comeback." The 1980 edition of the Kardiac Kids had deadlocked the pennant race on the last day of the season by completing a three-game sweep of the first-place Houston Astros. Another series of come-from-behind miracles, in 1981, rewarded the Los Angeles Dodgers with, first a Western Division title, then a National League pennant, and finally a World Championship.

The 1982 blue and white followed in the footsteps of their illustrious predecessors. In keeping with the tradition of "Team Comeback," Tommy Lasorda's boys left the gate more like the turtle than the hare. The surprising Atlanta Braves, meanwhile, came out with all guns blazing and, before anyone could react, they reeled off a record-breaking 13 wins in succession. By April 22, the Dodgers stood at 6-8 and were already mired in third place, 7 1/2 games behind Joe Torre's gladiators.

The Dodgers hobbled to a dreary 10-11 record in April, followed by 15-13 in May, and 16-12 in July. As the halfway mark approached on July 4th, L.A. was still in third place with an unexciting 41-38 record, and were still seven full games behind the Braves. Three and a half weeks later, things looked even bleaker. A 11-13 mark left them further behind, a distant 10 1/2 games out of first. To make matters worse, the battered Los Angeles contingent had to visit Atlanta for a four-game weekend series with the league-leaders.

Suddenly, as often happens in the mysterious game of baseball, the dark clouds drifted away and the sun came shining through. The two teams, Atlanta and Los Angeles, flip-flopped. One team, Atlanta, could do nothing right, and the other, Los Angeles, could do no wrong. L.A.'s extraordinary voyage to the top began with a double header on Friday evening, July 30.

Second baseman Davey Lopes, shown with manager Tommy Lasorda, anchored the infield and stole 23 bases during the season.

A raucous sellout crowd of 47,787 Atlanta fans crammed into Braves Stadium to watch their beloved Braves put away those awful Dodgers once and for all. Game One began like an Atlanta runaway. Torre's tigers rocked L.A. starter, Jerry Reuss, for six runs on nine hits in three innings. After four the Braves were up, 6-1. After five, it was 8-3. With Atlanta relief ace, Steve Bedrosian, on the hill, it looked like another easy Atlanta win. But such was not the case. In the seventh, Lasorda's somnolent sluggers suddenly awoke from a season-long sleep, and rose up to face their tormentors. A two-run pinch single by Ron Roenicke and Ken Landreaux's second two-run homer of the game highlighted a five-run Dodger uprising to give the west coast warriors the lead. Steve Howe, on in relief of eventual winner Terry Forster, shackled the Braves with one run over the last four innings to record his 11th save of the season.

Bob Welch made it a clean sweep for Los Angeles by throwing a six-hitter at Atlanta, winning easily, 8-2. Dodger bats came to life for the first time in weeks as Ron Cey hit a double and homer good for three RBIs, Steve Garvey stroked two singles and drove in three runs, Steve Sax hit a double and a home run and drove in two runs, and Dusty Baker hit three singles and scored three runs.

The next day, Fernando Valenzuela racked up his 14th victory of the season with a six-hit shutout, and the Dodgers prevailed again, 3-0. Dusty Baker provided all the offensive support El Toro needed when he deposited a Pascual Perez fastball into the left field seats in the top of the fourth inning. Rookie Steve Sax knocked in two insurance runs with a fifth-inning single.

The Braves were still confident as Sunday rolled around. They still had a comfortable 7 1/2-game lead and they could lengthen it to 8 1/2 with a victory in the finale. Four big runs in the first off the Dodger starter gave the tribe a big lift, but the Californians were unimpressed. Dusty Baker and Pedro Guerrero hit back-to-back home runs in the seventh to give L.A. the lead, and Baker hit another one in the eighth as the Big Blue Machine rolled, 9-4. Righthander Dave Stewart (6-6) got the victory with four innings of shutout relief.

It was apparent now that the Braves were enmeshed in their first slump of the season, while the Dodgers were beginning to get untracked. Atlanta's 6 1/2-game lead with 57 games remaining in the season was not nearly as secure as a 10 1/2-game lead would be. Tommy Lasorda's boys took a day off on Monday, August 2, and Mario Soto of the Cincinnati Reds made them pay for it with a 5-1 route-going effort. Atlanta's 7-3 drubbing of San Fransisco moved their lead back up to 7 1/2.

But it was all a mirage. By the time Thursday rolled around, the lead was back down to six, and Torre's embattled Braves had to enter the L.A. lion's den for a four-game weekend series. A full house packed Dodger Stadium to watch Fernando Valenzuela do battle with the Dodgers' east coast enemy in the opener. Fittingly, it was a pitchers' duel as the two adversaries maneuvered for

position. The game was tied at two all in the top of the sixth when Fernando had to leave the game after being hit by a line drive off the bat of Bob Horner. Dodger relievers, however, were up to the challenge, keeping the Atlanta bats silent through the seventh, eighth, ninth and tenth innings. When Steve Sax stepped into the batter's box to lead off the bottom of the tenth, the score was unchanged. The Dodger second baseman immediately spanked a single to right field and continued on to second when Atlanta rightfielder Claudell Washington bobbled the ball. Joe Torre ordered both Ken Landreaux and Pedro Guerrero walked intentionally to load the bases, but it was to no avail. Ron Cey drove a 1-2 pitch to center field, and Sax coasted home with the winning run.

The loss was a bitter pill for the Braves to swallow, opening up a crucial four-game series with their rivals. The slide continued the next day also as L.A. again eked out an extra-inning victory, this time 5-4 in ten innings. Torre's troops were reeling now, having lost four in a row and eight of nine. Their lead, a once-insurmountable 10 1/2 games, now stood at a shaky 3 1/2. And the Dodgers were charging hard, with two games yet to go in the series.

The Saturday game was another cliffhanger, with L.A.'s luck remaining intact. The Penguin, Ron Cey cracked his 15th home run of the season, and Steve Garvey hit three singles as the Blue and White took a 7-6, 11-inning thriller from the harried Tribe. Rookie Joe Beckwith was credited with his second victory of the season after hurling two innings of shutout relief.

Bob Welch completed the massacre the next day as he whitewashed the Georgians, 2-0, for his 13th win of the season. The Dodgers scored the only run Welch needed in the very first inning when Ken Landreaux singled, stole second, and came around on a single to right field by Pedro Guerrero. The L.A. centerfielder also scored the second run. He reached first on a force play in the eighth inning, stole second again, and raced home when Dusty Baker rifled a single to left field.

The entire southern California corridor was ecstatic at the recent turn of events. A drab, commonplace season had suddenly turned into a heated pennant race in the short period of ten days. Tommy Lasorda's darlings, once the embarrassments of the west coast, now found themselves only 1 1/2 games out of first place with 50 games left to go. The team had won 10 of 11 and six in a row, and there was no end in sight. Everything was jelling for the Big Blue Machine and they were geared for a big finish.

The good times continued to roll for L.A. on the day after the Atlanta series, as Russ Nixon's Cincinnati Redlegs came to town. The Reds were only a shadow of their former selves, having plummeted all the way from first place in 1981 to the celler in 1982. Their miseries continued in California as the Dodgers managed to salvage another squeaker, this time 3-2 in 13 inings. Big Dave Stewart, a flame-throwing right hander was the hero, stifling the Reds with six innings of hitless relief. His effort was rewarded when Pedro Guerrero hit the first pitch thrown to him for a game-winning home run in the bottom of the 13th. When the Braves were three-hit by Jim Barr of the San Francisco Giants 5-0, the lead was down to a mere 1/2 game.

Tuesday, August 8, was a red-letter day in Los Angeles as the Dodgers completed their dizzying dash to the top of the National League. The final assault came when Atlanta lost to San Francisco, 3-2,while Los Angeles routed Cincinnati. Milt May's seventh-inning home run spelled disaster for the Atlanteans, while the Dodgers toyed with Nixon's charges, 11-3. Fernando Valenzuela tossed a six-hit complete game at the Redlegs, and Dodger bats played havoc with Cincy pitchers. Monday hit homer #8, Garvey socked #12, Bill Russell recorded a single and a double and knocked in three runs, and Ron Roenicke had two RBIs. Two Dodger runs in the seventh and five more in the eighth broke open a close contest.

The rout continued on the 11th, 12th, and 13th. Two more Dodger wins and three Atlanta losses moved the L.A. lead to 2 1/2 games. In the most astounding turn-around in major league history, Tommy Lasorda's streaking sluggers had reeled off 14 wins in 16 games while, at the same time, Joe Torre's ineffective Injuns were dropping 15 of 16, a flip-flop of 13 full games in the standings. From a third-place position, 10 1/2 games behind the league-leading Atlanta Braves, on July 30, the blue and white found themselves leading the pack by 2 1/2 games on the morning of August 14.

Steve Howe had another strong year, with 13 saves and a 2.09 ERA in 66 games. (Los Angeles Dodger Photo)

Dodger fans were euphoric at the sudden turn of events. The general feeling throughout southern California was that the National League pennant race was as good as over. They forgot that there were still 45 games to play. They forgot, also, that Joe Torre's young charges were not about to roll over and play dead. Even after 11 straight losses, Brett Butler, Dale Murphy, Bob Horner, et al, kept focused on the job at hand–to get back into the hunt.

On Wednesday, August 18, L.A. extended their lead once again, which now stood four games to the good. A double victory over the Chicago Cubs included a marathon that took two days to complete. The Tucsday game was suspended after 17 innings with the score knotted at 1-1. A Cubby run in the first was offset by a second-inning Dodger score. For the next 15 innings, no one could dent the plate, and the game was carried over until the following evening. Jerry Reuss pitched the last four innings of the suspended game, then started the regularly scheduled game, going another five innings before retiring.

The suspended game took some strange twists before finally coming to an end. L.A. emptied its bench in the 20th inning when their 25th and last man, Fernando Valenzuela, was pressed into action in right field following the ejection of Ron Cey. Mercifully, Dusty Baker's sacrifice fly scored Steve Sax with the winning run in the 21st inning, ending the agony, and rewarding Jerry Reuss with his ninth victory. Three hours later, the blond southpaw picked up his tenth win, a 7-4 triumph. Pedro Guerrero's two-run homer in the first got the Dodgers off winging in the regular game, and his second round-tripper, #25, in the fifth, put the icing on the cake.

August was a torturous month for Joe Torre's beleagured Braves but, as the month headed toward its climax, the big bats of Murphy and Horner came to life again, and the aching pitching arms of Joe Niekro and Gene Garber became revitalized. The lines were drawn and the final battle for league supremacy got underway in earnest. On the 29th, the boys from Atlanta moved back into first place by the smallest of margins and, from then until the end of the season, the two teams jockeyed for position.

On the final Friday of the season, L.A., trailing Atlanta by one game, zipped Frisco, 4-0, behind Jerry Reuss, while the Braves kept pace with a win over the Padres. The following day, the Dodgers eliminated the Giants from the race as they rolled to a 15-2 victory behind Bob Welch's 16th win. Again the Braves won. On the last Sunday, Fernando Valenzuela got the nod in search of his 20th victory of the year. Ron Cey gave El Toro the lead in the second inning when he picked out a Bill Laskey fast ball and deposited it over the left-field wall with Steve Garvey on base. The Giants bounced right back. Aided by Fernando's wildness, they put two walks and two singles together to knot the count.

The 22-year-old Mexican southpaw settled down after his brief bout of wildness and pitched a strong game through six, when he was lifted for a pinch hitter. A loud scream went up around Candlestick Park in that inning when the scoreboard showed the Braves on the short end of a 5-1 score. The playoff was there for the taking as far as the Dodgers were concerned, but they couldn't pull the trigger. In the bottom of the seventh, with Tom Niedenfuer on to pitch, Bob Brenly singled and Champ Summers doubled, putting runners on second and third with no one out. Niedenfuer reared back and fanned both Minton and Wolford at that point, and the rally appeared over. When 39-year-old Joe Morgan stepped to the plate, Tommy Lasorda went to the bullpen for lefthander Terry Forster. Morgan was not intimidated. In fact, he got all of a 1-2 pitch and sent it on a line into the right-field stands for a 5-2 Giant lead.

That was the season. The Dodgers threatened in the seventh, loading the bases with one out, but Russell struck out and Jorge Orta grounded out to snuff out the rally. In the eighth, they pushed across one run to cut the deficit to 5-3, but that's where it stood when the final curtain came down.

It was a great pennant race, and one that typified the game of baseball. It showed once again that nothing can be taken for granted in baseball. When all was said and done, perhaps the best team won after all. Certainly Torres' Braves showed true character when they rebounded after their August debacle. After losing 19 of 21 games over a three-week span, the young warriors took 26 of their last 43 to clinch the pennant.

1983—HOW THE WEST WAS WON— BUT THE N.L. WAS LOST

The Los Angeles Dodgers of 1983 were a strange breed, a mixture of aging veterans and untested rookies. The L.A. all-time longest performing infield was a thing of the past. Davey Lopes had departed for Oakland after the '81 season. Now, Steve Garvey and Ron Cey were also missing. Garvey was attired in San Diego orange and brown when the season opened, while the Penguin cavorted around the infield in Chicago's Wrigley Field. In their places were names like Greg Brock, Steve Sax and Mike Marshall.

Tommy Lasorda's team was a Jeckyl-and-Hyde outfit. It was always a question of whether the Dodger pitchers could hold the opposition to fewer runs than the leaky L.A. infield would let in. Fortunately for L.A. fans, the pitching staff was, once again, the class of the league. They were led by Fernando Valenzuela (15-10, 3.75), Bob Welch (15-12, 2.65), Jerry Reuss (12-11, 2.94), and Alejandro Pena (12-9, 2.75). Tom "Buff" Niedenfuer was the mainstay of the bullpen, appearing in 66 games, with an 8-3 record, 11 saves, and a 1.90 earned run average. Steve Howe, in 46 games, was 4-7 with 18 saves and a 1.44 ERA.

On the other side of the ledger, the 2nd-3rd combination of Steve Sax and Pedro Guerrero was a disaster. Sax went through a torturous season where he couldn't even make a routine toss to first base. And Guerrero never did get comfortable at third. He eventually returned to the outfield early in 1984. But, in '83, every ball hit to the infield was an adventure. Guerrero was once quoted as saying, "Just before the pitcher throws the ball, I look up and say, 'please God, don't let the batter hit the ball to me.' Then I look around the infield and say, 'and don't let him hit it to Sax, either'."

Unfortunately, too many batters hit the ball to either Sax or Guerrero. The Dodgers finished next to last in errors in a 12-team league, committing 166 miscues in only 162 games. The infield contributed 91 errors to that total, including 29 by Guerrero and 30 by second baseman Sax.

In spite of the many defensive problems the Dodgers were confronted with, the team got away from the gate quickly, piling up a record of 18-5 by May 8, and settling into first place. A typical L.A. game was played at Dodger Stadium on May 6, against the St. Louis Cardinals. The Dodgers jumped on top early, 6-0, then saw their ace, Fernando Valenzuela, KO'd in the fourth as the Cards tied the count at 6-6. L. A. rallied again, recapturing the lead at 9-6, but again they couldn't hold it, and the Redbirds got even at 9-9. Finally, the blue and white added another three spot and held on to win, 16-10. All their games weren't that high scoring, of course, but they were all dog-fights. And the Dodgers were winning most of them.

Steve Garvey's successor, Greg Brock, was a major reason for the early Dodger surge. He got off to a blazing start, with nine home runs and 28 RBIs in the first 35 games. On May 18, the 25-year-old slugger hit two homers and drove in six runs in a 13-3 rout of the Montreal Expos. The win upped L.A.'s record to 25-10, and stretched their lead to three games over the Atlanta Braves. Many people accused Lasorda of doing it with mirrors, since the team didn't appear to be particularly impressive, especially in the infield. In spite of the shoddy defense, the Dodger manager said, "We're getting key hits, we're getting the big play on defense, and we're getting good relief pitching."

A sad footnote to the Dodger season saw relief pitcher Steve Howe miss six weeks, from May 17 to June 29, for drug rehabilitation. It was his second trip to "The Meadows" in Arizona in less than three months. He had missed most of spring training for the same problem.

June was no better than a .500 month for Lasorda's boys, as their 16-16 record left them in a flat-footed tie with the Braves. The miseries continued in July as Houston started off the month by stopping the blue and white three out of four in the Astrodome. After the Dodgers took a 10-inning thriller in the opener on Dusty Baker's bases-loaded double off the left-field wall, the Astro's copped the last three, by scores of 3-1, 8-1, and 5-4, knocking L.A. out of first place for the first time in over two months.

On July 27, after suffering through a depressing 4-15 slump, Los Angeles fell 4 1/2 games behind the Braves. By August 16, the deficit had reached 6 1/2. Then the momentum changed again, and the Dodgers got their second wind. A noisy, closed-door clubhouse meeting, following a 9-2 loss to Cincinnati, turned things around for the California team. First, manager Tommy Lasorda read the riot act to the team; then veterans Bill Russell and Rick Monday lectured the young players on team-work and dedication. The meeting brought the team to-gether as a unit, and they immediately went on an eight-game winning streak that catapulted them back into con-tention. By August 29, the surging Dodgers had moved back into first place.

Eleven days later, Joe Torre's Braves came to town for a crucial three-game series. Dodger pitching saved the day in Game One, as Alejandro Peña hurled seven scoreless en route to a 3-2 triumph. The tall, slim righty did most of the offensive damage himself, singling in two runs off Phil Niekro in the second inning. Steve Howe recorded his 18th save. Atlanta took Game Two, 6-3, but the Lasorda-men captured the rubber game, 7-6, with a four-run rally in the bottom of the ninth. Mike Marshall's two-run double tied the score, and rookie R.J. Reynold's squeeze bunt brought in Guerrero with the game winner.

The Braves had one more chance to overtake their west coast rivals, entertaining Lasorda's cohorts during the last week of the season. L.A. arrived in Atlanta Sta-dium sporting a 4 1/2-game lead, and it was imperative that Torre's crew sweep the series if they harbored any hopes of a pennant. The Dodgers ended that possibility quickly, when Jerry Reuss took the opener, and L.A. rolled, 11-2. Landreaux, Baker, and Guerrero all homered in the rout, with Dusty knocking in four runs. The Braves came back to take the last two games of the series, win-ning 3-2 with a run in the bottom of the ninth in Game Two, then taking the rubber game, 7-1. But it was too little, too late. L.A. took the Western Division title by three games.

For L.A., the title was a true team effort. There were no league leaders in any individual category. It was a case of well-balanced mediocrity combined with master personnel maneuvering by manager Tommy Lasorda. Pedro Guerrero, a rising superstar, was the most valuable Dodger, on the strength of a .298 batting average, 32 home runs and 103 runs-batted-in.

Steve Yeager belted 15 home runs in just 335 at bats to help the Dodgers edge out Atlanta for the Western Division title.

Steve Sax and Bill Russell were two valuable members of the Los Angeles inner defense. (W. McNeil)

Mike Marshall had his ups and downs during the first half of the year, but settled down and hit over .300 during the last half. Sax overcame his throwing prob-lems in time to thrill fans with great plays in August and September. Rookie catcher Jack Fimple came up mid-year to rescue a wounded Dodger catching staff and con-tribute mightily to the pennant drive. The pitching ran hot and cold. Valenzuela did well, but was not the Fernando of '81 or '82. Welch was the ace, and was the most consistent down the stretch. Peña came of age in time to keep the staff afloat. Reuss was in and out. Hooton and Howe were out of the lineup much of the season. Howe was suspended again on September 23, and entered the Care Unit in Orange County. Tom Niedenfuer was called upon to put out fire after fire, and did his job superbly. In the end, lots of guts and some timely plays brought the Dodgers home first in the West.

Their adversaries in the NLCS were the Philadelphia Phils, a team they had handled with ease during the season, winning 11 of 12 contests. Dodger pitchers blanked the Philadelphians five times, threw eight complete games at them, and outscored them, 49-15. Not to be overlooked, however, was the fact that the Dodgers caught the Phils during their two worst slumps of the year. In May and early June, when L.A. took six games from Pat Corrales' team, the Phils were in the midst of a 4-19 plunge. L.A. won two more in late August when the Phils were going 1-9.

Rookie Mike Marshall overcame an early-season slump, to finish the year with 17 home runs, 65 RBIs and a .284 batting average. (W. McNeil)

Under new manager Paul Owens, however, Philadelphia had won 47 of their last 77 games, including a 22-7 run in September. Having won 14 of their last 16 games, they were the hottest team in the majors when the regular season ended. And they were ready for L.A.

Both teams were confident, as lanky southpaw, Steve Carlton, faced off against Jerry Reuss in Dodger Stadium in Game One. With two out in the top of the first, third baseman Mike Schmidt took a Reuss offering downtown,

propelling the Phils to an early 1-0 advantage, and silencing the 49,963 Dodger rooters. The lead held up inning after inning as the 6'4" Carlton neutralized L.A.'s bats. Then, in the eighth, the Dodgers rallied. A one-out single by Steve Sax, and a two-out single by Dusty Baker brought the fans to their feet. When Steve Carlton walked Pedro Guerrero to load the bases, relief pitcher Al Holland was summoned to the mound. The stocky southpaw, who had racked up 25 saves during the season, did his job again, retiring Mike Marshall on a fly ball to center fielder, Garry Maddox.

Philadelphia Phils	1 0 0 000 000 -	1 - 5 - 1
Los Angeles Dodgers	0 0 0 000 000 -	0 - 7 - 0

Manager Tommy Lasorda handed the ball to his 22-year-old screwball artist, Fernando Valenzuela, to stop the slide. The portly Mexican lefty was up to the task as he kept the Phils in check for eight + innings. After L.A. pushed over the first run in the opening inning, Gary Matthews got the Phils even with a long home run into the left-field stands in the second. Pedro Guerrero delivered the eventual game-winning blow in the fifth inning when he tripled off 19-game winner, John Denny, for two runs. The Dodgers added another run in the eighth, on a Jack Fimple single, extending the lead to 4-1. The gutsy Valenzuela ran out of gas in the ninth, putting the first two men on base, but Tom Niedenfuer came on to retire three men in a row, two on strikes, to preserve the victory.

Philadelphia Phils	0 1 0 000 000 -	1 - 7 - 2
Los Angeles Dodgers	1 0 0 020 01x -	4 - 6 - 1

The best-of-five series was all even as the two teams broke camp and headed for the City of Brotherly Love for the final three games. The Dodgers had 15-game winner Bob Welch, their most consistent pitcher down the stretch, ready to do battle with rookie righthander Charles Hudson. The game turned out to be the pivotal game of the series. Welch lasted only into the second inning, when the Phils pushed over two runs without the benefit of a hit. With one out, Welch walked two men before a hip injury sent him to the bench, and sent the Dodgers into deep depression. A lackadaisical Alejandro Peña relieved the Dodger starter, and immediately watched both runs score on a wild pitch, a passed ball, and an infield grounder.

Down 3-0 in the fourth, L.A. narrowed the gap to 3-2 when Mike Marshall smashed a two-run homer off Hudson. That was it for the Dodgers, however, as Gary Matthews took control of the game. The fleet-footed leftfielder hit a solo home run in the bottom of the fourth off Peña, stroked a two-run single off Honeycutt in the fifth, and added another run-scoring single off Pat Zachry in the seventh, as the Phils rolled to a 7-2 triumph.

Mike Scioscia was a tough defensive catcher for 13 years. He has been rated by many experts as the all-time greatest catcher at blocking the plate. (Los Angeles Dodger Photo)

| Los Angeles Dodgers | 000 200 000 - 2 - 4 - 0 |
| Philadelphia Phils | 021 120 10x - 7 - 9 - 1 |

Tommy Lasorda's team was reeling and disorganized as they took the field for Game Four. Their confidence shattered, their concentration missing, they were ripe for the picking; and "Lefty" Carlton did the honors with help from Gary Matthews. Paul Owens' club pummeled Dodger starter Jerry Reuss in the very first inning, when Matthews blasted a three-run homer behind singles by Schmidt and Lezcano. Dusty Baker's home run accounted for L.A.'s lone run in the fourth. Then the flood gates opened again. Mike Schmidt doubled in one run in the bottom of the fifth, and came around to score himself on a ground ball by Maddox. Sixto Lexcano closed out the scoring with a two-run shot off Rick Honeycutt in the sixth.

Bob Welch, a 15-game winner during the season, was KO'd in less than two innings by Philadelphia in the playoffs.(Los Angeles Dodger Photo)

Ron Reed and Al Holland finished off Carlton's final-game victory, yielding only an unearned run in the eighth, as Philadelphia won the National League championship in convincing fashion, 7-2. Jerry Reuss' loss brought his NLCS record to a dismal 0-6.

| Los Angeles Dodgers | 000 100 010 - 2 -10 - 0 |
| Philadelphia Phils | 300 022 00x - 7 -13 - 1 |

Nineteen eighty-three had been a rollercoaster ride for Tommy Lasorda's rag-tag crew. Plagued by a porous defense, riddled by injuries, and hampered by inexperience, the Dodgers nevertheless gave their fans another exciting pennant race. In their typical never-say-die manner, L.A. scratched and clawed their way to the top of the National League West, and fought off the challenge of the defending champion Atlanta Braves, to represent their division in the Championship Series. Unfortunately, the proud Dodgers could not win it all. They had the heart. They just didn't have enough talent.

1985—THE OZZIE AND JACK SHOW

The 1985 Dodgers were a team of question marks as the season got underway. The 1984 club had plummeted to fourth place, compiling the unenviable record of 79-83. Their defensive problems continued as they finished next to last in fielding with 163 errors. The offense sputtered also, thanks to the season-long batting slumps of Sax, Brock, Marshall, and Landreaux, and the demise of Bill Russell as an everyday player. The team was last in the league in runs scored, and it was a credit to their pitching staff that they managed to finish as high as fourth.

Spring training got off to an inauspicious start for Lasorda's team when it lost Alejandro Peña, the league's ERA leader, for three months with a shoulder injury. Still, the Dodgers had an encouraging spring, compiling a strong 16-11 record in Florida. It all turned around, however, when the bell rang for the regular season. Injuries decimated the club from the start, with Sax, Russell, Welch and Brock all on the injured list. Forced to play Guerrero at third base again, and with a patchwork infield, the errors mounted as April came to an end. Twenty-three errors in 21 games, and a sputtering offense, resulted in a mediocre 11-10 record for the first month. Surprisingly, that still gave the Dodgers a share of first place.

Mariano Duncan, a 22-year-old second baseman from the Dominican Republic, was called up to the big club on April 15 to replace the injured Steve Sax. When Sax returned, Duncan was shifted to shortstop to spell aging veteran Bill Russell. Duncan was flashy but erratic, and his 30 errors contributed to the Dodgers' league-leading total of 166. His speed did pick up the offense, however, and he hit a game-winning home run in his major league debut, as L.A. beat Houston, 5-3.

Pitching, as usual, kept the Dodgers afloat early. Fernando Valenzuela began the season by pitching 41 1/3 innings without allowing an earned run. His 2-3 record for the month, in spite of a barely visible 0.23 earned run average, is directly attributable to L.A.'s poor defense and paltry offense. The L.A. whiffers managed to score just eight runs in his five starts.

Orel Hershiser, with a 3-0 record, and a 1.83 ERA, helped the Dodger pitching staff compile a 2.62 ERA for

The Dodgers' slugging duo of Mike Marshall and Greg Brock combined for 49 home runs and 161 runs batted in during the season.(W. McNeil)

turn to the outfield, Duncan's insertion at shortstop, and the third-base play of Bob Bailor and Dave Anderson.

The most noticeable difference was in Pedro Guerrero. Seemingly relaxed after being returned to his more familiar left field spot, the Dominican slugger immediately went on a hitting rampage. In 25 games, the 5'11" right-handed hitter crushed the ball at a torrid .344 clip, with 15 home runs, 26 runs-batted-in, and 27 runs scored, en route to winning the National League's Player of the Month award. Guerrero's home run binge, a new Los Angeles record, tied him with Babe Ruth, Bob Johnson, and Roger Maris, for the most home runs hit in the month of June.

For all intents and purposes, June was the beginning of the pennant race for Tommy Lasorda's cohorts. They bounced back with a 15-10 record, leaving them in second place, five games behind the Padres. The defense continued to improve, making only 15 miscues in 25 games, and the offense increased their runs-per-game average from 2.7 in April to 4.4. With Pedro Guerrero showing the way, the L.A. long-ball squad deposited 25 dingers into the distant reaches of the various National League parks.

the month "Bulldog" just missed a no-hitter on April 26 when he one-hit the San Diego Padres, 2-0. A ground ball through the right side of the infield by Tony Gwynn was the only blemish on Hershiser's performance. Pedro Guerrero's two-run double in the second provided all the runs the lanky righthander needed.

If April was discouraging, May was outright depressing. Tommy Lasorda's cohorts could do nothing right. The shoddy defensive play contributed 39 errors for the month, bringing the Dodgers total of miscues to 62 in just 47 games, a pace that would project to reach 207 by season's end. On May 3, with Bill Russell throwing three balls away, the west coast team was blitzed by the Pittsburgh Pirates, 16-2, their most humiliating defeat in 18 years. In one eight-game span, the bumbling Dodgers went 1-7 with 10 errors, gave up 13 unearned runs, and were outscored, 45-20.

Miraculously, in spite of their miserable defense and a sorry .230 team batting average, Los Angeles managed to finish the month with a so-so record of 23-24. Thanks to their courageous pitching staff, they were still within striking distance of the first-place San Diego Padres, sitting in fourth place, a mere 5 1/2 games from the top.

As the weather got hot, so did the Dodgers. The defense, which had all but scuttled the team ship during the first two months, suddenly settled down and played solid baseball. The team that had committed 62 errors in 47 games, made only 104 errors over the last 115 games! The improvement coincided with Pedro Guerrero's re-

Thrity-four-year-old Bill Madlock, a late-season pickup, helped power the Dodgers to the division title, by hitting a torrid .360 over the last 34 games.(W. McNeil)

A 20-7 surge, representing their best July in 22 years, propelled them to the top of the heap. The hitters continued to zero in on the opposing pitchers, stepping up their run production to a solid 5.1 runs per game. With the offense, defense and pitching all coming together for the first time, Tommy Lasorda's fired-up contenders, captured first place on July 13 with a convincing 9-1 win at Chicago. At the All-Star break, L.A. held a slim 1/2 game lead. By month's end, the lead was up to five.

The momentum continued through August as the Big Blue Machine became increasingly confident. Vice President Al Campanis added some late-season bench strength when he acquired Len Matuszek, Enos Cabell, and Bill "Mad Dog" Madlock. Madlock was immediately inserted into the lineup at third base, and went on a .360 tear for the rest of the season.

The September stretch run began with the Dodgers comfortably ahead by seven games. A potential catastrophe hit the team early in the month when Pedro Guerrero went down with a wrist injury, shelving him for 17 days. Big Mike Marshall stepped into the breach however, batting .422 with six homers and 20 RBIs over a 10-game span. Bill Madlock also picked up the slack, rattling off a 17-game hitting streak. By September 14, the Guerrero-less Dodgers had, nevertheless, won seven of 10, and opened up a 9 1/2 game bulge over Cincinnati. Pete Rose's fighting Redlegs closed to within 4 1/2 on September 20, but could get no closer as the mighty Dodger pitching staff kept the opposition at bay.

On October 2, in Dodger Stadium, Lasorda's cohorts captured their fifth Western Division title in nine years with a convincing 9-3 rout of the Atlanta Braves. Orel Hershiser had the honor of pitching the clincher.

L.A. had little time to savor the championship. They had to ready themselves for the National League Championship Series against the Eastern Division kings, the St. Louis Cardinals. Whitey Herzog's rambunctious Redbirds had rolled to 101 victories, to edge the New York Mets by three games. St. Louis was a well-balanced ballclub. Their defense was the pride of the National League. Led by shortstop Ozzie "The Wizard of Oz" Smith, they made only 108 miscues, 58 less than the Dodgers. Their offense, too, was outstanding, as they led the league in both batting average and runs scored. They were a team of rabbits, finishing last in home runs with 87, but stealing the amazing total of 314 bases, the most in the National League in 73 years. Rookie Vince Coleman was the #1 rabbit, as he stole 110 bases.

Game One of the NLCS was played in Los Angeles on Wednesday, October 9, before a packed house of 55,270. For awhile, it looked like the series would be a nice, easy stroll to the National League title for Lasorda's Dodgers. Fernando Valenzuela got the blue and white off and running with a workmanlike 6 1/3 inning effort, backed up by the omnipresent Niedenfuer. Surprisingly, the Dodgers beat St. Louis with speed and defense. They outstole Herzog's rabbits, 3-1, while making several scintillating

plays in the field. Rookie Mariano Duncan rose to the occasion with some magic of his own. In the third inning, he charged Herr's hopper over the mound, making a bare hand pickup and throwing the runner out by a step. In the seventh, he choked off a St. Louis rally by making an inning-ending unassisted double play.

St. Louis Cardinals	000 000 100	- 1 - 8 - 1
Los Angeles Dodgers	000 103 00x	- 4 - 8 - 0

Orel Hershiser maintained the momentum in Game Two as he outpitched Joaquin Andujar, 8-2. This time it was Dodger power and Mike Scioscia that did Whitey Herzog's Redbirds in. The L.A. catcher gunned down both Vince Coleman and Willie McGee trying to steal in the first inning, effectively shutting down the Cardinal of-

Carlos Diaz gave the Dodgers valuable left-handed strength out of the bullpen, appearing in 46 games, with a 2.61 earned run average.(W. McNeil)

fense. The Dodgers, meanwhile, rattled Andujar early. After St. Louis jumped to a 1-0 lead in the third, Lasorda's boys bounced right back. An error by the Cardinal pitcher, a single by Hershiser, a double by Landreaux, and a single by Madlock, accounted for three big runs. In the fourth, Greg Brock hit a two-run homer into the right-field pavillion, giving Hershiser a big 5-1 cushion. That was all the Dodger righty needed, although his teammates added three more runs to the onslaught, one in the fifth, and two in the sixth.

St. Louis Cardinals   0 0 1 0 0 0 0 0 1 - 2 - 8 - 1
Los Angeles Dodgers   0 0 3 2 1 2 0 0 x - 8 -13 - 1

The Dodgers were a loose crew as they departed for Cardinal country, confident that they would wrap the series up in four straight. They underestimated the courage of the Redbirds. Manager Whitey Herzog handed the ball to 18-game winner Danny Cox, and the big, 6'4", 235-pound righthander was more than ready. Bob Welch, in another of his postseason disasters, gave up two quick runs in the first. After Vince Coleman singled to left, Welch walked Willie McGee, then threw wild on a pickoff attempt at second. Coleman raced around to score with McGee going to third. He crossed the plate moments later on an infield out.

In the Cardinal second, they added two more runs to their cushion. Vince coleman walked with one out. A wild pickoff throw by Scioscia sent the Cardinal speedster racing around to third. Willie McGee singled in Coleman, but then was cut down at second on a steal attempt. Tommy Herr followed with a home run. The Dodgers pecked away with single runs in the fourth and seventh, but Cox and the Cardinal bullpen allowed them to get no closer. The 4-2 victory narrowed the L.A. lead in games to 2-1, and gave the Redbirds new life.

Los Angeles Dodgers   0 0 0 1 0 0 1 0 0 - 2 - 7 - 2
St. Louis Cardinals   2 2 0 0 0 0 0 0 x - 4 - 8 - 0

John Tudor, the loser to Valenzuela in Game One, was back on the mound in Game Four, to face L.A.'s big blond southpaw, Jerry Reuss. The Cardinals suffered a potentially crippling blow prior to the game when a freak accident sidelined their sparkplug Vince Coleman for the remainder of the series. The Cardinal outfielder injured his leg when a field tarpaulin rolled over it. Substitute Tito Landrum filled in admirably, including a four-hit effort in Game Four.

The Dodgers' well-rested 14-game winner didn't survive the second inning as the Cardinals raked him over the coals for seven runs, then continued the onslaught against reliever Rick Honeycutt, en route to an NLCS-record nine-run inning. The St.Louis 15-hit attack, in addition to Landrum's four hits, included three by Jack Clark and two each by Ozzie Smith and 34-year-old Cesar Cedeño. Landrum and Pendleton knocked in three runs apiece. Tudor, the Redbirds fiery southpaw, pitched a dominant seven innings, limiting the Big Blue Machine to three harmless hits and a single run. Bill Madlock homered for L.A.

Los Angeles Dodgers   0 0 0 0 0 0 1 1 0 - 2 - 5 - 2
St. Louis Cardinals   0 9 0 1 1 0 0 1 x -12 -15 - 0

Game Five was the key game of the series. It was also a shocker for Tommy Lasorda's gutty crew. Fernando Valenzuela, the Dodgers' magnificent Mexican southpaw, made his second start of the series, trying to stem the flow of Cardinal victories, and regain his team's momentum. He gave his usual courageous performance, reminiscent of his World Series victory in Game Three of the 1981 Series against the New York Yankees. Valenzuela had difficulty with his location in this game, as witnessed by his 8 bases on balls, but his coolness under fire got him out of trouble time after time.

The game was tied 2-2 through eight thanks to a Madlock home run in the fifth inning. The pitching on both sides dominated the hitters. As the bottom of the ninth got underway, Tom Niedenfuer relieved Valenzuela for Los Angeles. It was Niedenfuer's first appearance since he saved Game One. After retiring Willie McGee, the big Dodger righty faced little Ozzie Smith, a wizard on defense but a patty cake with the bat. This time, however, the Cardinal shortstop jerked a 1-2 pitch down the right field line for a game-winning home run, as both teams stared on in disbelief. It was the most unpredictable home run in NLCS history. Little Ozzie had only 13 career home runs in over 4,200 at bats—and none left-handed!

Los Angeles Dodgers   0 0 0 2 0 0 0 0 0 - 2 - 5 - 1
St. Louis Cardinals   2 0 0 0 0 0 0 0 1 - 3 - 5 - 1

Thirty-six-year-old Jerry Reuss gave Tommy Lasorda another sterling performance in 1985, as he tossed 212 innings, and came away a winner 14 times.

Tommy Lasorda's proud warriors had their backs to the wall as they returned to Dodger Stadium, their once impressive two-game lead gone. Now the outlook was victory or extinction. There were no more tomorrows. Orel Hershiser, the Dodger ace during the year, and the winner in Game Two, drew the starting assignment for the big one. His mound opponent was Joaquin Andujar, the tall, skinny righthander from the Dominican Republic. Whitey Herzog's 21-game winner battled the Big O for six innings. Neither pitcher had his best stuff, and they both struggled to stay alive. "Mad Dog" Madlock gave the Blue Crew a 4-1 lead in the fifth inning with a shot into the seats, his third home run of the series.

With Hershiser on the hill, the lead looked insurmountable. The Cardinals, however, had other ideas. They sent the Dodger starter to the showers under a three-run barrage in the top of the seventh to knot the game. The Dodgers un-tied it when big Mike Marshall hit a long home run over the right center field fence in the bottom of the eighth off Cardinal reliever Todd Worrell.

A confident Tom Niedenfuer took the mound in the ninth, for his third inning of work. The 6'5" 225-pound reliever disposed of pinch-hitter Cesar Cedeño easily to start the ninth. Willie McGee gave his team a life with a single, then proceeded to steal second. A walk to Ozzie Smith and an infield out by Tommy Herr put runners on second and third, and brought Jack Clark to the plate. Manager Tommy Lasorda opted to pitch to Clark rather than walk him to load the bases. That was a big mistake. Clark sent a Niedenfuer fastball 450 feet into the far reaches of Dodger Stadium. When it came to rest in the left center field stands, it gave the Cardinals a 7-5 lead. For the second day in a row, the Dodgers' top reliever was jolted for a late inning home run, and another L.A. victory slipped away. When Ken Dayley set the Dodgers down in order in the bottom of the ninth, the Cardinals were on their way to the World Series and the Dodgers were on their way home to their families.

St. Louis Cardinals	0 0 1 0 0 0 3 0 3 - 7 - 12 - 1
Los Angeles Dodgers	1 1 0 0 2 0 0 1 0 - 5 - 8 - 0

For the second time in three years, the Dodgers came close but couldn't grab the brass ring. After divisional play began in 1969, the Los Angeles Dodgers won their first three NLCS playoffs. Somehow it seemed natural. Then, in 1983, they were shocked by the Philadelphia Phils; their first NLCS loss. It was a crushing blow to a team looking ahead to the World Series. Now, two years later, they dropped another tough one, this time to Whitey Herzog's classy Cardinals. There was no looking ahead this time, however. No one took the St. Louis speedsters for granted. They were too talented, and they were favored to win the series. Still, the defeat hurt. A division title is nice, but if it doesn't lead to a World Series, the victory is hollow somehow.

Tom Niedenfuer was the Dodger closer for three years in mid-eighties. The hard-throwing righty pitched in seven postseason games, and was unscored on in five of them. He appeared in 440 games for the Dodgers, accumulating a superb career ERA of 2.76. (Los Angeles Dodger Photo)

The Dodgers, the Dodger fans, and particularly Tom Niedenfuer, would see those home runs by Ozzie Smith and Jack Clark in their dreams all winter long.

1991—THE UPSTART BRAVES RUIN THE SCRIPT

The baseball experts all picked the San Francisco Giants or the defending National League Champion Cincinnati Reds to walk off with the Western Division title in 1991. A few of them, out of respect for Tommy Lasorda's capabilities and Dodger tradition, opted for the Los Angeles entry. No one picked the Atlanta Braves to cop the crown. After all, Bobby Cox's boys had finished dead last in 1990, a full 26 games behind the Reds. And no one had ever gone from last to first in one year.

The first month of the season had its ups and downs for the Lasorda-men. The defense was porous, Strawberry couldn't hit his way out of a paper bag, and the bullpen lost its stopper when Jay Howell went down with an elbow injury. Still, the team won enough games to stay in contention. Martinez pitched his second-straight shutout to beat the Giants, 9-0, on the 26th, with Brett Butler punishing his old teammates with a 5-5 night.

The Dodgers picked up speed in May, running up a 17-10 record and slipping into first place by 1/2 game. Ramon Martinez was the team's bellwether, racking up a 7-2 record over the first two months. Mike Morgan was 5-4 with a 2.00 ERA, while Tim Belcher also had a 5-4 record and a 2.79 ERA. Orel Hershiser made his first start in over 13 months and, although he was beaten by Houston, 8-2, their were signs of optimism in his effort. After being touched up for four runs in the first inning, he blanked the Astros over his last three innings.

June was a banner month for L.A. as they widened their Western Division lead to four games on the strength of an 18-9 record. "Bulldog" Hershiser won his first game of the year with a 6-3 decision over the Chicago Cubs. Butler and Eddie Murray contributed three hits apiece to the Dodger attack, and the Big O chipped in with two hits of this own. Cincinnati was the main challenger to L.A.'s early season supremacy. The San Francisco Giants were struggling, and the Atlanta Braves were nowhere to be seen. In all encounters between the Braves and the Reds or Giants, Dodger fans rooted for Bobby Cox's team, feeling they were no threat to a Division title.

Pitchers Orel Hershiser and Kevin Gross chat during a quiet break in spring training. Hershiser, recovering from arm surgery, went 7-2 during the season. Gross was 10-11 in 46 games.(W. McNeil)

When the All-Star break arrived, the Big Blue Machine was securely ensconced in first place, a solid five games ahead of Lou Piniella's Redlegs, and nine games in front of the surprising Atlanta Braves. The first sign of trouble in Dodger-town came immediately after the break. Lasorda's cohorts dropped seven straight to the Montreal Expos and Philadelphia Phillies. Bad defense and inept relief pitching were the major causes of the slide. Despite the fact that the Dodgers won nine of their next 13 games, the pennant race began to heat up. The Reds stayed within range, the Giants began to kick up their heels a bit, and the Atlanta Braves, unnoticed by anyone, crept up on the leaders.

The Los Angeles contingent ran hot and cold during the dog days of August, more cold than hot. A ten game road trip to start the month brought near disaster, as the Californians dropped 7 of the 10. Along the way, they were swept by both the Astros and Giants, while taking three of four from the Redlegs. Outstanding pitching was wasted in three games as they dropped consecutive 2-1, 10-inning games to Houston, and a 1-0, 13-inning duel to the Giants. Mike Morgan and Tim Belcher (twice) were the victims of the lack of support. The final two games of the Giant series ended in 4-3 defeats when the bullpen failed again. The sweep pulled Roger Craig's Bay Area Bombers to within six games of the top, but the Braves were even closer, only 2 1/2 games out–still unnoticed and unrespected.

Dodger fans, in their ignorance, still rooted for Atlanta victories in their series against the Reds and Giants. The feeling was that the two favorites were the biggest threats to a Dodger title. Los Angeles players, and fans alike, were confident they could take the Braves any time they liked.

A 7-3 home stand, sparked by Darryl Strawberry's hot bat, picked up the Dodgers' spirits considerably. The former Met, after a sorry first half in which he batted a meager .230 with only eight dingers, found his batting stroke after the All-Star break and began to hit the ball with authority. On August 13, the big rightfielder hit a three-run homer in the bottom of the 13th off Jim Corsi to beat the Astros, 4-1. Eight days later, Straw smashed two homers (his 12th and 13th since the break), and drove in seven runs to propel the Dodgers to a 9-5 rout of the Padres.

All the while, the red-hot Atlanta Braves continued to narrow the gap between themselves and their cross-country rivals. Late in the month, with Lasorda's cohorts staggering again, Bobby Cox's fuzzy-cheeked kids captured the summit for the first time. After 134 days on top of the pack, the stunned Dodgers suddenly became contenders.

Ramon Martinez was part of the reason for the second-half Dodger collapse, although not by any means the entire cause. The L.A. ace, after an unbeatable first half in which he went 12-3, limped home with a horrible 5-10 record over the last 82 games. Many of the hitters also slacked off after impressive starts. Juan Samuel was most noticeable, plummeting from a .340 first half to a .216 second half. Others who slumped down the stretch included Brett Butler, Kal Daniels, Tim Crews, and John Candelaria.

The September stretch run was as exciting and unpredictable as any in National League history. The lead changed hands eight times, as first the Braves, then the Dodgers spurted. The mood in Dodgerdom, however, slowly changed from one of extreme confidence to one of impending doom. Dodger teams had been down this road countless times over the past 50 years, and they were very adept at reading the signs. At first, the Braves seemed to be just another weapon to help Lasorda's boys dispose of Cincinnati and San Francisco. Then they became pests, keeping the Dodgers from enjoying a well-earned Division title.

Finally, the upstart Braves became real threats to an L.A. championship. And they seemed to have the fates on their side to boot. The little things that decide a pennant race started to rear their ugly heads after the All-Star break. Untimely errors, seeing-eye hits, bad-bounce grounders, home runs that go foul, bad umpiring calls, and other freak happenings, favor one team over another, in the heat of a close pennant race. In '91 the scales were

Jim Gott pitched tough out of the bullpen, appearing in 55 games, with a 4-3 record, and a 2.96 earned run average.(W. McNeil)

tilted toward the state of Georgia. Bobby Cox's team had a penchant for late-inning heroics to turn certain defeat into glorious victory. They won several games they should have lost. On the other side of the coin, the Dodgers encountered the opposite situation. They couldn't win the close ones, and games they should have won, slipped away, often through no fault of their own.

Over the years, there have been many teams who seemed destined to win pennants, regardless of the odds. The Dodgers thrilled to the exploits of several "Teams of Destiny", including the Brooklyn World Champions of 1955, and the L.A. contingents of 1959, 1981, and 1988. Dodger fans knew the feeling, and the 1991 Atlanta Braves were beginning to feel like a "Team of Destiny."

The first "crushul" series of the year took place in Atlanta, September 13-15. In the opener, Mike Morgan, in a typical clutch performance, temporarily de-railed the Atlanta advance, 5-2. Darryl Strawberry, with four hits, including a homer, helped his team sneak back into first place by 1/2 game. After that brief glimpse of daylight, however, the series went downhill. Roger McDowell took a tough 3-2 loss in 11 innings in Game Two when a walk, a bloop double and a single did him in. Ramon Martinez was soundly thrashed by Bobby Cox's charges, 9-1, in the finale, throwing a grand slam home run to Sid Bream in the first.

Three days later, the Dodgers won an enormous victory that many thought would turn the tide of the race. A tight pitchers' duel between the Red's Scott Scudder and L.A.'s Orel Hershiser went to the ninth inning with L.A. on top, 2-1. Lou Piniella's crew rallied against five Dodger relievers to push over the go-ahead run in the top of the ninth, but clutch singles by Dave Hanson and Lenny Harris got the Dodgers even in the bottom of the inning. Cincinnati broke through again in the 12th to score two runs on a home run by Chris Jones and a bases-loaded walk to pitcher Ted Power. The Big Blue Machine fought back again. Strawberry drew a walk and, minutes later raced around to score L.A.'s third run on a triple by Eddie Murray. Rookie Eric Karros, following a walk to Mitch Webster, slammed his first major league hit, a ringing double to left to plate the tying run and put runners on second and third, with only one out. An intentional walk to Offerman loaded the bases for Jeff Hamilton. The third-sacker promptly sent a drive over the drawn-in infield, sending Dodger fans into delirium.

Three more L.A. victories set the stage for another nail-biting Braves-Dodgers series, this one in sunny California, amid the growing signs of increased pennant pressure. If the young, inexperienced Braves were to crack, now was the time. Atlanta arrived in town 1/2 game behind Tommy Lasorda's cohorts with but 14 games to play. Twenty-two-year-old Steve Avery, en route to an 18-8 season, got the Braves off on the right foot with an overpowering 3-0 shutout. Ron Gant's two-run homer off Tim Belcher in the sixth broke up a scoreless pitching duel, and enabled Bobby Cox's upstarts to move back into first place by the slimmest of margins.

In Game Two, Orel Hershiser tossed six innings, yielding one run on three hits. One of the hits was a fourth-inning triple that led to the only run of the game to that point. In the eighth, two Atlanta errors and a single by Mitch Webster tied the score. Then in the bottom of the ninth, Kal Daniels singled through the middle with one out; then carried the winning run across the plate moments later when Juan Samuel crashed a long triple up the right center field alley.

Ramon Martinez faced off against the Braves 6'1" southpaw, Tom Glavine, in the final matchup of the season between the two contenders. On this day, the eventual Cy Young Award winner was tagged early by Lasorda's sluggers. In the bottom of the first, Mike Sharperson reached on a bloop double, Darryl Strawberry sent him home with a scorching triple down the right-field line, and Eddie Murray drove the Strawman in with a sharp single to left. In the fourth, Martinez hit his first major league home run, sending a Glavine fastball over the fence in right center. The tall, skinny Dodger ace made those runs hold up as he two-hit the Braves over seven innings, winning 3-0.

After splitting a pair with the Padres, the Lasorda-men took two of three from San Francisco at home, taking the finale 3-2 on a two-run ninth. Singles by Sharperson and Strawberry proved to be the winning combination. After winning the opener of the Giant series, Lasorda's boys held a two-game lead with only eight games left to play. The second-game loss cut the lead to one.

Darryl Strawberry recovered from an early-season slump, to hit .265 with 28 homers and 99 RBIs. (W. McNeil)

The two key games of the 1991 season were played on October 1 and 2. The first game matched the Braves against the Cincinnati Reds at Riverfront Stadium. The Big Red Machine routed Atlanta starter Charlie Leibrandt in a six-run first inning, presenting their ace, Jose Rijo a, huge cushion to work with. Considering the stocky righthander was 15-5 for the season, and a perfect 9-0 at home, things looked bleak for Bobby Cox's team. To the Braves' credit, they never gave up. A lesser team might have called it quits for the season, and just played out the string, but the Atlanta players, displaying their character, sucked it in and fought back. They pecked away at the Dominican hurler, scoring two runs in the fourth, one in the fifth, and two more in the seventh. With Atlanta relievers holding the Reds scoreless after the first-inning uprising, the game moved into the ninth, a 6-5 spine tingler. Ron Dibble, the Cincinnati closer, facing Dave Justice with one on and two out, was rocked for a two-

Kal Daniels displays his dexterity at first base as he blows a bubble while keeping the runner close to first base.(W. McNeil)

run homer by the Atlanta right fielder, and the Braves pulled off a miraculous 7-6 come-from-behind victory. Meanwhile, the Dodgers protected their slim lead with a tough 3-1 win in San Diego. Bob Ojeda was the winning pitcher, and Darryl Strawberry hit #27 to pace the attack.

The next night, the Dodgers tangled with the Padres in the rubber game of the series, L.A. having won the first two. Game Three entered the eighth inning deadlocked at 3-3, when the fates intervened again. The Padres suddenly rose up and stunned the Los Angeles team with the wierdest six-run inning seen in these parts in many years. Five infield hits, including two bunts, a throwing error, and two bonafide singles comprised the San Diego assault. When the smoke cleared, the Padres had triumphed, 9-4, and the Dodgers and Braves were tied for the division lead with only three games left to play.

Lenny Harris was a super sub all year for Tommy Lasorda, filling in wherever necessary. Harris batted a solid .287 in 145 games. (W. McNeil)

It was a dispirited Dodger team that embarked for San Francisco for the final three-game series. Dodger players and Dodger fans alike, sensed the inevitable, now more than ever. With Atlanta at home against the last-place Astros, and L.A. in the Candlestick Park snakepit, the outlook was somber. On a cold and foggy Friday night, Will "The Chill" Clark put a Ramon Martinez fastball into orbit with one man on in the bottom of the first inning. One out later, Matt Williams drove #34 into the night and the Giants were off and running, 3-0. Bud Black and Jeff

Brantley scattered eight hits, Kevin Bass added a dinger in the seventh, and Roger Craig's boys pushed the Dodgers to the brink of extinction, 4-1. With Atlanta's 5-2 win over Houston, the Braves were up by one game with only two to play. The next day, the Giants put the final nail in L.A.'s coffin. Trevor Wilson tossed a masterful two-hitter, outdueling Mike Morgan, to win 4-0. With Atlanta's 5-2 win over Houston, the Western Division title went to the state of Georgia.

It was a thrilling pennant race that was not decided until the next to last day of the season, and one that both the Braves and Dodgers should be proud of. The Atlanta team, down by 9 1/2 games at the All-Star break, put on a stunning drive over the last 12 weeks, winning 55 times against only 28 losses. The Dodgers, after a sluggish August, finished with a rush themselves. From August 31 through October 2, Tommy Lasorda's warriors went 22-8, a sizzling .733 pace.

In the end, the script seemed to be pre-ordained. No matter what the Dodgers did, they could not contain the Atlanta Braves. Bobby Cox's team had supernatural help. They were a Team of Destiny.

1994—DODGERS WIN BUT BASEBALL LOSES

After the miraculous World Championship in 1988, and stirring pennant races in 1990 and 1991, the Los Angeles Dodgers self-destructed in '92. A combination of bad player deals, bad defense, and bad luck dropped the pride of L.A. into the cellar for the first time in 87 years.

The 1905 Brooklyn club, under Ned Hanlon, won only 48 of 154 games, to trail the league-leading New York Giants by a whopping 56 1/2 games. The '92 team didn't fare much better. Their 63-99 record left them 35 games behind the high-flying Atlanta Braves.

During the 1980s, and continuing into the 1990s, the Los Angeles front office made numerous questionable player deals, stripping the farm system of valuable talent, with a minimum return on their investment. Super closers like John Franco and John Wetteland left the fold, to be replaced by the likes of Rafael Landestoy and Kip Gross. Sid Fernandez was traded for Bob Bailor and Carlos Diaz. Juan Guzman went to Toronto for Mike Sharperson. And promising shortstop Jose Vizcaino was swapped for infielder Greg Smith.

After Tommy Lasorda's club finished a close second in both 1990 and 1991, the front office tried to strengthen the team with more strategic personnel moves. It seemed as if everything they tried backfired.

One of their first big moves, back in 1991, was to sign free agent Darryl Strawberry. The "Straw Man" had a decent season in '91, hitting .265 with 28 homers and 99 runs-batted-in. The '92 season, however, was a disaster. Limited to 43 games because of injuries the lanky slugger hit only five homers, with a .237 batting average.

The Dodgers signed Strawberry's buddy, Eric Davis, to a contract in 1992, but he too was a bust. He played only 76 games because of injuries and hit a paltry .228 with 5 homers. Other acquisitions, such as Todd Benzinger, Roger McDowell, Steve Wilson, and Cory Snyder, were disappointments. Overall, the Dodgers finished ninth in batting, and dead last in fielding. Rookie shortstop Jose Offerman booted 42 balls in 149 games. Journeymen infielders Lenny Harris and Mike Sharperson were not much better.

The '93 team showed a slight improvement, finishing fourth in the eight-team west. Home-grown products, Eric Karros and Mike Piazza, joined Brett Butler to give the punchless Dodgers a smattering of offense. The pitching was marginally better, thanks primarily to improved peformances by McDowell, Hershiser, and Ramon Martinez, and the development of Pedro Astacio. Third baseman Tim Wallach, an off-season acquisition from the Montreal Expos, provided valuable experience in the infield.

Giants were the division favorites, but L.A. had great hopes for graduates from their revitalized farm system. Over the winter they had strengthened their infield through the acquisition of second-baseman Delino DeShields from Montreal (but they lost Pedro Martinez in the process). Lasorda was hoping the smooth fielding DeShields would be a steadying influence on the flashy but erratic Offerman. Home-grown products Henry Rodriguez, Dave Hansen, and Raul Mondesi were given the opportunity to crash the lineup to bolster the efforts of Butler, Piazza, and Karros.

A healthy Todd Worrell was expected to be the closer on a strong pitching staff that included Hershiser, Martinez, Astacio, knuckleballer Tom Candiotti, and Kevin Gross.

Rookie Of The Year Raul Mondesi takes a crack at batting left-handed in a spring training game. He returned to batting right-handed during the season. (W. McNeil)

Second baseman Delino DeShields, obtained from Montreal to steady the infield, had an injury-plagued season. Here he is wearing a plastic face shield after suffering a fractured cheekbone in spring training. (W. McNeil)

As the 1994 season got underway, the experts were picking Lasorda's boys to finish second (out of four teams) in the newly created Western Division of the three-division alignment. Dusty Baker's powerful San Francisco

The season began on a high note for the Los Angeles contingent, as left fielder Cory Snyder slugged three home runs in a 19-2 rout of the Pittsburgh Pirates on April 17. Three days later, Brett Butler laced out five base hits, in a 6-5 win over the New York Mets. The jubliation was short lived however, as the Dodgers settled down to a .500 pace through April and May. On June 6, they held down first place in the weak Western Division, with a 29-28 record, two games ahead of San Francisco. The Dodgers' offense was potent, as their .282 batting average and 290 runs scored had them in second place in both categories, in the National League. Their defense was average, as was their pitching.

The big guns in the L.A. attack during the first third of the season, were Piazza (.338, 11 home runs), third baseman Tim Wallach (.263, 12 homers), Eric Karros (.288, eight HR), and surprising rookie Raul Mondesi (.330, eightHR). Pitching was a disappointment, as only Hershiser could show an ERA under 3.90 on the starting staff. Todd Worrell and Roger McDowell were marginally effective out of the bullpen, but the rest of the relief corps was a disaster. Their 12 blown saves were the most in the major leagues.

As the season progressed, another spector raised its ugly head; a possible player's strike. Negotiations between the players and the owners were going nowhere, as the players' executive director, Donald Fehr, and the owners' representative, Bud Selig, locked horns in an apparent power struggle. The main issue was the owners' contention that 19 of the 28 clubs would lose money in 1994, requiring a radical change in the way baseball did business. The owners wanted to institute a salary cap, but the players rejected the proposal. The union claimed that all the clubs were financially secure.

cisco, with 27 homers in 72 games, was not far behind. Frank Thomas of the Chicago White Sox was also in the hunt, with 28 homers in 67 games. Thomas, in fact, was in search of the triple crown, as his .371 batting average and 62 runs-batted-in, both challenged for the league lead.

Throughout July the Los Angeles Dodgers continued to struggle. They still could not divest themselves of the win one-lose one mentality they developed right out of spring training, but they still held the lead in the west. Their 48-45 record was three games better than the second-place Colorado Rockies' 46-49 showing. The favored Giants were mired in third place with an embarrassing 44-50 record.

The Dodger problems still centered around pitching and defense. Their 16 saves were last in the National League. Only two teams in the entire major leagues had a worse showing. The defense was still porous, in spite of the fact that Rafael Bournigal plugged the leaks at shortstop. Jose Offerman, with 11 errors in 72 games, and a barely visible .210 batting average, was shuttled off to Albuquerque. Piazza, Karros, Mondesi, and Cory Snyder, were all prone to fielding lapses.

On August 11, 1994, the hammer came down. At 12:45 AM, Randy Johnson of the Seattle Mariners fanned Ernie Young of the Oakland Athletics, nailing down an 8-1 Seattle victory, officially ending the 1994 baseball season. The owners and players could not settle their differences in a civilized manner, so the players walked.

Brett Butler gave the Dodgers another solid season, hitting .314 in 111 games, before the strike began.(W. McNeil)

Dave Hansen hit .340 in 40 games, most of them as a pinch hitter. Hansen had 18 pinch hits in 1993. (W. McNeil)

The saddest thing about the impending strike was that many outstanding performances that could have resulted in new records being established would be wasted. Seattle Mariner outfielder Ken Griffey, Jr., with 32 homers in 70 games, was on his way to breaking Roger Maris' single-season home-run record. Matt Williams of San Fran-

The childish behavior of the two sides prevented the fans from witnessing an assault on several of the major league's sacred records, particularly the single-season home run record. Ken Griffey's season came to a premature end with 40 home runs in 102 games. Frank Thomas had 38 in 99 games. And the leader of the pack, Matt Williams, had 43 home runs in 110 games, a figure that would have given him 63 homers for the season if he had maintained the same pace for 162 games.

Lost in the shuffle was the fact that the Los Angeles Dodgers were the 1994 Western Division champions, finishing with a 58-56 record, 3 1/2 games ahead of the San Francisco Giants. Mike Piazza paced the Dodger offense with a .319 batting average, 24 homers, and 92 runs-batted-in. Raul Mondesi, on his way to a National League Rookie Of The Year award, ran up a .309 average, with 16 homers, and 56 RBIs. And Tim Wallach chipped in with some timely offense on the strength of a .280 average, 23 homers, and 78 RBIs.

The bright spots in the pitching rotation were Ramon Martinez (12-7, 3.97 ERA), and rookie Ismael Valdes (3-1, 3.18 ERA).

The Dodgers won their division, but there was no joy in Mudville. Mighty Casey had struck out.

Tom Candiotti, the Dodgers' tough-luck pitcher, received the least run support in the National League. His 7-14 record is deceptive. The Dodgers scored just 2.9 runs a game in his last 25 starts. (W. McNeil)

1995—THE POST SEASON RETURNS, BUT THE DODGERS EXIT EARLY

The Atlanta Braves were the team of the nineties. Beginning with their stunning stretch run in 1991 that culminated in a National League pennant, Bobby Cox's boys captured another pennant in '92 and a Western Division title in '93. They finished second to Philadelphia in the newly structured Eastern Division in the strike-shortened season of '94.

In 1995, they were, once again, favored to go all the way in the Senior Circuit. Atlanta's pitching staff, led by their brilliant starters, three-time Cy Young-award winner Greg Maddux, former Cy Young winner Tom Glavine, John Smoltz, and Steve Avery, was the highest-rated staff in the major leagues. A tight defense helped keep opponents at bay, and the timely hitting of Fred McGriff, Dave Justice, and Roberto Kelly produced just enough runs to win most games.

The Braves' main competition was expected to come from the west coast, where the Los Angeles Dodgers continued their rebuilding process. Peter O'Malley shocked the baseball world in February when he signed Japanese superstar Hideo Nomo to a major league contract. The 6'2", 210-pound Nomo, led the Japanese Pacific League in both victories and strikeouts, his first four years in the league. His overall record in Japan was 79-46, with 1,204 strikeouts in 1051 innings.

Nomo joined a solid pitching staff that included Ramon Martinez, Tom Candiotti, rookie Ismael Valdes, and Pedro Astacio. The renowned Dodger farm system was in high gear again, producing three consecutive National League Rookies Of The Year; Eric Karros, Mike Piazza, and Raul Mondesi. Hopes were high in the Dodger organization, as winter turned to spring, and the smell of baseball filled the air.

All was not well with baseball, however. The players' strike continued into 1995. When the first day of spring training arrived, the major league players were nowhere to be seen. The owners, determined to present a full regular season schedule of games to their fans, filled their rosters with minor league players, and former major leaguers who either had retired or had returned to the minors. The Dodgers relied exclusively on young players from their own farm system. Several, like Jay Kirkpatrick and Mike Busch, sparkled in the Florida sunshine.

Just days before the regular season was scheduled to open, the players and owners reached a settlement in their long-standing feud. Opening day was delayed several weeks to give the big leaguers time to work out the kinks. The loyal replacement players, instead of fulfilling their dreams of playing in Dodger Stadium, made the long trek back to San Antonio, Vero Beach, and other minor league stations.

The season opened belatedly on April 25, with Ramon Martinez dumping the Florida Marlins, 8-7, behind two home runs by Raul Mondesi. The Dominican fireballer allowed only two runs in six innings, but the leaky Dodger bullpen almost blew the game. Relief pitching, it would turn out, would be L.A.'s achilles heel all year. Only closer Todd Worrell was dependable, but often the set-up men couldn't stem the tide, so Worrell was denied numerous save opportunities.

The Dodgers stumbled through the first month and a half of the season, crippled by injuries to Piazza, Todd Hollandsworth, and Tim Wallach. A 2-1 loss to the Phillies on June 11 dropped the Lasorda-men into the Western Division cellar, with a 20-23 record, five games behind the Colorado Rockies. Shortstop Jose Offerman, with 11 errors in 41 games, was a primary reason the L.A. contingent was last in defense in the National League.

Starting pitching came to the rescue in June, sparked by the two rookies, Hideo Nomo and Ismael Valdes. Between them, they went 11-1 during the month, with a combined 1.65 earned-run-average. Nomo, in particular, was brilliant. His perfect 6-0 record, and miniscule 0.89 ERA, included two shutouts and 60 strikeouts in just 50 innings.

Ramon Martinez picked up the pitching baton in July, running up a 4-0 record in six starts. The high point of his month came in Dodger Stadium on July 14 when the lanky right hander tossed a no-hitter at the Florida Marlins, winning 7-0. He retired the first 23 men in order before walking Tommy Gregg, with two out in the eighth. He finished off his gem by setting down the last four batters.

The baseball strike continued well into spring training. Dodger replacement players, like Jay Kirkpatrick (L) and Mike Busch (R), filled the gap until the strike was settled. (W. McNeil)

Rookie Todd Hollandsworth was the offensive star of the day, racking up his first three major league hits. His third-inning double ignited a two-run Dodger rally. In all, the 22-year-old center fielder went three for four, with two runs batted in, and two runs scored. He also made a fine running catch of a drive off the bat of Terry Pendleton, in the eighth, to preserve the no-no.

The Dodgers finished July in second place with a 45-42 record, 3 1/2 games behind the Rockies. In the other division races, the Cincinnati Reds held a four-game lead over the Houston Astros in the Central Division while, in the East, the surging Atlanta Braves went on a 20-7 spree in July, turning a four-game deficit into an eight-game lead, over the floundering Philadelphia Phillies.

L.A.'s problems continued to be a leaky defense and a shabby middle relief corps. Of the Dodgers' 85 errors in 87 games, Offerman's 24 miscues led the team. Mondesi and DeShields were next in line with six each. The inept Dodger set-up men included Greg Hansell (7.45 ERA), Willie Banks (10.38 ERA), Rudy Seanez (6.89 ERA), and Antonio Osuna (6.27 ERA).

Tommy Lasorda's crew got off to a fast start in August, whipping the division-leading Rockies, two out of three. Raul Mondesi hit two home runs into the friendly Colorado night, knocking in six runs in a 9-6 Dodger victory. The next night, it was more of the same. Karros hit two, Kelly one, and Hollandsworth one, as L. A. outlasted the Rockies, 10-7. Colorado took the final game, 9-4.

After San Francisco spanked Los Angeles and Tom Candiotti, 15-1, on August 4, Hideo Nomo got the Big Blue Machine back on track with a magnificaent 3-0 one-hitter, running his season record to 9-2. Karros' two-run homer in the top of the twelfth, two days later, gained the Dodgers a split in the four-game series.

Another Karros homer the next night beat St. Louis, 4-3, and his third in three days, on August 9, downed the Cards again, 4-2. Two days later, Los Angeles moved into a first-place tie by beating the Pittsburgh Pirates, 3-2. Ismael Valdes was touched up for a triple and two doubles in the first inning, then settled down to pitch seven shutout innings, for his ninth victory. Todd Worrell struck out the side in the ninth, for his 23rd save. The Dodgers came from behind with two runs in the bottom of the eighth to win. A single by DeShields, a walk to Fonville, and consecutive singles by Offerman and Piazza did the damage.

The west retained its reputation as a wild and wooly place, in a stranger-than-fiction 11-10 extra-inning victory over the Pirates on August 12. Eric Karros knocked in the tying runs in both the ninth and tenth innings, as the Lasorda-men overcame a 7-2 deficit, with five runs in the ninth, three in the tenth, and another in the eleventh, to win. The next night, Ramon Martinez pitched the Dodgers into first place, for the first time in six weeks, with a 4-1 victory over Pittsburgh.

The rest of the season was nip and tuck as Los Angeles and Colorado took turns holding down the top spot. On September 16, the Colorado Rockies held a two-game edge over the Dodgers, but from there to the end of the season Don Baylor's boys lost eight of their final 15 games, while the Dodgers took nine of 13, to win the Western Division by a single game.

Los Angeles played their final series of the year in San Diego. They blew a 5-2 lead in the opening game, losing 6-5, but still clinched a wild card spot when the Rockies also lost. The next night, Hideo Nomo and Raul Mondesi combined to bring the Western Division title home to Los Angeles. Nomo pitched a strong eight innings, fanning 11, and scattering six hits. Mondesi broke a 1-1 tie in the seventh with a two-run homer and a Piazza round-tripper, plus doubles by Kelly and Hanson, scored the final two runs in the eighth, in a 5-1 triumph.

Rookie pitcher Hideo Nomo breezed through June with a perfect 6-0 record, on his way to Rookie Of The Year honors. (W. McNeil)

The Los Angeles Dodgers were the Western Division champions, with the San Diego Padres the wild card choice. The Cincinnati Reds took the Central Division crown, and the Atlanta Braves romped in the east, winning by a 21-game margin.

The pennant excitement ended quickly in the playoffs for the Dodgers, as Davey Johnson's Cincinnati Reds swept Tommy Lasorda's boys, three straight. Dodger ace Ramon Martinez was rocked for four runs on four hits in the first inning, as the Reds crushed L.A. 7-2, in the opener, in Dodger Stadium. Mike Piazza had a single and a homer in a losing cause.

Game Two was a heartbreaker. The Dodger offense pounded out 14 hits, and Ismael Valdes held the Reds to three hits and two unearned runs in seven innings, but the Dodgers lost again, 5-4. An error by shortstop Chad Fonville in the fourth, gave the Reds two gift runs, when Reggie Sanders put a Valdes pitch into orbit. An Eric Karros double in the first and home run in the fourth accounted for two Dodger runs, as the two teams battled to a 2-2 tie through seven.

Los Angeles missed numerous scoring opportunities, leaving eight men on base in three innings–two in the fifth, three in the sixth, and three in the seventh. Cincinnati made them pay dearly for their ineptitude. In the top of the eighth, Barry Larkin took an Antonio Osuna fastball downtown, giving the Reds a 3-2 lead. In the ninth, Kevin Tapani walked the bases loaded, then yielded two runs on a force-out and a single, running the margin to 5-2. In the bottom of the ninth, the Dodgers staged a brief rally. Fonville singled, for his fourth hit of the night. Piazza fanned, but Karros drove a Jeff Brantley pitch into the left-field seats, cutting the margin to 5-4. That was the final score, however, as Brantley recovered to retire both Wallach and DeShields without a murmur.

The last hurrah for Los Angeles took place in Cincinnati. Hideo Nomo was clubbed for five runs in five innings, and the Reds romped, 10-1.

Twenty-two-year-old rookie Ismael Valdes put together a sterling season. His 13-11 record included a 3.05 ERA, six complete games and two shutouts. (W. McNeil)

It was a sad ending to a strange season. It began with a players' strike, and it ended with a three-game sweep in the first round of the playoffs. The Dodger team never did measure up to its potential. The much-maligned defense committed 130 errors in 144 games. The middle relievers were a disaster during the first half of the season, although there was some reason for hope for 1996 during the second half. Antonio Osuna showed promise when he returned from Albuquerque. John Cummings, Joey Eischen, Pedro Astacio, and Mark Guthrie all pitched well down the stretch.

The main bright spots in 1995 were the offense and Todd Worrell. The big closer saved 32 games for Tommy Lasorda during the season, finishing with a 4-1 record and a team-leading 2.02 earned-run-average. Mike Piazza arrived as a world-class hitter, pounding the ball at a .346 clip, with 32 home runs and 93 runs-batted-in. Eric Karros contributed a .298 average, with 32 homers and 105 RBIs, and Raul Mondesi hit .285 with 26 homers and 88 RBIs. Offerman hit a respectable .287, but he proved he is not a major league shortstop. His range and glovework are superior, but his arm is too erratic for the position.

The Los Angeles Dodgers did garner one postseason honor of note. Hideo Nomo walked off with the National League Rookie Of The Year award, the fourth successive R-O-Y trophy for L.A.

The Atlanta Braves captured the National League pennant, beating the Reds in four games. They completed their dream season by whipping the Cleveland Indians four games to two in the World Series, to capture their first World Championship. Tom Glavine pitched the finale, winning 1-0 on a Dave Justice home run.

1996–ANOTHER PLAYOFF, BUT NO CIGAR

The Los Angeles Dodgers entered the 1996 season with high hopes. Greg Gagne, a 13-year veteran, replaced the erratic Jose Offerman at shortstop. Mike Blowers, coming off a career season with Seattle, was picked up in a trade, to replace the aging Tim Wallach, at third. Second baseman Delino DeShields was healthy for the first time in several years. Piazza, Karros, and Mondesi, were all coming off outstanding years, and were sure bets to repeat–or improve upon–their 1995 performances. A healthy Todd Hollandsworth was expected to hold down right field, while big Billy Ashley was being counted on to supply a powerful bat in the middle of the lineup.

The defense was significantly improved by the addition of Gagne.

The pitching staff was considered to be one of the best staffs in the major leagues, with the addition of Mark Guthrie, Scott Radinsky, and Joey Eischen, the return of Darren Driefort, and the coming-of-age of Antonio Osuna. Todd Worrell, the closer, with 32 saves in 1995, was expected to beat that record by ten or more in '96 with a solid set-up team.

Manny Mota, driving his favorite form of transportation. Mota works with Dodger players in spring training, in hopes that his clutch-hitting mentality will rub off on Lasorda's hitters. (W. McNeil)

The starting staff of Ramon Martinez, Hideo Nomo, Ismael Valdes, Tom Candiotti, and either Pedro Astacio or Chan Ho Park was the equal of any starting staff in the major leagues, including the vaunted Atlanta staff.

As the season got underway, the division favorites were Atlanta in the East, Houston in the Central, and L.A. in the West. As usual, the Dodgers stumbled coming out of the blocks. After rookie Todd Hollandsworth beat Houston in the opener, 4-3, with a base-clearing double, Tommy Lasorda's crew proceeded to drop the next two to the Astros, and three out of four to Chicago. The pitching was bad, the defense was horrible, and the offense was non-existent.

They managed to turn things around at home, with Hideo Nomo throwing a three-hit shutout at the defending World Champion Atlanta Braves in the home opener, beating Tom Glavine, 1-0, on third-inning singles by Brett Butler, Piazza, and Mondesi.

The Japanese "Tornado" followed that gem with a three-hit, 17-strikeout performance against the Florida Marlins. He came within one strikeout of Sandy Koufax's Los Angeles record, when he fanned Jesus Tavarez to open the ninth, but he couldn't nail the equalizer. Home runs by Billy Ashley in the third and Raul Mondesi, with one on in the fourth, spelled the difference in the 3-1 Dodger victory.

The Dodgers' season of travail commenced in earnest on May 7 when center fielder Brett Butler, the team's sparkplug, was diagnosed with throat cancer. His future was uncertain, as a debilitating regimen of surgery, radiation, and chemotherapy was scheduled in order to destroy the dreaded disease.

Less than two months later, on June 25, manager Tommy Lasorda was felled by a heart attack. An angioplasty procedure was performed successfully the next day, clearing the blocked heart artery. While Lasorda's medical condition and future status with the team were being evaluated, coach Bill Russell took over as interim manager.

As the season approached the halfway mark, all the races were going according to form. The Braves held a five-game lead over the Montreal Expos, the Houston Astros were deadlocked with the St. Louis Cardinals, and the Dodgers trailed the San Diego Padres by a single game.

The Dodgers' 47-42 record was built on solid defense, strong starting pitching, and a deep, reliable bullpen. Greg Gagne had stabilized the inner perimeter of the Dodger defense, to the point where the L.A. contingent was third in the National League in fewest errors. The starting staff, led by Nomo (9-7) and Valdes (9-5), were the equal of any in the league. Pedro Astacio, the fifth starter, had a losing record, which was not indicative of his performances. He gave Tommy Lasorda quality starts most of the time, but couldn't seem to get the breaks.

The bullpen, unlike '95, sparkled. Antonio Osuna had a 1.95 ERA in 40 games. Southpaws Mark Guthrie (1.13 ERA in 36 games) and Scott Radinsky (2.42 ERA in 28 games), gave the Dodgers strong middle relief. Closer Todd Worrell, thanks to his set-up men, racked up 23 saves in 87 games, putting him on course to set a new Los Angeles record.

The soft underbelly of the Dodger demon was its offense. The anticipated high-scoring hitting machine never materialized. Their 370 runs scored in 89 games (an average of only 4.2 runs per game), left them in 12th place in the 14-team National League. Only Mike Piazza was powdering the ball as expected. His .363 batting average included 24 home runs and 63 runs-batted-in. Eric Karros, a .298 hitter in 1995, was sputtering along at .255, and grounding into double plays at a record clip. Raul Mondesi was 22 points below his '95 average, Mike Blowers was mired in a season-long slump, Roger Cedeno, Butler's replacement, was struggling at .258, and Billy Ashley was on the bench, thanks to a .153 batting average and 29 strikeouts in just 72 at bats. The overall free-swinging lineup accumulated too many strikeouts, picked up too few free passes, and left too many runners on base.

Greg Gagne, a strong defensive shortstop, made just four errors in the Dodgers' last 53 games. He also hit .255 and drove in 55 runners. (W. McNeil)

Twenty-three-year-old Chan Ho Park, in his first full season with the Dodgers, worked 48 games in middle relief. He struck out 119 batters in 109 innings. (W. McNeil)

More bad luck struck the team on July 17, when third baseman Mike Blowers tore a ligament in his left knee in a base-running mishap, and was lost for the season. Veteran Tim Wallach was quickly brought aboard to fill the void. Twelve days later, another shock wave went through the Dodger clubhouse. Manager Tommy Lasorda announced his retirement from the field. He was still a Dodger, however, staying with the Los Angeles organization in the capacity of Vice President. Lasorda's 20-year reign included five Western Division titles, four National League pennants, and two World Championships. His 1,599 career victories (against 1,439 losses) placed him in 13th place on the all-time managerial games-won list.

Los Angeles, true to its Hollywood tradition, finally produced a heart-warming story on September 6. Center fielder Brett Butler, out with throat cancer since May 1, returned to the Dodger lineup in triumphant fashion against the Pittsburgh Pirates. The courageous born-again Christian went one for three on his return, and scored the winning run in the eighth inning on a sacrifice fly by Eric Karros, and the Dodgers nipped the Pirates, 2-1. Valdes pitched brilliantly for seven innings, Osuna got the victory, and Worrell picked up his 39th save.

Unfortunately for the Dodgers, Butler's comeback was short lived. He went down with a broken thumb after only five games and was lost for the remainder of the season.

As the stretch drive heated up, so too did the Dodgers. Their pennant push, in fact, began on August 10. On that date, their record stood at 59-56, leaving them 2 1/2 games behind the division-leading San Diego Padres. From then until Wednesday, September 25, new manager Bill Russell had the Dodgers in high gear. They rolled up a scintillating 31-12 record, their hottest streak in over a decade.

The entire pitching staff was brilliant. Dodger ace Ramon Martinez went 7-0 from August 10 through the end of the season. Ismael Valdes was 4-1, with several quality, no-decision, starts. Hideo Nomo compiled a 6-2 record over the seven-week run, including a most unlikely no-hitter in homer-haven, Coors Field, on September 17. Nomo, working in a constant drizzle, pitched from the stretch after the second inning, and retired the last 17 Rockies in a row. He was ably supported by a 14-hit Dodger attack that included a home run by Tim Wallach, and three hits each, by Wayne Kirby and Raul Mondesi. Relief ace Todd Worrell ran off 16 saves in the 43-game run, bringing his total for the year to 44, a new Dodger record.

When the Dodgers defeated the San Francisco Giants on September 25, it gave them a 2 1/2 game lead over the Padres with only four games remaining. More than that, it guaranteed them at least a wild-card spot in the playoffs. Perhaps it was a coincidence. Or perhaps it was overconfidence. But whatever the reason, the 7-5 win over the Giants, their 90th victory of the season, was their last. They dropped the finale to Dusty Baker's boys, 6-1,

Pedro Astacio was 9-8 in 1996, with a 3.44 earned run average. He pitched 212 innings in 35 games. (W. McNeil)

then were unceremoniously swept by the San Diego Padres at home by scores of 5-2, 4-2, and 2-0. Once again, their offense failed to put in an appearance at the park, and their relief pitching went into premature hibernation. In the opener, Antonio Osuna was clipped for three runs in the tenth inning, to take the loss. The next day, Darren Driefort was rocked for two runs in just 2/3 of an inning.

Still, on the final day, Bill Russell's team could have captured the Western Division title with a victory. They had a golden opportunity to win it in the bottom of the ninth inning of a scoreless game, but they couldn't pull the trigger. Kirby and Hollandsworth reached base with no outs, setting the table for the big guns, Piazza and Karros. But Piazza whiffed, and Eric Karros hit into an inning-ending double play. Chan Ho Park, who entered the game in the tenth inning gave up the winning runs in the 11th, on two singles and a Chris Gwynn double.

The Dodger drought continued into the playoffs. Facing Atlanta, whom they had handled successfully during the season, they couldn't hit their way out of a paper bag. In Game One, in Dodger Stadium, they garnered only five hits off the slants of John Smoltz and Mark Wohlers. Still, the pitching kept them in a 1-1 game until the tenth inning, when Antonio Osuna gave up a game-winning home run to Javy Lopez. Game Two was not much better. This time, Ismael Valdes protected a precarious 2-1 lead into the seventh, when consecutive homeruns off the bats of Fred McGriff and Jermaine Dye did him in. The L.A. offense consisted of a Mondesi double and singles by Todd Hollandsworth and Mike Piazza. When the teams moved on to Atlanta, it was three and out for Bill Russell's crew. A four-run fourth against Hideo Nomo was all Tom Glavine needed as he coasted to a 5-2 victory. The Dodgers' six hits included a single and a double by Hollandsworth.

Nineteen ninety-six was a troubling and frustrating year for the Dodgers. The illnesses to Butler and Lasorda were difficult for the team to handle, leaving them physically and emotionally exhausted by the end of the season. Perhaps their collapse over the last seven games, was caused by the stress that pervaded the Dodger clubhouse during most of the season. In any case, the year 1997 will be another year of hope for the Los Angeles group. With any kind of luck, they could go all the way. They have the nucleus of a super team. They go into the season with ten solid pitchers, evenly divided between starters and relievers. The defense should continue to shine, and may even be better than 1996. The main needs are a second baseman, a third baseman, and one outfielder. If Butler can return to his former self, that will eliminate one hole in the lineup. The other positions may be filled from within the system–perhaps Wilton Guerrero or Juan Castro–perhaps both. Outfield support could come from Roger Cedeno or Karim Garcia. And then there is Paul Konerko, catcher/first baseman/third baseman, who may be heard from.

Dodger fans anxiously await the start of 1997. A World Championship is within their grasp. And hope springs eternal in Dodgerland.

1997—A SEASON TWO WEEKS TOO LONG

The key words were optimism and dedication as the 1997 spring training camp opened in Vero Beach, Florida, in late February. Everyone on the team—from Bill Russell to the trainers and coaches—was anxious to prove that the accusation that the Dodgers were underachievers was unfounded.

Russell, who assumed the managerial reigns from Tommy Lasorda in midseason in 1996, was beginning his first full year as the Dodgers field leader. He was determined not to repeat the disappointment of '96, when his club dropped their last seven games, including a season-ending three game sweep by the San Diego Padres—in Los Angeles—that knocked the Dodgers out of first place, followed by a three game sweep at the hands of the Atlanta Braves in the ensuing playoff. The team that met Russell in Dodgertown was solid from top to bottom. They had ten quality pitchers with previous major league experience. The starters, led by Ramon Martinez (15-6),

Ismael Valdes (15-7), and Hideo Nomo (16-11), had the lowest earned run average in the major leagues in 1996. The bullpen brigade, with Todd Worrell's 44 saves, ranked third in saves out of 28 teams.

Catcher Mike Piazza (36 home runs, 105 runs batted in, and a .336 batting average), first baseman Eric Karros (34, 111, .260), shortstop Greg Gagne (10, 55, .255), rightfielder Raul Mondesi (24, 88, .297), leftfielder Todd Hollandsworth (12, 59, .291), and centerfielder Brett Butler (who was on the disabled list most of 1996), anchored a potentially explosive lineup. Los Angeles signed free agent Todd Zeile to a three year contract during the off-season, giving them a solid third baseman with punch (25, 99, .263). Rookie Wilton Guerrero (.344 at Albuquerque) was expected to fill the void at second base, and outfielders Karim Garcia and Roger Cedeno, were ready to step in if needed.

Brett Butler surprised everyone by coming back for one final season in 1997, after battling cancer most of the previous year. Butler sparked the team over the first half of the season, batting .314 at the All-Star break. An injured shoulder curtailed his performance over the final three months. (W. McNeil)

When the bell rang, the Californians sprang from the starting gate like hungry greyhounds. After an opening day shutout loss to Philadelphia, the Dodgers took 11 of the next 14 games. The offense sputtered, but outstanding defense and spectacular pitching got the job done. The starting staff had an ERA of only 2.75, but what the bullpen did was even better. They put together a brilliant 1.29 ERA, at one point going more than 30 innings without yielding an earned run.

After 11 days of winning ball, however, the early season blahs set in, and the Big Blue Machine's tank went empty. For the next month, the pitching held the team together, but the hitting wasn't enough to pull them over the .500 mark. Hollandsworth (.248), Karros (.236), and Zeile (.224) barely hit their weight, and the team, as a whole, continued to have trouble driving in runners in scoring position. Through 34 games, the Dodgers averaged only 3.7 runs per game. Ismael Valdes was the biggest victim of the Dodgers invisible offense, losing four of six games, despite a brilliant 2.12 ERA. His teammates averaged only 2.13 runs in games he started.

The surprising San Francisco Giants, almost unanimously picked to finish in the West Division cellar in preseason polls, were leading the pack in mid-May. Their 21-13 record had them a half game in front of the Colorado Rockies, and one game ahead of the Dodgers. The 1996 West Division champion San Diego Padres couldn't get untracked, and were bringing up the rear, seven games out of first.

When the hitting finally began to pick up in mid-June, the pitching went into a slump, and the trials and tribulations of Russell-ville continued. At one point, the team lost 8 consecutive road games, and 10 of 11. As the month came to a merciful end, Los Angeles owned a 39-42 record (29-38 since April 18), and they were in third place, eight games behind San Francisco.

Roger Cedeno gave the Dodgers some outstanding outfield play until he broke his toe in late August. He supplemented his defensive contribution with a .273 batting average. (W. McNeil)

Chan Ho Park topped the Dodger staff with a record of 14-8 in only his second full major league season. (W. McNeil)

On July 1, the Dodgers whipped the Texas Rangers, 6-3, beginning an eight-game winning streak. The offense, defense, and pitching finally came together for the first time. At the All-Star break, on July 8, Eric Karros had his average up to .270, with 20 home runs. Raul Mondesi (.295, 17) and Mike Piazza (.357, 16) chipped in with some solid numbers. Pedro Astacio, Hideo Nomo, Chan Ho Park, and Tom Candiotti gave Bill Russell consistent quality starts, and the "Pen" boys of Guthrie, Radinsky, Dreifort, Osuna, Hall, and Worrell, did their job well.

The first "crucial" series of the year took place in Los Angeles on July 10–13, when the San Francisco Giants swaggered into town, leading the league by five games. Bill Russell's cohorts took Dusty Baker's boys to task in three out of four. Chan Ho Park, with help from Darren Dreifort and Antonio Osuna, routed the Giants 11-0 in the opener. Home runs by Mike Piazza and Tripp Cromer were the big blows. Cromer had three hits and three RBIs. The destruction continued the following day as Hideo Nomo bested Keith Foulke 6-2. Todd Zeile's three run homer in the fifth capped a six-run inning, and broke open a scoreless game. The Giants managed to salvage the third game, 8-5, blasting Todd Worrell for six runs in a seven-run ninth inning and erasing a 2-1 Dodger lead. L.A. came back to grab the getaway game 9-3, behind rookie Dennis Reyes. Roger Cedeno, with three hits including a two-run homer in the eighth, led a 13-hit Dodger attack. Reyes was the first left-hander to start a game for Los Angeles since Bob Ojeda took the mound on September 24, 1992—a span of 681 games.

After a short respite, where Russell's cohorts lost four of six games, they went on another tear, running off eight wins in a row to finish July with a brilliant 20-7 record. Their surge had wiped out an eight-game San Francisco lead and put them in a dead heat with the Giants for first place in the National League West. A 4-1 win over the Chicago Cubs on July 31 carried them to the top of the heap.

Bill Russell's cohorts went 19-11 in August, even though they played 20 of the 30 games on the road. The Los Angeles bullpen was spectacular during the surge, yielding only one run in 31 2/3 innings over one 12-game period. The streak came to an end when closer Todd Worrell threw consecutive home run balls to Joe Rando and Mark Smith, in the last of the ninth inning in Pittsburgh, turning a 3-1 Dodger lead into a heartbreaking 4-3 loss. Displaying considerable focus, however, L.A. rebounded the next night to defeat the Pirates 6-4 with two runs in the ninth, after Pittsburgh had tied the game at four all in the bottom of the seventh, aided by a two-run Dodger error.

The pennant races got serious as Labor Day arrived, with all the contests in the National League still up for grabs. In the East Division, Atlanta was holding on to a 4 1/2 game lead over the Florida Marlins. In the Central, the Houston Astros were 3 1/2 better than the surprising Pittsburgh team. The Pirates, under new manager Gene Lamont, after trading most of their expensive players and cutting their payroll to a major league low of less than $20 million, were making a run at the top spot with a young, relatively inexperienced team. The Marlins held a comfortable six game lead in the wildcard race.

And, in the West Division, it was like old times—another Dodger–Giant donnybrook, and one that looked like it would go down to the wire. Since the turn of the century, the two teams had finished one–two in the league a total of nine times. Six pennant races were decided during the last week of the season, two were decided on the final day, and two others ended in a flat-footed tie. The Giants led in the pitched battles, five pennants to four. In the American League, the leaders were Baltimore, Cleveland, and Seattle, with the Yankees having a lock on the wildcard spot.

An omen of things to come for Los Angeles reared its ugly head on September 2. Playing the Texas Rangers in Arlington Stadium, Bill Russell's boys went into the bottom of the ninth inning with a comfortable 12-7 lead, built on an explosive 18-hit attack, including a home run by catcher Tom Prince, and three hits each by Nixon, Piazza, and Gagne. Scott Radinsky was given the mop-up assignment, but the big southpaw couldn't retire anyone but himself. After four consecutive batters reached base, Russell rushed Todd Worrell into the fray. Unfortunately, the Dodger closer did no better. He blew his ninth save of the year, and was tagged with a numbing 13-12 defeat.

After another loss to Texas, the Dodgers righted themselves briefly, taking three out of four from the tough

Greg Gagne continued to provide Los Angeles with dependable inner perimeter defense. He committed only six errors after the All-Star game. (W. McNeil)

Florida Marlins in Los Angeles, but from there the Dodgers' fortunes ran hot and cold. Fortunately, the Giants were also experiencing a case of the blahs. On September 13, the Big Blue Machine pushed across four runs in the ninth inning against St. Louis closer Dennis Eckersley to beat the Cardinals. When San Fran lost to Atlanta, 6-4, the Dodger lead was two games.

Four days later, the Big Blue Machine moved into San Francisco to do battle with the orange and black. A two-game sweep would give the Dodgers a four-game lead and virtually lock up the title. The first game was a pitching masterpiece, as Kirk Reuter and Chan Ho Park were both on top of their game. Park made only one bad pitch, and Barry Bonds hit it out for a two-run homer in the first inning. Reuter and closer Roberto Hernandez made the runs stand up for a 2-1 victory, as they limited the L.A. hitters to just four hits, including Raul Mondesi's 27th homer of the season in the fifth inning.

In the second and final game of the two game series, the lead changed hands several times during the first seven innings, as the two starters, Candiotti and Mulholland, were hit hard. J.T. Snow and Barry Bonds took the Dodger knuckleballer downtown, as the Giants built a 5-1 lead after five innings. A two-run Dodger sixth and a two-run seventh knotted the count at five all, sending the game into extra innings.

The turning point of the game, and perhaps the season, came in the Dodger half of the tenth, when they loaded the bases off Rod Beck with no outs. After manager Dusty Baker made a quick trip to the mound, the Giant closer fanned the dangerous Todd Zeile, then induced pinch hitter Eddie Murray to ground into a second to home to first double play. Two innings later, San Francisco catcher Brian Johnson hit into the left field seats off

Mark Guthrie, to give the bay area boys a crucial 6-5 win, and a share of the division lead.

The series loss to San Fran was a major blow to the Los Angeles team's morale, but the next series, at home against the Colorado Rockies, was devastating. In the opener, Hideo Nomo blew a 3-1 lead in the seventh inning, with the go-ahead run crossing the plate on a wild pitch. Former Dodger Pedro Astacio was the recipient of the good fortune and came away the winner. The loss, coupled with San Francisco's 7-4 win over the San Diego Padres, gave the Giants a one-game lead in the West with eight games left to play.

Saturday was more of the same. The Dodgers' hard-luck pitcher Ismael Valdes threw another gem, but was once again betrayed by L.A.'s pop-gun offense, leaving after seven innings with a 1-1 tie. An RBI double by Jeff Reed off Antonio Osuna in the top of the eighth inning scored the game winner when Mike Piazza couldn't handle Juan Castro's relay from the outfield. The Giant lead stayed at one game, as they were bombed by the Padres, 12-2.

The Sunday evening finale started off on a brighter note for Bill Russell's embattled crew. After a scoreless first inning, the Dodgers put two on the board in the bottom of the second, and in the third, after a walk to Otis Nixon, Mike Piazza hit a towering 473-foot home run completely over the left field roof. It was the first ball in the 36-year history of Dodger Stadium ever hit out of the park to left field. Pirate legend Willie Stargell had hit the only two balls out of the park prior to Piazza's blow, and both balls went to right field.

As the sixth inning got underway, Ramon Martinez was coasting with a 5-2 lead. Then, disaster struck. Colorado put together four hits and two walks to score five runs and went on from there to win the game, 10-5. An 8-5 San Fran win over the Padres increased their lead to two full games and put the Dodgers on the brink of extinction.

A Giant win on Monday upped the margin to 2 1/2, but Dodger ace Chan Ho Park tossed a seven-hitter at San Diego on Tuesday, winning 6-2 on Todd Zeile's 28th and 29th home runs of the year and Eric Karros' 29th. Karros' round tripper was his first circuit clout of the month, after a drought of almost 80 at bats. The Dodger win, coupled with Colorado's 7-6 victory over San Francisco, cut the margin to 1 1/2 and, more importantly, to just one game in the loss column. The door was still open a crack for Bill Russell's cohorts, but they still had their work cut out for them. They needed to close out the season with a winning streak if they were to capture the division.

Wednesday, September 24, was the moment of truth for the boys from the City of Angels. They desperately needed another victory over the Padres before entering the snake pit in Denver for a season-ending, four-game series with Don Baylor's mighty sluggers. In an afternoon game, Dodger nemesis Brian Johnson had smashed a home run into the leftfield stands in the ninth inning at Coors Field to give the visiting Giants a dramatic come-from-behind 4-3 victory. Los Angeles should have been fired up with that score staring down at them from the scoreboard, but they weren't. They appeared listless and unmotivated, like cattle going to the slaughter.

Dodger starter Tom Candiotti was rocked for a line-drive homer off the bat of Steve Finley in the very first inning, putting the Padres on top early, 1-0. The Dodgers' big chance came and went in the bottom of the second when they loaded the bases against Joey Hamilton and had the big right-hander on the ropes. But they let him off the hook, and he made them pay dearly. A single by Karros, a hit batter, and a walk to Darren Lewis put Hamilton in a barrel of trouble. When Greg Gagne looped a single to right, it looked like a big inning for the Dodgers, but Todd Zeile got a poor jump off second base and couldn't score on the hit. The mistake came home to roost when the slow-footed Candiotti hit into an inning-ending double play, limiting the L.A. rally to a single run.

Joey Hamilton didn't falter again. He allowed only three more baserunners over his last six innings, and closer Trevor Hoffman retired the Dodgers 1-2-3 in the ninth, to end the game. Ken Caminiti's two run shot into the left center field seats off Candiotti in the fifth ended the scoring, as the Padres put another nail in the Dodger coffin, 3-1.

Mike Piazza, shown here as a rookie in 1992, developed into one of the greatest catchers in major league history. In 1997, his .362 batting average was the highest Dodger batting average since Lefty O'Doul hit .368 in 1932. His 40 home runs were the most by a Dodger since Duke Snider hit the same number in 1957. (W. McNeil)

Eric Karros gave the Dodgers another big year with the bat, with 31 home runs and 102 runs batted in. He also turned in a solid defensive performance. (W. McNeil)

The next day, Mike Piazza pounded out three base hits in the opener of the final series in Denver, and L.A. routed Pedro Astacio 9-5. Todd Zeile paced the Dodger attack with two home runs. Eric Karros and Darren Lewis also chipped in with homers to give Hideo Nomo his 14th victory. Piazza's three hits brought his season total up to 195, a new all-time record for major league catchers. It also brought his batting average up to .359, the highest average for a catcher since Bill Dickey hit .362 in 1936. Todd Zeile was the Dodgers' hottest hitter down the stretch. Over a 31-game span, the big third baseman rapped the ball at a .407 clip, with eight home runs and 25 runs batted in.

The Dodgers were still alive in the pennant race, though just barely. They trailed San Fran by two games with three left to play. They still needed a miracle to capture the West flag.

Friday, September 27, was a big day for L.A. Ismael Valdes, started for the Dodgers and received an unexpected present—some offense from the Dodger batsmen. For the season, Valdes received only 2.9 runs per game support from his teammates, the second worst support record in the entire National League. On this day, his buddies tried to make up for all the agony they caused him during the season, as they walloped six home runs en route to a 10-4 drubbing of Don Baylor's boys. Gagne, Young, and Karros all homered. Mike Piazza hit the longest home run in Coors Field's short history, a monstrous 496-foot shot to the concourse behind the center field seats. Raul Mondesi chipped in with two dingers, his 29th and 30th of the year. The last homer not only gave the

Dodgers another quartet of 30 homer players (Piazza, Karros, Zeile, Mondesi), it also made Raul the first 30–30 man in the club's history, with 30 homers and 32 stolen bases.

It was a big win for Los Angeles, but it didn't help in the pennant race. The Giants had their biggest scoring game in four years, as they pummeled the San Diego Padres 17-4. Another Giant victory on Saturday gave Dusty Baker's warriors a well-deserved West Division title. As noted in Baseball Weekly, the orange and black were an acknowledged group of castoffs and misfits, but they came together as a team and they played inspired baseball most of the season. They deserved their victory.

For the Los Angeles organization, it was a disappointing season. The team was widely favored to capture the National League West Division in preseason polls, but they never got untracked. The pitching was superior for most of the year, before faltering down the stretch. The staff finished second in the league in earned run average, with a mark of 3.62, but in September, both the starting staff and the bullpen had ERAs over 5.00. The hitting was sporadic, with long periods of inactivity. And they continued to have trouble driving in runners in scoring position. Three times during the last week of the season, they had the bases loaded with no one out, and they failed to score a single runner. One squeeze bunt would have been worth its weight in gold.

Baseball experts noted that the Dodgers had lost 14 consecutive key games. In 1995, they were swept in the playoffs. A year later, they were swept in the season-ending series by San Diego, costing them the West Division title. Then Atlanta took them three straight in the playoffs. In 1997, they went into San Francisco with a two-game lead, with only 11 games left to play in the season. They were swept by the Giants, then went home to L.A. where they were swept by the Rockies.

Individually, there were a few outstanding performers, particularly Mike Piazza, Raul Mondesi, Chan Ho Park, and Ismael Valdes. Piazza was sensational, hitting .362, with 201 base hits, 40 home runs, and 124 runs batted in. He was the first catcher ever to pound out 200 hits in a season, and the fourth catcher to hit 40 or more home runs. His .362 average tied him with Bill Dickey for the highest season batting average by a catcher. Over the last half of the season, Piazza led the entire major leagues in batting (.367) and runs batted in (73), while finishing second in home runs (24).

Raul Mondesi, with 30 home runs and 32 stolen bases, became the first 30–30 man in Dodger history. Mondesi was on the verge of becoming a true superstar. He was an exceptional outfielder with the strongest throwing arm in the major leagues, a daring and fleet-footed baserunner, and a .300 hitter with power. All he lacked was discipline and desire.

Chan Ho Park compiled a record of 14-8, with an ERA of 3.44. He gave the Dodgers consistently strong starts throughout the season. Ismael Valdes solidified his position as the most dependable pitcher on manager Bill Russell's staff. The big righty could show only a 10-11 record for the season, but he pitched like a 20-game winner. It was the inept Dodger bats that did him in. He averaged more than seven innings per start, while compiling a strong 2.65 earned run average. Over the last half of the season, he had the third lowest ERA in the league (2.23).

The 1997 season ended the O'Malley era. It is always a sad day for major league baseball when it loses such dedicated ownership. The O'Malley family had been a credit to the game for almost 50 years.

Now it was over.

2001—JIM TRACY'S BAPTISM OF FIRE

Davey Johnson brought the Los Angeles Dodgers home in second place in 2000, a distant eleven games behind the pennant-winning San Francisco Giants. The blue-and-white's 86-76 record was not enough to prevent Johnson from getting the axe, however. Management felt his team once again underachieved, and sent the feisty skipper into temporary retirement.

Kevin Brown's season was cut short because of recurring elbow miseries that finally required surgery. (Los Angles Dodgers)

Dodger manager Jim Tracy (Los Angeles Dodgers)

General Manager Kevin Malone selected bench coach Jim Tracy to succeed Johnson. Even though the Hamilton, Ohio native didn't have any major league managing experience, Malone was familiar with him from his Montreal tenure, where Tracy served as coach prior to coming to L.A., and Malone felt he had the necessary tools to be a successful major league manager. The low-keyed Tracy, who had paid his dues as a minor league manager for seven years before joining the Expos, seconded Malone's opinion: "I love the challenge of managing, of playing mental chess, of putting players in a position to win. . . . I spent a long time preparing for this."

When the season opened, the Dodgers were generally picked to finish first in the West, followed by Colorado, San Francisco, Arizona, and San Diego, in that order. But all was not well in Dodgerland. There was considerable tension, caused in part by Gary Sheffield's ultimatum to give him a lifetime contract or trade him. General Manager Kevin Malone promised to trade the malcontent by the end of spring training, but that didn't happen. Malone was forced to resign instead. He was replaced, on an interim basis, by Dave Wallace, a former Dodger pitching coach who was serving as a special assistant in charge of the farm system.

Paul Lo Duca loosens up before a game, with help from Dodger conditioning coach, Todd Clausen. (W. McNeil)

In spite of all the health problems, Jim Tracy kept his team in contention, although some people claimed he was doing it with mirrors. The most exciting game of the early going took place in Los Angeles on May 27 against the Houston Astros. A thrilling pitching duel between Darren Dreifort and Scott Elarton went into extra innings and, when Houston pushed across two runs in the top of the 12th, the situation looked bleak. But Tracy's boys came storming back. Walks to Grudzielanek and Green set the table, and Adrian Beltre's single brought home one run. Then Marquis Grissom lined a ball to the gap in right center field, sending the tying and winning runs across the plate.

The next night, Paul Lo Duca had a career day at the plate. In a game against the Colorado Rockies, the fiery backstop rapped six base hits in six at-bats, and the Dodgers needed them all to win the game 11-10. Fittingly, Lo Duca carried the winning run across the plate in the 11th inning on a single by Shawn Green.

The Dodgers 30-23 record on May 31, left them just one game back of the Arizona Diamondbacks, who were riding the brilliant pitching of Randy Johnson (6-4) and Curt Schilling (9-1) to a possible postseason position. Through June and into July, the L.A. injuries continued to mount, but Tracy always had a solution. When Ashby went down, he moved rookie Luke Prokopec into the rotation. Then, when Brown and Dreifort hit the wall, he pulled big, tough right-hander Terry Adams and husky Giovanni Carrara out of the bullpen and inserted them into the starting rotation. Both men stood up to the challenge and did a superb job.

The team highlight in July was a 22-7 drubbing of Colorado in Denver. L.A. put over five runs in the opening frame, and after the Rockies responded with a five spot of their own in the second, Tracy's sluggers tore into Buddy Bell's pitching staff, putting up six big ones in the sixth and nine in the eighth. Starter Eric Gagne was the beneficiary of the L.A. output, surviving the second inning Colorado rally and giving his manager six innings before turning the ball over to the bullpen. Gary Sheffield was the big gun for the Dodgers, hammering his 21st and 22nd homers, plus a single. Adrian Beltre ripped four singles, while Lo Duca, Grudzielanek, Green, and Christensen had three hits apiece, with Lo Duca and Green smashing home runs.

Sheffield settled down after Malone's departure and concentrated on playing baseball. As April came to an end, Jim Tracy had his team in first place, their 15-10 record one and a half games better than the Rockies. Sheffield was hitting only .279, but he had seven home runs and 21 RBIs to his credit. Shawn Green was close behind with six homers and 19 RBIs. On the mound, Kevin Brown was his usual dominating self, with a 3-1 record and a 1.03 ERA. Chan Ho Park's record stood at 3-2. The big surprise in the early going was the performance of rookie backstop Paul Lo Duca. The 193-pound right-handed hitter was slugging the ball at a .368 pace and had thrown out four of seven attempted base stealers.

As promising as the L.A. start was, the season quickly turned gloomy due to a growing hospital list. Kevin Brown, who came off the disabled list on April 10, would go back on it twice more during the season, and would eventually undergo elbow surgery on September 27.

Andy Ashby went on the disabled list on April 16, with a muscle strain in his right elbow. He would be lost for the season after going under the knife on June 15. And the number three starter, Darren Dreifort, would be cut down on June 30, and he would undergo his second Tommy John surgery in six years on July 9. On April 25, Mark Grudzielanek sprained his right thumb, and Sheffield tore a ligament in his left index finger—the injuries would hamper both players the rest of the season. Eric Karros, not to be outdone, went down with a lower lumbar sprain in his back. He would go on the DL from May 22 to June 15, but, in fact, he never fully recovered from the injury. Adrian Beltre, who had undergone two major surgeries over the winter, never regained his strength, and struggled through a painful and disappointing season.

Mark Grudzielanek talks with comedian Tom Arnold during a break in the filming of a television special in Vero Beach. (W. McNeil)

Surprisingly, maybe even shockingly, August 1 found the Big Blue Machine back atop the Western Division standings. Their 61-46 record gave them a half game lead over the Diamondbacks, and a three game bulge over Dusty Baker's Giants. Chan Ho Park was the new Dodger ace, piling up an 11-7 record, with an outstanding 2.83 earned run average. He was ably supported by Terry Adams at 7-4, Luke Prokopec at 8-8, long reliever Matt Herges at 6-6, and closer Jeff Shaw (3-2 with 33 saves). Sheffield (.303, 25, 60), Green (.290, 31, 87), and Lo Duca (.332, 17, 55), anchored the offense.

Eight days later, the Dodgers were riding the crest of a five-game winning streak and were on the verge of sweeping the lowly Pirates when the wheels suddenly came off the wagon. Chan Ho Park was battered unmercifully by Lloyd McClendon's troops, yielding seven earned runs in five innings of work as the Bucs took the getaway game, 8-5. Grudzielanek, Sheffield, and Beltre had three hits each for L.A., but 10 men left on base did them in. Later, Sheffield confided to Marquis Grissom, "That game's going to come back to hurt us. We let that game get away."

In fact, it was the turning point of the season. The team lost their next four games and struggled through the remainder of the season. They went 8-13 the rest of August and saw their 1 1/2 game lead in the Western Division turn into a five-game deficit. Even worse, they fell all the way to third place, one game behind San Francisco.

There was one bright spot during the August slump. Shawn Green smashed three home runs in a game against the Montreal Expos on August 15, sparking Tracy's warriors to a 13-1 victory. Green took Expos starter Carl Pavano downtown in the second inning, with two men on base, to give L.A. a comfortable 5-0 lead. He hit another homer off Pavano in the fourth, then drilled a two-run shot off Masato Yoshii in the 7th. Beltre and Grudzielanek each had four hits in the rout.

On September 11, the realities of life hit home for the Dodgers and their fans, as well as for millions of other people across the country, when terrorists hijacked four commercial airliners and flew two of them into the World Trade Center in New York City, with a third plane being flown into the Pentagon and the fourth crashing in a field in Pennsylvania, after passengers attacked the hijackers.

When play resumed a week later, the Dodgers found themselves in a hopeless situation. They trailed Arizona by four games and the Giants by two, with just 17 games remaining in the season. Although Bob Brenly was still riding his two big horses (Johnson 18-6, and Schilling 20-6) to a division crown, the big story of the season was turning out to be Barry Bonds' chase of the single-season home run record. When the season was interrupted, Bonds had sent 63 balls into orbit in 144 games, leaving

The Cinderella team of the year turned out to be the Arizona Diamondbacks. They enjoyed a rags-to-riches success story behind the dominant pitching of Curt Schilling (22-6) and Randy Johnson (21-6). After humbling the Giants and Dodgers in the Western Division race, Bob Brenly's cohorts swept through the postseason like a tidal wave. They knocked off the St. Louis Cardinals in five games in the Division Series, then took the NLCS four games to one against the aging Atlanta Braves. Moving on to the World Series to face the powerful New York Yankees, the D'backs showed their mettle by winning games six and seven to capture the World Championship. After scorching the Bronx Bombers 15-2 in game six to even the Series at three games apiece, Arizona came from behind in the bottom of the ninth inning of game seven, scoring two runs to win, 3-2. Facing All-World closer, Mariano Rivera with the bases loaded and two down, Arizona slugger Luis Gonzales dropped a bloop single into short left field, driving in Jay Bell with the championship run. Schilling and Johnson were co-MVPs, going a combined 4-0 with a scintillating 1.21 ERA.

Jeff Shaw saved 43 games in 77 appearances during the 2001 season. (W. McNeil)

him seven home runs behind Mark McGwire with 18 games left.

The Dodgers kept pace with the Giants and Diamondbacks through September, but couldn't close the gap. September finished as it began, with L.A. in third place, now six games out and two games behind Dusty Baker's club. Barry Bonds was sitting on 69 home runs, with six games to go, including three at home against Los Angeles. Barry didn't wait until he got home to hit #70 however. He put the big one into orbit in Houston on October 4. Then, returning to the cozy confines of Pac Bell a day later, the Giant slugger thrilled the home crowd with his record breaking theatrics. Coming to the plate in the bottom of the first inning against Dodger fireballer Chan Ho Park, Bonds tattooed a 1-0 pitch, sending it 442 feet into the dry California air. It splashed down in McCovey Cove for a new single-season home run record.

Barry Bonds hit #71 two innings later, but it wasn't enough to keep San Francisco in the wildcard race. Jim Tracy's bombers eliminated the Giants from contention by eking out an 11-10 victory. The next day, L.A. won again, 6-2, and in the season finale, Bonds took Dennis Springer deep, and the Giants prevailed, 2-1.

Adrian Beltre suffered through a pain-filled 2001 season after undergoing two major surgeries in the off-season. (W. McNeil)

The season was another disappointment for Dodger fans as the team missed the postseason play-offs for the fifth consecutive year, but there were a few highlights. Shawn Green has a sensational season, hitting .297, with a solid .311 batting average, with 36 home runs and an even 100 runs-batted-in. And rookie Paul Lo Duca sizzled behind the plate. He rapped the ball at a .320 clip, smashed 2 homers and drove in 90 teammates. Defensively, he shot down 39% of all would-be base stealers, 5% better than the league average. On the mound, Chan Ho Park was the ace, with a 15-11 record and a 3.50 earned-run-average. Terry Adams finished at 12-8, and Kevin Brown went 10-4 in limited duty.

As far as manager Jim Tracy was concerned, it was a brilliant debut for him. He kept the Big Blue Machine in contention throughout the season with masterful personnel decisions and game strategies. Unfortunately, the long list of crippling injuries were too much for the team to overcome.

2004—A NEW OWNER AND A DIVISION CHAMPIONSHIP

The Los Angeles Dodgers acquired a new owner and a new General Manager as the 2004 season got underway. Frank McCourt, Jr. purchased the club from The Fox Group in January and immediately put his own stamp on the organization by replacing General Manager Dan Evans with Paul DePodesta, making him the sixth General Manager in Los Angeles in less than six years. Prior to the sale of the Dodgers to the Fox Group in 1997, the team had only three General Managers in 36 years from 1951 to 1987. DePodesta, who had been the Assistant General Manager at Oakland, was a 31-year old executive whose teams had reached the playoffs seven times in his eight years in the game. And he was committed to bringing a World Championship to the west coast franchise.

The Dodgers had finished in second place in the tough Western Division of the National League in 2003, posting an 85-77 won-loss record but finish-

Gary Sheffield was the team's top clutch hitter in 2001. (W. McNeil)

Beltre's 48 home runs and 121 RBIs sparked the Dodgers to the Western Division pennant. (W. McNeil)

ing a hefty 15 ½ games behind the pennant-winning San Francisco Giants. They had relied primarily on pitching for their success in 2003, leading the league in ERA, saves, and fewest home runs allowed—offsetting a wretched offense that was last in home runs and runs scored. The pitching staff, that had long been a staple of the Dodger organization, lost some of its luster in 2004 with the departure of Kevin Brown to the Yankees and the lingering injuries to Hideo Nomo, but the arrival of Jeff Weaver from the Yankees and Jose Lima from Kansas City helped to keep the L.A. squad a step ahead of their west coast adversaries. They let Fred McGriff take his 13 home runs to Tampa Bay in the off season and bade 37-year old Brian Jordan a fond farewell. They moved Shawn Green to first base to fill the void there, hoping he could resurrect the 49 home run season he hammered out three years earlier, and they expected to see some improvement in the run production of third baseman Adrian Beltre who hit a mediocre .240 in 2003 with 23 homers and 80 RBIs. They had two open slots in the outfield after the departure of Jordan and the move of Green, and manager Jim Tracy filled those holes by acquiring Milton Bradley in a trade with Cleveland and picking up 6', 3", 215-pound slugger Jayson Werth from Toronto. The experts apparently had confidence in the Dodgers as they established them as the favorites to win the National League West.

The Dodgers broke from the gate quickly when the bell rang riding the hot hands of Lima and Ishii, and the ninth inning magic of Eric Gagne who was credited with saves in five of L.A.'s first nine victories, extending his streak of consecutive saves to a major league record 68. One of their more satisfying series took place from April 16 to 18 in AT & T Park in San Francisco when they swept the hated Giants by scores of 3-2 behind Odalis Perez, 5-4 behind Jose Lima, and 7-6 behind Jeff Weaver. The Dodgers, trailing in game three by a score of 2-1 in the top of the fifth inning came roaring back with a six spot to lead 7-2. Adrian Beltre was the main antagonist in the rally, taking an outside pitch from Brett Tomko and depositing it in the right field seats for a 4-2 Dodger advantage. Juan Encarnacion followed Beltre's blast with one of his own and David Ross made it a threesome with a homer to left. Eric Gagne saved all three games for Jim Tracy's charges who finished the month with a 14-8 record, giving them a first place tie with the San Diego Padres. Third baseman Adrian Beltre had a hot bat, caressing the ball at a .353 pace for the month with nine home runs, while homering in three consecutive games between the 18th and the 21st. In addition to his round tripper in game three of the Giant series, he sent one out of the park in a 9-4 win over the Colorado Rockies in Coors Field, and he gave his team their only run in a 7-1 loss to the Rockies. Cesar Izturis, in addition to giving his team exceptional defense at shortstop, stung the ball at a .329 clip, and Paul LoDuca had a .416 average to show for his first month behind the plate. Dave Roberts had a .416 on-base-percentage and was 15 for 15 in the stolen base department. Kazuhisa Ishii paced the mound corps with a 4-1 record, including a 5-1 victory over the Rockies in his first start. Roberts brought the big crowd to its feet several times during the game by stealing four bases. He scored the first run of the game after a walk, a stolen base, and a sharp single to right field by Paul LoDuca. Ishii also posted a 9-0 shutout against Felipe Alou's Giants in Dodger Stadium on April 25 before an enthusiastic home crowd of 54,235.

The game produced a number of Dodger heroes. Among them were Milton Bradley who launched two home runs, a leadoff homer in the third and a solo shot in the sixth, and Alex Cora, whose two-out, three-run homer in the second inning got the Dodger express off and running. In addition, Dave Roberts added three base hits to the Dodgers total.

From April 30 to May 12, the Dodgers ran off eight victories in ten games but then they hit the wall with a thud. Between May 13 and May 28 the west coast contingent managed to win just two games while losing twelve, dropping their record to 24-22. Their all-star third baseman managed just seven base hits in 49 at-bats for a .143 average with three RBIs during that period, and his counterpart, Shawn Green, was only slightly better, hitting .157 in 51 at-bats with two RBIs. They did however look

Kazuhisa Ishii contributed 13 victories to the Dodger pennant parade. (Los Angeles Dodgers)

like their old selves on May 29 and 30 against the visiting cellar-dwelling Arizona Diamondbacks. On the 29th, they blanked the Diamondbacks by a 10-0 count behind Jose Lima's fourth victory, as 35,343 D'Back fans sat in stunned silence. Green went two-for-four in the game with two RBIs, Beltre chipped in with a three-run homer, and Paul LoDuca had four base hits in four at-bats with two RBIs. The following night, Kazuhisa Ishii won his sixth game against three losses with a 3-0 shutout. Beltre, who was two-for-four on the day, crushed a two-run double to left field in the bottom of the first inning to send the L.A. crew on to victory.

As the end of June approached the Dodgers suffered through a six game losing streak, falling back into third place, 3½ games behind the Giants. Then, once again, the wind shifted and the team came together as a unit. On the 27th, Ishii defeated the Anaheim Angels 10-5 in Dodger Stadium much to the delight of the 54,235 National League fans who passed through the turnstiles at the ballpark in Chavez Ravine. They were down 2-1 after 3½ innings before exploding with a seven run fourth that included a three-run homer by Beltre.

Los Angeles put together an excellent 21-7 month in July to move to the top of the pack for the last time. They never relinquished the lead again. They enjoyed a 2½game lead at the end of July and a healthy 5½-game lead as August came to an end. And it was Beltre and Green who led the hit parade. The Dodger third baseman put ten balls into orbit

around the major leagues in July, including two in Anaheim during an 8-5 victory on July 3. And on the 24th he slammed a homer and drove in five runs in an 11-2 laugher over San Diego. He had two two-homer games in August, including a classic confrontation against the Atlanta Braves at home on the 20th of the month. In that contest, he smashed a ninth inning game-tying home run off Atlanta closer John Smoltz and then, with a flair for the dramatic, he launched an eleventh inning, walk-off homer to send the Dodger Stadium crowd home happy with a 3-2 victory. Counting that game, Beltre had three games with three or more RBIs over a period of five days. Shawn Green knocked in 20 runs in July and another 18 runs in August. On July 15, in Bank One Ballpark in Arizona, he hit a first inning, grand slam homer to give Wilson Alvarez all the runs he needed in a 4-3 victory, and on August 21, he homered twice, including another first inning grand slam homer, and drove in five runs in a 7-4 win over Atlanta.

July 5 was a historic day in Los Angeles Dodger history. On Sunday, the third of the month, when L.A. defeated Anaheim in eleven innings in the aforementioned 6-5 victory, Eric Gagne saved his 21st game of the year and his 84th consecutive save dating back to August 28, 2002. Two days later, in Dodger Stadium, the streak came to an end when Gagne surrendered two runs to Arizona in the ninth, erasing a 5-3 Los Angeles lead. When the last out was recorded in the inning, the crowd of 32, 929 stood as one and gave their world class closer a rousing cheer, causing Gagne to tip his cap in appreciation. Fortunately, L.A. won the game in the bottom of the tenth on a sacrifice fly by Shawn Green. And the next night, the Dodger closer was back on the mound to record his 22nd save of the year in a 4-1 win over the Diamondbacks.

Jim Tracy's cohorts entered September with a 5½-game lead over San Francisco and a six-game lead over San Diego, and they protected the leads reasonably well as the season wound down, although not without some concern. They had seven games remaining against San Diego and six against Felipe Alou's Giants, and they managed just five victories in those thirteen games, but they won eight of ten games against the rest of the division. Over a period of thirteen games between September 7 and September 19, the Dodgers had seven come-from-behind victories out of eight games won. The last game of the string, on the 19th, saw Tracy's charges fall behind by a 5-0 score at Coors Field before beginning their comeback in the seventh inning. They pushed over three runs in that inning on Beltre's bases-clearing double to left field, and plated the two tying runs in the eighth, one of them on Milton Bradley's monstrous 479 foot blast into the third deck in right field. After the Rockies recaptured the lead in the bottom of the eighth, the Dodgers forged one more comeback. Colorado closer Shawn Chacon struck out two men and walked one in the ninth, bringing up

The big Canadian saved 84 consecutive games in 2003-2004. Overall, Gagne saved 100 games in 102 save opportunities in those two years. (Los Angeles Dodgers)

Shawn Green who promptly unloaded on a two-strike pitch sending a 422 foot home run to dead center field for a 7-6 L.A. victory. The first critical series of the month, beginning on September 13, pitted the Dodgers against the Padres in Dodger Stadium and L.A. dropped three of four to reduce their lead over the Giants to 2½ games. Six days later, after losing two of three to Bruce Bochy's team in San Diego, the lead over San Fran was down to 1½, but it was still 5½ over the Padres who were having trouble beating any team that didn't have Los Angeles scripted across their chest. On September 24, L.A. invaded the Bay Area for a three game series with the Giants, with the division pennant hanging in the balance. Odalis Perez rose to the occasion, holding the Giants to two runs in eight innings while Green's two-run homer and Jose Hernandez's solo shot, both in the fourth inning, held up for a 3-2 Dodger victory, giving them a 2½-game lead and a little breathing room over the Giants. As the days dwindled down to a precious few, the Dodger lead stood at three games when the two teams locked horns one last time on October 1-3 in L.A. Game one went to the Giants 4-2 as Kirk Rueter won his ninth game of the season, besting

Jeff Weaver, and reducing L.A.'s lead to two games with two to play. Game two matched Brett Tomko against Elmer Dessens who was making his first start for Jim Tracy after being acquired from Arizona on August 19. The Giants jumped on Dessens for two runs in the fourth inning and they added a run in the seventh to increase the lead to 3-0. It was still 3-0 as the Dodgers came up for their last at-bats in the bottom of the ninth. Three walks, two singles, and an error later, brought Steve Finley up with the score tied, the bases loaded, and one out. It was, as Finley had stated after joining the Dodgers from Arizona on July 31, "the type of situation he wanted to be in." Wayne Franklin, a left-handed reliever appearing in his 43rd game, got a strike over on the first pitch but the second pitch never reached the plate. Finley caught it on the fat part of his bat and hit a towering drive to right field where it settled into the seats for a walk-off, pennant-winning, grand slam home run. The Dodger dugout emptied en masse, the stands erupted in a cacophony of whistles and screams, and the Dodgers had their first pennant in nine years.

Los Angeles finished the season with a record of 93-69 and they had to face the Central Division

Champion St. Louis Cardinals who won 105 games against just 57 losses, in the National League Division Series. Game one was in St. Louis where 38-year old right-hander Woody Williams, an eleven-game winner in the regular season met the Dodgers' Odalis Perez. The Tuesday afternoon game drew 52,127 fans to Busch Stadium III under sunny skies on a pleasant fall day with the temperature hovering around the 57 degree mark. The Redbirds took care of Perez in less than three innings, scoring one run in the first on a Pujols home run and five more in the third. Larry Walker, who came to the Cards on July 31, hit two home runs while catcher Tom Wilson's homer was the only bright spot for L.A., an 8-3 loser. Game two was a replay of game one, with St. Louis taking an 8-3 decision. Jayson Werth put Jim Tracy's charges on the board with a first inning home run, but the lead was short-lived as St. Louis struck back with a three-spot in the bottom of the second on two doubles and a triple. The Dodgers tied the game in the fourth on leadoff homers by Shawn Green and Milton Bradley, but Weaver quickly gave it back in the fifth when he was sent to the showers

Odalis Perez won twelve games for Jim Tracy's pennant-winners. (Los Angeles Dodgers)

under a barrage of base hits and hit batters. When the smoke had cleared Tony LaRussa's cohorts had pulled in front by a 6-3 score. They added two more runs in the seventh to close out the scoring for the day. The series moved to the west coast for game three, a Saturday night game matching the Cards 15-game winner Matt Morris against L.A.'s tall, lanky right-hander Jose Lima. The game started at 5:10 PM under sunny skies with 55,952 rabid Dodger fans in the stands, and it was all Lima. He shut down the heavy hitting Redbirds, pitching a complete game 4-0 shutout with four strikeouts and just one walk. Steve Finley gave the Dominican Dandy all the runs he needed with a two-run double in the third inning. Shawn Green completed the scoring for the day with solo homers in the fourth and sixth innings. Unfortunately, Los Angeles couldn't maintain the momentum and St. Louis sent them home for the winter with a 6-2 victory in game four. Jeff Suppan, the Cardinals 16-game winner, outpitched Perez and Wilson Alvarez, throwing seven innings of two-run ball, backed by a Reggie Sanders home run and a three-run homer off the bat of Albert Pujols. The Dodgers could muster only two runs on three base hits. The final stats told the story of the series. St. Louis had a team batting average of .254 and an ERA of 3.09 while L.A. checked in with an embarrassing .198 batting average and a lofty 5.82 ERA. Jason Werth with two homers and three RBIs and Shawn Green with three homers and three RBIs led the Dodger attack while Edgar Renteria with a hefty .455 batting average led all hitters. Pujols batted .333 with two homers and five RBIs.

A review of the Dodgers regular season gave some hope of success for the following season. Adrian Beltre, the league's Silver Slugger winner, had a breakout season, batting .334 with 48 home runs and 121 runs-batted-in. He was also a superb fielder, with soft hands, excellent range, a strong throwing arm, and he was particularly deadly on bunts. Shawn Green chipped in with 28 homers and 86 RBIs and gave the Dodgers excellent movement around first base. Cesar Izturis, an exciting defensive shortstop, who caressed the ball for a .288 average for the season, won a Gold Glove for his work in the field, Steve Finley, who had 13 homers after coming over from Arizona, was another Gold Glove recipient, and Eric Gagne, who saved 45 games in 47 chances, was named the Sporting News' National League Reliever of the Year.

2006—COLLETTI, LITTLE, AND ANOTHER WESTERN DIVISION PENNANT

Los Angeles Dodgers slipped from first place to fourth place in the Western Division in 2005, but once the season came to a merciful end, Dodger management went into high gear to put together a winning team, both on the field and in the front office. General Manager Paul DePodesta was fired on October 29, 2005 and Ned Colletti was hired to replace him. At the same time, Jim Tracy left to manage the Pittsburgh Pirates when Dodger management refused to give him an extension of his contract. Colletti got off to a running start in his new job, signing William "Grady" Little as manager, trading Milton Bradley for Andre Ethier, and signing free agents Nomar Garciaparra, Rafael Furcal, Kenny Lofton, and Bill Mueller. The trade of Bradley for Ethier was doubly important. The Dodgers disposed of a player who created problems in the clubhouse and they obtained in Ethier, a young man who was a .300 hitter with power in the Oakland A's minor league system and who looked ready to repeat the pattern at the Big League level. One overlooked addition to the team was Takashi Saito, a 14-year veteran of the Japanese league, who would turn out to be the key to the Dodgers' success. He had been both a successful starting pitcher and a successful closer in Japan at one time or another, and when Eric Gagne went on the Disabled List on April 1 Saito moved into the closer's position without losing a step and would solidify the bullpen situation down the stretch. The starting rotation seemed to be pretty well set as the season got underway, with opening day starter Derek Lowe joined by Brad Penny, Brett Tomko, Odalis Perez, and Aaron Sele. As the season progressed however, Perez would be traded to Kansas City in July, Tomko would spend a month on the DL, Colletti would trade for future Hall of Famer Greg Maddux on July 31, and rookie Chad Billingsley would move into the starting rotation the same month.

Opening day 2006, was celebrated in Dodger Stadium on April 3 with the visiting Braves throwing Tim Hudson at Dodger ace, Derek Lowe, but neither pitcher lasted past the fifth inning. Bobby Cox's Braves jumped on Lowe for four runs out of the gate and, after Atlanta put up another four-spot in the fifth inning, three of them coming on Andruw Jones three-run homer, L.A. KO'd Hudson with a four-spot of their own in the bottom of the inning to close the gap to 8-5, but they couldn't get any closer. Atlanta scored two runs in the sixth and one in the eighth for an 11-5 lead. The never-say-die Dodgers hung up a three-spot in the eighth and added another brace of runs in the ninth but they came up a run short. Actually the Dodgers out-hit the Braves 17 to 12 in the game, but 14 of their hits were singles with three doubles mixed in, while three of the Braves hits left the yard. Jose Cruz led all hitters with four base hits including a double, followed by Raphael Furcal who had three hits. According to news reports, the crowd of 56,000 was the largest single-game, regular-season crowd in Dodger Stadium history. Grady Little's charges bounced back to take game two, 5-4, behind right-hander Brad Penny, beginning an up-and-down month for the team.

The month ended with a shocking 6-5 ten-inning loss to San Diego on April 30. The Dodgers had the game well in hand after eight innings, lead-

Grady Little piloted the Dodgers to a Western Division tie with San Diego in his first year at the helm. (W. McNeil)

ing 5-0 on a Derek Lowe two-hitter, but the Dodger bullpen, particularly Danys Baez and Lance Carter, gave it away in the bottom of the ninth, surrendering five runs, and Tim Hamulack took the loss an inning later. The Dodgers record stood at 12-13 after that debacle, leaving them in third place, three games behind Clint Hurdle's Colorado Rockies. After dropping the first four games in May, the blue and white righted the ship and ran up a record of 18-6 the rest of the month, thanks to a perfect blend of pitching and hitting. L.A. averaged 6.4 runs per game during the streak while holding the opposition to just four runs per game. And except for two 10-4 losses to the Washington Nationals on the 26th and 28th of the month Dodger pitching held opposing teams to 3.4 runs per game. Colletti and Little made a number of strategic moves during the month that paid huge dividends as the season wore on. First, they recalled Aaron Sele from Las Vegas to replace Odalis Perez in the starting rotation, and the 35-year old right-hander won three of his five starts in May with two no-decisions. They also recalled Andre Ethier, Russell Martin, and Matt Kemp, from Las Vegas, and sent James Loney down to the same club for more seasoning. Just days after his arrival, Ethier had his biggest day of the season, pounding out five base hits in five at-bats, with his second career major league home run, four runs scored, and three RBIs, as the Dodgers routed the Anaheim Angels by a 16-3 margin.

The magic disappeared from the L.A. lineup in June and Grady Little's warriors limped home in second place on June 30, one game behind San Diego after winning just 11 of 26 games. The culprit in this case was the pitching that was tagged for an average of 5.3 runs per game. The offense averaged five runs per game but that was not enough to offset the shoddy mound work. Brad Penny and Derek Lowe pitched admirably in June with Penny going 4-1, holding the opposition to just seven runs in his four victories, and Lowe posting a 3-1 mark with the opposition scoring just six runs in his three victories. Aaron Sele won only one of three decisions in June, but that one was a 7-0 masterpiece against Pittsburgh. The other Dodgers starters were a combined 1-7.

L.A. won five of eight July games leading up to the All-Star Game, where Brad Penny, with a record of 10-2, got the starting assignment. He was joined on the All-Star team by Nomar Garciaparra. When regular season action resumed on July 13, the Dodgers went into the tank, losing 13 of 14 games, with Penny absorbing three of those losses. The last Dodger loss, on the 26th, was a 10-3 drubbing at the hands of San Diego that left them in last place with a 47-55 won-loss record, a distant 7½ games behind the Padres. After the game, manager Grady Little went into the clubhouse and told his team, "We have a day off on Monday when we fly to Cincinnati, and we're all going to dinner. All of us. Everybody. It's mandatory." Coincidentally or not, the team seemed to come together after that dinner. Greg Maddux joined the team within a few days, and Odalis Perez who had been a disruptive influence in the clubhouse, was shuttled off to Kansas City about the same time. The team went on a tear between July 28 and August 15, winning eleven in a row and 17 of 18, their best run since 1899.

The first game of the surge was a 13-1 blowout of the Washington Nationals in L.A on the 28th. Chad Billingsley was the recipient of the offensive explosion, tossing six innings of one-run ball. Andre Ethier's two-run homer in the second inning gave Little's troops a 2-0 lead and they gradually increased it inning after inning. Ethier added a triple to his output later in the game, J.D. drew hit a grand slam homer in the fourth, Russell Martin had three base hits, and Cesar Izturis cracked his first home run of the season. The Dodgers would go 41-19 after July 26, battling San Diego tooth and nail the rest of the way.

By the end of July, the Dodgers had closed the gap to five games, and by the end of their winning streak, they had moved into a one-half-game lead over San Diego. The rest of the season was a dogfight between the two teams, with first one, then the other, gaining an advantage. L.A. went 21-7 in August, ending the month with a three-game lead over the Padres. Greg Maddux made his first start as a Dodger on August 13 in a ten-inning 1-0 Dodger victory. Maddux, who left after holding San Francisco to two hits in eight innings, took a no-decision in the game. He beat San Francisco on the 19th of the month and took the measure of the Cincinnati Reds on the 30th.

The Dodgers increased their lead to four games with a 14-5 win over Colorado on September 2nd, but then lost four of five contests to see the lead shrink to a mere one-half game. The two teams battled back and forth over the next two weeks with L.A. falling one-half game behind San Diego after dropping two of three to the Padres, with one game remaining.

The game of September 18 may have been the defining game of the season. The Padres took the L.A. crowd out of the game in the first inning, pushing over four runs against Brad Penny. The Dodger

Russell Martin gave the Dodgers outstanding defense in 2006 and chipped in with ten home runs in 415 at-bats. (W. McNeil)

starter regrouped after the rough start and shut San Diego down over the next four innings while his teammates scratched and clawed their way back into contention, tying the game at four-all in the third. The Padres broke the tie with two runs in the eighth inning; L.A. got one back in the bottom of the inning, but San Diego pushed over three more runs in the ninth to open up a seemingly insurmountable 9-5 lead. After Jeff Kent and J.D. Drew had hit one-out homers to start the ninth, closer Trevor Hoffman was summoned from the bullpen, but he was rudely received by the Dodger hitting corps. His first two pitches were sent screaming out of the park, first by Russell Martin, then by Marlon Anderson, and suddenly the game was deadlocked at nine-all. The San Diego players did not seem to be discouraged by the Dodger rally as they came right back and scored another tie-breaking run in the top of the tenth inning. When Los Angeles came to bat in the bottom of the inning, they had to face hard-throwing right-hander Rudy Seanez who walked Kenny Lofton to start the inning. The next batter, Dodger first base-man Nomar Garciaparra, worked the count to 3-1 and then sat on a Seanez fastball. When it came as expected, Garciaparra put the wood to it and sent it screaming to the far reaches of the left field pavilion where Padre left fielder Dave Roberts could only watch and admire it as it settled into the seats for a game-winning two-run homer.

The season did not end there, but everything else was anti-climatic. L.A. fell two games behind after they lost three of their next five games, but they finished the season strong, winning their last seven games to finish in a tie with San Diego, with two of their victories coming from Greg Maddux. One of their final seven victories was particularly noteworthy. On September 28, James Loney, back from his Las Vegas exile, tied Gil Hodges' franchise record with nine runs-batted-in in a 19-11 donny-brook in the rarified atmosphere of Colorado. The Los Angeles first baseman had four hits in five trips to the plate with a double and two home runs. He hit a grand slam homer in the second inning to bring his team back from a 3-0 deficit, doubled home two more runs in the third as L.A. opened up an 8-3 lead, singled in a run in the fifth, and closed out his pyrotechnics with a two-run homer in the sixth. Los Angeles clinched a playoff spot two days later when Maddux defeated the San Francisco Giants 4-2 in AT & T Park. The six-foot tall, 180-pound right hander held Bruce Bochy's team to two runs on three hits in seven innings and Takashi Saito closed the game out with a rookie-record 24th save. The Dodgers were the wild card entry in postseason play based on their 5-13 record against San Diego in the regular season series.

The Dodgers drew the Eastern Division Champion New York Mets in the National League Division Series, and Willie Randolph's well-balanced squad made short work of their west coast rivals, sending them packing in three games. The opening game of the series in Shea Stadium, especially the goings-on in the second inning, reminded the New York faithful of the days when the Daffy Dodgers cavorted around Ebbetts Field in Brooklyn. With Jeff Kent on second and J.D. Drew on first in a scoreless game, Russell Martin hit a shot into the right field corner that looked like a two-run double when it was hit, but the ball caromed back into the glove of right fielder Shawn Green. He fired it to cutoff man, Jose Valentin who whirled and threw a bullet to catcher

Nomar Garciapara provided a big bat in the middle of the batting order, smashing 20 home runs with 100 RBIs. (W. McNeil)

Paul LoDuca who put the tag on the sliding Kent. When LoDuca looked up, he saw J.D. Drew bearing down on him and he casually tagged Drew out also, giving him a rare unassisted double play. It was the first time a Dodger batter had doubled into a double play since Babe Herman did it in 1926. The Mets went on from there to win the game by a 6-5 count with Brad Penny taking the loss in relief. Nomar Garciaparra went one for four for L.A. with a double and two RBIs and Kent, Marlon Anderson, and Wilson Betimit each chipped in with two hits. Hong–Chih Kuo, a fireballing southpaw who had just one victory to show for his efforts during the regular season, got the start for Los Angeles in game two and pitched well for four innings but ran out of gas in the fifth, leaving with one out and trailing by a 2-0 score. The Mets Tom Glavine, a silky-smooth southpaw who was a 15-game winner during the season and well on his way to 300 career victories, kept the Dodgers off balance by varying speeds and location on his repertoire of pitches. The final score was New York 4, L.A. 1.

The series moved to the west coast for Game Three with New York's Steve Trachsel opposed by the Dodgers' Greg Maddux and, unfortunately for the L.A. fans, it was not Maddux's day. New York jumped on him for three runs in the first inning and added another run in the third. Grady Little's troops came back with two runs in the fourth on James Loney's bases loaded single to left field, and three runs in the fifth, two of them on a Jeff Kent homer, to take a temporary 5-4 lead. Jonathan Broxton assumed the mound duties in the sixth inning, but he proved to be no mystery to the Mets as they ripped him for three runs on four base hits, essentially ending the Dodgers season. New York added two runs off Brett Tomko in the eighth to close out the scoring for the day. Jeff Kent had four hits, including a double and a home run, in the Dodger loss, and Russell Martin and James Loney had three hits apiece. Loney was the Dodgers leading hitter for the series, batting .750 in his only game. Kent was eight for 13 for a .615 average, and Wilson Betemit was four for eight for a .500 average. The pitching was the Achilles heel in their arsenal. Hong-Chih Kuo was the Dodgers leading starting pitcher with an ERA of 4.15 as the total staff ERA was an astronomical 5.76.

The 2006 season was a success for the Los Angeles ballclub in spite of their early departure from post season play. They broke their home attendance record with more than 3.75 million people making their way through the turnstiles. And many of their players had outstanding seasons they can build on for 2007. J.D. Drew batted .283 with 34 doubles, 20 home runs, and 100 RBIs in 494 at-bats. Thirty-three year old Nomar Garciaparra, a potential Hall-Of-Fame shortstop in the near future, stung the ball at a .303 clip with 31 doubles, 20 home runs, and 93 RBIs in 469 at-bats. Rafael Furcal in his first season in Dodger blue batted a solid .300 with 113 runs scored,

James Loney batted .284 in 48 games for L.A. and punched out three base hits in his only postseason appearance. (Los Angeles Dodgers)

32 doubles, 15 home runs, 63 RBIs, and 37 stolen bases, all-star numbers to be sure. Andre Ethier, fresh out of the Oakland farm system, celebrated with a .308 batting average, 20 doubles, 11 home runs and 55 RBIs in 396 at-bats. And Kenny Lofton hit .301 with 15 doubles, 12 triples, three home runs, 41 RBIs, and 32 stolen bases in 469 at-bats. On the mound, Brad Penny went 16-9 in 33 starts, Derek Lowe compiled a record of 16-8 in 34 starts, Chad Billingsley had a successful rookie season, winning seven games against four losses with a fine 3.80 ERA in 16 starts, Greg Maddux went 6-3 with a 3.30 ERA in 12 starts, and Aaron Sele went 8-6 in 15 starts. Former Japanese league star Takashi Saito took over the closer duties when Eric Gagne went down for the season and appeared in 72 games with a 6-2 won-loss record, 24 saves, and a 2.07 earned-run-average.

2008—NED COLLETTI AND JOE TORRE STRIKE WHILE THE IRON IS HOT

The 2007 Los Angeles Dodgers were expected to challenge for another Western Division title with their impressive Kiddie Korps of Kemp (age 23), Loney (24), Billingsley (23), Kershaw (20), Ethier (26), Broxton (24), and Martin (25), all now a year older and with major league experience, a strong pitching rotation, and a bullpen headed by Takashi Saito. The team started fast and held down first place on May 31 with a record of 31-22, but their good fortune deserted them as the season progressed. The Disabled List devoured several of the starting pitchers, and the middle relief corps was a disaster. Grady Little's charges went just 37-44 over the last three months of the season to finish in fourth Place, eight games behind pennant-winning Arizona.

As soon as the World Series was over, General Manager Ned Colletti took immediate steps to return the Dodgers to the top of their division in 2008. The first thing he did was fire manager Grady Little and replace him with 67-year old Joe Torre who had won six American League pennants and four World Championships as the manager of the New York Yankees. Pitching, as unusual, was the number one priority. Colletti had three outstanding starting pitchers, in Brad Penny (16-4 in 2007), Derek Lowe (12-14 with a 3.88 ERA), and Chad Billingsley (12-5). He expected a return to form from Jason Schmidt who missed most of the previous season after shoulder surgery, and he was counting on 20-year old Clayton Kershaw to step up and join the rotation. But to take the pressure off the youngster, he signed Japanese star Hiroki Kuroda to a three-year contract. Kuroda, a 6', 1", 210-pound right-handed pitcher, was an eleven-year veteran of the baseball wars in Japan with a good fastball and outstanding control. The catching

position was well covered with Russell Martin and the infield was set with Loney, Kent, Furcal, and Garciaparra. Andre Ethier and Matt Kemp covered two-thirds of the outfield. Colletti also signed free agent Andruw Jones, a former all-star and Gold Glove recipient, to patrol the center field pasture while keeping a fleet-footed Juan Pierre available for outfield duty and twenty-two year old Blake DeWitt waiting in the wings, ready to provide emergency help wherever needed in the infield. Unfortunately, the best laid plans of men often go awry through no fault of their own. And the Dodgers plans took an immediate hit in spring training when the injury bug sent Nomar Garciaparra to the Disabled List on March 21— the first of three times he would visit the list during the year. In all, he would play in just 55 games in 2008.

The 2008 National League season opened in Dodger Stadium at precisely 1:32 PM on Monday, March 31 with a temperature of 62 degrees, under sunny skies, and with a cool breeze blowing out to right field. Manager Joe Torre selected Brad Penny to toe the rubber for game one and he was opposed by San Francisco Giants left-hander, Barry Zito, an eleven-game winner in 2007. The Dodgers jumped on Zito early, scoring three runs before the late-arriving fans were settled in their seats. Raphael Furcal led off with a line drive down the left field line that skipped into the stands for a ground rule double. After Ethier popped to short, Matt Kemp singled

Chad Billingsley won a career-high 16 games in 2008 as L.A. edged Arizona by two games for the division title. (Los Angeles Dodgers)

to center field to drive in Furcal. Then Jeff Kent slammed a two-run home run to deep left-center field that exited the park at the 385 foot mark. L.A. added single runs in the second and sixth innings to complete a 5-0 victory. Penny pitched 6 2/3 innings of shutout ball, holding Bruce Bochy's Giants to four base hits while fanning three and issuing two walks along the way. Game two was just as satisfying as Derek Lowe handcuffed the Orange and Black, holding them to two runs over six innings as the Dodgers eked out a 3-2 victory.

Los Angeles ran hot and cold during the rest of April, finishing the month with a 14-13 record, leaving them 5½ games behind red-hot Arizona. The low point of the month occurred on April 24 when they were beaten at home by Arizona, dropping them seven games behind the D'Backs. Chad Billingsley absorbed his fourth loss of the season, yielding five runs in six innings. Two days later they whipped the Rockies by an 11-3 score that included a ten-run first inning. Matt Kemp knocked in five of the ten runs, with a sacrifice fly and a grand slam homer. Torre's troops ended the month on another high note with a 13-1 rout of the Florida Marlins in Dolphin Stadium before a quiet home crowd. Billingsley won his first game of the year as L.A. broke open a close 4-1 contest with four runs in the seventh inning and five more in the eighth. Russell Martin got the Dodgers started with a leadoff homer in the second inning, Matt Kemp added to the total in the third with a two-run single, and James Loney put the game away with a bases loaded triple to deep center field in the seventh.

Things went south for the blue and white in May as they lost 15 of the 28 games played, but they actually picked up two games on the Diamondbacks who were engaged in a struggle of their own. As manager Joe Torre pointed out to his team periodically, a major league season was not a sprint, it was a marathon; and the team that could handle the losing streaks without losing its confidence, and could take advantage of its winning streaks, would finish the season looking down at its competition.

May was a good example of what Torre was talking about. L.A. put together an eight game winning streak between April 25 and May 3, but then lost five in a row from the seventh to the thirteenth. Penny ran his record to 5-2 on May 2 with an 11-6 win over Colorado and Kemp provided the fireworks with a run scoring double to right field in the sixth and a bases clearing double to left field in the eighth. Brad Penny won his fifth game of the season on May 2 but would win only one more game in 2008, arm problems costing him most of the rest of the season. He would finally go on the DL on June 15 and would miss all but three weeks down the stretch. The next night, in the same venue, L.A. trounced the hometown Rockies again, this time by a 12-7 score. The visitors scored four runs in the top of the first inning,

three of them coming on a bases loaded double to deep left-center field by James Loney. Four innings later, the big first baseman took a 2-2 pitch over the right field wall with a man on, giving him six RBIs on the day, his biggest run production since September 28, 2006 when he knocked in a franchise high nine runs. The west coast contingent lost their shortstop to injury on May 6, and he would not return until September 24. Furcal played only 36 games in 2008, but hit a sizzling .357 with 34 runs scored when he was on the field.

June was a month manager Joe Torre would rather forget. His team went a disappointing 11-16

James Loney drove 90 runs with a .289 batting average and hit a lusty .438 in the NLCS. (W. McNeil)

wire-to-wire when the bats suddenly went cold. Starting pitching was strong as Billinglsey (3-1), Lowe (3-3), and company, tossed four shutouts and held opposing teams to 3.4 runs per game, but the Dodger bats could only score 3.1 runs per game, being shutout themselves five times. It was an exercise in futility, as they scored three runs or less in 15 of the 27 games. Clayton Kershaw lost his two decisions by scores of 2-0 and 2-1. Penny was beaten 3-0 and 3-1 before absorbing a 12-7 thrashing at the hands of the Detroit Tigers, being raked for seven runs in less than four innings. Andre Ethier's two-run homer in the sixth was L.A.'s only bright spot. Kemp lost 17 points off his .301 season batting average in June, while Ethier's average plummeted from .303 to .271.

With the advent of summer, the pennant races heated up, and Dodger bats heated up also. Dodger pitching was pounded for 20 runs on July 21-22, one of which they won, 16-10 but, except for those two games, the L.A. team scored an average of 4.2 runs per game to 3.3 runs per game for opposing teams. James Loney was the big gun in the 16-10 victory, going 3 for 6 at the plate with a bases loaded triple and five runs batted in. Chad Billingsley went 4-2 during the month, including a 9-1 victory over Florida on the 13th of the month, a 3-2 win over Washington on the 25th, and a 4-0, complete game shutout of the enemy Giants five days later. Clayton Kershaw, who started the season 0-3, finally won his first game, a 2-0 gem against Washington before a full house in Dodger Stadium on the 27th. The month was a good one for Joe Torre's contingent as they went 16-10, finishing the month with an overall record of 54-54, leaving them still in second place, two games behind Arizona.

Ned Colletti made some brilliant moves before the trade deadline expired, obtaining third baseman Casey Blake from Cleveland on July 26 and, in perhaps his key move, obtaining Boston Red Sox miscreant, Manny Ramirez in a three-team trade on July 31. L.A.'s record stood at 54-54 on that date, but from there to the end of the season they went 30-24, putting them over the top and bringing them the Western Division pennant by two games over Arizona. Manny set the pace for the Dodger team slugging the ball at a torrid .396 clip in 53 games with 17 home runs and 53 RBIs. The team didn't respond to him immediately, going just 13-16 in August in spite of Manny's blistering .415 attack on opposing pitchers. Or maybe they did respond to him and

Manny Ramirez's .396 batting average and 18 home runs in 53 games carried the Dodgers to the Western Division pennant. (W. McNei)

maybe he kept the Dodgers from going under for the third time. In the 13 games that he drove in two or more runs in August, L.A. won seven games and lost six. In games where he drove in less than two runs, the team went 6-10. He made his presence felt immediately on August 3, going 4 for 5 with a double, a home run, and three runs-batted-in, in a 9-3 victory over Arizona. Two weeks later, he homered and drove in three runs as L.A. defeated Milwaukee by a 7-5 score in Dodger Stadium. Andre Ethier, who went three-for-five with a double, two home runs, and three RBIs in the same game, hit a walk-off two-run homer to deep center field in the bottom of the ninth inning.

Manny slugged the ball at a .370 clip in September with eight home runs and 28 RBIs in 24 games as the Dodgers seized the moment, winning 17 games against 8 losses. The fun began on August 30 when Joe Torre's determined band whipped Arizona 6-4 to reduce Arizona's lead to 3½ games. They went on from there to win twelve of their next thirteen games, picking up nine games on the Diamondbacks in the process. And it was mainly a Manny and Ethier show over the final four weeks of the season. The Red Sox defector had a homer and three RBIs on September 2 to pace L.A. to an 8-4 victory over San Diego. Three days later, Andre Ethier went five-for-five with two doubles, a homer and five RBIs as the Dodgers drove another nail into the Diamondback's coffin with an impressive 7-0 win behind Derek Lowe's twelfth victory. And the following day, under sunny skies, L.A. beat Arizona for the fifth consecutive time, 7-2, behind Manny's three run homer to deep right field in the fifth inning and his two-run double in the sixth. On the 9th, as the Big Blue Machine continued its drive to the pennant, Ethier went two-for-four with a double and a triple, driving in four runs in a 6-2 romp over San Diego. One day later, Mr. Ramirez struck again, smashing two home runs and driving in four runs in a 7-2 romp over San Diego. Even Nomar Garciaparra and Chad Billingsley got into the act. The 24-year old Dodger righty, who went 3-0 in September, won his 16th game by a 10-1 margin over the Padres on the 23rd with help from Nomar who slammed a three–run homer to left-center field during a six-run uprising in the opening stanza. Manny batted .370 for the month as noted above and Andre Ethier stung the ball at a .462 clip with two homers and 18 runs-batted-in. And that was all the Dodgers needed as they won the pennant by two games.

The Dodgers opponent in the National League Division Series was the Chicago Cubs who won the Central Division pennant by 7½ games over Milwaukee. The series opened in Wrigley Field on October 1 with Derek Lowe facing the Cubs 17-game winner, Ryan Dempster. And Lowe was on the top of his game. After spotting the Cubs two runs in the second inning, he shut them down over the next four innings while L.A. put up a four spot in the top of the fifth on a James Loney grand slam homer following three bases on balls. L.A. won the game by a 7-2 score. In game two, Joe Torre's charges hammered Chicago's 6', 5", 255-pound right-hander, Carlos Zambrano, for five runs in the top of the second inning sparked by Russell Martin's bases clearing double. The final score was 10-3 with Chad Billingsley tossing 6 2/3 innings with seven strikeouts against a single walk. The series moved to Dodger Stadium on October 4 but the script was unchanged. The Dodgers scored all the runs they needed in the bottom of the first when Martin doubled, Manny singled, and Loney drove in both runners with a two-base hit to right field. Hiroki Kuroda pitched 6 1/3 shutout innings to win 3-1.

The Eastern Division champion Philadelphia was next up for Joe Torres troops and although they fell to the Phils in five games, they deserved a better fate. In the opener, consecutive doubles by Ethier and Ramirez gave the Dodgers a quick 1-0 lead in the first inning. They made it 2-0 in the fourth on a double by Kemp and a sacrifice fly by Blake DeWitt. Derek Lowe was sailing along nicely for five innings but in the sixth he hit the wall. An error and two home runs gave the Phils three runs, all they would need for a 3-2 win. The big guns came out in game two. Charlie Manuel's team chased Billingsley from the mound in less than three innings, scoring four runs in both the second and third innings to give the Phils an 8-2 lead. Manny Ramirez crushed a three-run homer in the fourth to close the gap to 8-5 but that would be all the scoring for the day as both bullpens put up goose eggs the rest of the way. When the series moved to L.A. the home team seemed to get a new life, as they pounded Jamie Moyer for five runs right out of the blocks, three of them coming on a bases loaded triple to right field by Blake DeWitt. That was all the support Kuroda needed as he held the powerful Phillies to two runs in six innings in a 7-2 Dodger victory.

On October 13, Philadelphia brought the feisty Dodgers back to earth with a 7-5 win. The game went back and forth with first one team then the other grabbing the lead. L.A. took a 5-3 lead in the fifth inning on a home run by Casey Blake, a double and an error, but the Phils came back one more time, pushing over four runs off Dodger reliever Corey Wade, to capture a 7-5 victory. The teams returned to the City of Brotherly Love for game five and Philadelphia closed out the Dodgers with an easy 5-1 win. L.A. starter, Chad Billingsley, lasted just 2 2/3 innings, yielding three runs. The Dodgers lone run came in the sixth on a Manny Ramirez home run.

Standouts for the Dodgers in the postseason were Manny Ramirez, James Loney, and Hiroki Kuroda. Manny slugged the ball at a .500 clip with two homers and three RBIs in the NLDS and .533 with two homers and seven RBIs in the NLCS. Loney hit a solid .438 with two doubles and two RBIs in the NLCS, and Kuroda won one game in both the NLDS and NLCS, yielding a total of just two runs in 12 1/3

innings.

National League statistics pretty much confirmed what Dodger fans already knew, that strong pitching carried the team to the National League Championship Series. L.A. ranked sixth in the league in runs scored with 4.32 runs scored per game, but were number one in pitching with a 3.68 ERA. It was strong starting pitching and effective middle relief pitching from Beimel, Kuo, Wade, and Park that made the difference. The Dodgers two closers were erratic most of the way with Broxton (14 of 22) and Saito (18 of 22) providing only a mediocre 73% save success rate.

Andre Ethier set the pace at the plate, hitting .305 with 20 homers and 77 RBIs. Matt Kemp checked in with a .290 average with 18 homers and 76 RBIs, Manny batted .396 with 18 homers and 53 RBIs, and Russell Martin hit .280 with 13 homers and 69 RBIs. Chad Billingsley led the mound corps with 16 victories against 10 losses, Derek Lowe went 14-11, and Hiroki Kuroda was 9-10 but he pitched much better than his record indicates.

2009—THE SEARCH FOR A NATIONAL LEAGUE CHAMPIONSHIP GOES ON

The 2009 edition of the Los Angeles Dodgers seemed poised to win it all, not only a National League Western Division pennant, but a league championship as well and perhaps even a World Championship. They were well stocked at every position. They had an outstanding catcher in Russell Martin, a solid inner defense with James Loney, Orlando Hudson, Rafael Furcal, and Casey Blake, and a stalwart outfield foursome of Andre Ethier, Matt Kemp, Manny Ramirez, and Juan Pierre. And on the mound they had a projected started rotation of Clayton Kershaw (5-5)—who seemed on the verge of a breakout season, Chad Billingsley (16-10), Hiroki Kuroda (9-10), Jason Schmidt, and 24-year old rookie, James McDonald, plus 6', 4", 290-pound fireballer Jonathan Broxton (14 saves) in the bullpen. Gone from the 2008 team were Nomar Garciaparra, Derek Lowe, Brad Penny, Jeff Kent, Andruw Jones, Chan Ho Park, and Takashi Saito.

The team opened their spring training routine in their new home at Camelback Ranch in Glendale, Arizona, after spending the previous 61 years in Dodgertown, located in Vero Beach, Florida. After the Dodgers moved to Los Angeles in 1958 it didn't make much sense to maintain a spring training facility 3000 miles from home, but old habits are hard to break and it took 50 years for the team to sever the umbilical cord.

The season opened to huge expectations on April 6 in PetCo Park in San Diego with Kuroda being designated as the opening day pitcher by manager Joe Torre. And the 34-year old right-hander justified his manager's decision by throwing a strong game at the Padres, pitching 5 2/3 innings and holding Bud

Black's team to a single run on four hits. The Dodgers flashed a preview of things to come in the first inning on consecutive singles by Pierre and Hudson, a double steal, a walk to Martin, and a two-out, two-run single to left field by James Loney. Ethier drove in a run with a single in the third inning, and L.A.'s powerful 6', 2", 230-pound slugger, Matt Kemp, closed out the scoring with a seventh inning home run off Jake Peavy. L.A.'s record stood at 2-3 after five games, but they quickly turned things around and ran off an eight-game winning streak and eleven of thirteen. The first victory in the streak was achieved in Chase Field in Arizona where Joe Torre's charges manhandled the Diamondbacks to the tune of 11-2 behind the strong pitching of Eric Stults and an offensive barrage that included a double, a home run, and three RBIs by Orlando Hudson.

The Dodgers home opener on April 13 was a historic event. L.A. crushed the hated San Francisco Giants by an 11-1 score and Orlando Hudson hit for the cycle. On a cloudy afternoon, with the temperature hovering around the 74 degree mark and a festive full house on hand to welcome their conquering heroes home, Hudson legged out an infield single in the first inning, launched a home run down the left field line in the third inning off the 6', 10" flame-throwing southpaw Randy Johnson to give his team a 1-0 lead, crushed a run scoring double to deep left-center field during a six-run rally in the fourth inning, and added a line drive triple down the right field line in the sixth. Andre Ethier hit two home runs and drove in four runs for the Dodgers and Chad Billingsley was the beneficiary of the explosion with seven innings of one-run ball liberally sprinkled with 11 strikeouts. The Dodger right fielder had another two-homer day on the 18th

Andre Ethier slammed 31 homers and drove in 106 runs in the Dodgers' drive to the pennant. (W. McNeil)

against the Colorado Rockies, hitting a three-run shot in the fourth inning and a leadoff homer in the seventh to lead his team to a 9-5 triumph. Billingsley (3-0) was touched up for three runs in six innings but emerged victorious.

Matt Kemp got into the act on Sunday afternoon, April 19 when he put together a three-for-five day with two home runs including a grand slam, leading Los Angeles to a 14-2 massacre of the Colorado Rockies. The 91 degree heat didn't slow down Kemp or Orlando Hudson who went three-for-four with three RBIs, or Andre Ethier who went two-for-four with three RBIs. The end of the month found L.A. on top of the Western Division of the National League with a 15-8 record and a 3½-game lead over San Diego. May was a good month in many respects, but it was a bad month for the team in general. They lost their slugging left fielder, Manny Ramirez, to a 50-game suspension for violating the league's drug policy. Manny proclaimed his innocence, saying he was taking a legal medication prescribed by his doctor, but that explanation fell on deaf ears. At the time of his suspension, he was stinging the ball at a .348 clip with six homers and 20 runs-batted-in, in 27 games, a lot of production that the team would have to overcome.

Somehow, the Dodgers filled the cracks beautifully, winning the first six games of the month, going 12-3 between May 13 and May 28, and finishing the month with a record of 20-9 and a healthy 8½-game lead over San Francisco. Using a well balanced attack with every member of the lineup contributing, and a stingy pitching corps that held the opposition to 50 runs in their 20 victories, an average of 2.5 runs per game, they proved to themselves that they were a good enough team to overcome the loss of their greatest hitter. They ended June with a overall record of 49-29, and July with a record 64-39, still maintaining an eight-game lead over San Francisco and a Colorado team that was beginning a push toward the top. And there were some big individual achievements along the way. Andre Ethier, the Dodgers classy right fielder, gave his team a victory over the Philadelphia Phillies on Saturday, June 6, in Dodger Stadium. As 41,412 fans enjoyed the comfortable 70 degree afternoon sun, the Dodgers and Phillies treated them to an old fashioned pitcher's duel between Hiroki Kuroda and big Joe Blanton—all 255 pounds of him.

Ethier put his team on the board first with a fourth inning home run into the right field seats, but Philadelphia took the lead in the seventh inning with two runs off the Dodger bullpen after Kuroda had tossed six shutout innings at them. L.A. was down to their last out when Raphael Furcal stepped to the plate and the Dodger shortstop jerked one of closer Brad Lidge's fastballs into the right field stands to deadlock the game at two-all. The game remained tied for another three innings until Ethier sent the big crowd home happy with a walk-off home run to straightaway center field off Chad Durbin.

That same Andre Ethier, batting out of the seventh slot in the batting order, had a career day on June 26 when he single-handedly demolished the Seattle Mariners in Dodger Stadium by an 8-2 score. As 50,752 loyal Dodger fans looked on, the sweet-swinging, left-handed hitter sent three balls out of the park, driving in six runs against the Washington-based club. He began his big night in the second inning, sending a three-run homer soaring into the southern California sky to break up a scoreless game. Four innings later he hit a two-run blast, and he ended his memorable day with a leadoff homer in the eighth. Clayton Kershaw was the beneficiary of the fireworks, pitching six innings and holding the Mariners to two runs while fanning eight and walking two. The victory left L.A. with a record of 48-26 and an eight-game lead over San Francisco. June was a big month for Ethier as he hit nine home runs in 26 games and drove in 22 runs.

Manny returned to the lineup on July 3 after his 50-game suspension and made an immediate impact on his team. He hit a hard .316 during the month with five home runs and 17 RBIs in 23 games, but his biggest hit took place on the 22nd during a 6-2 Dodger victory over the Cincinnati Reds in Dodger Stadium with the usual 56,000 fans cheering them on. The temperature was a balmy 83 degrees under sunny skies with a light wind blowing out to centerfield when the first pitch was thrown by Dodger starter Chad Billingsley at 7:11 PM. The Reds drew first blood when Joey Votto slugged a run-scoring double to right field, but Joe Torre's boys answered almost immediately on a long home run to deep center field by Andre Ethier in the bottom of the inning, and took the lead in the fourth on a run-scoring triple to right field by James Loney. Cincinnati pulled even in the top of the sixth inning on two singles, a stolen base, and a two-out wild pitch by Billingsley who eventually struck out the side. In the bottom the inning, L.A. loaded the bases with one out on two walks and a line drive single to short left field by Russell Martin. At that point Cincinnati manager Dusty Baker pulled starter Bronson Arroyo and brought in 6', 4", 240-pound right-hander Nick Masset to quell the storm. Manny Ramirez, the human hitting machine, who had been a spectator up to that point, was sent up to hit for Billingsley, and the big slugger jumped on the first pitch from Masset, a high fastball, and yanked it far down the left field line where it settled into the pavilion for a grand slam home run, giving the Dodgers a hard-fought victory and Billingsley his tenth win.

Los Angeles went 15-10 in July, giving them an overall record of 64-39 and an eight-game lead over both San Francisco and Colorado. And all eyes were now on the Rockies who were making a determined run for the top. Back on Wednesday, June 3, the Rockies were firmly settled in last place with a 20-32 record, and essentially out of the pennant race, a full 15½ games behind the Dodgers. But no one told

Juan Pierre hit .308 in the 145 games for Joe Torre's team. (W. McNeil)

the Rockies their season was over and they suddenly got as hot as the weather. Jim Tracy's crew went 21-4 the rest of June, to pull themselves up to third place, just 7½ games out of first, and the race was on. The Giants began to fade down the stretch and it would be the Dodgers and the Rockies jockeying for position. Colorado went 15-11 in July and 16-8 in August to close within 5½ games of L.A.

Ned Colletti, sensing that the Dodgers needed help in their starting rotation, signed 31-year old right-hander Vicente Padilla on August 19 and acquired Jon Garland in a trade with Arizona on the 31st. And both pitchers made major contributions in the pennant race down the stretch. Padilla went 4-0 in seven starts, including a clutch 3-2 victory in Colorado on August 27, wins over Arizona and San Francisco, and another win over the Rockies in Dodger Stadium on October 4. Garland won his first three starts for L.A., 4-2 over the Diamondbacks, 6-2 over the Pirates, and 12-1 over the Giants.

Matt Kemp had a big month in August as Joe Torre's charges struggled to maintain their stranglehold on first place. The team slipped under .500 for the month at 14-15 but still held a 5½-game lead as the month ended. And the right-handed hitting Kemp was a major factor in preventing a monumental collapse, spanking the ball at a .315 clip with nine home runs and 27 RBIs in 28 games. On August 2 in Turner Field in Atlanta, he went three-for-five with a three-run homer and five RBIs in a 9-1 Dodger victory. Two days later, at home, he had four base hits in five at-bats, with a double, a home run, and five RBIs as L.A. pounded the Milwaukee Brewers by a 17-4 score.

The month of September was a roller coaster ride for both Los Angeles and Colorado as the fast-closing Rockies made one last desperate push for the top of the Western Division and the Dodgers tried to hold them off. Jim Tracy's relentless warriors en-

Matt Kemp was a big gun in the Dodger attack, sending 26 balls into orbit and rescuing 101 teammates. (Los Angeles Dodgers)

dured a five-game losing streak as August ended but bounced back to run off a six-game winning streak from September 4th to the 11th, and a five-game winning streak as the season wound down. On September 26, Colorado trailed L.A. by six games, but six days later, after whipping Joe Torre's charges by a 4-3 score in Dodger Stadium, the lead was down to just one game with two games left to play. The most important game of the season was played in Dodger Stadium on Saturday night, October 3, with 54,531 of the Dodger faithful looking on. The weather was perfect, a mild 65 degrees with a light breeze blowing in from left field, and sunny skies as the first pitch was thrown. Dodger legend-in-the-making, 21-year old southpaw, Clayton Kershaw, was Torre's choice to wrap up the pennant, and he was opposed by Colorado ace, 16-game winner Jorge de

la Rosa. The game was scoreless for six innings, but in the bottom of the seventh the Dodgers exploded for five big runs to put the game out of reach and clinch the Western Division pennant. And it was a team effort, with pinch hitter Ronnie Belliard driving in the first run with an infield single, Mark Loretta sending another run scampering across the plate with a ringing double to deep right-center field, and three more runs scoring on RBIs by Pierre, Kemp, and Manny Ramirez

Los Angeles finished the season with a record of 95-67, giving them a three-game bulge over Colorado. Their opponent in the National League Division Series was the Central League Champion St. Louis Cardinals, and Joe Torre's crew made short work of them, disposing of them in three straight by scores of 5-3, 3-2, and 5-1. The Dodgers captured the opener in Dodger Stadium 5-3 on a two-run homer by Matt Kemp in the first inning, and single runs in the third, fifth, and sixth. The Cardinals sent Randy Wolf to an early shower in the fourth inning when they closed the gap to 3-2 but strong relief pitching kept them under control the rest of the game. The game-two getaway game was a pitcher's duel that went down to the last pitch. Andre Ethier hit a game-tying home run in the fourth inning, but the Cardinals added a run in the seventh to take a 2-1 lead into the bottom of the ninth when their defense let them down. The first two Dodger batters were retired and when the left-handed hitting James Loney sliced a line drive to left field, it looked like the game was over. But Matt Holliday dropped the ball for a two-base error and the Dodgers had a life. Blake walked, Belliard hit a fly ball to center field that dropped in for a run-scoring single, and Loretta smashed a line drive single to center that brought home the game-winner. Kershaw pitched the first 6 2/3 innings, holding St. Louis to two runs, and George Sherrill pitched a scoreless ninth to pick up the victory.

Los Angeles met their old nemesis, the Philadelphia Phillies in the National League Championship Series and the result was the same as 2008. Charlie Manuel's team took Joe Torre's cohorts down in five games. The Series opened in Dodger Stadium on October 15, with the usual 56,000 fans on hand, but the expected pitcher's duel between Clayton Kershaw and Cole Hamels never materialized. Kershaw was sent to an early shower, falling to a five-run barrage by the Phillies in the fifth inning, on two walks, a three-run homer by Carlos Ruiz, three wild pitches, and a two-run double by Ryan Howard. Hamels left shortly thereafter when the Dodgers pushed over three runs in the bottom of the inning, two on a home run by Manny Ramirez. Philly put up a three spot in the eighth and the Dodgers added two in the same inning to close out an 8-6 Philadelphia victory. The west coast contingent rebounded the following day as Vicente Padilla and Pedro Martinez gave the fans the pitcher's duel they expected. Padilla tossed 7 1/3 innings of one-run ball, but Pedro did him one better, throwing seven innings of shutout ball, holding L.A. to just two base hits. The Dodgers, happy to see Pedro leave, rallied for two runs in the bottom of the eighth and took game two, 2-1. Base hits by Casey Blake, Ronnie Belliard, and Jim Thome, scored the tying run and a bases loaded walk to Andre Ethier, brought in the game-winner. Ryan Howard's opposite field home run accounted for Philadelphia's only run. When the Series moved to the City of Brotherly Love, the Phillies took control. They won game three by the lopsided score of 11-0 behind a dominant Cliff Lee who held L.A. to three hits and struck out ten men. Jason Werth's two-run homer and Howard's two-run triple were the big blows in the game. Hiroki Kuroda lasted only 1 1/3 innings, yielding six runs. The Phillies took a play out of the Dodgers game-book to win game four. For L.A., Matt Kemp homered in the fifth inning and James Loney drove in two runs to give the Dodgers a 4-3 lead after eight innings with their closer, Jonathan Broxton, who had saved 35 games during the season, on the hill. But Broxton couldn't get the job done. A walk and a hit batter put two men on base with two out, leading to Jimmy Rollins' walk-off two-run double up the right-center field alley. The Game Five finale was almost anti-climatic after what happened in Game Four, but the Phillies jumped on Padilla early with three runs in the first inning another run in the second, and two more in the fourth, en route to a 10-4 victory and the League Championship. Ethier, Loney, and Hudson, homered in a losing cause.

The season ended in disappointing fashion but overall it was a successful season. They grabbed the lead in the pennant race on April 15 and were never headed, holding the top spot for 172 consecutive days. And several of their young players had outstanding seasons. Andre Ethier hit 31 home runs and drove in 106 runs with a .272 batting average. Matt Kemp hit 26 homers with 101 RBIs and a .297 batting average. Manny Ramirez hit 19 homers with 63 RBIs and a .290 average in 104 games, and James Loney hit 13 homers with 90 RBIs and a .281 average. On the mound, Clayton Kershaw went 8-8 with a 2.79 ERA and 185 strikeouts in 171 innings pitched, Chad Billingsley was 12-11 with a 4.03 ERA in 33 games, Randy Wolf went 11-7 with a 3.23 ERA in 34 games, Vicente Padilla went 4-0 with a 3.20 ERA, and Jon Garland went 3-2 with a 2.72 ERA.

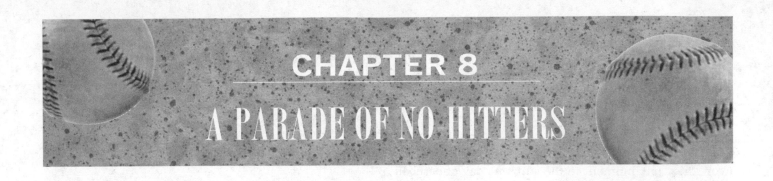

CHAPTER 8
A PARADE OF NO-HITTERS

DODGERS' NO-HIT HISTORY — 1884 TO 1997

DATE	PITCHER	OPPONENT	SCORE
BROOKLYN, AMERICAN ASSOCIATION			
October 4, 1884	S. Kimber	Toledo	0-0 (10 inn)
July 24, 1886	W. Terry	St. Louis	1-0
May 27, 1888	W. Terry	Louisville	4-0
BROOKLYN, NATIONAL LEAGUE			
June 22, 1891	T. Lovett	New York	4-0
June 2, 1894	E. Stein	Chicago	1-0 (6 inn)
August 1, 1906	H. McIntyre	Pittsburgh	0-1 (10.2 inn)
July 20, 1906	M. Eason	St. Louis	2-0
Sept. 5, 1908	N. Rucker	Boston	6-0
Sept. 13, 1925	D. Vance	Philadelphia	10-1
August 27, 1937	F. Frankhouse	Cincinnati	5-0 (7.2 inn)
April 30, 1940	T. Carlton	Cincinnati	3-0
April 23, 1946	E. Head	Boston	5-0
Sept. 9, 1948	R. Barney	New York	2-0
June 19, 1952	C. Erskine	Chicago	5-0
May 12, 1956	C. Erskine	New York	3-0
Sept 25, 1956	S. Maglie	Philadelphia	5-0
LOS ANGELES, NATIONAL LEAGUE			
June 30, 1962	S. Koufax	New York	5-0
May 11, 1963	S. Koufax	San Francisco	8-0
June 4, 1964	S. Koufax	Philadelphia	3-0
Sept. 9, 1965	S. Koufax	Chicago	1-0
July 20, 1970	W. Singer	Philadelphia	5-0
June 27, 1980	J. Reuss	San Francisco	8-0
June 29, 1990	F. Valenzuela	St. Louis	6-0
August 17, 1992	K. Gross	San Francisco	2-0
July 14, 1995	R. Martinez	Miami	7-0
Sept. 17, 1996	Hideo Nomo	Colorado	9-0

SAM KIMBER BECOMES #1

Brooklyn fielded its first major league team in 1884, when Charlie Byrne entered his club in the American Association. The debut season was not a happy experience for the Flatbush nine. Beginning with their opening-day 5-1 loss to the Cleveland Spiders, the Brooklyn performance was dismal. They won only 40 games out of 104, finishing ninth in a 12-team league. They did, however, enjoy one moment in the sun, one day of baseball glory. It occurred on October 4 as the season was nearing a merciful end.

The Brooklyn Grays met the seventh-place Toledo Blue Stockings at Washington Park in a battle of also-rans. On the mound for the Grays was right-hander Sam Kimber, #2 pitcher on manager George Taylor's staff. He was opposed by 19th-century pitching star, Tony "The Count" Mullane, an immigrant from Cork, Ireland. The good-natured Irishman went on to amass 285 victories over a 13-year professional career, including five years with 30 or more victories, and another three years with 20 or more. The 25-year-old Mullane was at the peak of his career in 1884, accounting for 37 of Toledo's 46 wins.

The erratic Kimber was struggling through a mediocre 17-20 season, his only full year of major league baseball. On October 4, however, it all came together for the tall, slim Brooklyn hurler. On that day, paired off against the brilliant Mullane, he was the superior pitcher. It was a great pitchers' duel from the start, as both men put a string of goose eggs on the scoreboard. The 31-year-old Kimber issued five bases on balls to Blue Stocking batters, but none of them were able to hit the ball safely. He fanned six batters.

As often happens, the dazzling pitching brought out the best in the defensive units, as well. In a rarity of 19th-century baseball, both teams played errorless ball. Glittering catches and great throws prevented any serious threat. Inning after inning, Sam Kimber sent the Toledo batters back to the bench hitless. Mullane, also known as "The Apollo of the Box," almost matched the Brooklyn right hander. He spaced four hits over the route, while striking out six batters and walking only three. Brooklyn first baseman Charlie Householder was the batting star of the day, collecting a single and a double in four at bats.

After ten innings, the game was called on account of darkness. It was officially recorded as a ten-inning no-hitter for Sam Kimber, the longest no-hitter in major league baseball history to that time. There had been 35 no-hitters prior to Kimbers, but all were of nine-inning duration or less.

The Brooklyn catcher, Jack Corcoran, and first baseman Householder accounted for 22 of the 30 putouts, a tribute to Kimber's masterful performance. Only five balls were hit to the outfield. Sadly, his Flatbush teammates could not push across the run that would give him a well-deserved victory, and the game ended in a scoreless tie after a titanic two-hour battle. For Sam Kimber, it was his grand finale. The 1884 season was almost over, as was his major league career. The Philadelphia native appeared in only one game in 1885, then he was gone.

TOLEDO					BROOKLYN				
NAME	POS	R	H	E	NAME	POS	R	H	E
Barkley	2B	0	0	0	Greenwald	2B	0	0	0
Miller	SS	0	0	0	Geer	SS	0	1	0
Welch	CF	0	0	0	Cassidy	RF	0	1	0
Poorman	RF	0	0	0	Walker	LF	0	0	0
Mullane	P	0	0	0	Remsen	CF	0	0	0
Meister	3B	0	0	0	Knowles	3B	0	0	0
Arundel	C	0	0	0	Householder	1B	0	2	0
McSorley	1B	0	0	0	Corcoran	C	0	0	0
Olin	LF	0	0	0	Kimber	P	0	0	0
Totals		0	0	0				0	4	0

TOLEDO	000 000 000 0	- 0 - 0 - 0	
BROOKLYN	000 000 000 0	- 0 - 4 - 0	

	IP	R	H	BB	SO
T. Mullane	10	0	4	3	6
S. Kimber	10	0	0	5	6

ADONIS TERRY NO-HITS ST. LOUIS, 1-0

Brooklyn fielded a respectable baseball team in 1886. They were still not pennant material, but they did finish in third place with a 76-61 record. Their success was built around a balanced approach to the game; above-average hitting and above-average pitching. Although lacking a single .300 hitter, the Grays managed to score runs through sheer teamwork. Second baseman Bill McClellan scored 130 runs and was second in the league in doubles with 33. His infield compatriot, George Pinckney, crossed the plate 119 times. He also tied for the league lead in walks with teammate outfielder Ed Swartwood, each drawing 70 free passes. Swartwood was fourth in the league in on-base percentage with .377. Of the regulars, only Pinckney would still be a member of the club when they captured the pennant in 1889.

The Grays owned one of the league's stronger pitching units in 1886. Right hander Henry Porter was the ace of the staff with a 29-19 record. Adonis Terry was #2 man at 18-16, and John Harkins finished at 16-15. Porter was coming off a "career season" in 1885 when he posted a brilliant 33-21 record with a sixth-place team. They were Porter's only winning seasons. After pitching over 900 innings in two years, his arm gave out, and he ended his six-year career in 1889, with a record of 96-107.

William "Adonis" Terry, on the other hand, was an outstanding major league pitcher, compiling a 205-197 record during a successful 14-year career. Terry was one of the game's first matinee idols. In addition to being one of the league's top pitchers, his handsome profile endeared him to thousands of female fans around the circuit. Whenever Terry pitched, the owners could count on an increase in female attendance at the game. He was one of the game's first bonafide drawing cards.

Pitching a no-hitter is always an exciting achievement. Pitching one in the heat of a pennant race is something special. On July 24, 1886, the Brooklyn Grays were locked in a tense struggle for first place with the powerful St. Louis Browns, who were on their way to the second of four successive American Association titles. The two teams met in St. Louis with 7,000 screaming Browns fans looking on. Adonis Terry was on the mound for the visitors. He was opposed by the ace of the St. Louis staff, 41-game winner Dave "Scissors" Foutz.

As might be expected, it was a pitchers' duel all the way. Foutz was in occasional trouble, thanks to seven base hits and four bases on balls, but for seven innings, he managed to shut the door on the Grays whenever it looked like they might push across a run. By that time, the Brooklyn right hander had thrown six hitless innings, and the crowd was on its feet in anticipation of an historic event. According to the *New York Times*, the game was marked by "sharp field work and clever base running."

After Adonis Terry had throttled the Browns offense for the seventh straight inning, Charlie Byrne's crew came to the plate still looking for a single run. With the entire Brooklyn bench on the edge of their seats, center fielder Ed Swartwood lined a clean single to right field. Then "Scissors" Foutz made his only mistake of the day. He threw a cripple to first baseman Bill Phillips, and the big 200-pound slugger promptly jumped on it. He ripped the ball to deep left center field, splitting the outfielders. As center fielder Curt Welch gave chase, Swartwood circled the bases to score the first run of the game, Phillips pulling into third with a triple.

William "Adonis" Terry

That was all the support Adonis Terry needed on this day. He proceeded to set the Browns down quietly in the eighth and ninth, preserving his hard fought 1-0 masterpiece.

BROOKLYN					ST. LOUIS				
NAME	POS	R	H	E	NAME	POS	R	H	E
Pinckney	3B	0	1	1	Latham	3B	0	0	1
McClellan	2B	0	1	0	Gleason	SS	0	0	0
Swartwood	CF	1	1	0	O'Neil	LF	0	0	0
Phillips	1B	0	1	0	Comiskey	1B	0	0	0
Burch	LF	0	1	0	Welch	CF	0	0	0
Smith	SS	0	1	2	Robinson	2B	0	0	0
Toole	RF	0	0	0	Caruthers	RF	0	0	0
Terry	P	0	1	0	Foutz	P	0	0	0
Peoples	C	0	0	1	Bushong	C	0	0	1
Totals		1	7	4			0	0	2

BROOKLYN   0 0 0   0 0 0   0 1 0 - 1 - 7 - 4
ST. LOUIS   0 0 0   0 0 0   0 0 0 - 0 - 0 - 2

	IP	R	H	BB	SO
W. Terry	9	0	0	2	2
D. Foutz	9	1	7	4	1

"ADONIS" TERRY PITCHES SECOND NO-HITTER

Eighteen eighty-eight was a big year for the Brooklyn American Association baseball franchise. It was a rebuilding year, and all indications pointed to a pennant in the not-too-distant future. The Brooklyn management had gone on the market and obtained two of the finest pitchers in the game, "Parisian Bob" Caruthers and "Scissors" Dave Foutz. Not satisfied with that, they also acquired two .300 hitting outfielders, Thomas "Oyster" Burns and Darby O' Brien. They were still a year away from grabbing the brass ring, but they were already a force to be reckoned with.

Once again, the St. Louis Browns were the class of the league. They even managed to survive the loss of their two top pitchers, Caruthers and Foutz, and went on to a fourth straight league championship. But Brooklyn was closing in. They would finish the season in second place, only 6 1/2 games behind the front-running Browns.

The Louisville Colonels, on the other hand, were mired deeply in the second division, barely keeping out of the cellar, 44 games behind St. Louis. On May 27, 1888, a festive Sunday gathering of the Flatbush faithful, 4800 strong, crammed into Ridgewood Park to watch their boys throttle the wretched Colonels. It was a pleasant spring day, with fair weather prevailing, and the temperature around 75 degrees. It was a perfect day for a no-hitter.

Louisville started southpaw Toad Ramsey on the mound. Ramsey, a 38-and 37-game winner the previous two seasons, was in the midst of a horrible 8-30 year. Manager Bill McGunnigle countered with right hander Adonis Terry. It was a well-pitched game on both sides for seven innings, as Ramsey matched Terry almost pitch for pitch. The same couldn't be said for the defense, however, which was as sloppy as the pitching was good. A total of 10 errors were committed by the two clubs, six by the winners, making Terry's job that much more difficult.

After five scoreless innings, the Grays finally broke the ice in the sixth, pushing across a single tally. They broke the game open in the bottom of the eighth, scoring three more runs. Brooklyn shortstop Germany Smith led the attack with three hits, including two triples. Big, burly first baseman Dave Orr, all 250 pounds of him, chipped in with two doubles, and Bill McClellan added a single and a double to the cause.

"Adonis" Terry, meanwhile, throttled the Colonel's efforts at every turn. Except for three bases on balls and the six errors, he was in command at all times. The right hander couldn't even fault his team's defense, since he committed four of the errors himself.

One unusual sidelight of the game was the fact that manager Bill McGunnigle had three pitchers in his starting lineup. In addition to Terry on the mound, Bob Caruthers was stationed in center field, and Dave Foutz patrolled the pasture in right.

LOUISVILLE					BROOKLYN				
NAME	POS	R	H	E	NAME	POS	R	H	E
Collins	LF	0	0	0	Pinckney	3B	0	0	0
Kerins	C	0	0	0	McClellan	2B	1	2	1
Browning	CF	0	0	0	Orr	1B	1	2	0
Mack	2B	0	0	1	Foutz	RF	1	0	0
Wolf	RF	0	0	1	G. Smith	SS	1	3	0
White	3B	0	0	0	O'Brien	LF	0	1	0
Smith	1B	0	0	0	Caruthers	CF	0	0	0
Werrick	SS	0	0	0	Terry	P	0	0	4
Ramsey	P	0	0	2	Peoples	C	0	0	1
Totals		0	0	4			4	8	6

```
LOUISVILLE   000 000 000 - 0 - 0 - 4
BROOKLYN     000 001 03x - 4 - 8 - 6
```

	IP	R	H	BB	SO
Ramsey	8	4	8	2	6
Terry	9	0	0	3	8

TOM LOVETT THROWS FIRST BROOKLYN NATIONAL LEAGUE NO-HITTER

Tom Lovett was one of the Brooklyn Bridegrooms' top pitchers between 1889 and 1891. He produced a solid 17-10 record in 1889; followed that with a dazzling 30-11 season and a league-leading .732 winning percentage in 1890; then capped off his fine string with a 23-19 year in 1891. He pitched in two World Series, going 0-1 against the powerful New York Giants in 1889, and picking up two wins against the same number of losses against the Louisville Colonels in 1890.

Although Lovett experienced many thrills on the mound during his three-year span of brilliance, none could compare with the thrill he experienced on the afternoon of June 22, 1891. It was a hot, muggy day in East New York, and the Grooms were hosting the hated Giants of manager Jim Mutrie. The New Yorkers had fallen on lean times since their pennant year of 1889, and were in the process of settling comfortably into third place, behind the first place Boston Beaneaters and Cap Anson's Chicago Cubs. Brooklyn's slide was even worse, as they struggled unsuccessfully to keep out of sixth place.

But, on this bright Monday afternoon, the two rivals squared off in Eastern Park, and it was a World Series atmosphere all over again. An enthusiastic crowd was on hand to lend vocal support to their heroes. And it wasn't all one sided. Train loads of Giant rooters made the trip across the river to harass their Brooklyn neighbors. "Long John" Ewing, the hard-throwing 21-game winner, was Mutrie's choice to quiet the Groom's bats. Monte Ward countered with his ace, right-hander Tom Lovett. New York had won three of the previous four encounters, and Brooklyn fans thirsted for revenge.

The tenor of the game developed quickly. After Lovett retired the Giants 1-2-3 in the top of the first, Brooklyn drew first blood in the bottom of the inning, thanks to some shoddy defensive play by the Gothamites. It was

Tom Lovett hurled 738 innings in 1890-91, winning 53 games along the way, but the strain ruined his arm. He only won 11 more games during his abbreviated career.

an omen of things to come. Hub Collins, the Groom's speedy little second baseman, reached first when third baseman Charley Bassett couldn't handle his hot smash down the line. Collins got another break when he attempted to steal second. A great throw by catcher Artie Clarke had Collins by five feet, but second baseman Danny Richardson muffed the throw. After a sacrifice by Captain Monte Ward moved Collins to third, a perfect squeeze bunt by Mike Griffin brought him home.

The Brooklyns struck again in the second, on a single, a hit batter, and a Giant error. They added single runs in the fifth and the sixth, to bring the final count to 4-0.

Lovett labored easily all afternoon. He was in complete command of his pitches, having, as the *New York Times* reported, "great speed and sharp curves." There was only one difficult play all afternoon, a long drive to right field that Darby O'Brien made a sensational catch on. On the other side of the ledger, the New Yorkers played more like school boys than professional ballplayers. They accumulated the embarrassing total of eight errors, three on batted balls, and five on errant throws. Catcher Artie Clarke was the main culprit, accounting for three of the errors all by himself. The Times reporter noted it all. "They were not Giants yesterday, either at bat or in the field. They were veritable pygmies."

There was, it turned out, only one giant on the field on June 22. His name was Tom Lovett, and he came away with a well-deserved 4-0 victory, a magnificent no-hit, no-run effort.

Playing manager, John Montgomery Ward, suffering through a 61-76 season, had his most enjoyable game of the year on June 22, as his team played like champions in support of Lovetts' no-hitter.

NEW YORK					BROOKLYN				
NAME	POS	R	H	E	NAME	POS	R	H	E
Tiernan	CF	0	0	0	Collins	2B	2	1	0
Richardson	2B	0	0	1	Ward	SS	0	0	0
Gore	RF	0	0	0	Griffin	CF	0	1	0
Connor	1B	0	0	0	Burns	LF	0	0	0
O'Rourke	LF	0	0	1	O'Brien	RF	2	3	0
Bassett	3B	0	0	1	Pinckney	3B	0	0	0
Whistler	SS	0	0	1	Foutz	1B	0	0	0
Clarke	C	0	0	3	Daly	C	0	1	0
J. Ewing	P	0	0	1	Lovett	P	0	0	0
Totals		0	0	8			4	6	0

```
NEW YORK     000 000 000 - 0 - 0 - 8
BROOKLYN     110 011 00x - 4 - 6 - 0
```

	IP	R	H	BB	SO
J. Ewing	8	4	6	0	5
T. Lovett	9	0	0	3	4

ED STEIN SHACKLES CUBS ON NO HITS

The last decade of the nineteenth century was one of rebuilding for the Brooklyn National League franchise. The pitching staff, in particular, was decimated. Lovett, Caruthers, and Foutz, all quickly disappeared from the scene, victims of having pitched too many innings in too short a period of time, although Foutz did hang on for awhile as a first baseman. Soon, even the defensive stars were gone. Hub Collins and Darby O'Brien died untimely deaths. Pinckney and Pop Corkhill were put out to pasture. New faces appeared on the scene, players like shortstop Tommy Corcoran, second baseman Tido Daly, and pitchers Brickyard Kennedy and Ed Stein.

In 1891, the team moved to a new ballpark in the East New York section of Brooklyn. In order for fans to reach Eastern Park, they had to ride the new electric trolley cars across town, then walk cross a myriad of trolley tracks to reach the gate. Sophisticated Manhattanites, amused by the sight of Brooklyn fans sidestepping trolley cars on their way to the game, dubbed the natives, "Trolley Dodgers." Within a short period of time, the name was passed on to the team itself. Eventually, it was shortened to just Dodgers.

In 1894, the Trolley Dodgers held down fifth place in the 12-team league, a respectable but not exciting position. Right hander Ed Stein was the ace of the staff, on his way to a 27-14 season. On Saturday, June 4, Cap Anson's hapless Chicago Cubs moved into Eastern Park to do battle with manager Dave Foutz's crew. The weather was threatening; a dark, overcast 65 degree day, with a chance of showers in the forecast.

A crowd of 4,223 die-hard Dodger fans sat huddled together under the wooden grandstand. Ed Stein was Foutz's selection to start the game. His opponent was journeyman Bert Abbey, a 2-7 hurler from Essex Junction, Vermont. Abbey's undistinguished career totaled just 22 wins against 40 losses.

After Stein set the Cubs down without a hit in the first inning, Brooklyn came to bat in hopes of driving Abbey to cover quickly. For awhile, it seemed as if they might do just that. With two gone in the bottom of the inning, left fielder George Treadway, en route to a .328, 102 RBI season, drilled a long triple to center field. When Mike Griffin followed with a single to right, the Dodgers were on the board, and things were looking up.

That was all they would get however, as the Chicago right hander settled down and gave one of his better pitching performances of the season. Unfortunately, he picked the wrong time to do it, as he caught Ed Stein in the middle of a magnificent season. And, on this day in particular, the 5'11", 170-pound Dodger hurler was simply overpowering. Never a strikeout pitcher, Stein had the Cubs hitting the ball into the dirt all day. He had his usual wild streaks as attested to by his five bases on balls, but otherwise was unhittable.

Abbey, after the first inning, held the Brooklyn contingent to only two other safeties, singles by Tido Daly and Treadway. As the game progressed, the weather worsened. A light drizzle turned into a steady rain until, by the sixth inning, the field looked more like a swamp than a ballfield. After a short huddle, the umpires decided it would be insane to try to continue. They halted the proceedings after six, giving Ed Stein an abbreviated 1-0 no-hitter.

CHICAGO					BROOKLYN				
NAME	POS	R	H	E	NAME	POS	R	H	E
Ryan	RF	0	0	0	Daly	2B	0	1	0
Dahlen	CF	0	0	0	Corcoran	SS	0	0	1
Decker	LF	0	0	0	Treadway	LF	1	2	0
Anson	1B	0	0	0	Griffin	CF	0	1	0
Lange	CF	0	0	0	Shoch	3B	0	0	0
Irwin	SS	0	0	1	Burns	RF	0	0	0
Parratt	2B	0	0	0	Foutz	1B	0	0	0
Abbey	P	0	0	0	Dalley	C	0	0	0
Kittredge	C	0	0	0	Stein	P	0	0	0
Totals		0	0	1			1	4	1

CHICAGO	000 000 - 0 - 0 - 1	
BROOKLYN	100 000 - 1 - 4 - 1	

	IP	R	H	BB	SO
Abbey	6	1	4	0	2
Stein	6	0	0	5	0

KID EASON NO-HITS ST. LOUIS, 2-0

The Brooklyn Superbas of 1906 were a pitiful lot. Gone were the sweet memories of the pennant-winning years of 1899 and 1900. Gone too, were the great players; Wee Willie Keeler and his .358 batting average, slugging outfielder Joe Kelley who hit .318, and 29 game winner, "Iron Man" Joe McGinnity. The upstart American League, that began operations in 1901, had siphoned off most of Brooklyn's most talented players.

Within five years of their last title, Pat Donovan's boys had plummeted all the way to the National League basement. They finished an eye-popping 56 1/2 games behind the pennant-winning New York Giants in 1905. There was little to cheer about around Washington Park in those days. The hitting was bad. The pitching was almost non-existent. And the defense was atrocious. The Superbas finished dead last in fielding in 1905, committing 411 errors in only 152 games.

The season of 1906 was more of the same, advanced mediocrity. Except for July 20. For, on that date, a 27-year-old right-handed pitcher named Malcolm "Kid" Eason strode to the mound in League Park, St. Louis, and made pitching history. He became the first Brooklyn pitcher to throw a no-hit, no-run game in the 20th century, shutting out the Cardinals, 2-0.

For Malcolm Eason, a mediocre pitcher on a mediocre team, this was his finest hour. For one hour and thirty-five minutes, he mesmerized St. Louis hitters. His curveball crackled like a buggywhip. His fastball moved like a snake. And his control was pinpoint perfect. At the end, he was carried off the field by his teammates, the hero of the day.

Center fielder Mike Griffin is shown making a fine running catch. The players around the turn of the century had rudimentary equipment and primitive playing fields to contend with. Note the skintight glove and the less-than-manicured outfield. (Transcendental Graphics)

Kid Eason's career lasted only two months after his no-hitter. A sore arm sent him into premature retirement at the age of 27. (Transcendental Graphics)

From the fourth inning on, the smooth working Brooklyn right hander retired 14 consecutive batters. St. Louis got one last life with one out in the ninth, when Superbas shortstop Phil Lewis threw wild to first on a ground ball by Lurch. No Matter. Kid Eason was in complete control, and he easily punched out Bennett and Mertes to preserve his gem.

Nineteen hundred and six was "Kid" Eason's swan song. He finished the season with 11 wins and 16 losses; then returned to his home in Brookville, Pennsylvania. He never played major league ball again. During his seven-year career, Eason won a total of 37 games. He lost 71. But for one brief shining moment, the Kid had no equal on the mound. For one hour and thirty-five minutes on a hot, sultry July afternoon in St. Louis, Malcolm "Kid" Eason was the finest pitcher in the major leagues.

The Superbas scored all the runs Eason needed in the second inning. Hard-hitting first baseman Tim Jordan ripped a line drive to right field for two bases. Minutes later, left fielder Jack McCarthy plated Jordan with a single. Subsequent hits by Phil Lewis and catcher Lew Ritter scored McCarthy with the second and final run.

Meanwhile, Kid Eason was mowing down the Cardinals with monotonous regularity. The only difficult fielding play of the game occurred in the fifth inning. With one out, Art Hostetter sent a long fly ball to left field. It had all the earmarks of a base hit when it left the bat, but the fleet-footed McCarthy got a great jump on the ball and made a spectacular running catch near the foul line.

BROOKLYN

NAME	POS	AB	R	H	E
Maloney	CF	4	0	1	0
Casey	3B	4	0	0	0
Lumley	RF	4	0	1	0
Jordan	1B	3	1	2	0
Alperman	2B	1	0	0	0
McCarthy	LF	3	1	1	0
Lewis	SS	3	0	2	1
Ritter	C	3	0	2	0
Eason	P	3	0	1	0
Totals		28	2	10	1

ST. LOUIS

NAME	POS	AB	R	H	E
Burch	CF	3	0	0	0
Bennett	2B	4	0	0	0
Mertes	LF	3	0	0	0
Grady	C	2	0	0	0
Noonan	1B	3	0	0	1
J.Marshall	RF	3	0	0	0
Hostetter	3B	3	0	0	0
McBride	SS	3	0	0	0
Thompson	P	2	0	0	0
Murray	PH	1	0	0	0
Totals		27	0	0	1

BROOKLYN	0 2 0 0 0 0 0 0 0	- 2 - 10 - 1
ST. LOUIS	0 0 0 0 0 0 0 0 0	- 0 - 0 - 1

	IP	R	H	BB	SO
M. Eason	9	0	3	3	5
G. Thompson	9	2	10	1	1

Tim Jordan started the winning rally with a leadoff double in the second inning.

"HARD LUCK" HARRY MCINTYRE LOSES
NO-HIT BID AND GAME

Harry McIntyre was another Superbas pitcher who could have sued his teammates for non-support in 1906. "Rocks," as he was fondly called, had a respectable 2.97 ERA for the season, but could only produce a 12-21 record to go along with it. The punchless Sueprbas, last in the league in batting average, and next to last in runs scored, wasted the efforts of a fine pitching staff all season.

The coup de grace, as far as McIntyre was concerned, took place on August 1, 1906, in front of 3,000 home fans in Washington Park. The Pittsburgh Pirates, under Fred Clarke, came into Brooklyn in second place, only five games behind front running Chicago. Pat Donovan's crew, meanwhile, was mired in sixth place, 26 1/2 games out.

Lefty Al Leifield, a 6'1" stringbean, took the hill for Pittsburgh, opposing McIntyre. The 23-year-old Leifield, on his way to a fine 18-13 season, and McIntyre, engaged in one of the most memorable pitching duels of the season. The Pirate southpaw scattered seven hits over the first nine innings, but he was outpitched by the classy Brooklyn curveballer.

The game was marked by brilliant pitching, dazzling fielding plays, and shoddy baserunning on both sides. The two shortstops sparkled. Honus Wagner made two leaping catches of line drives to kill rallies in the seventh and ninth innings. Phil Lewis also speared a line drive with a desperate lunge in the sixth inning, and acted as middleman on two exciting double plays.

Harry Lumley (Los Angeles Dodgers)

The 27-year-old McIntyre had the Pittsburgh Pirates chasing his low breaking ball all afternoon. Only two runners reached base on him over the first ten innings. In the second, a one-out walk to Nealon was erased on a lightning-fast McIntyre-to-Lewis-to-Jordan double play. Ritchey, leading off the fourth, reached second on an error by Alperman, but he was left stranded as McIntyre fanned both Phelps and Leifield, then retired Leach on a pop up to Tim Jordan. From that point until the eleventh inning, the Superbas righty retired 23 straight batters.

In the eleventh inning, "Rocks" McIntyre set down Nealon and Sheehan in succession. After a short rain delay, Pittsburgh second baseman Claude Ritchey, a tough little contact hitter, stepped in to face the tantalizing slants of the Brooklyn righty. He immediately slapped a single to left field to end McIntyre's quest for fame.

Neither team scored in the twelfth and, as the thirteenth inning got underway, the field was shrouded in darkness. It was obvious the game could not last much longer. Right fielder Bob Ganley was determined to end the contest then and there. He jumped on a McIntyre curveball and poked a single to center. The dangerous Honus Wagner, next up, smashed a hard double up the left center field alley, sending Ganley racing to third. The Pirates did not squander the advantage this time. Jim Nealon chased a McIntyre curve and dropped a Texas Leaguer into center field. Ganley raced across the plate with the first run of the game, with Wagner pulling up at third. The "Flying Dutchman" was later cut down on an abortive steal of home to end the inning.

Harry McIntyre pitched in the National League for nine years, winning 71 games while losing 117. His luck changed after he left Brooklyn. He had two winning seasons for Chicago, going 13-9 in 1910, and 11-7 in 1911. (Transcendental Graphics)

The Superbas were down to their last at bat. McIntyre, determined to win his own game, led off the bottom of the 13th with a solid single. He carried the tying run to second on a sacrifice, but got no farther as Casey fanned and Lumley hit an easy grounder to Wagner to end the game.

It was a disappointing day for "Rocks" McIntyre. He pitched 10 2/3 innings of hitless baseball. He faced only 33 batters over that period, one over the limit. It was, perhaps, the best pitching performance in the major leagues during the entire season. Yet the game Brooklyn right hander came away empty handed. He not only lost the no-hitter. He lost the game as well. It was a sad finish to a memorable achievement.

BROOKLYN

NAME	POS	AB	R	H	E
Maloney	CF	5	0	0	0
Casey	3B	5	0	1	0
Lumley	RF	5	0	1	0
Jordan	1B	5	0	1	0
Alperman	2B	5	0	2	1
McCarthy	LF	4	0	2	0
Lewis	SS	4	0	1	0
Bergen	C	4	0	0	0
McIntyre	P	5	0	1	0
Totals		42	0	9	1

PITTSBURGH

NAME	POS	AB	R	H	E
Leach	LF	5	0	0	0
Beaumont	CF	5	0	0	0
Ganley	RF	5	1	1	0
Wagner	SS	5	0	1	0
Nealon	1B	4	0	1	0
Sheehan	3B	5	0	0	0
Ritchey	2B	4	0	1	0
Phelps	C	4	0	0	0
Leifield	P	4	0	0	0
Totals		41	1	4	0

BROOKLYN	000 000 000 000 0	- 0 - 9 - 1
PITTSBURGH	000 000 000 000 1	- 1 - 4 - 0

	IP	R	H	BB	SO
McIntyre	13	1	4	1	8
Leifield	13	0	9	2	5

NAP RUCKER OVERWHELMS BOSTON WITH 6-0 NO-HITTER

The Georgia Cracker reached the pinnacle of his pitching career on September 5, 1908, in just his second major league season. In what some experts of the day referred to as the greatest game ever pitched, 23-three-year-old George Napolean "Nap" Rucker threw a 6-0 no-hitter at the Boston Beaneaters, in Brooklyn's Washington Park. The smooth Superbas southpaw so dominated the game that the only Boston baserunners reached on Brooklyn miscues.

Not only did Rucker hold Joe Kelley's team hitless, he also established a new National League single-game strikeout record by fanning 14 Boston batters. The old mark of 12 strikeouts was jointly held by Rucker and the great Christy Mathewson of the New York Giants. So overpowering was the Brooklyn ace that he didn't issue a single base on balls.

Seven thousand raucous Brooklyn fans saw Joe Kelley's boys capture the opener of a doubleheader, 4-3, with George Ferguson beating Kaiser Wilhelm. The winning runs crossed the plate in the eighth inning on Brooklyn errors. In the nightcap, Boston southpaw Patsy Flaherty squared off against Superbas ace Nap Rucker. Boston leadoff batter George Browne reached first when his ground ball was bobbled by shortstop Phil Lewis, ending any chance of a perfect game from the outset. The rally died quickly however, when Bates hit into a double play and 36-year-old Joe Kelley fouled to the catcher. Brooklyn gave Rucker all the offensive support he needed in the bottom of the second inning. Tim Jordan started the action with a single. Whitey Alperman, attempting to sacrifice, beat out a bunt. Phil Lewis walked to load the bases. Flaherty then hit Tom Sheehan with a pitch, forcing Jordan home with the first run of the game. The next hitter, catcher Bill Bergen, a lifetime .170 batter, hit a ball to Dan McGann at first base and, when McGann threw wildly to the plate, both Alperman and Lewis scored. Sheehan came around later in the inning on a sacrifice fly, and the Superbas were up, 4-0.

That was more than enough for the slick Georgian southpaw. After fanning only one man in the first two innings, Rucker picked up the tempo in the third. He struck out both Jack Hannifan and Flaherty. In the fourth, amidst the wild screams of the Brooklyn faithful, he whiffed the side. Dan McGann opened the fifth with a ground ball to third, and reached base when Sheehan booted it. Rucker then retired the next three men in order, striking out two of them.

His statistics after five innings were spectacular; no hits allowed, and eight men retired via the strikeout route. The sixth brought more of the same; a 1-2-3 inning with one strikeout. In the seventh, Bates and McGann went down swinging, bringing Rucker's total of strikeouts to 11, one shy of the record.

Nap Rucker joined the hapless Brooklyn Superbas in 1907, winning 15 games for Patsy Donovan's fifth-place club. In 1908, the Georgia Peach led the seventh place Superbas with 18 victories.

BOSTON

NAME	POS	AB	R	H	E
Browne	RF	3	0	0	0
Bowerman	PH	1	0	0	0
Bates	LF	3	0	0	1
Smith	PH	1	0	0	0
Kelley	CF	3	0	0	0
McGann	1B	3	0	0	1
Dahlen	SS	3	0	0	0
Sweeney	3B	3	0	0	1
Graham	C	3	0	0	0
Hannifan	2B	3	0	0	0
Flaherty	P	2	0	0	0
Ritchey	PH	1	0	0	0
Totals		29	0	0	3

BROOKLYN

NAME	POS	AB	R	H	E
Burch	CF	4	0	1	0
Lumley	RF	4	0	1	1
Hummell	LF	4	0	0	0
Jordan	1B	3	2	3	0
Alperman	2B	3	2	2	0
Lewis	SS	2	1	0	1
Sheehan	3B	3	1	0	1
Bergen	C	4	0	1	0
Rucker	P	4	0	0	0
Hannifan	2B	3	0	0	0
Flaherty	P	2	0	0	0
Ritchey	PH	1	0	0	0
Totals		31	6	8	3

BOSTON BEANEATERS	000 000 000	- 0 - 0 - 3
BROOKLYN SUPERBAS	040 000 02X	- 6 - 8 - 3

	IP	R	H	BB	SO
P. Flaherty	8	6	8	2	2
G. Rucker	9	0	0	0	14

The crowd yelled and stamped their feet, screaming for their beloved "Nap" to first break the strikeout record, then complete the no-hitter. Bill Dahlen led off the Boston eighth, and fanned for the third time. After Sweeney reached on an error by Lumley in right, Rucker retired Graham on a fly ball to Burch in center field for out number two. With 7,000 people on their feet, and the noise unbearable, the unperturbable Southerner proceeded to fan Jack Hannifan for the record. Hundreds of straw hats were thrown on the field in celebration, and the game was delayed for several minutes while the ground crew cleaned up the debris.

In the bottom of the eighth, the Superbas increased their lead to 6-0, sparked by a Tim Jordan home run. Three outs remained for Rucker's no-hitter. Manager Joe Kelley didn't make it easy for the Brooklyn lefty as he sent three right-handed pinch hitters up to the plate. Ritchey and Bowerman both grounded out, second to first. The last hitter, Englishman Harry Smith, fittingly went down on strikes, completing Rucker's no-hitter, and giving him a new strikeout record of 14.

It was George Napolean Rucker's finest hour.

VANCE NO-HITS PHILADELPHIA PHILLIES 10-1

Thirty-four-year-old Dazzy Vance, the ace of the Brooklyn Robins pitching staff, achieved a lifelong ambition on September 13, 1925, when he stopped the Philadelphia Phillies, 10-1, holding them without a hit the entire game.

Wilbert Robinson's mediocre ballclub, en route to a sixth-place finish, was holding down fourth place as the sun came up on September 13. Art Fletcher's Philadelphia Phillies were in town for a doubleheader, with Vance hurling the opener against former Robin Clarence Mitchell. It was a bright sunshiny fall day, and a festive crowd of 20,000 was on hand to cheer Vance and his teammates on. The Robin offense responded to the crowd support by knocking Mitchell out of the box in the very first inning. Johnny Mitchell led off with a double. Milt Stock singled, Jimmy Johnston tripled, and Mitchell was gone. Dick Cox greeted reliever Art Decatur with a double, eventually scoring himself, and the Robins were off and running, 4-0.

The Phils nicked Old Dazzy for a run in the top of the second without the benefit of a hit. Chicken Hawks, leading off, sent an easy fly ball to left field, but Jimmy Johnston boxed it around before finally dropping it as Hawks raced for second. The Robins' left fielder, trying to atone for his mistake threw wildly to second, and Hawkes continued on to third. He scored shortly thereafter when Barney Friberg skied to center.

Chicken Hawks was the Phils' last baserunner, as the big right-hander mowed down the last 24 batters to face him. Just one week earlier, against this same team, Vance had tossed a one hitter, with Hawks getting the lone safety in the second inning. When the last Philadelphia batter was retired, the Brooklyn ace had 16 consecutive hitless innings to his credit.

Fletcher's batters didn't come close to getting a base hit all afternoon. The freckle-faced veteran mixed fast balls with sharp-breaking curveballs and a tantalizing change of pace to keep the hitters continually off balance. Nine Phils went down on strikes, while only two men reached base against the Brooklyn strongman. In addition to the error, the only other baserunner was the game's leadoff man, Heinie Sand, who coaxed a walk from Vance. He was left stranded.

The Robins added four more runs to their total in the fourth when DeBerry, Mitchell, Stock, Johnston, and Cox all singled in succession following a walk to Tierney. Three hits and a walk produced another run in the sixth, and two hits and a sacrifice fly brought home the final tally in the seventh.

Dazzy Vance, working rapidly under an 84-degree sun, was drenched in his own sweat as the Philadelphia ninth got underway. With the noisy Brooklyn crowd screaming on every pitch, the Robins' ace blew pinch hitter Lou Fonseca away on strikes. Another pinch hitter, Wally Kimmick, also bit the dust via the strikeout route. The noise was almost unbearable as the last man to face the big redhead, Freddy Leach, hit a line drive to left field. For a brief instant it looked like a hit, but Johnston made a fine running catch to end the game and preserve the no-hitter. Straw hats showered the field as the big Brooklyn crowd paid homage to their Hall Of Fame pitcher.

Fittingly, it was the first no-hitter ever recorded in Ebbets Field, 13 years after its opening.

PHILADELPHIA

NAME	POS	AB	R	H	E
Sand	SS	1	0	0	1
Wrightstone	PH	1	0	0	0
Metz	SS	0	0	0	0
Kimmick	PH	1	0	0	0
Leach	CF	4	0	0	0
Williams	RF	3	0	0	0
Harper	LF	3	0	0	0
Hawks	1B	3	1	0	0
Huber	3B	3	0	0	0
Friberg	2B	2	0	0	1
Wilson	C	2	0	0	0
Wendell	C	1	0	0	0
C. Mitchell	P	0	0	0	0
Decatur	P	1	0	0	0
Betts	P	1	0	0	0
Fonseca	PH	1	0	0	0
Totals		27	1	0	2

BROOKLYN

NAME	POS	AB	R	H	E
J. Mitchell	SS	5	2	3	0
Stock	2B	4	3	2	0
Johnston	LF	4	2	3	2
Cox	RF	5	1	4	0
Brown	CF	4	0	0	0
Hargreaves	1B	4	1	1	1
Tierney	3B	3	0	1	0
Deberry	C	3	1	1	0
Vance	P	4	0	0	0
Totals		36	10	15	3

```
PHILADELPHIA PHILLIES  0 1 0  0 0 0  0 0 0 - 1 - 0 - 2
BROOKLYN ROBINS        4 0 0  4 0 1  1 0 X -10 -15 - 3
```

	IP	R	H	BB	SO
C. Mitchell	0	3	3	0	0
Decatur	4	5	7	2	0
Betts	4	2	5	1	4
Vance	9	1	0	1	9

Dazzy Vance was the dominant pitcher in the National League during the 1920s. From 1922 through 1932, the Brooklyn flamethrower averaged 17 wins a year.

FRANKHOUSE THROWS SEVEN–INNING NO-HITTER

Frederick Meloy Frankhouse was a fair-to-middling curveball pitcher who toiled in the major leagues for 13 seasons, first with the St. Louis Cardinals, then with the Boston Bees and Brooklyn Dodgers. Frankhouse had the misfortune to pitch for two of the worst teams in the National League during the '30s. The Bees and Dodgers, between them, finished in the second division 13 times in nine years, between 1931 and 1939. In one four-year period, his teams averaged only 61 wins a year against 93 losses, but the pride of Port Royal, Pennsylvania, chalked up an average 13-12 record over the same period.

After spending nine years with St. Louis and Boston, Fred Frankhouse moved on to Brooklyn, and won 13 games for a pitiful Dodger team that crawled home in seventh place. Frankhouse won almost 20% of the Dodger victories that year. The following season, the 34-year-old hurler, nearing the end of the trail, still had enough left to win 10 games for Burleigh Grimes' sixth-place entry. His persistence was finally rewarded when, on the afternoon of Friday August 27, 1937, he achieved the goal of all pitchers, a no-hitter. Never mind that the game was called after 7 2/3 innings because of rain. He pitched the complete game and the Reds are still looking for their first hit.

Fred Frankhouse's big game was played in Ebbets Field on a hot summer day, with the mercury hovering around the 84-degree mark. It was an unusual game for the Pennsylvania pitcher in more ways than one. Not only did he hold the Reds hitless, but the control pitcher issued an uncharacteristic six bases on balls. The only man to reach second base against the curveballer was leadoff man Hub Walker who drew a base on balls in the first inning. He advanced to second when the next batter, Ival Goodman was safe on an error, then held his base as Frankhouse retired the next three hitters.

The only difficult fielding play came in the fifth inning. With one out and Alex Kampouris on first, pitcher Al Hollingsworth sent a hot smash in the hole between first and second. Dodger second baseman Jimmy Bucher, racing to his left, made a sensational stop on the edge of the outfield grass, and threw Hollingsworth out by a step. No other Cincinnati batter came close to getting a base hit.

Brooklyn scored the only run it needed in the bottom of the second, when Cookie Lavagetto singled, stole second, and raced home on Gibby Brack's base knock. They added another run in the third on an RBI single by Lavagetto, and a run in the fourth on Bucher's single. The final two runs, in the sixth, came in on Lavagetto's third hit of the game and an infield out by Heinie Manush.

Frankhouse breezed through the sixth and seventh easily. In the top of the eighth, leadoff hitter Hub Walker went down on strikes. After Goodman grounded out to second, the skies opened and a heavy rain began to fall. Umpire Lee Ballanfant immediately called time and

Fred Frankhouse was a 5'11", 175-pound right-handed pitcher, who toiled in the major leagues for 13 years. He started 216 games, with 81 complete games and 10 shutouts.

waved the ground crew onto the field. While the downpour continued, the Dodger pitcher paced the clubhouse, anxious to complete his masterpiece. But fate ruled otherwise. After 30 minutes, with the field a quagmire, the umpires called the game, and Fred Frankhouse's no-hitter went into the book.

The right-handed pitcher won only four more games in the major leagues, retiring after an 0-2 start in 1939. His major league totals showed 106 victories against 97 losses, an outstanding record considering the quality of his supporting cast.

CINCINNATI

NAME	POS	AB	R	H	E
Walker	CF	2	0	0	0
Goodman	RF	3	0	0	0
Hafey	LF	3	0	0	0
Scarsella	1B	2	0	0	0
Campbell	C	3	0	0	0
Riggs	3B	3	0	0	1
Kampouris	2B	2	0	0	1
Myers	SS	2	0	0	2
Hollingsworth	P	3	0	0	0
Totals		41	1	4	0

BROOKLYN

NAME	POS	AB	R	H	E
Cooney	CF	4	2	2	0
Bucher	2B	4	1	1	1
Hassett	1B	3	1	2	0
Manush	RF	4	0	0	0
Lavagetto	3B	3	1	3	0
Phelps	C	3	0	0	0
Brack	LF	3	0	2	0
English	SS	4	0	0	0
Frankhouse	P	4	0	0	0
Totals		32	5	10	1

```
CINCINNATI REDS      0 0 0  0 0 0  0 0 - 0 - 0 - 4
BROOKLYN DODGERS     0 1 1  1 0 2  0 X - 5 -10 -1
```

	IP	R	H	BB	SO
Hollingsworth	7	5	10	3	2
Frankhouse	8	0	0	6	3

Thirty-four-year-old Tex Carleton pitched only one year in a Brooklyn uniform, but he made the most of it. His six victories included his first no-hitter. He retired at the end of the season. (Brace Photo)

TEX CARLETON SINKS THE REDS WITH A NO-NO

The 1940 Brooklyn Dodgers were a club on the move. Rejuvenated by General Manager Larry MacPhail, who joined the team in 1938, the Dodgers had climbed from seventh place to third place in one short year. Now, as the 1940 season opened, they were making noises like a pennant contender. Leo Durocher's conglomeration of seasoned veterans and minor league castoffs broke from the gate quickly, running off eight wins in a row.

The team was a well-balanced unit, finishing fourth in the league in runs scored, fourth in fielding, and second in pitching. Famous names abounded; names like Dolph Camilli, Ducky Medwick, Pee Wee Reese, Cookie Lavagetto, and Dixie Walker. At the plate or in the field, the Flatbush Flock could hold their own with most teams. But it was on the mound where they excelled. The patchwork pitching staff was headed by American League retread Whitlow Wyatt, minor league veteran Hugh Casey, former 20-game winner Luke "Hot Potato" Hamlin, 16-year veteran "Fat Freddie" Fitzsimmons, and 33-year-old James "Tex" Carleton, in the last year of an eight-year major league career.

The Brooklyn Dodgers, hoping to tie the National League record for most consecutive victories at the start of the season, visited Crosley Field on April 30, to tangle with the second-place Cincinnati Reds, the defending National League champions. Bill McKechnie's team was

off to a good start itself, having won six of its first eight games, but it still trailed the Dodgers by two. The starting pitcher for the Redlegs was "Milkman Jim" Turner, a 36-year-old southpaw with outstanding control. Turner had arrived in the major leagues three years before, as a 33-year-old rookie with the Boston Bees. He broke in with a brilliant 20-11 season for the sixth-place Bees, and walked off with the league earned run average title as well.

His mound opponent was Tex Carleton, a tall, slender right-handed pitcher with a good fastball and a good curve. Carleton was a seven-year veteran in the National League, having pitched for the Cardinals and Cubs previously. After a 16-8 season for the Cubs in 1937, Carleton, plagued with arm problems, struggled through a painful 10-9 campaign in '38. He spent the following season in the minors before being rescued by MacPhail. The experienced hurler gave the up-and-coming Brooklynites one good season, pitching in 34 games, equally divided between starting and relieving. The tall Texan hurled a total of 149 innings, threw four complete games, and finished with a 6-6 record. He retired permanently after the season.

His best game of the year and, indeed, his best game ever, was the April 30 game against the Reds. Tex Carleton put it all together one last time and pitched a masterpiece, shackling the hard-hitting Cincinnati contingent without a hit, and shutting them out, 3-0 before a small weekday crowd of 10,544. So overpowering was the Dodger righthander, that Bill McKechnie's boys could put only four men on base, two on walks and two on errors.

The quiet man from Comanche, Texas, didn't allow a baserunner after the fourth inning, retiring the last 17 men in order to complete his once-in-a-lifetime fantasy. After some loose fielding in the early innings, The Dodgers settled down and gave Carleton some outstanding defensive support later in the game. In the sixth, Lonnie Frey hit a long fly ball to right field, but Roy Cullenbine made a leaping catch against the wall to deprive him of a hit. One inning later, leadoff batter Frank McCormick drove a ball to left field that was ticketed for extra bases, but Vosmik ran it down at the left-field wall, making a leaping catch to keep the no-hitter intact. A near-disaster occurred in the eighth inning when Wally Berger, pinch-hitting for pitcher Jim Turner, hit a high pop fly in front of the mound. Carleton and catcher Herman Franks collided as they went for the ball. Fortunately, Carleton was not hurt in the mishap, and Franks held onto the ball to retire the side.

Brooklyn scored all its runs in the top of the fifth inning. Herman Franks led off the inning with a base on balls, and two outs later, Fred "Dixie" Walker also drew a walk, putting runners on first and second. The next batter, Pete Coscarart, never noted for his power, leaned into a Turner delivery and drove it over the left-field wall for a three-run homer.

Carleton made the three runs stand up. In the ninth inning, with most of the Cincinnati crowd now rooting for the visiting pitcher to complete the no-hitter, the Dodger veteran retired Werber, Frey, and Ival Goodman in order to reserve his niche in the Hall Of Fame.

BROOKLYN

NAME	POS	AB	R	H	E
Walker	CF	4	1	0	0
Coscarart	2B	4	1	2	1
Vosmik	LF	4	0	1	0
Lavagetto	3B	4	0	2	1
Camilli	1B	4	0	0	0
Cullenbine	RF	3	0	0	0
Franks	C	3	1	0	0
Reese	SS	4	0	0	1
Carleton	P	2	0	0	0
Totals		32	3	5	3

CINCINNATI

NAME	POS	AB	R	H	E
Werber	3B	2	0	0	0
Frey	2B	4	0	0	0
Goodman	RF	4	0	0	0
F. McCormick	1B	3	0	0	0
Lombardi	C	3	0	0	0
Craft	CF	3	0	0	0
M. McCormick	RF	3	0	0	0
Joost	SS	3	0	0	0
Turner	P	2	0	0	0
Berger	PH	1	0	0	0
Moore	P	0	0	0	0
Totals		28	0	0	0

BROOKLYN DODGERS	000 030 000 - 3 - 5 - 3			
CINCINNATI REDS	000 000 000 - 0 - 0 - 0			

	IP	R	H	BB	SO
Carleton	9	0	0	2	4
Turner	8	3	4	2	2
Moore	1	0	1	1	1

ED HEAD'S MOMENT OF GLORY

Edward Marvin Head was a promising pitcher in the Brooklyn Dodger organization in the late '30s. Brought up to the big club for a look-see in 1940, the native of Selma, Louisiana, posted a 1-2 record before being returned to the minors for more seasoning. Two years later, he became a fixture in the Dodger pitching rotation, going 10-6 in 1942 and 9-10 the year after. In 1944, with World War II blazing away, both in Europe and in the Pacific, the 26-year-old hurler entered the United States Army.

He returned from the war in 1946, along with dozens of other Brooklyn veterans and minor league hopefuls, and immediately won a spot in manager Leo Durocher's starting rotation, along with Joe Hatten, Kirby Higbe, and Vic Lombardi. On April 23, in the cozy confines of Ebbets Field, the 6'1", 175-pound Head started his first major league game in almost two years, facing Billy Southworth's Boston Braves. The handsome Cajun had a good feeling as he took the mound on that cool spring day. His wife had presented him with a son 24 hours before, and he was still walking on air. In addition to the excitement of his new paternal responsibilities, the Army veteran was keyed up for his 1946 pitching debut. He even had a pre-game premonition that he might throw a no-hitter.

The 30,287 fans that crowded into the little ballpark along Sullivan Place, gave Head a boisterous welcome as he took the mound. They became progressively noisier as inning after inning passed without the semblance of a Boston hit. Ed Head was in complete control throughout the game as he toyed with the visitor's lineup, keeping them off balance all afternoon with a wide assortment of curveballs, fast balls, and changeups. When the smoke cleared at the end of the day, Boston had been able to produce only four baserunners, three on walks and one on an error.

The Braves had only two opportunities to sabotage Ed Head's quest for glory. In the seventh inning, with many of the crowd on their feet cheering the youngster on, Tommy Holmes hit a long fly ball toward home run territory in the center field seats. As 30,287 hushed fans held their collective breaths, center fielder Carl Furillo, raced his left, and caught the ball on the run near the exit gate. The Beaneaters' last attempt to short-circuit the Head express came with two out in the eighth, when Boston shortstop Whitey Wietelmann, bidding for an extra base hit, drilled a line drive toward the left-field corner. The ball never got there. Dodger third baseman Pete Reiser, with cat-like reflexes, snared it in the webbing of his glove to end the inning.

The Dodgers gave Head more than adequate offensive support, combing Boston right hander Mort Cooper for five runs on ten hits. They broke a scoreless deadlock in the bottom of the third, scoring twice on a bunt by Dick Whitman, and consecutive singles by Herman, Reiser, and Walker. Two more runs crossed the plate in the fifth when Ed Stevens crashed a double off the right field wall, sending Herman who had walked and Reese who had singled scampering across the plate. Ferrell Anderson accounted for the final run when he homered into the left-field seats in the sixth inning.

Ed Head won only two more major league games after his no-hitter. A sore arm ended the slender right hander's career after only 465 innings pitched, over a five-year period. His career totals showed 27 victories against 23 losses.

Sadly, Ed Head pitched in only 11 more major league games. After compiling a 3-2 record early in the season, the talented righthander came down with a sore arm and was out of the league before the season ended.

BOSTON

NAME	POS	AB	R	H	E
Ryan	2B	3	0	0	0
Hopp	CF	4	0	0	0
Holmes	RF	3	0	0	0
Sanders	1B	3	0	0	0
Rowell	LF	3	0	0	0
Masi	C	2	0	0	0
Roberge	3B	3	0	0	0
Wietelmann	SS	2	0	0	0
Cooper	P	2	0	0	0
Workman	PH	0	0	0	0
Totals		25	0	0	0

BROOKLYN

NAME	POS	AB	R	H	E
Whitman	LF	4	1	1	0
Herman	2B	2	2	1	0
Reiser	3B	4	1	2	0
Walker	RF	3	0	2	0
Stevens	1B	4	0	1	0
Furillo	CF	4	0	0	0
Anderson	C	4	1	2	0
Reese	SS	4	0	0	1
Head	P	3	0	1	0
Totals		32	5	10	1

```
BOSTON BRAVES       000 000 000 - 0 - 0 - 0
BROOKLYN DODGERS    002 021 00X - 5 -10 - 1
```

	IP	R	H	BB	SO
M. Cooper	8	5	10	3	4
E. Head	9	0	0	3	2

REX BARNEY STUNS NEW YORK GIANTS WITH NO-HITTER

Once upon a time, in a far off land called Brooklyn, there was a baseball pitcher who was blessed with great strength, and a fast ball that was but a blur. This young man could have been the greatest pitcher in the world if, as one sports writer put it, "the plate was high and outside." For you see, this pitcher never knew where the ball was going when he threw it.

The pitcher's name was Rex Barney, and he was one of baseball's great talents. In a different era, under different conditions, he could have become another Sandy Koufax, but Barney had the misfortune to come of age during the second world war, and he was rushed into action prematurely. He was never given the time to mature and grow as Koufax was.

The 6'3", 185-pound right-handed pitcher with the blazing fast ball signed a professional contract right out of high school. With most able bodied men in the service in 1943, major league owners were desperate for players. As a result, the 18-year-old phenom was signed while playing American Legion ball in Omaha, and was shuttled off to the Dodger's minor league farm team in Durham, North Carolina in the Class B Piedmont League. Two months later he was whisked off to the AAA Montreal Royals and, after a short sojourn in Canada, he was called up to the National League Dodgers. From high school to the major leagues in just four short months. That's the way it was in 1943.

The first pitch thrown by Barney in each of the three leagues were reportedly three of the wildest pitches ever seen on a ballfield. One pitch hit the screen, one ended up in the grandstand, and there is no record of where the third pitch landed. Still, the kid from Omaha, Nebraska managed to finish his year in Brooklyn with a 2-2 record, a moral victory considering his 6.40 earned run average.

The next year, Rex Barney marched off to war with the rest of the men, and after three years of active service, two battle stars and a bronze star, the baseball hopeful returned to Brooklyn to pursue his career. Five frustrating seasons later, the likable youngster with the live pitching arm folded up his glove and moved on to another career. He was never able to harness his vast storehouse of talent.

For one brief season, however, it appeared as if Rex Barney would become the great pitcher that many experts had predicted. In 1948, the big righthander won more games than anyone on the Brooklyn staff, finishing with a 15-13 record and a 3.10 earned run average. His finest hour came on September 9, when he faced Leo Durocher's Giants in the Polo Grounds. Both teams were still in the pennant race at the time; the Dodgers 3 1/2 games behind the first place Boston Braves and the Giants 6 1/2 games in arrears. A big weeknight crowd of 36,324 vociferous New York rooters packed the big park at Coogan's Bluff to root for the home team. A small but noisy contingent of Flatbush residents provided the necessary support for their "Bums."

Barney's opponent was Monte Kennedy, a big left hander from Amelia, Virginia. The journeyman pitcher, who won a total of only 42 games in eight years in the majors, was in the throes of a miserable 3-9 season, and he was anxious to get the game started. Unfortunately, both he and Barney were trapped in the clubhouse for

Rex Barney had the world's greatest fast ball, but he couldn't control it. In his last major league season, 1950, he walked 48 men in 33 2/3 innings, before receiving a one-way ticket to the minors.

over an hour while rains drenched the field. When the evening's festivities finally did get underway, it looked like it might be a short night for Mr. Barney. The Giants loaded the bases in the bottom of the first inning with only one out, thanks to two walks and an error by Barney himself. The next batter, Willard Marshall, the Giants' slugging right fielder, obligingly hit a shot to the right side, where Jackie Robinson turned it into a lightning-fast 4-6-3 double play. That was it as far as New York was concerned. The only other Giant baserunner came in the third when Kennedy reached on an error by Robinson, but he was quickly erased on a double play, Barney to Reese to Hodges.

Rex Barney baffled Durocher's troops with a blazing fast ball, a good curve and a change of pace. He retired the last 21 men to face him in completing his gem. It was not an easy game for the big righthander, as the rain continued intermittently throughout, making the footing hazardous and the ball difficult to grip. In the ninth, with the crowd on its feet, the rain increased in intensity, causing some consternation in the Dodger dugout, but Barney rose to the occasion. He fanned Joe LaFata, got Lohrke on a pop to Hodges, and retired Whitey Lockman on a foul to Bruce Edwards.

Center fielder Carl Furillo was the defensive star of the game, making three outstanding catches to preserve the no-no. In the fourth, Johnny Mize, "The Big Cat," hit a sinking liner to center that Furillo grabbed after a long run. Three innings later, the Reading Rifle added two more saving catches. Sid Gordon, another member of Durocher's slugging machine smashed a 425-foot drive to left center field, but Furillo ran it down. One out later, he pulled in a 400-footer off the bat of Marshall.

Monte Kennedy pitched one of his better games against Brooklyn. Unfortunately, it was on a day when the Dodger flamethrower was unhittable. The 6'2" lefty limited Shotton's contingent to two runs and six hits, but that was all they needed. They scored one run in the second on a single by Furillo, a double by Reese, and an infield out. The second run came across an inning later on a leadoff walk to Billy Cox and two-out singles by Edwards and Furillo. The Reading Rifle had three of the Dodgers' six hits, all singles, while Edwards chipped in with a pair of singles and Reese had a double.

Barney's no-hitter was the first against a Giant team since 1915, when Jimmy Lavender of the Chicago Cubs blanked them by the same score in the same ballpark. The victory was the 13th of the season for the hard-throwing righthander, who seemed on the verge of greatness. It was all an illusion, however. He won only 13 more games for Brooklyn over the next three years. Unable to tame his wildness, he was shunted off to the minors in 1950 after a Memorial Day start against Philadelphia in which he walked six men and hit one in just 1 1/3 innings of pitching. He never returned.

BROOKLYN

NAME	POS	AB	R	H	E
Cox	3B	3	1	0	0
Robinson	2B	4	0	0	1
Reiser	LF	3	0	0	0
Shuba	LF	0	0	0	0
Edwards	C	4	0	2	0
Furillo	CF	4	1	3	0
Reese	SS	4	0	1	0
Hodges	1B	4	0	1	0
Hermanski	RF	3	0	0	0
Barney	P	3	0	0	1
Totals		32	2	6	2

NEW YORK

NAME	POS	AB	R	H	E
Lohrke	2B	3	0	0	1
Lockman	CF	4	0	0	0
Gordon	3B	3	0	0	0
Mize	1B	2	0	0	0
Marshall	RF	3	0	0	0
Mueller	LF	3	0	0	0
Cooper	C	3	0	0	0
Kerr	SS	2	0	0	0
Frey	PH	1	0	0	0
Rhawn	SS	0	0	0	0
Kennedy	P	2	0	0	0
Lafata	PH	1	0	0	0
Totals		27	0	0	1

BROOKLYN DODGERS	011 000 000 -	2 - 6 - 2
NEW YORK GIANTS	000 000 000 -	0 - 0 - 1

	IP	R	H	BB	SO
Kennedy	9	2	6	3	2
Barney	9	0	0	2	4

THE LITTLE HOOSIER JUST MISSES PERFECTION

Carl Erskine was one of the most courageous pitchers ever to don Brooklyn blue. The good-looking Hoosier pitched in the major leagues for a period of 12 years, most of the time with intense pain in his pitching shoulder, the result of an injury suffered during his rookie season. The shoulder never healed and, as a result, Erskine was unable to throw between starts, limiting his pitching to games only.

"Oisk," as he was fondly known in Brooklyn, carved his niche in baseball's Hall of Fame on Thursday, June 19, 1952, when his 5-0 no-hitter against the Chicago Cubs came within one out of a perfect game. A small weekday crowd of 7,732 paid fans witnessed the masterpiece in Ebbets Field, although an additional 5,000 kids were in the stands as guests of Happy Felton's "Knot-hole" club.

When Phil Cavaretta's Chicago Cubs entered the little ballpark along Sullivan Place on June 19, they were already 6 1/2 games behind Charlie Dressen's boys. The skies were overcast as the Bums took the field, and the threat of rain was of prime concern to all. Dodger ace Carl Erskine, with a 5-1 record, was paired against Cub righthander Warren Hacker (4-1), en route to his best season in the majors.

The Dodgers won the game, 5-0, but the big story was the pitching of Carl Erskine. He threw a gem, limiting Chicago to a single baserunner, and he might well have pitched a perfect game if not for the weather. The "Master of the Overhand Curveball" retired the first eight Chicago batters. With the weather rapidly deteriorating, and the Dodgers up, 4-0, Erskine rushed his delivery, trying to complete the five innings necessary to make it an official game. In his eagerness, he walked opposing pitcher Willard Ramsdell on four pitches before retiring the side in the third.

The rains came at the end of the inning, interrupting play for 45 minutes. When festivities resumed,

Erskine's quest for glory continued unabated. The Cubs never had another baserunner, as "Oisk" retired the last 19 batters in a row. He struck out only one batter as his overhand curveball had them hitting the ball into the ground all afternoon. Eighteen infield assists attested to the effectiveness of his bread-and-butter pitch, better known as a "drop" in the old days. Only five balls were hit to the outfield, and one man was retired on a foul pop to Campanella.

The Dodgers gave Erskine all the runs he needed in the very first inning when they jumped on Hacker for three runs. Reese hit a one-out, bad-bounce single over the head of former Dodger Eddie Miksis at short. One out later, Roy Campanella drilled a two-run homer into the left center field stands. Carl Furillo followed with a 360 foot shot into the same area. In the second inning, former Cub Andy Pafko slammed his tenth home run of the season, upping the count to 4-0. Dressen's boys pushed across their final tally in the eighth on singles by Reese and Campanella. Campy's three RBIs upped his total for the year to 47 in 55 games.

Dodger defense was outstanding in the game as they pulled off several eye-popping plays to protect the no-hitter. Erskine, Furillo and Bobby Morgan all flagged down potential hits to frustrate the Chicago crew. The Dodger pitcher made the first defensive gem himself when he intercepted a hot grounder through the middle by Dee Fondy in the fifth, to take a hit away from the big first baseman. Morgan made a scintillating pickup of a slow grounder toward third in the top of the sixth, and retired pitcher Willie "The Knuck" Ramsdell on a bang-bang play at first. The Emperor of Right Field took over in the sev-

enth. Carl Furillo was playing in right center field against National League home run leader Hank Sauer, when the big righthander smashed a long drive to the opposite field for what looked like an extra base hit. He didn't contend with Furillo, however, and the Dodger star thwarted the threat by making a fine running catch at the scoreboard as the crowd breathed a sigh of relief.

In the ninth, the cool-headed Erskine retired Bob Ramazzoti, Phil Cavaretta, and Eddie Miksis, all on routine plays, to nail down his sixth win of the season, and one he will never forget.

CHICAGO

NAME	POS	AB	R	H	E
Miksis	SS	4	0	0	0
Addis	LF	3	0	0	0
Hermanski	RF	3	0	0	0
Sauer	LF	3	0	0	0
Atwell	C	3	0	0	1
Fondy	1B	3	0	0	0
Jackson	3B	3	0	0	0
Ramazzoti	2B	3	0	0	0
Hacker	P	0	0	0	0
Ramsdell	P	1	0	0	0
Cavaretta	PH	1	0	0	0
Totals		27	0	0	1

BROOKLYN

NAME	POS	AB	R	H	E
Morgan	3B	4	0	0	0
Reese	SS	4	2	2	0
Robinson	2B	3	0	0	0
Campanella	C	4	1	2	0
Furillo	RF	4	1	1	0
Snider	CF	3	0	0	0
Hodges	1B	3	0	0	0
Pafko	LF	3	1	2	0
Erskine	P	3	0	0	0
Totals		31	5	7	0

CHICAGO CUBS   0 0 0 0 0 0 0 0 0 - 0 - 0 - 1
BROOKLYN DODGERS 3 1 0 0 0 0 0 1 X - 5 - 7 - 0

	IP	R	H	BB	SO
Hacker	1 1/3	4	4	0	1
Ramsdell	6 2/3	1	3	1	2
Erskine	9	0	0	1	1

Carl Erskine won 122 major league games with a golf-ball-size knot in his shoulder. His achievements included two no-hitters and a World Series strikeout record.

LIGHTNING STRIKES TWICE FOR ERSKINE

The little Hoosier from Anderson, Indiana, stepped to the head of the class as far as Dodger pitchers are concerned, becoming the first Brooklyn hurler in National League history to hurl two no-hitters. Only William "Adonis" Terry of the old American Association entry could match his performance.

Carl Daniel Erskine pitched his second no-hitter in four years when he stymied Bill Rigney's New York Giants 3-0 on May 12, 1956. The defending World Champions, en route to their second consecutive National League title, were ensconced in second place at game time, two games out of first. Their New York opponents were comfortably settled in sixth place, a position they also held at season's end.

Erskine, battling arm miseries, came into the game with a 1-2 record, while his opponent, righthander Al Worthington, was also at 1-2. A Saturday crowd of 24,588 Dodger enthusiasts hung on Erskine's every pitch as he threw his way to baseball immortality, joining a select circle of only seven other major league pitchers credited with two or more no-hitters. Rapid Robert Feller of the Cleveland Indians led the way with three.

Walter Alston's 165-pound dynamo issued a base on balls to the dangerous Willie Mays in the first inning, then set down the next seven men in a row, before walking Alvin Dark in the fourth. Not another Giant reached base as "Oiskin" retired the last 18 batters in a row. Along the way, he received some spectacular defensive play, particularly from Jackie Robinson and the omnipresent Carl Furillo. After Dark's walk in the fourth, Mays ripped an Erskine curve ball toward right field. The acrobatic Robinson, reacting instinctively, dove to his left and speared the ball in the webbing of his glove. After Dusty Rhodes was retired, second baseman Daryl Spencer hit a towering drive to right center field, but Furillo ran it down with an over-the-shoulder catch at the 352-foot mark.

The Giants went quietly from the fourth through the eighth, but they kicked up their heels again in the ninth. With one out, Whitey Lockman made a bid for a base hit with a smash through the middle, but Erskine knocked it down and threw to Hodges for the out. The final batter, Al Dark, ended the suspense with an easy bouncer to the mound, and was retired one to three.

It was not an easy game for the Dodger ace, as he was locked in a tight pitchers' duel with Worthington for seven long innings. The Dodgers broke the scoring ice in the bottom of the third inning, thanks to a temporary loss of control by the Giant starter. Alston's boys scored one run on a walk to Reese, a single by Snider, and one-out walks to both Hodges and Robinson. The slim 1-0 margin persisted into the seventh when the Bums gave their pitcher a little breathing room with two more scores. Once again Reese was the catalyst, singling to left. Duke Snider then smashed a long double up the alley in left center field, with Pee Wee scoring all the way from first. Campy brought the Duke in with a single to left.

Erskine threw only 102 pitches in his no-hitter, striking out three and walking two. Only seven balls were hit to the outfield, as the little Hoosier kept the New Yorkers off balance with a good fast ball, the league's best change of pace, and pin-point control. And the Dodger defense came to his rescue when they were needed.

The Dodger pitching staff, L to R. Don Newcombe, Billy Loes, Carl Erskine, Don Bessent, Clem Labine, and Roger Craig, unlimber their arms in Vero Beach, February 23, 1956.

NEW YORK

NAME	POS	AB	R	H	E
Lockman	LF	4	0	0	0
Dark	SS	3	0	0	0
Mays	CF	2	0	0	0
Rhodes	LF	3	0	0	0
Spencer	2B	3	0	0	0
White	1B	3	0	0	0
Castleman	3B	2	0	0	0
Mueller	PH	1	0	0	0
Thompson	3B	0	0	0	0
Katt	C	3	0	0	0
Worthington	P	2	0	0	0
Grissom	P	0	0	0	0
Wilson	PH	1	0	0	0
Totals		27	0	0	0

BROOKLYN

NAME	POS	AB	R	H	E
Gilliam	2B	4	0	1	0
Reese	SS	3	2	1	0
Snider	CF	3	1	2	0
Campanella	C	4	0	1	0
Hodges	1B	3	0	0	0
Robinson	3B	2	0	0	0
Amoros	LF	4	0	0	0
Furillo	RF	2	0	0	0
Erskine	P	4	0	1	0
Totals		29	3	6	0

```
NEW YORK GIANTS      000 000 000-0-0-0
BROOKLYN DODGERS     001 000 20X-3-6-0
```

	IP	R	H	BB	SO
Worthington	6 1/3	3	6	7	4
Grissom	1 2/3	0	0	0	0
Erskine	9	0	0	2	3

"THE BARBER" GIVES PHILLY A CLOSE SHAVE, 5-0

Sal "The Barber" Maglie, once the Brooklyn Dodgers most hated enemy, but now a key member of their vaunted pitching staff, pitched his Brooklyn mates closer to a National League title with a pressure-packed 5-0 no-hit win over the Philadelphia Phillies on Tuesday, September 25, 1956. The victory kept the Dodgers only 1/2 game behind the Milwaukee Braves with only three games to play.

On the final weekend, Brooklyn would capture the flag by sweeping their final three games from the hapless Pittsburgh Pirates. Maglie would pitch the Dodgers into first place with a 6-2 victory in the opener, while the Braves were stumbling against the St. Louis Cardinals, losing both Friday and Saturday, to blow the pennant.

Sal Maglie was a tough competitor, who had toiled in New York black and orange for six-and-a-half years, while piling up an enviable 95-42 won-loss record. He helped the Giants to pennants in both 1951 and 1954, leading the National League in victories in '51 with 23. The mean-looking righthander earned his nickname by throwing inside pitches under the batter's chin to keep him off the plate. He was once quoted as saying, "When I'm on the mound, the plate belongs to me." More than once "The Barber" had a run-in with his rivals from the other side of the river. Roy Campanella, the Dodgers good natured catcher, used to jokingly warn his teammates, "Better wear a helmet today. Maglie's pitching."

When Maglie joined Alston's forces in mid-1956, all was forgiven, however. He was quickly welcomed by Campy, Pee Wee and the rest of the team and became an important cog in the Brooklyn pennant machine. By the time Tuesday, September 25 rolled around, the Bums were in a nip-and-tuck battle with the Milwaukee Braves. Thanks in large part to "The Barber's" 11 victories in 14 weeks, the pennant was still up for grabs. A noisy midweek crowd of 15,204 turned Ebbets Field into a premature pennant party as Maglie faced the fifth place Phillies. After the 6'2", 180-pound righthander retired the first six batters to face him, the Brooklyn bats came to life. In the bottom of the second, Jackie Robinson stroked a double to left, leading off. An infield out and a walk to Hodges gave the Brooks two baserunners, and Robby scored on a slow grounder to short by Furillo. Big Gil brought in the second run ahead of Campanella's 19th homer, a 350-foot shot into the left-field seats.

The Dodgers added two more runs in the third, to close out the scoring. Maglie, meanwhile was cruising along. After walking pitcher Jack Meyer with two gone in the third, the 39-year-old hurler set down another 13 men in succession before walking Willie "Puddinhead" Jones leading off the eighth. With one out, Solly Hemus sent a sizzler down the first base line, but the slick-fielding Hodges quickly turned it into a 3-6-3 double play to end the inning.

After retiring the first two batters easily in the ninth, Maglie hit Ashburn on the foot with a pitch, the Phils' third and last baserunner. First baseman Marv Blaylock then hit an easy grounder to second where Junior Gilliam scooped it up and threw to Hodges to complete the no-hitter. Philadelphia's only threat of a base hit occurred in the second inning. "Puddenhead" Jones hit a hard shot back through the middle that had single written all over it, but Pee Wee Reese, darting to his left, gloved the ball cleanly and nipped Jones by a step. Other than that, it was an overpowering performance for the former New York pitcher. As Roy Campanella said, "We threw nothing but curves and fastballs. Sal's control was almost perfect. He put every pitch exactly where he wanted to."

Sal "The Barber" Maglie was one of baseball's greatest clutch pitchers. He was at his best when the chips were down. The former Dodger killer went 13-5 for the Brooks in 1956, as they nosed out the Milwaukee Braves by one game for the 1956 National League pennant.

PHILADELPHIA

NAME	POS	AB	R	H	E
Ashburn	CF	3	0	0	0
Blaylock	1B	4	0	0	0
Lopata	C	3	0	0	1
Ennis	LF	3	0	0	0
Jones	3B	2	0	0	0
Valo	RF	3	0	0	0
Hemus	2B	3	0	0	0
Kazanski	2B	0	0	0	0
Smalley	SS	2	0	0	0
Baumholtz	PH	1	0	0	0
Meyer	P	0	0	0	1
Miller	P	0	0	0	0
Bouchee	PH	1	0	0	0
Sanford	P	0	0	0	0
Haddix	PH	1	0	0	0
Totals		26	0	0	2

BROOKLYN

NAME	POS	AB	R	H	E
Gilliam	2B	3	1	1	0
Reese	SS	3	0	0	0
Snider	CF	2	1	0	0
Robinson	3B	2	1	1	0
Amoros	LF	4	0	0	0
Hodges	1B	2	1	1	0
Furillo	RF	3	0	0	0
Campanella	C	2	1	1	0
Maglie	P	3	0	0	0
Totals		24	5	4	0

```
PHILADELPHIA PHILLIES  000 000 000 - 0 - 0 - 2
BROOKLYN DODGERS       032 000 00X - 5 - 4 - 0
```

	IP	R	H	BB	SO
Meyer	2 1/3	5	3	3	0
Miller	2 2/3	0	0	1	2
Sanford	3	0	1	3	2
Maglie	9	0	0	2	3

SANDY KOUFAX NO-HITS METS 5-0

The Los Angeles Dodgers former bonus baby finally came of age on June 30, 1962, when he shackled the New York Mets, 5-0, without a single hit. Twenty-six-year-old Sandy Koufax, after six years of unrewarded promise, began to turn his career around in 1961. From a career won-loss record of 36-40, the stylish southpaw put together an 18-13 season. Strangely enough, while lowering the velocity of his fastball in order to improve his control, he still maintained his 9+ strikeout per game average; yet reduced his bases on balls from five per game down to two. By the time June 30, 1962, rolled around, the 6'2" hurler had developed into the best pitcher in the league. In addition to a 100-mph fastball, Koufax was also the possessor of the most vicious curve ball around, and he used them both with pinpoint accuracy.

Walter Alston's ace brought a 10-4 record into the game against the hapless Mets. Although it was still early in the season, Casey Stengel's hitless wonders were already 28 games behind the first-place San Francisco Giants, and 27 1/2 behind the Dodgers. Their 20-53 record was one of the worst in major league history.

From the outset, it looked like a bleak night for the visitors. As 32,769 blase Californians looked on, the Dodger lefty fanned the side in the top of the first. In the bottom of the same inning, the Big Blue Machine roughed up Met starter Bob Miller for four runs. After the big

Dodger speedster Maury Wills receives gifts from the L.A. Booster Club, in recognition of his achievements in 1962. Wills' spectacular defensive play on Frank Thomas in the second inning preserved Koufax's first no-hitter.

righthander retired the first two Dodgers, the roof caved in on him. Willie Davis tripled, Tommy Davis singled, Ron Fairly walked, Frank Howard singled, John Roseboro doubled, and Larry Burright singled, giving the Dodgers a comfortable cushion.

Koufax came close to losing his no-hitter three times along the way. In the second inning, Frank Thomas hit a shot through the hole in the left side, but Maury Wills made a dazzling backhand stop and threw out the slow-footed Thomas by a step. In the sixth, Richie Ashburn sliced a drive down the left-field line. Left fielder Tommy Davis momentarily lost the ball in the lights, but recovered in time to make a nice running catch. Then, in the ninth, Ashburn sliced another drive to left, but it curved foul by six feet. No other Met came close to a hit as the swift lefty overpowered them with his smoke.

The Dodgers extended their lead to 5-0 in the seventh when big Frank Howard sent a drive into the left-field seats for a home run. Then came the pressure-packed ninth. Even the laid back Angeleno fans were in a frenzy as the 210-pound lefty tried to nail down his masterpiece. They booed or cheered on every pitch, depending on whether the umpire called it a ball or a strike. Working

carefully, Koufax walked pinch hitter Gene Woodling, leading off. The raucous crowd let the umpire know they didn't agree with his call. Ashburn, after his drive curved foul in left, sent a skimmer to Wills to force pinch runner Joe Christopher. Rod Kanehl pulled an 0-2 pitch to third, where Gilliam gloved it and tossed to Burright for the force on Ashburn for out number two. Stillness filled the air as Felix Mantilla stepped to the plate; the Mets' last threat. Jumping on a 2-1 pitch the native of Puerto Rico hit a grounder to Wills, who flipped it to Burright for the third force play of the inning, ending the game and sealing Sandy Koufax's brilliant performance. The crowd gave Koufax a noisy round of approval as his teammates mobbed him on the mound.

The brilliant Dodger lefty struck out 13 New York batters during his no-hitter, giving him a league-leading 183 strikeouts in only 150 innings. Little did he know it at the time, but the great pitcher's season was almost over. Within a month, he was sidelined with Reynaud's Phenomenon, a circulatory problem in his pitching hand. Out of action for nine weeks, he was ineffective on his return and was unable to help his team fight off the San Francisco Giants. The Giants won a playoff between the two teams when they scored four runs in the ninth inning of the third game to capture the National League Championship.

Los Angeles Dodgers coach Leo Durocher discusses pitching mechanics with Dodger picher Sandy Koufax. The Koufax mechanics were almost perfect in 1962, as he went 14-7 before a circulation problem put him on the sidelines.

NEW YORK

NAME	POS	AB	R	H	E
Ashburn	LF	3	0	0	0
Kanehl	3B	4	0	0	0
Mantilla	2B	3	0	0	0
Thomas	1B	2	0	0	0
Cook	RF	3	0	0	0
Hickman	CF	3	0	0	0
Chacon	SS	2	0	0	0
Cannizzaro	C	3	0	0	0
Miller	P	0	0	0	0
Daviault	P	2	0	0	0
Woodling	PH	0	0	0	0
Christopher	PR	0	0	0	0
Totals		25	0	0	0

LOS ANGELES

NAME	POS	AB	R	H	E
Wills	SS	5	0	1	0
Gilliam	3B	3	0	1	0
W. Davis	CF	4	1	2	0
T. Davis	LF	4	1	2	0
Fairly	1B-RF	3	1	0	0
Howard	RF	3	2	2	0
Harkness	1B	0	0	0	0
Roseboro	C	3	0	1	0

Burright	2B		4	0	2	0
Koufax	P		4	0	0	0
Totals			33	5	11	0

```
NEW YORK METS      000 000 000-0- 0-0
LOS ANGELES DODGERS 400 000 10X-5-11-0
```

	IP	R	H	BB	SO
Miller	2/3	4	5	1	0
Daviault	7 1/3	1	6	5	7
Koufax	9	0	0	5	13

KOUFAX DOES IT AGAIN—GIANTS 0 RUNS, 0 HITS

Sandy Koufax, proving that his pitching hand was completely healed from the circulatory problem that plagued him in 1962, and silencing the skeptics who said his no-hitter against the Mets was a fluke, stopped the power hitting San Francisco Giants, 8-0, on a no-hitter. Alvin Dark's defending National League champions were loaded, boasting such sluggers as Willie Mays (.314, 38, 103), Orlando Cepeda (.316, 34, 97), and big 6'4" Willie McCovey (.280, 44, 102). But on May 11, they were completely overmatched when they faced the Brooklyn-born flame-throwing southpaw.

A big, anti-Giant crowd of 55,530 jammed Dodger Stadium to watch the fifth-place Dodgers tangle with the first place Giants. It was a big Saturday night extravaganza; the Dodgers against the Giants, Koufax against the San Francisco ace, Juan Marichal; Giant power against Dodger speed. Koufax set the first six men down in order. Marichal, after retiring the side, 1-2-3 in the first was touched up for a leadoff homer by Wally Moon in the second. The game moved at a rapid rate as both pitchers kept the opposition in check.

In the fifth, leadoff man Orlando Cepeda hit a slow grounder past the mound. As the crowd held their collective breath, Dick Tracewski made a bare-handed pickup and throw to nip the big first baseman by a step. One inning later, Walter Alston's boys jumped all over the Giants' high-kicking righthander, breaking the game open with a three-run rally. Jim Gilliam got the ball rolling with a leadoff single. Tommy Davis chipped in with a one-out single, and Wally Moon knocked in his second run of the game with a hit to right. After Frank Howard was intentionally walked to load the bases, Johnny Roseboro smashed a two-run single.

Felipe Alou almost broke up Koufax's no-hitter in the top of the seventh when he hit a long drive down the left-field line. With the stadium suddenly quiet, Tommy Davis backed up to the low barrier to make the catch for out number two. Willie Mays followed with a line drive to third, but Gilliam was right on it to retire the side.

Orlando Cepeda, leading off the eighth, hit a scorcher back to the mound. The Dodger lefty deflected the ball to second where Nate Oliver fielded it and threw to first for the out. The next batter, Ed Bailey, the big Giant catcher, walked to become San Francisco's first baserunner. Koufax had retired 22 men in a row to start the game. He still faced the minimum number of hitters when Jim Davenport hit into a fast 6-4-3 double play.

Los Angeles iced the game in the bottom of the eighth when they pushed across four runs at the expense of rookie reliever John Pregenzer. All the while the Dodgers were on the attack, Sandy Koufax sat alone with his thoughts in the dugout. His teammates avoided him and they also avoided any talk of a no-hitter, although the same thought was on everyone's minds.

The ninth inning began with the big crowd on it's feet, roaring support for their favorite Dodger. Second baseman Joe Amalfitano obliged them by making the first out on an easy pop fly to the infield. Jose Pagan followed with a long drive to center where Willie Davis gathered it in and, suddenly, the Dodger southpaw was only one out away from glory. Koufax faltered slightly at this point, as he started aiming the ball, and he walked Willie McCovey on four pitches. Just as quickly, he settled down again, as Harvey Kuenn, a lifetime .303 hitter, stepped to the plate. On a one-strike pitch, the Giant left fielder hit a soft tap back to the box. Koufax fielded it and tossed to Fairly for the game ender.

The great Dodger lefty breathed a sigh of relief, as teammates gathered around for the congratulatory handshake, and thousands of seat cushions sailed on the field in celebration. No-hitter number two was even sweeter

Sandy Koufax retired Joe Amalfitano, Jose Pagan, and Harvey Kuenn, in order in the ninth inning, to record his second no-hitter in two years.

than the first one for Koufax, who said, "This game gave me even greater satisfaction because I felt I had overcome my wildness problem."

SAN FRANCISCO

NAME	POS	AB	R	H	E
Kuenn	LF	4	0	0	0
F. Alou	RF	3	0	0	0
Mays	CF	3	0	0	0
Cepeda	1B	3	0	0	0
Bailey	C	2	0	0	0
Davenport	3B	3	0	0	0
Amalfitano	2B	3	0	0	0
Pagan	SS	3	0	0	0
Marichal	P	2	0	0	0
Pregenzer	P	0	0	0	0
McCovey	PH	0	0	0	0
Totals		26	0	0	0

LOS ANGELES

NAME	POS	AB	R	H	E
W. Davis	CF	5	1	0	0
Gilliam	2B-3B	3	2	2	0
Fairly	1B	5	0	3	0
T. Davis	3B-LF	4	1	1	0
Moon	LF	3	2	2	0
Oliver	2B	3	0	0	0
Howard	RF	3	0	0	0
Roseboro	C	4	0	2	0
Tracewski	SS	4	1	2	0
Koufax	P	3	1	0	0
Totals		35	8	12	0

SAN FRANCISCO GIANTS 0 0 0 0 0 0 0 0 0 - 0 - 0 - 0
LOS ANGELES DODGERS 0 1 0 0 0 3 0 4 X - 8 - 12 - 0

	IP	R	H	BB	SO
Marichal	5 1/3	4	9	1	5
Pregenzer	2 1/3	4	4	4	1
Koufax	9	0	0	2	4

From there, Koufax cruised in. The only difficult fielding play came in the bottom of the seventh when Richie Allen hit a slow grounder toward third, but Junior Gilliam, still quick on 35-year-old legs, took the ball on the run, and retired Allen on a bang-bang play at first.

The stylish L.A. Southpaw retired the last 16 men in a row, even making the pressure packed ninth look easy. He fanned Tony Taylor, retired Ruben Amaro on a soft foul pop behind first, and struck out Bobby Wine to wrap up his no-no.

Twelve-year veteran Junior Gilliam, shown here with Vin Scully and Walt Alston, sparked the Dodger victory. His leadoff single in the seventh inning ignited the winning rally. And his fielding gem in the bottom of the same inning, kept the no-hitter intact.

LOS ANGELES

NAME	POS	AB	R	H	E
W. Davis	CF	4	0	0	0
Wills	SS	4	0	1	0
Gilliam	3B	4	1	1	0
T. Davis	LF	4	1	2	0
Howard	RF	3	1	1	0
Fairly	1B	1	0	1	0
McMullen	1B	3	0	1	0
Parker	RF	1	0	1	0
Camilli	C	4	0	0	0
Tracewski	2B	3	0	1	0
Koufax	P	3	0	1	0
Totals		34	3	9	0

Frank Howard, shown here crossing the plate after hitting a home run off Whitey Ford in the 1963 World Series, pounded a three-run homer in the seventh inning, off Chris Short, to give Koufax the victory.

PHILADELPHIA

NAME	POS	AB	R	H	E
Rojas	CF	3	0	0	0
Callison	RF	3	0	0	0
Allen	3B	2	0	0	1
Cater	LF	3	0	0	0
Triandos	C	3	0	0	0
Sievers	1B	3	0	0	0
Taylor	2B	3	0	0	0
Amaro	SS	3	0	0	0
Short	P	2	0	0	0
Roebuck	P	0	0	0	0
Culp	P	0	0	0	0
Wine	PH	1	0	0	0
Totals		26	0	0	1

LOS ANGELES DODGERS   0 0 0 0 0 0 3 0 0 - 3 - 9 - 0
PHILADELPHIA PHILLIES 0 0 0 0 0 0 0 0 0 - 0 - 0 - 1

	IP	R	H	BB	SO
Koufax	9	0	0	1	12
Short	6 2/3	3	8	0	4
Roebuck	1/3	0	0	0	0
Culp	2	0	1	0	2

KOUFAX ACHIEVES PERFECTION AGAINST CUBS 1-0

The newspaper headlines on the morning of September 10, 1965, trumpeted the news.

"SANDY NOW GREATEST OF THEM ALL"

How right they were. The previous night, Sandy Koufax, the smooth-working 29-year-old southpaw of the Los Angeles Dodgers accomplished baseball's most difficult feat, pitching a perfect game, while blanking the Chicago Cubs, 1-0. In the long history of major league baseball, covering 90 years and over 300,000 individual pitching performances, only nine other pitchers had ever achieved perfection. John Richmond of the old Worcester Ruby Legs of the National League was the first pitcher to throw a perfect game, performing the feat way back in 1880, while Jim Bunning of the Philadelphia Phils was the most recent addition to the club, dispatching the New York Mets without a baserunner just one year ago.

Sanford "Sandy" Koufax went the other "perfect" pitchers one better, however. He preceded it with three other no-hitters, making him the only pitcher in baseball history ever to throw four hitless games. Only Bob Feller with three no-hitters was even close.

Koufax's feat, coming in the heat of a tight pennant race, was even more impressive. The Los Angeles Dodgers were 1/2 game behind the league-leading San Francisco Giants with only 13 games remaining in the season. At this point, every game was critical, especially for a second-place team.

Sandy's task was not an easy one. The 21-game winner faced 26-year-old Bob Hendley, a journeyman left hander with a good fastball and an adequate curve. As it turned out, the 6'2" Hendley pitched a career game against the Dodger ace, limiting Los Angeles to just one hit over the nine-inning distance, making this the greatest pitching duel of all time.

The pressure mounted from the first pitch, as 29,139 pennant-hungry Dodger fans kept Dodger Stadium rocking all night. For 4 and 1/2 innings, it was total perfection on both sides, with 27 batters up and 27 batters down. The Cubs hit two solid balls early in the game that could have ended Koufax's quest early, but fate deemed otherwise. A solid drive to left field by Glen Beckert in the first inning turned into a harmless foul, and a line drive to center field by Byron Browne in the second was hit right at Willie Davis who made a waist-high catch.

In the bottom of the fifth, the Chicago southpaw made his first mistake and it turned out to be a costly one. He walked leadoff batter Lou Johnson, an effervescent baserunner who was always looking for a way to win. Ron Fairly sacrificed Johnson to second base and, when Hendley failed to keep the Dodger left fielder close to the bag, Sweet Lou took off for third. Catcher Chris Krug's hurried throw sailed into left field, and Johnson carried home the first and, as it turned out, only run of the game.

The Chicago starter duplicated Koufax's no-hit exercise through six innings, but trailed the Dodger ace, 1-0. In the seventh, the dream of a double no-hitter ended abruptly when the omnipresent Johnson sliced a two-out pop fly into right field for two bases. It turned out to be the only hit of the game as Hendley retired the last four Dodger batters in order.

Koufax, fighting the painful effects of traumatic arthritis in his pitching elbow, relied on his sharp breaking curveball for the first few innings until his arm loosened up, then he swung over to his fastball. Once the seventh inning came around and his adrenaline was pumping at full tilt, the graceful southpaw threw nothing but fastballs in an effort to complete the perfect game. The normal Koufax hummer increased in velocity until it was little more than a blur to most hitters. Chicago third baseman Ron Santo was one batter who had difficulty seeing it. "He threw a fastball right by me (for a strikeout in the eighth), and I was waiting for it. He seemed to get a burst of energy in the late innings."

The Dodger ace took no chances with freak hits or errors late in the game. He fanned one man in the seventh, and retired another on a soft fly to left. In the eighth, he struck out Ron Santo, Ernie Banks, and Byron Browne in order, giving him a total of 11 strikeouts for the game.

Dodger manager Walter Alston, shown conducting infield practice, had an easy day managing on September 9, 1965. All he had to do was sit in the dugout and watch, as the world's greatest pitcher achieved perfection.

Then, in the pressure-cooker ninth, the cool-headed Koufax maintained control of the outcome. He fanned Chris Krug swinging on a 2-2 pitch. Pinch hitter Joe Amalfitano waved at strike three and sat down. That left it up to Harvey Kuenn, a tough contact hitter who, incidentally, had made the last out in Koufax's second no-hitter. This time, the right-handed hitting pinch hitter fought through a 2-2 count, then waved futilely at strike three as another Koufax fastball settled into catcher Jeff Torborg's glove.

It was over. The great Sandy Koufax had done it. Something no other pitcher in major league baseball had ever done, thrown four no-hitters including a perfect game.

As one Dodger teammate put it, "Sandy Koufax belongs in a higher league."

	IP	R	H	BB	SO
Hendley	8	1	1	1	3
Koufax	9	0	0	0	14

Second baseman Jim Lefebvre, after witnessing the greatest pitching duel in major league history, went on to capture the National League's Rookie Of The Year award.

CHICAGO

NAME	POS	AB	R	H	E
Young	CF	3	0	0	0
Beckert	2B	3	0	0	0
Williams	RF	3	0	0	0
Santo	3B	3	0	0	0
Banks	1B	3	0	0	0
Browne	LF	3	0	0	0
Krug	C	3	0	0	1
Kessinger	SS	2	0	0	0
Amalfitano	PH	1	0	0	0
Hendley	P	2	0	0	0
Kuenn	PH	1	0	0	0
Totals		27	0	0	1

LOS ANGELES

NAME	POS	AB	R	H	E
Wills	SS	3	0	0	0
Gilliam	3B	3	0	0	0
Kennedy	3B	0	0	0	0
Davis	CF	3	0	0	0
Johnson	LF	2	1	1	0
Fairly	RF	2	0	0	0
Lefebvre	2B	3	0	0	0
Tracewski	2B	0	0	0	0
Parker	1B	3	0	0	0
Torborg	C	3	0	0	0
Koufax	P	2	0	0	0
Totals		24	1	1	0

CHICAGO CUBS   0 0 0 0 0 0 0 0 0 - 0 - 0 - 1
LOS ANGELES DODGERS 0 0 0 0 1 0 0 0 X - 1 - 1 - 0

BILL SINGER NO-HITS PHILS 5-0

Bill Singer was born to be a Dodger. A native of Pomona, California, the baby-faced right-handed pitcher rolled up a 20-4 record as the ace of the Pomona High School team. Then, after pitching his American Legion team to the California state championship in 1961, he signed a lucrative $50,000 bonus contract with Los Angeles. He was immediately sent to Reno in the California League to begin his apprenticeship and, for the next four years, he alternately excited and dismayed his employers. The injury-prone hurler went from overpowering pitching performances to stints on the disabled list with alarming regularity.

In 1967, the tall, rangy fireballer moved up to the major leagues to stay. The winner of 12 and 13 games during his first two full seasons in L.A., Singer blossomed into a full-fledged 20-game winner in 1969, going 20-12 with a 2.34 ERA for the third-place Dodgers. Early in 1970, however, his bad luck returned, and the 26-year-old hurler was struck down with hepatitis, a debilitating illness that kept him on the sidelines for 53 days. He returned to the lineup on June 14, but appeared to be drawn and weak. Miraculously, the 6'4" 184-pound stringbean won six of his first seven decisions after coming off the disabled list.

Not even a blister could keep Bill singer from throwing a no-hitter against the Phillies. (Los Angeles Dodgers)

On July 20, Singer faced the fourth-place Philadelphia Phillies in Dodger Stadium in a rare afternoon game. Manager Walter Alston, fearing the California sun would keep Singer's effort to a minimum, had his bullpen warmed up and ready to go. In the first inning, the Dodger starter hit Philly right fielder Oscar Gamble on the right elbow with an errant inside pitch. Gamble made it to second base when Singer threw wild to first on an attempted pick-off play, but stayed there as the big righty retired Byron Browne on strikes and Don Money on a fly ball.

His mound opponent, big left-hander Woody Fryman was not as fortunate. Bill Grabarkewitz, hitting .337, and Ted Sizemore, led off the Dodger first with back-to-back singles. Willie Davis plated one run with a sacrifice fly, and a second run came across on a single by Jim Lefebvre.

The wiry Singer protected his slim lead as if his life depended on it. Mixing his overpowering fast ball with a darting slider, a baffling change of pace, and pinpoint control, he foiled Frank Lucchesi's boys inning after inning. His outstanding pitching was aided by two sparkling defensive plays. In the fourth inning, third baseman Steve Garvey made a nice play on a high bouncer by Gamble and, in the eighth, Maury Wills gunned out Larry Hisle by a step on a ball hit to the hole. Garvey, in commenting on his contribution, said, "The play was in self-defense. It hit my glove and stuck."

Alston's boys added to their lead in the third, pushing across another run on base hits by Davis and Parker. They padded the margin two innings later when Parker doubled, Lefebvre singled, and Bill Russell brought them both in with a two-base hit to left.

Midway through the game, the Dodgers' hard-throwing righthander developed a blister on his throwing hand, and had to have it drained between innings to keep the swelling down. The blister didn't hamper Singer's performance, however, as he kept the Phils at bay with little noticeable discomfort. He also kept his teammates loose in the dugout by kidding them about the progress of his no-hitter.

The 12,454 fans who attended the weekday afternoon game were on their feet urging Singer on during the last three innings. After his error allowed Money to reach base in the seventh, Singer retired the last eight batters in a row, to lock up his no-no.

The no-hitter was the high point of Bill Singer's major league career, as the injury jinx continued to plague the big pitcher wherever he went. In fact, just three weeks after his masterpiece, he was hit on the hand by a Bob Moose fastball and was sidelined for the remainder of the season.

PHILADELPHIA

NAME	POS	AB	R	H	E
Doyle	2B	4	0	0	0
Gamble	RF	1	0	0	0
Browne	RF	2	0	0	0
Money	3B	3	0	0	1
D. Johnson	1B	3	0	0	0
Briggs	LF	3	0	0	0
Hisle	CF	3	0	0	0
Bowa	SS	3	0	0	1
M. Ryan	C	3	0	0	0
Fryman	P	1	0	0	0
Palmer	P	1	0	0	0
Harmon	PH	1	0	0	0
Totals		28	0	0	2

LOS ANGELES

NAME	POS	AB	R	H	E
Grabarkewitz	SS	4	1	1	0
Sizemore	LF	4	1	1	0
Wills	3B	0	0	0	0
W. Davis	CF	3	1	1	0
W. Parker	1B	4	1	2	0
Lefebvre	2B	4	0	3	0
Garvey	3B	4	1	0	0
Joshua	LF	0	0	0	0
Russell	RF	4	0	2	0
Torborg	C	4	0	1	0
Singer	P	4	0	0	2
Totals		35	5	11	2

PHILADELPHIA PHILS   0 0 0 0 0 0 0 0 0 - 0 - 0 - 2
LOS ANGELES DODGERS 2 0 1 0 2 0 0 0 X - 5 - 11 - 2

	IP	R	H	BB	SO
Fryman	4 2/3	5	10	0	3
Palmer	3 1/3	0	1	0	5
Singer	9	0	0	0	10

JERRY REUSS COMES WITHIN ONE BATTER OF PERFECTION

Jerry Reuss, a 6'5" left-handed pitcher for the Los Angeles Dodgers had a reputation as the team prankster but, on Friday June 27, the big blonde was deadly serious as he battled his way into baseball's Hall of Fame with a superb 8-0, no-hit shellacking of the hapless San Francisco Giants.

Reuss, a native of St. Louis, Missouri, spent 11 years in the big leagues before coming to Los Angeles from the Pittsburgh Pirates in a trade for Rick Rhoden in 1979. The 227-pound fast ball pitcher, a 108-94 winner with the Cards, Astros, and Pirates, suffered through a miserable 7-14 season in his debut year in sunny California.

In 1980, however, the towering lefty turned it around. Breaking from the starting gate like a greyhound, the talented Reuss ran up a sizzling 8-1 record by the time the Dodgers moved into the Bay Area on Friday, June 27, to play a weekend series against Dave Bristol's San Francisco Giants. Starting the series opener against Giant southpaw Vida Blue, Reuss pitched well in the first inning, although an error by shortstop Bill Russell gave the home team a baserunner. Little did the Giants know it at the time, but Jack Clark, their first baserunner, was also their last baserunner, as Jerry Reuss came within one errant throw of a perfect game.

Tommy Lasorda's boys had given their starting pitcher a 1-0 lead in the top of the first in typical Dodger fashion. Davey Lopes led off the game with a single, stole second, continued on to third on an overthrow, and scored on an infield hit by Rudy Law. In the third, the Dodger second baseman cracked a triple to center field, and plated the game's second run on an infield out by Law, as 20,285 Giant fans groaned in anguish.

Anguish was a common characteristic of the long-suffering San Francisco fans. Their beloved Giants were en route to their sixth second-division finish in the last nine years. They had not risen above third place since Willie Mays and Bobby Bonds sparked them to their last pennant in 1971. With the demise of Mays, McCovey, Bonds, et al, the Bay Area team gradually sank into mediocrity.

The big Dodger lefty didn't improve the fan's disposition any, as he retired batter after batter without the semblance of a hit. His fast ball had exceptional movement on it on this day and, as a result, he threw the heat almost exclusively. Only in the eighth inning did Bristol's cohorts challenge the Los Angeles defense. Leadoff batter Larry Herndon sent a rocket to the left of Cey, but the "Penguin" made a diving stop and threw the Giant speedster out by a step. One out later, Johnnie LeMaster hit a hard grounder into the hole between short and third. Bill Russell, atoning for his first-inning error, made a slick backhand stop of the ball and retired LeMaster on a bullet to Garvey.

By now the Los Angeles lead had grown to 8-0 thanks to five big runs in the fifth and a singleton in the seventh. Dusty Baker's 17th home run of the young season, a three-run shot over the left-field fence, sparked the fifth inning uprising, and Steve Garvey closed out the scoring by slamming his 16th round-tripper into the same area two innings later.

As the ninth inning got underway, the home fans deserted their team and started rooting for Reuss to finish off his no-hitter. Jerry obliged them without working up a sweat. He retired Mike Sadek on an easy grounder to Ron Cey at third for out #1, then got pinch hitter Rennie Stennett on a bouncer to Russell at short. San Francisco's last hope, Billy North, poked an 1-0 pitch right back to the mound where Reuss speared it, tossed to Garvey for out #27, and raised his arms in a victory salute as his teammates rushed to the mound to congratulate him.

LOS ANGELES

NAME	POS	AB	R	H	E
Lopes	2B	5	2	3	0
Law	CF	5	1	3	0
Smith	RF	4	1	1	0
Guerrero	RF	1	0	0	0
Garvey	1B	5	2	2	0
Baker	LF	5	1	1	0
Cey	3B	5	1	2	0
Russell	SS	5	0	3	1
Yeager	C	4	0	2	0
Ruess	P	4	0	0	0
Totals		43	8	17	1

SAN FRANCISCO

NAME	POS	AB	R	H	E
North	CF	4	0	0	0
Evans	3B	3	0	0	0
Clark	RF	2	0	0	0
Wohlford	RF	1	0	0	0
Murray	1B	3	0	0	0
Herndon	LF	3	0	0	1
Strain	2B	3	0	0	0
Lemaster	SS	3	0	0	0

Jerry Reuss won another nine games after his no-hitter, finishing the year at 18-6. He led the league in shutouts with six.

Sadek	C	3	0	0	1
Blue	P	1	0	0	0
Griffin	P	0	0	0	0
Whitfield	PH	1	0	0	0
Lavelle	P	0	0	0	0
Stennett	PH	1	0	0	0
Totals		28	0	0	2

LOS ANGELES DODGERS 1 0 1 0 5 0 1 0 0 - 8 - 17 - 1
SAN FRANCISCO GIANTS 0 0 0 0 0 0 0 0 0 - 0 - 0 - 2

	IP	R	H	BB	SO
Blue	4 2/3	7	10	1	4
Griffin	1 1/3	0	2	0	0
Lavelle	3	1	5	0	0
Reuss	9	0	0	0	2

FERNANDO NO-HITS CARDS 6-0

Fernando. That single name is all Dodger fans need, to conjure up memories of a roly poly Mexican kid who captured the hearts of America's baseball fans in the early '80s. Fernando mania gripped the country like a steel vise in 1981, as the 20-year-old southpaw sparked Tommy Lasorda's team to one comeback victory after another, on their way to the World Championship.

Fernando blazed across the sky like a brilliant comet, piling up 99 victories and 26 shutouts in just six years, while hurling the Dodgers to three Western Division crowns. Then, just as rapidly as his skills matured, they began to deteriorate. His victory total dropped to 14 in 1987. The following year, shoulder miseries hampered the courageous screwball pitcher from the opening bell. When the injuries ended his season prematurely on July 31, his record stood at a mediocre 5-8.

The hero of southern California worked harder than ever to regain his lost skills, but it was to no avail. His fast ball was no more than a memory, and his screwball had difficulty locating the corners. In spite of a 13-13 season in 1989, the hand-writing was on the wall. Fernando was nearing the end of the trail.

As the 1990 season unfolded, it was apparent that it would be Fernando's last campaign in Dodger blue. Even hard-nosed fans cringed whenever the valiant Mexican pitcher took the mound, fearing that he would, once again, be mauled by the enemy batsman. More often then not, they were right. On Sunday, June 24, the Cincinnati Reds routed the once-great pitcher, 10-6, with the last five batters he faced, all hitting safely.

Three days later, Fernando stood in the Dodger locker room, pulling on his blue stirrups, while most of the team sat glued to the TV set, watching Oakland's Dave Stewart complete a no-hitter against the Toronto Blue Jays in the Skydome. As the last out was recorded, Fernando smiled and quipped, "You watch a no-hitter on TV. Now you can see one in person." Nervous laughter filled the room, as many of the players doubted El Toro's ability to contain the enemy.

From the opening pitch, it was obvious that Fernando was in top form on this night. He hit the corners with his famed screwball with uncanny accuracy, constantly getting ahead of the batters and making them hit from a defensive posture. With the exception of a two-base error by left fielder Kirk Gibson in the first inning, Cardinal hitters expired without a sound. After the miscue, 17 men in a row trudged back to the dugout without the faintest sign of a hit. Five of the 17 were strikeout victims.

The Dodgers meanwhile, had pecked away at Cardinal pitching, scoring single runs in the first, fifth, and sixth, adding two more in the seventh, and another one in the eighth. Hubie Brook's two-run homer led the L.A. attack. Juan Samuel hit his fifth round-tripper in the eighth.

As 38,583 Dodger fans roared with anticipation, a determined Fernando Valenzuela strode to the mound to start the ninth. He began the inning by painting the outside of the plate with a screwball to catch Vince Coleman looking, his seventh strikeout victim of the game. At this point, his pinpoint control deserted him momentarily, and he walked Willie McGee, bringing the dangerous Pedro Guerrero to the plate. The Cardinal first baseman, a former teammate and close personal friend of Fernandos, was determined to break up the no-hitter. He jumped all over a Valenzuela fastball, and sent it screaming back through the middle, an apparent hit. With cat-like reflexes however, the Dodger pitcher got a glove on the ball, deflecting it toward second base. In a flash, Juan Samuel pounced on it, touched second and fired to first for a game-ending double play.

The Dodger Stadium crowd pierced the still California air with their shrill screams. Fernando's family cried. And the kid from Sonora stood on the mound grinning as the entire Dodger team buried him under congratulatory hugs.

For the 29-year-old phenom from the Mexican countryside, it was the culmination of a dream, the crowning achievement in a spectacular career.

ST. LOUIS

NAME	POS	AB	R	H	E
Coleman	LF	4	0	0	0
McGee	CF	3	0	0	1
Guerrero	1B	3	0	0	1
Zeile	C	2	0	0	1
Pendleton	3B	3	0	0	0
Oquendo	2B	3	0	0	0
Horton	P	0	0	0	0
Hudler	LF	3	0	0	0
Smith	SS	3	0	0	0

ST. LOUIS CARDINALS   0 0 0 0 0 0 0 0 0 - 0 - 0 - 3
LOS ANGELES DODGERS 1 0 0 0 1 1 2 1 X - 6 - 12 - 1

	IP	R	H	BB	SO
Deleon	6 2/3	5	9	3	5
Horton	1 1/3	1	3	1	2
Valenzuela	9	0	0	3	7

KEVIN GROSS STIFLES SAN FRAN WITHOUT A HIT

Kevin Gross, a journeyman righthander, joined a select group of Los Angeles Dodger pitchers on the night of August 17, 1992 when he set the San Francisco Giants down without a hit, en route to a 2-0 victory.

Gross, a native of Downey, California, entered the major leagues in 1983 with the Philadelphia Phils. A big, strapping 6'5", 227-pound fireballer, he toiled for five years in Philly red and white, achieving a high of 15 victories in 1985.

Way stops in Pittsburgh and Montreal finally led the 29-year-old righty to L.A. in 1991. Gross came to California with a reputation of being a tireless workhorse, having thrown more than 200 innings in five of his previous seven seasons. In Dodgerland, however, the former starter was shifted to the bullpen, used as a setup man for Dodger closer, Jay Howell.

In 1992, after appearing in 46 games as both a spot starter and a middle reliever, the hard-luck pitcher was returned to the starting rotation. A fast ball hurler with tremendous talent, Gross always seemed to be on the other side of the fence from good luck. His 88-101 won-loss record over a nine year career, didn't reflect his tenacious attitude or his superior skills.

His luck didn't get any better in '92. In spite of an excellent 3.17 earned run average, Kevin Gross could do no better than an 8-13 record with the last place hitless wonders of Tommy Lasorda. The worst defensive team in the league allowed unearned runs to cross the plate in bunches, while the offense could muster only 3.4 runs per game when Gross was on the mound.

But, for one night in late August, the handsome Californian stood astride the baseball world, the greatest pitcher on the planet.

The Los Angeles Dodgers, on the way to their first last-place finish since 1905, had lost the first three games of the four-game series by scores of 3-2, 2-1, and 2-1, and were on the verge of being swept four straight at home by the San Francisco Giants for the first time in 69 years. Gross was given the assignment of stopping the bleeding, before a disappointing Monday crowd of only 25,561 frustrated Angelinos.

Roger Craig's Giants threatened early, as both Corey Snyder and Matt Williams drew bases on balls in the top of the second inning. Gross wriggled out of the jam by inducing Kirt Manwaring to hit an inning-ending double

Fernando Valenzuela, entering the twilight of an exciting career, reached back for a little extra on the evening of June 29, 1990, resurrecting Fernandomania one more time.

Deleon	P	2	0	0	0
Wilson	2B	1	0	0	0
Totals		27	0	0	3

LOS ANGELES

NAME	POS	AB	R	H	E
Harris	3B	4	3	3	0
Sharperson	3B	1	0	1	0
Javier	LF	3	0	1	0
Gibson	CF	4	0	1	1
Gonzalez	LF	1	0	0	0
Murray	1B	3	0	2	0
Brooks	RF	2	1	1	0
Scioscia	C	4	0	1	0
Samuel	2B	2	1	1	0
Griffin	SS	4	0	0	0
Valenzuela	P	4	1	1	0
Totals		32	6	12	0

play grounder to Jose Offerman at shortstop. The Dodger starter breezed through the next five innings, protecting a slim 2-0 lead. L.A. broke the scoring ice in the second when rookie first baseman Eric Karros smashed his 17th home run over the left center field fence. Another Dodger run crossed the plate in the fourth when Brett Butler doubled and came around on a single by Henry Rodriguez.

Robby Thompson, leading off the eighth inning, almost ended Gross' quest for glory when he pulled a line drive between third and short for an apparent hit. Offerman, reacting with the speed of youth, made a miraculous lunging back-hand grab to thwart the effort.

In the ninth, the tense Dodger hurler hit leadoff batter, Mark Leonard with a 1-2 pitch, breaking a string of 20 consecutive batters he had retired. Another pinch hitter, Greg Litton, sent a hot grounder back through the box. Once again, Dodger shortstop Jose Offerman came to the rescue. Racing to his left, he speared the ball, and turned another would-be hit into a force play at second. With one out, Giant left fielder Mike Felder sent a fly ball to his Dodger counterpart Mitch Webster, reducing Kevin Gross' magic number to one.

Pesky Willie McGee, always a thorn in Dodger sides, ended the agony when he sliced a ball down the left field line. Webster raced over and hauled it in for the game-ending out, as Dodger Stadium exploded in a wild celebration. Catcher Mike Scioscia raced out to congratulate his batterymate, but Kevin Gross, overwhelmed by the magnitude of the event, stood motionless on the mound, tears of joy streaming down his face.

For once in his life, the hard-luck pitcher of the Los Angeles Dodgers was the recipient of good fortune. And for once in his life, the talented righthander put it all together for nine straight innings. Of his 99 pitches, 71 were strikes. He struck out six Giants during his masterpiece, while walking only two and hitting one.

The night of August 17, 1992, produced beautiful memories that Kevin Gross will cherish forever.

Kevin Gross pitched in tough luck during his Los Angeles career, frequently receiving little or no offensive support. His 40-44 Dodger career record does not reflect his true value to the team. (W. McNeil)

SAN FRANCISCO

NAME	POS	AB	R	H	E
Felder	LF	4	0	0	0
McGee	CF	4	0	0	0
W. Clark	1B	3	0	0	0
Snyder	RF	2	0	0	0
Thompson	2B	3	0	0	0
M. Williams	3B	2	0	0	0
Manwaring	C	3	0	0	0
Benjamin	SS	2	0	0	0
Leonard	PH	0	0	0	0
Swift	PR	0	0	0	0
Oliveras	P	1	0	0	0
Wood	PH	1	0	0	0
Brantley	P	0	0	0	0
Righetti	P	0	0	0	0
Litton	PH	1	0	0	0
Totals		26	0	0	0

LOS ANGELES

NAME	POS	AB	R	H	E
Offerman	SS	4	0	1	0
Butler	CF	4	1	3	0
Rodriguez	RF	4	0	2	0
Karros	1B	2	1	1	0
Webster	LF	4	0	0	0
Scioscia	C	2	0	0	0
Hansen	3B	2	0	0	0
Young	2B	3	0	0	0
Gross	P	3	0	1	0
Totals		28	2	8	0

```
SAN FRANCISCO GIANTS  000 000 000 - 0 - 0 - 0
LOS ANGELES DODGERS   010 100 00X - 2 - 8 - 0
```

DOUBLES — Butler (12)
HOME RUNS — Karros (17)

	IP	R	H	BB	SO
Oliveras L, 0-2	5	2	4	2	2
Brantley	2	0	2	0	1
Righetti	1	0	2	1	1
Gross W, 6-12	9	0	0	2	6

HBP - Hansen, Leonard

RAMON MARTINEZ STIFLES FLORIDA'S MARLINS, 7-0

Ramon Martinez burst on the National League scene as a 19-year-old fireballer from the Dominican Republic. The year was 1988, and the 6'4" string bean turned in his first major league victory, pitching seven innings in a 2-1 decision at Montreal. Two years later, after additional seasoning with the Dodger AAA farm club in Albuquerque, the affable Martinez returned to take his place in the starting rotation. His blazing fast ball soon moved him to the front of the pack. As L.A.'s ace, he compiled a sparkling 20-6 record in 1990, with a 2.92 earned-run-average, and 223 strikeouts in 234 innings.

The following year, the 176-pound skyscraper bolted from the starting blocks like a world-class greyhound, running up a scintillating 12-3 mark by mid season.

Then, the bubble burst. Although Ramon was hesitant to make excuses, his arm apparently went dead. He struggled through the remainder of the season 5-10, and finished the year a disappointing 17-13. The next two years were sheer torture, as the youngster tried to win on nothing but guts and guile. His record for '92 was a sorry 8-11. '93 was not much better; 10-12.

Gradually, the strength returned to Martinez' arm– and with it, his 92-mile-per-hour fastball. In 1994, he won 12 games against seven losses, and struck out 119 men in 170 innings. As the 1995 season got underway, it became obvious that the Dominican flamethrower was his old self. His ball had its old zip back, and he developed more confidence with each passing game.

On a warm summer evening in Los Angeles, Ramon Martinez made it all the way back. It was Friday, July 14, and the Miami Marlins were in town to kick off the second half of the season after the All-Star break. The Marlins got Tommy Lasorda's boys off on the wrong foot the previous day, by white-washing the listless Dodgers 4-0. The Californians were in desperate need of a pick-me-up. They got it from Ramon.

The 27-year-old hurler, who had been booed off the mound in his previous Dodger Stadium start, after being pounded for 10 runs by the Colorado Rockies in less than five innings, retired the first nine Marlins in order. With the game still scoreless, the Big Blue Machine finally broke through in the bottom of the third, scoring two runs, on a double by rookie Todd Hollandsworth and a two-run triple by shortstop Jose Offerman.

The Dodgers added a single run in the fourth, then closed the scoring with four more markers in the sixth. Hollandsworth finished the night with three hits, two RBIs, and two runs scored. Offerman had a single to go with his triple, and knocked in a total of four runs.

But the night belonged to Ramon. His darting fastball had the Miami hitters off balance all night. Twenty-three visiting batters came to the plate, and 23 visiting batters went back to the dugout carrying their bats, as Martinez handed them nothing but goose eggs.

With two down in the top of the eighth, the Dodger ace walked right fielder Tommy Gregg on a 3-2 pitch. It was the Marlins only base runner of the night.

In the top of the ninth, the tension was unbearable. The crowd was on its feet, screaming at Ramon to finish his masterpiece. He obliged in championship fashion. He struck out the leadoff man, Charles Johnson, on four pitches. Jerry Browne followed with a one-hopper to second base, where Delino De Shields gobbled it up for out number two. Fellow Dominican Quilvio Veras was Florida's last hope, and Martinez disposed of him quickly. Veras lined a two-strike pitch to left field, where Roberto Kelly squeezed it to preserve the no-hitter.

Martinez was mobbed by his teammates as he stood on the mound, a sigh of relief on his face. The victory brought his record to 9-6, giving not only his team, but also himself a jump start.

Ramon went on from there to win 10 of his last 11 decisions, and finish the abbreviated season with a fine 17-7 record.

Ramon Martinez, at 29 years of age, has been the Dodger ace for eight years. (W. McNeil)

MIAMI

NAME	POS	AB	R	H	E
Veras	2B	4	0	0	0
Carr	CF	3	0	0	0
Conine	LF	3	0	0	0
Pendleton	3B	3	0	0	0
Colbrunn	1B	3	0	0	0
T. Gregg	RF	2	0	0	0
Nen	P	0	0	0	0
K. Abbot	SS	3	0	0	0
C. Johnson	C	3	0	0	0
Burkett	P	1	0	0	0
Diaz	PH	1	0	0	0
Weathers	P	0	0	0	0
Browne	RF	1	0	0	0
Totals		27	0	0	0

LOS ANGELES

NAME	POS	AB	R	H	E
DeShields	2B	2	2	0	0
Offerman	SS	4	0	2	0
Piazza	C	4	0	1	0
Karros	1B	4	0	0	0
R. Kelly	LF	4	1	2	0
Mondesi	RF	4	2	1	0
Wallach	3B	4	0	1	0
Hollandsworth	CF	4	2	3	0
R. Martinez	P	2	0	0	0
Totals		32	7	10	0

```
MIAMI MARLINS        0 0 0  0 0 0  0 0 0 - 0-0-0
LOS ANGELES DODGERS  0 0 2  1 0 4  0 0 X - 7-10-0
```

DOUBLES — Hollandsworth
TRIPLES — Offerman

PITCHER	IP	R	H	BB	SO
BURKETT, L 6-9	5	3	6	1	5
WEATHERS	1/3	2	2	0	1
MURPHY	1/3	2	1	1	0
MATHEWS	1/3	0	1	0	1
MANTEI	1	0	0	0	2
NEN	1	0	0	0	1
R. Martinez, W 9-6	9	0	0	1	8

HIDEO NOMO NO-HITS ROCKIES IN "THE MIRACLE OF COORS FIELD"

Hideo Nomo burst upon the National League scene much like Fernando Valenzuela, 15 years before. The Japanese fireballer had been a star pitcher in the Japanese Pacific League for five years before the Dodgers signed him. He led the Pacific League in victories and strikeouts for four years before arm miseries sidelined him for most of 1994.

The "Tornado," as he was called in Japan, because of his twisting, turning windup, was the first Japanese-born player to play in the major leagues. As a result, he was an immediate hero in his native country, and the ensuing media attention was suffocating, to say the least. Nomo-mania had Japanese Americans and Japanese nationals completely mesmerized. Every time Nomo pitched, hundreds of newspaper, radio, and television people were on the scene, following his every move, interviewing him, and documenting his daily activities. Every Nomo outing was a historic event in Japan. Even though the games started before the sun rose over the island empire, millions of people watched his performances on enormous television screens that were set up on streets and buildings in 13 Japanese cities.

Nomo had the bad luck to pitch in games when Dodger bats were silent, at the beginning of the season. His first five starts were no-decision affairs. Finally, on June 2, 1995, in Dodger Stadium, he won his first major league game, a 2-1 victory over the New York Mets. He went on to record a perfect 6-0 record for the month of June, with a sparkling 0.89 earned-run-average, and 60 strikeouts in just 50 innings. He fanned 16 Pittsburgh Pirate batters in one game.

Japanese fireballer Hideo Nomo pitched the most improbable no-hitter of them all, shutting down the powerful Rockies hitters in the rarefied air of Colorado. (W. McNeil)

Nomo finished his rookie season with a 13-6 record, 236 strikeouts in 191 innings, and the National League Rookie Of The Year award.

His 1996 season was just as impressive. He finished the year 16-11, and in one game fanned 17 Florida Marlins. But the highlight of his year came on September 17, in the most unlikely of places, homer-happy Coors Field. In the heat of a tension-packed pennant race, against a team with a home-field batting average of .348, the tall Japanese righthander put the Rockies away without a single hit.

The game was played in a constant drizzle, with the temperature hovering around the 46-degree mark. In the second inning, the Dodgers gave Nomo the lead, scoring two runs on base hits by Mondesi, Wallach, and Gagne. They added a run in the third, two more in the sixth, a singleton in the eighth, and three in the ninth, to make Nomo's job easier.

In the meantime, the "Tornado," being hampered in his windup by the wet mound, pitched from the stretch from the second inning, on. He wasn't perfect, walking four men, but his fastball and forkball were unhittable. He fanned eight, and retired the last 11 batters to face him, and 16 of the last 17.

The only difficult play occurred in the fourth inning, when Greg Gagne went into the hole to make a diving stop of a sharp hit ball off the bat of Andres Galarraga. Then, from a sitting position, he threw to DeShields at second to force Ellis Burks.

The final score was 9-0.

LOS ANGELES

NAME	POS	AB	R	H	E
Hollandsworth	LF	4	1	0	0
Kirby	CF	4	1	3	0
Curtis	CF	1	1	1	0
Piazza	C	4	1	0	0
Karros	1B	4	0	1	0
Mondesi	RF	5	3	3	0
Wallach	3B	4	2	2	0
DeShields	2B	5	0	1	0
Gagne	SS	4	0	2	0
Nomo	P	5	0	1	0
Totals		40	9	14	0

COLORADO

NAME	POS	AB	R	H	E
Young	2B	3	0	0	0
McCracken	CF	3	0	0	0
Burks	LF	3	0	0	1
Bichette	RF	3	0	0	0
Galarraga	1B	3	0	0	0
Decker	C	2	0	0	0
Jones	PH	1	0	0	0
J. Reed	C	0	0	0	0
Perez	SS	3	0	0	0
Swift	P	2	0	0	0
S. Reed	P	0	0	0	0
Rekar	P	0	0	0	0
Vanderwal	PH	1	0	0	0
Beckett	P	0	0	0	0
Totals		26	0	0	1

LOS ANGELES DODGERS 0 2 1 0 0 2 0 1 3 - 9 - 14 - 0
COLORADO ROCKIES   0 0 0 0 0 0 0 0 0 - 0 - 0 - 0

DOUBLES — Kirby, Mondesi
HOME RUN–Wallach

	IP	R	H	BB	SO
Nomo W, 16-10	9	0	0	4	8
Swift L, 1-1	5	5	7	2	2
S. Reed	2	0	1	1	3
Rekar	1	1	3	0	1
Beckett	1	3	3	2	1

1870–BROOKLYN ATLANTICS STOP CINCINNATI WIN STREAK

The Cincinnati Red Stockings were the first professional baseball team in the United States. Formed in 1869, the team was composed of the best players in the country, and they were paid to play baseball full time. For two years, these superstars, led by shortstop George Wright, the highest paid player at $1,400 per year, steamrollered all opposition. They went undefeated in their first season, winning 56 games, and outscoring the opposition by an average score of 36-9. The Buckeye Club of Cincinnati was buried, 103-8. Kekionga of Fort Wayne fell, 86-8, and Cream City of Milwaukee was thrashed, 85-7. The only blemish on their record was a 17-17 tie with the Haymakers of Troy, New York.

In 1870, the Cincinnati powerhouse picked up where it had left off the year before, sweeping their first 23 games and extending their record to 79-0-1. Their winning score margin now stood at 53-6. Oriental of Memphis was crushed, 100-2. Dayton was just as easy, 104-9. And Orion of Lexington was whitewashed, 75-0. As summer approached, the Red Stockings embarked on a 23-game road trip through the east. They swept the first ten games handily, beating teams like Flour City of Rochester, 56-13, Old Elm of Pittsfield, 65-9, and Fairmont of Worcester, 74-19. In early June they invaded Brooklyn, expecting to add the Atlantic's scalps to their impressive trophy belt. The previous year they had humiliated the pride of Flatbush, 32-10, and there was no reason to expect a different result this time. What transpired on June 14, 1870 turned out to be one of the most famous games in the annals of baseball.

The Brooklyn Atlantics were a force to be reckoned with in their own right. Their roster included some of the greatest baseball players of the nineteenth century. Pitcher George "The Charmer" Zettlein was one of the top hurlers of his day. Little Dickie Pearce revolutionized the shortstop position, stationing himself between sec-

This woodcut in Harpers Weekly is the only known image of the Atlantics-Red Stockings game. George Zettlein is shown pitching to an unidentified Red Stockings player. Note Dickey Pearce positioned between second base and third base. (Transcendental Graphics)

ond base and third base instead of in short left field as had been the practice. Bob "Death to Flying Things" Ferguson was an outstanding catcher and third baseman, noted for his defensive prowess.

Twenty thousand excited fans crowded into the Capitoline Grounds on Nostrand Avenue to view the mighty Cincinnati juggernaut in action, but also to root the home team on to victory. Cincinnati boasted an 80-game undefeated streak as the sun came up on June 14. Instead of making the Brooklyn nine their 81st victim however, Harry Wright's boys left town several hours later shackled with their first professional loss. The Atlantics pulled off the upset of the century, defeating the vaunted Red Stockings, 8-7 in 11 innings.

Asa Brainard joined the Cincinnati Red Stockings for a salary of $1,100. He was a thinking man's pitcher, according to The Ballplayers, who had good control and the ability to change speeds. (Transcendental Graphics)

Both teams dazzled the crowd with their natty attire. The Brooklyn contingent was decked out in their familiar dark blue trousers, white shirts with a large "A" on their chests, and white caps. The Red Stockings shocked the fans as they sauntered in from the clubhouse dressed in knickers and bright red stockings, their trademark. Cincinnati got off the mark quickly against Atlantic ace George (The Charmer) Zettlein, scoring a run in the first on two-out singles by catcher Doug Allison and Harry Wright, George's brother and the team captain. Two more runners crossed the plate in the third, as the Reds forged a 3-0 lead behind former Brooklyn Excelsior pitcher Asa Brainard. Undaunted, the Atlantics fought back. The gutty 25-year-old Zettlein cranked up his famed fastball and shut down the Red Stocking offense during the middle innings. Meanwhile, the Flatbush crew clawed and scratched to get back into the game. They pushed over

two runs in the fourth on hits by Pearce, Start, and Ferguson, and a Cincinnati error. Then, they grabbed the lead with two more runs in the sixth. Pandemonium broke loose in the grandstand as the noisy Brooklyn crowd sensed a glorious victory in the making. As the demonstration grew louder and wilder, the police had all they could do to keep the frenzied fans from storming onto the field.

Cincinnati was not dead, however. Like true champions, Harry Wright's sluggers zeroed in on the diminutive Brooklyn right-hander. George Wright, with a .518 batting average over 80 games, spearheaded a seventh-inning rally with a two-run single as the Reds recaptured the lead and silenced the big crowd. Once again the Atlantics retaliated. Third baseman Charlie Smith ripped a triple to the farthest corner of left field in the eighth, and scored on a sacrifice fly by "Old Reliable" Joe Start, to knot the score at five all. Now Zettlein and Brainard, both battered but unbowed, sucked in their guts and halted the onslaught. Each pitcher threw goose eggs at the opposing batters in the ninth, the game supposedly ending in a 5-5 tie. As fans swarmed onto the field, the Atlantic players gathered up their equipment and headed for the clubhouse. George Wright protested vehemently that the game should be played to a decision. A check of the rule book supported Wright's position. The field was quickly cleared, the players were called back from the clubhouse, and the game was resumed in the top of the tenth.

An unusual event occurred in the tenth inning, the first recorded "trap" double play in baseball history. Brooklyn had Jack McDonald on second, Dickie Pearce on first, and third baseman Charlie Smith at the plate. Smith hit a pop fly to shortstop, but Wright wisely let the ball drop instead of catching it. He then threw to Waterman at third for a force out, and Waterman's return throw to Sweasy at second doubled up Pearce. Wright's imaginative tactic eventually led to the introduction of the infield fly rule.

As the eleventh inning got underway, the 19th century's version of the Big Red Machine unleashed their big lumber. A double, a single, and an error brought home two runs, catapulting the Red Stockings into a 7-5 lead. An eerie stillness filtered through the grandstand as the Brooklyn fans saw their hopes of victory rapidly disappearing. Cincinnati was three outs away from extending their unbeaten streak to 81. But the Atlantics had something to say about that. And their bats spoke loud and clear on this hot summer afternoon. Charley Smith started the winning rally with a sharp single to left field. He raced around to third on a wild pitch, and subsequently scored the Atlantics' sixth run when Joe Start smashed a triple over the head of Red Stocking right fielder, Cal McVey. After Jack Chapman grounded out, Bob Ferguson strode to the plate. Not wanting to hit the ball to shortstop George Wright, Ferguson, a natural right-handed batter, turned around and batted left handed, thus becoming baseball's first switch hitter. The strategy paid off as Ferguson singled to right to tie the game. Zettlein jumped on a Brainard pitch and sent a scorcher between first and second. Cincinnati first baseman Charley Gould scooped up the hot grounder; then threw wildly to second, the ball going into short left field. Before left fielder Andy Leonard could retrieve the ball, Ferguson raced home with the winning run.

Joe Start, one of baseball's first clutch hitters, was in the middle of three Atlantic rallies, scoring three of their eight runs and driving in two. (Transcendental Graphics)

The Capitoline Grounds exploded in a wild display of emotion as fans met in joyous celebration on the field. The significance of the achievement was almost too much to comprehend. The mighty Cincinnati Red Stockings had gone down to defeat for the first time in 81 games. A determined group of Brooklyn baseball players had accomplished the impossible in a game that will be remembered as long as baseball is played.

CINCINNATI RED STOCKINGS

NAME	POS	OUTS	RUNS
G. Wright	SS	2	2
C. Gould	1B	6	0
F. Waterman	3B	4	0
D. Allison	C	2	1
H. Wright	CF	4	0
A. Leonard	LF	5	0
A. Brainard	P	3	2
C. Sweasy	2B	2	2
C. McVey	RF	5	0
Totals		33	7

BROOKLYN ATLANTICS

NAME	POS	OUTS	RUNS
D. Pearce	SS	3	2
C. Smith	3B	3	2
J. Start	1B	3	3
J. Chapman	LF	4	0
B. Ferguson	C	3	1
G. Zettlein	P	5	0
J. Hall	CF	4	0
L. Pike	2B	4	0
J. McDonald	RF	4	0
Totals		33	8

Cincinnati Red Stockings   201 000 200 02 - 7 -14 - 12
Brooklyn Atlantics   000 202 010 03 - 8 -14 - 11

WP - Zettlein   LP - Brainard

1890—BROOKLYN'S FIRST NATIONAL LEAGUE GAME

After six years of "proving themselves" in the American Association, and after capturing the Association's championship in 1889, the Brooklyn Bridegrooms were invited to join the more prestigious National League for the 1890 season.

Their first league contest took place in Boston on April 19 against Frank Selee's Beaneaters. The game began with great expectations for the Flatbush nine, as they had their sights set on another pennant. They got off the mark quickly in the first inning, scoring two runs against Boston starter John Clarkson. Left fielder Darby O'Brien was hit by a pitch, Hub Collins checked in with a single, and Dave "Scissors" Foutz rescued both runners with a ringing double to left. Manager Bill McGunnigle's cohorts extended the lead to 3-0 in the second on a double by "Parisian Bob" Caruthers and a single by Oyster Burns.

Then the roof caved in. Brooklyn ace Caruthers lost his stuff completely in the top of the third. Five Beaneater hits and three bases on balls plated eight big runs, wiping out the Brooklyn lead. Herman Long's home run capped off the rally.

The Grooms clawed their way back in the bottom of the third, scoring six runs for a 9-8 advantage. O'Brien, Collins, Burns, Germany Smith, Caruthers, and Tido Daly carried home the markers. That was it for Brooklyn however, as tiny Bob Caruthers proved to be no puzzle to the Beaneaters in the fourth. The 138-pound right-hander was driven from the mound under a four-run Boston barrage, as Selee's men opened up a comfortable 12-9 lead.

Boston added another brace of runs in the seventh, and Herman Long closed out the scoring with his second home run of the day in the eighth. As dusk settled over South End Grounds, the home team won going away, 15-9, sending 3,882 fans home happy.

Bob Caruthers, the ace of the Brooklyn staff, was pounded unmercifully by the Beaneaters in the league opener. He went on to finish the year at 23-11 as the Bridegrooms won the pennant. (Transcendental Graphics)

BROOKLYN

NAME	POS	AB	R	H	E
O'Brien	LF	5	2	0	1
Collins	2B	5	2	2	1
Burns	RF	4	1	3	0
Foutz	1B	5	0	1	2
Pickney	3B	5	0	0	1
Corkhill	CF	3	0	1	0
Smith	SS	4	1	1	2
Caruthers	P	2	2	2	0
Terry	P	2	0	1	0
Daly	C	3	1	0	3
Total		38	9	11	10

BOSTON

NAME	POS	AB	R	H	E
Long	SS	6	3	3	1
Donovan	CF	6	2	3	1
Sullivan	LF	6	2	2	0
Tucker	1B	5	2	2	1
Ganzel	RF	6	1	2	0
Lowe	3B	6	2	2	1
Smith	2B	2	2	0	0
Bennett	C	5	1	0	0
Clarkson	P	6	0	1	0
Total		48	15	15	4

```
BOSTON BEANEATERS     0 0 8  4 0 0  2 1 0 - 15 - 15 - 4
BROOKLYN BRIDEGROOMS 2 1 6  0 0 0  0 0 0 -  9 - 11 - 10
```

Fortunately for Brooklyn, the opener was not indicative of the season. The Bridegrooms went on to capture the National League flag by a comfortable six games over Cap Anson's Chicago White Stockings. The Beaneaters finished in fifth place, twelve games out.

1893—WILLIAM V. KENNEDY BECOMES AN "IRON MAN"

William V. "Brickyard" Kennedy was one of the great pitchers in Dodger history, piling up an envious 184-160 record from 1892 to 1903. The slightly built righthander surpassed the 20-victory mark four times, reaching 26 victories in 1893, in just his second season in the majors. Unfortunately for Kennedy, the Bridegrooms finished in the second division six times in his first seven years in the league.

In 1893, as the Grooms struggled home sixth with a 65-63 record, manager Dave Foutz had to rely on a two-man pitching staff of Kennedy and Ed Stein, for almost 60% of the innings pitched. During the season, Kennedy hurled 383 innings, finishing with a 26-20 won-loss mark. Stein chipped in with 298 innings, winning 19 games against 15 losses.

The pitching situation was so bad that Kennedy pitched both ends of a doubleheader against the last-place Louisville Colonels on Memorial Day. A small holiday crowd of 3,200 fans braved the trolley car ride to Eastern Park to view the pitiful Colonels who had lost 11 of their first 14 games.

"Brickyard" Kennedy faced 24-year-old Billy Rhines (1-4), in the first game of a morning-afternoon twin bill. Both pitchers were overpowering early in the game, and the score stood at 0-0 after seven innings of play. Kennedy limited the Colonels to just two singles, both by former Brooklyn third baseman George Pinckney. Rhines was almost as dominant, scattering six singles over seven innings. The Bridegrooms finally broke the scoreless deadlock with three runs in the bottom of the eighth.

34-game winner in 1890, was forced into retirement, with arm problems, before his 26th birthday. The 6', 180-pound right-hander kept the Bridegrooms at bay over the first five innings, scattering three harmless singles. Louisville, meanwhile, caught up with Kennedy in the top of the fourth. George Pinckney walked and came around to score the first run of the game on two infield outs and a single by catcher John Grim.

"Brickyard" Kennedy was the Brooklyn ace from 1892 through 1900. He pitched more than 200 innings in a season for eight consecutive years, five times surpassing the 300-inning mark. (Transcendental Graphics)

Tommy Corcoran smashed three hits in the opening game, in addition to supporting Kennedy with his usual flawless infield play. (Transcendental Graphics)

Harry Stovey led off the inning with a booming three-base hit. He carried home the first run of the game moments later when Dave Foutz hit a sacrifice fly to center fielder Tom Brown. Oyster Burns kept the rally going with a double, and was sacrificed to third by George Shoch. After Tido Daly drew a walk and stole second, both runners came around to score when second baseman Fred Pfeffer let Con Dailey's grounder go through his legs for an error.

Shortstop Tommy Corcoran led the Brooklyn attack with three hits.

Catcher Tom Kinslow and Kennedy added singles.

Dave Foutz's Grooms went ahead to stay in the bottom of the sixth. Third baseman George Shoch started the rally with a ringing double to left. Consecutive singles by Tido Daly, Con Dailey, Tommy Corcoran, and Tom Kinslow plated three big runs, and the Grooms never looked back. They added two more runs in the seventh on a leadoff walk to Oyster Burns, a two-out double by Con Dailey, and a two-run single by Tommy Corcoran. The final tally crossed the plate an inning later on a home run by Dave Foutz.

```
Louisville Colonels       0 0 0 0 0 0 0 0 0 - 0 - 2 - 4
Brooklyn Bridegrooms      0 0 0 0 0 0 0 3 x - 3 - 8 - 1
```

	IP	R	H	BB	SO
Rhines	8	3	8	3	0
Kennedy	9	0	2	4	5

The afternoon game drew a jovial crowd of 7,500 Flatbush fanatics, out for an afternoon in the sun. Kennedy was pitted against 23-year-old Scott Stratton, a righthander from Campbellsburg, Kentucky. Stratton, a

```
Louisville Colonels       0 0 0 1 0 0 1 0 0 - 2 - 6 - 1
Brooklyn Bridegrooms      0 0 0 0 0 3 2 1 x - 6 - 8 - 1
```

	IP	R	H	BB	SO
Stratton	8	6	11	6	2
Kennedy	9	2	6	3	0

1905—DOC SCANLON BECOMES AN IRON MAN

William D. "Doc" Scanlon was a journeyman righthander who toiled for Pittsburgh and Brooklyn during his eight-year major league career. During his Flatbush sojourn, the diminutive curveball artist won 65 games against 68 losses. He never pitched on a first-division team in Brooklyn, yet he managed to produce a 14-12 record in 1905 and a 19-14 record in 1906.

In 1905, Doc Scanlon etched his name in the Brooklyn baseball Hall of Fame, becoming the second and last Brooklyn hurler ever to pitch and win two games in one day. The Superbas and the St. Louis Cardinals were both finishing disappointing seasons. Stanley Robison's Redbirds limped home in sixth place, while Ned Hanlon's inept bunch had the basement all to themselves. Brooklyn's 44-103 record left them a full 58 1/2 games behind the pennant winning New York Giants. The fact that Doc Scanlon achieved a winning season with that team speaks volumes for his talents.

Twenty-five-year-old Doc Gessler was the hitting star of the day, lacing out five hits, including a first-game home run. (Transcendental Graphics)

The season ended on October 3, with the Superbas visiting Sportsman's Park for a season-ending doubleheader with St. Louis. Doc Scanlon with a 12-12 record faced Cardinal righthander Jack Taylor (15-20). Taylor was one of the top pitchers of his day, compiling a career record of 150-139. His 2.67 earned run average is #46 on the all-time list.

Only 2,200 fans turned out to bid farewell to the St. Louis entry. Most fans stayed home, trying to forget the miserable year the team had. One of the few bright spots on the Cardinal team was Jake "Eagle Eye" Beckley, a future Hall of Famer. The big first baseman spent 20 years in the majors, smashing 2,920 hits en route to a .308 batting average. His 244 triples are #4 on the all-time list.

Taylor matched Scanlon pitch for pitch for the first four innings, but in the fourth the Superbas pushed over

two runs to take a 2-0 lead. They upped the margin to 4-0 in the eighth, and Scanlon held on for the shutout. The slick Brooklyn curveballer needed only one hour and twenty-three minutes to whitewash the Redbirds. He yielded only three hits, and walked only two batters. Third baseman Emil Batch, with two singles and a home run, sparked the Brooklyn offense, while first baseman Doc Gessler added a homer and a single, and left fielder Jimmy Sheckard slapped a single and a double.

```
BROOKLYN SUPERBAS    000 020 200 - 4 - 10 - 1
ST. LOUIS CARDINALS  000 000 000 - 0 -  3 - 1
```

	IP	R	H	BB	SO
J. Taylor	9	4	10	0	1
Scanlon	9	0	3	2	8

Doc Scanlon, a decent major league pitcher, had the misfortune to pitch for a club that finished fifth, eighth, fifth, sixth, sixth, seventh. Still, he won 66 games with a fine 3.00 ERA. (Brace Photo)

Since the first game of the doubleheader was so easy on Scanlon's arm, Ned Hanlon came right back with his ace righthander in Game Two. This time, Doc's opponent was diminutive righthander Sandy McDougal. The Buffalo, New York native pitched a total of just six games in the majors, winning one and losing four. This was his last game.

The final game of the season was close throughout. The Superbas pushed over one run in the second, with the Cardinals countering in the fourth. Brooklyn scored two more runs in the eighth to take a 3-1 lead, but St. Louis edged back within one in its half of the same inning. Doc Scanlon then closed the door on any thoughts of a Cardinal rally in the bottom of the ninth, preserving his place in Brooklyn history.

Doc Gessler was the top Brooklyn batsman with three singles. Right Fielder Harry McIntyre and center fielder Charlie Malay had two hits each in the eleven hit barrage.

BROOKLYN SUPERBAS   0 1 0 0 0 0 0 2 0 - 3 - 11 - 2
ST. LOUIS CARDINALS 0 0 0 1 0 0 0 1 0 - 2 - 9 - 0

	IP	R	H	B	SO
McDougal	9	3	11	4	2
Scanlon	9	2	9	0	5

THE DAFFYNESS BOYS

Over the years, particularly from 1926 through 1938, the Brooklyn baseball team was jokingly referred to in the press as the Daffyness Boys. Baseball fans across the country adopted the phrase gleefully, bandying it about in everyday conversation, until the name Brooklyn became synonymous with lovable buffoons. The unflattering nickname was often associated with gangling outfielder Babe Herman and his Flatbush contemporaries but, the truth is, the birth of the Daffyness Boys myth goes back to 1914 when Brooklyn owner Charlie Ebbets hired portly Wilbert Robinson to manage the club.

Uncle Robby was a competent manager early in his career, but he was also something of a character. In 1916, the 52-year-old former catcher became the charter member in the Daffyness club. During spring training, after watching aviatrix Ruth Law do aerial acrobatics high above a Florida beach, Robby started bragging about how he could catch a baseball dropped from an airplane. Several players quickly challenged their leader to put his money where his mouth was. Bets came fast and furious, and arrangements for the momentous event were completed within a few days.

On the scheduled day, a large crowd gathered on the beach, and Ruth Law headed skyward carrying a Brooklyn coach and a baseball. Only the baseball wasn't a baseball. Casey Stengel, another of the team's oddballs, had substituted a large, ripe grapefruit for the ball. All eyes strained skyward as the plane began its decent over the beach. Robby positioned himself firmly in the sand, glove held high. At 400 feet, the plane leveled off and a round object hurtled groundward. Robinson waited intently and adjusted his position slightly to get directly beneath the ball.

The grapefruit exploded against his catcher's mitt like a small bomb, drenching him with grapefruit juice; the force of the impact sending him sprawling in the sand. As he felt himself oozing wet, he screamed, "My God.

I've exploded. The damn thing has blown me apart. Help me. I'm dead." Robinson lay on his back whimpering for several seconds, then slowly opened his eyes and looked up at the sea of faces that were staring down at him. The wide smiles all around told Uncle Robby he had been had.

Stengel was involved in another humorous incident as a player. One day in Ebbets Field, Casey strode briskly to the plate, tipped his cap to the crowd, then watched in silent admiration as a small bird flew out from under his cap and disappeared into the wild blue yonder. The crowd howled with delight. A reputation was being born.

The leaders of the "Daffyness Boys" were kindly manager Wilbert Robinson and star outfielder, Babe Herman. Both men were somewhat eccentric, but the stories of their antics were greatly exaggerated.

Ivy Olson, a compatriot of Stengel's, picked up the torch and carried insanity to the next level. Although a Brooklyn shortstop for ten years, his erratic defensive play often brought torrents of epithets from the stands at Ebbets Field. The abuse became so vicious at times that the native of Kansas City, Missouri, took to stuffing cotton in his ears whenever he played before the raucous home crowd.

Among other eccentricities, Olson had a strong aversion to bunting, considering it an unmanly act. The Brooklyn shortstop wanted to swing away on every pitch. One day, in an apparent sacrifice situation, manager Robinson attempted to give Olson the bunt sign several times, but the Robin shortstop refused to look in his direction. Finally, the frustrated leader just shook his head, muttered "Ah, the hell with it", and walked to the other end of the dugout.

The epitome of Brooklyn zaniness appeared on the scene in 1926. His name was Babe Herman, and he arrived in Ebbets Field carrying two bats and a cardboard suitcase. Whether the big, awkward outfielder was a clown or a serious ballplayer is still debated by baseball enthusiasts, but two things are certain. First, Babe was a colorful personality. And second, he could hit the baseball a mile, and hit it often as evidenced by his lifetime average of .324, number 34 on the all-time hit parade.

First and foremost, among the Herman tales, is the famous three men on third tale. It happened in Herman's rookie season of 1926. The Robins were playing the Braves in Ebbets Field. The score was tied 1-1 in the last of the seventh inning, and the Robins had the bases loaded with only one out. Hank DeBerry was on third, Dazzy Vance was on second, Chick Fewster was on first, and the mighty Babe was at the plate. Herman jumped on the first pitch and sent it screaming toward deep right center field.

Clarence "Pea Ridge" Day, champion hog caller and Brooklyn pitcher—briefly.

DeBerry scored easily, and the slow-moving Vance plodded plateward. Herman's ball hit the top of the right-field wall with such force that it bounced all the way back to the infield, directly to the surprised Braves second baseman, Doc Gautreau. The Dodger third-base coach,

seeing the turn of events, yelled to the baserunner, Chick Fewster, to hold up at third base. Vance, who strangely enough, still hadn't scored, stopped dead in his tracks and retreated to third. Herman, who was running with his head down, passed Fewster in the baseline, and slid into third at the same time that Vance slid in from the other direction. Fewster arrived shortly thereafter, and looked sheepishly at his two teammates.

Vance was smiling with relief. "I'm safe."

"If you are," said Herman, "You're the only one of us that is."

When the dust cleared, Herman and Fewster were both out. The Babe had doubled into a double play, but what went unnoticed in all the turmoil was that he had knocked in the winning run in the process.

A sequel to that story came some years later when a reporter had to leave a Dodger game in the ninth inning. By the time he made his way out of the ballpark and located a cab, the Dodgers had a rally underway. The excited cabbie brought him up to date. "The Dodgers have three men on base". "Yeh," replied the cynical reporter, "Which base?"

Herman was also accused of catching fly balls with his head from time to time, a charge he vehemently denied. "If a ball ever hit me on the head, I'd hang up my spikes." When asked if a fly ball ever hit him on the shoulder, Brooklyn's Babe immediately took offense. "Shoulders don't count."

Still another Herman story revolved around a reporter with a New York newspaper. The reporter, it seems, had been amusing his readers for several months with anecdotes about the colorful Babe. This didn't sit too well with Herman who was sensitive about his reputation as a buffoon. One day, after a game, Babe cornered the reporter in the runway leading to the clubhouse, and pleaded with him to find something else to write about. "You gotta stop writing about me, Joe. I'm no clown. And besides, I'm a married man with a family to support. Your articles are hurting my reputation and affecting my ability to earn a living."

The reporter was remorseful over the problems he had caused Herman, and promised not to write any more derogatory stories about his antics on the ballfield. With that, Babe, reaching into his coat pocket, pulled out a cigar butt, put it in his mouth, and started puffing on it. The reporter reached for matches. "Light?" "No, thanks," replied Herman as smoke curled skyward, "It's already lit."

Uncle Robby perpetuated the tradition of the Daffyness Boys by his own lax dugout regulations. One day, after a close play in the field, the manager, whose view was blocked, turned to the player next to him and asked, "What happened?" "I don't know, skipper," replied the player, "I was reading the newspaper."

Another time, when one of the players got particularly loud in the dugout, Robinson chastised him while pointing a finger toward pitcher Jess Petty, snoozing soundly on the bench. "Shh! Don't wake old Jess. He had a bad night last night."

Robby occasionally let the players make out the lineup for the game, but it never helped. The Robins kept losing. One time, the perplexed Brooklyn manager formed the bonehead club, designed to make the players more alert during the game by fining them for dumb plays on the field. The very first day, Robinson handed the wrong lineup card to the umpires, thereby becoming the first and last member of the club. It was immediately disbanded.

With the advent of the '30s, Dodger zaniness reached its zenith. Characters paraded in and out of Ebbets Field like they were in a revolving door. Clarence "Pea Ridge" Day, spent one season on the mound for Brooklyn. Day, from Arkansas, was a champion hog caller, and he enjoyed regaling audiences with his ear-piercing screams whenever possible. He would let go with his famous squeal after every strikeout, "Soo-eee. Soo-eee". The noise was so disagreeable that several of the infielders stuffed cotton in their ears whenever "Pea Ridge" was pitching. Fortunately for the infielders, and for the rest of the team as well, "Pea Ridge" wasn't around long. A person can listen to only so many hog calls in one lifetime.

Wally "Boom-Boom" Beck, friend to opposing batsmen.

Frenchy Bordagaray spent 11 years in the major leagues, six of them with Brooklyn. He batted .315 for the Dodgers in 1936, and .302 in 1943.

In the mid '30s, the Dodgers had colorful Frenchy Bordagaray patrolling centerfield for them. Bordagaray, a French Canadian, had thick, bushy eyebrows, a long, black flowing mustache, and a shiny, bald pate. He looked like the villain in a silent movie. And he fit right in with the Daffyness Boys. Frenchy was endowed with a streak of vanity that would eventually put his name near the top of the list of leading Dodger zanies. The native of Coalinga, California always wore a hat because his pride wouldn't allow anyone to gaze upon his bald head. One day in Brooklyn, in the middle of a ballgame, his vanity and his occupation clashed. Vanity won. Frenchy was stationed in centerfield as usual, when the opposing batter hit a long fly ball to his right. Bordagaray took off in hot pursuit, and had the ball clearly in his sights, when a gust of wind blew his hat off. He immediately applied the brakes, and turned to retrieve his hat, embarrassed that 30,000 fans should view his nakedness. The batter, meanwhile, gleefully circled the bases with a triple.

Bordagaray made the zany list a second time. He was called out by the umpire while he was standing on second base. "What the hell happened?" asked his frantic manager. "I was tapping my foot", said Frenchy. "I guess he got me between taps."

Every day was an adventure in Brooklyn during the thirties, but most of the adventures resulted from the mediocrity and incompetence of the pitiful Dodger crew. One day, a Brooklyn baserunner was tagged out at home plate when he went in standing up on a close play. When asked by the manager why he didn't slide, the runner

Hank Behrman, a 5'11", 174-pound right-handed pitcher, was 11-5 as a 25-year-old rookie in 1946. The following year, he pitched in five World Series games. According to The Ballplayers, manager Burt Shotton said poor work habits prevented Behrman from having a successful major league career. His final stats showed 24 victories against 17 defeats.

replied, "I didn't want to crush the cigars in my back pocket."

Another time, a Dodger baserunner stole second while it was already occupied. His explanation–"I couldn't resist. I had such a big jump."

Dodger centerfielder Hack Wilson was a member of the club. He was standing with his back to the plate during a pitching change, when a baseball flew over his head and careened off the centerfield wall. Not realizing that pitcher Wally "Boom-Boom" Beck had thrown the ball to the wall in disgust after being relieved, Wilson ran it down and made a perfect throw to the cutoff man as the crowd howled with glee.

Beck had earned his unusual nickname by giving up countless long hits to opposing batsmen. The "Boom-Boom" was intended to simulate, first, the sound of the ball making contact with the bat and, second, the sound of the ball striking the outfield fence.

Some of the zaniness even continued into the '40s and '50s. Pitcher Billy Loes, when asked how he had missed a ground ball during a World Series game, remarked with a straight face, "I lost it in the sun."

Hank Behrman, who pitched for the Dodgers from 1946 to 1948, was a throwback to the Daffyness Boys. One year the fans decided to throw a "day" in honor of Behrman, and collection cans were distributed in every saloon and Mom-and-Pop grocery in Brooklyn. When the big day arrived, Behrman strutted to the plate grinning from ear to ear, anticipating his gifts. The master of ceremonies made a short speech, then presented Hank with a $100 savings bond. Behrman stared at the bond in stunned silence, then looked around for a car or a boat. "Cut the crap. Where's my car?" "Sorry, Hank. We only collected $75." Furious, Behrman threw the bond on the ground and stomped it into the dirt. Then he turned and stormed back to the dugout. "Who needs a crummy bond, anyway".

Crazy antics followed the Dodgers to Los Angeles, thanks to the likes of Jerry Reuss, Don Stanhouse, Jay Johnstone, Mickey Hatcher, and Roger McDowell, but it wasn't the same. The new Dodgers had fun, but won games at the same time. In the old days, the Daffyness Boys hardly ever saw the light of day in the National League, finishing in the second division 14 times in 18 years.

The real Daffyness Boys were lovable losers.

1920–ROBINS PLAY 26-INNING GAME

The Brooklyn Robins and the Boston Braves played the longest game in major league history on May 1, 1920. It ended in a 1-1 tie, after 26 innings.

The visiting Robins started curveballer Leon Cadore on the mound. The 28-year-old righthander was the #2 hurler on manager Wilbert Robinson's staff, behind Burleigh Grimes. Cadore's opponent was Joe Oeschger, the ace of the Braves staff. The tall, lanky righthander, pitching for the Philadelphia Phillies the year before, had battled Grimes and the Robins to a 9-9 tie in 20 innings, so marathon efforts were nothing new for him.

The day was cold and damp as home plate umpire Barry McCormick put the ball in play. A small crowd of 3,000 hardy fans tried to lend support to their rag-tag team, unaware that they were witnessing history in the making. Oeschger's blazing fastballs and Cadore's tantalizing curves kept the game scoreless through four innings. Wilbert Robinson's boys finally broke the ice in the fifth when catcher Ernie Krueger drew a base on balls, advanced to second on an infield out and scored on a single to left by shortstop Ivy Olson.

George Stallings Braves bounced right back, tying the game in the bottom of the sixth. Right fielder Wally Cruise hit a one out triple to deep left field and came in to score on a single by third baseman Tony Boeckel. As it turned out, that would be the last run of the long afternoon.

As the innings passed, reporters began checking their records for the longest games ever played. The National League record was still fresh in the Robins' minds.

They had defeated the Pittsburgh Pirates, 6-5 in 22 innings in 1917. Eleven years before, the Boston Red Sox and Philadelphia Athletics set the major league record when the A's nipped the BoSox 4-1 in a 24-inning marathon.

The Robins appeared ready to blow the game wide open in the 17th inning. Zack Wheat led off with a sharp single to right, raced to second on a perfect sacrifice bunt by center fielder Wally Hood, and moved over to third on

Leon Cadore pitched in the National League for 10 years, eight of them with the Dodgers. He won 13-15 games four times for Wilbert Robinson's team, finishing his career with a 68-72 record.

an infield hit by Ed Konetchy. The bases were loaded when catcher Rowdy Elliott reached on a fielder's choice. Boston shortstop Rabbit Maranville, after fielding Elliott's grounder, tried to catch Wheat off third, but his throw was too late and everybody was safe. With a golden opportunity to put the game away, shortstop Chuck Ward, a .155 hitter, bounced to Maranville with the infield in. The Rabbit fired home to force Wheat at the plate, but Catcher Hank Gowdy's toss to first was wild, pulling Wally Holke off the bag. Ed Konetchy, seeing the errant throw as he rounded third, raced for home. Holke, a fine defensive player, quickly retrieved the ball and gunned it to Gowdy who put the tag on the sliding Konetchy for the third out.

As it turned out, that was the Robins' last gasp. Oeschger got stronger as the game progressed, retiring the side in order over the final nine innings. Counting the inning-ending double play in the 17th, the Boston fireballer recorded 29 consecutive outs.

Leon Cadore, although not perfect, was almost as good as his Boston counterpart. Beginning in the 14th inning, the Brooklyn hurler limited Stalling's crew to just two harmless singles, one by Leslie Mann in the 20th inning, and another by Wally Holke with two gone in the 26th.

After Cadore retired Tony Boeckel to end the 26th, plate umpiree McCormick stepped in and put a stop to the proceedings, declaring it too dark to continue. Seventy-two years later, the game remains the longest major league game ever played.

The day after the 26-inning marathon, Burleigh Grimes lost to George Smith of the Philadelphia Phillies in Brooklyn, 4-3, in 13 innings. On Monday, back in Boston, Robinson's crew was beaten by the Braves, 2-1, in 19 innings, as Sherry Smith and Dana Fillingim turned in route-going performances. Manager Wilbert Robinson's boys ended up with nothing to show for their three-day "Lost Weekend." They had played a total of 58 innings in three games, coming away with no wins, two losses, and one tie.

BROOKLYN

NAME	POS	AB	R	H	E
Olson	2B	10	0	1	1
Neis	RF	10	0	1	0
Johnston	3B	10	0	2	0
Wheat	LF	9	0	2	0
Myers	CF	2	0	1	0
Hood	CF	6	0	1	0
Konetchy	1B	9	0	1	0
Ward	SS	10	0	0	1
Krueger	C	2	1	0	0
Elliott	C	7	0	0	0
Cadore	P	10	0	0	0
Total		85	1	9	2

BOSTON

NAME	POS	AB	R	H	E
Powell	CF	7	0	1	0
Pick	2B	11	0	0	3
Mann	LF	10	0	2	0
Cruise	RF	9	1	1	0
Holke	1B	11	0	3	0
Boeckel	3B	11	0	3	0
Maranville	SS	10	0	3	0

O'Neil	SS		2	0 0 0
Christenbury	PH		1	0 1 0
Gowdy	C		6	0 1 0
Oeschger	P		5	0 1 0
Total			82	1 15 3

	IP	R	H	BB	SO
Cadore	26	1	15	5	6
Oeschger	26	1	9	4	7

1924–DAZZY VANCE WINS 15 GAMES IN SUCCESSION

Clarence Arthur (Dazzy) Vance began his career with Brooklyn at the ripe old age of 31 and, in eleven years, he established numerous Dodger pitching records, of which still stand after more than 70 years.

The one record that shines brightest in the Vance archives is the 15- game winning streak he put together during the torrid 1924 pennant race. Early in July of that year, the Robins found themselves in third place, eight games distant from the New York Giants. On July 6, the Boston Braves handed Dazzy Vance his fourth loss, 4-1. The big redhead would not taste defeat again for 79 days.

Four days after his embarrassment at the hands of the Braves, Vance cruised past the Chicago Cubs, 9-1. Before the month ended, he also posted victories over Cincinnati (5-4), Pittsburgh (6-2), and Cincinnati again (5-1).

The big Nebraska farmboy loved to pitch in the hot weather and, as the dog days of summer unfolded, the Vance fastball crackled as never before, and batter after batter bit the dust. In August his record was a perfect 7-0. In September he strung together four more victories before his luck ran out.

The Robin ace began August in fine style, blanking the second-place Chicago Cubs 4-0, with a 14-strikeout performance. His seven successive strikeouts tied a major league record. On the 6th, he whipped Pittsburgh, 5-3, for his 6th win in a row. Yet, in spite of Vance's overpowering pitching performances, his teammates were stumbling along in fourth place. Finally the team began to gel. Starting 12 1/2 games back on August 7, the Robins made their move. Their big bats came to life with a vengeance, and pitchers Bill Doak and Rube Ehrhardt began their own modest wins streaks that would reach eight and five respectively.

But it was Dazzy Vance who led the way down the stretch. On August 10, he stopped St. Louis, 8-4. Then Cincinnati (5-0), Pittsburgh (4-3), Chicago (6-5), and New York (3-1) fell in rapid succession. Every member of the Robin lineup contributed to the torrid offense. First baseman Jack Fournier won one game with a home run; then followed up with a two homer game. Center fielder Eddie Brown had several game-winning hits. Andy High punched out four hits in one game. Zack Wheat seemed to be in the middle of every rally. And Johnny Mitchell and Hank DeBerry both came through in the clutch.

Dazzy Vance pitched perhaps the greatest game of his career on August 23, a 6-5 win over Chicago. During that game he struck out 15 Cub batters, setting a new National League record, one behind Walter Johnson's Major League record. He set down six successive batters on strikes at one juncture. And, in the process, he broke Carl Mays' record of 9 straight wins. The 6'2",200-pound fireballer finished August with an 11-game winning streak, and an overall record of 22-4. Uncle Robby's boys were as hot as the weather as September got underway, sweeping four doubleheaders in four days. Vance was the winning pitcher in the seventh game of the streak, dumping the Boston Braves, 5-1, with a three hitter. The big redhead fanned 11 Braves en route to his 12 straight victory. Eddie Brown and Milt Stock gave Dazzy all the offensive support he needed, cracking big doubles to drive in runs.

By now, the Robins were considered serious threats to the Giant pennant hopes. Their blazing four-day run had left them only three percentage points out of first place. The Brooklyn tcam, like Dazzy Vance, was on a roll. On September 6, they edged Boston 1-0 in the first game of a doubleheader. It was their 15th straight win. In Game Two, their bubble finally burst. The Braves prevailed by a score of 5-4 in ten innings, dropping the Robins 1/2 game behind New York.

As fate would have it, the Giants visited Ebbets Field for the last series of the season on Sept. 7-8. New

Dazzy Vance walked off with most of the pitching honors in the National League in 1924. He led the league in victories (28), strikeouts (262), and earned run average (2.16). He was also voted the league's Most Valuable Player.

York took the first game of the series, 8-7, to extend their lead over the Flatbush flock to 1 1/2 games. Just when they seemed ready to wrap up the flag, the formidable figure of Arthur Clarence Vance stood before them. In a gallant pitching exhibition, the Nebraska farmboy outpitched Giant ace, Art Nehf, 7-2 to keep Robin hopes alive.

Time was running out on Dazzy Vance and the Robins, but a few thrills yet remained. On September 14, Vance threw goose eggs at Cincinnati, winning 2-0 in Ebbets Field. In rolling up his14th straight victory, he tossed a four hitter at the Reds, struck out nine and didn't walk a batter. His overall record stood at 26-4.

Victory no. 15 came on Vance's only relief appearance of the year. The Brooklyn star entered the game in the ninth inning against Branch Rickey's St. Louis Cardinals, and pitched four strong innings. He came away a winner when "Black Lightning," Zack Wheat, slammed a two-run homer in the 12th inning to give Uncle Robby's boys a hard-fought 7-5 victory. They still trailed New York by only 1/2 game.

The Pittsburgh Pirates moved into Ebbets field on the 19th for a critical series between contenders. Pirate ace Emil Yde nipped Rube Ehrhardt, 4-2, in the opener, dropping Brooklyn 1 1/2 back. Only seven games remained in the regular season, as Dazzy Vance strode to the mound to face the mighty Pirates. The lead changed hands several times as both teams jockeyed for position. As the 11th inning commenced, Pittsburgh Hall of Famer, Pie Traynor, slapped a two-out single to left. The next hitter, Rabbit Maranville, sent a Vance fastball into center field. Eddie Brown missed a shoestring catch and, before the ball could be retrieved, Traynor scored the winning run.

It was Dazzy Vance's first loss since July 6. His streak was over. But in a span of 79 days, the big redhead won 15 games in a row, a Brooklyn record that could live forever.

The Robins rebounded in Game Three of the series, winning 9-1, to keep their pennant hopes alive. Brooklyn finished the season with three wins in its final five games, but it wasn't good enough. The Giants went 4-1 to win the flag by 1 1/2 games.

1932–JOHNNY FREDERICK SETS PINCH HIT HOMER RECORD

Johnny Frederick played for the Brooklyn Dodgers from 1929 through 1934. The youngster from Denver, Colorado was an outstanding major league center fielder with extraordinary range. In fact, his great range places him with the top ten outfielders in major league history. He got a great jump on the ball, thanks to a combination of speed and anticipation.

Frederick was no slouch at the plate, either. He hit a solid .328 in his rookie season, leading the National

League with 52 doubles. In his sophomore year, the slightly built left-handed slugger batted .334 with 44 doubles, 11 triples, and 17 home runs. Like Pete Reiser after him, however, the 28-year-old's luck ran out near the end of his second year. He suffered a broken ankle on September 13, and was never the same again.

Although he continued to play in pain for another four years, his battered legs gave him more and more trouble, casting him in the role of part-time outfielder and pinch hitter extraordinaire. In 1932, Johnny Frederick set a pinch hitting record that still stands, 65 years later.

Johnny Frederick was a "Pete Reiser" type outfielder, with speed and range in the field, and power at the plate. Unfortunately, like Reiser, he fell to the injury jinx. (Brace Photo)

He slammed six home runs in crucial pinch-hitting roles.

The 5'11", 160-pound dynamo cracked his first pinch-hit home run on June 12 against the Pittsburgh Pirates in Forbes Field. The ninth-inning round-tripper tied the game at 7-7, and the Dodgers went on to win, 8-7 in 12 innings. Three days later, hitting for Van Lingle Mungo in the eighth inning, he took a Lon Warneke offering downtown in a losing cause. The Chicago Cubs won the game, 8-3.

Two months later, on August 10, the popular youngster hit his first pinch homer of the year in the friendly confines of Ebbets Field. His three-run shot in the seventh inning sparked a five-run, game-tying Brooklyn rally, and the Dodgers went on to win, 9-8, in 13 innings. His third-circuit clout tied the major league record held jointly by Ham Hyatt, Pat Crawford, and Fred Williams.

Johnny Frederick took sole possession of the record just four days later. Facing the immortal "King Carl" Hubbell of the New York Giants in the top of the ninth inning at the Polo Grounds, with Brooklyn down 1-0, the little left hander showed he could hit southpaws as he sent a game-tying drive into the right field seats. Max Carey's team went on to whip Hubbell and the Giants, 2-1 in the 10th.

Frederick still wasn't through with his late inning heroics, however. On Saturday September 10, he hit #5 against the Chicago Cubs in Ebbets Field in a losing cause. The Brooks were demolished by the National League champs, 9-2.

On September 12, the Brooklyn Dodgers finished out their season series against the Cubs. The Dodgers' third-place finish was their best effort in eight years. As a small Ebbets Field crowd rooted for the home team, the Chicagoans took a 3-2 lead into the ninth. A one-out double off the right field wall by shortstop Glenn Wright brought the determined Frederick to the plate to face former Dodger Burleigh Grimes. The 39-year-old Grimes was no match for the hot-hitting slugger on this day. Frederick pulled the second pitch over the right field wall for a home run, giving the Dodgers a 4-3 victory, and sending 5,000 fans home happy.

For the season, Johnny Frederick stepped to the plate in a pinch-hitting role 30 times. He smashed out nine hits in 29 at bats for a .310 batting average. He hit two doubles in addition to his six home runs, and drove home 13 runners.

1934—"IS BROOKLYN STILL IN THE LEAGUE" HAUNTS TERRY

Words said in jest frequently come back to haunt the speaker. A perfect example of this truism is Bill Terry's famous remarks made in the winter of 1934. Fresh from winning the 1933 World Championship, the outspoken manager of the Giants visited the city in February to make plans for the upcoming season. During a routine press conference, Terry was fed the perfect inflammatory question by Roscoe McGowen, a *Times* reporter who covered the exploits of the Brooklyn team.

"Do you think the Dodgers will be tough?"

Terry fell for it, hook, line and sinker. "Brooklyn? Haven't heard much about them lately. Is Brooklyn still in the league?"

As the season progressed, Terry's remark might not have seemed so out of place. The pathetic Brooklyn nine, now managed by a seemingly pathetic Casey Stengel, went through the motions of playing ball without ruffling anyone's feathers. They held down sixth

place in 1933, and were about to repeat the feat. They would finish some 23 1/2 games out of first place.

But they did have one bright, shining hour. It occurred during the last weekend of the season. The Giants were engaged in a dog fight with Frank Frisch's St. Louis Cardinals for the top spot in the league. A New York lead, which had stood at a comfortable eight games in mid August, had gradually disappeared. When Dizzy Dean blanked the cellar-dwelling Cincinnati Reds 4-0 on the last Friday of the season, the two teams were in a dead heat for first place.

The Dodgers moved into the Bronx for two season-ending games against Terry's Giants, while the Redbirds hosted the hapless Reds. It became apparent almost immediately that Bill Terry's comments regarding the talents of the Brooklyn Dodger ball club had not been forgotten.

Van Lingle Mungo, Brooklyn's flame-throwing right hander, won 18 games for the sixth-place Dodgers. His biggest victory was his last, a 5-1 triumph over the hated Giants that essentially scuttled New York's pennant hopes.

On Saturday, thousands of wild-eyed Dodger fans pushed their way into the Polo Grounds to root for their heroes, and to let Terry know that their team was still in the league. Hundreds of placards hurled the insult back at the New Yorkers. Signs reading, "Is Brooklyn Still in the League?" were visible all around the big park. Inning after inning, the Giant manager heard the same scornful question spit back at him in the dugout, "Hey, Terry. Is Brooklyn still in the league?"

Casey Stengel pitched big Van Lingle Mungo at the Gotham crew, and Mungo was devastating. The flame-throwing right hander won his 18th game of the year, 5-1, as he mowed down the Giant hitters with monotonous regularity. He also led the Dodger attack with two hits, scoring the first run in the fifth inning after singling, and knocking in the second run with a 6th inning single. The Dodger faithful went wild in the stands as the game ended. The loss, coupled with a 6-1 Cardinal victory, dropped the Giants into second place, one game behind. New York had to win the finale.

On the final Sunday, with 44,055 baseball fanatics screaming for Terry's blood, the Giants came out of the blocks with fire in their eyes. Jumping on Ray Benge for four big runs in the first inning, New York, with 18-game winner Freddie Fitzsimmons on the hill, appeared to be in control of the game. Not so. Casey Stengel's crew kept chipping away at the lead, while 25-year-old "Dutch" Leonard kept the Giants at bay, yielding only one run in almost seven innings of pitching. Brooklyn scored one run in the second, another in the fourth, and one more in the sixth, to cut the New York lead to 5-3 after seven innings.

The Dodgers made the most of two hits, a fielders choice, and a wild pitch to tie the score in the top of the eighth. Two innings later, they broke the game wide open, routing Giant aces Schumacher and Hubbell in the process. Three hits, a walk, and an error produced three runs as the Flatbush flock ended New York's pennant dreams once and for all.

Yes, Bill Terry. Brooklyn is still in the league.

1938—FIRST NIGHT GAME IN EBBETS FIELD, VANDER MEER THROWS SECOND NO-NO

Nineteen hundred and thirty-eight saw the birth of the modern Dodger baseball franchise. In that year, the Brooklyn board of directors hired Larry MacPhail as General Manager, and the brash baseball executive immediately put the club on the road to financial and professional success.

One of his first moves was to initiate night baseball in the bustling borough of Brooklyn. The date, June 15, was an historic day in Brooklyn and professional baseball annals, but not for the reason MacPhail envisioned. The Dodgers opponents were the rejuvenated Cincinnati Reds of Bill McKechnie. The Reds, long the doormat of the National League, and a last-place finisher in three out of the last five years, were a much improved, third-place ball club. The Dodgers, on the other hand, were comfortably ensconced in seventh place, still a year away from their move toward dynastic status.

MacPhail organized a spectacular program for his first night game. A festive Ebbets Field crowd of 38,748, 6,000 more than the rated seating capacity of the little park, jammed the aisles and hung from the rafters, welcoming in a new era in Brooklyn Dodger baseball. A band serenaded the fans for several hours prior to the first pitch, strutting lively and blaring loudly, more quantity than quality. The pre-game show also included a selection of musical routines by two fife and drum corps, a dazzling fireworks display over the Gowanus, and a track and field demonstration by Olympic hero Jesse Owens. The American superstar put on a long-jump exhibition, and competed against several players in the 100-yard dash and the 120-yard low hurdles.

Owens, the dominant athlete at the 1936 Olympic Games in Berlin, became the first American athlete in history to win three individual Olympic gold medals. Nazi dictator Adolph Hitler, who was promoting the superiority of the German race at the time, was thoroughly humiliated by Owens' overpowering performances.

At precisely 8:35 P.M., the lights were turned on in Ebbets Field for the first time, and night miraculously turned into day. One hour and ten minutes later, Brooklyn's Max Butcher fired the first pitch to Cincinnati second baseman, Lonnie Frey. Butcher's opponent on this momentous occasion was Johnny Vander Meer, a handsome 23-year-old southpaw who was coming off a sensational 3-0 no-hitter against the Boston Bees just four days previous.

Rookie Johnny Vander Meer won 15 games for the fourth-place Reds in 1938. In his 13-year major league career, Vander Meer won 119 games and lost 121, mostly for second-division teams.

The Redleg ace showed no signs of slowing down against Burleigh Grimes' crew. He was blazing fast and comfortably wild, preventing the Dodger hitters from getting a toe-hold. Bill McKechnie's team broke through first, scoring four runs against Butcher in the third, and driving the Brooklyn righty to cover.

As the game entered the seventh inning, Brooklyn was still without a hit, although they had coaxed three bases on balls from the Cincinnati fireballer. The Reds upped their margin to 5-0 in the top half of the inning on a single by Goodman, a stolen base, and a hit by Craft. Vander Meer dug himself a small hole in the bottom of the inning by issuing one-out walks to Cookie Lavagetto and Dolf Camilli. Working cooly under pressure, however, the kid from Midland Park, New Jersey, settled down to fan Ernie Koy and retire Leo Durocher on a grounder to second.

In the eighth, after the Reds added to their run total on a triple by Wally Berger, the Dodgers were retired in order, with pinch hitter Woody English and Johnny Hudson going down on strikes.

Tension gripped the tiny stadium as Vander Meer walked to the mound in the bottom of the ninth. The Brooklyn crowd had mixed emotions; on the one hand wanting to see the Cincinnati ace toss his second consecutive no-hitter, but on the other, not wanting to be on the losing side of such an historical event. In the end, the fickle crowd opted for history, and cheered for Johnny Vander Meer to complete his once-in-a-lifetime quest.

The ninth inning was not easy for the young southpaw. The first batter, Dodger left fielder Buddy Hassett, topped a ball down the first-base line, and was out. Then, without warning, the Cincinnati pitcher lost the location of the plate. He walked Babe Phelps, Cookie Lavagetto, and Dolph Camilli in succession, to load the bases with only one out. The crowd squirmed in their seats. Manager Bill McKechnie raced to the mound to settle his pitcher down.

The pep talk worked. The next batter, Ernie Koy, sent a grounder to Lew Riggs at third. Riggs fielded the ball cleanly and fired home to force Phelps at the plate. Then, with the stillness almost unbearable, Leo Durocher lifted an 0-1 pitch into short center field, where Harry Craft hauled it in to end the suspense. The big crowd exploded in a torrent of shrieks and whistles, and rose as one to applaud the conquering hero, the hated enemy who had silenced their beloved team with one of the greatest achievements in baseball history–a second consecutive no-hit game.

Vander Meer's teammates rushed the mound to bury their victorious pitcher in a pile of bodies. Thousands of fans, now become a frenzied mob, rushed the field to touch their new hero, but Vander Meer's teammates provided him with protective cover to the safety of the dugout. His parents, who were in the stands, were not so fortunate. They were surrounded by delirious fans for nearly 15 minutes before they could find their way to an exit.

CINCINNATI

NAME	POS	AB	R	H	E
Frey	2B	5	0	1	0
Berger	LF	5	1	3	0
Goodman	RF	3	2	1	0
McCormick	1B	5	1	1	0
Lombardi	C	3	1	0	0
Craft	CF	5	0	3	0
Riggs	3B	4	0	1	0
Myers	SS	4	0	0	0
Vander Meer	P	4	1	1	0
Total		38	6	11	0

BROOKLYN

NAME	POS	AB	R	H	E
Cuyler	RF	2	0	0	0
Coscarat	2B	2	0	0	0
Brack	PH	1	0	0	0
Hudson	2B	1	0	0	0
Hassett	LF	4	0	0	0
Phelps	C	3	0	0	0
Rosen	PH	0	0	0	0
Lavagetto	3B	2	0	0	2
Camilli	1B	1	0	0	0
Koy	CF	4	0	0	0
Durocher	SS	4	0	0	0
Butcher	P	0	0	0	0
Presnell	P	2	0	0	0
Hamlin	P	0	0	0	0
English	PH	1	0	0	0
Tamulis	P	0	0	0	0
Total		27	0	0	2

```
CINCINNATI REDS     004 000 110 - 6 - 11 - 0
BROOKLYN DODGERS    000 000 000 - 0 - 0 - 2
```

	IP	R	H	BB	SO
Vander Meer	9	0	0	8	7
Butcher	2 2/3	4	5	4	1
Presnell	3 2/3	1	4	0	3
Hamlin	1 2/3	1	2	1	3
Tamulis	1	0	0	0	0

1939–"PISTOL PETE" REISER EXPLODES ON THE MAJOR LEAGUE SCENE

Harold Patrick "Pistol Pete" Reiser, perhaps the greatest talent ever to don a Dodger uniform, exploded on the major league scene in the spring of 1939. The 20-year-old speedster had been signed by Larry MacPhail the year before when baseball commissioner Judge Landis, made him and 100 other St. Louis Cardinal farmhands free agents, declaring St. Louis general manager, Branch Rickey had signed them illegally.

Rickey and MacPhail were old friends, and the Brooklyn G.M. signed the 19-year-old youngster as a favor to his associate. MacPhail was supposed to trade Reiser back to St. Louis in a couple of years, but fate and the headlines the mercurial Reiser generated prevented the completion of the dark pact.

Pete Reiser spent his first year as a Dodger farmhand with Superior in the Northern League. He hit a comfortable .302 with 18 home runs, and was one of the league's top shortstops.

He was invited to the Brooklyn spring training camp the following spring as a favor, to allow him to get a jump on his conditioning program. The likable youngster was in camp only to get in shape for the upcoming minor league season, and to make himself useful around the training facility. He was not scheduled to participate in any grapefruit league games with the big club. His practice games would come later with his minor league teammates.

Pistol Pete so impressed manager Leo Durocher with his hustle and his hitting prowess in the batting cage that the Dodger field leader decided to view the budding phenom under actual game conditions. The Brooklyn baseball club travelled to St. Petersburg on March 22 to do battle with the St. Louis Cardinals. Reiser was inserted into the starting lineup as the shortstop, and a legend was born.

Facing Cardinal rookie left-hander Ken Raffensberger in the first inning, the switch hitting Reiser poled a long home run over the right-field wall with two men on base. He drew a base on balls from Raffensberger in his second at bat, then followed with two singles off right-handed pitchers, giving him a perfect 3-3 day. The Dodgers won the game, 6-4, with the rookie leading the hit parade.

The Dodger phenom started the next grapefruit league game also, facing the pennant-contending Cincinnati Redlegs. This time, he outdid himself. In a 9-1 romp, the 5'11", 185-pound slugger pounded two more home runs, and added two singles, driving in four runs on the day. Things started quietly enough for the kid from St. Louis, as righthander Dutch Gehrman held him to a harmless single in the second inning. Then, two innings later, facing 6'6", 230-pound righty, Big Jim Weaver, with runners at the corners, Reiser pulled a fastball over the right-field fence.

"Pistol Pete" Reiser had all the prerequisites of a superstar. He could hit, hit with power, run, field, and throw. In 1941, he became the youngest batting champion in major league history.

In the sixth, the speedster beat out a slow roller to short, beating Billy Myers throw easily. He closed out his sensational day by driving a fastball from Peaches Davis over the right-field wall for his third homer of the spring.

Manager Leo Durocher, staying with his hot property, started Reiser against the Detroit Tigers the next day. The youngster singled off 19-year-old Freddy Hutchinson to drive in a run in the first inning, as the Dodgers broke out on top, 3-0. While running the bases after his hit Pistol Pete pulled up lame, and spent the next couple of games on the bench.

During his torrid debut, the hell-bent-for-leather speedster reached base nine consecutive times, on five singles, three home runs, and a base on balls. He drove in eight runs in the outburst. Subsequent front-page publicity in several New York City newspapers, made any thoughts of returning Reiser to St. Louis impossible.

In spite of a .450 spring batting average, the 20-year-old budding superstar was sent back to the minors for further seasoning. He moved up to the big club to stay in 1940, exciting everyone with his vast talent. He could play the infield or the outfield, throw with either hand, hit for power from either side of the plate, and hit for average. He covered the outfield with effortless grace, and had a strong, accurate throwing arm.

Beginning in 1941, Pistol Pete Reiser dominated major league baseball. He won the batting title that year with an average of .343, becoming the youngest batting champion in major league history. The following year, he picked up where he had left off, rattling the fences at a .356 gait into mid July.

The rest is history. A collision with the outfield wall in Sportsmans Park, St. Louis, was the first act in a tragic, career-ending Greek drama. Additional injuries from collisions and beanings continued to drain his great skills, until there was nothing left but a shell.

As Leo Durocher once said, "Pete Reiser may have been the greatest ballplayer I ever managed. He had everything but luck."

MEMORIES OF EBBETS FIELD

Most people think of Brooklyn as one of the five boroughs of New York City. To the natives of the community during the first half of the twentieth century, however, Brooklyn was a city unto itself, a geographical entity of three million kindred souls; people who considered themselves to be Brooklynites, not New Yorkers. And, in the summer, when the heat rose in waves from the city streets, and boys in white uniforms roamed the pastures of Ebbets, the City of Churches became, more than anything else, a state of mind. Insanity ruled.

Citizens of Brooklyn are first identified by their quaint dialect. Nowhere else in America do people speak in that unique tongue known as "Brooklynese." The immigrants from other countries who sought shelter in and around Flatbush, developed their own jargon over the years. The 'er' sound became 'oi' in Brooklynese, and vice versa, and the 'th' sound became a 'd'. The resulting speech may have grated on the ears of strangers, but, to fellow citizens of Brooklyn, it sounded like heaven.

"Eatcha heart outcha bum."
"Dixie Walker is da peeple's cheerce."
"Dem Bums is our team."
"C'mon, Oisk, stick it in his ear."

Ebbets Field itself conjures up visions of past glories and strange inhabitants. It was a small ballpark, close and noisy, where the fans were personally involved in the game. One of the more familiar visitors to the old steel stadium on Sullivan Place was a plump, middle-aged matron named Hilda Chester. Blessed with a loud, penetrating voice, Hilda attended almost every home game for 30 years. She started watching her beloved Dodgers during the 1920s, and she continued cheering them on to the bitter end. She always sat in the left-field bleachers, carrying a big sign that read, "Hilda is here," making a racket with a large, brass cowbell, and spitting epithets at opposing players. Dodger management, in recognition of her years of loyalty, finally presented Hilda with a lifetime seat in her favorite section of the bleachers.

Howling Hilda, as she was called, loved to hang over the railing, clang the cowbell, and scream to the players. There is one story in Brooklyn Dodger lore that illustrates the whackiness that invariably pervaded Dodgerdom. It was recounted by Peter Golenbock, in his book, *Bums*. One day, as Pete Reiser patrolled center field, Hilda leaned over the grandstand railing and dropped him a note. "Hey Pete, give this to Leo." Reiser, thinking it was a personal note to the Dodger manager, handed it to Leo without comment when he returned to the dugout. Durocher opened the note and read it. "Get Casey ready. Wyatt's losing it." Thinking the note was from his pitching coach, Leo subsequently brought Hugh Casey in from the bullpen to relieve a bewildered Whitlow Wyatt, who couldn't understand why he was being taken out. This is the only case on record where a bleacher fan was responsible for making a pitching change during a major league game. It could only happen in Brooklyn.

Another inherent part of the Brooklyn mystique was a group of five musicians, dressed in tattered tuxedos with tails, patched trousers, black top hats and derbys. They comprised the famous Dodger Sym-phony, the Ebbets Field equivalent of the New York Philharmonic Orchestra. The Sym-phony stationed itself behind the Dodger dugout for every home game, keeping the park alive with musical selections. Occasionally they strolled through the stands single file, serenading the fans. The sounds the energetic quintet produced on their drums, cymbals, and brass instruments, were not of the highest quality, but they were loud. And in Brooklyn, that was good enough.

Hilda Chester, shown here at her place of employment, the concession stand at Monmouth Race Track, led the Brooklyn fans' vociferous attack on opposing players for over 30 years, from her "reserved" seat in the left-field bleachers. (Brooklyn Public Library)

Brooklyn's famous musical family, "The Dodgers Sym-phony," entertained the fans in Ebbets Field for 20 years. Occasionally, Dodger players joined in the fun. L to R Pat Palma, Spider Jorgensen, Bobby Bragan, Jerry Martin, Lou Soriano, Matty Pecora, and Jo Jo Delio. (Brooklyn Public Library Photo)

Dodger games in Ebbets Field would not have been the same if the Sym-phony were not there to add their special brand of music to the festivities.

The Sym-phony which was formed in 1938, had a variety of humorous selections, designed to tickle the funnybone of most fans, although sometimes irritating to opposing players and umpires. They always welcomed the men in blue to each game with a lively rendition of "Three Blind Mice." After an enemy strikeout, the Symphony serenaded the opposing batter all the way back to the dugout, with a frisky tune called "The Worm Crawls In." Da-dum-da-dum, da-dum-da-dum, da-dum-dum-dum-dum-dum-dum-dum-dum, in cadence with the batter's shuffling gait. When the embarrassed batter finally sat down on the bench, the big bass drum would sound to end the refrain.

Another favorite musician in Dodger-land was Gladys Goodding, who sang and accompanied herself on the organ. Miss Goodding, a native of Macon, Georgia, was well known around the New York area. A city resident since the 1920s, Gladys had played the organ in theatres at silent movies, as well as at Ranger hockey games and Knickerbocker basketball games in Madison Square Garden. In addition to playing the "Star Spangled Banner" prior to every Brooklyn home game, Goodding livened the seventh-inning stretch with some snappy foot-stomping music. She also entertained individual Dodger players with their favorite tunes.

Ebbets Field had its share of characters over the

Happy Felton enjoyed a long career in show business, hosting radio shows, appearing in movies, and performing on the Broadway stage. But he is best remembered as the leader of the Dodgers' Knot Hole Gang. (Brooklyn Public Library)

years, but none was more colorful than public address announcer Tex Rickard. In his early days, Rickard sat on a chair next to the Dodger dugout. When information had to be passed on to the crowd, Rickard would walk the field, from one end of the grandstand to the other, screaming his garbled news through a megaphone. Later, when he had the use of a microphone, his malapropisms gained widespread attention. Who can forget the time a child was separated from his parents? In Rickard's vernacular, the announcement became, "A little boy has been found lost." To a group of fans who had placed their coats over the grandstand railing, Rickard proclaimed, "Will the fans along the railing in left field, please remove their clothes."

Happy Felton, a 280-pound show business veteran, joined the Ebbets Field gang in 1950 to host a television show for youngsters on the Dodger pre-game broadcasts. The "Knot Hole Gang" show was shot in an area near the Dodger bullpen down the right-field line. It featured three youngsters, often little leaguers, their coach, and a Dodger player. The Dodger player put the boys through a simple competition, usually fielding drills. The kids got equipment as prizes, and the winner came back the following day to talk to his favorite Dodger player. The show was a big hit with the kids, who got to meet their heroes in person.

Walter Lanier Barber, the Old Redhead, was a living legend in Brooklyn. In the minds of many Dodger fans, Red Barber *was* the Dodgers. The erudite sportscaster, a Brooklyn fixture for 18 years, brought the game up close to thousands of people within receiving distance of his

An irate Dodger fan attacks umpire George Magerkurth in Ebbets Field after a questionable call.

voice. He introduced the first play-by-play radio broadcasts to the inhabitants of Brooklyn in the mid-thirties, later expanding into television–but it was radio that cast the magic spell. The pictures of the games flowing from the imaginations of the listeners were planted there by the vivid vocabulary of the young man from Florida.

Barber's down-home colloquialisms brought smiles to the faces of the Brooklyn faithful, and soon became part of the everyday Flatbush vocabulary. Some of the more colorful Barber-isms have become part of American lore.

- "They're tearin' up the pea patch," meant a big rally was underway.
- Being "In the catbird seat," was a sign that our team was way ahead.
- "A rhubarb on the field" identified a heated argument in progress.
- An "Old Goldie" named after one of the radio sponsors, Old Gold cigarettes, was a home run.
- When the bases were FOB, they were "Full of Brooklyns", or "Full of Bums."

Red Barber brought the game of baseball to life for fans all over the Brooklyn area, creating new fans every day. His colorful descriptions of the game have never been duplicated. He was an irreplaceable part of the Dodger myth.

Even the advertising was famous in Ebbets Field. Abe Stark, a Brooklyn clothier, had a sign at the base of the outfield wall, below the right field scoreboard, pushing his wares. It read, "Hit the sign, win a suit." With Snider and Furillo patrolling the outfield on either side of Abe's sign, it is doubtful if many suits were ever given away by the crafty haberdasher. The sign did make Abe Stark famous however. He eventually entered politics, first as President of the city council, then as Brooklyn Borough President.

Ebbets Field is gone now, and the demographics of Brooklyn have changed drastically over the past 36 years. The old times can never be recaptured. The Daffyness Boys, the Sym-phony, Hilda Chester, Tex Rickard, and Red Barber are only memories.

Ah, but what memories. In what other park could you see a sparrow fly out from under a batter's hat? Where else but Ebbets Field could you see three base runners on third base–all at the same time? Or see a disgruntled fan jump from the grandstand and pummel an umpire because he disagreed with the call?

Brooklyn was unique as a major league franchise. Its like will never be seen again. Perhaps the spirit of the community can best be expressed by an old newspaper cartoon. The cartoon, printed in 1947, showed a man slumped over a saloon bar, drinking heavily, and confessing his problems to the bartender. "What a day this has been. I lost my wallet. I lost my job. My wife left me. And the Dodgers lost to the Phillies. It's unbelievable, leading by three in the eighth and they lost to the Phillies."

1945–BROOKLYN DODGERS SIGN A BLACK BASEBALL PLAYER

The National Association of Professional Baseball Players, the first professional baseball league in America, was formed in 1871. Five years later, it was succeeded by The National Baseball League of Professional Baseball Clubs. In 1884, the National League was joined by a second major league, the American Association. One of the Association entries, the Toledo Blue Stockings, had a black catcher, Moses Fleetwood Walker. The bigots in baseball circles, of which there were many, created such an uproar during the season that the owners committee passed an unwritten law barring blacks from playing in the majors. The ban eventually extended to all of organized ball.

The exclusion of blacks from professional baseball lasted for almost 60 years. Finally, in 1945, after Happy Chandler was chosen to succeed Kenesaw Mountain Landis as Commissioner of Baseball, the mood changed. Chandler, a Southerner, supported the rights of blacks to play organized baseball, a platform that prompted Brooklyn Dodger General Manager, Branch Rickey to begin his search for the right man to break the color barrier.

The first black baseball player had to be a very special person. He had to be a man of consummate professional ability, but he also had to be a man who led an exemplary personal life, as well. Rickey knew that the racists in professional baseball would do everything in their power to discredit the black pioneer. They would attempt to create incidents on the playing field, hoping to get the black player expelled from the game. Additionally, they would scrutinize the player's personal life in minute detail to uncover any evidence of legal, ethical, or moral corruption. The man to carry the torch had to be above reproach.

Branch Rickey (Los Angeles Dodger Photo)

Jackie Robinson played one year in the Negro American League before joining the Brooklyn Dodger organization. He batted a hefty .387 for the Kansas City Monarchs. His teammates included future major leaguers Satchel Paige and Hank Thompson. (Larry Fritsch Cards)

Rickey's top scouts fanned out across the country, evaluating every black player in every black league from L.A. to Birmingham. Hundreds of reports flooded back into the Dodger corporate offices on Montague Street, discussing players like Satchel Paige, Josh Gibson, Roy Campanella, and Larry Doby. But the name most often mentioned was that of a 26-year-old Californian named Jack Roosevelt Robinson, a shortstop with the Kansas City Monarchs of the Negro American League. After months of sifting through all the data and carefully studying the personnel evaluations, Rickey was convinced that the All-American from UCLA was his man. He immediately sent his chief scout, Clyde Sukeforth, to Chicago to view the shortstop in action one more time. If Sukeforth liked what he saw, he was to invite the Monarch infielder to Brooklyn, ostensibly to interview for a position on the Brooklyn Brown Dodgers, a black baseball team supported by the Brooklyn organization.

Robinson arrived in Brooklyn on August 28, 1945, and met face to face with Branch Rickey. The historic meeting turned out to be an interview for a job with the Brooklyn Dodgers themselves, not the Brown Dodgers. The meeting was long and, occasionally heated. Rickey left no stone unturned to make sure that Robinson fully realized the difficult task that lay before him, should he accept the offer. At one point, the 63-year-old Mahatma, playing the part of a rival player, stuck his face close to Jackie's, and hurled the most vicious insults at his defenseless visitor. He cast dispersions on Robinson's race, his family, and his intelligence. He simulated on-field incidents where Robinson would be physically accosted, warning the 26-year-old that he could never retaliate, no matter what the provocation.

Finally, completely frustrated, Robinson pleaded with his tormenter, "Mr. Rickey. Do you want a player who's afraid to fight back?" Rickey exploded. "I want a player with guts enough not to fight back. You've got to win this battle with base hits and stolen bases."

Before the day was done, Jackie Robinson accepted the challenge. He agreed to play baseball with the Montreal Royals, the Dodgers' top minor-league affiliate, in 1946. The meeting was kept confidential for two months to give Jackie time to discuss the proposal with his mother and his girlfriend, and to give Rickey time to make all the necessary arrangements within the Brooklyn organization.

On October 23, 1945, the Montreal Royals called a news conference at their stadium to announce the signing of Jackie Robinson to a professional baseball contract. It was the major sports story of the year, perhaps the century.

The first step had been taken to recognize racial equality in professional baseball. It was a monumental event, the combined effort of three genuine heroes, Albert B. "Happy" Chandler, Branch Rickey, and Jack Roosevelt Robinson.

But the biggest hero of them all was Jackie Robinson.

1946—JACKIE ROBINSON'S FIRST GAME WITH MONTREAL

The hot stove league sizzled with the Jackie Robinson story all through the winter of 1945-46. The question of whether or not the Negro infielder could make the big time was the subject of many heated debates. For some people, it was a source of hope. For others, it was a threat to a racist life-style.

The discussions and arguments continued on into the spring. When the soft-spoken Robinson struggled through a mediocre spring training, the bigots smiled knowingly, "I told you so." It was a difficult six weeks for Jackie. The tension in the Royals training camp was almost unbearable, the loneliness depressing. No one on the team spoke to Robinson or to John Wright, a black pitcher Rickey signed to room with Jackie. Opponents addressed the pair only to taunt them with personal attacks.

Slowly, however, the 27-year-old Californian began to find his rhythm, both at the plate and in the field. Emotionally, he adjusted to his new mission, and he was prepared for the tortuous trials that lay ahead. By opening day, Robinson was ready to run the gauntlet. Physically and mentally he was focused.

Thursday, April 18, 1946, opening day in the International League, saw the Montreal Royals visiting the Jersey City Giants. The atmosphere around Roosevelt Stadium was charged with excitement as mobs of sportswriters descended on the ballpark from every major newspaper in the country. Opening day in Jersey City was a major news event in 1946. It was the first time in the twentieth century that a black man would play alongside white players in a professional baseball game. America nervously awaited the outcome.

Jackie Robinson played shortstop in the Negro American League. When he joined Montreal, he was converted into a second baseman.

A capacity throng of 25,000 patrons packed Roosevelt Stadium to witness the historic event. All eyes were focused on one man, a UCLA graduate, a four-sport star in college, a second lieutenant in the Army Air Force, a shortstop with the Kansas City Monarchs, and the Montreal Royals' new black second baseman, Jack Roosevelt Robinson.

The game started slowly with both teams going scoreless in the first inning. Robinson, batting second for the Royals, took the first five pitches, then grounded weakly to shortstop, in his first at bat. Montreal broke the ice the second time around, scoring two runs off Giants' starter, Warren Sandell. In the top of the third, with the score still 2-0, Clay Hopper's men put two men on base for Robinson, with no one out. Sandell, a southpaw, expecting a bunt, threw Jackie a letter-high fastball. Manager Clay Hopper had the Negro second baseman swinging away however, and the 230-pound slugger drove the ball over the 340-foot sign in left field for a three-run home run. It was as if a dam had burst. Roosevelt Stadium exploded with a roar that shook the old park to its foundations. The elated Robinson bounced around the bases, grinning from ear to ear and, when he crossed the plate, he was warmly greeted by his teammates. Suddenly color was no longer important in the Montreal dugout. The cloud that had enveloped the Canadian team for two months suddenly vanished. Now, it was only skill that counted. And the entire Montreal team realized that Robinson might possess the skills necessary to carry the team to a league championship.

His next time up, the mercurial second sacker beat out a bunt, then quickly stole second. After reaching third, he so unnerved the pitcher with his dancing lead that he was balked home. In the seventh, he singled to right field and later scored on a single by Spider Jorgensen. Then,

in his last at bat in the eighth, he beat out another bunt, and eventually scored on another balk.

When the smoke had cleared from the opening day fireworks, the Montreal Royals were easy winners over the Jersey City Giants, 14-1. Jackie Robinson was the batting star of the game, going four for five, with a home run, two stolen bases, four RBIs and four runs scored.

It was an omen of things to come. Montreal, sparked by their fiery second baseman, went on to win the International League championship by a whopping 19 1/2 games, then defeated the Louisville Colonels of the American Association in the Little World Series. Jackie Robinson led the International League in batting with an average of .349, and in runs scored with 113. He finished second in stolen bases with 40.

He was named the Most Valuable Player in the International League for 1946.

MONTREAL

NAME	POS	AB	R	H	E
Rackley	CF	5	2	1	0
Robinson	2B	5	4	4	1
Shuba	LF	4	1	0	0
Tatum	1B	5	2	3	0
Durrett	RF	5	2	2	0
Jorgensen	3B	5	1	2	1
Franks	C	3	0	0	0
Beard	SS	5	1	3	1
De Forge	P	2	1	0	0
Total		39	14	15	3

JERSEY CITY

NAME	POS	AB	R	H	E
Alm'dro		4	0	0	0
Roy		3	1	0	0
Thomson		4	0	2	0
Jaeger		4	0	1	0
Knickerbocker		4	0	1	0
Miggins		4	0	2	0
Wein		4	0	0	0
Bo'Knight		4	0	1	0
Sandell	P	1	0	1	0
Oates		1	0	0	0
Harpeeder	PH	1	0	0	0
Andrews		0	0	0	0
Kobesky	PH	1	0	0	0
Total		35	1	8	0

MONTREAL ROYALS	0 2 4 0 1 0 3 3 1 -	14 - 15 - 3
JERSEY CITY GIANTS	0 0 0 0 1 0 0 0 0 -	1 - 8 - 0

Jackie Robinson not only had to face all the racial tensions associated with his promotion to the Brooklyn team. He also had to learn a new position - first base - because Eddie Stanky held down second base, and the Dodgers needed a first baseman.

1947—JACKIE ROBINSON JOINS THE BROOKLYN DODGERS

Jackie Robinson's spectacular season in Montreal led to a busy rumor mill over the winter. Everyone was trying to guess whether or not Jackie would be moved up to the Brooklyn Dodgers in 1947. When spring training started, the young negro infielder was in the Montreal training camp in Cuba, but he was wearing a first baseman's glove, causing the rumor mill to heat up again.

The situation in the Brooklyn training camp in Havana, Cuba, in February 1947 was tense, yet exciting at the same time. Everywhere there was a beehive of activity; dozens of interviews by sportswriters looking for an exclusive; secret meetings between Dodger players; and strategy sessions between General Manager Branch Rickey and his lieutenants. In a little out-of-the-way hotel near the Montreal camp, Robinson and three other black players, Roy Partlow, Roy Campanella, and Don Newcombe, spent quiet evenings alone, contemplating the historical forces that were swirling uncontrollably all around them.

During a trip to Panama for exhibition games, several of the Dodger players, led by pitcher Kirby Higbe and outfielder Dixie Walker circulated a petition to bar Robinson from playing in Brooklyn. Dodger manager, Leo Durocher, learning of the maneuver, took swift action. He held a closed-door meeting with the instigators, and told them in no uncertain terms that they were wasting their time. Robinson would play in Brooklyn if his

Ben Chapman's Philadelphia Phillies made Jackie Robinson's life miserable during his rookie season. Crude comments, beanballs, and flashing spikes became a way of life for the black trailblazer.

skills merited it. He also told them that if they didn't like it, they could quit.

Branch Rickey had already decided that Jackie would play for the Brooklyn Dodgers in 1947, but he didn't want to put too much pressure on the young man too early, so he had him train with the Montreal squad during the spring. As opening day approached, the Dodgers played seven exhibition games with their top farm club. It was then that Rickey made his move.

Meeting with Robinson, he told the budding superstar, "Alright, Jackie, this is your time. I want you to go out there and dazzle these people. Hit, steal, drive them crazy. I want them to see the greatest player in baseball today. When the press gets finished sending their stories back to their papers, there will be such a demand for you, that I will be forced to promote you to the Dodgers."

Jackie Robinson responded to the challenge brilliantly. The black infielder smashed the ball at a .625 clip and stole seven bases in seven games.

The die was cast. On April 10, six days before the opening of the National League season, the Brooklyn Dodgers announced the promotion of Jackie Robinson to the big club. Ironically, on the same day, baseball commissioner Happy Chandler suspended Dodger manager Leo Durocher from baseball for one year, for keeping company with known gamblers.

Jackie's new manager, kindly old Burt Shotton, put him on first base for the opener against the Boston Braves, and had him batting second in the batting order, behind little Eddie Stanky. The most historic day in modern major league history was Tuesday, April 15, 1947.

It was a cold, dreary day in Brooklyn, but 26,623 excited fans, including more than 14,000 blacks, turned out to see the new major leaguer in person. The 14th Regiment Band was on hand to play the National Anthem. Everett McCooey sang. And borough president John Cashmore threw out the first ball. The Dodger Sym-phony carried a sign that read "Open the door, Chandler, and Let Our Leo In."

It was a glorious day for the Brooklyn franchise, but a disappointing day, personally, for Jackie Robinson. The rookie infielder went to the plate four times without the semblance of a base hit, but his team still came home a 5-3 winner.

In the first inning, number 42 was out on a routine grounder to third baseman Bob Elliott. In the third, he flied out to Johnny Litwhiler in left field and, in the fifth, he killed a Dodger rally by hitting into a double play. Actually the double play ball was a shot back through the middle that had "hit" written all over it, but Boston shortstop Dick Culler made a dazzling diving stop, and turned it into two quick outs. In the seventh inning, with the Braves clinging to a slim 3-2 lead, Eddie Stanky opened with his specialty, a base on balls. Robinson, up to sacrifice, reached base safely when Earl Torgeson made a wild throw to second. Moments later, the Dodger first-sacker carried home what proved to be, the winning run on a double off the right-field screen by Pete Reiser. "Pistol Pete's" blow came off Johnny Sain, the ace of manager Billy Southworth's staff. Eventually he scored the third run of the inning on a sacrifice fly by Gene Hermanski.

The early part of the season was not kind to Jackie Robinson. After getting his first hit two days later, a fifth-inning bunt against the Braves, Robby went on a painful 0-20 trip. He finally got hot in May, however, and by late June he was over the .300 mark.

The Dodgers went on to win the National League pennant by five games over the St. Louis Cardinals, and Jackie Robinson was a big part of the story. In addition to hitting a solid .297, the fleet infielder led the league in stolen bases with 29. He also hit 12 home runs, batted in 48 from the number-two spot in the batting order, and scored 125 runs himself, second in the league.

In appreciation of his outstanding achievements during the year, Jackie Robinson was voted the National League's Rookie of the Year.

BOSTON

NAME	POS	AB	R	H	E
Culler	SS	3	0	0	0
Holmes	PH	1	0	0	0
Sisti	SS	0	0	0	0
Hopp	CF	5	0	1	0
McCormick	RF	4	0	3	0
Elliott	3B	2	0	1	0
Litwhiler	LF	3	1	0	0
Rowell	LF	1	0	0	0
Torgeson	1B	4	1	0	1
Masi	C	3	0	0	0
Ryan	2B	4	1	3	0
Sain	P	1	0	0	0
Cooper	P	0	0	0	0
Neil	PH	0	0	0	0
Lanfranconi	P	0	0	0	0
Total		31	3	8	1

BROOKLYN

NAME	POS	AB	R	H	E
Stanky	2B	3	1	0	0
Robinson	1B	3	1	0	0
Schultz	1B	0	0	0	0
Reiser	CF	2	3	2	0
Walker	RF	3	0	1	0
Tatum	RF	0	0	0	0
Vaughan	PH	1	0	0	0
Furillo	RF	0	0	0	0
Hermanski	LF	4	0	1	0
Edwards	C	2	0	0	1
Rackley	PH	0	0	0	0
Bragan	C	1	0	0	0
Jorgensen	3B	3	0	0	0
Reese	SS	3	0	1	0
Hatten	P	2	0	1	0
Stevens	PH	1	0	0	0
Gregg	P	1	0	0	0
Casey	P	0	0	0	0
Total		29	5	6	1

BOSTON BRAVES   000 012 000 - 3 - 8 - 1
BROOKLYN DODGERS 000 101 30X - 5 - 6 - 1

WP - Hatten
LP - Sain

1948—DODGERTOWN OPENS

During their first 50 years in the National League, the Brooklyn Dodgers were baseball nomads, moving their spring training camp all over the western hemisphere, from Florida to Cuba to The Dominican Republic, and even to Bear Mountain, New York, during World War II.

When Branch Rickey assumed control of the Brooklyn franchise, he brought with him a master plan to create a new baseball dynasty within the Senior Circuit. A key ingredient of the plan was the existence of a vast training complex where all members of the Brooklyn Dodger organization, major leaguer and minor leaguer

The modern Dodgertown has tree-lined streets, and 90 comfortable, air-conditioned villas. (W. McNeil)

Holman Stadium, seating over 6,000 fans, has seen some of the greatest baseball players ever to walk on a ballfield–from Jackie Robinson, to Sandy Koufax, to Mike Piazza. (W. McNeil)

alike, could train together during spring training. Rickey believed it was essential for the success of his plan to have the minor league ballplayers room with, work out with, and live with, their varsity counterparts. He felt this would eliminate the intimidation factor that exists when a minor leaguer is in the presence of a major leaguer. He also thought the major leaguers would be good role models for their minor league brethren, who would subsequently develop strong baseball fundamentals from the experience.

Bud Holman, a Vero Beach businessman, helped make Rickey's dream a reality. When World War II ended, the United States Navy turned their Naval Air Station over to the city for whatever use the city wanted to make of it. All the city had to do was maintain the facility.

Holman, aware of the fact that the Brooklyn Dodgers had no permanent home, contacted Branch Rickey late in the fall of 1947. The Dodger president immediately dispatched Buzzie Bavasi to Florida to scout the potential training site. The Brooklyn official found a peaceful little town of 3,000 residents situated on the east coast of Florida, just north of Ft. Pierce, in an area known as the graveyard of ships. The black, turbulent waters off Vero, ominous at times, had dragged countless vessels onto the rocks over the years, including many treasure-laden galleons from the old pirate days.

The Naval Air facility, located just north of Vero Beach off route 60, consisted of two large, weather-beaten barracks, several secondary buildings, and hundreds of acres of prime Florida real estate. It was an ideal location for a large, expansive baseball facility. Rickey shrewdly picked up a 20-year-lease on the property for one dollar a year, and began to fit all the pieces of his baseball puzzle together.

Club engineers from New York laid out the first Brooklyn training complex. It consisted of four playing fields, batting cages, run-down areas, and sliding pits, in addition to the existing ramshackled living quarters. When the camp opened, in the spring of 1948, over 450 Brooklyn Dodger farmhands descended on Vero Beach, immediately increasing the local population by more than 20%. On March 31, 1948, prior to a spring training game between the Dodgers and their Montreal farm team, the facility was officially dedicated. Brooklyn president Branch Rickey gave the keynote address to 6,000 attendees, and Vero Beach mayor, Merrill Barber, in welcoming the organization to the city, christened the site, "Dodgertown."

The early years in Vero Beach were adventures in primitive survival. The Barracks rooms were small and uncomfortable; the floors were cold, the roof leaked, the communal toilet facilities were crude, and the alligators were unfriendly. But the food was good, and the baseball facilities were outstanding.

Over the years, the physical appearance of Dodgertown changed drastically. In 1953, a 6,000 seat concrete stadium was constructed. It was named Holman Stadium, after the Vero Beach businessman whose imagination fueled a dream. In the 1970s, the old barracks were finally torn down and 90 spanking-new air conditioned villas were constructed in their place. A modern 23,000-square foot administration building was erected to house major and minor league clubhouse facilities, trainers rooms, equipment rooms, press corps area, photo studios, the stadium lounge, a cafeteria, and a complete conference center. Paved roads popped up around the complex, first with names like Rickey Boulevard and Durocher Trail; later with identities like Sandy Koufax Lane, Jackie Robinson Drive, and Roy Campanella Drive.

Dodgertown expanded to a whopping 425 acres over the years. Recreational facilities were added to help the young players occupy their off-field time. These included a swimming pool, several tennis courts, and the Dodger Pines Country Club, complete with an 18-hole golf course. Naturally, friendly card sharks and pool hustlers could always find willing challengers in the lounge.

Today, the sleepy little town of Vero Beach has grown to a bustling community of more than 20,000 inhabitants. Dodgertown continues to be the envy of major league baseball, for its all-encompassing baseball programs. When the players leave Vero in the spring and make their way to their permanent summer addresses, Holman stadium becomes the summer home of the Vero Beach Dodgers, of the Class A Florida State League.

Even when the baseball season winds down, Dodgertown is alive with activity. Professional football teams have used the complex for their pre-season training camp. And major corporations reserve the conference center facilities during the winter to conduct marketing seminars for their professional staff.

1950–DUKE SNIDER HITS THREE HOME RUNS

Tuesday, May 30, 1950, was a gray overcast day in Brooklyn, with the temperature approaching the 77-degree mark. A morning-afternoon doubleheader in Ebbets Field pitted the beloved Dodgers against Eddie Sawyer's Philadelphia Phillies. As the Memorial Day festivities got underway, Brooklyn's defending National League champions held a slim one-game lead over the second-place St. Louis Cardinals, and a one-and-a-half game lead over the young upstart "Whiz Kids" from the City of Brotherly Love.

Duke Snider "arrived" as a major league slugger in 1950. He batted .321 with 31 home runs and 107 runs batted in. He also led the league in base hits with 199.

The Dodgers prevailed in the morning game, 7-6, behind Preacher Roe. Campy and Robinson homered. The Duke of Flatbush drew the collar in five trips to the plate. The afternoon game drew a full house of 34,700 noisy holiday celebrants. Brooklyn righthander Jack Banta faced the Phillies "Mad Monk," Russ Meyer. Snider got the Dodgers off and running in the first inning with a long home run over the right-field screen. After the two teams traded runs in the second and third, the Duke put the hurt on Meyer again, driving another ball over the right-field fence, onto Bedford Avenue.

Two Brooklyn runs in the fourth and a brace of Philly runs in the top of the fifth made the count 5-3. When "The Silver Fox" stepped to the plate for the third time, friendly Russ Meyer was long gone, and righthander Blix Donnely was serving them up for the Sawyer-men, but it didn't make any difference to the Duke. He picked out a fat pitch and sent it on a long arc to left center field. It fell untouched into the left center field stands for Snider's third consecutive home run. After each homer, the 23-year-old slugger regaled his teammates in the first-base dugout with play by play descriptions of his prodigious wallops.

The Dodgers were still leading 6-4 in the bottom of the seventh, when the Duke came up for his fourth at bat, against journeyman reliever Bob Miller. Snider wasted no time, jumping on the righthander's first delivery and hitting a vicious line drive to right field. The ball reached the right-field wall in a flash, hitting the screen one foot from the top. It was hit with such force that Dick Whitman's quick recovery and throw-in held the speedy Snider to a single.

Since the winning Dodgers didn't bat in the last of the ninth, the Duke had only four chances to tie the record. He didn't quite make it, falling twelve inches short.

PHILADELPHIA

NAME	POS	AB	R	H	E
Ashburn	CF	3	1	0	0
Hamner	SS	4	0	1	1
Waitkus	1B	5	1	3	0
Jones	3B	4	1	1	0
Sisler	LF	4	1	1	0
Whitman	RF	5	0	3	0
Goliat	2B	3	0	0	0
Seminick	C	3	0	0	0
Meyer	P	1	0	0	0
Ennis	PH	1	0	0	0
Church	PR	0	0	0	0
Donnely	P	0	0	0	0
Bloodworth	PH	1	0	0	0
Miller	P	0	0	0	0
Lopata	PH	1	0	0	0

Roy Campanella was the major league's premier receiver for ten years. In addition to being one of the greatest defensive catchers ever to play the game, he was also a powerful hitter, averaging 32 home runs for every 550 at bats.

Total   35 4 9 1

BROOKLYN

NAME	POS	AB	R	H	E
Cox	SS	5	0	0	1
Hermanski	LF	4	0	0	0
Snider	CF	4	3	4	0
Robinson	2B	2	0	0	0
Furillo	RF	4	0	1	0
Hodges	1B	4	1	2	0
Morgan	3B	2	1	0	0
Campanella	C	2	1	1	0
Banta	P	3	0	1	0
Branca	P	1	0	0	0
Total		31	6	9	1

PHILADELPHIA PHILLIES 0 0 1 0 2 0 0 1 0 - 4 - 9 - 1
BROOKLYN DODGERS   1 1 1 2 1 0 0 0 X - 6 - 9 - 1

DOUBLES - Hodges (2)
HOME RUNS - Snider (3)
WP - Banta
LP - Meyer

1950—ROY CAMPANELLA HITS THREE HOME RUNS

The Brooklyn Dodgers were engaged in a tough battle with the "Whiz Kids" of Philadelphia as they attempted to capture their second consecutive National League pennant. As August neared an end, Burt Shotton's boys were four games behind the surging Phils who had played at nine games over the .500 mark during the previous month.

The Dodgers caught fire midway through August, and were in the midst of a nine-game winning streak themselves, as they wrapped up a series against the seventh-place Reds in Cincinnati. It was a Saturday afternoon game, and the weather was hot and sticky, with the mercury hitting the 87-degree mark. It was the kind of weather Roy Campanella loved to hit in.

Twenty-two-year-old Erv Palica, Brooklyn's number-three starter, took the hill against the cagy veteran, Ken Raffensberger. The kid righty, nursing a sore elbow, was nicked for two runs in the first on two singles, a hit batter, and a sacrifice fly by Ted Kluszewski. Then Roy Campanella took over. After Gil Hodges drew a base on balls in the second inning, the roly-poly backstop creamed a two-strike pitch from the Cincinnati southpaw, bouncing a home run off the roof of the laundry behind the left-field fence. It was a low pitch, the kind Campy liked, and he went down a got it with his powerful stroke, lifting the ball in a high arc over the left-field wall.

In the fourth, with the Reds on top again, 4-2, thanks to Red Stallcup's two-run homer, Hodges beat out a bunt single, and Campy blasted another shot to left, this one clearing the laundry roof, to tie the game. Two innings later, with two men on and two out, he drew a full-count walk, as 10,342 Cincinnati fans breathed a sigh of relief.

Palica and Raffensberger were still pitching as the eighth inning rolled around. Gil Hodges singled ahead of Campanella, and the Dodger slugger did it again. He hit the first pitch from Raffensberger over the 18-foot fence in left field, bouncing it off the wall of the laundry, for home run number three. The blow gave the Dodgers a 6-4 lead. They extended it to 7-4 minutes later on an error, a sacrifice, and a single by Pee Wee Reese.

Cincinnati got one back in the bottom of the eighth on a single by big Klu and a double by Joe Adcock. In the bottom of the ninth, Palica ran out of gas, walking Grady Hatton and yielding a two-out single to Kluszewski. Ralph Branca came in from the bullpen to close the door on one pitch, an infield fly by Connie Ryan.

The three home runs gave Campanella 27 for the season, ten behind Gabby Hartnett's all-time home run mark for catchers.

Campy finished the season with 31 homers and 89 RBIs on a .281 batting average. He broke Hartnett's record three years later when he deposited 42 balls over various walls around the National League, en route to his second MVP season.

BROOKLYN

NAME	POS	AB	R	H	E
Reese	SS	5	0	1	0
Russell	LF	2	0	0	0
Abrams	LF	0	0	0	0
Brown	PH	1	0	0	0
Hermanski	LF	1	0	0	0
Snider	CF	4	0	1	0
Robinson	2B	4	0	1	0
Furillo	RF	5	0	1	0
Hodges	1B	4	3	2	0
Campanella	C	3	3	3	0
Morgan	3B	4	1	0	0
Palica	P	3	0	1	0
Branca	P	0	0	0	0
Total		36	7	10	0

CINCINNATI

NAME	POS	AB	R	H	E
Merriman	CF	5	1	2	0
Hatton	3B	3	1	1	0
Wyrostek	RF	5	0	1	0
Kluszewski	1B	4	0	2	1
Ryan	2B	5	0	0	0
Adcock	LF	4	1	1	1

Pramesa	C	4	1	4	0
Adams	PH	0	0	0	0
Howell	C	0	0	0	0
Stallcup	SS	4	1	2	0
Raffensberger	P	3	0	0	0
Litwhiler	PH	1	0	0	0
Erautt	P	0	0	0	0
Total		38	5	13	2

BROOKLYN DODGERS 0 2 0 2 0 0 0 3 0 - 7 - 10 - 0
CINCINNATI REDS   2 2 0 0 0 0 0 1 0 - 5 - 13 - 2

WP - Palica (8-4)
LP - Raffensberger (12-15)

1950—BIG GIL HODGES BLASTS FOUR HOME RUNS IN ONE GAME

Just five days after Campanella hit his three home runs in one game, teammate Gil Hodges went him one better. In a game against the Boston Braves, the Dodger strongman put four balls into orbit, tying the major league

Gil Hodges hit a total of 370 home runs during a distinguished 18-year major league career.

record. With Duke Snider having sent three balls out of the park on May 30, the Dodgers became the first team in major league history to have three players hit three or more home runs in a game in a single season.

Brooklyn, still trying to catch the Phils, found themselves six games out with only 35 games to play. The third-place Braves of Billy Southworth moved into Ebbets Field for a weekend series with Burt Shotton's crew. The Big Blue Machine had a fearsome offensive attack, averaging 5.5 runs per game, one full run per game more than the next best team. They were leading the league in runs, home runs, batting average, slugging average, stolen bases, fielding average, double plays, and fewest errors. Individually, Jackie Robinson was third in the league in hitting, with an average of .330, while Carl Furillo was fifth, at .323. On the power side, Roy Campanella was third in the league in home runs with 28, followed by Duke Snider with 23 and Gil Hodges with 19.

Carl Erskine, hampered by arm problems, started for the Dodgers. He was opposed by Warren Spahn, ace of the Boston staff. The smooth-working Spahn led the National League with 21 victories in 1949, and was about to repeat in 1950. Against Brooklyn however, the future Hall of Famer was not as successful. The Boys of Summer usually feasted on his southpaw slants. Coming into this game, Spahn's lifetime record against Brooklyn stood at 10-13.

Gil Hodges faced the high-kicking lefty in the bottom of the second inning with Carl Furillo on first and the Braves in front, 1-0, thanks to a Sid Gordon home run. The big right-handed slugger promptly gave his team the lead for good with a two-run shot into the left-field seats. In the third, Spahn was driven to cover before he could retire a single batter. Duke Snider got the ball rolling with his 24th homer, a high-towering drive over the scoreboard in right center field. The blow extended Snider's hitting streak to 18 games. Later in the Dodgers' seven-run inning, Hodges came up with two men on base. He laid into a Normie Roy curveball and sent it screaming into the left-field stands.

In the next inning, the big first-sacker was retired on a ground ball, 5-3. Things stayed quiet for a couple of innings, with the Dodgers still holding a comfortable 10-1 lead in the bottom of the sixth. With Carl Furillo on base, Hodges took a Bob Hall pitch down town, dropping it in the lower left field stands, running the count to 14-1.

Shotton's boys could do nothing wrong in this game. Hodges singled during a three-run seventh, giving him four for five for the day. The score mounted to 17-1.

Erskine eased up in the eighth, and the Braves pushed over two runs against the curveball artist. In the bottom of the same inning, Gil Hodges had one more chance to put his name in the record books. He didn't let it pass. For the fourth time in the game, Carl Furillo was on base when he came up. And for the fourth time in the game, big Gil brought him home. This time he put the ball into the upper left-field stands off left-hander Johnny Antonelli.

Hodges' fourth home run of the game tied a major league record first set way back in 1894 by little Bobby Lowe of the Boston Beaneaters. His 17 total bases also tied Lowe's record. Other players sharing a piece of the home run record included Ed Delahanty, Lou Gehrig, Chuck Klein, and Pat Seerey.

A small weekday night crowd of 14,226 Dodger rooters viewed the fireworks.

Hodges went on to finish the year with 32 home runs and 113 runs batted in, but the Dodgers could not catch the Phillies for the pennant. They made a gallant run at the end, making up nine games in the last two weeks but, in the end, they came up one inning short.

BOSTON

NAME	POS	AB	R	H	E
Hartfield	2B	5	0	1	3
Jethroe	CF	5	0	0	0
Torgeson	1B	4	1	1	0
Elliott	3B	3	0	1	0
Cooper	C	3	0	0	0
Crandall	C	1	1	0	1
Gordon	LF	4	1	3	0
Marshall	RF	4	0	2	0
Kerr	SS	3	0	0	0
Spahn	P	1	0	0	0
Roy	P	0	0	0	0
Haefner	P	0	0	0	0
Reiser	PH	1	0	0	0
Hall	P	0	0	0	0
Antonelli	P	1	0	0	0
Holmes	PH	1	0	0	0
Total		36	3	8	4

BROOKLYN

NAME	POS	AB	R	H	E
Brown	LF	4	0	1	0
Reese	SS	5	1	2	1
Snider	CF	5	1	1	0
Robinson	2B	5	1	1	0
Morgan	3B	0	0	0	0
Furillo	RF	5	4	2	0
Hodges	1B	6	5	5	0
Campanella	C	4	2	2	0
Edwards	C	1	1	1	0
Cox	3B	5	3	2	0
Erskine	P	5	1	4	0
Total		45	19	21	1

BOSTON BRAVES   0 1 0 0 0 0 0 2 0 - 3 - 8 - 4
BROOKLYN DODGERS 0 3 7 0 0 4 3 2 X - 19 - 21-1

DOUBLES —— Reese
HOME RUNS — Snider #24
                        Hodges (4), #23

WP — Erskine (2-3)
LP — Spahn (16-15)

1950–DON NEWCOMBE GUNS FOR IRON MAN TITLE

Wednesday, September 6, 1950, was a red-letter day in Brooklyn Dodger history. It was the day big Don Newcombe attempted to join the "Iron Man" club, whose last member was Doc Scanlon, back in 1905.

As the sun rose on the 6th, Burt Shotton's troops still trailed the pesky Phillies by 7 1/2 games. There were only 30 games left in the season, and time was running out. If the Dodgers were to make a move, it had to be soon.

Big Don Newcombe was a throwback to the old rough and tumble days of baseball, when players were tough and dedicated to the game. In addition to his iron man attempt, Newk pitched 32 innings over the last eight days of the 1951 season, as Brooklyn tried unsuccessfully to stave off the challenge of the New York Giants.

The Labor Day doubleheader in Philadelphia, pairing the mighty Dodgers against Eddie Sawyer's Kiddie Korps, created a lot of interest up and down the east coast. For the morning half of the twin bill, Shotton led with his ace, big Don Newcombe, his 16-game winner. Sawyer threw rookie righthander Bubba Church at the Flock. It turned out to be a classic pitchers' duel.

Brooklyn scored in the top of the first thanks to some early-game jitters on Church's part. The 25-year-old hurler walked both Reese and Hermanski with one out. A wild pitch advanced the runners to second and third, and Jackie Robinson's infield out brought Reese home with the first run of the game.

The score remained 1-0 through the seventh inning. Newcombe was spinning a masterpiece for Brooklyn, and Church was almost as good. In the Dodger eighth, Jackie Robinson singled, legged it all the way to third on Carl Furillo's sacrifice bunt, and carried home the second run of the game on Gil Hodges' long fly ball to Richie Ashburn in right center field.

Big Newk slammed the door on the Phils in the bottom of the ninth, finishing with a strong three-hitter, and a 2-0 shutout. He struck out two and walked only one in the two-hour, fifteen-minute gem. The victory cut Philadelphia's lead to 6 1/2 games.

Newcombe, with an easy game behind him, and realizing the many problems besetting the Dodger pitching staff, volunteered to start game two. Manager Burt Shotton quickly accepted the big guy's proposal.

Game Two was a toughie. Southpaw Curt Simmons, Sawyer's 21-year-old bonus baby, was on target all day. He shut down the big Blue Machine for eight long innings, and carried a 2-0 lead into the ninth. The Phils had nicked Newk for a tainted run in the first on a single by Ashburn and a pop fly double to right by Del Ennis. In the third, Eddie Waitkus tripled off the right-field wall when Furillo lost his footing, and came home on a sacrifice fly by Ashburn.

Things looked bleak for Shotton's boys as the ninth inning got underway. Newcombe's hope for glory had gone by the boards an inning earlier when Jim Russell batted for him. The big Dodger righty had thrown seven tough innings, allowing only two runs, both slightly tainted, on eight hits. He had struck out one and walked one in a fine effort.

In the Brooklyn ninth, Simmons walked Pee Wee Reese. When Tommy Brown singled to left, manager Eddie Sawyer quickly beckoned relief ace Jim Konstanty from the bullpen. Konstanty, who was to appear in a league-leading 74 games for the season, winning 16 games and saving another 22, couldn't stem the tide this time. Robinson smashed an infield hit off the pitcher's leg, loading the bases. Gil Hodges followed with a line drive single to left field. Reese and Brown scored and Robinson raced around to third. When "Puddinhead" Jones took the relay and tried to double Hodges rounding first, Robinson broke for home and slid across the plate with the winning run.

Righthander Dan Bankhead slammed the door on the Phillies in the bottom of the ninth, with his second shutout inning in relief.

Big Don Newcombe put forth a superhuman effort on this day, trying to ignite his team in their quest for another title. His effort succeeded, even if his attempt to become an Iron Man did not. The Dodgers won both games, cutting the Philadelphia lead to only 5 1/2 games. The pennant race remained nip and tuck the rest of the way—right up to the final pitch.

Newcombe's totals for the day showed:

GAMES	2
INNINGS PITCHED	16
RUNS ALLOWED	2
HITS ALLOWED	11
BASES ON BALLS	2
STRIKEOUTS	3

GAME ONE:

BROOKLYN DODGERS	1 0 0 0 0 0 0 1 0 - 2 - 6 - 0
PHILADELPHIA PHILLIES	0 0 0 0 0 0 0 0 0 - 0 - 3 - 0

WP - Newcombe (17-8)
LP - Church (8-3)

GAME TWO:

BROOKLYN DODGERS	0 0 0 0 0 0 0 0 3 - 3 - 4 - 1
PHILADELPHIA PHILLIES	1 0 1 0 0 0 0 0 0 - 2 - 8 - 1

WP - Bankhead (7-4)
LP - Konstanty (13-5)

1951—JACKIE ROBINSON SAVES THE DAY

The 1951 pennant race was one of the most thrilling pennant races in baseball history. The Brooklyn Dodgers, seemingly invincible, held a gigantic 13 1/2 game lead over the second-place New York Giants on August 12. Then, without notice, Leo Durocher's team began to come together as a unit. Imperceptibly at first, the Giants began to chip away at the Dodger lead. After winning three in a row, the New Yorker's swept a three-game series from the cocky Brooklynites, cutting the lead to ten. A short six weeks later, it was white-knuckle time.

A Dodger loss to the Phillies on the last Friday of the season dropped Chuck Dressen's crew into a flat-footed tie for the lead in the National League. The next day, Saturday, both teams won, with Don Newcombe blanking Robin Roberts and the Phils, 5-0.

The pennant race came down to the last day of the season, Sunday, September 30, 1951, with Brooklyn and New York deadlocked with 95 wins apiece. By the time the Dodgers took the field in Philadelphia, a near-capacity crowd of 31,755 frenzied fans packed little Shibe Park. Brooklyn starter Preacher Roe, possessor of a spectacular 22-3 record, was driven to cover in the second inning, under a four-run, five-hit barrage.

The Phils carried a 6-2 lead into the fifth, when the Dodgers bounced back with three runs. Jackie Robinson's triple to deep center field brought in one run, and the big

Jackie Robinson saved the pennant, at least temporarily, for the Dodgers, first with his glove, then with his bat. Historically, Jackie was the sparkplug that ignited the vaunted Dodgers' attack.

man scored another himself. Philadelphia got two of those runs back off Clyde King in the bottom of the inning, running the count to 8-5.

As the sixth inning got underway, things looked bleak for the Dressen-men. The scoreboard flashed a Giant victory, 3-2 over the Boston Braves and, with the Phils seemingly in command, the Flatbush faithful were sullen and subdued. The "Boys of Summer" were not subdued however. They came back one more time, pushing over three runs in the eighth to knot the count at eight all.

It was sudden death now, and both managers pulled out all the stops. Brooklyn had to win or their season was over. Philadelphia manager Eddie Sawyer was determined to derail the Dodger express. It was Robin Roberts and Don Newcombe face to face once again. The two adversaries had just pitched against each other less than 24 hours previous, but they were back at it one more time. They would have all winter to rest. Roberts hurled 6 2/3 innings of strong relief, while big Newk matched him with 5 2/3 tough innings of his own.

For awhile in the twelfth, it looked as if the Phils would scuttle the Dodger ship. They loaded the bases against a rapidly tiring Newcombe with two out. The next batter, Eddie Waitkus, smashed a low line drive back through the middle, ticketed for base-hit territory. Jackie Robinson, reacting instinctively, raced to his right and flung his body headlong over the second base bag. Miraculously, he speared the ball in the webbing of his glove and, even more miraculously, he held onto the ball as he crashed to earth in a heap. Reese, Furillo, Snider and Hodges all raced to their fallen hero, fearing a serious injury. Fortunately, the Dodger second sacker just had the wind knocked out of him, and he was able to continue in the game after a few minutes.

The tired Brooklyn crew struggled on. Newcombe was relieved by Bud Podbielan in the thirteenth, having pitched 14 2/3 innings in a 24-hour period. Roberts was still in the game as the fourteenth inning got underway. Philadelphia's 21-game winner retired both Reese and Snider easily. The next batter was Jackie Robinson. With a count of 1-1, Roberts threw the big right-handed slugger a curveball, and Jackie sent it screaming on a line into the left-field stands.

Chuck Dressen's crew prevailed 9-8 in 14 innings, pulling themselves back into a tie with the New York Giants as darkness descended over Shibe Park. They went on to lose the celebrated "Shot Heard Round The World" playoff, but they covered themselves with glory along the way.

Someone once said of Jackie Robinson, "If the game lasts long enough, Robinson will win it for you."

On this day, he won it several times.

BROOKLYN DODGERS   001 130 030 000 01 - 9 - 17 - 1
PHILADELPHIA PHILS 042 020 000 000 00 - 8 - 15 - 1

DOUBLES - Jones, Hamner, Pellagrini, Snider,

Walker, Campanella
TRIPLES - Reese, Campanella, Robinson
HOME RUNS - Robinson

WP - Podbielan (2-2)
LP - Roberts (21-15)

1952—THE DODGERS SCORE 15 RUNS IN ONE INNING

The Brooklyn Dodgers, after having lost the National League pennant to the New York Giants in 1951, were on a mission in 1952. They were determined to capture their rightful place at the top of the pack.

The first month of the '52 season was a dogfight, with no less than four teams battling for first place, and all eight teams in the league within five games of each other. The Dodgers were in a mild batting slump as May 21 arrived, but the sight of the hapless Cincinnati Reds visiting Ebbets Field cured all their ills. They jumped on Luke Sewell's team for 15 runs in the first inning, setting six major league records en route to a 19-1 romp.

Twenty-nine-year-old Ewell "The Whip" Blackwell, once the scourge of the National League with his buggywhip pitching motion, started on the mound for the Redlegs. The tall, skinny righthander had won a league-high 22 games in 1947 against only seven losses, before suffering arm problems. He managed to come back with two strong years in 1950 and '51, but now he was on the way down, washed up before the age of 30.

Blackwell's opponent was Chris Van Cuyk, a handsome 6'6", 215-pound southpaw. The 25-year-old flamethrower was fresh off a fine 11-4 season at Montreal, and was trying to claim a place in the Brooklyn starting rotation.

Van Cuyk retired the Reds in order in the top of the first, as the big Monday night crowd settled in for a pitchers' duel. Charlie Dressen's crew ended any thoughts of a low-scoring game almost immediately. After leadoff batter Billy Cox was retired on a nice defensive play by third baseman Bobby Adams, the Big Blue Machine put 19 consecutive batters on base.

Pee Wee Reese started the action by drawing a base on balls from Blackwell. Duke Snider followed with a high, towering home run over the scoreboard in right center field, and the Dodgers were off and running, 2-0. Jackie Robinson dropped a Texas league double into left. Andy Pafko walked. George "Shotgun" Shuba knocked in Robby with a single to right. That was all for Blackwell. Manager Sewell brought in Bud Byerly from the bullpen. "The Whips" record eventually totaled five runs on three hits and two bases on balls, in 1/3 of an inning.

Byerly fared no better, although Andy Pafko was cut down at third on the front end of a double steal, Dixie Howell to Bobby Adams. That was the only man the Cincinnati reliever retired. The next five Dodgers reached base. In rapid succession, Gil Hodges walked; Rube Walker singled to right, scoring Shuba; pitcher Chris Van Cuyk singled to left scoring, Hodges; Billy Cox singled to left scoring Walker; and Pee Wee Reese singled to left, driving in Van Cuyk. Out went Byerly, and in came reliever Herm Wehmeier.

Dodger rookie Chris Van Cuyk poses with four bats, representing his four base hits in the 19-1 shellacking of the Cincinnati Reds. Looking on are, L to R, manager Chuck Dressen, Bobby Morgan, and George "Shotgun" Shuba.

The journeyman righthander walked Snider to begin his journey into oblivion. Perhaps unsettled by the big Brooklyn onslaught in the first inning, he drove the next pitch into Robinson's ribs, forcing Cox home with the eighth run of the inning. The Dodger second sacker was the twelfth man in a row to reach base. With the bases loaded, Andy Pafko smashed a single to left, bringing in both Reese and Snider. Frank Smith got the call from the Cincinnati pen.

Like his two predecessors, Wehmeier and Byerly, Smith walked the first man he faced, "Shotgun" Shuba. He also walked Gil Hodges, forcing in Robinson with run number eleven. Rube Walker followed with a bad-bounce single over Grady Hatton's head at second, and both Pafko and Shuba trotted home. The Reds couldn't even get a lucky break in this inning. Chris Van Cuyk got his second hit of the inning, a one-base knock through the box, scoring Hodges. Billy Cox was hit by a pitch loading the bases for the fifth time. Reese walked forcing home Walker, before Snider mercifully ended the carnage by striking out.

Brooklyn's totals for the first inning showed 15 runs, 10 hits, seven bases on balls, two hit batters, and three men left on base. It was an inning to remember in Brooklyn Dodger history. Fifty-nine minutes of sheer ecstasy. Charlie Dressen's boys established six modern major league records in the process:

- Most runs in one inning (15).
- Most runs in the first inning (15).
- Most runs with two men out (12).
- Most batters to face pitcher in one inning (21).
- Most RBIs in one inning (15).
- Most consecutive batters reaching base in one inning (19).

In 1883, the Chicago Cubs scored 18 runs in one inning, sending 23 men to the plate for the all-time major league record.

Chis Van Cuyk coasted to an easy 19-1 victory, as Dodger fans reveled in the slaughter. Third baseman Bobby Morgan added to the humiliation by hitting two-run homers in both the third and fifth innings, both times with Van Cuyk on base. The towering rookie left-hander, in addition to shackling the Redlegs on five hits, had himself a 4-5 day at the plate, his four hits representing half his total for the entire year.

Brooklyn's explosion got the team moving in the right direction. They took over first place for good on June 1, and continually widened their lead over the Giants, winning the pennant handily, and establishing the "Boys of Summer" as one of the most productive wrecking crews in National League history.

CINCINNATI REDS   0 00 010 000 - 1 - 5 - 0
BROOKLYN DODGERS (15) 0 2 0 20 0 0 X - 19 - 17 - 1

HOME RUNS - Morgan (2), Dixie Howell

WP - Van Cuyk (3-2)
LP - Blackwell (1-6)

1954–"KING KARL" SPOONER DAZZLES NATIONAL LEAGUE

In 1954, the Brooklyn Dodgers were embroiled in a close pennant race with their cross-town rivals, the New York Giants. Walter Alston's boys made a fight of it until five days before the end of the season, when they were finally eliminated.

As the Dodger corpse lay cold and still, a warm breath of fresh air wafted across the body–and the Phoenix of Dodger baseball rose from the ashes–determined to redeem itself in 1955, and reclaim the National League throne.

The first breath of fresh air was borne on the left arm of a 23-year-old pitcher just up from Fort Worth of the Texas League. He was destined to make baseball history with the greatest major league debut in history. His name was Karl Benjamin Spooner, and all who saw him pinned a "can't miss" label on him.

Spooner possessed that rare weapon that all pitchers would kill for, a fast ball of mythical proportions. His "bat dodger" was favorably compared to that of the great Walter Johnson and the Dodgers own "Dazzy" Vance. Starting with the Brooklyn farm team at Hornell, New York, in the class D Pony League in 1951, Spooner toiled in such way stations as Newport News, Virginia, Greenwood, Mississippi, and Pueblo, Colorado. His explosive fast ball, that accounted for better than one strikeout per inning during his career, earned him a promotion to the Dodgers' AA farm team, the Fort Worth Cats of the Texas League, in 1954.

Karl Spooner arrived in the major leagues with more potential than any pitcher in Brooklyn Dodger history. Unfortunately, a sore arm ended his two-year career after just 29 games pitched, and a 10-6 won-loss record. He fanned 105 batters in just 99 innings. (Brace Photo)

The hard-throwing southpaw set the Texas League on its ear with a display of blinding speed never before seen south of the Mason-Dixon line. The 23-year-old phenom won 21 games for Fort Worth, and set a Texas-League record by striking out 262 batters in 238 innings of work. After winning two more games in Fort Worth's successful postseason playoff, Karl Spooner was brought up to the big club to finish the last week of the season on a major league bench.

Dodger manager Walter Alston had no plans to pitch the young minor league sensation down the stretch, since his club was locked in a tight pennant race with the New York Giants. But, as fate would have it, the Dodgers were eliminated from the race on Tuesday, September 21, 1954, and their scheduled starting pitcher, Billy Loes, went home.

Alston decided to give the young southpaw his baptism of fire against the National League champion Giants on Wednesday. A nervous Spooner took the mound in Ebbets Field before a scant gathering of 3,256 Dodger diehards. He immediately dug himself a huge hole, walking Lockman, Dark, and Mueller to load the bases with none out. The dangerous Wille Mays stepped to the plate, bringing 41 home runs and a .345 batting average with him. Campanella called time and went out to the mound to settle down his pitcher, telling him it was just another game. The strategy worked. Spooner reached back for his "bat dodger" and proceeded to strike out Mays, Monte Irvin, and Bobby Hofman to retire the side.

From then on, it was all Spooner. He did not walk another man the entire game. A total of 15 Giants went down on strikes before the Dodger rookie, a new major league debut record, as he limited New York to just three hits. At one juncture, Spooner fanned six batters in a row, tying another major league record. Brooklyn garnered only seven safeties off the slants of Johnny Antonelli and two relievers, but that was enough for a 3-0 victory. After the game, Campanella was ecstatic with his new batterymate, saying, "He's the greatest young pitcher I've ever seen. I couldn't believe it–and buddy–I put him to the test." Four days later, the kid from Oriskany Falls, New York, stood on the mound at Ebbets Field, poised to face the Pittsburgh Pirates. Like the Giants, the poor Bucs posed no problem for young Spooner. He overpowered them from the opening pitch. He had a no-hitter for four innings, and finished with a nifty four-hitter, winning 1-0 on a seventh-inning home run by Gil Hodges.

An even dozen Pittsburgh batters went down on strikes before "King Karl's" dazzling array of pitches; fastball, curve, and changeup. His 27 strikeouts, in his first two National League games, eclipsed the 32-year-old record of teammate Dazzy Vance, who fanned 25 men in two successive games back in 1922.

Brooklyn fans spent the following winter huddled around kitchen stoves, arguing whether the lightning-fast lefty would win 20 games in 1955–or 30. Spooner won only eight games, after suffering a sore arm in spring train-

ing. He did have the distinction of pitching and winning the pennant clincher however, as he handcuffed the Milwaukee Braves 10-2 on September 8. It was the earliest pennant clinching in National League history.

Karl Spooner never won another major league game. The zip never returned to his overpowering fastball, and he faded from the baseball scene forever, finished at the age of 24.

1955–SNIDER HITS THREE HOME RUNS AGAINST MILWAUKEE

Duke Snider hit three home runs and a single, with three RBIs, against the Philadelphia Phillies on May 30, 1950. Five years later, almost to the day, on June 1, 1955, the "Duke of Flatbush" outdid himself, cracking three home runs and a double, and driving in six big runs in an 11-8 slugfest with the Milwaukee Braves.

The year 1955 was the "Boys of Summer's" finest hour. They broke from the gate with a ten-game winning streak, won ten of their next twelve, and coasted home to the pennant by 13 1/2 games.

By Wednesday June 1, they held a 6 1/2 game lead over the second place Chicago Cubs, and a whopping 12-game lead over the fourth-place Braves. The entire Dodger team was on fire, slamming 67 home runs in only 44 games. Their leader, Edwin Donald Snider, was leading the major leagues in home runs with 15, to go along with 48 runs batted in, and a .319 batting average. Don Newcombe paced the pitching staff with a perfect 8-0 mark.

A typical mid-week crowd of 18,380 was spread around Ebbets Field to witness the first game of the series. The night was cool, with the temperature in the low 60s at game time. Carl Erskine was manager Walter Alston's choice to start the game. He was opposed by big Gene Conley, all 6'8" of him. Conley, a professional basketball player with the Boston Celtics, was an imposing presence on the mound. A 14-game winner in 1954, he was off to a sizzling start in '55, with a 7-1 record.

The fans anticipated a pitchers' duel between the two rightys, since they had already engaged in two 12-inning tussles earlier in the season, in which a total of five runs were scored. This night was different however. Neither man was around for the finish, as the two teams piled up a total of 19 runs on 25 hits, with five doubles, two triples, and six home runs. Most of the long-ball barrage, including all the home runs, came off Dodger bats.

Charlie Grimm's Braves nicked Erskine for a run in the first and two more in the second. The Bums answered back with one of their own in the home first, when Reese took Conley into the lower left-field seats, and the Duke pole axed one into the lower center field stands. In the bottom of the fourth, Brooklyn sent the Milwaukee hurler to an early shower under a six-run outburst, including a

Duke Snider was the most dominant player in the major leagues, from 1953 through 1957, outshining even the New York duo of Willie Mays and Mickey Mantle. Snider hit 40 or more home runs in each of the five years, knocked in 585 runs, and batted .311. He added another seven home runs in 24 World Series games.

home run by Jackie Robinson. Snider capped the scoring with a three-run shot over the screen in right, off southpaw Roberto Vargas.

Two innings later, with righthander Ernie Johnson on the hill for the Braves, Pee Wee Reese reached base on a walk, and Snider hit his third home run of the game, a towering drive onto Bedford Avenue. Milwaukee tried to make a game of it as they rallied in the eighth, scoring five big runs and driving Carl Erskine to cover. Johnny Logan's bases loaded triple spelled doom for the Dodger starter, and narrowed the Brooklyn lead to 10-8. The Braves could get no closer, however, as big Jim Hughes came on to shut them down over the last two innings.

Duke Snider had one more shot at home run #4, in the bottom of the eighth. As he strode to the plate to face lefty Chet Nichols, organist Gladys Goodding spurred him on with his favorite rendition of "California, Here I Come." He hit the ball good, but not good enough, coasting into second base with a double. Moments later, he was cut down trying to steal third. Campanella closed out the scoring with a circuit clout into the center field stands.

Once again, the Duke came up slightly short in his effort to capture a piece of the history book, but he had another outstanding game. His three home runs and a double gave him 14 total bases on the day, and his six runs batted in increased his season total to 54.

When the season finally came to an end four months later, Snider was one of the top players in the majors. His teammate Roy Campanella edged him out for the Most Valuable Player award, but the Duke was close behind. His .309 batting average produced 42 home runs and a league leading 136 runs batted in. He also led the league in runs scored with 126.

MILWAUKEE

NAME	POS	AB	R	H	E
Bruton	CF	5	1	4	0
Tanner	RF	3	2	0	0
Aaron	2B	5	1	1	2
Crowe	1B	5	0	1	0
Logan	SS	5	1	2	0
Thomson	LF	4	1	2	0
O'Connell	3B	4	0	1	0
Crandall	P	1	0	0	0
Conley	P	1	0	0	0
Vargas	P	0	0	0	0
Johnson	P	1	0	0	0
Adcock	PH	0	1	0	0
Burdette	P	0	0	0	0
Mathews	PH	1	0	0	0
Nichols	P	0	0	0	0
Total		38	8	12	2

BROOKLYN

NAME	POS	AB	R	H	E
Gilliam	2B	4	1	0	0
Reese	SS	4	3	2	1
Snider	CF	5	3	4	0
Campanella	C	4	1	2	0
Amoros	LF	3	0	1	0
Hodges	1B	3	0	0	0
Furillo	RF	2	1	0	0
Robinson	3B	3	1	2	0
Hoak	3B	1	0	0	0
Erskine	P	3	1	2	0
Hughes	P	1	0	0	0
Total		33	11	12	1

```
MILWAUKEE BRAVES    1 2 0 0 0 0 0 5 0 - 8 - 12 - 2
BROOKLYN DODGERS    2 0 0 6 0 2 0 1 X -11 - 13 - 1
```

HR - Reese, Snider (3), Robinson, Campanella

WP - Erskine (7-2)
LP - Conley (7-2)

Lefty Danny McDevitt pitched Brooklyn to their final win in Ebbets Field.

1957—BROOKLYN'S LAST HOME GAME

Ebbets Field opened on April 9, 1913. A crowd of 10,000 chilled fans watched silently as the Philadelphia Phillies defeated Nap Rucker and the Brooklyn Superbas 1-0. Forty-four years later, on September 24, 1957, a crowd of 6,702 dispirited Flatbush residents watched silently as the Dodgers bid goodbye to the City of Churches by blanking the Pittsburgh Pirates, 2-0, behind lefty Danny McDevitt. Within a few short months, the big cement ball from the contractor's crane crashed against the facade of the old stadium, and the walls came tumbling down, to make way for a new housing project.

The memories that were an integral part of the old steel and concrete ballpark were not destroyed with the structure. They live today within the heart of every surviving Brooklyn fan, in the written word of the sportswriters who covered the scene, and in the many books authored by men who keep the flame alive with new and exciting stories about the Daffyness Boys, the Boys of Summer, and their fellow Dodgers, Robins, Superbas, and Bridegrooms.

Brooklyn Dodger president Walter O'Malley had been trying to replace the old stadium since the early '50s. After years of fruitless negotiations with the Brooklyn city council, O'Malley decided to move the franchise to Los Angeles, California, where the city fathers gave him many financial incentives, plus a piece of choice real estate close to downtown L.A. Although the decision to move was not officially announced until October 8, 1957,

Jim Gentile, a 6'4", 210-pound first baseman, played in Brooklyn's last home game. He went on to a successful career with Baltimore. In 1961 he hit .302 for the Orioles, with 46 homers and 141 RBIs.

every baseball fan in the country knew about it months before. Hence, as the season wound down, a feeling of foreboding settled over the community, a sense of impending loss, like the death of a close relative.

September 24 was a cold fall day. The Dodgers playing their last home game of the season, hosted Danny Murtaugh's Pittsburgh Pirates. A small crowd of depressed Dodger rooters was on hand for the early evening wake. Twenty-four-year-old Danny McDevitt was Walter Alston's choice to write the final chapter of the history of Ebbets Field. Pirate rookie Bennie Daniels was the opponent.

It was a spiritless ballgame, particularly on the Dodgers' part, although the cellar-dwelling Bucs were already looking forward to the off season themselves. Happy Felton conducted the final Knot Hole Gang pre-game show, and Gladys Goodding bid adieu to her favorite ballplayers with a tearful rendition of Auld Lang Syne.

Brooklyn scored one run in the first inning on a double by Elmer Valo, and pushed across another in the third on a single by Gil Hodges. Both teams were held to five hits, with the Dodgers winning 2-0 on an outstanding pitching effort by young McDevitt. Brooklyn finished the season on the road, losing two out of three in Philadelphia, to finish the season in third place, 11 games behind the pennant-winning Milwaukee Braves.

PITTSBURGH

NAME	POS	AB	R	H	E
Baker	3B	4	0	0	0
Mejias	RF	4	0	0	0
Groat	SS	3	0	1	0
Skinner	LF	4	0	1	0
Fondy	1B	4	0	0	0
Mazeroski	2B	3	0	1	0
Clemente	CF	3	0	1	0
Peterson	C	3	0	1	0
Daniels	P	2	0	0	1
Freese	PH	0	0	0	0
Total		31	0	5	1

BROOKLYN

NAME	POS	AB	R	H	E
Gilliam	2B	3	1	0	0
Cimoli	CF	4	1	1	0
Valo	RF	3	0	1	0
Hodges	3B	4	0	1	0
Amoros	LF	3	0	0	0
Gentile	1B	2	0	0	0
Reese	3B	1	0	0	1
Campanella	C	2	0	0	0
Pignatano	C	1	0	0	0
Zimmer	SS	2	0	2	0
McDevitt	P	1	0	0	0

Total		27	2	5	1

```
PITTSBURGH PIRATES   0 0 0  0 0 0  0 0 0 - 0 - 5 - 1
BROOKLYN DODGERS     1 0 1  0 0 0  0 0 X - 2 - 5 - 1
```

DOUBLES — Valo, Zimmer

	IP	R	H	BB	SO
Daniel	7	2	5	3	2
Face	1	0	0	0	2
McDevitt	9	0	5	1	9

WP — McDevitt (7-4)

LP — DAaniels (0-1)

1959—DODGER FANS PAY TRIBUTE TO ROY CAMPANELLA

The years from 1947 through 1956 were the glory years for Brooklyn Dodger baseball. That was the decade dominated by the famed "Boys of Summer," perhaps the greatest array of offensive and defensive talent ever assembled on one team, in National League history.

The Brooklyn Dodgers captured six National League pennants over the ten-year period, losing two others on the last day of the season. One of the most dominating players to grace that lineup was catcher Roy Campanella, a squat fire-plug of a man, who "ran" the game from his position behind the plate. In addition to being the premier handler of pitchers in the major leagues, Campy had superior all-around defensive talents. Surprisingly quick and agile for his size, the Dodger backstop often beat the runner to first base while backing up the bag on a ground ball. He was death on foul popups, a block of granite to runners trying to score, and a waiting howitzer to base runners attempting to steal.

At the plate, his short, compact swing terrorized opposing pitchers. Three times during his brief ten-year career, Campanella was voted the Most Valuable Player in the National League. In 1951 he won his first MVP award, on the strength of his field generalship, as well as his offensive contributions, which included a .325 batting average, 33 home runs and 108 runs batted in. Two years later, his .312 batting average, 41 home runs, and league-leading 142 runs batted in, earned him another MVP award. His third trophy came in 1955, when he hit .318, with 32 homers and 107 RBIs for Brooklyn's first and only World Championship team.

Following the 1957 season, Dodger president Walter O'Malley moved the club to Los Angeles. Roy Campanella, although heartsick at the thought of leaving the site of so many triumphs, was looking forward to playing in the Coliseum, where the short 250 foot left-field wall was made to order for his long, towering fly balls.

Then tragedy struck. In the early morning hours of January 28, 1958, at 1:30AM to be exact, Roy Campanella locked the door to his New York liquor store, climbed into his Chevrolet sedan, and began the long drive home to Glen Cove, about thirty miles away. It was a cold, wintry night, with treacherous patches of ice dotting the roads. As Campy navigated an "S" curve only two miles from his house, the car hit a sheet of ice and went out of control, plowing into a telephone pole and shattering the seemingly indestructible body of the man behind the wheel.

Roy Campanella never walked again. The force of the crash nearly severed his spinal cord, leaving him paralyzed from the chest down. In typical Campanella fashion, however, the will to live, and the indomitable courage of the man saw him through the crisis, and returned him to the world, broken in body, but alive and well spirit.

Don Newcombe and Roy Campanella, former Negro League adversaries and Brooklyn Dodger teammates, reminisce about the good old days, during a reunion in Los Angeles.

A short 15 months after the near fatal accident, the Los Angeles Dodgers honored their future Hall of Fame backstop at a benefit game against his old enemies, the New York Yankees. The largest crowd ever to witness a major league baseball game, pushed their way into the Coliseum on the evening of May 7, 1959, to pay tribute to a great athlete and a courageous person. The official attendance was announced as 93,103, but several hundred "unofficial" attendees gained entrance when they overran one of the gates. The total attendance could easily have exceeded 100,000 if the seating capacity were available. Over 80,000 tickets were sold in advance, with an-

other 13,000 going on sale the day of the game. Still, another 15,000 fans were turned away after it was announced the game was sold out.

As the 93,000 misty-eyed fans held lighted matches in the silent, darkened stadium, the "Little Colonel" Pee Wee Reese, pushed Campanella's wheelchair onto the field in one of the most stirring moments in baseball history. Thunderous applause greeted the Dodger catcher as he sat before a microphone near second base. Choked with emotion at the great outpouring of love, the 36-year-old Campanella thanked everyone for attending. "I thank each and every one of you. This is something I'll never forget." Warren Giles, the president of the National League paid his tribute to Campy, as did Los Angeles councilwoman Rosalind Wyman, one of the moving forces behind the Dodgers transfer, and Dodger president Walter O'Malley.

In less than charitable fashion, Casey Stengel's Bronx Bombers failed to play the part of the patsy in the scheduled exhibition game following the ceremonies. They routed a still-developing Sandy Koufax with five runs in less than six innings, en route to a convincing 6-2 victory. Fortunately, exhibition games do not reflect the intensity of the pennant race. The Los Angeles contingent went on to capture the World Championship, while Stengel's crew finished third in the American League, 15 games off the Chicago White Sox pace.

Roy Campanella, renewed in spirit, and filled with a zest for life, continued to work for the Los Angeles organization for another 24 years. He served in the Los Angeles community relations department, giving inspirational speeches to civic groups, as well as to Dodger players and farmhands.

Although the valiant catcher's heart was finally stopped on June 26, 1993, he will never die. His spirit lives within all of us.

1962 — MAURY WILLS BREAKS TY COBB'S STOLEN BASE RECORD

Thirty-one years ago, a slightly-built 160-pound dynamo from Washington, D.C., revolutionized the game of baseball, making the stolen base a significant offensive weapon once again, after a 40-year hiatus.

Maurice Morning Wills seemed destined to be a career minor league baseball player, as he toiled for 8 1/2 long years in the Dodger farm system. Along the way, he learned to switch hit, adding a degree of versatility to his offensive capabilities. When the call from Los Angeles finally came, in June 1959, the 26-year-old shortstop and base stealer was ready. He proceeded to lead the National League in stolen bases his first six years in the league. After stealing 50 and 35 bases his first two seasons, he exploded in 1962.

As the season got underway, it was obvious to manager Walter Alston that he needed more offense if he wanted any chance of winning the championship. His pitching, headed by Don Drysdale and Sandy Koufax, was awesome, but his offense left something to be desired. He had eventual National League batting champion Tommy Davis, and towering Frank Howard, en route to a 31-homer season, but not much else.

Alston decided to turn the speedy Wills loose at every opportunity in an attempt to generate more offense. The lightning-quick Wills responded with abandon, swiping eight sacks in April, 19 in May, and 15 more in June. By the All-Star break, the Dodger shortstop had 46 steals, within four of his 1960 league-leading total, and more than

Maury Wills, shown stealing base #104, revolutionized the game of baseball, when he revived the lost art of base stealing. Before Will's explosion in 1962, no one had stolen more than 63 bases in a season since Ty Cobb swiped 96 in 1915. And no one had broken the century mark since Billy Hamilton stole 111 bases way back in 1891.

any other National Leaguer had accumulated in one season since 1927. Jokesters around the league categorized a Dodger rally as consisting of a single by Wills, a stolen base, a sacrifice, and a fly ball. It wasn't far from the truth.

When the stretch run began, the thief of L.A. turned on the after burners. The Dodger fans added to the excitement, filling Dodger Stadium with chants of "Go - Go - Go" every time little Maury got on base. As August drew to a close, his stolen base total stood at 73. By now his legs looked like two pieces of raw meat, covered top to bottom with bruises and open scrapes caused by a hundred slides into enemy territory. Wills just sucked it in a little more, and continued his charge.

Los Angeles suffered a disastrous blow to its pennant hopes in July when 14-game winner Sandy Koufax went down for the season with a circulation problem in his pitching hand. Somehow, Alston's charges maintained

their focus, holding the San Francisco Giants at bay throughout the summer, thanks primarily to the trio of Davis, Howard and Wills.

On September 7, before a packed house at Dodger Stadium, the Big Blue Machine routed the Pittsburgh Pirates, 10-1. Mousey, as he was called by his teammates because of his small stature, ignited the romp with four stolen bases, establishing a new National League stolen base record. The old mark of 80 was set by Bob Bescher back in 1911. Little Maury led off the game with a single, then quickly swiped both second and third, tying Bescher's 52-year-old record. Two innings later he walked and stole second. Play was halted temporarily while he was presented with the record-breaking base. Later in the game, the Dodger shortstop added number 82 to his total.

The final barrier looming before the audacious Wills was Ty Cobb's seemingly unbeatable mark of 96 stolen bases. The Detroit speedster's mark was considered to be one of baseball's untouchables, along with Babe Ruth's 60 home runs, and Joe DiMaggio's 56-game hitting streak. Maris had toppled the Babe's record in '61, and now Cobb's great achievement teetered on the brink.

Since Cobb's record was set over a 154-game schedule, Baseball Commissioner Ford Frick ruled that, like Ruth's, the record had to be broken in 154 games, even though the baseball schedule was now eight games longer. When Maris broke Ruth's home-run record, he did it in the 162nd game, causing his achievement to be marked by an asterisk.

The "Go-Go-Go" had, by now, spread around the National League, and every park the Dodgers visited was filled with invocations for little Maury to turn it on. Wills' body was beat black and blue, but he was running on adrenaline most of the time, and he pushed the pain to the back of his mind. He would have the long winter to heal.

The Dodger thief actually had 156 games to topple Cobb's record, since Detroit played two ties in 1915 when Cobb swiped 96. During the 15-day period from September 8 through September 22, Wills pilfered another 13 bases, giving him 95 for the season. On September 23, Los Angeles visited Sportsman's Park in St. Louis to tangle with Johnny Keane's Redbirds. As the "Go-Go-Go" chant echoed through the stands, Mousey victimized catcher Carl Sawatski twice, to establish a new modern major league mark of 97 stolen bases in one season. The two thefts gave Wills 40 stolen bases in his last 37 games. After his record-breaking attempt, the Dodger shortstop was presented with second base in honor of his brilliant achievement. The historic base now resides permanently in baseball's Hall of Fame in Cooperstown, New York.

On September 26, as Johnny Podres stifled the Houston Colt .45's 13-1, Wills thrilled the 25,813 fans in Dodger Stadium with two more stolen bases, running his total to an even 100, the first man to break the century mark since Billy Hamilton swiped 111 sacks in 1891. When the Dodgers fell to San Francisco in a heartbreaking three game playoff, the new stolen-base king swiped four more sacks, including three in the final game.

Wills achievement was the more remarkable when you realize he was caught only 13 times in 117 attempts. Ty Cobb, in his record-setting season, was cut down 38 times in 134 attempts.

In recognition of his outstanding achievement, Wills was voted the National League's Most Valuable Player for 1962. In addition to his 104 stolen bases, the Dodger shortstop batted .299, and scored 130 runs. He led the league in triples with 10.

1963—DICK NEN'S BIG HOME RUN

Richard Le Roy Nen played in the major leagues for six years, piling up a total of 185 base hits. A highly regarded Los Angeles Dodger farmhand, the 6'2", 200-pound first baseman, saw limited action with the big club. His L.A. career statistics totaled only one hit in eight at bats. His lone safety was a home run. It was a big one. It was hit in the heat of the pennant race, and helped the Dodgers ward off a furious assault by the St. Louis Cardinals. Dick Nen's only L.A. home run was probably the single most important base hit of 1963.

Walter Alston's Dodgers and Johnny Keane's St. Louis Cardinals were embroiled in a titanic struggle for first place in the National League as September 16 dawned. A 3 1/2-game Dodger lead on September 1 had dwindled to a single game under a withering St. Louis charge. The sizzling Redbirds reeled off 19 wins in 20 games, while the red-hot Dodgers carded a 19-6 record over the same period.

In the opening game of the year's most crucial series, Johnny Podres beat 18-game winner, Ernie Broglio, 3-1, in Sportsman's Park. The next day, the unhittable Sandy Koufax tossed his 11th shutout of the season, 4-0, to run his record to 24-5. A subdued crowd of 30,450 Cardinal fans quietly watched the execution. Frank Howard's 27th home run, a two-run shot off the right-field roof in the eighth, broke open a close game and spelled curtains for Lefty Curt Simmons.

The Cardinals suddenly found themselves with their backs to the wall. In spite of a sensational 19-3 run in September, Johnny Keane's cohorts now teetered on the brink of elimination. They trailed the Dodgers by three games with only ten to play. They had to win the final game of the series if they were to have any chance of copping the pennant.

Pete Richert got the call from manager Walter Alston, while "Old Reliable" Bob Gibson shouldered the burden for the beleaguered Redbirds. The Cards jumped on the 23-year-old Richert early, pushing over two runs in the second, and driving him to cover with three more in the third. Charlie James' two-run homer and Curt Flood's two-run double did the Dodger starter in. Gibson, meanwhile, was invincible. For seven innings, the big righty breezed along, limiting Alston's team to just four hits and no walks.

Nine L.A. batters went down on strikes over that period.

The score was 5-1 St. Louis after seven, and Cardinal fans were beginning to see a glimmer of hope. Then, the roof caved in. In the eighth, Gibson was driven to cover after retiring only one man. Singles by Wills and Gilliam put the Cardinal ace on the ropes, then a walk to Wally Moon and a two run single by Tommy Davis sent him to an unexpected shower. A base on balls to Howard and a sacrifice fly by Willie Davis cut the St. Louis lead to 5-4.

Dodger rookie Dick Nen, just up from Spokane, had opened the L.A. eighth with a pinch-hit line drive out. The 23-year-old left-handed slugger had played for the Dodgers' Pacific Coast League farm team in the playoffs against Oklahoma City the night before, and had just arrived in St. Louis hours before the game. After pinch hitting, he stayed in the game at first base.

Dick Nen got more mileage out of one home run than any Dodger except Kirk Gibson. He hit a total of 21 home runs in his career, but none was as big as his first one, on September 18, 1963. (Los Angeles Dodger Photo)

In the ninth, the 6'2", 200-pound youngster came up to bat again. This time there was one man out, and the Dodgers were still trailing 5-4. The pitcher was Ron Taylor, Johnny Keane's top right-handed reliever. Nen, nervous and anxious, unleashed a big swing on the first pitch a sent a long drive to deep right center field. The ball bounced off the top of the pavilion roof, sending the big crowd into a fit of depression. A certain Cardinal victory had been snatched away in an instant. Dick Nen's blast deadlocked the game at 5 all, and put his name in the history books at the same time.

Cardinal hopes flickered again in the bottom of the tenth when Dick Groat led off the inning with a triple. It all went for naught, however, when Dodger reliever Ron Perranoski slammed the door in their faces. The sinker ball artist struck out Gary Kolb, then walked Ken Boyer and Bill White intentionally to load the bases. Curt Flood hit a made-to-order ground ball to the drawn-in infield, and Wills forced Groat at the plate. Mike Shannon ended the inning with another grounder to Wills.

In the thirteenth, Willie Davis led off the Dodger half with a single. Perranoski bunted him to second. An error by Javier and a walk to Nen loaded the bases. Maury Wills slow ground ball to second base brought home the tie-breaking run.

Perranoski set the Redbirds down 1-2-3 in the bottom half of the inning to kill the St. Louis dreams once and for all. The Dodger reliever, on his way to a memorable 16-3 season, pitched three-hit ball for six innings, fanning three and walking only two in a brilliant pitching effort.

Dick Nen will forever be a Los Angeles legend. And he had only one hit in Dodger blue.

```
LOS ANGELES DODGERS   010 000 031 000 1 - 6 - 11 - 0
ST. LOUIS CARDINALS    023 000 000 000 0 - 5 - 11 - 3
```

	IP	R	H	BB	SO
RICHERT	2 1/3	4	4	1	2
MILLER	4 2/3	1	4	2	6
PERRANOSKI	6	0	3	2	3
GIBSON	7 1/3	4	7	1	9
SCHANTZ	1/3	0	0	1	0
TAYLOR	1 1/3	1	1	0	0
BURDETTE	4	1	3	1	3

WP — Perranoski (16-3)
LP — Burdette (9-12)

1965—LOU JOHNSON, "THE CINDERELLA MAN"

Louis Brown Johnson, a 5'11", 170-pound outfielder from Lexington, Kentucky, went from minor league vagabond to major league hero in the short span of five months.

The happy-go-lucky Johnson bounced around the minor leagues for 13 years, displaying his talents for 17 different franchises. Along the way, he failed three major league trials, with the Chicago Cubs, Los Angeles Angels, and Milwaukee Braves. In April 1964, he was traded by the Detroit Tigers to the Los Angeles Dodgers for relief pitcher, Larry Sherry.

Making the most of what might have been his last opportunity, the 30-year-old Johnson made a name for himself with the Dodgers' Spokane farm team, batting .328 with 18 homers, 93 runs scored, 70 runs batted in,

and 23 stolen bases. In addition to quality outfield play, "Sweet Lou" provided Spokane with a multi-faceted offensive blend of power and speed.

The following year, on May 1, Los Angeles left fielder Tommy Davis broke his ankle sliding into second base against the San Francisco Giants, and Dodger pennant hopes plummeted. An S.O.S. for an outfield replacement was quickly flashed around the Dodger minor league system. Lou Johnson, who was hitting .301 at Spokane at the time, and who was an experienced veteran with major league exposure, was Buzzy Bavasi's choice to fill Davis' shoes.

Shortly after arriving in L.A., Johnson was inserted into the lineup as a pinch runner in the bottom of the tenth inning of a 2-2 game with Houston. He promptly stole second base, continued on to third on a throwing error by the catcher, and scored the winning run on a single by Ron Fairly.

Lou Johnson, a perennial minor leaguer, was the right man at the right time. His daring base running, clutch hitting, and cheerful disposition, all contributed to a Los Angeles World Championship.

Five days later, his 10th-inning home run beat Houston. As important as his offensive contributions were, his clubhouse demeanor rallied the team. The effervescent outfielder brightened up Dodger Stadium with his infectious smile and spirited personality. His attitude was contagious, and soon pennant fever began to creep back into Dodgertown.

On May 13, near-disaster struck the Dodger team when Johnson was beaned by Houston southpaw Bob Bruce. Fortunately, Lou's batting helmet absorbed most of the impact, and he was back on the field in two days. An outfield collision with big Al Ferrara brought manager Walter Alston to his feet again, a few days later. The 210-pound Ferrara was carried from the field, but Johnson played on.

On June 2, little Al Jackson of the New York Mets broke Lou's right thumb with a pitch, sidelining him for two weeks. Back in the lineup with his digit in a cast, Johnson's .300 batting average nosedived, but the gritty left fielder refused to be benched. And the Dodgers kept winning.

Los Angeles moved into first place about the time "Sweet Lou" joined the club, and they held that spot until early September when they were overtaken by the Giants.

On September 9, trailing the Giants by 1/2 game in the standings, L.A. blanked the Chicago Cubs 1-0 on Sandy Koufax's perfect game. Lou Johnson scored the only run after walking in the fifth inning. He was sacrificed to second; then stole third and continued home on catcher Chris Krugs' wild throw. "Sweet Lou" was credited with the only hit of the game by either team, a seventh-inning double.

The stretch run was an exciting affair with first one team, then the other, getting hot. First it was the Giants who ran up a 14-game winning streak, opening up a 4 1/2-game bulge over the Dodgers. Then L.A. got hot. After the hapless New York Mets hung a shocking 5-2 loss on 26 game winner Sandy Koufax, Alston's boys went on a rampage, reeling off 15 wins in the final 16 games of the season.

Lou Johnson was sizzling down the stretch. His 15th-inning home run beat San Francisco in a crucial encounter. He singled in the winning run in a 12-inning 7-6 victory over the Milwaukee Braves. Another extra inning home run, this one in the twelfth, sunk the Cincinnati Reds.

During the last four games of the Dodgers' 13-game winning streak, the Cinderella Man pounded out 10 hits in 18 at bats, a torrid .556 clip. On October 2, Koufax fanned 15 Braves en route to a pennant-clinching 3-1 win at Dodger Stadium. Fittingly, Lou Johnson, the Dodger sparkplug, carried over the winning run.

In the World Series against the Minnesota Twins, Johnson stayed hot. After going 1-8 in L.A.'s two opening-game losses, he hit at a .368 clip over the final five games.

He was 2 for 2 with one RBI in game three, as Claude Osteen blanked the Twins, 4-0.

He singled and homered with one RBI in Game Four, sparking Drysdale's 7-2 victory.

He was 1-5 with an RBI in Game Five, as Koufax shut out Minnesota, 7-0.

He was 1 for 4 in Game Six, won by the Twins, 5-1.

He was 1 for 4 with a World Series winning home run in Game Seven, as Sandy Koufax came back with only two days' rest to dominate the Minnesota lineup, 2-0.

During the winter, Los Angeles councilman Thomas Bradley, at a special ceremony at city hall, presented Lou Johnson with the "Cinderella Man" award for his inspirational season.

Johnson played two more years with Los Angeles, helping Walter Alston and his staff win another pennant in 1966, but he will always be remembered for his once-in-a-lifetime season of 1965, when he rallied a demoralized Dodger team and carried them to a World Championship.

1966—SANDY KOUFAX RETIRES

Friday, November 18, 1966, was the saddest day in Dodger history. An era came to an end on that day when Sandy Koufax, the major league's greatest pitcher, retired prematurely at the age of 30. The handsome Dodger southpaw, plagued with an arthritic left elbow for the past three years, and fearing permanent damage if he continued pitching, called it quits at the peak of his career. Before a hushed crowd at a national news conference in Los Angeles, Koufax sent chills up the spines of Dodger rooters everywhere when he told the press conference, "A few minutes ago, I sent a letter to the Dodgers asking them to put me on the voluntary retired list."

A 12-year veteran of major league baseball, the product of the Brooklyn sandlots blossomed into a star in 1961 after receiving some pitching advice from catcher Norm Sherry that helped curb his wildness. During his last four years in Los Angeles, Koufax was almost unhittable, compiling a record of 97-27, with an earned run average of 1.87. He fanned 1,228 batters in just 1,192 innings, an average of 9.3 strikeouts per game. In his final season, the 6'2" 210-pound fireballer won 27 games against only nine losses, had an ERA of 1.73, and struck out 317 bat-

His story began on December 14, 1954, when he signed his first Dodger contract, for $6,000 plus a $14,000 signing bonus. Celebrating the historic event in the Brooklyn Dodger offices at 215 Montague Street, are L to R, Dodger scout Al Campanis, 19-year-old Sandy Koufax, and Brooklyn Vice President Fresco Thompson. Twelve years later, his story ended, prematurely and sadly. (Brooklyn Public Library)

ters in 323 innings. He led the league in complete games (27), victories, earned run average, strikeouts, and innings pitched.

During his brilliant career, Koufax threw four no-hitters, including a perfect game, against the Chicago Cubs in 1965. Twice he struck out 18 men in one game and, in 1963, he whiffed 15 New York Yankees to set a new World Series strikeout record.

At the time of his retirement, the 30-year-old super-star was the highest paid pitcher in history, earning a reputed $125,000 per year.

Sandy Koufax, he of the blazing fastball and the equally intimidating sharp-breaking curveball, was the greatest pitcher in Dodger history.

He just might have been the greatest pitcher of all time.

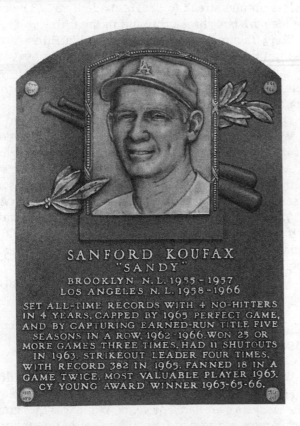

Sandy Koufax's plaque in the Baseball Hall Of Fame, in Cooperstown, New York, lists some of his numerous achievements. He remains the youngest person ever elected to the Hall Of Fame, entering the hallowed Hall at the tender age of 36.

1968 — BIG D THROWS 58 CONSECUTIVE SCORELESS INNINGS

Donald Scott Drysdale was an intimidating sight on the mound. Standing 6'5" tall and weighing a solid 190 pounds, the big right-hander threw his 90-mile-per-hour fastball from the direction of third base with a buggywhip motion that instilled fear in the hearts of most batsmen.

And to top it off, Big D was mean. He set a National League record of 154 hit batters during his career, leading the league in that dubious category five times.

The 32-year-old Drysdale was nearing the end of an illustrious 14-year career in 1968, when he put together the greatest pitching streak in major league history. From May 14 until June 8, the man with the explosive fastball threw six consecutive shutouts, a total of 58 2/3 consecutive scoreless innings.

The streak began on May 14. Drysdale entered the game with a record of 1-3, his teammates having scored only nine runs in his previous eight starts. His only victory in April was a 1-0 shutout of the Mets. On May 14, Big D handcuffed the Chicago Cubs 1-0 with a two-hitter. The high point of the game came in the fourth inning when the Dodger starter fanned both Billy Williams and Ernie Banks with the tying run on third.

Four days later, Drysdale repeated his Chicago effort with a 1-0 blanking of the Houston Astros. Wes Parker scored the only run of the game in the sixth inning, when he singled, and came around to score on two infield outs and an error. The Astros went down with their guns blazing, loading the bases in the top of the ninth on a single, a double, and a base on balls. Bob Watson finally ended the suspense by grounding out.

The St. Louis Cardinals were Big Don's next victim, going quietly, 2-0. In a game delayed 15 minutes by rain, the Dodgers drew first blood with a run in the third, on a walk to Paul Popovich, and a two-out double by Wes Parker. Parker's blow was the only hit allowed by Bob Gibson during his eight innings on the mound. The ace of Red Schoendienst's staff was overpowering in defeat.

Drysdale's shutout streak was in danger only twice during the game. The big right-hander struck out Mike Shannon with men on second and third, ending the seventh inning. After Los Angeles added an insurance run in the ninth, Lou Brock led off the Cardinal half with a double but was left stranded when Drysdale turned back the next three batters to preserve his shutout string of 27 straight innings.

On May 26, Big D tossed his fourth straight shutout, coasting to a 5-0 win over Houston. Once again, the Dodger starter had to fend off a late rally in order to protect the streak. With two men on and nobody out for the Astros in the bottom of the ninth, Leroy Thomas smashed a drive between first and second. Paul Popovich speared the ball going to his left, and turned it into a lightning-fast double play, leaving a runner on third with two out. A walk to Wynn and a hit batter re-loaded the bases before Drysdale retired Dave Adlesh on a ground ball to end the game.

Don Drysdale, in explaining his hot streak, said it required a certain amount of talent, establishing a "groove," outstanding assistance from your teammates, and a generous portion of good old luck.

The Van Nuys fireballer continued his fantastic performance in his next start against the San Francisco Giants. A crowd of 46,067 Dodger fans cheered his every pitch. L.A. scored in the second on a double by Rocky Colovito and a single by Bob Bailey. Willie Davis singled in the third and came around on a double by Parker to run the count to 2-0. Another two-bagger by the Dodger first baseman resulted in their third and final run when Ken Boyer scored him with a sacrifice fly.

The ninth-inning jinx almost did Drysdale in this time. A walk to Willie McCovey, a single by Jim Hart, and another walk to Dave Marshall loaded the bases with no outs. With a count of 2-2 on catcher Dick Dietz, the big righty threw an inside fastball that hit Dietz on the arm,

Don Drysdale teamed with Sandy Koufax during the 1960s to give the Dodgers the most overpowering pitching duo of the 20th century. In 1965, the two combined for a 49-20 record.

apparently forcing in a run. In a decision hotly disputed by the Giants, however, umpire Harry Wendelstedt ruled that Dietz made no effort to get out of the way of the pitch, calling it ball three.

After a ten-minute rhubarb, Drysdale retired Dietz on a short fly ball to right field, with the runners holding. The next hitter, Ty Cline, bounced into a force play at the plate. Then pinch hitter Jack Hyatt popped up, and the

game was history. The shutout, Drysdale's fifth in a row, tied the major league record for consecutive shutouts set by Doc White of the New York Highlanders back in 1904.

It was a tough outing for Big D. He labored throughout the game, throwing a total of 150 pitches before nailing down the victory. On June 4, Don Drysdale established two new pitching milestones. He set a new major league record for consecutive shutouts with six, and he broke Carl Hubbell's National League record of 46 1/3 consecutive shutout innings. After downing the Pittsburgh Pirates, 5-0 with a three-hitter, Drysdale's shutout string stood at 54 innings. The Dodger ace needed only 93 pitches this time to secure the shutout. His only trouble came in the sixth when Gary Kolb doubled and advanced to third with two out. Paul Popovich saved a run by charging Maury Wills' chopper and gunning him down on a bang-bang play at first.

Four days later, a Ladies Night crowd of 50,060 packed Dodger Stadium to root for their hero. Don Drysdale passed his last milestone, Walter Johnson's major league record of 56 consecutive scoreless innings, by blanking the Phils through four innings, extending his scoreless innings streak to 58. He made it 58 2/3 before Gene Mauch's boys broke through in the fifth.

Tony Taylor led off the Philadelphia fifth with a single, and went to third on another single by Clay Dalrymple. Drysdale fanned Roberto Pena, but Howie Bedell lifted a fly ball to Gabrielson in left field, scoring Taylor and ending Big D's streak.

Drysdale won the game, 5-3, running his record to 8-3. Wes Parker contributed a home run to the cause, and catcher Tom Haller added a double and two singles.

After his streak ended, the hard-luck pitcher resumed his losing ways, going 6-9 the rest of the season. The seventh-place Dodgers, with a team batting average of .230, failed to support their outstanding pitching staff, which finished second in ERA with a mark of 2.69. Drysdale's miniscule 2.15 earned run average was good enough for only a 14-12 record.

After going 5-4 in 1969, big Don Drysdale retired at the age of 33.

1969—WILLIE DAVIS HITS IN 31 STRAIGHT GAMES

Willie Davis was one of the fastest men ever to don Dodger blue. He was also one of the most enigmatic players the Dodgers ever had. For years, Willie was the "great experimenter" at the plate, unable to settle on any one batting stance. He changed his stance as many as six times a year, going from a Stan Musial-corkscrew-type stance to a Joe Dimaggio wide open-type almost overnight.

His season batting averages reflected his lack of confidence at the plate; bouncing from .245 in 1963, to .294 in '64, then dropping down to .238 in '65, and back up to .284 the following year. Life at the plate for Willie Davis was one big roller coaster ride during his first nine years in the league.

Finally, in 1969, at the age of 29, Davis found his hitting groove, and proceeded to put together a string of six straight years during which he averaged almost .300. His greatest hitting accomplishment occurred during that '69 season when he put it all together for a period of 34 days, hitting safely in 31 consecutive games, a feat exceeded by only 13 players in major league history.

On August 1, "Three Dog," as he was called because of his uniform number, his explosive speed, and his love for greyhound racing, was battling a prolonged batting slump. In an attempt to break out of his slump, the Dodger outfielder changed his batting stance (again), and switched to a heavier bat in an attempt to just meet the ball and hit it where it was pitched. The remedy worked as he drilled a double off the southpaw slants of Steve Carlton.

Willie Davis, one of the fastest men ever to wear Dodger blue, still holds the consecutive-game hitting record, set in 1969.

He continued his bombardment throughout the month of August, smashing out 15 hits in his first 27 at bats, and hitting safely in all 28 games during the month. On September 1, the fleet-footed left-handed hitter went two for five against the New York Mets, with a double and two runs batted in. The outburst tied Zack Wheat's 53-year-old Dodger mark of hitting safely in 29 consecutive games. After Davis' first hit, Dodger Diamond Vision flashed a message from the 81-year-old Wheat to his 29-year-old successor. "Congratulations. Keep going. You have done a good job. Good luck."

The following day, Willie D. established a new Dodger mark by singling against New York. He made it 31 straight in the finale of the Met series when he broke an 0 for 4 day with a game-winning double in the bottom of the ninth. Claude Osteen, the Dodgers' outstanding southpaw, had blown a 4-0 lead on two-run homers by Tommy Agee and Donn Clendenon in the eighth inning. In the ninth, Maury Wills led off with a single and was sacrificed to second. Manager Gil Hodges then summoned left hander Jack Di Lauro from the bullpen to face the red-hot Davis. The Dodger centerfielder slapped the first pitch, a sidearm curveball, to left for the game winning hit. Commenting on the pitch selection, Willie said, "I was looking for it because that's the pitch they got me out with the night before."

The following night, in San Diego, the streak came to an end during a 3-0 Los Angeles loss. After it was over, Willie seemed relieved, admitting, "I was bothered all day with an upset stomach." When asked about Joe DiMaggio's 56-game hitting streak, he just smiled and said, "Don't fool with Joe D."

During his 31-game hitting streak, Willie piled up 54 hits in 120 at bats, for an average of .435. He batted in 23 runs in 31 games.

The 1969 season was the beginning of the second half of Willie Davis' career. He batted .267 during his first nine years in the league, then slugged the ball at a .299 clip over the next six years. His lifetime average of .279 included a total of 2,561 hits, 2091 of them in a Dodger uniform. He still ranks number three on the all-time Dodger hit parade, behind Zack Wheat and Pee Wee Reese.

1973—"THE INFIELD" IS FORMED

On Wednesday, October 28, 1981, as the big night baseball crowd of 56,513 squirmed uneasily, New York Yankee first baseman Bob Watson lifted a fly ball to center field. When Ken Landreaux squeezed it for the last out, the Los Angeles Dodgers were champions of the whole world.

As Steve Garvey, Davey Lopes, Bill Russell and Ron Cey left the field, it marked the end of the longest-running infield in major league history. Just three months later, on February 8, second baseman Davey Lopes was traded to the Oakland Athletics to make room for rookie Steve Sax. Ron Cey and Steve Garvey left the following year.

In the beginning, all four kids were Dodger farm-hands, working their way up through the minor league system, with stopovers in places like Ogden, Bakersfield, Albuquerque, and Spokane. Bill Russell and Steve Garvey made their first appearance in a Los Angeles Dodger uniform in 1969. Ron Cey debuted in 1971, and Davey Lopes joined the gang in 1972. Russell was a centerfielder when he first joined the club. Garvey and Cey were third baseman, while Lopes was a recently converted outfielder, now learning the ropes at second base.

The multi-talented Russell was soon recruited by manager Walter Alston to fill a void at shortstop. The handsome blonde was afraid of ground balls at first, but soon settled in to become one of the Dodgers' all-time favorites at that position. Lopes didn't want to be an infielder, but when he realized his future was at second base, he buckled down and perfected the position through determination and hard work. Garvey didn't have a major league arm at third, and he was eventually shifted to the other side of the diamond where his natural talents made him the all-time major league fielding leader, with a lifetime fielding average of .996.

As the 1973 season got underway, the Los Angeles infield consisted of Bill Buckner at first, Lopes at second, Russell at short, and Cey at third. Steve Garvey was one of Alston's "super subs", pinch hitting when needed and spelling Buckner at first base occasionally. Garvey's shotgun-throwing arm, and Ron Cey's solid play had eliminated Garvey from contention for the third-base job the year before.

On June 13, in Philadelphia, Steve Garvey filled in for Buckner for the first time as a starter, giving the Dodgers a starting infield of Garvey, Lopes, Russell, and Cey. The L.A. contingent was buried by Danny Ozark's Phils, 16-3. Russell had a single and a homer in the game, while Garvey, Lopes, and Cey all drew the collar.

Ten days later, on June 23, the Dodgers hosted the Cincinnati Reds in a doubleheader before a big Dodger Stadium crowd of 52,831. In the opener, the Big Red Machine took the toll of Alston's boys, 4-1. Steve Garvey singled as a pinch hitter. In the nightcap, the 24-year-old Floridian was the starting first baseman, joining Lopes, Russell, and Cey in the infield. Tommy John tossed a three-hitter at the Redlegs, with the Dodgers winning easily, 5-1. Ken McMullen's three-run homer in the sixth provided the margin of victory. Garvey contributed two hits to the Los Angeles attack.

This game marked the beginning of "The Infield." Buckner was shifted to left field, and Garvey became a permanent fixture at first base. The foursome played together for a total of 8 1/2 years, longer than any infield in major league history. In fact, only three other combinations had ever stayed together for as long as five years; the Chicago Cubs of 1906-1910, the Cubs of 1965-1969, and the great Brooklyn combination of Hodges, Robinson, Reese, and Cox, who anchored the Dodger defense from 1948 through 1952.

The Dodgers' long-running infield individually went on to long and productive careers in the major leagues, with Garvey playing for 19 years, Lopes for 16, Russell for 21, and Cey for 17. The quartet sparked the Los Angeles franchise to four pennants and one World Championship between 1973 and 1981. All told, Garvey played 1,727 games in a Dodger uniform, including his last 1,104 games in succession. Lopes played in 1,207 games, and Cey in 1,481. Bill Russell played in 2,181 games, setting the all-time Los Angeles games-played record, and finishing second to Zack Wheat's 2,322 on the all-time Brooklyn list. All four infielders finished their Los Angeles careers in the top ten for at-bats, runs, and hits, and the top 11 for games played.

"The Infield" in action. Russell and Lopes team up for a double play against the New York Yankees in the 1981 World Series. Garvey was on the receiving end of Lopes' toss.

JUNE 23, 1973 — 2ND GAME

CINCINNATI

NAME	POS	AB	R	H	E
Rose	LF	4	1	1	0
Morgan	2B	4	0	1	0
Bench	C	4	0	0	0
Perez	1B	3	0	0	0
Concepcion	SS	3	0	0	0
Kosko	RF	3	0	1	0
Tolan	CF	3	0	0	0
Menke	3B	2	0	0	0
Hall	P	2	0	0	0
Borbon	P	0	0	0	0
Gagliano	PH	1	0	0	0
McGlothlin	P	0	0	0	0
Total		30	1	3	0

The major league's longest-running infield, L to R, Cey, Russell, Lopes, Garvey - 1973 to 1981. (Los Angeles Dodger Photo)

LOS ANGELES

NAME	POS		AB	R	H	E
Lopes	2B		3	2	1	0
Mota	LF		4	1	3	0
W. Davis	CF		4	0	1	0
Cey	3B		1	1	0	0
McMullen	3B		2	1	1	0
Garvey	1B		4	0	2	0
Paciorek	RF		3	0	0	0
Russell	SS		3	0	0	0
Cannizarro	C		3	0	0	0
John	P		3	0	0	0
Total			30	5	8	0

```
CINCINNATI REDS         000 001 000 - 1 - 3 - 0
LOS ANGELES DODGERS     000 013 10X - 5 - 8 - 0
```

HR - McMullen (1)
WP - John (7-3)
LP - Hall (5-4)

1976 AND 1981 — RICK MONDAY SAVES THE FLAG, THEN THE PENNANT

Rick Monday was a patriot. Also, one helluva baseball player. He played his collegiate ball at Arizona State University, the ultimate baseball factory. After graduation and a short stint in the United States Marine Corps, the 6'3" 190-pound slugger was drafted by the Kansas City Athletics. He became a fixture in the A's lineup after their move to Oakland. Following an off year in 1971, the 26-year-old outfielder was traded to the Chicago Cubs, where he plied his trade for the next five years.

In 1976, an incident occurred in Los Angeles that made Rick a national hero. It was Sunday, April 25, and the Chicago Cubs were closing out a weekend series with Walter Alston's Dodgers. Monday and the Cubs were both having a good day. Rick had rapped out three hits, and the Cubs were enjoying a 4-3 lead. As the slugging centerfielder trotted out to his position in Dodger Stadium to start the seventh inning, two figures jumped onto the playing field and prepared to make a political statement. The older man yanked an American flag from underneath his jacket and threw it on the ground. His son took out a can of lighter fluid and a box of matches, and the two prepared to burn the flag.

Not in front of a U.S. Marine, you don't. In a flash, the fleet-footed Monday raced to the scene, pushed the father to the ground, then snatched the flag and carried it to safety. When next he came to bat, Rick Monday was greeted with a standing ovation from an appreciative Los Angeles crowd, as Dodger organist Helen Dell burst into a rendition of "Mr. Wonderful." Even the message board got into the act, flashing congratulations to the heroic visitor, "Rick Monday, you made a great play." Unfortunately for Rick, the Cubs didn't fare as well. A single by Ron Cey drove in Ted Sizemore with the winning run in the bottom of the tenth.

After that display of patriotism, however, it was only fitting that Rick Monday should become a member of the Dodger organization, so in 1977, LA obtained the ballhawk in a trade for Bill Buckner and Ivan DeJesus. Monday gave Lasorda's team eight years of solid baseball, highlighted by his heroics in the 1981 National League Championship Series. As a member of "Team Comeback," Monday was used to seeing his team fight back from certain defeat to pull out a victory in story-book style.

The ultimate heroics occurred on Monday, October 19, in Montreal. It was a cold, raw, overcast day as the Dodgers and Expos fought for the right to meet the New York Yankees in the World Series. The playoff was deadlocked at two games apiece, and the winner of Game Five would be crowned the National League Champion. For eight long innings, Fernando Valenzuela and Ray Burris staged a courageous pitching duel, with neither team able to gain the upper hand. The game was deadlocked at one run apiece as Los Angeles came up for possibly their last at bat of the season. Montreal manager Jim Fanning decided to go with his best, and he summoned his ace, Steve Rogers, from the bullpen. It was Rogers' only relief appearance of the season. A crowd of 36,491 looked on nervously as the big right-hander faced Dodger clutch hitter Steve Garvey. Rogers retired the Dodger first baseman on a pop to second. He then disposed of the dangerous Ron Cey on a long drive to Tim Raines in left field. The big Canadian crowd breathed a sigh of relief and settled back in their seats anticipating the last of the ninth inning.

They overlooked one thing, however. The Dodgers had one out left. Right fielder Rick Monday, always a long-ball threat, stepped to the plate. Rogers, pitching carefully to the free-swinging Monday, ran the count to 3 and 1. The next pitch was supposed to be a low breaking sinker. The ball hung. Monday uncoiled his body like a rattler and struck with force. He could feel the bat make solid contact with the ball. He watched as the white blur began a graceful arc toward right center field. Andre Dawson, the Montreal center fielder, gave chase but ran out of room at the 375-foot mark, and watched dejectedly as the ball dropped over the barrier for a home run. Fernando Valenzuela and Bob Welch completed the formality of nailing down the pennant, but it was Rick Monday who was the hero of the day.

Rick Monday, in Los Angeles baseball lore, will always be known as the man who hit "THE pennant-winning home run."

Rick Monday, seconds after snatching the American flag from radical demonstrators intent on burning it. (Los Angeles Dodger Photo)

1977—RON CEY'S FANTASTIC APRIL

Ron Cey, known fondly as "The Penguin" to Dodger fans, because of his waddling gait, was a member of L.A.'s record-breaking, long-running infield, holding down third base in Dodger Stadium for ten years, 1973 through 1982. During his Dodger career, the chunky third baseman accumulated 228 home runs with 842 runs batted in. He was known as a dangerous clutch hitter who could put a low fast ball into orbit.

Cey helped the Dodgers win four National League pennants and one World Championship. In the 1981 World Series, he was co-MVP, along with Steve Yeager and Pedro Guerrero. He hit more than 20 home runs on six occasions, and twice drove in more than 100 runs. His peak year was 1977, when he hit 30 homers and knocked in 110 runs. In April of that year he sparked a Dodger charge that ran off 17 victories in the first 20 games of the season, paving the way for an easy route to the Western Division title. Along the way, he set a new major league record for runs batted in during the month of April, his 29 RBIs breaking the old mark of 27 set by Willie Stargell six years before.

"The Penguin" got off the mark quickly, knocking in two runs in the Dodgers opening three-game series against the San Francisco Giants at home. When the lowly Atlanta Braves moved into town and immediately knocked off Lasorda's team, 7-6, it looked like 1977 might be a long season. But there was a ray of sunshine standing in the wings. Cey had laced eight hits in the first four games, and had five RBIs. The next day, L.A. upped their record to 3-2 with a 14-10 slugfest victory over Dave Bristol's upstarts. Cey contributed a triple and a run batted in to the triumph. In the getaway game, won by the Dodgers, 4-3, the L.A. third baseman had a homer and an RBI.

The Big Blue Machine shifted into high gear when they moved into the bay area for a three-game series with Joe Altobelli's crew. Reggie Smith's two home runs sparked a 7-1 L.A. rout in the opener, with Cey getting one hit and one RBI. Reggie homered again the next night in support of Hooton's five-hit, 5-0 shutout. In the finale, the Dodgers came from behind in the late innings to win it, after "The Penguin" had tied the game in the sixth with a homerun.

Cey continued his torrid pace when the Dodgers faced the mighty Cincinnati Reds in Riverfront Stadium, in the first crucial series of the year. Both teams wanted to establish superiority on the field early, in order to grab the upper hand in the pennant race. Lasorda's boys did all the grabbing as they swept the Reds two straight, by scores of 7-3 and 3-1.

Los Angeles' record was now 9-2, and they were comfortably positioned at the top of the National League West. Ron Cey, who had hit in all 11 games, paced the attack with three home runs, 12 RBIs, and a .395 batting average.

Still on the road, the Californians moved into sunny Georgia to renew their battle with the Braves. Atlanta stopped L.A.'s seven-game win streak with a 6-5 win in the series opener, but Tommy Lasorda's warriors bounced back the next day to start a new winning streak. Ron Cey smashed a three-run homer early, then hit a ninth-inning sacrifice fly, as L.A. won the second game 7-6. The 29-year-old slugger was unstoppable. The next day, he blasted a grand-slam homer and added another RBI in a 16-6 Dodger runaway.

As the Los Angeles contingent headed for San Diego, they sported an impressive 11-3 record, and a 3 1/2-

Ron Cey sends a low fast ball into orbit, one of the nine home runs he hit during the month of April.

game bulge over second place Atlanta. Cey's contributions were impressive; five home runs and 22 RBIs in 14 games. The onslaught continued against the Padres, as Cey hit two homers and drove in three runs in a 7-3 Dodger triumph. He had two hits the following night, but failed to knock in any runs in a Dodger victory. In Game Three, however, he was back on track. A home run, two singles, and two runs batted in, helped Lasorda's team win their fourth game in a row, 7-6. His game-winning RBI in the eighth was his 27th of the season, tying him with Willie Stargell for the major league record for most RBIs during the month of April. He took a short breather the next day, going hitless to snap his 17-game hitting steak, but L.A. won anyway, defeating the Padres, 7-5, to complete a four-game sweep.

Cey wasn't through yet, however. Two games still remained in the month, and he was taking dead aim on the record. Back home again for the first time in two weeks, he went hitless for the second successive game, but he drove in a run in the 4-0 victory, giving him a new major league mark of 28. On April 30, playing against the Montreal Expos, the pride of Tacoma, Washington crashed a seventh-inning home run in the Dodgers 6-4 win.

It was an exciting month for both the Los Angeles Dodgers and for Ron Cey. L.A. finished the month in first place with a smart 17-3 record, good enough for a 7 1/2-game lead over Atlanta.

Cey had himself a once-in-a-lifetime month. His astronomical .425 batting average included nine home runs and a record-breaking 29 runs batted in. His average tailed off as the season progressed, but his run production didn't. In spite of a .241 season average, "The Penguin" hit a career-high 30 home runs and drove in a career-best 110 runs.

The Los Angeles Dodgers won the National League West title by ten big games.

1977—THE DODGERS' FOUR-MAN, 30 HOME RUN CLUB

Nineteen seventy-seven was a red-letter day in Dodger baseball. Tommy Lasorda's team produced four players with thirty or more home runs, a feat never before accomplished in major league history.

The exclusive club consisted of first baseman Steve Garvey, third baseman Ron Cey, and outfielders Reggie Smith and Dusty Baker. Only one of the foursome had ever hit as many as 30 home runs before. That was Reggie Smith who poled 30 for the Boston Red Sox in 1971. None of them ever reached that exalted plateau again.

When the 1977 season began, rookie manager Tommy Lasorda was cautiously optimistic. He felt his team could challenge for the pennant, but he knew they had an immense obstacle to overcome, the Big Red Machine of manager Sparky Anderson. The Cincinnati juggernaught had romped to the 1975 pennant by 20 games, and had carried off the '76 flag by a comfortable ten-length margin. The two-time World Champions, fresh off a 4 to 0 sweep of the New York Yankees in the World Series, had won a total of 210 regular-season games over the two-year span.

Garvey and Cey were established sluggers in Los Angeles, while veterans Baker and Smith were beginning their second season in a Dodger uniform. Reggie Smith, a 32-year-old slugger with over 200 major league home runs to his credit, and Dusty Baker, a polished outfielder who had played in the shadow of Hank Aaron in Atlanta, were counted on to add punch to the Dodger attack.

And add punch they did, as the Dodgers scored 161 more runs than they did the previous year. The revitalized offense, combined with their overpowering pitching staff of John, Rhoden, Sutton, Hooton, and Rau, which

led the league in ERA for the sixth straight year, made life easy for the new manager. Lasorda's boys broke away from the pack early, winning 17 of their first 20 games, and were never seriously challenged. Ron Cey led the breakaway by hitting the ball at a blistering .425 pace in April, with nine home runs and a major league-record 29 runs batted in. Sparky Anderson's Big Red Machine fell by the wayside as their starting pitching sputtered and their bullpen collapsed.

The Dodger lead reached 14 games by late July, and they coasted to a ten-game triumph over the Reds. Not only did the big four play long ball, but the entire lineup, with the exception of Bill Russell, flexed their muscles. By the time the season ended, the Dodgers had accumulated 191 round trippers, including 16 by catcher Steve Yeager, 15 by Rick Monday, and 11 by Davey Lopes.

Steve Garvey became the charter member of the 30 home run club when he took Manny Sarmiento of the Cincinnati Reds downtown in Riverfront Stadium on Sep-

The four members of the "30 Home Run Club" accomplished their most improbable feat while playing half their games in Dodger Stadium, a notorious pitcher's park.

tember 14. Four days later, at Dodger Stadium, "The Penguin," Ron Cey, joined the club with a circuit smash off southpaw Mickey Mahler of the Atlanta Braves. Reggie Smith followed suit the same day, off reliever Dave Campbell, giving L.A. three 30-homer men.

Dusty Baker carried the drama down to the last day of the season, with his home run production stalled at 29. Finally, in the sixth inning of the final game, Dusty caught a J.R. Richards fast ball and drove it into the left-field seats at Dodger stadium for the record setting home run. The crowd of 46,501 roared with delight and went home happy, in spite of the 6-3 loss to the Astros.

The 1977 Los Angeles Dodgers were the first team in major league history to have four men with 30 or more home runs. Steve Garvey finished the year with 33 homers, Reggie Smith had 32, and Cey and Baker hit 30 each.

1977 AND 1978–BILL RUSSELL, KING OF THE NLCS

The League Championship Series, begun in 1969, is the most pressure packed part of the baseball season. Winning the division title is satisfying, but it is accomplished over a 162-game schedule, where each game is important, but not critical. Today's mistake can be corrected tomorrow. Winning the World Series is gratifying, but even if you lose, you are still the league champion. Winning the LCS is a matter of life or death. The most important title in baseball is "league champion." A divison title is empty if it does not lead to a league championship. No one ever remembers who came in second in a league race.

From 1969 through 1984, the LCS was a five-game shootout. There was no margin for error. It was win or go home. The Dodger teams of the 1970s were deadly in the NLCS. Their lineup was loaded with clutch hitters. Dusty Baker laced the ball at a .373 clip in four championship series; Cey hit .302, Garvey .343, and Bill Russell .337. Russell's contributions were even bigger than his average showed. He gained a reputation for coming through in the clutch, getting the big hit when the title was on the line. That was never more evident than in the 1977 AND 1978 National League Championship Series against the Philadelphia Phillies.

In '77, the Dodgers and Phils split the first two games. In Game Three, L.A. starter Burt Hooton experienced severe growing pains in a pressure situation. With the Dodgers up 2-0 in the bottom of the second, Hooton slowly became unglued. Singles by Greg Luzinski and Bob Boone gave the Phils two base runners with two out. As the 63,719 raucous fans in Philadelphia's Veterans Stadium hooted and howled at the tall Texan, he lost the location of the plate, and walked Ted Sizemore to load the bases. The big park rocked. Hooton temporarily regained his composure with pitcher Larry Christensen at the plate, jumping ahead of the .143 hitter, 1-2 in the count. Then he proceeded to throw three straight balls, walking Christensen and forcing in the Phils' first run of the game.

Bill Russell, a dependable shortstop for the Dodgers for 18 years, was at his best when the chips were down. He helped his team win four pennants and one World Championship. (Los Angeles Dodger Photo)

Visibly upset, he walked both Bake McBride and Larry Bowa to force in two more runs before manager Tommy Lasorda rescued him from the living hell he had created. The experience, painful as it was, paid dividends four years later when Hooton paced the Dodgers to the National League Championship by winning two games in the big series against Montreal, and finishing with a perfect 0.00 ERA.

The game bounced back and fourth for eight innings, with Danny Ozark's team protecting a 5-3 lead. Then, in the ninth, the Dodgers and Bill Russell fought back. After the first two Dodgers were retired, pinch hits by Vic Davallilo and Manny Mota and a single by Davey Lopes tied the score and put the go-ahead run on second. Moments later, Bill Russell, the man of the hour, lined a base hit back through the box, giving Tommy Lasorda's team a thrilling 6-5 come-from-behind victory. L.A. clinched the Championship the next day when Tommy John tossed a seven-hitter for a 4-1 victory. Russell added another RBI to his trophy belt.

The following year, the same two adversaries squared off again. After Los Angeles took the first two games in the enemy's park, the Phils bounced back in L.A., winning Game Three ,9-4, behind lefty Steve Carlton. Game Four was nip and tuck, a typical nailbiter. The score was tied at 2-2 in the sixth when Steve Garvey hit a long home run to left field, his fourth round-tripper of the playoffs. Bake McBride tied it again for Philly with a seventh-inning homer. The game moved into extra innings with Terry Forster facing Philadelphia's eccentric reliever, Tug McGraw. In the Dodger tenth, McGraw retired the first two men in order. Then, like '77, Lasorda's team rallied. Cey, being very selective, walked on four pitches. Dusty Baker sent a line drive to center field for what should have been the final out of the inning, but McBride dropped the ball for an error, and the Dodgers had men on first and second. Russell, in a familiar position, came through again, lining a pennant-winning single to center field.

Russell went on to lead all Dodgers at the plate in the 1978 World Series with an average of .423.

1980—MANNY MOTA—PINCH HITTER EXTRAORDINAIRE

Manny Mota could always hit. A native of Santo Domingo in the Dominican Republic, Mota carried a sizzling bat, even in sandlot play. At the age of 19, he was signed to a professional baseball contract by the San Francisco Giants, along with Orlando Cepeda and Juan Marichal. First brought up to the major leagues by the Giants in 1962, the 25-year-old outfielder was traded to Pittsburgh the next year. He soon hit his way into the starting lineup for Danny Murtaugh's Pirates, compiling a .300 + average over the next six years. Never a long-ball threat, the 5'10", 160-pound outfielder eventually became a platoon player, starting against left-handers. He also began his "other" career, as a world-class pinch hitter.

Mota became a Los Angeles Dodger in 1969. The next five years found the smiling Dominican platooning for Smokey Alston as the Dodgers sought to rebuild their once-dominant team into another pennant contender. By 1974, Alston had his lineup in place and Mota was relegated exclusively to a pinch-hitting role. It was a role he relished, and one he excelled in. Coming up to bat late in the game with victory hanging in the balance, the confident Mota, more often than not, crashed the key hit to ignite a game-winning rally.

His most famous hit came in the 1977 National League Championship Series against Philadelphia. Having split the first two games of the series, the Dodgers and Phils were down to a best-of-three playoff. In Game Three at Philadelphia, Alston's charges found themselves down 5-3 in the ninth inning. Relief ace Gene Garber easily retired Baker and Monday on ground balls, and stood one out from victory. He got no closer. Little Vic Davalillo, another pinch-hitting magician, dragged a bunt down the first-base line, and beat it out for a hit. The Dodgers had a life. Alston motioned Mota to the bat rack, and Mr. Clutch responded brilliantly. After getting himself in a two-strike hole, Mota picked out an inside pitch and pulled it down the left-field line. Before Greg Luzinski could retrieve the ball, Davillilo was home with the fourth run, and Mota was comfortably into second. Seconds later, a single by Davey Lopes scored Mota with the tying run, and another

Manny Mota has been a valuable member of the Dodger organization since 1969. He still holds the Los Angeles career pinch-hit record, with 106 hits. (Los Angeles Dodger Photo)

single by Bill Russell brought home the game winner. L.A. went on to wrap up the series the next day when Tommy John stopped the Phils, 4-1.

In 1979, Manny Mota broke Smokey Burgess' record of 144 pinch hits, then retired to the coaching box. Twice, Mota was reactivated to help the Dodgers in pennant drives and, in 1980, he cracked his 150th and final pinch hit. Over his 20-year career, Manny Mota compiled a .304 batting average. As a pinch hitter, he was .297, with 150 hits in 505 at bats. As a Dodger, he was a .316 hitter in emergency roles.

Manny Mota is still the world's greatest pinch hitter.

1980—DODGER DIAMOND VISION MAKES ITS DEBUT

Diamond Vision, a Los Angeles Dodger innovation, is a mammoth 875-square foot television screen that sits atop the left center field grandstand at Dodger Stadium. Its purpose is to inform and entertain the fans during a ballgame. It measures 35 feet wide by 25 feet high.

Diamond Vision was the first full-color matrix board in the world. The system, which works on the same principle as a home color television set, was built by the Mitsubishi Corporation of Japan for the Dodgers in 1980. It was unveiled at the 51st All-Star game, played in L.A. on July 8 of that year.

The board is used to show replays and highlights of game action, outstanding defensive and offensive plays in slow-motion and freeze frame, as well as statistical information about the players. Diamond Vision is between-inning entertainment that does not interfere with the flow of the game.

The board consists of 38,400 red, green, and blue

lights, which produce a high-quality image. A new, state-of-the-art video display system, with advanced graphics, was installed in Dodger Stadium in 1991, further increasing the resolution of the picture.

Barry Stockhamer, at the time Director of Ticket Marketing and Promotions, spearheaded the Diamond Vision concept in the United States. Although the Dodgers were the first team to install Diamond Vision, many other teams followed suit after they viewed the Dodger system.

The control room, which is located in the pressbox area behind home plate, contains 27 monitors and a crew of 11. Three cameramen are constantly shooting game action, as well as capturing interesting sidelights in the stands. As the game proceeds, the directors select the shots to be viewed.

The producers of the Diamond Vision show arrive many hours before game time to prepare various programs to be shown that day. Game action is combined with musical selections, then edited to provide a brief entertaining interlude between innings. Additional selections are prepared during the game from humorous or exciting events on the field or in the stands. And there are always dozens of videocassettes on hand, most from "This Week in Baseball," that contain 90-second action sequences from around the major leagues.

The directors of Diamond Vision are careful not to interfere with the game action, which is the primary focus of the fans' attention. The video vignettes are used to fill the time between innings, or during a lull in the action. They complement the game, adding to the evening's overall entertainment.

Video selections include information about the Dodgers, news about the other major league teams, and current world events. As former producer Paul Kalil said, "It's really our own TV show, from three diversified locations, with a new script each game. We bring the fans closer to the players, who enjoy looking up and seeing a miracle catch they just made, too.

"After one recent playoff victory, we took our own cameras right into the clubhouse, permitting the fans at the park to celebrate with the players in the dressing room.

"When Pete Rose broke Stan Musial's record, we took the television feed from Philadelphia and showed it live on Diamond Vision.

"We had the space shuttle landing as it happened. We didn't want the fans wondering what they had missed in the world."

Diamond Vision, it seems, does it all. During an exciting game, Diamond Vision provides lighthearted entertainment between innings. During dull games, Diamond Vision is worth the price of admission all by itself.

1981–FERNANDOMANIA

Fernando Valenzuela stormed out of Sonora, Mexico, in 1981 to capture the hearts of the baseball world. With only 18 major league innings under his belt, the 20-year-old southpaw was thrust into the Los Angeles Dodgers' opening-day lineup as a last-minute replacement for scheduled starting pitcher, Jerry Reuss. Fifty-one thousand Dodger fans crowded into Dodger Stadium to see the new phenom in action. They witnessed history in the making.

The unflappable southpaw threw a 2-0 shutout, initiating a month and a half of craziness known around the southern California area as "Fernandomania." In his second start, five days later, the youngster faced the Giants in San Francisco. His famous screwball, which was death on right-handed batters, kept Jack Clark & Co. off balance all night. Ten of them went down on strikes, as he spun a neat 7-1 four hitter.

Dodger fans began to sit up and take notice of the chubby, baby-faced hurler after his victory over Frisco. When he blanked the Padres, 2-0, in his next outing, fanning ten more in the process, Fernandomania was born. The kid was 3-0, with two shutouts and a dazzling 0.33 earned run average. Would he ever lose a game? Romantic Angelenos didn't think so. Neither did Dodger fans around the rest of the country. They began to wink knowingly at each other whenever it was Fernando's turn to pitch. An "OK" gesture with their thumb and forefinger, coupled with a sly "Fernando goes tonight" whisper, was a sure guarantee of a Dodger victory.

And, for a time, that seemed to be the case. Another game against the Astros–another shutout–11 more strikeouts. The west coast was in a frenzy. Hordes of media people descended on Valenzuela's locker, on his apartment, cornered him on the street. Everyone wanted to know all the details of his early life. Where was he born? Did he have any brothers or sisters? Did he have a girlfriend?

America's appetite for gossip concerning the new pitching sensation was insatiable, particularly in southern California, where a large Mexican-American population had a new hero. The Latinos stormed Dodger Stadium to witness his historic march through the major leagues. They bought newspapers and magazines, crowded around radios and TV sets, and snatched up anything and everything that mentioned the kid from Sonora.

The Dodgers returned home to face San Francisco again on the night of April 11. It was Fernando's first home start since he blanked Houston in the opener, and the big Latino crowd turned it into a Mexican fiesta, screaming, singing, and dancing on every pitch their hero threw. Fernando didn't disappoint them. Giant manager Frank Robinson's boys went quietly to their execution, becoming victim number five, and the fourth to be humbled via the shutout route. The 20-year-old southpaw with the deadly screwball dazzled the up-staters with a 5-0, seven-strikeout performance. His ERA dipped to a paltry 0.20!!!

Fernando first burst upon the major league scene in the fall of 1980, when, as a 19-year-old rookie, he hurled 18 shutout innings in the heat of the pennant race, as the Dodgers overtook the Houston Astros on the last day of the season. (W. McNeil)

Five days later, the secret code words made the rounds of Dodgerland one more time, "Fernando goes tonight." All was well with the world. The Dodgers were assured a victory. Not unexpectedly, the rookie came through again, stopping the Montreal Expos, 6-1 in a tight, 10-inning thriller. Five big runs in the extra frame brought him home a winner. The Expos' run, coming with two men out in the eighth inning, snapped the Dodger lefty's scoreless-innings streak at 36.

Valenzuela's off-field schedule became more and more hectic as the days passed. Public Appearances. TV shows. Limousines to whisk him from one appointment to another. It was like a dream, but it was also emotionally tiring, and the 20-year-old peasant boy from south of the border began to feel the strain.

Still, in his next start, he rolled to victory number seven, blanking the New York Mets, 1-0, in an 11 strikeout performance. Now, Fernando's every pitch was news. Spanish-speaking radio stations beamed Dodger games to dozens of locations in Mexico and South America. Fernando Valenzuela suddenly became a household word in Dodgerland, and a hero to millions of poor Mexican-Americans, who needed a hero to emulate.

Victory #8 was a little tougher. The Dodgers pushed across a run in the bottom of the ninth inning to bring Fernando home a 3-2 winner over the Montreal Expos. After eight games, the southpaw's record stood at 8-0, with five shutouts and an earned run average of 0.50.

Then, on May 18, the dream ended. The kid with the explosive screwball proved he was human after all. Pitching in L.A. against right-hander Marty Bystrom of the Philadelphia Phillies, he was jolted for a first-inning home run by Mike Schmidt and suffered through a three-

run Philadelphia fourth. Bystrom blanked Fernando and his mates, 4-0. Strangely enough, as the *Cleveland Press* later reported, "...despite the doubts of 13 million residents in the LA metropolis, the sun came up, the Pacific Ocean didn't dry up, and the freeways were still jammed."

Fernando's season didn't end there, however. The young phenom went on to capture the National League Rookie of the Year award and the Cy Young award–the first time in history that a pitcher had won both awards in the same year. Capping off his fantasy year, his three postseason victories, including a courageous winning effort in the World Series against the New York Yankees, helped catapult Tommy Lasorda's "Comeback Kids" to a World Championship.

1983–STEVE GARVEY SETS NEW CONSECUTIVE GAME RECORD

On July 28, 1983, during the first game of a doubleheader against the Atlanta Braves, San Diego Padre first baseman Steve Garvey tried to score from third base on a wild pitch. In the ensuing collision, Garvey dislocated a thumb, sidelining him for two months. When he failed to play in the second game, it marked the first time since September 3, 1975, that the durable infielder had missed a game.

Steve Garvey's string of 1,207 consecutive games played established a new National League record, eclipsing the old mark of 1,117 set by Chicago Cubs outfielder Billy Williams on September 2, 1970.

Steve Garvey

Steve Garvey's crowning achievement was winning the 1981 World Championship. Here, he and teammate Ron Cey celebrate during the victory parade, through the streets of Los Angeles, on October 30, 1981.

The new Iron Man came up to the major leagues with the Los Angeles Dodgers in 1969. Originally a third baseman with an erratic arm, he was worked into the lineup at first base in 1972 to take advantage of his booming bat. Within a year he was the Dodgers' regular first baseman, displacing Bill Buckner, who was moved to the outfield.

Garvey adjusted to his new position easily, becoming one fourth of Los Angeles' longest-running major league infield, along with Lopes, Russell, and Cey. Known around the league as "Mr. Clutch" for his timely hits, Garvey sparked to Dodgers to four National League flags and one World Championship over an eight-year period.

His clutch hitting is reflected in his postseason batting averages; .368 in five Division Series games, .343 in 17 NLCS games, and .344 in 23 World Series games.

The Florida native began his consecutive-game streak on September 3, 1975. Six years later, on June 7, 1981, in a home game against the Atlanta Braves, the 5'10" slugger reached his first milestone when he played in his 1,000th consecutive game, becoming only the fifth player in major league history to reach that figure. The 44,714 Dodger fans in attendance gave their hero a standing ovation at the start of the game.

When the 1982 season ended, the Los Angeles management, committed to a youth movement, let the 34-year-old infielder test the waters in the free-agency market. His career in Los Angeles had covered a span of 14 years, encompassing 1,727 games. As a Dodger, he batted a consistent .301, with 211 home runs and 992 runs batted in, in 6,543 at bats. His consecutive game streak stood at 1,107 games when he departed L.A.

The handsome right hander returned to Dodger Stadium in early April, chasing Billy Williams' record of 1,117 games. He broke that record on April 17, 1983 before a pro-Garvey crowd of 50,800 joyous fans. In a 20-minute pre-game ceremony at home plate, Garvey received numerous gifts and posed for pictures with Williams. During the course of the game, the Padre first-sacker responded with a single and a double in four trips to the plate off Dodger starter Jerry Reuss but, in the end, the first-place Dodgers prevailed, 8-5.

Three months later, the record had reached 1,207 before his ill-conceived slide home. Steve Garvey's National league record of 1,207 consecutive games played, placed him third on the all-time major league list, surpassed only by Lou Gehrig's amazing 2,130 game streak, and Everett Scott's 1,307 games.

The gritty infielder came back from his injury to give San Diego four solid years of first-base play, before retiring in 1987.

Steve Garvey's consecutive-game National League record is still intact, although he has dropped to fourth place on the all-time major league list. Cal Ripken, the dependable shortstop of the Baltimore Orioles, surpassed Lou Gehrig's all-time major league mark of 2,130 games in 1995. By the time he retired, he had extended the record to 2,632 games.

1985—PEDRO GUERRERO SETS NATIONAL LEAGUE HOMERUN RECORD

June of 1985 is a month that Los Angeles Dodger outfielder Pedro Guerrero will never forget. And with good reason. He set a National League home run record by slamming 15 round-trippers during the month, breaking the record of 14, previously held jointly by Ralph Kiner and Mike Schmidt. His performance tied the major-league mark shared by Babe Ruth, Bob Johnson, and Roger Maris.

When the 1985 season got underway, Guerrero was Tommy Lasorda's designated third baseman and had been for over two years. After Ron Cey was traded to the Cubs in 1982, the Dodger manager tried to convert Guerrero to a third baseman. It was a disastrous two-year experiment. In 1983, the handsome Dominican booted 29 balls. The following year, he bobbled 22 more. Guerrero's defensive problems also carried over into the batter's box. His home run production plummeted from 32 in '83 to 16 in '84, while his RBIs dropped from 103 to 72.

As May, 1985, came to a close, Lasorda threw in the towel, and returned his number-one slugger to his favorite left-field position. In addition to another handful of errors at third, Pete was hitting only .268 with four homers and 16 runs batted in. His morale had deteriorated to an all-time low.

On June 1, the 5'11", 175-pounder found himself back in the outfield, with a new lease on life. He immediately celebrated by smashing a home run and going 2-5 in a losing effort. The next day, as the Dodgers nipped the Expos, 8-7, Guerrero went 1-5, and contributed an RBI to the cause.

The Mets followed Montreal into L.A. for a mid-week series. The Dodgers took two of three, and Pete had a home run and two runs batted in.

The Big Blue Machine left town after the Met series, stopping first in Atlanta to do battle with Ted Turner's Braves. Guerrero hit home run #7 in the opener, and the Dodgers won easily 7-2. In Game Two, the Braves blasted Hershiser for six runs in 1 2/3 innings, en route to a 7-3 victory. Pedro was the entire L.A. offense, pounding two hits in three at bats, with a homer and three RBIs. The fifth-place Tribe continued their bombardment the next day, routing Fernando Valenzuela during a 10-3 romp. The Dominican left fielder was 1-4.

Moving on to Cincinnati, Guerrero stayed hot. His home run and two runs batted in propelled Los Angeles to a 7-4 win. The Reds were up 3-0 in the fourth when Guerrero and Marshall hit round-trippers, igniting an L.A. comeback. The last two games of the series were postponed by rain.

In Houston, the big slugger picked it up a notch. His home run in the fifth knocked out Astro starter Joe Niekro as the Dodgers rolled 10-2 behind Jerry Reuss' eight-hitter. L.A. trailed 2-0 after three, but they bounced back with three runs in the fourth, two in the fifth, one in the sixth, one in the seventh, and three more in the ninth. Guerrero hit his second home run of the day in the seventh inning. It was his 11th of the season and seventh during the month of June.

Pete propelled #12 over the left-field fence the next day, adding a double in four trips to the plate. Orel Herhsiser's three-hitter stopped Houston, 3-0. In the getaway game, Fernando tossed a six-hitter, blanking the Astros again, 9-0. Pete was 2-5 with a double, a home run, and three RBIs. The homer was his eighth in the last ten games, and his feat of homering in four consecutive games tied a team record.

Coming back to home cooking didn't seem to do Pedro any good as he went homer-less in the next two games. Then, on June 19, the revitalized slugger punched #14 leading off the seventh inning to break open a 1-1 tie against San Diego. L.A. added three more runs in the inning, and won going away, 5-1. In the process, they shattered Andy Hawkins' winning streak. The San Diego pitcher was 10-0 coming into the game.

Two days later, Guerrero hit #15, and on June 23, against Houston, he tied Frank Howard's club record by depositing his 12th of the month into the seats. Howard's 12 homers had come in July 1962. The next day Guerrero hit #17 in the ninth inning, but it was too little, too late. Houston prevailed, 8-4.

After a one-game drought against San Diego, the red-hot slugger came back with his 18th of the season in the third inning against the Padres, but again it wasn't enough. The Padres roughed Hershiser up to the tune of 10-4.

Another drought, this one lasting three games, brought Guerrero and the Dodgers down to the last game of June, with Pedro stalled at 14 homers for the month. A big home crowd turned out to encourage their favorite player, and Pedro responded in grand style. With the Dodgers trailing, 3-2 in the bottom of the eighth, Guerrero followed a Ken Landreaux single with a big two-run homer off relief ace Bruce Sutter, rocketing L.A. into a 4-3 lead. The blow set a new National League home run record for June, eclipsing the mark of 14 set by Ralph Kiner in 1947, and matched by Mike Schmidt in 1977.

Ken Howell shut the Padres down in the ninth, with the help of an outstanding defensive effort by Guerrero. With one man out and Gerald Perry on second base, Albert Hall hit a sinking liner to left field. Guerrero raced in at full speed to make a sensational shoestring catch of the ball, and his quick throw to Steve Sax doubled Perry off second to end the game.

For the month, Pedro Guerrero batted .344 with 32 hits in 93 at bats. His totals included 15 home runs and 26 runs batted in. He also scored 27 runs. The onslaught raised Pete's season's average to an even .300, increased his home run total to 18, his runs scored to 44, and his RBIs to 40.

Pedro Guerrero was the Dodgers' top fence buster during the 1980s. He led Tommy Lasorda's club in most offensive categories, including home runs (171), runs batted in (585), and batting average (.309). (Los Angeles Dodger Photo)

Curiously, in spite of Guerrero's heroics, Tommy Lasorda's crew could do no better than compile a 14-10 record for the month, losing a half-game in the standings to the San Diego Padres.

Freed from his third-base worries most of the season, Guerrero put together a typical season, finishing with 33 home runs and 87 runs batted in, in just 487 at bats. A wrist injury put him on the shelf for 17 days in September, curtailing his explosive run production.

The Dodgers, led by the slugging left fielder, went 20-7 in July to move into first place in the west. They extended the lead throughout most of the summer, and won by 5 1/2 games over the Cincinnati Reds. The Padres came in a distant third, 12 games behind L.A.

1988—OREL HERSHISER TOPS DRYSDALE'S SCORELESS STREAK

Orel Hershiser, the tall, lanky sinkerball artist of the Los Angeles Dodgers, treated the 1988 California fans to a display of pitching excellence not witnessed in these parts since the days of Sandy Koufax. The 30-year-old right-hander rejuvenated the fourth-place Dodgers with his pitching superiority, and propelled them to the 1988 National League pennant. Hershiser finished the season with a record of 23 wins and eight losses, leading the league in shutouts (eight) and innings pitched (267), and tied for the lead in victories, and complete games (15). His efforts earned him the National League's Cy Young award.

In postseason play, the Dodger ace was voted the most valuable player in the NLCS after posting a 1-0 record, with one save, one shutout, and a 2.03 ERA. He went on to capture the World Series MVP trophy also, going 2-0, with one shutout, and a 1.00 earned run average, as the rag-tag Dodgers embarrassed the mighty Oakland A's in a five-game massacre.

The highlight of Hershiser's season, however, did not come in postseason play. His historic achievement was a demonstration of pitching superiority over an extended period of time, running from August 30 through the end of the season, in the heat of the torrid National League Western Division pennant race. His brilliant performances on the mound carried him to new heights, and gave him a permanent place in the baseball record book. For 4 1/2 weeks, the kid from New Jersey was unhittable, stringing together the greatest number of shutout innings in baseball history. When the smoke cleared on the evening of October 2, Orel Hershiser IV owned the major league record for consecutive scoreless innings, his 59 straight zeroes eclipsing Don Drysdale's old record by one.

His brilliant journey began innocently enough on the evening of August 30, during a 4-2 victory over the Montreal Expos. Tim Raines carried across a Montreal run in the bottom of the fifth inning, cutting a Dodger

lead to two runs. They would get no more as Tommy Lasorda's "Bulldog" blanked them over the final four innings, improving his record to a smart 18-8.

In his next start, five days later, Hershiser hurled his fourth shutout of the season, blanking the Atlanta Braves, 3-0. The Dodger starter struggled with his control over the first three innings, then settled down to pitch a neat four-hitter, retiring 16 men in a row at one time. Mickey Hatcher, with two singles and an RBI, led the Dodger attack.

Hershiser's next victims were the third-place Cincinnati Reds, who went quietly, 5-0. The Dodger ace tossed a seven-hitter and fanned eight, in winning his 20th game of the season. Mickey Hatcher's two singles and Rick Dempsey's two-run homer led L.A. at bat.

The last-place Braves visited Los Angeles on September 14, thirsting for revenge after Hershiser's whitewash eight days previous. They did no better this time, although southpaw Mickey Mahler kept them in contention right up to the end. The game went into the bottom of the ninth scoreless, with "Bulldog" tossing a six-hitter, and Mahler working on a four hitter. Kirk Gibson led off the Dodger ninth by drawing a base on balls, only the second issued by Mahler in the game. That was all L.A. needed. Gibby took off on the pitch to Mike Marshall, and raced around the bases to score the winning run

Orel Hershiser was nicknamed "Bulldog" by manager Tommy Lasorda, not because of any particular trait, but because Lasorda thought it would make him more tenacious on the mound. It did. (W. McNeil)

when the Dodger right fielder drilled the pitch into the corner for a double. The win brought Hershiser's record to 21-8, with six shutouts, 13 complete games, and 31 consecutive scoreless innings.

Next it was on to Houston where the pride of Los Angeles met the second-place Houston Astros, now nine games in arrears. After August 10, when the Dodgers' lead had dwindled to a mere 1/2 game, the Lasorda-men won 24 of their next 36 games, while the Astros could do no better than 16-21 over the same period. Things got worse for Hal Lanier's cohorts, facing Hershiser. The 6'3", 190-pound righty tossed his second consecutive 1-0 shutout, besting Nolan Ryan and Danny Darwin in a spectacular display of pitching pyrotechnics. The Dodgers managed only three hits and two walks off three Astro pitchers, but that was enough. Houston was held to four hits and no walks. John Shelby's leadoff home run in the top of the seventh was the margin of victory.

The shutout streak wasn't easy for Hershiser. In his four consecutive shutouts, his teammates were only able to score a total of ten runs. The last two games, both 1-0 victories, went into the seventh inning, scoreless. The script was the same in San Francisco, where the Dodger ace continued to chase Don Drysdale's record of 58 consecutive scoreless innings. After seven innings, it was a scoreless tie, with lefty Atlee Hammaker matching Hershiser pitch for pitch. In the top of the eighth, Lasorda's boys staged a rally. Singles by Woodson and Griffin set the table for Mickey Hatcher, and the Dodgers' self appointed cheerleader didn't disappoint. He slammed a three-run homer to bring L.A.'s Bulldog home a winner again.

The moment of truth for Orel Leonard Hershiser IV came in San Diego on September 28. It was Hershiser's last start of the year, and he still trailed Drysdale by nine shutout innings. The best he could do in a regulation game was to tie the record. The Dodger ace put zero after zero on the scoreboard in Jack Murphy stadium as 58,000 fans sat spellbound. The Dodgers, as usual, couldn't do much either, failing to dent the plate against 6'4" right-hander Andy Hawkins. Nine innings passed, and the game was still scoreless. As Hershiser stood on the mound in the bottom of the tenth, now owning a share of the record with Drysdale, he tipped his hat in the direction of the press box, where Big D. was broadcasting the game. The Dodger ace retired the first two men, Ready and Templeton. Keith Mooreland, the next batter, worked the count to one ball and two strikes before lifting a short fly ball to right field. Jose Gonzalez squeezed it for the record-breaking out. L.A. lost the game, 2-1, in 16 innings, but it was immaterial. Hershiser had his record, and the Dodgers had clinched the Western Division title two days before.

Orel Hershiser's September statistics were impressive.

GAMES	6
COMPLETE GAMES	5
INNINGS PITCHED	55
HITS	30
WINS	5
LOSSES	0
STRIKEOUTS	34
BASES ON BALLS	8
SHUTOUTS	5
EARNED RUN AVERAGE	0.00

Hershiser's consecutive scoreless innings record of 59 should last for many years. Certainly his September pitching performance will never be surpassed.

He was perfect.

1988– KIRK GIBSON–"THE NATURAL"

Roy Hobbs was a fictional baseball player who performed fantastic feats with the bat in the novel, *The Natural*. Kirk Gibson was the Roy Hobbs of 1988.

The Michigan native was the heart and soul of the Los Angeles Dodgers 1988 World Championship team. The former Michigan State flanker brought a winning attitude to his new team, a dedication to excellence he perfected under Sparky Anderson in Detroit. The 6'3", 215-pound slugger led the Steel City Tigers to a World Series victory over the San Diego Padres, in 1984. His 27 home runs and 91 RBIs spearheaded Detroit's 15-game runaway over Toronto in the American League Eastern Division race. In the ensuing three game sweep of the Kansas City Royals in the ALCS, the left-handed hitter led both teams at the plate with an average of .417. He climaxed his outstanding season in Game Five of the Series, his first-inning two-run homer propelling the Tigers to the World Championship. The big right fielder batted .333 with two home runs in the fall classic, and led both teams with seven runs batted in.

As he told the press upon his arrival in L.A., "I'll do whatever it takes to win. If it takes personal sacrifice, that's what I'll do. I always give 100%." That was an understatement. Gibson always gave 110%. His leadership qualities surfaced early in spring training when, after Jesse Orosco lined the inside of his hat with shoe black, causing streams of black perspiration to run down his face, he stormed off the field yelling, "No wonder this team finished fourth last year. I'm here to work, not play games."

Kirk Gibson's intensity gradually infiltrated the Dodger clubhouse, creating a new, positive atmosphere. Overnight he became the unofficial team leader, infusing his teammates with a burning desire to win. "I came to L.A. to win. That's my #1 goal every day. When I leave spring training, I'm leaving to be a World Champion." All

25 players heard his message, and they joined with him, dedicating themselves to winning the pennant.

After the Dodgers dropped the season's opener to San Francisco, 5-1, they reeled off five wins in a row. Orel Hershiser finished the first month of the season with a 5-0 record, as Tommy Lasorda's boys battled Houston for the top spot. By mid-July, the Dodgers enjoyed a seven-game lead over the second-place Astros. Kirk Gibson's victory cry, a familiar sight to members of the press corps, typified the new Dodger spirit. Standing next to his locker, half naked, after each victory, the 31-year-old slugger cupped his hands to his mouth, and bellowed his inspiring message, "How sweet it is; to taste the fruits of victory."

One of the key games of the season was played in Los Angeles on August 20. The Dodger lead was down to four games, and threatening to go even lower as they trailed the Montreal Expos, 3-2, in the bottom of the ninth. Then, as he had all season, Kirk Gibson raced to the rescue. He singled in the tying run, and immediately stole second base. When pitcher Joe Hesketh uncorked a wild pitch, Gibson had only one thought in mind; to score the winning run. He rounded third at full speed, and headed home. His surprise tactics caught Montreal catcher Nelson Santovenia off guard, and before he could retrieve the ball, the Dodger speedster slid across the plate with the winning run, as 46,743 Dodger fans went crazy.

The Dodger lead gradually increased from that point until the end of the season. The Cincinnati Reds finished in second place, seven games behind the front-running Dodgers. Houston dropped back to fifth, 12 1/2 games out. Kirk Gibson finished the season with 25 home runs, 76 runs batted in, and a .290 batting average. His contributions to the pennant drive couldn't be found in naked statistics, however, as demonstrated by his winning play on August 20. The Baseball Writers of America realized this also, and they voted him the Most Valuable Player in the league for 1988

In the NLCS against the New York Mets, a team that had beaten the Dodgers ten times in 11 meetings during the regular season, Gibson hit a key game-winning home run in the 12th inning of Game Four, deadlocking the series at two games apiece. The following day, the left-handed slugger pounded a three-run homer in the fifth inning, leading Tommy Lasorda's team to a 7-4 victory, and catapulting them into a three-games-to-two lead. They won the series, in seven games, as Orel Hershiser blanked the Mets, 6-0, in the finale.

Gibson, on the bench with a knee injury, was limited to one at bat in the World Series against the Oakland Athletics, but what an at bat it was. In true Roy Hobbs tradition, the crippled outfielder limped out of the dugout in the bottom of the ninth inning to pinch hit in one of the most dramatic moments in World Series history. The A's were leading, 4-3, the Dodgers had the tying run on first with two out, and the league's premier closer, Dennis Eckersley, was on the hill. Gibson, moving like a

fugitive from a hospital ward, hobbled around the plate, as he fouled off pitch after pitch. On one pitch, the Dodger star, after topping a ground ball down the first-base line, limped pathetically toward first on battered legs. Mercifully, the ball trickled foul.

With a count of three balls and two strikes on the big slugger, Eckersley tried to finesse him with a back-door slider, but Gibson was looking for the pitch. He lashed out at the ball with all the power he could generate with just his arms and wrists, and sent a high drive

Kirk Gibson had an exciting, glorious, and pain-filled major league career. He played 17 years, batted .268, with 1,553 hits in 1,635 games.

toward the right field stands. As right fielder Jose Canseco watched in stunned silence, the ball dropped into the crowd for a game-winning home run as Dodger Stadium exploded. The screams of 55,983 Dodger fans sent tremors up and down the west coast.

Gibson's fantastic blast ignited a Los Angeles World Series romp. The rag-tag Dodgers buried the mighty Oakland Athletics in five games, in one of the biggest upsets in World Series history.

Kirk Gibson was the Dodgers' magic ingredient during the 1988 "Miracle in Chavez." You had to forget the statistics when Gibson played. You had to throw out the scorebook. At bats, hits, runs, runs batted in, and batting average weren't important. His contributions were often found under "intangibles." He created a winning spirit on the ballclub. He led by example, taking the extra base, sacrificing his at bat to advance a runner, stealing a base at a critical time, making an impossible catch in the outfield with an extra effort.

Kirk Gibson's value to the 1988 Dodgers can be stated in one short sentence.

Kirk Gibson was a winner.

1988– MICKEY HATCHER, THE HUMAN BLOWOUT PATCH

If Orel Hershiser was the guts of the 1988 Los Angeles Dodger World Championship team and Kirk Gibson was its heart and soul, then Mickey Hatcher was, without a doubt its guiding spirit.

The 33-year-old Dodger outfielder had a reputation for being a clubhouse buffoon whose crazy antics drove managers back to the bottle. His reputation was well earned. The native of Arizona was, indeed, slightly eccentric. He maintained two boxes of props near his locker in L.A., one box filled with good luck charms (hats, glasses, toys), and the other box filled with charms whose good luck had worn off. It was not unusual to see the irrepressible Hatcher sitting on the bench playing with a slinky while wearing a propeller-topped beanie.

What separated Hatcher from a million other flakes around the world was his ability to play the game of baseball. Once he stepped on a ballfield, the 6'2", 205-pound dynamo went all out to win the game. No more fooling around. No more practical jokes. Inside the foul lines he was all business. And he played the game with the same boundless energy that he displayed in the clubhouse.

Mickey Hatcher, like the more intense Kirk Gibson, often looked less than graceful on the field, but he got the job done. Early in spring training, Hatcher devised the name "Stuntmen" for the Dodger bench; himself, Rick Dempsey, Franklin Stubbs, Dave Anderson, Mike Davis, Jeff Hamilton, Mike Sharperson, Danny Heep, and Tracy Woodson. Hatcher was the self-appointed leader.

The Stuntmen were named after their movie counterparts who came to the rescue of the stars when a dangerous scene needed to be filmed. The L.A. stuntmen rushed to Lasorda's rescue in strategic, late-game situations, where a clutch pinch hit or a speedy baserunner was required. The stuntmen also filled in for regulars full time when the injury jinx struck.

The leader of the stuntmen was one of a kind. He ran out bases on balls, raced around the bases on home runs, and was forever falling, sliding, and diving in the dirt. He always looked like he hadn't changed his uniform in a month. When not in the game, the peripatetic sub paced the dugout continually, eating sunflower seeds and yelling encouragement to his teammates.

Mickey Hatcher's vitality and spirit had as much to do with the Dodger success in 1988 as did Orel Hershiser's shutouts or Kirk Gibson's home runs. For the season, the Mick appeared in 88 games, filling in at first base, third base, and all outfield positions. He hit the ball at a brisk .293 pace, with 25 runs batted in, in 191 at bats.

"Mr. Everyman" scaled the heights in the World Series against the powerful Oakland Athletics. He set the tone for the entire Series in the bottom of the first inning of Game One in Los Angeles. With one man out and Steve Sax on first base, Hatcher jumped on a Dave Stewart fastball and drove it into the left-field seats for a two-run homer. As usual, he galloped around the bases at full speed as if he were afraid the umpire might change his mind and take the homer back.

In Game Three, filling in for the injured Mike Marshall in right field, the human blowout patch made a sensational diving, backhand catch of a line drive off the bat of Jose Canseco, rolling over several times before getting to his feet with his glove held high, the ball safe within. He did it ugly, but he did it.

In the fifth and final game of the fall classic, Hatcher put the last nail in the Oakland coffin. Stepping to the plate in the top of the first, with one out and Franklin Stubbs on first base, the leader of the stuntmen crushed a Storm Davis fastball and sent it six rows deep into the left-field stands. With Hershiser on the mound, that was all L.A. needed. They went on to capture the game and the World Championship, 5-2.

Mickey Hatcher was one of the sparks that ignited the Los Angeles World Championship drive. (W. McNeil)

Mickey Hatcher led both teams in hitting in the Series, slugging the ball at a .368 clip, with one double, two home runs, and five runs batted in, in five games.

Hatcher did what he had to do all year long. He pinch hit when needed, filled in at various infield and outfield positions when players were injured or needed a rest, and generally made himself available to the manager day after day. On the bench, he kept morale at a peak level, never letting a player get down after striking out or making a crucial error. A joke, a word of encouragement, a pat on the back; these were the unseen weapons of Mickey Hatcher.

The year 1988 was a glorious year in Los Angeles Dodger history. Never, in their long tenure in the National League have they accomplished so much with so little. Tommy Lasorda's gutty crew had many heroes during the season, but none of them shone any brighter than the zany outfielder from Arizona.

1990 — RAMON MARTINEZ FANS 18 BATTERS

In the summer of 1984, Dodger scout Ralph Avila spotted a tall, skinny right-handed pitcher with the Dominican Republic Olympic team in Los Angeles. The raw boned youth impressed Avila with his live arm; his sizzling fastball hurtling plateward at speeds in the mid '90s.

L.A. immediately signed 16-year-old Ramon Martinez to a minor league contract, sending him on a four-year odyssey through the Dodger farm system. The 6'4", 166-pound fireballer began his baseball education in 1985 with Bradenton in the Gulf Coast League. Two years later, he posted a terrific 16-5 record with a 2.17 ERA for Vero Beach. Moving rapidly through the minors, Martinez passed through San Antonio (8-4) of the AA Texas League, and Albuquerque (5-2) of the AAA Pacific Coast League before being promoted to the big club in August of 1988 to help the suddenly pitching-thin Dodgers in their historic pennant drive. Ramon's debut was nothing short of sensational. He started against the San Francisco Giants on August 13, and held the big Giant bats in check for seven innings, leaving with a 1-0 lead. Although he didn't get credit for the victory, the Dodgers winning 2-1 in 12 innings, he took a heavy load off the tired Dodger staff.

In mid-1989, the precocious pitcher completed his apprenticeship with a 10-2 start in Albuquerque, moving up to L.A. for good in mid-season. He went 6-4 for the Dodgers in 15 games, his 89 strikeouts in 99 innings giving promise of an exciting future. As the 1990 season blossomed, the tall, skinny kid with the blistering fastball was suddenly thrust into the spotlight as the Dodger's number one pitcher. Orel Hershiser went down early with an arm injury. Tim Belcher was erratic. And Fernando was still fighting his way back from his 1988 miseries. An undaunted Ramon Martinez picked up the gauntlet and defended the bastion.

Martinez racked up 135 victories against only 88 losses, in 14 major league seasons, 11 of them with the Dodgers. (W. McNeil)

On Monday night, June 4, in Los Angeles, his future became his present. Facing the Atlanta Braves, a club he had feasted on during his short career, Martinez discovered early that his pitches were all working to perfection, and his location had pinpoint accuracy, all the ingredients for an historic game.

With his fastball being clocked at 96 mph, the gangling right-hander sent one Brave after another back to the dugout in disgust. He struck out 14 of the first 19 batters to face him, mixing pitches and speeds like a battle-hardened veteran. In the eighth inning, slugger Dale Murphy waved vainly at the Martinez fastball, becoming strikeout victim #17. Minutes later, shortstop Jeff Blauser went down swinging for the third time, to become the 18th notch in Martinez' belt.

With four outs to go, the native of Santo Domingo stood on the threshold of immortality. He had already tied the Dodger strikeout record of 18, held by the great Sandy Koufax. He was within one strikeout of Tom Seaver's National League record, and within two K's of Roger Clemens' major league total of 20.

Ramon could not extend his total against the final four hitters, but he finished the game with a strong three hitter, issuing only a single pass to go with his 18 strikeouts. The Dodger offense meanwhile, tattooed Atlanta pitching for 12 hits, en route to a 6-0 victory. Jose Gonzalez led the L.A. attack with three hits and two runs batted in. Second baseman Juan Samuel chipped in with two hits, including a two-run homer.

The precocious 22-year-old fireballer went on to post a strong 20-6 record for the year. He finished the season with a 2.92 earned run average and struck out 223 batters in 234 innings.

At 22 years of age, Ramon Jaime Martinez held the future in the palm of his hand–a long bony hand that could throw baseballs through brick walls.

TODD HOLLANDSWORTH GIVES L.A. ANOTHER ROOKIE TROPHY

Todd Hollandsworth, a native of Dayton, Ohio, gave the Los Angeles Dodgers an unprecedented fifth consecutive National League Rookie Of The Year, with his sparkling 1996 season.

The 23-year-old Hollandsworth was always an over-achiever. He claimed he didn't have the natural talent to play in the big leagues, so he had to work harder than anyone else in order to succeed. Whatever the facts, he did work harder than anyone else, and he did succeed–in a big way.

Todd Hollandsworth has a dedicated work ethic that should produce a long and successful major league career for him. (W. McNeil)

Hollandsworth had an unusual amount of pressure put on him, by the media, when the season started. He was touted as the favorite to win the rookie award, and give the Dodgers a record five in a row. The intense young man, wanting desperately to break into the Dodger lineup, pressed in the early going, and hit only .125 over the first 11 games. Gradually he forced himself to relax, and by the middle of May, he had his batting eye back, and his average up to .286.

Down the stretch, as the Dodgers went 31-12, the 6'2", 193 pound southpaw swinger pounded the ball at a .367 clip, with 47 hits in 128 at bats, including 10 doubles, 3 triples, and 5 homers. Todd Hollandsworth, by the way, got the streak started by cracking out a single, double, and homer, driving in two runs, as the Dodgers beat the Reds 7-5 on August 10.

Cincinnati seemed to be Hollandsworth's favorite cousins. He spanked three hits against them on September 9, and again on September 10, sparking the Big Blue Machine to a three-game sweep. On the 14th, the tall lefty had a four-hit game against St. Louis, L.A. winning 9-5. His two-run homer in the ninth inning beat Colorado on September 16.

In the disappointing three-game sweep by the Reds in the first round of the playoffs, Hollandsworth led the Dodger attack, going 4 for 12, .333, with three doubles.

THE O'MALLEY ERA ENDS

The year 1997 got off to a shocking start when Los Angeles Dodger President Peter O'Malley announced at a January 6 press conference that his family was putting the team up for sale, ending a 48-year family ownership. Walter O'Malley, Peter's father, assumed control of the Dodgers in 1950, converting a successful baseball operation into the most lucrative enterprise in professional sports. During the Dodgers seven-year stay in the City of Churches under his ownership, they captured four National League flags and Brooklyn's only World Championship.

The elder O'Malley was forced to relocate his team to Los Angeles in 1958, after negotiations with New York City to construct a new baseball stadium in the borough of Brooklyn reached an impasse. Once situated in Los Angeles, the Dodgers proceeded to set attendance records, both home and away, for 45 years. Dodger Stadium attendance averaged well over 2,000,000 fans a year, with a high of 3,608,881 in 1982. In those same years, the team went over the 2,000,000 mark in 38 of 45 years, and the 3,000,000 mark 17 times.

The Dodgers on-field success contributed mightily to their elevated attendance figures. The Big Blue Machine stunned the baseball world in just their second season on the coast when they raced to the World Championship after having finished a disappointing seventh the previous year. They built on that success to capture three more National League pennants and two more World Championships between 1963 and 1966.

Peter O'Malley (SPI Archives)

Dodger Stadium, which opened in 1962, has been called the most beautiful stadium in the major leagues. The immaculately clean facility, with its well-groomed playing field and courteous and efficient stadium employees, is still the pride of the O'Malley family after 40 years.

Peter O'Malley, building on the empire his father created, continued to make the Dodgers a first-class enterprise. Almost single-handedly, he changed major league baseball from an American sport to a worldwide sport. He frequently invited foreign teams to train in Dodgertown during spring training, and he constructed a complete baseball academy in the Dominican Republic, as well as baseball fields in Managua, Nicaragua, and Tianjin, China.

The Dodger president added the first Korean-born player to a major league roster when he signed Chan Ho Park to a contract in 1994. Shortly thereafter, he secured the services of Hideo Nomo, making Nomo the first Japanese League veteran and the second Japanese-born player to play in the majors.

With a price tag of $311 million for the franchise, including the business, Dodger Stadium and land in downtown L.A., as well as Dodgertown, and the Campo Las Palma Academy in the Dominican Republic, the sale was the most lucrative event in baseball history at the time, more than double the previous record of $173 million, realized for the sale of the Baltimore Orioles in 1993.

The O'Malley era in Dodger history will be remembered for its class, stability, community involvement, and family atmosphere. The club had but one owner for 48 years, and it had only two managers for 43 of those years. Players were treated humanely and fairly, with a minimum of player movement between clubs during most of that time. The team's success is reflected in their 13 National League pennants, nine Western Division titles, and six World Championships. The O'Malley family were good friends. They will be sorely missed.

THE RUPERT MURDOCH ERA BEGINS

One era ended and another one began on March 19, 1998, when the O'Malley family sold the Los Angeles Dodgers to the FOX Group, owned by Australian media magnate Rupert Murdoch.

The new owner of the Dodgers was born in Australia in 1931. Shortly after graduating from Oxford University in England in 1953, the 23-year-old entrepreneur returned home and took control of News Limited and its major asset, the number-two daily newspaper in Adelaide. With inborn perspicacity and a generous helping of aggressiveness, Murdoch created a multi-billion dollar media empire over the next 45 years.

The Murdoch newspaper assets expanded to include the *Daily Mirror (1960)* and *The Australian (1964)* in his home country. Beginning in 1969 and continuing through the 1970s, he moved into England, acquiring *News of the World, The Sun, The Times,* and *Sunday Times.* A decade later he took over *The New York Post* and *The Weekly Standard* in the U.S. Along the way, he also acquired *Harper Collins Publishing* and *TV Guide.*

His company, News Corporation, purchased Twentieth Century Fox Film Corporation in 1985, projecting him into the visual mass media market. In the late '80s, he acquired six television stations, using them to create the Fox Television Station Group, which, in turn, helped launch the FOX Broadcasting Company. Today, FOX is a major American television network, reaching more than 40% of U.S. homes. Their heavy sports commitment includes broadcasts of games from the National Football League, the National Hockey League, and Major League Baseball.

During the decade of the '90s, Rupert Murdoch's group pioneered satellite broadcasting, with operations in England, Hong Kong, Japan, and Brazil, as well as the United States. It is now possible for FOX to televise almost any program worldwide.

News Corporation crowned its 1990s expansion program with the purchase of the Los Angeles Dodgers, thrusting the Australian media mogul into the field of professional sports ownership. Fittingly, Rupert Murdoch was named by The Sporting News as "the most powerful man in sports" in 1998.

Media mogul and Los Angeles Dodgers owner Rupert Murdoch (center) watches his Dodgers beat the Chicago Cubs on April 25, 1998. (AP/Wide World Photos)

Bob Graziano, a 14-year veteran with the Los Angeles Dodgers, was promoted to President of the team on March 19, 1998, by Peter O'Malley, who became Chairman of the Board. Graziano, a native of the City of Angels, graduated summa cum laude from the University of Southern California with a degree in Business Administration in 1980. After the usual pit stop with the accounting firm of Ernst & Young, he joined the Los Angeles Dodgers in 1986 as the club's Director of Financial Projects.

He was promoted to Vice President, Finance and Chief Financial Officer the following year, being responsible for Accounting, Human Resources, Stadium Operations, Ticketing and Management Information Systems departments. On February 13, 1997, he was appointed to the position of Executive Vice President, giving him full responsibility for the overall day-to-day functioning of the business side of the Los Angeles Dodgers.

After the sale of the Los Angeles franchise to News Corporation, Graziano reminded Dodger fans that the FOX Group's goal is to return the Los Angeles Dodgers to the top of the baseball world. FOX intends to make the Dodgers the dominant team of the first decade of the 21st century.

With that goal in mind, the management team took immediate steps to make the team a contender as quickly as possible. This was an approach that was both dynamic and unsettling. To say that the 1998 season was chaotic would be a gross understatement. Changes came fast and furious, both on the field and off. The first and most shocking change occurred on May 15 when all-world receiver Mike Piazza and third baseman Todd Zeile were shuttled off to Florida in exchange for five players, including potential superstar Gary Sheffield, gold glove catcher Charles Johnson, and three other players. The repercussions from that trade may be felt in Dodgerland for years to come

On June 4, Hideo Nomo, whose fastball had lost its zip, was traded to the New York Mets for Dave Mlicki. Seventeen days later, manager Bill Russell and General Manger Fred Claire were fired. They were replaced, on an interim basis, by Glenn Hoffman and Tommy Lasorda.

The trading frenzy continued into July. The Dodgers obtained closer Jeff Shaw from the Cincinnati Reds on the fourth of the month for rookies Paul Konerko and Dennis Reyes. Later in the month, infielder Wilton Guerrero was traded to Montreal for Mark Grudzielanek, in a seven player deal.

The quick fix didn't work as expected, however. The Dodgers struggled through another frustrating season, finishing in third place in the National League Western Division, a distant 15 games behind the pennant-winning San Diego Padres.

The rebuilding effort continued over the next four years, and by the end of the 2002 season, the Los Angeles Dodgers star was on the rise. Their 92 victories were the most games the team had won since 1991. The future once again looked bright.

Bob Graziano (Los Angeles Dodgers)

KEVIN BROWN—THE DODGERS $105 MILLION MAN

Los Angeles Dodger General Manager, Kevin Malone, stunned the baseball world on December 12, 1998, when he signed free agent pitcher Kevin Brown to a seven year, $105 million contract. It was unheard of to give a 34-year-old pitcher a long-term contract, but Dodger management was willing to assume the risk in order to bring the citizens of Los Angeles a winner during the first decade of the 21st century.

Brown, a native of Macon, Georgia, left Georgia Tech in 1986, after completing his junior year, to sign a professional baseball contract with the Texas Rangers. The 21-year-old fireballer had just six minor league appearances under his belt when he toed the rubber in Arlington Stadium for the first time on September 5. He beat the Oakland Athletics in his Big League debut, giving up two runs in five innings.

After two more years of seasoning in the minors, Kevin Brown moved up to the Rangers permanently on September 12, 1988. He spent the next six years in Texas, compiling a record of 78-64 for a team that went 467-457 over the same period. His record included a 21-11 season in 1992 for a team that won just 77 games. He led the league in innings pitched (266), as well as victories, that year.

Brown took advantage of the free agency rule to pitch for three different teams over the next four years. He spent one year in Baltimore where he won just 10 games against 9 losses. Then, in 1996, he moved on to Florida where he led the league in earned run average with a spectacular 1.89. After putting together successive seasons of 17-11 and 16-8 with the Marlins, Brown moved again in '98 to San Diego, where he went 18-7 for the pennant-winning Padres.

Kevin Brown reached the pinnacle of pitching proficiency on June 10, 1997, when he no-hit the pennant-winning San Francisco Giants, 9-0, in their own backyard. He struck out seven and didn't walk anyone, as he came within a whisker of tossing a perfect game. After retiring the first 23 batters to face him, Brown nicked Marvin Benard with a pitch before setting down the last four batters. The big right-hander also came close to a no-hitter on July 16 when he stopped the Los Angeles Dodgers, 5-1, on one hit.

The Georgia native won World Championships with both the Marlins and the Padres. He was particularly devastating in the Division Series and the League Championship Series, in which he compiled a 4-1 record over two years. His World Series mark, however, was a disappointing 0-3.

Superstar pitcher Kevin Brown. (Los Angeles Dodgers)

His career totals prior to coming to the Dodgers are particularly impressive. He yielded just one home run for every 18 innings pitched, the third best in the major leagues. His 51 victories between 1996 and 1998 was also the third best, as was his 727 innings pitched. His cumulative 2.33 earned-run-average led all pitchers, and was 2.14 runs below the major league average of 4.47.

Brown came to the Los Angeles Dodgers with a reputation for being a dedicated, tireless worker with pinpoint control. In his debut season in L.A., he confirmed that assessment, going 18-9, with a fine 3.00 earned-run-average, and averaging 7.2 innings per start. He pitched even better in 2000, leading the league with a 2.58 ERA and once again averaging seven innings per start, but a lack of offensive support left him with just a 13-6 record to show for his efforts. Then his luck turned bad. Arm problems limited him to 116 innings pitched in 2001, although he still racked up a 10-4 won-loss record. Elbow surgery on September 27 caused him to miss the first two months of the 2002 season, and a back operation in June, shut him down for good and probably prevented the Los Angeles Dodgers from participating in the postseason brawl.

2001—PAUL LO DUCA GOES 6 FOR 6

Paul Anthony Lo Duca was the forgotten man in the Los Angeles Dodger organization for nine long years. He had signed a professional contract to play for Los Angeles in 1993, after being selected as the national college player of the year, on the basis of his .446 average, 14 home runs and 88 RBIs at Arizona State University.

The All-American catcher began his professional career with Vero Beach in the Florida State League and hit a solid .313. He went on to hit .300 or better seven times in eight years in the Dodger farm system, but he always seemed to be overlooked when it came time to select two catchers for the big club.

He had been called up to the major league team three times for a cup of coffee, but was always sent back to Albuquerque for more seasoning. It was beginning to wear on the 29-year-old veteran, who considered retiring several times. Finally, in 2001, after enjoying a sensational year at Albuquerque, where he scorched the ball at a .351 clip, Lo Duca's bat sizzled to the tune of .459 in spring training, winning him the Dodgers catching position..

Paul Lo Duca got off to a fast start when the season got underway, batting .368 in April, with two homers and eight runs-batted-in over 13 games. As May drew to a close, the Dodgers 28-22 record put them in a tie for first place in the Western Division with the Arizona Diamondbacks. In the final game of a three-game series against the Astros in Los Angeles on May 27, Lo Duca's bat got hot, as he crushed three hits in six at-bats during a 5-4, 12-inning Dodger victory. The Big Blue Machine won the game by scoring three runs in the bottom of the 12th after Houston had tallied twice in the top of the inning.

The next night, Paul Lo Duca had a career night as the Dodgers hosted the Colorado Rockies. The right-handed hitter rapped three singles in his first three trips to the plate as the two teams tried to beat each other into submission. After five innings, the score stood Colorado 8, L.A. 4. But Lo Duca narrowed that lead by taking an 0-2 changeup from Pedro Astacio downtown, with two men on base. Two innings later, after each team had scored two more runs, he singled in the tying run, sending the game into extra innings. The game stood at 10-10 through the tenth inning. Then, Lo Duca stepped to the plate leading off the 11th and promptly drove the ball into left field for hit number six. Tom Goodwin followed with a base on balls, and Marquis Grissom laid down a perfect bunt to load the bases with no outs. Shawn Green ended the marathon quickly by dropping a fly ball single on the left field foul line, and Lo Duca scampered across the plate with the winning run.

It was the first time a Dodger had pounded out six hits in a game since Willie Davis did it in a 19-inning game against the New York Mets on May 24, 1973.

Lo Duca continued to spark the Dodger attack throughout the summer, and he completed his rookie sea-

The Dodgers are glad Paul Lo Duca didn't choose early retirement.
(Los Angeles Dodgers)

son batting .320, with 25 home runs and 90 runs-batted-in. And he struck out only 30 times in 460 at-bats. The stocky pepperpot was more than a hitter, however. He fielded .992 and threw out 39% of would-be base stealers, 5% more than the average National League catcher. He also displayed tremendous versatility, playing leftfield and first base when needed, doing an excellent job in all positions.

2001—SHAWN GREEN SMASHES THREE HOME RUNS

Shawn Green was obtained from the Toronto Blue Jays on November 8, 1999, in a trade for Raul Mondesi. After enjoying a sensational season in Toronto in 1999, batting .309 with 42 home runs and 123 RBIs, it took the big rightfielder a season to get adjusted to his new league and new team. He hit just .269 for L.A. with 24 homers and 99 RBIs, a big drop from his previous year.

But in 2001 he was ready. And he put together some exciting numbers for manager Jim Tracy. He batted .301 in April, with six homers and 19 RBIs, as the Dodgers held down the top spot in the Western Division, 1 1/2 games ahead of the Colorado Rockies. He continued to pound the ball in May and June, even though his sup-

porting cast, with the exception of Gary Sheffield, could not maintain the pace, and L.A. fell six games behind Arizona. Green's contribution to the Dodger offense was a .297 average, 20 home runs and 63 runs-batted-in over 81 games. He hit seven home runs in eight games from July 21 to July 28, giving him 30 home runs for the season, just the fourth Dodger left-handed hitter to hit 30 or more homers in a season, joining Duke Snider, Babe Herman, and Dolph Camilli.

He continued his bombarding into August, and on the 15th of the month he set the bar at a new height. Facing the Montreal Expos at home, the smooth-swinging, 6'4" slugger smashed three home runs in five at-bats to pace the Dodgers to an easy 13-1 victory. After striking out in the first inning, Green put the ball into the leftfield seats with two men on base in the second, putting L.A. on top, 5-0. In the fourth inning, he drove another Carl Pavano pitch into the rightfield seats with Mark Grudzielanek on base. After hitting into a fielders choice in the fifth, he came to the plate again in the seventh and put the frosting on the cake. Facing Masato Yoshii, he sent a ball deep into the right-centerfield seats for home run number three. In all, he drove in seven runs in the game.

Green's outstanding performance kept the Dodgers in the hunt, not only for a wildcard berth, but also for a Division title. This game kept Jim Tracy's crew within one game of San Francisco in the wildcard chase, and just three games out of the division lead. The Blue Crew continued to fight down the stretch, but came up short, finishing in third place, six games behind the Daimondbacks.

Shawn Green held up his end, though. Overall, he hit .297, with a franchise-record 49 home runs, and 125 runs-batted-in.

2002—SHAWN GREEN PUTS UP A FOUR SPOT

On May 23, 2002, Shawn Green did something that no player had ever done in the history of major league baseball. He hit four home runs, a double, and a single for a major league record 19 total bases. He also scored six runs and drove in seven, most definitely a day for the ages.

Shawn Green had a sensational year in 2001, and he was determined to repeat his performance the next year. But things don't always go as planned, and the Dodgers rightfielder got off to a slow start in April and early May. By May 19, when the Dodgers closed out a disappointing home stand, Green had gone homerless in more than 90 at-bats, and had suffered through an 0 for 18 slump that caused manager Jim Tracy to give him a day off to regroup. His .231 batting average, three home runs, and 21 runs-batted-in over 42 games brought the Los Angeles boo-birds out in force.

It was a relief for Shawn Green to play in Milwaukee, and the Brewers succeeded in bringing him out of his slump. In the opener of a three game series, the

Shawn Green set a new single-season Dodgers homerun record by driving 49 over the fence in 2001. (Los Angeles Dodgers)

Shawn Green joined the legends on May 23, 2002 with his fourth home run in a single game against the Milkwakee Brewers. (W. . McNeil)

to look like a softball moving in slow motion. Seymour Siwoff, President of the Elias Sports Bureau, was quoted in Baseball Weekly as saying, "You have to say that, on the basis of production, it's the greatest day in the history of baseball."

Shawn Green's sensational slugging didn't end with his history-making day. He homered off Curt Schilling the next night in Arizona and clocked two against All-World southpaw Randy Johnson two days later, making him the first major leaguer to hit seven home runs in three games. He went on from there to hit 24 home runs over a 44-game span, including four home runs in four consecutive at-bats over two games on June 14 and 15.

Dodgers dropped an 8-6 thriller to Davey Lopes' team , but Green went two for four and drove two balls out of Miller Park. The next night, he tripled in the only run of the game as Hideo Nomo stopped the Brew Crew, 1-0.

Japanese southpaw Kazuhisa Ishii squared off against Milwaukee lefty Glendon Rusch in the finale, and Ishii got the better of it. The Dodgers pushed across three big runs in the opening frame, and Shawn Green contributed a run-scoring double to the attack. In the second inning, the 6'4" slugger hit a 385-foot shot with two teammates on base, and the Big Blue Machine was off and running with an 8-1 lead. In the fourth, he hit a 415-foot solo homer, and in the fifth he sent an opposite-field homer 390-feet into the leftfield seats. He singled and scored a run in the eighth, as the score mounted to 12-2.

It didn't look as if Green would get a chance to hit a fourth home run, because two men had to reach base to bring him to the plate. But Chad Kreuter doubled and, after Williams and Reboulet were retired, Adrian Beltre hit a two-out home run to give the Dodger slugger one more shot. And Green didn't miss. Facing right-hander Jose Cabrera before a cheering throng of 26,728 Milwaukee fans hoping to see history made, Geeen took a mighty swing at a 1-1 fastball and put the ball into orbit. It was a monstrous, 450-foot home run that came to rest in a walkway beyond right centerfield.

Shawn Green commenting on his change in fortune said that, during his slump, the ball looked like a ping pong ball, but suddenly, in Milwaukee, it began

2004—ERIC GAGNE ESTABLISHES A MAJOR LEAGUE RECORD WITH HIS 84TH SAVE

When Eric Gagne arrived at Dodgertown in Vero Beach in the spring of 2002, he was there to compete for the fifth slot in the starting pitching rotation. The top four spots were already taken, by Kevin Brown, Andy Ashby, Kazuhisa Ishii, and Hideo Nomo. The other pitchers competing for the last spot were Odalis Perez and Omar Daal. As the season opener approached, Perez won the last starting pitching spot and Daal and Gagne were assigned to the bullpen. At the time, with Jeff Shaw having retired, manager Jim Tracy decided to go with "closer by committee," until a clear-cut winner emerged. The "committee" consisted of Paul Quantrill, who had been a mainstay in the Toronto Blue Jay bullpen in 2001, Giovanni Carrara, who went 6-1 with a 3.13 ERA in 47 games for L.A. in 2001, and Eric Gagne, who won six games against seven losses, with a 4.75 ERA in 33 games, in 2001.

Jim Tracy didn't get a chance to use his new "closer by committee" in the opening three-game series because the San Francisco Giants pummeled his boys by a combined score of 24-2. Finally, on Sunday April 7, in the Dodgers sixth game, Eric Gagne paraded out of the bullpen to register his first save of the year in L.A.'s 6-4 victory over Colorado. It was Gagne's fourth appearance of the year, covering 4 2/3 innings, and his slate was perfect. The Dodger manager, sticking with his hot gun, kept the big Canadian coming out of the pen when the game was on the line, and he wasn't disappointed. By the time April had come to an end, Gagne had appeared in 12 of the Dodgers 26 games, with nine saves and a 0.69 earned-run-average. The closer by committee concept was now history.

It was May 7th before the L.A. closer blew his first save, but the team recovered and beat the Atlanta Braves 6-5 in 16 innings. And Gagne bounced back the next night to pick up save number 11 by striking out the side in the bottom of the ninth inning, dumping the Braves, 3-1. He continued to provide superb relief for Jim Tracy's pitching staff throughout the season, becoming the fastest pitcher ever to record 20 saves, when he racked up number 20 in the team's 53rd game. He showed his mettle a week later, in a game against the Baltimore Orioles. With a runner on third base and no one out, he proceeded to retire the side without the run scoring, saving a 2-1 victory for Odalis Perez. And he got out of a bases loaded, no-out situation on July 5 to preserve a 6-5 win over the St. Louis Cardinals. It was save number 31.

On August 28, Eric Gagne combined with Odalis Perez to shut out the Arizona Diamondbacks, 1-0, registering his 45th save of the year, a new Dodger franchise record. His biggest game however, was September 21, when the Dodgers beat the Padres 5-3 in San Diego. It was his 50th save of the year, putting him in elite company, with John Smoltz who was having a career year himself. When the curtain came down on the 2002 season, Gagne had piled up 52 saves in 56 save opportunities, with a 4-1 won-loss record and a sensational 1.97 ERA. The hard throwing right hander appeared in 77 games during the season, holding opponents to a .189 batting average and striking out 12.46 batters for every nine innings pitched against just 1.75 bases on balls.

Eric Gagne's record included eight consecutive saves to end the 2002 season. The following year he was even better, saving 55 games with no blown saves, bringing his major league record for consecutive saves to 63, breaking Tom "Flash" Gordon's record of 54. He also established a new record for the most saves in a perfect season. The husky Canadian closer stayed hot for three months into 2004 before his streak came to an end. He saved 21 consecutive games to start the season, but he finally felt the sting of failure on July 4, when the Arizona Diamondbacks touched him up for two runs in the top of the ninth inning to knot their game with the Dodgers at five-all. Gagne was shocked when the 56,000 fans in attendance rose as one and gave him a standing ovation when the inning ended. A few minutes later, he had to come out of the dugout for a curtain call before the next inning could begin.

Happily for Gagne, and the fans, the Dodgers pushed over the game-winner in the bottom of the tenth inning on a sacrifice fly by Shawn Green. Gagne finished the season with 45 saves against just two blown saves.

2005—HEE-SEOP CHOI GOES DEEP THREE TIMES

Hee-Seop Choi, a native of Chun-Nam, South Korea, played major league baseball for four years, from 2002 through 2005. He was signed to a professional baseball contract as an amateur free agent by the Chicago Cubs on March 1, 1999, and worked his way through the Cubs minor league system over the next three years, finally settling in the Windy City in 2002. Two years later, he was traded to the Miami Marlins who sent him to the Los Angeles Dodgers along with Brad Penny for Paul LoDuca and two other players on July 30, 2004.

Hee-Seop Choi had a short but memorable major league career. (W. McNeil)

Choi played in 31 games for L.A. in 2004, hitting just .161 with six RBIs. The following year, he batted .253 in 320 at-bats with 15 homers and 42 runs-batted-in. He did have one day in the sun however where he was one of the greatest sluggers ever to put bat to ball. On June 12, an overcast Sunday afternoon in Dodger Stadium, with the temperature hovering around the 72 degree mark and with a slight breeze blowing out to center field, 54,368 would-be sun worshippers turned out to watch their heroes do battle with the Minnesota Twins. Choi did his part in the skirmish as he crushed three home runs to propel Jim Tracy's troops to a 4-3 victory. The 6', 5", 235-pound left-handed hitter, batting out of the second spot in the batting order, hit a towering fly ball into the right field seats in the first inning off Twins starter, Brad Radke. Minnesota touched the Dodgers D. J. Houlton for two runs in the top of the second inning on two walks, a sacrifice fly, and a double by Jacque Jones to grab a 2-1 lead, but the lead was short lived. In the Dodger fourth, Hee-Seop Choi launched a leadoff homer off the Twins right-hander to knot the score at two-all, and the next hitter, J.D. Drew gave the lead back to L.A. with a home of his own. The Twins tied it again in the sixth on a triple by Torii Hunter and another double by Jones. But, once again, it was Choi to the rescue. As he had done in the fourth inning, Choi led off with a blast into the California sky to plate the final run of the game. From June 10 to June 14, the big first baseman hit a total of seven home runs in four games becoming one of just three players to hit seven homers in four games. The only major league players to have a better home run streak than Choi's were Ralph Kiner who hit eight home runs in four games in 1947 and the Dodgers Shawn Green who hit seven home runs in three games in 2001. Choi was also the first player of Asian decent to hit three home runs in one game.

2006—DODGERS LAUNCH FOUR CONSECUTIVE HOME RUNS

The Dodgers, both the Brooklyn variety and the Los Angeles variety, have been known to do unusual things on a baseball diamond, some good and some bad, but they have also produced miracles at regular intervals—see Al Gionfriddo, Sandy Amoros, and Johnny Podres, in Broooklyn, and Lou Johnson, Orel Hershiser, and Kirk Gibson in L.A. The 2006 edition of the Los Angeles Dodgers joined that club on September 18, in the heat of an exciting pennant race. Grady Little's team was hosting the San Diego Padres with the two teams engaged in a knock-down, drag-out battle for the West Division pennant, and the Padres had won two of the first three games of the four game series to take a one-half-game lead over their California neighbors.

As game four got underway, the temperature was a comfortable 80 degrees, the sky was clear, and the wind was a light four mph blowing out to right field, as a full house of 55,831 die-hard Dodger fans pushed their way through the turnstiles for the 7:11 PM start. Sixteen game winner Brad Penny was on the hill for Los Angeles and he was opposed by Padre ace Jake Peavy, who was struggling through a rough 11-14 season, but neither pitcher was around to see the sixth inning. The score was deadlocked to four-all after three innings and remained tied through the seventh. By the time the bottom of the ninth arrived, Bruce Bochy's team seemed to have the game well in hand, leading

9-5, but the never-say-die Dodger crew showed their mettle against San Diego reliever Jon Adkins. The 6' tall, 200-pound right-hander was treated harshly by the home team. Jeff Kent hit a homer to left field on a 1-0 pitch to get the inning underway and when the next batter, J.D. Drew went the other way, launching a high drive into the right field stands, Adkins day was done. Bochy rushed his closer, Trevor Hoffman, into the game to put out the fire, but this was not Hoffman's night. The major league's all-time closer with 482 saves to his credit, served up his out pitch, his changeup, to Russell Martin and the Dodger catcher promptly deposited it into the left field seats to cut the Padre lead to one. That brought the usually laid-back Dodger fans into the game, cheering, clapping, and stamping their feet. In view of the disastrous result he got from his changeup, Hoffman decided it was time to go to his patented 88-mph fastball to Marlon Anderson, but the pitch never reached the catcher's glove. The Dodger left fielder was waiting for it and lofted it into the upper atmosphere for the fourth consecutive home run of the inning, tying the game again, this time at nine-all. The home run outburst was the fourth time in baseball history that a team had hit four consecutive home runs. The inning ended without further scoring and when the Padres came back with a run in the top of the tenth for a 10-9 lead, it was crunch time again for Grady Little's crew. Rudy Seanez, a hard-throwing right-hander took the mound in the bottom of the tenth and promptly walked leadoff hitter Kenny Lofton. That was a big mistake. Nomar Garciaparra worked the count to 3-1 and then jumped on a Seanez fastball and drove it into the left field pavilion for a walk-off home run to give the embattled Dodgers an 11-10 victory and a one-half-game lead in the pennant race.

2009—CAMELBACK RANCH OPENS

During the first half of the 20th century, the Dodgers, then housed in Brooklyn, were spring training nomads, training in such diverse locations as Jacksonville, Florida, Santo Domingo, Dominican Republic, Havana, Cuba and, during World War II when travel restrictions were in effect, in Bear Mountain, New York. When Branch Rickey became president of the team in the 1940s, he put his master plan into effect. One key element of the plan was to have all the Dodger players, major league and minor league alike, train in one location so they could get to know each other and so the major leaguers could serve as role models for their minor league counterparts.

Rickey selected a former Naval Air Station with two large barracks on a 425 acre site in Vero Beach, Florida, to construct his dream, "Dodgertown," a facility that would soon become famous as the shining example of a major league spring training facility. Eleven years after the Brooklyn Dodgers settled in Dodgertown, the major league franchise relocated to Los Angeles, California, 3,000 miles from its spring training base. It didn't make much sense for a team to train on the opposite side of the country from where the major league team played, but inertia being what it is, it took 41 years for the Dodgers to move their spring training facility to the west coast. Finally a site was located in the Phoenix, Arizona area, and Camelback Ranch was born.

Camelback Ranch, a joint venture between the Dodgers and the Chicago White Sox, is located just a six hour drive from Chavez Ravine, bringing the Dodger players in close contact with their thousands of fans west of the Pecos. The 141 acre complex, as noted in The Dodgers Guide, "includes more than 118,000 square feet of Major and minor league clubhouse space, 13 full baseball fields, and three half-fields. The site features walking trails, landscaped grounds with almost 5000 plants and trees, an orange grove and a stocked two-acre lake between the Dodgers and White Sox facilities." Frank McCourt said he wanted to keep the ambiance of the facility the same as it was in Florida, where walking trails and the absence of barriers allowed the fans to maintain close contact with the players.

Camelback Ranch opened officially on Sunday afternoon, March 1, 2009, under sunny skies, and the first spring training game was played there on that date, matching the host Dodgers with the visiting White Sox. The park, the largest park in the Cactus League with a seating capacity of more than 13,000, welcomed 11,280 baseball enthusiasts to the opening game. The Dodgers selected Hiroki Kuroda to kick off the Dodgers first Cactus League season, and he was opposed by Chicago's 15-game winner, southpaw Mark Buehrle. Both pitchers threw goose-eggs at the opposing batters during their two-inning stints, but over the course of the game Los Angeles paraded nine pitchers to the mound while the visitors relied on just six. Joe Torre's outfit scored single runs in both the fourth and six innings on RBIs by Mark Loretta and Blake DeWitt, to grab a 2-0 lead. The score was unchanged as the ninth inning got underway but Chicago's South-Siders staged a rally against L.A.'s bullpen, pushing over three runs to claim victory in the opening day encounter. Pinch hitter Jim Beckham took Strickland deep for Chicago's first run, and the tying and winning runs crossed the plate minutes later on two bases on balls, a base hit, and two infield outs.

CHAPTER 10

THE BALLPARKS—
FROM CAPITOLINE TO CHAVEZ

During the 140-some odd years of their recorded baseball history, Brooklyn-Los Angeles teams have played ball on every conceivable kind of field; from a cow pasture, to an Olympic track and field stadium. Their baseball parks have been called ramshackled relics and baseball monstrosities. One was even ridiculed as a "bandbox." But their most recent one, Dodger Stadium, is frequently referred to as the most beautiful park in the major leagues, a compliment it richly deserves.

A sampling of many of the baseball parks where Dodger players proudly displayed their talents over the past 140 years, presents a typical overview of the evolution of baseball in America.

THE CAPITOLINE SKATING LAKE AND BASE-BALL GROUND— 1862 TO 1878

During the early years of Brooklyn's baseball history, games were played on whatever open field happened to be available in town at the time. The Atlantics, for instance, usually played their home games on an open field at the corner of Marcy and Gates Avenues. There were no fancy stadiums or enclosed parks; no covered grandstands or outfield fences. Just a diamond scratched out of the grass, three bases, a home plate, and a couple of benches for the players. For important games, portable bleachers were erected along the first-and-third-base lines. The home team supplied the ball. Each team carried their own bats. Both teams wore uniforms. There was no other equipment. The fielders did not wear gloves. The catcher stood at least eight feet behind the batter to protect himself from bodily injury, because he did not have the luxury of a face mask or a chest protector (they hadn't yet been invented). Most teams carried only one pitcher, but they often had more than one man who could catch, since injuries frequently felled the poor defenseless man behind the plate. Such was the situation in 1862.

About this time, the owners of the Capitoline Skating Lake and Base-Ball Ground, located between Nostrand Avenue and Marcy Avenue in the Bedford-Stuyvesant section of Brooklyn, renovated their facility to make it more suitable for baseball. For many years, the Capitoline had been known primarily as a family winter skating rink. Each year, when the frost settled in for a long cold spell, the field was flooded, and the residents of Brooklyn came en masse to enjoy the good cheer and friendship of fellow skaters. Temporary fires were available to warm the hands and feet. Permanent facilities housed changing rooms, a restaurant, and a bandstand.

In 1862, the baseball field was improved. Bleachers were constructed along the first and third base lines, to accommodate up to 5,000 spectators. A clubhouse was provided for the players. Finally, a six-foot-high wooden fence was constructed around the outfield, making the Capitoline one of the country's first enclosed baseball grounds.

The Brooklyn Atlantics, one of the top amateur baseball clubs in the country, soon deserted their "home grounds" at Marcy Avenue, and became the Capitoline's first tenants. Within two years, the mighty Atlantics brought honor and glory to their new home. They captured the NABP national championships in 1864 and 1866, going undefeated both years.

Professional baseball came to Brooklyn in 1872, when the Atlantics joined the newly organized National Association. The glory days were behind them by that time, however, and the pride of Flatbush languished near the bottom of the league during the four years they participated.

When the National League was formed in 1876, Brooklyn was not even invited to be a member. Their reputation but a dim memory, the Atlantics were forced to compete in the minor leagues for eight years.

Located in the pleasant countryside just east of downtown Brooklyn, the Capitoline was eventually sacrificed to the cause of urban development. In 1879, the playing field was dug up, a new street was constructed on the spot where George Zettlein once dazzled Cincinnati batters, and sidewalks decorated the place where Dickey Pearce once ran down ground balls.

Coincidentally, the Capitoline Skating Lake and Base-Ball Ground was located only one mile from the subsequent site of Ebbets Field.

WASHINGTON PARK—1879 TO 1890

Washington Park became the home of the Brooklyn Atlantics upon the demise of the Capitoline Ground. The park, located on 5th Avenue, was so named because it was built on the site of a famous Revolutionary War battle between George Washington's Colonial Forces and the British Army. It was not impressive as parks go, a small wooden enclosure with bleachers for approximately 4,500 spectators. But it was the best field available in Brooklyn at the time.

A Brooklyn team played minor league ball in Washington Park for five years. Finally, after winning the In-ter-State League championship in 1883, the team was rescued for the new American Association, a league which had begun operations in 1882 to compete with the successful National League.

Brooklyn became a major league franchise for the first time in 1884. The team was called simply the Brooklyns, although out-of-town newspapers often referred to them as the Grays, after the color of their uniforms. Monday, May 5, 1884, was a red-banner day in the City of Churches. It was opening day, and Brooklyns first home game as a major league baseball team. The previous day had been miserable; cold and rainy. By morning however, the skies cleared, and the fans headed for the ballpark in large numbers. The *New York Times* reported that the crowd included "many ladies."

The Brooklyn nine was in top form for their major league debut, dominating the game from beginning to end. Their big bats whistled to the tune of 11 runs and 14 hits. It was a banner day for right fielder John Cassidy who led the attack with three hits, including a triple and a home run. Cassidy socked a total of only four home runs during an undistinguished ten-year career. Brooklyn's opponents, the Washington Senators, were unable to solve the slants of Brooklyn right hander Dick Conway, who tossed a seven-hitter. It was one of Conway's better efforts, as he finished the season with a record of 3-9. The final score was 11-3.

Washington Park was utilized by Brooklyn's professional teams from 1883 until 1889, when it was destroyed by fire. The Team played in Washington Park II for one year before moving into Eastern Park.

BROOKLYN

NAME	POS		R	H	E
Greenwood	2B		1	2	0
Cassidy	RF		2	3	0
Warner	3B		2	2	0
Benners	LF		0	1	0
Terry	CF		1	2	1
Householder	1B		1	1	2
Geer	SS		2	1	3
Farrow	C		1	1	0
Conway	P		1	1	0
Total			11	14	6

WASHINGTON

NAME	POS		R	H	E
Fennelly	SS		0	1	2
Kiley	LF		0	1	0
Gladman	3B		1	1	1
Humphries	C		1	1	2
Beach	RF		0	0	1
King	1B		0	1	3
Hawkes	2B		0	0	1
Morgan	CF		1	1	0
Hamill	P		0	1	0
Total			3	7	10

```
WASHINGTON   010 000 110 - 3 - 7 - 10
BROOKLYN     200 015 201 - 11 - 14 - 6
```

Brooklyn's joy was shortlived, however. They finished in tenth place in the 13-club league with a dismal 40-64 record. Their opening-day opponents fared even worse. The pitiful Senators dropped out of the league in mid-season, having won only 12 of 63 games.

The Brooklyn franchise persisted, improving their position every year until in 1889 they were crowned American Association Champions. The next year, 1890, the Brooklyns, now known as the Bridegrooms, moved into the National League, and began their long history of exciting and entertaining baseball.

EASTERN PARK—1891 TO 1897

George Chauncey, a Brooklyn businessman, purchased controlling interest in the Brooklyn franchise after the 1890 season, and immediately moved the team to East New York where he thought they would be more successful financially. Their new home park was Eastern Park, a similar old wooden structure to the one they just left. The seating capacity was more generous, however, and satisfied upwards of 18,000 spectators.

Since Eastern Park was located several miles from downtown Brooklyn, it was necessary to travel by horse drawn wagon or by trolley car to attend a game. Electric trolleys, which were new to Brooklyn, were very dangerous vehicles in their infancy, because the drivers, who were former horse and buggy jockeys, had difficulty controlling the big, electric beats. Accidents between trolleys and pedestrians were common, and fatalities frequent. By 1895, trolley cars were killing an average of one person a week.

This photo shows Eastern Park on opening day, May 3, 1894. Note the flags and bunting decorating the field. Brooklyn's player-manager Dave Foutz is leading off. (Transcendental Graphics)

The traffic was at its worst in front of the ballpark, where a confluence of trolley tracks made life particularly dangerous. Sophisticated Manhattanites, and other visitors to the fair city, were amused as they watched the natives dart around, in front of, and behind, the great electric monsters, as they crossed the street to the park. Soon, Brooklyn fans were being called "Trolley Dodgers," a name that was eventually passed on to the team itself. The shortened version, Dodgers, became their nickname in short order, and it has continued (with some minor diversionary periods), until the present day.

Opening day was a raucous occasion in East New York. By coincidence, the opponents were Jim Mutrie's New York Giants, and the enmity between the two teams was already at a fever pitch. Over 17,000 baseball zealots crammed into the little wooden park to participate in the festivities. As the *New York Times* reported, "All of the cranks of the two cities attended."

It was a noisy and riotous afternoon as Giant fans tried to out-yell Brooklyn fans, and vice versa. Mutrie's team, coming off four straight losses to the Boston Beaneaters, was looking for blood. And the Bridegrooms were always ready for a fight. Such was the setting for opening day.

Brooklyn got off winging in the first inning as little Mike Griffin crushed an Amos Rusie fast ball, and drove it between the fielders in right center field. Before the ball could be retrieved, the Bridegroom speedster had circled the bases with a home run. The lead was shortlived, however. New York pushed across two tallies in their next at bat on a Dick Buckley single.

The game was a nip-and-tuck affair, with first one team, then the other gaining the edge. Then, in the ninth inning, with Brooklyn protecting a slim 5-4 lead, the wheels came off the wagon. An infield error, a double, and a throwing error by Brooklyn catcher Tom Kinslow, gave New York the tying and winning runs.

BROOKLYN

NAME	POS	R	H	E
Collins	2B	0	2	0
Griffin	CF	1	1	0
Pinckney	3B	0	0	0
Burns	RF	0	0	0
Foutz	1B	1	1	0
O'Brien	LF	1	0	0
Daly	SS	2	2	3
Kinslow	C	0	1	2
Lovett	P	0	0	0
Total		5	7	5

NEW YORK

NAME	POS	R	H	E
Gore	RF	1	1	0
Tiernan	CF	1	1	1
Richardson	2B	0	0	1
Connor	1B	0	0	0
Glasscock	SS	2	1	0
O'Rourke	LF	1	3	1
Bassett	3B	0	0	0
Buckley	C	1	2	1
Rusie	P	0	1	0
Total		6	9	4

NEW YORK GIANTS	0 2 0 0 0 0 0 0 2 - 6 - 9 - 4
BROOKLYN BRIDEGROOMS	1 0 0 3 0 0 1 0 0 - 5 - 7 - 5

Charlie Ebbets gained full control of the Brooklyn franchise in 1898, and quickly bade farewell to East New York. He moved the club back to Flatbush, leased land at 4th Avenue and 3rd Street, and constructed his "new" Washington Park.

"NEW" WASHINGTON PARK—1898 TO 1912

Charlie Ebbets' "new" Washington Park was built between 3rd and 4th Avenues, and 1st and 3rd Streets. It was conveniently located to provide easy access from all sections of Brooklyn. New Yorkers, too, could reach the park within 20 minutes after crossing the Brooklyn Bridge.

Baseball parks had not widely progressed to the point of steel and concrete construction by this time, so the old familiar wooden facade still greeted spectators to Bridegrooms' games. Ebbets considered the park to be a temporary home for his ball club, until such time as he could construct his dream park, a modern, attractive, comfortable stadium that would entice more citizens of Brooklyn to games, particularly women.

Washington Park had a large covered grandstand that extended from first base around to third. Additional

Fielder Jones was an outstanding center fielder, who had a 15-year major league career. In addition to his sterling defensive play, Jones batted over .300 six times. He batted .314 in five years in Brooklyn, before jumping to Chicago in the new American League in 1901. (Transcendental Graphics)

bleachers down the left and right field foul lines brought the seating capacity up to a respectable 10,000. For important games, standing room was provided around the perimeter of the outfield, inside the fence.

Brooklyn was not able to enjoy the use of their home park until the eighth game of the season, the first seven having been played on the road. When opening day arrived, on Saturday, April 30, the Bridegrooms faced off against the Philadelphia Phillies. The weather was a warm 70 degrees, but the field was still soggy from the previous day's rain. In spite of the inclement weather, an overflow crowd of 14,000 fans paid their way through the turnstiles.

Elaborate pre-game festivities were presided over by Brooklyn club President Charles H. Ebbets. As the two teams lined up along the first and third base lines, Ebbets and his daughter, May, ascended the wooden platform near the flagpole. Shortly after 4 p.m., Charlie Ebbets unfurled a new American flag and, while the 23rd Regiment band offered a mournful rendition of the National Anthem, Miss May Ebbets raised the flag to the top of the pole. Pandemonium gripped the fans as the spirit of patriotism prevailed. Hundreds of miniature American flags were waved frantically in the stands as the last strains of the National Anthem faded into memory.

The Bridegrooms raced onto the field to take up their defensive positions as the big crowd screamed with delight. The deafening roar and shrill whistles could be heard a mile from the park. Ace pitcher "Brickyard" Kennedy, off a mediocre 18-20 season in 1897, was on the mound for Billy Barnie's boys. Philadelphia countered with George Wheeler, a journeyman right hander.

Much to the delight of the partisan crowd, the Bridegrooms scored in their very first at bat. Mike Griffin, a steady .300 hitter, led off with a single. He advanced to third on another single by Candy LaChance, and came across to score on a sacrifice fly by Jimmy Sheckard. The Phils bounced back to tie in the second on a home run over the left field wall by "Big Sam" Thompson.

After Philadelphia took a brief lead in the top of the third, the Bridegrooms rallied in their half of the inning on a double by LaChance and a long home run to left by Sheckard. Unfortunately, this was not Kennedy's day. Three hits, coupled with two Brooklyn errors, led to three unearned Philadelphia runs in the fifth.

Brooklyn closed to 5-4 on consecutive doubles by Fielder Jones and the omnipresent LaChance, but they could get no closer. Nap Lajoie and Lave Cross countered with two-baggers of their own to close out the days scoring. Both pitchers tightened up from the sixth inning on, and Philadelphia threw a damper on the Brooklyn home opener, walking off with a 6-4 victory.

The overflow crowd ringing the outfield had a decided effect on the play of the game. Nine balls disappeared into the mass of humanity for ground rule doubles, much to the chagrin of the pursuing outfielders.

BROOKLYN

NAME	POS	R	H	E
Griffin	CF	1	1	1
Jones	RF	1	3	0
LaChance	SS	1	4	1
Sheckard	LF	1	1	0
Shindle	3B	0	0	0
Tucker	1B	0	1	0
Hallman	2B	0	0	0
Ryan	C	0	1	0
Kennedy	P	0	1	0
Total		4	12	2

PHILADELPHIA

NAME	POS	R	H	E
Cooley	CF	0	1	0
Douglas	1B	0	1	0
Delahanty	LF	0	2	0
Lajoie	2B	1	1	0
Thompson	RF	1	1	0
Cross	SS	0	2	1
Nash	3B	1	0	0
McFarland	C	2	2	0
Wheeler	P	1	1	0
Total		6	11	1

```
PHILADELPHIA   011 031 000 - 6 - 11 - 1
BROOKLYN       102 010 000 - 4 - 11 - 2
```

Candy LaChance held down the first sack in Brooklyn for six years. His best year was 1895, when he hit .312 and drove in 108 runs. (Transcendental Graphics)

EBBETS FIELD—1913 TO 1957

Ebbets Field. The name conjures up memories of a caricature of a baseball park, populated by a zany group of mediocre ball players. It also conjures up visions of wild and exciting baseball games, where almost anything could be expected to happen at any time ... and usually did.

It didn't start out that way. Originally, Ebbets Field was the cherished dream of Brooklyn Club President Charles Hercules Ebbets. For 29 long years, the Brooklyn franchise played its home games in rickety old parks with flimsy wooden grandstands, and even flimsier outfield fences. Charlie Ebbets was embarrassed to be associated with such an operation. He felt the residents of Brooklyn deserved better. When he became president of the club in the early 1900s, Ebbets set about to construct a new stadium, one that would be the pride of the metropolitan area.

After a careful search of the entire borough, Ebbets located a four-and-a-half acre tract of land in a section of Flatbush known as Pigtown. The forlorn piece of property was home to a pitiful group of derelicts and their animals, pigs included. The center of the tract contained a large hole where the refuse of the day was dumped. The entire area was a blight on the landscape; the stench on a hot summer day, unbearable.

The Brooklyn president bought up the land, parcel by parcel. It took him nearly four years to complete the transaction, but by 1912, he owned the entire 4 1/2 acres. Almost immediately the big shovels came in and began the job of reclamation. The construction of Ebbets Field got underway.

The new ballpark was a gleaming maze of steel beams and cement foundations, a modern facility that would do justice to any bustling early 20th century metropolis. Charlie Ebbets spared no expense when he designed his masterpiece, the total bill topping the $750,000 mark. When completed, the stadium was a pitcher's delight. The right-field fence was a cozy 296 feet from home plate, but the rest of the outfield dimensions were enormous by any standards. The left-field wall stood 419 feet from home plate. Center field was a distant 476 feet away.

The right-field wall was the most unique feature of Brooklyn's new tourist attraction. It did not go straight up as most normal walls do. Instead, it sloped back at an angle of 15 degrees from the vertical until it reached a height of 9 1/2 feet, a concrete monster that sent baseballs ricocheting back to the infield faster than they left it. At the 9 1/2-foot mark, the wall suddenly changed direction, and rose in a vertical line for another 9 1/2 feet. Above the 19-foot wall, a large screen rose straight up for another 19-feet, making the entire complex a nightmare for visiting right fielders. As you can imagine, balls striking the screen would not rebound at crazy angles like balls that hit the concrete, but instead would drop straight down to the base of the wall. In the 45 years of the park's existence, only one man mastered the art of playing the wall. Carl Furillo, through hundreds of hours of practice, could mentally calculate where a particular ball would strike the wall, and at what angle. Ninety-nine times out of a hundred, when a ball caromed off the wall, Furillo was properly positioned to field it.

Charlie Ebbets' big day came on April 5, 1913. His magnificent stadium was unveiled for an exhibition game with the New York Yankees, and their manager, Frank Chance. Amidst all the pomp and pageant befitting the inauguration of a civic attraction, Genevieve Ebbets, daughter of the President, threw out the first ball. Nap Rucker, ace of the Superbas staff, toed the rubber for the first game. After the two teams battled through four scoreless innings, Casey Stengel gave the Flatbush flock their first lead with an exciting inside-the-park home run over center fielder Harry Wolter's head. The overflow crowd of 30,000 fanatical Brooklyn fans screamed with delight. An inning later, "Gentleman Jake" Daubert brought the crowd to its feet again as he legged out another round tripper.

The game stayed 2-0 in Brooklyn's favor into the ninth, when the New Yorkers tied it up against relief pitcher Frank Allen. But Bill Dahlen's boys were not about to lose their Ebbets Field opener. Brooklyn's favorite ballplayer, Zack Wheat, started a ninth inning rally with a leadoff single. Following an error and a sacrifice, "Black Lightning" carried home the game winner on a single by Red Smith.

BROOKLYN

NAME	POS	AB	R	H	E
Stengel	CF	3	1	1	0
Cutshaw	2B	4	0	1	2
Meyer	RF	3	0	1	0
Wheat	LF	3	1	2	0
Daubert	1B	3	1	1	0
Smith	3B	4	0	2	0
Fisher	SS	3	0	0	0
Miller	C	3	0	0	0
Rucker	P	1	0	0	0
Moran	PH	0	0	0	0
Allen	P	1	0	0	1
Total		28	3	8	3

Ebbets Field was a baseball showplace when it opened in 1913.

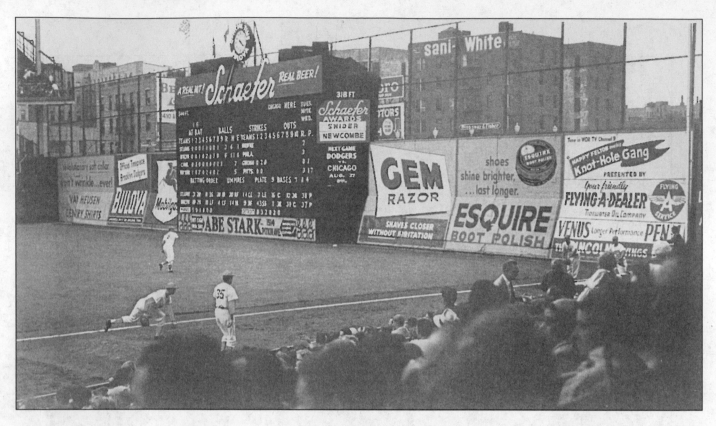

Ebbets Field's unique right-field wall towers over right fielder Gino Cimoil, in one of the last games ever played in the old park. The date was August 25, 1957, and the Cardinals were in town for their final visit. The southpaw warming up in the bullpen is 22-year-old Sandy Koufax. Number 35 is Sal Maglie. Both pitchers saw action in the ninth inning, with Maglie earning a save after relieving a beleaguered Koufax with the bases loaded and two out. Koufax had walked both men he faced, forcing in a run, to cut the Dodger lead to 6-5. (Copyright © 1987 Princeton Desktop Publishing, Inc. All rights reserved.)

NEW YORK

NAME	POS	AB	R	H	E
Daniels	RF	4	0	1	0
Wolter	CF	3	0	1	0
Hartzell	3B	3	0	1	0
Cree	LF	4	0	0	0
Chase	2B	3	0	1	0
Midkiff	PR	0	1	0	0
Stump	2B	0	0	0	0
Chance	1B	4	1	2	0
Sweeney	C	4	0	1	1
Derrick	SS	4	0	0	0
Caldwell	P	2	0	1	0
Fisher	P	2	0	0	0
Total		33	2	8	1

```
NEW YORK YANKEES      000 000 002 - 2 - 8 - 1
BROOKLYN SUPERBAS     000 011 001 - 3 - 8 - 3
```

The official opening day occurred four days later on April 9, when the Superbas hosted the Philadelphia Phillies under manager Red Dooin. Gaily colored bunting hung from the grandstand, dignitaries filled the places of honor, and the 23rd Regiment Band entertained the crowd with their extensive repertoire of marching music. Unfortunately, neither the weather nor the baseball skills of the Brooklyn players could match the pre-game festivities. Playing before a chilled crowd of 10,000 die hards, the Brooklyn bats were silent all afternoon. The Phillies spoiled Nap Rucker's Ebbets Field debut with a run in the first inning. Second baseman Otto Knabe doubled to right field with one out, and scored an unearned run when Superbas' right fielder, Benny Meyer, dropped a fly ball off the bat of Sherry Magee. Right hander Tom Seaton, en route to a 27-12 season, made the run stand up for a 1-0 Philadelphia victory, shackling the superbas on six hits.

BROOKLYN

NAME	POS	AB	R	H	E
Stengel	CF	4	0	0	0
Cutshaw	2B	4	0	1	0
Meyer	RF	2	0	0	2
Wheat	LF	4	0	0	1
Daubert	1B	3	0	1	0
Smith	3B	3	0	0	0
Fisher	SS	3	0	1	0
Miller	C	3	0	2	0
Rucker	P	2	0	1	0
Ragan	P	0	0	0	0
Erwin	PH	1	0	0	0
Callahan	PH	1	0	0	0
Total		30	0	6	13

PHILADELPHIA

NAME	POS	AB	R	H	E
Paskert	CF	4	0	1	0
Knabe	2B	3	1	2	0
Lobert	3B	3	0	0	0
Magee	CF	3	0	0	0
Doaln	RF	4	0	1	0
Luderus	1B	4	0	0	0
Doolan	SS	3	0	0	0
Dooin	C	3	0	2	0
Seaton	P	3	0	1	0
Total		30	1	7	0

```
PHILADELPHIA PHILLIES  1 0 0  0 0 0  0 0 0 - 1 - 7 - 0
BROOKLYN SUPERBAS      0 0 0  0 0 0  0 0 0 - 0 - 6 - 0
```

Brooklyn's first win at home didn't come until 17 days later, April 26, when they defeated the National League champion, New York Giants by a score of 5-3. Casey Stengel won the game with a two-run homer in the seventh inning. Nap Rucker was the winning pitcher.

Ebbets Field flourished for 45 years. Then it was over. After serving the residents of Brooklyn faithfully in more than 6,500 baseball games, the grand old park, like countless others before it, was deemed unsuitable for the modern game. President Walter O'Malley made the decision to relocate the team to Los Angeles, California for the 1958 season and, on September 24, 1957, the final act was played out in Ebbets Field. The Brooklyn Dodgers, behind southpaw Danny McDevitt, shut out the Pittsburgh Pirates, 2-0, as a slim turnout of 6,702 tearful fans looked on in stunned disbelief.

Within a few short years, the wrecking ball crashed against the Ebbets Field facade and concrete and steel fell in clumps inside the tile rotunda. The little ball park along Bedford Avenue slowly disappeared and, in its place rose a shiny new apartment complex.

LOS ANGELES COLISEUM—1958 TO 1961

If the average fan thought Ebbets Field was a baseball monstrosity, he should have attended a game in the Los Angeles Coliseum. The big stadium, originally constructed to host the track and field events of the 1932 Olympics, was an accountant's dream. It could seat 94,600 paying customers. But dimensionally it was a nightmare. The left-field fence cast a shadow on the third baseman, as it hovered a cozy 252 feet from home plate. Management erected a 40-foot-high screen atop the wall as a deterrent to the cheap home run, but players like Wally Moon, whose inside-out swing lofted many a "Moon-shot" into the seats, learned to uppercut the ball for maximum effect.

The right-field situation was just the opposite; acres and acres of open ground. The distant fence, which stood 440 feet from home, probably contributed to the early retirement of Carl Furillo. Dodger slugger Duke Snider, who averaged 42 home runs a year during the previous five years in Brooklyn, could muster only 15 round-trippers in the vast expanse of the Coliseum.

As bad as it was, the Coliseum served as home for Walter O'Malley's forces for four years, while a new Dodger Stadium was under construction. They even managed to win a World Series there in 1959, establishing World Series attendance records that should last for many years.

Opening day for the new Los Angeles Dodgers, on April 18, 1958, drew 78,672 excited fans, even though the 100-degree heat seared the skin in a few short minutes. Carl Erskine, the little Hoosier, got the call for Walter Alston's crew, while Al Worthington started for the visiting San Francisco Giants. The Dodgers brought the crowd to its feet in the fourth inning, scoring twice on a walk to Junior Gilliam and singles by Duke Snider and Charley Neal, to take a 2-1 lead. The Giants tied the score minutes later when Hank Sauer, one of the grizzled veterans who dotted both lineups, smashed a long home run to left center field. L.A. recaptured the lead for good in the bottom of the fifth with a three-run burst. A walk to Neal and singles by Dick Gray and Gino Cimoli brought one run home. A second run scored on an error and a third came in on a wild pitch.

San Francisco kept pecking away at Erskine, scoring another run in the sixth, to close the gap to 5-3. A Dick Gray circuit clout in the seventh gave Erskine a three-run cushion again and proved to be the eventual game winner. Sauer came back with his second homer of the game in the eighth with the bases empty, a 280-foot pop fly over the screen, making it a 6-4 game.

The Giants had a golden opportunity to ruin the Dodgers' home opener in the ninth, but some shoddy baserunning killed their chances. Rookie Jim Davenport opened the ninth with a line drive off the left field screen, and pulled into second with a double. Clem Labine relieved Erskine, and Willie Kirkland greeted the sinkerball specialist with a booming shot to dead center field. Gino Cimoli, after a long chase, saw the ball slide off his glove at the 430-foot mark. Davenport scored easily, and Kirkland coasted into third with a stand-up triple.

Or so it seemed. Dodger third baseman, Dick Gray, had noticed that Davenport failed to touch third base in his dash for home. He quickly called for the ball and stepped on third, as umpire Hal Dixon thumbed out the embarrassed Giant rookie. A harmless single by Mays brought in the fifth San Francisco run, but that was it. Labine shut the door on Rigney's crew after Willie's hit, preserving a 6-5 California debut victory.

SAN FRANCISCO

NAME	POS	AB	R	H	E
Davenport	3B	5	1	3	0
Kirkland	RF	5	1	3	0
Mays	CF	4	0	2	1
Spencer	SS	4	0	0	0
Cepeda	1B	5	0	0	0
Sauer	LF	4	2	2	0
Rodgers	SS	0	0	0	0
Schmidt	C	3	1	2	1
O'Connell	2B	2	0	0	0
King	PH	0	0	0	0
Gomez	PH	0	0	0	0
Bressoud	2B	0	0	0	0
Lockman	PH	0	0	0	0
Worthington	P	2	0	0	0
McCormick	P	0	0	0	0
Speake	PH	1	0	0	0
Antonelli	P	0	0	0	0
Jablonski	PH	1	0	0	0
Grissom	P	0	0	0	0
Total		36	5	12	2

The Los Angeles Coliseum opened for business on April 18, 1958. A festive opening day crowd of 78,672 viewed the historic event–the first major league game on the west coast. (Los Angeles Dodger Photo)

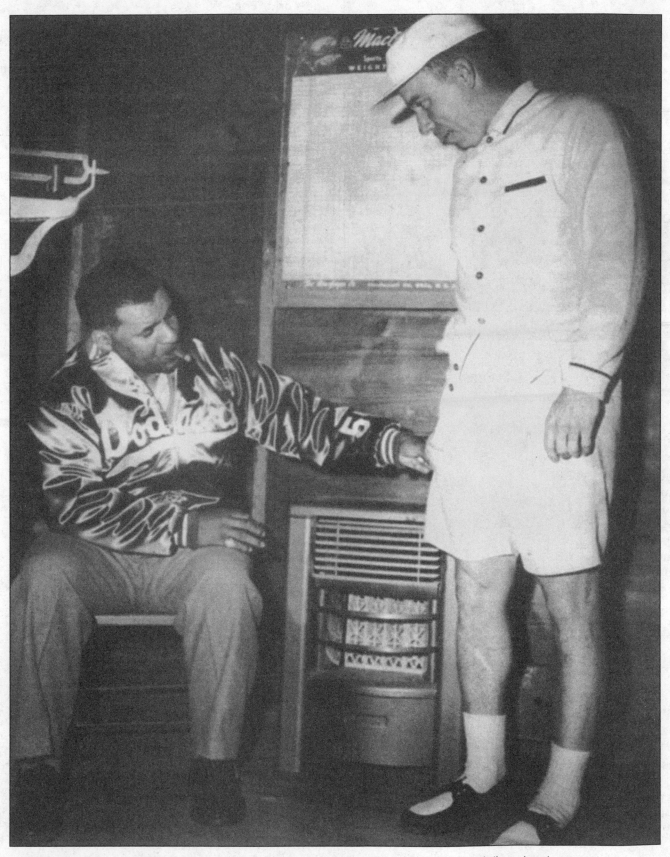

Roy Campanella inspects a dapper Pee Wee Reese, who models his "California" outfit, after learning of the Dodgers move to the west coast.

Pee Wee Reese selects a bat for his first at bat in California.

LOS ANGELES

NAME	POS	AB	R	H	E
Gilliam	LF	3	1	0	0
Reese	SS	4	0	1	0
Snider	RF	5	1	2	0
Furillo	RF	0	0	0	0
Hodges	1B	4	0	0	0
Neal	2B	3	1	2	0
Gray	3B	3	2	2	1
Cimoli	CF	3	1	1	0
Roseboro	C	1	0	0	0
Jackson	PH	1	0	0	0
Pignatano	C	1	0	0	0
Erskine	P	4	0	0	0
Labine	P	0	0	0	0
Total		32	6	8	10

```
SAN FRANCISCO   0 0 1 1 0 1 0 1 1 - 5 - 12 - 2
LOS ANGELES     0 0 2 0 3 0 1 0 x - 6 -  8 - 1
```

The statistics bore out the inhumanity of the Dodgers' new home field. In 1958, 172 balls were hit out of the Coliseum. Three home runs, all by Snider, left the park in dead center. Twelve balls disappeared over the right-field fence. The remaining 157 home runs sailed over or close to the Chinese screen in left.

The Dodgers did enjoy success in the Coliseum, however. In 1959, they surprised everyone in the National League by winning the pennant in a playoff with the Milwaukee Braves. They capped off their amazing year

by taking the Chicago White Sox in two in six games in the World Series.

Record-breaking crowds were common in the Coliseum. On May 7, 1959, 93,103 fans, still a major league record, fought their way into the park to honor Roy Campanella on his night. During the World Series that year, the Dodgers and White Sox drew successive crowds of 92,394, 92,650, and 92,706.

Three years later, in 1962, the Dodgers bid adieu to the Coliseum and moved into their new home, beautiful Dodger Stadium.

No mourners attended the wake.

DODGER STADIUM—1962 TO ?

When Walter O'Malley took his ball team west and settled in Los Angeles, he immediately set about to locate a suitable baseball park for his charges. He investigated several possibilities, including Wrigley Field, the former minor league park of the Chicago Cubs. They were all found wanting. Needing a home field quickly, he opted to house his team in the Coliseum while he scoured the area for a permanent residence.

After months of searching, he located a parcel of land not far from downtown Los Angeles. It was a rolling, wasteland of squatter's shacks and junkpiles, originally held by the city as a site for new housing projects. It was

A view from the left-field stands during the opening game of the 1963 World Series. A crowd of 69,000 saw Sandy Koufax shackle the New York Yankees, 5-2, on the way to a four-game Dodger sweep.

called Chavez Ravine. Negotiations between Dodger President Walter O'Malley, and Los Angeles Mayor, Norris Poulson, culminated in the Dodgers receiving 300 acres of land in Chavez Ravine in exchange for Wrigley Field.

Walter O'Malley constructed what has been called the most beautiful park in the major leagues. Aesthetically stimulating, with its sparkling clean surfaces, brightly colored grandstands, and view of the rolling hills in the distance, Dodger Stadium is a pleasure to behold, for player and fan alike. The size of the field favors neither pitcher nor hitter. The distances are 330 feet down the foul lines, 370 feet to the power alleys, and 400 feet to dead center. The seating design provides an unobstructed view for over 52,000 spectators.

On April 10, 1962, the Los Angeles Dodgers officially dedicated their new stadium in the season opener against the defending National League champion, Cincinnati Reds. Dodger lefty, Johnny Podres, won the honor of pitching the first game ever at Dodger Stadium. He was opposed by Cincinnati ace Bob Purkey.

No sooner had Kay O'Malley, wife of the Dodger President, thrown out the first ball, than Freddie Hutchinson's sluggers roughed up the Dodger starter. Leadoff man Eddie Kasko drilled a double down the left-field line and scored moments later on a single by Vada Pinson. The Dodgers came back to grab the lead in the last of the fourth. Gilliam stroked a single to right, and went to second on another single by Duke Snider. Both runners came around to score when Ron Fairly smashed a long double to left center field.

Cincinnati tied the game in the sixth on a walk and two singles. Then, in the seventh, they knocked Podres out of the box, icing the game in the process. With Pinson and Frank Robinson on base, Wally Post took a Podres pitch down town, cracking a 410-foot home run over the center field fence. That was all she wrote, as the Reds went on to spoil the Dodger home opener by a score of 6-3.

CINCINNATI

NAME	POS	AB	R	H	E
Kasko	SS	5	1	1	0
Rojas	2B	3	0	0	0
Lynch	PH	1	0	0	0
Blasingame	2B	0	0	0	0
Pinson	CF	4	3	4	0
Robinson	RF	4	1	1	0
Post	LF	5	1	3	0
Keough	RF	0	0	0	0
Coleman	1B	4	0	1	0
Harper	3B	4	0	3	0
Edwards	C	4	0	0	0
Purkey	P	4	0	1	0
Henry	P	0	0	0	0
Brosnan	P	0	0	0	0
Total		38	6	14	0

LOS ANGELES

NAME	POS	AB	R	H	E
Wills	SS	3	0	0	0
Howard	PH	1	0	0	0
Gilliam	2B	4	1	2	0
Moon	LF	3	0	0	0
Snider	RF	3	1	2	0
T. Davis	PH	1	0	0	0
Roseboro	C	2	0	0	0
Fairly	1B	4	0	1	0
Spencer	3B	4	1	1	0
W. Davis	CF	3	0	0	0
Walls	PH	0	0	0	0
Podres	P	2	0	1	0
L. Sherry	P	0	0	0	0
Harkness	PH	1	0	0	0
Perranoski	P	0	0	0	0
Carey	PH	1	0	1	0
Total		32	3	8	0

```
CINCINNATI    1 0 0  0 0 1  3 0 1 - 6 - 14 - 0
LOS ANGELES   0 0 0  2 0 0  0 0 1 - 3 -  8 - 0
```

Sandy Koufax pitched the Big Blue Machine to its first victory in its new home, the following night, winning 6-2 before 35,296 paying customers. Junior Gilliam hit the first Dodger home run in the new park.

The Los Angeles contingent won many games in the ensuing years, however. Pennants flew over Dodger Stadium in 1963, 1965, 1966, 1974, 1977, 1978, 1981, and 1988. World Championship banners were hoisted to the top of the stadium in five of those years, including the miracle year of 1988.

No one knows what lies in store for the Los Angeles Dodgers or their fans in the years to come. Or what dramatic events will unfold in beautiful Dodger Stadium. But based on their colorful 114-year history in the major leagues, you can bet it will be exciting and unexpected.

Dodger Stadium, called the most beautiful park in the country, opened its doors for the first time on April 10, 1962. (Los Angeles Dodger Photo)

MAJOR LEAGUE CAREER STATISTICS - BATTERS

NAME	G	AB	H	D	T	HR	RBI	SB	BA
ABRAMS, C.	567	1611	433	64	19	32	138	12	.269
ABREU, T.	146	367	92	25	2	3	31	2	251
ADERHOLT, M.	106	262	70	7	3	3	32	3	.267
AINSMITH, E.	1073	3048	707	108	54	22	317	86	.232
ALCARAZ, L.	115	365	70	9	2	4	29	2	.192
ALLEN, D.	1749	6332	1848	320	79	351	1119	133	.292
ALLEN, H.	4	7	0	0	0	0	0	0	.000
ALLEN, L.	8	9	1	1	0	0	0	0	.111
ALMADA, M.	646	2483	706	107	27	15	197	56	.284
ALOMAR, S.	1377	4530	1236	249	10	112	588	25	.273
ALPERMAN, W.	450	1632	387	60	36	7	141	27	.252
ALVAREZ, O.	25	51	8	2	0	2	8	0	.157
AMELUNG, E.	42	57	11	0	0	0	4	3	.193
AMOROS, S.	517	1311	334	55	23	43	180	18	.255
ANDERSON, D.	873	2026	490	73	12	19	143	49	.242
ANDERSON, F.	97	234	61	12	0	2	15	1	.261
ANDERSON, G.	2228	8640	2529	522	36	287	1365	80	.293
ANDERSON, J.	1635	6341	1841	328	124	48	976	338	.290
ANDERSON, M.	1151	3204	849	174	20	63	371	71	.265
ANDREWS, S.	70	149	32	2	1	1	12	2	.215
ANKENMAN, P.	15	29	7	1	0	0	3	0	.241
ANTHONY. E	682	1999	462	81	8	78	269	24	.231
ANTONELLO, B.	40	43	7	1	1	1	4	0	.163
ARCHER, J.	847	2646	660	106	34	16	296	36	.249
ARDOIN, D.	165	423	87	17	1	8	35	2	.206
ASHLEY, B.	281	618	144	23	1	28	84	0	.233
ASPROMONTE, B.	1324	4369	1103	135	26	60	457	19	.252
AUERBACH, R.	624	1407	309	56	5	9	86	36	.220
AUSMUS, B.	1971	6279	1579	270	34	80	607	102	.251
AVEN, B.	252	592	164	33	2	20	103	5	.277
AYBAR, W.	405	1219	315	68	2	33	157	7	.258
BABB, C.	347	1180	287	41	13	0	116	66	.243
BAILEY, B.	1931	6082	1564	234	43	189	773	85	.257
BAILEY, G.	213	634	156	16	7	2	52	13	.246
BAILOR, B.	955	2937	775	107	23	9	222	90	.264
BAIRD, D.	617	2106	492	86	45	6	191	118	.234
BAKER, D.	2039	7117	1981	320	23	242	1013	137	.278
BAKO, P.	789	2202	508	98	11	24	195	4	.231
BANCROFT, D.	1913	7182	2004	320	77	32	591	145	.279
BARAJAS, R.	1010	3139	746	176	1	125	449	2	.238
BARBER, T.	491	1531	442	47	21	2	185	28	.289
BARBIERI, J.	39	82	23	5	0	0	3	2	.280
BARKLEY, R.	63	163	43	9	0	0	21	2	.264
BARNES, L.	46	78	12	2	0	1	4	0	.154
BARRETT, B.	239	650	169	23	5	10	86	6	.260
BARTLEY, B.	9	21	1	0	0	0	1	0	.048

BASHANG, A.	8	17	2	0	0	0	3	0	.118
BASINSKI, E.	203	602	147	19	7	4	59	1	.244
BATCH, E.	348	1253	315	38	22	7	98	37	.251
BAXES, J.	88	280	69	12	0	17	39	1	.246
BEAN, B.	36	77	19	2	1	0	4	1	.247
BECK, E.	232	912	265	42	11	9	123	12	.291
BELANGER, M.	2016	5784	1316	175	33	20	389	167	.228
BELARDI, W.	263	592	143	13	5	28	74	1	.242
BELLIARD, R.	1484	5045	1377	328	24	114	601	43	.273
BELTRE, A.	1959	7361	2033	430	28	310	1113	114	.276
BENZINGER, T.	808	2518	644	122	16	56	343	19	.256
BERG, M.	663	1813	441	71	6	6	206	11	.243
BERGEN, B.	947	3028	516	45	21	2	193	23	.170
BERRES, R.	561	1330	287	37	3	3	78	4	.216
BERROA, A.	746	2575	665	118	21	46	254	50	.258
BETEMIT, W.	690	1721	463	106	6	61	240	9	.269
BILKO, S.	600	1738	432	85	13	76	276	2	.249
BISSONETTE, D.	604	2291	699	117	50	66	391	17	.305
BLAKE, C.	1265	4500	1186	264	18	167	616	36	.264
BLANCO, H.	3	5	2	0	0	1	1	0	.400
BLOWERS, M.	761	2300	591	116	8	78	365	7	.257
BLUE, L.	1615	5904	1696	319	109	44	692	150	.287
BOCACHICA, H.	272	535	115	28	1	15	37	16	.215
BOGAR, T.	701	1516	345	69	9	24	161	13	.228
BOHNE, S.	72	179	36	3	4	1	16	2	.201
BOLLING, J.	125	342	107	25	1	4	38	6	.313
BONILLA, B.	2113	7213	2010	408	61	287	1173	45	.279
BONNER, F.	246	949	244	44	8	4	115	28	.257
BOONE, I.	356	1160	372	79	11	26	194	3	.321
BORDAGARAY, F.	930	2632	745	120	28	14	270	65	.283
BORKOWSKI, B.	470	1170	294	43	10	16	112	2	.251
BOURNIGAL, R.	365	932	234	44	3	4	85	12	.251
BOYER, K.	2034	7455	2143	318	68	282	1141	105	.287
BOYLE, B.	366	1343	389	58	24	12	125	24	.290
BRACK, G.	315	980	273	70	18	16	113	13	.279
BRADLEY, M.	1042	3605	976	202	17	125	481	88	.271
BRAGAN, B.	597	1900	456	62	12	15	172	12	.240
BRANSON, J.	694	1555	383	72	11	34	156	9	.246
BREAM, S.	925	2770	726	172	11	81	413	46	.262
BREEDING, M.	415	1268	317	50	5	7	92	19	.250
BRESSLER, R.	1305	3881	1170	164	87	32	586	47	.301
BREWER, T.	24	37	4	1	0	1	4	1	.108
BRIDGES, R.	919	2272	562	80	11	16	187	10	.247
BROCK, G.	982	3142	777	137	6	109	456	40	.247
BRODERICK, M.	2	2	0	0	0	0	0	0	.000
BROOKS, H.	1536	5745	1546	276	31	147	786	63	.269
BROOKS, J	9	9	2	1	0	1	1	0	.222
BROUTHERS, D.	1673	6711	2296	460	205	106	1295	256	.342
BROWN, E.	790	2902	878	170	33	16	407	29	.303
BROWN, L.	48	115	31	3	1	0	6	1	.288
BROWN, T.	494	1280	309	39	7	31	159	7	.241
BROWNE, G.	1102	4300	1176	119	55	18	302	190	.273
BROWNING, P.	1183	4820	1646	295	87	45	353	258	.341
BRUMFIELD, J.	568	1575	404	91	14	32	162	74	.257
BRYANT, R.	79	150	38	6	3	8	24	2	.253
BUCHER, J.	554	1792	474	66	19	17	193	19	.265
BUCKNER, B.	2517	9397	2715	498	49	174	1208	183	.289

BURCH, A.	611	2185	554	48	20	4	103	96	.254
BURDOCK, J.	960	3873	944	131	40	15	390	32	.244
BURKE, G.	225	523	124	18	2	2	38	35	.237
BURNITZ, J.	1694	5710	1447	298	29	315	981	74	.253
BURNS, O.	1251	4920	1299	236	69	39	733	270	.303
BURRELL, B.	122	390	96	13	3	3	47	4	.246
BURRIGHT, L.	159	356	73	8	6	4	33	5	.205
BUSCH, M.	51	100	22	4	0	7	23	0	.220
BUSHING, D.	671	2392	511	58	12	2	106	39	.214
BUTLER, B.	2213	8180	2375	277	131	54	578	558	.290
BUTLER, J.A.	44	119	16	2	0	0	3	0	.134
BUTLER, J.S.	375	1251	315	48	12	3	146	17	.242
CABELL, E.	1688	5952	1647	263	56	60	596	238	.277
CABRERA, J.	561	1291	333	73	8	15	145	36	.258
CALDWELL, B.	25	38	7	1	1	0	5	1	.184
CALLAHAN, L.	114	276	61	17	5	1	12	5	.221
CAMILLI, DOLPH	1490	5353	1482	261	86	239	950	60	.277
CAMILLI, DOUG	313	767	153	22	4	18	80	0	.199
CAMPANELLA, R.	1215	4205	1161	178	18	242	856	15	.276
CAMPANIS, A.	7	20	2	0	0	0	0	0	.100
CAMPANIS, J.	113	217	32	6	0	4	9	0	.147
CAMPBELL, G.	295	708	186	30	2	5	93	5	.263
CANAVAN, J.	539	2064	461	63	48	30	287	114	.223
CANNIZZARO, C.	740	1950	458	66	12	18	169	3	.235
CAREY, A.	938	2850	741	119	38	64	350	23	.260
CAREY, M.	2476	9363	2665	419	159	69	800	738	.285
CARROLL, J.	1065	2974	826	121	26	12	214	63	.278
CARTER, G.	2201	7686	2030	353	30	319	1196	39	.264
CASEY, D.	1114	4341	1122	137	52	9	354	191	.258
CASSIDY, P.	101	382	98	15	1	3	48	11	.257
CASTRO, J.	869	2122	494	103	13	33	190	5	.233
CATTERSON, T.	28	86	17	1	1	1	3	0	.198
CEDENO, C.	2006	7310	2087	436	60	199	976	550	.285
CEDENO, R.	1100	3174	865	127	32	40	274	213	.273
CEY, R.	2073	7162	1868	328	21	316	1139	24	.261
CHAPMAN, B.	1717	6478	1958	407	107	90	977	287	.302
CHAPMAN, G.	67	93	26	5	1	1	10	1	.280
CHEN, C.F.	19	22	2	0	0	0	2	0	.091
CHERVINKO, P.	42	75	11	0	1	0	5	0	.147
CHOI,H. S.	363	915	220	54	3	40	120	3	.240
CIMOLI, G.	969	3054	808	133	48	44	321	21	.265
CISAR, G.	20	29	6	0	0	0	4	3	.207
CLABAUGH, M.	11	14	1	1	0	0	1	0	.071
CLANCY, B.	522	1796	504	69	26	12	198	19	.281
CLARK, B.	288	1011	233	25	11	1	63	71	.230
CLARK, B.W.	785	2015	559	97	7	36	210	48	.277
CLARK, D.	905	1964	518	81	8	62	284	19	.264
CLEMENT, W.	111	379	96	11	4	0	18	13	.253
COHEN, A.	29	67	13	2	0	0	2	0	.194
COLAVITO, R.	1841	6503	1730	283	21	374	1159	19	.266
COLLINS, B.	228	775	173	11	10	3	54	42	.223
COLLINS. H.	680	2779	790	127	38	11	243	328	.284
CONNORS, C.	67	202	48	5	1	2	18	4	.238
COOKSON, B.	22	35	5	1	0	0	5	1	.143
COOMER, R.	911	3019	827	151	8	92	449	13	.274
CORA, A.	1273	3408	828	140	39	35	286	47	.243
CORBITT, C.	215	630	153	22	1	1	37	8	.243

CORCORAN, T.	2200	8804	2252	289	155	34	1135	387	.256
CORGAN, C.	33	104	23	2	1	0	7	0	.221
CORKHILL, P.	1086	4404	1120	110	81	30	268	137	.254
CORRIDEN, J.	1	0	0	0	0	0	0	0	.000
COSCARART, P	864	2992	728	129	22	28	269	34	.243
COULSON, B.	197	692	163	28	12	1	67	43	.236
COUNSELL, C.	1053	3446	896	160	28	31	419	90	.260
COVINGTON, W.	1075	2978	832	128	17	131	499	7	.279
COX, B.	1058	3712	974	174	32	66	351	42	.262
COX, D.	246	832	261	40	14	8	109	10	.314
CRANE, S.	373	1359	276	30	18	3	45	26	.203
CRAWFORD, W.	1210	3435	921	152	35	86	419	47	.268
CROMER, T.	196	524	118	22	1	12	48	0	.225
CROSBY, B.	205	250	54	5	2	4	20	9	.216
CROSS, L.	2274	9068	2644	411	135	47	1345	301	.292
CROW, D.	4	4	0	0	0	0	0	0	.000
CRUZ, H.	171	280	64	7	3	8	34	1	.229
CRUZ, J.	1388	4724	1167	252	36	204	624	113	.247
CUCCINELLO, T.	1704	6184	1729	334	46	94	884	42	.280
CULLENBINE, R.	1181	3879	1072	209	32	110	599	26	.276
CULLOP, N.	173	490	122	29	12	11	67	1	.249
CURTIS, C.	1204	4017	1061	195	16	101	461	212	.264
CUTSHAW, G.	1516	5621	1487	195	89	25	653	271	.265
CUYLER, K.	1879	7161	2299	394	157	128	1065	328	.321
DAHLEN, B.	2443	9031	2457	413	163	84	1233	547	.272
DAHLGREN, B.	1137	4045	1056	174	37	82	569	18	.261
DAILY, C.	630	2222	541	74	22	2	262	94	.243
DALEY, J.	80	264	66	11	2	1	20	4	.250
DALTON, J.	345	1163	333	39	15	4	112	52	.286
DALY, T.	1564	5684	1582	262	103	49	811	385	.278
DANIEL, J.	12	27	5	1	0	0	3	0	.185
DANIELS, K.	727	2338	666	125	8	104	360	87	.285
DANTANIO, F.	50	135	33	6	1	0	12	3	.244
DAPPER, C.	8	17	8	1	0	1	9	0	.471
DAUBERT, J.	2014	7673	2326	250	165	56	722	251	.303
DAVALILLO, V.	1458	4017	1122	160	37	36	329	125	.279
DAVIDSON, B.	225	808	190	16	11	1	60	46	.235
DAVIS, B.	166	453	110	21	10	7	50	13	.243
DAVIS, E.	1626	5321	1430	239	26	282	934	349	.269
DAVIS, L.	348	1296	338	32	19	3	110	65	.261
DAVIS, M.	963	2999	778	161	16	91	371	134	.259
DAVIS, O.	1	0	0	0	0	0	0	0	.000
DAVIS, T.	1999	7223	2121	272	35	153	1052	136	.294
DAVIS, W,	2429	9174	2561	395	138	182	1053	398	.279
DEAL, L.	4	7	0	0	0	0	0	0	.000
DEAN, T.	215	529	95	15	3	4	25	3	.180
DEBERRY, H.	648	1850	494	81	16	11	234	13	.267
DEDE, A.	1	1	0	0	0	0	0	0	.000
DEDEAUX, R.	2	4	1	0	0	0	1	0	.250
DEISEL, P.	3	3	2	0	0	0	1	0	.667
DEJESUS, I.	1371	4602	1167	175	48	21	324	194	.254
DELMAS, B.	12	28	7	0	0	0	0	0	.250
DEMETER, D.	1109	3443	912	147	17	163	563	22	.265
DEMONTREVILLE	922	3615	1096	130	35	17	497	228	.303
DEMPSEY, R.	1758	4683	1092	223	12	96	471	20	.233
DESHIELDS, D.	1615	5779	1548	244	74	80	561	463	.268
DEVEREAUX, M.	1086	3740	949	170	33	105	480	85	.254

DEWITT, B.	404	1087	283	51	11	21	134	7	.260
DIETZ, D.	646	1829	478	89	6	66	301	4	.261
DILLON, P.	312	1181	298	44	16	1	116	34	.252
DOBBS, J.	582	2224	585	85	23	7	207	78	.263
DOLAN, C.	830	3174	855	99	37	10	315	114	.269
DONNELS, C.	450	798	186	36	5	17	86	5	.233
DONOVAN, P.	1821	7496	2253	207	75	16	737	518	.301
DOOLAN, M.	1728	5977	1376	244	81	15	554	173	.230
DOUGLAS, J.	5	9	0	0	0	0	0	0	.000
DOWD, S.	16	26	3	0	0	0	6	2	.115
DOWNEY, R.	19	78	20	1	0	0	8	4	.256
DOWNS, R.	241	790	179	30	11	3	22	13	.227
DOYLE, J.	1564	6039	1806	315	64	25	924	515	.299
DRAKE, S.	141	285	66	10	1	2	18	15	.232
DREW, J.D.	1566	5173	1437	273	48	242	795	87	.278
DUNCAN, M.	1279	4677	1247	233	37	87	491	174	.267
DUNN, J.	490	1622	397	54	10	1	164	56	.245
DUROCHER, L.	1637	5350	1320	210	56	24	567	31	.247
DURRETT, R.	19	48	7	1	0	1	10	0	.146
EARLE, B.	142	465	133	20	12	6	62	41	.286
EARYS, E.	114	271	83	5	2	1	26	4	.306
ECKHARDT, O.	24	52	10	1	0	1	7	0	.192
EDWARDS, B.	591	1675	429	67	20	39	241	9	.256
EDWARDS, H.	735	2191	613	116	41	51	276	9	.280
EDWARDS, M.	106	259	63	9	2	3	15	1	.243
EGAN, D.J.	917	3080	767	87	29	4	292	167	.249
EISENREICH, J.	1422	3995	1160	221	39	52	477	105	.290
ELBERFELD, K.	1292	4561	1235	170	55	10	535	213	.271
ELLIOTT, R.	157	402	97	15	5	1	44	5	.241
ELLIS, A. J.	87	206	54	6	1	2	28	0	.262
ELSTER, K.	940	2844	648	136	12	88	376	14	.228
ELY, B.	1341	5159	1331	149	68	24	586	164	.258
ENCARNACION, J.	1259	4685	1264	242	46	156	667	127	.270
ENGLISH, G.	240	791	194	22	7	8	90	5	.245
ENGLISH, W.	1261	4746	1356	236	52	32	422	57	.286
ERWIN, T.	276	635	150	23	3	11	70	10	.236
ESPY, C.	506	1188	290	41	16	7	103	101	.244
ESSEGIAN, C.	404	1018	260	45	4	47	150	0	.255
ESTERBROOK, D.	701	2837	741	120	34	6	203	55	.261
ETHIER, A.	854	2968	864	185	18	109	446	19	.291
FABRIQUE, B.	27	90	18	3	0	1	3	0	.200
FAIREY, J.	399	766	180	28	7	7	75	6	.235
FAIRLY, R.	2442	7184	1913	307	33	215	1044	35	.266
FALLON, G.	133	282	61	10	1	1	21	2	.216
FARMER, A.	12	30	5	1	0	0	0	0	.167
FARRELL, DUKE	1563	5679	1563	211	123	51	912	150	.275
FEDEROWICZ, T.	7	13	2	0	0	0	1	0	.154
FELIX, G.	583	2046	561	91	25	12	230	28	.274
FERGUSON, J.	1013	3001	719	121	11	122	445	22	.240
FERGUSON, B.	562	2306	625	76	20	1	226	236	.271
FERNANDEZ, C.	856	2778	666	91	19	40	259	68	.240
FERRARA, A.	574	1382	358	60	7	51	198	0	.259
FEWSTER, C.	644	1963	506	91	12	6	167	57	.258
FIMPLE, J.	92	197	45	9	1	2	28	1	.228
FINLEY, S.	2583	9397	2548	449	124	304	1167	320	.271
FINN, M.	321	1044	274	44	5	3	102	9	.262
FISCHER, B.	412	1099	301	50	15	10	115	20	.274

FISHER, T.	503	1742	480	61	26	11	170	48	.276
FITZSIMMONS, T.	4	4	1	0	0	0	0	0	.250
FLETCHER, D.	1245	3902	1048	214	8	124	583	2	.269
FLOOD, T.	231	816	190	26	6	3	86	23	.233
FLORES, J.	16	7	1	0	0	0	0	1	.143
FLOWERS, J.	583	1693	433	75	18	16	201	58	.256
FONVILLE, C.	244	546	133	10	2	0	31	30	.244
FORD, H.	1446	4833	1269	200	55	16	494	21	.263
FOURNIER, J.	1530	5208	1631	252	113	136	859	145	.313
FOUTZ, D.	1135	4533	1254	186	91	32	548	280	.277
FRANKS, H.	188	403	80	18	2	3	43	2	.199
FREDERICK, J.	805	3102	954	200	35	85	377	23	.308
FREIGAU, H.	579	1974	537	99	25	15	226	32	.272
FRENCH, R.	82	187	36	6	1	0	19	3	.193
FREY, L.	1535	5517	1482	263	69	61	549	105	.269
FRIAS, P.	723	1346	323	49	8	1	108	12	.240
FULLER, N.	3	9	0	0	0	0	1	0	.000
FURCAL, R.	1484	5965	1685	293	65	108	536	302	.282
FURILLO, C.	1806	6378	1910	324	56	192	1058	48	.299
GABRIELSON, L.	708	1764	446	64	12	37	176	20	.253
GAGNE, G.	1798	5673	1440	296	50	111	604	108	.254
GALAN, A.	1742	5937	1706	336	74	100	830	123	.287
GALLAGHER, J.	165	487	133	26	5	16	73	4	.273
GARCIA, K.	488	1463	352	44	13	66	212	10	.241
GARCIAPARRA, N.	1434	5586	1747	370	52	229	936	95	.313
GARNER, P.	1860	6136	1594	299	82	109	738	225	.260
GARVEY, S.	2332	8835	2599	440	43	272	1308	83	.294
GATKINS, F.	67	255	58	9	2	1	26	8	.227
GAUTREAUX, S.	86	81	20	4	0	0	18	0	.247
GENTILE, J.	936	2922	759	113	6	179	549	3	.260
GEORGE, G.	118	299	53	9	2	0	24	0	.177
GERAGHTY, B.	70	146	29	4	0	0	9	4	.199
GESSLER, D.	880	2969	831	127	49	14	363	142	.280
GETZ, G.	399	1114	265	22	9	2	93	41	.238
GIBBONS, J.	840	2917	759	166	7	127	427	2	.260
GIBSON, K.	1467	5241	1403	231	50	223	763	271	.268
GILBERT, C.	364	852	195	27	9	5	55	7	.229
GILBERT, P.	206	761	184	20	9	5	87	48	.242
GILBERT, S.	51	47	7	1	0	2	4	2	.149
GILBERT, W.	591	2317	624	112	17	7	214	21	.269
GILLENWATER, C.	335	1004	261	41	7	11	114	20	.260
GILLIAM, J.	1956	7119	1889	304	71	65	558	203	.265
GIMENEZ, H.	6	9	1	0	0	0	0	0	.111
GIONFRIDDO, A.	228	580	154	22	12	2	58	15	.266
GIULIANI, T.	243	674	157	18	3	0	69	1	.233
GLEASON, R.	8	1	1	1	0	0	0	0	1.000
GLOSSOP, A.	309	952	199	29	2	15	86	5	.209
GOCHNAUER, J.	264	908	170	32	8	0	87	18	.187
GONZALEZ, J.	461	676	144	30	7	9	42	33	.213
GONZALEZ, L.	2591	9157	2591	596	68	354	1439	128	.283
GOOCH, J.	805	2363	662	98	29	7	293	11	.280
GOODSON, E.	515	1266	329	51	2	30	170	1	.260
GOODWIN, T.	1288	3846	1029	125	39	24	284	369	.268
GORDON, D.	56	224	68	9	2	0	11	24	.304
GRABARKEWITZ, B.	466	1161	274	41	12	28	141	33	.236
GRABOWSKI, J.	190	301	59	8	1	11	33	1	.196
GRAHAM, J.	239	775	179	28	5	38	126	1	.231

GRAY, D.	124	305	73	7	6	12	41	4	.239
GREEN, N.	393	1000	237	53	5	16	96	6	.237
GREEN, S.	1951	7082	2003	445	35	328	1070	162	.283
GRIFFIN, A.	1916	6685	1668	242	78	24	524	192	.250
GRIFFIN, M.	1511	5914	1753	313	108	42	625	473	.296
GRIFFITH, B.	191	581	174	30	12	4	72	6	.299
GRIFFITH, D.	124	296	77	16	2	5	27	5	.260
GRIFFITH, T.	1401	4947	1383	208	72	52	619	70	.280
GRIM, J.	706	2638	705	119	37	16	296	82	.267
GRISSOM, M.	2165	8275	2251	386	56	227	967	429	.272
GROTE, J.	1421	4339	1092	160	22	39	404	15	.252
GRUDZIELANEK M.	1802	7052	2040	391	36	90	640	133	.289
GUERRERO, P.	1536	5392	1618	267	29	215	898	97	.300
GUERRERO, W.	678	1678	473	53	30	11	127	42	.282
GULDEN, B.	182	435	87	14	2	5	43	2	.200
GUZMAN, J.	24	56	13	1	2	0	7	0	.232
GWYNN, C.	599	1007	263	36	11	17	118	2	.261
GWYNN, T.	502	1236	305	38	18	7	78	64	.247
HAAS, B.	721	2440	644	93	32	22	263	51	.264
HALE, J.	359	681	137	25	2	14	72	10	.201
HALE, W. W.	333	575	159	27	1	7	78	2	.277
HALL, BOB	103	369	75	8	1	2	32	13	.203
HALLER, T.	1294	3935	1011	153	31	134	504	14	.257
HALLMAN, B.	1503	6012	1634	234	81	21	769	200	.272
HAMILTON, J.	416	1205	282	61	3	24	124	0	.234
HAMRIC, B.	10	9	1	0	0	0	0	0	.111
HANIFIN, P.	10	20	5	0	0	0	2	4	.250
HANSEN, D.	1230	1793	466	79	6	35	222	5	.260
HARGREAVES, C.	423	1188	321	44	11	4	139	6	.270
HARKNESS, T.	259	562	132	18	1	14	61	7	.235
HARRIS, J.	970	3035	963	201	64	47	517	35	.317
HARRIS, L.	1903	3924	1055	161	21	37	369	131	.269
HART, BILL W.	95	270	56	10	4	3	32	8	.207
HARTJE, C.	9	16	5	1	0	0	5	0	.313
HASSETT, B.	929	3517	1026	130	40	12	343	53	.292
HATCHER, M.	1130	3377	946	172	20	38	375	11	.280
HATFIELD, G.	317	1190	295	31	18	5	129	81	.248
HAYWORTH, R.	699	2062	546	92	16	5	238	2	.265
HEARNE, H.	94	293	83	13	2	0	35	5	.283
HECHINGER, H.	13	16	2	1	0	0	0	0	.125
HEEP, D.	715	1560	390	77	5	25	169	12	.250
HENDERSON, R.	3081	10961	3055	510	66	297	1115	1406	.279
HENDRICK, H.	922	2910	896	157	46	48	413	75	.308
HENLINE, B.	740	2101	611	96	21	40	268	18	.291
HERMAN, BABE	1552	5603	1818	399	110	181	997	94	.324
HERMAN, BILLY	1922	7707	2345	486	82	47	839	67	.304
HERMANSKI, G.	739	1960	533	85	18	46	259	43	.272
HERMANSON, C.	189	492	96	23	2	13	34	9	.195
HERNANDEZ, C.	488	1244	315	51	1	24	141	5	.253
HERNANDEZ, E.	714	2327	522	66	13	2	113	129	.224
HERNANDEZ, J.	1587	4618	1166	193	33	168	603	41	.252
HIATT, P.	170	422	87	20	2	12	52	7	.216
HICKMAN, D.	253	727	158	26	13	8	70	27	.217
HICKMAN, J.	1421	3974	1002	163	25	159	560	17	.252
HIGGINS, B.	13	35	5	0	0	0	2	1	.143
HIGH, A.	1314	4400	1250	195	65	44	482	33	.284
HILDEBRAND, G.	11	41	9	1	0	0	5	0	.220

HILL, K.	295	817	173	40	4	8	75	3	.212
HILLENBRAND, S.	943	3570	1014	202	15	108	490	16	.284
HINES, H.	2	8	2	0	0	0	1	0	.250
HOAK, D.	1263	4322	1144	214	44	89	498	64	.265
HOCKETT, O.	551	2165	598	112	21	13	214	43	.276
HODGES, G.	2071	7030	1921	295	48	370	1274	63	.273
HOFFMAN, G.	718	2059	502	103	9	22	207	5	.244
HOFFMANN, J.	16	26	4	2	0	1	7	0	.154
HOGG, B.	2	1	0	0	0	0	0	0	.000
HOLLANDSWORTH,	1118	3191	871	192	22	98	401	75	.273
HOLLINS, D.	8	15	3	0	0	0	2	0	.200
HOLMES, T.	1320	4992	1507	292	47	88	581	40	.302
HOOD, W.	67	80	19	2	2	1	5	5	.237
HOPKINS, G.	514	1219	324	47	6	25	145	6	.266
HOPP, J.	1393	4260	1262	216	74	46	458	128	.296
HOUSEHOLDER, E	12	43	9	0	0	0	9	3	.209
HOUSTON, T.	700	1805	479	84	6	63	263	10	.265
HOWARD, F.	1895	6488	1774	245	35	382	1119	8	.273
HOWARD, T.	929	2350	627	119	21	38	236	65	.267
HOWELL, D.	340	910	224	39	4	12	93	1	.246
HU, C. L.	118	193	34	4	3	2	18	4	.176
HUBBARD, T.	476	762	196	33	7	16	72	33	.257
HUDSON, J.	426	1169	283	50	11	4	96	17	.242
HUDSON, O.	1259	4565	1266	253	58	90	514	79	.277
HUFF, M.	174	383	90	16	2	4	35	15	.235
HUG, E.	1	0	0	0	0	0	0	0	.000
HUMMEL, J.	1161	3906	991	128	84	29	394	119	.254
HUMPHREY, A.	8	27	5	0	0	0	0	0	.185
HUNDLEY, T.	1225	3769	883	167	7	202	599	14	.234
HUNGLING, B.	51	137	33	3	2	1	15	2	.241
HUNT, R.	1483	5235	1429	223	23	39	370	65	.273
HUNTER, G.	45	123	28	7	0	0	8	1	.228
HURLEY, J.	10	23	1	0	0	0	0	1	.043
HUTCHESON, J.	55	184	43	4	1	6	21	1	.234
HUTSON, R.	7	8	4	0	0	0	1	0	.500
HUTTON, T.	952	1655	410	63	7	22	186	15	.248
INGRAM, G.	82	142	37	3	0	3	12	4	.261
IRWIN, C.	989	3679	981	144	46	16	488	180	.267
IZTURIS, C.	1185	4055	1036	162	32	15	290	109	.255
JACKLITSCH, F.	490	1344	327	64	12	5	153	35	.243
JACKSON, R.	955	3203	835	115	44	103	415	36	.261
JACOBSON, M.	133	331	76	9	2	0	24	7	.230
JAMES, C.	208	381	87	15	2	5	27	16	.228
JANVRIN, H.	757	2221	515	68	18	6	210	79	.232
JARVIS, R.	21	50	8	1	0	1	4	0	.160
JAVIER, S.	1763	5047	1358	225	40	57	578	246	.269
JENNINGS, H.	1285	4904	1527	232	88	18	840	359	.311
JOHNSON, C.	1188	3836	940	211	4	167	570	6	.245
JOHNSON, L.	677	2049	529	97	14	48	232	50	.258
JOHNSON, R.	997	3029	857	178	19	59	349	39	.283
JOHNSTON, F.	4	4	1	0	0	0	0	0	.250
JOHNSTON, J.	1377	5070	1493	185	75	22	410	169	.294
JOHNSTONE, J.	1748	4703	1254	215	38	102	531	50	.267
JONES, A.	2102	7366	1887	376	36	420	1255	152	.256
JONES, B.	10	37	4	1	0	0	2	0	.108
JONES, F.	1788	6747	1920	206	75	20	631	359	.285
JONES, M.	8	13	4	1	0	0	0	0	.308

JORDAN D.	165	519	108	21	3	0	40	16	.208
JORDAN, J.	376	1273	327	51	4	2	118	8	.257
JORDAN T.	540	1813	474	74	24	32	232	48	.261
JORGENSEN, S.	267	755	201	40	11	9	107	5	.266
JOSHUA, V.	822	2234	610	87	31	30	184	55	.273
JOYCE, B.	904	3304	970	152	106	71	607	264	.294
JUDGE, J.	2171	7898	2352	433	159	71	1012	213	.298
KAMPOURIS, A.	708	2182	531	94	20	45	284	22	.243
KARROS, E.	1755	6441	1724	324	11	284	1027	59	.268
KARST, J.	1	0	0	0	0	0	0	0	.000
KEELER, W.	2123	8591	2932	242	145	34	810	495	.341
KELLEHER, J.	235	703	206	29	8	10	89	9	.293
KELLERT, F.	122	247	57	9	3	8	37	0	.231
KELLEY, J.	1853	7006	2220	358	194	65	1194	443	.317
KELLY, G.	1622	5993	1778	337	76	148	1020	65	.297
KELLY, R.	1327	4772	1387	240	30	123	584	235	.291
KEMP, M.	787	2862	840	140	28	128	457	144	.294
KENNEDY, B.	1483	4624	1176	196	41	63	514	45	.254
KENNEDY, J.	856	2110	475	77	17	32	185	14	.225
KENT, J.	2298	8498	2461	560	47	377	1518	94	.290
KILDUFF, P.	428	1384	374	62	28	4	159	28	.270
KINKADE, M.	222	429	110	20	1	13	48	5	.256
KINSLOW, T.	380	1414	376	40	29	12	222	18	.266
KIRBY, W.	516	1198	302	51	9	14	119	44	.252
KIRKPATRICK, E.	203	528	125	20	6	3	46	32	.237
KLUGMANN, J.	77	187	47	11	3	0	17	3	.251
KLUMPP, E.	17	26	3	0	0	0	2	0	.115
KOCH, B.	33	96	21	2	0	0	1	0	.219
KOENECKE, L.	265	922	274	49	9	22	114	11	.297
KONERKO, P.	1998	7185	2024	364	8	396	1261	9	.282
KONETCHY, E.	2085	7649	2150	344	181	75	992	255	.281
KOSCO, A.	658	1963	464	75	8	73	267	5	.236
KOY, E.	558	1846	515	108	29	36	260	40	.279
KRESS, C.	175	466	116	20	7	1	52	6	.249
KREUTER, C.	944	2505	593	123	8	54	274	5	.237
KRUEGER, E.	318	836	220	33	14	11	93	12	.263
KUSTUS, J.	53	173	25	5	0	1	11	9	.145
LACHANCE, C.	1263	4919	1377	197	86	39	690	192	.280
LACY, L.	1523	4549	1303	207	42	91	458	185	.286
LAMAR, B.	550	2040	633	114	23	19	245	25	.310
LANDESTOY, R.	596	1230	291	32	17	4	83	54	.237
LANDREAUX, K.	1264	4101	1099	180	45	91	479	145	.268
LANDRUM, T.	607	995	248	40	12	13	111	17	.249
LARKER, N.	667	1953	538	97	15	32	271	3	.275
LAROCHE, A.	403	1180	267	53	6	22	113	8	.226
LARY, L.	1302	4603	1239	247	56	38	526	162	.269
LATIMER, T.	27	86	19	3	0	0	7	1	.221
LAVAGETTO, C.	1043	3509	945	183	37	40	486	63	.269
LAW, R.	749	2421	656	101	37	18	199	228	.271
LAZZERI, T.	1740	6297	1840	334	115	178	1191	148	.292
LEARD, B.	3	3	0	0	0	0	0	0	.000
LEDEE, R.	855	2030	494	120	17	63	318	29	.243
LEE, H.	752	2750	755	144	40	33	323	15	.275
LEE, L.	614	1617	404	83	13	31	152	19	.250
LEFEBVRE, J.	922	3014	756	126	18	74	404	8	.251
LEJEUNE, L.	24	84	14	0	1	0	4	6	.167
LEJOHN, D.	34	78	20	2	0	0	7	0	.256

LEMBO, S.	16	58	13	4	0	0	2	0	.224
LENNOX, E.	448	1383	379	70	25	18	185	38	.274
LEONARD, J.	1131	4001	1078	183	36	110	555	153	.269
LESLIE, S.	822	2460	749	123	28	36	389	14	.304
LEWIS, D.	1354	4081	1021	137	37	27	342	247	.250
LEWIS, P.	508	1775	429	33	13	4	130	55	.242
LEYRITZ, J.	903	2527	667	107	2	90	387	7	.264
LIEBERTHAL, M.	1212	4218	1155	257	10	150	610	8	.274
LILLIS, B.	817	2328	549	68	9	3	137	23	.236
LINDSEY, J.	11	12	1	0	0	0	0	0	.083
LINDSTROM, F.	1438	5611	1747	301	81	103	779	84	.311
LIRIANO, N.	823	2216	576	105	27	25	240	59	.260
LIVINGSTON, M.	561	1490	354	56	9	19	153	7	.238
LODUCA, P.	1082	3892	1112	222	8	80	481	20	.286
LOFTON, K.	2103	8120	2428	383	116	130	781	622	.299
LOFTUS, D.	97	212	53	12	0	0	21	3	.182
LOMBARDI, E.	1853	5855	1792	277	27	190	990	8	.306
LONEY, J.	782	2736	787	155	20	67	418	29	.288
LOPES, D.	1812	6354	1671	232	50	155	614	557	.263
LOPEZ, A.	1950	5916	1547	206	43	51	652	46	.261
LOPEZ, L.	6	6	0	0	0	0	0	0	.000
LORETTA, M.	1726	5812	1713	309	22	76	629	47	.295
LOUDENSLAGER, C.	1	2	0	0	0	0	0	0	.000
LUGO, J.	1352	4758	1279	238	34	80	475	198	.269
LUKE, M.	123	269	65	12	1	15	40	2	.242
LUMLEY, H.	730	2653	728	109	66	38	305	110	.274
LUND, D.	281	753	181	36	8	15	86	5	.240
LYONS, B.	109	230	54	11	2	4	37	0	.235
LYTTLE, J.	391	710	176	37	5	9	70	4	.248
MACGAMWELL, E.	4	16	4	0	0	0	0	0	.250
MACON, M.	226	502	133	17	4	3	46	9	.265
MADLOCK, B.	1806	6594	2008	348	34	163	860	174	.305
MAGEE, L.	1015	3741	1031	133	54	12	277	186	.276
MAGOON, G.	522	1834	439	62	16	2	201	47	.239
MALAY, C.	102	349	88	7	2	1	31	13	.252
MALDONADO, C.	1294	3824	974	206	16	132	576	32	.255
MALINOSKY, T.	35	79	18	2	0	0	3	0	.228
MALONE, L.	133	367	74	11	7	1	28	8	.202
MALONEY, B.	696	2476	585	54	42	6	177	155	.236
MANCUSO, G.	1460	4505	1194	197	16	53	543	8	.265
MANUEL, C.	242	384	76	12	0	4	43	1	.198
MANUSH, H.	2008	7654	2524	491	160	110	1183	114	.330
MARANVILLE, R.	2670	10078	2605	380	177	28	884	291	.258
MARRERO, O.	42	89	20	6	1	1	5	0	.224
MARRIOTT, B.	265	826	220	27	14	4	95	16	.266
MARSHALL, D.	261	756	159	23	8	2	54	15	.210
MARSHALL, M.	1011	3524	953	169	8	147	523	26	.270
MARTINEZ, R.	798	1952	512	98	10	29	242	10	.262
MARTINEZ, T.	657	1480	355	50	16	7	108	29	.240
MATUSZEK, L.	379	820	192	40	5	30	119	8	.234
MAUCH, G.	304	737	176	25	7	5	62	6	.239
MAUL, A.	410	1376	331	45	30	7	179	44	.241
MAURO, C.	167	416	96	9	8	2	33	6	.231
MAYNE, B.	1279	3614	951	178	8	38	403	18	.263
MAZA, L.	45	79	18	1	0	1	4	0	.228
MCCABE, B.	106	199	32	3	2	0	13	6	.161
MCCARREN, B.	69	216	53	10	1	3	27	0	.245

MCCARTHY, J. A.	1091	4195	1203	171	66	7	474	145	.287
MCCARTHY, J. J.	542	1557	432	72	16	25	209	8	.277
MCCARTHY, T.	1275	5128	1496	192	53	44	666	468	.292
MCCARTY, L.	532	1479	393	47	20	5	137	20	.266
MCCORMICK, M. J	105	347	64	5	4	0	27	22	.184
MCCORMICK, M. W.	748	2325	640	100	29	14	215	16	.275
MCCREDIE, J.	56	213	69	5	0	0	20	10	.324
MCCREERY, T.	799	2951	855	99	76	26	387	116	.290
MCDERMOTT, T.	9	23	3	0	0	0	0	0	.130
MCELVEEN, P.	171	502	105	16	4	4	56	12	.209
MCGANN, D.	1456	5295	1503	186	102	42	739	288	.284
MCGRIFF, F.	2460	8757	2490	441	24	493	1550	72	.284
MCGUIRE, D.	1781	6290	1749	300	79	45	787	117	.278
MCLANE, F.	1	2	0	0	0	0	0	0	.000
MCMANUS, F.	14	35	8	1	0	0	2	3	.229
MCMILLAN, T.	297	991	207	21	4	0	54	45	.209
MCMULLEN, K.	1583	5131	1273	172	26	156	606	20	.248
MEDWICK, J.	1984	7635	2471	540	113	205	1383	42	.324
MERCADO, O.	184	426	87	16	4	4	37	3	.204
MERKLE, F.	1638	5782	1580	290	81	61	733	272	.273
METCALFE, M.	4	1	0	0	0	0	0	2	.000
MEUSEL, I.	1289	4900	1521	250	93	106	819	113	.310
MEYER, B.	310	1041	276	29	17	7	84	46	.265
MEYER, L.	7	23	3	0	0	0	0	0	.130
MEYERS, C.	992	2834	826	120	41	14	363	44	.291
MICHAEL, G.	973	2806	642	86	12	15	226	22	.229
MIENTKIEWICZ, D.	1087	3312	899	221	11	66	405	14	.271
MIKSIS, E.	1042	3053	722	95	17	44	228	52	.236
MILES, A.	932	2827	793	110	18	19	229	30	.281
MILES, D.	8	22	4	0	0	0	0	0	.182
MILLER, H.	349	1200	387	65	11	38	205	10	.322
MILLER, J.	32	61	10	1	0	2	3	0	.164
MILLER, L.	8	12	2	0	0	0	0	0	.167
MILLER, O.	927	2836	695	97	33	5	231	40	.245
MILLER, R.	1	1	0	0	0	0	0	0	.000
MILLIES, W.	246	651	158	20	3	0	65	2	.243
MILLS, B.	415	1379	396	62	19	14	163	23	.287
MITCHELL, B.	202	617	150	15	8	3	43	9	.243
MITCHELL, C.	650	1287	324	41	10	7	133	9	.252
MITCHELL, D.	1127	3984	1244	169	61	41	403	45	.312
MITCHELL, F.	201	572	120	16	7	0	52	8	.210
MITCHELL, J.	329	1175	288	38	8	2	63	14	.245
MITCHELL, R.	40	93	14	1	0	4	7	0	.143
MOELLER, C.	501	1392	315	74	7	29	132	2	.226
MONDAY, R.	1986	6136	1619	248	64	241	775	98	.264
MONDESI, R.	1525	5814	1589	319	49	271	860	229	.273
MOON, W.	1457	4843	1399	212	60	142	661	89	.285
MOORE, D.	98	228	53	9	2	1	22	1	.232
MOORE, E.	748	2474	706	108	26	13	257	52	.285
MOORE, GARY	7	16	3	0	2	0	0	1	.188
MOORE, GENE	1042	3543	958	179	53	58	436	31	.270
MOORE, R.	749	2253	627	110	17	27	308	11	.278
MORALES, J.	733	1305	375	68	6	26	207	0	.287
MORAN, H.	595	2177	527	60	26	2	135	10	.242
MORGAN, B.	671	2088	487	96	11	53	217	18	.233
MORGAN, E.	39	66	14	3	0	1	8	0	.212
MORYN, W.	785	2506	667	116	16	101	354	7	.266

MOTA, M.	1536	3779	1149	125	52	31	438	50	.304
MOWE, R.	5	9	1	0	0	0	0	0	.111
MOWREY, M.	1276	4291	1099	183	54	7	461	167	.256
MUELLER, B.	1216	4223	1229	265	22	85	493	20	.291
MULLEN, B.	36	50	11	1	0	0	2	1	.220
MULVEY, J.	987	4063	1059	157	70	29	532	147	.261
MUNOZ, N.	2	1	0	0	0	0	0	0	.000
MURCH, S.	23	71	10	2	0	0	1	0	.241
MURRAY, E.	3026	11336	3250	560	35	504	1917	110	.287
MYERS, H.	1310	4910	1380	179	100	32	559	107	.281
NAKAMURA, N.	17	39	5	2	0	0	3	0	.128
NAVARRO, D.	602	1942	473	90	3	39	197	10	.244
NAYLOR, E.	112	290	54	6	1	3	28	2	.186
NEAL, C.	970	3316	858	113	38	87	391	48	.259
NEIS, B.	677	1825	496	84	18	25	210	46	.272
NELSON, R.	620	1394	347	61	14	31	173	7	.249
NEN, D.	367	826	185	23	3	21	107	1	.224
NIXON, A.	422	1345	372	60	13	7	118	19	.277
NIXON, O.	1709	5115	1379	142	27	11	318	620	.270
NOREN, I.	1093	3119	857	157	35	65	453	34	.275
NORTH, B.	1169	3900	1016	120	31	20	230	395	.261
NORTHEN, H.	164	584	159	29	8	3	63	14	.272
OATES, J.	593	1637	410	56	2	14	126	11	.250
O'BRIEN, D.	709	2856	805	147	47	20	321	321	.282
O'BRIEN, J.	501	1910	486	47	17	12	229	45	.254
OCK, W.	1	3	0	0	0	0	0	0	.000
O'DOUL, L.	970	3264	1140	175	41	113	542	36	.349
OFFERMAN, J.	1651	5681	1551	252	72	57	537	172	.273
OLIVER, N.	410	954	216	24	5	2	45	17	.226
OLMO, L.	462	1629	458	65	25	29	272	33	.281
OLSON, I.	1572	6111	1575	191	69	13	446	156	.258
OELTJEN, T.	99	164	36	6	3	5	11	9	.220
O'MARA, O.	412	1478	341	49	8	2	77	46	.231
O'NEIL, M.	672	1995	475	41	23	4	179	18	.238
ONIS, C.	1	1	1	0	0	0	0	0	1.000
ORENGO, J.	366	1120	266	54	8	17	122	12	.237
O'ROURKE, F.	1131	4069	1032	196	42	15	430	101	.254
ORTA, J.	1755	5829	1619	267	63	130	745	79	.278
OUTEN, C.	93	153	38	10	0	4	17	1	.248
OWEN, M.	1209	3649	929	163	21	14	378	36	.255
OWENS, R.	51	189	37	6	2	1	21	1	.196
PACIOREK, T.	1392	4121	1162	232	30	86	503	55	.282
PADGETT, D.	699	1991	573	111	16	37	338	6	.288
PAFKO, A.	1852	6292	1796	264	62	213	976	38	.285
PARKER, R.	160	225	55	9	0	2	24	9	.244
PARKER, W.	1288	4157	1110	194	32	64	470	60	.267
PARKS, A.	78	255	70	15	2	1	19	2	.275
PARTRIDGE, J.	183	645	167	17	7	7	52	11	.259
PASLEY, K.	55	122	31	7	0	1	9	0	.254
PATTEE, H.	80	264	57	5	2	0	9	24	.216
PAUL, X.	183	378	93	15	6	3	32	19	.246
PEACOCK, J.	619	1734	455	74	16	1	194	14	.262
PEARCE, R. J	257	1207	306	-	-	-	-	-	.254
PECK, H.	359	1092	305	52	13	15	112	10	.279
PEDERSON, S.	8	4	0	0	0	0	1	0	.000
PENA, A.	71	187	39	7	0	5	23	0	.209
PERCONTE, J.	433	1441	389	47	16	2	76	78	.270

PEREZ, A.	216	495	121	25	4	6	43	16	.244
PFISTER, G.	1	2	0	0	0	0	0	0	.000
PHELPS, E. G.	726	2117	657	143	19	54	345	9	.310
PHELPS, E. J.	633	1832	460	45	20	3	205	31	.251
PHILLIPS, J.	465	1382	344	77	0	30	168	0	.249
PIAZZA, M.	1912	6911	2127	344	8	427	1335	17	.308
PICINICH, V.	1037	2877	743	166	25	27	298	31	.258
PIERRE, J.	1751	6823	2020	234	86	16	484	554	.296
PIGNATANO, J.	307	689	161	25	4	16	62	8	.234
PINCKNEY, G.	1163	4610	1212	170	56	21	391	296	.263
PODSEDNIK, S.	1016	3707	1036	171	41	41	300	301	.279
POLLY, N.	14	25	5	0	0	0	3	0	.200
POPOVICH, P.	682	1732	403	42	9	14	134	4	.233
POST, S.	9	25	7	0	0	0	4	1	.280
POWELL, J. W.	2042	6681	1776	270	11	339	1187	20	.266
POWELL, P. R.	30	42	7	1	0	1	2	0	.239
PRINCE, T.	519	1190	248	66	4	24	140	9	.208
PYE, E.	14	18	1	0	0	0	0	0	.056
RACKLEY, M.	185	477	151	20	6	1	35	10	.317
RADTKE, J.	33	31	3	0	0	0	2	3	.097
RAMAZZOTTI, R.	346	851	196	22	9	4	53	15	.230
RAMIREZ, M.	2302	8244	2574	547	20	555	1831	38	.312
RAMSEY, M. JE.	394	786	189	26	6	2	57	14	.240
RAMSEY, M.JA.	48	125	29	4	2	0	12	2	.232
RANDOLPH, W.	2202	8018	2210	316	65	54	687	271	.276
REARDON, P.	55	14	1	0	0	0	0	0	.071
REBOULET, J.	1018	2229	536	100	6	20	202	22	.240
REDMOND, H.	6	19	0	0	0	0	1	0	.000
REED, J.	1284	4554	1231	263	10	27	392	40	.270
REESE, H.	2166	8058	2170	330	80	126	885	232	.269
REIS, R.	175	301	70	10	2	0	21	5	.233
REISER, H.	861	2662	786	155	41	58	368	87	.295
REPKO, J.	355	689	156	29	4	16	67	27	.226
REPULSKI, E. J.	928	3088	830	153	23	106	416	25	.269
REYES, G.	121	258	52	11	0	0	14	2	.202
REYNOLDS, R. J.	691	2055	543	111	16	35	275	97	.264
RHIEL, W.	200	519	138	26	8	7	68	2	.266
RICHARDS, P.	523	1417	321	51	5	15	155	15	.227
RICHARDSON, D.	1131	4451	1129	149	52	32	558	225	.254
RICONDA, H.	243	765	189	44	11	4	70	13	.247
RIGGERT, J.	174	558	134	18	14	8	44	20	.240
RIGGS, A.	9	20	4	1	0	0	1	1	.200
RIGGS, L.	760	2477	650	110	43	28	271	22	.262
RIPPLE, J.	554	1809	510	92	14	28	251	7	.282
RITTER, L.	462	1437	315	33	17	1	120	54	.219
RIVERA, G.	120	280	72	15	3	2	19	1	.257
RIVERA, J.	949	3159	874	168	4	123	492	16	.277
RIZZO, J.	557	1842	497	90	16	61	289	7	.270
ROBERTS, D.	832	2707	721	95	53	23	213	243	.266
ROBINSON, E.	170	421	113	20	5	12	44	7	.268
ROBINSON, F.	2808	10006	2943	528	72	586	1812	204	.294
ROBINSON, J.	1382	4877	1518	273	54	137	734	196	.311
ROBLES, O.	163	423	110	18	2	5	36	0	.260
ROBLES, S.	16	21	2	0	0	0	0	0	.095
ROCHELLI, L.	5	17	3	0	1	0	2	0	.176
RODRIGUEZ, E.	775	2173	533	76	6	16	203	17	.245
RODRIGUEZ, H.	950	3031	784	176	9	160	523	10	.259

ROENICKE, R.	527	1076	256	51	3	17	113	24	.238
ROETTGER, O.	37	66	14	1	0	0	6	0	.212
ROGERS, P.	23	37	7	1	1	0	5	0	.189
ROJEK, S.	522	1764	470	67	13	4	122	32	.266
ROMANO, J.	129	191	39	6	1	2	12	8	.204
ROSE, M.	27	54	11	2	0	1	2	0	.204
ROSEBORO, J.	1585	4847	1206	190	44	104	548	67	.249
ROSEN, G.	551	1916	557	71	34	22	197	12	.291
ROSENFELD, M.	42	57	17	4	0	2	7	2	.298
ROSS, C.	757	2436	636	152	11	100	371	28	.261
ROSS, D.	596	1525	360	82	5	75	225	0	.236
ROYSTER, J.	1428	4208	1049	165	33	40	352	189	.249
RUAN, W.	33	52	12	3	1	0	5	1	.231
RUSSELL, J.	1035	3595	959	175	51	67	428	59	.267
RUSSELL, W.	2181	7318	1926	293	57	46	627	167	.263
RYAN, J. B.	616	2192	476	69	29	4	154	32	.217
SAENZ, O.	733	1663	438	106	5	73	275	3	.263
SAMUEL, J.	1720	6081	1578	287	102	161	703	396	.259
SANDLOCK, M.	195	446	107	19	2	2	31	2	.240
SANDS, J.	61	198	50	15	0	4	26	3	.253
SANFORD, C.	19	36	6	1	1	0	5	0	.167
SANTANGELO, F.P.	665	1691	415	87	14	21	162	37	.245
SAVAGE, T.	642	1375	321	51	11	34	163	49	.233
SAX, D.	37	60	16	4	0	1	8	0	.267
SAX, S.	1762	6916	1943	278	46	54	549	444	.281
SCHEER, A.	281	931	262	48	20	5	105	41	.281
SCHLIEBNER, D.	146	520	141	23	6	4	56	4	.271
SCHMANDT, R.	317	1054	284	36	13	3	122	11	.269
SCHOFIELD, J.R.	1321	3083	699	113	20	21	211	12	.227
SCHOFIELD, R.C.	1368	4299	989	137	32	56	353	120	.230
SCHULTZ, H.	470	1588	383	85	7	24	208	15	.241
SCHULTZ, J.	703	1959	558	83	19	15	249	35	.285
SCIOSCIA, M.	1441	4373	1131	198	12	68	446	29	.259
SEBRING, J.	363	1411	368	51	32	6	168	52	.261
SEE, L.	26	43	8	2	0	0	2	0	.186
SELLERS, J.	36	123	25	9	0	1	13	1	.203
SHARPERSON, M.	557	1203	337	61	5	10	123	22	.280
SHEA, M.	439	1197	263	39	7	5	115	8	.220
SHECKARD, J.	2122	7605	2084	354	136	56	813	465	.274
SHEEHAN, J.	8	17	2	1	0	0	0	0	.167
SHEEHAN, T.	316	1009	238	26	8	1	88	32	.236
SHEFFIELD, G.	2576	9217	2689	467	27	509	1676	253	.292
SHELBY, J.	983	2947	717	120	23	67	305	98	.243
SHERIDAN, E.	5	6	1	0	0	0	0	1	.167
SHERLOCK, V.	9	26	12	1	0	0	6	1	.462
SHERRY, N.	194	497	107	9	1	18	69	1	.215
SHINDLE, W.	1422	5807	1560	226	97	30	758	318	.269
SHIPLEY, C.	582	1345	364	63	6	20	138	33	.271
SHIRLEY, B.	75	162	33	4	1	0	11	0	.204
SHOCH, G.	706	2536	671	89	28	10	323	138	.265
SHUBA, G.	355	814	211	45	4	24	125	5	.259
SIEBERT, R.	1035	3917	1104	204	40	32	482	30	.282
SIMPSON, J.	607	1397	338	54	12	9	124	45	.242
SIMS, D.	843	2422	580	80	6	100	310	6	.239
SINGTON, F.	181	516	140	36	5	7	85	2	.271
SIZEMORE, T.	1411	5011	1311	188	21	23	430	59	.262
SKAFF, F.	38	75	24	3	2	1	11	0	.320

SKOWRON, W.	1658	5547	1566	243	53	211	888	16	.282
SLADE, G.	437	1372	353	60	11	8	123	12	.257
SMITH, A.B.	287	955	252	30	11	1	130	37	.264
SMITH, C. W.	771	2484	594	83	18	69	281	7	.239
SMITH, R. A.	76	142	31	6	2	0	7	9	.218
SMITH, G.J.	1710	6552	1592	252	94	46	618	235	.243
SMITH, G. A.	27	52	11	2	1	0	7	1	.212
SMITH, H.J.	35	76	18	2	0	0	5	4	.237
SMITH, J. C.	1117	3907	1087	208	49	27	514	117	.278
SMITH, C. R.	1987	7033	2020	363	57	314	1092	137	.287
SMITH, A.	170	500	90	12	2	1	26	13	.180
SMYRES, C.	5	2	0	0	0	0	0	0	.000
SMYTH, J.D.	128	236	45	2	4	0	12	7	.191
SNIDER, E.D.	2143	7161	2116	358	85	407	1333	99	.295
SNYDER, J.C.	995	3503	866	172	13	143	470	27	.247
SNYDER, J.W.	8	11	3	0	0	0	1	0	.273
SOTHERN, D.E.	357	1355	379	80	9	19	115	38	.280
SPENCER, D. D.	1098	3689	901	145	20	105	428	13	.244
SPENCER, R. H.	636	1814	448	57	13	3	203	4	.247
STAINBACK, G.T.	817	2261	585	90	14	17	204	27	.259
STALLINGS, G.T.	7	20	2	1	0	0	0	0	.182
STANDAERT, J.J.	86	132	42	10	2	0	18	0	.318
STANKY, E.	1259	4301	1154	185	35	29	364	48	.268
STARK, M.R.	127	378	90	7	1	0	30	14	.238
STATZ, A.J.	683	2585	737	114	31	17	215	77	.285
STEELMAN, M.J.	43	142	31	3	1	0	15	6	.218
STENGEL, C.D.	1277	4288	1219	182	89	60	535	131	.284
STEVENS, E. L.	375	1220	308	59	17	28	193	7	.252
STEWART, J.F.	176	265	63	14	3	1	18	21	.238
STINSON, G.R.	652	1634	408	61	7	33	180	8	.250
STOCK, M.J.	1628	6249	1806	270	58	22	696	155	.289
STOVEY, H. D.	1486	6138	1769	347	175	121	547	509	.288
STRANG, S. N.	903	2933	790	112	28	16	252	216	.269
STRAWBERRY, D.E.	1583	5418	1401	256	38	335	1000	221	.259
STRIPP, J. V.	1146	4211	1238	219	43	24	464	50	.294
STUART, R.L.	1112	3997	1055	157	30	228	743	2	.264
STUBBS, F.L.	883	2475	573	98	12	102	329	74	.232
SUDAKIS, W. P.	530	1538	362	56	7	59	214	9	.234
SUKEFORTH, C. L.	486	1237	326	50	14	2	96	12	.264
SULLIVAN W.J.	962	2840	820	152	32	29	388	30	.289
SWEENEY, M.	1218	1830	464	101	9	42	250	16	.254
TATUM V.T.	81	194	50	6	2	1	17	7	.258
TAVERAS, A.A.	35	53	11	1	0	0	4	1	.208
TAYLOR, D. T.	674	2190	650	121	37	44	305	56	.297
TAYLOR, J.W.	918	2865	748	113	28	9	311	9	.261
TEED, R.L.	1	1	0	0	0	0	0	0	.000
TEPSIC, J.J.	15	5	0	0	0	0	0	0	.000
TERRY W.H.	668	2393	595	76	54	15	163	106	.249
TERWILLIGER, W.W.	666	2091	501	93	10	22	162	31	.240
THAMES, M.	640	1827	450	83	4	115	301	3	.246
THERIOT, R.	795	2894	816	122	17	17	229	108	.282
THOMAS, D.O.	1597	4677	1163	154	54	43	370	140	.249
THOMAS, R.J.	1	3	1	0	0	0	0	0	.333
THOMASSON, G.L.	901	2373	591	103	25	61	294	50	.249
THOME, J.	2485	8259	2287	444	26	604	1674	19	.277
THOMPSON, D.N.	217	307	67	8	0	1	19	4	.218
THOMPSON, L.F.	669	2560	762	149	34	13	249	69	.298

THOMPSON, C.L.	187	517	123	24	2	8	47	2	.238
THOMPSON, M.	1359	3761	1029	156	37	47	357	214	.274
THURSTON, J.	184	337	76	20	5	1	27	5	.226
TIERNEY, J.A.	630	2299	681	119	30	31	331	28	.296
TODD, A.C.	863	2785	768	119	29	35	366	18	.276
TOOLEY, A.R.	196	698	151	17	8	3	66	30	.216
TORBORG, J. A.	574	1391	297	42	3	8	101	3	.214
TRACEWSKI, R.J.	614	1231	262	31	9	8	91	15	.213
TREADWAY, G. B.	326	1283	364	56	46	12	224	60	.284
TREADWAY, H.J	762	2119	596	103	14	28	208	14	.281
TREMARK, N.J.	35	73	18	4	0	0	10	0	.247
TREMPER, C.O.	36	91	20	2	1	0	5	0	.220
TREVINO, A.	822	2213	547	105	9	20	215	19	.247
TUCKER, T.J.	1687	6479	1882	240	85	42	848	352	.290
TYSON, A.T.	199	704	197	34	4	5	73	14	.280
URIBE, J.	1333	4627	1169	243	41	155	627	41	.253
VAIL, M.L.	665	1604	447	71	11	34	219	3	.279
VALDEZ, W.	362	948	230	43	11	6	92	14	.243
VALENTIN, J.	1678	5539	1348	302	41	249	816	136	.243
VALENTINE, R.J.	639	1698	441	59	9	12	157	27	.260
VALLE, H. J.	9	13	4	0	0	0	2	0	.308
VALO, E. W.	1806	5029	1420	228	73	58	601	110	.282
VAN BUREN, E.E.	13	44	11	2	0	0	3	2	.250
VAUGHAN, J.F.	1817	6622	2103	356	128	96	926	118	.318
VELEZ, E.	259	663	160	31	14	8	72	31	.241
VENTURA, R.	2079	7064	1885	338	14	294	1182	24	.267
VERSALLES, Z.C.	1400	5141	1246	230	63	95	471	97	.242
VIZCAINO, J.L.	1820	5379	1453	204	47	36	480	74	.270
VOSMIK, J.F.	1414	5472	1682	335	92	65	874	23	.307
WAGNER, A.	74	261	59	12	3	1	34	4	.226
WALKER, F.	1905	6740	2064	376	96	105	1023	59	.306
WALKER, A.B.	608	1585	360	69	3	35	192	3	.227
WALL, J.F.	15	40	12	2	0	0	1	0	.300
WALLS, R.L.	902	2558	670	88	31	66	284	21	.262
WALLACH, T.C.	2212	8099	2085	432	36	260	1125	51	.257
WALTON, D.J.	297	779	174	27	4	28	107	4	.223
WANER, L.J.	1993	7772	2459	281	118	27	598	67	.316
WANER, P.G.	2549	9459	3152	603	190	113	1309	104	.333
WARD, C.W.	236	769	175	20	6	0	72	7	.228
WARD, D.	948	2234	588	131	5	90	379	1	.263
WARD, J.M.	1825	7647	2105	231	96	26	867	540	.275
WARD, P.M.	744	2067	522	83	15	50	262	7	.253
WARD, J.A.	13	31	9	1	0	0	2	0	.290
WARNER, J.R.	478	1546	387	52	20	1	120	32	.250
WARWICK, C.W.	530	1462	363	51	10	31	149	13	.248
WASDELL, J.C.	888	2866	782	109	34	29	341	29	.273
WASHINGTON, R.	557	1579	413	64	22	20	146	28	.262
WATKINS, G.A.	894	3207	925	192	42	73	420	61	.288
WEBSTER, M.D.	1129	3279	867	145	54	65	327	159	.264
WEISS, G.L.	22	19	2	0	0	0	1	0	.105
WELLMAN, B.E.	338	749	173	26	2	4	65	21	.231
WERHAS, J.C.	89	168	29	3	2	2	14	0	.173
WERTH, J.	925	3080	814	164	16	140	464	96	.264
WEST, M.E.	824	2676	681	136	20	77	380	19	.254
WHEAT, M.D.	225	602	123	23	5	4	35	7	.204
WHEAT, Z.D.	2410	9106	2884	476	172	132	1248	205	.317
WHEELER, E.	30	96	12	0	0	0	5	1	.125

WHITE, D.	1941	7344	1934	378	71	208	846	346	.263
WHITE, M.H.	7	4	2	0	0	0	1	0	.500
WHITE, W.B.	4	1	0	0	0	0	0	0	.000
WHITFIELD, T. B.	730	1913	537	93	12	33	179	18	.281
WHITMAN, D.C.	285	638	165	37	3	2	67	10	.259
WHITTED, G.B.	1025	3630	978	145	60	23	451	116	.269
WILKINS, R.	696	2062	506	94	7	80	265	9	.245
WILLIAMS, E.	395	1145	288	47	2	39	150	2	.252
WILLIAMS, R.H.	1023	2959	768	157	12	70	331	12	.260
WILLIAMS, R.D.	200	379	98	16	2	5	39	11	.259
WILLIAMS. R.B.	88	136	34	3	3	2	14	5	.250
WILLIAMS, W.W.	338	1255	314	40	5	1	79	14	.250
WILLS, M.M.	1942	7588	2134	177	71	20	458	586	.281
WILSON, E.F.	88	227	72	12	2	4	33	4	.317
WILSON, L.R.	1348	4760	1461	266	67	244	1062	52	.307
WILSON, R.	3	5	1	0	0	0	0	0	.000
WILSON, T.	214	554	140	29	0	15	76	0	.253
WINDHORN, G.R.	95	108	19	9	1	2	8	1	.176
WINSETT, J.T.	230	566	134	25	5	8	76	3	.237
WITT, L.W.	1139	4171	1195	144	62	18	302	78	.287
WOODSON, T.M.	215	506	125	22	2	5	50	2	.247
WRIGHT, F.G.	1119	4153	1219	203	76	94	723	38	.294
WRIGLEY, G.W.	239	861	222	25	20	5	117	18	.258
WYNN, J.S.	1920	6653	1665	285	39	291	964	225	.250
YALE, W.M.	4	13	1	0	0	0	1	0	.077
YEAGER, J.F.	574	1853	467	77	29	4	201	37	.252
YEAGER, S.W.	1269	3584	816	118	16	102	410	14	.228
YOUNG, D.	344	710	183	37	4	17	81	4	.258
YOUNG, E.O.	1730	6119	1731	327	46	79	543	465	.283
ZEILE, T.	2158	7573	2004	397	23	253	1110	53	.265
ZIMMER, D.W.	1095	3283	773	130	22	91	352	45	.235
ZIMMERMAN, W.H.	22	57	16	2	0	0	7	1	.281
ZIMMERMAN, E.D.	127	431	80	10	7	3	72	1	.204

CAREER STATISTICS - PITCHING AVERAGES

NAME	G	IP	W	L	PCT	SO	BB	H	ERA	SV
AASE D.W.	448	1109	66	60	.524	641	457	1085	3.80	82
ABBEY, B.W.	79	568	22	40	.355	161	192	686	4.52	1
ADAMS, T.	574	869	51	62	.451	691	380	890	4.17	42
AGUIRRE, H.J.	447	1376	75	72	.510	856	479	1216	3.24	33
AITCHISON, R.L.	34	206	12	12	.500	101	67	193	3.01	0
ALBOSTA, E.J.	19	53	0	8	.000	24	43	52	6.11	0
ALEXANDER, D.L.	528	3144	188	156	.547	1433	902	3131	3.71	3
ALLEN, F.L.	180	970	50	67	.427	457	373	893	2.93	3
ALLEN, J.T.	352	1951	142	75	.654	1070	738	1849	3.75	18
ALVAREZ, V.	9	16	0	2	.000	10	8	18	7.31	0
ALVAREZ, W.	355	1748	102	92	.526	1330	805	1624	3.96	4
APPLETON, E.S.	48	185	5	12	.294	64	84	182	3.26	1
ARNOLD, J.	50	108	2	7	.222	42	58	119	5.73	2
ASHBY, A.	309	1811	98	110	.471	1173	540	1857	4.12	1
ASTACIO, P.J.	392	2197	129	124	.510	1664	726	2292	4.67	0
BABICH, J.C.	112	591	30	45	.400	231	220	657	4.93	1
BAEZ, D.	533	697	40	57	.412	505	288	652	4.25	114
BAILEY, A.L.	52	137	4	7	.364	35	40	171	4.60	0
BAKER, T.C.	68	173	3	9	.250	58	92	195	4.73	2

BALDWIN, C.B.	118	1017	73	41	.640	582	233	921	2.86	1
BALDWIN, J.	226	1245	79	69	.534	807	461	1355	5.02	0
BALLOU, N.W.	99	330	19	20	.487	109	168	398	5.10	2
BANKHEAD, D.R.	52	153	9	5	.643	111	110	161	6.53	4
BANKS, W.A.	100	489	26	35	.426	344	241	532	5.03	0
BANTA, J.K.	69	204	14	12	.538	116	113	176	3.79	5
BARGER, E.B.	151	975	46	63	.422	297	334	1010	3.56	9
BARNES, B.K.	116	406	14	22	.389	275	204	364	3.94	3
BARNES, J.L.	422	2571	152	149	.505	653	515	2686	3.21	13
BARNEY, R.E.	155	599	35	31	.530	336	410	474	4.30	1
BARR, R.M.	158	1327	49	98	.333	588	363	1455	3.84	1
BARRIOS, M.	3	4	0	0	.000	1	4	4	2.45	0
BECK, W.W.	265	1034	38	69	.355	352	343	1119	4.30	6
BECKWITH, T.J.	229	422	18	19	.486	319	150	432	3.54	7
BEHRMAN, H.B.	174	430	24	17	.585	189	228	427	4.40	19
BEIMEL, J.	567	588	24	32	.429	332	242	631	4.21	4
BEIRNE, K.	34	57	1	3	.250	46	26	63	7.46	0
BELCHER, T.W.	394	2443	146	140	.510	1519	860	2423	4.16	5
BELISARIO, R.	128	126	7	4	.636	102	48	104	3.36	2
BELL, G.G.	160	1086	43	79	.352	376	305	1010	2.85	4
BENGE, R.A.	346	1877	101	130	.437	655	598	2177	4.51	19
BESSENT, F.D.	108	210	14	7	.667	118	88	196	3.34	12
BILLINGHAM, J.E.	476	2231	145	113	.562	1141	750	2272	3.83	15
BILLINGSEY, C.	192	1014	70	52	.574	903	441	949	3.68	0
BIRKOFER, R.J.	132	544	31	28	.525	224	175	618	4.19	2
BIRRER, W.J.	56	119	4	3	.571	45	37	129	4.39	4
BLACK, J.	172	414	30	12	.714	222	129	391	3.91	25
BLETHEN, C.W.	7	20	0	0	.000	2	10	33	7.20	0
BOCHTLER, D.	220	260	9	18	.333	215	166	231	4.57	6
BOEHLER, G.H.	61	202	6	12	.333	93	134	232	4.72	0
BOHANON, B.	304	1116	54	60	.474	671	489	1229	5.19	2
BORBON, P.	368	271	16	16	.500	224	134	259	4.68	6
BRADSHAW, J.S.	2	4	0	0	.000	1	4	3	4.50	0
BRAZOBAN, Y.	122	121	10	12	.455	108	59	117	4.76	21
BRANCA, R.T.	322	1485	88	68	.564	829	663	1372	3.79	19
BRANDT, E.A.	378	2268	121	146	.453	877	778	2342	3.87	17
BRENNAN, T.M.	64	220	9	10	.474	102	46	255	4.38	2
BRENNAN, W.R.	34	129	6	9	.400	104	57	149	5.23	0
BRETT, K.A.	349	1526	83	85	.494	807	562	1490	3.93	11
BREWER, J.T.	584	1041	69	65	.515	810	360	898	3.07	132
BROHAWN, T.	82	67	4	4	.500	46	28	70	4.86	1
BROWN, J.J.	1	5	0	1	.000	0	4	7	7.20	0
BROWN, K.	486	3256	211	144	.594	2397	901	3079	3.28	0
BROWN, L.A.	404	1693	91	105	.464	510	590	1899	4.20	21
BROWN, M.S.	387	1075	76	57	.571	435	388	1125	3.47	48
BROXTON, J.	386	392	25	20	.556	503	163	320	3.19	84
BRUBAKER, B.E.	2	3	0	0	.000	2	1	5	15.00	0
BRUNSON, W.	2	2	0	1	.000	1	2	3	11.57	0
BRUSKE, J.	90	127	8	1	.889	87	56	132	3.82	2
BUNNING, J.P.D.	591	3759	224	184	.549	2855	1000	3433	3.27	16
BURK, C.S.	52	218	4	11	.267	86	133	206	4.25	2
BUTCHER, M.S.	334	1787	95	106	.473	485	583	1935	3.73	9
CADORE, L.J.	192	1257	68	72	.486	445	289	1273	3.14	3
CALMUS. R.L.	22	48	3	1	.750	26	16	37	3.19	0
CANDELARIA, J.R.	576	2506	177	119	.598	1656	583	2374	3.29	28
CANDIOTTI, T.C.	451	2725	151	164	.479	1735	883	2662	3.73	0
CANTRELL, G.D.	38	99	2	7	.222	45	47	115	4.27	0

CANTWELL, B.C.	316	1533	76	107	.413	348	382	1640	3.91	21
CARLETON, J.O.	293	1607	100	76	.568	808	561	1630	3.91	9
CARLYLE, B.	112	253	11	12	.478	198	101	267	5.58	0
CARRARA, G.	313	472	29	18	.617	338	202	487	4.69	4
CARROLL, O.T.	248	1330	64	90	.416	311	486	1532	4.43	5
CARSEY, W.	294	2222	116	138	.457	484	796	2780	4.96	3
CARTER, L.	181	254	13	12	.520	127	73	245	4.15	29
CARUTHERS, R.L.	340	2829	218	99	.688	900	597	2678	2.84	3
CASEY, H.T.	343	941	75	42	.641	349	321	935	3.44	55
CASTILLO, R.E.	250	688	38	40	.487	434	327	623	3.95	18
CHANDLER, E.O.	15	30	0	1	.000	8	12	31	6.30	1
CHAPMAN, W.B.	25	141	8	6	.571	65	71	147	4.40	0
CHECO, R.	16	37	3	5	.375	30	21	47	7.61	0
CHENEY, L.R.	313	1880	116	100	.537	926	733	1880	2.70	19
CHIPMAN, R.H.	293	880	51	46	.526	322	386	889	3.72	14
CHRISTOPHER, M.W.	22	33	0	0	.000	23	15	33	2.94	0
CHURN, C.H.	25	48	3	2	.600	32	19	49	5.06	1
CLARK, W.W.	355	1748	111	97	.534	643	383	1897	3.66	16
CLONTZ, B.	272	278	22	8	.733	210	120	276	4.34	8
COLLUM, J.D.	171	463	32	28	.533	171	173	480	4.16	12
COLYER, S.	61	55	1	1	.500	51	37	64	5.04	0
COOK, D.B.	665	1011	64	46	.582	739	390	950	3.91	9
COOMBS, J.W.	354	2321	158	110	.590	1052	841	2034	2.78	8
COONEY, J.W.	159	796	34	44	.436	224	223	858	3.72	6
COREY, B.	91	98	4	4	.500	57	33	100	5.13	0
CORMIER, L.	290	469	24	28	.462	276	227	537	5.07	3
CRABLE, G.E.	2	7	0	0	.000	3	5	5	5.14	0
CRAIG, R.L.	368	1537	74	98	.430	803	522	1528	3.82	19
CRANE, E.N.	204	1550	72	96	.429	720	887	1525	3.99	2
CREWS, S.T.	281	424	11	13	.458	293	110	444	3.44	15
CROCKER, C.A.	3	5	0	0	.000	2	6	8	7.20	1
CRONIN, J.J.	128	924	43	57	.430	318	235	973	3.40	3
CROUCH, W.E.	50	155	8	5	.615	55	52	159	3.48	7
CULVER, G.R.	335	789	48	49	.495	451	352	793	3.62	23
CUMMINGS, W.A.	241	--	145	94	.607	--	--	--	----	--
CUMMINGS, J.R.	91	192	8	15	.348	106	92	219	5.31	0
CURTIS, C.G.	136	745	28	61	.315	236	317	707	3.31	6
DAAL, O.J.	392	1199	68	78	.466	806	441	1250	4.55	1
DARNELL, R.J.	7	15	0	0	.000	5	7	16	3.00	0
DARWIN, A.B.L.	4	7	0	1	.000	6	9	12	10.29	0
DAVIS, C.B.	429	2324	158	131	.547	684	479	2459	3.42	33
DAVIS, R.G.	481	746	47	53	.470	597	300	735	4.05	130
DAY, C.H.	46	122	5	7	.417	48	28	163	5.31	2
DECATUR, A.R.	153	539	23	34	.404	152	145	653	4.51	7
DE LA Rosa,R.	13	61	4	5	.444	60	31	54	3.71	0
DELL, W.G.	92	430	19	23	.452	198	171	367	2.55	3
DENT, E.E.	12	75	4	5	.444	21	26	81	4.44	0
DESILVA, J.	4	6	0	0	.000	6	1	8	7.11	0
DESSAU, F.R.	21	60	2	4	.333	25	39	80	6.60	1
DESSENS, E.	441	1174	52	64	.448	693	348	1300	4.44	5
DIAZ, C.A.	179	257	13	6	.684	207	97	249	3.22	4
DICKERMAN, L.L.	89	431	19	27	.413	135	218	443	3.99	1
DOAK, W.L.	453	2782	169	157	.518	1014	851	2676	2.98	16
DOCKINS, G.W.	35	131	8	6	.571	34	40	142	3.57	0
DONNELS, C.	1	0	0	0	.000	0	0	0	0.00	0
DONOVAN, W.E.	378	2966	186	139	.572	1522	1059	2631	2.69	8
DOSCHER, J.H.	27	145	2	10	.167	61	68	118	2.86	0

DOTEL, O.	695	888	54	47	.535	1077	396	705	3.74	108
DOUGLAS, P.B.	299	1709	94	93	.503	683	411	1626	2.80	8
DOWNING, A.E.	405	2269	123	107	.535	1639	933	1946	3.22	3
DOYLE, W.C.	51	224	6	15	.286	101	155	277	6.91	2
DRAKE, T.K.	18	40	1	2	.333	13	28	49	6.07	0
DRIEFORT, D.	274	873	48	60	.444	802	389	826	4.36	11
DRYSDALE, D.S.	518	3432	209	166	.557	2486	855	3084	2.95	6
DUDLEY, E.C.	100	421	17	33	.340	106	156	540	5.02	2
DUFFIE, J.B.	2	10	0	2	.000	6	4	11	2.70	0
DURHAM, L.R.	9	29	2	01	.000	6	12	37	5.28	1
DURNING, R.K.	2	3	0	0	.000	0	4	3	9.00	0
EARNSHAW, G.L.	319	1916	127	93	.577	1002	809	1981	4.38	12
EASON, M.W.	125	944	36	75	.324	273	289	1015	3.39	1
EGAN, R.W.	74	101	1	2	.333	68	41	109	5.17	2
EHRHARDT, W.C.	193	588	22	34	.393	128	200	633	4.15	10
EISCHEN, J.	70	89	1	2	.333	67	45	98	4.33	0
EISENSTAT, H.	165	480	25	27	.481	157	114	550	3.83	14
ELBERT, S.	77	60	2	2	.500	63	28	56	4.37	2
ELLINGSEN, H.B.	16	42	1	1	.500	16	17	45	3.21	0
ELLIOTT, J.T.	252	1206	63	74	.460	453	414	1338	4.25	12
ELLIS, R.	3	3	0	1	.000	0	0	6	0.00	0
ELSTON, D.R.	450	755	49	54	.476	519	327	702	3.70	63
ELY, J.	23	113	4	11	.267	89	47	117	5.35	0
ENZMANN, J.	67	270	11	12	.478	91	61	297	2.83	2
EOVALDI, N.	10	35	1	2	.333	23	20	28	3.63	0
EPPERLY, E.P.	14	36	2	01.	000	13	20	42	4.00	0
ERICKSON, S.	389	2361	142	136	.511	1252	865	2586	4.59	0
ERSKINE, C.D.	335	1719	122	78	.610	981	646	1637	3.99	13
EVANS, R.E.	41	111	1	11	.183	47	48	144	6.24	2
EVANS, R.	84	614	29	41	.414	211	233	673	3.66	0
EVELAND, D.	100	360	19	24	.442	238	180	429	5.52	1
FALKENBORG, B.	64	76	3	5	.375	62	36	91	5.59	0
FARRELL, R.J.	590	1704	106	111	.488	1177	468	1628	3.45	83
FAULKNER, J.L.	43	127	10	8	.566	34	47	146	3.76	3
FERGUSON, J.A.	257	1239	61	85	.418	396	478	1449	4.90	10
FERNANDEZ, C.S.	306	1862	113	96	.541	1740	713	1417	3.36	1
FERRELL, W.C.	374	2623	193	128	.601	985	1040	2845	4.04	13
FETTE, L.H.W.	109	691	41	40	.506	194	248	658	3.15	1
FETTERS, M.	620	717	31	41	.431	518	351	699	3.86	100
FINLAYSON, P.	2	7	0	0	.000	2	8	7	11.57	0
FISCHER, J.T.	6	17	0	1	.000	8	5	28	9.53	0
FISHER, C.B.	65	436	21	26	.447	80	140	583	5.37	3
FITZSIMMONS, F.L.	513	3225	217	146	.598	870	846	3335	3.51	13
FLETCHER, S.S.	3	19	0	1	.000	8	13	28	9.95	0
FLOWERS, C.W.	14	38	2	2	.500	11	23	49	5.45	0
FORSTER, T.J.	614	1105	54	65	.454	791	457	1034	3.23	127
FOSTER, A.B.	217	1028	48	63	.432	501	383	988	3.73	0
FOUTZ, D.L.	251	1998	147	66	.690	790	510	1843	2.84	4
FOWLER, J.A.	514	1025	54	51	.514	539	308	1039	4.02	32
FRANKHOUSE, F.M.	402	1889	106	97	.522	622	701	2033	3.92	12
FRANKLIN, J.W.	1	2	0	0	.000	0	4	2	13.50	0
FRENCH, L.H.	570	3152	197	171	.535	1187	819	3375	3.44	17
FUCHS, C.T.	47	167	6	10	.375	41	73	186	4.85	1
GADDY, J.W.	2	13	2	01	.000	3	4	13	0.69	0
GAGNE, E.	402	644	33	26	.559	718	226	518	3.47	187
GALLIVAN P.J.	54	175	5	11	.313	68	95	227	5.97	1
GALVEZ, B.	10	21	0	1	.000	11	12	19	3.86	0

GARLAND, J.	353	2083	132	119	.526	1124	700	2175	4.32	1
GARMAN, M.D.	303	433	22	27	.449	213	202	411	3.64	42
GARVIN, V.L.	181	1400	57	97	.370	612	413	1320	2.72	4
GASTON, W.T.	3	19	1	1	.500	0	13	20	2.84	0
GASTRIGHT, H.T.	171	1302	72	63	.533	514	584	1337	4.22	2
GIALLOMBARDO, R.P.	6	26	1	1	.500	14	15	29	3.81	0
GOLDEN, J.E.	69	208	9	13	.409	115	76	233	4.54	1
GORDINIER, R.C.	8	23	1	01	.000	9	16	23	7.04	0
GORECKI, R.	7	23	2	2	.500	13	16	24	7.54	0
GOTT, J.W.	492	1052	49	67	.422	789	434	997	3.73	86
GRANT, J.T.	571	2441	145	119	.549	1267	849	2292	3.63	53
GREEN, H.G.	2	1	0	0	.000	0	3	2	9.00	0
GREENE, N.G.	15	31	2	1	.667	7	9	59	8.71	1
GREENFIELD, K.	152	777	41	48	.461	242	297	871	4.53	1
GREGG, H.D.	200	826	40	48	.455	401	443	805	4.54	9
GRIMES, B.A.	616	4181	270	212	.560	1512	1295	4412	3.53	18
GRINER, D.D.	135	673	28	55	.337	244	202	700	3.49	6
GRISSOM, L.T.	162	702	29	48	.377	384	305	668	3.88	7
GROSS, K.F.	474	2488	142	158	.473	1727	986	2519	4.11	5
GROSS, K.L.	73	148	7	8	.467	81	66	168	3.90	0
GUERRA, J.	47	47	2	2	.500	38	18	37	2.31	21
GUERRIER, M.	463	538	23	28	.451	360	172	499	3.46	6
GUMBERT, A.C.	262	1985	124	102	.549	546	634	2321	4.28	1
GUTHRIE, M.	765	979	51	54	.486	778	381	989	4.05	14
HADDOCK, G.S.	204	1580	95	87	.522	599	714	1650	4.08	2
HAEGER, C.	34	83	2	7	.222	69	59	86	6.40	1
HALL, D.	130	126	5	9	.357	98	59	135	3.93	22
HALL, W.B.	3	5	0	0	.000	3	5	4	5.40	0
HALL, J.S.	3	4	0	0	.000	2	2	4	6.75	0
HALL, M.D.	119	115	5	9	.357	90	54	118	3.29	22
HAMLIN, L.D.	261	1405	73	76	.490	563	353	1442	3.77	9
HAMULACK, T.	39	36	0	3	.000	36	23	43	7.43	0
HANNAHS, G.E.	16	71	3	7	.300	42	42	76	5.07	1
HANSELL, G.	70	94	3	1	.750	59	37	112	6.05	3
HANSFORD, F.C.	1	7	0	0	.000	0	5	10	3.86	0
HARKEY, M.	10	15	1	01	.000	6	5	12	4.30	0
HARPER, G.B.	28	172	10	14	.417	46	88	234	5.44	0
HARPER, H.C.	219	1257	57	76	.429	623	582	1100	2.86	5
HARRIS, W.T.	2	9	0	1	.000	3	4	9	3.00	0
HART, W.F.	206	1583	66	120	.355	431	704	1819	4.66	3
HARTLEY, M.E.	141	224	17	11	.607	196	100	188	3.50	3
HATHAWAY, R.W.	4	11	0	1	.000	3	6	11	4.00	0
HATTEN, J.H.	233	1086	65	49	.570	381	492	1124	3.88	4
HAUGHEY, C.F.	1	7	0	1	.000	0	10	5	3.86	0
HAUGSTAD, P.D.	37	57	1	1	.500	28	41	51	5.53	0
HAVENS, B.D.	205	591	24	37	.393	370	246	624	4.81	3
HAWKSWORTH, B.	124	183	10	13	.435	124	67	187	4.07	0
HEAD, E.M.	118	465	27	23	.540	208	174	434	3.48	11
HEHL, H.J.	1	1	0	0	.000	0	0	0	0.00	0
HEIMACH, F.A.	286	1289	62	69	.473	334	360	1510	4.46	7
HEITMANN, H.A.	1	1/3	0	1	.000	0	0	4	(4)	0
HEMMING, G.E.	204	1587	91	82	.526	362	691	1799	4.56	6
HENDRICKSON, M.	328	1169	58	74	.439	666	345	1361	5.03	1
HENION, L.M.	1	3	0	0	.000	2	2	2	6.00	0
HENLEY, W.	97	722	32	42	.432	309	231	640	2.94	0
HENRY, F.J.	164	646	27	43	.386	169	190	809	4.39	6
HENSHAW, R.K.	216	742	33	40	.452	337	327	782	4.16	7

HERGES, M.	567	691	43	35	.551	473	257	735	3.91	34
HERRMANN, M.J.	1	1	0	0	.000	0	0	0	0.00	0
HERRING, A.L.	199	697	34	38	.472	243	284	754	4.33	13
HERSHISER, O.L.	510	3130	204	150	.576	2014	1007	2939	3.48	5
HEYDEMAN, G.G.	1	2	0	0	.000	1	1	2	4.50	0
HIGBE, W.K.	418	1954	118	101	.539	971	979	1763	3.68	24
HILL, W.C.	124	925	36	69	.343	280	406	994	4.17	3
HILLEGAS, S.P.	181	515	24	38	.387	332	238	521	4.61	10
HOLLINGSWORTH, A.	315	1519	70	104	.402	608	587	1642	3.99	15
HOLLINGSWORTH, J.	36	118	4	9	.308	50	81	127	4.88	0
HOLMES. D.L.	557	680	35	33	.515	581	256	709	4.25	59
HOLTON, B.J.	185	371	20	19	.513	210	125	401	3.62	3
HONEYCUTT, F.W.	795	2158	109	143	.433	1036	656	2178	3.71	38
HOOTON, B.C.	480	2652	151	136	.526	1491	799	2497	3.38	7
HOPPER, C.F.	2	11	0	2	.000	5	5	14	4.91	0
HORTON, E.E.	3	24	0	3	.000	3	15	38	9.75	0
HORTON, R.N.	325	673	32	27	.542	319	222	696	3.76	15
HOUGH, C.O.	858	3801	216	216	.500	2362	1665	3283	3.74	61
HOULTON, D.J.	53	157	6	11	.353	111	59	173	4.99	0
HOWE, S.R.	472	589	47	40	.540	323	133	567	2.93	90
HOWELL, J.C.	528	802	54	52	.509	644	275	738	3.22	153
HOWELL, K.	245	613	38	48	.442	549	275	534	3.95	31
HOYT, W.C.	674	3763	237	182	.566	1206	1003	4037	3.59	52
HUBBELL, W.W.	204	931	40	63	.388	167	225	1207	4.68	10
HUDSON, R.H.	1	2	0	0	.000	0	0	6	22.50	0
HUGHES, J.J.	135	1098	83	41	.669	370	376	1011	3.00	0
HUGHES, J.R.	172	297	15	13	.536	165	152	278	3.82	39
HUGHES, M.J.	75	623	39	28	.582	250	235	594	3.24	0
HULL, E.	5	7	0	0	.000	5	3	4	4.05	0
HUNTER, W.M.	69	114	4	9	.308	63	47	127	5.68	5
HUTCHINSON, I.K.	209	612	34	33	.507	179	249	628	3.75	13
INKS. A.P.	89	603	27	46	.370	167	266	603	5.54	1
ISHII, K.	105	564	39	34	.534	435	354	508	4.44	0
JACKSON, E.	203	1079	60	60	.500	801	439	1154	4.46	0
JANSEN, K.	76	81	3	1	.750	137	41	42	2.12	9
JEFFCOAT, G.E.	70	170	7	11	.389	86	100	159	4.50	3
JENKINS, W.W.	8	26	0	3	.000	16	19	28	4.85	0
JOHN, T.E.	750	4644	286	224	.561	2227	1237	4696	3.31	4
JOHNSON, J.	255	1357	56	100	.359	810	498	1521	4.99	0
JONES, A.L.	1	1	0	0	.000	0	1	2	18.00	0
JONES, O.W.	113	875	44	54	.449	257	225	904	3.20	1
JUDD, M.	28	75	4	.571	61	39	91	7.20	0	
KEHN, C.L.	3	8	0	0	.000	3	4	8	6.75	0
KEKICH, M.D.	235	860	39	51	.433	497	442	875	4.59	6
KENNEDY, W.P.	405	3021	187	159	.540	797	1201	3276	3.97	9
KENT, M.A.	23	100	5	5	.500	25	49	112	4.68	0
KERSHAW, C.	118	716	47	28	.627	745	278	562	2.88	0
KIDA, M.	65	96	1	1	.500	68	39	114	5.83	1
KIMBALL, N.W.	94	236	11	9	.550	88	117	219	3.78	5
KING, C.E.	200	496	32	25	.561	150	189	524	4.14	11
KIPP, F.L.	47	113	6	7	.462	64	48	119	5.10	0
KITSON, F.L.	303	2217	128	117	.522	729	488	2328	3.17	8
KLIPPSTEIN, J.C.	711	1970	101	118	.461	1158	978	1915	4.24	66
KNETZER, E.E.	220	1267	69	69	.500	535	484	1206	3.15	6
KNOLLS, O.E.	2	7	0	0	.000	3	2	13	3.86	0
KORWAN, J.	6	39	1	2	.333	14	33	56	6.92	0
KOUFAX, S.	397	2325	165	87	.655	2396	817	1754	2.76	9

KOUKALIK, J.	1	8	0	1	.000	1	4	10	1.13	0
KOUPAL, L.L.	101	336	10	21	.323	87	156	436	5.57	7
KRUEGER, W.C.	98	447	27	31	.466	190	231	481	4.57	1
KRUGER, A.	2	6	0	1	.000	2	3	5	4.50	0
KUBENKA, J.	12	17	1	1	.500	12	12	17	5.82	0
KUO, H.C.	218	292	13	17	.433	345	127	228	3.73	13
KURODA, H.	115	699	41	46	.471	523	163	667	3.45	0
LABINE, C.W.	513	1079	77	56	.579	551	396	1043	3.63	96
LAGROW, L.H.	309	778	34	55	.382	375	312	814	4.12	54
LAMANSKE, F.J.	2	4	0	0	.000	1	1	5	6.75	0
LAMASTER, W.L.	71	295	19	27	.413	173	116	352	5.83	4
LAMB, R.R.	154	424	20	23	.465	258	174	417	3.54	4
LANDRUM, J.B.	16	45	1	3	.250	22	11	58	5.60	1
LANKFORD, F.	224	490	33	36	.478	340	146	450	2.96	27
LASORDA, T.C.	26	58	0	4	.000	37	56	53	6.52	1
LEACH, B.	38	20	2	01	.000	19	12	16	5.75	0
LEARY, T.J.	286	1470	77	104	.425	879	524	1544	4.31	1
LEE, R.D.	269	493	25	23	.521	315	196	402	2.70	63
LEHMAN, K.K.	134	264	14	10	.583	134	95	273	3.92	7
LEONARD, E.J.	640	3220	191	181	.513	1170	737	3304	3.25	44
LEWALLYN, D.D.	34	80	4	4	.500	28	22	92	4.50	1
LILLY, T.	343	1911	125	110	.532	1632	632	1764	4.16	0
LINDBLOM, J.	27	30	3	01.000	28	10	21	2.73	0
LINDSEY, J.K.	177	431	21	20	.512	175	176	507	4.70	19
LINK, J.	9	9	0	0	.000	4	4	12	4.15	0
LOAIZA, E.	377	2099	126	114	.525	1382	604	2352	4.65	1
LOES, W.	316	1191	80	63	.559	645	421	1135	3.88	32
LOGAN, R.D.	57	223	7	15	.318	67	81	245	3.15	4
LOHRMAN, W.L.	198	992	60	59	.504	330	240	1048	3.68	8
LOMBARDI, V.A.	223	945	50	51	.495	340	418	919	3.68	16
LONG, T.F.	1	2	0	0	.000	0	2	2	9.00	0
LOWE, D.	634	2516	166	146	.532	1659	740	2563	3.94	85
LOVETT, T.J.	162	1306	88	59	.599	439	444	1341	3.93	1
LUCAS, R.W.	22	56	1	1	.500	5	32	58	5.79	1
LUCID, C.C.	54	375	23	23	.500	65	204	482	6.02	0
LUQUE, A.	550	3221	194	179	.520	1130	918	3231	3.24	28
MACDOUGAL, M.	400	388	18	23	.439	321	206	388	3.94	71
MADDUX, G.	744	5008	355	227	.610	3371	999	4726	3.16	0
MADDUX, M.A.	398	775	36	34	.514	502	250	779	4.00	20
MAGLIE, S.A.	303	1722	119	62	.657	862	562	1591	3.15	14
MAILS, J.W.	104	515	32	25	.561	232	220	554	4.11	2
MALLETTE, M.F.	2	1	0	0	.000	2	1	2	0.00	0
MALONEY, S.	11	13	0	1	.000	5	2	13	4.97	0
MAMAUX, A.L.	254	1294	76	67	.531	625	511	1138	2.89	10
MARICHAL. J.A.	471	3506	243	142	.631	2303	709	3153	2.89	2
MARQUARD, R.W.	536	3309	201	177	.532	1593	858	3231	3.07	19
MARSHALL, M.G.	723	1387	97	112	.464	880	514	1387	3.14	188
MARTIN, M.W.	250	605	38	34	.528	245	249	607	4.28	15
MARTIN, T.	376	317	11	9	.550	224	143	339	4.92	3
MARTINEZ, P.J.	476	2827	219	100	.687	3154	760	2221	2.93	3
MARTINEZ, R.J.	301	1896	135	88	.605	1427	795	1691	3.67	0
MASAOKA, O.	83	94	3	5	.375	88	62	78	4.23	0
MATTINGLY, L.E.	8	14	0	1	.000	6	10	15	2.57	0
MAURIELLO, R.	3	12	1	1	.500	11	8	10	4.50	0
MCBEAN, A.O.	409	1072	67	50	.573	575	365	1058	3.13	63
MCCANN, H.E.	9	64	3	5	.375	18	28	66	2.95	0
MCDEVITT, D.E.	155	456	21	27	.438	303	264	461	4.40	7

MCDONALD, J.	95	312	18	20	.474	266	142	311	4.04	0
MCDOUGAL, J.A.	6	48	1	4	.200	12	17	53	3.94	1
MCDOWELL, R.A.	723	1050	70	70	.500	524	410	1045	3.30	159
MCFARLAN, A.D.	40	264	8	25	.242	51	82	354	5.01	0
MCFARLAND, C.A.	106	840	34	61	.358	307	192	893	3.35	2
MCGINNITY. J.J.	465	3441	246	142	.634	1068	812	3276	2.66	24
MCGLOTHIN, E.M.	8	18	1	1	.500	13	6	18	5.50	0
MCGRAW, R.E.	168	591	26	38	.406	164	265	677	4.89	6
MCINTYRE, J.R.	237	1651	77	117	.378	626	539	1555	3.22	7
MCJAMES, J.M.	178	1361	79	80	.497	593	563	1414	3.43	4
MCKENNA, J.W.	22	146	4	9	.308	34	76	184	5.36	1
MCLISH, C.C.	352	1609	92	92	.500	713	552	1685	4.01	6
MCMAHON, J.J.	321	2634	173	127	.577	967	945	2726	3.51	3
MCMAKIN, J.W.	4	32	2	2	.500	6	11	34	3.09	0
MCMICHAEL, G.	402	473	30	28	.517	424	169	436	3.08	53
MCWEENY, D.L.	206	948	37	57	.394	386	450	980	4.17	6
MELOAN, J.	13	18	0	0	.000	20	11	11	4.58	0
MELTON, R.F.	162	704	30	50	.375	363	395	620	3.62	5
MESSERSMITH, J.A.	344	2230	130	99	.568	1625	831	1719	2.86	15
MICKENS, G.R.	4	11	0	1	.000	54	4	11	12.00	0
MIKKELSEN, P.J.	364	653	45	40	.529	436	250	576	3.38	49
MILJUS, J.K.	127	458	29	26	.527	166	173	526	3.91	5
MILLER, R.L.	694	1552	69	81	.460	895	608	1487	3.37	51
MILLER, F.H.	6	21	1	1	.500	2	13	25	3.01	4
MILLER, J.	216	376	24	14	.632	300	187	377	4.82	0
MILLER, R.D.	28	186	5	17	.227	46	99	203	5.27	0
MILLER, T.	694	523	18	17	.514	434	237	521	4.18	11
MILLER, W.W.	3	11	0	1	.000	0	6	16	6.55	0
MILLIKEN, R.F.	61	181	13	6	.684	90	60	152	3.58	4
MILLS. A.	474	636	39	32	.549	456	395	577	4.12	15
MILTON, E.	271	1582	89	85	.511	1127	453	1665	4.99	0
MINNER, P.E.	253	1311	69	84	.451	481	393	1428	3.94	10
MITCHELL, C.E.	390	2217	125	139	.473	543	624	2613	4.12	9
MLICKI, D.	262	1233	66	80	.452	834	472	1337	4.72	1
MOELLER, J.D.	166	583	26	36	.419	307	176	596	4.01	7
MOHART, G.B.	15	43	0	1	.000	14	8	41	2.09	0
MONASTERIOS, C.	32	88	3	5	.375	52	29	99	4.38	0
MOORE, W.A.	147	467	16	26	.381	181	168	547	4.86	3
MOORE, R.L.	365	1074	63	59	.516	612	560	935	4.06	46
MORGAN, M.T.	597	2772	141	186	.431	1403	938	2943	4.23	8
MORRISON, J.D.	297	1536	103	80	.563	546	506	1574	3.64	23
MOSS, R.E.	112	415	22	18	.550	109	189	474	4.97	2
MOSSOR, E.D.	3	2	0	0	.000	1	7	2	27.00	0
MOTA, G.	717	836	39	44	.470	672	323	738	3.91	10
MOULDER, G.H.	66	161	7	8	.467	50	98	188	5.20	4
MULHOLLAND, T.	685	2576	124	142	.466	1325	681	2833	4.41	5
MULLEN, S.	75	68	4	5	.444	35	35	76	4.66	0
MUNGO, V.L.	364	2111	120	115	.511	1242	868	1957	3.47	16
MUNNS, L.E.	61	181	4	13	.235	58	105	203	4.77	2
MUNOZ, M.A.	453	364	18	20	.474	240	174	408	5.19	11
MURPHY, R.	597	623	32	38	.457	520	247	598	3.64	30
MURRAY, J.F.	4	6	0	0	.000	3	3	8	4.50	1
MYERS, R.	167	240	7	5	.583	161	110	265	5.07	1
NAHEM, S.R.	90	225	10	8	.556	101	127	222	4.68	1
NEGRAY, R.A.	66	163	6	6	.500	81	57	170	4.03	3
NEIDLINGER, J.L.	12	74	5	3	.625	46	15	67	3.28	0
NEWCOMBE, D.	344	2154	149	90	.623	1129	490	2102	3.56	7

NEWSOM, L.N.	600	3762	211	282	.487	2082	1732	3769	3.98	21
NEWTON, E.J.	177	1200	54	72	.429	502	416	1179	3.23	3
NIEDENFUER, T.E.	484	653	36	46	.439	474	226	601	3.29	97
NITCHOLAS, O.J.	7	19	1	01	.000	4	1	19	5.21	0
NOMO, H.	320	1972	123	109	.530	1915	904	1758	4.21	16
NOPS, J.H.	136	989	72	41	.637	294	281	1083	3.69	1
NORMAN, F.H.	403	1938	104	103	.502	1303	815	1790	3.64	8
NUNEZ, J.	63	60	4	2	.667	60	26	62	4.50	0
OBRIEN, R.A.	14	42	2	2	.500	15	13	42	3.00	0
OESCHGER, J.C.	365	1818	82	116	.414	535	651	1936	3.81	8
OHMAN, W.	451	326	12	14	.462	323	154	299	4.11	3
OJEDA, R.M.	349	1881	115	98	.540	1125	670	1822	3.62	1
OLSON, G.	622	672	40	39	.506	588	330	598	3.46	217
OROSCO, J.	1252	1296	87	80	.521	1179	581	1055	3.16	144
ORTEGA, F.C.	204	952	46	62	.426	549	378	884	4.42	2
ORTIZ, R.	296	1423	86	84	.506	887	489	1532	4.93	0
OSORIA, F.	104	136	4	9	.308	72	37	175	5.48	0
OSBORNE, E.P.	142	646	31	40	.437	263	315	693	4.72	6
OSGOOD, C.B.	1	3	0	0	.000	0	3	2	3.00	0
OSTEEN, C.W.	541	3459	196	195	.501	1612	940	3471	3.30	1
OSTERMUELLER, F.	390	2069	114	115	.498	774	835	2170	3.99	15
OSUNA, AL.	208	189	18	10	.643	139	107	151	3.86	14
OSUNA, ANT.	411	489	36	29	.554	501	209	432	3.68	21
PADILLA, V.	330	1521	104	90	.536	1070	536	1553	4.31	5
PAGE, P.R.	31	69	3	3	.500	15	44	86	6.26	0
PALICA, E.M.	246	839	41	55	.427	423	399	806	4.23	10
PALMQUIST, E.L.	36	69	1	3	.250	41	36	77	5.09	1
PARK, C.H.	476	1993	124	98	.559	1715	910	1872	4.36	2
PARRA, J.	47	142	6	10	.375	86	55	181	6.59	0
PASCUAL, C.A.	529	2930	174	170	.506	2167	1069	2703	3.63	10
PASTORIOUS, J.W.	97	728	31	55	.360	205	278	705	3.12	0
PATTERSON, D.G	36	53	4	1	.800	34	22	62	5.26	6
PATTISON, J.W.	6	12	0	1	.000	5	4	9	4.50	0
PAYNE, H.F.	80	557	30	36	.455	148	136	678	4.04	0
PENA, A.	433	970	50	48	.510	743	301	878	2.95	67
PENNY, B.	319	1871	119	99	.546	1250	597	1954	4.23	0
PEREZ, C.	142	823	40	53	.430	448	211	900	4.44	0
PEREZ, O.	112	628	30	43	.411	673	344	576	4.67	0
PERKINS, C.S.	19	48	0	3	.000	20	29	62	7.50	0
PERRANOSKI, R.P.	737	1176	79	74	.516	687	468	1097	2.79	179
PERRY, W.P.	182	263	12	10	.545	131	99	215	3.46	6
PETERSON, J.N.	41	110	2	6	.250	29	42	140	5.24	0
PETTY, J.L.	207	1208	67	78	.462	407	296	1286	3.68	4
PFEFFER, E.J.	347	2408	158	112	.585	836	592	2320	2.77	10
PFUND, L.H.	15	62	3	2	.600	27	35	69	5.23	0
PHELPS, R.C.	126	602	33	35	.485	190	220	700	4.93	1
PIPGRAS, E.J.	5	10	0	1	.000	5	6	16	5.40	0
PLITT, N.W.	23	71	3	6	.333	9	38	85	4.82	0
PODBIELAN, C.A.	172	641	25	42	.373	242	245	693	4.49	3
PODRES, J.J.	440	2266	148	116	.561	1435	743	2239	3.67	11
POFFENBERGER, C.E.	57	267	16	12	.571	65	149	301	4.75	4
POOLE, E.I.	80	595	33	35	.485	226	238	585	3.04	1
POOLE, J.R.	431	363	22	12	.647	256	156	376	4.31	4
POSEDEL, W.J.	138	679	41	43	.488	227	248	757	4.56	6
POTTER, M.D.	2	2	0	0	.000	1	0	4	4.50	0
POUNDS, J.W.	1	6	0	0	.000	2	2	8	6.00	0
POWELL, D.C.	207	340	11	22	.333	199	159	360	4.95	3

POWER, T.H.	564	1160	68	69	.496	701	452	1159	4.00	70
PRESNELL, F.C.	154	526	32	30	.516	157	134	547	3.80	12
PROCTOR, S.	307	343	18	16	.529	291	167	337	4.78	1
PROKOPEC, L.	56	231	11	17	.393	144	74	255	5.30	0
PURDIN, J.N.	58	111	6	4	.600	68	52	93	3.89	2
QUINN, J.P.	756	3920	247	218	.531	1329	860	4238	3.29	57
RACHUNOK, S.S.	2	10	0	1	.000	10	5	9	4.50	0
RADINSKY, S.	557	482	42	25	.627	358	209	461	3.44	52
RAGAN, D.C.P.	283	1610	77	104	.425	680	470	1555	2.99	6
RAKOW, E.C.	195	760	36	47	.434	484	304	771	4.33	5
RAMSDELL, J.W.	111	479	24	39	.381	240	215	455	3.83	5
RATH, G.	8	8	0	1	.000	5	7	9	11.25	0
RAU, D.J.	222	1261	81	60	.574	697	382	1259	3.35	3
RAUTZHAN, C.G.	83	95	6	4	.600	45	47	98	3.88	7
REED, H.D.	229	516	26	29	.473	268	208	510	3.72	9
REGAN, P.R.	551	1373	96	81	.542	743	447	1392	3.83	92
REIDY, W.J.	79	601	27	41	.397	109	106	740	4.18	2
REISLING, F.C.	49	312	15	19	.441	100	75	303	2.45	1
REULBACH, E.M.	399	2633	182	106	.632	1138	892	2118	2.28	13
REUSS, J.	624	3661	220	191	.535	1906	1124	3726	3.64	11
REYES, A.	297	345	19	10	.655	333	164	270	3.60	6
REYES, D.	673	727	35	35	.500	642	400	724	4.21	4
RHODEN R.A.	413	2593	151	125	.537	1419	801	2606	3.60	1
RICHERT, P.G.	429	1164	80	73	.523	925	424	959	3.19	51
ROBERTS, J.N.	12	26	0	3	.000	10	8	42	7.27	0
RODAS, R.M.	10	10	0	0	.000	6	4	9	3.60	0
RODRIGUEZ, F.	563	586	38	26	.594	512	283	526	3.71	11
ROE, E.C.	333	1916	127	84	.602	956	504	1907	3.43	10
ROEBUCK, E.J.	460	789	52	31	.627	477	302	753	3.35	62
ROGERS, L.O.	12	24	0	2	.000	11	10	23	5.63	0
ROJAS, M.	525	667	34	31	.523	562	254	591	3.62	126
ROMANO, J.K.	3	6	0	0	.000	8	2	8	6.00	0
ROMO, V.	335	646	32	33	.492	416	280	569	3.36	52
ROWE, K.D.	26	45	2	1	.667	19	14	55	3.60	1
ROWE, L.T.	382	2218	158	101	.610	913	558	2330	3.88	12
ROY, J.P.	3	6	0	0	.000	6	5	5	10.50	0
ROY, L.F.	56	172	6	12	.333	36	92	231	7.12	0
RUCKER, G.N.	336	2375	134	134	.500	1217	701	2089	2.42	14
RUETHER, W.H.	309	2124	137	95	.591	708	739	2244	3.50	8
RUSH, J.H.	4	10	0	1	.000	4	5	16	9.00	0
RUSSELL, J.A.	21	90	2	7	.222	19	46	103	5.40	1
RUTHERORD, J.W.	22	97	7	7	.500	29	29	97	4.27	2
RYAN, J.	24	103	5	5	.500	32	26	101	2.88	1
RYAN, W.P.D.	248	881	52	47	.525	315	278	941	4.14	19
SAITO, T.	322	326	21	15	.583	389	103	233	2.18	84
SANCHEZ, D.	288	299	19	11	.633	214	126	292	4.10	8
SAVAGE, J.J.	20	29	0	2	.000	12	11	41	7.67	1
SAYLES, W.N.	28	79	1	3	.250	52	46	87	5.58	0
SCANLON, W.D.	181	1252	65	71	.478	584	608	1061	3.00	5
SCHARDT, W.	46	216	5	16	.238	84	97	215	3.67	5
SCHLICHTING, T.	16	25	1	01.000	16	15	21	3.55	0	
SCHMIDT, H.M.	40	301	22	13	.629	96	120	321	3.83	2
SCHMIDT, J.	323	1996	130	96	.575	1758	792	1846	3.96	0
SCHMITZ, J.A.	366	1812	93	114	.449	746	757	1766	3.55	21
SCHMOLL, S.	48	47	2	2	.500	29	22	47	5.01	3
SCHMUTZ, C.O.	19	61	1	3	.250	22	14	64	3.54	0
SCHNEIBERG, F.F.	1	1	0	0	.000	0	4	5	63.00	0

SCHREIBER, P.F.	12	20	0	0	.000	5	10	22	4.05	1
SCHUPP, F.M.	216	1054	61	39	.610	553	464	938	3.32	6
SCOTT, R.L.	12	16	0	0	.000	7	4	27	8.44	2
SEANEZ, R.	544	566	41	30	.577	574	285	515	4.10	12
SEARAGE, R.M.	184	220	7	9	.438	150	109	208	3.60	11
SEATS, T.E.	57	178	12	9	.571	69	58	194	4.45	1
SELE, A.	404	2153	148	112	.569	1407	798	2413	4.61	0
SELLS, D.W.	90	138	11	7	.611	49	67	146	3.91	12
SEXAUER, E.G.	2	1	0	0	.000	0	2	0	9.00	1
SHANAHAN, P.G.	11	23	0	0	.000	13	9	21	3.52	1
SHARROTT. G.O.	15	104	4	7	.364	26	63	121	5.97	1
SHAUTE, J.B.	360	1819	99	109	.476	512	534	2097	4.15	18
SHAW, J.	633	848	34	54	.386	545	234	821	3.54	203
SHERRILL, G.	440	323	19	17	.528	320	153		3.68	56
SHERRY, L.	416	799	53	44	.546	606	374	747	3.67	82
SHIRLEY, S.B.	11	13	1	1	.500	8	7	15	4.15	0
SHRIVER, H.G.	26	112	4	6	.400	39	48	122	3.13	0
SHUEY, P.	451	504	45	27	.625	534	256	438	3.57	22
SINGER, W.R.	322	2174	118	127	.482	1515	781	1952	3.39	2
SLOAT, D.C.	9	16	0	1	.000	4	11	21	6.75	0
SMITH, G.A.	229	1144	41	81	.336	263	255	1321	3.89	4
SMITH, J.H.	34	49	2	2	.500	31	17	48	4.59	1
SMITH, S.M.	373	2053	114	118	.491	428	440	2234	3.32	21
SMYTHE, W.H.	60	155	5	12	.294	33	62	232	6.39	4
SNYDER, G.W.	11	26	1	1	.500	20	20	32	5.54	0
SOLOMON, E.	191	718	36	42	.462	337	247	764	4.00	4
SOMMERVILLE, A.	1	1/3	0	1	.000	0	5	116	2.00	0
SOSA, E.	601	918	59	51	.536	538	334	873	3.32	83
SPOONER, K.B.	31	117	10	6	.625	105	47	86	3.08	2
SPRINGER, D.	130	655	24	48	.333	296	258	702	5.18	1
STACK, W.E.	102	491	26	24	.520	200	188	469	3.52	2
STANHOUSE, D.J.	294	761	38	54	.413	408	455	707	3.83	64
STEIN, E.F.	216	1664	110	78	.585	535	733	1697	3.96	3
STEPHENSON, J.J.	67	239	8	19	.296	184	145	265	5.69	1
STEWART, D.K.	485	2415	158	114	.581	1572	933	2247	3.74	19
STEWART, S.	214	181	11	6	.647	161	60	187	3.99	20
STRAHLER, M.W.	53	159	6	8	.429	80	79	149	3.57	1
STRICKLETT, E.G.	104	766	35	51	.407	237	215	755	2.84	6
STRYKER, S.A.	22	75	3	8	.273	22	23	98	6.60	0
STULTS, E.	41	157	8	10	.444	105	67	167	4.93	0
STURTZE, T.	272	797	40	44	.476	480	333	886	5.19	3
SUNKEL, T.J.	63	220	9	15	.375	112	133	218	4.54	2
SUTCLIFFE, R.L.	441	2630	165	135	.550	1653	1049	2569	4.02	6
SUTTON, D.H.	774	5282	324	256	.559	3574	1343	4692	3.26	5
SWIFT, W.V.	90	411	95	82	.537	636	351	1682	3.58	20
TAMULIS, V.C.	170	692	40	28	.588	294	202	758	3.97	10
TAPANI, K.	361	2265	143	125	.534	1482	554	2407	4.35	0
TASCHNER, J.	222	189	10	5	.667	160	104	208	5.14	0
TAYLOR, J.H.	90	358	19	21	.475	127	201	344	4.10	4
TEMPLETON, C.S.	10	21	0	2	.000	11	15	25	7.71	0
TERRY, W.H.	441	3522	197	195	.503	1555	1301	3521	3.74	6
THATCHER, U.S.	5	37	4	1	.800	13	9	42	3.16	0
THIELMAN, H.J.	31	246	9	19	.321	64	98	240	3.37	1
THOMAS, F.W.	81	229	9	20	.310	112	133	269	4.95	1
THOMPSON, D.	4	18	0	0	.000	13	10	16	3.50	0
THORMAHLEN, H.E.	104	565	29	30	.492	148	203	550	3.33	2
THURSTON, H.J.	288	1542	89	86	.509	306	369	1859	4.24	13

TOMKO, B.	397	1816	100	103	.493	1209	582	1898	4.65	2
TROMBLEY, M.	509	796	37	47	.440	672	319	800	4.48	44
TRLICEK, R.A.	87	126	5	8	.385	66	65	132	5.2	1
TRONCOSO, R.	175	197	8	8	.500	141	68	213	3.92	6
TUDOR, J.T.	281	1797	117	72	.619	988	475	1677	3.12	1
UNDERWOOD, F.T.	7	47	2	4	.333	10	30	80	7.85	0
VALDEZ, I.	325	1827	104	105	.498	1173	523	1872	4.09	1
VALDEZ, R.G.	5	13	1	1	.500	10	7	13	5.54	0
VALENZUELA, F.	435	2840	171	141	.548	2113	1105	2612	3.52	2
VANCE, C.A.	442	2967	197	140	.585	2045	840	2809	3.24	11
VANCE, G.C.	30	141	9	8	.529	56	46	147	3.83	0
VAN CUYK, C.G.	44	160	7	11	.389	103	63	170	5.17	1
VAN CUYK, J.H.	7	10	0	0	.000	3	3	12	5.40	0
VANDE BERG, E.J.	413	519	25	28	.472	314	200	572	3.92	22
VARGAS, C.	217	765	48	40	.545	544	294	801	4.83	1
VENAFRO, M.	307	253	15	10	.600	131	94	264	4.09	5
VICKERS, H.P.	88	458	22	27	.449	213	119	426	2.93	2
WACHTEL, P.H.	2	6	0	0	.000	3	4	9	10.50	0
WADE, B.S.	118	371	19	17	.528	235	181	364	4.34	10
WADE, C.	122	139	10	5	.667	99	33	112	2.86	0
WALKER, F.M.	61	297	7	23	.233	143	136	306	4.00	1
WALL, S.A.	66	98	4	6	.400	55	35	98	3.86	1
WARREN, T.G.	22	69	1	4	.200	18	40	74	4.96	0
WAYNE, G.A.	231	250	14	14	.500	164	104	237	3.93	4
WEAVER, E.	7	10	2	01	.000	5	6	5	0.93	0
WEAVER, J.	355	1838	104	119	.466	1214	516	1997	4.71	2
WEBB, H.G.M.	53	169	7	9	.438	71	91	159	4.31	0
WEBBER, L.E.	154	432	23	19	.548	141	201	434	4.19	14
WELCH, R.L.	481	3023	208	140	.598	1925	991	2815	3.38	8
WELLS, D.	660	3439	239	157	.604	2201	719	3635	4.13	13
WELLS, J.F.	4	15	0	2	.000	7	11	18	5.40	0
WETTELAND, J.K.	618	765	48	45	.516	804	252	616	2.93	330
WEYHING, A.	538	4324	264	232	.532	1655	1566	4562	3.89	4
WHITE, L.D.	11	19	0	1	.000	15	9	13	2.37	0
WHITING, J.W.	5	37	1	2	.333	9	15	42	4.14	0
WICKER, K.C.	40	141	10	7	.588	27	52	168	4.66	1
WILHELM, J.H.	1070	2253	143	122	.540	1610	778	1757	2.52	227
WILHELM, I.K.	216	1432	56	105	.348	444	418	1495	3.44	5
WILLHITE, J.N.	58	181	6	12	.333	118	75	195	4.57	1
WILLIAMS, J.	37	58	4	1	.800	30	41	65	7.49	0
WILLIAMS, L.T.	8	8	0	0	.000	3	2	16	5.63	0
WILLIAMS. S.W.	482	1763	109	94	.537	1305	748	1527	3.48	43
WILLIAMS, T.	16	19	2	2	.500	8	7	19	5.12	0
WILSON, S.D.	205	345	13	18	.419	252	130	348	4.40	6
WILSON, G.R.	2	4	0	0	.000	1	1	7	13.50	0
WINFORD, J.H.	68	276	14	18	.438	107	115	307	4.57	3
WINHAM, L.S.	6	39	3	1	.750	23	23	37	2.08	0
WINSTON, H.R.	15	39	1	3	.250	10	22	47	6.23	0
WOJEY, P.P.	18	33	1	1	.500	22	15	27	3.00	1
WOLF, R.	346	2110	127	107	.543	1663	758	2035	4.09	0
WORRELL, T.R.	552	633	48	46	.511	567	224	548	2.89	221
WRIGHT, C.E.	46	324	14	26	.350	140	152	361	4.50	1
WRIGHT, J.R.	55	103	3	3	.500	67	60	102	4.28	0
WUNSCH, K.	257	177	11	6	.647	145	97	136	3.76	1
WURM, F.J.	1	1	0	0	.000	1	5	1	36.00	0
WYATT, J.W.	360	1761	106	95	.527	872	642	1684	3.79	13
YARRISON, B.W.	21	45	1	4	.200	12	15	62	7.80	0

YINGLING, E.H.	94	568	25	34	.424	192	141	611	3.22	0
YOUNG, M.J.	333	1190	55	95	.367	857	565	1207	4.40	25
ZACHARY, A.M.	4	10	0	2	.000	3	7	10	9.90	0
ZACHARY, J.T.	533	3128	186	191	.493	720	914	3580	3.73	22
ZACHRY, P.P.	293	1179	69	67	.507	669	495	1147	3.52	3
ZAHN, G.C.	304	1848	111	109	.505	705	526	1978	3.75	1
ZETTLEIN, G.	217	125	90	.581						

DODGERS MAJOR LEAGUE STANDINGS, YEAR BY YEAR

YEAR	W	L	PCT	POS.	MANAGER
1884	40	64	.385	9	George Taylor
1885	53	59	.473	5	Joe Doyle
					Charlie Hackett
					Charlie Byrne
1886	76	61	.555	3	Charlie Byrne
1887	60	74	.448	6	Charlie Byrne
1888	88	52	.629	2	Bill McGunnigle
1889	93	44	.679	1	Bill McGunnigle

NATIONAL LEAGUE

YEAR	W	L	PCT	POS.	MANAGER
1890	86	43	.667	1	Bill McGunnigle
1891	61	76	.445	6	Monte Ward
1892	95	59	.617	3	Monte Ward
1893	65	63	.508	6	Dave Foutz
1894	70	61	.534	5	Dave Foutz
1895	71	60	.542	5	Dave Foutz
1896	58	73	.443	9	Dave Foutz
1897	61	71	.462	6	Bill Barnie
1898	54	91	.372	10	Bill Barnie
					Mike Griffin
					Charlie Ebbets
1899	101	47	.682	1	Ned Hanlon
1900	82	54	.603	1	Ned Hanlon
1901	79	57	.581	3	Ned Hanlon
1902	75	63	.543	2	Ned Hanlon
1903	70	66	.515	5	Ned Hanlon
1904	56	97	.366	6	Ned Hanlon
1905	48	104	.316	8	Ned Hanlon
1906	66	86	.434	5	Patsy Donovan
1907	65	83	.439	5	Patsy Donovan
1908	53	101	.344	7	Patsy Donovan
1909	55	98	.359	6	Harry Lumley
1910	64	90	.416	6	Bill Dahlen
1911	64	86	.427	7	Bill Dahlen
1912	58	95	.379	7	Bill Dahlen
1913	65	84	.436	6	Bill Dahlen
1914	75	79	.487	5	Wilbert Robinson
1915	80	72	.526	3	Wilbert Robinson
1916	94	60	.610	1	Wilbert Robinson
1917	70	81	.464	7	Wilbert Robinson
1918	57	69	.452	5	Wilbert Robinson
1919	69	71	.493	5	Wilbert Robinson
1920	93	61	.604	1	Wilbert Robinson
1921	77	75	.507	5	Wilbert Robinson
1922	76	78	.494	6	Wilbert Robinson
1923	76	78	.494	6	Wilbert Robinson
1924	92	62	.597	2	Wilbert Robinson

1925	68	85	.444	6	Wilbert Robinson
1926	71	82	.464	6	Wilbert Robinson
1927	65	88	.425	6	Wilbert Robinson
1928	77	76	.503	6	Wilbert Robinson
1929	70	83	.458	6	Wilbert Robinson
1930	86	68	.558	4	Wilbert Robinson
1931	79	73	.520	4	Wilbert Robinson
1932	81	73	.526	3	Max Carey
1933	65	88	.425	6	Max Carey
1934	71	81	.467	6	Casey Stengel
1935	70	83	.458	5	Casey Stengel
1936	67	87	.435	7	Casey Stengel
1937	62	91	.405	6	Burleigh Grimes
1938	69	80	.463	7	Burleigh Grimes
1939	84	69	.549	3	Leo Durocher
1940	88	65	.575	2	Leo Durocher
1941	100	54	.649	1	Leo Durocher
1942	104	50	.675	2	Leo Durocher
1943	81	72	.529	3	Leo Durocher
1944	63	91	.409	7	Leo Durocher
1945	87	67	.565	3	Leo Durocher
1946	96	60	.615	2	Leo Durocher
1947	94	60	.610	1	Clyde Sukeforth Burt Shotton
1948	84	70	.545	3	Leo Durocher Burt Shotton
1949	97	57	.630	1	Burt Shotton
1950	89	65	.578	2	Burt Shotton
1951	97	60	.618	2	Charlie Dressen
1952	96	57	.627	1	Charlie Dressen
1953	105	49	.682	1	Charlie Dressen
1954	92	62	.597	2	Walter Alston
1955	98	55	.641	1	Walter Alston
1956	93	61	.604	1	Walter Alston
1957	84	70	.545	3	Walter Alston
1958	78	83	.461	7	Walter Alston
1959	88	68	.564	1	Walter Alston
1960	82	72	.532	4	Walter Alston
1961	89	65	.578	2	Walter Alston
1962	102	63	.618	2	Walter Alston
1963	99	63	.611	1	Walter Alston
1964	80	82	.494	6	Walter Alston
1965	97	65	.599	1	Walter Alston
1966	95	67	.586	1	Walter Alston
1967	73	89	.451	8	Walter Alston
1968	76	86	.469	7	Walter Alston
1969	85	77	.525	4	Walter Alston
1970	87	74	.540	2	Walter Alston
1971	89	73	.549	2	Walter Alston
1972	85	70	.548	3	Walter Alston
1973	95	66	.590	2	Walter Alston
1974	102	60	.630	1	Walter Alston
1975	88	74	.543	2	Walter Alston
1976	92	70	.568	2	Walter Alston
1977	98	64	.605	1	Tommy Lasorda
1978	95	67	.586	1	Tommy Lasorda
1979	79	83	.488	3	Tommy Lasorda

1980	92	71	.564	2	Tommy Lasorda
1981	63	47	.573	1	Tommy Lasorda
1982	88	74	.543	2	Tommy Lasorda
1983	91	71	.562	1	Tommy Lasorda
1984	79	83	.488	4	Tommy Lasorda
1985	95	67	.586	1	Tommy Lasorda
1986	73	89	.451	5	Tommy Lasorda
1987	73	89	.451	4	Tommy Lasorda
1988	94	67	.584	1	Tommy Lasorda
1989	77	83	.481	4	Tommy Lasorda
1990	86	76	.531	2	Tommy Lasorda
1991	93	69	.575	2	Tommy Lasorda
1992	63	99	.389	6	Tommy Lasorda
1993	81	81	.500	4	Tommy Lasorda
1994	58	56	.509	1	Tommy Lasorda
1995	78	66	.542	1	Tommy Lasorda
1996	90	72	.556	2	Tommy Lasorda
					Bill Russell
1997	88	74	.543	2	Bill Russell
1998	83	79	.512	3	Bill Russell
					Glenn Hoffman
1999	77	85	.475	3	Davey Johnson
2000	86	76	.531	2	Davey Johnson
2001	86	76	.531	3	Jim Tracy
2002	92	70	.568	3	Jim Tracy
2003	85	77	.525	2	Jim Tracy
2004	93	69	.574	1	Jim Tracy
2005	71	91	.438	4	Jim Tracy
2006	88	74	.543	1T	Grady Little
2007	82	80	.506	4	Grady Little
2008	84	78	.519	1	Joe Torre
2009	95	67	.586	1	Joe Torre
2010	80	82	.494	4	Joe Torre
2011	82	79	.509	3	Don Mattingly

DODGERS MANAGERS RECORDS -- 1884 TO 2011

NAME	YEARS MANAGED	RECORD	PCT.
G. Taylor	1884	40-64	.385
J. Doyle	1885	13-20	.394
C. Hackett	1885	15-22	.405
C. Byrne	1885-87	174-172	.503
W. McGunnigle	1888-90	267-139	.658
J.M. Ward	1891-92	156-135	.536
D. Foutz	1893-96	264-257	.507
W. Barnie	1897-98	76-91	.455
M. Griffin	1898	1-3	.250
C.H. Ebbets	1898	38-68	.358
N. Hanlon	1899-1905	511-488	.512
P. Donovan	1906-08	184-270	.405
H. Lumley	1909	55-98	.359
W. Dahlen	1910-13	251-355	.414
W. Robinson	1914-31	1375-1341	.506
M. Carey	1932-33	146-161	.476
C. Stengel	1934-36	208-251	.453
B. Grimes	1937-38	131-171	.434

L. Durocher	1939-46, '48	738-565	.567
C. Sukeforth	1947	2-0	1.000
B. Shotton	1947-50	326-215	.603
C. Dressen	1951-53	298-166	.642
W. Alston	1954-76	2040-1613	.558
T. Lasorda	1977-96	1599-1439	.526
W. Russell	1996-1998	162-138	.540
G. Hoffman	1998	47-41	.534
D. Johnson	1999-2000	163-161	.503
J. Tracy	2001-2005	427-383	.527
G. Little	2006-2007	170-154	.525
J. Torre	2008-2010	259-227	.533
D. Mattingly	2011-	82-79	.509

DODGERS IN THE HALL OF FAME

NAME	YEARS IN BROOKLYN/LA	YEAR INDUCTED
Babe Ruth	1938	1936
George Sisler	1943, 1946-50	1939
Willie Keeler	1893, 1899-1903	1939
Dan Brouthers	1892-93	1945
Wilbert Robinson	1914-31	1945
Hughie Jennings	1899-1900, 1903	1945
Tom McCarthy	1896	1946
Joe McGinnity	1900	1946
Paul Waner	1941, 1943-44	1952
Rabbit Maranville	1926	1954
Dazzy Vance	1922-32, 1935	1955
Ted Lyons	1954	1955
Zack Wheat	1909-26	1959
Max Carey	1926-29	1961
Jackie Robinson	1947-56	1962
Burleigh Grimes	1918-26, 1937-38	1964
Heinie Manush	1937-38	1964
John M. Ward	1891-92	1964
Casey Stengel	1912-17, 1934-36,	1966
Branch Rickey	1942-50	1967
Lloyd Waner	1944	1967
Kiki Cuyler	1938	1968
Joe Medwick	1940-43, 1946	1968
Roy Campanella	1948-57	1969
Dave Bancroft	1928-29	1971
Joe Kelley	1899-1901	1971
Rube Marquard	1915-20	1971
Sandy Koufax	1955-1966	1972
George Kelly	1932	1973
Billy Herman	1941-43, 1946	1975
Fred Lindstrom	1936	1976
Al Lopez	1928, 1930-35	1977
Larry MacPhail	1938-42	1978
Red Barber	1939-53	1978
Hack Wilson	1932-34	1979
Duke Snider	1947-62	1980
Ernie Harwell	1948-49	1981
Vin Scully	1950-PRESENT	1982
Frank Robinson	1972	1982

Juan Marichal	1975	1983
Walter Alston	1954-76	1983
Don Drysdale	1956-69	1984
Pee Wee Reese	1940-42, 1946-58	1984
Arky Vaughan	1942-43, 1947-48	1985
Hoyt Wilhelm	1971-72	1985
Ernie Lombardi	1931	1986
Tony Lazzeri	1939	1991
Leo Durocher	1939-46, 1948,	1994
Jim Bunning	1969	1996
Ned Hanlon	1899-1905	1996
Tommy Lasorda	1954-56, 1973-1996	1997
Jaime Jarrin	1959-PRESENT	1998
Gary Carter	1991	2003
Eddie Murray	1989-91, 1997	2003
Walter O'Malley	1944-79	2008
Dick Williams	1951-54, 1956	2008
Rickey Henderson	2003	2009

INDIVIDUAL LEAGUE AWARDS

MOST VALUABLE PLAYER

YEAR	PLAYER	YEAR	PLAYER
1913	Jake Daubert	1956	Don Newcombe
1924	Dazzy Vance	1962	Maury Wills
1941	Dolph Camilli	1963	Sandy Koufax
1949	Jackie Robinson	1974	Steve Garvey
1951	Roy Campanella	1988	Kirk Gibson
1953	Roy Campanella		
1955	Roy Campanella		

CY YOUNG AWARD

YEAR	PLAYER	YEAR	PLAYER
1956	Don Newcombe	1974	Mike Marshall
1962	Don Drysdale	1981	Fernando Valenzuela
1963	Sandy Koufax	1988	Orel Hershiser
1965	Sandy Koufax	2003	Eric Gagne
1966	Sandy Koufax	2011	Clayton Kershaw

ROOKIE OF THE YEAR

YEAR	PLAYER	YEAR	PLAYER
1947	Jackie Robinson	1981	Fernando Valenzuela
1949	Don Newcombe	1982	Steve Sax
1952	Joe Black	1992	Eric Karros
1953	Jim Gilliam	1993	Mike Piazza
1960	Frank Howard	1994	Raul Mondesi
1965	Jim Lefebvre	1995	Hideo Nomo
1969	Ted Sizemore	1996	Todd Hollandsworth
1979	Rick Sutcliffe		
1980	Steve Howe		

WORLD SERIES MOST VALUABLE PLAYER

YEAR	PLAYER
1955	Johnny Podres
1959	Larry Sherry
1963	Sandy Koufax
1965	Sandy Koufax
1981	Ron Cey, Pedro Guerrero, Steve Yeager
1988	Orel Hershiser

LEAGUE CHAMPIONSHIP SERIES MOST VALUABLE PLAYER

YEAR	PLAYER
1977	Dusty Baker
1978	Steve Garvey
1981	Burt Hooton
1988	Orel Hershiser

ALL-STAR GAME MOST VALUABLE PLAYER

YEAR	PLAYER
1974	Steve Garvey
1977	Don Sutton
1978	Steve Garvey
1996	Mike Piazza

RAWLINGS GOLD GLOVE AWARD WINNERS

1957	Gil Hodges - 1B
1958	Gil Hodges - 1B
1959	Gil Hodges - 1B
	Charlie Neal - 2B
1960	Wally Moon - OF
1961	John Roseboro - C
	Maury Wills - SS
1962	Maury Wills - SS
1966	John Roseboro - C
1967	Wes Parker - 1B
1968	Wes Parker - 1B
1969	Wes Parker - 1B
1970	Wes Parker - 1B
1971	Wes Parker - 1B
	Willie Davis - OF
1972	Wes Parker - 1B
	Willie Davis - OF
1973	Willie Davis - OF
1974	Steve Garvey - 1B
	Andy Messersmith - P
1975	Steve Garvey - 1B
	Andy Messersmith - P
1976	Steve Garvey - 1B
1977	Steve Garvey - 1B
1979	Davey Lopes - 2B
1981	Dusty Baker - OF
1986	Fernando Valenzuela - P
1988	Orel Hershiser - P
1995	Raul Mondesi - OF

1997	Raul Mondesi - OF
1998	Charles Johnson - C
2004	Cesar Izturis – SS
	Steve Finley – OF
2006	Greg Maddux – P
2007	Russell Martin – C
2008	Greg Maddux – P
2009	Orlando Hudson – 2B
	Matt Kemp - OF
2011	Clayton Kershaw
	Andre Ethier
	Matt Kemp

SPORTING NEWS ALL-STAR TEAMS

MAJOR LEAGUE ALL-STAR TEAM

Dazzy Vance	Pitcher	1925
Lefty O'Doul	Outfield	1932
Dolph Camilli	First Base	1941
Pete Reiser	Outfield	1941
Whit Wyatt	Pitcher	1941
Mickey Owen	Catcher	1942
Billy Herman	Second Base	1943
Dixie Walker	Outfield	1944
Goody Rosen	Outfield	1945
Ralph Branca	Pitcher	1947
Jackie Robinson	Second Base	1949
Roy Campanella	Catcher	1949
Jackie Robinson	Second Base	1950
Jackie Robinson	Second Base	1951
Roy Campanella	Catcher	1951
Preacher Roe	Pitcher	1951
Jackie Robinson	Second Base	1952
Pee Wee Reese	Shortstop	1953
Duke Snider	Outfield	1953
Carl Furillo	Outfield	1953
Roy Capmanella	Catcher	1953
Duke Snider	Outfield	1954
Duke Snider	Outfield	1955
Roy Campanella	Catcher	1955
Don Newcombe	Pitcher	1955
Don Newcombe	Pitcher	1956

NATIONAL LEAGUE ALL-STARS

Maury Wills	Shortstop	1961
Maury Wills	Shortstop	1962
Tommy Davis	Outfield	1962
Don Drysdale	Pitcher	1962
Jim Gilliam	Second Base	1963
Tommy Davis	Outfield	1963
Sandy Koufax	Pitcher	1963
Sandy Koufax	Pitcher	1964
Maury Wills	Shortstop	1965
Sandy Koufax	Pitcher	1965
Sandy Koufax	Pitcher	1966

Willie Davis	Outfield	1971
Bill Russell	Shortstop	1973
Steve Garvey	First Base	1974
Jimmy Wynn	Outfield	1974
Andy Messersmith	Pitcher	1974
Steve Garvey	First Base	1975
Don Sutton	Pitcher	1976
Steve Garvey	First Base	1977
Steve Garvey	First Base	1978
Davey Lopes	Second Base	1978
Davey Lopes	Second Base	1979
Dusty Baker	Outfield	1980
Pedro Guerrero	Outfield	1981
Fernando Valenzuela	Pitcher	1981
Pedro Guerrero	Outfield	1982
Steve Sax	Second Base	1986
Fernando Valenzuela	Pitcher	1986
Orel Hershiser	Pitcher	1988
Eddie Murray	First Base	1990
Mike Scioscia	Catcher	1990
Mike Piazza	Catcher	1993
Mike Piazza	Catcher	1994
Mike Piazza	Catcher	1995
Eric Karros	First Base	1995
Mike Piazza	Catcher	1996
Mike Piazza	Catcher	1997
Eric Gagne	Pitcher	2003
Russell Martin	Catcher	2007
Matt Kemp	Outfield	2009
Clayton Kershaw	Pitcher	2011
Matt Kemp	Outfield	2011

INDIVIDUAL LEAGUE BATTING LEADERS

BATTING CHAMPION

1913	Jake Daubert	.350	1944	Dixie Walker	.357
1914	Jake Daubert	.329	1949	Jackie Robinson	.342
1918	Zack Wheat	.335	1953	Carl Furillo	.344
1932	Lefty O'Doul	.368	1962	Tommy Davis	.346
1941	Pete Reiser	.343	1963	Tommy Davis	.326

RUNS SCORED

1941	Pete Reiser	117	1953	Duke Snider	132
1943	Arky Vaughan	112	1954	Duke Snider	120
1945	Eddie Stanky	128	1955	Duke Snider	126
1949	Pee Wee Reese	132	1991	Brett Butler	112
			2011	Matt Kemp	115

BASE HITS

1900	Wee Willie Keeler	208
1919	Ivy Olson	164
1950	Duke Snider	199
1962	Tommy Davis	230

| 1978 | Steve Garvey | 202 |
| 1980 | Steve Garvey | 200 |

SINGLES

1900	Wee Willie Keeler	179
1911	Jake Daubert	146
1913	Jake Daubert	152
1919	Ivy Olson	140
1924	Zack Wheat	149
1925	Milt Stock	164
1932	Lefty O'Doul	158
1961	Maury Wills	150
1962	Maury Wills	179
1965	Maury Wills	165
1986	Steve Sax	157
1988	Steve Sax	147
1991	Brett Butler	162
1992	Brett Butler	143
1993	Brett Butler	149
2007	Juan Pierre	164

DOUBLES

1913	Red Smith	40
1929	Johnny Frederick	52
1941	Pete Reiser	39
1970	Wes Parker	47

TRIPLES

1901	Jimmy Sheckard	21	1945	Luis Olmo	13
1904	Harry Lumley	18	1953	Jim Gilliam	17
1907	Whitey Alperman	16	1959	Wally Moon	11
1918	Jake Daubert	15	1959	Charlie Neal	11
1919	Hy Myers	14	1962	Willie Davis	10
1920	Hy Myers	22	1962	Maury Wills	10
1941	Pete Reiser	17	1970	Willie Davis	16
1994	Brett Butler	9			

HOME RUNS

1903	Jimmy Sheckard	9	1924	Jack Fournier	27
1904	Harry Lumley	9	1941	Dolph Camilli	34
1906	Tim Jordan	12	1956	Duke Snider	43
1908	Tim Jordan	12	2004	Adrian Beltre	48
			2011	Matt Kemp	39

RUNS BATTED IN

1919	Hy Myers	73	1953	Roy Campanella	142
1941	Dolph Camilli	120	1955	Duke Snider	136
1945	Dixie Walker	124	1962	Tommy Davis	153
2011	Matt Kemp	126			

STOLEN BASES

| 1903 | Jimmy Sheckard | 67 | 1961 | Maury Wills | 35 |
| 1942 | Pete Reiser | 20 | 1962 | Maury Wills | 104 |

1943	Arky Vaughan	20	1963	Maury Wills	40
1946	Pete Reiser	34	1964	Maury Wills	53
1947	Jackie Robinson	29	1965	Maury Wills	94
1949	Jackie Robinson	37	1975	Davey Lopes	77
1952	Pee Wee Reese	30	1976	Davey Lopes	63
1960	Maury Wills	50			

INDIVIDUAL LEAGUE PITCHING LEADERS

VICTORIES

1921	Burleigh Grimes	22	1963	Sandy Koufax	25
1924	Dazzy Vance	28	1965	Sandy Koufax	26
1925	Dazzy Vance	22	1966	Sandy Koufax	27
1941	Kirby Higbe	22	1974	Andy Messersmith	20
1941	Whitlow Wyatt	22	1986	F. Valenzuela	21
1956	Don Newcombe	27	1988	Orel Hershiser	23
1962	Don Drysdale	25	2006	Brad Penny	16T
2006	Derek Lowe	16T	2011	Clayton Kershaw	21T

EARNED RUN AVERAGE

1924	Dazzy Vance	2.16	1964	Sandy Koufax	1.74
1928	Dazzy Vance	2.09	1965	Sandy Koufax	2.04
1930	Dazzy Vance	2.61	1966	Sandy Koufax	1.73
1957	Johnny Podres	2.66	1980	Don Sutton	2.21
1962	Sandy Koufax	2.54	1984	Alejandro Pena	2.48
1963	Sandy Koufax	1.88	2000	Kevin Brown	2.58
			2011	Clayton Kershaw	2.28

WINNING PERCENTAGE

1920	Burleigh Grimes	.676	1963	Ron Perranoski	.842
1940	F. Fitzsimmons	.889	1964	Sandy Koufax	.792
1942	Larry French	.789	1965	Sandy Koufax	.765
1949	Preacher Roe	.714	1966	Phil Regan	.933
1951	Preacher Roe	.880	1973	Tommy John	.696
1953	Carl Erskine	.769	1974	Tommy John	.813
1955	Don Newcombe	.800	1976	Rick Rhoden	.800
1956	Don Newcombe	.794	1985	Orel Hershiser	.864
1961	Johnny Podres	.783	2007	Brad Penny	.800

STRIKEOUTS

1921	Burleigh Grimes	136	1951	Don Newcombe	164
1922	Dazzy Vance	134	1959	Don Drysdale	242
1923	Dazzy Vance	197	1960	Don Drysdale	246
1924	Dazzy Vance	262	1961	Sandy Koufax	269
1925	Dazzy Vance	221	1962	Don Drysdale	232
1926	Dazzy Vance	140	1963	Sandy Koufax	306
1927	Dazzy Vance	184	1965	Sandy Koufax	382
1928	Dazzy Vance	200	1966	Sandy Koufax	317
1936	Van Lingle Mungo	238	1981	F. Valenzuela	180

| 1995 | Hideo Nomo | 236 |
| 2011 | Clayton Kershaw | 248 |

DODGER TEAM CAREER LEADERS - BROOKLYN AND LOS ANGELES

BATTING LEADERS

GAMES PLAYED

Zack Wheat	2322
Bill Russell	2181
Pee Wee Reese	2166
Gil Hodges	2006
Jim Gilliam	1956
Willie Davis	1952
Duke Snider	1923
Carl Furillo	1806
Steve Garvey	1727
Eric Karros	1601

AT BATS

Zack Wheat	8859
Pee Wee Reese	8058
Willie Davis	7495
Bill Russell	7318
Jim Gilliam	7119
Gil Hodges	6881
Duke Snider	6640
Steve Garvey	6543
Carl Furillo	6378
Maury Wills	6156

RUNS SCORED

Pee Wee Reese	1338
Zack Wheat	1255
Duke Snider	1199
Jim Gilliam	1163
Gil Hodges	1088
Willie Davis	1004
Jackie Robinson	947
Carl Furillo	895
Mike Griffin	881
Maury Wills	876

HITS

Zack Wheat	2804
Pee Wee Reese	2170
Willie Davis	2091
Duke Snider	1995
Steve Garvey	1968

Bill Russell	1926
Carl Furillo	1910
Jim Gilliam	1889
Gil Hodges	1884
Maury Wills	1732

DOUBLES

Zack Wheat	464
Duke Snider	343
Steve Garvey	333
Pee Wee Reese	330
Carl Furillo	324
Willie Davis	321
Jim Gilliam	304
Gil Hodges	294
Bill Russell	293
Eric Karros	302

TRIPLES

Zack Wheat	171
Willie Davis	110
Hy Myers	97
Jake Daubert	87
Duke Snider	82
John Hummell	82
Pee Wee Reese	80
Jimmy Sheckard	78
Tido Daly	76
Jimmy Johnston	73

HOME RUNS

Duke Snider	389
Gil Hodges	361
Eric Karros	270
Roy Campanella	242
Ron Cey	228
Steve Garvey	211
Carl Furillo	192
Mike Piazza	177
Pedro Guerrero	171
Willie Davis	154

RUNS BATTED IN

Duke Snider	1271
Gil Hodges	1254
Zack Wheat	1233
Carl Furillo	1058
Steve Garvey	992
Eric Karros	976
Pee Wee Reese	885
Roy Campanella	856
Willie Davis	849
Ron Cey	842

TOTAL BASES

Zack Wheat	4,003
Duke Snider	3,669
Gil Hodges	3,357
Willie Davis	3,094
Pee Wee Reese	3,038
Steve Garvey	3,004
Carl Furillo	2,922
Eric Karros	2,840
Jim Gilliam	2,530
Bill Russell	2,471

SLUGGING AVERAGE

Mike Piazza	.574
Babe Herman	.557
Duke Snider	.553
Jack Fournier	.552
Pedro Guerrero	.512
Raul Mondesi	.508
Roy Campanella	.500
Dolph Camilli	.497
Frank Howard	.495
Gil Hodges	.488

STOLEN BASES

Maury Wills	490
Davey Lopes	418
Willie Davis	335
Tido Daly	298
Steve Sax	290
Mike Griffin	264
Pee Wee Reese	232
Jimmy Sheckard	212
Jim Gilliam	203
Zack Wheat	203

BATTING AVERAGE (2000 AT BATS)

Wee Willie Keeler	.360
Babe Herman	.339
Mike Piazza	.331
Zack Wheat	.317
Fielder Jones	.313
Jackie Robinson	.311
Dixie Walker	.311
Pedro Guerrero	.309
Johnny Frederick	.308
Pete Reiser	.306

PITCHING LEADERS

GAMES PITCHED

Don Sutton	550
Don Drysdale	518
Jim Brewer	474
Ron Perranoski	457
Clem Labine	425
Charlie Hough	401
Sandy Koufax	397
Brickyard Kennedy	381
Dazzy Vance	378
Johnny Podres	366

GAMES STARTED

Don Sutton	533
Don Drysdale	465
Claude Osteen	335
Brickyard Kennedy	332
Dazzy Vance	326
Fernando Valenzuela	320
Sandy Koufax	314
Johnny Podres	310
Orel Hershiser	309
Burleigh Grimes	285

COMPLETE GAMES

Brickyard Kennedy	279
Dazzy Vance	212
Burleigh Grimes	205
Nap Rucker	186
Don Drysdale	167
Jeff Pfeffer	157
Don Sutton	156
Sandy Koufax	137
Ed Stein	136
Harry McIntyre	119

INNINGS PITCHED

Don Sutton	3814
Don Drysdale	3432
Brickyard Kennedy	2857
Dazzy Vance	2758
Burleigh Grimes	2426
Claude Osteen	2397
Nap Rucker	2375
Fernando Valenzuela	2349
Sandy Koufax	2324
Orel Hershiser	2181

GAME WON

Don Sutton	233
Don Drysdale	209
Dazzy Vance	190
Brickyard Kennedy	174
Sandy Koufax	165
Burleigh Grimes	158
Claude Osteen	147
Fernando Valenzuela	141

Johnny Podres	136
Orel Hershiser	135

GAMES LOST

Don Sutton	181
Don Drysdale	166
Brickyard Kennedy	150
Nap Rucker	134
Dazzy Vance	131
Claude Osteen	126
Burleigh Grimes	121
Fernando Valenzuela	116
Orel Hershiser	107
Johnny Podres	104

STRIKEOUTS

Don Sutton	2696
Don Drysdale	2486
Sandy Koufax	2396
Dazzy Vance	1918
Fernando Valenzuela	1759
Orel Hershiser	1456
Johnny Podres	1331
Bob Welch	1292
Nap Rucker	1217
Claude Osteen	1162

BASES ON BALLS

Brickyard Kennedy	1128
Don Sutton	996
Fernando Valenzuela	915
Don Drysdale	855
Sandy Koufax	817
Dazzy Vance	764
Burleigh Grimes	744
Ramon Martinez	704
Nap Rucker	701
Van Lingle Mungo	697

SHUTOUTS

Don Sutton	52
Don Drysdale	49
Sandy Koufax	40
Nap Rucker	38
Claude Osteen	34
Dazzy Vance	30
Fernando Valenzuela	29
Jeff Pfeffer	25
Orel Hershiser	24
Johnny Podres	23
Bob Welch	23

SAVES

Eric Gagne	161
Jeff Shaw	129
Todd Worrell	127
Jim Brewer	125
Ron Perranoski	101
Jay Howell	85
Jonathan Broxton	84
Clem Labine	83
Tom Niedenfuer	64
Charlie Hough	60
Steve Howe	59

EARNED RUN AVERAGE (1000 INNINGS)

Jeff Pfeffer	2.31
Nap Rucker	2.42
Sandy Koufax	2.76
George Bell	2.85
Whit Wyatt	2.86
Sherry Smith	2.91
Don Drysdale	2.95
Doc Scanlon	2.96
Tommy John	2.98
Orel Hershiser	3.00

WON-LOSS PERCENTAGE (100 DECISIONS)

Preacher Roe	.715 (93-57)
Tommy John	.674 (87-42)
Sandy Koufax	.655 (165-87)
Don Newcombe	.651 (123-66)
Kirby Higbe	.648 (70-38)
Whit Wyatt	.640 (80-45)
Hugh Casey	.631 (70-41)
Ramon Martinez	.615 (123-77)
Carl Erskine	.610 (122-78)
Dazzy Vance	.598 (190-131)

DODGER GAMES PLAYED BY POSITION - BROOKLYN AND LOS ANGELES

CATCHER

Mike Scioscia	1,395
John Roseboro	1,199
Roy Campanella	1,183
Steve Yeager	1,181
Otto Miller	891
Al Lopez	746
Mike Piazza	726
Bill Bergen	707
Hank DeBerry	546
Mickey Owen	510

PITCHER

Don Sutton	550
Don Drysdale	518
Jim Brewer	474
Ron Perranoski	457
Clem Labine	425
Charlie Hough	401
Sandy Koufax	397
Brickyard Kennedy	381
Dazzy Vance	378
Johnny Podres	366

FIRST BASE

Gil Hodges	1,851
Steve Garvey	1,672
Eric Karros	1,579
Jake Daubert	1,206
Wes Parker	1,108
Dolph Camilli	835
James Loney	755
Del Bissonette	598
Ron Fairly	557
Tim Jordan	510
Jake Fournier	495

SECOND BASE

Davey Lopes	1,150
Jim Gilliam	1,046
Steve Sax	1,070
George Cutshaw	833
Tido Daly	791
Jackie Robinson	751
Jim Lefebvre	613
Tom Hummell	547
Charlie Neal	523
Eddie Stanky	498

SHORTSTOP

Pee Wee Reese	2,017
Bill Russell	1,746
Maury Wills	1,497
Ivy Olson	827
Tom Corcoran	654
Bill Dahlen	649
Rafael Furcal	572
Jose Offerman	571
Cesar Izturis	553
Phil Lewis	505

THIRD BASE

Ron Cey	1,468
Adrian Beltre	957
Jim Gilliam	761
Billy Cox	700
Cookie Lavagetto	647
Billy Shindle	617
Joe Stripp	589
Wally Gilbert	476
Jimmy Johnston	434
Red Smith	390

OUTFIELD

Zack Wheat	2,288
Willie Davis	1,906
Duke Snider	1,769
Carl Furillo	1,739
Dixie Walker	1,176
Dusty Baker	1,092
Hy Myers	1,071
Raul Mondesi	912
Mike Griffin	847
Willie Crawford	823
Andre Ethier	810

DODGER TEAM CAREER RECORDS -- BROOKLYN AND LOS ANGELES

FIELDING LEADERS

FIELDING AVERAGE

CATCHER

Paul Lo Duca	.991
Tom Haller	.991
Russell Martin	.990
John Roseboro	.990
Mike Piazza	.989
Jeff Torborg	.989
Roy Campanella	.988
Mike Scioscia	.988
Steve Yeager	.987
Mickey Owen	.987

PITCHER

Freddie Fitzsimmons	.985
Curt Davis	.985
Clayton Kershaw	.985 (still active)
Odalis Perez	.980
Dutch Ruether	.979
Dazzy Vance	.979
Watty Clark	.974
Tom Candiotti	.974
Don Sutton	.972
Claude Osteen	.972
Fernando Valenzuela	.972

FIRST BASE

Steve Garvey	.996 (#2 all-time)
Wes Parker	.996 (#5 all-time)
Eddie Murray	.995
Greg Brock	.994
James Loney	.994 (still active)
Gil Hodges	.993
Eric Karros	.993
Dolph Camilli	.992
Jake Daubert	.991
Ron Fairly	.989

SECOND BASE

Jackie Robinson	.983
Grudzielanek, Mark	.983
Alex Cora	.981
Charlie Neal	.980
Delino DeShields	.980
Junior Gilliam	.979
Jim Lefebvre	.979
Davey Lopes	.977

SHORTSTOP

Cesar Izturis	.980
Dave Anderson	.970
Alex Cora	.969
Rafael Furcal	.967
Alfredo Griffin	.964
Maury Wills	.963
Pee Wee Reese	.962
Bill Russell	.960
Jose Offerman	.944
Ivy Olson	.936

THIRD BASE

Billy Cox	.965
Ron Cey	.961
Joe Stripp	.961
Adrian Beltre	.953
Junior Gilliam	.952
Jeff Hamilton	.948
Cookie Lavagetto	.938

OUTFIELD

Brett Butler	.992 (#4 all-time)
Dusty Baker	.987
Bill Buckner	.986
Shawn Green	.986
Andre Ethier	.986 (still active)
Matt Kemp	.985 (still active)
Duke Snider	.985
Ken Landreaux	.982
Ron Fairly	.981

Carl Furillo	.979
Wally Moon	.979
Mike Marshall	.979
Pete Reiser	.979

PUTOUTS

CATCHER

Mike Scioscia	8,335
John Roseboro	7,895
Roy Campanella	6,520
Steve Yeager	5,876
Mike Piazza	4,818
Otto Miller	3,870

PITCHER

Don Sutton	243
Orel Hershiser	235
Don Drysdale	188
Fernando Valenzuela	164
Bob Welch	141
Ramon Martinez	141

FIRST BASE

Gil Hodges	14,968
Steve Garvey	13,984
Eric Karros	13,216
Jake Daubert	11,545
Wes Parker	9,640
Dolph Camilli	7,736

SECOND BASE

Davey Lopes	2,578
Steve Sax	2,375
Junior Gilliam	2,279
George Cutshaw	2,126
Tido Daly	2,067

SHORTSTOP

Pee Wee Reese	4,040
Bill Russell	2,536
Maury Wills	2,464
Ivy Olson	1,920
Bill Dahlen	1,454

THIRD BASE

Ron Cey	1,196
Billy Shindle	817
Cookie Lavagetto	695
Billy Cox	640
Joe Stripp	625

OUTFIELD

Zack Wheat	4,891
Willie Davis	4,436
Duke Snider	3,916
Carl Furillo	3,322
Hy Myers	2,604
Mike Griffin	2,481
Dixie Walker	2,386
Dusty Baker	1,984
Jimmy Sheckard	1,830
Johnny Frederick	1,813
Matt Kemp	1,558 (still active)

ASSISTS

CATCHER

Bill Bergen	1,105
Otto Miller	1,053
Mike Scioscia	737
Steve Yeager	652
John Roseboro	565
Hank DeBerry	474
Al Lopez	398
Mike Piazza	364

PITCHER

Burleigh Grimes	763
Brickyard Kennedy	731
Don Drysdale	686
Nap Rucker	625
Dazzy Vance	535
Sherry Smith	433
Harry McIntyre	344

FIRST BASE

Eric Karros	1,295
Gil Hodges	1,241
Steve Garvey	734
Wes Parker	695
Jake Daubert	677
Dolph Camilli	546

SECOND BASE

Davey Lopes	3,174
Steve Sax	3,032
Junior Gilliam	2,724
George Cutshaw	2,499
Tido Daly	2,303

SHORTSTOP

Pee Wee Reese	5,891
Bill Russell	5,546
Maury Wills	4,630
Ivy Olson	2,616
Tommy Corcoran	2,343

THIRD BASE

Ron Cey	3,124
Junior Gilliam	1,265
Billy Shindle	1,253
Billy Cox	1,206
Cookie Lavagetto	1,124

OUTFIELD

Zack Wheat	224
Mike Griffin	153
Carl Furillo	151
Hy Myers	134
Jimmy Sheckard	128
Willie Davis	123
Dixie Walker	117
Duke Snider	116
Harry Lumley	97
Oyster Burns	93

BROOKLYN DODGERS TEAM CAREER LEADERS

BATTING LEADERS

GAMES

Zack Wheat	2,322
Pee Wee Reese	2,107
Carl Furillo	1,626
Gil Hodges	1,531
Duke Snider	1,425
Jackie Robinson	1,382
Jimmy Johnston	1,266
Roy Campanella	1,215
Jake Daubert	1,213
Dixie Walker	1,207

AT BATS

Zack Wheat	8,859
Pee Wee Reese	7,911
Carl Furillo	5,864
Gil Hodges	5,581
Duke Snider	5,317
Jackie Robinson	4,877
Jimmy Johnston	4,841
Jake Daubert	4,552
Dixie Walker	4,492
Hy Myers	4,448

RUNS SCORED

Pee Wee Reese	1,317

Zack Wheat	1,255		Jackie Robinson	137
Duke Snider	994		Zack Wheat	131
Jackie Robinson	947		Pee Wee Reese	122
Gil Hodges	916		Babe Herman	112
Carl Furillo	895		Johnny Frederick	85
Mike Griffin	881			
Tido Daly	787			
Jimmy Johnston	727			
Dixie Walker	666			

HITS

RUNS BATTED IN

Zack Wheat	2,804		Zack Wheat	1,223
Pee Wee Reese	2,137		Gil Hodges	1,049
Carl Furillo	1,762		Duke Snider	1,003
Duke Snider	1,609		Carl Furillo	961
Gil Hodges	1,556		Pee Wee Reese	868
Jackie Robinson	1,518		Roy Campanella	856
Jimmy Johnston	1,440		Jackie Robinson	734
Dixie Walker	1,395		Dixie Walker	725
Jake Daubert	1,387		Tido Daly	614
Hy Myers	1,253		Babe Herman	594

DOUBLES

TOTAL BASES

Zack Wheat	464		Zack Wheat	4,003
Pee Wee Reese	323		Pee Wee Reese	3,038
Carl Furillo	301		Duke Snider	2,974
Duke Snider	288		Carl Furillo	2,689
Dixie Walker	274		Gil Hodges	2,656
Jackie Robinson	273		Jackie Robinson	2,310
Gil Hodges	248		Roy Campanella	2,101
Babe Herman	232		Dixie Walker	1,982
Mike Griffin	210		Jimmy Johnston	1,827
Johnny Frederick	200		Jake Daubert	1,798

TRIPLES

SLUGGING AVERAGE

Zack Wheat	171		Duke Snider	.559
Hy Myers	97		Babe Herman	.557
Jake Daubert	87		Jack Fournier	.552
John Hummell	82		Gil Hodges	.501
Pee Wee Reese	78		Roy Campanella	.500
Jimmy Sheckard	76			
Tido Daly	76		Dolph Camilli	.497
Jimmy Johnston	73		Del Bissonette	.485
Babe Herman	66		Johnny Frederick	.477
Harry Lumley	66		Babe Phelps	.475
Duke Snider	66		Jackie Robinson	.474
Oyster Burns	66			

HOME RUNS

STOLEN BASES

Duke Snider	316		Pee Wee Reese	231
Gil Hodges	298		Jimmy Sheckard	209
Roy Campanella	242		Zack Wheat	203
Carl Furillo	174		Jackie Robinson	197
Dolph Camilli	139		Jake Daubert	187
			George Cutshaw	166
			Jimmy Johnston	164
			Bill Dahlen	146

Wee Willie Keeler   128
John Hummell   114

BATTING AVERAGE

Wee Willie Keeler   .358
Babe Herman   .339
Jack Fournier   .337
Zack Wheat   .317
Babe Phelps   .314
Fielder Jones   .314
Dixie Walker   .311
Jackie Robinson   .311
Johnny Frederick   .308
Pete Reiser   .306

PITCHING LEADERS

GAMES

Brickyard Kennedy   381
Dazzy Vance   378
Nap Rucker   336
Watty Clark   322
Burleigh Grimes   317
Clem Labine   304
Carl Erskine   294
Hugh Casey   293
Van Lingle Mungo   284
Ralph Branca   283

GAMES STARTED

Brickyard Kennedy   332
Dazzy Vance   326
Burleigh Grimes   285
Nap Rucker   272
Don Newcombe   222
Van Lingle Mungo   215
Carl Erskine   204
Jeff Pfeffer   201
Watty Clark   198
Ralph Branca   158

COMPLETE GAMES

Brickyard Kennedy   279
Dazzy Vance   212
Burleigh Grimes   205
Nap Rucker   186
Jeff Pfeffer   157
Ed Stein   136
Harry McIntyre   119
Van Lingle Mungo   114
Don Newcombe   110
Doc Scanlon   100

INNINGS PITCHED

Brickyard Kennedy   2,857
Dazzy Vance   2,758
Burleigh Grimes   2,426
Nap Rucker   2,375
Jeff Pfeffer   1,748
Van Lingle Mungo   1,738
Carl Erskine   1,598
Watty Clark   1,659
Don Newcombe   1,628
Ed Stein   1,406

GAMES WON

Dazzy Vance   190
Brickyard Kennedy   176
Burleigh Grimes   158
Nap Rucker   135
Don Newcombe   123
Carl Erskine   122
Jeff Pfeffer   113
Watty Clark   106
Van Lingle Mungo   102
Prescher Roe   93

GAMES LOST

Brickyard Kennedy   149
Nap Rucker   136
Dazzy Vance   131
Burleigh Grimes   121
Van Lingle Mungo   99
Watty Clark   88
Jeff Pfeffer   80
Carl Erskine   71
Sherry Smith   70
Don Newcombe   66
Ed Stein   66

STRIKEOUTS

Dazzy Vance   1,918
Nap Rucker   1,217
Van Lingle Mungo   1,031
Burleigh Grimes   952
Don Newcombe   913
Carl Erskine   912
Ralph Branca   757
Brickyard Kennedy   749
Jeff Pfeffer   656
Preacher Roe   632

BASES ON BALLS

Brickyard Kennedy   1,128
Dazzy Vance   764

Burleigh Grimes	744
Nap Rucker	701
Van Lingle Mungo	697
Carl Erskine	598
Ralph Branca	589
Doc Scanlon	582
Harry McIntyre	450
Joe Hatten	430

SHUTOUTS

Nap Rucker	38
Dazzy Vance	30
Jeff Pfeffer	25
Don Newcombe	22
Burleigh Grimes	20
George Bell	17
Whit Wyatt	17
Van Lingle Mungo	16
Doc Scanlon	15
Watty Clark	14
Carl Erskine	14
Harry McIntyre	14

SAVES

Clem Labine	59
Hugh Casey	50
Jim Hughes	39
Jack Quinn	23
Joe Black	20
Ralph Branca	18
Sherry Smith	16
Watty Clark	16
Nap Rucker	14
Van Lingle Mungo	14
Dutch Leonard	14
Les Webber	14

EARNED RUN AVERAGE

Jeff Pfeffer	2.31
Nap Rucker	2.43
Rube Marquard	2.58
Elmer Stricklett	2.77
George Bell	2.85
Whit Wyatt	2.86
Sherry Smith	2.91
Jay Hughes	2.93
Doc Scanlon	2.96
Hugh Casey	3.11
Leon Cadore	3.11
Harry McIntyre	3.11

WON-LOSS PERCENTAGE (100 decisions)

Preacher Roe	.715 (93-37)
Don Newcombe	.672 (123-60)
Kirby Higbe	.648 (70-38)
Whit Wyatt	.640 (80-45)
Hugh Casey	.631 (70-41)
Carl Erskine	.624 (118-71)
Dazzy Vance	.598 (190-131)
Jeff Pfeffer	.586 (113-80)
Ed Stein	.580 (91-66)
Ralph Branca	.580 (80-58)

LOS ANGELES DODGERS TEAM CAREER LEADERS

BATTING LEADERS

GAMES

Bill Russell	2,181
Willie Davis	1,952
Steve Garvey	1,727
Eric Karros	1,601
Maury Wills	1,593
Ron Cey	1,481
Mike Scioscia	1,441
Ron Fairly	1,306
Wes Parker	1,288
John Roseboro	1,254

AT BATS

Willie Davis	7,495
Bill Russell	7,318
Steve Garvey	6,543
Maury Wills	6,156
Eric Karros	6,002
Ron Cey	5,216
Davey Lopes	4,590
Mike Scioscia	4,373
Steve Sax	4,312
Jim Gilliam	4,157

RUNS

Willie Davis	1,004
Maury Wills	876
Steve Garvey	852
Bill Russell	796
Davey Lopes	759
Eric Karros	752
Ron Cey	715
Jim Gilliam	630
Steve Sax	574
Pedro Guerrero	561

HITS

Willie Davis	2,091
Steve Garvey	1,968
Bill Russell	1,926
Maury Wills	1,732
Eric Karros	1,608
Ron Cey	1,378
Steve Sax	1,218
Davey Lopes	1,204
Dusty Baker	1,144
Mike Scioscia	1,131

DOUBLES

Steve Garvey	333
Willie Davis	321
Eric Karros	302
Bill Russell	293
Ron Cey	223
Mike Scioscia	198
Wes Parker	194
Shawn Green	183
Dusty Baker	179
Jim Gilliam	176
Steve Sax	172

TRIPLES

Willie Davis	110
Bill Russell	57
Maury Wills	56
John Roseboro	44
Brett Butler	41
Davey Lopes	39
Steve Garvey	35
Wes Parker	32
Willie Crawford	29
Steve Sax	28

HOME RUNS

Eric Karros	270
Ron Cey	228
Steve Garvey	211
Mike Piazza	177
Pedro Guerrero	171
Shawn Green	162
Willie Davis	154
Dusty Baker	144
Mike Marshall	137
Matt Kemp	128 (still active)
Frank Howard	123

RUNS BATTED IN

Steve Garvey	992
Eric Karros	976
Willie Davis	849
Ron Cey	842
Bill Russell	627
Dusty Baker	586
Pedro Guerrero	585
Mike Piazza	563
Ron Fairly	541
Shawn Green	509
Mike Marshall	484
Wes Parker	470

TOTAL BASES

Willie Davis	3,094
Steve Garvey	3,004
Eric Karros	2,840
Bill Russell	2,471
Ron Cey	2,321
Maury Wills	2,045
Pedro Guerrero	1,843
Dusty Baker	1,779
Davey Lopes	1,744
Wes Parker	1,560
Mike Scioscia	1,557

SLUGGING AVERAGE

Mike Piazza	.574
Pedro Guerrero	.512
Shawn Green	.510
Raul Mondesi	.508
Matt Kemp	.496 (still active)
Frank Howard	.495
Andre Ethier	.479
Eric Karros	.473
Steve Garvey	.459
Mike Marshall	.449
Ron Cey	.445
Tommy Davis	.441

STOLEN BASES

Maury Wills	490
Davey Lopes	418
Willie Davis	335
Steve Sax	290
Brett Butler	179
Bill Russell	167
Ken Landreaux	119
Delino DeShields	114
Jim Gilliam	112
Mariano Duncan	97

PITCHING LEADERS

GAMES PITCHED

Don Sutton	550
Jim Brewer	474
Don Drysdale	459
Ron Perranoski	457
Charlie Hough	401
Orel Hershiser	353
Claude Osteen	339
Sandy Koufax	335
Fernando Valenzuela	331
Burt Hooton	322

GAMES STARTED

Don Sutton	533
Don Drysdale	424
Claude Osteen	335
Fernando Valenzuela	320
Orel Hershiser	309
Sandy Koufax	286
Bob Welch	267
Burt Hooton	265
Ramon Martinez	262
Johnny Podres	220

COMPLETE GAMES

Don Drysdale	156
Don Sutton	156
Sandy Koufax	133
Fernando Valenzuela	107
Claude Osteen	100
Orel Hershiser	65
Burt Hooton	61
Bill Singer	52
Johnny Podres	50
Bob Welch	47

INNINGS PITCHED

Don Sutton	3,814
Don Drysdale	3,112
Claude Osteen	2,397
Fernando Valenzuela	2,349
Orel Hershiser	2,181
Sandy Koufax	2,120
Burt Hooton	1,861
Bob Welch	1,821
Ramon Martinez	1,732
Jerry Reuss	1,408

GAMES WON

Don Sutton	223
Don Drysdale	187
Sandy Koufax	156
Claude Osteen	147
Fernando Valenzuela	141
Orel Hershiser	135
Ramon Martinez	123
Bob Welch	115
Burt Hooton	112
Johnny Podres	95

GAMES LOST

Don Sutton	181
Don Drysdale	152
Claude Osteen	126
Fernando Valenzuela	116
Orel Hershiser	107
Bob Welch	86
Burt Hooton	84
Sandy Koufax	77
Ramon Martinez	77
Bill Singer	76

STRIKEOUTS

Don Sutton	2,696
Don Drysdale	2,283
Sandy Koufax	2,214
Fernando Valenzuela	1,759
Orel Hershiser	1,446
Ramon Martinez	1,314
Bob Welch	1,292
Claude Osteen	1,162
Burt Hooton	1,042
Bill Singer	989

BASES ON BALLS

Don Sutton	996
Fernando Valenzuela	915
Don Drysdale	763
Sandy Koufax	709
Ramon Martinez	704
Orel Hershiser	667
Claude Osteen	568
Bob Welch	565
Burt Hooton	540
Johnny Podres	452

SHUTOUTS

Don Sutton	52
Don Drysdale	45
Sandy Koufax	38

Claude Osteen   34
Fernando Valenzuela 29
Orel Hershiser   24
Bob Welch   23
Burt Hooton   22
Ramon Martinez   20
Bill Singer   18

SAVES

Eric Gagne   161
Jeff Shaw   129
Todd Worrell   127
Jim Brewer   125
Ron Perranoski   101
Jay Howell   85
Jonathan Broxton   84
Clem Labine   83
Takashi Saito   81
Tom Niedenfuer   64

EARNED RUN AVERAGE (1000 innings)

Sandy Koufax   2.64
Clayton Kershaw   2.88 (still active)
Tommy John   2.97
Don Drysdale   2.98
Orel Hershiser   3.00
Bill Singer   3.03
Claude Osteen   3.09
Don Sutton   3.09
Jerry Reuss   3.11
Burt Hooton   3.14
Bob Welch   3.14

WON-LOSS PERCENTAGE (100 decisions)

Tommy John   .674 (87-42)
Sandy Koufax   .670 (156-77)
Ramon Martinez   .615 (123-77)
Doug Rau   .580 (80-58)
Bob Welch   .572 (115-86)
Burt Hooton   .571 (112-84)
Orel Hershiser   .558 (135-107)
Don Sutton   .563 (233-181)
Johnny Podres   .562 (95-74)
Don Drysdale   .552 (187-152)

DODGER TEAM SINGLE SEASON LEADERS - BROOKLYN AND LOS ANGELES

BATTING LEADERS

AT BATS

Maury Wills   695 (1962)
Carl Furillo   667 (1951)
Tommy Davis   665 (1962)
Steve Garvey   659 (1975)
Steve Garvey   658 (1980)
Ivy Olson   652 (1921)
Maury Wills   650 (1965)
Steve Garvey   648 (1979)
Steve Garvey   646 (1977)
Willie Davis   643 (1968)

RUNS SCORED

Hub Collins   148 (1890)
Babe Herman   143 (1930)
Mike Griffin   140 (1895)
Tido Daly   135 (1894)
Fielder Jones   134 (1897)
Pee Wee Reese   132 (1949)
Duke Snider   132 (1953)
Maury Wills   130 (1962)

HITS

Babe Herman   241 (1930)
Tommy Davis   230 (1962)
Zack Wheat   221 (1925)
Lefty O'Doul   219 (1932)
Babe Herman   217 (1929)
Wee Willie Keeler   215 (1899)
Zack Wheat   212 (1924)
Steve Garvey   210 (1975)
Steve Sax   210 (1986)
Wee Willie Keeler   209 (1901)

DOUBLES

Johnny Frederick   52 (1929)
Babe Herman   48 (1930)
Wes Parker   47 (1970)
Shawn Green   44 (2000)
Johnny Frederick   44 (1930)
Babe Herman   43 (1931)
Augie Galan   43 (1944)
Steve Sax   43 (1986)
Zack Wheat   42 (1925)
Babe Herman   42 (1929)
Dixie Walker   42 (1945)
Raul Mondesi   42 (1997)
Andre Ethier   42 (2009)

TRIPLES

George Treadway	26 (1894)
Hy Myers	22 (1920)
Dan Brouthers	20 (1892)
Tommy Corcoran	20 (1894)
Jimmy Sheckard	19 (1901)
Oyster Burns	18 (1892)
Harry Lumley	18 (1904)
Joe Kelley	17 (1900)
Pete Reiser	17 (1941)
Jim Gilliam	17 (1953)

HOME RUNS

Shawn Green	49 (2001)
Duke Snider	43 (1956)
Shawn Green	42 (2002)
Duke Snider	42 (1953)
Gil Hodges	42 (1954)
Duke Snider	42 (1955)
Roy Campanella	41 (1953)
Gil Hodges	40 (1951)
Mike Piazza	40 (1997)
Duke Snider	40 (1954)
Duke Snider	40 (1957)

RUNS BATTED IN

Tommy Davis	153 (1962)
Roy Campanella	142 (1953)
Duke Snider	136 (1955)
Jack Fournier	130 (1925)
Babe Herman	130 (1930)
Gil Hodges	130 (1954)
Duke Snider	130 (1954)
Oyster Burns	128 (1890)
Matt Kemp	126 (2011)
Glenn Wright	126 (1930)
Duke Snider	126 (1953)
Shawn Green	125 (2001)

TOTAL BASES

Babe Herman	416 (1930)
Duke Snider	378 (1954)
Duke Snider	370 (1953)
Shawn Green	370 (2001)
Tommy Davis	356 (1962)
Mike Piazza	355 (1997)
Matt Kemp	353 (2011)
Babe Herman	348 (1929)
Duke Snider	343 (1950)
Johnny Frederick	342 (1929)
Duke Snider	338 (1955)
Gil Hodges	335 (1954)

SLUGGING AVERAGE

Babe Herman	.678 (1930)
Duke Snider	.647 (1954)
Mike Piazza	.638 (1997)
Duke Snider	.628 (1955)
Duke Snider	.627 (1953)
Babe Herman	.612 (1929)
Roy Campanella	.611 (1953)
Mike Piazza	.606 (1995)
Duke Snider	.598 (1956)
Shawn Green	.598 (2001)
Roy Campanella	.590 (1951)
Jack Fournier	.588 (1923)

ON-BASE PERCENTAGE

Babe Herman	.455 (1930)
Jack Fournier	.440 (1923)
Jackie Robinson	.438 (1949)
Wally Moon	.438 (1960)
Babe Herman	.436 (1929)
Eddie Stanky	.436 (1946)
Jackie Robinson	.436 (1951)
Dixie Walker	.434 (1944)
Reggie Smith	.432 (1977)
Mike Piazza	.432 (1997)

STOLEN BASES

Maury Wills	104 (1962)
Maury Wills	94 (1965)
Monte Ward	88 (1892)
Hub Collins	85 (1890)
Davey Lopes	77 (1975)
Jimmy Sheckard	67 (1903)
Davey Lopes	63 (1976)
Davey Lopes	59 (1974)
Monte Ward	57 (1891)
Steve Sax	56 (1983)

BATTING AVERAGE

Babe Herman	.393 (1930)
Babe Herman	.381 (1929)
Wee Willie Keeler	.377 (1899)
Zack Wheat	.375 (1924)
Wee Willie Keeler	.368 (1900)
Lefty O'Doul	.368 (1932)
Mike Piazza	.362 (1997)
Oyster Burns	.361 (1894)
Zack Wheat	.359 (1925)
Dixie Walker	.357 (1944)

PITCHING LEADERS

GAMES PITCHED

Mike Marshall	106 (1974)
Paul Quantrill	86 (2002)
Jonathan Broxton	83 (2007)
Tom Martin	80 (2003)
Duaner Sanchez	79 (2005)
Charlie Hough	77 (1976)
Eric Gagne	77 (2002)
Jeff Shaw	77 (2001)
Guillermo Mota	76 (2003)
Scott Radinsky	75 (1997)
Matt Herges	75 (2001)

GAMES STARTED

Bill Terry	44 (1890)
George Haddock	44 (1892)
Brickyard Kennedy	44 (1893)
Tom Lovett	43 (1891)
Ed Stein	42 (1892)
Don Drysdale	42 (1963)
Don Drysdale	42 (1965)

COMPLETE GAMES

Brickyard Kennedy	40 (1893)
Tom Lovett	39 (1890)
Tom Lovett	39 (1891)
George Haddock	39 (1892)
Bill Terry	38 (1890)
Ed Stein	38 (1892)
Ed Stein	38 (1894)
Brickyard Kennedy	38 (1898)
Oscar Jones	38 (1904)

INNINGS PITCHED

Brickyard Kennedy	383 (1893)
George Haddock	381 (1892)
Ed Stein	377 (1892)
Oscar Jones	377 (1904)
Tom Lovett	372 (1890)
Bill Terry	370 (1890)
Tom Lovett	365 (1891)
Brickyard Kennedy	360 (1894)
Ed Stein	359 (1894)
Bill Donovan	351 (1901)

GAMES WON

Tom Lovett	30 (1890)
George Haddock	29 (1892)
Joe McGinnity	29 (1900)
Jim Hughes	28 (1899)
Dazzy Vance	28 (1924)
Ed Stein	27 (1892)
Ed Stein	27 (1894)
Don Newcombe	27 (1956)
Sandy Koufax	27 (1966)

WON-LOST PERCENTAGE

Phil Regan	.933 (14-1) 1966
Fred Fitzsimmons	.889 (16-2) 1940
Preacher Roe	.880 (22-3) 1951
Orel Hershiser	.864 (19-3) 1985
Ron Perranoski	.842 (19-3) 1963
Sandy Koufax	.833 (25-5) 1963
Jim Hughes	.824 (28-6) 1899
Dazzy Vance	.824 (28-6) 1924
Tommy John	.813 (13-3) 1974
Clayton Kershaw	.808 (21-5) 2011

STRIKEOUTS

Sandy Koufax	382 (1965
Sandy Koufax	317 (1966)
Sandy Koufax	306 (1963)
Sandy Koufax	269 (1961)
Dazzy Vance	262 (1924)
Don Drysdale	251 (1963)
Clayton Kershaw	248 (2011)
Bill Singer	247 (1969)
Don Drysdale	246 (1960)
Don Drysdale	242 (1959)

SHUTOUTS

Sandy Koufax	11 (1963)
Don Sutton	9 (1972)
Sandy Koufax	8 (1965)
Don Drysdale	8 (1968)
Fernando Valenzuela	8 (1981)
Orel Hershiser	8 (1988)
Tim Belcher	8 (1988)

SAVES

Eric Gagne	55 (2003)
Eric Gagne	52 (2002)
Todd Worrell	44 (1996)
Jeff Shaw	43 (2001)
Jonathan Broxton	36 (2009)
Todd Worrell	35 (1997)
Jeff Shaw	34 (1999)
Todd Worrell	32 (1995)
Jay Howell	28 (1989)
Jeff Shaw	27 (2000)

EARNED RUN AVERAGE

Rube Marquard	1.58 (1916)
Ned Garvin	1.68 (1904)
Sandy Koufax	1.73 (1966)
Sandy Koufax	1.74 (1964)
Kaiser Wilhelm	1.87 (1908)
Sandy Koufax	1.88 (1963)
Jeff Pfeffer	1.91 (1916)
Larry Cheney	1.92 (1916)
Jeff Pfeffer	1.97 (1914)
Orel Hershiser	2.03 (1985)

FIELDING LEADERS

FIELDING AVERAGE

CATCHER

Joe Ferguson	.996 (1973)
Mickey Owen	.995 (1941)
Paul LoDuca	.995 (2004)
Roy Campanella	.994 (1952)
John Roseboro	.994 (1965)
Russell Martin	.994 (2009)
Tom Haller	.994 (1968)
Mike Piazza	.992 (1996)
Paul Lo Duca	.992 (2002)
Paul Lo Duca	.991 (2001)

PITCHER

Dazzy Vance	1.000 (1928)
Hugh Casey	1.000 (1939)
Curt Davis	1.000 (1942)
Joe Hatten	1.000 (1947)
Fred Fitzsimmons	1.000 (1939)
Dutch Ruether	1.000 (1922)
Chad Billingsley	1.000 (2007)
Clayton Kershaw	1.000 (2009)
Clayton Kershaw	1.000 (2011)
Cy Barger	.990 (1910)

FIRST BASE

Steve Garvey	.999 (1981)
Wes Parker	.999 (1968)
Steve Garvey	.998 (1976)
Wes Parker	.997 (1965)
Wes Parker	.997 (1972)
Eric Karros	.997 (2002)
James Loney	.997 (2010)
Eric Karros	.996 (2001)
James Loney	.996 (2011)

SECOND BASE

Jody Reed	.993 (1993)
Jackie Robinson	.992 (1951)
Charlie Neal	.989 (1959)
Mark Grudzielanek	.989%(2002)
Orlando Hudson	.988 (2009)
Willie Randolph	.987 (1989)
Junior Gilliam	.986 (1957)

SHORTSTOP

Cesar Izturis	.985 (2004)
Cesar Izturis	.979 (2002)
Maury Wills	.978 (1971)
Pee Wee Reese	.977 (1949)
Cesar Izturis	.977 (2003)
Alex Cora	.977 (2002)
Alfredo Griffin	.975 (1989)
Mark Grudzielanek	.973 (1999)
Maury Wills	.970 (1965)
Pee Wee Reese	.969 (1952)

THIRD BASE

Adrian Beltre	.978 (2004)
Ron Cey	.977 (1979)
Tim Wallach	.976 (1995)
Casey Blake	.973 (2009)
Ron Cey	.972 (1980)
Joe Stripp	.968 (1936)
Dave Hansen	.968 (1992)

OUTFIELD

Andre Ethier	1.000 (2011)
Brett Butler	1.000 (1993)
Brett Butler	1.000 (1991)
Ken Landreaux	1.000 (1981)
Dave Roberts%	1.000 (2002)
Marquis Grissom	1.000 (2001)
Andre Ethier	.996 (2010)
Derrell Thomas	.996 (1979)
Matt Kemp	.995 (2009)
Brett Butler	.995 (1992)

PUTOUTS

CATCHER

Mike Piazza	1,055 (1996)
Mike Piazza	1,044 (1997)
Mike Scioscia	925 (1987)
John Roseboro	908 (1963)
John Roseboro	904 (1966)
Mike Piazza	899 (1993)
John Roseboro	877 (1961)

PITCHER

Orel Hershiser	37 (1987)
Ed Stein	36 (1892)
Orel Hershiser	32 (1988)
Fernando Valenzuela	29 (1986)
Orel Hershiser	28 (1992)
Ramon Martinez	28 (1993)

FIRST BASE

Steve Garvey	1,606 (1977)
Steve Garvey	1,583 (1976)
Steve Garvey	1,546 (1978)
Steve Garvey	1,539 (1982)
Steve Garvey	1,536 (1974)

SECOND BASE

George Cutshaw	455 (1914)
Eddie Stanky	429 (1945)
Junior Gilliam	407 (1957)
Eddie Stanky	402 (1947)
George Cutshaw	402 (1913)

SHORTSTOP

Charlie Babb	370 (1904)
Dave Bancroft	350 (1928)
Ivy Olson	.349 (1919)
Pee Wee Reese	346 (1941)
Ivy Olson	343 (1921)

THIRD BASE

Emil Batch	203 (1905)
Billy Shindle	192 (1894)
Billy Shindle	185 (1897)
George Pinckney	179 (1890)
Doc Casey	176 (1907)

OUTFIELD

Eddie Brown	449 (1925)
Johnny Frederick	410 (1929)
Willie Davis	404 (1971)
Hy Myers	399 (1922)
Johnny Frederick	398 (1931)
Johnny Frederick	394 (1930)
Goody Rosen	392 (1945)
Hy Myers	386 (1920)
Duke Snider	382 (1951)

ASSISTS

CATCHER

Bill Bergen	202 (1909)
Bill Bergen	151 (1910)
Bill Bergen	151 (1904)
Bill Bergen	149 (1906)
Otto Miller	148 (1913)

PITCHER

Elmer Stricklett	128 (1906)
Ned Garvin	117 (1903)
Doc Scanlon	112 (1905)
Brickyard Kennedy	109 (1893)
Henry Schmidt	109 (1903)
Kaiser Wilhelm	109 (1908)

FIRST BASE

Eric Karros	147 (1993)
Eric Karros	138 (2000)
Eddie Murray	137 (1989)
Gil Hodges	132 (1954)
Dolph Camilli	129 (1939)
Eddie Murray	128 (1991)
Eric Karros	126 (1992)
Eric Karros	126 (1999)
Eric Karros	121 (1996)
Eric Karros	121 (1997)
James Loney	121 (2008)

SECOND BASE

Tony Cuccinello	535 (1932)
Milt Stock	477 (1925)
George Cutshaw	473 (1915)
John Ward	472 (1892)
George Cutshaw	467 (1916)

SHORTSTOP

Bill Russell	560 (1973)
Maury Wills	535 (1965)
Bill Russell	533 (1978)
Bill Russell	523 (1977)
Bill Dahlen	517 (1900)

THIRD BASE

Ron Cey	365 (1974)
Ron Cey	346 (1977)
Ron Cey	336 (1978)
Ron Cey	334 (1976)
Ron Cey	328 (1973)

OUTFIELD

Jimmy Sheckard	36 (1903)
Mike Griffin	31 (1891)
Casey Stengel	30 (1917)
Tommy Griffith	27 (1921)
Harry Lumley	26 (1904)
Joe Kelley	26 (1899)
Hy Myers	25 (1921)
Mike Griffin	25 (1892)
Al Burch	24 (1908)
Babe Herman	24 (1931)
Carl Furillo	24 (1951)
Herbie Moran	24 (1912)
Jimmy Sheckard	24 (1905)

DODGERS WORLD SERIES INDIVIDUAL LEADERS

SERIES PLAYED

Carl Furillo	7
Jim Gilliam	7
Gil Hodges	7
Pee Wee Reese	7
Jackie Robinson	6
Duke Snider	6
Roy Campanella	5
Eight tied at	4

GAMES PLAYED

Pee Wee Reese	44
Carl Furillo	40
Gil Hodges	39
Jim Gilliam	39
Jackie Robinson	38
Duke Snider	36
Roy Campanella	32
Bill Russell	23
Davey Lopes	23
Steve Garvey	23
Ron Cey	%23

BATTING LEADERS

AT BATS

Pee Wee Reese	169
Jim Gilliam	147
Jackie Robinson	137
Duke Snider	133
Gil Hodges	131
Carl Furillo	128
Roy Campanella	114
Bill Russell	95
Steve Garvey	93
Davey Lopes	90

RUNS SCORED

Jackie Robinson	22
Duke Snider	21
Pee Wee Reese	20
Davey Lopes	18
Jim Gilliam	15
Gil Hodges	15
Roy Campanella	14
Carl Furillo	13
Steve Garvey	11
Dusty Baker	9

HITS

Pee Wee Reese	46
Duke Snider	38
Gil Hodges	35
Carl Furillo	34
Steve Garvey	32
Jackie Robinson	32
im Gilliam	31
Roy Campanella	27
Bill Russell	25
Ron Cey	20

DOUBLES

Carl Furillo	9
Duke Snider	8
Jackie Robinson	7
Roy Campanella	5
Billy Cox	5
Jim Gilliam	5
Steve Yeager	4
Steve Garvey	3
Ron Fairly	3
Pee Wee Reese	3
Many tied with %2	

TRIPLES

Tommy Davis	2
Gene Hermanski	2
Pee Wee Reese	2
Bill Russell	2
Several tied with	1

HOME RUNS

Duke Snider	11
Gil Hodges	5
Roy Campanella	4
Davey Lopes	4
Reggie Smith	4
Steve Yeager	4
Ron Cey	3

Dusty Baker   2
Ron Fairly   2
Pee Wee Reese   2

RUNS BATTED IN

Duke Snider   26
Gil Hodges   21
Pee Wee Reese   16
Ron Cey   13
Carl Furillo   13
Roy Campanella   12
Jim Gilliam   12
Jackie Robinson   12
Davey Lopes   11
Steve Yeager   10
Reggie Smith   10

STOLEN BASES

Davey Lopes   10
Jackie Robinson   6
Maury Wills   6
Pee Wee Reese   5
Jim Gilliam   4
Willie Davis   3
Bill Russell   2
Pedro Guerrero   2
Wes Parker   2
Several tied with 1

BATTING AVERAGE (10 GAMES)

Steve Garvey   .386
Billy Cox   .302
Ron Fairly   .300
Ivy Olson   .293
Duke Snider   .286
Lou Johnson   .286
Zack Wheat   .283
Wes Parker   .278
Pee Wee Reese   .272

PITCHING LEADERS

GAMES PITCHED

Carl Erskine   11
Clem Labine   10
Hugh Casey   9
Sandy Koufax   8
Don Drysdale   7
Joe Hatten   6
Burt Hooton   6
Johnny Podres   6
Don Sutton   6
Many tied at   5

INNINGS PITCHED

Sandy Koufax   57
Carl Erskine   42
Don Sutton   41
Don Drysdale   40
Orel Hershiser   40
Johnny Podres   38
Burt Hooton   32
Clem Labine   27
Don Newcombe   22
Claude Osteen   21

WON-LOSS RECORD

Johnny Podres   4-1
Sandy Koufax   4-3
Don Drysdale   3-3
Burt Hooton   3-3
Orel Hershiser   2-0
Larry Sherry   2-0
Tommy John   2-1
Preacher Roe   2-1
Hugh Casey   2-2
Carl Erskine   2-2
Clem Labine   2-2
Don Sutton   2-2

STRIKEOUTS

Sandy Koufax   61
Don Drysdale   36
Carl Erskine   31
Don Sutton   26
Burt Hooton   24
Don Newcombe   19
Johnny Podres   18
Orel Hershiser   17
Clem Labine   13
Tommy John   13

SHUTOUTS

Sandy Koufax   2
Burleigh Grimes   1
Preacher Roe   1
Johnny Podres   1
Clem Labine   1
Don Drysdale   1
Claude Osteen   1
Orel Hershiser   1

SAVES

Clem Labine   2
Larry Sherry   2

Jeff Pfeffer	1	Ron Cey	11
Hugh Casey	1	Davey Lopes	9
Ron Perranoski	1	Bill Russell	8
Mike Marshall	1	Steve Sax	8
Bob Welch	1	Mike Scioscia	6
Steve Howe	1	Andre Ethier	6 (still active)
Jay Howell	1	Rick Monday	5
		Mike Marshall	5
		Steve Yeager	5

EARNED RUN AVERAGE (18 INNINGS)

Claude Osteen	0.86
Sherry Smith	0.89
Sandy Koufax	0.95
Orel Hershiser	1.09
Clem Labine	1.65
Johnny Podres	2.12
Preacher Roe	2.54
Joe Black	2.54
Don Drysdale	2.95
Burt Hooton	3.74

HITS

Bill Russell	28
Steve Garvey	24
Dusty Baker	23
Davey Lopes	20
Ron Cey	19
Pedro Guerrero	19
Steve Sax	18
Mike Scioscia	14
Mike Marshall	14
James Loney	13 (still active)

DODGERS NATIONAL LEAGUE CHAMPIONSHIP SERIES

INDIVIDUAL LEADERS

BATTING LEADERS

DOUBLES

Ron Cey	6
Dusty Baker	5
Ken Landreaux	4
Mike Marshall	4
Steve Sax	3
Pedro Guerrero	2
Steve Garvey	2
Bill Russell	2
James Loney	2 (still active)
Andre Ethier	2 (still active)

GAMES PLAYED

Bill Russell	21
Steve Sax	19
Mike Scioscia	18
Dusty Baker	17
Ron Cey	17
Steve Garvey	17
Davey Lopes	17
Mike Marshall	17
Pedro Guerrero	15
Steve Yeager	15

TRIPLES

Davey Lopes	2
Mariano Duncan	1
Steve Garvey	1
Rick Monday	1
Pedro Guerrero	1
Mike Marshall	1
Reggie Smith	1
Bill Russell	1

AT BATS

Bill Russell	83
Steve Garvey	70
Davey Lopes	68
Mike Marshall	68
Steve Sax	66
Ron Cey	63
Dusty Baker	62
Mike Scioscia	53
Pedro Guerrero	51
Steve Yeager	45

HOME RUNS

Steve Garvey	7
Dusty Baker	3
Ron Cey	3
Bill Madlock	3
Mike Marshall	2
Mike Scioscia	2
Kirk Gibson	2
James Loney	2 (still active)

RUNS SCORED

Steve Garvey	14
Dusty Baker	12

RUNS BATTED IN

Dusty Baker	13
Steve Garvey	13
Ron Cey	11
Davey Lopes	11
Mike Marshall	10
Pedro Guerrero	8
Bill Russell	8
James Loney	5 (still active)

STOLEN BASES

Davey Lopes	9
Steve Sax	6
Kirk Gibson	2
Pedro Guerrero	2
John Shelby	2
Steve Yeager	2

BATTING AVERAGE (40 AT BATS)

Dusty Baker	.371
Steve Garvey	.343
Bill Russell	.337
Ron Cey	.302
Davey Lopes	.294
Steve Sax	.273
Mike Scioscia	.264
Ken Landreaux	.238
Mike Marshall	.206
Pedro Guerrero	.196

PITCHING LEADERS

GAMES PITCHED

Orel Hershiser	6
Tom Niedenfuer	6
Alejandro Pena	6
Bob Welch	6
Fernando Valenzuela	6
Jerry Reuss	4
Don Sutton	4
Rick Honeycutt	4
Rick Horton	4
Jesse Orosco	4

INNINGS PITCHED

Orel Hershiser	40
Fernando Valenzuela	37
Don Sutton	32
Tommy John	23
Burt Hooton	21
Jerry Reuss	21
Tim Belcher	15
Bob Welch	10

Clayton Kershaw	9
Chad Billingsley	8 (still active)
Rick Rhoden	8

WON-LOSS RECORD

Don Sutton	3-1
Fernando Valenzuela	3-1
Tim Belcher	2-0
Orel Hershiser	2-0
Burt Hooton	2-0
Tommy John	2-0
Lance Rautzhan	1-0
Andy Messersmith	1-0
Terry Forster	1-0
Alejandro Pena	1-1

STRIKEOUTS

Fernando Valenzuela	28
Orel Hershiser	20
Don Sutton	17
Tim Belcher	16
Tommy John	15
Burt Hooton	13
Chad Billingsley	12 (still active)
Bob Welch	9
Tom Niedenfuer	8
Jerry Reuss	7

SHUTOUTS

Don Sutton	1
Tommy John	1
Orel Hershiser	1
Jose Lima	1

SAVES

Tom Niedenfuer	2
Orel Hershiser	1
Brian Holton	1
Alejandro Pena	1
Mike Garman	1
Bob Welch	1
Jonathan Broxton	1 (still active)

EARNED RUN AVERAGE (10 INNINGS)

Tommy John	0.40
Don Sutton	1.73
Fernando Valenzuela	1.93
Orel Hershiser	2.03
Burt Hooton	3.43
Tim Belcher	4.11
Jerry Reuss	5.22
Bob Welch	5.40

APPENDIX C
GENERAL INFORMATION

BASEBALL FIELDS

Field	Dates Occupied	Capacity	Field Dimensions (in feet)				
			L	LC	C	RC	R
Capitoline Grounds	1865–1876	standing room	Open field—No fences				
Washington Park I	1884–1889	2,500	Fences were 400-500 feet. Spectators stood around the outfield.				
Washington Park II	1889–1890	8,000	Unknown				
Eastern Park	1891–1897	12,000	460 ft. X 860 ft. field				
Washington Park III	1898–1912	18,800	306	472	423	300	299
Ebbets Field	1913–1957	18,000	419		450		301
	1946	32,000	356	365	400	352	297
Los Angeles Coliseum	1958–1961	93,600	251	320–417	420	395	300
Dodger Stadium	1962–	56,000	330	385	400	385	330

TEAM NICKNAMES

Grays	1884–1888	From the color of their uniforms. They were also called The Brooklyns and the Church City Nine.
Bridegrooms (or Grooms)	1889–1891	Six players were married in the off season
Ward's Wonders	1891–1893	After Brooklyn manager John Montgomery Ward
Foutz's Fillies	1893–1897	After Brooklyn manager Dave Foutz
Trolley Dodgers	1896–1898	The heavy concentration of electric trolley car tracks in front of Eastern Park caused fans to dodge the trolleys to reach the park. Manhattanites and other visitors began calling the Brooklyn fans Trolley Dodgers. The name eventually was given to the team.
Dodgers	1899–	Shortened version of Trolley Dodgers. The Brooklyn National League Baseball Club referred to their team as the Dodgers on their World Series programs in 1916 and 1920.
Superbas	1899–1924	After a vaudeville group named Hanlon's Superbas. Ned Hanlon was the Dodger manager.
Robins	1915–1931	After Brooklyn manager Wilbert Robinson
The Flock	1931–1957	The Flatbush Flock—A nickname given to the team by newspaper writers.
Bums	1937–1957	More commonly known as "Dem Bums." An endearing nickname derived from the "Lovable Bum" cartoon of newspaper cartoonist Willard Mullin. This nickname could only be used by a rabid Dodger fan. If a non-Dodger fan called the Brooklyn team Bums, it was reason enough to fight.

UNIFORMS

- Brooklyn had gray uniforms in 1884

- Major league teams had both home and road uniforms by 1900. The home uniform was white and the road uniform was gray.

- In 1900, the Brooklyn home uniform was white with maroon trim and maroon stockings. The uniform had an Old English B on the left chest. The road uniform was gray with "Brooklyn" across the front in black block letters. The stockings were black.

- In 1902, the Brooklyn accent color was changed to navy blue. The home uniform was white with navy blue trim and a navy blue Old English B on the left chest. The cap was navy blue with a white B. The road uniform was gray with black trim and lettering. The uniform had 'Brooklyn' across the front in arched black block letters. The cap was gray with a black B.

- In 1906, the trim on the road uniform was changed to navy blue.

- The first team to have a nickname emblazoned across the front of their uniform was the Washington Nationals, in 1905.

- The first team to put numbers on their uniforms was the Cleveland Indians, who put numbers on the uniform sleeves in 1916.

- The New York Yankees put large numbers on the back of the uniform in 1929.

- In 1933, the name "Dodgers" was emblazoned across the front of both the home and road uniforms in block letters.

- In 1938 the accent color was changed to royal blue. The name "Dodgers" was emblazoned across the front of both the home and road uniforms in script letters.

- From 1939 until 1945, the team had "Brooklyn" across the front of the road uniform in script letters.

- The Brooklyn Dodgers put numbers on the front of the uniform in 1952.

- In 1959, the Dodgers road uniform had Los Angeles across the front in script letters.

- In 1970, the name Dodgers was emblazoned across the front of the road uniform in script letters.

- In 1999, the team reverted to Los Angeles, in script letters, across the front of the road uniforms.

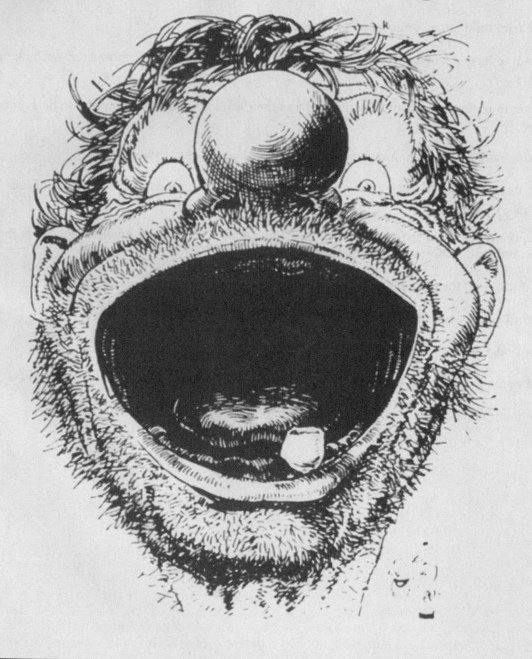

BIBLIOGRAPHY

Allen, M. (1979). *You could look it up*. New York: Time Books.

Alston, W., & Tobin, J. (1976). *A year at a time*. Waco, TX: Word Books.

Barber, R. (1970). *The broadcasters*. New York: The Dial Press.

Benson, M. (1989). *Ballparks of North America*. Jefferson, NC: McFarland & Company.

Best sports stories. (1952). New York: E.P. Dutton & Co., Inc.

Big blue review. (1991-1992). Stamford, CT: A Weston Communications Publication.

Bjarkman, P.C. (1990). *Baseball's great dynasties - the Dodgers*. New York: Gallery Books.

Bowman, J.S., & Zoss, J. (1986). *The National League*. London: Bison Books.

Brooklyn Dodger baseball 1901-1956. (1993). New York: Historical Briefs, Inc.

Brown, G., Keylin, A.,& Lundy, D. (Eds.).(1982). *Sports of the times*. New York, NY: Lundy, Daniel, Arno Press.

Campanella, R. (1959). *It's good to be alive*. New York: New American Library.

Carter, C. (Ed.). (1990). *Daguerreotypes (8th ed.)*. St. Louis, MO: *The Sporting News*.

Carter, C. (Ed.). (1989). *The series*. St. Louis, MO: *The Sporting News*.

Clark, D.,& Lester, L. (Eds.). (1994). *The Negro Leagues book*. Cleveland, OH: SABR.

Cohen, R.M.,& Neft, D.S. (1979). *The world series*.New York: Collier Books.

Cohen, S. *(1979). The Dodgers, the first 100 years*. New York: Carol Publishing Group.

Couzens, G.S. *(1973). A baseball album*. New York: Lippencott & Crowell.

Davenport, J. W. (1979). *Baseball graphics*. Madison, WI: First Impressions.

Davis, M. (1965). *Baseball's unforgettables*. New York: Bantam Books.

Dodger blue. (1983-1989). Los Angeles: *Los Angeles Press Telegram*.

Dodger yearbooks. (1950-1997). Brooklyn, NY & Los Angeles, CA.

Dodgers dugout. (1985-1997). Gothenburg, NE: Holmes Publishing.

Durant, J.(1948). *The Dodgers*. New York: Hastings House.

Durant, J. (1973). *The story of baseball in words and pictures*. New York: Hastings House.

Durocher, L. (1975). *Nice guys finish last*. New York: Simon & Schuster.

Frommer, H. (1985). *Baseball's greatest managers*. New York: Franklin Watts.

Gewecke, C. (1984). *Day by day in Dodgers history*. New York: Leisure Press.

Goldstein, R. (1991). *Superstars and screwballs*. New York: Penguin Group.

Golenbock, P. (1984). *Bums*. New York: G.P. Putnam's Sons.

Graham, F. (1948). *The Brooklyn Dodgers*. New York: G.P. Putnam's Sons.

Grayson, H. (1945). *They played the game*. New York: A.S. Barnes & Co.

Hershiser, O.,& Jenkins, J.B. (1989). *Out of the blue*. Brentwood, TN: Wolgemuth and Hyatt.

Holmes, T. (1990). *Brooklyn's Babe*. Gothenburg, NE: Holmes Publishing.

Holmes, T. (1979-1997).*Dodger blue book*. Gothenburg, NE: Holmes Publishing.

Holmes, T. (1988). *Brooklyn's best*. Gothenburg, NE: Holmes Publishing.

Holway, J.B. (1988). *Blackball stars*. Westport, CT: Meckler Books.

Honig, D.(1988). *The Brooklyn Dodgers-An illustrated tribute*. New York: St. Martin's Press.

Honig, D. (1988). *A Donald Honig reader*. New York, NY: Simon & Schuster, Inc.

Hoppell, J. (1988). *Baseball's Hall of Fame*. New York: Arlington House, Inc.

Johnstone, J.,& Talley, R. (1987). *Over the edge*. New York: Bantam Books.

Kahn, R. (1972). *The boys of summer*. New York: Harper & Row.

Lasorda, T.,& Fisher, D. (1985). *The artful Dodger*. New York: Avon Books.

Los Angeles Dodgers media guide. (1989-1997). Los Angeles, CA.

Lowry, P.J. (1992). *Green cathedrals*. Reading, PA: Addison-Wesley Inc.

McNeil, W.F. (1986). *Dodger diary*. Pittsfield, MA: The Celtic Publishing Organization.

Mitchell, J. (1966). *Sandy Koufax*. New York: Grosset and Dunlap.

Moreland, G.L. (1914). *Balldom*. New York: Balldom Publishing Co.

Neft, D.S., & Cohen, R.M. (1985). *The sports encyclopedia baseball*. New York: St. Martin's Press.

Nemec, D. (1987). *Great baseball feats, facts & firsts*. New York: New American Library.

Okrent, D., & Wulf, S. (1989). *Baseball anecdotes.* New York: Harper & Row Publishers.

Peary, D. (Ed.). (1990). *Cult baseball players.* New York: Simon & Schuster.

Peterson, R. (1970). *Only the ball was white.* New York: McGraw-Hill Book Co.

Reichler, J., & Clary, J. (1990). *Baseball's great moments.* New York: Gallahad Books.

Reichler, J.L. (Ed.). (1975). *The baseball encyclopedia.* New York: Macmillan Publishing Co., Inc.

Riley, D. (Ed.). (1992). *Dodger's reader.* Boston: Houghton Mifflin Co.

Riley, J.A. (1994). *The biographical encyclopedia of the Negro Baseball Leagues.* New York: Carroll & Graf Publishers, Inc.

Ritter, L. S. (1984). *The glory of their times.* New York: William Morrow.

Robinson, J. (1972). *I never had it made.* Greenwich, CT: Fawcett Publication.

Sahadi, L. (1982). *The L.A. Dodgers, the world champions of baseball.* New York: Quill Publishing.

Seymour, H. (1960). *Baseball, the early years.* New York: Oxford University Press.

Shatzkin, M. (Ed.). (1990). *The ballplayers.* New York: William Morrow & Co.,Inc.

Snider, D., & Gilbert, B. (1989). *The duke of Flatbush.* New York: Zebra Books.

Spalding, A.G. (1991). *Baseball–America's national game.* San Francisco: Halo Books.

Sullivan, N.J. (1987). *The Dodgers move west.* New York: Oxford University Press.

Thorn, J. (1987). *The National pastime.* New York: Bell Publishing.

Thorn, J., & Palmer, P. (1989). *Total baseball.* New York: Warner Books.

Who's Who In Baseball. (1916-1997). New York: Baseball Magazine Co.

Zimmerman, T. (1990). *A day in the season of the L.A. Dodgers.* New York: Shapolsky.